The Labor Relations Process

NINTH EDITION

William H. Holley, Jr.
Auburn University

Kenneth M. Jennings

Roger S. Wolters
Auburn University

SOUTH-WESTERN
CENGAGE Learning™

Australia • Brazil • Japan • Korea • Mexico • Singapore • Spain • United Kingdom • United States

SOUTH-WESTERN
CENGAGE Learning

The Labor Relations Process, 9th Edition
William H. Holley, Jr., Kenneth M.
Jennings, Roger S. Wolters

Vice President of Editorial, Business:
Jack W. Calhoun

Vice President/Editor-in-Chief: Melissa
Acuna

Executive Editor: Joe Sabatino

Developmental Editor: Jennifer King

Marketing Manager: Clint Kernen

Content Project Manager:
D. Jean Buttrom

Manager of Technology, Editorial: John
Barans

Technology Project Editor: Kristen Meere

Website Project Manager: Brian Courter

Manufacturing Coordinator: Doug Wilke

Production Service: LEAP, Inc. and
International Typesetting
and Composition

Copyeditor: Juli Cook

Art Director: Tippy McIntosh

Internal Designer: Craig Ramsdell,
Ramsdell Design

Cover Designer: Craig Ramsdell,
Ramsdell Design

Cover Image: Getty Images

For product information and technology assistance, contact us at
Cengage Learning Academic Resource Center, 1-800-423-0563

For permission to use material from this text or product,
submit all requests online at **www.cengage.com/permissions**
Further permissions questions can be emailed to
permissionrequest@cengage.com

ExamView® and ExamView Pro® are registered trademarks of
FSCreations, Inc. Windows is a registered trademark of the
Microsoft Corporation used herein under license. Macintosh and
Power Macintosh are registered trademarks of Apple Computer,
Inc. used herein under license.

© 2008 Cengage Learning. All Rights Reserved.

Library of Congress Control Number: 2008922452

ISBN-13: 978-0-324-42144-6

ISBN-10: 0-324-42144-3

South-Western Cengage Learning
5191 Natorp Boulevard
Mason, OH 45040
USA

Cengage Learning products are represented in Canada by
Nelson Education, Ltd.

For your course and learning solutions, visit
academic.cengage.com

Purchase any of our products at your local college store or
at our preferred online store **www.ichapters.com**

Printed in Canada
1 2 3 4 5 6 7 11 10 09 08

Brief Contents

Contents

Part 2: The Bargaining Process and Outcomes   240

Chapter 6: Negotiating the Labor Agreement   243

Chapter 7: Economic Issues   291

Chapter 8: Administrative Issues

Chapter 9: Resolving Negotiation (Interest) Disputes and the Use of Economic Pressure

Preface

This textbook is a culmination of more than 100 years of classroom teaching to more than 10,000 undergraduate and graduate college students. The ninth edition of *The Labor Relations Process* reflects our original objective in writing the book: to provide students with a textbook that will generate an understanding of and appreciation for core elements of union–management relationships. We have attempted to involve the student with the subject matter and to create an interest in related issues that will continue after the student completes the course. A model of the labor relations process (Exhibit 1.2) is presented in the first chapter and expanded in subsequent chapters through extensive references to academics and practitioners that focus on real-world situations and concerns. This provides a balance between concepts and applications for the reader.

As with the first and all subsequent editions, the ninth edition of *The Labor Relations Process* continues to be the most comprehensive text on the market.

FEATURES OF THE NINTH EDITION

The ninth edition approaches our student involvement objective by enhancing our commitment to application, an emphasis that is unmatched by other textbooks in this area. We believe that application generates student interest in the subject matter while enabling students to demonstrate their understanding of concepts and principles and apply this information to real-world situations. These opportunities and related efforts should sharpen readers' communication skills, a desirable skill for any student, regardless of his or her academic major or intended occupation.

Application has been enhanced through "Labor Relations in Action" features; National Labor Relations Board, court, or arbitration case studies at the end of most chapters; and "class activity" experiential exercises designed to promote active student participation in the learning process. There are updated Internet exercises called "Exploring the Web" at the end of each chapter to enhance student learning and application and to create interest in independent research. The negotiation exercise with computer applications and the arbitration cases have been prepared for role-playing experience to promote the reality of union-management relations. The book has also maintained many of the previous edition's features: a focus on currency, ethics, international issues, and real-world applications:

- **Currency.** This edition offers many opportunities for readers to become involved with the current applications of the labor relations process. For example, recent collective bargaining occurred with management and union officials in the auto industry, and recent bargaining subjects such as health care costs and technological change are given expanded coverage in this edition.

- **Ethics.** Ethical issues concerning such topics as bargaining behavior, union organizing, employee empowerment, and termination for union activities are addressed throughout the book.

- **International Labor.** Chapter 14 has been updated and expanded to include changes that have occurred in Canada, Mexico, China, Australia, and the European Union, as well as the effects of the North American Free Trade Agreement.

- **Real-World Applications.** The Labor Relations in Action boxes integrate current events in labor relations, and have been updated with several new applications.

Key Chapter-by-Chapter Changes in the Ninth Edition

Each chapter has been extensively updated with current research, laws and judicial decisions, studies, and statistics. Additional attention has been given to explaining the labor relations process and influences. Following are some of the key updates to this edition:

- Chapter 1 features updated union membership data, basic characteristics, and underlying assumptions of the U.S. labor relations system, and encourages online searches on current labor relations topics, supplemented by Internet exercises in every chapter.

- Chapter 2's labor history timeline chronicles important dates and events in labor's history and highlights expanded coverage of the unions' role in politics and campaign finance reform.

- Chapter 3 presents recent key decisions of the NLRB and courts affecting labor relations, such as classification of hospital interns and residents, graduate students in academic institutions, and supervisors for purposes of determining coverage as "employees" under the Labor Management Relations Act. The chapter also includes expanded coverage of the NLRB's unfair labor practice procedure and the concept of concerted and protected activity under the LMRA.

- Chapter 4 offers updates on "Change to Win," reasons why unions are withdrawing from the AFL-CIO, expanded coverage of "financial core" membership, and "right-to-work" legislation.

- Chapter 5 covers modern union-organizing tactics, such as union salting, card check and neutrality agreements, as well as approaches by the "Change to Win" unions and the renewed emphasis on union organizing led by AFL-CIO President John Sweeney.

- Chapter 6 explores collective bargaining preparation and behavior, including a comparison of distributive bargaining versus mutual gain (interest-based) bargaining approaches and contract ratification procedures.

- Chapter 7 features current information on wage and benefit trends and expanded coverage of wage incentive pay plans, such as skill-based pay, health care cost containment, and pension plans.

- Chapter 8 covers technological change issues, efforts to foster more cooperative labor–management relationships, safety and health issues, and the Americans with Disabilities Act.

- Chapter 9 reveals the role of the mediator as viewed through the eyes of one of the nation's prominent labor mediators. Coverage includes trends in strike activity; legal decisions affecting employees' and employers' rights during a work stoppage; and secondary strike, picket, and boycott activity.

- Chapter 10 provides the latest information on workplace investigations, grievance mediation, and a union's legal duty of fair representation.

- Chapter 11 offers a critique of employment arbitration, its advantages and shortcomings; explores the controversy over mandated employment arbitration as a condition of employment; explains Due Process Protocol; and reveals the arbitrator decision's potential conflict and accommodation with public policy.

- Chapter 12 provides guidelines used by arbitrators in determining "just cause," and features updates on *Weingarten* rights, such as the withdrawal of the NLRB's extension of *Weingarten* rights to nonunion (unrepresented) employees.

- Chapter 13 addresses current public-sector bargaining rights, dispute resolution, privatization of public services, and homeland security issues.

- Chapter 14 focuses on the labor relations systems of America's major trading partners, including NAFTA members and European Union countries, and covers major developments in Australia, Canada, China, Europe, and Mexico.

SUPPLEMENTARY MATERIALS
Instructor's Manual with Test Bank

(ISBN 0-324-585764)
This supplement includes chapter outlines, answers to end-of-chapter discussion questions, case notes, suggested student readings and term projects, and both instructors' and students' instructions for the Collective Bargaining Negotiations Exercise (available on our product support Web site). The Test Bank has been fully revised, updated, and expanded.

ExamView Testing Software

(ISBN 0-324-585772)
ExamView Testing Software contains all of the questions in the printed Test Bank. This easy-to-use test creation software is compatible with Microsoft® Windows. Instructors can add or edit questions, instructions, and answers to create custom tests for students. Instructors can also create and administer quizzes online.

Instructor's Resource CD-ROM

(ISBN 0-324-585756)
The Instructor's Resource CD-ROM contains all instructor materials cited previously: Instructor's Manual, Test Bank, and ExamView, plus a complete PowerPoint slide presentation.

Holley/Jennings/Wolters Product Support Website

(ISBN 0-324-585799)

Our product support website, academic.cengage.com/management/holley is a robust learning and resource center for both instructors and students. The self-assessment exercises on the site include:

- An Industrial Relations Orientation Self-Assessment that measures the degree of one's pro-union or anti-union sentiments.

- Bargaining Strategy Orientation Self-Assessment that measure one's preference for different bargaining strategies (e.g., distributive v. mutual gain).

- Mediator Effectiveness Potential Self-Assessment measures the degree to which one possesses the personal characteristics attributed to successful mediators.

Interactive Quizzes presented as multiple-choice and true-false questions allow self-assessments by students in understanding material related to each chapter's key terms and concepts.

Acknowledgments

We are especially grateful to the following professors for their reviews and suggestions on this revision:

Satish Desphande, Western Michigan University
Victor Devinatz, Illinois State University
Randyl D. Elkin, West Virginia University
Toni S. Knechtges, Eastern Michigan University
Douglas M. Mahony, University of South Carolina
Jonathan Monat, California State University, Long Beach
Carol F. Nowicki, California State University, East Bay
Machelle K. Schroeder, University of Wisconsin–Platteville
Donna M. Testa, Herkimer County Community College
Jeffrey L. Walls, Indiana Institute of Technology

We also extend our appreciation to those who made valuable suggestions for previous editions: Todd Baker, John C. Bird, Mollie Bowers, Gene Brady, James F. Byers, Joseph M. Cambridge, Anthony Campagna, James Chambers, William Chase, Boyd Childress, Milton Derber, Satish Desphande, James B. Dworkin, Geraldine Ellerbrock, Art Finkle, Paul Gerhart, Dennis W. Gibson, Carol L. Gilmore, Thomas P. Gilroy, David Gray, Charles R. Greer, Marvin Hill, Jr., Wayne Hochwarter, Janis Holden, Denise Tanguay Hoyer, Thomas Hyclak, H. Roy Kaplan, Zeinrab A. Karake, Katherine Karl, Philip Kienast, John Kilgour, Kenneth A. Kovach, Charles Krider, Thomas W. Lloyd, Eugene Lorge, Howard T. Ludlow, Karl O. Magnusen, Marick Masters, William Maloney, Pamela Marett, Douglas McCabe, Patrick McHugh, Frank Milman, Jonathan Monat, Roy Moore, William L. Moore, Thomas Noble, Lou Parrotta, Dane M. Partridge, Robert Penfield, Alex Pomnichowski, Roy R. Reynolds, Robert Rodgers, Richard L. Rowan, Sue Schaefer, Peter Sherer, David Shulenberger, Herman A. Theeke, Peter A. Veglahn, Suzanne M. Vest, William Werther, Elizabeth Wesman, and Carolyn Wiley.

We also wish to thank Sarah M. Philips and Charlie T. Cook for their aid in the preparation of this book.

Finally, we would like to thank Cengage Learning for its fine work on this book. We are especially grateful to Joe Sabatino, Executive Editor; Jennifer King, Developmental Editor; Jean Buttrom, Associate Content Project Manager; Tippy McIntosh, Art Director; and Clint Kernen, Marketing Manager.

William H. Holley, Jr.
Auburn University
Roger S. Wolters
Auburn University

About The Authors

William H. Holley, Jr., taught labor relations, collective bargaining, and arbitration for 32 years at Auburn University, and has served as an arbitrator for more than 30 years in most major industries, from airlines to professional sports to the postal service. He received his BS and MBA from Mississippi State University and his PhD from the University of Alabama. He has been active in the Southern Management Association, a division of the Academy of Management, where he has served as Secretary and President, and on the editorial board of the *Journal of Management* for three terms. He is a coauthor of *Personnel/Human Resource Management* with Ken Jennings and of *Labor Relations: An Experiential and Case Approach* with Roger Wolters. His research has been published in a wide range of journals, such as the *Academy of Management Journal, Labor Law Journal, Personnel Psychology,* and others. He is a member of the National Academy of Arbitrators, served as its Executive Secretary-Treasurer and on the Board of Governors, and now serves as Vice President.

Kenneth M. Jennings, Jr., was the Richard de Raismes Professor of Industrial Relations at the University of North Florida, where he taught undergraduate and graduate courses in labor relations and human resource management. After receiving his BS from Knox College and MS from the University of Illinois, he spent four years with Union Carbide in various industrial relations assignments. He received a PhD from the University of Illinois, and was a faculty member at the University of North Florida for more than 20 years. Ken was a prolific scholar and is remembered by his students as an exciting and engaging teacher. He wrote numerous books (*Balls and Strikes: The Money Game in Professional Baseball* and *Labor Relations at the New York Daily News*) and articles in journals such as *Industrial and Labor Relations Review, Industrial Management, Personnel Journal, Employee Relations Law Journal,* and *Transportation Journal.* He was a lifelong fan of the Chicago Cubs, and an avid collector of jazz recordings and baseball cards.

Roger S. Wolters is an Associate Professor in the Department of Management at Auburn University. Dr. Wolters received his BBA and MA from the University of North Florida and his PhD from the University of Illinois in Labor and Industrial Relations. Wolters' primary teaching interests include labor law, collective bargaining, and dispute resolution. He is the co-author of *Labor Relations: An Experiential and Case Approach* with William H. Holley, Jr. His research has been published in a variety of journals including *Labor Law Journal, Arbitration Journal, Employee Responsibilities and Rights Journal,*

Journal of Construction Engineering and Management, Industrial Relations, and others. He has engaged in consulting with private and public organizations and served as an Administrative Hearing Officer in the grievance procedure of the City of Auburn, Alabama. Dr. Wolters is a member of the Labor and Employment Relations Association (LERA). Outside interests include golfing and motorcycling.

Part 1: Recognizing Rights and Responsibilities of Unions and Management

Part 1 introduces the labor relations process that will be discussed throughout the book, placing it in historical and legal perspectives. It also examines the difference in union and management organization and labor relations strategies.

Copyright GettyImages

CHAPTER 1
Union–Management Relationships in Perspective

Today's global economy presents many challenges and opportunities for both employers and employees. The effective management of human resources is critical to maintaining an organization's competitiveness. Recognition of and respect for the legitimate interests of both labor and management are an important step in building and maintaining work relationships capable of adapting to change in the competitive environment facing most organizations.

Chapter 1 seeks to begin building a basic frame of reference for understanding the labor relations process by first defining the three phases of the labor relations process and then placing this process into an analytical perspective. Chapter 1 introduces the activities, focal point, participants, and influences of the labor relations process, which are discussed in detail in subsequent chapters. The chapter ends with a discussion of the current status of union membership and the relevance of labor organizations in today's economy.

PHASES IN THE LABOR RELATIONS PROCESS

The **labor relations process** involves managers (representing the ownership interests) and a labor organization (union) designated as the exclusive bargaining agent representing the interests of a group of employees engaged in the joint determination and administration of work rules. Union representation of employees' interests is not automatically granted in the workplace and the negotiation and administration of work rules demonstrate considerable variation across public- and private-sector organizations in the United States. Work rules in organizations where employees are unrepresented (no union) are typically determined unilaterally by management.

The labor relations process includes the following three phases:

1. **Recognition of the legitimate rights and responsibilities of union and management representatives.** The union selection phase includes the legal right of employees to join unions (see Chapter 3), union-organizing campaigns (see Chapter 5), and the rights and responsibilities of management and union officials to abide by applicable laws and labor agreement (contract) terms. From a labor organization's perspective, phase 1 may be the most important phase because, without successfully gaining legal recognition as the exclusive bargaining representative of a group of employees in phase 1, the process does not proceed to phases 2 or 3.

2. **Negotiation of the labor agreement, including appropriate strategies, tactics, and impasse-resolution techniques.** Contract negotiation involves union and management representatives jointly determining work rules (policies) governing the parties' rights and responsibilities affecting wages, hours, or other terms and conditions of employment (discussed in Chapters 6, 7, and 8). The outcomes of such negotiations have an important impact on a firm's labor costs, management's rights, and covered employees' standard of living. Most **interest disputes** (i.e., a dispute over what the terms or conditions of employment or work rules will be) are resolved voluntarily by union and management negotiators during the bargaining process. Strikes, lockouts, mediation, and interest arbitration are examples of impasse resolution techniques (discussed in Chapter 9) that can be used to resolve an interest dispute. Phase 2 of the labor relations process generally receives the most media attention even though phases 1 and 3 are equally essential.

3. **Administration of the negotiated labor agreement—the interpretation and application of labor contract terms on a daily basis.** Once contract terms have been settled in phase 2, there is a need to enforce those terms every day during the stated term or duration of the labor agreement. The contract enforcement phase of the labor relations process is generally accomplished through daily union and management interactions and, when necessary, the use of a grievance-arbitration procedure to resolve **rights disputes** (i.e., disputes over the interpretation or application of a contract's terms, discussed in Chapters 10, 11, and 12). Resolving rights disputes accounts for the most time and energy spent by union and management officials in the labor relations process and usually involves a larger number of these officials than the preceding phases.

Of course, not all labor-management relationships progress through these three phases smoothly. Indeed, employees and their chosen union representative at some public and private sector organizations have a difficult time moving from the recognition of an employee bargaining representative (phase 1) through the remaining two phases of the process.[1]

The phases of the labor relations process are subject to qualitative variation as well. In the first phase, for example, organizations vary in the amount of mutual trust and respect union and management officials have for each other's goals. In the second phase, negotiations are carried out with different levels of intelligence, preparation, and sincere desire to achieve results. The third phase may vary as to how well the negotiated labor agreement is understood and effectively administered in good faith by both parties. There are probably as many different relationships as there are union and management officials negotiating labor agreements.

Elements in the Labor Relations Process

Exhibit 1.1 provides a framework for the labor relations process. The elements shown can be applied to the labor relations activities at a single or multiple facilities owned by a single company, or in an entire industry. The exhibit cites three major categories: (1) the focal point of labor relations, which is the negotiation and administration of work rules; (2) the key participants in the process, who are the union and management organizations, employees, third-party neutrals, and branches of government (administrative, legislative, and judicial); and (3) constraints or influences affecting the parties in their negotiation and administration of work rules.

Focal Point of Labor Relations: Work Rules

Any academic discipline needs a focal point so that research, investigation, and commentary can generate applicable insights. "Labor" or "industrial" relations can become a very broad topic including many academic concerns. For example, sociologists have examined employee alienation; psychologists have investigated causes of job satisfaction; economists have studied wage determination; and political scientists have assessed the impact of union and management as interest groups attempting to influence government policy and legislative outcomes.

John Dunlop's book *Industrial Relations Systems* provided a useful focal point for these diverse academic approaches. Dunlop suggested that the center of attention in labor relations should be the work rules negotiated between management and union officials. Work rules facilitate the implementation of operational plans designed to accomplish an organization's strategic goals. Work rules determine employees' standard of living and the work environment within which employees will spend a substantial portion of their time.

It is important to understand the influences determining the creation and particular content of work rules.[2] **Work rules** can be placed in two general categories: 1) rules governing compensation in all its forms (e.g., wages, overtime payments, vacations, holidays, shift premiums), and 2) rules specifying the employees' and employers' job rights and obligations, such as no employee strike or employer lockout during the term of the labor agreement, performance standards, promotion qualifications and procedures, job specifications, and layoff procedures. Additional examples of work rules are furnished in Exhibit 1.2.

Compensation work rules, such as a negotiated wage rate, often capture the attention of employees and the media because they are negotiation outcomes easier for most people to understand and compare. Union and management officials, however, may attach equal or greater importance to work rules regarding the second work rule category, job rights and obligations. For example, managers might be very interested in obtaining a work rule which permits production employees to perform "minor repairs," instead of requiring higher-paid maintenance employees to do the tasks. About 30 percent of union contracts

Exhibit 1.1
Elements in the Labor Relations Process

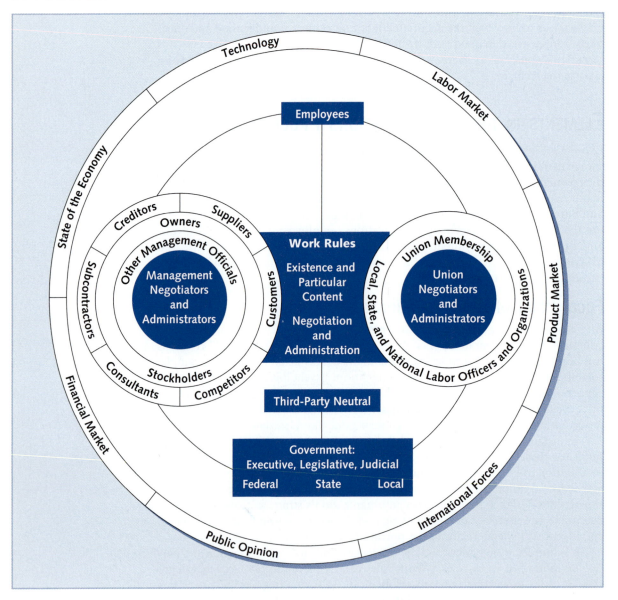

contain limitations on the right of management to require employees to work overtime, and some unions have sought work rules that would change the standard work week to less than 40 hours per week to earn full-time pay and benefits.[3]

Work rules can vary depending upon whether they are common or unique in the subject matter addressed and vague or specific in the wording used to express the rule. The wording or interpretation of work rules can also change over time in response to changes in operating environments and the need for greater flexibility.

For example, the work rules for airline flight attendants today would most certainly differ from the following three work rules formulated in the 1930s:

Job or Industry Classification	Work Rule
Government Installation	The employer agrees to furnish adequate protective clothing for employees required to work outside during rain, sleet, hail, or other atmospheric conditions detrimental to health or safety, provided the employee subjected to such assignments normally and historically performs the majority of his work assignment indoors. Employees who normally perform a majority of their work outdoors shall furnish their own protective clothing...
Electricians	Where the work assignment of employees who have been assigned a permanent reporting location requires travel to and be-tween other work locations and/or return to their permanent reporting location, the time consumed by the employees in such travel shall be counted as time worked.
Health Care	In situations where a department head determines that it is necessary for an em-ployee to use bilingual skills, those employees who have been previously deter-mined to possess those skills at a level necessary for the assignment, and who are so assigned by the department head, shall be eligible to receive additional compensa-tion of three percent above the applicable pay rate for the time period of the assignment.
Communications	The company subscribes to the principle that a well-informed union leadership pro-motes harmony and efficiency in union-man-agement relations. The company agrees to notify the union of any proposed changes af-fecting rates of pay, hours or work and other conditions of employment. It is understood that the company has the sole right to insti-tute all such changes as it may consider necessary, subject to the terms of this agreement. The union agrees to cooperate with the company at all times in maintaining a high degree of service to its customers and through conscientious endeavor and ap-plication of effort to strive for the lowest possible costs.
Professional Baseball	The player and the club recognize and agree that the player's participation in certain other sports may impair or destroy his ability and skill as a baseball player. Accordingly, the player agrees that he will not engage in professional boxing or

(Continued)

Exhibit 1.2
Examples of Work Rules

Exhibit 1.2
(Continued)

Job or Industry Classification	Work Rule
	wrestling, and that except with the written consent of the club, he will not engage in skiing, auto racing, motorcycle racing, sky diving or in any game or exhibition of football, soccer, professional league basketball, ice hockey, or other sport involving a substantial risk of personal injury.
Television	The latest version of the script will be made accessible to the player in the casting office 24 hours in advance of a scheduled reading or immediately after the scheduling of the interview, whichever last occurs.
Manufacturing	When employees are called to work at a time other than their regular reporting time, and after having clocked out, they shall be paid two hours plus one and one-half their straight time rate for all hours worked, but in no event will less than four hours at the straight rate be paid.
Cemeteries	In all cases where a grave is dug straight down, a second person shall be assigned to assist the digger after a depth of five feet is reached.

(1) swat flies in the cabin after takeoff, (2) prevent passengers from throwing lighted cigar butts out the windows, and (3) carry a railroad timetable in case of plane trouble. Today, the flight attendants' union is concerned with issues such as too much luggage stuffed into overhead compartments that may fall and hit a passenger and passenger use of cell phones during flights, which could pose a security risk by making it easier for terrorists to communicate with each other.[4]

An analysis of work rules helps to explain the complex output of the labor relations process. The formal labor agreement in this sense represents a compilation of jointly negotiated work rules. However, as discussed in Chapter 10, labor relations activities are not limited to the negotiation of work rules. The labor relations process also includes the everyday interpretation and application of work rules and the resolution of any disputes arising over such decisions.

Acquired Immune Deficiency Syndrome (AIDS) represents a working condition that has commanded employer and union concern, creating the need for appropriate work rules. Hospitals have written policies regarding occupational exposure to blood-borne infectious diseases such as AIDS. A nurses' union would seek to negotiate health and safety work rules aimed at protecting members from occupational exposure to the virus that causes AIDS.[5]

Companies and unions are also negotiating "no-smoking" rules in the work place both as a health benefit and a means of reducing health care costs associated with smoking related insurance claims. In 1908 a Columbia University professor insisted that "the deleterious effects of tobacco are greatly exaggerated," a belief that prevailed for the next 70 years.[6] Now, union and management officials and possibly arbitrators at thousands of facilities jointly determine whether the issuance of a no-smoking policy is reasonable and whether an employee was properly disciplined or discharged for violating the rule.

A majority of employers engage in one or more forms of electronic monitoring of employee work performance.[7] New technology such as computers and monitoring software, bar code scanners, and pressure-sensitive plates has enabled management to monitor employee performance in various ways, such as counting the number of keystrokes made on computer keyboards, listening to employees' telephone conversations with customers, or viewing computer files, e-mail messages, and Internet connections on company computers. Employers have a legitimate interest in evaluating employees' work performance and seeking to eliminate illegal employee misconduct. Employees have a legitimate interest in ensuring that their union representatives negotiate appropriate work rules to govern the time, place, and method of such electronic monitoring as well as the use of such information to reward or penalize employees' work performance.

Key Participants in the Labor Relations Process

Through the organization's structure, **managers** represent the interests of the ownership as well as their own self-interests. Managers include individuals who are delegated authority by the ownership to make decisions required to operate the organization and exist at various levels within the organization from first-line supervisors or department heads to the highest ranking management official (e.g., chief executive officer). Labor relations managers are typically found at corporate, divisional, and plant levels. Larger organizations that operate different facilities in different geographic locations may emphasize developing related objectives at upper organization levels to ensure that a particular work rule at one location, such as a wage rate for a particular job classification, does not adversely alter precedents or conditions set at another production facility.

Plant-level labor relations representatives implement these "corporate" directives, but they must also deal with other managers at each facility's location (particularly production and maintenance managers and first-line supervisors), who direct the daily work activities of hourly employees.

As will be further discussed in Chapter 10, first-line supervisors or department heads typically hear and attempt to resolve employees' grievances on the production floor. In some cases, lower-level managers are surprised to learn that higher-level management officials have overturned their decisions. Alert union leaders may use dissension or lack of clear communication among different levels of management officials to influence labor relations activities and the company's position toward unions.

Management consultants are individuals hired from outside the organization to provide some special service or expertise. The activities of management consultants in the labor relations process are varied and sometimes controversial, ranging from restructuring personnel practices in nonunion firms (in the absence of any active union-organizing campaign) to designing and presenting the employer's response throughout a formal union organizing campaign. Controversy occurs over the consultants' effectiveness and ethics. One union estimate found that consultants were involved in 75 percent of union-organizing campaigns.[8] "Employers who make threats of plant closings are more likely to hire outside consultants, discharge union activists, hold captive audience meetings and super-visor one-on-ones, establish employee involvement committees during the orga-nizing campaign, make unilateral changes in benefits and/or working conditions, use bribes and special favors, use electronic surveillance, threaten to report workers to the INS, and show anti-union films."[9] Research does show that the use of a management consultant can reduce the probability of a union win in very closely contested elections, but it does not appear to be as big an influence on union election outcomes as some other factors such as elec-tion-unit size or relevant labor market conditions.[10]

Management must be conscious of its competitors, who may challenge the company's product in quality, price, or service. Organizations with a good quali-ty labor–management relationship may gain a competitive advantage over firms that lack the ability to gain cooperation and consensus from employees in seeking to change to meet new competitive pressures.

Union representatives, usually elected by the members to represent their em-ployment interests, are a second key participant in the labor relations process. As elected representatives, union officials must consider the varied and sometimes conflicting interests of individual employees within the bargaining unit seeking to build a consensus for decisions that benefit the majority of constituents. Unlike managers who are appointed by higher-level managers, union officials are subject to the political pressure of majority rule if they wish to be re-elected to a union leadership position in the future. Unions as democratic organizations do experi-ence internal differences of view on policies and priorities that union officials must learn to effectively manage. Every union has its own history, traditions, per-sonalities, and accepted practices that can lead to observed differences across union organizations as well as within a particular union. While different unions may share common interests and positions on many issues of common concern, each union tends to value maintaining its own independence and sense of self-determination in representing the interests of its membership.

Certainly some of the most significant participants in the labor relations pro-cess are nonmanagerial **employees** because they often determine whether a union is even present in an organization (representation elections and union organizing drives are discussed in Chapter 5), whether a negotiated labor agreement is ac-cepted or rejected, and the extent to which a threatened strike is actually carried out (see Chapter 9).

Employees are treated here as a separate category because they may demon-strate **dual loyalty** to both their employer and union organization.[11] For example, public employees such as firefighters, police, and teachers may feel torn between the critical or professional nature of their jobs and the strategic advantages of a strike. Most employees want their organizations to be competitive and at the same time, they want to share in the rewards of competitive success. Employees' interests may shape the existence and content of particular work rules and thus, employees can be considered a third key participant in the labor relations process.

The **government** acting through its different branches—executive, legislative, and judicial—at the federal, state, and local levels represents a fourth key partic-ipant in the labor relations process. As discussed in Chapters 2 and 3, the govern-ment's role in regulating labor relations has gradually increased over time as the importance of labor relations to the effective functioning of the economy became more apparent. In the public sector, government officials also serve as managers in the labor relations process, representing both taxpayers and the general pub-lic's interests (discussed in Chapter 13).

In the private sector the federal government has traditionally played an indirect role in determining the outcomes of work rule negotiations, unlike the role of government in many other industrialized countries (see Chapter 14). The federal government's hands-off approach in most private-sector bargaining situations is based on the belief that most management and union officials are better equipped than their government counterparts to assess their needs and limitations and reach a mutually acceptable labor agreement.

Although the federal government does not dictate the terms of a negotiated labor agreement; laws, judicial decisions, and administrative agencies such as the National Labor Relations Board (NLRB) can influence work rules and the ability to exercise legally granted rights. For example, legislation to deregulate the trucking and airline industries has contributed to reduced union membership and economic gains for employees.[12]

Union and management officials cannot negotiate a mandatory retirement age of 60 years because this would conflict with the Age Discrimination in Employment Act. Although some coal miners have long believed that females working in mines would be bad luck, union and management officials would be violating sexual discrimination aspects of the Civil Rights Act if they negotiated a provision prohibiting female employees from working in the mines.

Third-party neutrals (i.e., mediators and arbitrators) represent a final key participant in the labor relations process. Differences between union and management officials that arise in negotiating the terms of a labor agreement (interest disputes) or administering its provisions (rights disputes) are often resolved with the aid of a third-party neutral. **Mediators** (discussed in Chapters 9 and 13) often supplied by the Federal Mediation and Conciliation Service (FMCS) or a state or private mediation agency may be used to help resolve interest disputes during contract negotiations. The mediator assists the union and management officials in resolving their differences to achieve a voluntary settlement themselves. The mediator does not possess any binding legal authority to require the parties to settle an interest dispute, but he or she will offer advice to help each party clarify their own priorities and assessment of costs or risks associated with failing to reach a voluntary agreement.

An **arbitrator** is a third-party neutral hired by union and management representatives to make a final and binding decision on a disputed issue. While final and binding arbitration may occasionally be used to resolve an interest dispute (see Chapter 9), most often it is used to resolve rights-type disputes arising during the term of a labor agreement over the interpretation or application of the contract's language (see Chapters 11 and 12).

THREE BASIC ASSUMPTIONS UNDERLYING U.S. LABOR RELATIONS

To better understand the U.S. labor relations system and the actions of its participants, it is helpful to bear in mind certain underlying assumptions that affect the thinking and behavior of most individuals within the system. Whereas the degree of support by some participants for these three basic assumptions has varied over the course of U.S. labor history, these assumptions have been the basis for a majority consensus for many years.

First, the adoption and support of a free enterprise (capitalist) economic system in the United States creates an inherent conflict of interest between employers (owners) and employees. Both employees and employers seek to advance their own self-interests. Employers seek to maximize their return on capital invested while employees seek to advance their pay, working conditions, and job security. Most of the interests employees seek to advance through the collective bargaining process represent an increased cost to the employer which, unless offset by cost savings elsewhere or higher productivity, may reduce the investment return desired by ownership. This creates a natural tension within a capitalist economic system between the pursuits of employees' and employers' legitimate interests. Such conflict should not be viewed in a negative light but rather as simply a reality of business operation which must be managed effectively. The presence of some degree of inherent conflict between employer and employee interests should also not be viewed as precluding opportunities for cooperation between the parties. Both employees and employers share a common interest in ensuring that the organization is competitive. Maintaining a sufficient number of qualified and motivated employees is necessary for an employer to attain desired organizational goals (e.g., productivity, product or service quality). Profits in turn permit an organization to provide competitive wages, benefits, and working conditions to help ensure the recruitment and retention of qualified employees. Ideally, employees perceive their own self-interest as best advanced by seeking to advance the interests of the organization as a whole.

A second underlying assumption of the U.S. labor relations system is that employees in a free and democratic society have a right to independently pursue their employment interests using lawful means. Employees should have a right to determine for themselves what is in their best interests and to pursue means of attaining such interests so long as the tactics used are legal. Only by allowing individuals to pursue their legitimate interests can a society foster the necessary support for prevailing economic, social, and political systems used to sustain the country. Employees may choose to pursue their legitimate interests on an individual basis or by joining together in a labor organization.

A third underlying assumption of the U.S. labor relations system is that collective bargaining provides a process for meaningful employee participation through independently chosen representatives in the determination of work rules. Employees in the U.S. labor relations system are not required to form or join a labor organization for the purpose of engaging in collective bargaining, but they are permitted to do so when a majority of the employee group expresses such a preference. In the absence of collective bargaining, individual bargaining may occur between an employer and his or her employee. Labor history suggests that most employees are at a relative bargaining power disadvantage in individual bargaining when confronted with the greater resources of their employer, but each employee is free to determine the degree of satisfaction that his own individual bargaining experience provides. Many unrepresented employees, for a variety of reasons, do not attempt to engage in individual or collective bargaining, thereby permitting the employer to unilaterally (without bargaining) establish work rules, setting the terms and conditions of employment. In limited cases, employment terms may be mandated by government action (e.g., minimum wage law, safety, and health conditions).

Exhibit 1.3 presents a list of some basic characteristics of the private-sector U.S. labor relations system. These characteristics will be discussed in further detail throughout the text.

- Primarily a *bilateral process* (union and management) governed by a *framework of labor laws.* For example, the Labor Management Relations Act (LMRA), Labor Management Reporting and Disclosure Act (LMRDA), Railway Labor Act (RLA), Occupational Safety and Health Act (OSHA), Family Medical Leave Act (FMLA), Employee Retirement and Income Security Act (ERISA), Americans with Disabilities Act (ADA), Norris-LaGuardia Act, and anti-discrimination laws.

- A *highly decentralized bargaining structure* that results in a large number of labor contracts negotiated most often between a single employer and a specific union to cover a defined group of employees (bargaining unit) at a specific geographic location.

- Recognition of the key legal principles of *majority rule* and *exclusive bargaining representation.* No union can gain the right to represent a group of employees for purposes of collective bargaining without first demonstrating the majority support (50% + 1) of the employees in that group. Once recognized, the union is the only legal representative authorized to negotiate work rules with the employer to establish the work group's terms and conditions of employment.

- Permits the *use of economic pressure* (e.g., strike, lockout, picketing, and boycott) to aid the parties (union and management) in reaching a voluntary negotiated settlement of interest disputes over what the terms and conditions of employment will be.

- Encourages the *use of final and binding arbitration,* if voluntary grievance negotiation efforts fail, to resolve rights disputes which arise during the term of a contract over the interpretation or application of the labor agreement's terms.

- Characterized by *significant employer opposition to employee efforts to organize and bargain collectively* through representation by an independent labor union chosen by the employees themselves.

Exhibit 1.3

Basic Characteristics of the U.S. Private Sector Labor Relations System

Constraints or Influences Affecting Participants' Negotiation and Administration of Work Rules

The labor relations participants who affect the development of work rules are influenced by external variables or constraints in their labor relations activities (see the outer circle of Exhibit 1.1). These constraints/influences can sometimes affect one another and may relate to a particular firm, local community, or society in general. The following discussion furnishes a few illustrations of how these constraints/influences can affect the existence and content of work rules.

State of the Economy: National, Industrial, and Firm-Specific Indicators

The state of the **economy** is usually referred to by indicating movement among such quantitative indicators as inflation, unemployment, and productivity. During the 1980s, the United States witnessed a rising inflation rate, which influenced the negotiation of work rules—notably, union insistence that a labor agreement include provisions to increase wages if increases occur in the cost of living (see Chapter 7). In the early 1990s, the focus of negotiations was on wage increases, enhancing employee benefits, and containing rising health care costs. However, in the late 1990s and the early 2000s, with slow economic growth, low inflation, and rising job losses, union and management negotiators returned to an emphasis on job security and other job protection issues. In recent years many employers have cited continued competitive pressure as a reason to address inefficient work rules and slow the growth in employee benefits cost such as pension and health care plans.

Two other economic indicators that can affect work rules are interest and unemployment rates. An increase in interest rates could slow home and industrial construction projects. The Federal Reserve Board voted to raise interest rates 17 times between June 2004 and June 2006 out of concern that too rapid economic growth might trigger an increase in consumer inflation.[13] More recently, the Federal Reserve Board has adopted a stable interest policy, believing that economic growth and inflationary pressures were in relative balance. If employees' wage gains do not at least match the rate of increase in consumer prices (inflation rate), the purchasing power of employees declines, adversely affecting employees' standard of living. If interest rates are raised to fight inflation, employees will pay more for consumer debt (e.g., credit cards, auto or home loans). A union might respond to such an interest/inflation rate environment by seeking to negotiate pay improvements which exceed the rate of inflation as well as offering group discount rates to members on benefits like credit cards or various types of consumer loans.

The unemployment rate affects work rules providing job protection. Chapter 6 discusses ways in which the unemployment rate can affect the bargaining power of union and management officials. If this and other economic measures pertaining to the gross national product, productivity, cost of living, compensation at all employee levels, and exports and imports are unfavorable, unions will be more likely to accept bargaining concessions. By the same token, strong product sales, economic growth, and low unemployment tend to strengthen union bargaining power as employers have more reason to compromise to avoid any disruption in the production of current products or services.

Over the period 1994–2004, annual job growth in the U.S. labor market averaged 1.2 percent, the same rate of growth that is projected for the next decade (2004–2014).[14] Annual unemployment rates over the period 1994–2006 have averaged between 4 percent (2000) and 6.1 percent (1994).[15] Manufacturing employment has been particularly hard hit, declining 16 percent over the 1994–2004 period and projected to decline another 5 percent over the next decade (2004–2014). Outsourcing of jobs to other countries, increasing global competition and domestic nonunion competition, and continued productivity growth through technological innovation are some of the factors that have contributed to job loss in the manufacturing sector and posed problems for national unions whose membership has traditionally been centered in basic manufacturing industries such as steel, auto, rubber, paper, textiles, chemicals, and plastics.[16]

With a loss of jobs, job security issues become a more important focus of many contract negotiations. A three-month strike involving 12 Goodyear Tire and Rubber Company plants and more than 10,000 union members represented by the United Steelworkers Union occurred over a management proposal to close two to four plants and shift production work overseas to plants owned by the company.[17] Striking workers returned to work in January 2007 with a new three-year contract under which the company committed to invest $550 million in existing U.S. plants to increase their ability to efficiently produce high value-added branded tires. One plant producing lower value-added, private-label tires will be closed under the new agreement, but the company agreed to delay that closure by 12 months to facilitate workers' transition to other employment opportunities. The company expects the new labor contract to produce savings of $70 million in 2007, $240 million in 2008, and $300 million in 2009.

As Goodyear's chairman and CEO Robert Kregan stated, "Our goal was always to reach a fair agreement that improves our ability to compete and win with customers. This agreement would accomplish that goal."[18]

The skills, wage levels, and availability of employees in a relevant **labor market** can affect negotiated work rules. Management is often concerned with ensuring that an adequate supply of labor of the skill levels required to operate is available in a particular community. For example, a firm needing skilled employees from a relatively low-skilled labor market supply would probably wish to negotiate work rules regarding apprenticeship programs or other forms of job training. Management would also consider negotiating a reasonable employee probationary period (e.g., 60–120 days) within which it could terminate a union-represented employee who cannot learn the job and perform adequately with no union right to protest the action through the labor contract's grievance procedure.

One effort being taken to assist employees in adjusting to changes in labor market forces is training. As far back as 1986, the Alliance for Employee Growth and Development, Inc. was created as a joint enterprise by AT&T, the CWA, and the IBEW to help displaced workers. By 1989, the focus had changed to preparing workers to handle new technologies. The Alliance set up Technicians for Tomorrow to train employees to qualify for future jobs with the company. Other outstanding examples include the UAW/General Motors Skills Centers and the joint training programs of Ford Motor Company and the UAW. In the building trades, unions have played a major role in training skilled workers. Because workers move from employer to employer on a regular basis, single construction companies have less financial incentive to train employees who may end up working for a competitor. Therefore, the unions, through their training and apprenticeship programs, provide an obvious contribution to the general national welfare. In fact, unions and their contractors outspend their nonunion counterparts by a ratio of 50 to 1 in training investments.[19]

Both management and union representatives should share an interest in establishing competitive compensation rates for comparably skilled employees within a relevant external labor market and internally within the firm itself. A job with higher skill or responsibility requirements should earn a higher compensation rate than jobs with less skill or job responsibility requirements. In some cases where the employer faces significant labor cost competition from nonunion or foreign employers, a union may have to agree to compensation or other flexible work rule changes which will permit a unionized employer to remain competitive in pricing goods or services sold in the firm's product or service markets.

The labor relations process can be affected by the **product or service market** where the company either sells its product or purchases key elements required for production of its products or services. Management would be more vulnerable if a strike occurred at a time when major customer sales were anticipated or on-time delivery of promised goods was critical to meet a customer's needs. For example, management at a brewery would prefer to avoid a labor agreement expiring, possibly leading to a strike, during the summer months when significant beverage sales are anticipated. A public school system would much prefer a contract expiration date in early summer after the regular school year has ended, rather than risk a possible work stoppage disruption if the contract expiration date coincided with the first day of the new school year.

A second dimension of the product market, the source of key elements for product manufacture, can be a factor affecting union members' perceptions of job security. For example, the United Auto Workers (UAW) union is concerned over the fact that many of the parts utilized in U.S. automobiles are being manufactured in other countries, creating job opportunities for foreign workers but not for UAW-represented employees.[20]

Another important consideration in the labor relations process is the **financial market,** the arena in which the employers (and unions) seek to borrow funds to finance their investment strategies. Companies must consider exchange rate money value differences among countries, which affect the profitability of plant location and sales marketing decisions. Exchange rates between countries (see Chapter 14) can alter companies' investment strategies because exchange rates affect comparative wage rates and, consequently, the comparative labor costs of production. As an example, when the peso in Mexico was devalued by as much as 50 percent of the U.S. dollar, the labor costs of production in Mexico declined dramatically and made producing goods in Mexico more attractive and economical for multinational corporations. A strong euro currency valuation in comparison to the U.S. dollar helped drive up labor production costs in European countries such as Germany, encouraging automakers such as Daimler AG (Mercedes) and Bavarian Motor Works (BMW) to build production plants in the United States.

When a company wants to expand its plant capacity and increase jobs, it often has to borrow money in the financial markets at the same time as it may request wage concessions from a union (see Chapter 7) or request the elimination of work rule restrictions to improve productivity (see Chapter 8). Unions must be able to perform financial valuation analysis in order to support, for example, an employee stock option plan (ESOP) (see Chapter 7) or anticipate the advantages or disadvantages of the sale or merger of an existing employer's operations with another competitor or private equity fund from the perspective of union-represented employees.

Labor unions have been able to use their financial resources and become active in the financial markets as a source of capital. With U.S. employee pension funds valued in excess of $7 trillion, many unions believe that decisions on how to invest those funds ought to take into consideration the effect of capital investments on the economic and job security interests of union members.[21] The United Steelworkers have created a regional investment fund of $100 million called the Heartland Labor Capital Project, which has the following objectives: 1) invest in regional business and protect jobs; 2) promote economic awareness as well as training workers and unions and raising the level of influence on economic development; 3) stimulate regional economies; 4) encourage regional business enterprises by involving both labor and its allies to support institutional development; 5) provide capital to enterprises where unions have created more democratic and sustainable practices; and 6) provide prudent returns to investors.[22] Other unions, including the AFL-CIO, have similar programs to promote jobs for union members.

Perhaps the most immediate and persistent influence on the creation of work rules is the **technology** of a particular workplace. Technology has four dimensions: 1) equipment used in the operation; 2) the pace and scheduling of work; 3) characteristics of the work environment and tasks to be performed; and 4) information exchange. Consider, for example, the major equipment found at a steel mill blast furnace, which requires a very high temperature for operation. Such a furnace cannot simply be turned on and off like a household oven. Often several days are required for either reaching the high operating temperature or for cooling the furnace for maintenance. This equipment characteristic affects the facility's work rules. In essence, steel mills must operate 24 hours a day, seven days a week—a situation prompting related work rules such as wage premiums for working the night shift, weekends, or holidays. Other continuous operating organizations like hospitals or large retail centers may face similar work rule issues.

In some cases the introduction of equipment reduces or eliminates employees in a particular job classification. This situation occurs when industrial robots handle tasks formerly performed by employees. A rather common application occurs in the auto industry, where mechanically joined arms perform spot welding, spraying, machine unloading, and assembly. Unions faced with having membership replaced by robots have increased related bargaining demands to protect their members' job security such as more paid time off; fewer hours comprising a regular work week (e.g., 35 or 38 hours versus a 40-hour week); or job transfer or retraining rights enabling displaced workers to fill available vacant employment opportunities.

Changes in technology have raised the level and type of skill requirements for many workers. While most competing firms have access to the same technology, the ability to apply that technology using the skills and brainpower of their employees ultimately determines whether any real competitive advantage is achieved. Technology improvements have created a greater demand for more highly skilled workers who are able to assume multiple responsibilities while reducing the demand for strictly manual labor. Although both profits and productivity growth have improved, average real hourly compensation for American workers has not changed significantly over the last 20 years, creating increasing stress on workers seeking to maintain a middle class standard of living.[23]

Technological change can also result in certain jobs requiring fewer skills to perform. In the supermarket industry, electronic scanners are used to change item prices, record customers' purchases, and maintain products' inventory counts. These activities result in a need for fewer employees to stock shelves and reduced skill requirements and compensation for cashiers.

The pace and scheduling of the workday also affect the work rules of certain occupations. For example, bus companies optimizing their productivity and revenue would concentrate on rush-hour traffic (6:00–9:00 A.M., 3:00–7:00 P.M.) when buses would be likely to be filled with passengers. However, problems would remain in scheduling work because many bus drivers might have a daily eight-hour work schedule of three hours on, three hours off, one hour on, two hours off, and four hours on. Because of the nature of the work, most labor agreements in related industries have provisions pertaining to the permissible number, length, and possible compensation of intervals (times off) between daily work assignments.

Computer operations can help both union and management officials in their daily labor relations activities. Union officers can use computer applications to maintain membership and dues records, as well as word processing for communication to the membership. Union and management officials can also use computer applications in the areas of contract negotiations (costing the various proposals, writing contract language) and administration (maintenance and research of grievances and arbitration decisions).[24] Union officers can use computer applications to maintain union records, union membership training, as well as word processing for communicating with the union's membership.[25] E-mail, Internet, and Web pages are used to keep employees and union members informed of progress during negotiations. Also, both unions and management are frequently using these communication tools during union organizing campaigns. (See Chapter 4, which discusses how unions are using computer technology.)

The American Federation of Labor–Congress of Industrial Organizations (AFL-CIO) has introduced two computer information networks, Labor-NET

LABOR RELATIONS IN ACTION

Getting Online with Labor Relations Research

The number of electronic sources for locating information on collective bargaining and labor relations is constantly increasing. The most efficient method for finding reports in journals, magazines, newspapers, and other periodical literature is through the use of online research databases, which are offered by most university and college libraries to their students, faculty, and staff members. You will choose your sources depending on the time period you want to cover, the amount of information you need, and the availability of resources in your area. Libraries still maintain a collection of print indexes, but most of these are being replaced by online versions, which allow for faster searching and less maintenance by the library.

Online databases have several advantages over print indexes, including currency, the ability to print in a variety of formats, the ability to combine terms and other qualifiers (e.g., date, language, and publication title) to broaden or narrow a search, the ability to e-mail or download articles, and availability by remote access. A few disadvantages are the commitment of time to become skilled in their use, the availability of only selected content in some databases, and overlapping titles from database to database.

Subscriptions to online databases that provide access to indexing or the full text of articles on business topics are being sold by a number of vendors, including Lexis-Nexis, ProQuest (formerly University Microfilms or UMI), OCLC (FirstSearch), Gale (part of Cengage Learning,

formerly Thomson Learning), EBSCO, and H. W. Wilson. Databases specifically devoted to labor relations cases and issues are provided by the Bureau of National Affairs (BNA) and Commerce Clearing House (CCH). Most of these databases are provided through the Web, although there are a few that are still available electronically only on CD-ROM.

Online databases that can be searched from university and college libraries also can usually be searched from a dorm room, home, or office with appropriate user authentication. Until a few years ago, the content of many of these databases was available only through mediated searches requested by a student or faculty member and performed by a librarian, who would then pass on the cost of the search to the requestor. These costs included a connection fee, ranging from $1.60 to $2.20 per connect minute, and charges for each record displayed, ranging from $0.50 per record to $1.40 per record. Web-based electronic resources have virtually eliminated the need for mediated searches and allow students to perform free searches with or without the assistance of a librarian.

General business indexes are extremely useful in locating articles on collective bargaining. *Business Periodicals Index,* published by the H. W. Wilson Company, is a print index that is still found in most libraries and, for many years, was the only business index in a small library. The online version of the index is *Wilson Business Abstracts,* which includes indexing and abstracting of the *The Wall Street Journal* and the business section of *The New York Times,* as well as more than 600 publications that date back to 1952. *Wilson Business Full Text* provides access to full text articles in more than 350 publications that date back to 1995.

(for members only) and Labor-WEB (public access), the organization's new "home page" on the Internet's World Wide Web that will enable practitioners and students of industrial relations to become well informed on current developments.[26] One AFL-CIO official contends that labor's message will be communicated to more people because most American families have computers at home or have access to computers at their work site. Many students needing to research a current labor relations topic for a class assignment may find the above "Labor Relations in Action" box helpful.

International Forces

The war in Iraq affected thousands of Americans, including union members called up as reservists. Although companies are required to retain the reservists' positions, some companies may be reluctant to hire and train new employees who may have to be laid off upon return of the reservists. Instead, companies may require other

Other general business periodical databases that are useful for finding trade publications are *ABI/INFORM Trade and Industry* (ProQuest), *Business and Industry* (Gale RDS), *Business and Management Practices* (FirstSearch), and the Business News portion of LexisNexis Academic. Trade journals such as *Automotive News, Supermarket News, Editor & Publisher,* and *Modern Healthcare* can provide related insights into labor issues and unions such as the United Autoworkers (UAW), United Food and Commercial Workers (UFCW), Newspaper Guild, and American Nurses Association, respectively.

ABI/INFORM Global, produced by ProQuest, was one of the first electronic databases to provide an index to the scholarly literature of business, although coverage is not limited to scholarly titles. Coverage also includes general business magazines and trade periodicals. *ABI/INFORM* contains abstracts and full-text articles published from 1971 to the present. Recently, ProQuest began to offer *ABI/INFORM Archive,* which provides full-text articles published from 1918 to 1986. EBSCO *Business Source Premier* is another comprehensive business periodical database that offers 2,300 scholarly journals and general business periodicals, including *BusinessWeek, Forbes, Fortune, American Banker,* and many others. EBSCO has exclusive rights to the electronic version of *Harvard Business Review.*

Newspapers are an excellent source of business information because of the detailed analysis of events not often found in other periodical literature. Because newspapers are often published daily, they offer the latest news about ongoing labor negotiations or work stoppages. Citations to articles in leading newspapers may be found in print indexes, whereas a rapidly increasing number of electronic indexes provide the complete text and indexing of national and regional newspapers. The major publishers of online full-text newspapers include Knight-Ridder, Lexis-Nexis, Newsbank, and ProQuest. Many major newspapers maintain online Web sites which offer free access to many stories (e.g., *The Washington Post, USA Today, Detroit Free Press,* and *Los Angeles Times*). The text of *The Wall Street Journal* is offered by several sources, and students can also sign up for a subscription to the online WSJ, which includes articles not found in the print copy of the newspaper. WSJ offers a special subscription for professors and students, which can be found on the Web site at http://www.wsj.com.

LexisNexis Academic and *Business Newsbank Plus* are reliable sources to consult for articles from regional newspapers about a particular event published in the city or region where the event took place. The regional publications often offer a different perspective from that of a national newspaper.

The *Daily Labor Report,* published by The Bureau of National Affairs in both print and online versions, is extremely useful in researching current labor relations topics. Coverage includes legislation pending in Congress, discussion of court cases, bargaining settlements, statistical information, and other items relating to labor. BNA also publishes the Labor and Employment Law Library, providing the full text of labor and employment cases and manuals for answering day-to-day labor and employment law questions. Exploring the Web Internet exercises at the end of each chapter in this book should also be helpful in exploring different labor relations topics further.

employees to work more overtime and temporarily reclassify employees (through promotions or transfers) to fill the positions left vacant by the call-up of the reservists.

Unions are concerned about the job security and economic impact of "free trade agreements" such as the North American Free-Trade Agreement (NAFTA; discussed more in Chapters 2 and 14) involving the United States, Canada, and Mexico. While imports from Mexico have clearly increased the U.S. trade deficit with Mexico since the enactment of NAFTA, the effect of NAFTA on U.S. employment and wages tends to be less clear.[27] Unions tend to stress "fair trade" rather than "free trade" in discussing ways to ensure that domestic companies can compete effectively in global markets. In addition to fostering more cooperation with foreign-based labor organizations, U.S. unions also seek to promote policies aimed at raising pay, working conditions, environmental and safety standards applicable to workers in foreign countries.[28] Not only does such an approach serve to raise the living standards of workers in their own countries, it also serves to reduce the labor cost advantage of moving work done by U.S. workers to those foreign countries, thus enhancing job security for U.S. workers.

International trade is a major influence in the labor relations process. Imports/exports, trade deficits, exchange rates, capital investments, and jobs are interconnected. As an example, Chinese exports to the United States have risen from $39 billion in 1994 to about $233 billion in 2006, accounting for approximately 25 percent of the total record $764 billion U.S. trade deficit.[29] Some economists claim that China's currency is undervalued by 15 to 25 percent. Coupled with a low-wage workforce, China has a competitive advantage in trade with the United States. At the same time, 63 percent of the rise in Chinese exports has come from foreign companies, including approximately 51,000 U.S. firms operating Chinese subsidiaries or engaged in joint ventures.[30]

Major retailers, like Target and Wal-Mart, depend on low-priced imports from China. Wal-Mart alone imported $18 billion worth of products from China in 2004, accounting for nearly half of all Chinese imports to the United States.[31] These imports help to keep inflation rates low and have helped the Federal Reserve to keep interest rates in the United States at their lowest levels in four decades.[32] A strong U.S. dollar has made imports appear cheap and contributed to the growing U.S. current account deficit (mainly comprised of the trade deficit but including capital income and transfers). "With large and persistent external deficits, the United States has swung from being the world's largest creditor nation to its largest debtor, with net foreign liabilities now at about one-fourth of GDP (gross domestic product)."[33]

The trend toward globalization has been characterized as free-market capitalism, which places enormous competitive pressures on all firms that become part of the global economy. Multinational firms that sell globally are pressured to produce globally by segmenting their production chains and outsourcing each segment to the country that can produce cheapest and most efficiently. Newly industrialized countries are able to compete in price-conscious markets by paying lower wages, offering fewer benefits, and providing less ideal working conditions than those available in the United States. In addition, due to the diversity and customization made possible by computer-based technology, the cost advantages of American-style mass production have been reduced.[34]

Labor unions have been active in the international arena since their beginning. American labor unions have a long history of resisting the importation of foreign products. Over the last two centuries, organized labor has been one of the more protectionist institutions in America. This position should not be a surprise because unions are democratic organizations that must reflect the interests and needs of their members, who believe that their jobs are endangered by foreign imports. Most union members have little inclination to accept assurances that they will find another comparable job or that in the long run, everyone will be better off. Organized labor unsuccessfully opposed trade legislation such as NAFTA and have consistently encouraged Congress to ensure that trade agreements with other countries contain safeguards for workers' rights and environmental protections applicable to foreign trading partners. American unions continue to support positions of the International Labor Organization (ILO), a United Nations-sponsored labor federation headquartered in Geneva, Switzerland, which has adopted "core labor standards" promoting basic workers' rights such as freedom of association, collective bargaining, rights to earn a living wage in a safe workplace, and the prevention of forced child labor.[35] Organized labor continues to engage in pressure tactics before the World Trade

Organization and the International Monetary Fund to forge links between international trading rights and labor standards.[36]

Public Opinion

Public opinion is a factor which affects the labor relations process. The mass media (television, radio, newspapers, movies, music) represent an important influence within a community, serving as both a generator and conduit of community opinion. Media sources often tend to perpetuate a negative stereotype of unions. "When put together, the collective media image portrays unions as greedy and corrupt institutions, eager to strike, protective of unproductive workers, heedless of America's need to compete internationally, and generally outmoded in a society that would have no disruptive class antagonisms were it not for a few self-aggrandizing union hot-heads."[37] The media are profit-making businesses, and at least one prominent union official contends that this orientation biases the reporting of labor relations activities:

> The media tend to cover collective bargaining as if it were a pier six brawl. The intricate moves and trade-offs that really make up bargaining aren't as newsy as impassioned rhetoric or a picket line confrontation. Reporters are given little training in covering collective bargaining. They are told to look for the "news"—the fist fight, the walkout, the heated exchange—and, as a result, frequently miss the "story," which is the settlement.... Every union proposal is a "demand," every management proposal is an "offer."[38]

An analysis of 40 years of *The New York Times* columns concerning labor unions agreed with the preceding quotation as it found that the newspaper had become increasingly concentrated on strike activities and had exaggerated the frequency of strikes.[39] Media coverage of labor issues often treat the subject matter as a consumer issue, focusing on how consumer prices or the availability of goods or services may be affected rather than focusing on the concerns of the workers affected by the labor issue.[40]

Public support for labor unions has remained positive over time. A 2006 Gallup survey reported 59 percent of Americans approve of labor unions.[41] Most Americans believe that unions are helpful to their members, to the companies where workers are organized, and to the U.S. economy in general. However, only one-third of survey respondents believe that unions help workers who are not members of a union. The general public has also in recent years sympathized more with unions than companies involved in labor disputes reported by the media.

Public opinion of institutions in general is low in the United States with a majority of the public currently expressing confidence in only 3 out of 15 surveyed American institutions (the military, the police, and the church or organized religion).[42] Only 24 percent of the public expressed a lot of confidence in organized labor, but this rating did rank ahead of the public's opinion of Congress (19 percent) and big business (18 percent).

Public opinion, like other external influences, can affect one or more phases of the labor relations process, as well as the content of negotiated work rules. After experiencing a bitter, well-publicized strike between Caterpillar and the UAW, the mayor of Peoria, Illinois, feared employers would not locate in his community: "We had worked so hard to make this a city with the image of having a cohesive relationship between labor and management, a place that people should think about expanding their businesses or opening new ones. Now comes this strike, which is going to damage our reputation."[43]

In some cases, a community may stress its low union membership level or the anti-union attitudes of citizens as a benefit to encourage business organizations to expand or relocate there.

Union officials are aware of the significant influence that public opinion can have on the labor relations process. Albert Shanker, former president of the American Federation of Teachers, indicated why he wrote the first of 1,000 columns entitled "Where We Stand." After strikes were conducted by his union, Shanker reflected,

> *I became one of the best-known figures in New York City, but people saw me only as a militant union leader—urging teachers to strike, refusing to settle, going to jail. In late 1968, I became convinced that I had been dead wrong in believing that the public's opinion of me didn't matter. Public schools depend on public support. And the public was not likely to support the schools for long if they thought teachers were led by a powerful madman....I decided to devote some time and energy to letting the public know that the union's president was someone who read books and had ideals and ideas about how to fix the schools.*[44]

Union officials seek to enhance public opinion in three general ways: monitoring and reacting to negative comments made in the media; getting organized labor's positive message out to the community; and forming alliances with various groups in the community. For example, the AFL-CIO recently supported a march sponsored by the Rainbow PUSH Coalition in New Orleans, Louisiana, to encourage faster government action to rebuild homes and communities devastated by Hurricanes Katrina and Rita.[45] The AFL-CIO has created its own Gulf Coast Revitalization Program, committing $1 billion dollars over seven years to fund housing and economic development initiatives. Organized labor continues to work with community-based religious, civil rights, and environmental groups on issues of shared interests, such as improving health care access and affordability, raising the minimum wage, and ensuring economic and social justice on the job and within the communities in which workers live.[46]

Unions have also become more sophisticated in creating their own media campaigns to support union membership and bargaining activities. Some efforts such as Wakeupwalmart.com or Walmartwatch.com are targeted at a specific company while others target a specific issue, such as the "Health Care Hustle" Web site sponsored by Working America, an affiliate of the AFL-CIO representing 1.5 million employees who currently are not members of an organized bargaining unit.[47]

In some cases, organized labor has cultivated alliances with business organizations. A coalition including Wal-Mart, AT&T Inc., Intel Corporation, the Service Employees International Union, and the Communications Workers of America is actively pushing public policy changes that would provide affordable health care coverage to all Americans, especially the 46 million citizens who currently have no health care coverage plan.[48] Another example is "Stand up for Steel," involving the AFL-CIO, United Steelworkers of America, and leading American steel companies who urged the public to ensure a "fair global trade environment" by swiftly and effectively dealing with foreign governments and companies that illegally or unfairly dump their steel products into U.S. markets.[49]

UNION MEMBERSHIP

Union membership in the United States has shown a steady gradual decline as a proportion of the total labor force (i.e., comprising all employed persons 16 years of age or older). In 2006, union membership was 15.4 million members

LABOR RELATIONS IN ACTION
Are Unions Still Relevant?

The answer to the provocative question of whether unions are still relevant in today's economy may depend on who you ask. Andrew Stern, president of the 1.8 million member Service Employees International Union (SEIU) believes the need for unions today may be greater than at any time in the past 75 years.

I think American workers want a voice on their job. The question is: Will unions change to become better partners with employers to respond to what is now a global economy where more people went to work in the U.S. in retail than in manufacturing? We want to find a 21st century new model that may look more like a European model, that is less focused on individual grievances, more focused on industry needs. We don't see our employers as enemies. We need to build successful employers [and] as a part of that you need to be involved and have a voice, and everyone needs to share in the success of an employer, not just the shareholders and executives.[a]

The AFL-CIO shares the belief that unions are just as important today as ever and views one important union role as safeguarding workers' past gains while seeking a fair share of future prosperity.

The nature of work in America is changing. Employers are trying to shed responsibilities—for providing health insurance, good pension coverage, reasonable work hours and job safety protections, for example—while making workers' jobs and incomes less secure through downsizing, part-timing and contracting out. Working people need a voice at work to keep employers from making our jobs like they did 100 years ago, with sweatshop conditions, unlivable wages and 70-hour work weeks.[b]

A survey of Canadian employees reported that the top three advantages of unions were that they made health and safety, job security, and benefits a lot better on the job.[c] While agreeing that it was important for workers to have a voice on the job, more Canadians preferred an employee association form of representation that would take up problems on behalf of workers with management than the traditional Canadian union model.

Employers, particularly those who currently are non-union, are more likely to argue that unions today are no longer necessary. "... the protections unions used to seek, such as from unfair dismissal and dangerous workplaces, have—with labor's ardent support—been taken over by government."[d] What were once considered significant employee pension and health care benefit gains under union contracts are now referred to as "high legacy costs" by unionized employers in industries such as airlines and autos, making those employers less competitive and threatening job security.[e]

Ultimately, what matters is how employees will answer the question of whether unions are still relevant. The issue of why employees join a union will be explored further in Chapter 5.

---

[a]Kris Maher, "Are Unions Relevant?" *The Wall Street Journal*, January 22, 2007, p. R-5.
[b]AFL-CIO, "What Is the AFL-CIO? Get the Union Facts," *Union Facts*, (accessed June 1, 2007), p. 2 at http://www.aflcio.org/aboutus/faq/.
[c]Uyen Vu, "Employees Want a Collective Voice, but Not Necessarily a Union, Survey Says," *Canadian HR Reporter*, 16 (20), November 17, 2003, pp. 3, 11.
[d]Robert J. Grossman, "Do Unions Pay?" *HR Magazine*, 50 (5), May 2005, p. 49.
[e]Michael Barone, "Big Labor, RIP," *The Wall Street Journal*, July 28, 2005, p. A-10.

---

or 12 percent of the 128.2 million wage and salary employees in the total U.S. labor force.[50] In 1945, union membership was about 36 percent of the total labor force. **Union density,** the proportion of a total group (e.g., national labor force, state labor force, industry, company, or geographic region), comprised of union members is one measure of relative union strength or potential influence. One estimate predicts that unions would need to organize one million new members annually to increase the union density level in the total labor force by one percent.[51] Exhibit 1.4 shows union membership data trends since 1975.

Unions typically represent a higher number of employees than are actually union members because a simple majority of employees must support a union

Exhibit 1.4

Union Membership Trends, 1975–2006 (in thousands)

Year	Total Employment	Union Members	Percent Union Members	Percent Represented for Bargaining
1975	75,703.9	16,778.3	22.2	—
1980	87,479.5	20,095.3	23.0	25.7
1985	94,5205	16,996.1	18.0	20.5
1990	103,904	16,739.8	16.1	18.3
1995	110,038.1	16,359.3	14.9	16.7
2000	120,785.6	16,258.2	13.5	14.9
2005	125,889.3	15,685.4	12.5	13.7
2006	128,237.2	15,359.1	12.0	13.1

Data is based upon information in the *Current Population Survey* (CPS) compiled by the Bureau of Labor Statistics, U.S. Department of Labor.

SOURCE: Barry Hirsch and David Macpherson, "Union Membership, Coverage, Density, and Employment among All Wage and Salary Workers, 1973–2006," *Unionstats.com*, 2007, p. 1 at http://www.trinity.edu/bhirsch/unionstats/.

in order for that union to gain the legal right to represent the entire employee group (bargaining unit) for purposes of collective bargaining. While no employee can legally be required to become a full active member of any union, if that employee is a member of an employee group whose majority has chosen to be represented by a union, then all members of that group would be covered by the labor agreement negotiated by that union and the employee group's employer.

In 2006, 7.9 million (7.4 percent) of 107.8 million private-sector employees were union members while 8.1 percent of private-sector employees were represented by a union for purposes of collective bargaining.[52] Slightly more than half of all union members are employed in the private sector. In 2006, 7.4 million public-sector employees were union members, representing a higher union density (36.2 percent) than in the private sector. Union density varies within the public sector with 46 percent of local government employees and 34 percent of federal and state level employees represented by a union for purposes of collective bargaining. Public-sector labor relations issues and trends will be discussed further in Chapter 13.

The decline in union membership has been attributed to three broad factors: structural changes in the labor force, improved management practices in business organizations, and political and legal conditions governing the workplace. Of these three explanations, research suggests that changes in the structure of the labor force may be the most important.[53]

Employment has shifted from traditionally unionized industries (manufacturing, railroads, mining) to professional and service-related industries (e.g., health care, legal, education, food preparation, personal care and service, building and grounds cleaning and maintenance, and protective services).[54] Many of the fastest growing occupations are on opposite ends of the level of education and skills required for effective job performance. "The problems of defending a shrinking number of high wage manufacturing jobs are different from organizing the growing ranks of lower-wage service workers. But what they have in common is the need to confront industry with one union that can bargain hard and solve problems."[55]

Most business organizations in the United States are small, with 88 percent of firms having fewer than 20 employees and 98 percent of firms having less than 100 employees.[56] Union membership has traditionally been concentrated in the 2 percent of firms which account for 43 percent of all jobs in the economy. Efforts to increase union membership in small firms is both time consuming and more expensive for labor organizations.

There has also been a demographic shift among those who are employed. More women, individuals 55 and older, and increasing racial and ethnic diversity are three trends that will affect the composition of the labor force over the next 50 years.[57] Unions will need to be able to attract and retain new members from these types of employees in order to maintain or increase current union density levels in the future.

Growth in part-time employment also has a small, but significant, negative impact on union density.[58] This negative effect declines as the number of hours of work increases to 20 or more hours per week. Part-time employment comprises approximately 17 percent of the total labor force, but only 6.3 percent of part-time employees are union members.[59]

More organizations are learning how to operate their businesses on a non-union basis. Sometimes this entails moving some or all operations to less-unionized sections of the United States (the West and South). Managers are also adopting human resource management practices, including anti-union campaigns (see Chapter 5), to keep their firms nonunion. Employers have become more sophisticated in understanding the reasons employees organize unions and more aggressive in presenting their firms' viewpoint opposing union organization to the employees.

Some union officials indicate that employers often use labor law loopholes to forestall or negate free employee union choices through secret-ballot elections. For example, pre-election time delays, contested elections, lengthy appeals, and delays in union attempts to negotiate a first contract settlement once union recognition is granted are possible under the LMRA (see Chapter 3). One analyst makes a comparison with the political process: Suppose U.S. political elections were legally structured so access to potential voters was denied to one political party (analogous to the union), while it was granted to the other one for eight hours a day at one's place of work. The second political party (analogous to management) could force the electorate to listen to campaign speeches (captive audience meetings), while the opposing party was denied access.[60]

Employment law changes that have expanded employees' rights through passage of the Americans with Disabilities Act, Equal Employment Opportunity Act, Occupational Safety and Health Act, Employee Retirement and Income Security Act, and other legislation have helped employers to argue that unions are less necessary today. Indeed, many unions appear to be committing more of their resources to serving the needs of their current members than to organizing new members.

There is an ongoing debate within the union movement regarding the proportion of resources that ought to be devoted to organizing new members versus providing enhanced services (e.g., negotiating contracts, researching wage, benefit, and working condition issues, processing contract grievances, monitoring political issues) to currently represented members. Each union's membership must decide if organizing new employees is in their best interests where these efforts would require the use of scarce union organization funds earmarked for present members' services. Because unions are political organizations and union leaders are elected by the current membership, the incentive to organize new members is often less than the incentive to provide services to current members.[61]

Although union membership has continued to decline as a percentage of the total labor force, many labor unions have responded by increasing their union-organizing activities. Unions are attempting to improve the ways in which they relate both to their own members and to employers with whom they have bargaining relationships.[62] The social significance of unions can also be assessed in general terms by considering what the consequences would be if unions were absent from our society. With no organized voice for workers' interests to counterbalance the economic interests of employers to reduce labor costs, would the improvements gained over the previous century continue or would they be subject to erosion and lax enforcement? Labor unions have historically functioned in the United States as a countervailing power necessary to maintain some balance between employer and employee rights and responsibilities.

Summary

Although unique to the particular labor-management activities, attitudes, and relationships at each organization (discussed more in Chapter 4), the labor relations process includes three key phases or steps: recognition of the legitimate rights and responsibilities of union and management representatives, negotiation of a labor agreement, and daily administration of the terms of that negotiated labor agreement.

The labor relations process focuses on jointly negotiated and administered work rules that pertain to compensation and employees' and employers' rights and responsibilities. These work rules can vary to accommodate the unique characteristics of a particular industry, job classification, geographic setting, or external environmental conditions. Labor relations is a dynamic process that provides the necessary flexibility to adapt bargaining relationships to changing competitive conditions.

Union and management officials represent two key participants in the labor relations process along with employees, government, and certain third-party neutrals like mediators and arbitrators who aid in resolving interest and rights-type disputes. Employees are particularly important in the labor relations process because they determine whether a union will be chosen to represent their employment interests. Employees also typically have loyalties to both their union and employer, which help to determine the organizational effectiveness of each.

Participants in the labor relations process are influenced by several variables such as technology (equipment, pace and scheduling of work, the work environment and tasks to be performed, and information exchange); labor and product markets; international forces such as the North American Free Trade Agreement (NAFTA); public opinion; and the state of the economy.

The current status of labor unions can be assessed from both statistical and general standpoints. A prolonged decline in the proportion of the total labor force comprised of unionized employees has occurred in the United States. However, this trend and its related general explanations (employment shifts, business organizational practices, and legal and political conditions) do not indicate that unions have lost their societal significance.

Key Terms

Labor relations process, p. 5
Interest dispute, p. 6
Rights dispute, p. 6
Work rule, p. 7
Manager, p. 11
Union representative, p. 12
Employees, p. 12

Dual loyalty, p. 12
Government, p. 12
Third-party neutral, p. 13
Mediator, p. 13
Arbitrator, p. 13
Economy, p. 15
Labor market, p. 17

Product or service market, p. 17
Financial market, p. 18
Technology, p. 18
International forces, p. 20
Public opinion, p. 23
Union density, p. 25
Employment-at-will, p. 33

Discussion Questions

1. Exhibit 1.1 illustrates the focal point of the labor relations process and many variables that affect the process. Select an academic discipline such as political science, economics, or sociology, and indicate three specific ways the discipline could add insights into the labor relations process.

2. Discuss the different dimensions of technology, indicating how this variable might contribute to two unique and specific work rules for unionized employees at a grocery store. Also indicate with examples how two other external constraints or influences (see the outer circle of Exhibit 1.1) could affect the work rules at a grocery store.

3. The text outlines three basic assumptions underlying the labor relations process in the United States. To what extent do you agree or disagree with these assumptions? Does your response differ any depending on whether you think about the question from the perspective of an employer or an employee?

4. Discuss your opinion regarding whether unions are still relevant and necessary in today's work environment. What other means might be used to ensure "employee voice" in the workplace?

5. Can an individual be both pro-union and pro-employer, or does being pro-union mean one has to be anti-employer? Can an individual be anti-union and still legitimately claim to support pro-employee views?

Exploring the Web

Labor Relations from Several Points of View

1. Public Opinion Polls

Chapter 1 discusses the effect that public opinion may have on the labor relations process. Public opinion polls can provide an indication of the backing or support by the public during a strike.

The Gallup Organization's Web page, which requires a subscription to read most of their full reports, provides abstracts to the results of polls conducted by the organization. The abstracts can provide some insight into the attitudes of the public on labor issues. Go to the Gallup page and determine if the public backed the UPS workers or the company during the strike of 1997.

The Harris Poll provides portions of their reports without charge on the Harris Interactive page. Search for the site for the results of a 2005 poll on American adults' attitudes toward labor unions. What positive things did the majority of the adults interviewed credit labor unions with doing? How have attitudes changed since a similar survey was conducted in 1993?

2. Reports from Labor and Management Web Sites

Good sources of information on strikes and labor relations can be found by searching the Web pages of labor unions and management as well as reports from newspapers and newswires. This will allow you to see examples of the reporting of the strikes from both sides.

Go to the Web site maintained by the United Steelworkers Union and search for the "Summary of the Agreement between Goodyear and the United Steelworkers, ratified December 22, 2006." Point out the main provisions of the Agreement as discussed in the Introduction.

Looking at a strike through articles published by the management side may give a different perspective. Go to the Goodyear site and read documents on the strike and tentative agreement. The agreement was ratified at the end of December.

3. Newspapers

The Library of Congress provides a Web page that lists links to online newspapers and new services— News & Periodical Resources on the Web. You may know of other free news services that you search on a daily basis. Search online news sources to find articles that were published in reporting news of the International Association of Machinists and Aerospace Workers union and a possible strike at the Kennedy Space Center in 2007. Did the workers strike?

References

1. See, for example, AFL-CIO, *The Silent War: The Assault on Workers' Freedom to Choose a Union and Bargain Collectively in the United States.* Washington, D.C.: AFL-CIO, June 2002, pp. 1–24; Kate Bronfenbrenner, et.al., "Introduction" in *Organizing to Win: New Research on Union Strategies.* Ithaca, N.Y.: ILR Press, 1998, pp. 1–8; William N. Cooke, "The Failure to Negotiate First Contracts: Determinants and Policy Implications," *Industrial and Labor Relations Review* 38 (January 1985), pp.162–178.

2. John Dunlop, *Industrial Relations Systems,* rev. ed. (Boston: Harvard Business School Press, 1993), pp. 13–16.

3. "2006 Employer Bargaining Objectives," *Collective Bargaining Bulletin,* 11 (2), January 19, 2006, p. s24; "VW Wants 35-Hour Workweek, but Union Says No," *The Wall Street Journal,* June 13, 2006, p. A-11; "Pilots' Duty and Flight Hours Continue to Divide Industry," *Air Safety Week,* 20 (9), February 27, 2006, pp. 1–4; Jeremy Smerd, "Gulf Seen between Blue-Collar Workers, Firms over Flextime," *Workforce Management,* April 24, 2006, pp. 14–16.

4. "AFA-CWA Applauds Anticipated FCC Decision to Keep Cell Phones Off Aircraft," *News Release,* March 22, 2007, p. 1 at http://www.afanet.org; Nancy Keates, "Rising Concern: Falling Luggage Inside Airplanes," *The Wall Street Journal,* November 10, 1997, pp. B-1 & 10.

5. Bureau of National Affairs Inc., *Daily Labor Report,* September 10, 1992, p.A-12.

6. Sandra M. Tomkowicz and Susan K. Lessack, "Where There's Smoke: Employer Policies on Smoking," *Employee Relations Law Journal,* 32 (3), Winter 2006, pp. 48–65; Mollie H. Bowers, "What Labor and Management Need to Know about Workplace Smoking Cases," *Labor Law Journal,* January 1992, pp. 40–49.

7. G. Daryl Nord, Tipton F. McCubbins and Jeretta H. Nord, "E-Monitoring in the Workplace: Privacy, Legislation, and Surveillance Software," *Communications of the ACM,* 49 (8), August 2006, pp. 73–77; Donald J. Petersen and Harvey R. Boller, "Hidden Surveillance Cameras: A Mandatory Bargaining Subject?" *Employee Relations Law Journal,* 31 (3), Winter 2005, pp. 56–64.

8. "The System for Forming Unions Is Broken," AFL-CIO, 2007, p. 1 at http://www.aflcio.org/joinaunion/voiceatwork/brokensystem.cfm.

9. Kate Bronfenbrenner, "Raw Power: Plant Closing Threats and the Threat to Union Organizing," *Multinational Monitor,* December 2000, p. 28.

10. John J. Lawler, "The Influence of Management Consultants on the Outcome of Union Certification Elections," *Industrial and Labor Relations Review* 38 (1), October 1984, pp. 38–51; Bruce E. Kaufman and Paula E. Stephan, "The Role of Management Attorneys in Union Organizing Campaigns," *Journal of Labor Research,* Fall 1995, pp. 439–455; Bureau of National Affairs Inc., Special Report, *Labor Relations Consultants: Issues, Trends, and Controversies* (Washington, D.C.: Bureau of National Affairs Inc., 1985).

11. William A. Ward, "Manufacturing Jobs, 2005-2010," *Economic Development Journal,* 5 (1), Winter 2006, pp. 7–15; Louis Uchitelle, "A Missing Statistic: U.S. Jobs That Have Moved Overseas," *The New York Times,* October 3, 2003, p. 21. For a more thorough discussion, see: Erica L. Groshen and Simon Porter, "Has Structural Change Contributed to a Jobless Recovery?" *Report of the Federal Reserve Bank of New York,* 9 (8), August 2003, pp. 1–7 at http://www.ny.frb.org/research.

12. Pierre-Yves Cremieux, "The Effects of Deregulation on Employee Earnings: Pilots, Flight Attendants, and Mechanics, 1959–1992," *Industrial and Labor Relations Review,* 49 (2), January 1996, pp. 223–242; Michael H. Belzer, "Collective Bargaining after Deregulation: Do the Teamsters Still Count?" *Industrial and Labor Relations Review,* July 1995, pp. 636–655.

13. Barbara Hagenbaugh, "Fed Holds Rates Steady Again," *USA Today,* May 9, 2007, pp. 1–2 at http://www.usatoday.com/money/2007-05-09-fed_N.htm.

14. U.S. Department of Labor, "BLS Releases 2004-14 Employment Projections," *Press Release,* December 7, 2005, pp. 1–8 at http://www.bls.gov/emp.

15. U.S. Department of Labor, "Employment Status of the Civilian Noninstitutional Population, 1940 to date," *Labor*

Force Statistics from the Current Population Survey, May 16, 2007, p. 207 at http://www.bls.gov/cps/cps_over.htm#news.

16. William A. Ward, "Manufacturing Jobs, 2005-2010," *Economic Development Journal*, 5 (1), Winter 2006, pp. 7–15; Louis Uchitelle, "A Missing Statistic: U.S. Jobs That Have Moved Overseas," *The New York Times*, October 3, 2003, p. 21. For a more thorough discussion, see: Erica L. Groshen and Simon Porter, "Has Structural Change Contributed to a Jobless Recovery?" *Report of the Federal Reserve Bank of New York*, 9 (8), August 2003, pp. 1–7 at http://www.ny.frb.org/research.

17. Timothy Aeppel, "Steelworkers Strike Tests Goodyear's Recovery," *The Wall Street Journal*, October 6, 2006, p. A-3; Terry Kosdrosky, "Goodyear Union Plans to Terminate Contract Thursday," *The Wall Street Journal*, October 3, 2006, p. A-10; Jim Mackinnon, "Strike Punctures Goodyear Earnings for 2006," *Knight Ridder Tribune Business News*, February 17, 2007, p. 1.

18. Frederick Kiel, "Goodyear Resumes Tire Production as Union Approves New 3-Year Deal," *Transport Topics*, January 8, 2007, pp. 2, 24.

19. Hoyt N. Wheeler, *The Future of the American Labor Movement* (Cambridge, U.K.: Cambridge University Press, 2002), pp. 80–81.

20. James R. Healey, "Tangled Web of Rules Obscures Autos' Origins," *USA Today*, March 2, 1992, pp. 1, 3B.

21. Jill Andresky Fraser, "Capital: State of the Union," *Inc. Magazine*, July, 2002, pp. 1–2 at http://www.heartlandnetwork.org/pressarticles/article9.htm; Emma Blackwell, "Asset Managers Launch Labor-Friendly Private Equity Vehicles," *Corporate Financing Week*, April 24, 2006, p. 1; *Working Capital: The Power of Labor's Pensions*, ed. by A. Fung, T. Hebb, and J. Rogers. Ithaca, NY: Cornell University Press, 2001.

22. Wheeler, *The Future of the American Labor Movement*, pp. 176–177; "The Heartland Labor Capital Network: What Is the Heartland Network?" 2007, p. 1 at http://www.heartlandnetwork.org/whatis.htm.

23. David Wessel, "Politics & Economics; Capital: Fishing Out Facts on the Wealth Gap," *The Wall Street Journal*, February 15, 2007, p. A-10; David Wessel, "Fed Chief Warns of Widening Inequality," *The Wall Street Journal*, February 7, 2007, p. A-6; Kevin G. Hall, "Health Care, Wages, Energy Cost Put Squeeze on Middle Class," *Knight Ridder Tribune Business News*, October 22, 2006, p. 1; Wheeler, *The Future of the American Labor Movement*, pp. 25–27.

24. Neil De Clereq, Alec Meiklejohn, and Ken Mericle, "The Use of Microcomputers in Local Union Administration," *Labor Studies Journal* 10 (Spring 1985), pp. 3–45.

25. Cynthia G. Wagner, "Cyberunions: Organized Labor Goes Online," *The Futurist*, 34 (1), Jan./Feb. 2000, p. 7; Chuck Moozakis, "Portals Give Perks to Autoworkers," *Internet Week*, November 13, 2000, p. 11; John Lund, "Using Microcomputer Spreadsheets to Teach Industrial and Labor Relations Applications," *Labor Studies Journal*, 20 (Summer 1995), pp. 22–38.

26. "AFL-CIO Goes On-Line with New Labor NET," *AFL-CIO News*, July 26, 1993, p. 6; "Labor Unions Are Getting Off to a Slow Start in Cyberspace," *The Wall Street Journal*, May 30, 1995, p. A-1; Montieth M.

Illingworth, "Workers on the Net, Unite!" *Information Week*, August 22, 1994, pp. 27–36.

27. Mihal Nica, Ziad Swaidan, and Michael M. Grayson, "The Impact of NAFTA on the Mexican-American Trade," *International Journal of Commerce & Management*, 16 (3&4), 2006, pp. 222–233.

28. Andrew Batson, "How U.S. Labor Leaders Chart a Global Course," *The Wall Street Journal*, May 23, 2007, p. A-6; Anya Sostek, "USW Joins Effort to Form Superunion," *Knight Ridder Tribune Business News*, April 19, 2007, p. 1.

29. Martin Crutsinger, "Trade Deficit Rises to Record $763.6 Billion," *The Washington Post*, February 13, 2007, pp. 1–2 at http://www.washingtonpost.com/wp-dyn/content/article/2007/02/13/AR20007021300368_pf.html; Dean Calbreath, "U.S. Trade Deficit Isn't Just about the Chinese," *Knight Ridder Tribune Business News*, May 13, 2007, pp. 1–3 at http://proquest.umi.com/pqdweb?did=1270628781&sid=2&Fmt=3&clientid=1997&RQT=309&VName=PQD.

30. "Hot Topic: Sorting Out U.S.-China Relations," *The Wall Street Journal* (Eastern edition), May 26, 2007, p. A-7; John Kitchen, "U.S. International Deficits, Debt, and Income Payments: Key Relationships Affecting the Outlook," *Business Economics*, 42 (1), January 2007, pp. 7–16.

31. Gordon Fairclough, "Wal-Mart Sneezes, China Catches Cold," *The Wall Street Journal*, May 29, 2007, pp. B1–2.

32. Rich Miller, Pete Engardio, Dexter Roberts, and Michael Arndt, "Is It China's Fault?" *BusinessWeek*, October 13, 2003, pp. 32–35.

33. William R. Cline, "Why the U.S. External Imbalance Matters," *Cato Journal*, 27 (1), Winter 2007, p. 53.

34. Wheeler, *The Future of the American Labor Movement*, p. 25.

35. International Labor Organization, *ILO Declaration on Fundamental Principles and Rights at Work*, 1996-2003, pp. 1–2 at http://www.ilo.org.

36. Wheeler, *The Future of the American Labor Movement*, pp. 81–82.

37. David Porreca, "Through Jaundiced Eyes: How the Media View Organized Labor," *Journal of Communications*, 46 (3), Summer 1996, p. 198.

38. Lane Kirkland, "Labor and the Press," *American Federationist* 82 (December 1975), p. 3; John A. Grimes, "Are the Media Short Changing Organized Labor?" *Monthly Labor Review* 110 (August 1987), pp. 53–54.

39. Diane E. Schmidt, "Public Opinion and Media Coverage of Labor Unions," *Journal of Labor Research* 13 (Summer 1992), pp. 151–165; William J. Puette, *Through Jaundiced Eyes: How the Media View Organized Labor* (Ithaca, NY: ILR Press, 1992); Paul Jarley and Sarosh Kuruvilla, "American Trade Unions and Public Approval: Can Unions Please People All of the Time," *Journal of Labor Research* 15 (Spring 1994), pp. 97–117; Geoff Walsh, "Trade Unions and the Media," *International Labour Review*, 127 (2) 1988, pp. 205–220.

40. Christopher R. Martin, *Framed: Labor and the Corporate Media* (Ithaca, NY: Cornell University Press, 1994).

41. "Poll Analyses: Labor Union," *The Gallup Poll*, August 7–10, 2006, pp. 1–5 at http://www.galluppoll.com/content/?ci=12751&pg=1.

42. "Poll Analyses: Confidence in Institutions," *The Gallup Poll*, June 1-4, 2006, pp. 1–3 at http://www.galluppoll.com/?ci=1597&pg=1.

43. Jonathan P. Hicks, "Dreams and City Image Put at Stake in Strike," *The New York Times,* April 10, 1992, p. A-31.

44. Albert Shanker, "Where We Stand," *The New York Times,* December 16, 1990, p. 7; Sandra Feldman, "The Big Lie," *The New York Times,* June 7, 1998, p. 7.

45. "Statement by AFL-CIO President John Sweeney on Rainbow PUSH Coalition Reclaiming Our Land March in New Orleans," *News Release,* April 27, 2007, p. 1.

46. Steve Early and Larry Cohen, "Jobs with Justice: Mobilizing Labor Community Coalitions," *Working USA,* 1, no. 4 (November–December 1997), pp. 49–57; James Craft, "The Community as a Source of Union Power," *Journal of Labor Research* 11 (Spring 1990), p. 149. For a detailed account of a community effort involving religious institutions in an attempt to restore closed steel mills as a community- and employee-owned enterprise, see Thomas G. Fuechtmann, *Steeples and Stacks: Religion and Steel Crisis in Youngstown* (New York: Cambridge University Press, 1989).

47. Anya Sostak, "Unions Take a Closer Look," *Knight Ridder Tribune Business News,* March 22, 2007, pp. 1–2; http://www.wakeupwalmart.com/ and http://walmartwatch.com.

48. Kris Maher, "Politics & Economics: Wal-Mart Joins Health Care Call; Unlikely Coalition of Labor, Business Pushes for Overhaul," *The Wall Street Journal,* February 8, 2007, p. A-6.

49. "Take the Pledge," *The New York Times,* October 1, 1998, p. A-19.

50. United States Department of Labor, "Union Members in 2006," *News Release,* January 25, 2007, pp. 1–12.

51. Gary Chaison, "The AFL-CIO Split: Does It Really Matter?" *Journal of Labor Research,* 28 (2), Spring 2007, p. 305.

52. United States Department of Labor, "Union Members in 2006," p. 8.

53. *Justice on the Job: Perspectives on the Erosion of Collective Bargaining in the United States,* ed. by Richard N. Block, Sheldon Friedman, Michelle Kaminski, and Andy Levin (Kalamazoo, MI: W. E. Upjohn Institute for Employment Research, 2006); C. Timothy Koeller, "Union Activity and the Decline in American Trade Union Membership," *Journal of Labor Research* 15 (Winter 1994), pp. 19–31.

54. Daniel E. Hecker, "Occupational Employment Projections to 2014," *Monthly Labor Review,* 128 (11), November 2005, pp. 70–101.

55. Rik Kirkland, "The New Face of Labor," *Fortune,* 154 (8), October 2006, p. 122; Steven Greenhouse, "Union Leaders See Grim News in Labor Study," *The New York Times,* October 13, 1999, p. A-23.

56. Shail J. Butani, Richard L. Clayton, Vinod Kapani, James R. Spietzer, David M. Talan, and George S. Werking Jr., "Business Employment Dynamics: Tabulations by Employer Size," *Monthly Labor Review,* 129 (2), February 2006, p. 4; Brian Headd, "The Characteristics of Small-Business Employees," *Monthly Labor Review,* 123 (4), April 2000, pp. 13–18.

57. Mitra Toossi, "A New Look at Long-Term Labor Force Projections to 2050," *Monthly Labor Review,* 129 (11), November 2006, pp. 19–39; Abraham Mosisa and Stephen Hippie, "Trends in Labor Force Participation in the United States," *Monthly Labor Review,* 129 (10), October 2006, pp. 36–57.

58. Arleen Hernandez, "The Impact of Part-Time Employment on Union Density," *Journal of Labor Research,* 16 (4), Fall 1995, pp. 485–491.

59. U.S. Department of Labor, "Labor Force Statistics from the Current Population Survey," *Current Population Survey,* May 2007, at http://www.bls.gov.

60. Bruce Nissen, "The Recent Past and Near Future of Private Sector Unionism in the U.S.: An Appraisal," *Journal of Labor Research* 26, no. 2 (Spring 2001), p. 325.

61. Joseph B. Rose and Gary N. Chiason, "New Measures of Union Organizing Effectiveness," *Industrial Relations* 29 (Fall 1990), pp. 457–468.

62. Peter Fairbrother and Glynne Williams, "Unions Facing the Future: Questions and Possibilities," *Labor Studies Journal,* 31 (4), Winter 2007, pp. 31–53; Paul F. Clark and Lois S. Gray, "Changing Administrative Practices in American Unions: A Research Note," *Industrial Relations,* 44 (4), October 2005, pp. 654–658.

Discharge for Whistleblower Activity

CASE STUDY 1-1 Janet Broom and Darla Miller were employed as a certified medication aide and cook, respectively, at the employer's residential care facility located in Norman, Oklahoma. Both employees suspected another employee of stealing and using drugs intended for use by residents of the facility from the facility's medication room. Broom and Miller decided to report the suspected employee based on their observation that she had falsified medical drug log books to conceal her theft from facility managers.

The facility's *Employee Handbook* clearly outlined a procedure employees were to follow when making complaints involving other employees. The *Employee Handbook* called for the initial complaint to be filed with the accused employee's immediate supervisor. Because the two employees making the complaint believed that the immediate supervisor in this case, Sarah Dutton, was a close personal friend of the accused, Broom and Miller chose to make their complaint to another manager, who was the medication consultant at the facility.

Upon learning of the complaint from the medication consultant, supervisor Dutton discharged Broom and Miller for "not following the proper chain of command in raising an issue about another employee." Both Broom and Miller are nonunion employees unrepresented by a union. After being discharged, Broom and Miller's only recourse was to file a wrongful discharge state court claim, arguing that they were engaged in internal whistleblowing activity and thus protected from discharge as a matter of Oklahoma public policy.

The employer argued that Broom and Miller were subject to the Oklahoma common law **employment-at-will** doctrine, which permits an employer to discharge an at-will employee at any time for any or no stated reason. The employer sought and received a summary judgment in state district court declaring Broom and Miller's discharge to be lawful under the state's common law employment-at-will doctrine.

Broom and Miller appealed the state district court's decision to a federal Court of Appeals, seeking to reverse the district court's decision.

In *Groce* v. *Foster,* 880 P.2d902 (Okla. 1994), the Oklahoma Supreme Court recognized five types of public policy exceptions to the common law employment-at-will doctrine. Under Oklahoma law, an at-will employee may not be lawfully discharged for (1) refusing to participate in an illegal activity; (2) performing an important public service (e.g. jury duty); (3) exercising a legal right or interest of the employee; (4) exposing some wrongdoing by his or her employer; and (5) performing an act that public policy would encourage or refusing to perform an act public policy would discourage, when the discharge action is coupled with a showing of bad faith, malice, or retaliation.

Broom and Miller argued that their discharge fell under the fifth public policy exception to the employment-at-will doctrine. By reporting to management a co-worker who they honestly believed was engaged in stealing drugs intended for administration to residents of the facility, Broom and Miller believed they were engaging in conduct that Oklahoma public policy encourages.

The Oklahoma Supreme Court mandates that to be recognized and enforced, public policy exceptions must be clearly stated in state constitutional, regulatory, or case decision law. To that end, Broom and Miller cited three statutory laws that they believed provided a clear statement of public policy supporting their action.

The first law is the *Nursing Home Care Act,* which governs safeguards and procedures for the storage, safekeeping, monitoring, dispensing, and, when necessary, destruction of patient prescription drugs. The employer argued that the act specifically applies only to licensed nursing homes operating within the state. The employer's facility is licensed as a residential care facility and thus is excluded from coverage under the *Nursing Home Care Act.* The state of Oklahoma grants operating licenses for several different types of elder-care facilities, including nursing homes, assisted living homes, and residential care facilities.

The second law is the *Residential Care Act,* which the employer admitted does apply to the facility in this case. Broom and Miller noted that the law authorizes the Oklahoma State Department of Health to "develop and enforce rules and regulations...to implement the provisions of the *Residential Care Act.* Such rules and regulations shall include but not be limited to governing temperature limits, lighting, ventilation, and other physical conditions which shall protect the health, safety, and welfare of the residents in the home." The employer argued that Broom and Miller did not raise the issue of the *Residential Care Act*'s applicability to their case when the case was before the district court and therefore could not legally raise it as a supporting argument on appeal. It is a well-settled legal principle that issues or arguments not clearly presented and considered at a prior legal proceeding cannot be subsequently raised as a legal basis for argument on appeal. The employer also noted that the language referred to by Broom and Miller in the *Residential Care Act* is very general and not specific enough to rise to the level of a clear statement of public policy supporting intent to make an exception to the prevailing Oklahoma employment-at-will doctrine.

The third law cited by Broom and Miller as a basis for their appeal is the *Uniform Controlled Dangerous Substances Act*. Although this law does make it a criminal offense to steal a controlled dangerous substance, Broom and Miller made no specific argument as to how this law established a clear mandate of public policy applicable to their discharge case. The employer argued that Broom and Miller again failed to meet the required showing of a clear and compelling public policy in favor of restricting an employer's right to discharge an at-will employee for failing to follow the established procedure for bringing a serious complaint against a co-worker.

Questions

1. Should the federal appeals court deny Broom and Miller's appeal and enforce the decision of the state district court finding upholding the discharge of the two whistleblowers? Explain your reasoning.

2. How might this case have been handled differently if Broom and Miller had been members of a bargaining unit represented by a union for purposes of collective bargaining?

Classroom Exercise

1.1
Work Rules

Directions: This activity can be performed as an individual or group assignment using either an oral or written report format. Select a recent (not more than one year old) news story or article and explain how the information in the story could affect the negotiation or administration of a particular work rule. An appropriate news story or article should contain information on one or more of the possible constraints or influences affecting the negotiation or administration of work rules identified in the text (e.g., state of the economy, labor market conditions, product market conditions, financial market conditions, technology, and international forces or events).

1.2
Union Membership Trend

Directions: This activity can be performed as an individual or group assignment using either an oral or written report format. Select a recent (not more than one year old) news story or article and explain how the information in the story could affect future union membership growth in a positive or negative manner. Your explanation should clearly indicate why or how you think the information in your story will have the predicted effect on future union membership growth.

1.3
Word Association

Directions: Divide the class into groups of 3–5 students. Presented below are 25 words or phrases. Each group should classify each listed word or phrase as primarily applicable to *UNIONS* (U) or *MANAGERS* (M), *BOTH* U & M (B), or *NEITHER* U nor M (N). Groups may compare their results and discuss their reasoning for associating particular words or phrases with the term **Union** or **Management**. Groups may also list additional descriptive terms or phrases that they would strongly associate with the term **Union** or **Management**.

Words or phrases to classify:

1. POWERFUL
2. EDUCATED
3. DEMOCRATIC
4. PROFIT-ORIENTED
5. PRODUCTIVE
6. FAIR
7. VIOLENCE
8. TRUSTWORTHY
9. JOB SECURITY
10. COMPETITIVE
11. POLITICAL
12. AUTHORITY
13. REASONABLE
14. WORK STOPPAGE
15. PROFESSIONAL
16. EMPLOYEE COMPENSATION
17. ETHICAL
18. INNOVATIVE
19. FLEXIBLE
20. QUALITY IMPROVEMENT
21. RISK TAKER
22. NECESSARY
23. JOB SAFETY & HEALTH
24. WORK RULES
25. GROWTH-ORIENTED

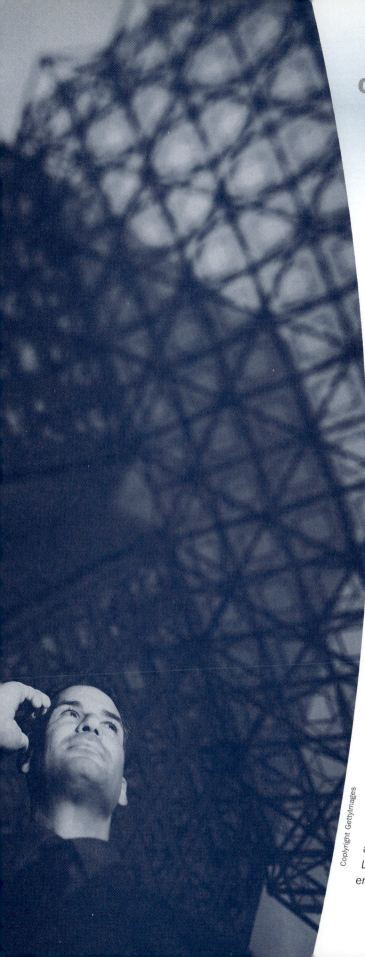

CHAPTER 2

Evolution of Labor-Management Relationships

The American labor movement as we know it has adjusted to changing social and economic events, employers' attitudes and actions, and employee preferences for more than 100 years. A historical perspective is necessary to better understand current union behavior and helps us predict how most unions might react to sudden and dramatic change.

There is no best way to obtain this perspective.[1] Insights from many academic disciplines (sociology, economics, political science, and so forth) have to be considered, and many focal points can be assessed. Our discussion focuses on what has worked and not worked for organized labor through two interrelated historical dimensions: (1) relationships between labor and management organizations, and (2) organizational characteristics of labor organizations.

This second dimension is important to labor relations students and practitioners because the current American Federation of Labor–Congress of Industrial Organizations (AFL-CIO, with 55 national and international unions representing over 10 million union members) and the newer Change To Win Federation (with 7 national unions representing 6.4 million union members) have both been historically affected by four major labor organizations: the Knights of Labor, the Industrial Workers of the World, the American Federation of Labor, and the Congress of Industrial Organizations.

The strength of any labor organization depends on four criteria:

- *Its structural and financial stability*

- *Its ability to work within the established political and economic system, particularly the wage system*

- *The degree to which the broader social environment such as legislation, media, and public opinion are supportive or opposed to a labor organization's goals and tactics*

- *The ability of union leaders to identify and satisfy members' goals and interests*

Readers can use these criteria to assess why some labor organizations failed in the past and to predict the likelihood of current unions posing a strong challenge to management. The chapter is organized into three time periods: 1869 to World War I, World War I to World War II, and World War II to the present.

1869 TO WORLD WAR I

Unions as we know them today did not exist before 1800. There were small guilds, joint associations of employers and craftspeople, that pressed for professional standards and restriction of outside competition.[2] These guilds pressed concerns that typically benefited employees and employers alike. By 1820 there had been only a few scattered strikes, usually over wages, because only two industries, shoemaking and printing, had even the semblance of collective bargaining. There was also no general labor philosophy or labor movement in the United States at this time, as labor organizations were principally small groups of craft employees located in major metropolitan areas along the Eastern coast of the United States.[3]

The 1850s and 1860s saw development of the U.S. factory system (industrial revolution), improved transportation, and increased product mobility—factors that extended a company's (and potential unionized employees') organization beyond the local community. For example, an employer could produce shoes at lower wages in Baltimore and ship them to Boston, where they could be sold at a higher price. Negotiating similar terms and employment conditions for labor was viewed as a means to take wages out of competition; but to do so would require labor organizations capable of operating on a national rather than local basis. The Civil War (1861 to 1865) refined and encouraged mass-production techniques, creating large concentrations of semiskilled and unskilled employees under a single factory roof—a situation that created conditions conducive to the organization of labor.

During the period of 1869 to World War I, three national labor organizations emerged: the Knights of Labor (KOL), the American Federation of Labor (AFL), and the Industrial Workers of the World (IWW). Each of these organizations is discussed in terms of its orientations and goals, organizational structure, and strategies and tactics. Reasons suggested for the demise of the KOL and the IWW and other issues discussed illustrate the previously mentioned criteria for a labor organization's strength. Three prominent labor episodes of this period are also discussed: the drive for an eight-hour workday (including the Haymarket Riot of 1886), the Homestead strike (1892), and the Pullman strike (1894).

These three events and other union-management confrontations through the 1930s reflect a degree of unbridled violence that has been unmatched in contemporary times. The "Labor Relations in Action" box gives brief examples of steps companies often took to keep out unions and what employees were

LABOR RELATIONS IN ACTION

Labor History Time Line—Selected Events

Year	Event
Late 1700s	Emergence of local craft unions in large East Coast cities (e.g., New York, Philadelphia).
1842	The Massachusetts Supreme Court in *Commonwealth v. Hunt* establishes a legal precedent that workers have a right to combine together for the purpose of pursuing lawful end (goals) using lawful means (tactics).
1850	U.S. economy begins to shift from an agricultural base to a manufacturing (industrial) base. Regional and national product markets emerge with larger firms able to use new technology and improved transportation modes (roads, rail) to mass produce goods.
1869	Noble Order of the Knights of Labor organized.
1880s	Use of the labor injunction to prohibit or restrict employees' concerted activities replaces reliance on criminal or civil conspiracy trials as a management legal strategy.
1886	Eight-hour day movement gains momentum; Haymarket Square Riot occurs in Chicago, IL; American Federation of Labor (AFL) is organized, electing Samuel Gompers as president.
1892	The Homestead strike involving the Amalgamated Association of Iron, Steel & Tin Workers and steel mills owned by Andrew Carnegie occurs.
1894	Eugene Debs leads the American Railway Union in a strike against the Pullman Company resulting in federal troop intervention in the labor dispute.
1898	Congress attempts to extend mediation and voluntary arbitration of labor disputes to the railroad industry by passing the Erdman Act. The law was declared unconstitutional by the U.S. Supreme Court in 1908.
1905	The Industrial Workers of the World (IWW) organized.
1908	U.S. Supreme Court declares a national product boycott by the United Hatters' Union to be a violation of the Sherman Antitrust Act.
1911	Triangle Waist Company fire in New York City leads to the death of 146 clothing workers. Focuses national attention on the poor working conditions facing many industrial employees.
1913	Congress creates the U.S. Department of Labor and the department's head (Secretary of Labor) is designated a member of the President's Cabinet.
1926	Railway Labor Act enacted granting employees in the private sector railroad industry the right to form unions and bargain collectively.
1932	The Norris-LaGuardia Act enacted placing restrictions on the issuance of labor injunctions during labor disputes and making a "yellow-dog" contract unenforceable in court.
1933	U.S. Secretary of Labor Frances Perkins becomes of the first woman to serve as a member of the President's Cabinet.
1935	National Labor Relations (Wagner) Act enacted granting most private sector employees the right to form unions and bargain collectively. The Committee for Industrial Organization created by several AFL unions to encourage efforts to organize workers in the mass production industries (auto, steel, rubber, etc.).
1936	Railway Labor Act amended to add coverage of the airline industry.
1938	The Committee for Industrial Organization is reorganized as the Congress of Industrial Organizations (CIO), electing John L. Lewis as its first president. Fair Labor Standards Act enacted, establishing a federal minimum wage of 25 cents per hour and requiring time and one-half pay for hours worked in excess of 40 hours in a regular work week.
1947	Labor Management Relations (Taft-Hartley) Act enacted over the veto of President Truman. Retains NLRA protections for employee collective activity but adds protection for the right of individual employees not to engage in collective activity and imposed restrictions on union conduct similar to restrictions imposed on management conduct by the NLRA.

(Continued)

Year	Event
1952	Presidents of both the AFL and CIO die of natural causes in the same month, setting the stage for new leadership by AFL president George Meany and CIO president Walter Reuther.
1955	AFL and CIO labor organizations merge to form the AFL-CIO electing George Meany as president and Walter Reuther as vice president.
1959	Labor Management Reporting and Disclosure (Landrum-Griffin) Act enacted to regulate the internal affairs of unions and their relationship with individual union members.
1962	President John F. Kennedy issues Executive Order 10988, permitting federal employees to organize and engage in collective bargaining. Encourages states to enact similar legislation, granting state and local public employees bargaining rights.
1963	Equal Pay Act enacted, prohibiting different wage rates based on sex for workers performing the same job who are subject to coverage under the Fair Labor Standards Act.
1964	Civil Rights Act enacted, prohibiting discrimination based upon race, color, religion, sex, or national origin in hiring, apprenticeship, compensation, terms or conditions of employment, and union membership.
1968	Public sector employee unrest leads to increased organizing, bargaining, and strikes involving public employees (e.g., police, firefighters, teachers, and sanitation workers). Martin Luther King is assassinated while helping to lead a sanitation workers strike in Memphis, TN. Age Discrimination in Employment Act enacted making it illegal to discriminate against individuals 40 years of age or older in regards to hiring, discharge, or other employment decisions on the basis of the individual's age.
1970	Occupational Health and Safety Act enacted to provide a safe and healthy work environment for American workers.
1974	Employee Retirement Income Security Act (ERISA) enacted to protect the assets of private sector employees provided for under employer established benefit plans (e.g., pension plan).
1975	Economy begins to transition from an industrial-based to a service-based economy.
1978	Civil Service Reform Act enacted converting previous presidential executive orders establishing bargaining right for federal employees into permanent legislation.
1980	Increasing global competition ushers in a decade in which many U.S. firms are forced to undergo dramatic change in order to remain competitive. Concession bargaining involving

willing to do to force management to recognize their working concerns and independent union representative.

The Knights of Labor (KOL)

Goals and Organizations of the KOL

Founded by Uriah S. Stephens as a secret society in 1869, the **Knights of Labor (KOL)** operated in secrecy until 1882 so that the members would not be discharged by their employers for participating in a labor organization. There are two major reasons for discussing the KOL. First, it was a national union in scope, larger than any previous union in American history. In the early 1880s, it had a steady growth, reaching a membership of more than 100,000 in 1885. Between 1885 and 1886, the organization's membership increased sharply, to 700,000. The KOL achieved more power, prestige, and notoriety than any other previous labor organization.[4] However, its goals and strategies also

Year	Event
	management demands for union cost concessions in exchange for promises of improved job security becomes common. Flexible work rules take on increased importance in efforts to improve productivity and product/service quality. Some bargaining relationships stress increased labor-management cooperation as a means to improved competitiveness that can benefit management's and labor's interests.
1981	Members of the Professional Air Traffic Controllers Union (PATCO) engage in an illegal strike to support bargaining demands and are discharged by the Reagan administration. This act was widely interpreted by practitioners in the private and public sectors as evidence of a new employer "get tough" policy in labor relations. Organized labor is forced to expend its resources fighting to defend established legal rights and employment conditions, rather than expanding or improving employment interests.
1988	Worker Adjustment and Retraining Notification Act enacted (made effective Feb. 1989). Requires employers who employ 100 or more employees to provide 60 days advance notice of any plant closing or major layoff, but enforcement of the Act requires an employee or their representative to sue the employer in court.
1991	Americans with Disabilities Act enacted to protect disabled persons from discrimination in regards to hiring, discharge, or other terms and conditions of employment. Civil Rights Act of 1991 enacted, amending Title VII of the Civil Rights Act to permit suits for punitive damages for violations involving intentional discrimination and endorsing the use of alternative dispute resolution methods to resolve employment discrimination claims.
1992	North American Free Trade Agreement enacted (effective January 1, 1994) intended to promote trade between the United States, Canada, and Mexico.
1993	The Family and Medical Leave Act enacted, permitting employees of employers who employ 50 or more employees to take up to 12 weeks of unpaid time off in the event of a birth, adoption, or foster care of a child; or to care for a child, parent, spouse, or themselves involving a serious health condition.
2001	September 11 terrorists attack on U.S. targets occurs. Organized labor and business interests join in efforts to rebuild and provide aid to victims of the attack. Negative impact on travel-related industries leads to layoffs and renegotiation of labor contract terms.
2005	Formation of the Change To Win labor federation to focus more resources on organizing unrepresented employees.

contributed to its demise as an effective organization. So the Knights served as an important negative lesson to the American Federation of Labor and other contemporary labor organizations that followed in establishing goals, policies, and an organizational structure necessary to survive and grow as a labor organization.

The Knights strongly objected to many features of the new industrial revolution, which dramatically altered work practices and relationships beginning during the Civil War. This view led the KOL to establish two major interrelated goals:

1. Change the existing labor–management relationship so that the depersonalized and specialized aspects of mass production could be avoided.

2. Attain moral betterment for employees and society.

The KOL's goals can best be understood through the views of **Terence V. Powderly,** its leader and chief spokesman from 1879 to 1883. Powderly felt that mass production reduced employees' feelings of pride and personal accomplishment.[5] During the Agricultural Economy era prior to 1850, work occurred in relatively small shops where employees gained satisfaction and pride from their craftsmanship in creating high-quality customized products from beginning to end. The Industrial Economy (1850–1975) utilized mass production techniques and job specialization so that different jobs only focused on a relatively few tasks which, when combined with other employees' job output, could produce a complete product. Because the time and skill level required to learn and perform a limited set of job tasks were less than previously required to produce the entire product, less costly labor could be employed and more easily replaced when necessary. Powderly placed this situation in perspective by considering the shoemakers' situation: "The man who was called a shoemaker 30 years ago made shoes; the man who claims to be a shoemaker today makes only part of a shoe. What was once a trade in itself is a multiplicity of trades. Once there were shoemakers, now we have Beaters, Binders, Bottomers, Buffers, Burnishers, Channellers, Crimpers, Cutters, Dressers, Edge Setters . . . and several other workers at the shoe trade, and they all consider themselves shoemakers."[6]

Employees working in these specialized classifications could not obtain meaning or satisfaction from their fragmented work tasks. Powderly also felt that bankers and owners of gold were the villains of industrial society, causing higher taxes for employees and creating monopolies that further depersonalized the individual employee.[7]

The KOL believed that changing the existing industrial and societal system would help accomplish a second goal, moral betterment and increased dignity for their members. Powderly claimed that members must place their concerns on a "higher" ground than material working conditions, as these physical effects were but stepping stones to "a higher cause, of a nobler nature . . . the more exalted and divine nature of man, his high and noble capabilities for good."[8] The leadership of the KOL were continually concerned that its members would devote too much attention to improving working conditions and ignore the goal of moral betterment—to make every man his own master.[9]

The moralistic overtones of the Knights guided their membership policies, organizational structure, and strategies and tactics. Because moral betterment affected all members of society, the KOL adopted a **One Big Union** approach encouraging people of all job types and skill levels to join the organization except professional gamblers, stockbrokers, lawyers, bankers, and those who lived in whole or in part by the sale or manufacture of intoxicating liquors.[10] Employers were also encouraged to join the KOL, the rationale being that they along with employees were being duped by financiers and lawyers and once educated to this fact would join hands with the employees in improving society.

The local assembly, the basic unit in the KOL, could consist of employers and employees from several different trades. By 1886 there were 1,100 KOL local assemblies. However, the formal authority and power of the KOL remained centralized in the hands of the General Executive Board headed by Powderly.[11] As seen later in this section, the top-down pyramid structure of the KOL later led the AFL to adopt a dramatically different organizational structure.

Strategies to Accomplish the KOL's Goals

The Knights used at least four strategies to accomplish their goals. First, political action was viewed as important, particularly because the Knights felt that previous legislation had led society down the wrong road. The Knights believed that politicians were motivated by self-interest and therefore required careful watching. However, the Knights believed in operating through existing political parties. The KOL actively lobbied for legislation to restrict the immigration of foreign labor for the purpose of expanding the labor supply, lessening labor's value. The KOL lobbied for increased funding of public school systems to give every individual an opportunity to become better educated.

A second strategy was the encouragement of producer and consumer cooperatives. Unlike the socialists, the Knights did not want the cooperatives to be owned by the state. Instead, the KOL wanted employees to save enough from their wages to either purchase established operations or create their own cooperative ventures. Because factories would then be owned by the employees, KOL leaders reasoned that conflict between employees and employers would cease.[12] Cooperatives would also enable the employees to become their own masters, granting employees a voice in decision making, including the determination of a fair distribution of profits.

The Knights' leadership believed cooperatives would affect the established wage-profit system most directly; yet they made little attempt to establish cooperatives or to financially support the approximately 100 cooperatives which were established by KOL local or district assemblies during the mid-1880s. Most of these cooperatives failed because of "inefficient managers, squabbles among shareholders, lack of capital, and injudicious borrowing of money at high rates of interest."[13]

The KOL pursued a third strategy when it actively avoided the use of strikes to obtain its goals. Indeed, the KOL's leadership often actively discouraged strikes and, in some cases, demoralized local assembly members with their statements.[14] Some leaders viewed strikes as a last resort that could result in labor violence and lessen the common interests of employers and employees, serving to distract members from the major goal of moral betterment. The General Executive Board set up a complicated procedure that local assemblies had to follow before they could obtain strike funds.[15] Powderly believed that no employee should be able to enter a strike that would result in other employees losing their jobs; therefore, a procedure was needed to ensure that every employee possibly affected by a strike would have a voice in the strike decision.[16] Yet the red tape involved in obtaining strike funds caused great dissension between the KOL leaders and members.[17] Local assemblies that conducted strikes were often left on their own to financially support work stoppages or KOL-approved funds arrived too late to effectively support a strike.

The Knights' leadership preferred a fourth strategy as an alternative to the strike: namely, the education of the members and citizens as to the perceived evils of the existing industrial system, as well as the Knights' goals for societal improvement. Usually the leaders would meet with members of local assemblies in private sessions to inform them of the organization's goals and objectives. The emphasis on education instead of job action efforts (strikes and boycotts) is further discussed in the next section.

Reasons for the KOL's Failure and Demise

Despite tremendous growth, the KOL experienced a sudden demise. One reason for its growth was a successful strike initiated by local assemblies against Jay Gould's railroads in 1885, in which the Knights showed the public that an aggressive, well-disciplined group could take on one of the most powerful financiers of the day and win. Yet the effect of this strike may have been limited because neither the Knights nor the newspapers highly publicized the events. Another reason for the KOL's growth was its identification with the eight-hour workday, an issue of growing importance to the nation's workforce.[18] However, as discussed in the next section, the KOL's actions in support of the eight-hour workday were rather weak.

The KOL's leadership operated under several faulty assumptions. The advantage of hindsight makes it clear that the KOL's leadership erred in assuming that technological advancement could be halted and possibly reversed. The KOL also overestimated the extent to which employers and employees share common interests. Although some common ground exists, each group is motivated by self-interest, which in a profit-oriented economic system, makes labor gains a cost factor to be minimized in order to enhance ownership's interest. Employers are concerned about increased operating efficiency and profitability, whereas employees are concerned about job security and improving working conditions.

The KOL's third faulty assumption was that all types of employees shared identical employment interests. The KOL was ahead of its time in its attempt to organize less-skilled employees—a goal eventually accomplished by unions within the Congress of Industrial Organizations (CIO) in the late 1930s. However, employees do not all have the same employment interests, particularly if they have different skills, work classifications, or are employed in different industries or occupations. The "one big union" approach (enrolling nearly anyone who expressed an interest in the Knights) was further complicated by many immigrant members whose differences in race, language, and religion presented barriers to effective communications and achieving consensus regarding goals and tactics.[19]

The KOL's success was further hampered by a lack of legislation protecting the rights of employees to join unions and engage in collective bargaining. This point is further discussed in the next chapter. Suffice it to say that the Knights, as well as other labor organizations before 1935, did not have a legal right to engage in many of the collective activities necessary for effective representation of workers' interests.

The inability of the KOL's leadership (particularly Powderly) to identify with members' goals also presented a problem. The Knights insisted on adopting a middle-class program for the American labor force, which they refused to contemplate in industrial, working-class terms. Almost all local assembly meetings required the members to dress up after a day's work to engage in intellectual discourse. In essence, the members had nothing to do except "ceremonialize, play politics, and study."[20] Powderly felt his position was above that of the membership. Instead of understanding members' needs, Powderly imposed his own goals, on his terms: "I will talk at no picnics. . . . When I speak on the labor question I want the individual attention of my hearers and I want the attention for at least two hours and in that two hours I can only epitomize. At a picnic where . . . the girls as well as the boys swill beer I cannot talk at all."[21] The preference for intellectual deliberation over immediate action is perhaps best illustrated by Powderly's approach to the eight-hour workday movement.

The Eight-Hour Workday Movement and the Haymarket Riot

One of the more important reforms desired by many employees in the late 1800s was reducing the prevalent ten-hour workday to eight hours. Samuel Gompers, who was a Knights member and an official of other labor organizations (Federation of Organized Trades and Labor Unions and the Cigar Makers' Union), pressed Powderly to support a nationwide general strike on May 1, 1886, in support of the eight-hour workday. Powderly was receptive to the goal of an eight-hour workday, as it would give employees more leisure time to pursue intellectual activities. However, Powderly did not join Gompers' call to action because he did not believe the length of the workday was the major problem: "To talk of reducing the hours of labor without reducing the power of machinery is a waste of energy."[22]

Supporters of the eight-hour workday believed that, if instituted, employers would have to hire more employees to perform the current total hours worked, thereby reducing the unemployment problem. On May 3, 1886, some workers striking over this issue in Chicago were involved in a skirmish with the police, and at least four strikers were killed. A leader of this dispute published an inflammatory circular urging "Revenge!" and "Workingmen to Arms!" The circular also indicated that a mass rally would be held the next day at Haymarket Square in Chicago. The stage was set for an event (known later as the **Haymarket Riot**) that virtually eliminated the KOL's effectiveness.

On May 4, 1886, approximately 3,000 people attended the scheduled meeting, which began peacefully. Police who monitored the meeting were ordered by their chief to return to the station. However, Police Captain Bonfield, whom the governor of Illinois later charged as being responsible for the incident, ordered them back to the meeting. During a speech a bomb was thrown into the gathering of police, killing seven and wounding sixty. What happened next is uncertain. The *Chicago Tribune* reported that "anarchists and rioters poured in a shower of bullets before the first action of the police was taken."[23] Yet another report in the same article stated that the police opened fire on the crowd immediately after the bomb exploded. Regardless of the order of events, the police did shoot into the crowd, killing several and wounding 200.

Eight individuals allegedly responsible for the incident were arrested. Four of the eight were hanged, one committed suicide in prison, and three were eventually pardoned by the governor of Illinois after serving some of their sentences. The trial of these eight individuals contained a number of irregularities. For example, the hand-picked jury included a relative of one of the bombing victims.[24] The trial never did establish who threw the bomb; however, the accused were judged guilty by the *Chicago Tribune* before the trial took place. More specifically, the paper stressed that the "mob" was led by "two wirey whiskered foreigners,"[25] who were "Nihilistic Agitators."[26]

The Knights were not directly labeled in the immediate press accounts of the strike nor in the subsequent series of unsuccessful strikes over the eight-hour workday, which involved nearly 340,000 employees. However, the strikes contributed to the organization's demise for at least two paradoxical reasons. A substantial body of public opinion did label the Knights as being involved in the strikes. Yet many of the Knights' own members criticized their leadership for not participating enough in the events during and after the Haymarket Riot.[27] Indeed, Powderly strongly discouraged strikes over the eight-hour workday, believing instead that members should write essays on the subject. Thus, the Haymarket Riot dramatically reflected the split between the KOL and the newly formed American Federation of Labor led by Samuel Gompers, a labor organization that was to flourish and endure.

Origin and Goals of the American Federation of Labor (AFL)

An outgrowth of the Federation of Organized Trades and Labor Unions of the United States and Canada, the **American Federation of Labor (AFL)** was formed in 1886 after some of its member national unions (most notably the Cigar

Makers) were expelled from the Knights of Labor.[28] As previously mentioned, **Samuel Gompers**, a major founder of the AFL, was a member of the Knights but became disenchanted with the KOL leadership's long-range social reform philosophy. Gompers was also upset about KOL activities involving the cigar makers—in particular, the KOL's raiding of its members and supplying of strike-breakers to employers when the cigar makers struck firms.

Gompers met with the Knights in December 1886 to discuss these problems, but the meeting did not resolve the situation. Indeed, Gompers became incensed when a pamphlet was circulated among KOL representatives that attacked Gompers personally by indicating "the General Executive Board has never had the pleasure of seeing Mr. Gompers sober."[29] Also, in retrospect, KOL leaders blundered when they focused on recruiting skilled craft employees already members of an existing craft union (e.g., Cigar Makers Union), a move that resulted in bitter reactions from those trade unions. The Knights might have been better off (and still consistent with their goals) if they had devoted more attention to recruiting lesser skilled employees, where the skilled trades unions did not have any argument.[30]

Unlike the KOL, the AFL was not established as one big union. (The current organizational structure of the AFL-CIO is discussed more fully in Chapter 4.) The AFL represented a federation of national unions cooperating for mutual gain while permitting each national union to maintain independent control over its own identity and operations. Craft unions, such as the Cigar Makers, dominated the early stages of the AFL. The AFL influenced its member unions through its services, particularly organizing activities, philosophies, and strategies.

It is impossible to discuss the AFL apart from Gompers because "in the early years, the AFL existed only in the person of Gompers and in the annual conventions."[31] With the exception of 1895, Gompers was president of the AFL from its founding in 1886 until his death in 1924. Therefore, much of the discussion of the goals, strategies, and organization of the AFL is from the perspective of Gompers, a point of view that still relates strongly to the thinking of organized labor.

Gompers placed little emphasis on intellectual betterment, and he scorned other union leaders' pretensions to show labor union members the course of action they should pursue.[32] Gompers criticized the KOL as representing "a hodge-podge with no basis for solidarity with the exception of a comparatively few trade assemblies."[33] Gompers believed that the goals and organization of unions should flow directly and naturally from the members' needs, not from the pronouncements of top leaders who structured unions based on their views of what should have been, rather than what was.

Gompers particularly scorned those union leaders who tried to change the existing social system through revolutionary means.[34] Although Gompers was a socialist in his early years, he grew to despise this philosophy, contending that it was economically unsound, socially wrong, and impossible to apply in an industrial setting.[35] Gompers believed that union members should work for equitable treatment within industrial society rather than revolt against it.[36]

Thus, the AFL's major, if not sole goal was to improve the material conditions of members through the existing capitalistic system. This goal was attacked by the critics of the AFL as representing pure and simple unionism. Gompers embraced this intended insult; indeed, he seemed to devote most of his attention to ensuring that the AFL's "pure and simple" approach to collective bargaining successfully differentiated it from other labor organizations.

Pure and simple unionism had two major objectives. The primary objective was economic betterment of the organization's members. Gompers believed the "truth," or essence, of labor unions should be measured in terms of their economic accomplishments:

> Economic betterment—today, tomorrow, in home and shop, was the foundation upon which trade unions have been built. Economic power is the base upon which may be developed power in other fields. It is the foundation of organized society. Whoever or whatever controls economic power directs and shapes development for the group or the nation.[37]

Thus, the AFL's notion of "employee dignity" equated with measured economic gains. This view differed from the KOL's contention that employee dignity is attained by participation as equals in meaningful work and in other societal concerns.[38]

Gompers also stressed a second objective of pure and simple unionism—the enhancement of the capitalistic system, which could benefit both employees and employers. Workers could obtain more only if capitalism continued to flourish. Without capitalism, neither employees nor employers would receive revenues. The AFL therefore believed labor and management shared some similar interests. However, Gompers did not agree with Powderly that this situation would lead to complete employer–employee agreement on all issues. Gompers realized that major differences of opinion would occur over the distribution of revenues and that employees would probably have to pressure employers to receive their fair share.

Strategies and Tactics of the AFL

This realization prompted the AFL to rely on using economic pressure tactics in support of its collective bargaining efforts. Unlike the KOL, Gompers believed the strike was a viable collective bargaining tactic: "A workman must convince his employer that he is entitled to an advance in wages.... Why should the wage-earner work for less than living wages, which he would have to do if he could not strike? The worker is expected to continue to work at whatever wages his employer is willing to give in order to save the public from inconvenience."[39]

A second AFL tactic (particularly when its headquarters moved to Washington, D.C.) was that of involvement in the political arena. Gompers, an aggressive lobbyist, attempted to translate election votes of AFL members into "rewards" for political friends of labor and "punishments" for political enemies of labor. However, political efforts during Gompers's leadership were neither intense nor widespread throughout the AFL.[40] AFL political efforts were directed at influencing the existing two-party system instead of forming a third political party. Gompers felt that establishing a third party would divert too much time from fundamental collective bargaining efforts and was concerned that any new political party might fall under the socialists' control.[41]

A third AFL tactic was to enhance the public status and reputation of organized labor and the collective bargaining process. Gompers devoted much attention to the National Civic Foundation (NCF), formed in 1899 to promote industrial peace through collective bargaining. The NCF, composed of prominent labor, management, and political officials, attempted to guide public opinion toward the positive aspects of collective bargaining. However, at least one observer of industrial relations has questioned the success of this tactic, believing that "its rhetoric surpassed its performance."[42]

Organization of the AFL

The AFL's organizational structure was based on two related principles: **exclusive union jurisdiction** and **decentralized authority**. The AFL avoided the concept of "one big union" which had proven ineffective for the KOL, and insisted on using the principle of exclusive union jurisdiction. This principle rested on the twofold observation that (1) each craft or trade had unique working conditions and job interests and (2) combining members of different trades into one organization would jeopardize those interests and cause unnecessary dissension. The AFL believed in one union representing each identifiable skilled craft; for example, separate unions to represent carpenters, painters, and cigar makers. Because membership in the AFL was restricted to established skilled crafts, many semi-skilled workers did not meet the qualifications for membership in an AFL-affiliated union.

Gompers also strongly believed the AFL was a voluntary organization held together by the mutual self-interests of its members. Unlike Powderly, who believed that centralized authority was necessary to achieve the Knights' objectives, Gompers viewed the central AFL as a "rope of sand," dependent entirely on the acceptance of its members. Thus, the real authority rested with AFL's affiliated national unions and their member locals. As is further discussed in Chapter 4, these principles continue to influence contemporary union organizations.

Gompers was a most active union organizer who claimed to have helped in organizing 28 unions representing different crafts such as painters, papermakers, firefighters, and post office clerks.[43] Much of this effort was due to Gompers's view of himself as "one of the boys"—he took pride in his ability to socialize with the members on their own terms.

Despite Gompers's efforts, the AFL's early growth was not spectacular. Its original membership of 150,000 had increased to only 250,000 six years later. The initial slow growth was due to the counterattack of industry (discussed in the section on World War I to World War II), the generally repressive attitude of the government and the courts toward collective employee activities, and the difficulties created by the depression of 1893. Yet Gompers could view these modest membership gains as a tribute to the AFL's powers of "stability and permanency."[44]

From its formation until World War I, the AFL was directly or indirectly involved in three prominent events: the Homestead and Pullman incidents and the formation and demise of the Industrial Workers of the World.

The Homestead Incident

The Carnegie Steel Works, located in Homestead, Pennsylvania, was ironically the scene of one of the more violent episodes in labor history. The founder of the works, Andrew Carnegie, was a renowned philanthropist who gave every indication of being receptive to organized labor. In one article, written before the Homestead Incident, Carnegie stated that a strike or a lockout was a "ridiculous affair" because it represented only a test of strength instead of determining what was "fair and just."[45] Carnegie also believed that labor–management problems would occur in large firms run by salaried managers instead of owners because the former group had no permanent interest in the desires of the employees.

Carnegie's remarks proved prophetic in the **Homestead Incident** of July 6, 1892. Although many have labeled the incident a strike, one labor historian has noted that no strike vote was ever taken by the membership, and the employer prohibited the employees from working which would be more consistent with an employer lockout.[46] During negotiation between the mill and the Amalgamated Association of Iron, Steel, and Tin Workers (an affiliate of the AFL), a 15-foot-high solid board fence, topped with barbed wire, was constructed around the building. Andrew Carnegie was vacationing in Scotland during negotiations and had delegated these duties to a management official named Henry Clay Frick. The union labeled the structure around the steel mill "Fort Frick." Union members were undoubtedly aware that Frick was negotiating with Pinkerton detectives as a potential strike intervention force at the same time negotiations were being conducted with the Union. Frick intended to use Pinkerton detectives inside the facility to protect the company's property and as strikebreakers should a work stoppage occur.

On June 30, 1892, the company made its last offer, which represented a substantial reduction of previous wages and locked out its 4,000 employees.[47] Workmen then began an around-the-clock surveillance of the plant. One newspaper account indicated, "The line of pickets covers the river, roads, and railways so tightly that no stranger can enter the town without being known to the strikers."[48] On the morning of July 5, 300 Pinkertons gathered at Ashtabula, Ohio, and proceeded by rail to Youngstown, Ohio. They then traveled up the Monongahela River by barge. On July 6, word had reached the townspeople that the Pinkertons would be entering the plant from the river. Six thousand people lined the river banks at 2:00 A.M., and employees prepared two small cannons, one on each side of the river, to be used on the Pinkertons.[49]

The Pinkertons attempted to land by the company's beach at 5:00 A.M.; shots were exchanged, and three Pinkertons were killed. Shooting by both sides continued for 12 hours, with an additional seven townspeople killed and fifty wounded. The Pinkertons surrendered to the townspeople and were forced to run a bloody gauntlet before being locked up for their protection. The townspeople had taken the weapons from the Pinkertons, a situation that resulted in 8,700 National Guard militiamen being sent to secure the town. There were few further attempts to occupy the mill by Pinkertons or strikebreakers.[50] The incident ended for all purposes approximately five months later (November 20, 1892) when the Amalgamated lifted its prohibition against returning to work.

Homestead has been labeled the Waterloo of unions in the steel industry. After the Homestead Incident, membership in the national union dropped from 24,000 in 1892 to 8,000 in 1894. On the local level, only 800 of the original Homestead employees were reinstated. Carnegie's mills showed a dramatic increase in profits when the union was eliminated, a message that must have encouraged other employers to take an anti-union stance.[51]

Although Homestead represented a victory for management, the AFL and organized labor did benefit to some extent from the situation. First, Gompers demonstrated to existing and potential union members his very real concern about the Homestead situation.[52] The funds contributed by the AFL to help defray the employees' legal expenses also demonstrated that the AFL was interested in helping its member unions in a material sense.[53] Finally, the Homestead situation received more sympathetic newspaper accounts than did the Haymarket Riot. The press charged Carnegie with provoking the situation. For example, the *Chicago Tribune* strongly criticized the company's use of Pinkertons and contended that Carnegie's company, as well as any large industrial organization, "has duties and obligations toward society which it must not forget, and not the least of them is to do all in its power, and make all of the concessions it can, to preserve civil and industrial peace."[54]

The Pullman Strike

In the late 1800s and early 1900s strikes were common in the railroad industry. For example, the Great Upheaval of 1877 involved independent railroad employee associations protesting wage cuts. It was a bitter and violent confrontation in which more than 100 employees were killed and several hundred were badly wounded.[55]

Yet the **Pullman Strike** of 1894 assumes significance because of the principal personalities involved (Eugene Debs and George Pullman) and an organization (the American Railway Union) that had the potential to challenge the AFL for union members. It also approached being the only revolutionary strike in the United States, progressing from a nationwide strike in one industry to nearly involving all industries.[56]

As a result of the 1893 depression, the Pullman Company laid off 3,000 of its 5,800 employees and cut wages 25 to 40 percent. Both actions were important because they occurred in the milieu of George Pullman's company town. This town represented a social, paternalistic experiment by the owner of the Pullman Palace Car Company. The company owned all the houses, buildings, and services in the town, which were built to provide living space for company employees who were not allowed to own their own homes.[57] Pullman did not correspondingly reduce rents and charges for other services when wages were cut; thus, the wage cuts resulted in some employees having a net two-week pay of $1 to $6 during the winter of 1893 to 1894.

This situation generated much hostility among employees, many of whom were members of the American Railway Union (ARU), formed in 1893. The ARU was completely independent from the AFL and competed for members with the AFL-affiliated railway craft unions. The ARU accepted any white employee, regardless of specific job classification, so that railroad employees could present a unified front to the railroad companies.[58] The ARU was attractive to many employees because its inclusion of all types of railway workers served to counter employers' previously successful strategy of creating dissension among the different specialized craft unions by playing one against the other in wage negotiations.

The ARU's local unions had sole authority to call a strike, and the Pullman strike began on May 11, 1894. Eugene Debs, the ARU's leader, informed the strikers that the strike should represent a protest against philosophical issues rather than just for mere material betterment: "The paternalism of Pullman is the same as the interest of a slave holder in his human chattels. You are striking to avert slavery and degradation."[59]

At first the strikers followed Debs's orders not to damage railroad property. The ARU instead adopted a strategy of not operating any train that included a Pullman sleeping car—the common practice was to cut these cars from the train and move them to the side tracks. If any employee was discharged for this action, then the entire crew would quit, leaving the train immobilized. This tactic, employed in 27 states and territories, was intended to make railroad carriers put pressure on Pullman to agree with the ARU's bargaining position.

The railroad employers rallied behind Pullman and countered the union's strategy by hiring strikebreakers. Railroad employers also decided to include federal mail on nearly every train as a way of getting support from the federal government to ensure the mail was delivered. Owners were able to obtain a labor injunction on July 2, 1894 (subsequently upheld by the Supreme Court), to prevent any employee from interfering with the delivery of the mail. Employees could no longer engage in their strike strategy of rendering the trains inoperative. Some 16,000 troops, dispatched by President Cleveland to enforce the injunction, either delivered the mail and operated the trains or protected strikebreakers so that food and other perishable items could be delivered throughout the country.

The strike then took a particularly ugly turn when employees burned at least 700 railroad cars in Chicago on July 7, 1894. Management was also criticized for this incident for failing to take minimum security measures, such as guarding or locking the railroad cars, to prevent such damage. There were allegations that some management officials may have even provoked the incident to receive additional support from the government. This possibility is suggested because all the burned cars were old (the newer, more expensive Pullman sleeping cars were not on the property), and very few of the cars were loaded with any product.[60]

The resulting negative public opinion and increased action by the federal troops forced Debs to seek Gompers's cooperation. Debs wanted Gompers to call a national strike to help enforce Debs's last offer to settle the strike, which was simply management's agreement to reinstate the striking employees. Gompers refused to support Debs, contending that he did not have the authority to call a general strike. Gompers also believed that the proposed settlement would, in effect, admit to the public that the ARU had failed to win material benefits for its members. Much of Gompers's reluctance was based on his view of Debs as being "a leader of irregular movements and lost causes."[61] However, Gompers's inaction might also have been caused by his desire to eliminate a potential rival to the AFL and bolster his reputation in the business community.

Debs was eventually convicted and sentenced to federal prison in Atlanta, Georgia, for failing to abide by the court's injunction. The ARU, which had grown to 150,000 members in one year, quickly faded from existence. Organized labor did learn an important lesson from the Pullman strike: It would be difficult to alter existing terms and conditions of employment when confronted by a persistent, if not exceptionally stubborn, owner (Pullman), the federal government (troops, injunctions, legislation), and negative public opinion (fueled by exaggerated and dramatic newspaper articles).

The Industrial Workers of the World (IWW)

The **Industrial Workers of the World (IWW)** was formed as an alternative to the AFL on June 27, 1905. **William "Big Bill" Haywood**, one of the initial organizers of the IWW, proclaimed the organization's goals in calling the convention of 209 delegates to order with the following remarks:

> *"Fellow Workers... We are here to confederate the workers of this country into a working class movement that shall have for its purpose the emancipation of the working class from the slave bondage of Capitalism.... The aims and objects of this organization should be to put the working class in possession of the economic power, the means of life, in control of the machinery of production and distribution without regard to capitalist masters."*[62]

The initial goal of the IWW was to overthrow the existing capitalistic system by any means necessary because it felt the employers and employees had nothing in common. The IWW's radical political ideology was a marked departure from the pure and simple unionism approach of the AFL, which extolled the virtues of the capitalist system. While the Knights of Labor had also stressed that the existing wage and profit system needed to be changed, the KOL believed that employees and employers shared similar interests and that change must be peaceful and gradual. The IWW, on the other hand, had no reservations about using any method that would result in the quick destruction of capitalism.

The IWW also wanted to remove any societal aspect or group that supported capitalism. This approach placed the IWW in direct opposition to the AFL. The IWW regarded the AFL as an "extension of the capitalist class" because it advocated "pure and simple unionism," which was dependent on capitalism.[63] Haywood believed that Gompers had sold out the ARU when he failed to support Debs in the Pullman strike, and he viewed Gompers as an arrogant, power-hungry leader.[64] Thus, the IWW appeared to have two general enemies: capitalism and the AFL, which did not recognize a working-class movement of hourly employees as being a class-conscious group apart from the rest of society.

An analysis of the IWW reveals that establishing goals can be an easier task than accomplishing them. The IWW never did establish an effective organization; in fact, its leaders never made up their minds about precisely what kind of organizational structure it should adopt.[65] Most of the IWW officials agreed with Haywood's objective of organizing "every man that earns his livelihood either by his brain or his muscle."[66] This was similar to the One Big Union approach previously tried by the KOL. However, major differences arose among IWW leaders over how to organize one big union into an effective organization. Some members felt that the IWW should work slowly, for example, infiltrate the established AFL unions and gradually persuade members that the IWW cause was best. Others felt that this temporary acceptance of collective bargaining with the capitalists only made employees "better paid slaves" and would hinder the quick and necessary overthrow of the capitalistic system.[67] In addition to organizational differences, there were at least four reasons for the decline of the IWW, reasons that served as negative lessons for contemporary organized labor.

1. **Lack of permanent membership and financial base.** A large proportion of the IWW consisted of itinerants—individuals who either were unemployed or traveled from job to job, particularly in the agriculture, mining, and lumber industries. This contributed to an unstable financial base. Many IWW leaders thought the members' dues should not be mandatory but instead, should be paid out of a voluntary "inner conviction." For example, in 1907 only 10,000 members out of the total 31,000 members paid any dues. The lack of revenues resulted in meager strike funds, and by 1909 the organization was deeply in debt.

2. **Inability of the IWW to appeal to members' interests.** The IWW did not consider the short-run material interests of its members. Its major emphasis on long-term political and philosophical goals and its focus on propaganda as a means to achieve these goals failed to demonstrate tangible signs of success on a continuous basis.[68] The average trade unionist, inside or outside the IWW, had no desire to help the underdog. Indeed, it was all he could do to look out for himself.[69]

3. **Identification of the IWW with sabotage and violence.** The relationship between the IWW and sabotage and violence was ambiguous. The IWW in 1914 became the only labor organization to ever officially endorse sabotage at its convention. Yet no local, state, or federal authority could ever establish legal proof of any IWW-instigated violence. A strike in 1917 closed the logging camps and sawmills of the Pacific Northwest but did not record any violent acts of sabotage by the IWW.[70] The IWW often stated that sabotage does not always equal destruction of equipment. For

example, employees could "sabotage" a company by "malicious obedience" (following the work rules to the letter, thereby creating a slowdown) and by informing customers that the company's product was of inferior quality. However, at least one article in the IWW's paper, the *Industrial Worker,* indicated how emery dust and ground-up glass could cause the destruction of machinery. Evidence suggests that the IWW's leadership did not generally advocate physical violence.[71] Yet, there are some accounts of incidents in which IWW members and leaders pledged a "life for a life" or "an eye for an eye."[72] At a minimum, it would appear that the IWW did not actively discourage its link with violence.

4. **Alienation of the news media and government officials.** The newspapers enhanced the IWW's reputation for violence by labeling members as "desperate villains who set fire to wheat fields, drove spikes into sawmill-bound logs, derailed trains, destroyed industrial machinery, and killed policemen."[73] Part of this negative image was enhanced by leaders of IWW factions who would damn one another in the press. The IWW also engaged in several "free speech fights"—soapbox speeches in local communities. This strategy, which has since been copied by various protest groups, including students, relied on there being more participants than there were available jail spaces. City officials, faced with such a situation, typically allowed the "unlawful" demonstration to continue.[74] In many of these speeches, members of the IWW would shout anti-social comments such as "There is no God."[75]

The press, never enthusiastic about unions in general, reserved a special hatred for the IWW. One editorial against the IWW stated: "They would be much better dead, for they are absolutely useless in the human economy; they are the waste material of creation and should be drained off into the sewer of oblivion there to rot in cold obstruction like any other excrement."[76]

The IWW also remained alienated from the government. It did not actively use the existing political system because many of its transient members could not meet voter registration requirements. The IWW also incurred the wrath of the federal government when it refused to support involvement in World War I, proclaiming instead that the war represented a plot to allow capitalists to profit from the sale of war materials, while working-class individuals served as soldiers in the armed conflict. The government responded to the IWW's anti-war stance by arresting more than 100 leaders for sedition and sentencing most of them to prison terms ranging from 5 to 20 years. In effect, the IWW went out of existence in 1918, even though the organization remains today with a handful of members.

The onset of World War I found the AFL confronting several challenges. The AFL had been the first national labor organization to withstand a severe economic depression, a hostile press, reluctant or hostile employers, and three rival labor organizations (KOL, ARU, and IWW). Yet the AFL also faced internal pressures from at least three sources: 1) socialists and other related political groups that advocated independent political action and the organization of low-skilled industrial employees; 2) pacifist members who wanted the AFL to remain neutral or take a stand against the war; and 3) member unions that became involved in jurisdictional disputes caused by increased specialization and technological change (for example, the plumber was no longer responsible for the complete installation of the water and heating system for a building).[77] Perhaps the most lingering concern of the AFL was that the largest proportion of unrepresented workers in the

Copyright GettyImages

"Unions are first and foremost, organizations seeking to improve the lives of those they represent by improving their conditions of work and by insuring respect for their dignity as workers. Organized labor believes that each worker is entitled to a fair day's pay for a fair day's work. That pay should include a share in the profits the worker helps to create and, thus, unions seek a larger share of those profits than 'market forces' might dictate.... those profits can only be created in a well-managed enterprise, where both capital and labor contribute to the result. Since its earliest days, the labor movement has sought to improve the quality of work-life, create workplace democracy and participate in joint employer-employee decision-making...we understand that confrontation and conflict are wasteful and that a cooperative approach to solving shared present and future problems is desirable."

SOURCE: AFL-CIO Committee on the Evolution of Work, *The Changing Situation of Workers and Their Unions* (Washington, D.C.: AFL-CIO, 1985), pp. 5–7.

"The industrial union organizing drive of the 1930s was a movement for democracy. Talk to the mass production workers who took part in it, and they will tell you that what they wanted more than anything else was dignity. They wanted freedom from the petty harassment of a foreman who could send a man home at will and regard those who curried his favor with steady work, preferred jobs, and promotion. They wanted unions of their own choosing which could stand up to the power of corporate employers and bargain on equal terms. Like democratic movements in America before and

labor force, low- or semi-skilled industrial employees, remained essentially outside the ranks of organized labor.[78]

WORLD WAR I TO WORLD WAR II

The period from World War I to World War II witnessed several important phenomena:

1. The inability of unions, particularly the AFL, to make substantial membership gains in the 1920s.
2. The further development of employer strategies to minimize union growth.
3. Increased union concern over organizing semi-skilled industrial employees, which led to a bitter rivalry between the AFL and the Congress of Industrial Organizations (CIO).

Union Organizing after World War I: Problems and Prospects

The AFL overcame its initial reluctance toward participating in World War I and eventually pledged its cooperation when the United States became directly involved in the war. The government, aware of the need to ensure uninterrupted production of war materials, responded to the AFL by attempting to meet some its concerns. Government agreements with the AFL provided for the enforcement of trade union standards in all government contracts; labor representatives were appointed to all government agencies, including the War Labor Board; and Gompers was made a member of the Advisory Commission of the National Council of Defense. In short, organized labor was elevated to a more prominent status than had ever been witnessed before. Accordingly, the

since, they believed that the human right to a job should take precedence over the property right to manage an enterprise as the employer sees fit."

SOURCE: *Rank and File,* ed. by Alice and Staughton Lynd (Boston: Beacon Press, 1973), p. 1.

"...the contemporary union may be viewed primarily as a response to modern industrialism....

Central to modern industrialism is the principle of rationality in the planning of enterprise decisions according to some cost-output standard. The application of this principle introduces tensions and strains in the management-worker relationship whenever it leads to decisions which in the eyes of the workers conflicts with their interest in job security, work satisfaction, and sense of equity."

SOURCE: Jack Barbash, *American Unions: Structure, Government, and Politics* (New York: Random House, 1967), p. 3.

"The present day union leader is likely to carry a briefcase, look like a business executive, and sport an undergraduate or professional degree."

SOURCE: Arthur R. Schwartz and Michele M. Hoyman, "The Changing Guard: The New American Labor Leader," *The ANNALS,* 473 (May 1984), p. 65.

"The problem with history is that it's written by college professors about great men. That's not what history is. History's a hell of a lot of little people getting together and deciding they want a better life for themselves and their kids."

SOURCE: Bill Talcott, organizer, as quoted in Studs Terkel, *Working* (New York: Avon Books, 1974), p. 468.

"Like it or not, these challenges aren't the kind that can be ridden out. They demand new and farsighted solutions, and we must be an integral part of developing those solutions."

SOURCE: Ron Gettelfinger, President of the United Auto Workers as quoted in Dina ElBoghadady, "UAW Chief Warns Workers of Tough Changes Ahead," *Washington Post,* June 13, 2006, D1.

AFL had a sizable growth in membership during this period (an increase from 2,370,000 members in 1917 to 3,260,000 members in 1919). Legislative gains also occurred. A long-time AFL goal of severely restricting the number of new immigrants entering the country was accomplished.

The rather sharp increase in the cost of living that followed World War I, coupled with the newly recognized status of labor, resulted in an unprecedented number of strikes. For example, the Seattle General Strike of 1919, along with other strikes by actors, New York waterfront employees, and coal miners. The most widespread strike in 1919 occurred in the steel industry, where some 367,000 employees walked off the job in 70 major cities.

This strike actually resulted in a setback to organized labor in the steel industry. Many possible factors contributed to the setback. Some were notably similar to those found in the Homestead and Pullman incidents, whereas others reflected a typical situation unions faced in the 1920s and early 1930s. Of crucial importance to the outcome of the 1919 steel strike were internal union difficulties: an organizing campaign conducted by 24 unions instead of one common industrial union; improvised leadership rather than a consistent union approach to the issues; and poor financial resources. U.S. Steel was also successful in withstanding the strike by using strikebreakers and maintaining strong ties with other companies and social institutions, such as the press and church leaders. The strike ended without a labor agreement and another 15 years would elapse before organized labor would make any significant progress in organizing the steel industry.[79]

Although the steel industry did not reflect all industrial reactions to collective bargaining, apparently many other unions were similarly powerless to organize companies like U.S. Steel, that firmly believed unions were not in the firm's best interests. For example, another 1919 strike almost paralyzed the coal industry when no miners returned to work until President Wilson persuaded them to accept a temporary wage increase and submit all other issues to a newly appointed Bituminous Coal Commission. In 1920 the commission awarded increases ranging from 20 to 30 percent, but this was the last victory for mine employees for several years.

Despite increased status and militancy, something went wrong for organized labor in the 1920s; the "Golden Twenties" for the majority in the United States was a dreary decade for labor—both for hourly employees in terms of real income and for labor unions in terms of membership.[80] Between 1920 and 1924, total union membership declined from 5,110,000 to 3,600,000; membership in AFL unions dropped from 4,078,000 to 2,866,000. By 1930 total union membership had declined to 3,400,000, and AFL membership dropped to 2,700,000.[81] This decline was caused by at least two major factors: (1) aggressive counteractions by employers and (2) organized labor's inability to overcome anti-union sentiment among potential union members.[82]

Counteractions by Employers

Concerned with the increased status given labor during the war, employers actively engaged in efforts to roll back union membership gains, beginning in the 1920s and continuing through the 1930s. These tactics took the form of either 1) aggressive opposition toward labor unions or 2) providing an acceptable alternative to independent unions.

Employers actively opposed unions throughout the **open-shop movement**, which is discussed in more detail in Chapter 4. The stated purpose of this movement was to ensure that employees had the freedom to determine whether they would choose to join a union. Another rationale for this movement, also called the **American Plan**, was employers' desire for employees to adhere to the traditional American value of "rugged individualism" instead of the "foreign," "subversive," and "corrupt" principles of labor unions. Many employers equated the attainment of an open shop status with the absence of an independent union controlled by employees.

Other tactics were also used by employers to prevent employees from joining or forming an independent union. For example, some employers would hire **industrial spies** to determine which employees had pro-union sentiments.[83] Identified employees would then be discharged and possibly **blacklisted**, meaning that their names would be given to other employers in the area who would then refuse to hire anyone whose name appeared on the list. Employer violence against participants in union-organizing drives was also a potential strategy to counter unions during this period.[84]

A variation of the open shop or American Plan, appeared in the 1930s, with the development of the so called **Mohawk Valley Formula**. This approach formulated specific steps which could be used by an employer to defeat an organizing drive or strike action by a union. The Mohawk Valley Formula consisted of the following steps: "Form a citizens' committee in the community, label the union leaders as outside agitators, stir up violence or the fear of violence, have a 'state of emergency' declared, organize a back-to-work movement, and finally have the back-to-work employees march into the plant protected by armed police."[85]

Employers also countered unions by providing an alternative model to unionism. The 1920s saw widespread employer **paternalism**, a management style in which the employer was viewed as the wise parent figure and employees were expected to rely upon the employer to know what was in their best interest and trust the employer to protect employees' interests. Paternalistic practices implemented by some companies included free lunches, baseball fields, vacations, pensions, and employee counseling.[86] Employers felt that employees receiving these benefits would be indebted to the employer and realize that a union would be unnecessary.

An **employee representation plan**, or **company union** as it was also called, provided another substitute for an employee-controlled independent union. Employee representation plans (ERPs) covered as many as 1.5 million employees and appeared superficially similar to independent unions in that employee representatives (typically selected by the employer) would discuss working conditions with management officials. ERPs differed from independent unions in two major respects. First, independent unions had more autonomy than ERPs. Employers strongly influenced the decisions of ERPs, provided the funding, space, and time for their operation, and could veto any decision made by the joint labor-management committee. The employer typically controlled the agenda of items discussed with ERP leaders, and ERPs did not engage in economic pressure tactics like strikes or boycotts to persuade the employer to modify decision outcomes. ERPs were usually limited to a single facility, and employees under ERPs could neither press for work rules that would remove unfair competition from other facilities nor push for legislation at the local, state, or federal level.[87] ERPs did provide employees more communication with management than existed in their absence and most importantly, an employee need not fear discharge for participating in an organization created by their own employer.

Labor's Inability to Overcome Anti-Union Sentiment

The lack of organizing gains during the 1920s also has to be attributed to the anti-union sentiment of potential union members and the activities and attitudes of organized labor. Part of this problem may have been caused by the relatively good economic conditions that prevailed: "While job insecurity may have deterred some employees from joining unions in the face of employer opposition, many of them apparently felt that unions were no longer as necessary as they had formerly believed them to be. What profit strikes or other agitation for collective bargaining when the pay envelope was automatically growing fatter and a more abundant life seemed to be assured with our rapid approach to the final triumph over poverty?"[88]

There was also a public perception fostered by employers and media accounts that much of organized labor was corrupt and subject to control by the socialists and communists. Racketeering had become a feature of some local union–employer relationships. For example, in one incident a union official signed a two-paragraph agreement with three major employers guaranteeing no wage increase for three years and requiring all employees to join the union or be discharged. None of the employees had ever contacted the union about joining, nor did they ever see a union official during the life of the contract. This type of **sweetheart contract** was often coupled with financial kickbacks from the employer to the union official, meaning the employer paid the union official a portion of the labor cost savings achieved by the employer.[89]

Some labor unions were also accused of harboring communists and other political radicals. Many prominent union leaders would occasionally accept help from almost any group that would devote time and effort in organizing employees, believing that they could control these political elements once the local union had been established. However, union leaders sometimes overestimated their ability to control such elements. One former president of the Steelworkers Union recalled how communists could dominate local union meetings by using the **V technique**, whereby the leader would find a seat in the center of the auditorium in about the second or third row. Then the following would ensue: "A few rows back, two of his associates would locate about ten seats apart, and this same pattern would be followed all the way to the rear of the hall. When the chief spokesman opened debate, his line would then be parroted all the way through the V behind him, giving an illusion of widespread strength. The radical groups would also wait until other union members, tired and bored, had gone home before trying to push through their own proposals."[90]

Organized labor, particularly the AFL, devoted much of its attention during the 1920s to overcoming its negative public image.[91] These efforts detracted from active organizing efforts, particularly because Gompers had lost much of his former physical enthusiasm for this activity. In 1924 Gompers died, and his successor, William Green, did not revive any major organizing activities, as he had to maintain the AFL's existing organization in an adverse atmosphere.[92] The AFL's preference for simply maintaining the status quo among its member unions rather than seeking to actively grow the labor movement eventually led to the formation of the **Congress of Industrial Organizations (CIO)**.

Rise of the CIO and Industrial Unionism

Major disagreement occurred within the AFL over organizing the growing number of semi-skilled employees in the labor force. Tremendous technological shifts occurring during and after World War I reducing the demand for highly skilled employees. This increased the percentage of the labor force comprised of semi-skilled production workers. In 1926, for example, 85 percent of the hourly employees at Ford Motor Company required less than two weeks of training.[93] Because craft employees no longer dominated the industrial scene, the AFL needed to organize production employees if it wanted to increase membership.

Many of the AFL unions did not want to enroll semi-skilled production employees. Some AFL leaders believed these employees were inferior to craft employees and possessed less bargaining power. Other AFL leaders thought the inclusion of production workers would confuse and distort the AFL's organization. William Green himself did not view industrial employees as being compatible with the AFL's organizational principle of exclusive jurisdiction by skilled craft.

Some AFL leaders thought that a separate union would be needed for each company's or industry's products. Thus, if General Electric had 50 different products, then 50 different AFL unions (each having exclusive jurisdiction over its members' interests) would be needed for effective collective bargaining. In other words, at least 50 separate collective bargaining agreements could be negotiated by GE and its unions. The president of one AFL union urged his members to stamp out "the awful serpent of industrial trade unionism that would destroy this International and weaken the entire structure of the Labor Movement."[94]

The issue came to a head in 1935 under the direction of John L. Lewis, president of the AFL's United Mine Workers Union. The AFL rejected the concept of industrial unionism through three separate votes at its 1935 convention.[95] On November 9, 1935 the Committee for Industrial Organizations was formed. Its purpose was allegedly "educational and advisory," but in reality it was intended to promote organizing among unrepresented employees, particularly those semi-skilled workers in the mass-production industries.[96]

In January 1936, AFL leaders were shocked to find that the Committee for Industrial Organizations had been formed by some AFL unions. AFL President Green thought the industrial unionism issue had been buried once and for all at the 1935 convention. The Committee for Industrial Organizations not only discussed the industrial unionism concept but also requested the immediate granting of industrial union charters to a number of industries such as the rubber workers and the autoworkers. The Committee further insisted that an organizing campaign be started at once in the steel industry.

The AFL, confronted with the most serious challenge in its history, ordered the Committee for Industrial Organizations to disband or get out. Personalities intensified the issue. John L. Lewis, a powerful man in voice and action, sought and obtained power and publicity in his union activities.[97] Lewis managed to provoke AFL leaders into a confrontation while at the same time whipping his United Mine Workers members into a "lather of rage" against the AFL.[98] Lewis believed that the future success of the American labor movement was dependent on the ability to organize production workers in the fast growing mass production industries. In 1938, the split over the industrial unionism issue resulted in seven unions with almost a million members being expelled from the AFL. These seven unions joined with newly established industrial unions in some of the mass production industries to quickly form a rival and completely independent labor federation, the Congress of Industrial Organizations (CIO), electing **John L. Lewis** (then president of the United Mine Workers union) as the first CIO president.[99]

The development of the CIO coincided with a significant upsurge in union membership. By November 1937, the CIO's affiliated unions had already organized 75 percent of the steel industry, 70 percent of the automobile industry, 65 percent of the rubber industry, and about one-third of the maritime and textile industries.[100] The AFL also saw rapid growth in membership during the late 1930s and the 1940s. The AFL organized the skilled trade employees in mass production industries into local labor unions and national councils assigned to various craft unions. The steady growth of the AFL during the late 1930s was also aided by employers' preference to deal with the more conservative organization instead of taking their chances with the new, unpredictable, and more politically radical CIO.[101]

Why did union membership increase dramatically in the 1930s and 1940s? At least five factors seem to account for the growth in unionism during this period: strong CIO leadership, the CIO's realistic goals, the CIO's effective use of sit-down strikes, passage of the National Labor Relations (Wagner) Act of 1935, and changes in employees' attitudes toward a more favorable view of unions.

Strong CIO Leadership

The aggressive and effective CIO leaders (John L. Lewis, Sidney Hillman, and David Dubinsky, among others) infused new life into a union movement previously content with resting on its laurels. Most of the CIO union leaders had extensive organizing experience and prided themselves on keeping in touch with their membership.[102] Union leaders' accomplishments should not be overstated, however, because organizing drives involved the tireless efforts of many individuals who typed up circulars, contacted prospective members, and provided routine services that ensured union election victories. One biographer of

John L. Lewis indicated he lacked involvement in many routine organizing chores by noting that Lewis preferred "arriving only in time for the triumphant finale."[103] Much organizing effort in the steel, mining, automobile, and other industries was effectively directed toward second-generation immigrants. Some 30 percent of the CIO leadership came from a "new immigrant" background. One historian notes, "The success of the CIO was based on the mobilization of ethnic workers and on their willingness to join unions."[104]

Realistic Goals

The CIO shared only a superficial similarity with the KOL's and IWW's "one big union" approach to union membership. The CIO believed that grouping all employees by chartering one union for each particular industry (e.g., auto, steel) would still provide sufficient membership similarity to reflect the common interests of employees even though within that industry non-managerial employees of all skill levels were welcome to join. More importantly, the CIO dramatically differed from the Knights and the IWW in its goal of focusing on short-run economic gains instead of long-range reform, which paralleled the AFL's "pure and simple unionism" approach, including support for the existing capitalist system. John L. Lewis remarked: "I think most people have come to realize, that we cannot progress industrially without real cooperation between workers and management, and that this can only be brought about by equality in strength and bargaining power of labor and management. Labor is sincere in its desire to help. It looks forward to an industrial procedure which will increase productive efficiency and lower prices to the consumer."[105]

The Effective Use of Sit-Down Strikes

The CIO used a successful tactic for encouraging employer's to recognize and bargain with its member national unions—the **sit-down strike**, in which employees stayed inside the plant instead of picketing outside. This technique was successful because employers were reluctant to physically remove the employees from the plant for fear that their equipment could be damaged in the confrontation.

The tactic was initially applied by the IWW at a General Electric facility in 1906, but the most famous of this strike tactic occurred in December 1936 at a General Motors facility in Flint, Michigan. At one time, 26,000 General Motors employees had belonged to a union, but in early 1936, there were only 122 union members, many of whom were management spies.[106] A local grassroots organization was secretly established to build up the union at Flint. The sit-down strike was locally planned by autoworkers as Lewis and the CIO were focused on organizing the steel industry before launching any major effort to organize the automobile industry. The CIO, however, did lend its active support to autoworkers once the strike was under way.

The sit-down strike at Flint lasted 44 days and received widespread community support while hindering GM's efforts to reverse its negative profit situation of previous years.[107] The strike resulted in employer recognition of the union, a fact that was noticed by many employees in other trades. Between September 1936 and June 1937, some 500,000 employees in the rubber, glass, and textile industries engaged in sit-down strikes. Although effective, the sit-down strike was short-lived because public opinion eventually frowned on this tactic, and a subsequent decision by the Supreme Court declared such strikes represented an illegal seizure of the employer's property.

Passage of the National Labor Relations (Wagner) Act

Another (and perhaps the most significant) reason for the increased number of union members was the passage of the **National Labor Relations Act (NLRA) of 1935** (discussed more in Chapter 3). The federal government indicated through this law that collective bargaining was a public policy in the national interest. Private-sector employees covered by the law were granted a legal right to form or join unions, bargain collectively, or engage in other concerted acts for mutual aid or protection. Many previously common employer tactics used for preventing union growth were declared illegal (e.g., black listing, spies, employee discharge for union activity, and company unions). A new federal agency, the National Labor Relations Board (NLRB), was created to administer union representation elections, define employer unfair labor practices, and enforce the legal rights of employees to join independent unions and bargain collectively.

Changes in Employees' Attitudes

Many employees' previously negative attitudes toward organized labor changed dramatically. Employees had experienced the Great Depression of the 1930s and realized that job security could not be achieved solely through hard work and loyalty to the employer. These employees now viewed unions as a mechanism to promote job security and provide other material economic benefits.

By the onset of World War II, organized labor had reversed its membership decline of the 1920s, rising to almost nine million members in 1940. Yet the rivalry between the CIO and the AFL was intense and sometimes violent as AFL and CIO organizers clashed over the right to represent mass production industry employees. James Hoffa, a former president of the International Brotherhood of Teamsters (then an AFL union), recalled violent organizing drives in 1941 between CIO affiliated unions and his union: "Through it all the members wore two pins, putting on a Teamsters button when we were around and switching to a CIO button when those guys showed up. They were waiting to see which union was going to win the battle. You couldn't really blame them. They were scared out of their britches because they didn't want to get caught in the bloody middle."[108] The AFL and CIO rivalry existed in almost every industry and extended to the local level, where it was common for an employer to have both AFL and CIO unions representing the same employees.[109] Even employers with the best intentions had difficulty in building an effective labor–management relationship in such an environment.

WORLD WAR II TO THE PRESENT

The AFL at first did not want the United States to become involved in World War II; however, this attitude changed after the bombing of Pearl Harbor. Concern over providing for the nation's defense prompted increased union–management cooperation. For example, both union and management officials participated on War Production Board subcommittees. Such panels weighed employee suggestions, which saved 31 million work hours and $44 million during World War II.[110]

The cooperative spirit was not total, particularly from the standpoint of strikes taken during wartime. In February 1943, organized labor complained to President Roosevelt that the cost of living during wartime had increased far beyond wage increases permitted by the government under the 1942 government imposed wage controls known as the Little Steel Formula.[111] The United Mine Workers conducted a series of strikes to obtain wage increases of $2 a day in 1943. These actions resulted in President Roosevelt seizing the mines to ensure continued production, but eventually a compromise wage settlement was obtained.

The public viewed these and other strikes with anger and alarm, considering them violations of the no strike pledge announced by organized labor in 1941. Negative public sentiment increased when some unions continued to call strikes. After 1942, the number of strikes increased every year of the war. In perspective, however, the number of employee days lost to strikes was estimated to be the equivalent of no more than one day per year per worker for the four war years.[112] Yet, the mere act of participating in a strike was viewed by some as unpatriotic.

Labor's collective bargaining concerns shifted at the end of the war to the issues of full employment and further wage increases in order to sustain national purchasing power and thereby create an expanding market for industrial goods. Labor, remembering the reconversion period following World War I, was concerned about employer policies aimed at restricting union growth and wage gains.

Unions backed their postwar concerns with strikes. "During no period in the history of the United States did the scope and intensity of labor–management conflicts match those recorded in the year following VJ Day, August 14, 1945."[113] In this one-year period, more than 4,600 strikes, involving 5 million employees and resulting in almost 120 million workdays of idleness, affected almost every major industry. These strikes were basically nonviolent, representing essentially economic tests of strength and endurance. With many soldiers returning to the private-sector labor force and increasing the labor supply, many employers saw little need for improving wages to be able to fill necessary job vacancies. Generally, both labor and management prefer to be free to resolve their differences through the collective bargaining process without the type of government interference and wage restrictions that were present during the war years.

Developments in Organized Labor Since World War II

Four major developments have occurred in organized labor since World War II: increased concern over new collective bargaining issues; organizing drives aimed at white-collar, service-, and public-sector employees; the merger of the AFL and CIO in 1955; and the formation of the Change to Win labor federation in 2005.

New Collective-Bargaining Issues

The return to peacetime after World War II and, particularly, the Korean War saw increased efforts to extend the provisions of the labor agreement to include all aspects of the collective bargaining relationship. In the late 1950s and early 1960s, the relative scarcity of jobs coincided with the need for price stability to ease the deficit in international payments. Unions directed their collective bargaining efforts toward guaranteeing members job security in the face of possible technological advances and wages that would compensate for inflation. Organized labor's response toward technological change (discussed in more detail in Chapter 8) brought notable results during this period, including the Automation Fund Agreement between Armour and Company and the Packinghouse Workers and Meat Cutters' unions (1959), the Mechanization and Modernization Agreement in the Pacific Coast longshore industry (1960), and the Long-Range Sharing Plan negotiated between Kaiser Steel and the United Steelworkers (1962).

Employee benefits represented a second new bargaining area. Before World War II, labor cost was overwhelmingly comprised of straight-time hourly pay for time actually worked.[114] Subsequent bargaining efforts by labor unions (and personnel policies of nonunion firms) have resulted in a substantial increase in the proportion of labor costs comprised of employee benefits (pensions, insurance plans, and so forth), which are currently around 37 percent of payroll costs for unionized employers.[115] Wage and benefit issues will be discussed further in Chapter 7.

The trend toward multi-year labor agreements after World War II put pressure on union leaders to safeguard wage increases against the possibility of increases in the inflation rate. In 1948, General Motors and the United Auto Workers negotiated a long-term agreement with a cost-of-living (COLA) provision that adjusted wages for inflationary changes during the life of the contract. This contract provision spread to other labor-management negotiations. In 1952, almost 3 million employees (approximately 20 percent of the employees covered by labor agreements) had cost-of-living provisions in their contracts.[116] Since the mid-1970s increased global competition from foreign companies and non-union organizations in the United States have produced periods of **concession bargaining** in some industries (e.g., auto, airline, steel, rubber), in which management seeks to obtain more flexible work-rule modifications or other labor cost reductions (wage rates, pension, or health care benefits). Work rule modifications include scheduling changes, fewer rest breaks, and combining job classifications to give management more flexibility in employee work assignments. Some employers (e.g., United Airlines, Northwest Airlines, Delphi Automotive) have declared bankruptcy and sought to use the bankruptcy process as a means to pressure unions representing the firm's employees to agree to significant concessions as a part of management's reorganization plan, resulting in a lower, more competitive labor cost operating structure. Wage concessions represent the most significant organized labor development since World War II. Audrey Freedman of the Conference Board notes that, "wages, even under union bargaining pressures, are far more responsive to economic conditions at the industry and firm level and even the product level. . . ."[117] Examples of wage flexibility include:

- "Two-tiered wage plans," where employees hired after a negotiated labor agreement takes effect receive a lower hourly pay rate (and/or benefits) than their counterparts for performing similar work.

- "Lump sum" pay usually associated with a firm's economic performance for a given time period. This wage payment does not necessarily occur in every year of a contract's term and does not alter the employee's hourly wage rate, thus avoiding any increase in employee benefit costs which use an employee's wage rate to calculate the size or amount of the benefit (e.g., holiday or vacation pay).

Organization of Public-Sector, White-Collar, and Service Employees

A second major development in organized labor since World War II involves the organization of different types of employees. More specifically, public-sector (government) employees (discussed in Chapter 13) and white-collar and service employees (discussed in Chapter 5) have received increased attention from union organizers and are now an increasing segment of union membership.

Merger of the AFL and CIO

Perhaps the most dramatic postwar development in organized labor was the merger of the AFL and CIO in 1955. The presence of three influences during the 1950s resulted in the eventual merger.[118] First was the change in the presidents of the AFL and CIO. Phillip Murray of the steelworkers' union became president of the CIO in 1940 when Lewis resigned and Murray continued the verbal feud against the AFL and its president, William Green. In November 1952, both Green and Murray died. Walter Reuther from the autoworkers union was elected to head the CIO and George Meany from the plumbers' union was elected president of the AFL. Although neither new leader had any particular fondness for the other, unlike Green and Murray, the new leaders had not previously gone on the record as being opposed to each other. Therefore, a merger could occur without either leader losing face.

Another influence contributing to the **AFL-CIO** merger was the recognized ineffectiveness of union raiding. The two labor organizations investigated employee representation elections in which the AFL tried to organize employees affiliated with CIO unions, and vice versa. During a two-year period (1951 to 1952), 1,245 such elections involved some 366,740 employees, with only 62,000 employees changing union affiliation. This figure overestimates the number affected because it does not consider the offsetting nature of elections. An AFL union could organize a CIO represented factory of 1,000 employees only to have a CIO union organize an AFL factory of 1,000 employees—the net change being zero. In fact, the extensive raiding during 1951 and 1952 resulted in a net gain for the AFL of only 8,000 members, or only 2 percent of the total number of employees involved in the elections.[119] Both the AFL and CIO finally realized that organized labor would benefit if the energies devoted to raiding each other were spent on organizing unrepresented employees. Accordingly, many of the AFL and CIO unions signed a no-raiding agreement in 1954. Instead of concentrating on differences emphasized in raiding activities, the two major federations could now look at similar goals that might be more easily attained by a merger.

One similar goal was the desire of both organizations to reward their political friends and punish political enemies.[120] In many instances, the independent organizations failed to achieve this goal. For example, the AFL and CIO were unable to defeat the re-election of Senator Taft (one of the authors of the Taft-Hartley Act, who was perceived as being anti-labor) and failed to elect Adlai Stevenson (supporter of organized labor) over Dwight D. Eisenhower for U.S. president. Both organizations believed that a merger might increase their effectiveness in the political arena.

The AFL-CIO merger on December 12, 1955, involved 15,550,000 members, making the new organization the largest trade union federation in the world. George Meany became the president of the merged organization due to the longer history of the AFL as an established organization. Walter Reuther, the former president of the CIO became the vice president of the merged AFL-CIO. George Meany believed the merger would lead to more employees becoming unionized and to a greater political influence for labor within the American two-party system.[121]

The merger resulted in the continued reduction of union raiding. It also reduced the influence of union locals within the national unions because they could no longer threaten to affiliate with the rival national organization.[122] However, as discussed further in the next section, the AFL-CIO merger has not resulted in a tremendous increase in union membership or political influence. It did reduce the former divisiveness within organized labor, but it cannot be concluded that the merger was a significant impetus for growth and change.

Formation of the Change to Win Federation

Reminiscent of the split among AFL unions which led to the formation of the CIO in the late 1930s, several national unions affiliated with the AFL-CIO voluntarily chose to leave in order to form a new federation of national unions called the **Change to Win federation** (discussed further in Chapter 4). After failing to achieve reforms within the AFL-CIO intended to focus more resources on organizing new union members, seven national unions representing approximately 6.4 million members, many of whom work in service-related industries, formed their own independent federation to foster more emphasis on organizing new union members.[123] The Change to Win federation, although less formally structured than the AFL-CIO, still shares many of the same basic principles and philosophies as unions affiliated with the AFL-CIO. Member unions of the Change to Win federation are encouraged to devote 50 percent of their annual operating budget toward union organizing activities compared to a goal of 30 percent for AFL-CIO affiliated unions. The Change to Win federation also plans to spend less time and money working through the established political parties (principally the Democratic Party) and instead focus more resources on grass-roots direct political action by the member unions themselves. Whether the formation of a new labor federation will spur union membership and political gains or as critics charge, further sow disunity and weaken the ranks of organized labor remains to be seen.

Aspects of Organized Labor Unchanged Since World War II

Organized labor as it existed at the end of World War II compared with its present state appears to have more similarities than differences:[124]

- Exclusive union representation, in which one union is given a job territory and selected by a majority of the employees represented.

- Collective bargaining agreements that embody a sharp distinction between the negotiation and contract administration phases of the labor relations process. Once the contract is negotiated, the no-strike, no-lockout, and grievance procedure clauses ensure that the parties will use an arbitrator instead of job action to resolve any disputes that may arise over the labor agreement's interpretation or application.

- Government policies which favor a basically hands-off or non-intervention role in the conduct of labor relations based on the principle that the parties involved should decide bargaining outcomes for themselves.

  Additional major labor relations similarities from World War II to the present are organized labor's continued effort to advance workers' interests through the political process; difficulty in achieving consensus on key issues among unions and union members; and continued emphasis on economic and job-security–related bargaining goals.

Unions and Politics

Samuel Gomper's political dictum of "reward your friends and punish your enemies" still conveys the political philosophy of organized labor today. Politicians or political parties that support the issues and outcomes favored by unions will be rewarded with support while those who oppose union prefer-ences will be denied such support. Historically the Democratic Party and its candidates have been more supportive of labor's agenda and have thus garnered the majority of union support. The current decade has seen a Republican presi-dent and Republican-controlled Congress control the legislative agenda and ju-dicial appointments to the detriment of organized labor's interests. Within the ranks of labor there are unions such as those in the new Change to Win federa-tion who believe that the AFL-CIO has been too supportive of the Democratic Party in the past, even when party leaders did not stand with organized labor on key issues, such as opposition to the North American Free Trade Agreement and subsequent proposed trade pacts. The AFL-CIO's Executive Council did not endorse Bill Clinton in the 1992 presidential election, although members of union households supported Clinton and Democratic senators and members of Congress in the 1992 and 1994 elections (67 percent and 63 percent, respec-tively). President Clinton subsequently obtained legislative passage of the North American Free Trade Agreement (NAFTA) over organized labor's strenuous opposition.[125] Moreover, the Republicans made widespread gains on Election Day 1994, capturing control of both houses of Congress for the first time in 40 years.

In early 1998, the AFL-CIO leadership altered its political strategy by focus-ing more on voter registration (four million more by 2000) and voter education on labor-related issues.[126] In the 2000 election, union households accounted for 26 percent of the overall votes cast, up from 19 percent in 1992.[127] The AFL-CIO reaffirmed its policy of supporting any candidate (Republican or Democrat) who supports organized labor's position on issues such as increasing the minimum wage, creating a patients' bill of rights with health maintenance organizations (HMOs), fair trade policies, and ensuring the future of the Social Security pro-gram. In the 2004 presidential election union households accounted for 24 per-cent of the total votes cast with the Democratic candidate John Kerry receiving 59 percent of those votes compared to 40 percent for the incumbent candidate George Bush.

Difficulty in Achieving Consensus among Unions and among Members

Whether the subject is politics or bargaining issues, there has always been a di-versity of opinions and responses within the U.S. labor movement. While many unions share some basic organizational and philosophical similarities, each union has its own unique history and membership characteristics that help to shape the organization's response to specific issues. Understandably, complete agreement among the diverse national unions within the AFL-CIO federation and among all members within a particular national or local union is rare. This problem occurs in any large organization, particularly one that grants a large amount of autonomy to its members. The AFL-CIO is always subject to na-tional unions withdrawing from it if they become dissatisfied. The federation also realizes that many national unions are strong enough to get along quite well with-out its support. For example, the expulsion of the Teamsters and the United Auto Workers (UAW) from the federation did not hinder these organizations' ability to increase their membership, grow in influence, and engage in collective bargain-ing. (Both the Teamsters and the UAW subsequently reaffiliated with the AFL-CIO with the Teamsters voluntarily withdrawing in 2005 to participate in the Change To Win federation.)

Lack of consensus is also found at the local union level, especially when younger employees become members. Most labor unions have a long tradition of struggle and sacrifice; their leaders have risked physical hardships merely to gain employer recognition of their union. However, many of the younger members have little appreciation for labor history and are more likely to be asking local leaders, "What have you done for me lately?"

Pursuit of Short-Range Economic and Job Security Goals Instead of Long-Range Reform

The KOL likely taught organized labor a permanent lesson—that goals should relate to members' needs instead of being abstract attempts to change the existing societal system. The period since World War II has witnessed tremendous economic growth and technological change; therefore, union leaders believe these issues deserve more attention than other societal concerns. Even when unions make bargaining concessions due to recessionary economic conditions, the concessions are viewed as short-term and economically related—lower wages in exchange for job security, for example.

Summary

In obtaining a contemporary perspective of organized labor, one must be aware of the evolution of labor–management relationships and of the various labor organizations that have attempted to influence those relationships. Current labor organizations have learned important lessons from their historical counterparts. Criteria for comparing the effectiveness of a labor organization are the union's structural and financial stability; its ability to work within the established political and economic system; the presence of supportive or disruptive features in the social environment, such as mass media and legislation; and the ability of union leaders to identify and satisfy members' goals and interests.

Organized labor did not exert much influence before 1869, although employees became increasingly concerned with working and market conditions associated with mass production. The active years of organized labor can be grouped into three time periods: 1869 to World War I, World War I to World War II, and World War II to the present. Three major labor organizations developed in the period from 1869 to World War I: the Knights of Labor (KOL), the American Federation of Labor (AFL) under Gompers, and the Industrial Workers of the World (IWW). These organizations had different goals, strategies, and organizational characteristics, which in part furnished reasons for the demise of the KOL and IWW. The Haymarket Riot, the Homestead Incident, and the Pullman Strike hurt organized labor, although AFL President Gompers managed to derive some benefit from each of these events.

The period immediately following World War I saw limited growth in union membership. Factors contributing to this situation included several strategies used by employers to counter union-organizing campaigns. Internal differences occurred within the AFL regarding the advantages of organizing the heretofore unrepresented semi-skilled employees working in the nation's mass production industries. This disagreement led to the formation of a rival labor organization, the Congress of Industrial Organizations (CIO), whose major objective was to organize industrial employees. The CIO achieved substantial membership gains in the late 1930s and 1940s.

Three major developments have occurred in organized labor since World War II. Concern has increased over new collective-bargaining issues; organizing drives have been aimed at public-sector employees and private-sector service workers; and the AFL and CIO have merged. It is still too early to tell what lasting impact the formation of the new Change to Win federation will have on union membership levels or success for labor through the political process. More similarities than differences are apparent when comparing the state of organized labor at the end of World War II with its present state. Despite representing a relatively small proportion of the total labor force, organized labor remains an influential economic and social movement in U.S. society. The emphasis on advancing employees' short-term economic and job security interests have remained the focus of organized labor since World War II.

Key Terms

Knights of Labor (KOL), p. 40
Terence V. Powderly, p. 41
One Big Union, p. 42
Haymarket Riot, p. 45
American Federation of Labor (AFL), p. 45
Samuel Gompers, p. 46
Pure and simple unionism, p. 47
Exclusive union jurisdiction, p. 48
Decentralized authority, p. 48
Homestead Incident, p. 48
Pullman Strike, p. 50

Industrial Workers of the World (IWW), p. 51
William "Big Bill" Haywood, p. 51
Open-shop movement, p. 56
American Plan, p. 56
Industrial spies, p. 56
Blacklisted, p. 56
Mohawk Valley Formula, p. 56
Paternalism, p. 56
Employee representation plan, p. 57
Company union, p. 57

Sweetheart contract, p. 57
V technique, p. 58
Congress of Industrial Organizations (CIO), pp. 58–59
John L. Lewis, p. 59
Sit-down strike, p. 60
National Labor Relations Act (NLRA) of 1935, p. 61
Concession bargaining, p. 63
AFL-CIO, p. 64
Change to Win federation, p. 65

Discussion Questions

1. Discuss the similarities and differences between the Knights of Labor (KOL) and the Industrial Workers of the World (IWW).

2. Use the four criteria mentioned in the introduction of this chapter for evaluating the strength of a labor organization, and discuss why the AFL survived and the IWW faded into obscurity as labor organizations.

3. Explain how the Haymarket Riot, Homestead strike, and Pullman strike helped as well as hurt the AFL.

4. Discuss some employer tactics used to prevent or minimize union membership growth prior to the passage of the National Labor Relations (Wagner)

Act in 1935. Which, if any, of these tactics would be lawful today?

5. Discuss some key similarities and differences between the AFL and the CIO.

6. Discuss some key similarities and differences between the AFL-CIO and the Change to Win federation. What impact do you think the Change to Win federation will have on union membership growth and union involvement in politics over the next 5 to 10 years?

7. In the future there are likely to be fewer but larger labor organizations. Discuss some advantages and disadvantages of the so called One Big Union approach to representing employees' interests.

Exploring the Web

History of the Labor Movement

1. **Key People.** Go to the Web site for the Bureau of Labor Statistics and look for "Birth of a federation: Mr. Gompers endeavors 'not to build a bubble'," an article published in the *Monthly Labor Review,* November 1981. Why is the event described in the article significant to the history of the labor movement?

The U.S. Department of Labor has a Labor Hall of Fame. Find the DOL Web site and comment on why you think the following people were chosen:

Eugene V. Debs, Mother Jones, John L. Lewis, George Meany, Frances Perkins, Terence V. Powderly, A. Philip Randolph, and Walter Reuther.

Locate Labor History on the Web made available by the AFL-CIO. Try your hand at Vital Pursuits, which provides a different question on labor history each day.

2. **Labor Unions.** Locate the preambles to the constitutions of the Knights of Labor (Hint: Chicago Historical Society) and the Industrial Workers of the World (Hint: Culture link on the IWW Web site). Compare the structure and mission of the two groups. Who were the wobblies, and what is the origin of the term?

3. **The Pinkertons.** What role did the Pinkerton Detective Agency play in labor relations in the 1880s? Find "The Strike at Homestead Mill: The Hated Men in Blue," a Web account published by the Public Broadcasting Service (PBS).

4. **Pullman Strike.** In the Illinois Labor History pages hosted by the Chicago-Kent College of Law Web site, read the Parable of Pullman. What events led up to the Pullman Strike? See also the PBS Online NewsHour with Jim Lehrer transcript on the "The Origins of Labor Day" and the discussion of the Pullman Strike.

5. **Haymarket Riots.** The Chicago Historical Society offers The Haymarket Digital Collection, composed of photographs and narrative related to the Haymarket Riots that occurred in Chicago on May 4, 1886. Enter the Drama of Haymarket and read about the "sequence of events that ignited the Haymarket bomb." Who were August Spies and Albert Parsons, and what part did they play in the events leading up to the riots?

References

1. Robert Ozanne, "Trends in American Labor History," *Labor History* (Fall 1980), p. 521. See also Barry Goldberg, "A New Look at Labor History," *Social Policy* 12 (Winter 1982), pp. 54–63; Robert H. Zieger, "Industrial Relations and Labor History in the Eighties," *Industrial Relations* 22 (Winter 1983), pp. 58–70.

2. Henry Pelling, *American Labor* (Chicago: University of Chicago Press, 1960), pp. 12–13.

3. Edward B. Mittelman, "Trade Unionism 1833–1839," in *History of Labor in the United States,* John R. Commons et al., eds. (1918; reprint ed. New York: Augustus M. Kelly, Publishers, 1966), vol. 1, p. 430.

4. William C. Birdsall, "The Problems of Structure in the Knights of Labor," *Industrial and Labor Relations Review* 6 (July 1953), p. 546.

5. For a discussion of how the expansion of the markets affected unionization among the shoemakers, see John R. Commons, *Labor and Administration* (New York: Macmillan, 1913), pp. 210–264.

6. T. V. Powderly, *Thirty Years of Labor: 1859–1889* (Columbus, Ohio: Excelsior Publishing House, 1889), p. 21.

7. Ibid, pp. 58–59.

8. Ibid, p. 163.

9. Philip Taft, *Organized Labor in American History* (New York: Harper and Row, 1964), p. 90.

10. Gerald N. Grob, *Workers and Utopia* (Evanston, Ill.: Northwestern University Press, 1961), p. 35. Powderly was most concerned about the evils of drinking; for example, he spent almost 50 pages of his autobiography, *Thirty Years of Labor,* discussing this issue.

11. Birdsall, "The Problems of Structure," p. 533.

12. Melton Alonza McLaurin, *The Knights of Labor in the South* (Westport, Conn.: Greenwood Press, 1978), p. 39.

13. Joseph G. Rayback, *A History of American Labor* (New York: Macmillan, 1968), p. 174.

14. Joseph R. Buchanan, *The Story of a Labor Agitator* (1903; reprint ed. Westport, Conn.: Greenwood Press, 1970), pp. 318–323.

15. For details of these procedures, see Taft, *Organized Labor,* p. 91.

16. Powderly, *Thirty Years of Labor,* pp. 151–157.

17. It should be noted that local assemblies were somewhat responsible for this situation as they contributed only

$600 to the General Assembly's strike funds in 1885–1886 (McLaurin, *The Knights of Labor,* p. 54). For more details of KOL strike activities, see Norman J. Ware, *The Labor Movement in the United States, 1860–1895* (1929; reprint ed. Gloucester, Mass.: Peter Smith, 1959), pp. 117–154. It should be further noted that the Knights made more effective use of boycotts than any previous union. However, as was true with strikes, the boycotts were instigated by the local assemblies and forced on the Knights' national leaders (Grob, *Workers and Utopia,* p. 61).

18. Donald L. Kemmerer and Edward D. Wickersham, "Reasons for the Growth of the Knights of Labor in 1885–1886," *Industrial and Labor Relations Review* 3 (January 1950), pp. 213–220.

19. Foster Rhea Dulles, *Labor in America: A History,* 3d ed. (New York: Thomas Y. Crowell, 1966), p. 127.

20. Ware, *The Labor Movement,* p. 96.

21. Dulles, *Labor in America,* p. 135.

22. Powderly, *Thirty Years of Labor,* p. 514. It should also be noted that Powderly believed Gompers misled employees by advocating the eight-hour workday without telling them that their wages would be proportionately reduced. Most workers thought they would receive ten hours' payment for eight hours of work.

23. "A Hellish Deed!" *Chicago Tribune,* May 5, 1886, p. 1.

24. For additional details of the rigged nature of the trial, see Samuel Yellen, *American Labor Struggles* (1936; reprint ed. New York: Arno Press, 1969), pp. 60–65.

25. "A Hellish Deed!" *Chicago Tribune,* May 5, 1886, p. 1.

26. "Their Records," *Chicago Tribune,* May 5, 1886, p. 1. See also Paul Avrich, *The Haymarket Tragedy* (New Jersey: Princeton University Press, 1984).

27. Sidney Lens, *The Labor Wars: From the Molly Maguires to the Sitdowns* (Garden City, N.Y.: Doubleday, 1973), p. 67.

28. The origination of the AFL was changed between 1881 and 1889 to include activities under the Federation of Organized Trade and Labor Unions. At least one historian has claimed that the revised date is regrettable because the parent organization (Federation of Organized Trades and Labor Unions) had little similarity to the AFL in terms of effective organization and broad-based support (Ware, *The Labor Movement,* p. 251). See also Glen A. Gildemeister, "The Founding of the American Federation of Labor," *Labor History* 22 (Spring 1981); and Harold C. Livesay, *Samuel Gompers and Organized Labor in America* (Boston: Little, Brown and Company, 1978), pp. 75–86.

29. Samuel Gompers, *Seventy Years of Life and Labor* (New York: E. P. Dutton, 1925), p. 266.

30. Ware, *The Labor Movement,* pp. 70–71.

31. Norman J. Ware, *Labor in Modern Industrial Society* (1935: reprint ed. New York: Russell and Russell, 1968), p. 262.

32. Dulles, *Labor in America,* p. 155.

33. Gompers, *Seventy Years of Life and Labor,* p. 245.

34. Samuel Gompers, *Labor and the Employer* (1920; reprint ed. New York: Arno Press, 1971), pp. 33–34.

35. Stuart Bruce Kaufman, *Samuel Gompers and the Origins of the American Federation of Labor: 1848–1896* (Westport, Conn.: Greenwood Press, 1973), p. 173. For details of this relationship, see Gompers, *Seventy Years of Life and Labor,* pp. 381–427.

36. Louis Reed, *The Labor Philosophy of Samuel Gompers* (1930; reprint ed. Port Washington, N.Y.: Kennikat Press, 1966), p. 20. See also an editorial by Gompers in the *American Federationist,* June 1924, p. 481; and Sarah Lyon Watts, *Order Against Chaos: Business Culture and Labor Ideology in America 1880–1915* (New York: Greenwood Press, 1991), pp. 9–10.

37. Gompers, *Seventy Years of Life and Labor,* pp. 286–287, 381–427.

38. Alice Kessler-Harris, "Trade Unions Mirror Society in Conflict between Collectivism and Individualism," *Monthly Labor Review* 110 (August 1987), p. 33.

39. Gompers, *Labor and the Employer,* p. 202.

40. Marc Karson, *American Labor Unions and Politics: 1900–1918* (Carbondale, Ill.: Southern Illinois University Press, 1968), p. 29; and Julia Green, "Strike at the Ballot Box: The American Federation of Labor's Entrance into Election Politics, 1906–1909," *Labor History* 32 (Spring 1991), pp. 165–192.

41. Reed, *The Labor Philosophy of Samuel Gompers,* pp. 106–110.

42. Milton Derber, *The American Idea of Industrial Democracy: 1865–1965* (Urbana, Ill.: University of Illinois Press, 1970), p. 117.

43. Gompers, *Seventy Years of Life and Labor,* p. 342. For additional details regarding early AFL organizing, see Philip Taft, *The AF of L in the Time of Gompers* (1957; reprint ed. New York: Octagon Books, 1970), pp. 95–122.

44. Dulles, *Labor in America,* pp. 163–164.

45. Andrew Carnegie, "An Employer's View of the Labor Question," in *Labor: Its Rights and Wrongs* (1886; reprint ed. Westport Conn.: Hyperion Press, 1975), pp. 91, 95. For a recent collection and analysis of material pertaining to the situation, see David P. Demarest Jr., ed., *The River Ran Red* (Pittsburgh: University of Pittsburgh Press, 1992).

46. Yellen, *American Labor Struggles,* p. 81.

47. For details of the wage package, see Ibid, pp. 77–80. See also E. W. Bemis, "The Homestead Strike," *Journal of Political Economy* 2 (1894), pp. 369–396; and Linda Schneider, "The Citizen Striker: Workers' Ideology in the Homestead Strike of 1892," *Labor History* 23 (Winter 1982), pp. 47–66. For some additional insights into Frick's background, see Carol Aymowitz, "Frick's Homey Mansion," *The Wall Street Journal,* September 24, 1990, p. A-12.

48. "Surrounded by Pickets," *The New York Times,* July 4, 1892, p. 1.

49. "Mob Law at Homestead," *The New York Times,* July 7, 1892, p. 1.

50. "Leader O'Donnell Is Glad," *The New York Times,* July 12, 1892, p. 2; and "Bayonet Rule in Force," *The New York Times,* July 13, 1892, p. 1.

51. Lens, *The Labor Wars,* p. 77.

52. "A Talk with Gompers," *The New York Times,* July 7, 1892, p. 2; and "Provoked by Carnegie," *The New York Times,* July 7, 1892, pp. 2, 5.

53. Taft, *The AF of L in the Time of Gompers,* p. 136.

54. "Arbitrate the Homestead Strike," *Chicago Tribune,* July 8, 1892, p. 4. See also "The Origin of the Trouble," *The New York Times,* July 8, 1892, p. 2.

55. Yellen, *American Labor Struggles,* p. 3.

56. Lens, *The Labor Wars,* p. 81. See also Susan Kay Morrison's unpublished paper, "Eugene V. Debs: His Ride on the Pullman," 1981.

57. For additional details about the town, see Almont Lindsay, *The Pullman Strike* (Chicago: University of Chicago Press, 1967), pp. 38–60.

58. For more details regarding ARU's organization, see Philip S. Foner, *History of the Labor Movement in the United States,* vol. II (New York: International Publishers, 1955), p. 256.

59. Lindsay, *The Pullman Strike,* p. 124.

60. Ibid, p. 215.

61. Gompers, *Seventy Years of Life and Labor,* p. 403.

62. *Proceedings of the First Convention of the Industrial Workers of the World* (New York: Labor News Company, 1905), p. 1.

63. Ibid, p. 143.

64. Bill Haywood, *Bill Haywood's Book: The Autobiography of William D. Haywood* (New York: International Publishers, 1929), p. 73.

65. Melvyn Dubofsky, *We Shall Be All: A History of the Industrial Workers of the World* (Chicago: Quadrangle Books, 1969), p. 481.

66. Haywood, *Bill Haywood's Book,* p. 181.

67. For additional details pertaining to these differences, see Dubofsky, *We Shall Be All,* pp. 105–119; Joseph Robert Conlin, *Bread and Roses Too* (Westport, Conn.: Greenwood Publishing, 1969), pp. 97–117; and Lens, *The Labor Wars,* pp. 154–155.

68. David J. Saposs, *Left-Wing Unionism* (1926; reprint ed. New York: Russell and Russell, 1967), p. 148.

69. Louis Adamic, *Dynamite: The Story of Class Violence in America* (1934; reprint ed. Gloucester, Mass.: Peter Smith, 1963), p. 174.

70. Robert E. Ficken, "The Wobbly Horrors, Pacific Northwest Lumbermen, and the Industrial Workers of the World, 1917–1918," *Labor History* 24 (Summer 1983), p. 329.

71. Conlin, *Bread and Roses Too,* pp. 97–117. See also Fred Thompson, *The IWW: Its First Fifty Years* (Chicago: Industrial Workers of the World, 1955), pp. 80–87.

72. Adamic, *Dynamite,* pp. 163–164.

73. Conlin, *Bread and Roses Too,* p. 96.

74. Philip S. Foner, ed., *Fellow Workers and Friends: I. W. W. Free Speech Fights as Told by Participants* (Westport, Conn.: Greenwood Press, 1981), p. 15.

75. Foner, *History of the Labor Movement,* vol. III, p. 465.

76. Conlin, *Bread and Roses Too,* p. 68.

77. For additional details, see Frank L. Grubbs, Jr., *The Struggle for Labor Loyalty: Gompers, the AFL, and the Pacifists, 1917–1920* (Durham, N.C.: Duke University Press, 1968).

78. James O. Morris, *Conflict within the AFL: A Study of Craft versus Industrial Unionism, 1901–1938* (1958; reprint ed. Westport, Conn.: Greenwood Press, 1974), pp. 9–10.

79. Taft, *Organized Labor,* pp. 355–358; and Francis Fox Piven and Richard A. Cloward, *Poor People's Movements* (New York: Pantheon Books, 1977), p. 104. For details of this strike, see Lens, *The Labor Wars,* pp. 196–219.

80. Frank Stricker, "Affluence for Whom? Another Look at Prosperity and the Working Classes in the 1920s," *Labor History* 24 (Winter 1983), pp. 5–34.

81. Lens, *The Labor Wars,* pp. 222, 296, 312.

82. Derber, *The American Idea,* p. 246. For an application of these reasons to a specific industrial situation during this time period, see Stephen L. Shapiro, "The Growth of the Cotton Textile Industry in South Carolina: 1919–1930" (Ph.D., diss., University of South Carolina, 1971), pp. 168–171.

83. For additional details regarding this tactic, see Clinch Calkins, *Spy Overhead: The Story of Industrial Espionage* (1937; reprint ed. New York: Arno Press, 1971).

84. Violence was limited neither to this time period nor to the employer. One of the more publicized episodes of employer violence was the Ludlow Massacre of 1914. The mining camps in Colorado were involved in a strike for union recognition when, on April 20, militiamen opened fire on a tent colony, killing two strikers and one boy. They then set fire to the tents, killing two women and eleven children. For more details of this event, see Leon Stein, ed., *Massacre at Ludlow: Four Reports* (reprint ed.; New York: Arno Press, 1971). Perhaps one of the more vivid examples of union violence occurred in Herrin, Illinois (1922), where miners tortured and killed at least 26 management officials and strikebreakers. For details of this episode, see Saul Alinsky, *John L. Lewis: An Unauthorized Biography* (New York: Vintage Books, 1970), pp. 43–50.

85. Richard C. Wilcock, "Industrial Management's Policies toward Unionism," in Milton Derber and Edwin Young, eds., *Labor and the New Deal* (Madison: University of Wisconsin Press, 1957), p. 293.

86. For a case study of paternalism, see "Welfare Work in Company Towns," *Monthly Labor Review* 25 (August 1927), pp. 314–321. For a more thorough discussion of employer counteractions during this time period, see Larry J. Griffin, Michael E. Wallace, and Beth A. Rubin, "Capitalist Resistance to the Organization of Labor before the New Deal: Why? How? Success?" *American Sociological Review* (April 1986), pp. 147–167.

87. Derber, *The American Idea,* pp. 220–221; and Morris, *Conflict within the AFL,* pp. 40–41. For more details on ERPs, see Ware, *Labor in Modern Industrial Society,* pp. 414–435. For a contemporary assessment of the problems and prospects facing the single-firm, independent union, see Arthur B. Shostak, *America's Forgotten Labor Organization* (Princeton: Industrial Relations Section, Department of Economics, Princeton University, 1962).

88. Dulles, *Labor in America,* p. 245.

89. This example was drawn from a more detailed account of racketeering during this period found in Sidney Lens, *Left, Right, and Center: Conflicting Forces in American Labor* (Hinsdale, Ill.: Henry Regnery, 1949), pp. 86–108.

90. David J. McDonald, *Union Man* (New York: E. P. Dutton, 1969), p. 185. See also Max Gordan, "The Communists and the Drive to Organize Steel, 1936," *Labor History* 23 (Spring 1982), pp. 226–245. For further historical insights into the relationship between

organized labor and communism, see Harvey A. Levenstein, *Communism, Anticommunism and the CIO* (Westport, Conn.: Greenwood Press, 1981).

91. James O. Morris, "The AFL in the 1920s: A Strategy of Defense," *Industrial and Labor Relations Review* 11 (July 1958), pp. 572–590.

92. See, for example, "William Green: Guardian of the Middle Years," *American Federationist* 88 (February 1981), pp. 24–25.

93. Bruce Minton and John Stuart, *Men Who Lead Labor* (New York: Modern Age Books, 1937), pp. 14–15.

94. Morris, *Conflict within the AFL,* p. 216.

95. For additional details pertaining to the background of this historic convention, see Herbert Harris, *Labor's Civil War* (1940; reprint ed. New York: Greenwood Press).

96. Lens, *The Labor Wars,* p. 284.

97. Cecil Carnes, John L. Lewis: *Leader of Labor* (New York: Robert Speller Publishing, 1936), p. 299.

98. David Dubinsky and A. H. Raskin, *David Dubinsky: A Life with Labor* (New York: Simon and Schuster, 1977), p. 226.

99. The seven unions were the United Mine Workers; the Amalgamated Clothing Workers; the International Ladies Garment Workers Union; United Hatters; Cap and Millinery Workers; Oil Field, Gas Well and Refinery Workers; and the International Union of Mine, Mill, and Smelter Workers.

100. Benjamin Stolberg, *The Story of the CIO* (1938; reprint ed. New York: Arno Press, 1971), p. 28.

101. Milton Derber, "Growth and Expansion," in Derber and Young, *Labor and the New Deal,* p. 13; and Steve Rosswurm, ed., *The CIO's Left-Led Unions* (New Brunswick, N.J.: Rutgers University Press, 1992).

102. See, for example, John Hutchinson, "John L. Lewis: To the Presidency of the UMWA," *Labor History* 19 (Spring 1978), pp. 185–203; and Steven Fraser, *Sidney Hillman and the Rise of American Labor* (New York: The Free Press, 1991).

103. James Arthur Wechsler, *Labor Baron: A Portrait of John L. Lewis* (New York: William Morrow, 1944), p. 71; and Robert H. Zieger, "Leadership and Bureaucracy in the Late CIO," *Labor History* 31, no. 3 (1990), pp. 253–270.

104. Thomas Gobel, "Becoming American: Ethnic Workers and the Rise of the CIO," *Labor History* 29 (Spring 1988), p. 174.

105. S. J. Woolf, "John L. Lewis and His Plan," in Melvyn Dubofsky, ed., *American Labor Since the New Deal* (Chicago: Quadrangle Books, 1971), pp. 110–111.

106. Lens, *The Labor Wars,* p. 295.

107. Sidney Fine, *Sit-Down: The General Motors Strike of 1936–1937* (Ann Arbor: The University of Michigan Press, 1969), pp. 156–177. For another perspective of the sit-down strike, see Daniel Nelson, "Origins of the Sit-Down Era: Worker Militancy and Innovation in the Rubber Industry, 1934–1938," *Labor History* 23 (Winter 1982), pp. 198–225.

108. James R. Hoffa and Oscar Fraley, *Hoffa: The Real Story* (New York: Stein and Day Publishers, 1975), p. 65.

109. For a detailed account of the AFL-CIO rivalries in several industries, see Walter Galenson, *The CIO Challenge to the AFL* (Cambridge, Mass.: Harvard University Press, 1960).

110. Richard B. Morris, ed., *The U. S. Department of Labor Bicentennial History of the American Worker* (Washington, D.C.: U.S. Government Printing Office, 1976), p. 236.

111. For details of this formula and the extent that cost-of-living estimates exceeded this formula, see Taft, *Organized Labor in American History,* pp. 549–553 and 557–559.

112. Dulles, *Labor in America: A History,* p. 334.

113. Arthur F. McClure, *The Truman Administration and the Problems of Postwar Labor, 1945–1948* (Cranbury, N.J.: Associated University Press, 1969), p. 45.

114. George H. Hildebrand, *American Unionism: An Historical and Analytical Survey* (Reading: Addison-Wesley, 1979), pp. 36–37.

115. U.S. Department of Labor, "Employer Cost for Employee Compensation—March 2005," *News Release,* June 16, 2005, p. 11.

116. Robert M. MacDonald, "Collective Bargaining in the Postwar Period," *Industrial and Labor RelationsReview* 20 (July 1967), p. 568.

117. Audrey Freedman, "How the 1980s Have Changed Industrial Relations," *Monthly Labor Review* (May 1988), p. 37.

118. For a more detailed discussion of historical attempts at the merger of the AFL and CIO, see Joel Seidman, "Efforts toward Merger 1935–1955," *Industrial and Labor Relations Review* 9 (April 1956), pp. 353–370.

119. "Document: AFL-CIO No-Raiding Agreement," *Industrial and Labor Relations Review* 8 (October 1954), p. 103.

120. "A Short History of American Labor," *American Federationist* 88 (March 1981), p. 14.

121. George Meany, "Merger and the National Welfare," *Industrial and Labor Relations Review* 9 (April 1956), p. 349.

122. Richard A. Lester, *As Unions Mature* (Princeton, N.J.: Princeton University Press, 1958), p. 25.

123. Aaron Bernstein, "Is Labor Headed For Splitsville?" *BusinessWeek,* May 30, 2005, p. 32.

124. John T. Dunlop, "Have the 1980s Changed Industrial Relations?" *Monthly Labor Review* 111 (May 1988), pp. 29–33.

125. Ken Jennings and Jeffrey W. Steagall, "Unions and NAFTA's Legislative Passage: Confrontation and Cover," *Labor Studies Journal* (Spring 1996), pp. 61–80; and Jefferson Cowie, "National Struggles in a Transnational Economy: A Critical Analysis of U.S. Labor's Campaign against NAFTA," *Labor Studies Journal* 21 (Winter 1997), pp. 3–32.

126. Steven Greenhouse, "Labor Tries New Strategy in '98 Elections," *The New York Times,* May 16, 1998, p. A-9.

127. Jeanne Cummings, "Unions Recast Their Political Role; Fracturing of AFL-CIO Could Boost Labor's Influence over Election Campaigns in Long Run," *The Wall Street Journal,* July 27, 2005, p. A4.

CHAPTER 3

Legal Influences

Labor relations law provides a framework for defining the legal rights and responsibilities of the parties engaged in the labor relations process. This chapter introduces the basic legal foundation regulating the major phases of the labor relations process: organizing unions, negotiating labor agreements, and ensuring employee rights in contract administration. It is essential today not only to know the law but to understand and appreciate the interrelationships between the law and the labor relations process. Practitioners should recognize that having a legal right to act does not always mean it is one's practical best interest to exercise that legal right.

This chapter logically follows the one on historical development of unions in the United States because labor relations law and union development go hand in hand. Law as it pertains to labor is traced from the first major court case involving union activities, through the application of common law and the use of antitrust legislation that inhibited the growth of unions, to passage of laws that pertain to most private firms today: the Norris–La Guardia, Wagner, Taft-Hartley, and Landrum-Griffin Acts. Because these acts cover the major portion of private-sector U.S. industries and businesses, a substantial amount of space is devoted to their content. The Railway Labor Act, which principally covers railroads and airlines, is also explained and assessed. A final section briefly considers several other employment laws that can affect the labor relations process.

ORIGIN OF LABOR RELATIONS LAW

Article I, Section 8 of the **U.S. Constitution** grants Congress the right to pass laws regulating interstate and international commerce. Labor relations activities can affect interstate commerce and therefore have been the focus of many statutory laws to regulate various aspects of the employment relationship since the late 1800s. The First Amendment of the U.S. Constitution, which ensures the rights of peaceful assembly, freedom of association, and free speech, usually has been interpreted as allowing employees to form and join unions and has provided the justification for union picketing (to communicate information to possible union members or supporters). The Fifth Amendment contains due process protections, and the Fourteenth Amendment prohibits state laws from depriving citizens of their constitutional rights providing equal protection under the law. These constitutional provisions play an important role in defining the basic framework of American labor law.

Few statutory labor laws were enacted prior to the late 1800s, so early U.S. history was governed by the application of **common law**. Common law is only used to resolve a legal dispute when no constitutional or statutory law applies to that dispute. In such situations, judges develop legal principles or procedures to resolve these types of disputes, which over time, are adopted by other judges in similar disputes and come to represent the common law. Early U.S. common law was based upon English common law principles as modified by local custom and practice.

One example of a common law doctrine that is still often used today is the **employment-at-will (EAW) doctrine**. The EAW doctrine states that employment relationships established for an indefinite duration may be terminated by either the employer or employee at any time for any or no stated reason. Arising from the English common law governing master-servant relationships, employers have historically relied upon this common law doctrine as a basis for terminating employees for a wide variety of reasons without permitting the terminated individual to legally challenge whether management's decision or reasoning was correct or justified. Although the doctrine has been modified by the passage of laws and court interpretations intended to prohibit employers for discharging individuals for certain protected reasons (e.g., joining a union; an individual's race, sex, religion), in many states the EAW doctrine remains the primary protection of management's right to discharge employees. This doctrine is more thoroughly discussed in Chapter 12.

Modern U.S. labor relations law relies primarily on federal and state statutory laws or local government ordinances; judicial decisions interpreting and applying statutory laws and local ordinances; and decisions by administrative agencies (e.g., National Labor Relations Board (NLRB), U.S. Department of Labor, Occupational Safety and Health Administration) responsible for administering specific labor laws. Congress has enacted numerous labor relations laws in the interest of employees and employers, public welfare, and the furtherance of interstate commerce. Three major laws—the Norris–La Guardia Act, the Labor Management Relations Act, as amended, and the Railway Labor Act—are discussed at length later in this chapter. Under the **preemption doctrine**, federal law takes precedent over state law or local ordinances whenever both seek to regulate the same conduct and there is a conflict between them.[1] The preemption doctrine underscores the importance of labor relations as an area that affects the national economy and therefore benefits from the uniformity and stability that federal regulation of issues can provide. State legislatures may pass laws and local municipalities may enact ordinances to fill voids in federal laws or to extend regulation to issues not regulated by federal laws, such as the right of state and local public employees to engage in collective bargaining.

The judicial branch of government, with its court system at the federal, state, and local levels, functions to determine a law's constitutionality and conformity to legal standards; to assess the accuracy of interpretations by administrative agencies; and to issue injunctions that restrict or require certain activities. In addition, the courts must decide issues not covered by existing laws and make rulings under the general guide of "equity." These decisions constitute case law which has developed over the years, establishing precedents and providing guidance for future legal decisions.

The executive branch includes various administrative agencies created by Congress to interpret and administer some labor laws. These government agencies establish policies and make rules to guide the administration of labor laws. Although administrative agency decisions may be appealed to federal courts, the courts are encouraged by Congress to give great deference to the expertise of agencies in interpreting and applying an applicable labor law. Some of the more important administrative agencies mentioned include:

- **National Labor Relations Board (NLRB)**: Administers the National Labor Relations (Wagner) Act as amended by the Labor Management Relations (Taft-Hartley) Act and certain aspects of the **Labor Management Reporting and Disclosure (Landrum-Griffin) Act;** involving the supervision of union representation elections and determination of unfair labor practice (ULP) charges.

- **Federal Mediation and Conciliation Service (FMCS)**: Provides mediation services to unions and employers engaged in collective bargaining and assists these parties in selecting arbitrators in grievance administration; provides training programs to encourage more cooperative labor management relations.

- **U.S. Department of Labor (USDOL)**: Performs many employment-related services, such as research and data-collecting functions; administers federal wage and safety laws; and enforces federal contract compliance under equal employment opportunity requirements. In addition, the USDOL's head (Secretary of Labor) serves as a member of the President's Cabinet, responsible for employment-related matters.

- **National Mediation Board (NMB)**: Handles union representation issues under the Railway Labor Act; provides mediation services to parties in negotiations; assists in resolving disputes over contract interpretation; and in cases involving emergency disputes, proposes arbitration and certifies the dispute to the President as an emergency.

- **National Railroad Adjustment Board (NRAB)**: Hears and attempts to resolve railroad labor disputes growing out of grievances and interpretation or application of labor agreements.

- State and local administrative agencies: Are responsible for the enforcement and administration of state laws and local ordinances involving labor relations topics.

Early Legal Interpretations Involving Labor-Management Relationships (1806–1931)

As discussed in Chapter 2, early labor unions in the United States had to struggle for their existence. The legal system was primarily focused on protecting employer property rights to advance the economic growth of the nation with little importance placed on protecting the rights of employees within the emerging free enterprise economic system. Employer property rights were defined in broad terms to include both the right to control tangible property (e.g., plant, equipment, employees) as well as intangible property (e.g., right to engage in normal business, right to make a profit). Due to the absence of statutory laws regulating labor relations, the judicial system exerted great control over conflicts of interests between employers and employees from the early 1800s to the 1930s.

Criminal Conspiracy Doctrine

Under English common law it was illegal for two or more workers to join together for the purpose of pressuring their employer to improve their wages or working conditions. In 1806, one of the first major labor law cases in the United States, known as the "Cordwainers case," occurred when a group of journeymen shoemakers in Philadelphia were indicted, convicted, and fined $8 each for forming an illegal criminal conspiracy. The shoemakers had joined together in an attempt to raise their wages and refused to work with nonmembers or at a wage rate less than they demanded. Twelve jurors (all businessmen) found the shoemakers guilty of forming an illegal combination for the purpose of raising their own wages while injuring those who did not join the coalition.[2]

The prosecutor in the trial stated: "Our position is that no man is at liberty to combine, conspire, confederate and unlawfully agree to regulate the whole body of workmen in the city. The defendants are not indicted for regulating their own individual wages but for undertaking by a combination, to regulate the price of labor of others as well as their own. It must be known to you, every society of people are affected by such confederacies; they are injurious to the public good and against the public interest."[3]

The application of the common law **criminal conspiracy doctrine** to attempts by employees to organize unions aroused much public protest, not only from employees but also from factory owners who feared the closing of their factories if their employees' dissatisfaction grew too strong. These concerns were undoubtedly a consideration when the Supreme Judicial Court of Massachusetts in *Commonwealth v. Hunt* (1842), set aside the criminal conspiracy conviction of seven members of the Journeymen Bootmakers' Society, who refused to work in shops where nonmembers were employed at less than their scheduled rate of $2 per pair of boots.[4] While not rejecting the criminal conspiracy doctrine, the court instituted an ends/means test to be applied on a case-by-case basis to determine if the ends (goals) sought by the combination of workers was legal and if the means (tactics) used by the workers were also lawful. The court concluded it was not illegal for workers to seek to protect their own economic interests in maintaining a desired wage rate nor was it illegal to refuse to work as a means of encouraging an employer not to hire an individual at a lower wage rate, thus undercutting the current established rate of pay for a particular type of labor. Of course the employer was free to replace any employee who refused to work in order to continue normal business operations.

Civil Conspiracy Doctrine

The *Commonwealth v. Hunt* decision virtually ended the use of the common law criminal conspiracy doctrine in labor relations. However, the courts continued to apply the **civil conspiracy doctrine**, which held that a group involved in concerted activities could inflict harm on other parties (e.g., customers or other employees) even though the workers were pursuing a valid objective in their own interest.[5] In the *Vegelahn v. Guntner* (Mass. S.Ct. 1896), an injunction was issued against a union that was picketing their employer to obtain higher wages and shorter hours.[6] Although the court agreed that higher wages and shorter work hours were legitimate ends for workers to pursue, the court concluded that picketing, accompanied by threats of violence, could unlawfully intimidate individuals who desired to continue to work for the employer or customers who sought to do business with the employer and therefore, was an unlawful means to accomplish an otherwise lawful end. Only where both the workers' ends and means were lawful would the concerted activity be permitted.

Breach of Contract (Contractual Interference) and Use of the Labor Injunction

Around 1880 many states began loosening restrictions on who could serve on juries (e.g., removing property ownership requirements), which permitted more hourly workers to perform jury duty service. As a consequence, juries became less willing to convict workers of criminal or civil conspiracy charges. Employers turned to the courts for a quicker and more reliable means of restricting employee concerted activities which the legal system provided in the form of a labor injunction.[7] A **labor injunction** is a court order prohibiting or restricting certain activities in conjunction with a labor dispute. The advantage of a labor injunction over a jury trial was that a preliminary labor injunction could be issued by a judge without a formal jury hearing and was often based solely on statements or evidence provided by the employer intended to demonstrate the need for the labor injunction. It might be weeks or months before the labor organization enjoined might get a chance to challenge the credibility of the employer's evidence or offer alternative evidence at a hearing to show why a labor injunction was not necessary or appropriate. By that time the employer had often prevailed in ending the labor dispute on terms favorable to the employer's interest aided by the labor injunction's restrictions on workers' ability to use effective economic pressure tactics against the employer.

The courts' long-standing interest in enforcing the terms of contracts led many employers to require their employees to sign a **yellow-dog contract**—an agreement stating that they would neither join a union nor assist in organizing one.[8] Because this contract was a condition of continued employment, any violation would allow the company to discharge the employee. More importantly, if any outside union organizer attempted to solicit employees to join a union or engage in other concerted activity such as a strike to improve wages or working conditions, such activity could be enjoined by a judge on the grounds that it was an attempt to interfere with a legal contractual relationship between the employer and its employees. Union organizers who violated the court order could then be charged with contempt of court and fined or imprisoned.

Application of Antitrust Legislation to Labor Unions

Another legal obstacle confronting labor organizations in the late 1800s was the application of antitrust law to restrict union organizing and bargaining activities. Congress passed the **Sherman Antitrust Act** in 1890 to regulate the increasing power of large corporations to engage in anti-competitive practices (e.g., cutthroat pricing; restricting competitor's access to necessary raw materials), which tended to drive smaller firms out of the market.[9] The Sherman Antitrust Act neither explicitly included nor excluded labor unions from coverage as an illegal combination in restraint of interstate commerce. All of the congressional debate and testimony leading to passage of the bill focused on the business practices of employers, not labor organizations.

The U.S. Supreme Court decided to apply the Sherman Antitrust Act to labor organizations in the 1908 landmark decision, *Loewe v. Lawlor* (better known as the *Danbury Hatters* case).[10] The United Hatters of North America (UHU), having organized 70 of 82 firms in the hat manufacturing industry, wanted to organize Loewe & Co., one of the few remaining nonunion employers located in Danbury, Connecticut. As a part of the UHU's campaign to gain union recognition as the bargaining agent for employees at Loewe & Co., the union organized a nationwide boycott assisted by the American Federation of Labor (AFL) directed at persuading all retailers, wholesalers, and customers not to buy, sell, or handle hats produced by Loewe & Co. The boycott was successful, which prompted Loewe & Co. to sue, alleging that the UHU's boycott interfered with Loewe & Co.'s ability to engage in its normal interstate commerce of selling hats. The Supreme Court ruled that unions were covered under the Sherman Act and that the union's boycott did illegally obstruct Loewe & Co.'s ability to engage in its normal interstate commerce. The court awarded the employer triple damages ($252,000) as provided for under the Sherman Antitrust Act and ruled that individual union members could be held liable for paying the damage award if the labor organization itself did not have sufficient funds to pay the claim.

The *Loewe v. Lawlor* decision had several important impacts on labor relations. First, the decision essentially eliminated the use of the boycott which had previously been considered a very effective union tactic for bringing economic pressure against an employer in order to persuade an employer to agree to union proposals. It also raised concerns in the minds of some union leaders as to whether the courts might extend the ruling on boycotts in future legal cases to include other union tactics (e.g., picketing, strikes, or handbilling) also intended to impose economic pressure on an employer's business operations. Second, the court's decision to hold individual union members personally liable for damages resulting from the actions of their labor organization dealt a serious blow to union organizing efforts. Not only could an employee face discharge for participating in union organizing activity, but if the organizing activity was declared to be an antitrust violation, the employee might also risk loss of personal assets acquired over the individual's work career, as some UHU members experienced.

One positive aspect for unions of the *Loewe v. Lawlor* decision was that it clearly demonstrated to AFL president Samuel Gompers and other labor leaders the need to expand state and local union political efforts to include Congress and other federal branches of government. An aggressive campaign led by the AFL to address labor concerns about the court's interpretation of the Sherman Antitrust Act led to the enactment of the **Clayton Antitrust Act** in 1914. Included among the Clayton Act's amendments to the Sherman Antitrust Act were the following provisions:

> [The] labor of a human being is not a commodity or article of commerce. Nothing contained in the antitrust laws shall be construed to forbid the existence and operations of labor [unions]...nor shall such organizations...be held or construed to be illegal combinations or conspiracies in restraint of trade.
>
> No restraining order or injunction shall be granted...in any case between an employer and employees...growing out of a dispute concerning terms or conditions of employment, unless necessary to prevent irreparable injury to property....
>
> No such restraining order...shall prohibit any person or persons...from ceasing to perform work...recommending, advising, or persuading others by peaceful means so to do...peacefully persuading any person to work or abstain from working...peacefully assembling in a lawful manner, and for lawful purposes.[11]

When AFL president Samuel Gompers read the provisions of the Clayton Act, he proclaimed it U.S. labor's Magna Charta because it would free organized labor from the restraints of antitrust prosecution. Gompers's joy, however, was short-lived; as a series of Supreme Court decisions in the 1920s left no doubt that the Clayton Act was not labor's Magna Carta.[12] Rather than viewing the Clayton Act as a repudiation of the court's prior interpretation of the Sherman Antitrust Act, the Supreme Court interpreted Congress's intent in passing the Clayton Act as only reaffirming a labor organization's right to exist so long as it sought to achieve lawful ends using lawful means. In fact, the Clayton Act hurt union growth and development more than it helped because under the act, employers could now seek labor injunctions for alleged antitrust violations on their own, whereas under the Sherman Act only a U.S. district attorney could seek such an injunction from a court.

Some states attempted to address perceived labor law deficiencies on their own by enacting state labor legislation to grant legal bargaining rights to employees or restrict the circumstances under which a state court judge could issue a labor injunction to ban employee activity during a labor dispute. For example, in 1921, the U.S. Supreme Court declared a law enacted by the Arizona legislature and upheld by the Arizona state supreme court unconstitutional in violation of the Fifth and Fourteenth Amendments.[13] The Arizona law sought to deny a judge the right to issue a labor injunction to halt otherwise peaceful picketing during a labor dispute. The Supreme Court majority declared the Arizona law unlawfully denied the employer being picketed during a wage dispute his due process and equal protection right to obtain a labor injunction to prevent the picketing from damaging normal restaurant operations. The dissenting opinion argued that states such as Arizona ought to be free to determine for themselves whether some restrictions on employer property rights (e.g., limiting access to injunctive relief) might not be imposed if necessary to protect other legitimate rights of employees to participate in bargaining over work conditions.

The 1920s were a difficult period for organized labor. Although this was a period of general economic growth and prosperity, unions confronted an environment where labor injunctions were easier to obtain; the court system strongly supported employer property rights; favorable legislation protecting employees' right to organize and bargain collectively was absent; and employers commonly used anti-union tactics (such as "goon squads," yellow-dog contracts, discharge, and blacklisting). Although the Railway Labor Act (covered later in this chapter) was passed in 1926 granting bargaining rights to railroad employees, this was primarily a time of regrouping, self-analysis, and trying to preserve the status quo for most unions.

THE NORRIS–LA GUARDIA ACT

The 1929 stock market crash and ensuing economic depression forced a reassessment of the extent to which private-sector employers could be trusted to manage the economic welfare of the country. As unemployment rose and individual's savings declined, political pressure mounted on Congress to take a more active role in regulating the economy, including providing more protection for basic workers' rights. In 1932, Congress passed the **Norris–La Guardia Act** (also called the Federal Anti-Injunction Act) to accomplish three basic public policy goals.[14] First, to allow employees a greater voice in seeking to advance and protect their legitimate job interests, Congress limited the power of federal courts to intervene in labor disputes through the issuance of a labor injunction. Activities that previously had been routinely enjoined to the benefit of employer interests were now protected by law (e.g., peaceful picketing or publicity; encouraging employees to join a union; union economic or legal aid provided to employees during a labor dispute). A temporary restraining order (TRO) obtained solely on the basis of an employer's statements to restrict some alleged unlawful employee conduct could only be effective for five days. During that time period the judge was required to conduct a hearing at which both sides could present basic arguments and evidence as to whether the TRO should be converted to a temporary labor injunction after the initial five-day period expired. An employer seeking to have the court issue a labor injunction had the burden of proving that the following conditions existed: 1) Unlawful acts have been threatened or committed; 2) substantial and irreparable injury to the employer's property has or will likely occur as a result of such unlawful acts; 3) greater injury would be inflicted on the employer by denial of an injunction than on the union (employees) by granting an injunction; 4) the employer had no other adequate legal remedy; 5) public safety officers were either unable or unwilling to adequately protect the employer's property; and 6) the employer had satisfied any existing legal duty to bargain in good faith in an effort to settle the labor dispute (including the offer of mediation, voluntary arbitration, etc.) before going to court. Any labor injunction issued by a court was required to describe the specific conduct being enjoined, eliminating the previous abuse of general or vaguely worded "blanket injunctions."[15]

The Norris–La Guardia Act also declared that a yellow-dog contract would be unenforceable in federal court and thus no longer could be used as a basis for obtaining a labor injunction to prevent conduct which might breach such an employment contract.[16] However, many employers continued to discharge or otherwise discriminate against employees for engaging in union activities.

A second public policy goal of the Norris-La Guardia Act was to encourage the courts to adopt a more impartial or neutral role in seeking to protect and enforce the legitimate rights of employers and employees. Courts were encouraged to balance the legitimate rights of employers and employees, a difficult task in an economic system where the parties' interests inevitably conflict to some extent. Acts for which a labor injunction was not obtainable under the Norris-La Guardia Act were no longer considered to be antitrust violations under the Clayton Antitrust Act.[17] Rejecting the Supreme Court's interpretation and application of the antitrust laws during the 1920s, Congress reinstated the use of the economic boycott as a legitimate means of worker protest so long as it was used to pursue a lawful purpose in a lawful manner.

A third public policy goal of the Norris–La Guardia Act was to express congressional support for the process of collective bargaining as an appropriate means for employees to improve and protect their employment interests. Through the collective bargaining process, both labor and management could voice their concerns and present evidence to support the adoption of reasonable work rules which fit the particular circumstances and resources of each bargaining relationship. While conflict or the threat of conflict was a part of such a bargaining process, the presumption was that in most cases the parties would see it to be in their own self-interests to peacefully resolve disputes over what the terms and conditions of employment would be.

Although the passage of the Norris–La Guardia Act signaled a change in U.S. labor relations policy, the act did not establish an independent administrative agency to enforce the act's provisions. This meant that organized labor had to pursue enforcement through the judicial system, which historically had not been responsive to labor's needs and interests. Another deficiency of the Norris–La Guardia Act was that no specific employer unfair labor practices were identified and prohibited. These deficiencies were not resolved until three years later.

THE NATIONAL LABOR RELATIONS (WAGNER) ACT OF 1935

Franklin D. Roosevelt, who was backed strongly by labor unions, was elected president in 1932 along with a new Congress receptive to labor legislation as a means of ending a long economic depression. President Roosevelt promised Americans a "new deal" based upon a belief that market forces alone were incapable of putting the public's interests ahead of private ownership's interests. This created a need for more active government involvement in managing the economic welfare of the country. One of the first acts of the Roosevelt administration was to encourage Congress to pass the National Industrial Recovery Act (NIRA), a law designed to stabilize economic activity by allowing businesses to form associations that would draw up codes of fair competition to standardize marketing, pricing, financial, and other practices.[18] Upon approval of the codes by the National Recovery Administration, firms could display the "Blue Eagle" symbol that supposedly signified compliance and identified firms from which customers should purchase their goods and services. Section 7 of the NIRA required the codes to guarantee employees the right to unionize without employer interference, and a National Labor Board (NLB) was later established to help settle disputes and to determine violations under Section 7.

Because the NIRA did not require employers to bargain with unions and the NLB could not enforce its orders effectively, the law was not very effective in protecting employees' rights to organize and bargain collectively. In 1934 Congress issued a joint resolution calling for the president to establish a National Labor Relations Board (NLRB) to investigate violations under Section 7, NIRA and to conduct elections to determine whether employees wanted independent union representation.[19] The new board, created like its predecessor by executive order of the president, had trouble enforcing its orders and determining appropriate employee organizational units for conducting elections. In 1935, the Supreme Court ruled the NIRA unconstitutional when one of its codes of fair competition was applied to an employer engaged in intrastate commerce going beyond Congresses' authority to regulate interstate commerce.[20]

One month later, Senator Robert Wagner, chairman of the NLRB and an active participant in labor law matters, steered through Congress a separate labor relations law—the National Labor Relations (Wagner) Act (NLRA).[21] The NLRA established a new national labor policy that sought to ensure the free flow of commerce, labor peace and stability, and protection of the public's interests by encouraging the process of collective bargaining and preventing employer interference with the exercise of employee rights defined in the act. The National Labor Relations Board (NLRB) was authorized to investigate and decide unfair labor practice charges and conduct representation elections (other provisions are covered later in the chapter).

Congress perceived that without legal protection for employee rights, the economic power of employers far exceeded that of individual employees and inevitably led to labor unrest which had a detrimental effect on economic growth and the public's interests. "The Wagner Act is premised on an industrial relations model that there are two classes in the industrial world, labor and management, and that these two classes have very different, in fact opposing interests."[22]

Employee rights protected from employer discrimination in Section 7 of the NLRA included the right to form or join a union, bargain collectively, or engage in other concerted activity for mutual aid and protection (see Exhibit 3.1). Common employer tactics used previously to discourage union activity such as discharge or refusal to hire for union activity, company spies, blacklisting, employee representation plans (company unions), and yellow-dog contracts were declared to be unfair labor practices by the NLRA.

Many employers believed the NLRA would be ruled unconstitutional like the National Industry Recovery Act.[23] However, the Supreme Court declared the NLRA constitutional in 1937 recognizing the important impact labor relations can have on interstate commerce and thus endorsing Congress's right to regulate labor relations.[24] With Supreme Court approval of the NLRA and improved economic conditions in the United States, unions experienced tremendous growth, almost tripling union membership to 8.4 million members by 1941.[25]

Union activities in the decade following passage of the NLRA caused many to believe that the labor relations pendulum had swung too far in favor of unions and the exercise of collective employee rights. Examples of union actions which precipitated much public concern were strikes over union representation rights between competing AFL and CIO unions, union strikes or boycotts over bargaining issues, a union refusal in some cases to negotiate in good faith with an employer, and pressure on job applicants to become union members at companies where the employer and union negotiated a **closed shop union security clause** under which

Exhibit 3.1
Rights of Employees

> **Sec. 7**—Employees shall have the right to self-organization, to form, join, or assist labor organizations, to bargain collectively through representatives of their own choosing, and to engage in other concerted activities for the purpose of collective bargaining or other mutual aid or protection, and shall also have the right to refrain from any or all such activities except to the extent that such right may be affected by an agreement requiring membership in a labor organization as a condition of employment as authorized in section 8(a)(3).
>
> SOURCE: Labor-Management Relations Act, 1947, as amended.

an employer agreed to hire only job applicants who were members of a union representing the firm's workers.

As a reaction to employer criticisms of the NLRA and growing public concern over organized labor's actions, in 1947 Congress amended the NLRA by enacting the Labor Management Relations (Taft-Hartley) Act (LMRA).[26] Leaving the original language of the NLRA virtually unchanged, the LMRA added language intended to address certain identified deficiencies and direct more attention to the legitimate rights of individual employees and employers involved in the labor relations process. Calling it a "slave labor act," labor groups immediately mounted a successful campaign to have President Truman veto the bill; however, Congress easily overrode Truman's veto.

Significant Changes under the LMRA

To emphasize Congress's intent to fairly balance labor relations policy, the **National Labor Relations Act (NLRA)** was renamed the **Labor Management Relations Act (LMRA)**. Similar to employer prohibitions included in the NLRA, a section of unfair union labor practices was added to the LMRA, making it illegal for a union to engage in actions that discriminated against any employee's exercise of rights protected under Section 7 of the LMRA. Language was added to Sec. 7 granting individual employees a right to refrain from engaging in otherwise protected concerted activity (except as that right might be limited by a lawful union security clause requiring membership or support of a labor organization).

Congress agreed that membership in a particular labor organization should not be a precondition for employment and therefore made the closed shop union security clause illegal. However, Congress recognized that some level of union security was necessary in order to ensure that employees who desired union representation could achieve a reasonably effective voice in protecting and advancing their workplace interests. Employers and unions were permitted under the LMRA to negotiate voluntary agreements to either require an employee join a union within 30 days after hire (**union shop union security clause**) or pay a fee equivalent to regular union dues and initiation fees (**agency shop union security clause**) if the employee held a job in a bargaining unit represented by the union. As a political compromise, Congress did agree to permit individual states to pass a more restrictive ban on union security agreements applicable to their state (a so called **right-to-work law**). Union security issues will be discussed further in Chapter 4.

The LMRA addressed employer criticism of an NLRB policy that severely restricted an employer's right to speak out on the question of union representation during an organizing campaign. The Supreme Court declared that NLRB policy to be an unconstitutional prohibition of employers' First Amendment free speech rights.[27] Congress essentially incorporated the court's decision into the language of Sec. 8 (c), LMRA, which protects the expressing of any opinions or arguments about labor relations issues *so long as such expression contains no threat of reprisal or promise of benefit.*

To encourage unions and employers to live up to negotiated contract terms, Sec. 301, LMRA permitted the parties to a collective bargaining agreement to sue in court for breach of contract if necessary to obtain the other party's compliance with the terms of the labor agreement. Prior to this change an employer was forced to sue individual union members separately who participated in a work stoppage in violation of a contractual no strike agreement, which was both time consuming and expensive. While permitting an employer to sue a union directly for economic damages under Sec. 301, LMRA, Congress removed the right to sue individual union members to recover economic damages for a breach of a labor contract's terms.

Since 1959, there have been two successful legislative attempts to enact major changes in the LMRA. The LMRA was first extended to cover the U.S. Postal Service in 1970 (see Chapter 13) and then to cover private-sector profit and nonprofit health care institutions in 1974.

LABOR MANAGEMENT REPORTING AND DISCLOSURE (LANDRUM-GRIFFIN) ACT

In the late 1950s, a special Senate committee headed by Senator John McClellan vigorously pursued the abuses of power and corruption by some union leaders, particularly those of the Teamsters and specifically of Dave Beck and James Hoffa.[28] Exposing shocking examples of union corruption and abuses of power, Congress reacted in 1959 by passing the Labor-Management Reporting and Disclosure (Landrum-Griffin) Act (LMRDA).[29] The LMRDA is primarily designed to protect the rights of individual union members in their relations with their own union and to ensure that labor organizations operate in a democratic and financially responsible manner. Unlike the LMRA, which applies to both union and nonunion employees, the LMRDA only covers individuals who are members of a labor organization.

For example, the LMRDA requires all local union officers to be elected by secret ballot vote of union members at least once every three years and national union officers at least once every five years. Union members must approve any increase or decrease in the amount charged for union membership dues, initiation fees, or other special assessments. A union's constitution and by-laws approved by a vote of the membership is considered to be a binding contract between the union and its members enforceable in court. Unions are required to file annual reports with the U.S. Department of Labor available to the public containing information on union assets and liabilities, union officer salaries, and current union operating rules. Labor organizations are among the most regulated organizations in U.S. society today.

Title VII of the LMRDA also contained some amendments to the LMRA. Of most importance was the addition of Sec. 303 to the LMRA granting neutral, secondary employers harmed by unlawful secondary strike, boycott, or picket activity a right to sue the guilty labor organization to recover economic damages.

NATIONAL LABOR RELATIONS BOARD (NLRB)

The rights of employees provided by the LMRA are not self-enforcing and a weakness of the previous NIRA had been the lack of any effective enforcement mechanism. Confronted with a prior history of relatively weak court enforcement of employee rights, Congress took the extraordinary step of designating an independent federal administrative agency, the National Labor Relations Board (NLRB), to be the primary interpreter and administrator of the newly created NLRA. To ensure the constitutionality of the NLRA, Congress provided that unfair labor practice decisions of the NLRB could be appealed for review to an appropriate federal Circuit Court of Appeals. The courts were instructed by Congress to pay great deference to the policies of the NLRB in interpreting what Congress intended the law to accomplish.

The NLRB is headquartered in Washington, D.C. and headed by a five-member panel termed **the Board**.[30] Board members are nominated by the president to serve a five-year term and must be confirmed by the U.S. Senate. Terms of Board members are staggered to ensure that not all vacancies occur at the same time although due to delays in the nomination and confirmation process, there have been periods where several Board seats were vacant at the same time, affecting the ability of the NLRB to function effectively.

As political appointees, Board members generally reflect the basic labor relations philosophy of the president who nominated them. The nomination process is subject to intense lobbying by employers, unions, and other outside interest groups (e.g., National Right To Work Committee) who recognize the important role the Board serves in determining the balance between protection for employer and employee interests, particularly on legal issues where such interests may conflict. "Interpretations of the facts and law governing union-management relations is ... dependent in part on the makeup of the board."[31] One study reported finding an apparent pro-employer or pro-union bias in only 20 percent of Board case decisions.[32] Recent decisions shown in the "Labor Relations in Action" box demonstrate the importance of presidential appointments to the Board and courts.

The Board has two primary responsibilities. One responsibility is to prevent employer and union unfair labor practices as defined by the LMRA, as amended, which interfere with the exercise of employee rights protected by the act. This responsibility is carried out primarily through the investigation, prosecution, and remedy of unfair labor practices. The second responsibility is to determine if employees covered under the LMRA desire representation by an independent labor organization for purposes of collective bargaining. The Board establishes and conducts certification procedures to determine if a majority of eligible employees desires a specific labor organization to represent them for purposes of collective bargaining. Approximately two-thirds of the Board's case load involves unfair labor practice cases and one-third involves representation determination cases. The Board exercises final administrative decision-making authority in all unfair labor practice and representation cases, although ULP decisions may be appealed for review by a federal court.

The Board delegates authority to the General Counsel and staff attorneys to investigate and prosecute unfair labor practice charges. The General Counsel is nominated by the president to serve a four-year term and must be confirmed by the U.S. Senate. As with Board members, the General Counsel's nomination and confirmation process is subject to interest group politics.

A major responsibility of the General Counsel's office is to conduct a preliminary investigation of each unfair labor practice charge to determine if sufficient (*prima facie*) evidence exists to conclude an unfair labor practice may have occurred. If insufficient evidence of a violation is found, the General Counsel has the authority to dismiss an unfair labor practice charge and there is no appeal of that decision. This gives the General Counsel tremendous influence in helping to determine the policy making agenda of the Board because the Board announces new policies or alters existing policies through the issuance of unfair labor practice case decisions. The only cases in which the Board will have an opportunity to render a ULP decision are those cases in which the General Counsel's investigation concluded that evidence of an unfair labor practice existed.

LABOR RELATIONS IN ACTION

Selected Labor Relations Cases Decided by the U.S. Supreme Court and the NLRB

Liability for Filing a Retaliatory Lawsuit

In a 5-4 decision, the Court concluded that the NLRB could not impose liability on an employer who filed an unsuccessful lawsuit against several unions alleging unlawful acts if the employer could prove there was a reasonable basis for filing the lawsuit. *BE & K Construction Company v. NLRB,* 122 S.Ct. 2390 (2002)

Back Pay Remedy

In a 5-4 decision, the Court ruled that the Immigration Reform and Control Act prevents the NLRB from awarding a back pay remedy to an undocumented alien even though an employer can be found guilty of committing an unfair labor practice in violation of the undocumented alien's employee rights under the LMRA. The NLRB could impose other remedies for the employer's unfair labor practice such as a cease-and-desist order and an order to post notices admitting the unlawful conduct and informing company employees of their basic employee rights under the LMRA. *Hoffman Plastic Compounds, Inc. v. NLRB,* 122 S.Ct. 1275 (2002)

Determination of Supervisory Status

The party asserting that an employee is a supervisor and thus excluded from coverage under the LMRA has the burden of proving the employee's supervisory status. To be a supervisor under the LMRA, an individual must 1) perform at least one of the 12 specified supervisory functions (e.g., hiring, performance evaluation); 2) use independent judgment that is not merely routine or clerical in nature; and 3) exercise authority in the interests of the employer. Supervisory status must be made on a case-by-case basis. See: *Oakwood Healthcare, Inc. and United Auto Workers of America,* 348 NLRB No. 37 (2006); *Beverly Enterprises-Minnesota, Inc. d/b/a Golden Crest Healthcare Center and Untied Steelworkers of America,* 348 NLRB No. 39 (2006; *Croft Metals, Inc. and International Brotherhood of Boilermakers, Iron Ship Builders, Blacksmiths, Forgers and Helpers,* 348 NLRB No. 38 (2006); and *NLRB v. Kentucky River Community Care, Inc.,* 121 S.Ct. 1861 (2001).

Union Recognition

The Court unanimously upheld the NLRB's decision that an employer may not refuse to bargain with an incumbent union on the grounds that the union had lost majority status shortly after the employer had previously entered into a contract with such union. *Auciello Iron Works, Inc. v. NLRB,* 116 S. Ct 1754 (1996)

Definition of "Employees" under LMRA

Even though the majority of work duties performed by members of a "live chicken catching crew" were performed on site of chicken farmers who subcontracted with the chicken processing plant to raise the chickens to a marketable age (size), crew members were "employees" of the chicken processing plant and not excluded from coverage under the LMRA as agricultural laborers. *Holly Farms Corp. v. NLRB,* 116 S. Ct. 1396 (1996)

Union Organizers

The Court unanimously upheld the NLRB's decision that paid union organizers are "employees" within the meaning of the LMRA when applying for a job or after being hired by the employer. Therefore, individuals acting as "salts" are protected against employer retaliation in the form of discharge or discipline for participating in any protected activity under Section 7 of the act, such as attempting to organize a union among employees. *NLRB v. Town & Country,* 116 S. Ct. 450 (1995)

Partial Lockout

The 7th U.S. Circuit Court of Appeals reversed an NLRB decision permitting an employer to lock out employees who had initiated a lawful economic strike on June 28, but abandoned that strike on August 31 and sought immediate reinstatement to their bargaining unit jobs. Still without a negotiated collective bargaining agreement, the employer initiated a lockout applicable to striking workers who had not abandoned the strike prior to August 31 in order to put pressure on those employees to agree to the employer's proposed contract terms. The court found no evidence in the case record supporting a legitimate business reason for the lockout and further found the lockout to be an unfair labor practice under the LMRA because it discriminated against employees who had exercised their lawful right to engage in an economic strike in furtherance of their bargaining interests. *Local 15, International Brotherhood of Electrical Workers v. NLRB,* 429 F.3d 651 (7th Cir. 2005)

Failure to Pay Required Union Dues

Employees covered by a valid union security clause are subject to discharge for failing to pay the amount of union dues owed after proper notification by the union and a reasonable opportunity to meet the employee's dues obligation. A refusal by an employer to honor a union's request to discharge bargaining unit employees who have failed to meet their lawful union dues obligation represents an employer unfair labor practice violation under the LMRA. *St. John's Health Systems v. NLRB,* 436 F.3d 843 (8th Cir. 2006)

Successor Employer Bargaining

Overruling a 1999 Board policy, the Board returned to the previous policy, which holds that an incumbent union in a successor employer situation is entitled to a rebuttable presumption of continuing majority support. This would permit employees to file a valid decertification petition or another union to file a valid representation petition or a successor employer to file an employer election petition challenging the union's presumption of continuing majority support. A successor employer's duty to bargain with an incumbent union continues until the date on which a lack of majority employee support for the union can be established. *MV Transportation,* 337 NLRB 770 (2002)

Inclusion of Leased Employees in a Bargaining Unit with Regular Employees

On a 3-2 vote, the Board held that it was not permissible to combine an employer's own employees in the same bargaining unit with employees performing similar job tasks obtained from another employer (e.g., company supplying leased labor) without the consent of both the user employer and the supplier employer. This will make it more difficult for leased employees to gain union representation rights at the firm where they actually perform their job duties. *Oakwood Care Center,* 343 NLRB No. 76 (2004)

Unilateral Employer Withdrawal of Union Recognition

Applying legal principles established by the U.S. Supreme Court in *Allentown Mack Sales & Service v. NLRB,* 522 U.S. 359 (1998), the Board held that an employer may unilaterally withdraw union recognition of the exclusive bargaining unit representative only if the employer can prove the union has lost majority employee support as of the date of the employer's unilateral withdrawal of recognition. Alternatively, an employer may obtain an NLRB supervised election to determine if the majority of bargaining unit employees supports the incumbent union if the employer can demonstrate a good-faith reasonable uncertainty regarding the union's continued majority support. The Board would prefer employees directly express their desire for or against union representation through a secret ballot representation election rather than an employer acting unilaterally to withdraw union recognition. *Levitz Furniture Company of the Pacific, Inc.,* 333 NLRB 717 (2001)

Duty to Bargain

When an employer has been found guilty of bad-faith bargaining and issued a remedial order to bargain in good faith, such bargaining must occur for a "reasonable time" before the union's majority status as bargaining representative can be challenged. "Reasonable time" refers to a period no less than six months nor longer than one year. The exact length time good-faith bargaining would be required is determined on a case-by-case basis based on several factors including: whether the negotiations are for an initial contract or seek to amend an existing agreement, the complexity of the issues being negotiated and the parties bargaining procedures, the total amount of time elapsed since the start of bargaining and the number of bargaining meetings held, the amount of progress the parties have made and how close the parties appear to be to reaching a settlement, and whether the parties have reached a good faith bargaining impasse. *Lee Lumber and Building Material Corp.,* 334 NLRB 399 (2001)

Employer Use of Employees in Pro-Company Union Representation Election Campaign Videos

While finding that the employer in the instant case unlawfully solicited employees to appear in a campaign election video, the Board established four clear conditions which if met, would permit employers to solicit employees to appear in a union election campaign video. To be lawful: 1) the solicitation to participate in the campaign video must be in the form of a general announcement, which discloses the purpose of filming and assures employees that participation is voluntary;

no retaliation will occur against employees who do not voluntarily choose to participate, and no rewards or benefits will be provided to those employees who do participate; 2) employees may not be pressured to make a decision regarding their participation in the presence of a supervisor; 3) there can be no unlawful conduct connected with the employer's solicitation for voluntary participants; and 4) the solicitation cannot occur in a coercive atmosphere created by the employer's commission of other unfair labor practices. *Allegheny Ludlum Corporation,* 333 NLRB 734 (2001)

Coverage of Teaching and Research Graduate Assistants

The Board reversed, by a 3-2 vote, a 2000 Board decision extending coverage to teaching and research graduate assistants at a private university and ruled that such graduate student assistants do not meet the definition of "employee" and thus are not entitled to exercise protected employee rights under the LMRA. Compare *Brown University,* 342 NLRB No. 42 (2004) to *New York University,* 332 NLRB 1205 (2000).

Coverage of Medical Interns, Residents, and Fellows (House Staff)

Reversing previous policy, the Board ruled that hospital interns and residents in a private hospital are employees covered by the LMRA even though they are students. Therefore, these employees have the right to organize and join a union and participate in other protected concerted activities. *Boston Medical Center Corp.,* 330 N.L.R.B. 152 (1999) [Note: If the Board follows its reasoning in *Brown University* discussed above, then the *Boston Medical Center Corp.* decision could be reversed in the future.]

Weingarten Rights Applied to Unrepresented Employees

Continuing a long running dispute over the interpretation of what constitutes protected activity for mutual aid or protection, by a 3-2 vote, the Board reinstated a previous policy denying nonunion (unrepresented) employees covered by the LMRA a right to have a co-worker present during an investigatory interview with management where the employee had reason to believe that he or she might be subject to disciplinary or discharge action as a result of the investigation. Exercise of such a right is viewed as a form of concerted activity for mutual aid or protection when exercised by union represented employees but not when exercised by unrepresented employees. So-called *Weingarten rights* also permit a union-represented employee to know the general nature of the alleged violation being investigated and a reasonable opportunity to meet with his or her union representative prior to any investigatory meeting with management. Compare *IBM Corporation,* 341 NLRB 1288 (2004) to *Epilepsy Foundation of Northeast Ohio,* 331 NLRB 676 (2000) enforced in part, *Epilepsy Foundation of Northeast Ohio v. NLRB,* 268 F.3d 1095 (D.C. Cir. 2002). See also *NLRB v. Weingarten,* 420 U.S. 251 (1975).

Voluntary Employer Recognition Does Not Create an Election Bar

In a 3-2 decision, the Board overturned the established precedent and ruled that an employer's granting of a union's request for voluntary recognition as the exclusive bargaining representative of an employee group does not bar the filing of a decertification or rival union petition within 45 days of the date notice is provided to effected parties that voluntary employer recognition has been granted. The previous policy precedent established in 1966 required an election bar for a "reasonable period of time" following voluntary employer recognition to permit the parties to focus on efforts to negotiate a first labor agreement. The new policy would appear aimed at weakening the credibility of voluntary employer recognition based upon a showing of majority employee support for a union using union authorization card signatures. *Dana Corporation,* 351 NLRB No. 28 (2007)

The General Counsel is also responsible for representing the NLRB whenever a Board decision or order is appealed to a federal court or when the Board seeks a court order to enforce its decision. The General Counsel also serves as a legal advisor to Board members on matters pertaining to the interpretation or application of the LMRA or how past Board policies and procedures have fared upon review by the federal courts. The General Counsel relies upon staff attorneys located at the NLRB's headquarters in Washington, D.C., as well as each regional NLRB office to help carry out the responsibilities of the General Counsel's office.

For employees, a union, or management practitioner, contact with the NLRB typically occurs at the regional or resident office level. The NLRB maintains 32 regional, 3 sub-regional and 17 resident offices located throughout the country to handle unfair labor practice and representation election cases.[33] Each regional office is headed by the Regional Director who also manages any sub-regional or resident offices located within the regional office's geographic jurisdiction. The Regional Director and staff work with the General Counsel to investigate unfair labor practice charges and are delegated authority by the Board to administer all representation election procedures. Most meritorious unfair labor practice cases get resolved at the regional office level with the settlement rate ranging between 91.5 and 99.5 percent over the previous ten year period. NLRB regional and field office locations handled more than 216,000 public inquiries for information in FY 2005, and the NLRB's Web site's "Frequently Asked Questions" page received 518,325 visits in its first nine months of operation.

Employer and Employee Coverage under the LMRA, as Amended

In order to promote the public policy goals of the LMRA, as amended Congress sought to include as many employers and employees as possible under the statute's coverage. The U.S. Constitution permits Congress to regulate private-sector employers whose operations have *the potential to vitally affect interstate commerce*. If an employer is subject to coverage under the statute, the employer's employees are also covered (protected) by the statute unless they fall into an employee category specifically excluded from coverage (e.g., agricultural workers). The term **NLRB jurisdiction** refers to those employers and employees to whom the NLRB can apply the language of the LMRA.

The NLRB may refuse to assert jurisdiction in cases where it believes the effect on interstate commerce is minor (*de minimus*). For example, state regulated industries such as real estate, horse and dog racing. Individual states may assert jurisdiction over any case where the NLRB has declined to do so.[34]

From 1935 to 1950 the Board relied upon the judgment of individual Regional Directors to determine an employer's ability to affect interstate commerce on a case-by-case basis. To reduce the inconsistencies inherent in this approach and improve the objectivity of decisions, the Board adopted a set of monetary standards (guidelines) applicable to different types of employer operations (see Exhibit 3.2). In 1959 as part of the LMRDA, Congress prohibited the Board from refusing to apply or altering the monetary standards then in effect without congressional approval.

The standards measure the total dollar volume of an employer's operations (gross revenue) and the dollar value of products or services sold (outflow) or purchased (inflow) over a 12-month period (e.g., most recent calendar or business tax year or 12 months immediately preceding the filing of an unfair labor practice charge or representation election petition). Meeting the specified dollar threshold using any one of the available measurements is sufficient to permit the NLRB to assert jurisdiction over the case and apply the terms of the LMRA.

Exhibit 3.2

NLRB Jurisdictional Standards Determining Employer Coverage under the LMRA

- **NonRetail Business**—Direct or indirect sales through others of goods to consumers in other states (called *outflow*) of at least $50,000 a year; or direct or indirect purchases through others of goods from suppliers in other states (called *inflow*) of at least $50,000 a year.

- **Retail Business**—At least $500,000 total annual volume of business.

- **Office Building**—Total annual revenue of $100,000, $25,000 or more of which is derived from organizations which meet any of the standards except the indirect outflow and indirect inflow standards for nonretail firms.

- **Public Utility**—At least $250,000 total annual volume of business, or $50,000 direct or indirect outflow or inflow.

- **Newspaper**—At least $200,000 total annual volume of business.

- **Radio, Telegraph, Television, and Telephone Firms**—At least $100,000 total annual volume of business.

- **Private Health Care Institutions** (e.g., hospital, HMO, clinic, nursing home)—At least $250,000 total annual volume of business for hospitals; at least $100,000 for nursing homes, visiting nurses associations, and related facilities; at least $250,000 for all other types of private health care institutions.

- **Hotel, Motel, Residential Apartment Houses**—At least $500,000 total annual volume of business.

- **Transportation Enterprises, Links, and Channels of Interstate Commerce** (e.g., interstate bus, truck)—At least $50,000 total annual income from furnishing interstate passenger and freight transportation services OR performing services valued at $50,000 or more for businesses which meet any of the jurisdictional standards except the indirect outflow and inflow standards established for nonretail firms. [**NOTE:** Airline and Railroad operations are covered under the Railway Labor Act (RLA), not the LMRA and thus are not subject to NLRB jurisdiction.]

- **Transit Systems**—At least $250,000 total annual volume of business.

- **Taxicab Companies**—At least $500,000 total annual volume of business.

- **Associations**—The annual business of each association member is totaled to determine whether any of the standards apply.

- **Private Universities and Colleges**—At least $1 million gross annual revenue from all sources (excluding contributions not available for operating expenses due to limitations imposed by the donor).

- **Any Firm with a Substantial Impact on National Defense.**

- **U.S. Postal Service** by enactment of the Postal Reorganization Act of 1970.

- **Symphony Orchestras**—At least $1 million gross annual revenue from all sources (excluding contributions not available for operating expenses due to limitations imposed by the donor).

- **Social Service Organizations Not Covered under Any Other Standard**—At least $250,000 gross annual revenue.

SOURCE: Office of the General Counsel, NLRB, *A Guide to Basic Law and Procedures under the National Labor Relations Act* (Washington, D.C.: U.S. Government Printing Office, 1997), pp. 35–37.

Congress excluded some individuals from the definition of an employee subject to coverage under the LMRA, as amended. Specifically excluded by statutory language are:

- Agricultural laborers—An employee whose primary duties involve ordinary farming operations performed prior to a product's readiness for initial sale.[35] Some states (e.g., AZ, CA, HI, ID, KS, MA, WI) have enacted a collective bargaining law to cover agricultural laborers in their state.

- Individuals employed by an employer covered under the Railway Labor Act (rail and airline industries).

- Individuals employed as a domestic by a private household (e.g., cook, nanny, butler, chauffeur, gardener, personal assistant).

- Individuals employed by a parent or spouse are excluded from coverage under the LMRA. On a case-by-case basis, other individuals may be excluded from a particular bargaining unit because evidence demonstrates their self-interests to be more closely aligned with that of ownership rather than other employees included in a bargaining unit.

- Individuals employed by a public-sector employer (federal, state, or local). Public-sector labor relations issues are discussed further in Chapter 13. U.S. Postal Service employees are the only exception to the public employee exclusion rule. As part of a settlement to end an illegal strike by postal workers, Congress enacted the **Postal Reorganization Act of 1970** which placed postal workers under coverage of the LMRA, greatly expanding the number and types of issues over which workers could legally bargain. Unlike other private-sector employees covered by the LMRA, postal workers have no legal right to strike but may invoke final and binding arbitration as a means of resolving interest disputes that may occur during the labor agreement negotiation process. Interest arbitration will be discussed further in Chapter 9.

- Independent contractors are considered self-employed and thus are treated as an employer, not an employee under the LMRA. Merely calling someone an independent contractor is not sufficient evidence to establish their employment status. In general, an independent contractor is an individual who offers a service for a fixed fee to provide a specified result. The wages of an independent contractor are at risk in the sense that any profit is dependent upon the contractor's ability to deliver the agreed-upon work product at a cost below the fixed fee agreed upon in advance. An independent contractor controls the manner in which work is performed and generally furnishes his own training, tools, or other work materials.

- Supervisors were not originally excluded from coverage under the 1935 NLRA, but Congress added the exclusion as part of the LMRA (Taft-Hartley) amendments in 1947. Sec. 2 (11), LMRA defines a supervisor as "any individual delegated management authority to perform or effectively recommend one or more of the following functions affecting employees: to hire, transfer, suspend, lay off, recall, promote, discipline, discharge, adjust grievances, assign work, or reward employees so long as the exercise of such authority requires the use of independent judgment which is note merely routine or clerical in nature."[36] To be a supervisor the evidence must show that the individual 1) performs at least one of the specified supervisory functions, 2) has been delegated authority to perform such supervisory functions in the interests of the employer (as opposed to performance as a routine part of the individual's professional responsibilities), and 3) exercises independent judgment when performing his or her supervisory duties (as opposed to merely carrying out the decisions of some other manager or applying established policies). The supervisory exclusion has since been extended to include any manager who participates in the formulation or execution of management policies and procedures so long as such activity involves the exercise of independent judgment or discretion.[37]

The mere fact that a professional employee (e.g., nurse, teacher, engineer) exercises some independent judgment or discretion in performing job duties does not automatically exclude that individual from coverage under the LMRA. In *Oakwood Healthcare Inc.* (NLRB 2006), cited in the Labor Relations in Action section earlier in this chapter, the Board ruled that 12 permanent charge nurses met the definition of a supervisor whereas 169 other registered nurses whom the employer had sought to exclude from a bargaining unit as supervisors were *not* supervisors even though on some occasions they were labeled as charge nurses by the employer.[38]

Concerted and Protected Employee Activity

Concerted activity implies some action taken by or on behalf of two or more employees to express a complaint or grievance relating to conditions of employment under the employer's control, for example, work procedures, staffing levels, pay or benefits, safety conditions, hours of work, discipline or other matters affecting wages, hours, or other terms and conditions of employment. The LMRA does not protect complaints or grievances of a purely personal nature (i.e., of concern to a single employee).

To be protected under the LMRA, the concerted activity must be for a protected purpose described in Sec. 7 of the act and engaged in using lawful means. For example, tactics used to form or join a union or engage in collective bargaining or other mutual aid or protection cannot involve violence, sabotage, or a disproportionate loss or disruption to the employer relative to the seriousness or importance of the employees' complaint or grievance. On a case-by-case basis, the National Labor Relations Board must decide if the act is concerted and if so, is the act for a lawful purpose using lawful means?

Employees are not required to provide management with an opportunity to resolve a complaint or grievance prior to engaging in some form of **concerted and protected activity** to express a complaint or grievance.[39] Nor are employees required to accept any management proposal for resolving a complaint or grievance even though management believes the proposed settlement terms are fair and appropriate. Although unrepresented (nonunion) employees covered under the LMRA have a right to engage in concerted and protected activity, they do not have a right to require their employer to engage in collective bargaining with them over a solution to the grievance dispute. The duty to bargain cannot be lawfully imposed until a labor organization has been legally certified as the exclusive bargaining representative of an employee group. The union recognition (certification) step is discussed further in Chapter 5, and the duty to bargain in good faith is discussed in Chapter 6.

The *Interboro* doctrine represents an exception to the requirement that an employee be able to prove that he or she acted with or on the express authorization of one or more other employees in order to be considered engaged in concerted activity.[40] A single bargaining unit member can be implied to be acting in concert with other bargaining unit members covered under the same contract terms whenever the individual acts alone to enforce a term or condition of a collective bargaining agreement. Even if the employee has not previously discussed the issue (e.g., safety concern, denial of pay or promotion) with other employees or no other employee is present at the time the employee expresses the grievance complaint to a member of management, no adverse action could be taken against the individual merely for expressing the grievance so long as the complaint concerned a term or condition of the existing collective bargaining agreement.

The exercise of Sec. 7 rights through concerted activities is not unlimited. For example, reasonable restrictions on the right to strike can occur based upon a strike's objective, its timing, or the conduct of the strikers. If a strike's purpose was to achieve a closed shop contract provision forcing the hiring of only union members, its purpose would be illegal; therefore, the strike would be illegal. If a strike occurs in violation of a no-strike provision in the contract, the timing of the strike is inappropriate, and all striking employees may be disciplined. Further, strikers do not have the right to threaten or engage in acts of violence. Neither sit-down strikes nor refusals to leave a plant are protected strike activities. Strikers also exceed their rights when they physically block persons from entering a struck plant or when threats of violence are made against employees not on strike. Strike issues are further explained in Chapter 9.

NLRB Unfair Labor Practice Procedure

The procedure for an unfair labor practice (ULP) charge (Exhibit 3.3) starts when an employee, employer, labor union, or individual files a charge with an NLRB office within six months of the date the alleged violation occurred. The party filing the charge is termed the **Charging Party** and the party accused of committing the violation is termed the **Respondent**. An employer was named the Respondent in 74 percent of ULP cases filed in FY 2005, with most charges being filed by a union on behalf of one or more employees.[41] Refusal to bargain in good faith or illegal discharge or other discrimination against employees were the most commonly alleged employer ULPs. Of ULP charges filed against unions, the two most common allegations were illegal restraint or coercion of employees or unlawful secondary boycotts and jurisdictional disputes.

The General Counsel's Office with the aid of the NLRB regional office staff will investigate the ULP charge to determine if sufficient evidence exists to believe a ULP violation may have occurred. The investigation may involve interviews with potential witnesses, examination of documents, or other necessary steps. A ULP charge may be settled or withdrawn at any point in the ULP procedure prior to a final Board decision. If insufficient evidence to support the charge is found during the preliminary investigation, the General Counsel will dismiss the ULP charge and there is no further appeal of this decision. In cases alleging an unlawful boycott or strike, the NLRB must request a federal district court to issue a temporary restraining order while the case is investigated.

If the General Counsel's investigation confirms the ULP charge has **merit** (i.e., there is sufficient evidence found to believe a ULP appears to have been committed), a reasonable effort will be made to get the Respondent to agree to a voluntary settlement of the charge. If no voluntary settlement is reached, a formal ULP complaint and notice of a hearing date will be issued before the **Administrative Law Judge (ALJ)**.

In FY 2005, there were 24,726 ULP charges filed (down 9.2 percent from the previous year), of which 36.5 percent were found to have merit resulting in the issuance of 1,440 ULP complaints in a median time of 93 days.[42] In FY 2005, the NLRB obtained 8,232 ULP case settlements representing 97.2 percent of all merit cases. The voluntary settlement rate for ULP charges with merit has ranged

Exhibit 3.3
Unfair Labor Practice Procedure

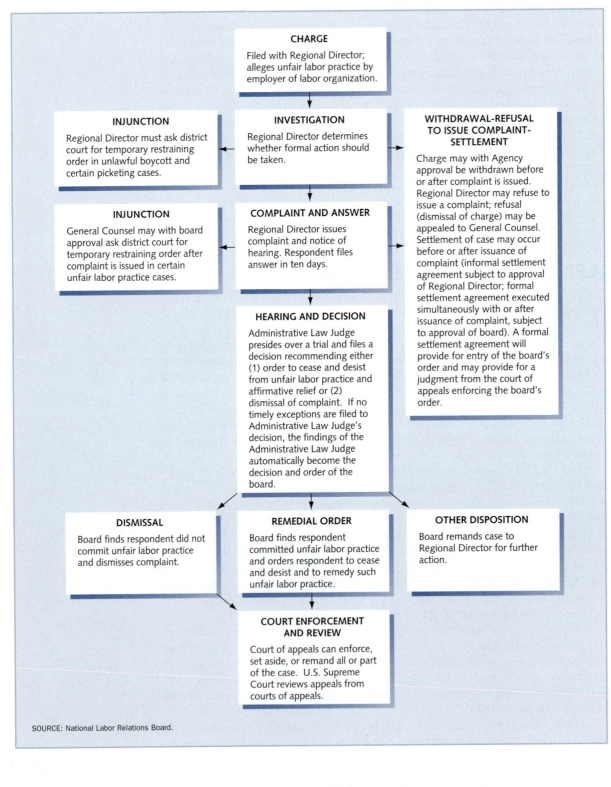

CHARGE

Filed with Regional Director; alleges unfair labor practice by employer of labor organization.

INJUNCTION

Regional Director must ask district court for temporary restraining order in unlawful boycott and certain picketing cases.

INVESTIGATION

Regional Director determines whether formal action should be taken.

WITHDRAWAL-REFUSAL TO ISSUE COMPLAINT-SETTLEMENT

Charge may with Agency approval be withdrawn before or after complaint is issued. Regional Director may refuse to issue a complaint; refusal (dismissal of charge) may be appealed to General Counsel. Settlement of case may occur before or after issuance of complaint (informal settlement agreement subject to approval of Regional Director; formal settlement agreement executed simultaneously with or after issuance of complaint, subject to approval of board). A formal settlement agreement will provide for entry of the board's order and may provide for a judgment from the court of appeals enforcing the board's order.

INJUNCTION

General Counsel may with board approval ask district court for temporary restraining order after complaint is issued in certain unfair labor practice cases.

COMPLAINT AND ANSWER

Regional Director issues complaint and notice of hearing. Respondent files answer in ten days.

HEARING AND DECISION

Administrative Law Judge presides over a trial and files a decision recommending either (1) order to cease and desist from unfair labor practice and affirmative relief or (2) dismissal of complaint. If no timely exceptions are filed to Administrative Law Judge's decision, the findings of the Administrative Law Judge automatically become the decision and order of the board.

DISMISSAL

Board finds respondent did not commit unfair labor practice and dismisses complaint.

REMEDIAL ORDER

Board finds respondent committed unfair labor practice and orders respondent to cease and desist and to remedy such unfair labor practice.

OTHER DISPOSITION

Board remands case to Regional Director for further action.

COURT ENFORCEMENT AND REVIEW

Court of appeals can enforce, set aside, or remand all or part of the case. U.S. Supreme Court reviews appeals from courts of appeals.

SOURCE: National Labor Relations Board.

between 91.5 and 99.5 percent over the past decade. The percentage of ULP charges filed found to have merit has ranged from 32 to 40 percent since 1980. Thirty-six percent of cases were settled before the issuance of an ALJ report, 30.2 percent of charges were withdrawn voluntarily before the ALJ had completed the preliminary investigation, and 29.4 percent of cases were dismissed after completion of the ALJ's preliminary ULP investigation. Employers were the named Respondent in 90.2 percent of cases that resulted in the issuance of a formal ULP complaint.

The ALJ presides over a formal ULP hearing conducted under federal court rules of evidence during which the General Counsel (representing the Charging Party) has the initial burden of proving by a preponderance of the evidence that a ULP was committed. The Respondent (typically an employer) would have an opportunity during the hearing to present evidence and arguments attempting to prove that no ULP violation occurred. Based upon the evidence presented at the hearing, the ALJ sends a written report to the Board containing findings of fact regarding the alleged ULP charge and recommendations on an appropriate remedy for any ULP violations found to have occurred.

The Board has final agency authority to decide all ULP charges. The ALJ's written report is sent to all parties involved in the case as well as the Board. The Board rarely hears oral arguments or testimony from any of the parties in a ULP case and therefore places a great deal of importance on the ALJ's findings regarding key issues such as the credibility and demeanor of witnesses who testified during the hearing.

Unfair labor practice cases can be classified into two broad categories or types: routine or lead cases. A **routine ULP case** involves charges that do not raise any new or novel issues of labor law and can be determined by application of existing relevant Board policies and legal principles. Such cases are typically decided by a three-member panel of Board members and comprise 80 to 90 percent of all Board decisions. The high percentage of routine cases has been cited by some as evidence that the Board's current remedial powers are not adequate to prevent typical discriminatory acts involving supposedly protected employee rights under the Act.[43]

A **lead ULP case** involves a charge that either raises a new or novel labor law issue or presents the Board with an opportunity to initiate a new policy or change a significant established policy interpreting the LMRA, as amended. Because of the precedent-setting nature of lead cases, a decision requires the participation of all Board members. The Board adopts the recommended decision and order of the ALJ in approximately 85 percent of ULP cases but has the authority to reject or alter the ALJ's recommendations in every ULP case.

Unfair Labor Practice Remedies

Sec. 10 (c), LMRA grants the Board broad authority to fashion an appropriate remedy for ULP violations.[44] At a minimum, the Board will issue a **cease-and-desist order**, instructing the Respondent to stop committing the ULP violations immediately and in the future. It is common for the Board to order a Respondent to **post written notices** at places where employees will see them to inform employees about the ULP violations that have occurred, the Respondent's pledge not to commit such violations in the future, and the basic rights of employees protected by Sec. 7 of the LMRA. Such notices must remain on display for a period of time ranging from six weeks to six months. Additional remedies fall under the heading of **affirmative action** necessary to provide a make-whole type remedy to individuals adversely affected by the occurrence of a ULP. Depending upon the specific type of ULP committed, affirmative action could include one or more of the following types of actions: reinstatement, back pay, promotion, restoration of seniority rights or other benefits to which the individual should have been entitled had the ULP not occurred, expunging any reference to the illegal action from an individual's personnel file, an order to bargain in good faith, an order to re-open an illegally closed plant or return illegally relocated work, decertification or disestablishment of a union as the employees' exclusive bargaining representative, union repayment of illegally withheld or overcharged dues or fines.

The Board has no authority to award punitive damages in any case no matter how many separate or intentional ULP violations were committed by a Respondent. An employee alleging unlawful discharge is under an affirmative duty to seek comparable employment to mitigate the Respondent's potential back-pay liability while awaiting a final determination of the merit of the ULP charge. Although the Board can order a party to bargain in good faith, the Board has no authority to order either union or management representatives to accept any specific change in a term or condition of employment. The Board could rule that a current employment policy or practice is unlawful and cannot continue to be enforced but could not order the guilty party to change the policy or practice in a way to make it lawful.

Parties may appeal a Board ULP decision to an appropriate federal appeals court as shown in Exhibit 3.3. While the Board relies primarily on voluntary compliance by Respondents with its ordered remedies, when necessary to the Board may also petition an appropriate federal appeals court for an order enforcing the Board's ULP decision. An unfair labor practice decision can be appealed to the District of Columbia Circuit Court of Appeals, which has jurisdiction over where the Board is located; an appeals court having jurisdiction over the location where the ULP occurred; or an appeals court having jurisdiction over the location of the appealing party's principal residence or business headquarters.

Upon review of the Board's ULP decision, a court of appeals may enforce the order as written, modify the decision, remand the case back to the Board for further consideration, or refuse to enforce the Board's decision. Approximately 50 percent of final ULP Board decisions (or approximately 1 percent of all ULP charges filed) are appealed annually to federal courts, making the NLRB one of the most active federal agencies involved in federal court litigation. In FY 2005, 156 ULP cases were appealed to the federal courts with private parties initiating the appeal in 82 (53 percent) cases and the NLRB seeking a court enforcement order in the other 74 cases.[45]

A federal court must enforce the Board's ULP decision if 1) the decision is a reasonable interpretation of congressional intent as expressed in the language of the LMRA, as amended and 2) the decision is supported by substantial evidence (facts and reasoning) contained in the case record.[46] It is the lack of substantial evidence in the case record to support the Board's decision which is cited most frequently when a court refuses to enforce all or part of a Board ULP decision. The courts were encouraged by Congress to pay deference to the Board's interpretations of the LMRA and to witness credibility determinations by an Administrative Law Judge during the ULP hearing. On balance, the NLRB has a very successful track record of having its decisions enforced by federal appeals courts. In FY 2005, U.S. Courts of Appeal decided 73 cases of which 78.1 percent of Board decisions were enforced entirely; 16.4 percent were enforced in part; 1.4 percent were remanded to the Board for further consideration; and 4.1 percent of Board case decisions were denied enforcement.[47]

A court of appeals decision in a ULP case can be appealed for possible review by the U.S. Supreme Court (**petition for *certiorari***). To be reviewed, four of the nine Supreme Court justices must agree to hear a case. Cases most likely to be accepted for review are those which raise a new or novel labor law question not previously addressed by the court or which raise an issue on which lower courts of appeal having rendered different interpretations thus creating a so-called legal split amongst the courts of appeal. Agreeing to hear such a case on appeal would allow the Supreme Court to resolve the legal question and establish a binding precedent which lower courts and administrative agencies (e.g., NLRB) would have to follow in deciding future similar cases. The Supreme Court agrees to review less than one percent of all *petitions for certiorari* it receives.

Assessment of the LMRA, as Amended and NLRB Administration

The LMRA and its administration have critics in the academic community. Professor James Gross, an authority on the LMRA, has stated: "The current national labor policy favors and protects the powerful at the expense of the powerless. In the essential moral sense, therefore, the current national labor policy is a failure."[48] Professor Janice Bellace has suggested that most labor commentators find the current application of labor laws has actually discouraged unionism.

"Current labor law tolerates long delays in getting to an election and in having the election results certified. Labor supporters will also point out that even when there is a union at a work place, labor law permits the threatened and actual replacement of strikers from the first day of the strike. They will decry this, particularly because rules on the labor contract do not maintain the status quo when the contract expires, thus enabling employers demanding concessions to take back in a flash those contract items gained by the union over the years. Finally, labor supporters deride a statute with remedies so weak they do not deserve the label 'remedy'."[49]

While admitting that the Bush Board has favored employer interest in recent decisions, management attorney Kenneth Dolin views recent policy changes as returning the Board to the mainstream and correcting the excesses of the Clinton-era Board.[50] Other commentators express concern that such frequent policy interpretation shifts may cause the courts to pay less deference to the Board's interpretation of the LMRA, viewing the opinions as more reflective of changing economic and political climates than a consistent view of congressional intent in passing the law.[51]

The language of the LMRA has remained relatively unchanged by congressional action since 1959 even though the labor relations environment has undergone substantial change over the same time period. The labor force has become substantially more diverse with increased labor force participation by women and racial and ethnic minorities. The economy has transformed from a manufacturing base to a service-information technology base, creating a truly global economy where products, information, and monetary resources are easily transported across national boundaries, expanding product/service markets and increasing competitive pressures on both employers and employees. Emphasis by Congress and the legal system on protecting individual employees right to equal treatment and the establishment of minimum employment standards has also deemphasized the role of collective bargaining as a means of providing employees a voice in determining employment interests.[52]

The lack of congressional action to address labor law reforms has been attributed to the fact that "for many decades, both organized labor and especially employers have had enough support in Congress to block any significant amendment that either group strongly opposes. Enough support does not mean a majority; it means a minority that is big enough, well organized enough, and committed enough to tie up a bill through the arcane supermajority requirements of the Senate—for example through filibuster—or to sustain a presidential veto."[53]

Labor union advocates would like to see several reforms of the LMRA enacted. Among desired reforms are greater access by union organizers to communicate with employees during organizing campaigns and stronger penalties for unfair labor practices committed by employers against union supporters (e.g., elimination of offsets for interim earnings in computing back-pay awards for unlawful discharge). Union advocates have also sought unsuccessfully to eliminate management's right to permanently replace otherwise lawful economic strikers during a labor dispute. Union advocates have also opposed efforts to weaken the unfair labor practice provision in Sec. 8(a)(2), LMRA, which prohibits employer domination or interference with the operation of a labor organization under the guise of promoting cooperative labor relations as a means of improving productivity and employee involvement in work decisions.[54]

Some employer advocates would clearly favor an expansion of an employer's right to create work teams and have those teams deal with a wide range of employment issues involving work processes, compensation, productivity, safety, and other work rules.[55] Many employers are interested in efforts to expand the application of so-called *Beck rights,* which reinforce the basic right of an employee not to become a full member of a union in order to meet the requirements of a negotiated union security clause and to pay a bargaining unit representative where required by contract, only for those regular charges associated with the duties of representing the bargaining unit.[56] *Beck rights* will be discussed further in Chapter 4.

The NLRB also has its critics among labor and management officials. One area of concern over the years has been the amount of time required to complete ULP case decisions by the Board. Both administrative law judges and Board members share the responsibility for administrative delays which have occurred.[57] The General Accounting Office (GAO) released a damaging report to Congress entitled Action Needed to Improve Case-Processing Time at Headquarters. This report revealed that between 1984 and 1989 only about 67 percent of the 5,000 cases appealed to the Board in Washington were decided within one year. Ten percent of the cases took from three to more than seven years to decide. Such time delays existed even though the number of cases assigned was only 874, compared with 1,875 in 1980. Between 1984 and 1989, the medians for processing unfair labor practice cases ranged from a low of 273 days to a high of 395 days—two to three times higher than medians during the 1970s. For representation cases, the medians ranged from 190 to 256 days, higher than the medians during the 1970s. The GAO report identified several reasons for the excessive delays: 1) lack of standards and procedures for preventing excessive delays; 2) lack of timely decisions on leading cases; and 3) Board member turnover and vacancies (the highest in history during the 1980s).[58]

Beginning in 1994 under the leadership of NLRB Chairman William Gould, several initiatives were undertaken to make the NLRB more efficient. These included:

- Creating a "super panel" system for processing certain cases, whereby a panel of three Board members meets each week to hear cases involving issues that lend themselves to quick resolution without written analysis by each Board member's staff.

- Creating "speed teams," which are used to reduce the amount of staff time devoted to cases in which the Board is adopting the recommended decision of an administrative law judge.

- Providing "settlement judges" who are assigned in select cases to conduct settlement discussions.

- Permitting "bench decisions" in certain cases in which oral arguments are heard in lieu of written briefs. After the oral arguments are presented, the administrative law judge reads the decision into the record and later certifies the transcript that contains the decision.

- Creating advisory panels composed of distinguished labor and management attorneys to provide the Board and the office of the General Counsel with practical input on a wide range of topics.

- Increasing the use of the injunction as a means of stopping certain violations quickly and providing an incentive for voluntary compliance.[59]

The current Board and General Counsel continue to address the case backlog issue. In FY 2005, regional offices processed cases from the initial charge filing date to the issuance of a ULP complaint in a median of 95 days, which included a 15-day period after the conclusion of the General Counsel's preliminary investigation in which the Respondent was given an opportunity to voluntarily settle meritorious charges.[60] If no settlement occurs, a formal ULP complaint, ALJ hearing, and a review and decision by the Board will ensue requiring additional time to resolve cases. At the end of FY 2005, there were 14,558 unfair labor practice cases at some stage in the unfair labor practice procedure.

TRANSPORTATION-RELATED LABOR RELATIONS LAW (RAILWAY AND AIRLINES)

Rail and air transportation labor relations are covered by the **Railway Labor Act (RLA) of 1926**. Enacted with bipartisan labor and management support to apply only to the railway industry, the RLA was actually the first comprehensive collective bargaining law. In 1936, the RLA was amended to extend coverage to a new and developing transportation industry—airlines. Like other labor laws, the RLA did not develop overnight; it resulted from years of union activity and attempts to pass laws accommodating railway labor relations.[61] The primary goal of the RLA is the avoidance of disruption in transportation services by encouraging collective bargaining.

Under the RLA, if a union and employer are unable to resolve their differences over negotiating terms of their labor agreement (termed a **major dispute under the RLA**), the dispute is subject to mandatory mediation through the National Mediation Board (NMB). If mediation does not succeed, the parties have the option of proceeding to final and binding arbitration. If either party declines to submit the dispute to arbitration, there is a 30-day status quo period invoked during which the president may appoint an emergency board to investigate the dispute and make recommendations on a settlement.

Since the enactment of the RLA, over 97 percent of the collective bargaining disputes mediated by the NMB have been resolved without a strike or other form of interruptions of commerce. Historically, about 85 percent of presidential-appointed emergency boards (PEB) established have dealt with disputes in the railroad industry. In recent years, there has been a dramatic drop in the use of emergency boards. In FY 2005, there were no presidential emergency boards established involving the airline or railroad industries.[62]

The National Railroad Adjustment Board (NRAB), a bipartisan group of 18 union and 18 management representatives, was established to assist in resolving grievances arising during the term of a labor agreement over the interpretation or application of the contract's terms (termed a **minor dispute under the RLA**). Where the board cannot agree to a settlement, the grievance may be settled by an arbitrator selected by the parties.[63]

Over the past five years, the NMB has closed an average of 5,592 arbitration cases and 67 representation cases annually.[64] The NMB is empowered to conduct representation elections and to help resolve interest disputes that develop during negotiations between union and management representatives over what the terms and conditions of employment will be as stated by contract language. Under the RLA, labor agreements never expire but do become amenable for negotiation of proposed changes as of a specified date. In 2002, the NMB began using a new method for conducting representation elections called Telephone Electronic Voting (TEV). Eligible voters are given two passwords to use in casting their representation election ballot by telephone rather than using a mail-in paper ballot. The NMB believes the system is very secure and will save the agency substantial time and expense in conducting representation elections.

There are several differences between the RLA and the LMRA:

1. The RLA covers the railway and airline industries, whereas the LMRA covers most other private-sector employers engaged in interstate commerce.

2. Union representation under the RLA requires a showing of support from the majority of all employees in the particular craft or class who are eligible to vote. Union representation under the LMRA requires a showing of support from the majority of eligible voters who actually cast a valid ballot on Election Day. If there were 50 eligible voters of whom 44 cast a valid ballot, under the RLA a union would need 26 "Yes union" votes to be certified as the exclusive bargaining representative for the 50 employees. Under the LMRA, a union would only require 23 "Yes union" votes to be certified as the exclusive bargaining representative for the same size (50 employees) unit.

3. A significantly higher percentage of employees in the railway and airline industries are organized by unions under the RLA compared to other private-sector employees covered under the LMRA.

4. Under the RLA, a union cannot strike and an employer cannot lock out until they have exhausted the impasse resolution procedures required by the NMB. Under the LMRA, the parties can engage in self-help actions if a) the dispute involves a mandatory subject of bargaining; b) there is no current contract language barring the action; and c) good faith bargaining responsibilities have been met.

5. Under the RLA, arbitration of minor disputes (grievances) in the railway industry is mandatory, and the government bears the expense of arbitration. Under the LMRA, grievance arbitration procedures are negotiated by the parties, and the parties pay for the arbitration (airline grievance arbitration is similar to arbitration under the LMRA).[65]

Assessment of the RLA

Faced with such problems as changing markets for freight transportation, severe competition, government regulation, and public interest in uninterrupted rail service, labor relations in the railway industry are unique. Complicating the situation further are the chronic financial instability of the numerous independent railroads; the presence of strong, competing craft unions; and tradition-bound work rules. These factors can affect labor relations in the following ways. First of all because the public depends on rail transportation for many essential goods, much effort has been made to avoid strikes (five interventions by Congress). Second, due to the large number of craft unions involved, the labor relations process takes much time and creates many opportunities for disputes. Union mergers and consolidation have reduced the total number of rail unions by about half to approximately 20 unions since 1970. Finally, the tradition-bound work rules of the operating crafts strictly control not only how a particular job will be performed, but also which craft will be assigned the job. These work rules slow the introduction of new technology and magnify the problems of a declining industry.[66] Any assessment of the RLA must be kept in proper perspective. There are over 7,000 labor agreements in the railroad and airline industries, and about 1,000 railroad and 200 airline agreements (mostly local) are in negotiations during any given year.[67] Further, any measure of the RLA's effectiveness must be made with reference to its objectives—to promote free collective bargaining and protect the public from interrupted flows of commerce.[68]

Regarding negotiations, mediation has been the most important method of intervention under the RLA; however, few nationwide railroad wage cases have been settled by mediation since 1936. Its greatest success has been in settling minor controversies after the major issues have been resolved. This does not mean that mediation is unimportant—minor disputes left unresolved could easily lead to major strikes in future negotiations.

Deregulation Legislation

The Airline Deregulation Act of 1978 ended government controls of fares and routes, and the Motor Carrier Act of 1980 reduced the amount of economic regulation of the industry by the Interstate Commerce Commission. The Staggers Rail Act of 1980 gave railroads more flexibility in setting rates and service levels.[69] Initial concerns that deregulation might result in only a relatively few large carriers, thereby reducing competition within the industry, have largely proved unfounded. Airline deregulation prompted the introduction of 128 nonunion carriers, but by 1987 only 37 had survived. There has been increased merger activity by the major airlines, ticketing agreements between major carriers and regional and commuter airlines, hub-and-spoke airports, and frequent flier programs to promote airline customer loyalty.[70] Deregulation also encouraged price competition, with 90 percent of passengers traveling at discount prices averaging 60 percent below the coach price. During the same time, accident rates have not increased, and service to small communities has not deteriorated; however, there have been increased congestion at airports and in the airways, delays in departures and arrivals, threats to safety, and a general decline in the quality of air service.[71] Profitability in both the railroad and airline industry has been reduced by the slow pace of economic recovery although large (Class 1) railroad operators appear to be making a faster recovery than most major airlines.

Airlines were particularly hard hit by the terrorists' attacks of September 11, 2001. Not only were air operations suspended or significantly reduced for several days following the attacks, but in subsequent months the public demonstrated an increased reluctance to fly and additional security costs have imposed a significant cost burden on airlines.[72] Congress created the Air Transport Stabilization Board (ATSB) and funded a $10 billion loan program to aid airlines' economic recovery. Most airlines have adopted a variety of cost cutting strategies to cope with revenue declines, including significant employee layoffs, postponement or cancellation of equipment orders, reduced flight schedules, and negotiated economic concessions from employees. A study by the General Accounting Office (GAO) reported that since airline industry deregulation in 1978, the average length of time to negotiate new contracts has increased, the number of strikes has declined, but the frequency of nonstrike work actions (e.g., sickouts) have increased.[73]

Promising Developments Regarding the RLA

Despite problems, several events and developments provide the basis for some optimism:

- Recent negotiations have been characterized by greater union-management cooperation, which has resulted in fewer conflicts and outside interventions.

- Emergency board procedures have been drastically improved, and the ritualism and legalism so prevalent in the 1960s have been reduced.

- Encouraging progress has been made on some long-standing manning and work-rule issues, such as the fireman on diesel trains, combined road and yard service, and interdivisional runs.

- New leadership has had a positive influence on both management and unions, and neutrals and government officials have provided capable assistance in the bargaining and dispute-resolution processes.

Critical issues remain to be resolved, including secondary picketing, bargaining stalemates, restrictive work rules in some agreements, intercraft wage structure problems, crew size disputes, and the use of bankruptcy law to force labor cost concessions from employees, including the abandonment of traditional defined pension benefit plans.[74]

On balance, the RLA appears to have accomplished its primary goal of facilitating cooperative labor relations in the airline and railroad industries and avoidance of significant service disruptions. Whereas both labor and management might create their own wish list of labor law reforms, as a joint airline labor-management committee concluded "... the potential for disruption far outweighs the marginal gain that any legislative refinements might provide."[75]

Additional Laws That Affect Labor Relations

Other statutes and executive orders, more narrow in scope, influence labor relations either directly or indirectly. The following section highlights only their major provisions; however, practitioners find that detailed knowledge of them is essential to most business operations. (Related legislation is summarized here, but its specific implications for labor relations activities and unions are discussed in the appropriate chapters.)

Employee Retirement Income Security Act of 1974

The **Employee Retirement Income Security Act (ERISA)** establishes minimum standards for the operation of voluntarily established private-sector pension and health benefit plans (covered further in Chapter 7). Standards define plan participation, vesting rights, benefit accrual and funding, fiduciary responsibilities of plan administrators, and guaranteed payments of benefits accrued under a defined benefit plan through a federally chartered corporation called the **Pension Benefit Guaranty Corporation (PBGC)**, should the plan be terminated. There are approximately 44.1 million U.S. employees currently enrolled in 30,330 defined benefit plans. There is a maximum monthly pension benefit adjusted by law each year, which the PBGC is allowed to pay to a beneficiary. This means that some private-sector employees covered under a generous defined benefit plan (e.g., airline pilots) may lose some portion of their expected benefits if their private employer-sponsored plan is terminated and their benefits are determined by the PBGC's mandated benefit cap. The PBGC is currently responsible for the paying the pension benefits of 1.3 million workers previously covered under 3,595 terminated private-sector defined benefit plans. The PBGC receives its funding from insurance premiums paid by employers whose plans are covered, investment revenues, and the remaining assets of pension plans, which are terminated and taken over by the PBGC.[76]

The Americans with Disabilities Act of 1990

The **Americans with Disabilities Act (ADA)** of 1990, which covers an estimated 40 million disabled Americans, went into effect in January 1992. Considered a "Bill of Rights" for Americans with a wide variety of disabilities, the act applies to employment, public accommodations, transportation, and telecommunications. The employment provisions cover virtually every aspect of the employment process. The act prohibits discrimination in advancement, discharge, compensation, training, and other terms and conditions of employment which are usually included in collective bargaining agreements. The act requires employers to make reasonable accommodations for disabled employees, except when doing so would subject the employer to undue hardship. This subject will be addressed more fully in Chapter 8.

Bankruptcy Act

The **Bankruptcy Act of 1984** includes standards for the rejection of collective bargaining agreements by companies for obtaining modifications in labor agreements. It requires companies to provide relevant information to unions and engage in good-faith efforts to reach an agreement, which could avoid the necessity to declare bankruptcy. In cases where no agreement can be reached, the act specifies the requirements for terminating or altering provisions of an existing labor agreement. (See Chapter 6 for more details.)

Worker Adjustment and Retraining Notification Act

Triggered by major plant closings without notification, the **Worker Adjustment and Retraining Notification Act (WARN)** was passed in 1988. WARN requires employers with 100 or more employees to give 60 days' advance notice to employees (excluding those employed less than 20 hours per week) who will be affected by a plant closing or major layoff. Also, the union, the chief elected local government official, and the state government must be notified. The law permits a union and employer to negotiate language in their collective bargaining agreement that could require more than 60 days of advance notice be provided.

Situations where WARN Act notice requirements would apply include the following:

- A "plant closing" resulting in an employment loss for 50 or more workers at one site within a 30-day period.

- A "mass layoff" of at least 33 percent of the workforce (minimum of 50 employees) within any 30-day period.

- A "mass layoff" involving at least 500 employees within any 30-day period.

Remedies available to affected employees for employer violations include back pay and benefits for up to 60 days and payments (maximum of $500 per day) to local communities for a period of up to 60 days. One criticism of the statute is that it requires the injured party to bear the economic cost of initiating enforcement action by filing a lawsuit in a federal district court rather than having the U.S. Department of Labor initiate such legal action.

WARN ties in closely with the Job Training Partnership Act (JTPA), which provides funds to state and local governments for training and retraining. In cases of plant closing and mass layoff, state "rapid response" teams are available to work with labor and management officials to set up retraining and reemployment programs for the affected workers.

Racketeer Influenced and Corrupt Organizations Act of 1970

The **Racketeer Influenced and Corrupt Organizations Act (RICO)**, part of the Organized Crime Control Act of 1970, forbids anyone involved in racketeering from investing in or controlling through racketeering activity any enterprise (business or labor union) engaged in interstate commerce. The law provides for penalties of up to $25,000, 20 years of imprisonment, and forfeiture of all relevant property. A person found guilty of a RICO violation may be required to divest himself of all interests in the organization and may be restricted from any future activities in that or a related organization. In addition, any persons who suffered damages from the prohibited activities are entitled to recover triple the amount of damages.

Employment Discrimination Laws and Executive Orders

The **Civil Rights Act of 1991** prohibits any form of employment discrimination by companies, labor unions, and employment agencies on the basis of race, color, religion, sex, or national origin. The Equal Employment Opportunity Commission is a federal administrative agency created to enforce the statute through investigating complaints, attempts at conciliation, and law suits filed on behalf of the complainant.

The **Age Discrimination in Employment Act of 1967**, as amended in 1978, 1984, and 1986, prohibits employment discrimination against those over the age of 40, permits compulsory retirement for executives who are entitled to pensions of $44,000 per year or more, and authorizes jury trials in covered cases.

Executive Order 11246, as amended by **Executive Order 11375**, prohibits employment discrimination in the federal government and by federal government contractors and subcontractors receiving $50,000 or more. Those having contracts of $50,000 or more and employing 50 people or more are required to establish affirmative action plans that prescribe specific goals and procedures for increasing the percentage of minority employees. Firms that fail to comply could lose part or all of their contracts.

The **Vocational Rehabilitation Act of 1973** (Section 503) requires holders of federal government contracts in excess of $2,500 to take affirmative action to employ and advance in employment qualified physically and mentally disabled individuals. Further, if any disabled individual believes that a federal contractor has failed or refused to comply with the act, he or she may file a complaint with the Department of Labor, which will investigate the complaint and take any warranted action. In addition, Section 504 extends coverage to organizations receiving federal financial assistance and is enforced by the Department of Health and Human Services.

Other Related Labor Relations Laws

The **Uniformed Services Employment and Reemployment Rights Act (USERRA) of 1994** clarifies and extends the Veterans' Reemployment Rights Act of 1940 to protect the job rights of individuals called to perform military service on behalf of the United States. Also, the Vietnam Era Veteran Readjustment Assistance Act requires employers with government contracts of $10,000 or more to take affirmative action to employ and advance disabled veterans and qualified veterans of the Vietnam War.

The **Social Security Act of 1935**, as amended, established two national systems of social security for protection against loss of income resulting from unemployment, old age, disability, and death: 1) retirement, survivors, and disability insurance, and health insurance for persons over age 65; and 2) unemployment insurance, which operates under a state-administered, federal-state plan whose operating costs are paid by the federal government. The **Fair Labor Standards Act of 1938** administered by the U.S. Department of Labor covers a variety of employment issues including minimum wage and overtime pay requirements, child labor, and migrant and seasonal agricultural worker protections.

Other important laws include state wage laws, the federal **Occupational Safety and Health Act of 1970** (covered in Chapter 8), the **Family and Medical Leave Act of 1993** (covered in Chapter 7), and federal and state laws and local ordinances that pertain to public-sector labor relations and equal employment opportunity.

Summary

This chapter has presented the major provisions of federal labor relations laws in the United States. These legal influences must be understood to fully appreciate the remaining chapters in this book because nearly all issues in labor relations are either directly or indirectly influenced by labor law. The legal question of whether one has a right to act is separate and distinct from the practical question of whether it is in one's best interest to exercise such a right under the prevailing circumstances. Union and management practitioners should give consideration to the legal and practical costs, benefits, and risks of actions in making operational decisions.

Although many think of law in terms of statutes passed by the U.S. Congress or state legislatures, labor relations and other types of law proceed not only from statutes but also from the U.S. Constitution, judicial decisions, and administrative decisions of government agencies. Similarly, case law and administrative law develops at the state and local government levels.

Developing the legal influences historically, this chapter began with the early struggles of labor unions to exist as they faced an unsympathetic judiciary and lack of legislation intended to protect workers' rights. Several hurdles included the criminal conspiracy and civil conspiracy doctrines, as well as the breach-of-contract rulings. Then the Sherman Act, passed primarily to control business monopolies, was applied to restrict labor unions' activities also. With the support of labor, the Sherman Act was amended by the Clayton Act; however, this act in initial court decisions also proved unfavorable to unions.

The 1920s did bring passage of the Railway Labor Act (RLA), but little legislative action occurred in other sectors. However, the 1930s, during which the country confronted a severe economic depression, brought about major changes. The enactment of the Norris–La Guardia Act removed many legal restrictions on the types of employee-concerted activity that could be used to peacefully pressure employers to grant favorable employment improvements. Federal courts began to take a more neutral stance in labor disputes attempting to balance the legitimate exercise of employee and employer rights.

Congress passed the National Labor Relations Act in 1935, covering most private-sector employees, to control employer unfair labor practices and established the National Labor Relations Board to enforce the right of employees to form and join unions, bargain collectively, and engage in other concerted activities for mutual aid or protection. Then, in 1947 and again in 1959, Congress amended the National Labor Relations Act with passage of the Labor Management Relations (Taft-Hartley) Act and the Labor Management Reporting and Disclosure (Landrum-Griffin) Act, respectively. The LMRA's amendments added union unfair labor practices and restrictions on union security clauses. The LMRDA added regulations governing the internal operations of unions and restrictions on secondary strike, picketing, and boycott activities.

Starting in 1863, union activity in the railroad industry played a key role in the legislative arena. The Railway Labor Act of 1926, whose major purpose is to provide for stable and effective labor relations without major interruptions in commerce, established procedures for resolving labor disputes and created the National Mediation Board and National Railroad Adjustment Board to accomplish the act's purposes. The airline industry was added to coverage under the RLA in 1936.

While the legal rights of employers and employees to pursue their respective interests in a free enterprise system will inevitably create certain conflicts and stress, on balance the legal environment has provided reasonable stability in U.S. labor relations, encouraging economic growth. The acceptance of collective bargaining, wide-spread use of no strike or lockout clauses, final and binding arbitration of rights disputes, improved employer–union cooperation on important issues, and infrequent need to use national emergency dispute procedures provide support for progress in protecting the legitimate rights of both employers and employees.

Key Terms

U.S. Constitution, p. 74

Common law, p. 74

Employment-at-will (EAW) doctrine, p. 74

Preemption doctrine, p. 74

National Labor Relations Board (NLRB), p. 75

Labor Management Reporting and Disclosure (Landrum-Griffin) Act, p. 75

Federal Mediation and Conciliation Service (FMCS), p. 75

U.S. Department of Labor (USDOL), p. 75

National Mediation Board (NMB), p. 75

National Railroad Adjustment Board (NRAB), p. 75

Criminal conspiracy doctrine, p. 76

Commonwealth v. Hunt (1842), p. 76

Civil conspiracy doctrine, p. 77

Labor injunction, p. 77

Yellow-dog contract, p. 77

Sherman Antitrust Act, p. 78

Loewe v. Lawlor, p. 78

Danbury Hatters, p. 78

Clayton Antitrust Act, p. 78

Norris–La Guardia Act, p. 80

Closed shop union security clause, p. 82

National Labor Relations Act (NLRA), p. 83

Labor Management Relations Act (LMRA), p. 83

Union shop union security clause, p. 83

Agency shop union security clause, p. 83

Right-to-work law, p. 83

The Board, p. 85

NLRB jurisdiction, p. 89

Postal Reorganization Act of 1970, p. 91

Concerted and protected activity, p. 92

Interboro doctrine, p. 92

Charging Party, p. 93

Respondent, p. 93

Merit, p. 93

Administrative Law Judge (ALJ), p. 93

Routine ULP case, p. 95

Lead ULP case, p. 95

Cease-and-desist order, p. 95

Post written notices, p. 95

Affirmative action, p. 95

Petition for *certiorari*, p. 97

Railway Labor Act (RLA) of 1926, p. 99

Major dispute under the RLA, p. 99

Minor dispute under the RLA, p. 100

Employee Retirement Income Security Act (ERISA), p. 103

Pension Benefit Guaranty Corporation (PBGC), p. 103

Americans with Disabilities Act (ADA), p. 103

Bankruptcy Act of 1984, p. 103

Worker Adjustment and Retraining Notification Act (WARN), p. 103

Racketeer Influenced and Corrupt Organizations Act (RICO), p. 104

Civil Rights Act of 1991, p. 104

Age Discrimination in Employment Act of 1967, p. 104

Executive Order 11246, p. 105

Executive Order 11375, p. 105

Vocational Rehabilitation Act of 1973, p. 105

Uniformed Services Employment and Reemployment Rights Act (USERRA) of 1994, p. 105

Social Security Act of 1935, p. 105

Fair Labor Standards Act of 1938, p. 105

Occupational Safety and Health Act of 1970, p. 105

Family and Medical Leave Act of 1993, p. 105

Discussion Questions

1. How have the major labor relations laws helped or hindered the development of unions?

2. How were yellow-dog contracts and labor injunctions used to limit the activities of union organizers or slow union growth?

3. Why did the 1914 Clayton Act, called U.S. Labor's Magna Charta by AFL president Samuel Gompers, fail to live up to union leaders' expectations?

4. What was the intent or purpose of Congress in passing a) the 1932 Norris–La Guardia Act; b) the 1935 National Labor Relations (Wagner) Act; and c) the 1947 Labor Management Relations (Taft-Hartley) Act?

5. Although the National Labor Relations Act gives employees certain rights, these rights are not unlimited. Discuss.

6. Should the NLRB's administration of the LMRA be termed a success? Why or why not?

7. Why is there still a separate labor relations law for the railway and airline industries?

8. Should the LMRA be amended to a) cover agricultural laborers or b) index the NLRB's jurisdictional standards (i.e., monetary threshold for affecting interstate commerce) to take into account the effects of inflation?

Exploring the Web

Exploring the Web
Labor Relations and the Law

1. Case Law. Go to the Web site for the Supreme Judicial Court of Massachusetts and locate the landmark case, *Commonwealth v. Hunt*. Why is this case important?

Find a recent (2002) Supreme Court opinion involving the National Labor Relations Board in which the case *Loewe v. Lawlor* is cited.

Suggestions for searching:

Cornell University's Law School offers the Supreme Court Collection through their Legal Information Institute.

Findlaw Legal Information Center is a good commercial site.

You may also use electronic databases offered by your university's library; for example, LexisNexis or Westlaw.

2. National Labor Relations Board. Go to the Web site for the National Labor Relations Board to see the NLRB's current organization, rules and regulations, decisions, and manuals. Read the section that describes the National Labor Relations Act. Which groups of workers are not covered by the NLRA and why?

Included also on the site are press releases, public notices, and a weekly summary of current events.

Find a recent Board decision on Caterpillar, Inc. Search the press releases to read former chairman William Gould's speech delivered on June 18, 1998, in which he discussed enforcement of the NLRA and NLRB administrative reform. Gould was chairman from 1994 through 1998. Who is the current chairman of the NLRB?

You can also search the Internet for articles made available by law firms that distribute bulletins and newsletters to keep their clients informed on changes in labor law. Use the Martindale Hubbell site to search for a law firm that specializes in labor law in your area. Search the law firm's Web site for updates on NLRB activity.

3. U.S. Code. When legislation becomes law, it is incorporated into the U.S. Code in the appropriate sections. Identify sections of the Code affected by these acts related to labor relations: Railway Labor Act, Norris La-Guardia, Taft-Hartley, and Landrum Griffin.

Searching hints:

Search by Popular Names of Acts in Cornell University's Law School U.S. Code Collection or the U.S. Code search provided by the U.S. House of Representatives.

References

1. Walter E. Oberer, Kurt L. Hanslowe, and Timothy J. Heinsz, *Labor Law: Collective Bargaining in a Free Society*, 4th ed. (St. Paul, MN: West Publishing Co., 1994), pp. 358–359.

2. J. R. Commons and E. A. Gilmore, *A Documentary History of American Industrial Society* (Cleveland, Ohio: A. H. Clark, 1910), p. 68.

3. Quoted by John Fanning in "The Balance of Labor-Management Economic Power under Taft-Hartley," *Proceedings of the 40th Annual Meeting of the Industrial Relations Research Association*, ed. Barbara D. Dennis (Madison, Wis.: IRRA, 1988), p. 70.

4. *Commonwealth v. Hunt*, 45 Mass. 111 (1842).

5. E. E. Herman and G. S. Skinner, *Labor Law* (New York: Random House, 1972), p. 21.

6. *Vegelahn v. Guntner*, 44 N.E. 1077 (1896). See Herbert L. Sherman, Jr., and William P. Murphy, *Unionization and Collective Bargaining*, 3d ed. (Washington, D.C.: Bureau of National Affairs Inc., 1975), p. 3.

7. John R. Commons, *History of Labour in the United States*, Vol. 2 (New York: The Macmillan Company, 1946), p. 504. See also *Sherry v. Perkins*, 147 Mass. 212 (1888).

8. *Hitchman Coal & Coke Company v. Mitchell*, 245 U.S. 229 (1917).

9. *Sherman Antitrust Act*, 26 Stat. 209 (1890).

10. *Loewe v. Lawlor*, 208 U.S. 274 (1908).

11. 38 Stat. 731 (1914).

12. *Duplex Printing Press Co. v. Deering*, 254 U.S. 443 (1921).

13. *Truax v. Corrigan*, 257 U.S. 312 (1921).

14. 47 Stat. 70 (1932).

15. A labor dispute was defined as "any controversy concerning terms or conditions of employment, or concerning the association or representation of persons in negotiating, fixing, maintaining, changing, or seeking to

arrange terms or conditions of employment regardless of whether the disputants stand in the proximate relation of employer and employee." 47 Stat. 70 (1932).

16. *United States v. Hutcheson*, 312 U.S. 219 (1941).

17. Ibid.

18. Irving Bernstein, *Turbulent Years: A History of the American Worker, 1933– 1941* (Boston: Houghton Mifflin, 1971), pp. 1–36. See also Bruce Nelson, "Give Us Roosevelt: Workers and the New Deal Coalition," *History Today*, 40 (1), January 1990, pp. 40–48.

19. Alvin L. Goldman, *The Supreme Court and Labor-Management Relations Law* (Lexington, Mass.: D.C. Heath, 1976), pp. 22–28; and Sherman and Murphy, *Unionization and Collective Bargaining*, pp. 7–9.

20. *Schecter Poultry Corporation v. United States*, 295 U.S. 495 (1935).

21. *National Labor Relations Act*, 49 Stat. 449 (1935).

22. Janice R. Bellace, "The Future of Employee Representation in America: Enabling Freedom of Association in the Workplace in Changing Times through Statutory Reform," *University of Pennsylvania Journal of Labor & Employment Law*, 5 (Fall 2002), p. 5 at http://web.lexis-nexis.com. See also Bruce E. Kaufman and David Lewin, "Is the NLRA Still Relevant to Today's Economy and Workplace?" *Labor Law Journal*, 49 (September 1998), pp. 1113–1126.

23. Goldman, *The Supreme Court*, pp. 28–31.

24. *NLRB v. Jones & Laughlin Steel Corporation*, 301 U.S. 1 (1937).

25. Bernstein, *Turbulent Years*, pp. 769–771.

26. *Labor Management Relations Act*, 61 Stat. 136 (1947).

27. *NLRB v. Virginia Electric & Power Company*, 314 U.S. 469 (1941).

28. Goldman, *The Supreme Court*, pp. 31–39.

29. *Labor Management Reporting and Disclosure Act*, 73 Stat. 519 (1959).

30. *Fact Sheet on the National Labor Relations Board* (Washington, D.C.: NLRB Division of Information, 2006), pp. 1–2 at http://www.nlrb.gov/nlrb/press/facts.asp. Additional information regarding the NLRB's organizational structure, procedures, and decisions are available at the NLRB's home page at http://www.nlrb.gov.

31. William N. Cooke and Frederick H. Gautschi III, "Political Bias in NLRB Unfair Labor Practice Decisions," *Industrial and Labor Relations Review*, 35, July 1982, p. 549.

32. William N. Cooke, Aneil K. Mishra, Gretchen M. Spreitzer, and Mary Tschirhart, "The Determinants of NLRB Decision-Making Revisited," *Industrial and Labor Relations Review*, 48, January 1995, pp. 254–256.

33. Arthur F. Rosenfeld, "Summary of Operations FY 2005," *Memorandum GC 06-01*, November 28, 2005, pp. 1–11.

34. Bruce S. Feldacker, *Labor Guide To Labor Law*, 4th edition (Upper Saddle River, NJ: Prentice-Hall, 2000), pp. 12–14.

35. *Holly Farms Corporation v. NLRB*, 116 S.Ct. 1396 (1996).

36. Sec. 2 (11), LMRA 61 Stat. 136 (1947). See also *NLRB v. Kentucky River Community Care, Inc.*, 532 U.S. 706 (2001).

37. *NLRB v. Bell Aerospace Company*, 416 U.S. 267 (1974).

38. *Oakwood Healthcare Inc. and United Automobile Workers International Union*, 348 NLRB No. 37 (2006).

39. *NLRB v. City Disposal Systems, Inc.*, 465 U.S. 822 (1984); *NLRB v. Washington Aluminum Company*, 370 U.S. 9 (1962).

40. *NLRB v. City Disposal Systems, Inc.*, 465 U.S. 822 (1984).

41. *Seventieth Annual Report of the National Labor Relations Board for the Fiscal Year Ended September 30, 2005* (Washington, D.C.: NLRB, 2006), pp. 6–7.

42. Office of the General Counsel, "Summary of Operations (Fiscal Year 2005)," *Memorandum GC 06-01*, November 28, 2005, pp. 4–6 and *Seventieth Annual Report of the National Labor Relations Board for the Fiscal Year Ended September 30, 2005* (Washington, D.C.: NLRB, 2006), pp. 8–9.

43. Leonard R. Page, "The NLRA at 70: Perspectives from the Office of the General Counsel," *Labor Law Journal*, 56 (3), Fall 2005, pp. 188–189; Fredrick L. Feinstein, "The NLRA at 70: Perspectives from the Office of the General Counsel," *Labor Law Journal*, 56 (3), Fall 2005, pp. 192–195; and Risa L. Lieberwitz, "Labor Law in the United States: The Continuing Need for Reform," *Managerial Law*, 46 (4/5), 2004, pp. 53–70.

44. *H.K. Porter Company v. NLRB*, 397 U.S. 99 (1970). See also *BE & K Construction Company v. NLRB*, 536 U.S. 516 (2002) and *Hoffman Plastic Compounds, Inc. v. NLRB*, 535 U.S. 137 (2002).

45. Office of the General Counsel, "Summary of Operations (Fiscal Year 2005)," *Memorandum GC 06-01*, November 28, 2005, pp. 7–8.

46. *Ford Motor Company v. NLRB*, 441 U.S. 488 (1979); *Charles D. Bonanno Linen Service v. NLRB*, 454 U.S. 404 (1982).

47. Office of the General Counsel, "Summary of Operations (Fiscal Year 2005)," *Memorandum GC 06-01*, November 28, 2005, p. 8.

48. James A. Gross, "The Demise of the National Labor Policy: A Question of Social Justice," in *Restoring the Promise of American Labor Law*, ed. Sheldon Friedman et al. (Ithaca, N.Y.: ILR Press, 1994), pp. 57–58.

49. Janice R. Bellace, "Labor Law Reform for the Post Industrial Workplace," *Labor Law Journal* 45 (August 1994), p. 460.

50. Kenneth R. Dolin, "Analyzing Recent Developments at the National Labor Relations Board," *Labor Law Journal*, 56 (2), Summer 2005, pp. 120–138.

51. "Bush Labor Board Decisions: Pendulum Shift or Permanent Changes?" *Labor Law Journal*, 56 (3), Fall 2005, p. 222.

52. James J. Brudney, "The Changing Workplace: Reflections on Group Action and the Law of the Workplace," *Texas Law Review*, 74, June 1996, pp. 1563–1599.

53. Cynthia L. Estlund, "The Ossification of American Labor Law," *The Columbia Law Review*, 102, October 2002, p. 1540.

54. Estlund, "The Ossification of American Labor Law," pp. 1536–1158. See also William B. Gould, *Agenda For Reform: The Future of Employment Relationships and the Law* (Cambridge, MA: MIT Press, 1993) and Paul C. Weiler, *Governing the Workplace: The Future of Labor and Employment La* (Cambridge, MA: Harvard University Press, 1990).

55. Michael C. Harper, "The Continuing Relevance of Section 8 (a)(2) to the Contemporary Workplace," *Michigan Law Review*, 96 (8), August 1998, pp. 2322–2383.

56. Jeff Canfield, "Note: What a Shame: The Broken Beck Rights System in the Real World Workplace," *The Wayne Law Review*, 47, Fall 2001, 1049–1074; Peter Capelli, "Old Laws Hobble the New Economy Workplace," *Sloan Management Review*, 42 (2), Winter 2001, pp. 110–111.

57. Samuel Estreicher and Matthew T. Bodie, "Review essay—Administrative Delay at the NLRB: Some Modest Proposals," *Journal of Labor Research*, 23 (1), Winter 2002, pp. 87–105. See also Edward B. Miller, *An Administrative Appraisal of the NLRB*, 4th ed. (Fairfax, VA: John M. Olin Institute for Employment Practice and Policy at George Mason University, 1999).

58. United States General Accounting Office, *National Labor Relations Board: Action Needed to Improve Case-Processing Time at Headquarters* (Washington, D.C.: Superintendent of Documents, 1991), pp. 1–7.

59. *Three-Year Report by William B. Gould IV, Chairman, National Labor Relations Board* (Washington, D.C.: National Labor Relations Board, March 7, 1997), pp. 2–5; "Press Release" (Washington, D.C.: National Labor Relations Board, August 26, 1998).

60. *Seventieth Annual Report of the National Labor Relations Board for the Fiscal Year Ended September 30, 2005* (Washington, D.C.: NLRB, 2006), pp. 10–13. See also Douglas S. McDowell and Kenneth Huhn, *NLRB Remedies for Unfair Labor Practices* (Philadelphia: Industrial Research Unit, University of Pennsylvania, 1976), pp. 245–246 and William N. Cooke, Aneil K. Mishra, Gretchen M. Spreitzer, and Mary Tschirhart, "The Determinants of NLRB Decision-Making Revisited," *Industrial and Labor Relations Review* 48 (January 1995), pp. 254–256.

61. Lisa Catherine Tulk, "Comment: The 1926 Railway Labor Act and the Modern American Airline Industry: Changes and "Chaos" Outline the Need for Revised Legislation," *Journal of Air Law and Commerce*, 69 (Summer 2004), pp. 615–645; Nancy Brown Johnson, "Airlines: Can Collective Bargaining Weather the Storm?" in *Collective Bargaining in the Private Sector*, ed. by Paul F. Clark, John T. Delaney, and Ann C. Frost (Champaign, IL: Industrial Relations Research Association, 2002), pp. 16–20; Charles M. Rehmus, "Evolution of Legislation Affecting Collective Bargaining in the Railroad and Airline Industries," in *The Railway Labor Act at Fifty*, ed. Charles M. Rehmus (Washington, D.C.: U.S. Government Printing Office, 1977), p. 4.

62. *2005 Annual Performance and Accountability Report* (Washington, D.C.: National Mediation Board, 2005), p. 21.

63. Rehmus, "Collective Bargaining," in *The Railway Labor Act at Fifty*, pp. 14–15.

64. *2005 Annual Performance and Accountability Report* (Washington, D.C.: National Mediation Board, 2005), pp. 24 & 29.

65. *Fact Finding Report, Commission on the Future of Worker-Management Relations* (Washington, D.C.: U.S. Departments of Labor and Commerce, May 1994), pp. 99–100.

66. Charles M. Rehmus, "Emergency Strikes Revisited," *Industrial and Labor Relations Review*, 43 (2), January 1990, pp. 175–190; and Douglas M. McCabe, "The Railroad Industry's Labor Relations Environment: Implications for Railroad Managers," *ICC Practitioners' Journal* 49 (September–October 1982), pp. 592–602.

67. Charles M. Rehmus, "The First Fifty Years—And Then," in *TheRailway Labor Act at Fifty*, ed. Rehmus, p. 246.

68. Beatrice M. Burgoon, "Mediation under the Railway Labor Act," in *TheRailway Labor Act at Fifty*, ed. Rehmus, p. 23.

69. "Deregulation in Three Transport Industries Has Produced Widely Diverse Labor Market Results," *Daily Labor Report*, May 13, 1986, p. A-13.

70. Mark Kahn, "Introduction," *Cleared for Takeoff: Airline Labor Relations Since Deregulation*, ed. Jean T. McKelvey (Ithaca, N.Y.: ILR Press, 1988), p. 3.

71. Alfred Kahn, "In Defense of Deregulation," *Cleared for Takeoff: Airline Labor Relations Since Deregulation*, ed. Jean T. McKelvey (Ithaca, N.Y.: ILR Press, 1988), pp. 344–345. For a legal analysis, see Beth Adler, "Comment: Deregulation in the Airline Industry: Toward a New Judicial Interpretation of the Railway Labor Act," *Northwestern University Law Journal* 80 (Winter 1986), pp. 1003–1006.

72. Annual Performance Report for the Fiscal Year Ending September 30, 2002 (Washington, D.C.: National Mediation Board, 2003), pp. 16–17.

73. United States General Accounting Office, *Airline Labor Relations: Information on Trends and Impact of Labor Actions* (Washington, D.C.: Government Accounting Office, 2003), pp. 3–4; Andrew von Nordenflycht and Thomas A. Kochan, "Labor Contract Negotiations in the Airline Industry," *Monthly Labor Review*, 126 (7), July 2003, pp. 18–28.

74. Johnathan E. Collins, "Comment: Airlines Jettison Their Pension Plans: Congress Must Act to Save the PBGC and Protect Plan Beneficiaries," *Journal of Air Law and Commerce*, 70, Spring 2005, pp. 289–317; Daniel P. Rollman, "Comment: Flying Low: Chapter 11's Contribution to the Self-destructive Nature of Airline Industry Economics," *Emory Bankruptcy Developments Journal*, 21, 2004, pp. 381–418; and Donald E. Cullen, "Emergency Boards Under the Railway Labor Act," in *The Railway Labor Act at Fifty*, ed. Rehmus, pp. 176–183. Also see "The Railroads Lose Their Bargaining Unity," *Business Week*, April 10, 1978, pp. 31–32.

75. Nancy Brown Johnson, "Airlines: Can Collective Bargaining Weather the Storm?" in *Collective Bargaining in the Private Sector*, eds. Clark, Delaney, and Frost, 2002, p. 20.

76. Pension Benefit Guaranty Corporation, "Who We Are," 2006, pp. 1–2 at http://www.pbgc.gov and U.S. Department of Labor, "Retirement Plans, Benefits and Savings: Employee Retirement Income Security Act (ERISA)," 2006, p. 1 at http://www.dol.gov.

The Great Temperature Debate

CASE STUDY 3-1 The Employer is a small, non-union furniture manufacturer with 15 employees engaged in interstate commerce. Both of the employees involved in this case worked in the machine shop building as band-saw operators. Because the band saws were located near the shop's large overhead door, to facilitate the disposal of sawdust, the band-saw operators were often subject to lower temperatures and drafts on cool or cold days, whereas other employees farther from the overhead door often felt too warm. To resolve this long-standing problem, the plant manager established a rule that stated: "The overhead door will remain open when the temperature in the shop exceeds 68 degrees and closed when the temperature is at or below 68 degrees."

On the day in question, employees Drake and Keeler, who were both band-saw operators, complained to the shop supervisor that they were too cold and requested that the overhead door be closed. When questioned by the shop supervisor, the majority of the other shop employees present responded that they thought the door should be left open. The thermometer on the wall of the shop supervisor's office, located in approximately the center of the machine shop building, read 72 degrees.

On this day, employee Drake was wearing a sleeveless shirt and shorts. Employee Keeler was dressed in blue jeans, a short-sleeved shirt, a flannel shirt, and a heavy sweater. Both Keeler and Drake claimed it was too cold and drafty at their workstation near the open overhead door. The shop supervisor refused to close the overhead door because the majority of employees wanted it left open. During a scheduled lunch break, Drake and Keeler discussed their problem and decided to walk off the job for the remainder of the day to protest the cold temperature at their workstation.

Upon returning to work the following morning, Drake and Keeler were informed by the plant manager that they had been fired for leaving work the previous day without management's permission. Drake and Keeler subsequently filed an unfair labor practice charge with the NLRB alleging their discharge represented unlawful discrimination of their right to engage in concerted and protected activity under Sec. 7 of the LMRA. Drake and Keeler requested a remedy to include reinstatement with full back pay and restoration of any lost privileges.

Questions

1. Because Drake and Keeler's employer meets the standard for coverage under the LMRA by engaging in interstate commerce, which specific employee right protected by Sec. 7 of the LMRA could Drake and Keeler argue they were engaged in which at least partially motivated the employer's decision to discharge them?
2. On what grounds might the Employer try to argue that the discharge of Drake and Keeler was an appropriate (legal) exercise of management's rights?
3. Was the Employer's discharge of Drake and Keeler an unfair labor practice under the LMRA, as amended? If so, what should be the appropriate remedy?

A Matter of Timing

CASE STUDY 3-2 Ramon Ortiz had been employed for six years as a waiter in the employer's restaurant at the time of his June 19 discharge. On May 11, Ortiz was scheduled to work from noon until 10 P.M. After clocking in, Ortiz requested and received permission from restaurant manager Hildago to leave work early if Ortiz would return in time to work the 4:30 P.M. dinner period. Ortiz left work but later claimed that he "forgot to clock out."

When Ortiz's brother Juan reported for work at 6 P.M. he clocked himself in and clocked his brother Ramon out at 6:04 P.M.

A week later, manager Susan Post noticed while reviewing time card records that both Ortiz brothers had clocked in and out at virtually the same time (6 P.M.) on May 11. Manager Post interviewed both Ortiz brothers to solicit their explanation of the time card entries. Ramon Ortiz claimed that he had worked on May 11 but had left work early with the permission of his restaurant manager. Juan Ortiz stated that he was simply doing a favor for his brother, who had asked Juan to clock him (Ramon) out when Juan arrived for work. Juan stated he assumed his brother (Ramon) was calling him from the restaurant and Juan was unaware that his brother had actually left work much earlier in the day (shortly after noon). Manager Post informed Ramon Ortiz that his time record for which he was responsible falsely claimed pay for hours worked on May 11 between noon and 6:00 p.m. which was a violation of company policy regarding use of time cards to report paid hours worked.

The following day manager Post placed an undated "Employee Communication Record" form in Ramon Ortiz's personnel file. Such forms are used at the restaurant to record written warnings to employees concerning work rule violations.

The Hotel and Restaurant Employees Union had begun an organizing campaign targeting the hotel's restaurant employees sometime in the spring of 2003. Ramon Ortiz was an active union supporter and member of the union's in-plant organizing committee. The Union cautioned supporters like Ortiz that they should confine their union authorization card solicitation activities to times when away from the restaurant so that management would be less likely to be able to identify union supporters and possibly take adverse action against them for their union activity.

On June 15, Ramon Ortiz approached the restaurant's front desk manager, Louis Gaines. The conversation began with manager Gaines informing Ortiz that this was Gaines' last day at the restaurant as he had already turned in his resignation to management effective the following day. After further conversation, Ortiz told manager Gaines about another employee who claimed she had been threatened with discharge the previous day by her manager for something she did not do. Ortiz asked manager Gaines if he would write a letter to the corporation that owned the restaurant, setting up a meeting between the corporation's human resource (HR) manager and several restaurant employees without any restaurant managers being present. The purpose of the meeting was to give restaurant employees an opportunity to present their concerns to the corporation's HR manager about various working conditions at the restaurant, including discipline and discharge practices, in a confidential manner without having restaurant managers know which employees had made what statements. Ortiz and other restaurant employees were not sure whether the corporation really understood how the restaurant was currently being managed. Ortiz had previously met with several employees who had authorized him to seek manager Gaines's help to arrange the meeting because Gaines was more fluent in English than the restaurant employees and could help draft a letter to the corporation's HR manager which clearly explained the employees' request. Initially manager Gaines said he would help draft the letter but later in the work shift informed Ortiz that it would be better if employees contacted the corporation directly without a member of restaurant management (Gaines) being involved.

Four days later on June 19, Ortiz was called into manager Post's office and informed that he was being terminated immediately because of the incident on May 11 involving the falsified time card. Ortiz asked manager Post for one last chance because he had a previous good work and disciplinary record at the restaurant, but manager Post informed him it was out of her hands and the discharge decision was final. On July 11, the Union filed a valid representation election petition with the National Labor Relations Board to conduct a secret ballot election to decide if restaurant employees wanted union representation. On July 16, the Union filed several unfair labor practice charges against the restaurant owner, including a charge that the discharge of Ramon Ortiz was illegal. A representation election was held in September in which the majority of restaurant employees did vote to elect the Union as their exclusive bargaining representative.

Positions of the Parties

The NLRB's General Counsel representing the charging party (the Union on behalf of Ramon Ortiz) argued that Ramon Ortiz was discharged for engaging in concerted and protected activity under the LMRA. Specifically, the meeting between manager Gaines and Ortiz on June 15 represented concerted activity for the protected purpose of expressing employee grievances to management. Ortiz was acting on behalf of several other employees who had authorized him to contact manager Gaines to arrange a meeting with higher level company representatives who could receive and respond to job related employee concerns. The General Counsel argued that the real reason or motive behind Ortiz's discharge was that restaurant management did not like the idea that Ortiz was stirring up trouble by going over their heads and contacting corporate management directly about alleged problems at the restaurant. The previous incident on May 11 involving the time clock could not have been the real reason for discharge (as the employer claims) because management had already disciplined Ortiz for that incident weeks before by placing a written warning in Ortiz's file. One likely effect of permitting the company to discharge a recognized employee leader in the union organizing campaign on the basis of a pretext would be to intimidate other restaurant employees from risking the exercise of their legitimate right to form or join a labor organization under Sec. 7 of the LMRA, a result not intended by Congress.

The respondent (employer) argued that management had no knowledge of any union organizing campaign until being informed by the NLRB of the union's representation election petition filed on July 11. The employer also denied any knowledge of concerted and protected activities in which

Ortiz might have engaged prior to his discharge on June 19. The employer stated former manager Gaines had never disclosed to other managers at the restaurant that he had met with Ortiz on June 15. The employer argued that the investigation into the May 11 time clock incident had been a continuing affair and was concluded on June 19 with the decision to terminate Ortiz's employment. The employer did not call former manager Gaines or any other restaurant managers as a witness to testify at the unfair labor practice hearing and provided no written evidence to support the claim that the investigation of the May 11 incident had continued beyond the date the warning notice was placed in Ortiz's file.

Questions

1. Evaluate the employer's decision not to call any management witnesses or offer any written evidence to support the employer's stated position in the case. What are some examples of testimony or written documentation that an employer in a similar situation could use to prove the employer's theory of the case?

2. Was Ramon Ortiz unlawfully discharged in violation of Sec. 8 (a) (1) and (3) of the LMRA, and if so, what should be the appropriate remedy? Explain your reasoning.

Determination of Supervisory Status

CASE STUDY 3-3 The union sought to become the exclusive bargaining representative for a group of five harbor pilots employed by Pacific Coast Docking Pilots (the Employer). The Union won a National Labor Relations Board (NLRB)–supervised secret ballot election by a vote of 5-0. The employer refused to recognize and bargain with the union in an effort to force a federal court to determine if the five harbor pilots who composed the bargaining unit were supervisors or employees. The Union filed an unfair labor practice against the Employer for a refusal to bargain in good faith. The Board granted

summary judgment in favor of the Union, which the Employer then appealed to a federal court of appeals for review.

The Employer argued that the harbor pilots should be classified as "supervisors" and therefore excluded from the definition of "an employee" covered under the LMRA, as amended. The burden of proving the supervisory status of an employee is on the party asserting such a status. Under Section 2 (11), LMRA defines a supervisor as: "any individual having authority, in the interests of the employer, to hire, transfer, suspend, lay off, recall, promote, discharge, assign, reward, or discipline other employees, or responsible to direct them, or to adjust their grievances, or effectively to recommend such action, if in conjunction with the foregoing the exercise of such authority is not of a merely routine or clerical nature, but requires the use of independent judgment."

The Supreme Court has established a three-part test for determining the supervisory status of an individual under the LMRA, as amended (*NLRB v. Health Care & Retirement Corp.*, 511 U.S. 571 [1994]). First, an employee must perform at least one of the 12 specific functions outlined in the statutory definition of a supervisor under Section 2 (11) of the LMRA. Second, in performing one of the 12 specified supervisory functions, the individual must be required to exercise independent judgment. Third, the exercise of independent judgment in performing one or more of the 12 listed supervisory functions must be "in the interest of the employer." The third test is typically the easiest to prove because virtually any action related to the attainment of a legitimate business goal or purpose of the firm will be considered an act "in the interest of the employer." Most cases involving the determination of supervisory status will rest on an analysis of the evidence related to parts one and two of the three-part supervisory status test.

The Employer maintains that the docking pilots make recommendations on hiring and promotion decisions, assign work to employees, and are responsible for directing employees' work during the docking process. More specifically, the Employer states that the advice of docking pilots is almost always followed in making decisions regarding who to hire or promote into a docking pilot position or relief docking pilot position. U.S. Coast Guard regulations require that docking pilot trainees make trips with licensed docking pilots before becoming eligible to obtain a docking pilot's license. Docking pilots are required to evaluate the performance of trainees on such trips and provide a recommendation as to the suitability of each trainee for the job position of docking pilot. Docking pilots do not discipline other employees, adjust employee grievances, or

evaluate the job performance of non-trainee pilots. The final authority for all hiring and promotion decisions rest with the president and vice president of the employer.

When a large ship enters a port, it requires the assistance of tugboats to maneuver into a position to dock or undock. The docking pilot receives from the Employer a list of the ships scheduled to arrive or depart the port on a given day. The information provided by the Employer includes such items as the current location and dimensions of each ship. The docking pilot uses this information together with current information on other factors (e.g., current wind speed, water current speed, existing navigation hazards in the channel), to determine the number of tugboats required to accomplish the docking procedure. Once a ship's captain has entered the port, a tugboat delivers the docking pilot to the ship. The docking pilot then assumes command of the ship from the ship's captain and directs the docking procedure. The docking pilot communicates directly with the captain of each tugboat involved to ensure that each tugboat will render the necessary assistance to ensure a safe and accurate docking experience. Essentially, the docking pilot communicates what must be accomplished to each tugboat captain, who then determines what actions his tugboat crew must take to accomplish the defined objective. Each tugboat captain is responsible for directing his or her own boat crew to carry out the instructions of the docking pilot. Tugboat captains have been previously determined by the NLRB to be supervisors under the LMRA. Once the docking procedure is completed, the docking pilot returns control of the ship to the ship's captain and reboards one of the tugboats to prepare for the arrival or departure of the next ship on the daily schedule.

The Employer argued that the docking pilot's determination of how many tugboats will be required to perform a particular docking operation constitutes an assignment of work using independent judgment, which is a supervisory function under the LMRA's definition of a supervisor. The Employer also notes that a docking pilot "responsibly directs" others during the docking procedure by giving orders to the tugboat captains regarding the number and placement of towing lines to ensure a safe and efficient docking procedure.

The Union argued that the five docking pilots were professional employees covered by the

LMRA, not supervisors. The docking pilots have no authority to hire anyone, although they may be asked to give a professional opinion regarding the qualifications of an applicant for a vacant docking pilot position. Compliance with Coast Guard regulations, which requires less-experienced pilots to ride along with a more experienced pilot to learn information about a particular port before assuming responsibility for docking procedures in that port, represents a discharge of professional responsibility, which is a job duty of being a docking pilot. The docking pilots do not discipline other employees, handle grievances, or formally evaluate other employees' job performance.

The Union further argued that instructions given by docking pilots to other tugboat captains (who are supervisors) during docking procedures are part of the job duties of a professional docking pilot. The docking pilot has no authority to order members of a tugboat captain's crew to perform any specific job duties. The determination of the number of tugboats required to perform docking procedures is a function of the size of the ship to be docked and prevailing sea and weather conditions. This determination does not require the exercise of significant independent judgment on the part of the docking pilot.

Questions

1. Should the docking pilots be classified as supervisors and thus excluded from participating in a bargaining unit for purposes of collective bargaining? Explain your reasoning.

Challenge of Employer Policy on "Inquiries by Government Representative"

CASE STUDY 3-4 Sec. 8 (a) (1), LMRA makes it an unfair labor practice for an employer to interfere with, restrain, or coerce employees in the exercise of rights guaranteed in Sec. 7 of the Act. Sec. 8 (a) (4), LMRA makes it an unfair labor practice for an employer to discharge or otherwise discriminate against an employee for filing an unfair labor practice charge or giving testimony in any NLRB proceeding. The employer's employee handbook provided to every company employee contained the following written policy entitled "Inquiries by Government Representative":

From time to time, management may be called, visited or sent written communication by a representative of a federal, state, or local government agency investigating a possible violation of law or seeking other information.

It is our policy to cooperate with all authorized government agencies in the legitimate pursuit of their regulatory or enforcement functions. The following procedures must be followed for all such contact other than those regarding routine forms and other communications relating to sales taxes, business licenses and permits, and routine local health inspections.

If you are the person contacted, immediately notify the person in charge of your Facility. If the visit is made after hours, contact the department vice president. If this fails, call the Emergency Phone number which is posted at all company facilities. Additionally, these guidelines should be followed:

Be cordial to the person making the request. The visitor should be treated with the same courtesy as any guest at the Facility.

Do not volunteer any information, or admit or deny the truthfulness of any allegation or statement the inspector may make, nor sign any written statements, such as reports or affidavits, without express approval from a company attorney.

During the course of an investigation into the alleged unlawful discharge of two employees at the company's nonunion facility for union activity, several employees expressed a reluctance to be interviewed by NLRB staff investigators or to testify at any unfair labor practice hearing out of concern that such action on their part could be viewed by management as a violation of the above stated company policy thus subjecting them to possible disciplinary action.

A separate unfair labor practice charge was filed alleging that the company's "Inquiries by Government Representative" policy was unlawful under the LMRA.

The employer presented three arguments why the current policy should be considered lawful under the LMRA. First, the policy states that it only applies to members of management as indicated by the first sentence "From time to time, management may be called...." Second, the policy does not mention union activity or the NLRB. Third, no employee was disciplined for participating in the NLRB's ULP investigation of the alleged unlawful discharge of two employees for union activity.

Questions

1. Does the employer's policy "Inquiries by Government Representative" represent a violation of Sec. 8 (a) (1), LMRA? If so, what should be the appropriate remedy?

2. Does the employer's policy "Inquiries by Government Representative" represent a violation of Sec. 8 (a) (4), LMRA? If so, what should be the appropriate remedy?

CHAPTER 4

Unions and Management: Key Participants in the Labor Relations Process

As noted in Chapter 1, two key participants in the labor relations process are the union, which as the exclusive bargaining agent represents employees in the bargaining units, and management, which represents the owners or stockholders of the company. This chapter first provides a general explanation of the goals, strategies, and organizational structure of the company and the union for labor relations purposes. Because companies and unions are organized differently to meet different purposes, basic goals, strategies, and organizational structures will be presented that may be adjusted to meet respective differences. The second part of the chapter focuses on union governance and structure by describing the characteristics of unions, government at the various levels, organizational structure, and problems with corruption and misuse of power within a few unions. The final section covers union security, a subject vital to the union's role in gaining bargaining strength and meeting members' expectations.

GOALS AND STRATEGIES: MANAGEMENT AND UNIONS

Unions and management of companies have goals that are similar and those that may at times conflict. Their goals provide direction and serve as the basis for their

Exhibit 4.1
Goals of the Company
and the Union

The Company Wants	The Union Wants
To survive and remain competitive	The company to survive and remain competitive as well as for the union to survive and remain secure
To grow and prosper	The company to grow and prosper as well as the union
To achieve a favorable return on its investment	The company to achieve a favorable return on its investment and return "fair" wages to employees
To effectively use human resources	The company to effectively use human resources within the rules and policies of the agreement and to achieve job security and employment opportunities for members
To attract, retain, and motivate employees	The company to attract, retain, and motivate employees within the rules and policies of the agreement
To protect management's rights to make decisions and retain flexibility	To protect union and employee rights that were negotiated and included in the labor agreement
To obtain a commitment from the union that there will be no strike for the duration of the agreement	To obtain a commitment from the company that there will be no lockout for the duration of the agreement

organization's strategies, plans, and organizational structure. Exhibit 4.1 displays some major goals for both companies and unions, which in several cases are similar and consistent and in others have potential for conflict. The areas of potential conflict create possibilities for an adversarial relationship, and the areas of agreement create possibilities for cooperation and labor peace. As will be noted, most of the time unions and management are able to settle their differences without resorting to a work stoppage (0.0002 of total man-days are lost to work stoppages). The collective bargaining process itself is a mechanism designed by the parties and confirmed by the U.S. Congress as the preferred method for resolving differences between unions and management.

Both the company and the union want the company to survive and remain competitive. Union agreement with this goal is logical because the employees would lose their jobs and the union would not survive without the company. Likewise, the union wants to survive as the representative of the employees of the company and will take steps to retain this designation. When a company wishes to remain nonunion or to have the union decertified, an inevitable conflict occurs.

The company wants to grow and prosper—a sign of success of its management. The union agrees with this goal and supports it because it creates more opportunities and benefits for employees, adds union members, allows more funds for union activities, and strengthens the union as an institution. Likewise, both company and union want the company to achieve a favorable return on its investment. Although they may disagree on what is meant by "favorable," both parties understand the mechanics of the financial side of the business. However, the union also wants to achieve a favorable or "fair" return for the employees' efforts, input, and contribution. Here, there may be a disagreement over what is a favorable return to the investors and a "fair" return to the employees.

Two related goals of the company are to achieve the effective use of its human resources and to attract, retain, and motivate employees. The union accepts these company goals as long as the company abides by the provisions that were negotiated and included in the collective bargaining agreement. For example, the company may wish to have the most productive employee work on an overtime assignment to be able to ship a rush order; however, the agreement may require that overtime assignments be made on a rotating basis. The presence of the union does not prevent making overtime assignments to the most productive employee; however, the overtime provision is a negotiable subject, and the parties must live by the provisions that they agree on.

The company wants to protect its rights to make decisions and retain the flexibility to operate the business. The union accepts the philosophy that some decisions are best made by management, including the type of products, the price of the products, financial policies, customer relations, advertising and promotion decisions, product design, and plant layout. At the same time, the union represents the interests of employees and attempts to provide protection and guarantee job opportunities for them by negotiating provisions in the labor agreement, such as contracting out work, use of seniority, and promotions and transfers to provide these rights.[1]

The company wants a union commitment to have no work stoppage for a specified period; this guarantees a stable workforce and allows the company to make production promises to customers. This commitment comes in the form of a "no-strike" clause in the labor agreement. The union may want a commitment from the company that employees have the right to have their grievances heard by management and may appeal them to a third-party neutral (arbitrator) when necessary to resolve differences.

Once the union and the company decide on their respective goals, they determine the appropriate strategies to reach these goals. Companies have been involved in strategic planning much longer than unions, and their strategic plans are usually more detailed and sophisticated. Only in recent times have unions started to think and operate in terms of strategic planning.

Company Strategic Planning

A company's strategy in labor relations is determined by its managerial philosophy, the ethics of its management, its economic condition, the composition of the workforce, competition in the industry, the time in the life of the company, and the capabilities of management. Management has choices about its strategy. It may believe that the company is better off remaining nonunion and devote much time and effort to ensuring positive human resources management. Some employers resist unions bitterly to ward off the large wage gap between union and nonunion employees (weekly earnings averaged $827 for union members versus $642 for nonunion workers in 2006, according to the Bureau of Labor Statistics). Management members who are in a highly competitive industry may be willing to do almost anything to keep unions out. Management at other companies may choose to change from a hard-bargaining approach to one of labor-management cooperation after it finally accepts the philosophy that both parties would gain more by cooperating than by conflicting. Exhibit 4.2 shows the range of company strategies in labor relations, from union suppression to labor–management cooperation.

Nonunion Companies' Strategies

Some authorities believe that profound changes in labor relations began in the 1980s and were brought on by forces external to union–management

Exhibit 4.2

Company Strategies in Labor Relations

Union Suppression	Union Avoidance	Union Substitution	Codified Businesslike	Accommodation or Labor-Management Cooperation
Union busting Illegal acts Refusal to bargain Decertification Filing for bankruptcy Encouraging strikes	Positive human resources management Double-breasting	Company paternalism Company-sponsored employee organizations Forms of employee participation and employee involvement	Neutral in union campaign Straight-forward approach	Gain-sharing Union involvement Employee empowerment Employee stock option plans

relationships. These forces include competition from abroad, deregulation, and competition from nonunion companies. More and more companies are finding that their labor relations strategies are driven by economic choices and their need to adapt to new, more competitive business conditions. Because union suppression, union-avoidance, and union-substitution strategies have existed in different forms since the Industrial Revolution, a company may choose to attempt to maintain its nonunion status by preventing or supplanting unions. Another company may choose one of the nonunion strategies as a legitimate response that has been forced on it to cut costs, innovate, enter new markets, and devise flexible labor force strategies. This latter approach focuses on costs and productivity of human resources and the management of human resources.[2]

A company may use a more aggressive approach, called the *union suppression* strategy, to maintain its nonunion status or to destroy the union. Human Rights Watch conducted research on Wal-Mart labor relations practices between 2004 and 2007 by interviewing 41 former employees, meeting with labor lawyers and union organizers, analyzing cases against Wal-Mart which charged the company with violating U.S. labor laws, and reviewing company publications that addressed working conditions at the company (Wal-Mart officials did not respond to three requests from Human Rights Watch researchers). Human Rights Watch concluded: "Wal-Mart employs a sophisticated and multifaceted strategy to prevent union activity at its U.S. stores and, when that strategy fails, quashes organizing wherever it starts."[3]

Another company that has received much national media attention is the Smithfield Packing Company in Wilson, North Carolina. The United Food and Commercial Workers began a union organizing drive in March of 1999 and a representation election was held on July 8, 1999. Smithfield opposed the Union's organizing efforts from March until July. In the course of the union organizing campaign, the union alleged that Smithfield committed multiple unfair labor practices and filed charges with the National Labor Relations Board. An Administrative Law Judge of the NLRB rendered a decision on January 23, 2001, and Smithfield appealed the decision. The Board did not render its decision until August 31, 2006 and found numerous unfair labor practices, which are highlighted in Exhibit 4.3.[4]

1. Threats of plant closures by company president and plant manager.

2. Directing video security cameras to record employees and union organizers passing out union information.

3. Interrogation of employees about support for the union by supervisors.

4. Unlawful loss of benefits by announcing that employees would lose their 401(k) program if they voted for the union.

5. Threats of a pay cut if employees signed union authorization cards that supported the union.

6. Discharge of employees because of their union activities.

SOURCE: Decisions and Order of the National Labor Relations Board, 347 NLRB No. 109, August 21, 2006.

Exhibit 4.3

Unfair Labor Practices of Smithfield Packing Company, Wilson, North Carolina

Other extreme—and in some cases illegal—tactics used by some companies to avoid unionization include the following:

- Developing a spy network (tattletales) to identify union supporters

- Refusing to hire former employees of unionized companies (but giving the applicant a reason other than prior union affiliation for employment denial)

- Establishing a case for discharge (including documentation) of known union advocates

- Seeking to determine prospective employees' attitudes toward unions from interviews, references, and so on, and then refusing to hire them (again giving another reason) if they are pro-union

- Giving psychological tests (job-interest questionnaires) to determine the likelihood that an applicant will be interested in a union

- Locating new plants in areas where union membership is low and expanding the company's nonunion plants

- Using a standard application of a State Employment Service that asks applicants whether they have been a member of a union and using the application as part of the preemployment inquiry[5]

Some employers facing union-organizing campaigns have committed unfair labor practices deliberately, with the expectation of economic returns to them.[6] One study of employers led to this disappointing conclusion:

> [I]n the past, the compliance system [of the National Labor Relations Act] has been inadequate to the extent that some employers have found it profitable to commit unfair labor practices in order to forestall unionization. Those employers obeying the law because "it's the law" have faced a greater probability of incurring costs of unionization and may have been at a competitive disadvantage to employers who violated the law. Such inequities do not encourage compliance with the law and provide evidence of the need for labor law reform.[7]

When illegal practices yield economic returns to the violators, ethical questions are raised as to the fairness of the law and its application. Some companies that select a *union-avoidance* strategy take a strong stance against union representation, even in facilities where unions already exist. They open nonunion facilities and attempt to keep them nonunion. They shift their capital investments away from the unionized facilities and make plant improvements in the nonunion plants. Where a union represents its employees, the company attempts to reduce the labor costs by lowering wages and benefits, modifying traditional work practices, and encouraging decertification to the point of committing illegal actions. In these situations, the labor relations environment is highly adversarial, and union-management collaboration is not considered an option.[8]

One company, Ingersoll-Rand Company, was reported as initiating an anti-union corporate strategy. Its strategy included the following: (1) concentrate on building or buying new U.S. plants in open-shop states, and acquire other firms whose plants are partly or wholly nonunion, (2) relocate production from union plants to nonunion plants, and (3) use labor and community relations techniques that bypass local union officers, encourage union decertification, and oppose union-organizing efforts. As a result of the company's union-avoidance strategy, union representation declined from 100 percent to 25 percent of Ingersoll-Rand's eligible work force. Top company officials were reported as saying that the company wanted to remain "union-free," to listen to employees as individuals, not through a third-party union, and to stop unions from forcing the company to take actions with which it disagreed.[9]

Some companies adopting the union-avoidance strategy practice *positive human resources management* or operate *double-breasted*. Company officials who adopt positive human resources management recognize the importance and necessity of maximizing "employee voice." Moreover, such firms implement the claim that people are the most important asset of the organization. Such organizations involve their employees in the decision-making processes of their organizations. These efforts are included under the general umbrella of "participative management," "total quality management," and "total quality control" programs.[10] In unionized organizations, the union is sometimes involved; those efforts are covered in Chapter 7.

Companies such as IBM, Texas Instruments, and Eastman Kodak have essentially adopted this strategy. Positive human resources management programs include the following elements:

- The absence of symbols of rank and status such as parking spaces, company cars, or country club memberships for managers

- Carefully considered surroundings—locating near high-quality schools and universities and keeping individual facilities small

- Overall corporate strength—high profits, fast growth, high technology, or dominant market position

- Programs to promote employment security, such as work sharing or overall reduction in pay to avoid layoffs in hard times

- Promotion from within—job posting, career development, and training and education programs

- Influential human resources management programs, for example, having the human resources manager report directly to top management

- Competitive pay and benefits, especially having compensation that is equitable externally and internally and comparable to the pay at unionized companies

- Management that listens—using systematic approaches such as attitude surveys, open-door policies, and appeal procedures

- Careful grooming of managers—focusing on long-term results, using assessment centers, and appraising in terms of competence and employee relationships[11]

Double-breasting exists when one company has two or more subsidiaries, one unionized and the others nonunion or open shop. These arrangements take several forms: (1) a holding company has financial control of one or more operating subsidiaries, (2) a unionized company buys a nonunion subsidiary and continues to operate it as nonunion, and (3) a nonunion company buys a unionized subsidiary and continues to operate it unionized. At present, the law requires the open-shop and unionized units of a holding company to be separately managed and operated as distinct entities. The National Labor Relations Board (NLRB) determines whether two seemingly separate companies should be treated as one by considering the following guidelines: interrelation of operations, centralization of control of labor relations, common management, and common ownership or financial control.[12] The Board stated:

> No one of these factors has been held to be controlling, but the Board opinions have stressed the first three factors, which go to show "operational integration," particularly centralized control of labor relations. The Board has declined in several cases to find integration merely upon the basis of common ownership or financial control.[13]

A third company strategy to maintain nonunion status is the *union substitute* strategy. Some firms seek to avoid or ward off unionization of their employees by providing a substitute for unionism. Two companies, Northrup-Grumman Corporation (which has only three percent of its employees in unions) and Federal Express (whose pilots are the only group in unions) explicitly state that their adoption of nonunion employment dispute resolution procedures was due in large part to their desire to avoid additional employees in unions. In addition to union avoidance, nonunion employers have adopted formal workplace dispute procedures primarily for strategic reasons, such as avoidance of legal suits, identification of workplace problems, generation of information about these problems, diagnosis of the underlying reasons for these problems, and specification of solution to these problems. In fact, about 45 million employees in nonunion companies are covered by individual employment contracts and about 80 percent of these contracts contain a formal dispute resolution procedure (arbitration as the final step in one half). In comparison, about 12 million employees are covered by grievance procedures in collective bargaining agreements (nearly all have arbitration as the final step).[14]

Many nonunion companies have initiated employee involvement programs to restore the sense of working in a small business, to gain employee commitment to the enterprise, to dissuade union organizing, and to provide feedback to enhance motivation and productivity. Over 85 percent of companies in a Conference Board survey have a system for giving nonunion employees information about the competitive conditions or economic circumstances of their company. The majority have employee participation programs, such as quality circles and small-group discussions of production and quality of work, and have provided formal complaint and grievance systems.[15]

The most common system for resolving employee grievances is the open-door policy, wherein employees may present their grievances to management representatives. The success of this system depends on how conscientious managers at all levels are in fulfilling this policy and whether employees fear that presenting their grievances to managers above their immediate supervisor will have undesirable consequences.

Other forms of nonunion grievance procedures include grievance appeal boards, appeal steps up to top management, and peer review committees.[16] The grievance appeal board allows employees to present their grievances to a board for a final decision. In this system, three management members and two employees might hear the grievance and decide the outcome. Although the system is sometimes called a "jury of one's peers," management representation is usually greater than that of employees and can outvote employee board members if necessary.[17]

Unionized Companies' Strategies

The labor relations function in unionized companies differs from that in nonunion companies in several ways. First, in the unionized setting, two parties, the union and management, are involved. Instead of decisions being made by management alone, many decisions, such as wages, hours, promotion, layoffs, and other terms and conditions of employment, are made bilaterally through negotiations. Second, the presence of the union formalizes the employee-representation activities because employees may file a grievance if they believe that the company has violated terms of the negotiated agreement. Third, the negotiated rules and policies that govern the employment relationship for those employees covered under the collective-bargaining agreement essentially become company policy because both parties have to abide by the terms that they have negotiated.[18]

One strategy adopted by unionized companies is the *businesslike, codified strategy*. These companies accept unions as the legitimate representative of the employees and conclude that if the employees want a union, they will deal with it. They do not attempt to have the union decertified, do not commit flagrant unfair labor practices, and do not try to substitute participative groups for unions. Company managers respect and trust their union counterparts and expect the same in return. For the relationship to last, both parties must realize that respect and trust are fundamental to both their futures. The approach of these companies is to deal directly and bargain with the union over wages, hours, and terms and conditions of employment at the appropriate times. When the labor agreement negotiations are complete, managers of these companies administer the agreement as they interpret it. In other words, they "go by the book." Although General Electric was known in the 1950s for its take-it-or-leave-it approach to labor negotiations, its strategy today can be categorized as a businesslike approach. The remaining chapters explain this approach to labor relations. Also, as noted previously, strategies of companies and unions change during their lifetimes and with economic conditions, changes in leadership, and personalities of participants.

The fifth strategy shown in Exhibit 4.2 is one of *accommodation and labor-management cooperation*. This strategy entails the union cooperating with management, rather than the parties having an adversarial relationship. Management and unions actively work together to create an organizational climate and a way of operating that will allow employees to participate directly in decisions in their work areas as members of task teams and as members of problem-solving groups. Unions represent their members in decision making and in collective bargaining.[19]

Over 1,000 collective bargaining agreements have contract clauses that provide for cooperation between unions and management. Some agreements establish joint committees, such as safety committees that focus of an interest to both parties—improving safety in the workplace. More extensive cooperative arrangements include joint decision making to improve quality and productivity. An even further degree of cooperation includes a partnership between the union and management about all or most decisions in the production process.[20]

Frequently, multiple companies and multiple unions join together to meet a challenge of common interests. For example, in 2005, industrial users, power generating companies, contractors, and labor unions in the Southeast United States formed the Southeastern Manpower Tripartite Alliance to provide programs to meet a projected 50 percent increase in demand for craft labor between 2005 and 2010.[21]

Unions can contribute to companies' strategic planning and implementation activities. For example, a union can provide input from a clearly defined group of employees, as well as transfer information about corporate plans and direction to those represented employees. The union leaders can help the rank-and-file employees better understand the business plan and lend credibility to the plan. Although these contributions are clearly positive, union involvement in strategic planning takes more time because the union leadership must meet with the membership to explain planned actions. Also, to retain a competitive edge, upper management often does not want to reveal new directions and planned actions. As a result, unions typically have a greater opportunity to have a role in strategy implementation rather than in strategy formulation. For example, if a company is facing increasing losses because of foreign competition, the company may enlist the assistance of the union in finding ways to reduce costs. Alternatives include cooperative approaches to job design or developing a new reward system, such as gain-sharing, to encourage labor-management cooperation. Another possibility is the introduction of new technology to improve productivity, which may include restructuring existing jobs.[22]

For organizations and unions to achieve a more collaborative relationship, managers, unions, and employees must overcome their resistance to change. Managers must develop a more open, less authoritarian managerial style; unions must abolish their traditional "us versus them" approach and adopt the team concept; and employees must accept a greater worker commitment and more involvement in determining how to get the job done and how to get it done right.[23]

Employee empowerment is reflected in employee involvement and participation programs, which include quality circles, quality-of-work-life efforts, labor–management participation teams, and autonomous work units. These efforts address such issues as product quality, work-unit performance, new technology, safety and health, and supervision. Here, union leaders and members accept responsibility for success of the organization. Unions demonstrate their capacity to confer value to their members and create wealth for all of the organization's stakeholders.[24]

This relationship ensures that unions and management focus on common goals, which include the health of the business in a changing economic environment, and new issues, such as adopting new technology to ensure competitiveness and business survival. Management accepts unions as stakeholders in an ongoing complex, multistakeholder organization designed to ensure survival and provide an equitable return for all involved in the process. Several companies and unions have already proceeded in this direction. Harley Davidson and its two unions comanage the Kansas City plant.

To achieve this new union role, management and union leaders must develop different skills. Union leaders need business decision-making skills; they must understand the business and the problem-solving process. At the same time, union leaders must maintain contact with the membership to better represent members' interests. Management must take steps to reorient its views from seeing unions and labor agreements as constraints to recognizing a more cooperative union-management relationship. Management must provide the union and its leadership with a secure position as the legitimate, permanent representative of the bargaining unit employees. This means abandoning efforts to decertify the union or to reduce the union's importance at the workplace. It means developing a mutual trust between parties at every level of the organization.[25]

Companies may choose a mixed strategy, which can encompass union avoidance, union-substitution, or labor–management cooperation, at various sites in a multi-plant operation. For example, a company may operate double-breasted and strongly oppose the union at one of its nonunion plants while at the same time engaging in labor–management cooperation at another plant. Such strategic choices are made at the highest levels of the organization, and the advantages and disadvantages of each strategy are seriously debated and deliberated before any strategy is adopted by the company.

Upper management considers the market pressures, operational and financial factors, and collective bargaining relationships in its deliberations. If market pressures are intense as a result of import penetration, management may be inclined to choose union avoidance in the nonunion sector. However, if a high proportion of the plants are unionized, management may choose the labor–management cooperation strategy. Researchers continue to examine which factors lead to certain strategies.[26]

Union Strategic Planning

Labor unions, like other organizations, define their operational goals, determine their organizational strategies and plans, develop policies and procedures, and manage their resources to reach their goals and maximize their performance. Unions also are involved in long-range planning, establishing procedures for budgeting, attracting able staff members, communicating with members to provide information and to obtain reliable feedback, and establishing controls for financial accountability.[27]

Labor unions in the United States have been involved in strategic planning for only a short time. For years, unions as a rule reacted to managerial decisions with little concern for long-range implications. Today, more and more unions are finding it essential to become involved in strategic planning. Several unions, such as the Communications Workers, the Auto Workers, and the Steelworkers, have recognized the need for long-range strategic planning and created strategic planning committees. To survive, all unions must develop such plans. A typical union's strategic plan includes: (1) a mission statement, (2) analysis of the external environment, (3) internal analysis of the union's strengths and weaknesses, (4) long-term and short-term objectives, and (5) strategy development. A survey of American Federation of Labor–Congress of Industrial Organizations (AFL-CIO) unions found the following:

1. Typical mission statements are to organize workers for the purpose of collective bargaining; to foster legislation of interest to the working class; and to disseminate economic, social, and political information affecting workers' lives and welfare. As an example, see Exhibit 4.4 for the AFL-CIO's mission statement.

Exhibit 4.4
AFL-CIO's Mission
Statement

What We Stand for: Mission and Goals of the AFL-CIO
The mission of the AFL-CIO is to improve the lives of working families—to bring economic justice to the workplace and social justice to our nation. To accomplish this mission we will build and change the American labor movement.

We will build a broad movement of American workers by organizing workers into unions.
We will recruit and train the next generation of organizers, mass the resources needed to organize and create the strategies to win organizing campaigns and union contracts. We will create a broad understanding of the need to organize among our members, our leadership and among unorganized workers. We will lead the labor movement in these efforts.

We will build a strong political voice for workers in our nation.
We will fight for an agenda for working families at all levels of government. We will empower state federations. We will build a broad progressive coalition that speaks out for social and economic justice. We will create a political force within the labor movement that will empower workers and speak forcefully on the public issues that affect our lives.

We will change our unions to provide a new voice to workers in a changing economy.
We will speak for working people in the global economy, in the industries in which we are employed, in the firms where we work, and on the job everyday. We will transform the role of the union from an organization that focuses on a member's contract to one that gives workers a say in all the decisions that affect our working lives—from capital investments, to the quality of our products and services, to how we organize our work.

We will change our labor movement by creating a new voice for workers in our communities.
We will make the voices of working families heard across our nation and in our neighborhoods. We will create vibrant community labor councils that reach out to workers at the local level. We will strengthen the ties of labor to our allies. We will speak out in effective and creative ways on behalf of all working Americans.

SOURCE: AFL-CIO Mission Statement at www.aflcio.org. Reprinted by permission.

2. The analysis of the external environment includes an examination of the changing demographics of the workforce (toward more worker diversity), appraisal of current and future political and legislative concerns, consideration of labor's image, and analysis of employer practices and industry trends.

3. The internal analysis includes an examination of the union's internal functioning, such as union governance, openness for discussion of diverse opinions, and appraisal of the professional staff whose jobs are to provide service to the members.

4. Organizational objectives are set for short-term and long-term activities. Short-term objectives may include meeting membership needs through collective bargaining, reducing substance abuse, improving pensions, and enhancing job security. The most common long-term objective is simply the survival of the labor organization.

5. Further work is needed to define strategies for addressing labor unions' long-term concerns for continued survival and growth as institutions.[28]

Some unions, like the UAW, have established internal commissions to participate in strategic planning. The report of the Commission on the Future of the UAW, entitled "A Strong Union in a Changing World," addressed the union's major economic concern about the erosion of the nation's industrial base and related problems of corporate flight and disinvestment. It also urged more effective use of the media in presenting the union's public positions on tax policy and fairness, dislocated employees, the changing workforce, issues of sexism and racism, and rapid change in technology and methods of work.

The Communications Workers of America is one union that has effectively instituted strategic planning for its success. Over the last two decades, the CWA has faced serious challenges as a result of product market deregulation and technological change.

Union density in the telecommunications industry fell from 56 percent in 1983 to 24 percent in 2001 due to downsizing by the Bell companies, reclassifying jobs from technical and professional to managerial (not eligible for union membership), and creation and growth in mostly nonunion companies, such as MCI. The CWA was faced with organizational uncertainty and complexities with a membership accustomed to easy contract victories and predictable, paternalistic labor relations. The CWA decided to transform itself from a telephone workers union to the "union of the information age," which would focus on information services. Instead of being a union predominantly of telephone employees, the CWA would expand to printing and publishing, radio broadcasting, journalists, computer programmers, software specialists, and others. The CWA made adjustments at the bargaining table; it began negotiating retraining provisions for its members, pension enhancements, and early retirement bonuses. To ward off health insurance concessions, it had to mobilize its members for contract fights. Mobilizations included one-on-one postcard messages, work-to-rule (following rules and instructions in excessive detail) campaigns, wearing common colors or arm bands on certain days of the week to show solidarity, public rallies, and campaigns of letter writing to state and local politicians. The CWA negotiated company neutrality pledges, expedited elections, and card checks for union recognition, through which the CWA gained over 30,000 members. Through mergers with eight smaller national unions, the CWA has gained over 227,000 new members. The CWA agreed to support regulatory changes by use of its political influence in exchange for explicit benefits guarantees and job security. Thus, over the last 20 years, the CWA has taken strategic steps to transform itself from a telephone workers union to a "union of the information age" and has intertwined its collective bargaining, political, and organizing activities to make it one of America's most effective and successful unions.[29]

Several other international unions, such as the Air Line Pilots Association, Steelworkers, Service Employees International Union, American Federation of Teachers, and the Bakery, Confectionery, and Tobacco Workers have undertaken strategic planning efforts. These international unions have added new terms to their operational language, such as strategy development, organizational assessment and planning, and implementation. Unions have used surveys, interviews, and focus groups for building participation and consensus. The results have been mission statements, goals and priorities, assignment of responsibilities, funding activities and budget allocations, dues split between the local and international unions, and measures for evaluating success.[30]

With the decline of union membership as a percent of the total labor force and subsequent reduction in dues income, unions at every level have attempted revitalization efforts. The Service Employees International Union (SEIU) and the United Brotherhood of Carpenters (UBC) have taken a mission-driven strategic approach, which includes a strategic plan with time-bound goals promoted aggressively by their national union leaders. The SEIU allocated 50 percent of its national budget to organizing new members; engineered mergers among locals, which were deemed too small to pursue an effective organizing agenda independently; and removed old-line, heavy-handed local leaders who resisted change. The UBC cut the national office staff by half, eliminated departments, outsourced some work, rented out a substantial part of its national headquarters, eliminated many small locals, and shifted control of resources to regional councils. These cost-cutting efforts helped to fund a shift of 50 percent of the union's resources to union organizing. While most of the national and international unions experienced a decline in overall membership, the SEIU and UBC experienced growth.[31]

Creation of the Change to Win (CTW) Federation.

Changes in directions and strategic plans of unions at the national and international levels can influence the directions and strategic plans at the federation level. In 1995, John Sweeney had won the presidency of the AFL-CIO in its first contested election and promised to lead a resurgence within organized labor with a strategic program that emphasized organizing new members. In the first five years, Sweeney made every effort to promote his priority—he introduced the Union Summer program for young student activists, he expanded the AFL-CIO's Organizing Institute's recruitment and placement activities, and he urged affiliates to organize employees who were unrepresented. With limited authority over the affiliated national unions, Sweeney's efforts were stalled because few unions were willing to allocate 30 percent of their resources to union organizing. By 2001, AFL-CIO officers and key staff began to deemphasize organizing and began concentrating on how to build a political agenda for labor law reform. This change in strategy frustrated those unions—SEIU [service employees], UNITE [needle trades and textiles], HERE [hotel employees], and UBC [carpenters]—who were committed to organizing new members and had embraced the Changing to Organize agenda. The UBC left the AFL-CIO in 2001 and by 2002, the other three unions were calling for open debate within the federation to halt the continuing decline in union density. By 2003, these unions were joined by the Laborers' International Union and formed the New Unity Partnership (NUP). In 2004, UNITE and HERE merged and became UNITE-HERE. By the time of the AFL-CIO convention in July 2005, the IBT (teamsters), the UFCW (food and commercial workers), and UFW (farm workers) had joined NUP. By September 2005, seven national unions with six million members (close to 40 percent of the AFL-CIO membership at the time) had withdrawn from the AFL-CIO and formed a new union federation, Change To Win (CTW). The unions included several national unions with over one million members; these were the Teamsters and Service Employees International Union, and several with over 500,000—the Carpenters, the United Food & Commercial Workers, and UNITE-HERE.

On September 27, 2005, the CTW held its founding convention in St. Louis and elected Anna Burger of the SEIU as chair and Edgar Romney of UNITE-HERE as vice chair. The CTW unions decided to shift substantial resources to organizing, conduct joint organizing campaigns, and promote strategic support among members. The CTW unions declared they had no desire to fight with the AFL-CIO and would be content to build power in those industries already within their core jurisdiction. In other words, the key leaders of the CTW publicly voiced their opposition to raiding AFL-CIO unions for new members. Although the AFL-CIO has stated that it wanted to continue emphasizing union organizing, there was a definite emphasis on political activities, as shown in Exhibit 4.5, which includes items from the AFL-CIO strategic plans for 2006.

Exhibit 4.5

Items from AFL-CIO's
Strategic Plans for 2006

To concentrate on political action with the centerpiece being its Voice@Work campaign for labor law reform and passage of the Employee Free Choice Act, which would establish union certification based on signed authorization cards, provide for arbitration in bargaining first contracts, and increase penalties for employer unfair labor practices violations. In the 2006 elections, a total of 205,000 members from AFL-CIO unions, CTW unions, and Working America visited 8.25 million households, distributed 14 million flyers, and made 30 million phone calls.

To have a year-round Get Out the Vote (GOTV) program.

To establish a communication link, including Internet and door-to-door campaigns, to workers who support labor's political philosophy but who are not currently union members through Working America.

To continue to form Industry Coordinating Committees designed to coordinate bargaining and organizing activities among unions with substantial membership in a particular industry. The first ICC was formed in October 2005 and brought together 11 unions in the arts, entertainment, media, and information industries. Another ICC representing nurses was formed in 2006, and another joins state and local unions.

To establish a $22.5 million Strategic Organizing Fund (a $10 million increase in annual spending in this area) and to rebate $15 million to affiliated unions who met high standards in changing their unions to organize.

To create a Blue Ribbon Panel to recommend mergers among affiliated unions.

SOURCE: Richard W. Hurd, "U. S. Labor 2006: Strategic Developments across the Divide," *Journal of Labor Research*, 38, No. 2 (Spring 2007), p. 313–324; Marick F. Masters, Ray Gibney and Tom Zagenczyk, "The AFL-CIO v. CTW: The Competing Visions, Strategies, and Structures," *Journal of Labor Research*, 27, No. 4 (Fall 2006), p. 473–503.

In contrast, Exhibit 4.6 shows items from the CTW's strategic plans, where the emphasis is definitely on organizing new members.[32]

It will be interesting to follow the efforts of the CTW and AFL-CIO to determine whether these federations reach their respective objectives. In 1955, the merger of the AFL and CIO significantly reduced, if not fully eliminated, the competition for unionism among what had been two separate, vigorous organizations. Those unions affiliated with the AFL sought to organize workers on the basis of their particular occupation, job titles, or skills set (craft unionism) and unions affiliated with the CIO sought to organize workers on the basis of their common employment with a single firm or industry (industrial unionism). One researcher noted that just as mergers among business firms tend to reduce competition for customers, so too did the merger of these two dominant labor organizations reduce competition for workers to become union members/customers. As evidence, it was pointed out that union membership in the United States reached its peak of about 35 percent of the labor force in 1955 the same year of the AFL and CIO merger. Since 1955, union membership as a percent of the labor force has continued to decline.[33]

COMPANY ORGANIZATION FOR LABOR RELATIONS ACTIVITIES

There are many organizational structures for labor relations activities in U.S. companies. The following discussion introduces some of the basic organizational considerations, although different company characteristics will alter these designs.[34]

Exhibit 4.6
Items from CTW's Strategic
Plans for 2006

To emphasize organizing by reallocating resources on a grand scale away from other union activities and devoting 75 percent of the CTW budget to organizing.

To rebate one-half of union affiliates' per capita dues if they adopt aggressive organizing programs and to create a $25 million Strategic Center that will target notable anti-union employers.

To target for organizing those industries that will remain in the United States. These include the health care, hospitality, retail, building services, transportation, and construction industries.

To conduct joint campaigns to recruit new members. As examples, SEIU and the Teamsters are partnering to recruit school bus drivers; UFCW and UNITE-HERE are developing a retail apparel and distribution initiative; all unions are joining the Wake Up Wal-Mart campaign, a public awareness offensive to provide information about the world's largest retailer.

To build global partnerships with unions in other countries in support of organizing multinational corporations. Andy Stern, president of the SEIU, has established informal global alliances with key union leaders in at least a dozen countries.

To cooperate with the AFL-CIO in national election campaigns. In addition, to operate field offices in several states in hopes of electing labor-friendly governors and elect legislators who are committed to take actions that will facilitate organizing.

SOURCE: Richard W. Hurd, "U. S. Labor 2006: Strategic Developments across the Divide," *Journal of Labor Research,* 38, No. 2 (Spring 2007), p. 313–324; Marick F. Masters, Ray Gibney and Tom Zagenczyk, "The AFL-CIO v. CTW: the Competing Visions, Strategies, and Structures," *Journal of Labor Research,* 27, No. 4 (Fall 2006), p. 473–503.

In larger corporations, the labor relations function is usually highly centralized, with policy, strategic planning, and bargaining decisions made at the corporate level. In fact, the final economic decisions are usually made by the chief operating executive with the advice of corporate-level labor relations managers. In smaller companies with only one or a few facilities, these decisions are made at the plant level and shared by plant management with the plant labor relations manager, who offers advice.

In larger companies, at the operations or plant level, the plant manager and plant labor relations manager play the key roles in certain labor relations activities, such as contract administration, grievance handling, and monitoring labor relations activities. In smaller companies, activities at the plant level also include bargaining, strategic planning, and policy formulation.[35]

The duties and responsibilities of all labor relations managers and specialists are determined in large part by the organizational structure and its degree of centralization or decentralization of authority. The duties typically include corporate-wide responsibility for policies, procedures, and programs ranging from union organizing drives at nonunion facilities to negotiations with the union at others.

Exhibit 4.7 shows the organizational chart for the labor relations function in a large, complex company. As shown in the organizational chart, the vice president of personnel and industrial relations reports directly to the president and has the director of labor relations reporting to him or her. Each of the company's six product lines has its own labor relations organization.

A large, diversified company having several divisions or product lines will typically have a vice president of industrial relations, which includes human resources and labor relations activities, who reports directly to the president and has the director of labor relations reporting to him or her.

Exhibit 4.7
Labor Relations Organization: Dotted-Line Relationships

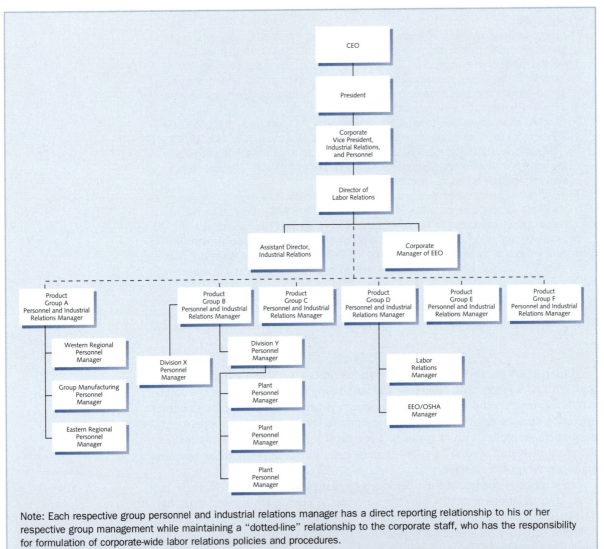

Note: Each respective group personnel and industrial relations manager has a direct reporting relationship to his or her respective group management while maintaining a "dotted-line" relationship to the corporate staff, who has the responsibility for formulation of corporate-wide labor relations policies and procedures.

As each group is dependent upon the corporate function as the formulator of this policy, the lines of communication and working relationships are strong, and the level of communication is very high. Their function is to administer corporate policies and procedures as formulated by the vice president of personnel and industrial relations and his or her staff.

SOURCE: Audrey Freedman, Managing Labor Relations (New York: The Conference Board, 1979), p. 28.

Labor relations managers at the plant level also typically have responsibilities for both human resources and labor relations activities. They help implement related corporate and divisional policies, participate in contract negotiations, and resolve employee grievances over daily labor agreement administration. They typically are accountable both to the plant manager for daily labor relations activities and to divisional or corporate industrial relations officials for approval of negotiated labor agreements.

Exhibit 4.8 suggests relationships between labor relations managers and other managers at the plant level (operations B, C, D, and E are not delineated in detail for the sake of brevity). The facility's operations can be grouped in

Exhibit 4.8

Management Organization at the Plant Level (Approximately 1,100 Hourly Employees)

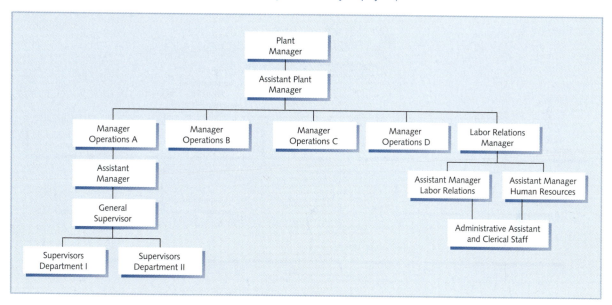

one or more of the following ways: by location (furnace room one versus furnace room two at a steel mill, for example), by product (manufactured valves versus gaskets, for example), by function (such as maintenance), or by technology (electroplated and chemical plated processes, for example).

The labor relations manager is on the same level as managers of the operations, but neither individual has authority over the other. Instead, plant labor relations managers have *line-staff* relationships with other managers. Line-staff relationships occur when two or more organizational members from different lines of authority work together on a particular policy (a no-smoking policy, for example) or activity (such as grievances). Neither has authority over the other; therefore, resolution or output of this relationship is often determined by past perceived benefits each has derived from the other.

Relationships between labor relations managers and other management officials at the plant level can be tension laden. Consider, for example, the attitude a shift supervisor might have toward a labor relations manager who has awarded to the union a grievance against him or her for performing bargaining unit work (Chapter 10) or who has overturned a discharge decision made by the supervisor (Chapter 12).

Union Governance and Structure

Unions as organizations are fundamentally different from business organizations. Business organizations are built on the assumption that power, authority, and legitimacy flow downward from the owner or stockholders through management. Union organizations, on the other hand, have mechanisms such as a written constitution and bylaws that ensure an opportunity for members to participate in the governance of the organization—hold office, attend meetings, vote in elections, or express dissatisfaction with the leadership. Thus, in the democratic

Exhibit 4.9
Organizational Chart of an International Union

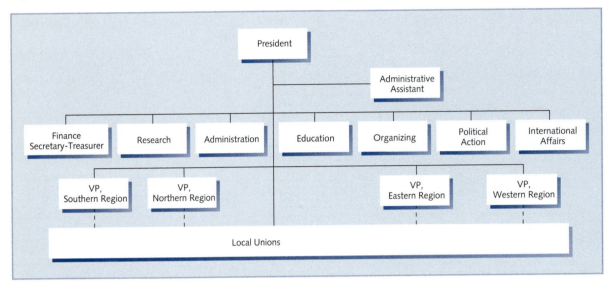

organization of a union, power, authority, and legitimacy ultimately flow upward from the consent of the governed. If the leadership of a union wishes to move in a new direction, such as toward greater union–management cooperation, the new direction ultimately depends on the approval of the membership. If elected leaders do not consider new initiatives in terms of the political realities, they will be rejected by the vote of the members. For example, in cases where the members do not trust management's actions in a joint cooperative effort, the leadership must put forth the appropriate effort to build a trusting relationship before developing the joint effort.[36]

Nearly a hundred different international (an international union has local unions outside the United States, such as Canada) and national unions and over 60,000 local unions exist in the United States; their governance is discussed in this chapter following a brief description of their organizational structure. As with companies, unions' organizational structures reflect their activities. Exhibit 4.9 shows the organizational chart of an international union, which includes the various officers, operational departments and staff, regions, and local unions. In this case, the basic functions include financial activities handled by the secretary-treasurer, research, administration, education, organizing, political action, and international affairs. These activities are usually carried out at the union's national headquarters, with some headquarters' staff members possibly working in the field. The regional offices are headed by a vice president, who has an advisory relationship with the local unions in the region. Regional offices are established to better serve the needs of the local unions and to represent the national office in the region.

At the local union level, the organizational structure is fairly simple, as illustrated by Exhibit 4.10 In most small unions, officer and shop steward positions are all part-time; only in larger unions does the financial support allow full-time union leaders. Most local unions have at least one vice president, a secretary, and a treasurer. The addition of any other officer, such as the sergeant-at-arms in Exhibit 4.10, depends on the needs of the union. Shop stewards are usually elected to represent the membership in their respective departments.

Exhibit 4.10
Organizational Chart for a Local Union

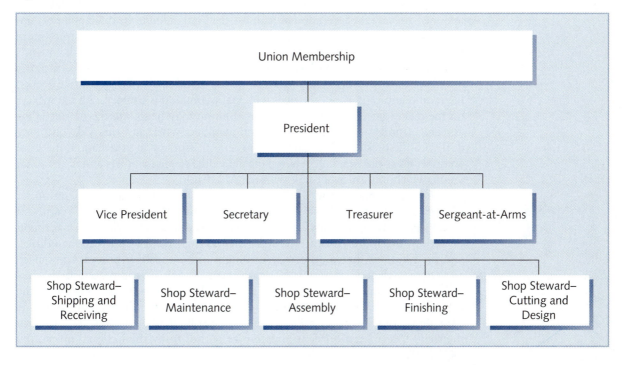

The following section explains how unions are governed at the different levels and presents some of the major problems in the governing process.

To understand union governance, one can compare the union with a unit of state or federal government. The executive, legislative, and judicial activities occur at various levels. The local union meetings and national conventions are the legislative bodies; the officers and executive boards comprise the executive bodies; and the various appeal procedures serve the judicial function. A union can also be compared with a private organization because it is a specialized institution having a primary purpose of improving the economic conditions and working lives of its members.

Unions claim the democratic ideal, but realistically, they must rely on a representative form of government. On the whole, they seem to be as democratic as local, state, and federal governments. In fact, a union's membership has more of a say in the way the union operates than most citizens have in their governments or most stockholders have in their corporations.[37]

To appreciate unions as organizations, one must recognize their wide diversity, the organizational relationships of the various levels, the functions of the officers, and the varying degrees of control. The next section explores the characteristics of craft and industrial unions, the functions of local union officers, and the government and operations of local unions. The national or international union, which is composed of the local unions within a craft or industry, is explained in a similar framework. Not to be overlooked are the various intermediate levels of union organizations that provide specific functions for their affiliated unions. A fourth level for many union organizations is the federation. The AFL-CIO's organizational structure, functions, and officer responsibilities are discussed since the CTW structure is still developing.

The Local Union

Although there are generally four levels of unions—local, national (or international), intermediate, and the federation of unions—the local union is the main point of contact for the individual employee. The typical union member often identifies more closely with the local union than with the other union levels. He or she attends and sees local officers at the local meetings and workplace. When the union member has a grievance, the local union officers are the first to assist. When a strike occurs, the local union officers are the ones who make continuous contact with the strikers on the picket line. Although the national union may negotiate the master labor agreement under which the local union members work and the AFL-CIO may deal with the president and Congress on certain issues facing the nation, the local union serves as the vital link between the individual union members and the national union, which in turn might link with the AFL-CIO.

Organizationally, the local union is a branch of the national union. It receives its charter from the national union and operates under the national union's constitution, bylaws, and rules. The constitution of the national union prescribes the number and types of officers, their duties and responsibilities, and the limits of their authority. Although union constitutions vary in length and content, they often mandate certain financial reports and require that a certain number of meetings be held, that the local labor agreement conform to the master labor agreement negotiated by the national union if there is companywide bargaining, and that approval to call a strike be obtained by the local union. With the trend toward greater centralization of authority by the national union, the local union over the years has lost much of its operational flexibility.

Differences between Local Craft and Industrial Unions

The operation of the local union in large part depends on the type of employees making up its membership. Although there is not a clear-cut division between them, unions can be divided generally into two groups: craft and industrial.

Differing Union Organizations.
The **craft unions** are composed of members who have been organized in accordance with their craft or skill, for example, bricklayers, electricians, carpenters, or ironworkers. **Industrial unions** have been organized on an industry basis, for example the Steelworkers, Auto Workers, Chemical Workers, Mine Workers, and so on. This, of course, does not mean that there are no skilled employees in the steel, auto, or rubber industries; but it does mean the electricians in a steel plant would likely be members of the Steelworkers.

Differing Scope of the Labor Agreement.
The craft and industrial unions differ in other ways that have an effect on their operations. First, the craft unions, who frequently represent the building trades, usually negotiate short labor agreements (supplemented by detailed agreements on special topics, such as apprenticeship programs and safety) that cover a defined geographical region, and each has considerable independence from the national union compared with industrial unions. Because of the nature of their work, craft union members may work on several job sites for several employers in a given year under the same labor agreement. The labor agreement covers the construction companies and a number of building trades' unions in the particular geographical area.

The industrial union, on the other hand, may be covered by a national labor agreement negotiated between the company and the national union, which covers all of the company's unionized plants. For example, GM plants in Atlanta,

Detroit, and Los Angeles are covered by the same master agreement. Well over 100 pages long, the agreement explains in detail the wage plan, transfers, pensions, layoffs, and so on. A separate local agreement is negotiated to cover matters of concern to the specific local plant and its employees, which must be consistent with the master agreement. For example, the local agreements may address rotating overtime assignments, use of plant bulletin boards, visits by international union representatives and other issues applicable to the local plant. In plants having no national labor agreement, a plant-wide agreement covering production and maintenance employees is typically negotiated.

Differing Skills.

Types of skills help demonstrate another difference in local union operations. The craft members are highly skilled artisans who have completed formal training, usually in a formal apprenticeship program. Many industrial employees, on the other hand, do not require much prior job training. Therefore, the craft union members often feel that they have higher status than their industrial counterparts. The training programs available for the industrial union members are usually offered by the company, whereas the training received by members of craft unions is organized and operated by the unions. So craft unions select those who will be offered the apprenticeship training, whereas companies alone select the trainees in the plants. Such an arrangement has allowed the craft unions to limit the numbers in the craft, sometimes giving preference to their families and friends.

Differing Job Characteristics.

The nature of their work creates a unique opportunity for craft unions to operate under conditions that approximate a closed shop. Because many of the work assignments last only a short period, the craft members, such as electricians on a building project, return to the union hiring hall for their next assignment after their part of a project is completed. Upon receiving the assignment, the union members could report to another job site and work, possibly for another company. Usually, these arrangements are worked out in advance by the business agent of the craft union and the companies who agree to operate under the existing labor agreement. In other words, the union hiring hall serves as a clearinghouse or placement office for the construction companies as well as the union members. Because the hiring hall must be operated in a nondiscriminatory manner, nonunion employees may also use its services; however, use by nonunion employees is still quite rare. In comparison, the typical member of the industrial union is hired by the company and will work for the same employer—usually at the same facility—until retirement or employment is terminated.

Differing Leadership Roles.

Another difference between craft and industrial unions pertains to the roles of the business agent and shop stewards of the craft union and the local union officials of an industrial unions. The **business agent**, the full-time administrator of the local craft union, provides many of the same services as the local union president of a large industrial union. Both are considered the key administrative official of their respective local union halls, and they lead the local union negotiations and play a key role in grievance administration. However, the business agent has additional duties, such as administering the union hiring hall, serving as the chief "watchdog" over the agreement at the various work sites, and appointing an employee on each job site to serve as the shop steward. The **shop steward**, who may be the first person on the job or a senior employee, handles employee grievances, represents the business agent on the job, and contacts the business agent if anything goes wrong.

The shop steward is the personification of the union to the members; the impressions of the steward greatly influence the members' perceptions of the union. Where impressions of the steward are positive, members also have positive views of grievance procedures and have greater union commitment. Stewards spend about 12 hours per week on labor relations matters; between 50 and 80 percent of this time is spent on grievance handling. Therefore, training of shop stewards in grievance handling is important because it results in less time required to process grievances, an increased likelihood that the shop steward will seek re-election, and the ability of the steward to devote more time to improving relations between the union and management.[38]

Most unions have ongoing steward training programs, which include such subjects as enforcing the contract, filing grievances, and monitoring health and safety violations. However, some unions have made arrangements with universities to offer college-credit courses specifically designed to provide a broader understanding of organized labor's role in achieving social justice and to increase the effectiveness of stewards as advocates in the workplace and the community. As one example, Queens College in New York City began offering the course "Labor at the Crossroads" for stewards of Local 1180 of the Communications Workers of America. With its success, Queens College began offering an Urban Leadership Program, which is a special sequence of college-credit courses that could be applied to a bachelor's or master's degree. Today, over 150 Local 1180 members are enrolled in Urban Leadership courses every year.[39]

In local industrial unions, the president may or may not serve full-time. If the position is full-time, the salary comes from union dues. If the position is part-time, the president is compensated from the union treasury only for the time taken off his or her company job (at the regular rate of pay). Presidential duties include participating in local negotiations, maintaining the local union office, chairing local union meetings, assisting in grievance administration, and ensuring that management abides by the agreement. On many occasions, a staff member of the international union (usually the **international union representative**) assists local officers in negotiations and in administering the labor agreement and ensures that the local's activities conform to the national constitution and directives. The shop steward, the elected representative in each department in a plant or facility, represents the members at local union meetings, handles grievances at the shop level, and collects dues, if necessary.[40] Union officers who are involved in the day-to-day administration of the collective bargaining agreement may be granted preference in shift assignment and protected from layoffs.

Involvement in union leadership depends on individuals being convinced of the importance of the cause of the union. This is necessary because the union leadership, whether a shop steward or a local union president, will be devoting a certain number of hours each month without pay to provide services to co-workers. Employees who take on the role of union officer tend to do so because they are concerned about the well-being of their co-workers and have received encouragement from these peers. They are more likely to have been employed for a longer period and tend to have a lesser degree of job satisfaction.[41]

Many unions today are neither pure craft unions nor pure industrial unions in nature. Unions are likely still concentrated in their traditional sector (that is, the core of the UAW is the automobile industry and the United Steelworkers, the steel industry, for example). Many unions are more appropriately described as "diversified unions" because of their multi-jurisdictional organizations. As an example, both the UAW and the Steelworkers' now represent employees in manufacturing, in the service industry, and in wholesale and retail trades.[42]

Government and Operation of the Local Union

There are several common ways for union members to participate in union activities: holding office, participating in meetings, attending conventions, voting (elections, ratification, and strike vote), and helping with the monthly newsletter.

Union members whose growth needs are not fulfilled on their job are usually more willing to become involved in union administration. Also, individuals are usually more willing to participate in union administration when their values are closely aligned with their role in the union.[43]

Participation in Meetings.

Attendance at local union meetings often varies between five and ten percent of the membership; however, attendance is higher among union members who perceive a potential payoff for participation.[44] When a union is confronted with important business or a crisis, such as during union elections, taking a strike vote, negotiations, or ratifying a negotiated agreement, attendance rises. Unions and their members have been criticized for their lack of attendance, but formal attendance cannot be taken as the real measure of membership participation. Much membership participation takes place on an informal basis at the plant level among employees, among friends during lunch, or between shop stewards and members during rest breaks. Concerns are channeled to the union leadership through these stewards, who regularly attend local meetings. The influence of these information channels over union policies and actions should not be underestimated. Local unions are learning to use survey methods and interviewing techniques to gather information about such issues as safety and health, contract provisions, promotional opportunities, job stress, perception of the union, recruitment of new members, and so on, not only to prepare for negotiations, but also to improve the operations of the union and assess membership attitudes.[45]

Unions have much potential for increasing participation of local union members. For example, unions could allow members to provide volunteer services to the local union in lieu of paying local union dues; make full use of electronic information services, like the Internet, Web sites, and e-mail, to communicate and pursue union objectives; and find new ways to involve the rank-and-file members in organizing, bargaining, and political activities.[46]

Interestingly, union participation does not always lead to greater job dissatisfaction. In fact, active union membership in less adversarial climates will not be a source of increased job dissatisfaction. Therefore, if the labor-relations climate is less adversarial, management should not fear or discourage employees to take an active role in their unions.[47]

The union leaders almost always attend local union meetings, as do departmental representatives, "hard-core" members, pressure groups, social groups, and aspirants to union leadership positions. Union stewards are expected to attend local union meetings and represent the interests of those in their unit. Although direct votes occur only on major issues, the union steward can usually reflect the membership views.[48]

Locals have tried numerous ways to increase attendance of regular members, such as providing beer, sandwiches, movies, and door prizes; fining members who miss a specified number of meetings; or refusing to let them seek an elected office. Although some gimmicks may increase the attendance in the short run, many members still feel the meetings are "long, boring, and frustrating affairs."[49]

Local meetings are held at a time that meets with the approval of the majority. Although they often start late and last too long, the average length is about two hours. The content inspires little attendance because much of the time is devoted to reading reports from the treasurer, project leaders, and committee chairpersons. Opportunities are provided for members to discuss these reports, but this procedure itself takes time, especially when a grievance involving someone in attendance is presented or when a controversial issue is raised before the meeting as a whole. Parliamentary procedure is used at times to excess by quasi-parliamentary experts who may want to tie up the meeting. Although the meeting may stray from the ideal, generally the business of the local is accomplished.

Functions of the Meeting. The local union meeting may seem boring and not well attended; however, it serves several vital functions in the local union government. First, the meeting is the union's single most important governmental activity, and all authority at the local level is derived from it. Second, the meeting provides an opportunity for members to communicate with union leaders, express gripes directly, and call attention to their concerns. Likewise, it is an opportunity for leaders to give information to members, present results of activities, seek union support, and give direction to the membership. Finally, the meeting is the supreme legislative body; this is where decisions are made on such items as disposition of grievances, approval of expenses and constitutional changes, election of officers, and ratification of the contract.[50]

Unions exist not only to better workers' economic conditions, but to give them a voice. Democratic unions provide that voice. A democratic union provides members an opportunity to exert influence over their workplace environment and to participate in decisions which affect them at work through such activities as attending local union meetings, voicing their opinions, participating in ratification and strike votes, running for office, and voting in local and national union elections. The processes in democratic unions, such as officer elections, make the union leaders more responsive to the membership.

Research has shown that positive union–management relations lead to members voting in line with the political objectives of the union leaders, such as contract ratification and re-election of the incumbent union leaders. In local union officer elections, greater effectiveness in processing grievances increases the likelihood that an incumbent union leader will be re-elected. Confidence in using the grievance procedure to resolve problems and the fairness of the collective bargaining agreement lead to increased support for the local union leader's political goals and re-election of the incumbent. Interestingly, members who are more senior were found more likely to exercise their vote against the incumbent union leader. Thus, it must be concluded that the more senior union members might not believe that the union officers are doing as much for them as they are for the more junior members.[51]

Because elections are so important to the democratic process, the U.S. Department of Labor has been authorized by Congress to develop rules governing union elections. (These rules are shown in the Labor Relations in Action on page 140.)

The National or International Union

The national or international (these terms are used interchangeably in this chapter) union in the United States occupies the "kingpin" position in organized labor "because of its influence in collective bargaining—the core function of American unions." Size alone (Exhibit 4.11) indicates the magnitude of the influence of

Organization	Members (in thousands)
National Education Association[*]	3,200
Service Employees International Union[**]	1,575
American Federation of State, County and Municipal Employees[**]	1,400
International Brotherhood of Teamsters[**]	1,400
United Food and Commercial Workers[**]	1,400
United Steelworkers[***]	1,200
American Federation of Teachers[***]	1,300
International Brotherhood of Electrical Workers[***]	750
United Auto Workers[***]	538
Communication Workers of America[***]	700
International Association of Machinists[**]	730
Laborer International Union of North America[**]	550

[*]Independent union
[**]Affiliated with Change To Win
[***]Affiliated with AFL-CIO

SOURCE: LM-2 Reports by U.S. labor unions, which may be found at http://www.dol.gov/esa, the home page of the U.S. Department of Labor.

Exhibit 4.11
Twelve Largest National and International Unions

national unions—millions of members work under labor agreements that are directly or indirectly the result of national union actions. The local union operates under its constitution and directives, and the federation (AFL-CIO) derives its influence, prestige, and power from the affiliated national unions.

The national union operates under a **constitution** adopted in a convention by representatives from locals. These constitutions have evolved over time through three stages: first, the locals were initially careful to restrict the power of the national union; second, as national unions became more active in collective bargaining, political action, and so on, the locals became subordinate bodies; and third and currently, the constitution includes provisions that not only authorize the major national union functions but also protect union member's individual rights and rights of local unions in relation to the national union.[52]

The Convention

The supreme governing body of the national union is its **convention**, which is usually held annually or biennially.[53] The convention serves the national union in many ways: as the constitutional assembly, the legislature of the national union, the final court for union decisions, and the means for nominating officers (and the election in many cases). The convention provides the time and place for national officers to report to the members their accomplishments and failures. It provides the agenda for policy formulation, program planning, and rule making. It represents the time in which the voice of the membership holds leaders accountable for their actions. However, not all activities are official; the convention provides a reward for drudgery work at the local, an opportunity for politicking and public relations, and a time and place for the members to "let their hair down."

The convention makes use of the *delegate system,* in which the number of delegates allowed depends on the number of members in the local. Because even the smallest union is allowed one delegate, the number of delegates is not

LABOR RELATIONS IN ACTION
Rules Governing Union Elections (U.S. Department of Labor)

1. All local unions must elect officers at least once every three years; international unions every five years.

2. Local unions are required to have direct elections by manual or mail ballots; international unions are permitted to elect officers by delegates.

3. Proper safeguards must be prepared for mail balloting, for example, insurance that all members received a ballot and have sufficient time to vote and return the ballot. With manual balloting, procedures for voter secrecy (private voting booths, a private table where the view is blocked by cardboard or a private room), and voter identification (driver's license or company badge) must be established.

4. The location, date, and time of the election must be convenient for all of the members.

5. Notice of the election, which contains the date, time, place, etc., must be mailed to every member 15 days prior to the election.

6. There must be reasonable notice of the rules governing nominations mailed to or posted for the membership. Nominations may be done orally at a union meeting or by mail, but every member must have a reasonable opportunity to nominate.

7. Requirements for voter eligibility are the same as the requirements for membership. Voter eligibility must be verified.

8. After the ballot is marked, it should be placed in a nearby ballot box by the voter and the voter should leave the area by a door different from the entrance of members who have not voted.

9. Neutral persons should conduct the elections and count the ballots.

10. Observers are a necessary part of the election process, and each candidate is entitled to one or more observers (depending on the polling hours, polling sites, and size of the election).

11. Each candidate has a right to have campaign materials mailed. Some unions do the mailing at the candidate's expense; some unions provide computer printouts of the membership lists or mailing labels of membership addresses.

12. The use of union or employer funds is prohibited. This ban applies to copying machines, campaigning in a union publication, use of union or employer cars, any property of the union or an employer, assistance by any employer or a relative who owns a business and just wants to help a family member get elected, etc.

SOURCE: Helen Boetticher, "How to Hold a Union Election and Stay Out of Trouble," *Labor Law Journal*, Vol. 51, No. 4 (Winter 2000), pp. 219–224.

in direct proportion to the size of the local, although larger locals usually have more delegates. The convention conducts its business similarly to Congress and various state legislatures in that much committee work (including the possible holding of hearings) is performed before debate and vote on the convention floor. However, much discussion also takes place in the convention hotel bars and in meeting rooms.[54]

Although many subjects may go before the convention, several continue to emerge year after year, such as the following:

- Internal government: dues; financial matters; and authority of the president, executive board, and locals

- Collective bargaining: problems with current agreements, membership requests for future negotiations, establishment of bargaining priorities, determination of strategy for future negotiations

- Resolutions in support of or against domestic and international public policies: labor law reform, inflation, interest rates, unemployment, international balance of payments, loss of jobs to foreign countries[55]

Leadership and Democracy

Between conventions, the national union is led by its executive board, whose members are elected by the membership. In some cases, executive board members are elected on a regional basis, and they are responsible for regional intermediate organizations that maintain contact between the locals in the regional and the national unions. The relationship between the executive board and the national union president is usually specified in the constitution. For example, some national union presidents primarily carry out the policies of the executive board; others direct the affairs of the national union, subject to the approval of the board. However, the largest group of presidents has virtually unrestricted authority to appoint staff, regulate locals, and direct the activities of the national union. The rationale for allowing such great authority to be vested in the chief executive is that the union often finds itself in struggles with employers or in other situations where it must act decisively and quickly. Thus, a strong executive is needed, and a single spokesperson for the union is required. However, the concentration of power creates opportunities for misuse of power, and an internal system of checks and balances must be devised to ensure democracy and adequate representation. Experiences that led to the passage of Titles I to VI of the Landrum-Griffin Act (covered later in this chapter) have shown that internal control often does not work effectively, making that government regulation essential. Members' rights to participate in union elections and governance include the right to nominate candidates in elections, vote in elections, attend membership meetings, participate in the deliberations, and vote on the business at these meetings, such as setting dues and assessments.[56]

Democracy within the union can improve its overall efficiency and effectiveness. Union leaders will better represent the members because they will know what the members want. Democracy will make it easier to eliminate corrupt and ineffective officers who do not represent the members' interests. Furthermore, paid union officials cannot do all the tasks needed within a union and have to rely on the efforts of unpaid leaders. These volunteer leaders will have a greater commitment to the union if they are involved in it democratically.

The components of democracy should include (1) shared sovereignty in decision making; (2) opportunities to participate in decision making; (3) access to complete information necessary for decision making; (4) guaranteed equal rights for individuals and respect for individual dignity; (5) the right to minimum economic, health and safety, and environmental standards; and (6) the right to a fair share of the value created by one's work.[57]

One slight sign of democracy and active participation by members has been the turnover rates of national union presidents. Some former international union leaders maintained their positions for extended periods (Dan Tobin, Teamsters, 45 years; John L. Lewis, Mine Workers, 39 years). In the 1950s and 1960s, the turnover rate for union presidents was about 20 percent, rising to 25 percent in the 1970s. Then, in the late 1980s, the turnover rate reversed to ten percent. Although turnover is not the necessary prerequisite for union democracy, the general rule is that a union leader must be responsive to the membership and satisfy the membership's objectives to remain in office.[58] The president's tenure in office tends to be longer in larger unions, with formalized communication networks, centralized bargaining, and heterogeneous rank-and-file members.[59]

Profile of Union Leaders

Most union leaders come from working-class families; 62.1 percent of their fathers were hourly employees and have an average of 14.1 years of formal education. Over 70 percent of union leaders have some college experience; 17 percent have postgraduate education; and another 27 percent are college graduates. They first joined a union for the same reasons most union members do today: 40 percent joined because it was a condition of employment, 33 percent joined because they believed in the goals of organized labor, and 25 percent wanted better pay and working conditions. Their reasons for pursuing union leadership positions included the following (80 percent or more responded positively to these survey items): challenging work, interesting work, extended my range of abilities, opportunity to learn new things, achieve something I personally valued, believed in the goals of the union, and opportunity to improve working conditions of fellow employees.[60]

A recent survey of national union leaders revealed some new directions, which included the following:

- Centralizing some of the national union's functions while pushing other decisions closer to the membership, such as taking a case to arbitration

- Broadening the scope of bargaining to include a more holistic approach, such as negotiating child-care and elder-care issues and member education

- Studying and learning from business organizations on subjects like strategic planning, clear objectives, a clear chain of command, and established rules and procedures

- Improving union and member effectiveness through goal setting, team building, and member surveys

- Improving communication with members by use of information technology, such as video conferences, Web sites, and e-mail[61]

Administration

The operational departments of international unions vary in kind and number, but the typical international union will have at least the following departments: (1) executive and administration; (2) financial and auditing; (3) organizing and servicing; and (4) technical staff, which includes research, education, economics, law, publications, and public relations.

Likewise, international unions create operating departments to serve various special interests among their membership. For example, the UAW established the Transnational and Joint Ventures Department for the 8,000 UAW members who were employed by three Japanese-managed vehicle makers at U.S. sites: the Toyota-General Motors, Ford-Mazda, and Chrysler-Mitsubishi joint ventures (Nissan remains nonunion).

The executive and administrative group includes the president, vice president(s), secretary-treasurer, and their assistants. This group is chiefly responsible for the activities of the overall union. In some cases, the vice president may concentrate on organizing or collective bargaining, whereas the secretary-treasurer will focus on financial matters.

Presidents of U.S. national and international unions are well-paid. Four earned more than $400,000 per year and four earned over $300,000. However, the average annual salary is about $125,000.[62] These salaries did not approach the average earnings of CEOs of the Standard & Poor's 500 companies, which was $14.78 million in 2006.[63]

There are thousands of union members, union stewards, and local union officials who receive no compensation for their union work and are reimbursed only for time lost from their jobs when involved in union business.

Policies on union compensation vary as well, and there is no correlation between the size of a union in terms of the number of members or assets under its control and the salary of the highest elected officer. For example, the president of United Auto Workers (UAW) earned $158,530 in 2006, and the UAW has $1.3 billion of assets. The total compensation of the president of the National Education Association (NEA) was $ 417,858 in 2006. The subject of salaries is addressed in unions' constitutions or governing documents either directly by setting the level of pay or indirectly by granting authority to elected delegates or executive board members who then establish salaries. The Communications Workers of America vests authority for setting salaries in delegates to its annual convention; The Electrical Workers give significant weight to compensation levels of other organizations of similar type and size; the Auto Workers link salaries of officers and staff to compensation earned by UAW members. In addition, the annual salary increases in a majority of unions are linked to the increase in average hourly earnings of members.[64]

Professional Staff Members

Unions have two kinds of professional staffs. The first group is either appointed or elected and holds such titles as international union representative, staff representative, business agent, or organizer. These staff members work away from the international union headquarters and assist local unions in bargaining, contract administration, and organizing. The second group performs more technical, specialized functions at the union headquarters. This group includes such professionals as industrial hygienists, physicians, economists, attorneys, accountants, computer operators, and specialists in education, media, public relations, and so forth. Interestingly, the staff members have formed staff unions, mostly to promote their job security and equitable salary schedules. Most staff unions are independent, but 13 of the 40 bargaining units have affiliated with a national labor union, such as the Communications Workers of America, the Steelworkers, or the Newspaper Guild. In addition, an association of these unions, called the International Congress of Staff Unions (ICSU), was formed in 1988 to share information and provide mutual support and assistance.

National unions have traditionally selected their staff through political processes by rewarding demonstrated leadership and loyalty at the local level. Union officers traditionally have been suspicious of college-educated persons and have believed that the staff should work its way up the ranks. More recently, national unions are using human resource practices used by business and government.

A survey of national and international unions showed that American unions are increasingly adopting more formal, systematic administrative practices, which are similar to those used in businesses and government. American unions are placing less emphasis on union membership status in their hiring of professional staff; the emphasis is on professional qualifications. Most unions now create budgets and allocate resources by function; they have formal organizational charts, strategic planning processes in place, and an evaluation process. Larger unions are likely to employ a human resource director and have written personnel policies. Also, there has been an increase in the employment of outside consultants to perform such functions as economic analysis, financial planning, organizational analysis, computer services, public relations, training, and personnel recruitment. American unions are responding to membership pressure for increased accountability, declining financial resources, and aggressive employer[65] opposition.

In the past there has been no recognized sequence of professional training for union officials, and experience and performance have been stressed in appointments and elected office. However, training has increased significantly over the last several years. Most national unions provide in-house training for their professional staff. Numerous universities have labor education programs that offer professional development for union members. The George Meany Center for Labor Studies in Silver Springs, Maryland, has an annual enrollment of several thousand. The Center, in cooperation with Antioch College, sponsors a college degree program designed for union staff, and several hundred union officials have graduated from this program.[66]

Services to and Control of Locals

As indicated earlier, the locals are constitutionally subordinated to the national union, but the degree of subordination varies with the union. The national union provides services to the local union in several ways while at the same time controlling local union leaders. For example, where a national product market exists, a **master labor agreement** with one firm might be negotiated to cover all its facilities (such agreements have been negotiated in the steel, auto, rubber, aircraft, and electrical appliance industries). Also, a union such as the UAW may negotiate an agreement with a company like GM at the national level, and this agreement may establish a pattern for negotiating with other auto companies such as Ford and Chrysler. Following the negotiations of the master agreement between the national union and each company, the local union will negotiate a local agreement with officials at each plant, covering local rules, policies, and benefits. Deviations from the master agreement must be approved by the national union. (See Chapter 6 for further coverage.)

The national union assists locals in collective bargaining, grievance administration, strike activities, and internal financial administration. These services also provide an opportunity for national union staff members to ensure that the local unions are conforming to national policies.

The international union representative, in addition to organizing new unions, also helps the local unions in grievance administration and labor arbitration. The national union supports the local union in strike situations, but the local union must get approval to qualify for strike benefits. The national union provides counseling and consultation for internal financial administration (bookkeeping, dues collection, purchases, financing union lodges, and so on), but trusteeship (receivership) procedures are available whereby the national union can suspend local union control for abuses such as malfeasance, corruption, and misuse of funds. The national union could replace local leaders with a trustee appointed by the national union.

Dues, Fees, and Distribution of Funds

Although all union members pay dues or fees to their national unions, the amount and form vary considerably. Such dues are the chief source of revenue for unions. Typically, the monthly dues are typically between $20 and $30, and the initiation fee is about $40. Some unions set a single rate, but most allow the local union some flexibility in making the final determination. Frequently, dues are collected via a dues checkoff system. The member agrees to a payroll deduction of union dues, which are collected by the employer and paid directly to the union.

Several specialized unions with small memberships, such as the Director's Guild, Football Players, Mine Workers, and Iron Workers, charge over $100 for an initiation fee, and the Radio Association charges $2,000. Usually when dues are higher than average, the payments include premiums for insurance, pension payments, and other benefits.

The local unions forward a portion of the monthly dues for each member to the national union. The national unions use these funds for various purposes beneficial to the membership. Although the largest percentage of funds goes to the general fund, which covers administrative and operational costs and salary expenses, allocations are also made to accounts such as a strike fund, a convention fund, union publications, educational activities, and a retirement fund.[67]

Use of union dues and fees for political purposes and non–collective-bargaining activities has come under fire in the last few years. Union members who disagree with the manner in which their unions contribute or use their funds have challenged their unions. Recent court decisions have caused several unions, such as the Machinists, Auto Workers, Communications Workers, and American Federation of State, County, and Municipal Employees, to adopt dues rebate plans. These plans allow a rebate of a portion of member dues spent on political activities if the member requests it in advance (usually annually).

The U.S. Supreme Court has ruled that if a union uses dues and fees of protesting employees for non–collective-bargaining activities and purposes, it breaches its fiduciary duty of fair representation.[68] Unions can continue to solicit volunteer contributions through such units as the AFL-CIO Committee on Political Education (COPE), the UAW's Community Action Program (CAP), and the United Mine Workers' (UMW's) Coal Miners' Political Committee (COMPAC), but collections may be more difficult.

Although union membership has not increased over the past two decades, unions have prospered financially, and their influence has increased in recent years. The level of unions' assets and income has enhanced their ability to finance strikes and other union activities. For example, in 1960, private-sector union membership was 14.6 million, and its receipts were $1.4 billion. By 1987, union membership was 10.9 million, and its receipts were $11.8 billion. This is a drop in membership of more than 25 percent and an increase in receipts of more than 700 percent. Taking inflation into account, receipts increased 220 percent. On a per-member basis, the receipts in real dollars were more than doubled.[69]

Finances of unions are considerably decentralized across union levels, with a few local unions having more wealth and income than their national unions. Likewise, union finances are highly concentrated with a few unions dominating the scene. For example, the National Education Association generates about $800 million in annual revenue, and the UAW has assets of $1.3 billion.[70]

The unions' financial performance has improved considerably in the last 15 years. In fact, unions have a collective capacity to fund nearly a full year of prior-year services without the infusion of any new income. Furthermore, unions' decline in bargaining power and strike activity over the past two decades has not been due to any diminished financial capacity of unions to withstand strikes.[71]

Mergers of National Unions

Encouraged by the AFL-CIO merger, but mostly spurred by rising costs, the need for stronger bargaining positions, expensive jurisdictional disputes, decline for some U.S. industries, economies of scale, avoidance of external controls, and the need for self-preservation, mergers of national unions have occurred at a quickening pace.

Mergers occur through amalgamation, absorptions, and affiliations. An **amalgamation** occurs when two or more unions of roughly equal size form a new union. An **absorption** occurs when a small union merges into a larger union and the smaller union loses its separate identity. An **affiliation** occurs when a single-plant, single-company, or regional union merges into a national union. Although unions do not report the number of affiliations, absorptions are far more common. Since the AFL and CIO merger in 1955, there have been 22 mergers through amalgamations and 149 absorptions. There has been an increase in the rate of mergers since the 1950s. In the four-year period between 1955 and 1959, there were nine mergers, or a 1.8 percent increase. During the 1990–1994 period, there were 21 mergers, or 4.2 percent, and during the 1995–1999 period, there were 17 mergers, or 3.4 percent.[72] In 1995, the Clothing and Textile Workers merged with the Garment Workers Union to form UNITE. In 2005, UNITE merged with HERE (hotel & restaurant employees), and the Rubber Workers and Paper Workers united with the Steelworkers.

Mergers appear to play an important role in some national unions' strategies for growth and diversification. However, the rising trends in mergers are best understood within the context of escalating employer opposition to unionism during negotiations and organizing, growth of nonunion competition, declining political and economic influence of unions, declining industries where unions are strong, foreign competition, and propensity of workers not to join unions.[73]

Typically, mergers have not succeeded immediately in welding together functions, organizational units, and staff members. They have required the time, patience, and goodwill of all parties, as officers and staff members who have different personalities and modes of operation are meshed. The local unions must be accommodated as well as the employers and the collective bargaining relationships. Mergers have been particularly difficult when one of the unions feels a loss of its autonomy, and when the merger occurs between unions whose prior dealings have been characterized by intense rivalry. Often members' pride is hurt, and fear surfaces when they find out that their union may be submerged by another.

In a more positive vein, the resulting larger unions gain more clout with industrial giants and can negotiate more as equals. The greater size generates resources to provide better training in collective bargaining, grievance administration, and steward leadership; to offer greater strike benefits; to lobby more effectively for legislation; and to maintain a staff to combat unfair labor practices. Moreover, successful mergers reduce the risks to smaller unions from technological change, economic recessions, declines in membership, unemployment, and financial strains. Also, fewer, but larger unions, will ultimately move the United States toward more centralized, industry level bargaining structure.

Most officers of unions with 50,000 or fewer members (includes more than half of AFL-CIO affiliates) believe that mergers have the best prospects of providing and maintaining member services. The benefits include more effective lobbying, increased bargaining power, expertise, economies of scale, and more effective strikes. The trade-offs are reduction in membership participation and less attention to needs of special interest groups. The potential advantages of a merger, coupled with the risks of not merging, suggest that mergers of national unions will be continued in the future.

Intermediate Organizational Units

Structurally, between national headquarters and the locals lie the intermediate organizational units—regional or district offices, trade conferences, conference boards, and joint councils. These units usually operate under the guidance of their various national units, but their activities are important to the union members and employers in their areas.

The regional, or district, offices house the regional or district officers, the staff, and the international union representatives for the geographical area served. For example, Michigan has a number of Auto Workers' district offices; the Steelworkers have district offices in Pittsburgh, Birmingham, and elsewhere. The offices are established for national unions to better serve their respective locals.

Trade conferences are set up within national unions to represent a variety of industrial groups. For example, the Teamsters have established 11 trade conferences for such groups as freight, laundry, airlines, and moving and storage. These groups meet to discuss various mutual problems and topics of interest.

Conference boards are organized within national unions in accordance with the company affiliation to discuss issues that pertain to the union and the particular company. For instance, each of the national unions within the steel, auto, rubber, and electric industries has established conference boards that meet to discuss negotiations and related problems. Delegates are chosen from the local unions to represent the interests of their constituents at meetings, to plan the next negotiations, and then to relay these plans to the local union members.

Joint councils involve groupings of local unions that have common goals, employers, and interests. Examples are the building trades councils established in most metropolitan areas in the United States. Joint councils negotiate with the association of construction employers in the area, coordinate their activities, and assist in resolving jurisdictional disputes between unions.

Independent Unions

There are 41 independent unions (not affiliated with the AFL-CIO or Change To Win). These unions represent mostly service and health care providers. The largest union in the United States, the National Education Association (3,200,000 members), is among these independent unions. Other independent unions include the American Nurses Association (149,000 members), American Physicians and Dentists (1,690 members), Life Insurance Agents (1,150 members), National Labor Relations Board Union (1,370 members), Professional Engineering Association (510 members), and United Plant Guard Workers of America (26,000 members).[74] There are also approximately 1,500 independent local unions that have nearly half a million members. Independent local unions are found in a few large organizations such as DuPont, Texaco, Exxon, AT&T, and Procter & Gamble; in several medium-sized firms such as Dow-Jones, Weirton Steel, and Zenith; and in numerous small companies in a variety of industries.[75]

Employee Associations

Unions are supporting new employee associations that provide a wide range of services to their members. In Cleveland, 9 to 5: The Association for Working Women, which is a 15,000-member affiliate of the Service Employees International Union, provides a toll-free hotline, offers courses on sexual harassment and VDT injuries, and lobbies on workplace issues. In New York, AIM (Associate ILGWU Members), a 2,500-member affiliate of the International Ladies Garment Workers Union (now part of UNITE HERE), provides English classes for its members; graduate-equivalency diploma classes; skills training; and legal assistance with immigration, minimum wage, safety and health, sexual harassment, disability, and pensions laws. In Montana, the 1,400-member Montana Family Union, sponsored by the AFL-CIO and made up of government employees, small business owners, and even priests, offers its members major medical benefits at less than 50 percent of their individual rates. Although critics refer to these employee associations as "watered-down unions," they are serving important social functions, and their membership has grown to 500,000 nationally while total membership in unions has declined to approximately 13 percent of the labor force.[76]

Managerial and Professional Organizations. Even though 43 percent of the total U.S. labor force is classified as managers, supervisors, or professional employees and therefore, not eligible for coverage under the National Labor Relations Act, these groups are interested in having a greater voice at work. Sidney and Beatrice Webb recognized in their classic book "Methods of Trade Unionism" published in 1902 that there were three methods of unionism: (1) collective bargaining, (2) mutual aid and insurance, and (3) legal enactment. Many managers, supervisors, and professional employees have joined organizations to represent their work-related interests, that is, for their mutual aid and insurance. Many of these organizations use union-like tactics, such as collective action, mutual aid, skill certification, and political activity to achieve their goals. They provide group insurance and discounts and special rates for university courses, books, video tapes, and products, assist members in their career development, and engage in legal-enactment strategies. One survey identified 37 of these types of organizations in a variety of industries and businesses.[77]

The American Federation of Labor and Congress of Industrial Organizations (AFL-CIO)

The AFL-CIO, while not including all U.S. labor unions, is composed of 55 national and international unions that have 60,000 local unions and about 10 million members. Members represent a diversity of occupations, such as actors, construction workers, barbers and hairdressers, steelworkers, bus drivers, railroad workers, telephone operators, newspaper reporters, sales clerks, garment workers, engineers, schoolteachers, and police. These AFL-CIO affiliates maintain day-to-day relationships with several thousands of employers and administer about 160,000 labor agreements. Most (over 99 percent) of these agreements are negotiated without strikes or other forms of conflict and serve as the basis of employment conditions under which many work.

Established in 1955 when the American Federation of Labor and the Congress of Industrial Organizations merged, the AFL-CIO recognized the principle that both craft and industrial unions are appropriate, equal, and necessary parts of U.S. organized labor. The federation accepts the principle of autonomy—each affiliated union conducts its own affairs; has its own headquarters, offices, and staff; decides its own economic policies; sets its own dues; carries out its own contract negotiations; and provides its own services to members.

No national union is required to affiliate with the AFL-CIO. About 40 unions remain outside the AFL-CIO. Member unions are free to withdraw at any time; however, their voluntary participation plays an essential role that advances the interest of every union. National unions continue their membership because they believe that a federation of unions serves purposes their own individual unions cannot serve as well.

Examples of AFL-CIO services include the following:

- Speaking for organized labor before Congress and other branches of government

- Representing U.S. labor in world affairs and keeping in direct contact with labor unions throughout the free world

- Coordinating activities such as community services, political education, lobbying, and voter registration with greater effectiveness

- Helping to coordinate efforts to organize nonunion employees throughout the United States

Another vital service enhances the integrity and prestige of AFL-CIO unions—they must operate under established ethical practice codes covering union democracy and financial integrity. The federation also assists in minimizing conflicts that cause work interruptions by mediating and resolving disputes between national unions, such as organizing disputes and conflicts over work assignments.[78]

Organizational Structure

The AFL-CIO organizational structure, shown in Exhibit 4.12, illustrates the importance of the convention. Meeting every two years and at times of particular need, delegates decide on policies, programs, and direction for AFL-CIO

Exhibit 4.12
Organization Chart of AFL-CIO

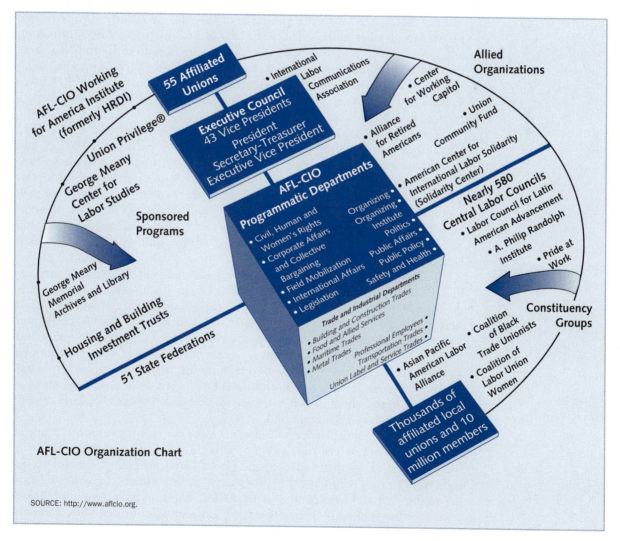

AFL-CIO Organization Chart

SOURCE: http://www.aflcio.org.

activities. Each national or international union is authorized to send delegates to the convention. Each union's representation of delegates at the convention is determined by the number of dues-paying members. In addition, other affiliated organizations, such as state labor councils, are represented by one delegate each.

Between conventions, the governing body is the Executive Council, composed of the president, secretary-treasurer, and 43 vice presidents. The AFL-CIO's first president, George Meany, was succeeded in 1979 by Lane Kirkland, whose unexpired term was concluded by Thomas R. Donahue. In 1995, the biennial convention elected President John J. Sweeney, Secretary-Treasurer Richard Trumka, and Executive Vice President Arlene Holt-Baker. They have been reelected three times since then, most recently in 2005 for four-year terms.

The other members of the Executive Council are likely to be current or previous presidents of international unions affiliated with the AFL-CIO. The Executive Council meets at least three times a year and handles operational duties involving legislative matters, union corruption, charters of new international unions, and judicial appeals from member unions.

Between meetings of the Executive Council, the president, who is the chief executive officer, has authority to supervise the affairs of the federation and to direct its staff, and the secretary-treasurer handles all financial matters. To assist his administration, the president has appointed 15 standing committees on various subjects, which, with the assistance of the AFL-CIO staff, provide related services to member unions. The staff, located at headquarters in Washington, D.C., corresponds closely to these standing committees in order to better serve the member unions. (See Exhibit 4.12 on pg. 151 for a listing of standing committees and staff divisions.) The General Board, composed of the Executive Council and one officer from each member union, is available to act on matters referred to it by the Executive Council.

The AFL-CIO has established 51 state central bodies (plus one in Puerto Rico) to advance the statewide interests of labor through political, lobbying, and organizing activities, which involve attempts to elect friends of labor, to have favorable legislation passed, and to organize nonunion workers, respectively. Each local union of the AFL-CIO–affiliated unions in a particular state may join the state organization and participate in and support its activities. In addition, 580 *local central bodies* have been formed by local unions of the national affiliates to deal with civic and community problems and other matters of local concern.

To accommodate and serve the interests and needs of various trade and industrial unions, the AFL-CIO has established eight trade and industrial departments. The Industrial Union Department represents the interests of industrial unions, mostly members of the former CIO. Another department, the Union Label Department, promotes the purchase and sale of union-made goods and services. The remaining departments represent the interests of such union groups as the building trades, food and beverage trades, maritime employees, metal trades, public employees, and professional employees. In addition, throughout the United States where there is sufficient interest and support, 976 *local department councils* have been organized.[79]

These local central bodies have become more active in recent years, particularly in the northeastern states. As an example, 60 percent of the councils in the northeast region have adopted the Union Cities program, which contains eight steps toward rebuilding the labor movement from the bottom up and helping to improve the lives of working families. These steps include mobilizing against anti-union employers, organizing grassroots lobbying/political action committees, creating strategies to create jobs and improve economic growth, sponsoring economic education, persuading city and county officials to pass resolutions supporting worker rights, and increasing union membership.[80]

The AFL-CIO established a no-raiding clause for its affiliated unions in 1962 to keep one affiliated union from attempting to draw members from another or seeking to represent a group of employees at a work site where a union already exists. Then, in 1962, the AFL-CIO set up an Internal Dispute Plan to adjudicate conflicts among its affiliated unions.[81]

The AFL-CIO's operations are financed through regular member dues, called *per capita taxes,* which are paid by affiliated unions on behalf of their members. Currently, the per capita tax is $0.65 month, or $7.80 per year, for each member. Thus, the AFL-CIO's operating budget is over $70 million, of which nearly all covers regular operating expenses. A major portion of the budget goes to the salaries of the staff. The detailed financial report of the AFL-CIO is submitted to the delegates at each convention.[82]

The AFL-CIO recently recognized the potential of maintaining contact with employees who are not members of unions by establishing an **associate membership program**. Eligibility for associate membership are those who voted for the union in elections where the union did not win, employees in nonunion companies who would vote for the union if given a choice, and employees who are represented by the union but have not joined it. There are over 400,000 associate union members, and the number continues to grow steadily. This program helps the AFL-CIO maintain contact with these employees.

The AFL-CIO offers Internet access to 17 million union members and retirees and offers computers at low cost. This new service is an extension of the Union Privilege Benefit Program (see Exhibit 4.13), which was offered in the 1980s. The benefits provide reduced attorney fees, lower-cost life and accident insurance, participation in a motor club, car repair discounts, travel club services, a Walt Disney discount, a parents' college advisor, reduced prices for educational books and software, mortgage and real estate advice, and a dental program. This program was also offered to nonunion members for a small fee who become "associate members," The AFL-CIO hoped that the associate members would later become union members. In 1995, the AFL-CIO added a credit card with no annual fee and a low monthly interest for which the AFL-CIO received $75 million each year for five years.[83]

Other AFL-CIO activities are educational and informational, presenting the federation's stance on a variety of issues. For example, the AFL-CIO publishes a weekly newsletter, the *AFL-CIO News,* which keeps members up to date on current events that pertain to them and presents various reports on problems and policies of organized labor. The AFL-CIO maintains the George Meany Center for Labor Studies, which offers short courses in union leadership development, and a Speaker's Bureau to provide labor speakers for high school and college classes. They also make educational films available to interested groups for a nominal fee.

In the political arena, the AFL-CIO receives much attention. As a representative of organized labor, it serves as the focal point of political activities. Not only does it lobby aggressively for favorable legislation, but it publishes the voting records of each senator and representative at both federal and state levels. It attempts to influence appointments, such as Supreme Court judges, the Secretary of Labor, and NLRB members, who are important to organized labor. Its policy of "reward your friends, punish your enemies" has not changed much since Samuel Gompers's day. The AFL-CIO's COPE has a network in each state and in most

Exhibit 4.13
Union Plus Benefits from Union Privilege

Union Plus Benefits from Union Privilege

Benefits for Life

Union Plus benefits stand for quality and service with prices working families can live with.Best of all, Union Plus programs are designed specifically for working families. Our benefits have added features that are especially helpful in cases of disability or layoffs.

Who can use these benefits?

You don't have to join Union Plus or Union Privilege; as a member of an AFL-CIO union, you and your family are automatically eligible for our benefits. Most unions participate in most Union Plus benefits, but some international unions elect not to offer all the programs. Click here to find out which Union Plus benefits your union participates in.

Our Secret? Union Power.

Just as unions provide strength in the workplace, Union Privilege provides strength in the marketplace. We deliver the best benefits through the collective buying power of over ten million AFL-CIO union members. And we do so without using union member dues.

Programs available outside the U.S.

Calculate your annual savings with Union Plus benefits

Money & Credit
- Credit Card
- Loans
- Mortgage & Real Estate
- Union-Made Checks
- Credit Educational Information
- Your Credit Score

Insurance Deals
- Accident Insurance
- Life Insurance
- Auto Insurance
- Pet Insurance

Health & Well Being
- Health Savings
- Health Club Discounts

Education Services
- Union Plus Scholarship
- Union Plus National Labor College Scholarship
- Education Loan Program
- "Go to College" Process

Entertainment Discounts
- Theme park discounts
- Movie ticket discounts

Auto Advantages
- Care Rentals
- Auto Insurance
- Auto Buying Service
- Goodyear Tire & Service Discounts

Member Satisfaction & Advocacy

To guarantee the quality of our benefits, we only work with industry leading providers.

Our relationships don't stop after the Initial provider selection. We continuously update programs and monitor performance closely to ensure that they satisfy union members' needs time and time again.

Our member advocates also use the collective strength of union consumers to ensure members get prompt, courteous service and high-quality benefits—as well as help resolve any problems. With Union Plus programs, union members can rest assured their needs will be addressed and their voice will be heard.

CONSUMER CORNER

Sign up for updates

Save time and money with the tips and deals offered in the Union Plus e-mails. Click here to sign up.

For other benefits, visit the links below. Union Plus products and services help save money—a nd headaches.

House & Home
- Mortgage & Real Estate
- North American Van Lines

Legal Resources
- Immigration Legal Service

Pet Service
- Pet Insurance
- Pet Savings
- PETCO Discounts

Gift Shop
- Flower Discounts

Travel & Recreation
- Car Rentals
- Vacation Tours
- Bahamas Getaways
- Disney Hotel Savings

Computers & Tech
- Cingular Wireless Discount
- IBM Computer Discount
- Dell Computer Discount

Union-Made
- Auto Buying
- Cingular Wireless Discounts
- Goodyear Tire 7 Service Discounts
- Disney Hotel Savings
- Powell's unionized bookstore
- Union-Made Checks

PROVIDER EXCELLENCE

Union Privilege only works with top quality companies you can trust. Our program providers:

- Are respected specialists in their field
- Offer first-rate products and services nationwide
- Share our worker-friendly philosophy
- Demonstrate outstanding customer service
- Understand the importance of privacy and security

SOURCE: http://www.unionplus.co m/benefits/. Note: Visit www.unionplus.org for updated information.

large communities. COPE seeks voluntary contributions to provide funds for its activities, which include voter registration, "get-out-the-vote" campaigns, preparation of leaflets and posters, and research on behalf of its candidates.

Although the Federal Election Campaign Act of 1971, amended in 1974, has restricted financial contributions to federal candidates, the AFL-CIO, COPE, and state and local bodies can still amass amazing support to help their candidates for office, especially when the candidate is clearly the choice of organized labor. Organized labor and corporations have become major players in the funding of political campaigns at the federal level, primarily through Political Action Committees.

However, business groups outspend organized labor by 10 to 1. Although organized labor has played a major role in U.S. politics, it remains independent of a national political party. Over the years it has been more closely aligned with the Democratic Party, both philosophically and politically. It has become perhaps the single most important political force that has supported government programs to help the socially and economically disadvantaged. It has supported consumer and environmental protection and safety and health legislation that have benefited all employees, union and nonunion alike.

Organized labor has accumulated much power and influence through its own established network and has also been instrumental in organizing other politically active groups with socially oriented objectives, such as minorities and senior citizens. However, organized labor's overall political strength and effectiveness should not be exaggerated. In some states and municipalities, union membership is so negligible that its influence is inconsequential. In others, where union membership is high, its influence is significant, and political candidates must actively solicit its support.[84] The AFL-CIO does not control the membership's votes, and members frequently have multiple reasons for voting for candidates.

In May 2006, the AFL-CIO and CTW coordinated member mobilization efforts for 2006 elections, which contributed to a Democratic majority in both the U.S. Senate and House of Representatives.[85]

Use of Information Technology by Unions

Virtually every international union in the United States uses the World Wide Web and other information technologies in the major areas of union activity:

1. Internal communications between union officers, staff, and members, particularly when they are geographically dispersed. Within every union, there are international union representatives who are employed throughout the country and represent members in organizing and representational activities. E-mail communication serves as an immediate means of communication throughout the organization. Other unions provide an e-mail alert system that gives weekly updates to union members and their representatives.

2. External communications, such as to inform the public about union issues potentially affecting the public, workers, and unions. The AFL-CIO Web site (www.aflcio.org/) gives members and nonmembers valuable information on matters dealing with worker rights, pensions, and benefits during layoffs, provides useful links to other resources, and provides a system allowing interested persons to receive e-mail updates about labor events from across the United States and the world. By the fall of 2002, the number of e-mail addresses in the AFL-CIO database was 600,000, and it is anticipated to reach several million in a few years.

3. Facilitation of bargaining activities, such as in negotiations, and informing members about employer practices. During 2007, members of the Auto Workers were able to keep up with the negotiations on wage concessions and plants shutdowns between the UAW and Delphi Corporation via UAW's home page. Members of the Communications Workers of America were able to be informed of the AT&T's purchase of BellSouth via CWA's home page.

4. Contract administration, such as communicating grievances and tracking decisions of arbitrators. Unions are better able to communicate with members in preparation for grievance meetings and arbitration hearings via e-mail communication. The American Postal Workers Union has a database of thousands of arbitrator decisions readily accessible to its arbitration advocates.

5. Union organizing, such as making contact with potential union members and providing a means for interested employees to communicate with the union. The United Food and Commercial Workers (UFCW) is currently using the Internet in its attempt to organize employees at Wal-Mart. Its Web site (www.UFCW.com) keeps up-to-date information on the UFCW campaign activities.

6. Political action, such as informing potential voters about union views and those held by organized labor's friends and adversaries. Nearly every union Web site has political messages for the reader.

Union leaders see the Web as an important avenue for modernizing unionism and for bridging the gap between an increasingly heterogeneous work force and collective activity and solidarity. One Web site (www.labourstart.org/) collects daily labor news from newspapers from around the world and posts it. LaborNet (www.labornet.org/) promotes computer communications for strengthening and building organized labor. Some unions have created member-only "chat rooms" and forums; others have organized voting over particular issues in order to obtain membership input on issues facing the union. If the unions continue to adopt these technological innovations at their current pace, unions in advanced countries will be truly transformed organizations.[86]

The use of e-mail and the Internet has caused some concerns among organized labor. Among the concerns are the erosion of face-to-face contact, worry about "loudmouths" and "troublemakers" monopolizing the communications, the generation gap between older "precomputer" leaders and the younger "computer techies," loss of confidentiality by "computer hackers" and "snoops," and worry that e-mail messages will overload the system and consume an extraordinary amount of time that could be used more effectively elsewhere.[87]

One of organized labor's greatest concerns is use of company intranets (computerized e-mail and Web site systems within a company). These add new communication possibilities to employer's union-substitution strategies by linking workers to their supervisors and human resource specialists who are able to quickly disseminate company information and focus attention on resolving employee grievances. Employers' use of intranets is already widespread and has among its explicit objectives improved communication between workers and human resource departments and closer identification with the company.

Unions will also find themselves competing with alternative advocacy and workers' rights organizations that are attempting to organize and represent workers. For example, the Professional Association of Contract Employees provides its members with group benefits and assistance with record keeping and contracting. Working Today is an organization that promotes the interests of freelancers, independent contractors, temporary and part-time workers, and people who work from their homes. It offers group health insurance, legal aid, financial services, and discounts on travel, computers, and office supplies.[88]

UNION CORRUPTION AND THE LANDRUM-GRIFFIN ACT

Like some business executives, a few union officials have encountered problems with law enforcement officials. Unethical and illegal practices, including corruption, racketeering, and embezzlement, have been discovered in some local and national unions. Union abuses of power were exposed by the McClellan hearings of the late 1950s. Large amounts from Teamsters pension funds had been misused. Union officials have been indicted for conspiracy to bribe a U.S. senator and for embezzlement. Indictments have been rendered where "ghost workers" were maintained on payrolls even though no services were performed. Although union corruption cannot be condoned, its magnitude is diminished by the billions of dollars lost to shareholders and retirees from the corporate corruption scandals at Enron, HealthSouth, Tyco International, and WorldCom.

J. Thieblot researched database sources which provide an overview of union corruption in the United States and found 1,238 documented instances of corruption in 137 different labor unions between the middle of 1998 and the end of 2005. Financial corruption, the most common of which was embezzlement, included forms such as submitting fictitious expense reports and diverting members' dues to one's own pocket. Other examples of corruption were longstanding association with organized crime, suppression of internal dissent, nepotism, selling of labor peace, and approving freedom from contract obligations. Specific examples include:

- President of a grocery store employees' local union of baggers and checkers made was paid $547,000 annually and relatives who were vice presidents were paid $174,000 and $143,000.

- A local union created an unreasonable requirement, making attendance at union meetings mandatory, in order to disqualify 90 percent of the members from running for election.

- A president of an international union steered pension funds to various banks in exchange for more than $5 million in personal loans.

- Five trustees of a union pension fund misused funds by investing in a hotel project that lost millions of dollars.[89]

An accurate assessment of union corruption is reflected by the following conclusion:

> Union corruption stories are front-page news. They create images that tend to linger and are reinforced each time new allegations are raised. Certainly, Jimmy Hoffa's lasting notoriety is evidence of this phenomenon. In fact, the level of corruption among unions and union leaders is negligible. The Labor-Management Reporting and Disclosure Act ... insures this. Very few institutions in American society are as closely regulated or as open to scrutiny as are American unions.... The evidence is clear that all but a minute fraction of American union leaders are honest and dedicated in the performance of their duties. Supporting this conclusion is an investigation by a former Attorney General that found serious problems of corruption in less than one-half of one percent of all local unions.[90]

The AFL-CIO established the Ethical Practices Committee in its efforts to control corrupt practices and racketeering of its member unions, and its Executive Council was given the authority to suspend any affiliated union with corrupt practices. In 1959, the U.S. Congress showed its concern with union abuse and the potential misuse of union power through passage of the Landrum-Griffin Act (the Labor-Management Reporting and Disclosure Act), which has several provisions governing union operations and government. For example, it governs the following:

- Disclosure by union officers and employees (and employers and their agents) about financial dealings, trusteeships, and any private arrangements made with any employees.

- Regulation of union trusteeships, including rules for their establishment and maintenance, and the protection of the rights of members of unions under trusteeship.

- Fiduciary responsibilities of union officers and representatives. It also disqualifies criminals and former communists from holding union offices, and it requires certain union officers to be bonded to ensure the faithful discharge of their duties and responsibilities.

- Rights to participate in union elections and governance, such as the right to nominate candidates in elections, to vote in elections, to attend membership meetings, to participate in the deliberations, and to vote on the business, such as setting dues and assessments.

The law was intended to promote union democracy and financial integrity. Success in the administration of the law requires initiative on the part of union members and availability of necessary information to union members.

The Landrum-Griffin Act requires unions to report and file financial information (LM-2 Reports) with the Department of Labor and to make these reports available to members. The act's intent was to allow rank-and-file union members to hold union officials accountable by letting members know how their union leaders were spending their dues. For many years after the passage of the act, these LM-2 reports were not readily accessible to union members and the general public. In the summer of 2002, the U.S. Department of Labor began addressing this problem about union financial reporting and began making these LM-2 reports available online via its Web site. Still, there has been criticism that even when accurately reported information fully complies with the law, it is "hard to obtain, too complicated to understand, and difficult for members to use."[91]

In 1984, the Comprehensive Crime Control Act, containing the Labor Racketeering Amendments, was passed. These amendments, backed by the AFL-CIO, closed the loopholes in the existing laws against labor malfeasance. Convicted labor officials cannot hold any union position for up to 13 years; the previous law allowed for elongated appeals during which the officials might remain in office. Any convicted management official must be transferred outside the labor relations function and cannot serve as a consultant or advisor in labor relations.

UNION SECURITY

A **union security clause** in the labor agreement makes it easier for the union to enroll and retain members. A reasonable level of union security is necessary for a labor organization to survive and effectively represent the interests of bargaining unit members. Upon National Labor Relations Board (NLRB) union certification under the LMRA, a union is granted an *irrebuttable presumption of majority status support* for one year. This provides the certified union a reasonable time in which to negotiate a first labor agreement with the employer without being concerned that it might be replaced by a rival union or by a decertification election. Any additional form of union security (e.g., union shop or dues checkoff clause) must be obtained by a union through negotiation with the employer.

Union security provisions tend to strengthen the union's financial resources by increasing the number of dues-paying members. Unions seek to recoup their initial time and money investments spent on organizing employees at a facility by subsequently obtaining dues from the eligible members. Union leaders believe they are morally justified in asking bargaining unit members to help pay for services provided by the union because they are legally obligated to represent all bargaining unit employees.

Union security provisions can offer benefits to the employer and the union. Many might contend that employers prefer dealing with a weak rather than a strong union. A weak union can aid an employer's effort to terminate a union–management relationship, but it can frustrate an employer who earnestly tries to resolve working condition disputes through an established union–management relationship. It is commonly the union, not the employer, who sells the collective-bargaining agreement to the membership. A union has difficulty in accomplishing this objective when there are nonunion member factions within the bargaining unit that seek to undermine support for union policies.

Union officials contend that union security provisions also offer other advantages to the employer, such as less time spent recruiting new members and collecting dues of existing members during the workday. However, management officials counter that this time savings will not result in more production because union officials might use the extra time to police the labor agreement and formulate additional grievances. Unions also maintain that morale can be improved if all employees are union members. Tensions arise when some employees do not pay for the services shared by all (the so-called *free rider* issue). However, a counterargument could be made that tensions are not reduced by union security, merely redirected. The possible anger of union members working with nonunion employees is replaced by the anger of nonunion bargaining unit members who feel forced to pay for unwanted union services.

Union Security Provisions

In view of their potential advantages and disadvantages, union security provisions have taken one or more of the following forms.

Closed Shop

For an employee to obtain a job in a **closed shop,** the employee must first become a member of a union. The closed shop was made unlawful by the LMRA in 1947.

Union Shop

The most common form of union security clause, the union shop clause, is found in about 64 percent of private-sector labor agreements.[92] Under a **union shop** contract provision, the employee does not have to be a union member to be hired by the company. However, after being hired, the employee must become a union member within a period of not more than 30 days (seven days in the construction industry) to remain employed by the company.

An example of a union shop clause is found in Exhibit 4.14.

The U.S. Supreme Court in *Communications Workers v. Beck* (487 U.S. 735 [1988]), held that a union shop clause only requires a bargaining unit member to become a **financial core union member**. This term refers to an individual who meets the minimum (core) union membership requirement of paying regular union dues and initiation fees. A union may impose additional lawful conditions for obtaining **full union membership** status (e.g., individual must be willing to comply with the union's constitution and bylaws). Under a union shop provision, an employer does not always have to honor a union request to discharge an employee who is not a union member if (1) the employer believes union membership was not offered to the employee on the same terms as other employees or (2) membership was denied for any reason other than the failure to tender dues.[93]

The *Beck* decision created a group of so-called "*Beck* rights" for bargaining unit employees. These *Beck* rights cover (1) notices to employees, (2) accounting of funds by unions, and (3) procedure for implementation. Unions are required to notify current members annually of their *Beck* rights. For example, this notice requirement may be met with a notice in the December edition of the union's monthly magazine. Newly hired employees receive notice at the time the union seeks to have the employees pay dues. An employee may choose between being a nonmember agency fee payer (a financial core employee) or a "union member in good standing" who will become a full union member. The union is required to maintain an accounting system (subject to audit) that determines the percentage of employees' dues used for collective bargaining purposes (known as "chargeable fees") and those used for other activities not related to collective bargaining (known as "nonchargeable fees"). The union notifies employees that those who wish to exercise their *Beck* rights must do so annually, and the union then provides a "window period" (a certain time period each year) for application for a refund of a portion of dues (nonchargeable fees) for employees who exercise their *Beck* rights. In other words, employees who exercise their *Beck* rights must file once per year during a specific period designated by the union.[94]

On February 17, 2001, President George W. Bush issued Executive Order 13201 entitled "Notification of Employee Rights Concerning Payment of Union Dues or Fees." The Executive Order requires federal government contractors to post notices to employees informing them of their *Beck* rights. On January 2, 2002, the U.S. District Court for the District of Columbia held that the new rules would regulate a core labor–management area that is already regulated

Exhibit 4.14

An Example of a Union Shop Clause

All present employees who are members of the union of the effective date of the execution of this Agreement shall remain members of the Union in good standing as a condition of employment. All present employees who are not members of the Local Union and all employees who are hired hereafter shall become and remain members in good standing of the Union as a condition of employment within thirty (30) calendar days following the beginning of their employment, or within sixty (60) calendar days following the effective date of this Agreement. An employee who has failed to acquire, or thereafter maintain, membership in the Union, as herein provided, shall be terminated seventy-two (72) hours after the Employer has received written notice from the Principal Officer of the Local Union certifying that member has been and is continuing to be offered to such employees on the same basis as all other members, and further that the employee has had notice and an opportunity to make all dues or initiation fee payments.

by the National Labor Relations Act and would impose a duty on employers that the National Labor Relations Act does not impose. Therefore, the Court ruled that the new rules were preempted by the National Labor Relations Act and were unenforceable. This ruling was appealed and the Court of Appeals over-turned the lower court's decision. Subsequently, the Labor Department began the regulatory process to implement Executive Order 13201.

Agency Shop

More commonly found in public-sector labor agreements, an **agency shop** clause does not require an employee to join the union but does require the employee to pay the union a sum equal to membership dues to remain employed. This provi-sion assumes that employees should not be forced to join a union but nonetheless should help defray the bargaining and grievance costs. The U.S. Supreme Court has determined that the minimum legal requirements for union membership imposed by a union or agency shop clause are essentially the same.[95]

Before seeking to impose an agency shop provision on a bargaining unit member, the union must inform the employee of his or her right to become a financial core rather than full union member.[96] A union may not charge a finan-cial core member for the cost of union expenditures unrelated to collective bar-gaining, contract administration, or grievance resolution activities if the financial core member notifies the union of his or her objection to such expenditures.[97] A union must notify all financial core members annually of the percentage of union dues assessments spent on nonchargeable activities, as well as the reason-able procedure by which the financial core member can object to such expendi-tures. If the financial core member objects, the union must reduce the amount of the financial core member's dues obligation by the percentage amount spent on nonchargeable activities. A financial core member who disagrees with the union's calculation of chargeable and nonchargeable expenditures may either appeal the dispute to final and binding arbitration or file an unfair labor practice charge with the NLRB. Some examples of chargeable union activities would be the costs of conducting contract negotiations, investigating and resolving grievances, conducting union business meetings, union publications such as newsletters intended to inform the union's membership about contract issues or grievance disputes, litigation costs incurred in the course of representational activities, social events or member benefits available to all bargaining unit members, and attendance at national or state union conventions. The NLRB recently ruled that the cost associated with union organizing is a chargeable expense as long as the employees being organized work for an employer in the same competitive markets as bargaining unit members already represented by the union.[98] Exam-ples of nonchargeable union activities would be the cost of legislative lobbying, union benefits not available to financial core members, and charitable contribu-tions such as a donation to the local United Way campaign.

The U.S. Supreme Court in another decision also applied *Beck* guidelines to similar expenses paid by public-sector employees' union dues.[99] The Court stated that public employees did not have to pay the portion of union dues that paid for any union activities that were not oriented toward the ratification or implemen-tation of the dissenters' collective bargaining agreement. This decision was not clear cut, however, as it indicated, for example, that dues payments can properly go toward a teacher union's strike preparation activities even if a strike is illegal under state law. In essence, the Court agreed with the public-sector union that a strike threat represented a reasonable, albeit illegal, bargaining tactic in pursuit of legitimate bargaining unit objectives.

Contingency Union Shop

Some labor agreements in right-to-work states (covered on pg. 163) have a contingency union shop provision stating that the union security provision currently in force will automatically convert to a union shop provision if the state's right-to-work laws are eliminated.

Union Hiring Hall

According to a **union hiring hall** provision, employers hire employees referred by the union if the union can supply a sufficient number of qualified applicants. This provision is found in about 23 percent of all labor agreements but is much more common in certain industries such as construction (90 percent) and maritime (88 percent).[100] Unions are required to operate hiring halls in a nondiscriminatory manner, making them equally available to union members and nonunion employees. In reality, most nonunion individuals do not choose to seek employment through union-operated hiring halls. A hiring hall provision helps to strengthen union security by encouraging current union members to associate their union more closely with the provision of job opportunities.

Preferential Treatment Clause

A negotiated labor agreement provision that indicates current employees who may be union members will be given employment preference over nonemployees when a new facility is opened is called a **preferential treatment clause**. This arrangement was negotiated between the United Auto Workers and General Motors for the new Saturn manufacturing plant located in Spring Hill, Tennessee, and was upheld by the NLRB. Such an arrangement permitted General Motors to take advantage of the skilled labor pool represented by employees already on the payroll, some of whom were laid off for lack of work at the time the new plant was seeking to fill employment positions.

Dues Checkoff

A provision commonly used in conjunction with one of the previously cited union security provisions, a **dues checkoff** makes the collection of union dues more convenient for both the union and union members. It is not a union security clause in the strict sense of the word because it does not guarantee that some or all employees will become union members. However, a dues checkoff clause in the labor agreement allows a union member to have dues automatically taken out of his or her paycheck (similar to any other payroll deduction) and transferred to the union. In addition to the dues checkoff clause agreed to by the employer and union in the labor agreement, each individual union member must sign a separate document authorizing the deduction to be made before any union dues can be automatically deducted from the employee's paycheck. This provision is important to the union because it assures the union of an uninterrupted flow of income. Without a systematic dues deduction, union officers would have to spend a great deal of time contacting recalcitrant members who kept delaying their dues payments. In many cases, the employer automatically agrees to this provision in the first contract negotiation on the assumption that every other labor agreement contains it. The employer may charge a reasonable administrative fee to the union for the cost of dues collection and other paperwork associated with administering this contract provision. In negotiations, astute management officials usually bargain for something in return for this provision, such as flexibility in making work assignments, subcontracting, or writing job descriptions.

Right-to-Work Laws: Controversy and Effects

Employers, some employees, and the courts have long been concerned with union security provisions.[101] Efforts to have Congress impose a national ban on union security agreements as part of the LMRA (Taft-Hartley Act) in 1947 were unsuccessful. Congress believed that providing a reasonable opportunity to achieve union security aided in the effective representation of employees' interests in collective bargaining between their union representative and the employer. As a political compromise, Congress did enact Section 14(b) of the LMRA, which states:

> Nothing in this Act shall be construed as authorizing the execution or application of agreements requiring membership in a labor organization as a condition of employment in any State or Territory in which such execution of application is prohibited by State or Territorial law.

Under this provision, a state may initiate legislation prohibiting union membership as a condition of employment. Currently 22 states (44 percent) have a **right-to-work law** (Exhibit 4.15).

Right-to-Work States	Average Weekly Pay	Non–Right-to-Work States	Average Weekly Pay
Alabama	$654	Alaska	$ 746
Arizona	$724	California	$ 879
Arkansas	$592	Colorado	$ 800
Florida	$694	Connecticut	$1,032
Georgia	$760	Delaware	$ 858
Idaho	$585	District of Columbia	$1,185
Iowa	$628	Hawaii	$ 665
Kansas	$659	Illinois	$ 843
Louisiana	$645	Indiana	$ 682
Mississippi	$562	Kentucky	$ 649
Nebraska	$615	Maine	$ 617
Nevada	$728	Maryland	$ 823
North Carolina	$688	Massachusetts	$ 970
North Dakota	$569	Michigan	$ 791
Oklahoma	$607	Minnesota	$ 788
South Carolina	$623	Missouri	$ 696
South Dakota	$551	Montana	$ 537
Tennessee	$690	New Hampshire	$ 789
Texas	$786	New Jersey	$ 945
Utah	$631	New Mexico	$ 603
Virginia	$807	New York	$1,019
Wyoming	$627	Ohio	$ 708
		Oregon	$ 697
		Pennsylvania	$ 755
		Rhode Island	$ 713
		Vermont	$ 647
		Washington	$ 774
		West Virginia	$ 587
		Wisconsin	$ 675

US Average Weekly Pay: $779

SOURCE: http://www.bls.gov/cew/state2005.pdf (U.S. Bureau of Labor Statistics).

Exhibit 4.15
Private Sector Average Weekly Pay by State and Right-to-Work Status, 2005

As noted in Exhibit 4.15, workers in the 13 of the 28 states which allow the parties to negotiate union shop agreements have average annual pay greater than the U.S. average; only two states, Virginia and Texas, which do not allow the parties to negotiate union shop agreements, has average annual pay above the U.S. average.

In 2001, Oklahoma became the 22nd "right-to-work" state. During the political campaign, proponents of the change argued that Oklahoma would become more competitively positioned to create jobs if the state adopted the labor policies of neighboring states and argued for liberty, free choice, and individual initiative. Unions promoted the principle of majority rule as essential to workplace democracy and urged allowing parties to negotiate the union security issue without intervention from the state. Unions also claimed that the other Sunbelt states offered lower wages, tax relief, and other subsidies in order to attract jobs.[102]

Unfortunately, one study found that Oklahoma residents were uniformed or misinformed about their rights under the law. Similar results had been found in studies of residents of Virginia and Idaho.[103]

Efforts to promote so-called state right-to-work laws are mainly conducted by the National Right to Work Committee, founded in 1955, whose stated purpose is to protect the employee's right to determine whether to join a union. Funded principally by employer contributions, the committee does not regard itself as being against unions but merely against union security provisions that compel employees to become members. However, allegedly, the committee's "pro-union, antiunion security" stance has been modified to a flat "anti-union" approach in recent years. A related, but separate organization, the National Right to Work Legal Defense Foundation, provides legal representation in right-to-work cases.

There has been a long-running debate on the effects of right-to-work laws on wages and union membership. Because there is no single explanation for wage rates or union density rates and no cause-and-effect relationship has been identified, one cannot conclude that "right-to-work" laws cause lower wages or low union density rates. However, Exhibit 4.15, which compares the average pay of employees in right-to-work states with that of employees in "non–right-to-work" states, certainly shows a wage disparity in favor of employees in the latter.

Even more impressive is the comparison of union density rates between right-to-work states and non–right-to-work states (see Exhibit 4.16). Only two of the 22 (9 percent) right-to-work states have union density rates above ten percent, whereas 25 (89 percent) of non–right-to-work states (those states that allow the union and management tonegotiate union security clauses) have union density rates of ten percent or more.

Meaning and Morality of Right to Work

Supporters of right-to-work laws contend the underlying definition affirms the right of every U.S. citizen to work for a living, despite whether he or she belongs to a union. In their view, compulsory unionism in any form (union shop, agency shop) contradicts a fundamental human right—freedom to join or not to join a union. Even Samuel Gompers, former president of the American Federation of Labor (AFL), occasionally stressed the necessity for "voluntarism" in labor unions:

The workers of America adhere to voluntary institutions in preference to compulsory systems which are held to be not only impractical but a menace to their rights, welfare, and their liberty.[104]

Supporters further contend that nobody should be required to join a private organization, particularly if that organization uses the individual's dues to

Right-to-Work States	Employed Union Members (%)	Represented by Unions (%)	Non-Right-to-Work States	Employed Union Members (%)	Represented by Unions (%)
Alabama	8.8	10.0	Alaska	22.2	23.8
Arizona	7.6	9.7	California	15.7	16.9
Arkansas	5.1	6.0	Colorado	7.7	8.6
Florida	5.2	6.5	Connecticut	15.6	16.5
Georgia	4.4	5.8	Delaware	10.8	11.4
Idaho	6.0	7.2	District of Columbia	10.3	12.2
Iowa	11.3	14.0	Hawaii	24.7	25.9
Kansas	8.0	9.3	Illinois	16.4	17.2
Louisiana	6.4	7.2	Indiana	12.0	13.0
Mississippi	5.6	7.3	Kentucky	9.8	11.2
Nebraska	7.9	9.5	Maine	11.9	13.5
Nevada	14.8	17.0	Maryland	13.1	14.8
North Carolina	3.3	4.1	Massachusetts	14.5	15.3
North Dakota	6.8	8.0	Michigan	19.6	20.4
Oklahoma	6.4	7.7	Minnesota	16.0	16.8
South Carolina	3.3	4.2	Missouri	10.9	11.9
South Dakota	5.9	7.2	Montana	12.2	13.1
Tennessee	6.0	6.8	New Hampshire	10.1	11.3
Texas	4.9	5.9	New Jersey	20.1	21.6
Utah	5.4	6.1	New Mexico	7.8	11.5
Virginia	4.0	5.2	New York	24.4	25.4
Wyoming	8.3	10.0	Ohio	14.2	15.5
			Oregon	13.8	14.7
			Pennsylvania	13.6	14.7
			Rhode Island	15.3	16.0
			Vermont	11.0	12.9
			Washington	19.8	21.0
			West Virginia	14.2	15.5
			Wisconsin	14.9	16.1
US Average	12.0	13.1			

SOURCE: Bureau of Labor Statistics, U.S. Department of Labor, "Union Affiliation of Employed Wage and Salary Workers by State," January 25, 2007, at http://stats.bls.gov/news.release/union2.t05.htm.

Exhibit 4.16

Employees Who Are Union Members and Who Are Represented by Unions by State and Right-to-Work Status, 2006

support causes that the individual believes are morally unjust or contrary to his or her religious beliefs. This attitude has been reinforced by Section 19 of the LMRA and actions by the U.S. Supreme Court, which, in effect, permit an employee to refuse to pay union dues because of a legitimate religious objection.[105]

Opponents of right-to-work laws contend the term *right-to-work* represents a gimmicky public relations slogan designed to restrict union security and related bargaining power. Opponents argue that unions do not deny anyone the fundamental freedom to seek work. Union security represents one of many negotiated employment conditions, such as work schedules, type of work performed, or wages, which a job applicant may choose to accept or reject if a job offer is made. If an employee does not like a particular working condition, that employee is free to seek employment elsewhere. This argument can also be supported by a quotation from Samuel Gompers:

> [T]he union shop, in agreement with employers, mutually entered into for the advantage of both employees and unions and the maintenance of industrial peace ... is to the economic, social, and moral advancement of all our people.[106]

Opponents further believe that union security provisions requiring some union attachment are moral because a person is a member of society with a responsibility to contribute to the common good. Because a union is legally required to represent all members of the bargaining unit in a fair and nondiscriminatory manner, it only seems fair that a bargaining unit member be required to help defray the costs of providing those services.

Impact of Right-to-Work Laws on the Union Organization and Employees

Research studies suggest that state right-to-work laws have a mixed effect on union membership levels and bargaining outcomes.[107] The presence of a right-to-work statute would appear to reduce union membership levels within a state 3 to 8 percent over the long term. Right-to-work laws appear to have no significant effect on employee wage rates but do appear to be positively associated with perceptions of a "better business climate," which in turn is positively correlated with greater industrial development activity over the long term. Of course, the presence of a right-to-work statue is typically one of several factors (e.g., tax structure, labor supply) used to measure the favorability of a state's business climate, making it difficult to determine the precise contribution of a right-to-work law to the overall perception of a favorable business climate and industrial development location decisions.

The bargaining unit members who choose not to join or financially support the union representing them for purposes of collective bargaining are referred to as **free riders**. Delaney (1998) notes that individuals with a college education are more likely to be free riders than less-educated employees. This poses a challenge to unions seeking to expand union membership levels among workers in occupations requiring increasing levels of education and skills to effectively use available technologies.[108] It is also important to note that most bargaining unit employees do not choose to be "free riders" even in right-to-work states that would legally permit it.

Right-to-work advocates claim that voluntary union membership increases union democracy by making leaders more responsive to members. With compulsory union membership, the members must remain "captive passengers" of the union if they wish to keep their jobs. Union leaders can become indifferent or even corrupt because members have no economic way of voicing their displeasure, such as by withdrawing their union membership dues support. Union leaders should have to earn their dues through their responsive, diligent actions. "Good unions don't need compulsory unionism—and bad unions don't deserve it."[109]

Opponents of right-to-work laws stress that under the LMRA, unions may be sued for lack of fair representation by bargaining unit employees who are nonmembers. The law also permits bargaining unit members to rectify ineffective or unresponsive union leadership problems by either electing new union leaders or electing to decertify the status of the current bargaining unit representative.

One research effort examined union members at a police organization in a right-to-work state. Dues-paying members were more likely to be male, married with more financial dependents, and have longer organizational tenure.[110] Another study also found that females as a group were more likely not to be union members, a finding possibly related to their lower wages, concentration in occupations with large proportions of nonunion members (e.g., professional specialties), and less employment in job categories having larger proportions of union members (e.g., precision production, craft, and repair).[111]

Summary

This chapter discussed two of the major participants in the labor relations process: unions and management. First, the goals of unions and management were presented, with emphasis on where the goals are the same and where they have potential for conflict. Companies' labor relations strategies, ranging from union suppression to labor-management cooperation, were explained.

Union strategic plans, which are at the embryonic stage in most unions, were discussed, and examples from the AFL-CIO and CTW were presented. Companies and unions are structured according to their goals; typical examples of company labor relations organizations and organizations at various levels of unions were displayed.

The chapter also discussed union governance. First, general characteristics of craft and industrial unions were explained. Then, the government and organizational activities of the local union, the national or international union, the intermediate bodies, and the federation (the AFL-CIO) were discussed. Because unions, like businesses and government, have experienced corruption and misuse of power and authority, examples of these problems and of steps that have been taken to seek a resolution were provided. Unions show concern for the long-term survival and growth of their organizations when they attempt to negotiate a union security provision (such as union shop, union hiring hall, or agency shop) into the labor agreement. However, certain union security provisions cannot be negotiated in states having right-to-work laws, permitted under Section 14(b) of the LMRA. Controversy occurs over the meaning, morality, and impact on union organizations of a right-to-work law.

Key Terms

Craft unions, p. 136
Industrial unions, p. 136
Business agent, p. 137
Shop steward, p. 137
International union representative, p. 138
Constitution, p. 141
Convention, p. 141
Master labor agreement, p. 146
Amalgamation, p. 148

Absorption, p. 148
Affiliation, p. 148
Conference boards, p. 149
Joint councils, p. 149
Associate membership program, p. 153
Union security clause, p. 158
Closed shop, p. 159
Union shop, p. 159

Financial core union member, p. 160
Full union membership, p. 160
Agency shop, p. 161
Union hiring hall, p. 162
Preferential treatment clause, p. 162
Dues checkoff, p. 162
Right-to-work law, p. 163
Free riders, p. 166

Discussion Questions

1. Compare the steps companies may take to implement a positive human resources management program with principles of effective management.

2. What suggestions can you offer to emphasize common goals of companies and unions as opposed to conflicting goals?

3. Assess the strategic plans of the AFL-CIO and CTW, and determine whether these plans provide direction for growth.

4. Locate a local union and a local plant, and draw an organizational chart for each.

5. Select a craft union and an industrial union and point out differing characteristics of these two types of unions.

6. Compare the government of the local union with student governments and municipal governments, paying special attention to participation by members.

7. Explain why and how national unions' presidents have been able to accumulate so much authority and power.

8. Differentiate among the business agent of a local union, a shop steward, and an international union representative. How do their roles differ?

9. Because the AFL-CIO does not negotiate labor agreements on behalf of national unions, how can it claim to be the "spokesperson for organized labor" in the United States?

10. Compare the requirements for union democracy to any student organization with which you are familiar.

11. Formulate a one- or two-sentence argument for or against the right-to-work philosophy. Fully defend your statement from arguments that could be made against your position.

Exploring the Web

Labor Unions, Mergers and Union Security

1. UNITE and the History and Merger of Textile Unions

UNITE (formerly the Union of Needletrades, Industrial and Textile Employees) and HERE (Hotel Employees and Restaurant Employees International Union) merged on July 8, 2004, forming UNITE HERE. Part of the history of UNITE includes a fire at the Triangle Shirtwaist Factory in New York City in 1911 which killed 146 workers and led to the first workplace health and safety laws. The Kheel Center for Labor-Management Documentation and Archives at Cornell University provides reproductions of moving accounts of the fire. From the Cornell site, read newspaper articles published in 1911 and selections from the book by Leon Stein, *The Triangle Fire,* and view photographs and drawings depicting the fire.

2. Merger of the USW and the AFGWU

The tenth merger for the United Steelworkers took place when the USW and the American Flint Glass Workers Union (AFGWU) agreed to merge. Look on the USW's Web site for the story of the merger and a short history of the Flint Glass Workers. Search, also, for a history of other USW mergers with international unions.

3. Bureau of Labor Statistics and Current Union Membership

The Bureau of Labor Statistics publishes an annual report on union membership. Find and read the summary for the 2006 report to discover more about the current status of labor unions. What percentage of the total people employed in protective services were members of labor unions in 2006?

Read an article by David Denholm, "Unions Turn to Public Sector as Membership Declines." The article is available on the Web site of the Capital Research Center. Comment on whether the decline in membership has continued since the article was published in 2002.

4. Articles on Union Mergers

Read the article, "Falling Union Membership Prompting Mergers," excepted from Laura M. Litvan's "Unions Have an Urge to Merge," published in *Investor's Business Daily,* August 8, 1997, and reproduced on the Web page for the National Center for Policy Analysis. What is one of the reasons that the author gives for the surge in mergers?

If your university or college has access to the *Journal of Labor Research,* either in print or online, locate an article published in 2004 by Gary Chaison, "Union Mergers in the U.S. and Abroad." What does the author say are the two basic forms of union mergers? What does he gives as the reasons for and barriers to mergers?

5. Union Security Provisions in Labor Agreements

Search the Web for examples of labor agreements. In the examples, which forms have been taken by the union security provision? (Forms are closed shop, union hiring hall, union shop, agency shop, maintenance of membership, quasi-union shop, contingency union shop, preferential treatment clause, dues checkoff.) Examine the rights of the employer (management) and the employees (union) as set forth in the agreements.

References

1. Audrey Freedman, "How the 1980s Have Changed Industrial Relations," *Monthly Labor Review* 111 (May 1988), pp. 35–39.
2. Martin M. Perline and David J. Poynter, "Union Orientation and Perception of Managerial Prerogatives," *Labor Law Journal* 40 (December 1989), p. 781.
3. http://hrw.org/english/docs/2007/05/01usdom 1597. Human Rights Watch, 350 Fifth Avenue, 34th Floor, New York, NY 10118-3299.
4. *Decisions and Order of the National Labor Relations Board,* 347 NLRB No. 109, August 21, 2006.
5. Alan Balfour, "The Unenforceability of the UAW's 'Neutrality Pledge' from General Motors," paper presented at the *Second Annual Meeting of the Southern Industrial Relations Association,* 1981.
6. Charles R. Greer and Stanley A. Martin, "Calculative Strategy Decisions during Organization Campaigns," *Sloan Management Review* 19 (Winter 1978), p. 73.
7. Ibid.
8. William N. Cooke and David G. Meyer, "Structural and Market Predictors of Corporate Labor Relations Strategies," *Industrial and Labor Relations Review* 43 (January 1990), pp. 280–282.
9. Keith Knass and Michael Matuszak, "An Antiunion Corporate Culture and Quality Improvement Programs," *Labor Studies Journal* 19 (Fall 1994), pp. 21–39.
10. Douglas M. McCabe and David Lewin, "Employee Voice: A Human Resource Management Perspective," *California Management Review* 34 (Spring 1992), pp. 112–114.
11. Fred K. Foulkes, "How Top Nonunion Companies Manage Employees," *Harvard Business Review* 59 (September–October 1981), pp. 121–125.
12. Herbert R. Northrup, "Construction Doublebreasted Operations and Pre-Hire Agreements: Assessing the Issues," *Journal of Labor Research* 10 (Spring 1989), pp. 219–227.
13. *Twenty-First Annual Report of the NLRB* (Washington, D.C.: U.S. Government Printing Office, 1956), pp. 14–15.
14. David Lewin, "Workplace ADR: What's New and What Matters," *Keynote Address at the Annual Meeting of the National Academy of Arbitrators.* May 24, 2007, pp. 1–6.
15. Audrey Freedman, *The New Look in Wage Policy and Employer Relations* (New York: The Conference Board, Inc., 1985), pp. 16–18.
16. Richard B. Peterson and Douglas M. McCabe, "The Nonunion Grievance System in High Performing Firms," *Proceedings of the 1994 Spring Meeting, Industrial Relations Research Association,* Paula B. Voos, ed. (Madison, Wis.: Industrial Relations Research Association, 1994), p. 529.
17. Douglas M. McCabe, "Corporate Nonunion Grievance Arbitration Systems: A Procedural Analysis," *Labor Law Journal* 40 (July 1989), pp. 432–438.
18. John E. Butler, Gerald Ferris, and Nancy K. Napier, *Strategy and Human Resources Management* (Cincinnati, Ohio: South-Western, 1991), pp. 147–158.
19. William N. Cooke and David G. Meyer, "Structural and Market Predictors," pp. 280–282.
20. Barbara Haskew, "A New Model for Labor-Management Relations, *Tennessee Business,* Vol. 13, No. 2, 2004, p. 8.
21. Barbara Haskew, "Southeastern Manpower Tripartite Alliance," *Tennessee Business,* Vol. 16, No. 3, 2007, pp. 25–26.
22. Butler, Ferris, Napier, pp. 147–158.
23. Francis A. O'Connell, Jr., "The Changing Character of Industrial Relations: Comment," *Journal of Labor Research* 12 (Fall 1991), p. 323.
24. Robert T. Thompson, "The Changing Character of Employee Relations," *Journal of Labor Research* 12 (Fall 1991), pp. 316–317.
25. Edward E. Lawler III and Susan A. Mohrman, "Unions and the New Management," *The Academy of Management Executive* 1, no. 3 (1987), pp. 293–300.
26. William N. Cooke and David G. Meyer, "Structural and Market Predictors," pp. 292–294.
27. John T. Dunlop, *The Management of Labor Unions* (Lexington, Mass.: Lexington Books, 1989), pp. xii–7.
28. Christine L. Scheck and George W. Bohlander, "The Planning Practices of Labor Organizations: A National Study," *Labor Studies Journal* 15 (Winter 1990), pp. 69–84.
29. Harry C. Katz, Rosemary Batt, and Jeffrey H. Keefe, "The Revitalization of the CWA: Integrating Collective Bargaining, Political Action, and Organizing," *Industrial and Labor Relations Review* 56, no. 4 (July 2003), pp. 573–589.
30. Tracy Fitzpatrick and Weezy Waldsteing, "Challenges to Strategic Planning in International Unions," *Proceedings of the 46th Annual Meeting of the Industrial Relations Research Association,* Paula B. Voos, ed. (Madison, Wis.: IRRA, 1994), pp. 73–84.
31. Richard Hurd and Martin Behrens, "Structural Change and Union Transformation," *Proceedings of the 55th Annual Meeting of the Industrial Relations Research Association,* Adrienne E. Eaton, Editor, 2003, pp. 113–121.
32. Richard W. Hurd, "U. S. Labor 2006: Strategic Developments across the Divide, "*Journal of Labor Research,* 28, No. 2 (Spring 2007), pp. 313–324; Gary Chaison, "The AFL-CIO Split: Does It Really Matter?" *Journal of Labor Research,* Vol. 28, No. 2 (Spring 2007), pp. 301–310; Marick F. Masters, Ray Gibney and Tom Zagenczyk, "The AFL-CIO v. CTW: The Competing Visions, Strategies, and Structures," *Journal of Labor Research,* 27, No. 4 (Fall 2006), pp. 473–503; Jack Fiorito, "The State of Unions in the United States," *Journal of Labor Research,* Vol. 38, No. 1 (Winter 2007), pp. 44–60.
33. David Lewin, "Workplace ADR: What's New and What Matters," *Keynote Address at the Annual Meeting of the National Academy of Arbitrators,* May 24, 2007, pp. 1–6.
34. John T. Dunlop, "Have the 1980s Changed U.S. Industrial Relations?" *Monthly Labor Review* 111 (May 1988), p. 33.

35. Audrey Freedman, Managing Labor Relations (New York: *The Conference Board, Inc.,* 1979), pp. 7–33.

36. Bert Spector, "Transformational Leadership: The New Challenge for U.S. Unions," *Human Resource Management* 26 (Spring 1987), pp. 3–11.

37. Alice H. Cook, *Union Democracy: Practice and Ideal* (Ithaca, N.Y.: Cornell University, 1963), pp. 19–26.

38. James E. Martin, John Christopher, and John M. Magenau, "A Longitudinal Examination of Union Steward Behaviors and Behavioral Intentions," *Proceedings of the 46th Annual Meeting of the Industrial Relations Research Association,* Paula B. Voos, ed. (Madison, Wis.: IRRA, 1994), pp. 422–431; Paul F. Clark, Daniel G. Gallagher, and Thomas J. Pavlak, "Member Commitment in an American Union: The Role of the Grievance Procedure," *Industrial Relations Journal* 21 (1990), pp. 147–157.

39. Gregory Mantsios, "Developing Rank-and-File Leaders: A Union/University Collaboration," *Labor Studies Journal* 26, no. 4 (Winter 2000), pp. 72–81.

40. Allan Nash, *The Union Steward: Duties, Rights, and Status* (Ithaca, N.Y.: New York State School of Industrial and Labor Relations, 1977), pp. 20–22.

41. Renaud Paquet and Isabelle Roy, "Why Do People Get Involved in Local Union Office?" *Journal of Collective Negotiations in the Public Sector* 27, no. 1 (1998), pp. 73–75.

42. Victor G. Devinatz, "From Industrial Unionism to General Unionism: A Historical Transformation?" *Labor Law Journal* 44 (April 1993), pp. 252–256.

43. Steven L. McShane, "A Path Analysis of Participation in Union Administration," *Industrial Relations* 25 (Winter 1986), pp. 72–78.

44. John C. Anderson, "Local Union Participation: A Reexamination," *Industrial Relations* 18 (Winter 1979), p. 30.

45. John Lund, "Using Surveys to Learn More about Membership Attitudes," *Labor Studies Forum* 4, no. 4 (1991), pp. 1–4.

46. John T. Delaney, Paul Jarley, and Jack Fiorito, "Planning for Change: Determinants of Innovation in U.S. National Unions," *Industrial and Labor Relations Review* 49 (July 1996), p. 612.

47. J. Bryan Fuller and Kim Hester, "The Effect of Labor Relations Climate on the Union Participation Process," *Journal of Labor Research* 19 (Winter 1998), pp. 184–185.

48. James E. Martin and John M. Magenau, "An Analysis of Factors Related to the Accuracy of Steward Predictions of Membership Views," *Labor Law Journal* 35 (August 1985), pp. 490–494.

49. Leonard R. Sayles and George Strauss, *The Local Union,* rev. ed. (New York: Harcourt, Brace & World, 1967), pp. 96–100.

50. Ibid, pp. 93–105.

51. James E. Martin and Michael P. Sherman, "Voting in an Office Election: Testing a Model in a Multi-Site Local," *Journal of Labor Research,* Vol. 26, No. 2 (Spring 2005), pp. 281–294.

52. Jack Barbash, *American Unions* (New York: Random House, 1967), pp. 69–72.

53. The Landrum-Griffin Act requires a convention at least every five years, and some unions, such as the Teamsters, take the limit of five years.

54. George Strauss, "Union Government in the U.S.: Research Past and Future," *Industrial Relations* 16 (Winter 1977), p. 234.

55. Barbash, *American Unions,* pp. 76–80.

56. Marick F. Masters, Robert S. Atkin, and Gary W. Florkowski, "An Analysis of Union Reporting Requirements Under Title II of the Landrum-Griffin Act," *Labor Law Journal* 40 (November 1989), pp. 713–722.

57. Susan J. Schurman and Adrienne E. Eaton, "Labor and Workplace Democracy: Past, Present and Future," *Labor Studies Journal* 21 (Summer 1996), p. 8.

58. Shulamit Kahn, Kevin Long, and Donna Kadev, "National Union Leader Performance and Turnover in Building Trades," *Industrial Relations* 25 (Fall 1986), pp. 276–289.

59. Lawrence French, David A. Gray, and Robert W. Brobst, *Political Structure and Presidential Tenure in International Unions: A Study of Union Democracy,* paper presented at the annual meeting of the Academy of Management, Detroit, 1980, 16.

60. Phillip L. Quaglieri, "The New People of Power: The Backgrounds and Careers of Top Labor Leaders," *Journal of Labor Research* 9 (Summer 1988), pp. 271–283.

61. Jack Fiorito, Lee P. Stepina, Paul Jarley, John Thomas Delaney, and Mike Knudstrup, "Visions of Success: National Leaders' Views on Union Effectiveness," *Labor Studies Journal* 22 (Spring 1997), pp. 14–16.

62. Labor Union Leaders Well-Paid," *The Enquirer,* June 29, 2004, http://www. enquirer.com. Current salaries may be obtained from the Forms LM-2 Reports by U.S. labor unions, found at http://www.dol.gov/esa, the home page of the U.S. Department of Labor.

63. http://www.aflcio.org/corporatewatch/paywatch/

64. "How Much Pay Union Presidents Receive Varies Widely, Latest LM-2 Forms Show," *Daily Labor Report* (December 17, 2003), pp. C-1–C-8.

65. Paul F. Clark and Lois S. Gray, "Changing Administrative Practices in American Unions: A Research Note," *Industrial Relations,* Vol. 44, No. 4, pp. 654–658.

66. Paul F. Clark and Lois S. Gray, "Union Administration," in *The State of Unions,* eds. George Strauss, Daniel G. Gallagher, and Jack Fiorito (Madison, Wis.: Industrial Relations Research Association, 1992), pp. 179–193.

67. Charles W. Hickman, "Labor Organizations, Fees and Dues," *Monthly Labor Review* 100 (May 1977), pp. 19–24.

68. Ibid., pp. 117–118.

69. James T. Bennett, "Private Sector Unions: The Myth of Decline," *Journal of Labor Research* 12 (Winter 1991), pp. 1–5.

70. Marick F. Masters and Robert S. Atkin, "The Finances of Major U.S. Unions," *Industrial Relations* 36 (October 1997), pp. 502–503.

71. Marick F. Masters, "Union Wealth: The Bargaining Power," *Journal of Labor Research* 18 (Winter 1997), pp. 106–107.

72. Gary Chaison, "Union Mergers and Union Revival," *Rekindling the Movement: Labor's Quest for Relevance*

in the 21st Century, eds. Lowell Turner, Harry C. Katz, and Richard W. Hurd (Ithaca, N.Y.: ILR Press, 2001), pp. 238–240.

73. Gary N. Chaison, "The Form and Frequency of Union Mergers," *Labor Law Journal* 46 (August 1996), pp. 493–497.

74. James W. Robinson, "Structural Characteristics of the Independent Union in America Revisited," *Labor Law Journal* 43 (September 1992), pp. 567–575.

75. Sanford M. Jacoby and Anil Verma, "Enterprise Unions in the United States," *Industrial Relations* 31 (Winter 1992), p. 140.

76. Dana Milbank, "Labor Broadens Its Appeal by Setting Up Associations to Lobby and Offer Services," *The Wall Street Journal,* January 13, 1993, pp. B-1, B-5.

77. Adrienne E. Eaton and Paula B. Voos, "Managerial Unionism: Prospects and Forms," *Labor Studies Journal,* Vol. 29, No. 3 (Fall 2004), pp. 25–56.

78. *This is the AFL-CIO* (Washington, D.C.: American Federation of Labor and Congress of Industrial Organizations, 1992), pp. 1–10.

79. U.S. Department of Labor, Bureau of Labor Statistics, *Directory of National Unions and Employee Associations,* 1975 (Washington, D.C.: U.S. Government Printing Office, 1977), pp. 1–4.

80. Jill Kriesky, "Structural Change in the AFL-CIO: A Regional Study of Union Cities' Impact," *Rekindling the Movement: Labor's Quest for Relevance in the 21st Century,* eds. Lowell Turner, Harry C. Katz, and Richard W. Hurd (Ithaca, N.Y.: ILR Press, 2001), pp. 129–154.

81. Joseph Krislov, "The AFL-CIO Effort to Minimize Union Membership Conflicts: 1962–1987," *Labor Studies Journal* 16 (Summer 1991), pp. 3–5.

82. *This is the AFL-CIO,* pp. 8–10.

83. Leo Troy, "Is the Future of Unionism in Cyberspace?" *Journal of Labor Research* 24, no. 2 (Spring 2003), pp. 268–269.

84. David Greenstone, *Labor in American Politics* (Chicago: University of Chicago Press, 1977), pp. xiii–xxix.

85. Jack Fiorito, "The State of Unions in the United States," *Journal of Labor Research,* Vol. 38, No. 1 (Winter 2007), p. 44–60.

86. Charles R. Greer, "E-Voice: How Information Technology is Shaping Life within Unions," *Journal of Labor Research* 23, no. 2 (Spring 2002), pp. 215–235; Richard Freeman, "Can the Internet Help Unions Rebound?" *Perspectives on Work* 7, no. 1 (2003), pp. 43–49.

87. Arthur B. Shostak, "Today's Unions as Tomorrow's CyberUnion: Labor Newest Hope," *Journal of Labor Research* 23, no. 2 (Spring 2001), pp. 242–243.

88. Gary Chaison, "Information Technology: The Threat to Unions," *Journal of Labor Research* 23, no. 2 (Spring 2002), pp. 251–256.

89. G. A. J. Thieblot, "Perspectives on Union Corruption: Lessons from the Databases," *Journal of Labor Research,* Vol. 27, No. 4 (Fall 2006), pp. 514–531.

90. Paul F. Clark, "Union Image-Building at the Local Level," *Labor Studies Journal* 15 (Fall 1990), p. 55.

91. Phillip B. Wilson, "Conquering the Enemy Within: The Case for Reform of the Landrum-Griffin Act," *Journal of*

Labor Research, Vol. 26, No. 1, Winter 2005, pp. 135–150.

92. Bureau of National Affairs, Inc., *Basic Patterns in Union Contracts* (Washington, D.C.: Bureau of National Affairs Inc., 1995), p. 97.

93. Billie Ann Brotman and Thomas J. McDonagh, "Union Security Clauses as Viewed by the National Labor Relations Board," *Labor Law Journal* 37 (February 1986), pp. 104–115.

94. Jeff Canfield, "Note: What a Sham(e): The Broken Rights System in the Real World Workplace," *Wayne Law Review* 47 (Fall 2001), pp. 1049–1055.

95. *NLRB v. General Motors,* 373 U.S. 734 (1963); *Retail Clerks International Association Local 1625 AFL-CIO v. Schermerhorn* et al., 373 U.S. 746 (1963); and *D. Louis Abood et al v. Detroit Board of Education,* 431 U.S. 209 (1977).

96. *California Saw and Knife Works,* 320 NLRB 224 (1995), enf'd. 133 F.3d 1012 (7th Cir. 1998). See also: "Guidelines Concerning Processing of *Beck* Cases," *Memorandum from the Office of the General Counsel,* August 17, 1998.

97. For further discussion of this issue, see Kenneth A. Kovach and Peter Millspaugh, "Implementing the *Beck* and Lehnert Union Security Agreement Decisions: A Study in Frustration," *Business Horizons* 39 (May/June 1995), pp. 57–65; Jan W. Henkel and Norman J. Wood, "Limitations on the Uses of Union Shop Funds after Ellis: What Activities Are Germane to Collective Bargaining?" *Labor Law Journal* 35 (December 1984), pp. 736–746; Peter Florey, "Fair Share Proceedings: A Case for Common Sense," *Arbitration Journal* 44 (March 1989), pp. 35–44; and David A. Lebowitz, "Limits on the Use of Agency Fees: The Revival of *Communications Workers of America v. Beck,* " *Employee Relations Law Journal* 18 (Winter 1992–1993), pp. 437–461.

98. *UFCW, Locals 951, 7, & 1036 (Meijer, Inc.) and Various Individuals,* 329 NLRB No. 69 (1999).

99. *Lehnert v. Ferris Faculty Association,* 500 U.S. 507 (1991).

100. Bureau of National Affairs, Inc., *Basic Patterns in Union Contracts,* p. 99.

101. For further historical insights into the right-to-work issue, see Gilbert J. Gall, *The Politics of Right to Work* (New York: Greenwood Press, 1988); and William Canak and Berkeley Miller, "Gumbo Politics: Unions, Business, and Louisiana Right-to-Work Legislation," *Industrial and Labor Relations Review* 43 (January 1990), pp. 258–271. For a classification system of right-to-work laws' various dimensions and related bibliography, see Thomas R. Haggard, "Union Security and the Right to Work: A Comprehensive Bibliography," *Journal of Labor Research* 11 (Winter 1990), pp. 81–106.

102. Raymond L. Hogler and Robert LaJeunesse, "Oklahoma's Right to Work Initiative: Labor Policy and Political Ideology," *Labor Law Journal* 53, no. 2 (2002), pp. 109–113. Also see Stan Greer and Charles W. Baird, "Reply to Hogler and LaJeunesse's 'Oklahoma's Right to Work Initiative: Labor Policy and Political Ideology,'" *Labor Law Journal* 54, no. 2 (2003), pp. 89–100.

103. Marc Singer, "Knowledge of the Right-to-Work Law among Residents of the State of Oklahoma," *Journal of*

Collective Negotiations in the Public Sector, Vol. 31, No. 1, 2006, p. 85–99.

104. National Right to Work Committee, "The Voluntarism of Samuel Gompers," (Fairfax, Va., n.d.), p. 1.

105. See, for example, "Supreme Court Reviews Objection to Agency Fee," Bureau of National Affairs Inc., *Daily Labor Report,* May 3, 1982, pp. 2–3. Amendments to the NLRA put restrictions on religious reasons and can require a donation to a charity (other than the religion) equivalent to a fair share of union costs.

106. *The Truth about "Right-to-Work" Laws* (Washington, D.C.: American Federation of Labor and Congress of Industrial Organizations, January 1977), p. i.

107. For related complexities, see William J. Moore, "The Determinants and Effects of Right-to-Work Laws: A Review of the Recent Literature," *Journal of Labor Research* 19 (Summer 1998), pp. 445–469; William J. Moore and Robert J. Newman, "The Effects of Right-to-Work Laws: A Review of the Literature," *Industrial and Labor Relations Review* 38 (July 1985), pp. 571–575; Joe C. Davis and John H. Huston, "Right-to-Work Laws and Union Density: New Evidence from Micro Data," *Journal of Labor Research* 16 (Spring 1995), pp. 223–230; and David T. Ellwood and Glenn Fine, "The Impact of Right-to-Work Laws on Union Organizing," *Journal of Political Economy* 95 (April 1987), pp. 250–274.

108. John T. Delaney, "Redefining the Right-to-Work Debate: Unions and the Dilemma of Free Choice," *Journal of Labor Research* 19 (Summer 1998), pp. 425–442.

109. Reed E. Larson, "Are Right-to-Work Laws Desirable? Yes," in *Contemporary Labor Issues,* eds. Walter Fogel and Archie Kleingartner (Belmont, Calif.: Wadsworth, 1968), p. 272.

110. John M. Jermier, Cynthia Fryer Cohen, Kathleen J. Powers, and Jeannie Gaines, "Paying Dues: Police Unionism in a Right-to-Work Environment," *Industrial Relations* 25 (Fall 1986), pp. 265–276.

111. Gary N. Chaison and Dileep G. Dhavale, "The Choice between Union Membership and Free-Rider Status," *Journal of Labor Research* 13 (Fall 1992), pp. 355–369.

Employee Rights under the Landrum-Griffin Act

CASE STUDY 4-1 Background

Paul Sanchez, a member of Local 1 of the Bartenders Union, speaks Spanish and is not sufficiently bilingual to understand the English language in either written or spoken form. Local 1 has 16,500 members, 48 percent of whom understand Spanish only.

For several years Local 1 has had its collective bargaining agreements, monthly newsletters, and various notices printed in Spanish to accommodate its Spanish-speaking members. At meetings held to nominate union officers and contract ratification meetings, which occur once every three years, English and Spanish translations are provided for the discussion that takes place. Monthly union meetings are conducted primarily in English and are attended by 50–75 members (less than one percent of the Union's total membership). Subjects debated during local union meetings include such topics as union expenditures, salaries of officers, general complaints with particular employers, and various other operational matters. Such debate is commonly referred to as "shop talk."

Spanish translation at monthly meetings is provided whenever union officer nominations take place or whenever Spanish-speaking members request their comments or those of others be translated for the benefit of other members attending the meeting. Such translation duties are typically performed by a bilingual local union officer, rather than hiring an outside, professional translator to be present at each monthly meeting.

Paul Sanchez, along with several other employees, petitioned Local 1's officers to provide a qualified translator who was not a member of the Union at all monthly membership meetings. This person would simultaneously translate all meetings proceedings and discussion into Spanish and English. The Union officers brought the petition request before the members at the next monthly meeting. With the union members in attendance acting as a legislative body in accordance with the Union's constitution and by-laws, Sanchez's proposal to hire a full-time outside translator for the monthly meetings was debated and defeated by a majority vote of those members in attendance. The majority of the members in attendance felt that the cost of hiring an outside translator for every monthly meeting was not justified based on the number of members who typically attended and the availability of bilingual union members who could perform the necessary translation duties upon request.

Union member Sanchez then filed a civil suit in federal court. Sanchez alleged the Union's failure to provide simultaneous translation at the regular monthly union meetings by an independent professional translator was a violation of his equal participation and freedom of speech rights under Title I of the Landrum-Griffin Act.

Relevant Statutory Language—Title I, Sec. 101 (a) Landrum-Griffin Act

(1)*Equal Rights*—*Every member of a labor organization shall have equal rights and privileges within such organization to nominate candidates, to vote in elections or referendums of the labor organization, to attend membership meetings, and to participate in the deliberations and voting upon the business of such meetings, subject to reasonable rules and regulations in such organization's constitution and by-laws.*

(2)*Freedom of Speech and Assembly*—*Every member of any labor organization shall have the right to meet and assemble freely with other members; and to express any views, arguments, or opinions; and to express at meetings of the labor organizations his views, upon candidates in an election of the labor organization or upon any business properly before the meeting, subject to the organization's established and reasonable rules pertaining to the conduct of meetings: Provided, that nothing herein shall be construed to impair the right of a labor organization to adopt and enforce reasonable rules as to the responsibility of every member toward the organization as an institution and to his refraining from conduct that would interfere with its performance of its legal or contractual obligations.*

Title IV, Section 401 (e) Landrum-Griffin Act states in relevant part, "In any election ... a reasonable opportunity shall be given for the nomination of candidates and every member in good standing shall be eligible to be a candidate and to hold office (... subject to reasonable qualifications uniformly imposed)."

Questions

1. Did the Union violate Title I, Section 101 (a) of the Landrum-Griffin Act in this case? If so, what should be the appropriate remedy?

2. Would it be legal under Title IV of the Landrum-Griffin Act for the union in this case to adopt a rule that required all candidates for union office to be proficient in both Spanish and English? Why or why not?

Financial Core Membership Rights under the *Beck* Decision

CASE STUDY 4-2 Background

The company and union are parties to a collective bargaining agreement that contains the following valid union security clause:

> *It shall be a condition of employment that all employees of the company covered by this agreement who are members of the union in good standing on the date of this agreement shall remain members in good standing, and those who are not members on the effective date of this agreement shall, on the ninety-first (91st) day following the effective date of this agreement, become and remain members in good standing in the union.*
>
> *For purposes of this Agreement, an employee shall lose his good standing in the Union only for failure to tender periodic dues and initiation fees uniformly required of all members. The Business Manager of the Union shall notify the Company by certified mail of any employees the union deems to have lost "good standing" within the meaning of this Article.*

On July 6, an employee named Budnik sent a letter to the union informing the union officers that he was resigning his union membership and claiming financial core member status. Budnik requested the union to begin charging him the "new appropriate amount" of dues in compliance with *Beck* (1988). Budnik did not pay any dues money to the union after he mailed the July 6 letter.

On July 28, the company sent a letter to all bargaining unit members informing them that financial core membership status was available to them and that full union membership was not a legal requirement under the parties' current union security contract language. The union sent a letter to Budnik on or about August 5 acknowledging receipt of Budnik's resignation letter. The union informed Budnik that his insistence on financial core membership status would result in the loss of valuable membership privileges and benefits and that, as a financial core member, he would still be required "to pay the financial obligations of membership germane to the costs of collective bargaining, contract administration, and grievance adjustment." The union encouraged Budnik to reconsider his decision to resign his union membership. The union's letter closed with the disclosure that the union was currently undergoing its annual financial audit and that, when that process was completed, all the expenses germane to collective bargaining duties would be identified.

The following February 23, the Union sent a letter to Budnik and advised him that, despite his resignation from the union, he was still required to comply with the terms of the current union security clause. The union offered to let Budnik pay a sum equal to current monthly union dues to a "mutually agreed upon charity." The union listed three charitable funds acceptable to it. Budnik did not agree to the Union's proposal and, instead, quit his job at the company and filed an unfair labor practice against the union alleging a violation of Sec. 8 (b)(1)(A) of the Labor-Management Relations Act (LMRA). Specifically, Budnik alleged that the union failed to meet the requirements set forth in *Beck* regarding a union's duty to furnish information about the amount of dues money spent for legitimate collective bargaining purposes or to provide a procedure by which employees like himself could challenge the amount charged or the basis for calculating such charges.

In *Communications Workers v. Beck*, 487 U.S. 735 (1988), the Court upheld an interpretation that the LMRA does not permit a union, over the objection of a dues-paying nonmember, to expend funds collected from them under a union security agreement on activities not related to collective bargaining, contract administration, or grievance adjustment. In *California Saw & Knife Works*, 320 NLRB 222 (1995), the Board held that if a nonmember employee chooses to file a *Beck* objection to the payment of full union dues, the employee must be informed by the Union of the following information: the percentage of the reduction in fees for objecting nonmembers, the basis for the union's calculation, and the right to challenge these figures. Any union-provided procedure for challenging the amount or method of dues calculation is appropriate so long as the procedure is not shown to be arbitrary, discriminatory, or in bad faith.

The Union cited the NLRB decision *Laborers Local 265 and Fred A. Newmann Co.*, in which the Board held that a union did not breach its duty of fair representation by failing to provide a *Beck* objector with *Beck*-related financial information, where the union expressly waived the objector's obligations under the union security clause and informed the objector that he would not be required to pay any dues or fees. The union noted that Budnik is the only employee, out of the 300

bargaining unit members the union represents, to request financial core membership status. The union believed that the cost burden of gathering *Beck*-related financial information for use by a single employee would be prohibitive and detrimental to the union's obligation to use resources wisely to represent the bargaining interest of all bargaining unit members. The union believed that it had offered Budnik a reasonable accommodation that did not require him to pay any dues money to the union, thus ensuring that none of the objecting member's funds would be used for union expenditures. At the same time, the reasonable accommodation offered by the union avoided the necessity of spending union funds to gather *Beck*-related financial information for only one employee. The union requested that the unfair labor practice charge be dismissed.

Questions

1. What are the union's legal obligations?
2. Did the union commit an Unfair Labor Practice in this case? If so, what should be the appropriate remedy?

CHAPTER 5

Why and How Unions Are Organized

This chapter focuses on the essential elements of unionization: why unions are formed, the procedures for organizing employees into unions, new union strategies for obtaining union recognition, and union decertification.

The chapter highlights employees' choices: (1) whether to become involved in union formation where there is no union, and (2) whether to vote for or against union representation if and when there is a representation election. Although an employee's choices to assist in the formation of a union, to vote for a union, and to join a union are highly interrelated, they are separate decisions. Employees may join unions voluntarily or be required to join. The circumstances in which an employee may be required to join a union were covered in Chapter 4. Employees who vote for union representation in an election in which the union loses are nevertheless left without union representation.

WHY UNIONS ARE FORMED

Unions are not present in every organization; in many instances, employees have chosen to remain nonunion. This section provides explanations of employees' collective behavior that cut across many organizations; the following section attempts to explain what motivates employees at a particular facility to vote for a union.

Work and Job Conditions Explanation

Alienation Theory

The **alienation theory** is based on the belief that employees might seek collective action to relieve their feelings of alienation, which have resulted from the extensive use of machinery in manufacturing operations. Employees became alienated from their work because of the following reasons:[1]

- They lost contact with their own labor when the products they created were taken away from them, thereby reducing their spirit and status.

- They lost involvement in their work when the machine dominated, separating the work of the hand from the work of the brain.

- They became estranged from fellow employees when their work made them so tired and competitive that they were incapable of having authentic relationships.

As a result, employees might become aware of their common plight, and class consciousness could compel them to join together in a union or to engage in collective activities to improve their working situation. Unions can and do address a possible aspect of employee alienation, namely the employees' desire to speak their minds without fear of management reprisal. In other words, "intertwined with the motives for union membership is the almost universal desire to tell the boss to 'go to hell.' "[2] A union typically indicates to its potential members that the employees' rights to voice their opinions on a managerial action are protected by negotiated grievance procedures and disciplinary policies (see Chapters 10 and 12).

Employees might be dissatisfied with some aspect of their jobs while not being alienated from their work. Some research has shown that employees might join unions if they (1) are dissatisfied with physical characteristics of the workplace, low wages, or lack of benefits and (2) believe that a union will help them achieve the job-related conditions important to them.[3]

Employees who are not satisfied with their pay, supervision, and/or work may view the union as the instrument to satisfy their job needs. Some researchers have argued that job dissatisfaction is the beginning of employees' efforts to start a union formation campaign. They argue that job dissatisfaction sets in motion a search to end the uncomfortable dissonance between what is desired (good pay, effective supervision, and so on) and what they are experiencing. Job dissatisfaction results in the formation of a coalition of employees designed to bring about changes in economic and working conditions.[4]

A survey of 3,372 unrepresented employees and union members showed that "employees who are less satisfied with the companies for which they work have greater desire to join a union." The researchers also found a negative relationship between work attitudes, such as company commitment, and desire to join a union.[5]

Scarcity Consciousness Theory—The Need for Job Security

In his classic book, *A Theory of the Labor Movement,* Selig Perlman suggested that employees are attracted to unions on the assumption that unions will protect their jobs. Many employees, particularly manual workers, strongly believe they are living in a country of limited opportunity and become scarcity conscious— the employees collectively believe that jobs are difficult to obtain and retain. This belief is particularly true today for some industries, such as auto, steel, and coal. Thus, employees turn to unions for job protection.[6]

Unions therefore are attractive to the many employees concerned about job security, regardless of their skill or occupational level. Few employees, including white-collar employees and managers, are currently immune from the possibility of a layoff. Also, unions do offer several ways of strengthening employees' job security: For example, a union can negotiate work rules which prescribe procedures for performing a job, thereby ensuring that a certain number of employees will be assigned work. Unions can negotiate apprenticeship programs, which ensure that qualified people are available for certain skilled jobs or negotiate seniority and layoff provisions, which require the company to lay off employees by their seniority and to recall the most senior ones first. A union can negotiate grievance procedures, which include a final step of arbitration to protect them against unjust discharges, unfair treatment, and violations of the labor agreement. Unions can also lobby for legislation protecting employees' job rights, in regard to such issues as plant closings and employment discrimination, which has been a viable alternative used by unions throughout the years. Legislation or administrative policies can restrict employer access to cheap labor, strengthen job security by pressing for restrictions—foreign citizens, child labor, prison labor—impose quotas or restrictions against imported products such as steel, automobiles, and textiles, and provide adjustment assistance to employees who are displaced as a result of foreign competition.

Wheeler Model of Union Formation

Hoyt Wheeler has provided a theoretical basis for union formation that entails a two-stage process. The first stage consists of the worker's readiness to take some form of aggressive action; the second stage represents that worker coming together with other workers as a group and deciding to take some form of collective action. A single employee usually begins to move toward unionization when he or she experiences feelings of deprivation about pay, security, and/ or respect. The individual employee's thought process can be viewed as taking the individual along one or more possible paths toward readiness to take some form of aggressive action to demonstrate anger at the employer. The employee may take the path toward collective action and supporting the union under certain conditions.

Deprivation at work may occur when there is a gap between what employees expect from their work and what they receive in return. Three paths connect deprivation and readiness to take action. The first path is a "threat" or an "attack"; this results when the employer takes away or threatens to take away something the workers already have. The second path is "frustration," which results when workers try to act on their own behalf. Their action is blocked or ignored and they have no voice and see no way of achieving effective voice as individuals. The third path is "rational calculation," which does not involve anger, but the workers become convinced that the benefits of unionization outweigh its costs.

Even though workers may mobilize along one of these paths, they may not choose unionization. Instead, they may choose some form of withdrawal, such as quitting their job, or revenge behavior, such as sabotaging the company's products. The conditions that promote collective action or unionization are love, hope, and saliency. Love is essentially the cohesion and solidarity wherein workers care enough for each other to act together and share good relationships. Hope prevails when workers believe that the union can do what is necessary to bring an end to their deprivation and frustrations. Saliency is recognition that problems exist and workers perceive that dramatic events and good leadership would contribute to facilitating action toward resolution.

Along with each of these conditions, which promote the union option, there are inhibiting conditions. One such condition is the fear of punishment for supporting the union, such as losing one's job or being laid off. Another is the general belief that "unions are wrong in principle." Either of these beliefs may dissuade a worker or a group of workers from taking action. The interaction of the workers' beliefs, their chosen paths, and the existing conditions may lead a group of workers toward collective action and unionization.[7]

Employees' Backgrounds and Needs

Employees' previous experiences with unions can strongly affect their attitudes toward unions and their decision to join one. Eighty-seven percent of those who have had experience with unions, usually as members, said they would vote for a union if given a choice; only 27 percent of those who have had no experience with unions would vote for the union if given the choice.[8]

Many might even be influenced by parental attitudes and family experiences with unions. One active union member stated, "I attended union meetings with my father before I was ever inside a church." Another commented, "My dad was a great union man and that's where I got it—if it wasn't union, it wasn't no good."[9] Of course, parental comments about unions may be unfavorable as well.

Unions, like all formal organizations, potentially satisfy the members' needs by providing a means of enhancing a sense of identity and maintaining self-esteem. Thus, unions can appeal to three interrelated social needs of members: the need for affiliation, or belonging; the need for status; and the need to belong to something purposeful, useful, and creative that is on a higher level than improved wages and working conditions.

The union's possible benefit of social affiliation is strengthened or weakened by the degree of prestige or self-esteem it offers its members. Some employees join a union for the same reason they would join any social organization, namely, to enjoy the responsibility and status associated with being a member of that organization. This feature can be particularly attractive to employees whose jobs are basically interchangeable and carry very few elements of prestige or room for advancement.

Employees who become union officers can often attain prestige or self-esteem in their dealings with management officials:

> As a shop steward or union officer or member of the grievance committee, a worker can become "a fellow your buddies look to." Such positions give him the opportunity to win other workers' approval by being "a fellow who stands up to the boss" with impunity. The role of "a fellow who stands up to the boss" is made more significant because the definition of the boss has been enlarged to include not merely the foreman but "the head office in Pittsburgh." He can win prestige as "a guy that gets results" in such matters as the distribution of work, assignment to jobs, seniority policy, and protection from discrimination.[10]

Chapter 10 discusses the notion that union officers and management officials are equals in their day-to-day administration of the labor agreement. However, as the preceding quotation suggests, the union steward can often emphatically disagree with a management official six levels above the steward on the organizational chart. This ability to challenge without fear of reprisal is not usually afforded nonunion employees or even management officials when they deal with their organizational superiors.

Studies of employee characteristics associated with employee votes have been mixed. Some have shown that employees' characteristics such as age, gender, and education are not closely associated with favorable union votes or attitudes.[11] Race appears to be the one exception—several studies have suggested that more black employees have positive attitudes toward potential union advantages than their white counterparts.[12] Other studies indicate that young people are more likely to support unions, and women are less likely to support unions.[13]

PROCEDURES FOR ORGANIZING UNIONS

In forming and joining a union, employees mainly consider whether the union will improve their personal situations in terms of wages and benefits, promotional opportunities, and job security. Can the employees expect to satisfy their job-related goals and needs by supporting a union? Will the union provide the means for achieving these goals? If employees perceive that a union will help them attain their goals, they will likely vote for it in an election and support its activities afterward. If they are not convinced, they will not vote for the union and will not support its activities.

The union's campaign to secure employee support may contribute to a union vote, especially among those who are familiar with the union's positions and who attend union campaign meetings. Employees who are satisfied with working conditions are less likely to attend union campaign meetings, but if they attend, they often become more favorable toward the union.

The company's campaign can affect the vote because it affects employees' belief in the anticipated influence of the union. If the company campaigns hard, some employees will believe that the employer has "seen the light" and will now improve conditions without the union. A strong anti-union campaign may convince some employees that the employer is so anti-union that the union cannot improve working conditions.[14]

Although there may be many reasons why a particular group of employees votes for or against the union in a specific election, several influences have been identified that affect union votes generally. Exhibit 5.1 shows the relationships among the general influences on employees.

Researchers have argued that social pressure influences employee votes. When employees know a number of union supporters within a work group,

Exhibit 5.1
Influences on Employees on Whether to Vote For or Against a Union

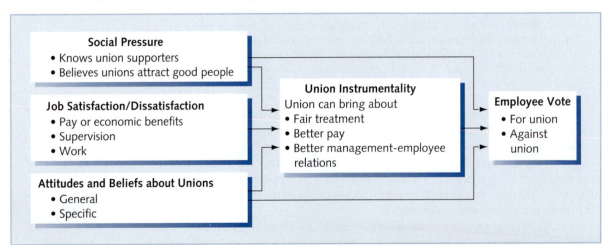

this knowledge helps to form group cohesion. When this group of employees is regularly blocked by employer actions, they respond as a group, and their actions can lead to union formation. As union supporters, they are better able to convince others that the union has the power to bring about changes in the workplace and are more convincing in influencing other employees' votes.

General beliefs about unions mean that an employee believes, for example, that a union will improve wages, benefits, and working conditions; provide a return to the employee for the dues paid; and secure pro-employee legislation. These general beliefs include whether an employee believes unions are autocratic, increase the risks of a plant closing, stifle individual initiatives, or ignore the members in strike decisions. To influence employees' general beliefs about unions, union organizers should place more effort on national campaigns, such as the "Union Yes" campaign of the American Federation of Labor–Congress of Industrial Organizations (AFL-CIO).

Specific beliefs about unions are more related to an individual's job and workplace. To influence employees' specific beliefs about unions, union organizers should focus attention on communicating the union's unique characteristics and its impact at the workplace. Specific beliefs that can be focused on include expectations about improvement in pay, benefits, and job security as a result of unionization.[15] Other beliefs include expected improvement in recognition, job advancement, worker participation, treatment by supervisors, and reduction in sexual and racial discrimination on the job.

In an organizing campaign, unions need to show employees that significant positive results will occur at their workplace if they vote for and join a union. Unions must promote the union's ability not only to improve wages and benefits but to help make work more meaningful and increase employee participation. At the same time, the employer will attempt to show that it has acted reasonably toward employees and has been fair and sincere in dealings with employees.[16]

Social pressure, job dissatisfaction, and general and specific beliefs about unions interact with **union instrumentality**, which is the employees' perception of whether the union will be instrumental in attaining desired outcomes, such as higher wages, improved working conditions, job security, and protection from arbitrary treatment by management.[17] In general, if these interactions are positive, the employee will vote for the union; if not, the employee will vote against it.[18] For the individual employee, any one of the influences may cause the employee to vote a certain way. For example, if an employee believes his or her supervisor is considerate and supportive, this belief may be enough to cause a vote against union representation.[19]

An individual's decision on whether to vote for union representation depends on his or her subjective assessment of the benefits to be obtained as weighed against the subjective assessment of the cost. If the expected benefits are higher than the cost, the employee will vote for the union. Otherwise, the vote will be against representation. If employees have a good chance of promotion, can expect a higher wage based on their present level of effort, and are pleased with their supervisor, they probably will not vote for union representation.

The Union's Challenge of Organizing the Diverse Workforce

Unions recognize that some occupations, such as retail sales, registered nursing, janitorial services, and food services, are expected to expand. In addition, one-fourth of all workers in the United States are part-time employees; these employees are hired on a temporary basis (referred to by many as "contingent workers"), are independent contractors, and are hired as subcontractors or leased workers. As noted earlier, minorities and skilled employees will also become a larger percentage of the work force. In fact, in 2000, one-fourth of the work force was minorities, and the greatest increases came from the Hispanic and Asian populations. Unions must design organizing strategies to attract these employees.[20]

Organizing Professional Employees

Professional employees provide a challenge to unions and an opportunity to increase union membership. Although unions have made significant inroads in many professions, such as acting, professional sports, writing, music, nursing, and teaching, debate continues over the compatibility of unionism with professionalism. Excellent arguments have been conveyed on both ends of the continuum, and unions must successfully address these concerns before they will increase the memberships of professional employee unions. On one side is the argument that the selection of a union entails the rejection of key professional values, such as collegial participation in organizational decision making, professional independence, and a merit-based performance and reward system. On the other side is the argument that collective bargaining is often the most effective method of achieving and maintaining these same professional values.[21]

Professional employees provide a fertile ground for increased unionization because professional employment has been growing rapidly. Between 1983 and 2003, the number of professional employees (excluding teachers) grew 78.7 percent, while the number of all employees grew by 35.9 percent. During the same period, union membership among professionals grew by 38.2 percent, while union membership among all employees fell by 9.8 percent. A survey of 2,014 members of the American Pharmacists Association revealed that general beliefs (such as benefits of a free labor union in a democratic society or the market imperfections brought about through collective bargaining) about unions have a stronger direct effect on union voting intentions among professionals than specific beliefs. (What will I gain if my workplace becomes unionized?) Among other employees, both general and specific beliefs are important in predicting how an individual will vote in a union election; however, specific beliefs have a stronger effect. In addition, the researchers found that co-worker support among professionals had a large impact on union voting behavior. This supports the notion that unions should focus their organizing efforts on cultivating support among incumbent employees and develop a stronger positive presence within a profession (such as union's involvement in the leadership and governance in the profession and active participation as an advocate for the profession).[22]

Evidence drawn from a study of collective bargaining agreements covering professional employees reveals that the overwhelming majority of contract provisions include subjects quite similar to those traditionally held in industrial sector agreements. These provisions include wages, fringe benefits, grievance-arbitration procedures, and so on. In addition to those traditional subjects, these agreements also address professional issues. These issues can be categorized into six groups: (1) professional standards, (2) mechanisms for professional participation in policy making, (3) regulation of professional work, (4) training and professional development, (5) commitment of organizational resources to professional goals, and (6) criteria for personnel decisions and the role of professionals in making these decisions. The conclusion was that, although there is variation in the collective bargaining agreements among professional employee unions, unionism and professionalism are not inherently incompatible. Moreover, professional values and interests can be incorporated into the bargaining process along with the economic and job security issues of professional employees. With concrete evidence of compatibility between professionalism and unionism, the opportunity is present for unions to promote their product and services.[23] A successful union organizing campaign of professional employees is presented in the Labor Relations in Action feature on page 216.

Activities of the Union in Organizing Employees

Employees' initial interest in unionization is usually based on their present dissatisfaction with some work-related situation coupled with a belief that each employee acting alone cannot change the current situation. The union does not create this dissatisfaction with working conditions among employees; instead, it is in the union's interest to improve job satisfaction among employees by negotiating to improve working conditions. Therefore, during an organizing campaign, the union advertises the benefits that would flow from a negotiated collective bargaining agreement and successful handling of grievances.[24]

Most managers of nonunion companies incorrectly believe that labor unions initiate union organization drives; instead it is usually the employees themselves who begin the process by contacting the union. This contact with union organizers usually occurs after the employees believe that there is sufficient support for the union and that the union's expertise and representation will help them.[25]

Union organizers enter the campaign by playing three general roles that influence employees' decisions on whether to vote for unionization. First, organizers try to educate the workers on the benefits of the union, labor movement traditions, and protections afforded by union representation and the present laws. Next, union organizers attempt to persuade workers to vote for unionization and respond to statements and allegations made by management during the organizing campaign. Third, organizers try to support workers in their individual and collective actions.[26] To ensure that these roles are carried out capably, unions recruit and select union organizers with the appropriate education, competencies, and personality characteristics.

Unions, especially those in the service industries, are hiring union organizers who have different characteristics from the traditional union organizers in manufacturing. Service union organizers are almost 15 years younger on average, ten times more likely to be female, average almost four more years of education, and have an average of about seven fewer years of union-organizing experience. They are six times less likely to have held elected positions in local unions and are less than half as likely to have served in appointed positions in local or national unions. Although nearly all of the union organizers in manufacturing were rank-and-file members early in their careers, only about half of the union organizers in the service industries were rank-and-file members.[27]

Union organizers must recognize that the workforce has changed sharply and has become more complex. Employees do not typically have a homogeneous set of problems; they are widely diverse. As well, the growth industry sectors and occupations are different from those that have been traditional strongholds for unions, such as manufacturing, mining, trucking, shipping, railroads, and construction. As a result, the selection of staff members to work as union organizers has changed. Instead of appointing staff members as political rewards, unions are selecting union organizers not only from the rank-and-file members but also from colleges, law schools, Volunteers in Service to America (VISTA), and other sources. Unions are then investing funds in training union organizers at the AFL-CIO's George Meany Center and improving their organizing capability through training at the newly created AFL-CIO's Organizing Institute (Exhibit 5.2).[28]

Exhibit 5.2

AFL-CIO Organizing Institute Informational Flier

Answers to Common Questions about the AFL-CIO Organizing Institute

What is the Organizing Institute?

The Organizing Institute was created in the fall of 1989 to promote and foster union organizing. In November of that year, we held the first weekend training session for people interested in a career as union organizers. Since then, we have developed a highly selective program to recruit and train a new generation of union organizers, to place them for training on the campaigns of designated unions, and to facilitate job matches for graduates into full-time, paid positions as union organizers with international unions affiliated with the AFL-CIO. In addition to this program, this Institute also has a variety of other programs designed to assist unions in the area of external organizing.

What does a union organizer do?

Union organizers assist workers in gaining union recognition at their work site. Where workers do not currently have a union, a union organizer will work with employees to build support and leadership to form their own local union, usually in the face of intense employer opposition. The union must prove it represents a majority and get recognition from the employer. This often, but not exclusively, happens through a secret ballot election held at the workplace. Ultimately, the goal is to win a binding agreement between the workers and their employer that includes real improvements in the living and working conditions of the employees.

What unions are participating in the Organizing Institute training program?

The following unions directly participate in the training program by providing internship and apprentice campaigns and hiring graduates: American Federation of State, County, and Municipal Employees (AFSCME), American Federation of Teachers (AFT), Communications Workers of America (CWA), International Longshoremen's and Warehousemen's Union (ILWU), United Auto Workers (UAW), United Mine Workers of America (UMWA), and United Steelworkers of America (USWA), Oil, Chemical, Atomic Workers (OCAW.

How often are the three-day training weekends held?

The three-day trainings are held each month in various locations. They are held regularly in Washington, D.C., and in San Francisco. Other sites where we have held trainings include Chicago, Los Angeles, New York, and Atlanta.

What is the weekend session like? What are the costs?

The three-day training is an intense and fascinating look at what it takes to be a union organizer. The sessions themselves are led by senior organizers from among the unions in the program. The talent and enthusiasm of the participants are a large part of the overall success of the weekend. Institute staff meet individually with participants on Sunday afternoon. The cost of the training, including housing and meals, are paid by the Organizing Institute. Travel to and from the training is the responsibility of the applicant.

How does job placement work?

The unions have told us that they are in need of talented and committed organizers to wage the battle for union recognition. Our track record on job matches for graduates bears out this claim. Over 95 percent of Institute graduates have been

(Continued)

Exhibit 5.2

(Continued)

placed. The unions in the program are notified of all graduates. They then contact the apprentice to arrange interviews. You should notify the Institute if you
have any preferences in selecting a position. This program works because it is directly linked to employment opportunities in union organizing. Unions and applicants alike are interested in the program because of the job-match component.

How much travel is involved?
The jobs vary by union and by location within a union. However, most jobs require
the organizer to be available to work on the road at times, and in some jobs the
organizer will work away from home most of the time. Even when working from
home, long days, including regular evening and weekend work, is standard. Most
unions look for flexibility in travel and relocation. The pay ranges from $18,000
to $30,000 per year plus benefits.

SOURCE: http://www.aflcio.org/.

The union organizer does not create job dissatisfaction but rather assists in
transforming this employee dissatisfaction into collective action. The union organizer tailors the organizing approach to employee concerns and problems and focuses on the special needs of various groups, such as older workers, female or
minority workers, or white-collar workers. The organizer tries to sell the idea
that group action via the union provides the instrument through which employee
concerns and dissatisfaction can be most effectively addressed.[29]

The influence of union organizers should never be underestimated by a company. The union organizers may be first seen distributing handbills to employees
as they leave the company parking lots. Union organizers dress like the target employee group so that the employees will identify with them. Although their dress
may be misleading, management should realize that union organizers are professionals at what they do. Like their counterparts in management, contemporary
union organizers must understand the psychology of the workplace and the
labor relations climate in which employees work. Union organizers must be
able to (1) sort out these complex factors for the employees on a group or individual basis and (2) communicate in the employees' language how the union can
assist in fulfilling their needs in the specific work environment.

As an example, Exhibit 5.3 lists a number of work-related concerns and problems. To the right of each is a possible course of action the union could take to
satisfy the concern or to alleviate the problem. The union organizer would bring
to the employees' attention outcomes that could result from such activities by
the union on their behalf.

The union enters the organizing campaign knowing that it must convince the
uncommitted employees that the union is composed not of outsiders but of concerned fellow employees, that the changes the union proposes are worth fighting
for, that the union will be able to protect employees against reprisals, and that
union officials can be trusted. The union realizes that its success depends on
the development of a strong inside organizing committee to convey the message
directly to employees who do not attend union meetings, and on the ability of the
union organizer to convey his or her own personal commitment and concern, get
to know the employees, listen to employees about their job concerns, and have
employees themselves speak at public meetings to express their feelings and
their commitment to the cause.

Researcher Kate Bronfenbrenner has identified union campaign tactics
characterized as the "rank-and-file intensive strategy," which yields a higher
union win rate than other tactics. This strategy focuses on representative

Exhibit 5.3

Union Strategy and Courses of Action to Achieve Employee Goals and Resolve Job-Related Concerns

Examples of Work-Related Problems and Employee Concerns	Actions by Unions to Encourage Employees to Join Union
Relations between employees and management are poor. Employees do not trust their employer's promises.	Union will represent the interests of employees to management. Union will negotiate a contract requiring management to abide by its agreements.
Employees prefer to deal with management as a group.	Union provides an opportunity for individual employees to deal as a group with the employer.
Employees want to have more influence in workplace decisions.	Union provides a mechanism for influence by collective bargaining and administering the agreement.
Employees feel that productivity improvement would be more effective if employees had more say in how programs are run. Employees question the effectiveness of the company's system for resolving employee problems and grievances.	Union provides a mechanism in which employees can provide input into those issues that affect the workplace. Unions typically negotiate a grievance procedure that provides representation of employees at each step and hearings before an outside, neutral arbitrator.

SOURCE: Richard B. Freeman and Joel Rogers, *Worker Representation and Participation Survey*, Princeton, N.J.: Princeton Survey Research Associates, 1994.

leadership, personal contact, dignity and justice, and building an active union presence in the workplace. This strategy generates the worker participation and commitment necessary to withstand aggressive employer anti-union campaigns and to counteract any anti-union aspects of the economic, political, and legal climate. The components of the strategy are associated with union win rates, which are 12 to 26 percent higher than union win rates that do not employ this strategy (Exhibit 5.4).[30]

Activities of the Company in Union Organizing

The employer realizes that the keys to its success are whether it is able to sustain and increase employees' concern about how the union would perform if chosen and whether it can convince employees that the employer's past record shows that it deserves their support or at least a second chance.

Positive human resource management practices, such as job enrichment/enlargement, internal promotions, learning opportunities, bonus and merit pay, and employee involvement programs, seem to reduce nonunion workers' desire to vote for a union in a representation election.[31] The employer enters the campaign with three advantages: (1) it has instant and prolonged access to the employees; (2) although it can make no promises during the election campaign, it informs employees of the possibility of improvement without cost and without the creation of a new bureaucracy; and (3) it can take advantage of the fact that most people find the thought of substantial change in their lives frightening.[32]

Employer campaign tactics attempt to avert an employee vote in favor of unionization. Usually more than one campaign activity must be used. The

Exhibit 5.4

Components of "Rank-and-File Intensive Strategy" That Are Associated with Higher Union Win Rates

1. Use of representative committees to be more in touch with concerns of the bargaining unit as a whole, to have better access to employees at the workplace, and to demonstrate to the employees that the union is a democratic and inclusive organization

2. Person-to-person contact, house calls, and small-group meetings

3. Conducting union bargaining surveys, selection of the bargaining committee, and working with rank and file to develop proposals before election

4. Focus on issues, such as dignity, justice, discrimination, fairness, or service quality

5. Serious commitment of staff and financial resources to organizing, involvement of the international in union local campaigns, and training, recruitment, and effective utilization of rank-and-file volunteers from already organized bargaining units

6. Use of solidarity days (designated days to wear union buttons, hats, T-shirts, arm bands, etc.)

SOURCE: Kate Bronfenbrenner, "The Role of Union Strategies in NLRB Elections," *Industrial and Labor Relations Review* 50 (January 1997), pp. 195–211; Kate Bronfenbrenner and Tom Juravich, "It Takes More Than House Calls: Organizing to Win with a Comprehensive Union-Building Strategy," *Organizing to Win*, eds. Kate Bronfenbrenner, et al. (Ithaca, N.Y.: Cornell University Press, 1999), pp. 33–34.

most commonly used employer tactics are hiring a labor lawyer, spreading rumors about loss of jobs, and spreading rumors about store or plant closings. In terms of making a difference in the outcome of the election, employees are more likely not to choose the union when the employer spreads rumors about a store or plant closing. However, employees are more likely to choose the union when the employer intentionally delays the election and when the unions work closely with community leaders to facilitate community acceptance of the union. Two employer tactics that have backfired and are associated with employees' vote for the union are shifting work and jobs to other facilities and testing applicants to identify union sympathizers.[33]

Employers frequently use the "second chance" strategy. When the employer's past record has not been good for employees and problems clearly exist, the "second chance" strategy encourages the employer to admit that conditions could be better and request employees to give the employer a "second chance" to do better. Often, employees are inclined to give management another chance now that management is listening. This is a one-time-use only strategy. If the employees vote "no union" and the employer does not make necessary changes, then another election will follow after 12 months and the second time employees won't be listening to much of any thing from management.

Also, certain employer practices have their effect on the election. For example, the employer can influence the election outcome by changing the election unit composition and the date of the election, but only modestly influence the election outcome by such activities as publicizing the disadvantages of the union, displaying posters, and making campaign speeches. Companies must be cautious in election campaigns because they may overdo their resistance and cause a negative reaction from employees, especially when both attorneys and management consultants are used.[34] Thus, if employers overreact to a union's campaign with suppressive tactics, such overreaction may create a more favorable climate for unionization.[35]

LABOR RELATIONS IN ACTION

A Union Organizing Success: A Story of the Organization of Home Care Professionals (OHCP)

The story of the OHCP is a compelling example of the potential for unionizing professional employees when they experience the restructuring of labor markets and reorganization of their work. The impetus for collective action was the desire for a voice in key decisions about the organization of work and the delivery of professional services.

The OHCP was formed by a group of 80 physical therapists, occupational therapists, and speech therapists who worked for a hospital-based home care company. These therapists spend most of their working hours alone in their cars or with their patients at their homes. They go to the office once a month for staff meetings and drop off paperwork every other day. Before the organizing campaign, only a few knew each other personally.

In the summer of 2000, the company announced changes in procedures and workload; these changes concerned the therapists because of their impact on their work and the quality of patient care. Then, the company announced a 20 percent cut in pay. The therapists asked for a meeting with management, but the therapists were told that the pay cut would stand and there was nothing more to discuss.

The following month, about 60 therapists met in a borrowed church basement to consider forming a union. A labor lawyer attended and explained their legal rights and the procedures for establishing a collective bargaining unit. The therapists elected an executive committee and adopted a dues structure. A set of bylaws was adopted, and the executive committee composed a letter to the company CEO informing her

of the OHCP's existence and asking for recognition of the OHCP.

After five days and no response from the company, the OHCP sent a petition to the NLRB. Then, the CEO called and asked for a meeting with the executive committee. At the meeting, the HR manager asked, "What would it take for you to abandon this whole project?" Afterwards the OHCP filed an unfair labor practice charge because the OHCP leaders felt like the HR manager was attempting to bribe the OHCP leaders and interfere with employees exercise of their rights under the LMRA. (The NLRB ruled that the company had committed an unfair labor practice.)

A representation election was scheduled by the NLRB. The company hired an out-of-state lawyer to advise its management during the campaign. During the campaign, therapists were called to the manager's office and questioned about loyalties, relationships, beliefs, and interests in the union. The CEO made frequent visits to team meetings. The company sent printed materials to the therapists' homes; one piece warned of what might happen in case of a strike. Managers telephoned individual therapists, asking them to vote no and telling therapists how sad it would be to create a division between management and employees if a union came into play. The OHCP continued to hold meetings and formed needed committees, such as a fund-raising committee that held garage sales to pay for campaign literature and pay the attorney's fee.

On the weekend before the election, all bargaining unit members were called and reminded to vote. In October 2000, the NLRB held the election; the OHCP assembled at the company headquarters to observe the vote counting by the NLRB official. When the votes were counted, the OHCP won with 83 yes to 16 no.

After its victory, the OHCP set up a listserve for members for rapid communication. A college-aged child of one of the members set up and maintained the OHCP Web site,

---

The use of consultants in organizational campaigns has increased dramatically. One study reported that most elections studied were directed by consultants. In these campaigns, employer unfair labor practices were committed in over half of the elections, and companies actively resisted the union by making captive audience speeches and writing letters to employees in nearly all of the cases.[36] Use of consultants to advise employers how to persuade employees not to vote for a union requires reports to be filed with the Secretary of Labor, even though the consultants have no direct contact with employees.[37]

Attorneys who specialize in union avoidance campaigns are often employed either to offer advice on questions of labor law or to devise strategy and conduct the union avoidance campaign. In addition, attorneys may offer legal advice; plan

which contained a secure portion with a password for members only. During the negotiations, the negotiating team put out bargaining bulletins after each bargaining session. The OHCP was able to obtain addresses of 400 referring physicians; they received a letter explaining the OHCP's goals and asking for their support. National and local professional organizations were informed of the OHCP, and one executive director wrote a personal letter to the CEO to express his concern about the pay cut and its impact on quality of care. An article was printed in a professional journal that was mailed to about 100,000 members. Members attended meetings of local professional groups to share information. A letter was written to all licensed therapists in the area, asking them not to be replacement workers in case of a strike. Assistance from local established unions, such as picketers and the printing of handbills, was obtained. The OHCP handbilled the hospitals to inform staff members and patients of OHCP's goals.

By September 2001, there was still no collective bargaining agreement. The members of the OHCP decided to affiliate with the Communications Workers of America (CWA), and the CWA furnished two experienced bargainers, legal advice, printing resources, a toll-fee telephone number, mailings, and office space. After two more months of negotiations and no agreement, a strike authorization vote was taken. Members of the executive committee met several times per week in each other's homes. There were daily e-mail and phone contacts. Bulletin board messages that responded to management messages were posted. There was a "thought of the day" posted to address a specific issue that may arise. The OHCP used its Web site and obtained e-mail addresses from most members in the unit.

After 12 months of negotiations, an agreement was reached and then ratified on January 3, 2002. The agreement restored the pay cut, established a formal grievance procedure, set up seniority rules, provided union access to internal mail service and voice-mail, allowed the union to meet with new hires during orientation, lifted productivity quotas, and set up a practice advisory committee to address quality issues.

During all of these events, the OHCP members gained strength through solidarity and developed friendships through these activities. At the monthly meetings, the members were able to share opinions and ideas and maintained their focus on quality and professional development of their work as therapists. The members identified talent not known before. Some members were "good at writing or public speaking; others were great at photography, graphic design, public relations, and press contacts, and getting members involved and staying in touch. Some simply offered their help with mailings, and opened their homes when we needed meeting space. We have also had some good parties and events for supporting family members."

The president of the OHCP wrote the following in the November 2001 newsletter:

> We are not accustomed to making waves. We are accustomed to and prefer to work cooperatively and gently with people. Forming a union was certainly not something we had anticipated. We did it because we felt that we had no other way to maintain our personal and professional dignity and integrity. Our struggle for fairness at our workplace is something we can be proud of the rest of our lives, and it is a valuable lesson and example for our children.

SOURCE: Richard W. Hurd and Elisabeth Tenenholtz, "Charting Their Own Future: Independent Organizing by Professional Workers," *Proceedings of the 54th Annual Meetings of the Industrial Relations Research Association*, Ed. Paula B. Voos, Urbana, IL: Industrial Relations Research Association, 2003, pp. 172–179. Reprinted by permission of the Labor and Employment Relations Association.

the week-to-week campaign strategy; interview supervisors to identify sources of employee discontent and to ameliorate the discontent that led to the organizing campaign; raise the perceived costs of union representation by such tactics as publicizing major layoffs and closings at unionized plants; train supervisors in how to effectively present the employer's position to the employees; prepare and edit campaign literature and speeches for company officials; and build support and sympathy for the employer in the local community. An inexpensive campaign in a small to medium-sized firm with one attorney could cost up to $30,000 in legal fees. An "all-out" campaign with several attorneys using all of the latest campaign tools, such as slick videotapes, visits by prominent politicians and civil rights leaders, and so on, could easily exceed $100,000. The cost of a campaign in a large, multi-plant firm involving a dozen attorneys could exceed $1 million. These costs are incurred at the rate of $150 to $300 per hour for attorneys from specialized labor law firms ($400 per hour or more for "big name" attorneys).[38] Illegal discharge and other forms of discrimination against union activists, used by employers to affect the outcome of the election, have increased dramatically in the past several years. Such discrimination reduces the probability of an organizing success by 17 percent and nearly cuts in half the likelihood of a first contract being obtained. Nearly all these illegal activities occur during an organizing drive, just before an election, or during the first contract negotiations. Such violations generally occur when employers perceive the financial gains of keeping unions out are far greater than the cost of back-pay awards and reinstatement of union advocates, and such is often the case. One study reported that less than half of illegally discharged workers were offered reinstatement, and only 69 percent of those ever returned to work. Because it takes so long to settle a case, and reinstatement comes so long after the organizing drive, some employers have been able to frustrate the legal process and use it against the union and employees interested in the union.[39]

Some companies use as their guide the book *Winning Union Campaigns*, by Robert Pearlman, a former staff attorney with the National Labor Relations Board (NLRB). In the book, management is advised that the "consequences of illegal labor practices must be kept in perspective," and they must be "subordinated to the prime objective, which is remaining union free." Management is advised that the best bet is to "campaign aggressively" and avoid "playing the union's game" by allowing "fear of the NLRB to stifle communications." Pearlman advises that in the event the company loses the election after an aggressive campaign, the bargaining order won't be issued until two to four years after the election. By that time, employees will be too intimidated to support the union, and the union will not be in a position to take employees out on strike if negotiations reach an impasse.[40]

Two relevant questions are: How do employers reconcile their personal ethics when either they or their representatives knowingly commit illegal practices by discharging an employee or a group of employees for exercising their legal right to support a union? Moreover, why does the U.S. Congress continue to tolerate such an imbalance in the legal procedures governing the exercise of statutory rights that have existed in the United States since 1935? (See the discussion of the Employee Free Choice Act later in this chapter.)

Methods for Organizing Unions

The three basic ways for organizing unions are through (1) voluntary recognition, (2) NLRB directives, and (3) secret-ballot elections (Exhibit 5.5).

Voluntary Recognition

By far the simplest and least confrontational path to union recognition is voluntary employer recognition often based on union authorization cards.

Several unions, particularly the Service Employees International Union and UNITE/HERE, have been successful in organizing tens of thousands of employees under these neutrality/card check agreements. The current agreements between the Big Three automakers and the UAW contain provisions for employer neutrality and card check. With such success, opposition groups, such the National Right to Work Committee and other groups, are challenging these agreements in court and before the NLRB.[41] Within the voluntary

Exhibit 5.5
Basic Union Representation Procedures

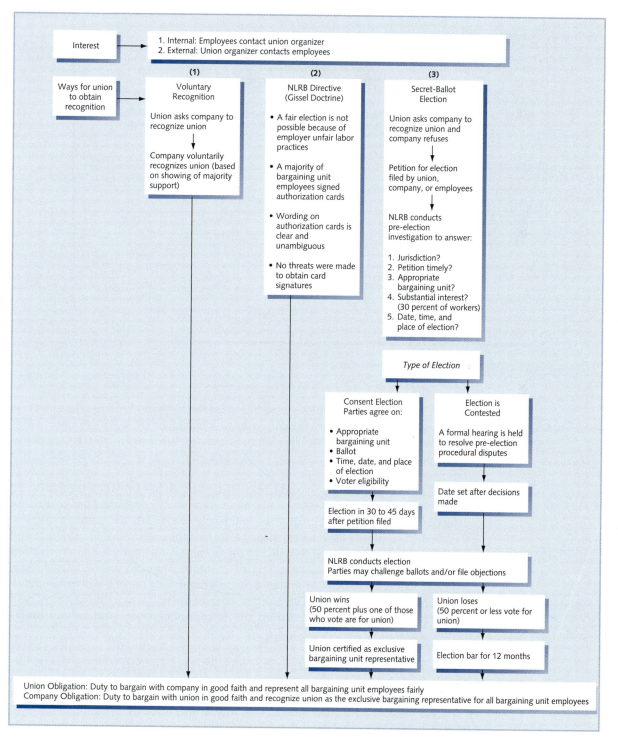

Interest
1. Internal: Employees contact union organizer
2. External: Union organizer contacts employees

Ways for union to obtain recognition

(1)
Voluntary Recognition

Union asks company to recognize union

↓

Company voluntarily recognizes union (based on showing of majority support)

(2)
NLRB Directive (Gissel Doctrine)

• A fair election is not possible because of employer unfair labor practices

• A majority of bargaining unit employees signed authorization cards

• Wording on authorization cards is clear and unambiguous

• No threats were made to obtain card signatures

(3)
Secret-Ballot Election

Union asks company to recognize union and company refuses

↓

Petition for election filed by union, company, or employees

↓

NLRB conducts pre-election investigation to answer:

1. Jurisdiction?
2. Petition timely?
3. Appropriate bargaining unit?
4. Substantial interest? (30 percent of workers)
5. Date, time, and place of election?

Type of Election

Consent Election
Parties agree on:

• Appropriate bargaining unit
• Ballot
• Time, date, and place of election
• Voter eligibility

Election in 30 to 45 days after petition filed

Election is Contested

A formal hearing is held to resolve pre-election procedural disputes

↓

Date set after decisions made

NLRB conducts election
Parties may challenge ballots and/or file objections

Union wins (50 percent plus one of those who vote are for union)

Union loses (50 percent or less vote for union)

Union certified as exclusive bargaining unit representative

Election bar for 12 months

Union Obligation: Duty to bargain with company in good faith and represent all bargaining unit employees fairly
Company Obligation: Duty to bargain with union in good faith and recognize union as the exclusive bargaining representative for all bargaining unit employees

Exhibit 5.6
Example of a Union Authorization Card

United Food & Commercial Workers International Union
Affiliated with AFL-CIO-CLC
AUTHORIZATION FOR REPRESENTATION

I hereby authorize the United Food & Commercial Workers International Union, AFL-CIO-CLC, or its chartered Local Union(s) to represent me for the purpose of collective bargaining.

_____	_____
(Print Name)	(Date)
_____	_____
(Signature)	(Home Phone)

| _____ | _____ | _____ | _____ |
| (Home Address) | (City) | (State) | (Zip) |

| _____ | _____ |
| (Employer's Name) | (Address) |

| _____ | _____ | _____ |
| (Hire Date) | (Type Work Performed) | (Department) |

	Day _____	Night _____	Full _____	Part _____
_____	_____	Shift	Shift	Time	Time
(Hourly Rate)	(Day Off)

Would you participate in an organizing committee?   Yes _____   No _____

SOURCE: Courtesy of the United Food and Commercial Workers International Union.

---

recognition procedure, unions have increased the likelihood of organizing success by negotiating a pledge by the employer to remain neutral in the organizing process and/or through the establishment of card check (see Exhibit 5.6 for an example of a Union Authorization Card) procedures to avoid National Labor Relations Board elections.

The Federal Mediation and Conciliation Service has provided mediation assistance in first contract negotiations an average of 275 occasions per year in the last 10 years where a company has voluntarily recognized the union.[42]

Most neutrality agreements also specify that the employer will recognize and bargain with the union if a majority of its employees sign valid authorization cards.[43] Neutrality agreements typically contain language stating that the employer will neither help nor hinder a union's organizing efforts, will not communicate opposition to the union, will not refer to the union as a "third party," will not attack or demean the union or its representatives, and other similar provisions.

The language in the card check agreements typically calls for a third-party neutral to validate the cards to determine whether a majority of the bargaining unit employees want the union to represent them. Most of these agreements allow union access to the physical property of the employer and set limits on the union's behavior, most commonly not to attack management. In over 90 percent of the agreements, some form of dispute resolution, most frequently arbitration, is set up to resolve alleged violations or disputes that may occur during the term of the agreement. An example of a dispute is disagreement over the composition of the bargaining unit and eligibility of employees to sign union authorization cards.

The union success rate with neutrality and card check agreements, as measured by the percentage of campaigns resulting in recognition, are high:

- Neutrality-agreements-only success rate was 45.6 percent.

- Card-check-procedure-only success rate was 62.5 percent.

- Card-check-procedure with neutrality agreements was 78.2 percent.

Two other types of language that appeared to increase the union's organizing success are (1) the requirement that employers provide the union with lists of employees and (2) an agreement that the parties place time limits on the campaigns. Problems in the administration of these agreements are most likely to occur in large, multi-plant companies where the local managers fail to honor the language negotiated by their far-removed superiors at corporate headquarters.[44]

When employers sign neutrality agreements, the signing is likely to be negotiated within the context of a broader labor–management partnership. In addition to limitations on employer and union actions during the campaign, the union and its members agree to assist the company in meeting its performance goals and the union leadership spends more time communicating the positive contributions of the union, rather than responding to the employer's anti-union messages or attacking the employer. Typically the card check/neutrality agreements improve the relationship between the union and the company, and after the union is recognized, the union is more willing to accept flexible agreements to help companies in highly competitive environments.[45]

Thomas A. Kochan, a noted labor relations scholar, has concluded: "It is understandable why unions turn to neutrality, card check, and other nonelection processes to gain recognition. The law simply no longer works to protect workers' right to join a union or gain access to collective bargaining. So unions are forced to work around the NLRB's election procedures...." Why would a company sign on to a neutrality agreement? Kochan gives two reasons: The first is union power, and the second is union value. The UAW has been strong enough in the auto industry to reach neutrality agreements with GM, Ford, and Chrysler. The Service Employees International Union has relied on employer pressure from corporate and capital campaigns and coordinated pressures from other unions such as the Teamsters who controlled key points in the supply chain or product/service delivery process. Unions also have potential to bring value to the company. As example, Continental Airlines, which experienced attempts in the 1980s to break the union by cutting wages and benefits and using bankruptcy protections, brought in a new team of managers in the 1990s. The new team created a positive labor relations culture with greater employee support, and Continental Airlines became one of the most successful airlines in America.[46]

Most employers still refuse to voluntarily recognize a union even when union organizers present signed authorization cards (see Exhibit 5.6) from a majority of employees. Management might be concerned that these cards were obtained through inappropriate means (such as after drinking parties, under threats of violence, or through forgeries, for example). Employers also realize that authorization cards are not very accurate predictors of union success in representation elections.

NLRB Directive

In rare and very controversial cases, the NLRB may direct the employer to recognize and bargain with the union. Although the NLRB considers secret-ballot elections superior, it has discretionary authority to use alternative means to determine the majority interests of employees. In the landmark *Gissel* case, the NLRB decided (and the Supreme Court agreed) that a company may be ordered to recognize and bargain with a union under the following conditions:

1. Evidence reveals that a fair, impartial election would be impossible because of serious or numerous employer unfair labor practices.

2. Wording on the authorization cards is clear and unambiguous (Exhibit 5.6).

3. Employee signatures on the cards were obtained without threat or coercion.

4. A majority of employees in the bargaining unit had indicated their interest in having the union represent them by signing the authorization cards.[47] (Card signatures are valid for 12 months unless voluntarily withdrawn by the employee who signed the card prior to a union's use of that card as evidence of employee support.)

In essence, the NLRB and the courts have concluded that holding another election in certain situations where the employer had made a fair and impartial election impossible would not be a realistic remedy because a rerun election would favor the party that had interfered with the first election.

NLRB *Gissell* bargaining orders do not occur very frequently. During a ten-year span from 1987 to 1996, the NLRB issued an average of ten per year. Then, if appealed by the company to the U.S. Circuit Court of Appeals, only about 50 percent of the bargaining orders were enforced.[48]

An analysis of NLRB opinions issued since 1969 reveals a measure of predictability in deciding whether the NLRB will issue a *Gissel* bargaining order. The NLRB is more likely to issue a bargaining order:

- When it believes that an employer's illegal acts are deliberate or calculated.

- If the employer's conduct threatens the employees' economic interests.

- If the employer's actions are characterized as vengeful and the NLRB does not believe the actions can be remedied without a bargaining order.

- When an employer promises to correct the grievances that led to union organizing and the NLRB finds that the only way to remedy the illegal promise is to issue a bargaining order.

- When the employer engages in a series of unfair labor practices rather than a single incident.

A NLRB-ordered bargaining order has little value without federal judicial enforcement (see Chapter 3) through the U.S. Circuit Courts of Appeal, which tend to rely on a case-by-case analysis. Before enforcing the NLRB's bargaining order, the courts require the NLRB to provide a "reasoned explanation" of why a rerun election would be futile. In general, if an employer's unfair labor practices seem reprehensible or egregious, the courts will be more likely to enforce the NLRB's bargaining order. For example, if a company takes unlawful actions, such as terminating employees, because of their union activities or making threats about the consequences of unionization, the courts will likely enforce the bargaining order.[49] Threats of an actual plant closing to deny employees an opportunity to exercise their Section 7 rights is also considered a very serious unfair labor practice which could justify a *Gissel* doctrine bargaining order from the NLRB.

NLRB Secret Ballot Election

Pre–NLRB-Election Union Campaigns. The union preelection campaign is not simply a process of exchanging letters and handbills and then holding an election. The campaign usually goes through several stages[50]:

1. Contacting employees as a result of either employee requests for help or distribution of union literature (handbilling) at the workplace by the union.

2. Determining interest by calling meetings, visiting homes, and counting responses to handbills. (See the Labor Relations in Action feature above for an array of responses received by union organizers who were seeking support from employees.)

3. Setting up an organizing committee by identifying leaders and educating them about the benefits and procedures of the union, the law, and the issues likely to be raised by management.

4. Building interest by soliciting signatures on authorization cards (see Exhibit 5.6 on pg. 192). (Most organizers will wait to announce that the union represents a majority until over 50 percent, and usually 60 to 80 percent, have signed cards.)

During this time the union discovers and highlights employees' problems, compares wages at their facility to wages at unionized facilities, and explains the role of the union in helping to satisfy their job-related needs. In other words, the union will attempt to convince the workers that they need a union and then that they should sign union authorization cards and should support the forthcoming organizing campaign by wearing union buttons, attending meetings, and signing up members. Although various means are available to gain support, research indicates that one-to-one contact, peer contact and persuasion, and high-quality, professionally designed written communications are most effective.[51] Other efforts used by unions include television and radio advertising, "hotline" telephone numbers, group meetings, and handbilling.

Organizing new locals is costly. Evidence shows that the cost of each additional union member is about \$600.[52] These costs include direct, out-of-pocket expenditures for such items as the printing and mailing of leaflets and other literature, rent for office space, salaries for staff hired, and legal fees. These efforts take time from the union staff that could be devoted to providing services to present union members (handling grievances, arbitration, and negotiation).

The costs of organizing new members must be compared with the returns:

- Extra compensation made possible by increased bargaining power

- Additional dues and fees paid by new members

- Enhanced political influence

- Social benefits and satisfaction derived from extending membership to others[53]

Companies often learn of union-organizing attempts from supervisors or rank-and-file employees and through observing handbilling at the work site before they receive official notification (by letter or telegram) from the union demanding recognition. Some companies react vigorously, whereas others do little to acknowledge any union's attempt to organize the employees. Some employers tell their employees about their opposition and urge them not to sign union authorization cards. Because the cards may specifically state that the signee favors union representation, any employee signature assists the union in establishing itself in the company. See the Labor Relations in Action feature on page 197 for typical employer messages during a union campaign.

Filing a Petition for the Election.

Before 1935, to obtain recognition, the union usually had to show its strength and employee interest in representation by such actions as strikes. The Wagner Act and the NLRB changed this situation by developing procedures and guidelines for peacefully determining the majority interest of employees through elections or some other comparable demonstration. The procedure is initiated when the potential bargaining representative for the employees files a petition for an election.

The NLRB is authorized to conduct an election only when a valid petition has been filed by an employee, group of employees, an individual or labor organization, or an employer. Usually the petition is filed by the union after it has requested union recognition from the employer and the request is denied. The petition must be supported by evidence (usually authorization cards) that a substantial interest in union representation (at least 30 percent of the anticipated bargaining unit) exists. Further, the union may request voluntary recognition and that the employer declined this request that the union be recognized as the exclusive bargaining agent. An employer cannot petition for an election until the union seeks recognition. If the employer could, it would petition at the time when the union's support was weakest. After receiving a petition, the NLRB will first determine whether it has jurisdiction and the petition is valid. If so, it will promptly notify the company and request a listing of employees. Companies are not required to submit this list but usually comply with the request as an act of good faith. Next, the NLRB will arrange a conference with the company and union to discuss the possibility of a *consent election*. Here, if both sides agree to the appropriate bargaining unit, voter eligibility, ballot, date, time, and place for the election, a **consent election** will be held. If either party refuses to agree on any of these items, a formal hearing to settle these matters will be conducted.

Election Investigation and Hearing. If the union and management officials cannot agree to a consent election, the NLRB will investigate the petition, hold a hearing, and then direct an election (**directed elections**) if it finds that there is substantial interest in union representation. This investigation will secure answers to the following questions:

1. What is the anticipated appropriate bargaining unit?
2. Does substantial interest in representation (30 percent) exist among employees in the unit?
3. Are there any barriers to an election in the form of existing unions, prior elections, or present labor agreements?

The formal hearing permits both parties to present evidence on issues in dispute, e.g. composition of the bargaining unit, date of election, voter eligibility, etc. Based on the evidence presented, the NLRB Regional Director will issue a directed election order which includes his decision on disputed issues at the hearing and prior voluntary agreements between the parties about other election issues.

Appropriate Bargaining Unit. An appropriate bargaining unit is a grouping of jobs or positions in which two or more employees share common employment interests and conditions (community of interests) and which may reasonably be grouped together for collective bargaining purposes. Determination of an appropriate bargaining unit is left to the discretion of the NLRB, which decides in each representation case how employee rights can best be protected under the act. The Board's decision has, however, been limited by law in several ways. The statute includes the following:

- Professional employees cannot be included in a unit composed of both professional and nonprofessional employees unless a majority of the professional employees vote to be included in a mixed unit.
- A proposed craft unit cannot be ruled inappropriate simply because a different unit has been previously approved by the NLRB unless a majority

of employees in the proposed craft union vote against being represented separately.

- Plant guards cannot be included in any bargaining unit that has nonguard employees in the unit because of the potential conflict of interest, such as searching a fellow union member's locker for stolen property.

- Supervisors and managers are not considered employees covered under the act and may not be in any bargaining unit. Supervisors are defined as "individuals who have authority in the interest of the employer, to hire, transfer, suspend, lay off, recall, promote, discharge, assign, reward, or discipline other employees, or responsibility to direct them, or to adjust their grievances, or effectively to recommend such action, if in connection with the foregoing the exercise of such authority is not of a merely routine or clerical nature, but requires the use of independent judgment."

- Excluded are agricultural laborers, public employees (except postal employees), and independent contractors, although some of these may be covered in separate state statutes.

- Confidential employees (individuals with access to confidential information, e.g. bargaining strategies, etc.) and some family members (e.g., son, daughter, spouse) are excluded.

The interplay between a professional employee and a supervisor becomes more complicated when the professional employee exercises some supervisory responsibility over less-skilled employees. For example, nurses often direct the work of less-skilled aides and others in clinics and hospitals. In 1994, the Supreme Court made it more difficult for nurses in nursing homes to organize when it ruled that licensed practical nurses (LPNs) were not employees under the NLRA because they attended to the needs of nursing home patients and therefore acted in the interests of their employer. Then, in 2001, the Supreme Court ruled that six registered nurses were not employees under the NLRA because these nurses exercised a sufficient degree of discretion when they directed less-skilled employees to provide services to patients.[54] Then, in 2006, the National Labor Relations Board found that permanent charge nurses, as a regular part of their duties, assigned nursing personnel to the specific patients for whom they would care during their shift and, as a result, were supervisors under the NLRA. In the same decision, the Board found that rotating charge nurses did not exercise supervisory authority and, as a result, were employees under the NLRA. Therefore, the rotating charge nurses could be part of the bargaining unit and could seek union representation.[55] The NLRB considers the facts in each case to determine whether or not supervisory authority exists.

The NLRB's determination of the appropriate bargaining unit influences whether the union will win the election, who will vote in the election, whether one union will prevail in an interunion contest, whether craft employees will have their own union or be included in a plant-wide unit, who the union must represent, who will be covered by the collective bargaining agreement, or whether the union will include key employees who could give direction and leadership for the bargaining unit employees.

Analysis of NLRB representation elections indicates that the success of a union campaign depends on the composition of the appropriate bargaining unit. When the appropriate bargaining unit is composed of similarly skilled groups, the union will likely succeed. This may be so because decisions within unions are made through a democratic process, and a degree of consensus is necessary to facilitate decision making and to win the support of the majority. However, when different skill groups comprise the bargaining unit, achieving consensus is more difficult, and majority support for the union likewise is harder to achieve and maintain. Thus, the NLRB's policy of including in a bargaining unit all "production and maintenance" employees within a plant (which would include a diversity of skills) may have contributed to the decline in union membership as a percentage of the total labor force. A more narrowly defined bargaining unit composed only of employees of similar skills (such as electricians) would favor the union winning the representation election and sustaining the continuation of the union.[56]

If the union wins, the appropriate bargaining unit may determine who will be required to join the union. Therefore, the composition of the bargaining unit is important to the employer, the union, and the public.

Some companies pay attention to these considerations and take preventive steps regarding management structure, employee interactions, and personnel policies and practices. For example, if the company prefers a large multiunit bargaining unit, it will retain centralized control on management practices and decisions. If it prefers smaller, independent units, it will decentralize decision making in these independent units. Because the union has no control over management structure and the authority-responsibility relationship, it can try to convince the NLRB that the bargaining unit should be composed only of those employees who are supporting the union.[57]

Should a plant have several small bargaining units, the employer may face different unions in negotiating several times throughout the year, which could cause continuous instability in labor relations. Separate units concerned with similar jobs may cause disputes over rights to jobs, leading to strikes or slowdowns. Should a small bargaining unit be merged with a nationwide bargaining unit, any confrontation that resulted in a strike could cause a nationwide shutdown and complications for customers in need of the companies' products. Chapter 6 covers the various bargaining structures and their implications.

The bargaining unit itself may cover employees in one plant or in two or more facilities of the same employer. The NLRB considers the "community of interests" in determining the composition of an appropriate bargaining unit. It evaluates the following factors:

- Interests of employees and employers

- Commonality of wages, working conditions, training, and skill

- History of collective bargaining either at the location in question or another facility owned by the company

- Transfers of employees among various facilities

- Geography and physical proximity of the workplaces

- Employer's administrative or territorial divisions

- Degree of separation (or distinctiveness) of work or integration (or interrelatedness) of work[58]

When the relevant factors do not give a clear indication for the composition of an appropriate bargaining unit, an election (commonly called a *Globe* election, from the original NLRB case) may be held to determine employee interests. For example, one group of electricians in a steel plant might wish to be represented by the International Brotherhood of Electrical Workers (IBEW) instead of the United Steelworkers of America (USWA). The USWA wants to include all electricians in a bargaining unit composed of all production and maintenance employees in the plant. Under such circumstances, the electricians' vote will determine whether they will be members of USWA, a separate electricians' union (IBEW), or no union.

The U.S. Supreme Court supported the NLRB's first rule-making effort to determine appropriate bargaining units for private acute-care hospitals. Eight standard bargaining units were established for approximately 4,000 acute-care hospitals: (1) all registered nurses, (2) all physicians, (3) all professionals except registered nurses and physicians, (4) all technical employees, (5) all skilled maintenance employees, (6) all business office clericals, (7) all guards, and (8) all other nonprofessional employees. Such rule-making practices reduce the number of cases in which employers are able to contest the number and composition of the appropriate bargaining unit. Employers sometimes intentionally use this tactic to delay the election and thereby increase the chances that the union will not win representational rights.[59]

In 2000, the Board ruled that, under the National Labor Relations Act a group of medical interns, residents, and fellows were employees and formed a proper bargaining unit, even though they were students. This ruling overruled a previous ruling that had excluded such individuals from bargaining units of employees. The Board reasoned that the interns, residents, and fellows were similar to apprentices, who had been considered statutory employees for a long time. Later in 2000, the Board extended its ruling and found that a group of graduate assistants (including teaching and research assistants) at New York University were employees. The Board rejected the university's contention that the graduate assistants were predominately students, not employees.[60]

In 2004, with a Bush-appointed majority, the Board made a significant reversal and ruled that graduate students were students, not employees under the National Labor Relations Act. This reversal came at a time when graduate student unionization was on the rise in the United States. Over the last decade, graduate student unions had grown from 10 to 30. New graduate student unions existed at several major universities such as Temple, Michigan State University, University of Rhode Island, and Columbia. It is estimated that 20 percent of all graduate students are now covered under collective bargaining agreements.[61] Most of these graduate student unions were organized and recognized in the public sector, which is governed by state labor relations laws (covered in Chapter 13).

Eligibility of Voters. Before an election is conducted, voter eligibility must be determined. An employee is eligible to vote in a representational election if he or she is (1) employed in a bargaining unit job; (2) employed during the eligibility period, which is usually the payroll period immediately preceding the date a consent agreement is signed or a directed election order is issued; and (3) employed on the date of the election. However, employees who are on sick leave, vacation, temporary layoff, or temporary leave, such as military duty, may vote in the election. In addition, the NLRB will occasionally consider irregularity of employment, such as in the construction, food processing, and longshoring industries. Economic strikers who have been replaced by permanent employees are allowed to vote in any election within 12 months after the strike begins. This policy ensures that management does not provoke a strike and hire replacements who could vote out the union. Employees hired after the union files its petition but before the election may be challenged for their eligibility by the union.

Untimely Petitions. Several rules make a petition for a representation election untimely. The *election bar* doctrine is a legal requirement that prohibits any NLRB representation election where one has been held in the last 12 months or where a petition for election covers a group of employees who are already covered by an existing contract and already members of a legally certified union.

The second rule and potential barrier to elections is an administrative determination that was made in the interest of stable and effective labor relations. The NLRB rule, called the **contract bar doctrine**, specifies that a valid, signed agreement for a fixed period of three years or less will bar any representation election for the life of the agreement. Thus, the contract bar doctrine could extend the 12-month statutory limitation on elections to three years. To do otherwise would be unfair to union and management officials who have negotiated a multiyear labor agreement in good faith. Longer term (four years or more) contracts bar the employer and union for the life of the agreement, but would only bar bargaining unit members or an outside party, e.g. a rival union, for a maximum of three years.

"Names and Addresses" (Excelsior Rule). Within seven days after the regional director of the NLRB has approved a consent election or after an election has been directed, the employer must file a list of names and addresses of all eligible voters with the regional director. This information is then made available to the union. Refusal to comply could be identified as a bad faith act on the part of the employer and cause the election to be set aside or the NLRB to seek the names and addresses by subpoena. The purpose of this disclosure rule is to give the unions involved in an election access to employees' contact information that management already possesses.[62]

The Election. The representation election, acclaimed as one of the great innovations of American labor law, is conducted by NLRB officials and is typically held within 48 days (median) of the initial request. NLRB data show that about 90 percent of the eligible voters usually participate in NLRB elections, as compared with about 50 percent in major political elections.

The high voter turnout in union representation elections might be due to the convenient voting procedure (usually carried out on company property) and the belief of many employees that their vote more directly affects their lives (at least their working conditions) than do political elections. Finally, both unions and management realize that an employee could express union preference to a union representative and an opposite preference to the management representative to avoid a confrontation during the election campaign. Neither side is sure of employee voting preferences when faced with a secret ballot; therefore, union and management officials work to get out the vote.

Voter participation tends to decline the longer it takes for the NLRB to conduct the election. Thus, some employers are motivated to refuse to consent to an election in hopes of increasing the chances of the union losing the election. Also, because most single-unit elections are close, the number of nonparticipants affects the outcome of many elections.[63] Also, a small number of votes greatly influences the outcome of the election; research shows that a switch of eight votes would have changed the outcomes of half the elections.[64] Furthermore, small increases in the time to process cases are important; a delay of ten days has proven to be a significant factor in differentiating employer wins from employer losses. The number of pre-election days has also been linked to union losses. During the first six months of delay, there is an average drop-off in union victories of 2.5 percent per month. Consent elections have the highest victory rate.[65]

The size of the election unit has tended to be negatively related to union victories. The larger election unit is closely related to delay because it takes longer to process and is more likely to result in a hearing than in a voluntary settlement.[66] Recent research has also revealed that success in union organizing has been influenced positively by the size of the union and democracy within the union and negatively influenced by the union's propensity to strike and centralization of the union's decision making.[67]

A study of NLRB elections revealed that independent unions (those unions not affiliated with the AFL-CIO) have had a higher union win ratio than AFL-CIO affiliates. Thus, the AFL-CIO's "big labor" image may be a liability, and the AFL-CIO may need to encourage union autonomy, as did the AFL before the merger of the AFL and CIO in 1955, the year when union density reached 35 percent of the private work force.[68]

Using a ballot with the appropriate company and union designations (Exhibit 5.7), a secret-ballot election is conducted under NLRB supervision, usually during working hours on payday at the employer's location. However, the NLRB has discretionary authority to conduct it by mail ballot. In 1998, the Board (the majority of members appointed by President Bill Clinton) approved a new procedure that encouraged the use of mail ballots in representation elections under any of the following conditions: (1) eligible voters were widely dispersed geographically, (2) eligible voters worked differing schedules and were not present at common locations at common times, or (3) where there was strike, lockout, or picketing.[69]

The NLRB must determine whether the majority of the employees in an appropriate bargaining unit want to be represented by a union for collective bargaining purposes. It defines majority as the simple majority rule generally accepted in democratic elections, which means that those choosing not to vote in the election have decided to assent to the wishes of the majority who did vote. Therefore, a majority of the employees who vote (50 percent plus one of those casting valid ballots in the election) must favor representation before a union will be certified by the NLRB.

If two or more choices are placed on the ballot, a runoff election may be necessary between the choices receiving the two highest numbers of votes in the initial election. If the majority votes "no union," no representation election can be held for 12 months. If a union receives the majority of the votes, the NLRB will certify it as the exclusive bargaining agent of the employees in the bargaining unit. Interestingly, where more than one union has vied for representation rights in the same election, unions have fared extremely well.

Although only four percent of representation elections are multi-union elections (choice between two unions), one of the competing unions is more likely to win representation rights than in a single-union election. Also, multi-union elections bring out a substantially high number of voters.[70] The major reason for this positive vote is that two unions would have to gain support from a sufficient number of the bargaining unit's employees to be placed on the ballot. Such support usually indicates that the employees have already decided to vote for a union; the election is conducted to determine which union will receive the majority vote.

UNITED STATES OF AMERICA
National Labor Relations Board
OFFICIAL SECRET BALLOT
FOR CERTAIN EMPLOYEES OF
CONTAINER CORPORATION

Do you wish to be represented for purpose of collective bargaining by
METAL PRODUCTS MACHINERY AND RELATED
EQUIPMENT WORKERS OF AMERICA
AFL-CIO

MARK AN "X" IN THE SQUARE OF YOUR CHOICE

YES ☐   NO ☐

DO NOT SIGN THIS BALLOT. Fold and drop in ballot box.
If you spoil this ballot return it to the Board Agent for a new one.

UNITED STATES OF AMERICA
National Labor Relations Board
OFFICIAL SECRET BALLOT
FOR CERTAIN EMPLOYEES OF
CONTAINER CORPORATION

This ballot is to determine the collective bargaining representative, if any,
for the unit in which you are employed.

MARK AN "X" IN THE SQUARE OF YOUR CHOICE

(Name of Union A)   NEITHER   (Name of Union B)

☐   ☐   ☐

DO NOT SIGN THIS BALLOT. Fold and drop in ballot box.
If you spoil this ballot return it to the Board Agent for a new one.

Exhibit 5.7

Examples of Secret Ballots for Union Representation Election

After the votes have been counted, either party has seven calendar days to file objections alleging misconduct or to challenge the ballots of voters whom one party believes should not have voted in the election. This part of the representation process receives considerable criticism because of the delay in assessing ballot challenges and objections concerning misconduct often seems excessive.

In 2005, the NLRB conducted 3,649 representation elections involving 146,822 employees. Over eighty percent of the eligible voters cast ballots—far more than in any presidential election, or for any other political election. The election is usually conducted on the employer's premises during working hours and involves a subject about which most employees are vitally interested—whether or not they will be represented by a union. In 2005, unions won 1,505 representation elections, or 56.8 percent, compared with 54.1 percent of the 2,522 elections held in 2001. In every year since 2002, unions have won more than 50 percent of the NLRB-conducted representation elections. The most active unions involved in representation elections have been the Teamsters, the United Food and Commercial Workers (UFCW), and the Service Employees International Union (SEIU). The SEIU was the most successful union. The states in which the most NLRB elections were held in 2005 were California, New York, Illinois, Pennsylvania, and Washington.[71]

Several trends in union representation elections over the last half century can be identified. First, the number of union representation elections has fallen sharply since the mid-1970s, despite showing an increase between the mid-1950s and mid-1970s. The number of elections reached a height of 8,799 in 1973, but has slowed to average less than 3,000 per year. Between 1980 and 1983, there was a precipitous drop of over 50 percent. Second, union success rates in representation elections have steadily declined since the 1940s, when union win rates averaged about 75 percent compared with the present win rate of just over 50 percent. Third, unions continue to be less likely to win NLRB-supervised representation elections involving bargaining units of over 100 employees.[72] Today, the majority of representation elections occur in bargaining units of 50 or fewer employees.

After the Election

As noted in Chapter 1, the first step of the labor relations process, the recognition of legitimate rights and responsibilities of unions and management representatives, includes more than the representation election. After unions win bargaining rights in a representation election, they attempt to negotiate a labor agreement; however, they fail to secure a first contract 25 to 30 percent of the time. Several factors increase the likelihood of reaching agreement: existence of relatively high wages already at the company, presence of other bargaining units within the company, large election victories, and active participation of international union representatives. Factors that reduce the chances of attaining a first contract include location in a southern state with right-to-work laws, the national union having to approve the local union's contract, presence of outside labor-management consultants hired by the company,[73] NLRB delays in resolving employer objections and challenges to election results, employer refusal to bargain in good faith, and discrimination against employees after the election.[74]

Delays associated with filing objections to campaign conduct have increased threefold over the last 20 years, and the median amount of delay time is now about 210 days. Then, employers fail or refuse to bargain in good faith 13 percent of the time. This unfair labor practice adds approximately 140 days. Additional delay can occur if appeals are made to the full Board in Washington, D.C., or to a federal court of appeals or the Supreme Court.

In addition to the delays, there has been a six-fold increase in the number of unfair labor practice charges for firing union supporters and an eleven-fold increase in the number of back-pay awards. Research has discovered that employers discharge union activists or union supporters for two main reasons: (1) to get the key union organizers out of the facility, and (2) to send a chilling message to the rest of the work force. With such trends in statistics, it does not appear that ethical considerations prevent all employers from breaking the law.

One researcher has found that unions are prompted to file unfair labor practices in 20 percent of the representation elections in which they participate. However, surprisingly, one study found no measurable differences in the outcome of the elections whether the unfair labor practices were filed or whether the unfair labor practices that were filed actually had merit.[75]

Duties of the Exclusive Bargaining Agent and Employer

The exclusive bargaining representative (the union) chosen by the majority of the employees in an appropriate unit has the duty to represent equitably and fairly all employees in the unit regardless of their union membership and to bargain in good faith with the employer. The employer has a comparable obligation, that is, to bargain in good faith with the exclusive bargaining agent and to refuse to bargain with any other union seeking to represent the employees. Further, any negotiated labor agreement will cover all employees in the bargaining unit, regardless of their union membership status.

After Election Loss by Union

After losing a representation election, typically the union reduces its activities because there can be only one election every 12 months. However, there are some creative ways in which the union can maintain contact with employees, particularly those who supported it during the campaign, and provide a representational service to those included in the bargaining unit. Exhibit 5.8 includes alternative activities that could increase the chances of success of any future unionization drive.

Mandatory Secret Ballot Elections Versus Employee Free Choice Act

In 2005, legislation (*Secret Ballot Protection Act of 2005*) was introduced in the U.S. Congress to require secret ballot elections for union certification. This bill would make it an unfair labor practice for an employer to recognize or bargain with a union that has not been selected by a majority of employees in a secret ballot election conducted by the National Labor Relations Board and for a union to cause or attempt to cause an employer to recognize or bargain with a union that has not been chosen by a majority of employees in a secret ballot election. In other words, voluntary union recognition by card check would be a prohibited practice.

The bipartisan *Employee Free Choice Act* passed by the U.S. House of Representatives (244 to 185) in 2007 contained three major provisions:

- The NLRB would be required to certify a union if a majority of employees signed union authorization cards which stated that the employee wants the union to represent him/her (see Exhibit 5.6 on pg. 192).

- A procedure for reaching the first collective bargaining agreement could be invoked by either party if the two parties have not reached an agreement with 90 days (or longer if both parties agreed) to request mediation by the Federal Mediation and Conciliation Service. If mediation is not successful, after 120 days a first contract would be subject to binding arbitration, resulting in a first contract in effect for a two-year period.

- Penalties for employer violations of certain unfair labor practices committed during the union organizing campaign or the negotiation of the first contract would be increased.[76]

1. Maintain in-plant committees, designate employees as union stewards, identify them with steward buttons, and through them, maintain contact with member and nonmember employees.

2. Distribute employment-related union literature in the plant during non-working time and serve as the voice of employees on all matters of common employment-related matters of concern.

3. Union stewards can present employee grievances to management. If management refuses to meet with the union committee, employees may leave their work as a group to request a discussion of their employment-related problems directly with management. If the response is unsatisfactory, the union may engage in a work stoppage; however, striker replacement rules apply.

4. A nonmajority union can provide a shield of concerted activity for an individual employee who refuses to drive a faulty truck, reports Occupational Safety and Health Administration (OSHA) violations, refuses to act in violation of personal ethics or morality, or sues for unpaid overtime.

5. Help employees know and enforce their individual employment rights concerning workers' compensation, third-party tort claims, wage and hour violations, and so on.

6. In-plant committees help employees know and receive their entitlements, such as medical benefits, sick leave, severance pay, pensions, unemployment compensation, disability pay, and social security.

7. Inform employees of rights under common-law doctrines and exceptions to employment-at-will doctrine, including employee manuals, employment contracts, public policy exceptions, good faith exceptions, and tort suits involving outrageous conduct, defamation, and invasion of privacy.

8. Reinforce OSHA statutory procedures: (1) establish in-plant safety committees; (2) file complaints through the union; (3) serve as representative of employees to accompany compliance officer on plant "walk-around," discuss claims, and participate in conferences; (4) act as representative of employees in the proceedings before the OSHA; (5) enforce the Hazard Communication Standard by filing complaints if employer fails to provide toxic training to employees and has not prepared a written communication program; and (6) petition for information contained on Material Safety Data Sheets.

9. Represent employees under plant closure laws, pregnancy leave acts, polygraph and privacy acts, and whistle-blowing statutes.

10. Represent employees under unjust discharge procedures modeled after labor arbitration.

SOURCE: Clyde W. Summers, "Unions without Majorities: The Potentials of the NLRA," *Proceedings of the 43rd Meeting of the Industrial Relations Research Association* (Madison, Wis.: IRRA, 1991), pp. 154–162.

There are several arguments from the proponents of union recognition via card check as well as proponents of mandatory secret ballot elections (see Exhibit 5.9 for the common arguments).

The card check procedure for union recognition has experience in other countries. A system of card check union recognition has operated successfully in the United Kingdom under the Employment Relations Act since 2000. The UK's equivalent to the National Labor Relations Board will certify a union when over 50 percent of the workers sign union membership cards or it may

Proponents of Card Check Recognition	Proponents of Mandatory Secret Ballots
Card check recognition requires signatures from over 50 percent of bargaining unit employees (subject to verification by the NLRB). A secret ballot election is decided by a majority of workers voting.	Casting a secret ballot is private and confidential. A secret ballot election is conducted by the NLRB. Under card check recognition, authorization cards are controlled by the union.
During a secret ballot campaign, the employer has greater access to employees.	Under card check recognition, employees may only hear the union's point of view.
Because of potential employer pressure or intimidation during a secret ballot election, some workers may feel coerced into voting against a union.	Because of potential union pressure or intimidation, some workers may feel coerced into signing authorization cards.
Employer objections can delay a secret ballot election.	Most secret ballot elections are held within two months after a petition is filed.
Allegations against a union for unfair labor practices can be addressed under existing law. Existing remedies do not deter employer violations of unfair labor practices.	Allegations against an employer for unfair labor practices can be addressed under existing law. Existing remedies do not deter union violations of unfair labor practices.
Card check recognition is less costly for both the union and employer. If only secret ballot elections were required, the NLRB would have to devote more resources to conducting elections.	Unionization may cost workers union dues; higher union wages may result in fewer union jobs.
Card check and neutrality agreements may lead to more cooperative labor–management relations.	An employer may be pressured by a corporate campaign into accepting a card check or neutrality agreement. If an employer accepts a neutrality agreement, employees who do not want a union may hesitate to speak out.

SOURCE: E: Gerald Mayer, "Labor Union Recognition Procedures: Use of Secret Ballots and Card Checks," Congressional Research Service, The Library of Congress, 2005 (http://digitalcommons.ilr.cornell.edu/key workplace/237).

Exhibit 5.9

Most Common Arguments Made by Proponents of Union Recognition via Card Check and Proponents of Mandatory Secret Ballot Elections

call for an election if it believes the election would be in the interest of good industrial relations. However, the practice has been that the Board rarely requires an election when a majority of workers has signed the union membership cards.[77]

In Canada, five provinces require secret ballot elections and five provinces allow card check union recognition. The province of British Columbia allowed card checks until 1984; then from 1984 to 1992, secret ballot elections were required. In 1992, card checks were allowed again. During the period when card checks were allowed, the union success rate was 91 percent; when secret ballot elections were required, the success rate was 73 percent. Also, during the period where card checks were allowed, there was an average of 531 union organizing drives per year; during the period when secret ballot elections were required, the average was only 242.

In June 2007, the Senate failed to end a Republican filibuster by a vote of 51 to 48, thereby preventing a vote on the merits on the Employee Free Choice Act.

Exhibit 5.10

Examples of Handbills Distributed During Representation Election Campaigns

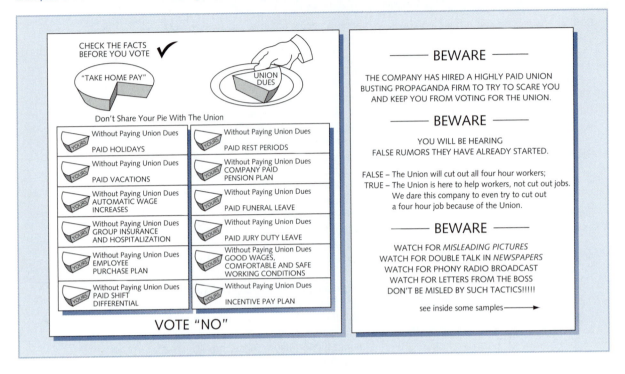

Thus, it appeared that although a majority of senators would have voted for the act, they needed 60 votes to end the filibuster. Still, if the act had passed, it would have faced a certain veto by President Bush. As a result, the union strategy appears to be focused on the 2008 election.[78]

CONDUCT OF THE REPRESENTATION ELECTION CAMPAIGN

All elections are conducted according to NLRB standards, which are designed to ensure that employees in the bargaining unit can indicate freely whether they want to be represented by a union for collective bargaining purposes. However, election campaigns differ substantially, and the strategies of individual unions and employers vary widely. For example, handbills similar to those in Exhibit 5.10 are often used in addition to speeches, informal talks, interviews, and films. Thus, the election campaign, one of the most interesting and controversial activities in labor relations, has led to a body of doctrines and rules. Because of changes in NLRB philosophy, those doctrines and rules are subject to change.

Campaign Doctrines and NLRB Policies

The **totality of conduct doctrine** guides the NLRB interpretations of unfair labor practice behavior. This doctrine essentially means that isolated incidents such as campaign speeches must be considered within the whole of the general circumstances of the campaign and with the possibility that other specific violations have occurred.

Employer statements to employees may seem harmless on the surface, but under the circumstances that exist at the time of the statements, they may carry implied threats. For example, if an employer stated that a third-party intervention could make it economically impossible for it to continue in business, it would be making an illegal statement during a union election campaign. However, if the employer made the same statement during an attempted leveraged buyout, there would be no legal violation.

The NLRB concluded that it would no longer probe into the truth or falsity of the parties' campaign statements but would intervene in cases where a party had used forged documents that render voters unable to recognize propaganda for what it is. The Board concluded that today's voters (employees) are more educated and sophisticated than their historical counterparts and can analyze materials more accurately. This assessment was influenced by a research study involving over 1,000 employees in 31 elections in five states. This study cast doubt on the previously held assumption that employees are unsophisticated about labor relations and are swayed easily by campaign propaganda. In fact, votes of 81 percent of the employees could have been predicted from their precampaign intent and their attitudes toward working conditions and unions in general. The study concluded that employees' votes appeared to be the product of attitudes that resulted from their everyday experiences in the industrial world and not from the campaign itself.[79]

The data used in the study were later reanalyzed, and the following additional (some different) conclusions were made[80]:

- Employee predisposition favoring the union is a very important determinant of voting behavior.

- Written communications distributed later in the campaign and meetings held early in the campaign most probably have an effect.

- Threats and actions taken against union supporters are effective in discouraging support for the union.

Thus far, these later analyses have not influenced the Board's position on election campaigns.

Captive Audience—24-Hour Rule

One legal approach used by employers to discourage union support includes presenting "captive audience" speeches, which are delivered to employees during working hours and that employees are required to attend. The speeches, authorized by the Taft-Hartley amendments in 1947, must not be presented within 24 hours of an election, and the speech's content must not include threats of reprisal or promises of benefits. However, if the union has no acceptable means of communicating with the employees, as in the lumber and logging industry, where employees live on company property, or if the employer's unfair labor practices have created a serious election campaign imbalance, the NLRB and the courts may grant the union access to plant bulletin boards, parking lots, and entrances so that it may communicate with the employees. Still, it is extremely difficult for the union to respond effectively by using its traditional means of contacting employees, such as plant employee solicitations, distribution of literature before or after work, house calls, and union meetings.[81]

Polling or Questioning Employees

Polling employees or asking questions about their interest in unions was considered unlawful interference with employee rights in early days. In 1984, the NLRB announced that it would no longer automatically consider an employer interrogation about an employee's union sentiment an unlawful inquiry in violation of section 8(a)(1). It announced that it would examine the totality of the circumstances surrounding such interrogations in light of the following:

1. The background of the interrogation
2. The nature of the information sought
3. The identity of the questioner
4. The place and method of the interrogation

Therefore, an employer's questioning of open and active union supporters and other employees about their union sentiments in the absence of threats or promises does not necessarily violate the law. However, NLRB decisions since 1984 reveal that employers are still at risk in these interrogations because it is necessary only to establish that the questions asked may reasonably be said to have a tendency to interfere with the free exercise of an employee's rights under the act.[82]

Distribution of Union Literature and Solicitation by Employees on Company Property

Distribution of union literature can be banned in work areas at all times. Union solicitation can only be banned during work time, e.g. the time when the employee is expected to be engaged in performance of regular job duties.

The NLRB and the courts have long held that except in special circumstances, employees may not be prohibited from distributing union-organizing materials or soliciting union support in nonworking areas during nonworking time[83] unless the employer can show that such activity would disrupt production, employee work, and plant discipline. For example, employees of restaurants and retail establishments cannot distribute union materials in customer areas, and employees of health care institutions cannot distribute materials in areas designated strictly for patient care.[84] However, distribution of materials by employees in such places as hospital cafeterias predominantly patronized by hospital employees cannot be prohibited.[85] In addition, the employer cannot prohibit distribution of union materials if the basis for the prohibition is that part of its content includes political issues, such as right-to-work laws and minimum wages.[86] Nor can the employer prohibit employees from wearing buttons, hats, or T-shirts promoting the union.

Some employers publish no solicitation rules that prevent employees from discussing union organizing on working time. However, to be enforceable, these no solicitation rules must be posted in advance of the organizing drive, and these rules must prohibit all types of solicitation by employees with limited exceptions for broad-based community charities such as the United Way.

The employer may limit the type of information distributed to employees by classifying company data as "confidential." The NLRB has upheld the discharge of five employees who distributed wage data comparing the company's wage scale with that of other plants in the area. The NLRB found that the company had declared this wage information to be confidential and that it had not been obtained in the normal course of employment.

For 35 years, the NLRB traditionally weighed the union's right to access employees in a unionizing campaign against the private property rights of an employer. In the 1992 *Lechmere* decision, the Supreme Court ruled (Justice Clarence Thomas wrote the court's opinion) that a company can ban a union organizer who is not an employee of the company from the property if the union has a reasonable alternative means of reaching individual employees with the union message, such as through newspaper advertising and home visits. The court would restrict exceptions to extraordinary situations in which the work site is isolated geographically and the union could not easily contact potential members except at the work site. Thus, the Supreme Court has made a distinction between employee and nonemployee access to individual employees during an organizing campaign and has made the union's efforts to communicate with employees more difficult, as well as more costly.[87]

The *Lechmere* decision applied to a store's parking lot designated for customer and employee use, and the store had strictly enforced a no solicitation rule to parties. Since the *Lechmere* decision, the NLRB has been faced with the application of the Supreme Court's decision in similar situations. Although decided on a case-by-case basis, nonemployee handbillers have access to a neutral third party's property, specifically from the entrance of the store and not merely the entrance to the parking lot. The union was able to show that handbilling at the entrance of the parking lot was dangerous and that the use of media was cost prohibitive.[88] Also, nonemployee union handbillers may be allowed on company property when and if the employer has allowed church and school groups, fundraisers, Boy Scouts, Little League teams, and so on, to solicit on company property.[89]

Showing Films during Election Campaigns

Films presented to discourage workers from joining unions have taken on new dimensions, especially since the 1950s, when the movie *And Women Must Weep* was produced by the National Right-to-Work Committee. This movie portrays union violence, strikes, vandalism, phone threats, a house bombing, and even the shooting of a baby of a dissident union member. Frequent use of the film by employers prompted the International Association of Machinists to produce a rebuttal film, entitled *Anatomy of a Lie,* which claims no evidence exists of a connection between the shootings and other misconduct and the union's activities. On-site interviews with persons involved in the strike are shown to reveal an opposite view of the employer film, and the president of the union is filmed, stating that nearly 99 percent of the union members voted to strike. The NLRB's position on the showing of these films has varied; its current position is that their showing alone does not constitute an unfair labor practice and is not sufficient cause to have the results of an election set aside.[90]

Use of E-Mail and Internet

All major unions and the two major federations use Internet technology in reaching out to unrepresented employees.[91] For example, the AFL-CIO (http://www.alfcio.org) allows individuals to sign up for e-mail messages from the AFL-CIO and has information of "How to Join a Union," "Find Your Union," and "State and Local Labor Contacts" as a link to the AFL-CIO's Organizing Institute. Change To Win (CTW) (http://www.changetowin.org) allows individuals to sign up for e-mail messages about organizing campaigns and also allows individuals to "Join the Movement."

The use of e-mail by employees and employer e-mail policies have been an issue before the NLRB. In a controversial 3–2 decision, the Board majority upheld an employer policy which banned employees from using the company's e-mail system to urge support for groups or organizations (e.g., a union) while permitting employees to send personal e-mails during non-work time (e.g., for sale notices, wedding announcements). The e-mail system was viewed as employer property which employees have no statutory right to use under Sec. 7, LMRA.[92]

New Union Strategies

In response to employers' strategies to maintain nonunion status, unions have had to be creative in their actions. Some well-publicized strategies by unions include instituting cyberspace organization with the Internet, whereby employees can simply enter the search words "how to organize" and receive on-line information on union organizing; and hiring "union salts," whereby an union organizer applies for a job within a targeted company, goes to work, and solicits for union membership as an employee (see the Labor Relations in Action feature on pg. 216).

Some recent union successes have come from corporate campaigns such as Justice for Janitors, which mobilized thousands of janitors across the country, many of whom were immigrants. In Los Angeles, the campaign relied on tactics such as marches and civil disobedience, which required extensive participation by the membership. Through boycotts, mobilization of immigrant community organizations, public awareness campaigns, and support from the Department of Labor, UNITE-HERE was able to organize immigrants workers who were employed by contractors who provided supplies to fashion designers. It was discovered that the traditional NLRB procedure was a completely ineffective approach.[93]

As noted in Chapter 4, one of the major reasons for the creation of Change To Win (CTW) was its emphasis on union organizing. CTW has reallocated resources on a grand scale away from other union activities and is devoting 75 percent of its budget to organizing. It will rebate one-half of union affiliates' per capita dues if they adopt aggressive organizing programs and has created a $25 million Strategic Center that will target notable anti-union employers. CTW's target for organizing will be those industries that will remain in the United States, such as health care, hospitality, retail, building services, transportation, and construction industries. The AFL-CIO has responded by establishing a $22.5 million Strategic Organizing Fund (a $10 million increase in annual spending in this area) and providing a plan to rebate $15 million to affiliated unions who met high standards in union organizing. The AFL-CIO has established a Union Plus program that provides consumer benefits for members and retirees and informs unrepresented employees of the benefits of union membership[94] (see Exhibit 5.11).

Also, there have been suggestions that new forms of unions be created. Richard Freeman has proposed a new form of unionism—"open source unionism"—wherein union membership does not depend on unions proving that they have majority support of employees and negotiating collective bargaining agreements. Open source unionism builds a common collaborative platform, language, and practice among workers who may operate at some distance from each other and at different work sites. Union membership would be defined more in terms of shared values and actions than collective bargaining with an employer. Representation would be extended to individual workers rather than members of a bargaining unit and would continue to extend to the members as they move

Exhibit 5.11
AFL-CIO
Union Plus

Click to Print

Union members have access to a wide array of members-only benefits, including low-interest cards, scholarships, mortgages, legal services and more. Most of the products and services listed here are members-only. But if you're not represented by a union, you can access some great services and products as well.

Watch Video

Watch this video (Windows media) to see how the AFL-CIO Is helping Katrina survivors.

Union Plus

Union Plus is brought to you by Union Privilege established by the AFL-CIO, to provide consumer benefits to members and retires of participating labor unions. Union Plus offers many products and services, including travel discounts on hotels, car rental and more. Below are details on some of their services; for more information and to see the full list, please visit the Union Plus website.

- *Retirement Planning*—Concerned about planning for retirement? Get help at the Union Plus Retirement Planning website.

- *Mortgage and real estate*—This Union Plus program makes refinancing and home buying more affordable for working families, offering an easy application process, closing cost assistance, and more.

- *Consumer credit counseling*—Certified consumer credit counseling advisers work with union members to help them eliminate their debt.

- *Credit card*—Carry the card that works as hard as you do: the Union Plus® Credit Card, exclusively for working families. Explore the many reasons to apply today.

- *Everyday savings, including health club discounts, 20 percent off flower service, discounts on union-made clothing and more.*

Scholarships

Union members and their children can tap into a range of education benefits. Union Plus Scholarship Program—A program offered through the Union Plus Education Foundation provides scholarships ranging from $500 to $4,000 to members of unions participating in any Union Plus program, their spouses and dependent children.
Union Scholarship Database—A searchable database of union-sponsored scholarships.

The Union Shop

The AFL-CIO's online store for union-made products is a one-stop for a variety of clothing, publications, music, videos, cards, buttons and more. Includes links to other union stores online.

Union Label

The AFL-CIO Union Label and Service Trades Department website provides information on union-made goods and services, featuring a national Do Not Buy list, the *Label Letter* newsletter and a new website, www.ShopUnionMade.org.

AFL-CIO Employees Federal Credit Union

A non-profit financial cooperative providing union members, union staff, and their families with a range of savings, checking and loan services.

Amalgamated Bank—The nation's only fully union-owned bank, in operation since 1923, provides a full menu of individual and commercial banking services.

SOURCE: http://www.aflcio.org/aboutus/benefits/.

from employer to employer. With the Internet, unions will be able to connect with this diverse and dispersed membership. This form of open unionism could appeal to a tremendous source of untapped union members who may be organized away from their workplace and away from their employer's opposition. There are 42 million workers who have expressed a need for some form of representation, and open source unionism could appeal to professional workers and others who need assistance with their employment contracts, overtime regulations, pensions, and health care benefits, but who do not believe that the traditional form of union representation through collective bargaining is appropriate from them.[95]

DECERTIFICATION PROCEDURE

Whenever employees believe that the union is not representing their interests, they may turn to a decertification procedure. In the last decade, decertification elections have nearly doubled, and researchers have identified a variety of reasons:

- Fair treatment of employees by employers

- Poor job by unions (especially smaller unions) of providing services to members

- Inability of unions to negotiate an effective first contract after winning bargaining rights

- Striking employees having skills that can be readily replaced[96] so that when a strike occurs, the employer hires replacements

Any employee, group of employees, or employee representative may file a petition for a decertification election 12 months after the union has been certified or upon expiration of the labor agreement (see "contract bar doctrine" discussed earlier). This petition must be supported by at least 30 percent of the bargaining unit employees.

Although employers cannot initiate the petition or assist in filing a petition for a decertification election, a company may raise a "good faith" doubt as to whether the union represents the majority of employees. The NLRB and the courts have developed presumptions and rules related to determining good faith doubt. First, there is a presumption of majority status for one year following certification by the Board. The second presumption is that majority status continues for up to three years if the collective bargaining agreement extends for three years. At the end of the certification year or the expiration of the three-year collective bargaining agreement, the employer may rebut the presumption of the union's majority status by presenting objective evidence—that the union does not continue to represent the majority of bargaining unit employees.

Examples of this evidence include a reduction in dues-paying members, a high percentage of employees crossed a union picket line during a strike, resignations from the union, or a petition by employees without company involvement.[97] (See Exhibit 5.12 for other examples of objective evidence.)

If the employees choose to decertify their union, another representation election cannot be held for 12 months. However, after a valid petition is filed with the NLRB, but before the election, the employer must still bargain with the union until the question of union representation is resolved.

Exhibit 5.12

Examples of Objective Evidence* of Union's Lack of Majority Status

1. Unsolicited communications from employees expressing a desire to become unrepresented

2. Any material change in the size or composition of the unit, such as a reduction in the number of employees

3. Date of union certification

4. Failure of the union to appoint a shop steward or committee

5. Failure of the union to process grievances

6. Failure of the union to actively represent employees on matters arising under the contract

7. Failure of the union to hold meetings that could be attended by the employees

8. Failure of the employees to attend union meetings

9. Failure of a majority of employees to authorize a dues checkoff if the contract provides for one

10. Whether the union has communicated a lack of interest in representation to either the company or the employees

11. Whether employees have filed or attempted to file a decertification petition of their own.

*"Objective evidence" is defined as "reasonable grounds" to believe that an incumbent union no longer represents a majority of bargaining unit employees.

SOURCE: Clyde Scott, Kim Hester, and Edwin Arnold, "Employer-Initiated Elections, 1968–1992," *Journal of Labor Research* 18 (Spring 1997), p. 317.

Although employers must be careful of their role in the decertification process, they have exhibited growing interest in it. For example, a one-day seminar, "The Process of Decertification" by Executive Enterprises is designed to teach management representatives about the entire process of decertification. Many employers have concluded that they should become more involved, especially because they are becoming aware that they do not necessarily have to play a passive role in the decertification process.

Companies have used several deunionization approaches in recent years. One is the withdrawal of recognition of the incumbent union on the grounds that it no longer holds majority status. In these cases, the employer must be able to show through objective evidence that a majority interest in the union no longer exists. Employers have been able to do this by showing that only a few employees are having their dues deducted through a "checkoff" system, a strike was called and few employees participated, and/or employees on their own signed a petition denouncing their union membership.[98]

From 1951 to 2001, an employer could lawfully withdraw recognition from an incumbent union if it could show that the union no longer had the support of a majority of the bargaining unit or had a good-faith doubt, based on objective evidence, of the union's majority status. The Board has indicated that it is "entirely appropriate" to place the burden of proof on the employer to show that there is an actual loss of majority support for the union. Another option is for an employer to petition for a Board-conducted representation election. In 2001, the NLRB changed its policy. Where there have been no unfair labor practices that tended to undermine the employees' support for the union, loss of majority now is the sole legal basis for withdrawing recognition from an incumbent union. The Board eliminated the good-faith requirement and now provides for the employer

LABOR RELATIONS IN ACTION
Union Salting: A New Union-Organizing Tactic

Town & Country Electric, a nonunion electrical contractor, needed to hire several licensed Minnesota electricians for construction work within Minnesota and advertised the positions through an employment agency. Eleven union applicants, including two professional union staff members, applied for jobs. Only one union applicant was interviewed; he was hired but was subsequently dismissed after only a few days on the job.

The IBEW filed a complaint with the NLRB against Town & Country. The complaint was that the company refused to interview applicants and refused to retain union members because of their union membership, which was in violation of the National Labor Relations Act (NLRA).

An administrative law judge and the board determined that all of the union applicants were "employees" under the language of the NLRA. Although the applicants had not been hired, applicants are covered under the prohibition of "discrimination in regard to hire" under the NLRA. The board found it immaterial that the union applicants intended to try to organize Town & Country employees upon securing employment, as well as the fact that the union would be paying these employees to organize a union.

The U.S. Court of Appeals for the Eighth Circuit reversed the NLRB and held that the board had incorrectly interpreted the definition of "employee" in the NLRA. The Court ruled that the NLRB did not protect employees who were working for a company while simultaneously being paid by the union to attempt to organize employees of the company.

The U.S. Supreme Court determined that the NLRA sought to improve labor-management relations by granting employees the right to organize, form unions, join unions, and assist in organizing unions. The high Court ruled that the meaning of the word "employee" was critical and that the language and definition of "employee" includes paid union organizers. The Court noted that the NLRB was created to administer the NLRA and will be upheld when its rulings are "reasonably defensible." The Court indicated that it relied on the NLRB's expertise and congressional intent in its ruling. Furthermore, the Court ruled that Congress had delegated the primary responsibility for developing and applying national labor policy and that the board's views are entitled to the greatest deference by the courts. The principal difference between **salting** and the traditional organizing is that salting is a "top-down" approach and traditional organizing is a bottom-up approach. Union salting may be called covert or overt. Covert salting is like a Trojan horse in that a full-time union organizer applies to a help-wanted ad placed by nonunion businesses. The union organizer does not reveal that he or she is employed by the union. The employer does not conduct a background or reference check, and the union organizer is hired by the employer. Once employed, the union organizer initiates

to seek a representation election if the employer can show a reasonable uncertainty that a majority of employees support the union. The logical conclusion is that employers should not be allowed to withdraw recognition of the union short of a representation election.[99] Employers may become active participants in the decertification efforts after the petition is filed; however, they should do so only after analyzing the costs and benefits of such a strategy. For example, if the company actively campaigns against the present union and the union wins the election and continues to represent employees, the long-term relationship with the union may be irreparably damaged. Moreover, if the company's relationship with the present union is reasonable and productive, it might be wiser to retain it than chance a later replacement by a more militant union.

If the employer chooses to become engaged in the decertification campaign, similar representation election rules and policies apply. For instance, after the petition is filed with the NLRB, the employer may communicate with employees and forcefully state its opposition to the present union, lawfully respond to employee questions, and inform them about the decertification election process. The employer may conduct captive audience speeches,

an organizing campaign. Overt salting occurs when the union organizer reveals in the application process that he is employed by the union. If he is denied employment due to his union affiliation, he files a charge of an unfair labor practice against the employer for discriminating against him because of his union membership.

Since the *Town & Country* Decision

Since the *Town & Country* decision, there has been a 53 percent increase in overt salting activities and a 47 percent increase in covert salting. By 2001, there were 55 union salting unfair labor practices cases before the NLRB. Of the 55 cases, 6 were dismissed and 3 were remanded to the administrative law judge. In 43 cases, the charges were upheld by the NLRB. These charges were associated with monetary penalties of back pay. These charges included unlawful discharge, unlawful layoff, refusal to consider for employment, refusal to recall from layoff, unlawful suspension, and refusal to reinstate strikers. Interestingly, nonunion contractors may join the Associated Builders and Contractors and take out salting insurance, which pays legal fees and up to 90 percent of back pay awards issued by the NLRB.

The appellate courts have cut back on some union salting activities by finding that an employer may fire a "union salt" if he falsified his employment application to obtain a job or the "union salt" violated a lawful "moonlighting" policy that does not allow employees to hold two jobs at the same time. In other words, the court found that the dual employment rule was lawful if applied in a nondiscriminatory manner.

Legal proceedings

The NLRB has ruled that two factors must be present for a finding of guilt in a "refusal-to-consider" case. The general counsel must prove that the employer excluded "salts" from the hiring process and that an anti-union animus contributed to the employer's decision not to consider the salts. If these facts are established, then the burden of proof shifts to the employer to prove that it would not have considered the "salts" even in the absence of their union activity.

In "refusal-to-hire" cases, the general counsel must (1) show that the employer was hiring or had concrete plans to hire at the time the salting took place, (2) demonstrate that the "salts" had appropriate experience and training and were qualified for the position for which they applied, and (3) prove that anti-union animus was present and contributed to the decision not to hire the salts. If successful, the burden of proof shifts to the employer to prove that it would not have hired the salts even in the absence of their union activity. Justification by the employer includes the hiring of other better qualified applicants or proof that the "salts" were not qualified for the vacant positions.

SOURCE: Jeffrey A. Mello, "The Enemy Within: When Paid Union Organizers Become Employees," *Labor Law Journal* 47 (October 1996), pp. 677–679;NLRB v. *Town & Country Electric, Inc.*, 116 S. Ct. 450 (1995); NLRB has developed guidelines in FES (*A Division of Thermo Power*) 331 N.L.R.B. No. 20, 5/11/00. See also Cory R. Fine, "Union Salting: Reactions and Rulings since *Town and Country*," *Journal of Labor Research* 23 (Summer 2002), pp. 475–483.

send letters to employees, and conduct small group discussions during the decertification election campaign. Management may tell employees about the employer's perception of the disadvantages of the union and that the employer prefers to deal directly with individual employees instead of through a third party and wants to build a "trusting, team-oriented" relationship with employees, not an adversarial one. At the same time, employers must be careful not to plant the idea of decertification in the minds of employees by offering unsolicited advice, distributing booklets that explain how to decertify the union, or circulating a decertification petition. During the union decertification campaign, union officials will attempt to convince employees of the benefits of continued union representation.[100]

Decertification campaigns are conducted by unions and management in a manner similar to certification campaigns. Decertification elections are usually initiated by a group of employees who are not satisfied with the working conditions and economic provisions achieved by the union through collective bargaining. During the campaign period, the union officials prefer to use handbills, conduct personal visits, and make special pleas with members to refuse signing any decertification petition. Management prefers to rely on legal counsel and small group meetings with employees. Researchers have found both management and the unions have been successful in their campaigns when they emphasize personal contacts with employees and listen genuinely to their concerns, instead of mailing letters and giving out handbills.[101]

Employers must be aware of related unlawful activities, such as the following:

- Obtaining NLRB forms for employees who may be interested in union decertification

- Providing services such as typing, assistance in phrasing the petition for decertification, and use of company stationery by employees who are interested in launching a decertification campaign

- Initiating discussions on how or whether to decertify the union

- Allowing supervisors or any other persons identified with management to promote the decertification process[102]

Unions respond to any challenge to their existence as the certified representative of the bargaining unit employees by attempting to convince the employees that there are reasons to continue their union membership and representation and not to seek decertification. Unions do this by improving the level of services to the employees and by attempting to gain improvements in benefits through negotiation.[103]

The number of decertification elections, the number of employees in the bargaining units, and the percentage of elections lost by unions have remained steady over the last five years. The number of elections is less than 400 per year, the number of employees eligible to vote was 22,690 (less than .0014 of all union members), and 35 percent of the elections were won by unions.[104]

Research has identified several explanations for union decertification. First, the affiliation status of the local union involved in the union decertification election is important because affiliated unions have greater resources available to hold membership support and ultimately to retain union representation. A second factor affecting decertification is the availability of local employment and income opportunities. As employment opportunities increase, there is a decreased likelihood of support for the retention of the union. However, as income opportunities exceed the average, there is increased support to retain the union. Furthermore, where employees face income and employment opportunities that are limited to part-time, low-wage employment, support for union retention is significantly lower. For those employees whose income from part-time employment is relatively small, the expense of continuing to support the union is reduced. These reasons may help to explain such corporate strategies as moving to small southern towns where alternative employment is relatively sparse and increasing the number of part-time employees.[105]

The employees, like the employer, must be aware of possible consequences of their activities attempting to decertify the union. Decertification advocates must be prepared for pressure from union officials and isolation from fellow employees who are pleased with the union. The NLRB has upheld the union's right to discipline union members who actively participate in the campaign to decertify the union, as long as the disciplinary action does not affect the employee's employment status.

In addition to decertification elections, there are the "raid" elections or multi-union elections. These elections occur when a different union (a challenger) attempts to replace an incumbent union. The bargaining unit employees are given a choice between (1) the incumbent union, (2) the challenger union, and (3) no union. Like other types of elections, the employer may campaign in an attempt to persuade employees to vote "no union," and the union in effect will be decertified. In those elections, the incumbent unions wins most of the time.[106]

Summary

This chapter provides insights into reasons unions are formed. It discusses the most important theories and explanations ranging from alienation and class consciousness to the employees' backgrounds and personal desires. The role of a union is to fulfill employees' perceived needs and answer job-related concerns. Unionization efforts progress from first contacts with employees to signing the authorization cards, petition for election, hearings, determination of the appropriate bargaining unit, and the eventual representation election. Within this framework numerous rules, regulations, and legal requirements govern the union certification process. The procedures by which employees can be formed into unions through voluntary recognition, NLRB directives, and secret-ballot elections are explained.

The chapter presents the arguments for and against the Employee Free Choice Act and the Mandatory Secret Ballot Protection Act. The Employee Free Choice Act was passed by the U.S. House of Representative and had a majority of senators who supported its passage, but there was not enough support to bring the act to a vote. Even if the act had passed, President Bush would have vetoed it. As a result, supporters of the Employee Free Choice Act are focusing on the 2008 elections.

Recently, unions have launched new strategies to organize nonunion employees. The AFL-CIO and CTW have introduced several new programs.

Finally, in those cases where the union is judged by employees as not representing their interests, a decertification procedure is available through the election process. Generally, only a few employees and only small bargaining units have been involved in decertification elections.

Key Terms

Alienation theory, p. 177
Scarcity Consciousness Theory, p. 177
Union instrumentality, p. 181

Consent election, p. 196
Directed elections, p. 197
Contract bar doctrine, p. 201

Totality of conduct doctrine, p. 208
Salting, p. 216

Discussion Questions

1. Refer to the reasons why employees become members of unions to assess the means used by union organizers to meet these needs.

2. Select an organization with which you are familiar, and determine the number of bargaining units that would be appropriate for its structure.

3. Explain the contract bar doctrine. How would it influence the negotiation of the first labor agreement?

4. Discuss the shifting position of the NLRB on representation election campaigning. Appraise each position.

5. Prescribe a "do" and "don't" list for supervisors involved in unionization campaigns so that they will not commit any unfair labor practices.

6. Why do you believe employers are becoming more interested in decertification elections?

7. Explain the following statement: "It is not the union that organizes the employees; it is management."

8. What would be a good response from a union organizer for each statement in the Labor Relations in Action feature on page 195?

9. Review the arguments for and against the Employee Free Choice Act and the Mandatory Secret Ballot Protection Act. How would you vote? Give your reasons.

Exploring the Web

Salting

1. Definition

What is salting? Go to the Web site of the Industrial Workers of the World (IWW) and read a definition published from a union's point of view.

On the Web site for the Associated Builders and Contractors, a national trade association, locate "ABC's Legislative Position on Salting." What impact, according to the position paper, does salting have on industry, consumers, taxpayers, and the federal budget?

2. Salting and the Courts

Use Cornell's law pages or OYEZ to locate a major 1995 Supreme Court case in which the Court overturned an Eighth Circuit Court of Appeals holding and affirmed an earlier opinion by the National Labor Relations Board. The NLRB had ruled that a worker may be a company's "employee" as defined by the NLRA and may also be paid by a union to organize the company's workers.

National Labor Relations Board v. Town & Country Electric, Inc., 516 U.S. 85 (1995)

Check with your college or university library to see if you can locate "Union Salting: Reactions and Rulings since *Town and Country*," an article by Dr. Cory Fine published in the *Journal of Labor Research* in 2002.

3. Salting and Congress

Go to THOMAS, the Library of Congress Web site that provides legislative information and locate the text of two bills that were introduced in Congress in June 2007 to "amend the National Labor Relations Act to protect employer rights." This is the "Truth in Employment Act of 2007." The Senate bill is S.1570 and the companion bill in the House is H.R. 2670. What do the bills say about "salting"? What is the current status of each bill? Locate references to these bills in the *Congressional Record*.

Similar legislation has been introduced, but not passed, for the last several years. Locate Congressional testimony and hearings related to the legislation for any year. What are the main points of debate from each side?

References

1. Kai Erikson, "On Work and Alienation," *American Sociological Review* 51 (February 1986), p. 2. For examples of this situation, see Michael Hanagan and Charles Stephenson, *Confrontation, Class Consciousness, and the Labor Process* (New York: Greenwood Press, 1986).

2. Clinton S. Golden and Harold Ruttenberg, "Motives for Union Membership," in *Unions, Management, and the*

Public, eds. E. Wight Bakke, Clark Kerr, and Charles W. Anrod (New York: Harcourt, Brace, 1948), p. 49.

3. M.D. Dunnette and W.K. Kirchner, *Psychology Applied to Industry* (New York: Appleton-Century-Crofts, 1965), pp. 199–200; and Henry S. Farber and Daniel H. Saks, "Why Workers Want Unions: The Role of Relative Wages and Job Characteristics" (Working Paper, Cambridge, Mass.: M.I.T., 1978), pp. 27–28. See also W. Clay

Hamner and Frank J. Smith, "Work Attitudes as Predictors of Unionization Activity," *Journal of Applied Psychology* 63 (1978), p. 415; William J. Bigoness, "Correlates of Faculty Attitudes toward Collective Bargaining," *Journal of Applied Psychology* 63 (1978), pp. 228–233; Chester A. Schreisheim, "Job Satisfaction, Attitudes toward Unions, and Voting in a Union Representation Election," *Journal of Applied Psychology* 63 (1978), pp. 548–552; J. G. Getman, S. B. Goldberg, and J. B. Herman, *Union Representation Elections: Law and Reality* (New York: Russel Sage Foundation, 1976); Edward L. Harrison, "Employee Satisfaction and Voting Behavior in Union Representation Elections," In *Toward Renewal of Management Thought and Practices,* eds. Dennis F. Ray and Thad B. Green (State College, Miss.: Southern Management Association, Mississippi State University, 1978), p. 169.

4. Jeanette A. Davy and Frank Shipper, "Voter Behavior in Union Certification Elections: A Longitudinal Study," *Academy of Management Journal* 36 (February 1993), pp. 187–199.

5. Barry A. Friedman, Steven E. Abraham, and Randall K. Thomas, "Factors Related to Employees' Desire to Join and Leave Unions," *Industrial Relations,* Vol. 45, No. 1 (January 2006), pp. 102–110.

6. Selig Perlman, *A Theory of the Labor Movement* (1928; reprinted New York: Augustus M. Kelley, 1968), p. 242.

7. Roger D. Weikle, Hoyt N. Wheeler, and John A. McClendon, "A Comprehensive Case Study of Union Organizing Success and Failure: Implications for Practical Strategy," *Organizing to Win,* ed. Kate Bronfenbrenner et al. (Ithaca, N.Y.: Cornell University Press, 1999), pp. 199–203.

8. Hoyt N. Wheeler and John A. McClendon, "The Individual Decision to Unionize," in *The State of the Unions,* ed. George Strauss, Daniel G. Gallagher, and Jack Fiorito (Madison, Wis.: IRRA, 1991), pp. 65–67.

9. Joel Seidman, Jack London, and Bernard Karsh, "Why Workers Join Unions," *Annals of the American Academy of Political and Social Sciences* 274 (March 1951), pp. 775–784.

10. E. Wight Bakke, "Why Workers Join Unions," *Personnel* 22 (July 1947), p. 3.

11. J.G. Getman, S.B. Goldberg, and J.B. Herman, Union *Representation Elections: Law and Reality* (New York: Russel Sage Foundation, 1976). See also Henry S. Farber and Daniel H. Saks, "Why Workers Want Unions: The Role of Relative Wages and Job Characteristics," *Journal of Political Economy* 88 (April 1980), pp. 349–369; and Jack Fiorito and Charles R. Greer, "Gender Differences in Union Membership, Preferences and Beliefs," *Journal of Labor Research* (Spring 1986), pp. 145–164.

12. Farber, *Why Workers;* and Stephen M. Hills, "The Attitudes of Union and Nonunion Male Workers toward Union Representation," *Industrial and Labor Relations Review* (January 1985), pp. 179–194.

13. Hoyt N. Wheeler and John A. McClendon, "The Individual Decision to Unionize," pp. 64–67.

14. J.M. Brett and T.J. Hammer, "Organizational Behavior and Industrial Relations," in *Industrial Relations Research in the 1970s: Review and Appraisal,* eds. T. A.

Kochan, et al. (Madison, Wis.: Industrial Relations Research Association, 1982), pp. 245–251.

15. Satish P. Deshpande and Chockalingam Viswervaran, "Predictors of Unionization: The Role of Specific Beliefs, General Beliefs, and Normative Pressures," *Labor Studies Journal* 19 (Fall 1994), pp. 68–69.

16. Satish P. Deshpande and Jack Fiorito, "Specific and General Beliefs in Union Voting Models," *Academy of Management Journal* 32 (December 1989), pp. 883–895.

17. Thomas A. DeCottis and Jean-Yves Le Lovarn, "A Predictive Study of Voting Behavior in a Representation Election Using Union Instrumentality and Work Perceptions," *Organizational Behavior and Human Performance* 27 (February 1981), pp. 103–118. Also see Stuart A. Youngblood, Angelo S. DeNisi, Julie L. Molleston, and William H. Mobley, "The Impact of Work Environment, Instrumentality Beliefs, Perceived Labor Union Image, and Subjectivity Norms on Union Voting Intentions," *Academy of Management Journal* 27 (December 1984), pp. 576–590; Masoud Hemmasi and Lee A. Graf, "Determinants of Faculty Voting Behavior in Union Representation Elections: A Multivariate Model," *Journal of Management* 19 (November 1, 1995), pp. 13–32.

18. Stuart A. Youngblood, William H. Mobley, and Angelo S. DeNisi, "Attitudes, Perceptions, and Intentions to Vote in a Union Certification Election: An Empirical Investigation," *in Proceedings of the Thirty-Fourth Annual Meeting: Industrial Relations Research Association,* ed. B.D. Dennis (Madison, Wis.: Industrial Relations Research Association, 1982), pp. 244–253; Tom Langford, "Involvement with Unions, Union Belief Perspectives, and Desires for Union Membership," *Journal of Labor Research* 15 (Summer 1994), pp. 257–270.

19. Edward L. Harrison, Douglas Johnson, and Frank M. Rachel, "The Role of the Supervisor in Representation Elections," *Personnel Administration* 26 (September 1981), pp. 69–70.

20. Dorothy Sue Cobble, "Union Strategies for Organizing and Representing the New Service Workforce," in *Proceedings of the 43rd Annual Meeting of the Industrial Relations Research Association* (Madison, Wis.: IRRA, 1991), p. 76.

21. David M. Rabban, "Is Unionism Compatible with Professionalism?" *Industrial and Labor Relations Review* 45 (October 1991), pp. 97–112.

22. Heejoon Park, Patrick P. McHugh and Matthew M. Bodah, "Revisiting General and Specific Union Beliefs: The Union-Voting Intentions of Professionals," *Industrial Relations,* Vol. 45, No. 2 (April 2006), pp. 270–289.

23. David M. Rabban. "Is Unionism Compatible with Professionalism?" *Industrial and Labor Relations Review* 45 (October 1991), pp. 97–112.

24. Michael E. Gordon and Angelo S. DeNisi, "A Re-examination of the Relationship between Union Membership and Job Satisfaction," *Industrial and Labor Relations Review* 48 (January 1995), p. 234.

25. John J. Hoover, "Union Organization Attempts: Management's Response," *Personnel Journal* 61 (March 1982), pp. 214–215.

26. Thomas F. Reed, "Do Union Organizers Matter? Individual Differences, Campaign Practices, and

Representation Election Outcomes," *Industrial and Labor Relations Review* 43 (October 1989), pp. 102–117.

27. Thomas F. Reed, "Profiles of Union Organizers from Manufacturing and Service Unions," *Journal of Labor Research* 11 (Winter 1990), pp. 73–80.

28. Charles McDonald, "U.S. Union Membership in Future Decades: A Trade Unionist's Perspective," *Industrial Relations* 31 (Winter 1992), pp. 19–21.

29. James A. Craft and Marian M. Extejt, "New Strategies in Union Organizing," *Working Paper Series* (Pittsburgh, Penn.: University of Pittsburgh, 1982), p. 304.

30. Kate Bronfenbrenner, "The Role of Union Strategies in NLRB Elections," *Industrial and Labor Relations Review* 50 (January 1997), pp. 195–211.

31. Jack Fiorito, "Human Resource Management Practices and Worker Desires for Union Representation," *Journal of Labor Research,* Vol. 22, No. 2 (Spring 2001), p. 340–350.

32. Julius G. Getman, "Ruminations on Union Organizing in the Private Sector," *The University of Chicago Law Review* 53 (Winter 1986), p. 59.

33. Richard B. Peterson, Thomas W. Lee, and Barbara Finnegan, "Strategies and Tactics in Union Organizing Campaigns," *Industrial Relations* 31 (Spring 1992), pp. 370–374.

34. John J. Lawler and Robin West, "Impact of Union-Avoidance Strategy in Representation Elections," *Industrial Relations* 24 (Fall 1985), pp. 406–420.

35. Satish P. Deshpande and Chockalingam Viswervaran, "Predictors of Unionization: The Role of Specific Beliefs, General Beliefs, and Normative Pressures," *Labor Studies Journal* 19 (Fall 1994), pp. 68–69.

36. Donna Sockell, "Contemporary Challenges of Labor Law," in *Proceedings of the Fortieth Annual Meeting of the Industrial Relations Research Association,* ed. Barbara D. Dennis (Madison, Wis.: Industrial Relations Research Association, 1988), pp. 85–90.

37. *United Autoworkers v. Secretary of Labor,* 678 F. Supp. 4 (D.C., 1988).

38. Bruce Kaufman and Paula E. Stephan, "The Role of Management Attorneys in Union Organizing Campaigns," *Journal of Labor Research* 16 (Fall 1995), pp. 439–454.

39. William N. Cooke, "The Rising Toll of Discrimination against Union Activists," *Industrial Relations* 24 (Fall 1985), p. 437.

40. "Adherence to Labor Laws Not in Management's Interests, Says Ex-NLRB Staff Member," *Report on Union Busters, RUB Sheet* (Washington, D.C.: AFL-CIO, March/April, 1990), p. 1.

41. Wilma B. Liebman, "Discussion," *Proceedings of the 57th Annual Meeting of the Labor and Employment Relations Association,* Champaign, IL: LERA, 2005, pp. 114–116.

42. *Annual Reports, Federal Mediation and Conciliation Service,* (http://www.fmcs.gov).

43. James J. Brudney, "Contractual Approaches to Labor Organizing: Supplanting the Election Paradigm?" *Proceedings of the 57th Annual Meeting of the Labor and Employment Relations Association,* Champaign, IL: LERA, 2005, pp. 105–113.

44. Adrienne E. Eaton and Jill Kriesky, "Union Organizing Under Neutrality and Card Check Agreements," *Industrial and Labor Relations Review* 55 (October 2001), pp. 42–57.

45. Adrienne E. Eaton and Jill Kriesky, "No More Stacked Deck: Evaluating the Case Against Card-Check Union Recognition," *Perspectives on Work* 7, no. 2 (2003), pp. 19–21.

46. Thomas A. Kochan, "Employer's Stake in Union Neutrality," *Proceedings of the 58th Annual Meeting of the Labor and Employment Relations Association.* Andrienne E. Eaton,Editor, Champaign, IL: LERA, 2006, pp xx.

47. *NLRB* v. *Gissel Packing Co.* 385 U.S. 575 (1969). An authorization card signifies that the employee desires to be represented by the union in collective bargaining. The employee thereby authorizes the union to represent him or her with his employer. The signed card may be used later by the union as proof of majority representation, as support to demand recognition, and as evidence that there is "substantial interest" among the bargaining unit to support a petition to the NLRB for representation election. Schlossberg and Sherman, *Organizing and the Law,* p. 50.

48. Peter J. Leff, "Failing to Give the Board Its Due: The Lack of Deference Afforded by the Appellate Courts in *Gissel* Bargaining Order Cases," *The Labor Lawyer* 79 (2002), pp. 109–111.

49. Gil A. Abramson, "The Uncertain Fate of *Gissel* Bargaining Orders in the Circuit Courts of Appeal," *The Labor Lawyer* 18 (2002), pp. 121–136.

50. Harry E. Graham and Karen N. Neilsen, "Union Representation Elections: A View From the Heart of It All," *Labor Law Journal* 42 (July 1991), pp. 438–441; William E. Fulmer, "Step by Step through a Union Campaign," *Harvard Business Review* 59 (July–August 1981), pp. 94–95; Clyde Scott, Kim Hester, and Edwin Arnold, "Employer-Initiated Elections, 1968–1992," *Journal of Labor Research* 18 (Spring 1997), pp. 315–331.

51. David R. Stephens and Paul R. Timm. "A Comparison of Campaign Techniques in Contested Faculty Elections: An Analysis of the Florida Experience," *Journal of Collective Negotiations in the Public Sector* 7 (1978), pp. 167–177.

52. Paula B. Voos, "Does It Pay to Organize? The Cost to Unions," *Monthly Labor Review* 107 (June 1984), pp. 43–44.

53. Paula Voos, "Union Organizing: Costs and Benefits," *Industrial and Labor Relations Review* 36 (July 1983), pp. 576–580. Also see Paula Voos, "Trends in Union Organizing Expenditures, 1953–1977," *Industrial and Labor Relations Review* 38 (October 1984), pp. 52–66.

54. Steven E. Abraham and Paula B. Voos, "The Market's Reaction to Two Supreme Court Rulings on American Labor Law," *Journal of Labor Research,* Vol. 26, No. 4 (Fall 2005), pp. 677–681.

55. *Oakwood Healthcare, Inc.* 348 NLRB No. 37 (September 29, 2006).

56. Rebecca S. Demsetz, "Voting Behavior in Union Representation Elections: The Influence of Skill Homogeneity and Skill," *Industrial and Labor Relations Review* 47 (October 1993), pp. 99–113.

57. Robert Sebris, Jr., and Robert D. McDonald, "Bargaining Unit Determination Case Trends of the NLRB," *Labor Law Journal* 37 (June 1986), pp. 378–382.

58. Robert J. Alberts, "The Appropriate Bargaining Unit, Geographic Proximity, and The 'Nearest Neighbor': An Alternative Analysis," *Labor Law Journal* 41 (July 1990), pp. 424–426.

59. Clyde Scott and Nicholas A. Beadles II, "Unit Placement Decisions in Acute-Care Hospitals," *Labor Law Journal* 44 (March 1993), pp. 143–152; Satish P. Deshpande and David J. Flanagan, "Union Certification Elections in Hospitals," *Labor Studies Journal* 21 (Fall 1996), pp. 56–71.

60. Kenneth R. Dolin and Ross H. Friedman, "Recent Developments and the Likely Effect of Changes at the National Labor Relations Board," *Labor Law Journal* 54, no. 1 (2003) p. 15.

61. Debroah M. Zinni and Anne F. MacLennan, "Graduate Student Unions in the United States," *Journal of Labor Research,* Vol. 27, No. 1 (Winter 2006), pp. 55–70.

62. *Excelsior Underwear, Inc.,* 156 NLRB 1236 (1966).

63. Richard N. Block and Myron Roomkin, "Determinants of Voter Participation in Union Certification Elections," *Monthly Labor Review* 105 (April 1982), pp. 45–47.

64. Myron Roomkin and Richard N. Block, "Case Processing Time and the Outcome of Representation Elections: Some Empirical Evidence," *University of Illinois Law Review* 1981, reprinted in *Oversight Hearings on the Subject"Has Labor Law Failed?"* (Washington, D.C.: Committee on Education and Labor, 1984), pp. 844–845.

65. Marcus H. Sandver and Herbert G. Heneman III, "Union Growth through the Election Process," *Industrial Relations* 20 (Winter 1981), pp. 109–115.

66. William N. Cooke, "Determinants of the Outcomes of Union Certification Elections," *Industrial and Labor Relations Review* 36 (April 1983), pp. 402–414.

67. Cheryl L. Maranto and Jack Fiorito, "The Effect of Union Characteristics on the Outcome of the NLRB Elections," *Industrial and Labor Relations Review* 40 (January 1987), pp. 225–238.

68. Victor G. Devinatz and Daniel P. Rich, "Representation Type and Union Success in Certification Elections," *Journal of Labor Research* 15 (Winter 1995), pp. 85–92.

69. Dolin and Friedman, "Recent Developments and the Likely Effect of Changes at the National Labor Relations Board," p. 13.

70. Marcus Hart Sandver and Kathryn J. Ready, "Trends in and Determinants of Outcomes in Multi-Union Certification Elections," *Journal of Labor Research* 19 (Winter 1998), pp. 164–171.

71. *Seventieth Annual Report of the National Labor Relations Board, for the Fiscal Year ended September 30, 2005,* (http://www.nlrb.gov).

72. Henry S. Farber, "Union Success in Representation Election: Why Does Unit Size Matter?" *Industrial and Labor Relations Review* 54 (January 2001), pp. 329–345.

73. "Study Calls for Labor Law Reform to Aid Unions Seeking First Contracts," *Daily Labor Report,* July 10, 1985, p. A-10.

74. William N. Cooke, "The Failure to Negotiate First Contracts: Determinants and Policy Implications," *Industrial and Labor Relations Review* 38 (January 1985), pp. 163–178.

75. Karen E. Boroff, "Unfair Labor Practice Filings in Organizing Elections: New Data and Analysis," *Labor Law Journal* 47 (November 1997), pp. 655–661.

76. Gerald Mayer, "Labor Union Recognition Procedures: Use of Secret Ballots and Card Checks," Congressional Research Service, The Library of Congress, 2005 (http://digitalcommons.ilr.cornell.edu/key_workplace/237).

77. John Logan, "No Choice for Workers," June 26, 2007, TomPaine.com.

78. Gerald Mayer, "Labor Union Recognition Procedures: Use of Secret Ballots and Card Checks," Congressional Research Service, The Library of Congress, 2005 (http://digitalcommons.ilr.cornell.edu/key_workplace/237).

79. *Shopping Kart Food Market,* 94 LRRM 1705 (1977); Julius G. Getman, Stephen B. Goldberg, and Jeanne B. Herman, Union Representation Elections: Law and Reality (New York: Russell Sage Foundation, 1976); and Neal Orkin and Mara Landberg, "Election Campaign Propaganda: Board Policy Then and Now," *Labor Law Journal* 46 (July 1995), pp. 440–446.

80. William T. Dickens, "The Effect of Company Campaigns on Certification Elections: Law and Reality Once Again," *Industrial and Labor Relations Review* 36 (July 1983), pp. 574–576.

81. Richard N. Block, Benjamin W. Wolkinson, and James W. Kuhn, "Some Are More Equal Than Others: The Relative Status of Employers, Unions, and Employees in the Law of Union Organizing," *Industrial Relations Law Journal* 10, no. 2 (1989), p. 220.

82. David P. Brenskelle, "Questioning Employees Concerning Union Sentiment Remains a Risky Proposition," *Employee Relations Law Journal* 13 (Summer 1987), pp. 141–147.

83. *Republican Aviation Corp. v. NLRB,* 324 U.S. 793 (1945).

84. "Justices Twice Back Right to Distribute Union Literature on Company Property," *The Wall Street Journal,* June 23, 1978, p. 6; Peter G. Kilgore, "No- Solicitation/No-Distribution Rules: The Word Battle of 'Time' Versus 'Hours' Continues," *Labor Law Journal* 35 (November 1984), pp. 671–672.

85. *Beth Israel v. NLRB,* 46 U.S.L.W. 4765 (June 22, 1978).

86. *Eastex, Inc. v. NLRB,* 46 U.S.L.W. 4783 (June 22, 1978).

87. "NLRB Member Oviatt Says Lechmere Creates Presumption Against Union Access," *Daily Labor Report,* February 3, 1992, p. A-5; "Employers and Union Foresee More Costly Organizing Tactics," *Daily Labor Report,* January 29, 1992, p. A-15; and "*Lechmere* Decision Makes Organizing More Difficult for Unions, NLRB Attorney Says," *Daily Labor Report,* June 5, 1992, p. A-1.

88. Karen E. Boroff, "Shopping for Access after Lechmere," *Labor Law Journal* 46 (June 1995), pp. 366–370; Eileen P. Kelly, Owen Seaquest, Amy Oakes, and Lawrence S. Clark, "NLRB v. Lechmere: Union Quest for Access," *Journal of Labor Research* 15 (Spring 1994), pp. 155–167.

89. Kevin Conlon and Catherine Voight, "Distinguishing *Lechmere*: Union Organizers' Access to Employers' Property," *Labor Law Journal* 44 (August 1993), pp. 496–501.

90. Joseph A. Pichler and H. Gordon Fitch, "And Women Must Weep: The NLRB as Film Critic," *Industrial and Labor Relations Review* 28 (April 1975), pp. 395–410.

91. Anthony M. Townsend, Samuel M. Demarie and Anthony R. Hendrickson, "Information Technology, Unions, and the New Organization: Challenges and Opportunities for Union Survival," *Journal of Labor Research,* Vol. 22, No. 2 (Spring 2001), p. 285.

92. *The Guard Publishing Company, d/b/a/ The Register-Guard,* 351 NLRB No. 70 (December 16, 2007).

93. Andrew W. Martin, "Why Does the New Labor Movement Look So Much Like the Old One? Putting the 1990s Revitalization Project in Historical Context," *Journal of Labor Research,* Vol. 27, No. 2 (Spring 2006), p. 176.

94. Richard W. Hurd, "U.S. Labor 2006: Strategic Developments across the Divide," *Journal of Labor Research,* 38, No. 2 (Spring 2007), p. 313–324; Marick F. Masters, Ray Gibney and Tom Zagenczyk, "The AFL-CIO v. CTW: the Competing Visions, Strategies, and Structures," *Journal of Labor Research,* 27, No. 4 (Fall 2006), p. 473–503.

95. Gary Chaison, "The Changing Role of Unions: A Review Essay," *Journal of Labor Economics,*" Vol. 27, No. 3 (Summer 2006), 423–424.

96. James B. Dworkin and Marian Extejt, "Why Workers Decertify Their Unions: A Preliminary Investigation," paper presented at the Annual Meeting of the Academy of Management, August 1979.

97. Robert W. Schupp, "When Is a Union Not a Union? Good Faith Doubt and Its Limitations in Collective Bargaining," *Labor Law Journal* 48 (June 1997), pp. 369–370.

98. Clyde Scott, Kim Hester, and Edwin Arnold, "Decertification Elections: An Analysis of Recent Activity," *Labor Law Journal* 46 (February 1995), pp. 67–74.

99. David M. Savino and Nealia S. Bruning, "Decertification Strategies and Tactics: Management and Union Perspectives," *Labor Law Journal* 43 (April 1992), pp. 201–208.

100. William A. Krupman and Gregory I. Rasin, "Decertification: Removing the Shroud," *Labor Law Journal* 30 (April 1979), pp. 234–235.

101. Trevor Bain, Clyde Scott, and Edwin Arnold, "Deauthorization Elections: An Early Warning Signal to Decertification?" *Labor Law Journal* 39 (July 1988), pp. 432–436.

102. *Seventieth Annual Report of the National Labor Relations Board, for the Fiscal Year ended September 30, 2005,* (http://www. nlrb.gov).

103. David Meyer and Trevor Bain, "Union Decertification Election Outcomes: Bargaining-Unit Characteristics and Union Resources," *Journal of Labor Research* 15 (Spring 1994), pp. 117–136.

104. *Tawas Tube Production, Inc.* 151 NLRB 9 (1965).

105. Edwin Arnold, Clyde Scott, and John Rasp, "The Determinants of Incumbent Union Victory in Raid Elections," *Labor Law Journal* 43 (April 1992), pp. 221–228; Clyde Scott and Edwin Arnold, "Raid Elections: An Analysis of Employer Campaigns," *Labor Law Journal* 41 (September 1990), pp. 641–648. Also see Robert W. Schupp, "When Is a Union Not a Union? Good Faith Doubt by an Employer," *Labor Law Journal* 42 (June 1991), pp. 357–364.

106. Martha B. Perdrick, "Withdrawal of Recognition: NLRB Toughens, Loosens Standards," *Labor Law Journal* 52 (Fall 2001), pp. 166–169.

Who Should Be in the Bargaining Unit?

CASE STUDY 5-1 Oakhurst Hospital, an acute care hospital with 257 licensed beds, has approximately 181 staff registered nurses (RNs) who provide direct care to patients in 10 patient care units. The patient care units are behavioral health, emergency room, intensive care, intermediate care, medical/surgical east, medical/surgical west, operating room, pain clinic, post-anesthesia care/recovery, and rehabilitation. The RNs report to the on-site nursing manager, clinical managers, clinical supervisors, and assistant clinical managers—all supervisors. In providing patient care, RNs follow the doctors' orders and perform tasks such as administering medications, running blood tests, taking vital signs, observing patients, and processing admissions and discharges. RNs may direct less-skilled employees to perform tasks such as feeding, bathing, and walking patients. RNs may also direct employees to perform tests that are ordered by doctors for their patients.

Many RNs at the hospital serve as charge nurses. Charge nurses are responsible for overseeing their patient care units, and they assign other RNs, licensed practical nurses (LPNs), nursing assistants, technicians, and paramedics to patients on their shifts. The charge nurses do not assign employees to the shifts; that function is done by a staffing office at the hospital. Charge nurses also monitor the patients in the unit, meet with doctors and the patients' family members, and follow up on unusual incidents. Charge nurses may also take on their own patient load, but those who do assume patient loads will sometimes, but not always, take less than a full complement of patients. When serving as charge nurses, RNs receive an additional $1.50 per hour.

Twelve RNs at the hospital serve permanently as charge nurses on every shift they work, while other RNs take turns rotating into the charge nurse position. In the patient care units of the hospital employing permanent charge nurses, other RNs may serve as charge nurses on the permanent charge nurses' days off or during their vacations. Behavioral health, intensive care, intermediate care, medical/surgical east, and medical/surgical west are units with both permanent and rotating charge nurses. Most of the permanent charge nurses work in behavioral health unit. Emergency room, post-anesthesia care/recovery, and rehabilitation units only have rotating charge nurses, while operating room and pain clinic units do not have any charge nurses. Depending on the patient care unit and the work shift, the rotation of the charge nurse position may be worked out by the RNs among themselves, or it may be worked out by the RNs among themselves, or it may be set by higher-level managers. The frequency and regularity with which a particular RN will serve as a "rotating" charge nurse depends on several factors (i.e., the size of the patient care unit in which the RN works, the number of other RNs who serve as rotating charge nurses in that unit, and whether the unit has any permanent charge nurses). However, some RNs do not serve as either rotating or permanent charge nurses at the hospital. Most individuals who fit in this category are either new employees at the hospital (After approximately one year, new RNs are usually deemed eligible to serve in the charge nurse role) or those who work in the operating room or pain clinic units. There are also a handful of RNs at the hospital who choose not to serve as charge nurses.

The Union has petitioned to include all the charge nurses (permanent and rotating) in the RN unit. Oakhurst seeks to exclude the permanent and the rotating charge nurses from the bargaining unit on the basis that they are supervisors within the meaning of the Section 2(11) because they use independent judgment in assigning and responsibly directing employees. Oakhurst also argues that the charge nurses have the authority to adjust employee grievances within the meaning of Sec. 2(11).

Questions

1. What are the Union's best arguments?
2. What are Oakhust's best arguments?
3. Should charge nurses be included in the bargaining unit?
4. Should rotating charge nurses be included in the bargaining unit?
5. Why does it matter to the Union and Oakhurst?

Are Teaching Assistants (TAs), Research Assistants (RAs), and Proctors Employees Under the NLRA?

CASE STUDY 5-2 Yellowstone University (YU) is a private university and within the jurisdiction of the NLRA. Its mission is to serve as a university in which the graduate and undergraduate schools operate as a single integrated facility. YU has over 50 academic departments, approximately 37 of which offer graduate degrees. YU employs approximately 550 regular faculty members and has an unspecified number of short-term faculty appointments. Although student enrollment levels vary, over 1,300 are graduate students, 5,600 are undergraduate students, and 300 are medical students in various degree programs. Most graduate students seek PhDs, with an estimated 1,132 seeking doctorates and 178 seeking master's degrees.

Each semester many of these graduate students are awarded a teaching assistantship (TA), research assistantship (RA), or proctorship; others receive a fellowship. Approximately 375 of these graduate students were TAs, 220 served as RAs, 60 were proctors, and an additional number received fellowships.

Although varying somewhat among the departments, a teaching assistantship generally is assigned to lead a small section of a large lecture course taught by a professor. Although functions of research assistants vary within departments, these graduate students, as the title implies, generally conduct research under a research grant received by a faculty member. Proctors perform a variety of duties for university departments or administrative offices. Their duties depend on the individual needs of the particular department or the university administrative office in which they work and, thus, include a wide variety of tasks. Unlike TAs and RAs, proctors generally do not perform teaching or research functions. Fellowships do not require any classroom or departmental assignments; those who receive dissertation fellowships are required to be working on their dissertation.

YU's charter describes the school's mission as "educating and preparing students to discharge the office of life with usefulness and reputation." To educate and prepare its students, YU uses the university/college model, which "furnishes the advantages of both a small teaching college and a large research university," according to YU's Bulletin of the University. The Bulletin describes the PhD as "primarily a research degree" and emphasizes that "[t]eaching is also an important part of most graduate programs." Nearly 20 department heads and the contents of numerous departmental brochures and other brochures all pointed to graduate programs steeped in the education of graduate students through research and teaching.

In their pursuit of a PhD, graduate students must complete coursework, be admitted to degree candidacy (usually following a qualifying examination), and complete a dissertation, all of which are subject to the oversight of faculty and the degree requirements of the department involved. In addition, most PhD candidates must teach in order to obtain their degree. Although these TAs (as well as RAs and proctors) receive money from YU, that is also true of fellows who do not perform any services. Thus, the services are not related to the money received.

The faculty of each department is responsible for awarding TAs, RAs, or proctorships to its students. To receive an award, the individual usually must be enrolled as a student in that department.

TAs generally lead small groups of students enrolled in a large lecture class conducted by a faculty member in the graduate student's department. The duties and responsibilities vary with the department involved. In the sciences, TAs typically demonstrate experiments and the proper use of equipment, and answer questions. In the humanities and social sciences, TAs lead discussions of what was discussed in the lecture by the professor. All the TAs' duties are under the oversight of a faculty member from the graduate department involved.

During semesters when these students do not act as TAs, RAs, or proctors, they enroll in courses and work on dissertations. Even during those semesters when they are acting in one of these capacities, they nonetheless participate in taking courses and writing dissertations.

The content of the courses that the TAs teach, and the class size, time, length, and location are determined by the faculty members, departmental needs, and YU's administration. Although undergraduate enrollment patterns play a role in the assignment of many TAs, faculty often attempt to accommodate the specific educational needs of graduate students whenever possible. In addition, TAs usually lead sections within their general academic area of interest. In the end, decisions over who, what, where, and when to assist faculty members as a TA generally are made by the faculty member and the respective department involved, in conjunction with the administration. These are precisely the individuals or bodies that control the academic life of the TA.

Research assistantships are typically generated from external grants from outside YU, i.e., federal agencies, foundations, and corporate sponsors. A faculty member, referred to as the "principal investigator," typically applies for the grant from the government or private source, and funds are included for one or more RAs. The general process is for students to work with or "affiliate with" a faculty member, who then applies for funds and awards the student the RA. The students supported by the grant will work on one of the topics described in the grant. The faculty member who serves as a principal investigator most typically also serves as the advisor for that student's dissertation. Although technically the principal investigator on the grant, the faculty member's role is more akin to teacher, mentor, or advisor of students. Although the RAs in the social sciences and humanities perform research that is more tangential to their dissertation, the students still perform research functions in conjunction with the faculty member who is the principal investigator.

Proctors perform a variety of duties for university departments or administrative offices. A representative list of these duties include working in YU's museums or libraries, editing journals or revising brochures, working in the office of the dean, advising undergraduate students, and working in various university offices. Although a few perform research and at least one teaches a class in the Hispanic studies department, they generally do not perform research or teaching assistant duties.

The vast majority of incoming and continuing graduate students receive financial support. Eighty-five percent of continuing students and 75 percent of incoming students received some financial support from YU. YU gives assurances to some students that additional support will be available in the future. Thus, at the discretion of each department and based on the availability of funds, some incoming students are told in their award letters that, if they maintain satisfactory progress toward the PhD, they will continue to receive some form of financial aid in their second through fourth years of graduate study at YU, most probably as a teaching assistant or research assistant. YU's ultimate goal is to support all

graduate students for up to five years, typically with a fellowship in the first and fifth years, and TA or RA positions in the intervening years. As noted above, the financial support is not dependent on whether the student performs services as a TA, RA, or proctor.

YU considers academic merit and financial need when offering various forms of support, although support is not necessarily issued to those with the greatest financial need. This support may include a fellowship, TA, RA, or proctorship, which may include a stipend for living expenses, payment of university health fee for on-campus health services, and tuition "remission" (payment of tuition). Priority is given to continuing students when awarding financial support.

The amount of funding for a fellowship, TA, RA, and proctorship generally is the same. The basic stipend for a fellowship, TA, RA, or proctorship is $12,800, although some fellowships, RAs, and TAs are slightly more. Tuition remission and health fee payments generally are the same for TAs, RAs, proctors, and fellows, although the amount of tuition remission depends on the number of courses taken by a student.

YU treats funds for TA, RAs, proctors, and fellowships as financial aid and represents them as such in university-wide or departmental brochures. Graduate student assistants receive a portion of their stipend award twice a month, and the amount of stipend received is the same regardless of the number of hours spent performing services. The awards do not include any benefits, such as vacation and sick leave, retirement, or health insurance.

The Union seeks to represent a unit of approximately 450 graduate students employed as TAs, RAs in certain social sciences and humanities departments, and proctors at YU.

YU contends that the relationship between a research university and its graduate students is not fundamentally an economic one, but an educational one. YU contends that the support to students is part of a financial aid program that pays graduate students the same amount, regardless of work, and regardless of the value of those services if purchased on the open market (i.e., hiring a fully-vetted PhD). YU also emphasizes that "[c]ommon sense dictates that students who teach and perform research as part of their academic curriculum cannot properly be considered employees without entangling the…Act into the intricacies of graduate education." YU argued that, at a minimum, teaching and research are required for a graduate degree and graduate assistants are only temporary employees.

The Union contends that TAs, RAs, and proctors clearly meet the statutory definition of "employee" because they meet the common law test. The Union disputes YU's contention that TA and RA stipends, like fellowship stipends, are "financial aid." The Union argued that YU's contention that TAs or RAs lose their status as employees because the TAs and RAs are academically required to work is based on the false notion that there is no way to distinguish between a graduate student's academic requirements and the

"work appointments" of the TAs or RAs. Further, even assuming that these individuals usually are satisfying an academic requirement, this is not determinative of employee status.

Questions

1. Why would a labor union want to organize and represent TAs, RAs, and proctors?
2. Why would TAs, RAs, and proctors want union representation?
3. What rights would TAs, RAs, and proctors have if the NLRB rules they are "employees" under the NLRA?
4. Which group(s), if any, would be "employees" under the NLRA and, thereby, be allowed to form a union?

May Union Members Wear Union Insignia to Support the Union?

CASE STUDY 5-3 Wingfield Hotel operates a 250-room downtown hotel in Santa Fe. The Company recognized the Union in 2007, pursuant to a card-check agreement. The parties had negotiated, but not yet executed, a collective bargaining agreement.

The Company markets itself as providing an alternate hotel experience referred to as "Wonderland" where guests can fulfill their "fantasies and desires" and get "whatever [they] want whenever [they] want it." To further the hotel's hoped-for ambience, it commissions special uniforms for its public-contact employees in order to achieve a trendy, distinct, and chic look. During the first 11 months of 2006, the Company spent $28,000 to purchase new uniforms and spent $60,000 to clean these uniforms. The Company's 2006 budget included $100,000 to replace all existing uniforms. The list price of the in-room dining server uniform T-shirt is $28.49. As part of their uniform, employees must wear a small (½ inch) "W" pin on the upper left chest. The Wingfield attire policy prohibits all other uniform adornments, including

sweatbands, scarves worn as belts, and professional association pins.

Wingfield encourages employees to "express themselves" in a manner consistent with the trendy atmosphere. It also encourages employees to interact with guests on a personal level, and requires employees to introduce themselves by name to each guest. In its training program for new employees, Wingfield teaches: "Every interaction with our guests must be Genuine, Authentic, Comfortable, Engaging, Conversational, with Personality, Fun."

In-room delivery (IRD) servers deliver food orders from the kitchen to guest rooms. The IRD server uniform is a black T-shirt, black slacks, and a black apron. When delivering an order, the IRD servers start in the hotel kitchen (a nonpublic area), take a service elevator to the guest's floor, deliver the order to the guest's room, and return to either the hotel kitchen or another nonpublic area to await the next order. If the service elevators are unavailable, the IRD servers must get permission to use the guest elevators. Use of the guest elevators occurs on only 20 to 25 percent of deliveries. The IRD servers' contact with the public varies widely on a daily basis. IRD server Hector

Gomez stated that there were nights where he had delivered only one order and had seen only one guest. On the other hand, there were also nights when he had delivered as many as 50 orders to as many guests. Gomez has no contact with the public other than during food deliveries. Gomez also stated that only 30 to 40 percent of his time (less than a majority) is spent in contact with the public.

Gomez regularly worked the night shift. At approximately midnight on July 10, 2006, Gomez put on a button distributed by the Union. The button was two inches square. It contained the wording: "JUSTICE NOW! JUSTICIA AHORA! H.E.R.E. Local 120" in blue or red letters on a yellow background. At about 3 A.M., while Gomez was on a meal break in a nonpublic area, supervisor John Black ordered Gomez to remove the button. After a brief discussion, Gomez removed the button.

The Union filed a charge with the National Labor Relations Board and claimed that it is well established that employees have a statutorily protected right to wear union insignia. An employer may lawfully restrict the wearing of union insignia where "special circumstances" justify the restriction. Special circumstances justify restrictions on union insignia or apparel "when their display may jeopardize employee safety, damage machinery or products, exacerbate employee dissension, or unreasonably interfere with a public image that the employer has established, or when necessary to maintain decorum and discipline among employees." The employer bears the burden of proving such special circumstances.

The Company argued special circumstances—interference with Wingfield's public image—justified the no-button order while Gomez was in public areas where he would come in contact with guests. These special circumstances did not apply while Gomez was in nonpublic areas where he would not come on contact with guests. Gomez spent the majority of his work time in nonpublic areas. The Company had issued the no-button order while Gomez was in a nonpublic area, and that the Company's no-button order was not limited to public areas.

The Company stated that the union button interfered with the Company's use of a particular IRD server uniform (professionally designed, all-black shirt, slacks, and apron) to create a special atmosphere for hotel customers. Therefore, Wingfield could lawfully prohibit the button with regard to the time that Gomez was in public areas.

Questions

1. Discuss the burden of proof in this case.
2. To what extent do employees have the right to express their support for the Union on the job?
3. How should the NLRB rule? Give your reasons.

Did the Company Violate the Section 8(a)(1) of the LMRA When It Discharged the Employee?

CASE STUDY 5-4 DCP manufactures data collection products. The chief operational officer is Barry Marks. Larry Leiner is one of 23 employees located in two buildings and was hired in April 2005 as a "software engineer" who prepared computer programs.

On December 1, Marks sent a message to all employees by e-mail about "proposed plans" for an incentive-based bonus system (as to which employees were told to "reply with your comments or stop by to see me. A response to this is required.") and changes in vacation policy ("Your comments are welcome, but not required"). The incorporated memorandum on the proposed vacation policy changes stated, "Please give me your comments (send me an e-mail or stop in and talk to me) by Tuesday, 12/5." The suggested policy changes were to close the offices on December 23 and reopen on January 2 and to adjust the number of paid days off over a five-year period, the effect of which Marks asserted, was that the employees "actually get more days off each year, compared to our present system."

Marks received a number of employee responses on his vacation proposals, including one on December 1, by e-mail, from Larry Leiner. Leiner's response demonstrated that, in fact, the change referred to by Marks would result in the same number of vacation days per year, and less flexibility as to their use. Marks conceded to the accuracy of Leiner's correction and claimed that he had inadvertently erred and had not intended to deceive the employees. On December 4, Leiner, having checked his calculations over the weekend, discovered another minor error, and notified Marks by e-mail.

Marks did not reply to Leiner's communications. On December 5, Tom Dunn, a member of the engineering team, sent an e-mail to Marks, with copies to other engineering team members (which would include Leiner), which stated: "In response to the proposed vacation plan, I have only one word, GREAT!" Promptly, Leiner sent an e-mail to Dunn telling him that the proposed policy did not, in fact, work to the advantage of the employees.

Also, on December 5, Leiner sent a lengthy e-mail message to all employees, including Marks. The message spelled out in detail Leiner's calculations on the result of the proposed vacation policy change. It contained, as well, some flippant and rather grating language. The salutation was "Greetings Fellow Travelers." In his initial remarks, Leiner wrote, "the closing statement in Barry's memo: 'The effect of this is that you actually get more days off each year, compared to our present system,' will be proven false." This declaration was reiterated in the final thought of the memo: "Thus, the closing statement in Barry's memo ... is proven false." The paragraph preceding that statement read: "Assuming anyone actually cares about the company and being productive on the job, if Christmas falls on Tuesday or Wednesday as it did in 1996 and 1997, respectively, two work weeks of one and two days each produced by the proposed plan will replace the fragmented weeks." In closing, Leiner asked that the recipient "please send errata to Larry."

Also on December 5, after reading the e-mail message from Leiner, Dunn e-mailed again Marks and also the engineering team (as shown on the e-mail address). Dunn said in part, "After reading Larry's E-mail(s) of this date[,] I realized I had made a mistake in calculating the vacation days and wish to change my comment from 'GREAT' to 'Not so Great' on the proposed vacation policy." Dunn also noted in his message that the proposals had "generated more E-mail than any other plan in the company."

Marks became angry that Mr. Leiner sent his e-mail messages to all employees. He prepared a December 5 memorandum to Leiner. The memo stated that Marks was "saddened and disappointed" by Leiner's e-mail, which was "inappropriate and intentionally provocative" and beneath "someone as talented and intelligent as you are." Marks then wrote:

> Our employment manual states: "Certain actions or types of behavior may result in immediate dismissal. These include, but are not limited to:
> Failure to treat others with courtesy and respect."

Marks went on to "direct" Leiner to write him by 5 P.M. that day: "In light of the above, why this e-mail message was inappropriate; How sending an e-mail message like this hurts the company; How this matter should have been handled." Marks continued:

> If your response is acceptable to me, you will post it by e-mail today to those who received your other messages.
> If you decline to do so, or if your response is unacceptable to me, your employment will be terminated immediately. Otherwise, your employment will continue on a probationary basis for six months, during which time your employment may be terminated at any time and for any reason.
> Larry, I am very disappointed in you. Barry.

Marks stated that what upset him about the e-mail messages was their "tone": it was a "slap in the face" of employees with good attitudes and a "personal attack" upon him.

At least twice in the afternoon on December 5, Leiner approached Marks. In Marks' words, Leiner wanted Marks to "tell him what to write." In Marks view, Leiner was "profess[ing] not to understand what was wrong with the e-mail message, the confusion of which Marks seriously doubted." He nonetheless tried to give Leiner some appropriate suggestions. Leiner gave a different version of these conversations: portraying himself as admitting to an "honest mistake" after Marks told him that Leiner should have contacted him, not the other employees, because "it was up to him to decide what to say to other people"; Leiner described Marks as refusing to offer any assistance in preparing the requested memo and stated that Marks had branded Leiner a "troublemaker."

Marks admonished Leiner for having contacted employees; his December 6 e-mail to the employees picked up the theme that the "right way" for Leiner to have proceeded was to approach management. Marks stated that, on December 5, he "may have" told Leiner that he should have pursued the matter privately."

Leiner said that in his last meeting with Marks on December 5, they agreed to extend the memo deadline to 8 A.M. the next day. Leiner further stated that he stayed up well into the morning as he attempted to compose an appropriate letter, but he was unable to come up with anything he deemed satisfactory. When the two men met at 8 A.M., and Marks asked if Leiner had produced a memo, Leiner said, "No, I couldn't really write anything incriminating because it could be used against me later." Marks wished him luck in his future endeavors and bade him farewell.

Later that day, Leiner called his supervisor and asked for a discharge letter. The December 9 letter received by Leiner citing as the "Reason [sic] for termination" two of the grounds for dismissal given in the employee manual:

Failure to treat others with courtesy and respect

Failure to follow instructions or to perform assigned work

Early on December 6, Marks e-mailed all the employees. After discussing the vacation proposal, he turned to "Larry's memo" and how to "address our grievances." He wrote of the impropriety of using "sarcasm or disrespect"; he pointed out that the "long or provocative" e-mail messages had taken up everyone's time; that reading, printing, discussing, and dealing with these messages had "unnecessarily cost our company time and money." Marks noted that "the right way" to handle a "grievance, or a question, or a comment, or a complaint" was to discuss it with a team leader or Marks. Marks admitted that he had erred in explaining the proposed vacation policy, and he asked employees to inform him if that had changed their minds. He closed by saying that, while he welcomed disagreement, he also demanded that everybody be treated with courtesy. No specific mention was made of Leiner's discharge.

The records showed that in September 2005, Marks had sent a memo to the members of the engineering team requiring them to work at least 50 hours per week because of production necessities. Leiner sent a two-word reply: "I refuse." Leiner said that he expected this to lead to a dialogue with Marks, which it did. Leiner explained to Marks that his free time was important to him and that he would rather accept a paycut than work additional hours. Marks eventually agreed that Leiner need not work the extra time, but Marks told Leiner "don't tell anybody." Marks said that he spoke to Leiner and asked him simply to "do what he can."

Marks stressed that it was the "tone" of Leiner's e-mail, and the ramifications of that tone, which played a dominant role in the discharge. This is reflected in his December 5 memorandum to Leiner, which mentioned only "Failure to treat others with courtesy and respect." While his December 6 communication makes a point of the time and expense wasted by Leiner's lengthy e-mail to the employees, no other message (including the "reason for discharge" set out in the December discharge letter) mentions that issue. Marks agreed that he had no objection to both "simple" e-mailings and personal telephone calls being made by employees and that he was aware that, among the employees, "there is a certain amount of time during the workday that is not devoted strictly to work." Marks acknowledged that he knew that Dunn's e-mails to him had been directed also to the other members of the engineering team, and Dunn had not been admonished or otherwise disciplined.

On December 10, Leiner filed a charge with the National Labor Relations Board.

Questions

1. Was this matter within the jurisdiction of the National Labor Relations Board?

2. Were Leiner's actions considered a protected activity under the Labor Management Relations Act?

3. How should the NLRB rule? Give your reasons.

The T-Shirt Offer and Picnic Photographs

CASE STUDY 5-5 On the day before the Union election, the Union hosted a free picnic luncheon for employees during the first and second shifts' meal breaks in a parking lot adjacent to the Young Skin's plant. At the picnic, the Union took 88 snapshots. During the luncheon, union representatives distributed "Union Yes" T-shirts carrying the slogan, "The Best Things in Life Are Negotiable. Union Yes." Between "Union" and "Yes" was a square containing a checkmark. To receive a T-shirt, employees were required to sign a pro-union petition titled, "We Are Voting Yes on August 2nd!" which stated that the undersigned employees agreed to openly support the Union and asked their co-workers to join them. This petition was to be used as a handbill on election day.

By requiring signing as a condition of receiving a free T-shirt that cost the union $4 to $5 each, the Company contended that this represented an unlawful grant of benefit that the Union used to induce employees to sign the pro-Union petition. The Company compared the T-shirt offer to a union's offer to waive union initiation fees contingent on an employee's signing a union authorization card. The Supreme Court found such a fee waiver unlawful in a previous case because it "allow[ed] the Union to buy endorsements and paint a false portrait of employee support during its election campaign." The Company said the monetary value of the T-shirts was irrelevant, noting that the waived initiation fee in the Supreme Court case was a "nominal" $10.

The Union stated that it was clear to all concerned that the T-shirts were inexpensive and that their free distribution would not interfere with employee free choice. They further stated that it was a considerable leap to conclude that the offer of these "Union Yes" T-shirts contingent on employees' signing a pro-union petition was an inducement tantamount to buying endorsements.

The Supreme Court in the previous case ruled that all employees, regardless of their views on unions, had an economic interest in obtaining the fee waiver that was offered as an inducement to sign union authorization cards. The inducement here—the "Union Yes" T-shirt—however, would reasonably be desirable only to employees who favored the Union and wanted to proclaim their pro-union view. Thus, the requiring employees to sign a pro-union petition to obtain a pro-union T-shirt would not reasonably induce nonsupporters to sign the petition and thereby allow them to paint a false portrait of employee support.

Even if the T-shirts might be desirable to nonsupporters, the Union in that event had a justifiable interest in trying to ensure that T-shirts were distributed only to employees who would wear them as campaign paraphernalia in support of the Union. Requiring employees desiring T-shirts to sign a pro-union petition was a reasonable means for the Union to try to accomplish this objective.

The Company also contended that the Union created an atmosphere of fear and coercion by photographing employees at the picnic luncheon. In many of the photographs, employees posed for the camera, sometimes displaying their Union T-shirts. The photographs were taken for the purpose of memorializing the chicken meal and perhaps to publish in a Union newspaper. Two employees later said they were "concerned" or "felt funny" about their pictures being taken.

The Company contended that the employees who were photographed might well have thought that their responses to the Union campaign activity were being recorded for the purpose of future retaliation. The Union responded that, although photographing some activities might suggest retaliatory purpose, the Union photographed employees enjoying a picnic, which each employee voluntarily chose to attend. When a company security guard attending the picnic asked why a Union representative was taking photographs, the Union representative stated, "You are all going to make the front page of *USA Today*," and "We want to remember this fun-filled memory." Union representatives stated that the photographs were taken for submission to the Union's newspaper. Copies of the photographs were later given to employees at a party celebrating the Union's victory in the election (217 in favor of the Union, 200 against it, and 16 challenged ballots). The Company now seeks to overturn the election results based on its objections to the Union's T-shirt distribution and the photographing of employees at the Union picnic.

Questions

1. Must illegal conduct occur to overturn the results of a Union representation election?

2. Compare the present case to the following ones:

   - *NLRB v. Savair Mfg. Co.,* 414 U.S. 270 (1973); 84 LRRM 2929 (1973)

   - *Pepsi Cola Bottling Co.,* 289 NLRB 736 (1988); 128 LRRM 1275 (1988)

   - *Mike Yurosek & Sons, Inc.,* 292 NLRB 1074 (1989); 130 LRRM 1308 (1989)

3. Did the Union interfere with the outcome of the election by offering the T-shirts? Why or why not?

4. Did the Union interfere with the outcome of the election by taking the photographs at the picnic? Why or why not?

5. How will the NLRB rule?

The Loudspeaker Campaign Tactic

CASE STUDY 5-6 Acoustical Enterprises (the Employer) manufactures commercial acoustic sound-proofing material at a plant in Echo, South Dakota. On December 20, the Union filed a petition with the NLRB seeking certification as the exclusive bargaining representative of Acoustical's production and maintenance employees. An election was set for 2:00 P.M. on February 18.

As the election approached, the main issue became the wages and benefits received by the non-union employees at the Echo plant versus those received by unionized employees at a Bronx, New York, plant owned by the Employer. Acoustical made divergent statements about the extent of any difference between the two plants, and the election rhetoric became quite heated. In particular, the Union repeatedly made disparaging remarks about Acoustical's main spokesperson, Fran Orange. On the day before and day of the election, the Union parked a car mounted with a loudspeaker system 25 to 30 yards from Acoustical's main entrance. From approximately 6:50 A.M. to 7:05 A.M. and from just before 12:00 noon to 12:35 P.M. on both days, the Union broadcast music and campaign messages focusing on wage and benefit issues and also on Ms. Orange. In addition, on February 17 from 3:25 P.M. to 3:40 P.M. and just before and after 5:30 P.M., the Union broadcast the same content. These broadcasts were intentionally made to coincide with the beginning and ending of the day shift (7:00 A.M.–3:30 P.M.) and with lunch breaks (12:00–12:30 P.M.) at the plant. The February 17, the 5:30 P.M. broadcast coincided with the end of an overtime day shift.

The loudspeaker system had a range of well over 100 yards, and the Union's messages were clearly heard on the plant grounds. Because of industrial noise, however, the broadcasts were inaudible inside plant buildings when machinery was in use. However, at the lunch break, when no machinery was in use and when employees were outside the plant buildings, the broadcasts were more easily heard. Employees were not free to leave the plant area during their lunch break.

The election was held as scheduled, and the Union won by an 81-to-71 vote. The Employer filed election objections, including one over the Union's sound car broadcasts. The Employer contended that the broadcasts violated the long-standing rule of *Peerless Plywood Co.,* 107 NLRB 427 (1953), which prohibits speeches by either the Union or the Employer to massed assemblies of employees, on company time, within 24 hours of an election.

On March 17, the Union requested Acoustical to bargain. The Employer refused. On April 11, the Union filed an unfair labor practice charge under Section 8(a)(1), (5) of the LMRA. The Employer admitted refusing to bargain but contended that the Union had been improperly certified, and therefore no legal duty to bargain could be imposed.

Questions

1. Review the captive-audience, 24-hour rule. Should the rule apply in this case, although the Union was not on the Employer's property and

had no legal authority to require employees who were on the employer's property to listen to the Union's broadcasts?

2. Why does the Employer typically have a significant advantage over a Union in conveying its message during a representation election campaign?

3. Did the Union's broadcast violate the captive-audience rule? If so, should the results of the election be overturned and a rerun election scheduled? Why or why not?

Bulletin Board Use

CASE STUDY 5-7 The Employer operates a merchandise catalog distribution center in Wichita, Kansas, employing 1,000 workers. The Union began an organizing campaign among distribution center employees. For many years, the Employer has published an employee handbook that contained the following bulletin board policy:

> Bulletin boards are located throughout the Center [distribution center], generally near time clocks. Company announcements, such as policy changes, holiday schedules and Company news of general interest, are posted on these boards. Personal postings are not permitted.

Employees who supported the Union placed printed material on the bulletin boards advertising upcoming Union meetings and soliciting Union support. On discovery, managers removed the union material from the bulletin boards. The Union subsequently filed an unfair labor practice charge, alleging the Employer's removal of the Union materials from the bulletin board represented unlawful interference with employees' right to solicit for the purpose of organizing a Union under the LMRA.

The Employer maintained that managers were simply enforcing a nondiscriminatory policy barring all solicitation materials from company bulletin boards that were not approved by the company. The Employer noted that management had given employees permission to post on bulletin boards a company-approved newsletter that did include a section advertising employee

personal items for sale (e.g., car, television set, golf clubs). Certain other company-sponsored solicitations for the United Way and March of Dimes charities had also previously been approved for posting on company bulletin boards.

Several employees testified that other employee communications had also been posted on several company bulletin boards in the past, such as thank-you notes, party announcements, Christmas cards, a solicitation for maid service, and donation requests when an employee was hospitalized or died. Such unapproved announcements were often posted for several weeks before being removed from bulletin boards. The Employer responded that items such as those mentioned by the employees who testified were, for the most part, connected to company-sponsored events or charities.

Questions

1. Is an Employer required to have bulletin boards at the workplace?

2. If an Employer did not provide bulletin boards at the workplace, would employees have a right to provide and mount their own bulletin boards?

3. If there are company-provided bulletin boards at the workplace, does the Employer have a right to restrict the purpose or type of material that can be posted on such boards?

4. In this case, did the Employer unlawfully deny union supporters access to use company bulletin boards for Union solicitation purposes? Explain your reasoning.

Nonemployee Union Solicitation Activity

CASE STUDY 5-8 In October, the Union began an organizing drive involving nursing personnel employed at the Medco Hospital (the Employer). In November, Medco's management revised a portion of the existing no-solicitation and distribution policy to read as follows: "Visitors, patients and other nonemployees may not solicit or distribute literature on any hospital property for any purpose at any time."

The hospital operates a cafeteria that is open to serve employees, patients, and the general public. On December 4, two (nonemployee) union organizers entered the hospital cafeteria accompanied by some off-duty nursing employees. The off-duty nursing employees proceeded to distribute union literature provided to them by the two union organizers. The two union organizers did not personally hand out any union literature or attempt to solicit any employees to sign a union authorization card. The two union organizers did remain seated in the cafeteria for approximately five hours and answered questions about the Union initiated by interested employees. Sitting on the table where the two (nonemployee) union organizers were seated was an open box containing union literature.

On December 10, the two union organizers accompanied by several off-duty nursing employees again entered the hospital cafeteria and engaged in the same actions as those previously described as occurring on December 4. After approximately 30 minutes, the human resources (HR) manager

for the hospital entered the cafeteria and spoke to the two union organizers. The HR manager informed the two union organizers that they were in violation of the hospital's no-solicitation and distribution rule. The HR manager gave the two union organizers permission to stay for 15 minutes to have a drink or 30 minutes to eat a meal, after which time they would be arrested if they refused to leave. The two union organizers left the hospital cafeteria voluntarily and proceeded to file an unfair labor practice charge, alleging the hospital unlawfully barred their access to the hospital cafeteria. There was no evidence to show that the Employer had ever allowed solicitation or distribution activity by nonemployees to occur on its premises in the past.

Questions

1. Did the Employer unlawfully deny the two nonemployee union organizers access to the hospital's cafeteria? If so, what should be the appropriate remedy?

2. Would the Employer's no-solicitation policy prohibit the two nonemployee union organizers from entering the hospital's property anywhere at any time?

Campaign Threats or Implied Promise of Benefit?

CASE STUDY 5-9 Do the oral or written statements made by employer representatives during a representation election campaign contain any unlawful threats or implied promises of benefit in violation of Section 8(a)(1) of the LMRA?

In early June, the Union filed a petition with the NLRB requesting a representation election be held in a bargaining unit comprising 880 employees of the Jackson Equipment Company (the Employer). The Employer had previously rejected the Union's request for voluntary recognition. The Union's election petition was supported by 426 (52 percent) valid union authorization card signatures. There were 880

employees declared eligible to vote in the election, which the Union lost by a vote of 391 for to 489 (55.5 percent) against union representation. The Union filed several objections to the Employer's conduct during the election.

The Union charged that the Employer's statements made during the election campaign threatened that, if the Union won the election, the employees' benefits would be reduced. Such a threat tends to discourage employees from freely exercising their Section 7 rights under the act. The Employer contended that these statements were merely a factual response to Union's promises to increase employees' wages. The Employer cited 22 out of 33 leaflets distributed by the Union that referred to improved employee benefits at some unionized plants. Here are the Employer's statements:

> Neither the Company nor the Union can predict what will be in the contract. Your wages and benefits could turn out to be higher, lower, or the same as they are....I'm sure the Union will try to tell you there is some sort of law that will prevent the Company from negotiating for anything less than you now receive. That statement is simply not based on facts. I've given your supervisors copies of a decision in which the court upheld the Employer's right to inform his employees that he may not even have to agree to the continuance of existing wages and benefits. These facts may seem harsh, but I think it's important that you know the truth about the collective-bargaining process before you vote.
>
> Remember, bargaining means putting everything on the table, including the benefits you already have. Bargaining with a union can be a complicated and time-consuming process during which the Union and the Company negotiate to get an agreement that both sides are satisfied with. And bargaining starts from scratch, which means that everything is negotiable. As I have told you, we would bargain in good faith. But, I would not sign a contract that I did not believe was in this plant's best interest. Sometimes, when a company takes this position, the Union tries to force a settlement. This usually leads to a breakdown in bargaining and can result in a strike—which hurts everyone.
>
> You should know, however, that the benefit package given our plant employees from the time the plant opened was better than those at other unionized plants owned by the Company. You were given greater benefits voluntarily by the Company. Those in unions bargained repeatedly with the Employer for more than 20 years for their benefits....Your pay increases are a result of the fair and responsible compensation policy we follow. There is no question in my mind that our wages are better than the Union wages I've seen in contracts of other companies in our area. A vote of "no union" is a vote to

continue the pay practices we have been committed to at our plant since the day we began operations.

The Union also objected to other Employer statements on the grounds that they implied a promise to do things differently or better if the employees voted against the Union. Such a promise, conditioned on whether an employee does or does not choose to exercise his or her lawful Section 7 rights to select a bargaining representative, is in the Union's view a form of "positive coercion" and destructive of an atmosphere in which employees may freely decide the bargaining representation issue.

The Employer contends it was only informing employees of how good conditions were at the plant. The conditions referred to were changes that had begun at the plant before the onset of the Union organizing campaign. The statements made by the plant manager were as follows:

> I admit, no employer is perfect. However, I am totally convinced that we can best resolve our differences without the Union and the adversarial relationship the organizers have tried to develop. In order to move ahead, we must work together, not fight each other.
>
> Unions are known chiefly for extracting dues from you, calling strikes, making promises, and causing confusion among employees. I am asking for a vote of confidence and a chance to prove what we can accomplish by working together, without interference by a Union. I am asking for a chance to continue the improvements we have underway at our plant, without interference by the Union.
>
> I know that mistakes have been made. The fact that we are having a Union election at this time indicates to me that some of you felt it was necessary, at one time, for an outsider to represent you, that management was unresponsive to your needs and concerns. It has been difficult to bring back to the plant the positive feelings that most of you had about the Company, but I sincerely feel we have turned the corner. I am aware of your frustrations with machine problems, material flow problems, overtime problems, inconsistent interpretation of company policies, pay inconsistencies, and management in general. Also, the personnel function has not been as sensitive to your needs as it should have been or could be. I admit that these things could have been diagnosed sooner and acted upon. However,

we all know it is easy to quarterback Friday night's football game on Monday morning.

I believe today we are building a management team that is willing to recognize its shortcomings and is actively working to correct them. It is not an easy job, but with your help it can be done. Programs have been developed to: (1) improve scheduling in the plant, (2) reduce scrap, (3) provide foremen training development, (4) improve the quality of our product, (5) purchase required machinery, and (6) improve our housekeeping.

Finally, the Union charged that a company supervisor unlawfully questioned and threatened two open and active Union supporters. About two weeks before the election, supervisor Bates asked employee Culp what he thought the Union could do for him, and then told Culp, "If it came down to where you all went out on strike and they had people out, they could go out and hire because the Company had 100 to 200 people waiting for jobs....They would use us as an example for the Company's other plants here in the South."

Approximately one week before the election, supervisor Lofton asked employee Rogers how he was going to vote. When Rogers replied, "For the Union," Lofton inquired whether Rogers was sure he was doing the right thing. Supervisor Lofton further asked Rogers if he knew that if the Union won he could lose his benefits and told him he should think twice about voting for the Union.

Questions

1. Do these employer statements constitute an unlawful threat in violation of Section 8(a)(1) of the LMRA? Why or why not?

2. Do the employer statements constitute an unlawful promise of benefits in violation of Section 8(a)(1) of the act? Why or why not?

3. Did the questioning or statements by either supervisor Bates or supervisor Lofton constitute unlawful interrogation in violation of Section 8(a)(1) of the act? Why or why not?

4. Should the NLRB give consideration to its "Totality of Conduct" doctrine in reaching a conclusion about the alleged violations in this case? Explain your answer.

5. Develop some guidelines for managers who may be talking with employees about the Union during an organizing campaign.

6. How should the NLRB rule?

Classroom Exercise

5.1
Designing Union Election Campaign Literature

Purpose

The purpose of this exercise is to allow students to use creativity and gain experience in designing legal election campaign materials that effectively communicate common employer or union themes.

Instructions

This exercise may be completed on an individual or group basis. Using one or more of the common employer and union representation election campaign themes described in Exhibit 5.3, design a poster to encourage employees to vote either for or against union representation. Some students (groups) may be assigned to create a poster stressing employer campaign themes, while other students may design a union campaign poster. Students should be allowed to view the finished poster and choose a winner for "Best Company" and "Best Union" poster. The best poster is the one that the group majority judges would be most likely to lawfully influence (persuade) employees to vote in the intended direction.

Students may wish to develop a description of the type of company or bargaining unit employees that are the target of the union's organizing campaign as a focus for their poster design. A local firm's description may be used as a mock organizing target, or news items concerning a recent organizing campaign reported in newspapers, business periodicals (e.g., *Business Week, BNA's Daily Labor Report*), or other sources.

Note: The same type of exercise may be used to give students experience in preparing and presenting a brief five- to ten-minute oral presentation on the advantages or disadvantages of union representation.

Part 2: The Bargaining Process and Outcomes

Part Two pertains to key activities and issues involved in the labor relations process of negotiating a labor agreement (contract), setting forth work rules pertaining to wages, hours, terms and conditions of employment, and the rights and responsibilities of the parties governed by the contract's terms. These topics are approached from the vantage point of legal and practical proscriptions on related behavior as well as with an eye to the realities forged out of the relationships between union and management representatives.

Copyright GettyImages

CHAPTER 6

Negotiating the Labor Agreement

Negotiation is a common feature of everyday life. Although this chapter covers negotiations between union and management representatives over terms and conditions of employment, many aspects of negotiations or collective bargaining have broader applications to other bargaining activities in society. This chapter first defines collective bargaining and explains initial influences affecting this activity. Subsequent sections consider negotiation preparation activities, such as bargaining team selection, proposal formulation and cost estimates, bargaining strategies and tactics, and legal requirements. The chapter places these diverse collective bargaining considerations in perspective by describing a "bargaining power model" as a likely resolution framework.

COLLECTIVE BARGAINING: DEFINITION AND STRUCTURE

Collective bargaining is an activity whereby union and management officials attempt to resolve conflicts of interest by exchanging commitments in a manner intended to sustain and possibly enrich their continuing relationship. Collective bargaining is a special form of interdependent social interaction, in which the attainment of desired outcomes by one party is dependent on the behavior of another party. A dispute that arises between union and management representatives over what the terms and conditions of employment will be is termed an **interest dispute**. The basic objective of collective bargaining is to resolve such interest disputes by reaching an agreement acceptable to both parties (union and management).[1]

Attitudes of union and management officials toward collective bargaining and the negotiated settlement influence their relationship during the term or duration of the labor agreement. The fact that both parties generally understand that they will return to the bargaining table in future negotiations affects their strategic choices regarding acceptable tactics and outcomes in any current negotiation.

Defining success in collective bargaining often entails both objective and subjective evaluation criteria. Objectively measuring the economic value or cost of specific settlement terms to each bargaining party is one way to measure success. Comparing settlement outcomes to industry or area averages is another way. Depending on the prevailing bargaining conditions, maintaining the status quo or conceding less than one might have been expected to concede under the circumstances could be defined as a successful bargaining outcome. Union leaders seeking re-election may consider the extent to which the interests of key constituent groups within the bargaining unit (e.g., skilled employees or women) are satisfied as one measure of success. One other criterion for measuring negotiation success is whether a bargaining settlement contributes to building a positive relationship between union and management representatives that is necessary for the effective implementation of contract terms on an everyday basis.

It is not unusual for both union and management negotiators to claim success at the conclusion of contract negotiations. This may be possible due to the different priorities each party may place on achieving a desired outcome on specific bargaining subjects or a reflection of different criteria being applied by each party to measure success. A successful bargaining settlement reinforces a labor-management relationship, whereby the parties, although not always agreeing, nonetheless trust each other to be honest and straightforward in their positions without trying to unnecessarily damage the other party.[2]

Bargaining Structure

Bargaining structure has two general dimensions: (1) employee groupings that can affect the collective bargaining outcome and (2) the employees and employers who are subject to the provisions of the negotiated labor agreement. Unions are responsive to several groups within and outside their organizations. Every organization has informal work groups (the night-shift crew or the company bowling team, for example) who have unique preferences and place pressures on union officers to achieve their preferences in collective bargaining. Other examples of groups within a bargaining unit who may seek to press special bargaining interests during negotiations include skilled craft employees, women, minorities, high- or low-seniority employees, and part-time employees.

In some cases, union and management officials are influenced by other collective bargaining settlements. For example, a labor settlement between city government and the police might influence subsequent negotiations between the city and firefighters. The term **pattern bargaining** is used to describe a situation where union or management negotiators informally attempt to extend a negotiated settlement from one formal structure to another. Pattern bargaining may occur among similar companies in the same industry. For example, the United Auto Workers (UAW) has traditionally designated one auto manufacturer in each cycle of contract negotiations as the lead firm with whom the union will attempt to achieve a contract settlement. Terms of the "lead" contract are then used as a pattern for negotiating labor agreements with other auto makers during the same time frame. For example, in the 2007 auto negotiations the agreement reached between the UAW and General Motors became the pattern for subsequent settlements between the UAW and Chrysler, LLC and Ford Motor Company (see further discussion of 2007 auto negotiations in the Labor Relations in Action feature on page 256). Pattern bargaining might also occur if union or management negotiators attempt to apply a settlement obtained for one segment of an industry (automobile manufacturing) to another company that produces related products, such as tires or headlights.

Management and union negotiators might prefer pattern bargaining as a way to take wages out of competition between unionized employers operating in the same product or service market. The objective of standardizing wages through pattern bargaining is beneficial for management because it will reduce concern about competitors receiving a labor cost advantage. Pattern bargaining is also beneficial to union negotiators because it builds a perception among similar types of workers (represented by the same union under contracts at different firms) that they are receiving equal and fair treatment from their union in securing negotiated improvements desired by the union's membership.[3] Sometimes management negotiators actively resist pattern bargaining in order to try to negotiate contract settlement terms which will provide the firm with a labor cost competitive advantage over other firms with whom the same union bargains. Increased competition by nonunion firms not covered under union-negotiated contracts (both domestic and international competitors) has also forced some unionized employers to resist pattern bargaining.

The Bargaining Unit

The second dimension of the bargaining structure, the **bargaining unit,** refers to the employees and employers who will be bound by a negotiated labor agreement. As discussed further in Chapter 5, any appropriate bargaining unit (ABU) determined by the National Labor Relations Board (NLRB) for representation election purposes is, by definition, a unit appropriate for negotiating purposes (see the first example in Exhibit 6.1). Once a union has been certified as the representative of an ABU, two or more ABUs may be combined together for the purpose of negotiating a single labor agreement to cover all ABUs if such a combination is acceptable to both the union and the employer. Most often this involves two or more ABUs at an employer's operation represented by the same union, but it could involve ABUs represented by different unions. For example, Harley Davidson Motor Company operates a manufacturing plant in Kansas City, MO, where the International Association of Machinists & Aerospace Workers (IAM) and the United Steel, Paper and Forestry, Rubber Manufacturing, Energy, Allied Industrial & Service Workers International Union (USW) were elected to represent two separate groups of plant workers but, with the employer's agreement, have chosen to negotiate a single contract to cover both groups of workers. Whether to combine ABUs together for negotiation purposes is a **non-mandatory** subject of bargaining.[4]

Choosing to combine ABUs for negotiation purposes is a form of **centralized bargaining** (see the remaining examples in Exhibit 6.1), of which there are two major types. *Single employer/multi-plant bargaining* may be used when one company has several separate facilities, each having a separate ABU.

Exhibit 6.1

Possible Structures for
Collective Bargaining

Structure	Example
1. Single employer—single union	
Single location	ABC Manufacturing Co.—UNITE
Multiple locations	General Motors—UAW
2. Single employer—several unions	
Single location	Johnson Metal, Buffalo, New York—all crafts and industrial unions
Multiple locations	General Electric—IBEW and IUE
3. Multiple employers—single union	Trucking Management Incorporated—Teamsters
4. Multiple employers—several unions	Association of General Contractors of North Alabama—Birmingham Trade Council

A **multi-employer bargaining unit** involves more than one employer combining together to negotiate a single contract covering employees at each of the participating employer's firms who are typically represented by the same union. Multi-employer bargaining may be found in industries such as trucking, motion picture and television, construction, longshore, newspaper, and professional sports. Some union-management bargaining relationships choose to combine ABUs under a master contract to negotiate certain issues (e.g., wages, pension plans) that are equally applied to employees throughout an industry or at different locations of the same employer (*industry level bargaining*). Working conditions or terms specific to an individual ABU may then be bargained separately at the local facility (*local level bargaining*) and incorporated as a local addendum to the master contract.

One or both parties might prefer centralized bargaining because of product interdependence, market factors, or legal considerations. For example, a company may have three manufacturing facilities, each having a separate ABU. If the products at the facilities are *interdependent* (Facility A's product is needed for Facility B, whose product is in turn completed with products at Facility C), then management would probably prefer centralized bargaining producing a single contract expiration date and only one risk of a possible strike at all facilities—instead of three different contract expiration dates and possible separate strikes at different times at each of the facilities if each ABU negotiated a separate contract. Of course, should a work stoppage actually occur, the potential magnitude of the impact would be greater under centralized bargaining because all three covered plants would be affected immediately.

If the three facilities operate *independent* of each other—each facility producing a complete product or service itself (e.g., three steel mills, each producing steel beams; or three facilities producing unrelated products such as baseball gloves, cereal, and marbles)—management would probably prefer to negotiate a separate contract to cover the ABU at each independent facility. Separate negotiations would probably result in different contract expiration dates for the three facilities. Although each separate contract would involve the risk of a work stoppage when it expired, if one facility went on strike, the others could still continue production. In the case of facilities that produce similar products, management could transfer some of the orders from the striking facility to other non-striking facilities where labor contracts had not expired.

Some believe that conglomerate companies with a wide range of products have too much bargaining power over unions. One sample of nine conglomerates revealed 846 different manufacturing products sold. A union threatening a strike to shut down one of these manufacturing facilities or even an entire product line might not be able to put sufficient pressure on a conglomerate to reach a bargaining settlement.[5] A union would prefer centralized bargaining in this situation, realizing that a strike could effectively shut down the company's entire operations, thereby increasing union bargaining strength. Market factors also influence the degree of centralization of the bargaining unit. In a highly competitive product/service market, a multi-employer (centralized) negotiating unit would be desirable to employers who fear being placed at a competitive disadvantage if other employers subsequently negotiate lower labor cost terms. This would be particularly true for an employer with fewer resources (less bargaining power) than the union with whom the employer must bargain and whose firm also exhibited a high **degree of labor intensiveness** (i.e., the proportion of an employer's total operating costs comprised of labor costs). Combining with other employers into a multi-employer bargaining unit strengthens an individual employer's bargaining power and also minimizes another potential problem—the loss of customers to competitors should a work stoppage occur.

Unions are also concerned about market problems in some industries (construction, coal, trucking, ladies' garments, longshore, and others) and attempt to extend the bargaining unit to include all unionized employers in a geographic area producing the same competitive product. This approach is taken to prevent a few employers with above-average bargaining power from separately negotiating lower wages, which could provide them lower production costs, thereby attracting customers from other unionized firms, which could result in layoffs at higher labor cost firms for some union members. In essence, unions are attempting to standardize wages, hours, and other terms of employment to reduce the importance of labor costs as a competitive factor and force employers to compete on the basis of other non-labor factors, such as product design, product quality, customer service, and so on.

Multi-employer bargaining also has other advantages and disadvantages. A union engaged in multi-employer bargaining has a powerful advantage over rival unions because the NLRB holds that while a multi-employer bargaining unit is intact, it is the only appropriate bargaining/election unit.[6] Thus, the NLRB will dismiss a rival union's petition for an election in a single firm as long as the incumbent union and the firm are participants in a multi-employer bargaining unit. Both labor and management can benefit from the cost savings that accrue from having to prepare for fewer contract negotiations when separate ABUs are combined to form a centralized bargaining unit. The costs of preparing for and conducting negotiations can also be shared among employers participating in a multi-employer bargaining unit.

Centralized bargaining tends to become more formal and less flexible in terms of meeting employee and employer concerns at an individual workplace. Because terms must be applied across different employee groups often at different locations, bargaining outcomes tend to reflect a broader regional, corporate, or industry level perspective rather than emphasizing local conditions prevailing at any particular plant location. For example, wage and benefit trend data used to identify an appropriate bargaining outcome are more likely to reflect prevailing industry or national averages rather than local labor market conditions.

Finally, multi-employer bargaining can create tensions among the member employers. An employer might consider pulling out of a multi-employer group if it feels it can get a better deal negotiating separately with the union. To legally withdraw from an existing multi-employer bargaining unit, an employer must provide both the union and other unit employers with reasonable advance notice (e.g., prior to the expiration date of the current agreement and before negotiations have commenced on a new contract to replace the expiring agreement).[7] Where there is a clear disparity in the size of the participating firms, larger employers may attempt to control the decisions of the multi-employer group. This may become a problem for smaller employers within the group whose perceptions may differ from larger employers regarding the affordability or administrative burden of accepting certain union bargaining proposals.

The decision to engage in centralized bargaining can also be affected by legal guidelines. The size and makeup of each party's bargaining team are non-mandatory subjects of bargaining.[8] A union representing a particular bargaining unit could permit representatives from other unions who also bargain separately with the same employer to sit in on negotiations as part of the union's bargaining team. Although the employer cannot control who sits on the union bargaining team, the employer could legally require that only the legal union representative of the bargaining unit covered by the contract under negotiation be permitted to decide whether to accept or reject management's bargaining proposals.[9] Union representatives from other bargaining units could function as observers in the negotiation process but could not exercise any authority over determining settlement terms.

The NLRB has also ruled as unlawful a **lock-in agreement** between unions which prohibits any union represented bargaining unit covered by an agreement from reaching a final contract settlement until all unions who bargain contracts with the same employer are willing to settle.[10] The intent of such a lock-in agreement is to prevent an employer with multiple bargaining units covered under separate contracts from using a **whip-saw bargaining strategy** to obtain concessions from one bargaining unit which could then be used as leverage to seek similar or additional changes in contract terms in subsequent negotiations with other bargaining units. The lock-in agreement forces the employer to address the concerns of all bargaining units at the same time rather than selectively choosing the order in which negotiations with particular bargaining units will proceed. It is lawful for two or more separate bargaining units to share information with each other about bargaining priorities, strategies, or employer-specific information (so-called **coordinated bargaining**).

The U.S. Supreme Court ruled that it was unlawful for an employer to withdraw from an established multi-employer bargaining arrangement during a bargaining impasse without the union's consent.[11] The employer's withdrawal was not allowed, and the employer was bound to any subsequent agreement reached by the union and the multi-employer bargaining group. An employer may legally withdraw from a multi-employer negotiating unit before the onset of bargaining preparations by notifying the other employers and union(s) involved in the unit of the withdrawing employer's intention and the effective date of such withdrawal.

Negotiation Preparation Activities
Selection of the Negotiating Team and Related Bargaining Responsibilities

The selection of the number and type of individuals who will make up the bargaining team for each party is an important decision that can affect the outcome of negotiations. Exhibit 6.2 suggests some characteristics of an effective negotiator, although few individuals are likely to possess all of these characteristics to the ideal degree. "A skilled negotiator is not just someone who can make

- Able to say *no* effectively.
- Has integrity and the ability to inspire confidence in his or her judgment ability.
- Able to plan effectively and conduct research necessary to become thoroughly knowledgeable about bargaining issues and trends.
- Able to discern the *bottom line interests* of other parties.
- Even-tempered and able to tolerate conflict and ambiguity.
- An excellent communicator (i.e., able to speak, write, and listen effectively).
- Self-confident and pragmatic (able to establish realistic bargaining expectations and accurately assess the benefits, costs, and risks of insisting on specific settlement terms).
- Good physical and mental stamina.
- Able to understand the short- and long-term implications of specific bargaining proposals on the parties' interests.
- Understands the importance of *face saving* and is willing to provide opportunities to the other party to do so (or conversely, knows when to take advantage of such opportunities when offered by the other party).
- Willing to take calculated risks in order to achieve desired bargaining outcomes without seriously jeopardizing constituents' best interests.
- Knows how and when to ask relevant questions and interpret the other party's responses (even no response to a question or action may, in fact, represent a meaningful response).
- Has a sense of humor to relieve stress or establish rapport with the other party. Always laughs with the other party, never at the other party.

Exhibit 6.2

Some Common Characteristics of an Effective Negotiator

deals, a skilled negotiator is someone who can make deals that can be implemented. Skilled negotiators anticipate implementation issues before the deal is agreed. Less skilled negotiators make deals that others find difficult or impossible to implement."[12]

Management generally selects negotiating team members based on the perceived need for each individual's skills and experience. Management generally wants at least one line manager who supervises bargaining unit employees on its team to either interpret or answer negotiating issues related to daily work operations.

In determining the size of each negotiating team, smaller teams are generally preferable, with a maximum suggested size of nine.[13] Teams larger than nine tend to experience increasing coordination problems (e.g., task assignment, delegation of authority, pressure to conform) and require additional time to reach consensus on bargaining issues. Sometimes bargaining team size is influenced by a desire to match the size of the other party's team. A bargaining structure that emphasizes centralized industry or corporate-level bargaining or multiple parties (on either the employer or union side) tends to expand the size of negotiating teams.

Unions apply selection criteria similar to those of management, but in addition, they must weigh certain political considerations. For example, an elected union leader may think it is important to appoint at least one or more representatives from key constituent groups within the bargaining unit (e.g., skilled trade, largest department or occupation, women, minorities) to serve on the union's negotiating team. This choice helps to ensure that the special interests of key constituent groups will be considered in negotiating settlement terms, which will enhance the probability that tentative contract settlement terms will be approved by a majority of the union's membership.

The union negotiating team may be elected by the membership or appointed by elected union officers depending on the wording contained in the union's constitution and bylaws. Where direct election of negotiating team members is permitted, there is always a risk to current leaders that one or more rivals for union leadership may be elected to serve on the team. This can create some problems in attempting to achieve consensus on bargaining priorities, strategies, tactics, and acceptable settlement terms.

Union and management negotiators seek bargaining team members who can keep their emotions and opinions in check. An indiscreet negotiating team member can unintentionally reveal confidential settlement positions and strategies to the other team. In some cases, union and management negotiators may agree to release information in the form of a joint statement to outside third parties (e.g., news media) during negotiations. This tactic helps to reduce rumors or misleading claims that can damage progress being made toward a settlement at the bargaining table. Where no such agreement exists, there may be a risk that one or both parties may choose to leak certain information about the contents of specific proposals, perceived road blocks to settlement, or a perceived lack of honest effort to reach an acceptable agreement. While such leaks may sway public opinion or shore up political support for negotiating team members, they can also damage the existing level of trust between the bargaining parties and delay progress on substantive issues as the leaks themselves become a topic of conversation at the bargaining table. One party may fear mentioning a possible alternative settlement approach on an issue for fear the other party may disclose the remark publicly as a firm and final position of the initiating party, rather than the idea starter or "trial balloon" it was intended to be.

Proposal Determination and Assessment

Management relies on several sources to determine a union's likely bargaining goals in contract negotiations. A review of recent settlements negotiated by the company's competitors and other local firms may help to identify likely bargaining subjects as well as possible settlement outcomes. The company and union may have negotiated settlements at other facilities that might also be used as a starting point in the current negotiations. Some management officials obtain bargaining insights by reviewing the proceedings of a national union's convention or visiting a union's Internet Web site.

One study of local union officials reported that staff representatives, business agents, and organizers were more likely to rely upon formal information sources (e.g., libraries, union research departments, databases) than informal sources (e.g., personal networks, telephone inquiries) to gather information for use in contract negotiations.[14] Formal training in research methods also increased the number of information sources used by a union official in preparing to perform role functions such as contract negotiations.

Attention should be given to the parties' previous negotiations, particularly to those issues that one party actively sought and reluctantly dropped. Compromise settlements on previous issues also generate valuable clues because compromise does not always mean permanent resolution of the issue. An analysis of previous grievances at the facility can also identify certain trouble spots. GM, for example, uses a computerized analysis of number, type, and resolution status of grievances in their negotiation preparations. However, caution must be taken not to overemphasize these grievances. Unions often increase the number of grievances filed in the six months prior to negotiations to dramatize widespread concern over certain bargaining issues—concerns perhaps more tactical than real.

Formulating Proposals and the Bargaining Range

Management negotiators need to be proactive rather than reactive in preparing for contract negotiations. Traditionally, many management negotiators chose to wait for the union to present its bargaining proposals before determining management's bargaining response. Often, this approach permitted the union to control the bargaining agenda and left management negotiating over how many or to what extent to grant union demands for improvements in employment terms of interest. Increased competitive pressures have caused many unionized employers to initiate proposed work-rule changes to decrease labor costs and improve productivity and quality, which would not likely have been a part of the bargaining agenda if management negotiators did not take a more proactive stance at the bargaining table. Rather than waiting for the union to raise every issue, management negotiators should put forward their own proposals concerning issues, such as health care cost containment, revising pension benefits, broadening job descriptions, and subcontracting or outsourcing of certain bargaining unit work.

Since the union will normally present its bargaining proposals first as the party initiating the request to renegotiate a current contract set to expire soon, management negotiators may prefer to defer presenting proposals on any issues the union is expected to initially address (e.g., wage rate improvement) so as not to "tip their hand" to the union. See Exhibit 6.3 for some advice on wording contract language proposals.

Exhibit 6.3
Practical Advice on Wording Contract Language

- Whenever possible, use common words, terms, or phrases that are easy to read and understand.

- Consider the types of individuals who will use the contract (e.g., employees, managers, union representatives, arbitrators) and write contract language with this audience in mind.

- Anticipate questions or circumstances that might arise in implementing the intent of the proposal and include contract language that would answer or address such issues or concerns.

- Use consistent terminology throughout the contract to refer to the same concept or item to enhance consistency of meaning and interpretation.

- Write concisely using only the words necessary to clearly convey the meaning or intent of the contract clause.

- Use appropriate section numbers or headings to organize contract language by specific bargaining subjects or topics.

- Use numbered lists to highlight criteria or factors relevant to a particular subject (e.g., steps in a grievance procedure, promotion eligibility criteria).

- Be clear and specific when specifying time frames or numbers (e.g., length of employee probationary period, length of regular work shift or break-time, effective and expiration time and date of the contract).

SOURCE: Marc Boulanger and Brian H. Kleiner, "Preparing and Interpreting Collective Bargaining Agreements Effectively," *Management Research News*, 26 (2/3/4), 2003, pp. 193–197.

In formulating bargaining proposals, managers often perform a close analysis of the current labor contract to determine desirable changes in language that will reduce labor costs and increase management flexibility in making operating decisions. Assume, for example, that the current contract prohibits managers from performing any bargaining unit work. Management might propose allowing supervisors to perform bargaining unit work under at least three conditions: (1) when training new employees, (2) in emergency situations (usually interpreted to mean when employees' lives or production equipment are at immediate risk), and (3) when experimental production efforts are involved.

Management and union officials may propose contract language intended to nullify the impact of prior adverse arbitration decisions. For example, an arbitrator's decision that the company will pay for an employee's safety shoes could be nullified by negotiating new contract language that reads, "The Company will provide the employees with safety shoes and deduct the cost of these shoes from the employee's paycheck." Both union and management will typically contact union stewards and first-line supervisors or department heads, respectively, to determine if any contract language has been difficult to administer during the term of the current labor agreement and thus, ought to be modified.

Efforts will also be made to research data from government reports, especially from the U.S. Departments of Commerce and Labor, and from various labor relations services such as the Bureau of National Affairs, Commerce Clearing House, and Prentice-Hall. Data pertaining to wages, benefits, safety and health, technological change, job security, productivity, legal developments, and so on, from these and other sources, give both parties substantial information with which to prepare for negotiations. Being over-prepared to conduct contract negotiations is a rarity, but the negotiator who enters bargaining under-prepared is taking a sizeable risk.

The Bargaining Range

Union and management officials enter collective bargaining with their own ideas of an acceptable settlement, although both parties know the other will not agree entirely with their position. Therefore, both parties usually enter negotiations with a range of acceptable positions that give them some room for maneuvering. These positions can be given priorities and grouped into a **bargaining range**, one for management and the other for the union. Exhibit 6.4 illustrates bargaining ranges for a few issues; however, it is common for the parties to negotiate a hundred or more bargaining issues.

Both management and union representatives have upper and lower limits on their respective ranges. Management's upper limit is usually determined by its objectives, such as profitability and productivity growth. Settlement terms that are too costly or restrictive on management's right to make operating decisions would be incompatible with the company's objectives. The point beyond which a party would prefer no settlement to settlement on unacceptable terms represents that party's **resistance point** on a particular bargaining issue. For example, management might prefer to close, move its operations, or bring new employees into its existing facility rather than agree to a settlement that would make operations less profitable. On the other hand, management may not want to be known as the cheapest employer in the area, nor would it want to be unable to recruit, retain, and reward its productive employees. These concerns help place a lower limit on management's bargaining range— a minimum offer that management feels is necessary to maintain employee morale and output.

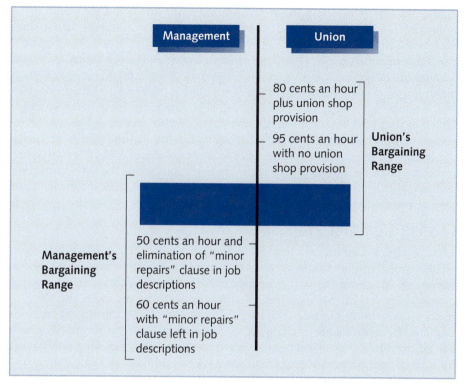

Exhibit 6.4
Bargaining Ranges for Union
and Management
Negotiators

A union's upper limit is usually shaped by two factors: (1) desired employ-ment levels and (2) the ability to promote and sustain a strike. A union realizes that there is often a trade-off between pressing for economic gains (higher wages and improved benefits) and the number of jobs that may be available at that higher labor cost. Higher labor costs increase management's incentive to look for ways to substitute capital for labor (e.g., technological innovation), use less labor (e.g., layoffs), or find a less costly labor supply (e.g., subcontracting bar-gaining unit work to nonunion employers or moving work operations to lower-cost domestic or international labor markets). Unrealistic union bargaining proposals are likely to be discounted by management and can serve as a hin-drance to serious negotiation over meritorious issues. Also, a strike cannot be ini-tiated, let alone successfully concluded, if union leaders call a strike over an unrealistic bargaining demand (e.g., $3/hour wage increase when union members recognize that management could realistically afford a raise of only $.80/hour). Bargaining unit members are not likely to risk a work stoppage over issues of minor importance to their interests or proposed settlement terms that they view as unrealistic under the prevailing circumstances.

On the other hand, union leaders realize that there is a lower limit on the bargaining range and that a settlement below this limit would result in member-ship dissatisfaction. Because union leaders are strongly influenced by their de-sire to ensure the survival of the union and their continued election as union officers, they seldom accept a settlement below this perceived resistance point. It is important for union leaders to solicit input from members about their bargaining interests and priorities and to inform members about current bargaining conditions and trends, thereby encouraging the members to form realistic bargaining expectations. Union members obtain their knowledge about current economic conditions, bargaining trends, and estimates of union bargaining power not only from their union organization, but also from many public information sources (e.g., television, newspapers, Internet, discussions with other employees).

The bargaining range, although bound by upper and lower limits, represents a multitude of issues. Assigning priorities to these issues and their possible combinations produces bargaining ranges of an almost infinite number of possibilities. Bargaining ranges can change during negotiations as bargaining issues get linked in package proposals (see Exhibit 6.4) covering several subjects or in response to new information, usually becoming finalized as the parties approach the contract expiration date or a strike/lockout deadline. A party's bargaining resistance point on a particular issue generally remains stable during negotiations, and any drastic alteration of a party's resistance point indicates insufficient bargaining preparation on the part of that bargaining party.

Costing Contract Proposals

Management has an overriding concern about the eventual cost of a labor agreement's terms because it has the responsibility of paying for those terms of employment. Management will generally need to estimate the cost of contract proposals at several points during the negotiation process including prior to the first bargaining meeting (pre-bargaining preparation), during negotiations as counter-proposals are exchanged, and after final contract terms have been agreed on. Management negotiators often use two general costing approaches in negotiations: preparation of employee background data and calculation of a cents-per-hour wage increase. Unions also engage in costing efforts for the purpose of either determining the value of management proposals or helping to persuade management that it can afford to grant union proposals.

Management usually obtains statistical summaries of employees, cross-tabulated by several variables (age, sex, marital status, seniority, job classification). These summaries provide immediate information necessary to cost out a variety of contract proposals, such as health insurance, vacations, funeral pay, and pensions.

One of the most important calculations is the cost of a cents-per-hour wage increase. The **cents-per-hour cost** of any contract item can be obtained by dividing the annual total cost of the item by the number of bargaining unit hours worked during the year. If an employer has 100 employees who work a standard 40 hour week and the firm operates 52 weeks per year then the total bargaining unit hours worked would be $100 \times 2,080$ hours = 208,000 hours. Calculating the cents-per-hour cost of an item allows for realistic cost comparisons across bargaining units of different sizes (number of employees).

The true cost of a wage increase includes the cost of the wage increase itself, plus the increased costs of all benefit items paid on the basis of an employee's straight-time hourly wage rate (e.g., holiday and vacation pay, sick leave and jury duty pay, paid rest and lunch periods, overtime pay, call-in pay). The **roll-up factor** is an estimate of the total cents-per-hour costs of employer benefit items affected by a change in the straight-time hourly wage rate as a proportion (percentage) of the current average hourly bargaining unit wage rate. For example, if the total cents-per-hour costs for the employer benefit items affected by a wage rate change amounted to $3.60, and the current average hourly bargaining unit wage rate was $10, then the roll-up factor or cost would equal $3.60 ÷ $10 = $.36 or 36 percent. The actual cost of the wage increase calculated in the following example would be $20,800 plus the roll-up factor cost [$20,800 × .36 = $7,488] for a total annual wage cost of $28,288.

An illustrative calculation of a one cent-per-hour wage increase for a bargaining unit of 1,000 employees is as follows:

$20,800 *Straight-time pay* (1,000 employees × 40 hours a week × 52 weeks × $.01).

7,488 *Roll up cost* for benefit items directly affected by the wage increase (profit sharing, pensions, life insurance, employer contributions to social security, shift differential if paid on a percentage basis, unemployment insurance, workers' compensation, and so on), estimated for illustrative purposes at 36 percent of the average bargaining unit straight-time hourly wage rate.

_____

$28,288 True cost of a one cent-per-hour wage increase.

A negotiator should be prepared to bargain on either a cents-per-hour wage increase or a percentage wage increase. Since the union will normally introduce the wage issue first when presenting its initial bargaining proposals, the union will initially determine whether the format for wage negotiations will be cents-per-hour or a percentage increase in the current hourly wage rate. If bargaining on a percentage basis, it is important to remember the magnitude difference between a given size percentage wage increase versus a similar size cents-per-hour wage increase.

Assuming the average hourly straight-time wage rate for the 1,000-member bargaining unit in the previous example was $10 per hour, the cost of a *one percent* wage increase for this bargaining unit would be calculated as follows: .01 × $10 = .10¢ per hour × 1,000 employees × 2,080 hours = $208,000 straight-time pay + roll-up cost of $74,880 ($208,000 × .36) = $282,880. This compares to the $28,288 total cost of a *one cent-per-hour* wage increase for the same group of employees.

Union officials may submit proposals that are difficult to cost, thereby weakening management's related objections based on cost estimates during negotiations. Assume, for example, that a current contract provision provides a Sunday work premium of 75¢ an hour if the employees have no absences during their regularly scheduled work week. The union proposes that employees working on Sunday receive this premium pay regardless of their attendance record during the week. Management can examine past payroll records to estimate the added cost of this proposal, which is a difficult task if there are thousands of employees involved and it is uncertain if extra absences might occur if this proposal is accepted. Other proposals, such as extending a previous labor agreement's three-day paid leave for the death of an immediate family member to include first cousins, are nearly impossible to precisely estimate cost because it is very difficult to accurately gather the data needed to cost the item (i.e., the number of living first cousins of each employee). In addition, using past payroll records and anticipated future production and staffing requirements may not always be a perfect predictor of future operating experience.

Union negotiators may formulate proposals that benefit members' interests while saving management money, a difficult task requiring much ingenuity. Examples include the following:

- Allowing police to keep a squad car for personal use, thereby reducing crime statistics and related expenses.

- Allowing sabbaticals for which professors receive one-half their salaries for nine months, and management uses any surplus funds elsewhere if a replacement teaches the professors' classes at a lower pay rate.

LABOR RELATIONS IN ACTION
Bargaining in the Auto Industry

In July 2007, the United Auto Workers (UAW) union opened negotiations with the "Big Three" U.S. automobile manufacturers—C hrysler Holding LLC (CH), General Motors Corp. (GM) and Ford Motor Co. (Ford)— to replace the current contract scheduled to expire on September 15, 2007.[a] The outcome of these negotiations will be critical to the future competitiveness of both the auto companies and the UAW as a national union. Declining market share, high gasoline costs, changing consumer preferences for more fuel-efficient and environmentally friendly vehicles, and unrelenting pressure from international auto manufacturers such as Toyota, Honda, Nissan, and Hyundai combine to make this one of the most difficult periods in the history of the so-called Big Three auto manufacturers.

In 1985 major U.S. auto makers accounted for 74 percent of U.S. auto sales.[b] By the first quarter of 2007, the Big Three's market share had declined to 52.1 percent and is predicted to decline an additional seven percent by 2012.[c] Some of the decline in market share is the result of a conscious decision by the Big Three firms to reduce production levels in order to focus more on improving bottom-line profits. Labor costs under contracts currently in force at domestic operations of the Big Three total approximately $73 dollars per hour compared to $43 dollars per hour at U.S. plants of Japanese auto makers.[d] Hourly wage rates are fairly comparable between the Big Three firms and foreign-owned firms, averaging about $27 per hour. Most of the current $30 per hour labor cost disadvantage born by the Big Three is comprised of higher health care and pension benefit costs.[e] In 2006, Asian auto makers such as Toyota and Honda averaged $1,200 profit per vehicle sold compared to an average loss per vehicle sold by CH, GM, and Ford of $1,072, $1,436, and $5,234 respectively. The Big Three firms have, with the UAW's cooperation, been making work rule changes to improve productivity, which has resulted in reducing the number of hours required to make a vehicle by an average of two percent.[f] Production quality of vehicles has also improved, although the marketing campaign to successfully get that message across to consumers will take additional time.[g]

Each of the Big Three firms has embarked on programs to reduce the size of its work force as a key step in reducing wage, health care, and pension benefit costs.[h] GM has reported a reduction of 34,400 employees through early retirement or buyout packages. CH will eliminate 13,000 jobs (including 4,700 U.S. hourly wage jobs) over a three-year period, and Ford will eliminate 10,000 salaried jobs and up to 30,000 hourly wage jobs through early retirement and buyout incentive packages offered to workers.

GM is under particular cost pressure with more retirees and dependents than active workers entitled to health care benefits, which cost $55 billion in 2006 compared to $22 billion at Ford and $16 billion at CH.[i] This equates to approximately $1,500 additional cost per vehicle. Pension and health care costs tend to be lower at many transplant competitor firms because such operations in the United States employ a labor force whose average age is younger and has few individuals with sufficient years of service to be eligible for pension benefit payments.

The UAW is a union struggling to cope with a declining membership level where most members are employed at companies facing downsizing and intense cost competition. In 1979, UAW membership was 1.5 million but has since declined to a current level of 576,000 members.[j] Unable to make significant organizing gains at foreign transplant auto operations in the United States and facing continued elimination of jobs at the Big Three, the UAW has sought to diversify its membership base by increased organizing of service and professional workers in education, health care, insurance, and casino gambling.

The president of the UAW, Ron Gettelfinger, has developed a reputation as a pragmatic consensus builder who understands the competitive environment in which the Big Three operate. "Like it or not, these challenges aren't the kind that can be ridden out. They demand new and far-sighted solutions, and we must be an integral part of developing these solutions."[k] The 2007 talks will be the second time Mr. Gettelfinger has led the UAW in national bargaining with the Big Three. The year 2007 will mark the first time in the UAW's over 70-year history that more cars and trucks are likely to built in the United States by non-UAW members than UAW members.[l]

Historically, the UAW has selected one of the auto companies as its primary negotiating target in an attempt to negotiate a favorable settlement whose terms could then form a pattern agreement for settlement talks at remaining auto firms. Faced with a need to maintain stable operating environments at the Big Three in 2007, the union opened negotiations with all three auto companies but quickly designated GM as the primary target for negotiation of a new agreement. By emphasizing settlement rather than confrontation, the UAW hoped to forge a working partnership with auto firms that would recognize the legitimate interests of both ownership and employees in determining final settlement terms. The UAW's bargaining strategy permits it to coordinate bargaining positions across the three separate companies while still affording an opportunity for each bargaining relationship to structure final contract settlement terms to best meet the needs of that firm's competitive position.

While attempting to shape UAW members' expectations regarding realistic bargaining outcomes under current auto industry conditions, union leaders also sounded a cautionary note to industry employers who may believe that current conditions strengthen their bargaining power to demand significant labor cost concessions. "Collective bargaining is not collective begging. It would be a grave mistake to equate our actions to capitulations."[m] There is a small but extremely vocal group of UAW members who believe significant concessions have already been granted to auto makers and to prevent further erosion of hard fought previous bargaining gains, the union must draw the line at further significant wage, benefit and work rule concessions. No elected union leader likes to hear the word "sell out" used to describe their bargaining efforts to represent members' interests.[n] Careful planning, effective communication, creativity, and courage was required for UAW negotiators to serve their members' bargaining interests effectively during the 2007 auto negotiations.

Key bargaining issues in the 2007 auto negotiations focused on health care and pension benefits, eliminating or restructuring the Jobs Bank program, and continuing to address plant-level work rule changes to provide more flexible work structures, scheduling, and the use of lower cost labor to perform some types of jobs not directly involved in the assembly of vehicles (so-called non-core jobs like custodians or fork lift operators). Employers sought changes to enhance profitability and the UAW evaluated proposed changes from the standpoint of how changes might impact members' job security from both a short- and long-term perspective.

In 2005, the UAW voluntarily negotiated mid-term contract changes to lower health care costs at GM and Ford for current retirees by up to 25 percent or $15 billion per year and further reduced annual health care costs for current employees by $1 billion per year.[o] At the time the UAW did not agree to similar health care cost concessions at CH because the union viewed CH's financial position as stronger than GM's or Ford's. The UAW has recently indicated to private equity firm Cerebus Capital Management, which recently acquired CH from Daimler-Chrysler, that the union is now ready to address additional

health care cost reduction changes in the 2007 negotiations to help CH cope with its estimated $19 billion per year health care cost obligation.[p] Like many union contracts, auto industry agreements typically contain a variety of features designed to help reduce health care costs, such as employee co-payments or deductibles, requiring generic drugs be used when available, delaying new hire eligibility for health care coverage, requiring outpatient surgery when medically possible, wellness programs, utilization review, pre-admission testing, or requiring a second opinion in certain cases.

Rather than continuing to represent the "Gold Standard" in employee health insurance programs, UAW members will continue to enjoy above-average benefits but benefits that begin to more closely resemble those offered by competing employers. Long term, the UAW believes the health care cost crisis in America is too great to resolve in bargaining on a firm-by-firm basis and requires a national, single payer, comprehensive health care plan covering adults and children.

The Big Three auto companies with an estimated combined $95 billion retiree health care cost obligation have expressed interest in negotiating a plan similar to the recently negotiated plan between Goodyear Tire & Rubber Company (Goodyear) and the United Steelworkers Union (USW), which shifts the responsibility for paying future employee and retiree health care cost to the union.[q] In exchange for a $1 billion cash and stock contribution from Goodyear to establish a health care trust fund (Voluntary Employee Beneficiary Association—VEBA) administered by the Union to pay current employee and retiree future health care costs, the company was able to remove $1.2 billion in health care liability costs from the firm's balance sheet.

It is estimated that establishing a VEBA health care plan in the auto industry would require the Big Three firms to contribute between $55 and $65 billion in assets and make the UAW one of the largest private sector health care providers in the United States.[r] Investment earnings on the original trust fund balance and future health care cost savings would be relied upon to ensure that future health care obligations for UAW members were met.

The **Jobs Bank program** was created during the 1982 round of auto negotiations as a job security measure for union members affected by a temporary downturn in the industry. Companies benefited from maintaining a ready pool of experienced workers who could easily be added back into the work force as industry conditions improved and production levels rose. While in the Jobs Bank program, an employee continues to earn full wages and benefits and is required to report for work at their assigned plant to perform some company-approved activity (e.g., training, community service), although how much workers are asked to do and how often appears to vary within the industry from plant to plant.[s]

Employees who are laid off initially receive state unemployment benefits and supplementary unemployment benefits provided by the company under the terms of the contract. After 48 weeks when unemployment benefits have typically been exhausted, the employee can enter the Jobs Bank program and remain in the program indefinitely under current contract terms. There are approximately 14,700 employees in the Jobs Bank program, representing a cost of $1.4 to $2 billion in 2006. GM has the largest number of employees (5,000–6,000) in the Jobs Bank program at an estimated cost of $700 to $800 million annually.[t] While total elimination of the program is unlikely, management negotiators will likely propose contract language aimed at reducing the cost of the program, such as imposing a time limit for remaining in the program, tightening eligibility requirements, and providing employers more flexibility in the type or amount of approved activities workers can be required to perform while in the program.

The Big Three auto makers are likely to continue to pursue plant level work rule changes that allow more jobs to be performed by non-bargaining unit labor at lower costs (e.g., forklift operators, custodial services).[u] The UAW will continue to insist on application of its long standing principle of "equality of sacrifice," requiring managers and ownership to share proportionally in the sacrifices that cost cutting entails. There will likely be an effort to increase the proportion of employee compensation tied to productivity and profits although profit-sharing agreements may be a hard sell given recent poor returns received by employees under current profit sharing plans.[v] Lump sum payments instead of hourly wage improvements may be an acceptable alternative that would not increase an employer's roll-up costs for fringe benefits paid on the basis of hourly wage rates.[w]

Although a work stoppage was not deemed likely during the 2007 auto negotiations because both sides would be significantly damaged by any disruption in production, leading to possible further loss of market share and union member job loss, a brief work stoppage did occur at both GM (two days) and CH (seven hours).[x] In both cases the UAW indicated that the strike was called to change the current bargaining dynamic between the parties at the bargaining table and remind employers of the need to address remaining differences between the parties' bargaining positions as quickly as possible. No doubt the UAW's willingness to strike at GM and CH facilitated the efforts of UAW and Ford negotiators to reach an agreement in subsequent negotiations without the necessity of a work stoppage. Strike or lockout threats often help the parties to focus on the fact that they need each other to achieve their respective interests, and they have much more to gain by reaching a reasonable agreement than facing the alternative of failing to reach agreement. It is important that both labor and management continue to forge a partnership that recognizes and addresses the legitimate needs of all parties to encourage business growth and profitability capable of sustaining improving compensation levels and job security.

Although there are differences between the final contract settlement terms at each auto company, the UAW was successful in maintaining a pattern of settlement terms in the CH and Ford agreements initially established in the GM contract agreement.[y] Some key features of the new labor agreements include the following: an immediate $3,000 pay bonus per employee upon ratification of the tentative contract agreement; lump sum payments in each of the remaining three years of the four-year contract's term; establishment of a VEBA initially funded by employer contributions but administered by the UAW; establishment of a two-tier wage and benefit plan applicable to new hires; establishment of a two-tier wage and benefit plan for current employees classified as performing "non-core" production jobs at an initial wage rate of approximately half the $28 per hour rate of current production employees; and an expressed commitment from employers to use

- Using outpatient surgery for minor procedures or requiring second medical opinions before scheduling major surgical procedures.

When presenting cost analyses information at the bargaining table, it is important to clearly explain how cost estimates were obtained and any underlying assumptions on which estimates may rest.[15] Using current and credible sources for data used in preparing cost estimates can increase the credibility and thus, persuasiveness of such information when used in support of bargaining proposals.

the more competitive labor cost terms in the new agreement to maintain production opportunities in U.S. plants. Both GM and Ford were more specific than CH in terms of discussing future model production plans targeted for specific existing auto plants and the time frame for specific models' expected production cycle.

UAW members were not unanimous in their support of the new contract terms. Opposition centered around the introduction of a two-tier wage and benefit plan, which some union members feared would, over time, drive a wedge between union members on different tiers and likely increase turnover rates among lower-tier employees. Some UAW members were also critical of the fact that employers were not more specific about future job guarantees. Whether or not the new labor agreements at GM, Ford, and CH will be truly transformational in ushering in a new, more competitive era for unionized U.S. auto companies is yet to be determined. Whether or not these new labor agreements will permit the parties to develop a more cooperative bargaining relationship which builds mutual trust and respect between the parties will also be determined by the future, but the opportunity to do so does exist.

SOURCES: [a]Joe Guy Collier, "1,500 Will Shape UAW's Priorities: Session in Detroit to Begin Tuesday," *Knight Ridder Tribune Business News,* March 26, 2007, p. 1.
[b]Federal Reserve Bank of Cleveland, "The American Auto Industry," *Economic Trends,* May 2006, pp. 1–3.
[c]John K. Teahen, Jr., "Import Brands Steal the First-Quarter Thunder," *Automotive News,* April 9, 2007, p. 49; James B. Treece, "Forecaster: Sales Will Bounce Back; Detroit 3 Might Not," *Automotive News,* May 28, 2007, p. 6; and Jean Halliday, "GM Finds Profit Religion as Toyota Overtakes It; After 76 Years, Will No Longer Focus on Market Share," *Advertising Age,* 78 (18), April 30, 2007, p. 1.
[d]John D. Stoll, "U.S. Auto Makers Narrow Productivity Gap," *The Wall Street Journal,* June 1, 2007, p. A-2.
[e]Gina Chon, Jason Singer, and Jeffrey McCracken, "Chrysler Deal Heralds New Direction for Detroit," *The Wall Street Journal,* May 15, 2007, pp. A-1,14.
[f]Chris Woodyard, "Carmakers, Union Working Hand-in-Hand," *USA Today,* February 5, 2007, pp. 1–4.
[g]Sarah A. Webster, "Quality? It's Ford," *Detroit Free Press,* June 7, 2007, pp. 1–2 at http://www.freep.com; Joe Guy Collier, "Domestics Gain Ground on Japanese," *Detroit Free Press,* June 7, 2007, p. 1 at http://www.freep.com; Jamie LaReau and Dave Barkholtz, "GM to UAW: Let's Cut Costs," *Automotive News,* April 16, 2007, pp. 1–2; and Norihiko Shirouzu, "Big Three Gain on Japanese Rivals," *The Wall Street Journal,* June 2, 2006, p. A-6.

[h]John D. Stoll, "GM Pares Obligations for Pensions, Health Care," *The Wall Street Journal,* August 9, 2006, p. B-8; Tim Higgins, "6,400 Jump For Chrysler Buyouts," *Detroit Free Press,* June 8, 2007, pp. 1–2 at http://www.freep.com; Sholnn Freeman and Amy Joyce, "Ford To Cut 14 Plants and Up to 30,000 Jobs," *The Washington Post,* January 24, 2005, p. A-1; and Associated Press, "Ford Cuts Health Benefits, Merit Pay," *Findlaw,* November 2, 2006, pp. 1–2 at http://news.findlaw.com.
[i]John D. Stoll, "GM Pares Obligations for Pensions, Health Care," *The Wall Street Journal,* August 9, 2006, p. B-8; Tim Higgins, "6,400 Jump For Chrysler Buyouts," *Detroit Free Press,* June 8, 2007, pp. 1–2 at http://www.freep.com; Sholnn Freeman and Amy Joyce, "Ford To Cut 14 Plants and Up to 30,000 Jobs," *The Washington Post,* January 24, 2005, p. A-1; and Associated Press, "Ford Cuts Health Benefits, Merit Pay," *Findlaw,* November 2, 2006, pp. 1–2 at http://news.findlaw.com.
[j]Tom Krisher, "UAW Head: Union Has Plenty of Fight Left," *The Associated Press,* March 27, 2007, pp. 1–2.
[k]Dina ElBoghdady, "UAW Chief Warns Workers of Tough Changes Ahead," *The Washington Post,* June 13, 2006, p. D-1.
[l]Jeffrey McCracken, "Detroit Pursues Sweeping Cuts in Union Talks," *The Wall Street Journal,* June 14, 2007, pp. A-1,9.
[m]Sholnn Freeman, "Autoworkers Ready for a Fight," *The Washington Post,* March 28, 2007, p. D-1, and Micheline Maynard, "No Retreat, No Surrender (They Hope)," *The New York Times,* June 18, 2006, pp. 1–5 at http://www.nytimes.com.
[n]Jerry Flint, "Sellout!" *Forbes,* May 21, 2007, p. 58.
[o]Dee-Ann Durbin, "GM, UAW Reach Deal as GM Posts $1.6 Billion Loss," *Associated Press,* October 17, 2005, pp. 1–2 at http://www.washingtonpost.com; Michael Ellis, "GM Deal: Cries of Pain Mix with Sighs of Relief," *Detroit Free Press,* October 21, 2005, pp. 1–2 at http://www.freep.com; and Tim Higgins, "Zetsche: Don't Blame UAW: Health Care Didn't Force Chrysler Sale," *Knight Ridder Tribune Business News,* May 17, 2007, p. 1.
[p]Tom Krisher, "United Auto Workers Assures Members that Chrysler Pensions Are Safe," *Findlaw,* May 16, 2007, pp. 1–2 at http://news.findlaw.com.
[q]Jeffrey McCracken, "Detroit Pursues Sweeping Cuts in Union Talks," *The Wall Street Journal,* June 14, 2007, pp. A-1,9 and Kris Maher, "Now Someone Else Has to Tell Retirees No," *The Wall Street Journal,* January 29, 2007, pp. B-1,4.
[r]Gina Chon, Jason Singer, and Jeffrey McCracken, "Chrysler Deal Heralds New Direction for Detroit," *The Wall Street Journal,* May 15, 2007, pp. A-1,4.
[s]Jeffrey McCracken, "Detroit's Symbol of Dysfunction: Paying Employees Not to Work," *The Wall Street Journal,* March 1, 2006, pp. A-1,12.
[t]Michael Ellis, "Pre-Contract Negotiations: GM to Look for More Concessions," *Detroit Free Press,* January 9, 2006, pp. 1–2 at http://www.freep.com.
[u]Jamie LaReau and Dave Barkholz, "GM to UAW: Let's Cut Costs," *Automotive News,* April 16, 2007, pp. 1–2.
[v]Joe Guy Collier, "Autoworkers Take More Hits," *Detroit Free Press,* February 6, 2006, pp. 1–2 at http://www.freep.com.
[w]Jeffrey McCracken, "For UAW Chief, a Bid To Forestall 'Waterloo'," *The Wall Street Journal,* June 19, 2007, pp. A-1,14.
[x]"GM-UAW Reach Tentative Deal; Strike Ends," *USA Today,* September 26, 2007, pp. 1–3 and Sholnn Freeman and Howard Schneider, "UAW Calls Off Strike Against Chrysler," *The Washington Post,* October 10, 2007, pp. 1–2.
[y]Katie Merx, Tim Higgins, Sarah A. Webster and Joe Guy Collier, "UAW, GM Tentative Deal Ends 2-Day National Strike," *Detroit Free Press,* September 26, 2007, pp. 1–3; Sholnn Freeman, "Ford, Union Agree on Contract," *The Washington Post,* November 4, 2007, p. A17; and Dee-Ann Durbin, "UAW Approves Pact with Chrysler," *The Washington Post,* October 28, 2007, pp. 1–2.

COLLECTIVE BARGAINING BEHAVIOR
Two Bargaining Approaches

Although each bargaining situation is unique and depends on the negotiators' personalities and the issues involved, collective bargaining behavior generally falls into one of two strategic approaches: **distributive bargaining** or **mutual gain bargaining** (also referred to as *interest-based* bargaining or *win-win* negotiation).[16]

Each of these approaches can lead to a voluntary settlement of bargaining issues, and neither approach guarantees that either party will get everything it wants.

A distributive bargaining approach tends to view the two parties' interests as being in conflict, making the negotiation process a win-lose (zero sum) exercise. Gains for one party's interests must come at the expense of the other party because there is a finite amount of resources available to the parties with which to meet bargaining goals. Bargaining issues such as wages, for which the economic gain or cost of proposed settlement terms can be estimated by the parties, lend themselves to a distributive bargaining approach. The primary focus of a distributive bargainer is to maximize his or her own party's interests, although to accomplish this may require some consideration and satisfaction of the other party's key interests.

A distributive bargainer seeks to achieve settlement at (or as close as possible to) the other party's **resistance point** (i.e., the point beyond which the other party would prefer no settlement to settlement on the other party's proposed terms). Each negotiator tries to discover where the other party's resistance point lies on each issue and to modify the other party's position and perceptions to achieve a settlement on preferred bargaining terms. An effort is made to restrict and structure communications for strategic advantage (e.g., control of the bargaining agenda). A distributive bargainer's persuasive efforts focus on convincing the other party that the distributive bargainer's proposal is more acceptable than the other party's or that settlement on the distributive bargainer's proposed terms is preferable to the costs or risks of non-settlement. Distributive bargainers often respect each other's abilities more than they trust each other's intentions. Finally, there is a greater willingness to rely on bargaining power, if necessary, to force the other party's acceptance of proposed settlement terms.

Mutual gain bargaining is sometimes referred to as **win-win bargaining** or the more recent popular term **interest-based bargaining**.[17] Mutual gain bargaining differs from traditional distributive bargaining in a number of important ways. Negotiators approach the bargaining process as a mutual problem-solving exercise. Open and honest communication about each party's interests, intentions, and the merits of specific bargaining proposals is encouraged. Mutual gain bargaining lends itself particularly to bargaining issues in which both parties perceive a common threat or need, and successfully resolving the problem can benefit the interests of both parties. For example, resolving problems such as maintaining competitiveness, adapting to technological change, and meeting employee health care needs might lead negotiators to a mutual gain bargaining approach.

Mutual gain bargaining encourages and values mutual trust and respect between the parties. In addition to concern for the parties' respective substantive interests, there is concern about the effects of the negotiation process and outcomes on the quality of the parties' continuing bargaining relationship. Efforts are made to identify multiple alternatives to each negotiating problem that are capable of meeting both parties' key interests. Negotiators focus less on narrowing the gap between each party's position and more on expanding the number of mutually satisfactory solutions. Bargaining power is a less important determinant of bargaining outcomes because the parties agree in advance on what objective criteria or standards to use in evaluating the merits of specific bargaining proposals. For example, the industry or local area average might be agreed on to determine the number of paid holidays that employees should receive. This approach encourages mutual trust and an understanding of the other party's needs and objectives and emphasizes the commonalities between the parties instead of their differences.[18]

Strategies and Tactics

Some bargaining strategies and tactics may be appropriate for use in either a distributive or mutual gain approach to bargaining. *Using persuasive arguments and objective evidence* in support of bargaining proposals or *painting a picture of the loss or gain* to ensure that negotiators understand what is at stake for the parties' interests, as well as the relative costs/benefits of reaching agreement versus continued disagreement, are two examples. *Summarizing bargaining progress* to date often helps to clarify perceptions and direct future negotiations on specific subjects. *Presenting a bargaining proposal in writing,* as well as explaining it orally, helps to ensure the other party understands the proposal. *Listening carefully* for ideas and emotions, not just facts, and noting *nonverbal cues* (e.g., eye contact, tone of voice, facial or hand expressions, reaction of other team members) can often provide information about the importance and degree of commitment to statements made at the bargaining table.

Use of a *bargaining caucus* provides time away from the bargaining table to discuss bargaining proposals or strategies, conduct costing, gather additional information, or simply avoid making a statement at the bargaining table that one is not prepared to make. *Use of positive reinforcement,* such as expressing appreciation for specific bargaining behavior or acknowledging the acceptable portions of the other party's proposal, can help to establish a positive environment in which to continue negotiations. *Linking issues (package proposal),* such as the example in Exhibit 6.4, is another strategy that can be used to resolve a large number of issues in a fairly short time or aid in resolving the few remaining unsettled issues late in the negotiation process. As different types of issues become linked, it may become more difficult to evaluate the relative value of different proposed packages.

Two final strategies or tactics that may be appropriate in either a distributive or mutual gain approach to bargaining are *matching concessions* and *splitting-the-difference*. Many negotiators operate under the assumption that concessions granted by one party will be reciprocated or matched by concessions of relatively equal value from the other party, although not necessarily involving the same bargaining issue. Most negotiators prefer to leave all settlements reached during the negotiation process as tentative settlements until all issues have been resolved. What a party finds acceptable in the later stages of bargaining may be determined in part by the prior pattern of concessions and whether that established concession pattern is perceived to have been equitable or fair. The acceptability of simply splitting the difference as a means of resolving settlement terms, particularly near the end of negotiations where the prior concession pattern is known, may depend on a party's perceived equity in the tentative contract terms already reached and the priority of the unsettled bargaining issues to that party's key bargaining interests. In addition to the general strategies and tactics mentioned above, Exhibit 6.5 presents a list of bargaining strategies or tactics appropriate for use in distributive bargaining.

Exhibit 6.6 presents a list of bargaining strategies and tactics appropriate for mutual gain (win-win or interest-based) bargaining.

The Bargaining Power Model

Bargaining power is an important concept that can affect the process and outcomes of negotiations, particularly when the parties adopt a distributive bargaining approach. Because negotiation is an interdependent activity, it is important to focus on the difference between the bargaining power of each bargaining party rather than simply assessing the amount of bargaining power possessed by a single party. Evidence of

Exhibit 6.5

Some Strategies and Tactics for Use in Distributive Bargaining

- Undermine the other party's position. Question the validity of assumptions, facts, or conclusions; focus on omissions, inconsistencies, or other perceived weaknesses in the other party's reasoning or information.

- Offer initial proposals well removed from your party's resistance point on each bargaining subject.

- Concede slowly from initial bargaining positions. The other party will value more highly (and thus reciprocate in kind) those concessions that it has to work hard to get.

- Attempt to appear firmly committed to bargaining proposals.

- Threaten the other party's key interests (e.g., job security, sales, public image) to impose pressure by increasing the other party's perceived costs of failing to settle on your party's proposed terms. For a threat to be perceived as credible, the party receiving the threat must believe that the party making the threat is both able and willing to perform the threatened act.

- Offer to reward key interests of the other party (e.g., increase job security, grant greater access to information, grant economic incentive) to persuade them to settle on your preferred terms. This approach is intended to lower the other party's costs of agreeing to your party's proposed terms.

- Seek opportunities to delay negotiations as a means of imposing time pressure on the other party before a settlement deadline (e.g., contract expiration date, strike/lockout date).

- Seek to maximize the perceived value of your party's concessions while minimizing the value of concessions granted by the other party.

- Threaten to withdraw a proposal if it is not accepted within a reasonable time. Alternatively, make the initial proposal contingent on acceptance by a specified deadline. This approach can also be used to counter another party's delay tactics when addressing proposals.

- Schedule marathon bargaining sessions in an effort to wear down the other party's resistance or concentration level. Time pressure during the late stage of bargaining may make such marathon bargaining sessions necessary if the parties seek to reach an agreement before a strike or lockout deadline is reached.

- Make a final offer. Whether a so-called "final offer" is really final depends on the perceived credibility of the negotiator making the offer.

a party's greater bargaining power is the ability to obtain settlement on that party's preferred terms rather than less favorable terms proposed by another party.

Chamberlain and Kuhn present one of the better-known bargaining power models.[19] One party's bargaining power can be conceptualized as equal to the other party's cost of disagreeing with proposed settlement terms divided by their cost of agreeing to such terms. These union or management bargaining power equations can be applied to assess the parties' relative bargaining power regarding specific bargaining proposals or to a post hoc analysis of final settlement terms to assess which party possessed greater bargaining power. Although the bargaining power model is presented as an equation, it is an imprecise formula based on two major assumptions: (1) Union and management negotiators cost issues in a similar manner and are rational individuals, and (2) if it costs more for party A to disagree than to agree with party B, then party A will agree to party B's proposal. Each side can increase its bargaining power

- Set realistic bargaining objectives.

- Clarify the interests underlying each party's proposals on specific issues. Avoid becoming fixated on another party's stated position. Focus instead on understanding a party's key interests at stake regarding the issue being negotiated.

- Use brainstorming to generate alternative proposals designed to meet the parties' respective interests on each subject.

- Identify the bargaining subject where the parties share mutual interests and those subjects where the parties' interest may conflict. Begin negotiations on subjects of mutual interests, seeking to establish a bargaining pattern that can later be used as a model to address more difficult issues which involve conflicting interest.

- Exhibit empathy toward the other party's interests and concerns.

- Identify and mutually agree on objective standards for evaluating the merits of specific bargaining proposals.

- Open negotiations with a clear statement of your party's intent to negotiate cooperatively and invite the other party to participate in such an approach. For a win-win bargaining approach to succeed, both parties must be committed to the process.

- Ask questions to clarify the substantive content or intent behind specific bargaining proposals.

- Share objective information about specific bargaining subjects with the other party.

- Seek to incorporate as much of the other party's proposal as possible into your party's counterproposal on a bargaining subject. This helps to demonstrate a willingness to accommodate the other party's interests and helps to focus subsequent bargaining on those aspects of the proposal where a conflict of interests remains.

- Explain how or why your party's proposal meets an important need or interest of the other party.

- Openly discuss perceived obstacles or barriers to achieving a voluntary settlement (e.g., personalities, tactics, competitive environment, or status of the bargaining relationship).

- Minimize emotional outburst.

- Avoid strategies or tactics that might undermine your credibility as a negotiator or damage the level of mutual trust and respect between the bargaining parties.

Exhibit 6.6

Some Strategies and Tactics for Use in Win-Win (Mutual Gain) Bargaining

by either increasing the other party's costs of disagreement or reducing the other party's cost of agreement to proposed contract terms.

To illustrate this strategic framework, consider a union bargaining proposal for a ten minute cleanup time before the end of the work shift. First, the union could reduce management's cost of agreeing with the cleanup time proposal by eliminating some of its other bargaining proposals in exchange. The union negotiator might also reduce management's perceived agreement costs by demonstrating that there are currently many different cleanup practices at the firm. Some departments do not have cleanup time, whereas other departments let their employees stop work a half-hour early to clean up. If the total cleanup time in the plant were calculated, it would probably amount to 15 minutes per employee. It would be difficult for management to discipline employees who are abusing cleanup time because no consistent policy regarding this issue is enforced in the plant. This contract provision would enable management to wipe the past practice slate clean and establish a consistent policy. Management could instruct supervisors to enforce a ten minute cleanup time policy, which could actually save the company money.

If management does not accept this argument, the union could try the second strategic approach—increasing management's cost of disagreeing with the union's proposal. A union might threaten to withhold approval of some management-proposed contract term or publicize poor working or safety conditions at the plant that could harm employee recruitment efforts or customer relations. A strike threat might carry some credibility if management knew that widespread dissatisfaction existed over this issue and given current product demand, any disruption in current production would economically harm the firm.

Factors Potentially Affecting Both Bargaining Power Equations

Some factors that may affect union and management bargaining power are prevailing economic conditions (e.g., unemployment rate, labor supply, sales volume), goodwill, public image, and government intervention. For example, high unemployment in the labor market increases the union's cost of disagreeing with management because strikers could find it difficult to find employment at other firms while reducing management's disagreement costs by making striker replacements easier to hire.

One factor that can influence the decision to strike, especially in small plants, is goodwill, which pertains mostly to internal relationships. Management and union negotiators do not want antagonistic attitudes that may develop during negotiations or a subsequent strike, to linger when operations are resumed. Negotiators also do not want their activities labeled irresponsible or insensitive to the public interest, thereby adversely impacting each party's public image. Possible government intervention for vital industries (e.g., airline, railroad) or in the case of a national emergency dispute (discussed in Chapter 9) must also be considered, especially if management or the union believes government intervention will weaken its bargaining position.

Factors Affecting a Union's Disagreement and Agreement Costs

Financial supplements given to union members can lower both a union's disagreement costs and management's bargaining power. Employees might be able to supplement their incomes during a strike through their spouses' employment, union strike benefits, personal savings, aid from other labor organizations, or public aid. Union strike benefits rarely are intended to cover all lost income resulting from strike participation and usually average $50 or less per week. Whether a union provides strike benefits may often determine whether union members will vote to strike, as well as how long they will stay out on strike. Although the amount that each union member receives during a strike is minimal, the total amount of annual strike payments can be large. Most unions pay strike benefits when funds are available and the strike has been sanctioned by the national union leadership, but often additional stipulations may require that the member be in good standing, complete a waiting period, or establish a need for the payments.

Public aid (e.g., welfare, food stamps, and unemployment compensation) can also reduce union members' disagreement costs by supplementing their incomes when they go on strike. These assistance programs might exist at the federal or state level and are subject to various qualifications, such as a waiting period for striking employees to qualify for unemployment compensation. Many arguments can be made for and against public aid being given to union members on strike. Proponents of public aid might claim the following:

- Strikers are taxpayers when they work, so when they do not work, they should receive aid.

- Tax dollars are used to feed hungry people in other countries and prisoners in this country, so strikers who are needy should receive the same consideration.

- Even though some persons may be against public aid for strikers, they should not be against public aid for the families of strikers who are directly affected.

- Eligibility for public support should be based on need as determined by law, not on whether a person is on strike.

    Opponents of public support to strikers also make several arguments:

- Legislators never intended to provide public aid to strikers, particularly because strikers have voluntarily chosen to cease work and refuse to go back to work in furtherance of their bargaining position.

- Giving public aid to strikers violates a traditional policy of government neutrality in labor-management relations.

Factors Affecting Management's Agreement and Disagreement Costs

Management's costs of agreeing to union proposals can be reduced if it can pass on the cost of a negotiated settlement to customers. Increased global competition in many product and service markets makes it increasingly difficult for employers today to simply pass costs on to consumers in the form of product or service price increases. Some regulated firms, such as electric utilities, operate under pricing guidelines, which permit the company to raise prices to cover legitimate increases in business operating costs. Management's disagreement costs (and union bargaining power) could be increased if any of the following conditions prevail: low inventories combined with high customer demand; fear of permanent loss of customers (market share) during a work stoppage; or high fixed costs, such as rent, interest on loans, payments for equipment, and salaries of nonunion personnel, that could continue to accrue even if production were reduced or eliminated by a work slowdown or stoppage.

Complexities Associated with the Bargaining Power Model

Bargaining power "costs" are often imprecise figures associated with calculation difficulties, large and sudden change, and other complexities. Negotiators often over-estimate the extent to which their bargaining preferences are clearly communicated to the other party during negotiations.[20] Some issues are difficult to cost, such as inserting a job requirement that the employees must "perform minor repairs." Such contract language could save the company money by having lower skilled, non-craft employees perform some duties previously performed by more expensive, higher skilled maintenance employees, particularly when minor repairs are performed at overtime or other premium wage rates. However, management cannot calculate the precise dollar cost savings associated with this provision, particularly if the union negotiator fears that agreeing with such a "minor repairs" clause would incur imprecise yet large political costs, such as skilled maintenance members rejecting the proposed labor contract or the union leader's re-election bid.

Perceived or estimated costs associated with use of the bargaining power model are subject to change during negotiations. The government may suddenly announce wage-price controls or guidelines, forcing unions to agree to wage settlements comparable to the limits set by the government. Or, management could receive a sudden influx of rush orders from a major customer near the contract expiration date. Management's disagreement costs may sharply increase, particularly if the customer indicates that he or she will take unfilled orders to a competitor.

The limitations of the bargaining power model do not eliminate its usefulness. Union and management officials do assign costs, however crudely, and direct their strategies toward increasing the other party's disagreement costs relative to agreement costs.

Intraorganizational Bargaining

Another important aspect of the bargaining process is **intraorganizational bargaining**, which refers to the negotiations that occur within each bargaining party as management and union negotiators attempt to achieve consensus within their respective organizations.[21] Sometimes the most difficult bargaining is that which occurs within each party's negotiating team rather than between union and management negotiators.

Management's chief negotiator sometimes takes a back seat to other management officials, particularly lawyers, at the bargaining table. Often the need to comply with corporate policy may complicate local plant negotiations by reducing a management negotiator's flexibility to deviate from a policy intended to cover a variety of different plant settings. When a settlement is reached, it is also subject to second-guessing by other managers, who usually contend that management negotiators could have obtained a better deal. The union is not exempt from internal disputes either, particularly because its chief negotiator is seldom given a free hand in selecting the negotiating committee. In many cases, at least one member of the union's negotiating team is a political rival of the chief negotiator. More prevalent are factions that attempt to obtain various bargaining demands regardless of the chief negotiator's preferences.

Management and union negotiators spend much time resolving differences within their respective organizations. One observer of labor-management negotiations noted: "[A] large share of collective bargaining is not conflict but a process by which the main terms of the agreement, already understood by the negotiators, are made acceptable, not to those in charge of the bargaining but to those who will have to live with its results."[22]

Ethical and Legal Considerations in Collective Bargaining

Union and management negotiators' bargaining behavior often involves at least two general ethical dimensions. The first ethical dimension, moral or ideal behavior, is subject to varying definitions instead of an either/or distinction. However, negotiator behaviors such as bribing the opponent to reach a settlement, stealing an opponent's confidential information, publicly demeaning or humiliating another negotiator, or using electronic surveillance to "bug" an opponent's meeting areas are clearly at the unethical end of the continuum.

Some bargaining behaviors have more general and longer-range ethical implications. Consider, for example, the reflections of Lee Iacocca, former chief executive officer of Chrysler Corporation:

> As long as Detroit was making money, it was always easy for us to accept union demands and recoup them later in the form of price increases. The alternative was to take a strike and risk ruining the company. The executives at GM, Ford, and Chrysler have never been overly interested in long-range planning. They've been too concerned about expediency, improving the profits for the next quarter—and earning a good bonus. They? I should be saying "we." After all, I was one of the boys. I was part of that system. Gradually, little by little, we gave in to virtually every union demand. We were making so much money that we didn't think twice. We were rarely willing to take a strike, and so we never stood on principle. I sat there in the midst of it all and I said: "Discretion is the better part of valor. Give them what they want. Because if they strike, we'll lose hundreds of millions of dollars, we'll lose our bonuses, and I'll personally lose half a million dollars in cash." Our motivation was greed. The instinct was always to settle quickly, to go for the bottom line. In this regard, our critics were right—we were always thinking of the next quarter. "What's another dollar an hour?" we reasoned. "Let future generations worry about it. We won't be around then." But the future has arrived, and some of us are still around. Today we're all paying the price for our complacency.[23]

The second ethical dimension, conforming to professional standards, is more complicated when applied to negotiators' behaviors. Top union and management bargaining team officials would likely agree on at least three professional commitments in their bargaining behaviors:

1. To obtain the best possible settlement benefiting their party's interests.

2. To convince their respective bargaining team members and other constituents that they are effective negotiators.

3. To communicate with the other negotiating team in an honest, respectful fashion to enhance the parties' continuing labor relations relationship after the collective bargaining agreement is reached.

All three of these standards are attainable, although maximizing the first two may strain and alter the third. In other words, it is difficult to convince one's bargaining constituents that the best settlement possible was obtained after revealing the complete truth to the negotiating opponent. This perhaps helps explain why distributive bargaining is still more common than mutual gain bargaining in labor negotiations. A completely honest and open negotiator may be exploited by his or her opponent, commit to a position that allows no further concessions, or sacrifice what might have been successfully gained through a less-candid approach. Many successful negotiations feature ritualistic elements, such as describing elaborate but irrelevant statistics, using histrionics, or staging false fights or temper tantrums.

Successful negotiators realize that credibility is a necessary personal attribute, and lying or uttering a deliberate falsehood can destroy credibility and ruin a negotiator's effectiveness. However, a fine line exists between lying and withholding the complete truth. Negotiators are not generally going to volunteer information that could damage their bargaining positions. Negotiators may also exaggerate or bluff on occasion, although this is risky behavior if a negotiator is not prepared to have his or her bluff called by the other party:

> The principled negotiator doesn't resort to trickery, but that doesn't mean he naively gives away his position. Not all principled negotiators agree on just how

principled you have to be. It's OK to mislead the other side as to your intentions, [one principled negotiator] argues. You can say I'm not going to give in, and then give in five minutes later. But never give the other side misinformation about the facts.[24]

The Legal Duty to Bargain in Good Faith

Union and management officials are not completely free to shape or ignore ethical considerations in collective bargaining. The government, through the Labor Management Relations Act, as amended, requires that both union and management organizations negotiate in good faith in an effort to voluntarily settle bargaining disputes. **Good faith bargaining** essentially means each party must demonstrate a sincere and honest intent to reach a labor agreement and be reasonable in their bargaining positions, tactics, and activities.

In attempting to decide the merit of a bad faith bargaining unfair labor practice charge, the NLRB must assess the totality of each party's conduct, which includes both overt behavior and underlying motivation or intent. However, good faith represents a state of mind which is difficult to define precisely. For example, the duty to bargain in good faith does not require a party to reach a settlement, agree to a specific proposal, or make a particular concession to the other party. Yet for settlement to occur, an underlying presumption in collective bargaining prevails that concessions will typically be made by both parties. Violations of good faith bargaining can come from four sources: the type of the bargaining subject, specific bargaining actions (called *per se* violations), the totality of a party's conduct, and successor employer bargaining obligations.

Type of Bargaining Subject

Over the years, the NLRB and the courts have categorized bargaining subjects or issues as illegal, mandatory, or voluntary (also referred to as non-mandatory or permissive). **Illegal bargaining subjects** involve a violation of law, and there is no legal duty to bargain over such an issue. If the parties were to include such an illegal term in their contract (e.g., permitting management to pay less than the federal minimum wage for covered employees), that portion of the parties' contract would be unenforceable in court. Other examples of illegal terms would include a closed-shop union security clause, a "whites only" employment clause, mandatory retirement at age 62, and compensation terms that violate the provisions of the Fair Labor Standards Act (e.g., not paying covered employees overtime pay for hours worked in excess of 40 hours per week).

There is a duty to bargain in good faith over **mandatory bargaining subjects**, which are subjects that may have a direct effect on bargaining unit members' wages, hours, or other terms and conditions of employment; including the willingness to meet at reasonable times for the purpose of negotiating and the willingness to reduce oral agreements to writing. Exhibit 6.7 presents a list of some mandatory subjects of bargaining, although new bargaining subjects continue to arise in response to changing bargaining conditions so any such listing should never be considered as an all inclusive list. Mandatory bargaining subjects compose the bulk of the bargaining agenda during labor contract negotiations.

Management may not legally change current contract language governing an existing employment term involving a mandatory bargaining subject unless the current contract clearly gives management the right to do so; the union has clearly waived its right to bargain over the subject; or both parties have bargained in good faith and reached a voluntary agreement about the change. Either party may request the other party to voluntarily agree to negotiate a current contract

Exhibit 6.7

Some Mandatory Subjects of Bargaining[*]

Hourly wage or incentive (piece) rate of pay	Vacation pay
Identity of the insurance carrier	Layoff and recall procedure
Bonus pay	Holiday pay
Health-care cost containment plan	Seniority rights
Profit-sharing plan	Paid rest periods
Clothing or tool allowance	Length of job probationary period
Employee stock ownership plan	Paid lunch period
Hours of work	Grievance-arbitration procedure
Lump-sum pay	Employee discounts on company products or services
Mandatory overtime policy	Management rights
Two-tier wage plan	Child-care assistance plan
Pension plan	Subcontracting of bargaining unit work
Call-in pay	Dental insurance
Tax deferred (e.g., 401k) savings plan	Joint union-management cooperation plan
Shift differential pay	Life insurance
Job or income security guarantee	Employee testing procedures (e.g., drug test)
Jury duty pay	Effective and expiration time and date of the contract
Job classification system	Performance evaluation methods and procedure
Overtime pay	Waiver of right to bargain (e.g., "zipper clause")
Job duties and qualifications	Safety and health standards and procedures
Cost-of-living adjustment clause	Leave of absence
Job transfer rights and procedure	Successorship clause
Funeral leave pay	Health and accident insurance
Job promotion criteria and procedure	No strike or lockout clause

[*]The subjects listed are not intended to represent an all-inclusive list of possible mandatory bargaining subjects.

provision early (so-called **mid-term bargaining**), but there is no legal duty to engage in good faith bargaining over existing contract terms until—at the earliest—60 days prior to the scheduled expiration date of the current contract. If a mandatory bargaining subject not covered by the parties' existing contract language arose during the mid-term of a labor agreement, then management could implement a change in such a subject after bargaining in good faith to an impasse or reaching an agreement with the union about the subject. A **good faith bargaining impasse** occurs at the point in negotiation where neither party is willing to modify its position on a bargaining subject any further. Interest disputes involving a mandatory bargaining subject are also the only disputes over which a lawful strike or lockout may occur.

There is no duty to bargain over a business decision that involves a fundamental change in the nature, scope, or direction of the firm.[25] This would include decisions to sell the firm or buy another firm, major equipment purchases, the number or types of products or services to produce, financing sources or terms to meet operating needs, and marketing decisions. Even though not required to bargain about a business decision itself, an employer is required to bargain over the *effects* of that business decision on bargaining unit employees' job security or economic interests (e.g., severance pay, transfer rights, seniority rights, layoff or recall rights).[26] An employer may be required to bargain over a decision to transfer or relocate bargaining unit work if the business decision does not involve a substantial change in the nature of the employer's operation (e.g., same work being performed under similar work conditions at a new location but using different [non-bargaining unit] employees).[27]

Union and management officials may also negotiate **voluntary bargaining subjects** (also termed *non-mandatory* or *permissive*) which do not directly affect bargaining unit members' terms or conditions of employment and are not illegal. Examples include a jointly funded industry marketing promotion plan, strike insurance, an interest arbitration clause, or improved pension benefits for retired (former) bargaining unit members. Unlike mandatory subjects, voluntary bargaining subjects do not require either party to bargain. In fact, insisting on their bargaining and inclusion in a labor agreement to the point of impasse would be an unfair labor practice. For example, when Dupont Company managers asked employees to participate in a promotional videotape, the NLRB determined this action was a voluntary bargaining subject that did not have to be negotiated with the union because it was not part of the employees' day-to-day responsibilities, employees were not compelled to participate, and the taping was not shown to be a matter of deep concern to the employees.[28]

Specific Bargaining Actions

In some cases a single, specific action by an employer constitutes an unfair labor practice in bargaining. For example, management commits a per se violation whenever it does the following:

- Refuses to meet with the union to negotiate its proposals.

- Implements a wage change without consulting the union.

- Insists to a point of impasse on a provision requiring that a secret-ballot election be held before a strike can be called.

- Refuses to furnish requested information to the union that is relevant and necessary for the union to perform its legal bargaining duty (e.g., supply cost and other data relating to a group insurance plan administered by the employer).

If an employer claims an **inability to pay** for a union's bargaining proposal, the union is entitled access to company financial information necessary to validate the employer's inability to pay claim. An inability to pay is legally distinct from expressing an *unwillingness to pay* the cost of a union bargaining proposal, and thus this obligation is sometimes complicated to apply.[29] In one case, the NLRB found the employer did not commit a violation when it refused a union's request for information because the employer's stated desire to bring its labor costs in line with its competitors, who might be nonunion, was a legitimate bargaining goal and not a statement of the employer's inability to pay.[30] Yet in other cases, although the employer tries to couch its refusal to furnish information requested by a union as a competitive issue rather than a claim of inability to pay, the NLRB has found that the employer's intent was to claim an inability to pay.[31]

Any information request by a union from management must meet the following requirements:

1. The union must make a good faith demand or request for the information.

2. The information sought must be *relevant and necessary* for negotiations. This typically means the information sought must pertain to a mandatory bargaining subject and is information not reasonably available to the union from any other source.

3. The information must be supplied to the union promptly and in a form reasonably useful for negotiation purposes although not necessarily in the exact format requested by the union.

A union commits a *per se* violation when it engages in the following:

- Insists on a closed-shop or discriminatory hiring clause.

- Refuses to meet with a legal representative of the employer about negotiations.

- Refuses to negotiate a management proposal involving a mandatory subject.

Totality of Conduct

In evaluating the underlying intent behind specific bargaining actions, the NLRB and the courts often apply the **totality of conduct doctrine**. This legal doctrine states that even though individual acts when viewed separately do not constitute a bargaining violation, such acts may constitute an unfair labor practice when viewed as a pattern of conduct in the totality of the circumstances surrounding the negotiations. A prominent and controversial example of this legal consideration involved a bargaining strategy used by the General Electric Company (GE) called **Boulwarism** after the late vice president of General Electric, Lemuel Boulware.[32]

GE contended that it simply approached bargaining in a manner similar to its product marketing—by researching the employees' desires and the firm's competitive position and then presenting a fair bargaining proposal to the union. GE would refuse to modify its original proposal unless the union could present new and significant information bearing on the issues at the bargaining table, which the union, in the company's view, was rarely able to do. GE management contended that this approach was not capricious, but "fair and firm," because management's bargaining position was based on a careful examination of the "facts." This approach, the company maintained, represented a sincere bargaining effort aimed not at destroying the union but rather at eliminating a time-consuming and unnecessary ritual from collective bargaining (such as initial unrealistic offers that both parties know will not be accepted). GE coupled its bargaining table strategy with a separate communication campaign aimed at convincing bargaining unit employees that the company's offer was fair and reasonable and implying that any delay in reaching agreement would be the responsibility of union leaders, not management.

Unions representing General Electric employees termed the company's approach "hard bargaining" which was not flexible enough to reasonably consider alternative union views on bargaining subjects. GE unions believed that the company's communication campaign directed at bargaining unit members represented an effort by management to undermine the union's legal status as the employees' bargaining agent by attempting to bypass dealing with union negotiators at the bargaining table in favor of dealing directly with employees.

GE's Boulwarism strategy was found, based on the totality of conduct doctrine, to be a violation of good faith bargaining primarily because it attempted to bypass the employees' exclusive bargaining agent (the union) with a direct communication campaign intended to persuade employees to pressure their union representative to accept management's terms.[33] The U.S. Supreme Court was careful to point out that "hard bargaining" *without other condemning evidence* was not, per se, an unfair labor practice itself. Other condemning evidence present in the GE case included a refusal to supply cost information on an insurance program, vague responses to the union's detailed proposals, a prepared lecture series instead of counteroffers, and a "stiff and unbending patriarchal posture" even after it was apparent that the union would have to concede to the employer's terms. Management can legally communicate to employees its own bargaining proposals and the reasons for them, as well as explain why management opposes specific union bargaining proposals, as long as such communication is not intended to undermine the status of the union as the employees' bargaining agent.[34]

Other rulings involving employer or union conduct have provided the following examples of conduct that may constitute bad faith bargaining:

- *Surface bargaining:* A party is willing to meet at length and confer but merely goes through the motions of bargaining without any evidence of a sincere desire to reach an agreement. Surface bargaining includes a party making proposals that it knows the other party cannot accept, taking an inflexible attitude on important issues, or offering no alternative proposals.

- *Dilatory tactics:* Unreasonable procrastination in executing an agreement, unreasonable delay in scheduling meetings, willful avoidance of meetings, evasive tactics, unreasonable delay in providing data for bargaining, and similar tactics are evidence of bad faith.

- *Imposing unreasonable conditions:* Attempts to specify conditions on bargaining or the administration of a labor contract will be scrutinized closely to determine whether such conditions are onerous or unreasonable (e.g., insisting that all grievances be resolved before collective bargaining can start). In addition, the requirement of agreement on a specific item as a prerequisite to negotiating other issues may reflect a bad faith bargaining intent.

- *Unilateral changes in conditions:* Such actions as changing the compensation or fringe-benefit package unilaterally during bargaining without having reached a good faith bargaining impasse is a strong indicator of bad faith bargaining.

- *Commission of unfair labor practices:* Committing unfair labor practices (such as promoting withdrawal from the union, reducing work hours without economic justification, or engaging in discriminatory layoffs) during negotiations is indicative of bad faith.

Managerial Rights. One very important mandatory subject of bargaining of interest to employers is the subject of **management's rights.** Before the passage of the National Labor Relations Act (NLRA) in 1935, management rights and discretion in operating facilities were seldom questioned, and managers were virtually free to run their operations as they saw fit. In many cases, unions were considered intruders into managerial prerogatives because there were few laws regulating managers' actions toward employees. Although unions have become more accepted today, managers remain concerned over the gradual erosion of their rights in the labor relations process.

Under common law, management officials were relatively free to manage their businesses and their employees. In unilaterally running the operation, the employer drew from the concepts of property rights and the laws of agency, as well as the legal and social acceptance of "private enterprise," "ingenuity," and the "profit motive." Hence, management assumed the right to manage as derived from the property rights of the owner. The authority of the owner is delegated to management, which in turn directs the employees in achieving the goals of the company. Following this line of reasoning, management contends it cannot share its prerogatives with employees or any other group because such an action would represent a dereliction of legal responsibility to the ownership.

Most unions in the United States, unlike their European counterparts (see Chapter 14), have typically been reluctant to become "partners with management"—directly involved in managerial rights pertaining to layout of equipment, financial policies, sources of materials, and so forth. Union officers realize that often union members prefer to second-guess or challenge the wisdom of management decisions instead of supporting or echoing them. It is more difficult for union leaders to effectively criticize business policy decisions that they have jointly participated in deciding with management representatives.

Yet a union's desire to avoid involvement in traditional areas of management decision making is not absolute. Management rights are exercised to achieve significant managerial goals of organizational flexibility and efficiency. Unions are concerned about managerial actions to achieve these goals, which appear arbitrary, inconsistent, or entail adverse consequences for union members' jobs or economic security.[35] Some research has found that craft and industrial unions have become more interested in joint determination of traditional management issues (e.g., products to be manufactured, services to be performed, and customer relations) over the past 20 years. This new emphasis is largely attributed to competitive pressures, which have influenced union officials to evaluate a broader range of managerial decisions that could reduce union members' job opportunities.[36]

Until 1960, management rights clauses contained in labor agreements tended to be based solely on the **reserved rights doctrine**, which essentially holds that all rights to manage the firm are reserved to management except to the extent management has voluntarily agreed to limit or restrict such rights through language found in a labor agreement. For example, if the labor agreement is silent on overtime administration, then under the reserved rights doctrine, management can assign overtime to whomever it sees fit. A typical **short-form management's rights clause** prior to 1960 based on the reserved rights doctrine might state the following: *Employer retains all rights to manage, direct, and control its business in all particulars, except as such rights are expressly and specifically modified by the terms of this agreement or any subsequent agreement.*

Many managers assumed that the broad language of the short-form management's rights clause guaranteed management's complete discretion in those matters not specifically included in the labor agreement. Primary reliance by management on the reserved rights doctrine to protect its managerial prerogatives was dealt a setback by the U.S. Supreme Court's 1960 decision in *United Steelworkers v. Warrior and Gulf Navigation Company* (as discussed in Chapter 11).[37] In this case, the employer refused the union's request to take a grievance dispute to final and binding arbitration because the employer argued that the issue involved was not covered under the parties' labor agreement, and therefore the right to determine the outcome of that issue was reserved to management. The Court stated that where there isn't clear evidence of the parties' intent to cover a specific subject under a labor agreement's terms, the arbitrator could determine whether an issue was covered under the parties' agreement to arbitrate contract disputes, and any doubts about coverage should be resolved in favor of permitting the grievance dispute to be arbitrated.

In response to the U.S. Supreme Court's decision in *Warrior and Gulf Navigation Company* (1960), many management negotiators sought to bargain a more specific, detailed list of subjects over which management intended to reserve the unilateral right to control. Such contract language became known as a **long-form management's rights clause** and is the most common form of management's rights clause found in labor agreements today (see Exhibit 6.8). Presumably, arbitrators, upon seeing such a detailed list of management prerogatives clearly stated in the labor agreement, would rule in management's favor on whether the grievance is subject to arbitration. However, the long-form management's rights clause has its problems. First, it is difficult to anticipate and clearly list every item over which management might seek to maintain unilateral discretion. Arbitrators tend to view a detailed long-form management's rights clause as expressing management's intent to define all of its prerogatives. A detailed listing of management's rights in a labor agreement makes it more unlikely an arbitrator would permit management to retain exclusive control over any otherwise mandatory subject of bargaining that management might claim it merely forgot to include in the negotiated management's rights clause. Second, because the union must agree to all wording contained in the management's rights clause of the labor agreement, it may be necessary for management negotiators to give the union a concession on another issue to obtain a strongly worded management's rights clause. For example, management may have to allow the union a strong union security clause, such as a *union shop* clause, previously discussed in Chapter 4.

Both long and short forms of a management's rights clause can cause additional problems. By insisting on including the management's rights clause in the labor agreement, management runs the risk of stirring up ideological differences with the union. Rights included in the management's rights clause may also influence union bargaining goals in subsequent negotiations.

For managers, the advantages of a long-form management's rights clause outweigh the potential risks. Approximately 80 percent of labor agreements contain a management's rights clause that helps remind arbitrators, union officials, and other managers (particularly first-line supervisors) that management retains its administrative initiative to establish the status quo.[38]

Successor Employer Bargaining Obligations

The increased level of merger and acquisition activity among firms in recent years has raised several concerns about the duty to bargain. Whether a change in ownership at a unionized firm results in a "new" versus "successor" employer depends on the degree of continuity in the business enterprise after the ownership change occurs.[39] Purchasers would generally prefer to be classified as a **new employer**, who has no legal duty to automatically recognize any former union as the bargaining representative of current employees and thus is under no duty to bargain over the establishment of employment terms or to abide by the terms of any prior labor agreement negotiated by the former owner.

Where there is *substantial continuity in business operations*, the purchaser is classified as a **successor employer**, whereas a lack of substantial continuity in business operations characterizes a new employer. Degree of business continuity can be evaluated based on a preponderance of the evidence by examining factors

Article 2 Management Rights

The company has, retains and shall possess and exercise all management functions, rights, powers, privileges and authority inherent in the company as owner and operator of the business, excepting only such rights that are specifically and expressly relinquished or restricted by a specific Article or Section of this Agreement.

The company shall have the exclusive right to manage facilities; to direct the working forces; to fix or change the number, hours, and duration of work shifts; to establish or alter work schedules or standards; to control the use of scheduling of operations; to allocate and assign work to employees; to schedule overtime; to hire, classify, train, promote, transfer, suspend, demote, discipline; to discharge employees for just cause, ... and to discipline or discharge employees for violation of such rules and regulations; to determine safety, health, and property protection measures for any and all employees, operations, and facilities; to select and to change tools, equipment, machinery, material, layout, and facilities with which it shall carry on its operations; to determine the products to be manufactured or sold or the services to be rendered; to determine at all times the number and composition of the work force as a whole or of any unit, shift, job classification, or work within such job classification; to create new organization groups deemed appropriate by the company and to determine the organization and structure of each; to determine, implement, modify, or eliminate techniques, methods, processes, means of manufacture, maintenance, and distribution, schedules, crew, or production team sizes, and line speeds; to control raw material; to shift types of work and production or maintenance in and out of any facility; to place production, service, maintenance, or distribution work with outside contractors or subcontractors; to use labor-saving devices; to determine and implement actions necessary to operate as economically and efficiently as possible when and where the company deems the same necessary or desirable, including layoff of employees; to determine the qualifications and duties of employees; to establish or modify reasonable quality and quantity standards; to judge the quantity and quality of workmanship required and discipline or discharge employees whose work does not meet such standards; to establish or revise pay grades for jobs; to change the method of compensation of employees, to establish or modify job classifications and related rates of pay, or revise or eliminate existing jobs; to transfer and assign work and duties to job classifications when the company deems the same necessary or desirable; to select, demote, promote, or transfer bargaining unit employees from one unit, section, department, division, plant, or other unit to another; to transfer work from one job to another; to determine the location of the business, including the establishment of new plants, departments, divisions, or subdivisions and the relocation, closing, selling, merging, or liquidating of any plant, department, division, or subdivisions thereof either permanently or temporarily; to determine financial policy, including accounting procedures, prices of goods or services rendered or supplied, and customer relations; to determine the size and character of inventories; to determine the policy affecting the selection and training of new employees; to determine the amount of supervision necessary; and generally to control and direct the company in all of its affairs and operations.

SOURCE: Excerpted from a labor agreement.

Exhibit 6.8

Example of a Long-Form Management's Rights Clause

such as what percentage of the post-ownership change work group continues to be comprised of former union-represented employees; whether there is any substantial change in the location of the firm, type of customers served, or products produced; degree of change in equipment or other technological processes; and the percentage of managers under the former owner who continue to manage employees after the change in ownership.

A successor employer has a legal duty, upon request, to recognize the union that represented bargaining unit members under the former owner as continuing to represent the same bargaining unit structure under the current ownership. A successor employer must also be willing, upon request, to engage in good faith bargaining over the terms of a new labor agreement covering bargaining unit employees. A successor employer is not generally obligated to continue to enforce the terms of a previously existing labor agreement unless the contract contained a **successorship clause** that the purchaser knew about at the time of the ownership transfer. A successorship clause represents a mandatory subject of bargaining and requires an employer not to sell or merge the firm unless the purchaser is willing to take on the terms of any existing labor contract. Approximately 28 percent of labor agreements contain some type of a successorship clause.[40]

Collective Bargaining under Bankruptcy Proceedings

Turbulent operating environments in some industries (e.g., airlines and auto) have led some employers to threaten or actually declare bankruptcy as a means to radically restructure debt, eliminate or consolidate operations by reducing excess plant capacity, and lower labor cost in order to increase competitiveness. The negative stigma once attached to a bankruptcy filing implying management failure has seemingly been replaced by a view of bankruptcy as a strategic economic shortcut to implementing transformational change that might otherwise take years or be entirely impossible to accomplish without the protection afforded by the bankruptcy court. What happens to an existing bargaining agreement if management files for bankruptcy and contends that it can no longer honor the terms of the labor agreement? This question was addressed in the U.S. Supreme Court's 1984 *Bildisco* decision, which involved a building supply distributor who filed a petition for reorganization under Chapter 11 of the bankruptcy code.[41] After filing the bankruptcy petition, the company failed to pay the scheduled wage increases specified in the labor agreement and also failed to give collected union dues to the union. The company also moved to reject the collective bargaining agreement entirely.

The NLRB agreed with the union that this unilateral action violated the good faith bargaining duty under the Labor Management Relations Act (LMRA). However, the Supreme Court disagreed with the NLRB and determined that management's behavior in this situation did not violate the good faith provision. The Court's decision in *Bildisco* gave management more discretion in its collective bargaining efforts with a union. Because many members of Congress did not fully agree with the *Bildisco* decision, the Bankruptcy Reform Act of 1978 was amended (P.L. 98-353) in June 1984 to make it more difficult for employers to abandon the terms of an existing labor agreement after filing a petition for bankruptcy. Under current law, an employer cannot reject the terms of a valid labor agreement before obtaining approval of the employer's petition for bankruptcy from a federal bankruptcy court judge.[42] To obtain the approval of a bankruptcy court judge, the following conditions must be proven:

1. The debtor in possession (the employer) must have made a proposal to the union to modify the collective bargaining agreement based on the most complete and reliable information available at the time.

2. The proposed modifications must be necessary to permit the reorganization of the firm and must ensure that all the creditors, the debtor, and all other affected parties are treated fairly and equitably.

3. The debtor must provide the union with requested information it needs to evaluate the employer's proposed contract modifications. The union cannot demand information simply for the purpose of making a counter-proposal.

4. The debtor must meet at reasonable times with the union and bargain in good faith in an effort to reach an agreement on proposed modifications to the collective bargaining agreement.

5. The union's refusal to accept the employer's proposed modifications must demonstrate a lack of good cause for the union's rejection of the employer's terms.

6. In the bankruptcy court judge's view, the balance of equities in the case must clearly favor permitting the debtor (employer) to reject the collective bargaining agreement.

Legal Remedies Associated with Violations of the Duty to Bargain in Good Faith

NLRB remedies in unfair labor practice cases are designed to stop further violations and return any adversely affected parties to the position they would have been in had the unfair labor practice violation(s) not occurred. As discussed in Chapter 3, a typical Board remedial order might consist of one or more of the following:

1. A *cease and desist order* to halt any further unfair labor practice violations (e.g., cease enforcement of an illegally adopted change in contract language).

2. A requirement that the Respondent (guilty party) *post written notices* for a reasonable period (e.g., four to six weeks) in the workplace informing employees of their basic rights under the LMRA, the specific unfair labor practices committed by the Respondent, and the Respondent's pledge not to commit such violations in the future.

3. Whatever affirmative actions might be necessary to remedy the adverse effects of any unfair labor practices, often referred to as a *make-whole remedy*. For example: reinstatement with back pay; restoration of lost seniority rights or other benefits denied an employee because of the unfair labor practice violation; requirement to furnish necessary and relevant bargaining information upon proper request by another bargaining party; discontinuance of any policy found to be a violation of employees' protected rights; removal from employee records of any reference to unlawful disciplinary action taken against an employee; return of unlawfully transferred work to its previous location; or an order to begin or resume bargaining in good faith.

The Board has no authority to award punitive damages, regardless of the Respondent's willful intent, the number of specific violations committed, or the Respondent's history of committing similar violations in prior cases.[43] The Board also lacks the authority to order an employer or union to agree to any specific term or condition of employment. Even where back pay is awarded, the amount owed by the Respondent would be reduced by the amount of interim earnings the employee (charging party) may have received while the unfair labor practice charge was pending (e.g., income from another job, unemployment compensation) and the discharged employee is required to seek comparable employment while pursuing his or her unfair labor practice charge.

Union officials have contended that present NLRB remedies are inadequate, particularly in cases of bad faith bargaining. Because NLRB decisions can be appealed to the courts, it might take two or three years for a final determination to occur. During the interim period the employer's ability to delay labor cost increases by postponing negotiations results in lost economic benefits for bargaining unit members. Once the employer is found guilty of bad faith bargaining, the Board can only issue an order to stop bargaining in bad faith and begin good faith negotiations. No remedy is available for the lost income opportunities or possible deterioration in a union's bargaining power caused by the unlawful time delay in reaching a voluntary settlement of bargaining issues.

The General Counsel of the NLRB has recently responded to the failure of employers to engage in good faith bargaining during initial or first contract negotiations following certification of a union as the employees' lawful bargaining representative by recommending additional remedial actions to be taken in these cases. "Initial contract bargaining constitutes a critical stage of the negotiation process in that it provides the foundation for the parties' future labor-management relationship. Unfair labor practices by employers and unions during this critical stage may have long-lasting, deleterious effects on the parties' collective bargaining and frustrate employees' freely exercised choice to unionize."[44] Among the additional ULP remedies available in these cases are requiring parties' to bargain on a set schedule until either agreement is reached or a good faith bargaining impasse occurs; a minimum six-month extension of the normal 12-month time period following initial certification when a union's status as bargaining representative may not be lawfully challenged; reimbursement of bargaining costs incurred as a result of bad faith bargaining; and the filing of periodic reports with the NLRB, updating the status of bargaining and the implementation of Board-ordered ULP remedies.

Contract Ratification

Unlike management negotiators, union negotiators are typically only authorized to reach a tentative agreement on contract terms at the bargaining table. The union's constitution and by-laws typically require that union members be given an opportunity to approve or disapprove proposed tentative settlement terms before a final contract agreement can be achieved. For example, the Steelworkers, Auto Workers, and United Mine Workers use a direct referendum. Some unions may require a simple majority approval from union members voting whereas other unions might require a higher percentage of votes for approval (e.g., 60 percent). In recent years, union members have shown increasing interest in participating in the **contract ratification process** and more ratification elections have been held.

The ratification process provides union leaders with an indication as to whether union members can live with the proposed agreement, even though they may not be completely satisfied with all of its provisions. Acceptance of the proposed contract's terms by a majority of the union's membership also provides management some assurance that the employees will comply with the letter and spirit of the agreement during its term. A vote to accept therefore is considered a commitment or willingness to be bound by the agreement.[45] Union members typically approve tentative contract settlement terms negotiated by their union representatives, rejecting such terms in only about ten percent of cases.[46]

Explanation of Voting Behavior

It is overly simplistic to say that union members vote for the contract when they like it and against it when they don't like it. Researchers have attempted to explain why and when union members will vote to accept or reject the tentative agreements. When employees perceive that alternative employment opportunities are limited, members are more likely to approve proposed settlement terms. Satisfaction with the economic terms of the proposed settlement and a perception that their union has represented members' interest effectively also increases the probability a union member will vote to approve proposed contract settlement terms.[47] For example, when employees with the most seniority are to become eligible for a guaranteed income security plan, those employees could be counted on to favor ratification.

A "no" vote in a ratification election confronts employees with the potential costs of lost income and the uncertainty of when they will begin work again. Although the potential for contract rejection may create incentives for union negotiators to try to get a little extra for the members, such extras come with increased anxiety as the strike deadline approaches.[48]

Reasons for Rejection of Tentative Contract Agreements

The most common reason why union members reject proposed settlement terms is genuine dissatisfaction with one or more of those terms. Union members may feel shortchanged in comparison with other agreements in their geographic area or industry. Internal union politics is another reason contract rejection may occur. Sometimes union leaders are elected by slight majorities, and their rivals will campaign against any labor agreement negotiated by the incumbent leaders. This problem can be exacerbated if the union permits members to select the union's negotiating team, and current leaders find rivals for union leadership elected to serve as part of the negotiating committee.

Communication problems between union leaders and members can sometimes play a role in contract rejection, although good communication can also facilitate contract approval. Upward communication flows are important because union leaders must understand what issues are most important to the majority of the union's membership if bargaining proposals and tentative agreements reached are to reflect those interests. For example, in industrial unions, individuals holding skilled-trade positions (electrician, carpenter, painter, machinists) usually represent a minority of the total membership. Such skilled-trade members might vote to reject a contract if their wages did not compare favorably with those of similar skilled-trade individuals employed in the same geographic area.

Downward communication flows are particularly important in keeping members informed of progress toward achieving a settlement during negotiations and in explaining how members will be affected by contract language changes contained in the tentative contract settlement proposed for ratification. Particular care must be given to explaining changes in contract terms of high importance to members, such as the adoption of new wage payment methods and alterations in pension or health care benefit plans.

Some groups (women, racial minorities, and younger employees) within the bargaining unit may base their contract ratification vote on the outcome of one or more very specific issues directly impacting them. Although equal employment opportunity laws have been passed, wage differentials continue to exist for racial minorities and women and eliminating perceived intra-plant inequities may be the primary determinant of how an affected employee votes on the contract ratification question. Moreover, young employees with low seniority often view pension and layoff issues, which are usually based on seniority or retirement age, differently from older employees, causing additional internal friction within a bargaining unit. Unless members in these subgroups believe that the agreement reflects their own personal needs, they may vote to reject it.[49]

Contract rejection can sometimes be used as a bargaining strategy by a union, although the effectiveness of such a strategy would tend to diminish over time as management negotiators adapted by being less willing to propose their best offer during initial negotiations in case they had to go back to the bargaining table after the initial tentative agreement was rejected. One research study reported that a subsequent contract settlement obtained after an initial contract settlement was rejected by the union's membership did contain additional economic gains for union members in 65 percent of cases.[50] It is important that union leaders and managers attempt to keep members' expectations of bargaining success as realistic as possible during the negotiation process in order to avoid a negative reaction to proposed contract settlement terms that fall below unrealistically high expectations.

Obtaining the union negotiating team's strong endorsement of a proposed contract settlement can usually ensure that the majority of union members will support the negotiation team's recommendation.[51] Some contract concessions by management negotiators may be necessary in some cases to obtain the endorsement of a union's bargaining team. Management negotiators must carefully weigh the costs of any required concessions against the probability that contract rejection will occur without such an endorsement and the additional costs such a rejection might entail before any final contract settlement could be achieved (e.g., probability that contract rejection could trigger a strike).

Summary

Collective bargaining occurs when union and management attempt to resolve conflicting interests by mutually agreeing to acceptable terms or conditions of employment. Sometimes this activity is centralized and more than one appropriate bargaining unit can be combined to form the negotiation unit, encompassing the employees and employers who are subject to the provisions of the labor agreement. Most often the structure of bargaining in the private sector is decentralized, with a separate contract negotiated to cover employees in each separate bargaining unit of an individual employer at a specific location.

Management and union negotiators are involved in three general pre-negotiation activities: selecting the negotiating team, researching and formulating proposals and the bargaining range, and costing these proposals. Bargaining behavior during collective negotiations can be extremely varied, but choosing a distributive or mutual gain approach to bargaining will dictate which specific bargaining behaviors are likely to be effective. Intraorganizational bargaining is also an important and challenging part of achieving success in labor negotiations.

The relative distribution of bargaining power between the parties can be an important determinant of bargaining outcomes, especially in a distributive bargaining approach. Raising the other party's costs of disagreement or lowering the other party's costs of agreement with your proposals aids in attaining a bargaining settlement on your party's proposed terms and thus increases your party's bargaining power. Bargaining costs can and should be calculated in negotiations, albeit sometimes rather imprecisely.

Collective bargaining occurs within a legal framework, which regulates the parties' bargaining responsibilities and behavior. Both union and management negotiators have a legal duty to bargain in good faith, demonstrating both reasonableness and a sincere effort to reach a voluntary settlement of interest disputes affecting employees' wages, hours, and other terms or conditions of employment. Good faith bargaining enhances the opportunity for labor peace and stability necessary for the production of goods and services. The need to remain competitive and to successfully attain the respective interests of employers and employees helps to ensure the parties have a common goal to promote realistic and ethical conduct during the negotiation process.

Key Terms

Collective bargaining, p. 243
Interest dispute, p. 244
Pattern bargaining, p. 244
Bargaining unit, p. 245
Non-mandatory, p. 245
Centralized bargaining, p. 245
Multi-employer bargaining unit, p. 246
Degree of labor intensiveness, p. 247
Lock-in agreement, p. 248
Whip-saw bargaining strategy, p. 248
Coordinated bargaining, p. 248
Bargaining range, p. 252
Resistance point, p. 252
Cents-per-hour cost, p. 254
Roll-up factor, p. 254

Jobs Bank program, p. 257
Distributive bargaining, p. 259
Mutual gain bargaining, p. 259
Resistance point, p. 260
Win-win bargaining, p. 260
Interest-based bargaining, p. 260
Intraorganizational bargaining, p. 266
Good faith bargaining, p. 268
Illegal bargaining subjects, p. 268
Mandatory bargaining subjects, p. 268
Mid-term bargaining, p. 269
Good faith bargaining impasse, p. 269
Voluntary bargaining subjects, p. 270
Inability to pay, p. 270

Totality of conduct doctrine, p. 271
Boulwarism, p. 271
Management's rights, p. 272
Reserved rights doctrine, p. 273
Short-form management's rights clause, p. 273
Long-form management's rights clause, p. 274
New employer, p. 274
Successor employer, p. 274
Successorship clause, p. 276
Contract ratification process, p. 278
Funeral leave policy, p. 285

Discussion Questions

1. What are some situations in which management or the union would prefer centralized bargaining? In what situations might both prefer centralized bargaining? Discussion should take into account specific legal considerations affecting centralized bargaining.

2. Using the information provided in the Labor Relations in Action segment on auto industry bargaining, analyze the relative bargaining power of union and management in those negotiations. What factors appear to increase each party's bargaining power or weaken their bargaining power and why?

3. Assume that you are a management negotiator and the union presents the following proposal: Any overtime assignment will be guaranteed a minimum of two hours at time-and-a-half the base hourly rate for the classification. Previously, employees working overtime received time-and-a-half pay for the hours they worked but no two-hour guarantee. Indicate in some detail how you would cost out this proposal. Also, discuss some arguments the union might use to make it easier for management to accept this proposal (i.e., to reduce management's agreement costs).

4. Identify some sources of information a union or management negotiator could consult to get timely and relevant information about the following:

   a. recent bargaining settlements in a particular industry

   b. current wage rates for specific types of labor in a specific geographic area

c. health care cost and bargaining trends

d. pension benefits plans and trends

5. Good and bad faith bargaining might be easier to define than implement. Discuss different types of evidence that might be used prove or disprove a charge of bad faith bargaining.

6. Are current legal remedies for bad faith bargaining adequate to promote compliance with the LMRA's goal of good faith bargaining? Why or why not? What recommendations would you suggest for improving compliance with the goal of promoting good faith bargaining?

Exploring the Web

Collective Bargaining

1. **Definitions.** How does the U.S. Department of Labor define "collective bargaining"? Check the Glossary on the Department of Labor's Web site.

Find a good definition of "good-faith bargaining" in the online glossary of the U.S. Office of Personnel Management.

Go to the Communications Workers of America's Web site and read articles on the NLRB's charges of "bad-faith bargaining" against the York, Pennsylvania newspapers. What was the final outcome of these charges?

2. **Bankruptcy and Collective Bargaining.** The *Bildisco* decision is a landmark Supreme Court case dealing with bankruptcy and collective bargaining. Use the Oyez Web site to read the opinion and discuss the significance of the case. Search for other cases involving bankruptcy and collective bargaining that have been decided since 1984. What legislation was amended as a result of the Bildisco decision?

NLRB v. Bildisco & Bildisco. 465 U.S. 513 (1984)
Use Web pages from Cornell's Legal Information Institute to examine a section of the U.S. Code affected by the Bildisco case.

Bankruptcy Rejection of collective bargaining agreements 11 U.S.C. § 1113 (1996)

Go to Cornell's overview of labor law and, in the case of conflict between the National Labor Relations Act and the Bankruptcy Code, find out which generally prevails.

Using the House of Representatives' Web site, Thomas, search for Public Law 98-353, Bankruptcy Amendments of 1984.

From the Web site of Paul K. Rainsberger, Director of the University of Missouri's Labor Education Program, read an overview of bankruptcy law and how it has affected collective bargaining. What was the Packwood-Rodino bill?

3. **Auto Industry and Collective Bargaining.** Listen to audio clips from National Public Radio on the 2007 United Auto Workers' (UAW) negotiations with the Big Three in the automobile industry. On the UAW site, explore articles on the negotiations in "Solidarity Magazine." Then go to the corporate Web sites of the three automobile manufacturers, Chrysler Holding LLC (DaimlerChrysler), General Motors, and Ford and see what you can find on the negotiations. Comment on the main issues and the different perspectives presented from all sources.

References

1. For a more detailed conceptualization of various behavioral and situational aspects of negotiation behavior and a thorough bibliography, see Leonard Greenhalgh and Roy J. Lewicki, "New Directions in Teaching Negotiations: From Walton and McKersie to the New Millennium," in *Negotiations and Change*, ed. by Thomas A. Kochan and David B. Lipsky (Ithaca, NY: Cornell University Press, 2003), pp. 20–34 and James A. Wall and Michael W.

Blum, "Negotiations," *Journal of Management* 17, no. 3 (June 1991), pp. 273–303.

2. "Interest-Based Bargaining: Evidence from Quebec," *Worklife Report* 14, no. 4 (Winter 2003), p. 2; and Ira B. Lobel, "Realities of Interest-Based (Win-Win) Bargaining," *Labor Law Journal* 45 (December 1994), p. 771.

3. For related considerations, see Kathryn J. Ready, "Is Pattern Bargaining Dead?" *Industrial and Labor Relations*

Review 43, no. 2 (January 1990), pp. 272–279; discussions of Ready's article by Peter Cappelli, Daniel J. B. Mitchell, and Kathryn J. Ready, *Industrial and Labor Relations Review* 44, no. 1 (October 1990), pp. 152–165; John W. Budd, "The Determinants and Extent of Pattern Bargaining," *Industrial and Labor Relations Review* 45, no. 3 (April 1992), pp. 523–539; and John W. Budd, "The Intrepid Union Political Imperative for UAW Pattern Bargaining," *Journal of Labor Research* 26 (Winter 1995), pp. 43–57.

4. *Don Lee Distributor, Inc., et. al.* v. *NLRB,* 145 F.3d 834 (6th Cir. 1998).

5. For a discussion of several factors associated with centralized bargaining in the United States and other countries, see Harry C. Katz, "The Decentralization of Collective Bargaining: A Literature Review and Comparative Analysis," *Industrial and Labor Relations Review* 47 (October 1993), pp. 3–22.

6. Douglas L. Leslie, "Labor Bargaining Units," *Virginia Law Review* 70 (April 1984), p. 414; Douglas L. Leslie, "Multiemployer Bargaining Rules," *Virginia Law Review* 75 (1989), pp. 241–178.

7. Bruce Feldacker, *Labor Guide to Labor Law,* 4th edition (Upper Saddle River, NJ: Prentice-Hall, Inc., 2000), pp. 54–55.

8. *General Electric Company and International Union of Electrical, Radio and Machine Workers,* 173 NLRB 253 (1968).

9. *Utility Workers Union of America and Ohio Power Company et. al.,* 203 NLRB 230 (1973).

10. *United Paperworkers International Union, Locals 620, 14, and 197 and International Paper Company,* 309 NLRB 44 (1992).

11. *Charles D. Bonanno Linen Supply* v. *NLRB,* 454 U.S. 404 (1982).

12. Ian Newall, "Is Win-Win Just Pie in the Sky?" *Strategic Direction,* 22 (6), June 2006, p. 4.

13. Leigh Thompson, *The Mind and Heart of the Negotiator* (Saddle River, NJ: Prentice-Hall, 1998), pp. 160–161.

14. Margaret A. Chaplan and Edward J. Hertenstein, "The Information Needs of Local Union Officials," *Library Trends* 51 (Summer 2002), 50–69.

15. Sam Ashbaugh, "The Art and Science of Costing Labor Contracts," *Government Finance Review,* 18 (December 2002), pp. 33–34.

16. For a discussion of distributive bargaining, see Richard E. Walton and Robert B. McKersie, *A Behavioral Theory of Labor Negotiations* (New York: McGraw-Hill, 1965). For a discussion of mutual gain bargaining, see Roger Fisher, William Ury, and Bruce Patton, *Getting to Yes: Negotiating an Agreement Without Giving In,* 2nd ed. (Boston: Houghton Mifflin, 1991) and William Ury, *Getting Past No: Negotiating with Difficult People* (New York: Bantam Books, 1991).

17. Leib Leventhal, "Implementing Interest-Based Negotiation: Conditions for Success with Evidence from Kaiser Permanente," *Dispute Resolution Journal,* 61 (3), Aug.-Oct. 2006, pp. 50–58; Nils O. Fonstad, Robert B. McKersie and Susan C. Eaton, "Interest-Based Negotiations in a Transformed Labor-Management Setting," *Negotiation Journal,* 20 (1), January 2004, pp. 5–11; and Joel Cutcher-Gershenfeld, "How Process

Matters: A Five-Phase Model for Examining Interest-Based Bargaining," in *Negotiations and Change: From the Workplace to Society,* ed. by T. Kochan and D. Lipsky (Ithaca, NY: Cornell University Press, 2003), pp. 141–160.

18. Roy J. Lewicki and Joseph A. Litterer, *Negotiation* (Homewood, Ill.: Richard D. Irwin, 1985), p. 108.

19. Neil W. Chamberlain and James W. Kuhn, *Collective Bargaining,* 2nd ed. (New York: McGraw-Hill, 1965), pp. 162–190.

20. Eva Zellman and Simon Kemp, "Estimating the Other Party's Preferences and Trust in Trade Union and Employer Negotiations: A Comparison between NZ and Sweden," *New Zealand Journal of Employment Relations,* 29 (2), June 2004, pp. 17–31.

21. Dudley B. Turner, "Intraorganizational Bargaining: The Effect of Goal Congruence and Trust on Negotiator Strategy Use," *Communication Studies,* 41 (Spring 1990), pp. 54–75 and Richard E. Walton and Robert B. McKersie, *A Behavioral Theory of Labor Negotiations* (New York: McGraw-Hill, 1965), pp. 281–351.

22. Albert Blum, "Collective Bargaining: Ritual or Reality?" *Harvard Business Review* 39 (November-December 1961), p. 65.

23. Lee Iacocca, *Iacocca: An Autobiography* (New York: Bantam Books, 1984), p. 304.

24. Jeremy Main, "How to Be a Better Negotiator," *Fortune* 108 (September 19, 1983), p. 143; see also, Roy J. Lewicki and Joseph A. Litterer, *Negotiation* (Homewood, Ill.: Richard D. Irwin, 1985), p. 8.

25. *First National Maintenance Corporation* v. *NLRB,* 452 U.S. 666 (1981).

26. *Fibreboard Paper Products Corporation* v. *NLRB,* 379 U.S. 203 (1964).

27. *Dubuque Packing Co and UFCE, Local 150-A,* 303 NLRB 386 (1991); enf. in *UFCW, Local 150-A* v. *NLRB,* 1 F.3d 24 (DC Cir. 1993); Roger Wolters and Stuart Langdon, "The Duty to Bargain over Business Decisions: The Dubuque Case," *Labor Law Journal* 43 (September 1992), pp. 579–587.

28. *E. I. Dupont de Nemours & Company and Chemical Workers Association Inc., a/w International Brotherhood of Dupont Workers,* 301 NLRB 155 (1991).

29. See, for example, Katrina L. Abel, "Current Developments in Labor-Management Relations," *Employee Relations Law Journal* 15, no. 2 (Autumn 1989), pp. 281–289; and "Union Attorney Sees NLRB As More Willing to Inquire Whether Bargaining Is Serious," Bureau of National Affairs Inc., *Daily Labor Report* no. 24 (February 5, 1991), pp. A-6, A-7.

30. *Graphic Communications International Union, Local 508* v. *NLRB,* 977 F.2d 1168 (7th Cir. 1992).

31. *ConAgra Inc. and Congreso de Uniones Industriales de Puerto Rico,* 321 NLRB 944 (1996); and *Stroehmann Bakeries Inc. and Bakery, Confectionery and Tobacco Workers Local Union No. 116,* 318 NLRB 1069 (1995).

32. Virgil B. Day, "Bad Faith Bargaining?" *Contemporary Labor Issues,* ed. Walter Fogel and Archie Kleingartner (Belmont, Calif.: Wadsworth Publishing, 1968), pp. 388–392; and Lemuel R. Boulware, *The Truth about Boulwarism* (Washington, D.C.: Bureau of National Affairs, Inc., 1969).

33. *NLRB* v. *General Electric Company,* 418 F.2d 736 (1969); *General Electric Company* v. *NLRB,* 397 U.S. 965 (1970).

See also Thomas P. Brown IV, "Hard Bargaining: The Board Says No, the Courts Say Yes," *Employee Relations Law Journal* 8, no. 1 (Summer 1982), pp. 37–51.

34. Francisco Hernandez-Senter, Jr., "Closing the Communication Gap in Collective Bargaining," *Labor Law Journal* (July 1990), pp. 438–444.

35. Marvin Hill, Jr., and Anthony V. Sinicropi, *Management Rights* (Washington, D.C.: Bureau of National Affairs Inc., 1986), p. 6.

36. Martin M. Perline and David J. Poynter, "Union Orientation and the Perception of Managerial Prerogatives," *Labor Law Journal* 40 (December 1989), pp. 781–788.

37. *United Steelworkers of America v. Warrior & Gulf Navigation Company*, 363 U.S. 574 (1960).

38. Bureau of National Affairs, Inc., *Basic Patterns in Union Contracts* (Washington, D.C.: Bureau of National Affairs Inc., 1995), p. 79.

39. *NLRB v. Burns Security Services*, 406 U.S. 272 (1972); *Fall River Dyeing & Finishing Corp. v. NLRB*, 107 S.Ct. 2225 (1987); *Golden State Bottling Co. v. NLRB*, 414 U.S. 108 (1974). See also Clyde Scott, Trevor Bain, and John Robb, "The Successorship Doctrine: Fall River Dyeing and Beyond," *Labor Law Journal* 45 (April 1994), pp. 230–239.

40. The Bureau of National Affairs, Inc., "2006 Employer Bargaining Objectives," *Collective Bargaining Bulletin* 11 (January 2006), p. s-24.

41. *NLRB v. Bildisco & Bildisco*, 104 S.Ct. 1188 (1984).

42. Jennifer J. Froehlich, "Bankruptcy Brinkmanship: Employer's Threats of Bankruptcy in the Context of Collective Bargaining and the National Labor Relations Act," *Labor Law Journal*, 57 (2), Summer 2006, pp. 89–116 and John Wren and Kent Murrmann, "Chapter 11 and Collective Bargaining Agreements," *Employee Relations Law Journal* 16, no. 1 (Summer 1990), pp. 17–27.

43. *H. K. Porter Co., Inc. v. NLRB*, 397 U.S. 99 (1970).

44. Office of the General Counsel, "Additional Remedies in First Contract Bargaining Cases," *Memorandum GC 07-08*, May 29, 2007, p. 1.

45. Clyde W. Summers, "Ratification of Agreements," in *Frontiers of Collective Bargaining*, eds. J. T. Dunlop and N. W. Chamberlain (New York: Harper & Row, 1967), pp. 82–83.

46. Herbert J. Lahne, "Union Contract Ratification Procedures," *Monthly Labor Review* 91 (May 1968), pp. 7–10; and Federal Mediation and Conciliation Service, *Thirty-Fourth Annual Report* (Washington, D.C.: Government Printing Office, 1982), p. 21. (The FMCS no longer collects data on contract ratification outcomes.)

47. James E. Martin and Ruth D. Berthiaume, "Predicting the Outcome of a Contract Ratification Vote," *Academy of Management Journal* 38 (June 1995), pp. 916–928.

48. Peter Cappelli and W. P. Sterling, "Union Bargaining Decisions and Contract Ratifications: The 1982 and 1984 Auto Agreements," *Industrial and Labor Relations Review* 41 (January 1988), pp. 195–209.

49. William E. Simkin, "Refusal to Ratify Contracts," *Industrial and Labor Relations Review* 21 (July 1968), pp. 528–529.

50. William E. Simkin, "Refusal to Ratify Contracts," *Industrial and Labor Relations Review* 21 (July 1968), pp. 528–529.

51. D. R. Burke and Lester Rubin, "Is Contract Rejection a Major Collective Bargaining Problem?" *Industrial and Labor Relations Review* 26 (January 1973), pp. 832–833.

The Funeral Leave Policy Proposal

CASE STUDY 6-1

Purpose

To provide each student practice in drafting and negotiating contract language. For a more in-depth bargaining experience, refer to the bargaining simulation exercise in Appendix A.

Instructions

1. Each student will be assigned the role of either a union or management negotiator. Students may also be assigned to either a union or management bargaining team.

2. Taking into consideration the relevant interests of your assigned role and the advice contained in Exhibit 6.3, prepare a written bargaining proposal to establish a **funeral leave policy**. Your proposal should address the following issues:

    *   How many days (hours) of funeral leave will be provided?

    *   Will time off from work for funeral leave be paid or unpaid? If paid, at what rate of pay?

    *   Will part-time employees qualify to receive the funeral leave benefit?

    *   Whose death would qualify as an occurrence permitting an employee to take funeral leave? Be sure to be specific when defining terms such as "immediate family member" or "relative."

    *   Should funeral leave be granted upon the death of a "domestic partner," "significant other," or "personal friend"?

    *   If paid leave is granted for a specified period of time, could an employee extend their leave time by using either other paid-leave time (e.g., vacation days, holidays, sick-leave days) or by using unpaid-leave days?

    *   Must an employee actually attend the funeral in order to receive funeral leave? If so, what might constitute adequate proof of an employee's attendance at a funeral?

    *   Must an employee offer any proof to verify a death has occurred in order to receive funeral leave? If so, what type of evidence or proof would be acceptable?

    *   What is the procedure an employee must follow to request funeral leave?

    *   How far in advance must an employee request funeral leave to cover a period of absence from work?

    *   Who has authority on behalf of the employer to grant or deny an employee's funeral leave request?

3. Union and management role players may be provided an opportunity to negotiate any differences in contract language that may exist between each party's initial written funeral leave policy proposals. Any final agreement reached within the allotted bargaining time should be reduced to writing and signed by the respective parties.

Additional Background Information

The employer operates a large retail store in a popular shopping mall that serves a surrounding three-county area. There are 100 employees in the bargaining unit who currently earn an average hourly wage rate of $8.00. There is no current language in the parties' labor agreement that addresses the issue of funeral leave. The company was recently purchased by another owner and employees are very concerned that informal policies which may have been used in the past are likely to undergo significant change with the change in ownership. The union has requested management bargain over creating a formal funeral leave policy, and the company has agreed to do so.

The past company practice on an employee's request for funeral leave has been to handle each request on a case-by-case basis with the employee's department head having the authority to authorize varying amounts of unpaid time off from work depending on the circumstances. During the previous 12-month period there have been 20 requests for funeral leaves, of which 16 were granted. Three of the four funeral leave requests denied were from part-time employees, and no reason was given by the individual department head involved for denying the employee's request. The average length of time off from work for the 16 funeral leave requests that were granted (10 full-time and 6 part-time employees) was 2.8 days.

Each full-time employee's regular work schedule consists of eight hours a day, five days per seven-day work period. Part-time employees work eight to 32 hours per seven day work period and comprise 45 percent of the bargaining unit members. The geographic area served by the store has seen tremendous growth in the past eight years and unemployment rates in the area are among the state's lowest, averaging 1.5—2.5 percent per month. The store's regular hours of operation are seven days a week from 10 A.M.–10 P.M.

Classification of a Bargaining Subject

CASE STUDY 6-2 The company and union have had a bargaining relationship for more than 20 years. On July 11, bargaining unit member Allan Engle was performing his assigned work duties of cleaning the bathroom on the second floor of the company's administrative building when he glanced up and observed a camera approximately six to eight feet away located in an air vent and pointed directly at him. Engle reported his discovery to three other bargaining unit members, including union steward Luther Hall, who went to the second-floor bathroom in question and confirmed that the hidden camera was there. The following day the local union president was notified, but when she went to investigate, the hidden camera had been removed.

On July 15, local union president Wanda Jackson was asked to meet with the company's HR Manager Susan Albright. Albright asked Jackson if she had heard about the camera that was discovered in the sanitation department's restroom. Albright went on to say that the camera had been installed by the company because of a reported theft problem in that area, and the company's legal counsel had advised her that it was lawful as long as the company had a legitimate business reason for doing so. Albright stated that once the camera had been discovered and union members appeared irate over the issue, the camera was immediately removed by management.

Local union president Jackson believed the company could have accomplished its theft investigation through less intrusive means, and the union did not approve of management's invasion of employees' privacy. The union sent a letter to the company, dated August 1, indicating that an internal investigation by union members had also uncovered hidden cameras being used in the employees' physical fitness room. On August 16,

Jackson sent a hand-delivered letter to HR manager Albright demanding that the company bargain over the subject of video camera use in the workplace. The company refused to bargain over the subject, whereupon the union filed an unfair labor practice charge, alleging that the company's action violated Section 8 (a)(5) and (1) of the LMRA, as amended.

Positions of the Parties

The union argues that the use of surveillance cameras in the workplace for providing evidence of work-rule violations by employees for which they could be subject to discipline or discharge is clearly an issue that is germane to the working environment and job security interests of union members. Therefore, the union believes management has a legal duty to bargain in good faith, upon request, over issues such as the number and location of video cameras within the workplace. Other issues over which bargaining unit members might have an interest in bargaining include whether employees will be given prior notice that their conduct may be subject to filming; who will have access to the video recordings made; for what purposes the video recordings may be used; and the circumstances under which the cameras can be required to be removed.

The company essentially makes two arguments. First, the company believes it has an absolute right to engage in actions (like using cameras) to protect the legitimate business-related interests of the ownership. The company noted that it had for many years used 17 video cameras located both inside and outside company buildings to observe activity for protecting company property from theft or damage and to discourage other work-rule violations (e.g., drug use, sleeping on the job). These 17 cameras were in plain sight, and their existence had been known to the union's membership for many years without any prior objection from the union. In recent years, eleven additional hidden video cameras had been installed inside the company to observe specific areas where employee misconduct was suspected. To require management to bargain in advance over the use or placement of such surveillance equipment would significantly reduce the effectiveness of this method of monitoring employee conduct on the employer's premises.

Second, management argues that even if the Board were to find that a duty to bargain existed, based on the circumstances in this case, the union waived its right to bargain over the subject of surveillance cameras. The company points to the length of time it has used video cameras without any objection by the union as evidence that the union has acquiesced in this practice and essentially acknowledged management's right to use surveillance cameras for legitimate business reasons. The company acknowledges that the union has a right to file a contractual grievance over any alleged misuse or abuse of surveillance methods leading to a lack of just cause for disciplinary or discharge action against a bargaining unit member. However,

the right to grieve a management discipline or discharge decision is not equivalent to a right to require management to bargain, in advance, over the right to use camera surveillance as a legitimate investigatory technique.

Questions

1. What is a mandatory subject of bargaining?

2. Can a union waive its right to bargain over a mandatory subject of bargaining?

3. Was management's refusal to bargain over the subject of surveillance camera usage in the workplace a violation of the duty to bargain in good faith under the LMRA, as amended? If so, what should be the appropriate remedy? Discuss the merits of the parties' respective positions in this case.

Unilateral Work Rule Changes

CASE STUDY 6-3 Over the years, the company had unilaterally implemented several plant rules (e.g., use of company telephones, excused absences from work), including the following two rules:

1. **Perfect attendance**—All employees who have a perfect attendance record in a 12-month calendar year will receive special recognition from the Company. (Note: There was no evidence introduced to show that any employee had ever received any special recognition under the announced rule before the implementation of the new attendance bonus rule.)

2. **Discharges**—The company has the right to discharge or discipline any employee for just cause. The term "just cause" shall include ... drinking or possessing any alcoholic beverage on company property or company time or reporting for work while under the influence of alcohol or drugs.

During the term of the current labor agreement, the company announced the implementation of two new work rules:

1. As of March 1, any injuries requiring treatment will now be accompanied by a drug/alcohol test.

2. As of March 1, any employee who achieves perfect attendance for a week will receive a wage bonus of $1 per hour for that week. Any employee who achieves perfect attendance for an entire month will receive a total wage bonus of $1.50 per hour for the month.

Three days after the two new work rules were announced; the union contacted management and requested to bargain over the two new work rule changes. The company representative refused the union's request to bargain on the grounds that the subjects at issue were not mandatory subjects of bargaining and even if they were, the current contract language gave management the right to unilaterally implement the two rule changes. Management cited the following portions of the parties' current labor agreement as evidence:

- **Section 3: Management's Rights**—The management of the plant, direction of the working forces, and work affairs of the Company, including but not limited to the right ... to discipline or discharge for just cause; to issue, enforce and change Company rules ... is reserved to the Company.

- **Section 8: Wages**—The rates of pay and classifications set forth are agreed upon by the parties and are attached hereto and made a part of this Agreement. The wage rates set forth are the minimum rates under this Agreement and are not to be construed as preventing the employer from paying or the employee from accepting pay or benefits.

- **Zipper clause**—Except as provided herein, this Agreement resolves all the bargainable issues for the term thereof.

Questions

1. What is the purpose of a zipper clause?

2. Which, if any, of the two new rules involve a mandatory subject of bargaining? Explain your reasoning.

3. Did management's unilateral implementation of the two new work rules without providing the union with prior notice or an opportunity to bargain constitute a violation of the duty to bargain in good faith under the LMRA, as amended? If so, what should be the appropriate remedy?

Refusal to Furnish Requested Information

CASE STUDY 6-4 The employer operates a large electrical utility company serving three states in the northeastern region of the United States. The bargaining unit consists of two types of employees. Meter readers (MR) are required to visit each customer's location monthly to physically read the electric meter measuring electricity usage for billing purposes. Meter worker associates (MWA) perform the duties of a meter reader, but in addition, make collections on delinquent customer accounts. If the delinquent account is not paid, the MWA locks out the electric meter or turns off the power. When the bill has been paid, the MWA returns to the location and unlocks the electric meter or turns the power back on.

In a meeting between company and union officials on June 1, management indicated to the union representatives that due to current inadequate staffing levels of MWAs the company was unable to collect a growing number of delinquent accounts in a timely manner. The company wanted the union to consider the possibility of allowing the use of temporary employees at 75 percent of the normal pay rate to collect these "excess delinquent accounts." Union officials were told the company had prepared a Request For Proposals (RFP) document to be circulated to private, outside contractors

for the purpose of having such firms bid to perform the excess collections work.

Union representatives indicated a willingness to discuss the excess account collections issue but wanted to see a copy of the RFP to clearly understand what work and terms the company anticipated requiring of outside contractors and their employees. The Union was particularly concerned with how the hiring of outside personnel to perform bargaining unit work might affect their members' pay, working conditions, and job security. Management representatives responded that they would check the RFP to determine if there was any relevant information in it that the employer needed to share with union representatives.

On June 8, union and management representatives met, at which time the company representative presented the union with a one page summary of information which in management's view addressed the questions and concerns raised by the union at the previous meeting. The company did not present the union with a copy of the actual RFP document. Union officials responded that the summary sheet did not address all of the prior questions raised in the previous meeting and again renewed a request for the RFP document itself so the union could confirm the accuracy of statements in the company-provided summary, as well as determine what information the company may have left out of their one-page summary.

On June 20, the Company sent a letter to the Union declaring that the parties were at an impasse over the issue of the excess collections work and therefore, the Company had decided to have such work performed by outside contractors. Union representatives responded by indicating they were still evaluating the Company's previous proposal on the issue but needed to see the RFP document sent to contractors as a part of that evaluation process. The Company did not provide the union with a copy of the RFP document.

On July 20, the Union filed an unfair labor practice charge with the NLRB, alleging the Company's failure to provide a copy of the original RFP document constituted bad faith bargaining on the Company's part, denying the Union relevant information necessary to administer the terms of the current labor agreement and engage in collective bargaining over the Company's proposal to subcontract the bargaining unit work to outside contractors.

Question

1. Does the Company's refusal to furnish the Union a copy of the RFP document represent a violation of the duty to bargain in good faith under Sec. 8 (a) (5) and (1) of the LMRA, as amended? If so, what should be the appropriate remedy?

Duty to Bargain over a Work Relocation Decision

CASE STUDY 6-5 The employer operates a meat slaughtering, processing, and packing business at several U.S. plant locations, including Hog Heaven, Nebraska, where this labor dispute occurred. The company and union have been engaged in a bargaining relationship for many years, with the most recent contract covering a three-year period (subsequently extended one additional year). Before the Hog Heaven plant's closing, the union represented 1,900 to 2,000 employees at the plant.

Five years ago the Hog Heaven plant began experiencing economic difficulties. As profit losses mounted, the company began to receive pressure from its financial lenders and finally sought some labor cost concessions from the union. After voluntary mid-term negotiations with the union, employees voted to accept productivity standards for use in determining incentive pay increases to aid the company's financial situation. Despite the work-rule changes, the company's financial problems continued to mount. In June, management notified the union of its decision to close the "beef kill" and related departments effective December 12. The company also notified the union that in order to remain competitive, high productivity levels would have to be maintained in the "hog-kill-and-cut" department. In August of that year, the parties agreed to eliminate all incentive pay options while continuing to require employees to meet the higher productivity standards previously jointly agreed to in mid-term bargaining. In exchange, the company agreed that it would not seek any further cost concessions from the union for the remaining two years of the contract's term. The company's estimated cost savings from the August concession by the union was approximately $5 million annually.

In December, the company sought a $5 million loan from the firm's financial lenders to modernize the Hog Heaven plant. The loan application was rejected by the firm's financial lenders. In January of the new year, the company's primary bank called due a $10 million loan and indicated it intended to revoke the company's $45 million line of credit. The company immediately instituted several cost-saving measures and was able to raise the necessary funds to pay off the $10 million loan.

In March, management asked the union to agree to a speed-up (i.e., an increase in the number of animals slaughtered per hour) on the hog-kill line to raise productivity. The union rejected this proposal citing safety concerns, prompting the company to announce on March 31 that it intended to close the hog-kill-and-cut department within six months. The union did not immediately request to bargain over management's announced intent to close the hog-kill-and-cut department.

In early June, the company proposed letting the hog-kill-and-cut department continue operating until the end of the contract's term (September 1) if the union would agree to grant a wage freeze by July 1. The company later expanded its proposal to include a profit-sharing plan in exchange for a wage freeze by July 1. The union's membership rejected the company's proposal in a vote on June 9.

On June 10, after learning of the union members' rejection, the company issued a press release confirming that the hog-kill-and-cut department would be closed. The press release also announced for the first time that the company planned to relocate the hog-kill-and-cut operation to an unspecified new location. On June 16, the company obtained a new $50 million line of credit from its lender with the stipulation that the bank could withdraw from the financial arrangement at any time.

On June 23, the union requested extensive corporate-wide information from management to verify the company's need for labor cost concessions affecting the hog-kill-and-cut department employees. The company objected to the union's information request on the grounds of relevancy and confidentiality. In a letter to the union, the company stated: "Your request for this information appears to be related to a desire to negotiate with the Company as to its decision to close part of its operations." The company denied that it had any legal duty to bargain over a decision to close part of its business and thus was under no duty to provide information for facilitating such negotiations.

Another vote on the wage freeze/profit-sharing proposal was scheduled by the union for June 28. On June 24 the company advised the union's membership that a favorable vote on the wage freeze/profit-sharing proposal would save the hog-kill-and-cut department. Nevertheless, on June 28, union members voted once again to reject the wage freeze/profit-sharing proposal.

On July 1, the company notified the union that the decision to close the hog-kill-and-cut department was final. Ten days later, the company announced the purchase of a plant in Bacon, Illinois, as a replacement for the plant in Hog Heaven, Nebraska. The Bacon, Illinois, plant opened on October 1. On October 3, the hog-kill-and-cut department at the Hog Heaven plant was closed, eliminating 530 jobs.

Negotiations between the union and company concerning the possible relocation of other Hog Heaven plant operations were conducted during the July–October period of that same year. The company sought labor cost concessions in exchange for a promise not to relocate remaining operations at the Hog Heaven plant. During these negotiations, the union was rebuffed each time it tried to bring up the relocation of the hog-kill-and-cut department as a bargaining subject. The company's position was essentially that the hog-kill-and-cut department had already been closed, and there was no duty to bargain over the decision to close it. On October 19, an agreement on wage concessions was reached between the company and union, affecting 900 remaining workers at the Hog Heaven plant. Early the next year, the company lost its bank financing. On October 15, unable to obtain additional operating capital investment, all operations at the Hog Heaven, Nebraska, and Bacon, Illinois, plants ceased, and the assets at both plant locations were subsequently sold.

Questions

1. What is the difference between so-called *decision* bargaining and *effects* bargaining?

2. Did the company's refusal to bargain over the decision to relocate the hog-kill-and-cut operation from the Nebraska plant to a new plant in Illinois violate the employer's duty to bargain in good faith? If so, what should be the appropriate remedy? Explain your reasoning.

CHAPTER 7

Economic Issues

The ability to achieve economic gains in the form of higher wages and improved benefits is one important criterion workers use to gauge the effectiveness of a union. From an employee's perspective, the economic rewards from work largely determine his or her standard of living. When management adopts a goal of minimizing operating costs as a means of optimizing profits, this creates an inevitable conflict of interests between employees' desire for economic gains and an employer's desire to minimize higher operating costs. This chapter discusses a number of factors that help to determine the economic terms of employment, as well as current wage and benefit trends and issues.

As the new century began, the U.S. economy appeared to be among the best in the world, experiencing strong growth, low inflation, and a steady creation of new jobs. Much of the increase in family net worth was attributed to gains in the stock market as a record 48.8 percent of families owned stock directly or indirectly through mutual funds and retirement savings accounts in 1998.[1] From 2000 to 2005, productivity rose 16 percent while median family income declined 2 percent.[2]

The 2001 economic recession was attributed to several factors, including structural changes in some industries accounting for almost 80 percent of job losses (e.g., manufacturing, information technology); the bursting of the dot-com bubble, causing investors to lower valuations on a wide range of U.S. firms; corporate scandals (e.g., Enron, WorldCom, Health South, Arthur Andersen); lower consumer confidence levels; cost-cutting strategies employed by firms to improve productivity and profitability, often resulting in permanent job losses; and heightened security concerns due to terrorist activity.[3] The 2001 economic recession was officially declared over in November 2001 and was followed by a period dubbed the *jobless recovery* because unlike previous economic recessions since World War II, job growth did not recover quickly even though productivity rates and company profits improved.[4] Increasing competition from global competitors and rising employment costs (e.g., health care, defined benefit pension obligations), coupled with an inability to simply raise product or service prices to offset such increased costs have made companies reluctant to add permanent workers to payrolls and encouraged strategies to reduce labor requirements through technological innovation or outsourcing jobs to lower-cost suppliers often in other countries.

Wages and other economic benefits represent income necessary to attain a desired standard of living to an employee, a cost to be minimized by an employer, and a basis for creating tax revenue for a government. Wages also serve as a factor in the allocation of resources. For example, wages influence an individual's selection of an occupation and movement from one firm, industry, or location to another. Wages influence managers' decisions on plant location, investments in machinery and capital equipment, and employment levels. As wage and benefit costs rise, at some point it becomes more cost effective for an employer to invest in production or service delivery technologies that require less labor. Thus, employees may price themselves out of certain labor markets in which substitutes for labor are available to an employer at lower costs.

Wage and benefit issues represent mandatory subjects of bargaining as discussed previously in Chapter 6. Under the Labor Management Relations Act (LMRA), union and management negotiators are required to bargain in good faith over subjects such as pensions, health care insurance, shift differential, overtime pay, job evaluation, and incentive pay or profit-sharing plans if either party presents a bargaining proposal on such a topic during negotiations. Union and management negotiators spend many hours annually bargaining over wages and wage-related issues. This chapter focuses on the methods of wage determination and factors used by negotiators in determining the wage package—wages and other economic benefits.

Union and management officials have to agree on what the term *wages* means before they can successfully bargain over this issue. For instance, wages may refer to an employee's base hourly wage rate, average gross hourly earnings, average weekly earnings, or incentive pay (payment per product completed). Basic wage rates for each job class are usually listed in the labor agreement; however, other wage payments (overtime, incentive pay, shift differentials, and other compensation earned in the regular work week) may have to be computed in accordance with provisions in the labor agreement.[5] After agreeing on the language for the basis of wage negotiations, the parties consider various factors in determining specific wage rates for different jobs or wage ranges covering different job classes.

INDUSTRIAL WAGE DIFFERENTIALS

The existence of wage differentials among individuals, jobs, industries, or geographic regions can be explained in a variety of ways. However, any explanation must consider the interrelationships between labor and capital as factors of production and as contributors to productivity. Jobs with varying duties and responsibilities are often assigned different wage rates. Besides these occupational wage differences within a firm, there are regional, industry, and shift differences that may affect an employee's wage rate. Retail employees in the South generally earn less than those in the North; electricians and laborers in the building trades generally have higher wage rates than electricians and laborers in manufacturing firms. Industrial wage differentials may be explained in terms of three interrelated factors: (1) the degree of competition or monopoly in the product market, (2) the value added by workers in a particular industry, and (3) the percentage of total costs that labor costs represent.

- **Competition in the product market.** First, if a firm has a monopoly or near monopoly (the product is essential, with no or few available substitutes), then increased labor cost can easily be passed on to the consumer by raising the product price. In such cases, the employer may resist higher wages less vigorously in negotiations because higher labor costs do not necessarily adversely impact the firm's competitiveness or profit margins. Conversely, many firms today who are affected by global competition in their product or service markets find it increasingly difficult to simply pass along increased labor costs in the form of higher product or service prices unless other competitors are also absorbing similar labor costs increases. Nonunion or foreign competitors are unlikely to pay compensation terms equal to or greater than those terms required under union labor agreements. Under highly competitive market conditions, unionized employers must bargain harder to ensure that labor cost increases do not force higher product prices that might make the firm less price competitive. In industries where employers face fewer competitive threats, wages tend to be proportionately higher.

- **Value added by employees.** The term *value added* refers to the contribution of factors of production to the value of a final product. Comparing the value added by labor's contribution in different industries helps to explain industrial wage differentials. For example, the value added by labor in sawmills, cotton weaving, clothes manufacturing, and the mobile home industry is significantly lower than corresponding figures in the steel, petrochemical, and paper industries. However, because employees must use machines, which represent capital investments, and because such a close interrelationship exists between labor and capital investments in machinery and equipment, exact determination of labor's contributions has become a complicated process. It is sometimes difficult to accurately measure the value added by an individual employee when that person functions as part of a "team" or performs only one or a few tasks required to create the final product or service delivered to customers. In unionized settings, negotiations between union and management representatives ultimately determine the amount of value added attributed to labor.

- **Labor costs as percentage of total costs.** A firm's **degree of labor intensiveness**, a measure of the proportion of total operating costs comprised of labor costs, must also be considered in determining employee wage rates. More labor-intensive organizations, such as health care facilities, professional sports, and government, have high labor costs in relation to total costs. Any upward adjustment in labor costs will have a bigger impact on such a firm's competitiveness when compared with the effect on a less labor-intensive firm who may grant an equal size increase to their employees. Less labor-intensive firms, such as petroleum refining, chemical, and electricity-generating firms, can afford to offer relatively high wage and benefit levels because fewer workers are employed. Thus, the impact of labor costs on the firm's total operating costs affects the firm's competitiveness less.

Usually, firms with a high ratio of labor costs to total costs are more likely to resist wage increases in contract negotiations than less labor-intensive firms. For example, if a hospital where labor costs are 60 percent of total costs grants a 10 percent wage increase, it must raise prices about 6 percent to cover the cost increase. A petroleum refining plant where labor cost is only five percent of total costs would only have to raise its price about 0.5 percent to cover a similar ten percent wage increase. If competitive conditions preclude or limit an employer's ability to raise product prices, the wage increase cost must be funded from other sources, such as firm profits; cost savings from other operating areas (e.g., finance, marketing); higher labor productivity; finding more cost-effective ways to employ less labor (e.g., outsourcing, new technology); or some combination of these strategies. Nonetheless, the relation of labor cost to total cost can be an important factor in explaining differences in wages for similar jobs across different employers or industries.

Occupational Wage Differentials and the Role of Job Evaluation and Wage Surveys

Within a company or industry, maintaining rational and fair wage relationships among various jobs is important. These relationships are often maintained using a **job evaluation** program, but in other cases, they are determined by individual or collective bargaining.[6] The process of determining the relative importance of each job to the organization helps in understanding occupational wage differentials; therefore, the following steps in a job evaluation program are presented.[7]

Evaluating Jobs within the Organization

Before conducting a job evaluation program, an organizational analysis should be conducted to evaluate the organization's objectives, structure, and authority and responsibility relationships. The findings from this analysis help ensure that the job content is up to date.

The organization then selects and measures the job factors that are found at least to some extent in all of the organization's job classifications. Job factors can vary substantially depending on the type of organization, but skill (education and training), effort, responsibility (for people and equipment), and working conditions (hazards, surroundings) are typically selected. Management must consider the minimum amount of each job factor or qualification necessary to adequately perform a particular job. For example, it may be nice to employ a typist who can edit, interpret, and make complex economic subjects understandable, but few organizations can find or are willing to pay wages needed to attract such a qualified person.

Next, an appropriate job evaluation system for appraising jobs according to the established job factors is selected.[8] Three common job evaluation methods used are ranking, classification, or a point system. The ranking method compares jobs nonquantitatively in terms of each job's relative value to a firm's success, ranking jobs from most to least valued. The classification and point-system methods compare jobs to predetermined numerical rating scales designed to measure one or more job factors about each job. A job evaluation system may use 10 to 15 different job factors, with these factors often divided into subfactors. For example, effort may be divided into physical and mental effort.

The foundation of job evaluation is **job analysis,** which is a process of systematically securing information and facts about the jobs to be evaluated. The job evaluation process focuses on the job, not the employee in the job, for analysis. A well-written job description can aid management in proving that a selection decision regarding which individual holds a particular job was legally nondiscriminatory based on an assessment of the requirements of the job and the candidate's qualifications.

The job classifications resulting from job analysis will receive the same rating whether the employee holding the job has a master's degree or high school diploma, is lazy or ambitious, or is a high or low performer. Job analysts use observation, interviews, and questionnaires to gather data about specific jobs and then use that data to formulate job descriptions and job specifications. Job descriptions include written summaries of a job's duties and responsibilities. Job specifications include the personal characteristics that an employee must possess to qualify for the job. Both are used in the job evaluation process. As firms try to relate wages to various degrees of duties and responsibilities, they must also pay more to hire employees who have higher qualifications in education, training, and skills.

Lawler has noted that as work structures continue to be altered and employees' job responsibilities become more varied and complex, it becomes increasingly difficult and perhaps less relevant to focus compensation systems on an analysis of job titles as opposed to focusing on the contributions of individuals or teams who actually perform those jobs.[9] Some combination of job-based evaluation and individual or group-based performance evaluation may provide a more comprehensive compensation system designed to enhance the competitiveness of the firm and employees' perceived equity in the effort-reward exchange between the individual and the organization.[10]

Management often prefers to conduct its job evaluation independently of the union. Management may prefer not to share its weightings of job factors, particularly when it believes certain factors (such as training, skill, and responsibility for equipment) should receive more compensation than others. Excluding union participation in the job evaluation process may reduce the time required to complete the process; however, subsequent application of job evaluation results may generate grievances that then must be resolved on a case-by-case basis. Some companies seek to encourage union participation in the job evaluation process both to benefit from the insight of workers who actually perform different jobs and to increase the acceptance of the results of job evaluation by bargaining unit members.

Some union leaders view job evaluation with disfavor because it tends to limit bargaining and freeze the wage structure.[11] Unions prefer to establish wage scales through collective bargaining where both internal and external labor market factors can be considered in determining the value or worth of a job. Although unions reserve the right to file grievances to resist or express dissatisfaction with job evaluation results, they seldom show strong opposition unless firms attempt to use job evaluation as the sole criterion for wage determination or try to use it as a substitute for collective bargaining.[12] In fact, some unions regard job evaluation techniques as a useful guide in negotiating wages and a means to more effectively explain the negotiated wage settlement outcome to their members.[13]

Regardless of the job-evaluation method used, the objective is to develop a wage structure that prices jobs with less skill, effort, and responsibility at lower wage rates than jobs with greater skill, effort, and responsibility. Exhibit 7.1 presents an example of a wage structure for a firm that includes job titles, labor grades, point ranges, and starting wage rates for each labor grade. Because a numerical score should indicate the relative value of the job, the greater the score, the higher the labor grade and the hourly wage rate.

Surveys to Compare Firms' Wage Structures

Wage surveys are conducted to ensure that external labor market considerations, such as comparable wages, are included in the wage structure. Such a market-based approach has become an increasingly important determinant of wage rates in many firms.[14] Although firms attempt to rationalize their wage structure internally through job evaluation, they must also maintain competitive wages externally to ensure that the firm can recruit and retain qualified employees. Usually a wage analyst either visits, sends a questionnaire, or conducts a telephone interview with the wage analysts of similar organizations to obtain current wage rates for comparable jobs.[15] Some trade or professional groups conduct annual wage surveys among their member firms and share the information with participating firms. Unions often conduct independent wage surveys as part of their preparation for collective bargaining.

The U.S. Department of Labor also periodically conducts area wage surveys and publishes the results.[16] Two of these publications are the National Compensation Survey (NCS) and the Occupational Pay Relatives (OPR) survey, which provide wage data by occupation for different geographical areas. The OPR survey covers a larger number of geographical areas and provides information on the relative pay differences between specific occupations in those locations. The NCS survey provides more detailed information about specific occupations based on the duties and responsibilities of the job (e.g., knowledge, complexity, scope of responsibility).

The party conducting the survey provides the responding firms with titles, descriptions, and specifications of the jobs in the wage survey. Participating

Exhibit 7.1

Typical Wage Structure for a Manufacturing Firm

Job Titles	Labor Grade	Points	Starting Hourly Wage Rate
Janitor	I	200–249	$6.55
Material handler	II	250–299	8.30
Shipper	III	300–349	9.45
Tool room keeper	IV	350–399	10.20
Machinist B	V	400–449	10.50
Maintenance worker	VI	450–499	11.80
Mechanic	VII	500–549	12.00
Painter	VIII	550–599	13.30
Carpenter	IX	600–649	14.10
Truck driver	X	650–699	14.68
Electrician	XI	700–749	17.19
Tool and die maker	XII	750–799	17.42
Machinist A	XIII	800–849	18.49

SOURCE: Adapted from Collective Bargaining Negotiations and Contracts (Washington, D.C.: Bureau of National Affairs Inc., 1992), p. 18:331.

firms supply the starting wage rate and the economic benefits paid individuals in these job classifications (Exhibit 7.2). After the wage survey is complete, the firm must determine how the data will be used. For example, does it want to lead the industry, compete with a specific competitor, or pay the industry average? The final wage plan should contain a certain number of job classes; wages for each job class; wage ranges (from starting to top wages) for each class; policies and procedures for wage adjustments (seniority, merit, and so on); procedures for job changes to a different class, including temporary job changes; procedures for dealing with jobs that pay above or below their wage range; and a policy on union involvement.

Production Standards and Wage Incentives

Unions and management sometimes negotiate provisions in the labor agreement that cover wage-related issues such as production standards, time studies, and wage-incentive payments. Production standards refer to the expected employee output that is consistent with workmanship quality, operational efficiency, and reasonable working capacities of normal operators. These standards are often determined by time studies that involve analyses of the time and motions of workers on a job, and the resulting standards are used to assess performance and determine the wage incentives for individual employees or groups of employees.

Performance standards that are not accepted as realistic by both labor and management can be demoralizing and adversarial when used to determine workers' pay.[17] Unrealistically high performance standards will ensure lower performance ratings for many workers, thereby reducing pay and motivation levels. Unrealistically low performance standards will ensure that many workers easily meet or exceed work requirements, encouraging some workers to slack off during remaining scheduled work hours and discouraging workers from seeking to improve performance beyond the established norm. Performance standards also should be periodically updated to reflect changes that occur in materials and methods used to perform job tasks.

When incentive wage plans are negotiated, the structure and design are included in the contract, although specific details may not be included. Contract language defining the role of the union in setting and challenging production standards and wage rate changes and its right to be consulted on related issues is also usually included. Some contracts include provisions about time studies and the involvement of unions. A small number permit a union observer during the time study, and a few provide special training for the union time study

Job Title	Firms						Average Wage
	A	B	C	D	E	F	
Janitor	$6.00	$6.25	$6.75	$6.80	$7.00	$6.20	$6.50
Assembler	10.00	10.60	10.30	10.70	9.90	10.30	10.30
Shop clerk	11.00	10.00	10.75	10.25	10.40	10.60	10.50
Welder	12.60	12.30	12.00	12.00	12.30	12.60	12.30
Electrician	16.50	17.00	17.50	17.00	16.75	17.25	17.00
Tool and die maker	18.00	17.00	17.75	17.25	17.50	17.50	17.50
Machinist	19.00	18.50	18.00	18.75	18.25	18.50	18.50

Exhibit 7.2

Typical Results from a Wage Survey

representative. Other provisions include procedures used for timing an employee, specification of the meaning of typical employee, advance notice to the employee holding the job being studied, and specification for fatigue and personal allowances in setting production standards.[18]

Although wage incentive plans such as gain sharing, piece-rate pay, and profit sharing vary in structure and specific content, their goals are essentially the same: (1) to increase employee productivity, (2) to attract prospective employees to the company, and (3) to reward employees monetarily for their increased productivity. A typical individual wage incentive plan is one in which employees are paid for the number of pieces or jobs completed. Others pay bonuses or premiums to employees for production above the standard. Many varieties of incentive plans exist, but all are similar in concept.

The majority of production employees are paid an hourly wage rate. A major reason for an hourly-based compensation plan is that many production jobs are machine paced, so employees have limited control over the pace of work and thus the number of items produced during scheduled work hours. Many companies and unions have investigated the additional use of various incentive pay plans as a way to stimulate employee productivity. Increased interest in incentive plans has resulted from increased foreign and domestic competition, adoption of various employee involvement (EI) and total quality management (TQM) practices, heightened interest in labor-management cooperation, and employer efforts to obtain wage concessions from unions.

Approximately 35 percent of firms pay employees individual monetary incentives and 15 to 20 percent provide some type of group economic incentive, but few firms cover the majority of their employees under any single incentive plan.[19] A sample of 105 employers involved in negotiating a labor agreement in 2007 reported the following incidence of incentive or variable pay plans in their current contracts: individual incentive plan (six percent), group incentive plan (ten percent), profit-sharing plan (five percent), and gainsharing plan (four percent).[20] Although companies tend to report that plans such as profit sharing, employee stock ownership, gain sharing, skill-based pay, team incentives, and open pay information are successful, evidence is less clear over the ability of such plans to sustain initial productivity or pay satisfaction improvements over time.[21]

Employees may not be as enthusiastic about reward-incentive plans as employers. A survey of 1,500 employees reported that most workers preferred rewards based on individual performance, rather than team, group, or company performance and preferred to receive rewards in the form of a base pay rate increase rather than a one-time, lump-sum bonus or incentive payment.[22] Lack of employee support along with previously mentioned employer concerns have led to a slowdown in the rate at which companies are adopting reward incentive plans.

Profit-sharing plans cover between 6 and 27 percent of employees in most industrialized countries where government tax policies often encourage the adoption of such plans.[23] Approximately 20 percent of U.S. firms have a profit-sharing plan, although larger firms are more likely to participate.[24] Plans typically provide an annual cash payment or some payment into a pension plan. Most U.S. and international labor organizations today do not oppose profit sharing and other incentive systems as a matter of general policy, although opposition may arise in the context of negotiating a specific labor agreement.[25]

Some companies have negotiated profit-sharing plans that provided cash bonuses based on the company's profit to partially or totally take the place of hourly base-wage increases (e.g., American Airlines, Ford, General Motors

[GM], and International Harvester). In 2006, Ford and GM workers received no profit-sharing payout compared to 2005 results, which provided U.S. union employees of DaimlerChrysler AG average profit-sharing checks of $1,500; union-represented employees at Ford Motor Company an average of $600; and union workers at GM an average of $195.[26] Profit-sharing payouts under UAW contracts are based on a formula that takes into consideration company profits, productivity gains, and the firm's market share.

Profit sharing does have some management critics. First, some are concerned that union participation in profit sharing could lead to more union influence on other major management decisions beyond just wages. Second, a costly profit-sharing plan could drain company funds that could otherwise be used for capital improvements or research and development. Third, although initial firm performance gains may occur after the adoption of a profit-sharing plan, this positive effect appears to dissipate fairly quickly over time.[27]

In a group incentive or **gain-sharing plan**, companies make monetary payments to a specific group or groups of employees for producing more output or generating cost savings beyond some established goal. Incentives may include group bonuses, group piece rates, profit sharing, production sharing, and cost-reduction sharing. In some cases, plans may be limited to a few employees, to specific departments, to other organizational divisions, or extended to cover the entire company work force. Although group incentives aim to increase production and reduce costs, they are also designed to increase teamwork, provide greater job security, and achieve acceptance of new technology.

Many national unions adopt a neutral position toward gain-sharing plans, preferring to allow local unions to address such proposals on a case-by-case basis.[28] Union leaders may be wary of including gain-sharing plans as part of wage negotiations out of concern that management might tend to treat such plans as a substitute for traditional, negotiated hourly wage improvements during a contract's term. It may be easier to adopt gainsharing or other variable incentive plans if such plans are negotiated in addition to, rather than instead of, traditional straight-time hourly wage improvements.

There are a variety of group incentive plans. One of the most popular is the **Scanlon plan**, a group plan for sharing labor cost savings that was developed by former union leader Joseph Scanlon in the late 1930s. A Scanlon plan provides bonus payments based on a computed ratio of total labor costs (TLC) to total production values (TPV), which typically equal monthly sales, plus or minus inventory adjustments. A reduction in the ratio would be a labor cost savings. For example, if the employees were to reduce costs by working harder, producing more efficiently, and saving on wastes and the TLC/TPV ratio declined from 50 to 40 percent, the 10 percent labor cost savings would be shared with the employees.[29]

The **Rucker plan** is based on a change in the ratio between labor costs and dollar value added. The value added equals sales less purchased materials. Under this plan, if employees lower the ratio between labor costs and dollar value added, the productivity gains are shared. Under both the Scanlon and Rucker plans, employees receive between 25 and 75 percent of the available bonus pool, which is often distributed in the form of a percentage of each employee's hourly wage.[30]

The term **improshare plan** is derived from "improved productivity through sharing."[31] Improshare productivity measurements use traditional work measurement standards for a selected base period. A monetary reward is granted whenever the number of labor hours required to produce the output during a measured period (e.g., week or month) is less than the number of hours required during the base period. Both blue- and white-collar employees are typically included in an improshare plan, and all participants share equally in the bonus pool created. A study of improshare programs in 34 unionized companies showed an average productivity gain of 26.9 percent after the first year, whereas the average gain for 38 nonunion plants was 21.5 percent.[32] Another study of 112 firms that had introduced improshare found that the median increase in productivity in the first year was 8 percent and that cumulative productivity gains had risen to 17.5 percent by the third year, after which productivity gains leveled off.[33]

A review of several studies reports that gainsharing and profit-sharing plans generally provide a sustainable three to six percent increase in productivity.[34] Keys to the successful implementation of alternative reward systems in a unionized firm include (1) developing a cooperative relationship between union and management, which is based on genuine mutual trust and respect for each party; (2) involvement of the union in the development and implementation of the reward system; (3) effective communication of the program to covered employees; (4) flexibility to adapt the reward system to operating conditions and changing business needs; and (5) establishment of realistic achievable goals, particularly with respect to group incentive plans.[35] Employees' ability to understand the goals of a reward system and how those goals were established, how the attainment of plan goals will be measured, and how payouts are determined have a strong effect on covered employees' perceptions of both procedural and distributive justice under a reward system.[36]

Group incentive programs are based on the assumption that by linking earnings to performance, employees will adjust their efforts to optimize income. Because bonuses are tied to group effort, employees should have more incentive to work cooperatively. Considerable evidence suggests that the combination of employee participation programs and group incentive programs can exceed the gains made by either program alone. Employees have little incentive to share their performance-enhancing ideas with management without corresponding rewards. In addition, employees with no participation in decisions cannot respond effectively to such incentive programs. A union can provide more direct and open channels of communication for a collective voice in decisions enhancing employee input. Contract language with rigid wage classifications and a confrontational negotiating style may inhibit cooperation and employee response to reward incentives. Thus, in general, unionized firms may provide an environment more conducive to employee participation because of the collective bargaining process, but nonunion firms may have an environment more conducive to implementing group incentive programs.[37]

One additional alternative reward plan that has received attention in recent years is **skill-based pay (SBP)**.[38] Rather than setting base pay on the job an employee performs, SBP systems base compensation on the skills or knowledge an employee possesses that are valued by the employer. Sixty percent of Fortune 1000 firms report using SBP, although it typically applies to less than 20 percent of employees in a firm.[39] Changes in operating methods or the introduction of new technology requiring employees to acquire new skills or enhance existing skills may serve as an impetus for adopting an SBP plan. A proliferation of different job classifications may be reduced by grouping employees into a smaller number of skill blocks. Skill blocks can be defined based on natural work groups (e.g., assembly, painting), a set of existing job classifications, normal skill progression within a particular trade (e.g., welder), or team based. Each block has a defined set of skills, and employees can acquire skills through training and work experience both within a block and in preparation to qualify for a different skill block. An SBP plan encourages a more flexible labor force, enhances employee skills acquisition, and aids a company in adapting to a changing competitive environment.[40]

SBP plans can be successfully implemented in a unionized company as demonstrated by such firms as GM, Ford Motor Company, AT&T, Corning, Maxwell House, and Harley-Davidson Motor Company.[41] Establishing the initial composition of skill blocks, determining individuals' access to training opportunities, and creating an appeals procedure for handling disputes over the administration of the plan are key issues affecting the success of SBP plans. Union representatives may initially prefer to handle the implementation of an SBP plan as a trial project governed by a negotiated memorandum of understanding separate from the parties' negotiated labor agreement. An SBP plan is typically one part of a broader effort to introduce work-practice changes to enhance a firm's competitiveness. As with the introduction of other alternative reward systems, union involvement in planning, implementing, and administering an SBP plan can help to ensure employees' acceptance of the plan and attainment of the plan's potential benefits.

Arguments Used by Management and Union Officials in Wage Determination

Union and management representatives recognize that no single causal factor determines wage outcomes; however, both parties will use any identifiable factor to support their arguments for or against a wage increase. Related factors often used to bolster wage claims include differential features of the work performed (usually determined by job evaluation), wage comparability (external market-based pay), the employer's ability to pay (financial condition of the organization), productivity, cost of living, and legal requirements.[42] Union and management officials do not always favor the same criteria for wage determination. Moreover, each may emphasize different criteria at different times, particularly if using a distributive bargaining strategy. During prosperous times, unions tend to emphasize the employer's ability to pay. During recessions, management may emphasize its poor financial position as a reason to justify a wage cut, freeze, or lower rate of increase than in past contract negotiations. Similarly, during periods of rapid inflation, unions emphasize cost-of-living adjustments. When prices are stable, management places much weight on the lack of necessity for cost-of-living adjustments.

Pressure from domestic and international competition has reduced management's ability to simply pass increased labor costs on to the customer in the form of higher prices for goods and services. This has caused employers to place more emphasis on operating efficiency, cost-cutting measures, and productivity improvement. During difficult economic times, employers tend to deemphasize industry wage patterns and focus more attention in wage negotiations on their firm's specific labor costs, expected profits, and labor market conditions.

DIFFERENTIAL FEATURES OF THE WORK: JOB EVALUATION AND THE WAGE SPREAD

The job evaluation process described previously can influence the wages assigned to various job classifications in an organization. The relative influence of job evaluation can be seen in the **wage spread**, which represents the internal distribution of the proposed or negotiated wage increase to the bargaining unit employees (Exhibit 7.3).

The six employee job classifications in Exhibit 7.3 range in skill and pay from Classification A (highest) to Classification F (lowest), which conform to the results of management's job evaluation procedure. Management would generally prefer the wage spread in example 2. It gives more highly skilled employees a higher hourly wage increase, which could maintain or increase their wage differential over less-skilled employees, while at the same time utilizing fewer employee classifications than example 1, which simplifies administration of the pay system. Maintaining this wage differential is important to management for two reasons: (1) It helps ensure that current skilled employees do not leave because of higher wages offered by other firms, and (2) it offers some motivation to employees in lower-paid classifications to train for higher skill-level classifications within the company.

Unions support the job evaluation principle that higher-rated jobs should receive a higher rate of pay than lower-rated jobs. However, job evaluation ratings are not the only factor unions believe should be considered in determining the size or amount of wage improvements. One concern of union negotiators (which should be shared by management) is to ensure that the negotiated wage spread will result in sufficient votes by bargaining unit members to ratify the proposed labor agreement. Satisfied union members will also enhance a union leader's reelection prospects. Assume, for example, that Classification C in Exhibit 7.3 represented a politically influential group of employees. To satisfy this important group of bargaining unit constituents, union negotiators might prefer the wage spread illustrated by example 1, which grants Classification C employees a 48 cents-per-hour wage increase, or example 3, which grants a 47.2 cents-per-hour increase, rather than management's preferred wage spread (example 2), which only grants classification C employees a 44 cents-per-hour increase. The union might even propose a different wage spread that would give the employees in Classification C a much higher wage increase.

To encourage employees to ratify a tentative contract agreement and foster employees' perception of equity in wage adjustment, management might agree to an across-the-board increase to all employees regardless of their job classification. Granting an equal cents-per-hour increase in wages to all bargaining unit employees has the effect, over several contract renegotiations, of narrowing the

Exhibit 7.3

Three Examples of Internal Wage Spreads

Example	Number of Employees	Employee Classification	Percentage of Plants Total Employees	Increase in Cents Per Hour
1	184	A	16%	57.0
	197	B	18	50.0
	165	C	15	48.0
	237	D	21	46.0
	149	E	13	44.0
	193	F	17	42.0
	1,125			
2	381	A and B	34	60.0
	402	C and D	36	44.0
	342	E and F	30	34.0
	1,125			
3	1,125	A through F	100	47.2

wage spread between differently rated job classifications. If the wage spread narrows too much, management could experience increased dissatisfaction among employees holding higher-rated jobs, thereby leading to problems of increased turnover, absenteeism, or lower productivity among these workers. Union and management negotiators might attempt to address the potential problem of narrowing wage spreads over time by agreeing to an equal percentage increase in hourly base wage rates (rather than an equal cents-per-hour increase), which would maintain existing wage spreads. Another alternative to maintain a desired wage spread between higher- and lower-skilled employees would be to negotiate a special cents-per-hour increase only applicable to certain higher-rated jobs (**skill pay differential**) in addition to an equal cents-per-hour wage improvement granted to all job classifications.

Within the same or similar job classifications, one of the principal goals of unions is to reduce wage dispersion among employees with satisfactory job performance. This goal can be summarized in the phrase "equal pay for equal work." Unions seek to achieve this goal by negotiating a single rate of pay for each job classification and a seniority-based progression of wage rates within a defined employee classification up to some defined maximum rate. This approach is commonly used in job classifications that have two or more steps or grades that an employee may advance to over time based on some established criteria (e.g., work experience, demonstration of advanced job skills, or successful completion of training). A single wage rate (one pay grade for all employees in a given classification) eliminates wage dispersion between employees in the same classification, and seniority rules help control overall wage rates by requiring similar treatment of workers who have the same plant or company-wide seniority. Because of the "spillover" effect of union wage practices, even non-union firms experience less wage dispersion over time than one might expect.[43]

Contract language that specifies a newly hired employee will be paid less than other employees performing a similar job is referred to as a **two-tier pay plan**. Of 105 union contracts sampled, 25 percent contained a temporary and 6 percent a permanent (duration of the contract) two-tier wage plan with manufacturing firms more likely than nonmanufacturing firms to have one.[44] A temporary two-tier wage plan permits a new hire over time (e.g., the term of the contract) to rise to the same pay level as other similarly classified workers. Some bargaining relationships extend the two-tier concept to include eligibility for some employee benefits. Exhibit 7.4 presents an example of a two-tier pay schedule.

A two-tier wage plan achieves immediate labor cost savings as job openings are filled by lower-paid "new hires," and it may facilitate a favorable contract ratification vote since the wages of current bargaining unit members are not adversely affected by implementation of a two-tier plan. A union may legally negotiate a wage differential based on factors such as skill, type of work, or seniority so it would appear to have ample latitude to negotiate two-tier wage levels if the union does so in a "good faith and honest" effort to meet an employer's demand for lower labor costs in a manner that best protects the economic interests of current bargaining unit members. Auto parts suppliers Visteon and Delphi are two examples of firms that have negotiated two-tier wage and benefit plans with the United Auto Workers union.[45] In exchange for a $120 million plant expansion and the creation of 100 new jobs, Harley-Davidson Inc. employees represented by the United Steelworkers union agreed to lower the top-tier wage rate of more than $27 per hour by $7 per hour, establishing a lower-tier wage rate that would match the wages the company would pay if it chose to move the production of motorcycle powertrains to another location.[46]

Exhibit 7.4

Examples of Two-Tier
Pay Scales

Job Classes and Hourly Rates for Employees on Payroll Prior to March 1, 2003	
Job Classes	**Wage Rate**
0	$9.40
1	9.60
2	9.80
3	10.00
4	10.20
5	10.40
6	10.60
7	10.80

All employees hired after March 1, 2003, shall be considered new hires and...
shall be paid according to the [following] bracket rate:

Job Classes and Hourly Rates for Employees Hired After March 1, 2003	
Bracket	**Wage Rate**
0	$6.00
1	6.10
2	6.20
3	6.40
4	6.60
5	6.80
6	7.00
7	7.20

Some bargaining relationships have found that the costs of increased friction over time between lower- and upper-wage tier employees outweighs the initial labor cost savings of a two-tier wage plan and in subsequent negotiations have eliminated such language from their labor agreement.[47] If lower-tier employees view the pay situation as inequitable, they may vote to remove union leaders responsible for negotiating the wage terms or support union decertification. Likewise, lower-tier employees may feel less commitment to their employer, thereby increasing turnover rates and lowering productivity, which results in higher relative labor costs to the company.[48]

Wage Comparability

A common argument in wage negotiations is that wage rates in one bargaining unit should be equal or related to the wage rates in comparable bargaining units. **Wage comparability** is given considerable weight in wage determination, although these comparisons can become quite complicated and may be based on biased information.[49] Wage surveys can be helpful, but they do not measure how the job content, method of payment, regularity of employment, supplemental unemployment benefits, vacations, pensions, and holidays vary from company to company. Fundamental considerations such as the size of the appropriate labor market and occupational and geographic differences must be recognized. At first glance, it appears that bus drivers in Miami would have duties identical to those of bus drivers in Chicago. However, many differences in these similar jobs can exist, such as weather conditions, number of scheduled stops, location of scheduled stops, number of passengers, and so on. Furthermore, a major difference could arise in situations in which the bus drivers are required to make change for passengers. In such cases, a union could claim that this job responsibility creates a safety hazard by increasing the likelihood of robberies and would seek adequate compensation for this additional risk.

The relative importance of wages to total costs (degree of labor intensiveness) is also a significant factor in wage comparability. For example, if a modern, highly automated textile mill pays wages that account for 30 percent of total costs, a 10 percent increase in wages would equal a 3 percent change in the sales price. However, in an old textile mill with out-of-date machinery, where wages account for 65 percent of total costs, a 10 percent increase in wages would equal a 6.5 percent change in sales price. Even though wage data are often largely fragmented or deficient, negotiators still have to rely on wage comparability in arguing for or against certain levels of wages. Therefore, both parties continue to look for commonalities with other companies, local firms, or similar jobs that can provide a base from which to present their proposals.

Ability to Pay

The **ability to pay,** or the financial condition of the organization, is a commonly used standard for wage determination given much weight by unions during periods of high profitability.[50] Management rarely claims a true "inability to pay," except in extreme cases where the firm is losing money or is otherwise financially threatened. If management claims an inability to pay, the union has a legal right to independently examine the company's financial records under the duty to bargain in good faith for the purpose of verifying the employer's claim. Management more commonly responds to union wage demands by expressing an "unwillingness to pay" based on factors such as productivity rates, wage survey data, other capital needs, industry settlement patterns, or other relevant factors.

Ability to pay has limited usefulness as the sole criterion for wage determination for several reasons:[51]

1. Wages based solely on the ability to pay would create a chaotic wage structure and would cause a change in the wage-costs-price relationships that have evolved over time.

2. To be consistent, the ability to pay must work both ways, causing wage reductions when profits are nonexistent or inadequate. Such an approach would be generally unacceptable to unions.

3. It is extremely difficult to determine the share of profits that should be used for wage increases. If the profit is distributed to employees in the form of higher wages and an insufficient amount is shared with stockholders, there will be no incentive for investment, thereby limiting the firm's growth potential.

4. Wages supposedly are paid to employees in accordance with their relative value to the firm, their contribution to its goals, and the relative importance of their services. If ability to pay is the major factor, the relationship between actual pay and actual value could become distorted.

5. Wages are negotiated for future application. Basing wage changes on past profits is no guarantee that future profit levels will remain high enough to sustain a firm's profitability at the higher agreed-on wage levels.

Productivity

In 2006, the average annual business productivity rate for U.S. workers in the nonfarm business sector rose 1.7 percent compared to an increase in unit labor costs of 3.2 percent.[52] Manufacturing productivity over the same period rose four percent compared to a rise in unit labor cost of only 0.1 percent. **Labor productivity** represents a measure of the value of output created relative to the hourly costs of the labor necessary to produce that output (see Exhibit 7.5 for an international comparison of manufacturing productivity).

Although no argument has been advanced with more conviction or sophistication than that wages should vary with changes in productivity, union and management negotiators often experience difficulty in attempting to apply the principle to specific negotiations. For example, the rate of change in productivity varies widely from industry to industry, firm to firm, and even plant to plant. Not only is productivity itself difficult to measure accurately, but any change in productivity (usually measured in output per employee-hour) results from many causes, only one of which is labor.[53]

Those who study productivity have generally agreed that new capital investment and mechanization have been the primary causes for greater productivity, but there are still important issues to reconcile. Who should share in the revenue resulting from increased productivity—the employees, stockholders, or consumers? What is the proper balance among the contributing factors of production—labor and capital investments? Any use of productivity data must be handled carefully because the available data are only approximate estimates. Output per employee-hour often overstates gains attributed to labor and understates the relative contributions of advanced technology, improved methods, better machines, product quality, and so on to the value created by an hour of paid labor.

To remain competitive, companies and employees must be more productive. Union negotiators often argue that productivity gains may be used to pay for higher wage or benefit costs. Conversely, rising labor costs without offsetting

Exhibit 7.5

Average Annual Rates of Change in Manufacturing Output per Hour for the United States and Selected Countries

Country	1979–2005	2005
United States	4.1%	5.1%
Canada	2.5	5.7
France	4.3	3.9
Germany (unified)	2.8	5.3
Italy	1.8	.1
Sweden	4.3	0.0
Australia	2.9	1.9
United Kingdom	3.5	2.5
Japan	3.5	2.4
Korea	—	8.5
Taiwan	5.6	6.4

Productivity data is affected by factors such as the amount of output (product or service produced), number of hours worked, hourly compensation costs, value of goods/services produced, and the currency exchange rate. Productivity data represent the combined contributions of labor, management, new technology, capital investment, capacity utilization, and energy use.

SOURCE: U.S. Department of Labor, "International Comparisons of Manufacturing Productivity and Unit Labor Cost Trends, 2005," *News Release*, September 26, 2006, p. 6.

gains in productivity may act as an incentive for management to find lower-cost substitutes for employing additional labor (e.g., outsourcing, mechanization, and plant relocation). The International Longshoremen's Association (ILA) has agreed to work rules with shipping firms, allowing the use of cargo containers, global-positioning, satellite-system technology to track the movement of cargo, and other innovations that have increased productivity and job security, which benefits employers and union members.[54] Average annual wages for West Coast longshoremen working 2,000 hours per year are $123,464. The same principle applies to other industries; high productivity is the only way to warrant high wages. However, as witnessed in many manufacturing industries over the past 15 years, steady productivity growth has not led to a comparable increase in employment opportunities or significant real wage gains. One possible explanation for the inverse relationship between productivity growth and growth in real wages is that workers in the United States lack sufficient power to encourage or require employers to share a sufficient proportion of productivity gains with workers.[55]

A gain-sharing plan was previously discussed as one way to share productivity gains with employees who help create them. More than one-third of large companies have implemented some type of gain-sharing program.[56] In addition to providing an economic incentive for workers to improve the quantity and quality of outputs, productivity sharing plans may also serve to reduce grievances, absenteeism, and turnover, and to improve labor-management relations.[57]

Problems with Productivity Sharing

Although productivity sharing offers an innovative approach for mutual gain sharing and cooperative activity, it, too, has its problems. A large percentage of gain-sharing programs (43 percent) fail to achieve the positive returns expected by managers.[58] Most often this results from managers setting productivity-quality goals unrealistically high. There are also problems associated with the measurement of productivity. Some jobs do not lend themselves to precise measurement of output. It is much easier to measure bricks laid per hour by a worker than the value of that same worker spending one hour in a meeting discussing safety issues affecting the job. In jobs that are not routine or repetitious, exact measures are impossible.

Another problem is locating and organizing productivity data in such a manner that it may be useful to a firm. Serious arguments over the contribution of specific factors to increased productivity can inhibit the success of any productivity bargaining. What is the chief contributor to productivity gains? Is it the skill, efforts, or attitudes of the employees? Or is it the advanced technology of the machinery and equipment, efficiency of the operations, or the scale of operations? Or is it the interaction between these sets of factors?[59]

Because productivity gains are shared by labor and management under the productivity bargaining concept, they will certainly give rise to rigorous and complicated negotiations. Evidence suggests that many unions do not consider gain-sharing plans a substitute for traditional hourly wage gains but rather an additional pay benefit, a trade-off for wage concessions, or a means of maintaining parity with an industry wage pattern.[60]

Examples of bargaining for productivity improvement have occurred in the construction industry. Negotiations there have resulted in agreements to reduce work stoppages and contract language covering jurisdictional disputes, inefficient work rules, illegal featherbedding, and the duties of nonworking union stewards. Interestingly, the stimulus for productivity bargaining in the construction industry was the loss of work that increasingly went to nonunion contractors, along with the desire of union members to protect or expand their employment opportunities, particularly during unfavorable economic conditions.[61]

Effect of Unions on Productivity and Efficiency

Recently, there has been considerable debate and research about the effect of unions on productivity and efficiency. Labor productivity appears to be higher in unionized firms, particularly in manufacturing and construction. Explanations vary but the following reasons are often cited: improved morale brought about by higher wages, benefits, and improved working conditions; less employee turnover at unionized firms; higher levels of firm-specific skills, resulting in part from more training opportunities and greater employee longevity on the job; more pressure on management to invest in better methods, such as technological improvements to reduce unit labor costs; more effective grievance procedures, which help to resolve employee problems more quickly and therefore improve productivity; and the ability to negotiate subjects related to industrial accidents and diseases that can reduce lost work time and consequently increase productivity.[62]

A union can also promote efficiency when employees, through their union power, ensure that managers treat them fairly and gain a voice to influence decision making that leads to higher morale and greater productivity. Productivity is also enhanced by the fact that unionized workplaces attract and retain more highly skilled and experienced employees because of higher wages, the opportunity to be heard, and the assurance of fair treatment, which can also increase employees' loyalty to the firm.[63] Unionized firms are just as likely as nonunionized firms to adopt advanced manufacturing technologies as a means of enhancing productivity growth and competitiveness.[64]

On the other hand, it may be argued that unions can decrease productivity by reducing managerial flexibility, limiting the use of merit-based compensation, imposing work-rule restrictions, such as limits on work loads or tasks performed, and increasing the size of work crews.[65] To what extent unions are shown to have a positive or negative effect on productivity is often determined by the researchers' methodology used to measure productivity.[66]

On balance, unions generally have a positive effect on productivity. However, productivity gains are not generally sufficient to completely offset the higher labor costs (higher distribution of profits to meet employees' interests) attributable to unionization. Therefore, unionization may lower the rate of return per dollar of capital invested (one measure of profitability). This effect is most likely to be noticeable in unionized firms operating in product or service markets with relatively little competition and high profit margins.[67]

Cost of Living

During periods of rising prices, unions support wage demands in part by referring to the cost of living. Union negotiators argue that a rise in the cost of living without a commensurate wage increase is equivalent to a cut in real wages or a drop in purchasing power. Thus, the proposition that wages should be raised at least in proportion to the rise in living costs may seem quite fair and reasonable, especially to employees.

Employers are often concerned that a firm has little control over how much inflation may increase over a specified time period, making the employer's liability for pay more unpredictable. Wage payments based solely on an increase in the cost of living are also not tied to the need for increased labor productivity or the actual operating experience (profit/loss) of the firm. Where contract negotiations cover two or more plants, the additional concern is that the cost of living may vary by geographical location, either overestimating or underestimating the true cost of living if regional or national inflation rates are used in computing cost-of-living wage adjustments.[68]

Cost of living usually refers to the **Consumer Price Index (CPI)** computed by the U.S. Labor Department's Bureau of Labor Statistics, which measures changes in the price of goods and services purchased by a typical American household on a monthly basis.[69] The index covers 207 categories of goods or services (e.g., food, housing, health care, entertainment) sampled from 44 urban geographical areas around the country. During the first five months of 2007, consumer prices rose at a 5.5 percent seasonally adjusted rate, fueled by higher energy and food costs.[70] This compares to a 2.5 percent increase in consumer prices for all of 2006.

Wage Adjustments During the Term or Duration of the Labor Agreement

Because most negotiated labor agreements have a term of more than one year, it is common to include contract language that allows the adjustment of wages during the term of the contract. The most common term or duration of a labor agreement is three years (55 percent of 882 contracts surveyed), followed by more than three years (32 percent), two years (8 percent), and one year or less (5 percent).[71] There has been a trend in some basic goods manufacturing industries (e.g., auto, textiles, petroleum, paper) to negotiate longer-term contracts (four to six years) in an effort to stabilize labor conditions and avoid any threat of a work stoppage. Several different methods may be used to adjust employee base wage rates during the term of a labor agreement such as a **cost-of-living adjustment (COLA)** clause, **deferred wage increase** (also called an *annual improvement adjustment*), or a **wage re-opener** clause.

A COLA clause imposes a contractual obligation on an employer to change rates of pay in accordance with a collectively bargained formula and appears in approximately 21 percent of labor contracts.[72] When negotiating COLA provisions, union and management representatives usually consider the following issues:

1. *Selection of the particular price index and base point.* Most labor agreements use the all-cities CPI-W (consumer price index for urban wage earners and clerical workers). The beginning date of the contract is usually specified as the base point. The CPI-W is used to measure the rate of inflation from the base point to the end of the period when the COLA adjustment is scheduled to be paid.

2. *Frequency and timing of the wage adjustment.* Quarterly adjustments are more common in manufacturing industries, whereas annual adjustments are most common in nonmanufacturing firms. Employers would generally prefer less-frequent adjustment periods (e.g., annual rather than quarterly) to delay the time when the employer must expend the funds, thus permitting the firm to use that money in the interim and delaying the imposition of roll-up costs (as discussed in Chapter 6) incurred whenever an employee's base wage rate is adjusted upward. Unions would generally prefer quarterly (more frequent) COLA payments because it puts the money into the hands

of bargaining unit members sooner and increases the value of benefit items affected by the roll-up factor.

3. *COLA formula.* The most common negotiated formula for COLA adjustments is a 1 cent-per-hour increase for each .3 point increase in the CPI-W during the specified base period. For example, if during the base period the CPI-W rose 1.3 points, then the employer on the specified adjustment date would increase a covered employee's base wage rate by 4 cents per hour ($1.3 \div .3 = 4.33 \times \$.01 = 4¢$ rounded off to nearest whole cent). Some contracts negotiate an alternative formula, specifying a percentage change in wages in accordance with a specified percentage change in the CPI-W.

4. *Effect of COLA on other elements of the compensation package.* There is little uniformity found in labor contracts on this issue. Some agreements may include COLA adjustments only for the purpose of computing gross hourly earnings to avoid roll-up costs. Other labor contracts may use the COLA adjusted base wage rate in computing all items related to wages and benefits (e.g., holiday pay, vacation pay, sick leave pay).

One means of reducing the uncertainty of the amount of upward adjustment in wages under a COLA clause is to negotiate a maximum and minimum cap for such payments. A cap would guarantee a specified minimum or maximum adjustment during the term of the labor agreement regardless of the actual rise in the rate of inflation during the period. A minimum guarantee would benefit bargaining unit members in that management generally insists on negotiating smaller base hourly wage increases when a COLA clause is included in the labor agreement because part of the employee's wage gain is expected to be provided by the COLA payment during the contract's term. A maximum cap would reduce management's wage liability risk should an unexpected rapid escalation in inflation occur (e.g., an oil crisis) during the contract's term. Despite the apparent advantage of a cap to both parties, only an estimated 25 percent of COLA clauses contain any form of caps, indicating the difficulty encountered in reaching a mutual agreement on what constitutes a reasonable minimum or maximum guaranteed COLA payment.

Deferred wage increases are negotiated in multi-year contracts to provide some adjustment in base wage rates beyond the first contract year. Contracts are sometimes referred to as being **back-loaded, front-loaded,** or **even-loaded** as a means of indicating in which years of the contract most of the wage improvement occurs. For example, a three-year contract that averaged a three percent annual wage gain could provide annual wage adjustments of five, three, and one percent (front-loaded); one, three, and five percent (back-loaded); or three, three, and three percent (even-loaded). As with the timing of COLA adjustments, unions generally favor transferring cash into the hands of bargaining unit members as quickly as possible (front loading), whereas management prefers delaying the transfer of money as long as possible (back loading). The loading of economic improvements in a labor agreement can be used as one measure of the relative bargaining power between the parties.

A wage re-opener clause is written to permit wages to be renegotiated at a specified point in time during the term of the contract or whenever some predetermined event occurs (e.g., profits exceed a certain level, the CPI has risen by a specified amount). A wage re-opener clause may be necessary in order to get both parties to agree to a contract settlement whenever the future operating environment of the firm is unclear or the term of the contract is longer than one year or both bargaining parties believe they can reasonably predict what constitutes an adequate (acceptable) wage settlement. Some labor agreements may also contain re-opener contract language which permits certain nonwage items to be renegotiated during the term of the contract (e.g., health care insurance costs).

Lump-Sum Pay Adjustments

Lump-sum pay adjustments appeared in approximately 15 percent of labor contracts in 2007, up from 12 percent in 2004.[73] The most common payment was a flat dollar amount, an average of $1,362 in 2005.[74] Only 20 percent of contracts provide a lump-sum payment in the second year, and only 11 percent provide a third-year lump sum payment. Lump-sum pay adjustments are popular with management because they do not change the employee's base hourly wage rate and thus have no impact on increasing roll-up costs. Unions generally favor lump-sum pay only as an alternative to a wage freeze or cut when economic conditions prevent an employer from paying a straight-time hourly wage increase.

EMPLOYEE BENEFITS

In 2007, unionized U.S. employers paid benefit costs averaging $13.35 per hour worked (37.8 percent of each payroll dollar) compared with nonunion employers' benefits expenditures of $6.90 per hour worked (27.8 percent of each payroll dollar).[75] Exhibit 7.6 presents a complete breakdown of employer cost per hour worked by bargaining status. Benefits are an important part of an employee's compensation and include insurance costs, pension payments, payments for time not worked (such as vacations, sick leave, holidays, paid rest and lunch breaks), supplemental pay (e.g., bonuses, shift differential, overtime pay) and legally required payments. Legally required payments (e.g., social security, workers' and unemployment compensation) for many years constituted the single largest category of benefit expense incurred by both union and nonunion employers.

Type of Compensation	Union	Nonunion
Total Compensation (wages + benefits)	**$35.27 (100.0%)**	**$24.82 (100.0%)**
Wages and salaries	**21.92** (62.2%)	**17.92** (72.2%)
Total Benefits	**13.35** (37.8%)	**6.90** (27.8%)
Individual Benefit Categories		
Paid Leave (e.g., vacation, holiday, sick leave)	**2.79** (7.9%)	**1.66** (6.7%)
Supplemental Pay (e.g., overtime, shift differential, lump-sum pay)	**1.13** (3.2%)	**.72** (2.9%)
Insurance (e.g., life, health, short- and long-term disability)	**4.08** (11.6%)	**1.72** (6.9%)
Retirement & Savings (e.g., defined benefit plan, defined contribution plan, cash balance plan)	**2.25** (6.4%)	**.71** (2.8%)
Legally required benefits (e.g., social security, unemployment compensation, workers' compensation)	**3.10** (8.8%)	**2.10** (8.5%)

SOURCE: U.S. Bureau of Labor Statistics, "Employer Cost for Employee Compensation—March 2007," *News Release,* June 21, 2007, p. 11.

Exhibit 7.6
Employer Costs per Hour Worked by Bargaining Status, March 2007

In 2003, health insurance became the highest single benefit cost item for unionized employers, thus making it an important bargaining topic in labor negotiations. Unionized employers incur substantially higher cost than nonunion employers for health insurance because policies provided for under union contracts generally cover a greater proportion of employees and provide a wider range and higher dollar amount of health care coverage. The following sections present major areas of employee benefits, relying largely on an analysis of 105 collective bargaining agreements by the Bureau of National Affairs.[76]

Insurance

Of 105 union contracts surveyed, 91 percent provided life insurance and 97 percent covered hospitalization and surgical expenses. Other common health care benefits found in union contracts are doctor visits (95 percent), prescription drugs (96 percent), mental health (90 percent), dental care (82 percent), vision care (76 percent), and domestic partner coverage (32 percent). Approximately 33 percent of union employers participate in multi-employer health insurance plans that enable plan participants to negotiate lower insurance rates and fee schedules with health care providers, as well as spread administrative costs over a large number of plan participants.

Tight labor market conditions in the late 1990s caused many employers to improve health insurance benefits as an incentive to attract and retain qualified workers. This was a change from the bargaining trend of the early and mid-1990s when employers often sought to shift a greater proportion of health care costs onto employees or reduce health care benefits as a means of controlling rising health care costs. During recent years generally weak demand for labor and increased pressure on company profits have once again focused employers' attention on managing health care costs effectively. Health care benefits have been a principal issue in several major strikes that have occurred in recent years at companies such as General Electric, Hershey Foods Corporation, and Lockheed Martin Corporation.[77]

Health Care Cost Containment

In 2003, 48.8 million individuals (19.2 percent of the U.S. population) lived in a family who spent more than ten percent of family income on medical care, an increase of 11.7 million individuals since 1996.[78] Over seven percent of individuals live in families spending more than 20 percent of family income on medical care. In 2006, health care insurance premium costs rose 7.7 percent, more than twice the average increase in wages and other consumer prices.[79] The average annual health insurance premium cost for individual coverage was $4,242 and family coverage averaged $11,480. On average employers pay 74 percent of family coverage annual insurance premium costs and 85 percent of individual coverage annual insurance premium costs. Both union and nonunion employers have been active in recent years in efforts to either reduce the costs of health care coverage or shift a greater portion of that cost burden to employees. Such an employer strategy often conflicts with employees' pressure on their union to maintain or expand the type and quality of health care benefits while minimizing any additional cost to bargaining unit members.

Unions and employers jointly recognize the importance employees place on the provision of health care benefits and the need to cooperate in seeking cost-effective means of providing such benefit coverage. The availability and quality of health care benefits is an important factor in the recruitment and retention of quality employees. A number of contracts contain provisions designed to lower health care costs including co-payments (88 percent), deductibles (80 percent), and premium contributions by employees (71 percent). Union-represented employees typically pay a smaller proportion of such expenses under negotiated contracts compared to similar types of provisions under nonunion employer-promulgated employment terms. Raising co-payments per doctor's office visit or deductible amounts paid by the employee before insurance coverage begins can impact employees differently, depending on how frequently they use medical services. Increasing the proportion of insurance premium costs paid by the employee affects all employees covered under the same policy provision equally, and therefore is sometimes preferred as a cost-sharing mechanism over raising employee co-pay or deductible amounts. Other cost-containment provisions found in union contracts include a generic drug requirement (71 percent), pretax spending account (55 percent), utilization review (47 percent), preadmission testing (46 percent), outpatient surgery requirement (44 percent), delayed new hire eligibility (42 percent), wellness program (42 percent), spousal eligibility (24 percent), required second opinion (24 percent), hospice care requirement (24 percent), home health care requirement (22 percent), gatekeeper system requirement (18 percent), and two-tier plan (9 percent).[80]

Many union contracts provide more than one type of health care plan. Traditional **fee-for-service plans** have declined in use over the past decade and currently are found in 26 percent of contracts.[81] Most popular are **preferred provider organization (PPO)** health care plans (84 percent of contracts), which permit an employee to pay a lower rate for health care services if the employee agrees to use health care providers approved by the PPO plan. To become an approved health care provider, a doctor or hospital must agree in advance with the insurance provider to accept a lower reimbursement rate than the traditional fee-for-service rate for most health care services provided. A **health maintenance organization (HMO)** plan restricts an employee's choice of health care provider to the HMO and is available in 43 percent of contracts. A few union contracts (eight percent) offer a **consumer-directed health care plan**, which typically involves a high deductible insurance policy combined with a health savings account into which an employee may place pre-tax dollars to spend for later health care needs until the high deductible has been paid and the insurance policy begins to pay for health care needs. Some employers may make a defined contribution to an employee's health savings account, matching an employee's contribution up to a specified dollar amount. Most employees when presented with a choice of plans do not prefer a consumer-directed plan because of the high out-of-pocket expense of meeting deductibles and confusion over how the plans are supposed to work.[82]

Income Maintenance

Income maintenance provisions usually involve issues such as work or pay guarantees, **severance pay** (separation or termination pay), or a **supplemental unemployment benefit plan (SUB)**. Severance pay plans provide a lump-sum payment on termination and are included in 31 percent of manufacturing contracts but only in 22 percent of nonmanufacturing labor agreements.[83] More senior workers and those who earn higher wages are generally entitled to a proportionally larger severance payment. In most cases, severance pay is only extended to an employee whose job has been terminated as a result of permanent shutdown, is subject to a lengthy layoff extending beyond an established minimum period, or who has no reasonable prospect for recall. For example, The Hershey Company recently decided to shift production of some candy products to Mexico, resulting in employment reductions at its U.S. plants.[84] Hershey and the Teamster's union negotiated an early retirement and severance pay package, which included two weeks of severance pay for each year of an employee's service. If the current contract does not specifically provide for severance pay, as a mandatory subject of bargaining, a union will generally request to bargain over the subject should a significant layoff or plant closure occur.

A SUB plan provides pay in addition to unemployment compensation to which the individual would be entitled and is found in seven percent of labor contracts. A few SUB plans provide individual accounts in which the employee has a vested right and from which he or she may withdraw money for reasons other than lack of work. The most common method provides payment of an amount equal to a percentage of the employee's take-home pay with unemployment compensation deducted. Other issues to be negotiated as part of a SUB plan include the duration of benefits, length of service requirements to qualify for coverage, and employer financial requirements to fund the plan.

Work sharing provisions are found in three percent of labor contracts. As a means of avoiding or minimizing layoffs among bargaining unit members, qualified employees agree to share the available work opportunities by having each employee work a reduced number of hours. An employer may benefit from such an arrangement by retaining quality workers who, if laid off, might accept employment elsewhere and not return to work when future work opportunities become available.[85]

Premium Pay—Overtime and Other Supplements

Most labor agreements specify daily or weekly work schedules and provide **premium pay** for hours worked beyond regularly scheduled hours. Most agreements call for an eight-hour day and a work week of 40 hours, Monday through Friday. Overtime premiums are usually paid for work over eight hours per day at a time-and-a-half rate, which is more beneficial to the worker than the Fair Labor Standards Act (FLSA) requirement of time-and-a-half payment for work in excess of 40 hours in a week. For example, employees on a four-day, 40-hour work week would receive eight hours of overtime pay under typical union contract language, whereas the FLSA would require no overtime pay. Payment of double-time for hours worked on certain days such as Sunday or holidays has declined in union contracts as employers have successfully bargained to eliminate such special pay incentives. Employers who operate on a continuous basis (e.g., retail stores open 24 hours per day, seven days per week) typically negotiate work schedules which do not require the use of premium pay in order to meet normal operating schedules.

Many labor agreements also contain provisions for overtime administration. For example, overtime assignments may be restricted to qualified employees within a specific job classification, department, or work shift. Management may be required to offer overtime work assignments to workers who have the greatest seniority first, or a contract might specify overtime opportunities to be awarded on a rotating basis regardless of seniority. In some cases, when management has had difficulty getting employees to voluntarily work overtime, a provision making overtime work mandatory may be negotiated. Excessive use of overtime as a means of avoiding the additional employment costs associated with hiring additional full-time workers can lead to a labor dispute. Most employees (and union leaders) understand the necessity for overtime work periodically and usually value the additional income opportunity.

Some labor agreements that provide equalization of overtime hours count the hours whenever an overtime opportunity is offered even though the employee refuses the offer. For example, if an employee is offered four hours of Saturday morning overtime and he or she turns it down, those four hours for overtime-equalization purposes would still be counted as if the employee had worked them. Likewise, unions have sought provisions in a labor agreement that would enable their members to better plan their off-the-job activities, such as a minimum advance notice of required overtime work or the right to refuse overtime work for certain specified reasons.

Various other forms of premium pay are also included in most labor contracts. For instance, **shift differentials** (e.g., premium payments for working the night shift) are provided in most of labor agreements. Other forms, such as **reporting pay** (which guarantees some minimum number of hours' pay for employees who report for scheduled work but find no work) and **call-in pay** (which typically guarantees four hours' pay for employees called in to work during nonscheduled work hours) are also usually included. Other pay supplements may include pay for temporary transfer, hazardous work, travel, work clothing, tool allowance, or bonus pay for certain specified purposes (e.g., annual bonus, good attendance, or safety record).

Pay for Time Not Worked—Holidays, Vacations, and Rest Periods

Labor agreements often contain payments for various time during which the employee is not required to work such as vacation leave (95 percent), holiday leave (93 percent), bereavement leave (90 percent), jury duty leave (84 percent), sick leave (69 percent), military leave (50 percent), personal leave (46 percent), and voting leave (18 percent).[86] The two most expensive paid-leave benefit provisions deal with holiday and vacation pay. The average number of paid holidays provided under union contracts was 10, although 40 percent of bargaining unit members receive 11 or more.[87] This compares to nonunion employees who receive on average eight paid holidays annually.

Nearly all union contracts provide holidays for Labor Day, Independence Day, Thanksgiving, Christmas, New Year's Day, and Memorial Day. Good Friday, Christmas Eve, the day after Thanksgiving, and Martin Luther King, Jr.'s birthday are also often granted. Contracts generally contain some eligibility requirements for holiday pay (e.g., specified length of service [usually four weeks] or a requirement that the employee must perform any scheduled work the day before and after the holiday). Other issues which should be covered in contract language include payment for holidays falling on a regularly scheduled day off or during a paid vacation period and premium pay for hours worked on a paid holiday.

In many industrialized countries employees are guaranteed a paid vacation by law; however, in the United States there is no such legal guarantee.[88] For example, after one year of service, workers receive 25 paid vacation days in France; 24 days in Germany; 22 days in Spain; and 20 days in Belgium, Ireland, the Netherlands, Australia, and the United Kingdom. Not only do U.S. workers receive less paid vacation, a survey of 1,003 workers by the independent Families and Work Institute reported that 36 percent of respondents did not plan to use all of their vacation entitlement.[89]

The U.S. Bureau of Labor Statistics reports that both union and nonunion workers receive on average, nine paid vacation days after one year of service.[90] After three years of service, union workers begin to earn more vacation days than their nonunion counterparts with the divergence continuing to increase over time until after 25 years of service. Union workers receive on average 24 days of paid vacation compared to a nonunion worker's 19 days. Part-time status, an average wage of less than $15 per hour, and employment in a firm with less than 100 employees are all factors which result in a below-average number of paid vacation days being granted an employee.

Vacation scheduling provisions appear in almost all labor agreements, covering issues such as annual plant shutdowns and consideration of employee seniority and employee preference in vacation scheduling decisions. Such provisions are essential in large organizations to reduce potential disputes between employees and to ensure that adequate qualified personnel are available to meet planned operating schedules.

Pensions

As the life expectancy of U.S. workers has increased (to 77.9 years in 2004), pension benefits have taken on added importance as a source of income to sustain an individual's standard of living after leaving the labor force.[91] In 2006, 84 percent of private-sector union members participated in some type of employer- or union-sponsored pension plan compared to 57 percent of nonunion employees.[92] Only 36 percent of private-sector employees earning less than $15 per hour were covered under a pension plan.

Nearly all labor agreements make some reference to pension plans, whether in the form of a general statement mentioning the plan or a fully detailed provision. Items usually mentioned include age for retirement (normal and early), disability retirement, benefits available and requirements for qualifying, vesting provisions, administration procedures, and financial arrangements. The presence of a union tends to greatly increase pension coverage and alter the provisions of pension plans in ways that benefit senior employees and equalize pensions among bargaining unit members.[93] Union members typically receive larger pension benefits than nonunion employees at the time they retire and also receive larger increases in such benefits in the years after their retirement. Union members also retire at an earlier age than nonunion employees.

In 1987, the *Age Discrimination in Employment Act* (ADEA) was amended to prohibit any mandatory retirement age (with limited exceptions for certain occupations such as airline pilots), ending the common pension plan use of 70 as a mandatory retirement age. Although this amendment helped extend the career of senior employees, the Supreme Court's controversial *Betts* decision in 1989 ruled that virtually all employee benefit programs are exempt from challenge under the ADEA unless the employee can prove "intentional discrimination" on the part of the employer.[94]

The majority (64 percent) of union contracts include a **defined benefit pension plan**, which guarantees a specified dollar benefit payment per month to a covered employee on retirement and is typically funded by the employer. Knowing the amount of pension benefit to be received in advance aids an employee in retirement planning, and having the pension benefit amount guaranteed reduces the investment risk incurred by the employee. Some younger employees who have grown up in an era of generally rising stock market values express a preference for a tax-deferred 401(k) plan as a retirement savings vehicle (a type of **defined contribution pension plan** discussed later in this chapter). However, the stock market declines experienced in recent years have served to remind employees of the risk and volatility associated with investing for long-term security in a stock market that historically has had periods of growth and decline.

Most union contracts (69 percent) contain a 401(k) savings plan often as a supplement to a member's defined benefit pension plan whereby an employee can invest his or her own dollars in a retirement savings account and often have the contribution matched by an employer's contribution up to a specified limit (e.g., 50 cents per dollar invested by the employee up to an amount equal to three percent of the employee's salary).[95] During a period of economic stress, employers often suspend discretionary company matching contributions to employee 401(k) plans as a cost savings measure, although employees are still eligible to contribute to their individual accounts.[96]

Unions generally oppose efforts by an employer to use an **employee stock ownership plan (ESOP)** as a basic pension plan.[97] Investing pension savings in a single company greatly increases the risk to the employee's investment should the firm experience poor future performance (and thus a decline in the value of its stock price). Enron, WorldCom, Global Crossing, Polaroid, Kmart, and Lucent are just some of the firms whose financial difficulties have resulted in significant 401(k) plan losses for covered employees.[98] Firms in some industries such as airlines, steel, and trucking have negotiated ESOPs as a management trade-off for union wage concessions.[99] Employee stock ownership plans under union contracts are more likely to permit union employees to vote their own shares of stock, have some direct representation on the governing board of the plan, and be more involved in the development and implementation of the plan.

Research on the effects of ESOPs on labor relations is tentative at this time because of the lack of widespread or long-term experience. However, a few preliminary conclusions may be reported:[100]

- Labor-management cooperation does not emerge automatically when publicly traded companies move into employee ownership.

- Employee ownership leads to greater identification of the employees with the company, and employees receive more information about the company; supervisor-employee relations become more cooperative; and employees and managers express positive attitudes about employee ownership and the organizational climate.

- No evidence supports the concern that employees want to take over companies with ESOPs and restructure management roles and authority from top to bottom.

- Employee ownership does not have an automatic effect on employees' motivation, work effort, absenteeism, or job satisfaction; however, greater integration of the employee into the organization and more employee participation in decisions do have positive results.

- Generally, the role of the union does not change except when the union made an early and ongoing effort to become involved in the change process, and unions initiate few changes in labor-management relations.

- Companies with an active employee ownership philosophy that try to translate it into concrete cooperative efforts have the strongest effect on positive employee attitudes.

- The presence of an ESOP does not make a firm more productive, efficient, or profitable; however, most studies show that employee-owned firms performed successfully on a number of financial variables, such as profits, stock appreciation, sales, and employment growth.

The proportion of private-sector employees who participate in a defined benefit pension plan has declined since 1985 to 20 percent in 2006.[101] Unionized workers (68 percent) are much more likely to participate in a defined benefit plan than nonunion workers (14 percent). Only 47 percent of nonunion employees participate in any type of pension plan compared to 80 percent of union represented employees. Forty-three percent of nonunion employees participate in a defined contribution pension plan compared to 44 percent of union represented workers. In a defined contribution plan, an employer establishes an account in an employee's name and promises to contribute a specified amount to the account on an annual basis. The employer's contribution may be contingent on certain factors such as sufficient operating revenue to make the payments or a matching contribution from the employee. An employee may also contribute as many of his or her own dollars to the account's balance as desired. A negative personal savings rate and a high level of consumer debt (on average equal to 129 percent of disposable family income in June 2006) often make it difficult for employees to find personal funds to invest in their pension savings account. Most experts suggest that an employee will need to generate 70 to 85 percent of their preretirement income to maintain a comparable lifestyle in retirement.[102]

The ultimate value of an employee's retirement benefit under a defined contribution plan depends on the amount of employer and employee contributions to the account, along with the investment gains or losses experienced by the account. A defined contribution plan shifts the investment risk from the employer to the employee for ensuring at the time of actual retirement that pension funds available will be sufficient to fund the individual's retirement lifestyle. Allowing the employer to determine the amount of the firm's contribution rather than guarantee the value of the account at the time of retirement permits the employer to control the cost of providing a pension benefit.

Defined contribution plans are not insured unlike defined benefit plans whose value is insured by the federal government through the Pension Benefit Guaranty Corporation (PBGC) should the employer default on pension obligations. The PBGC has estimated that defined benefit plans are under-funded by $450 billion with many problem plans contained in airline and auto-related industries.[103] When the value of a defined benefit pension fund's investments decline, an employer must make additional contributions to the pension fund to ensure pension fund liabilities are met. This can create a financial burden on a firm faced with declining profits and lower sales revenues and has led many firms to terminate their defined benefit plans and institute a defined contribution plan.

A **cash balance plan** represents a retirement savings approach that combines features of both defined benefit and defined contribution plans.[104] Under a cash balance plan, an employer typically agrees to make a specified contribution to an employee's retirement account, which is guaranteed to earn a specified rate of interest generally pegged to an index such as the one-year treasury bill rate. On reaching retirement age, a retiree may generally choose to accept an annuity payment (e.g., $10,000 per year for life) based on the value of the account balance or receive a lump-sum distribution equal to the value of the account balance. Because the amount of benefit earned each year of employment is steady under a cash balance plan, an employee who does not anticipate remaining with the employer for an extended period might earn a greater pension benefit during a shorter employment tenure compared with an employee covered under a traditional defined benefit plan, which typically computes the amount of pension benefit earned based on the average of an employee's three highest salary years, which typically would not occur until late in a worker's career. Conversely, a more senior employee covered under a defined benefit plan might actually experience a 30 to 50 percent reduction in pension benefits if the pension plan were converted to a cash balance plan.[105]

In the late 1980s and early 1990s during a period of high interest rates and stock market returns, many companies found their defined benefit plans were over-funded (i.e., plan assets exceeded liabilities). By terminating the existing defined benefit plan, the employer was able to shift the excess funds to other employer uses, resulting in a cash bonanza for employers. Defined contribution or cash balance plans were then adopted to provide a pension benefit for covered employees. More than 300 firms, including AT&T, IBM, Citigroup Inc., Bell Atlantic, Sun Co., Hallmark Cards, and Eastman Kodak, have adopted cash balance plans; however, such plans are found in only nine percent of union contracts.[106] Passage of the **Pension Protection Act of 2006** and a recent federal appeals court ruling upholding the legality of IBM's cash balance plan have eliminated most legal concerns surrounding the implementation of cash balance plans.[107]

Pension plans under union contracts often offer several early retirement options to the employee. For example, agreements provide such options as retirement at age 60 after ten years of service; retirement at age 55, but only when the combined age and service years equal 85; or retirement after 30 years of service, without regard to age. Although nearly all of the contracts contain vesting provisions stating that an employee whose service is terminated continues to be entitled to earned benefits, the **Employee Retirement Income Security Act (ERISA) of 1974** as modified by the Pension Protection Act of 2006 has very specific regulations governing vesting requirements of pension plans.[108] Under a **cliff vesting schedule**, a qualified retirement plan must, at a minimum, permit a participant to earn a nonforfeitable right to 100 percent of his or her accrued benefit derived from the employer's contributions after five years of service. Alternatively, under a **graded vesting schedule**, a plan participant would be 20 percent vested after three years of service, 40 percent after four years, 60 percent after five years, 80 percent after six years, and 100 percent vested after seven years of service. Special vesting rules apply to elective deferrals and matching contributions. Elective deferrals must be immediately vested. Matching contributions generally must vest at least as rapidly as under one of the two minimum vesting schedules described above. Although management and labor may negotiate provisions covering pensions that are more favorable than the law requires, most agreements for the time being will no doubt closely correspond to the legal minimum.

Family and Child-Care Benefits

After an eight-year effort in the U.S. Congress, the **Family and Medical Leave Act (FMLA) of 1993** was passed.[109] The FMLA requires private-sector employers of 50 or more employees to provide eligible employees up to 12 weeks of unpaid leave for their own serious illness; the birth or adoption of a child; or care of a seriously ill child, spouse, or parent. For eligibility, an employee must have been employed for at least one year and worked at least 1,250 hours within the previous 12 months. The Department of Labor (DOL) is assigned administrative responsibility for the act, and civil suits by employees are allowed. The small employer exemption from coverage under the FMLA means the law only covers 10.8 percent of private-sector employers but these covered firms employ 58.3 percent of all private-sector employees.[110]

Now more than ten years after the FMLA's enactment, it is clear that the law has served to make employers more aware of family work/life issues without imposing any significant costs or administrative burdens on employers.[111] The U.S. Department of Labor reports that 16.5 percent of eligible employees actually take leave time provided under the FMLA with a median length of ten days' leave.[112] The most common reason for taking leave is for the employee's own health (52.4 percent), followed by care for a newborn, newly adopted, or newly placed foster child (18.5 percent). Among employees who needed to take leave but did not, the most common reason cited for not taking leave was they could not afford to do so (77.6 percent). This has prompted some advocates to encourage Congress to amend the FMLA to provide paid, rather than unpaid, leave, although employer opposition to such a change and federal budget deficits makes enactment unlikely at the federal level in the near future.[113] In 2004, California became the first state to authorize partially paid family and medical leave benefits under the state's disability insurance fund and legislation to provide paid family leave benefits have been introduced in 27 other states.[114]

Some employers have expressed concern over the broader definition of "serious medical condition" being applied by the U.S. Department of Labor and some courts, in comparison to how that term has typically been defined in cases under the *Americans with Disabilities Act* (ADA).[115] Another employer concern is what constitutes proper employee notice to their employer of a need to take FMLA leave. Some employers also report administrative difficulty in managing FMLA intermittent leave requests where an employee is absent for a block of time (e.g., four hours each Friday for treatment) or works a reduced daily or weekly work schedule. Intermittent leaves comprise 27.8 percent of all employee leave requests. Approximately 23 percent of employers report providing additional leave time beyond the 12 weeks specified under the FMLA and a majority of employers report granting leave time for one or more reasons beyond those covered by the FMLA (e.g., attending school functions—68 percent; routine medical care—73 percent).[116]

Unions are free to negotiate family and medical benefits that exceed those provided by the FMLA. Because family and medical leave is a mandatory subject of bargaining, the employer is legally obligated to bargain with the union over these subjects.[117] Negotiable issues might include the amount of leave provided and reasons for taking leave, paid or unpaid status of leave time granted, substitution of other paid leave (e.g., sick leave, vacation days) for unpaid FMLA leave, or the method used to determine what 12-month period is used to calculate the 12 weeks of unpaid FMLA leave available within a 12-month period (e.g., calendar year, 12-month period beginning with the employee's date of hire, 12-month period beginning when the employee's first FMLA leave starts). If the company and union have negotiated a general nondiscrimination clause, it is important to ensure that specific laws, such as the FMLA to which the contract clause applies, are included in the contract language. This would permit the resolution of FMLA disputes under the parties' contract grievance-arbitration procedure rather than requiring an employee to file a complaint with the U.S. Department of Labor or pay a private attorney to pursue a court claim.

OTHER BENEFITS

Companies and unions also bargain over a wide range of other benefits. The American Bar Association estimates that half of all U.S. citizens need the services of an attorney annually.[118] **Prepaid legal service plans** are a relatively inexpensive means of providing legal assistance to employees without imposing substantial administrative burdens on an employer. An estimated 19 million individuals were covered under such plans in 2002, a 20 percent increase during the previous two-year period. Prepaid legal service plans operate in a manner similar to HMOs. In exchange for a monthly premium ($16 to $26), subscribers are entitled to free legal advice, representation, and document reviews from a network of approved attorneys who provide the service for a fixed fee paid by the plan's provider. Some plans offer a full array of services, ranging from counsel for criminal offenses to routine matters such as a will, divorces, house closings, and landlord-tenant problems.

Approximately 70 percent of union contracts provide some type of **employee assistance plan (EAP)**, which provides counseling services to employees, covering a wide range of problems such as personal finance, marital relationships, stress management, or substance abuse.[119] The U.S. Labor Department estimates that employers save $14 in costs related to employees' problems for every one dollar invested in an EAP program.[120] Many employers and unions view an EAP plan as another means of effectively managing employee health care costs in a proactive manner by providing employees with timely assistance in identifying and resolving problems.

The need to improve employee job skills to match changing job requirements has led to more firms providing **education tuition aid**.[121] Found in 59 percent of labor agreements sampled, education tuition aid helps to cover expenses incurred by an employee who seeks additional education and training related to the employee's career. A slight majority of Fortune 500 firms offer similar benefits to both married spouses and domestic partners of employees, up from less than one percent of similar firms in 1992.[122] Larger bargaining units with more than 1,000 members are likely to offer a wider variety of benefits than smaller bargaining units, including benefits such as a **transportation subsidy** to offset travel expenses to and from work, which is more common in nonmanufacturing (20 percent), a free or subsidized **home computer** (13 percent), and **child-care assistance** (7 percent).[123]

UNION EFFECTS ON WAGES AND BENEFITS

The degree to which unions influence wage and benefit levels is a commonly debated subject among labor economists. In a 1963 classic book, *Unionism and Relative Wages in the United States,* Greg Lewis concluded that union wages ranged between ten and 15 percent higher than nonunion wages.[124] By the 1970s the union wage differential had climbed to 20 to 30 percent in most industries. Further analysis reveals a greater impact on wages of blue-collar employees, younger employees, and less-educated employees. Since the 1980s an increasingly competitive global economy has served to narrow the union-nonunion wage differential.[125]

The data in Exhibit 7.7 present the union-nonunion wage differential by industry. A positive union wage advantage is present in every industry listed except professional/business services and finance/insurance. Unlike in Europe where narrower union-nonunion wage differences appear to foster more cooperative labor relations, there does not appear to be any significant lessening of employer opposition to unions in the United States, despite the narrowing wage gap. Perhaps this merely indicates that the gap has not narrowed sufficiently in the view of many employers to warrant a change in their labor relations philosophy. Unions also have a **spillover effect** on wages and benefits in nonunion companies. Union wage and benefit changes "spill over" into nonunion companies because nonunion employers who want to retain their nonunion status will respond to union wage increases by raising the wages of their employees.[126] Such increases are provided not only to reduce the threat of unions but to provide equity and maintain morale and productivity.

Exhibit 7.7

Union Versus Nonunion
Employee Median Weekly
Earnings, 2006

Industry	Union	Nonunion	Annual Union $ Advantage
Manufacturing	$755	$692	$3,120
Construction	969	610	18,668
Transportation and warehousing	831	661	8,840
Information	998	841	8,164
Wholesale trade	780	720	3,120
Retail trade	583	518	3,380
Health care and social assistance	703	614	4,628
Professional and business services	744	749	−260
Finance and insurance	657	799	−7,384
Public sector (federal, state, local)	871	717	8,008

Nonunion data include the earnings of managers and other salaried (nonbargaining unit) employees.

• Data for both union and nonunion groups exclude employer-paid benefits although union members typically enjoy an even greater advantage in fringe benefit comparisons (See data in Exhibit 7.6, on pg. 311.

SOURCE: U.S. Department of Labor, "Union Members in 2006," *News Release*, January 25, 2007, p. 10.

Summary

Economic issues include wages and a variety of economic benefits that make up what is commonly called the economic package. The negotiation of economic issues consumes a substantial amount of time, and outcomes on such issues affect both parties' satisfaction with the negotiation process. Wage differentials between jobs result from several industrial, occupational, and regional factors. Job evaluation is one method used to determine the worth of a job to an organization and helps to ensure internal wage equity among jobs in an organization. To attract and retain qualified employees, an employer must also maintain external equity between similar jobs in the organization and other organizations competing to hire such labor.

In addition to a base wage, some firms also provide either individual or group wage incentives as a means of tying employee job performance more closely to the attainment of organizational objectives. Negotiators use a variety of criteria to determine an acceptable wage structure. Commonly accepted criteria include differential features of jobs, comparable wages, ability to pay, productivity, and cost of living.

Because labor agreements usually are negotiated for periods greater than one year, provisions are commonly negotiated to adjust wages during the life of the contract. Such adjustments include a fixed cents-per-hour or percentage increase in base wages at specified time intervals and/or a cost-of-living adjustment (COLA), which adjusts wages in accordance with changes in the consumer price index at specified intervals during the contract's term. Another less common form of wage adjustment during the term of a contract is the wage reopener clause, which permits wages to be renegotiated at a predetermined time typically contingent on the occurrence of some specified event (e.g., sales or revenue target goal being achieved).

Employee benefits account for 38 percent of a unionized employer's payroll dollar. Numerous types of benefits exist. The major ones include insurance, income maintenance, premium pay, paid time off (e.g., rest period, lunch period, vacation, holiday), pensions, and legally required payments (e.g., Social Security, workers' and unemployment compensation). Employee demands to improve wages and benefits are being evaluated at the bargaining table in light of the impact such employer expenditures will likely have on a firm's ability to compete. Economic outcomes achieved in negotiations will vary across and within industries, reflecting the different operating environments unions and employers confront in today's global economy.

Key Terms

Degree of labor intensiveness, p. 293
Job evaluation, p. 294
Job analysis, p. 295
Profit-sharing plans, p. 298
Gain-sharing plan, p. 299
Scanlon plan, p. 299
Rucker plan, p. 299
Improshare plan, p. 299
Skill-based pay (SBP), p. 300
Wage spread, p. 301
Skill pay differential, p. 303
Two-tier pay plan, p. 303
Wage comparability, p. 304
Ability to pay, p. 305
Labor productivity, p. 306
Consumer Price Index (CPI), p. 309
Cost-of-living adjustment (COLA), p. 309
Deferred wage increase, p. 309
Wage re-opener, p. 309

Back-loaded, p. 310
Front-loaded, p. 310
Even-loaded, p. 310
Lump-sum pay, p. 311
Fee-for-service plans, p. 313
Preferred provider organization (PPO), p. 313
Health maintenance organization (HMO), p. 313
Consumer-directed health care plan, p. 313
Severance pay, p. 313
Supplemental unemployment benefit plan (SUB), p. 313
Work sharing, p. 314
Premium pay, p. 314
Shift differentials, p. 315
Reporting pay, p. 315
Call-in pay, p. 315
Defined benefit pension plan, p. 316

Defined contribution pension plan, p. 316
Employee stock ownership plan (ESOP), p. 317
Cash balance plan, p. 318
Pension Protection Act of 2006, p. 319
Employee Retirement Income Security Act (ERISA) of 1974, p. 319
Cliff vesting schedule, p. 319
Graded vesting schedule, p. 319
Family and Medical Leave Act (FMLA) of 1993, p. 319
Prepaid legal service plans, p. 320
Employee assistance plan (EAP), p. 321
Education tuition aid, p. 321
Transportation subsidy, p. 321
Home computer, p. 321
Child-care assistance, p. 321
Spillover effect, p. 321

Discussion Questions

1. List the main factors that may help to explain the wage differential between three jobs in an organization with which you are familiar.

2. Explain why job evaluation plans must take into consideration external and internal factors if they are to be successful.

3. Assume that labor and management are negotiating a labor agreement and the wage spread becomes an issue of disagreement—management wants a wider wage spread, and the union wants a smaller wage spread. Why should management be cautious about the union's proposal, even though the total costs may be the same?

4. For each of the wage criteria given in the chapter, state the union's expected arguments and management's expected counter-arguments, given the following conditions:

a. High profits, a growing firm, a healthy economy, and the cost of living rising at four percent per year.

b. Low profit, sales growth is stagnant, uncertain economic conditions, and the rise in cost of living is fluctuating by three to four percent each month.

5. Assuming that a firm's costs for employee benefits are 38 percent of payroll, why doesn't the firm just let the union determine the manner in which the amounts are apportioned to various benefits, such as insurance, holidays, and vacations, without negotiating each specific clause?

6. Which type of pension plan would you prefer to be covered under (i.e., defined benefit, defined contribution, or cash balance) and why if you were an employee? An employer?

7. To what extent can a union exploit benefit issues (e.g., health care insurance, pension, child-care benefits, and family leave) in an effort to organize more union members? Explain your reasoning.

8. What type of control should an employee have over shares issued under an employee stock ownership plan? For example, should an employee have a right to sell their plan shares at any time or vote

those shares in shareholder meetings to elect Board of Director candidates or approve a merger or bankruptcy plan?

9. Is early retirement (prior to age 62) still a realistic option for most employees to achieve without experiencing a substantial decline in their preretirement standard of living?

Exploring the Web

Economic Issues

1. Sources of Economic Data. It is important to know how to find information on economic indicators that affect wages and benefits. Using the Web site for the Bureau of Labor Statistics, answer the following questions.

What was the annual inflation rate at the end of 2006? (Remember that the inflation rate is the percent change in the Consumer Price Index over a specific period of time.)

During the first quarter of 2007, what were the median weekly earnings for males aged 25 and over?

Locate the Economic Report of the President to answer these questions and use the link for statistical tables to answer the following questions. What was the civilian unemployment rate in 2006 for all civilian workers? What was the exchange rate, in U.S. dollars, for the euro in the fourth quarter of 2006?

2. Comparable Worth. Deborah Walker, a research fellow at the Center for the Study of Market Processes at George Mason University, presents an argument against comparable worth policies in an article published on the Cato Institute Web site. The Cato Institute is a nonpartisan public policy research foundation. The article is "Value and Opportunity: The Issue of Comparable Pay for

Comparable Worth." Find the article and comment on Deborah Walker's suggested alternative.

What is the American Federation of State, County, and Municipal Employees (AFSCME) doing in the areas of pay equity for women? See "We're Worth It" on the AFSCME Web site.

3. NCS and OPR. Find the latest National Compensation Survey (NCS) published by the U.S. Department of Labor. What is the Employment Cost Index and when and why was it developed? In March 2007, what was the figure for the average employer costs for employee compensation per hour worked. What percentage of this amount accounted for employee benefits?

Locate the Occupational Pay Relatives (OPR). What data are used to calculate the pay relatives? Are construction workers in Brownsville, Texas, paid more or less than the national average?

4. Gain Sharing. Locate a working paper, "Productivity Gainsharing" by C. Bernolak on the Web site of the International Labour Organization and scan down to Chapter 3. Define "gain sharing" and discuss the histories and differences in the four basic types: Scanlon Plan, Rucker Plan, Improshare, and profit sharing.

References

1. Mary William Walsh, "Boom Time a Bad Time for Poorest, Study Finds; Economy: New Worth Rose for Middle-Income Families, but Lowest Earners Were Worse Off, a Federal Survey Says," *The Los Angeles Times*, January 19, 2000, p. 1; Albert B. Crenshaw, "Net Worth of U.S. Families Up Sharply; Stock Surge Spurred 17.6 percent Gain for 'Typical' Household from '95 to '98," *The Washington Post*, January 19, 2000, p. E-1.

2. Greg Ip, "Not Your Father's Pay: Why Wages Today Are Weaker," *The Wall Street Journal*, May 25, 2007, p. A-2; Eileen Appelbaum, "Economic Challenges Facing the Middle Class," Testimony before the House Education and Labor Committee, *Congressional Quarterly*, January 31, 2007, pp. 1–8 at http://web.lexis-nexis.com.

3. Mortimer B. Zuckerman, "So Where Are All the Jobs?" *U.S. News & World Report* 135 (September 22, 2003), p. 86.

4. Justin Fox and Anna Bernasek, "Things Are Looking Up—Unless You Want a Job: This Economic Recovery Is Different and That Has a Lot of People Worried. Should They Be?" *Fortune,* 148 (September 29, 2003), p. 73; James C. Cooper and Kathleen Madigan, "A Jobs Recovery, Yes. A Hiring Boom, No. Intense Cost Pressures and Weak Pricing Will Keep Payrolls from Surging," *BusinessWeek,* October 20, 2003, p. 33; Jared Bernstein, "The Young and the Jobless: Why Those New to the Workforce Stand to Lose the Most," *The American Prospect* 14 (October, 2003), pp. A17–19.

5. Susan Jackson and Randall S. Schuler, *Managing Human Resources through Strategic Partnerships* 8th ed. (Mason, OH: South-Western, 2003), pp. 416–445; John W. Budd, "Union Wage Determination in Canadian and U.S. Manufacturing," *Industrial and Labor Relations Review* 49 (July, 1996), pp. 673–690; Jules Bachman, *Wage Determination: An Analysis of Wage Criteria* (Princeton, NJ: D. Van Nostrand, 1959), pp. 1–21.

6. Bachman, Wage Determination: An Analysis of Wage Criteria, p. 58.

7. For further reference, see Thomas Bergmann and Vida Scarpello, *Compensation Decision Making,* 4th ed. (Mason, OH: South-Western, 2001); George T. Milkovich and Jerry M. Newman, *Compensation,* 6th ed. (Boston: Irwin McGraw-Hill, 1999).

8. Roger J. Plachy and Sandra J. Plachy, *Building A Fair Pay Program,* 2nd ed. (New York: American Management Association, 1998), pp. 124–210; David W. Belcher, "Wage and Salary Administration," in *Motivation and Commitment,* eds. Dale Yoder and H. G. Heneman, Jr. (Washington, D.C.: Bureau of National Affairs, Inc., 1975), pp. 6–95.

9. Edward E. Lawler III, *Rewarding Excellence: Pay Strategies for the New Economy* (San Francisco: Jossey-Bass Inc., 2000), pp. 116–119.

10. For a review of alternative methods, see Robert L. Heneman, "Job and Work Evaluation: A Literature Review," in *Strategic Reward Management: Design, Implementation, and Evaluation* (Greenwich, CT: Information Age Publishing, 2002), pp. 275–301.

11. Harold D. Janes, "Issues in Job Evaluation: The Union View," *Personnel Journal* 51 (September 1972), p. 675; see also Research Department, International Association of Machinists, *What's Wrong with Job Evaluation?* (Washington, D.C.: International Association of Machinists, 1954).

12. Harold D. Janes, "Comparative Issues in Job Evaluation: The Union View, 1971–1978," *Personnel Journal* 58 (February 1979), pp. 80–85.

13. David Belcher and Thomas J. Atchison, *Compensation Administration,* 2nd ed. (Englewood Cliffs, N.J.: Prentice-Hall, 1987), pp. 154–155.

14. David Barcellos, "The Reality and Promise of Market-Based Pay," *Employment Relations Today,* 32 (1), Spring 2005, pp. 1–10.

15. Belcher and Atchison, *Compensation Administration,* pp. 107–124.

16. U.S. Bureau of Labor Statistics, *National Compensation Survey: Occupational Wages in the United States, June 2005,* Bulletin 2581, August 2006 at http://www.bls.gov/ncs/ocs/sp/ncbl0832.pdf and U.S. Bureau of Labor Statistics, "Occupational Pay Relatives, 2005", *News Release,* September 28, 2006 at http://www.bls.gov/ncs/ocs/home.htm.

17. Royal J. Dossett, "Work-Measured Labor Standards—The State of the Art," *Industrial Engineering* 24 (April 1995), pp. 21–25.

18. "Return of the Stopwatch," *The Economist* 326 (January 1, 1993), p. 69; Herbert G. Zollitsch, "Productivity, Time Studies and Incentive-Pay Plans," in *Motivation and Commitment,* eds. Dale Yoder and H. G. Heneman, Jr. (Washington, D.C.: Bureau of National Affairs, Inc., 1975), pp. 6–61.

19. Heather M. McGee, Alyce M. Dickinson, Bradley E. Huitema, and Kathryn M. Culig, "The Effects of Individual and Group Monetary Incentives on High Performance," *Performance Improvement Quarterly,* 19 (4), 2006, p. 107 and Gerald E. Ledford, Jr., and Edward E. Lawler III, "Reward Innovations in Fortune 1000 Companies," *Compensation and Benefits Review* 27 (July/August 1995), pp. 76–80.

20. The Bureau of National Affairs, Inc., "2007 Employer Bargaining Objectives," *Collective Bargaining Bulletin* 12 (February 1, 2007), p. S-13.

21. Woodruff Imberman, "Gainsharing: A Lemon or Lemonade?" *Business Horizons* 39 (Jan.–Feb. 1996), pp. 36–40; Adrienne E. Eaton and Paula B. Voos, "Unions and Contemporary Innovation in Work Organization, Compensation, and Employee Participation," in *Unions and Economic Competitiveness* (Armonk, N.Y.: M. E. Sharpe, Inc., 1992), pp. 176–177.

22. Robert J. Paul, Brian P. Niehoff, and William H. Turnley, "Empowerment, Expectations, and the Psychological Contract—Managing the Dilemmas and Gaining the Advantages," *Journal of Social Economics* 29 (2000), pp. 471–485; Peter V. LeBlanc and Paul W. Mulvey, "How American Workers See the Rewards of Work," *Compensation and Benefits Review,* 30 (January/February 1998), pp. 24–28.

23. "Sharing the Spoils," *The Economist* 341 (November 30, 1996), p. 80; Edward M. Coates III, "Profit Sharing Today: Plans and Provisions," *Monthly Labor Review* 114 (April 1991), pp. 19–25.

24. Michel Magnan, Sylvie St.-Onge, and Denis Cormier, "The Adoption and Success of Profit-Sharing Plans in Strategic Business Units," *International Journal of Productivity and Performance Management,* 54 (5/6), 2005, p. 356.

25. Daryl D'Art and Thomas Turner, "Profit Sharing, Firm Performance and Union Influence in Selected European Countries," *Personnel Review,* 33 (3), 2004, pp. 338–339 and John Zalusky, "Labor's Collective Bargaining Experience with Gainsharing and Profit Sharing," *Proceedings of the 39th Annual Meeting of the Industrial Relations Research Association* (Madison, Wis.: Industrial Relations Research Association, 1987), pp. 177–178.

26. Joe Guy Collier, "Autoworkers Take More Hits," *Detroit Free Press,* February 8, 2006, pp. 1–2 at http://www.freep.com.

27. Michel Magnan, Sylvie St.-Onge, and Denis Cormier, "The Adoption and Success of Profit-Sharing Plans in Strategic Business Units," pp. 362–363 and "Potential Dangers in Expansion of Current Auto Profit Sharing Plans Cited by Attorney," *Daily Labor Report*, March 24, 1982, p. C-1.

28. Timothy L. Ross and Ruth Ann Ross, "Gainsharing and Unions: Current Trends," in *Gainsharing and Employee Involvement*, ed. by Brian Graham-Moore and Timothy L. Ross (Washington, D.C.: The Bureau of National Affairs, Inc., 1995), pp. 179–191.

29. Timothy L. Ross and Ruth Ann Ross, "Gain Sharing: Improved Performance," in *The Compensation Handbook*, ed. by Lance A. Berger and Dorothy R. Berger (New York: McGraw Hill, 2000), pp. 227–240; Theresa M. Welbourne and Luis R. Gomez Mejia, "Gainsharing: A Critical Review and a Future Research Agenda," *Journal of Management* 21, no. 3 (1995), pp. 562–564; J. Kenneth White, "The Scanlon Plan: Causes and Correlates of Success," *Academy of Management Journal* 22 (June 1979), pp. 292–312.

30. Welbourne and Gomez Mejia, "Gainsharing: A Critical Review," p. 563.

31. Mitchell Fein, "Improshare: Sharing Productivity Gains with Employees," in *The Compensation Handbook*, ed. by Lance A. Berger and Dorothy R. Berger (New York: McGraw Hill, 2000), pp. 217–226.

32. Mitchell Fein, "Improved Productivity through Workers' Involvement," *Hearings before the Subcommittee on General Oversight of the Committee on Small Business* (Washington, D.C.: U.S. Government Printing Office, 1982), pp. 118–123.

33. Roger T. Kaufman, "The Effects of IMPROSHARE on Productivity," *Industrial and Labor Relations Review* 45 (January 1992), pp. 311–315.

34. Matthew H. Roy and Sanjiv S. Dugal, "Using Employee Gainsharing Plans to Improve Organizational Effectiveness," *Benchmarking*, 12 (3), 2005, pp. 250–259; Roger T. Kaufman and Raymond Russell, "Government Support for Profit Sharing, Gainsharing, ESOPs, and TQM," *Contemporary Economic Policy* 13 (April 1995), pp. 38–39.

35. Glenn Dalton, Jennifer Stevens, and Robert Heneman, "Alternative Rewards in Union Settings," in *Strategic Reward Management: Design, Implementation, and Evaluation* (Greenwich, CT: Information Age Publishing, 2002), pp. 153–161; Glenn Dalton, "The Glass Wall: Shattering the Myth That Alternative Rewards Won't Work with Unions," *Compensation and Benefits Review* 30 (November/December 1998), pp. 38–45; Douglas P. O'Bannon and Craig L. Pearce, "An Exploratory Examination of Gainsharing in Service Organizations: Implications for Organizational Citizenship Behavior and Pay Satisfaction," *Journal of Managerial Issues* 11 (Fall 1999), pp. 363–378.

36. James H. Dulebohn and Joseph J. Martocchio, "Employee Perceptions of the Fairness of Work Group Incentive Pay Plans," *Journal of Management* 24 (July–August 1998), pp. 469–488.

37. William N. Cooke, "Employee Participation Programs, Group-Based Incentives, and Company Performance: A Union-Nonunion Comparison," *Industrial and Labor Relations Review* 47 (July 1994), pp. 594–608.

38. Gerald E. Ledford, Jr. and Robert L. Heneman, "Pay for Skills, Knowledge, and Competencies," in *Strategic Reward Management: Design, Implementation, and Evaluation* (Greenwich, CT: Information Age Publishing, 2002), pp. 409–423.

39. Ledford, Jr., and Lawler III, "Reward Innovations in Fortune 1000 Companies," pp. 76–80.

40. Brian Muray and Barry Gerhart, "An Empirical Analysis of a Skill-Based Pay Program and Plant Performance Outcomes," *Academy of Management Journal* 41 (February 1998), pp. 68–78.

41. Kenneth Mericle and Dong-One Kim, "From Job-Based Pay to Skill-Based Pay in Unionized Establishments: A Three-Plant Comparative Analysis," *Relations Industrielles* 54 (Summer 1999), pp. 549–578.

42. Irving Bernstein, *Arbitration of Wages* (Berkeley: University of California, 1954), pp. 26–27; Craig Overton, "Criteria in Grievance and Interest Arbitration in the Public Sector," *Arbitration Journal* 28 (1973), pp. 159–166; Howard S. Block, "Criteria in Public Sector Interest Disputes," in *Arbitration and the Public Interest*, eds. G. G. Somers and B. D. Dennis (Washington, D.C.: Bureau of National Affairs, Inc., 1971), pp. 161–193.

43. Richard B. Freeman, "Union Wage Practices and Wage Dispersions within Establishments," *Industrial and Labor Relations Review* 36 (October 1982), pp. 3–21.

44. The Bureau of National Affairs, Inc., "2007 Employer Bargaining Objectives," p. S-13.

45. Katie Merx and Jewel Gopwani, "Delphi Workers Get Choices," *Detroit Free Press*, June 24, 2007, pp. 1–2 at http://www.freep.com, Julie M. McKinnon, "Auto Union to Consider Two-Tiered Wage Structure," *The Blade*, September 25, 2003, pp. 1–2; Joann Muller, "You Sure I Agreed to That?" *Forbes* 172 (October 27, 2003), p. 66.

46. Avrum D. Lank, "Harley Union Members Approve Deal: Company Will Expand Here with Two-tier Wages," *Knight Ridder Tribune Business News*, November 15, 2006, pp. 1–2 at http://proquest.umi.com/pqdweb?did=1162295381& sid=1& Fmit=3&clientid=1997& RQT=309VName=PQD.

47. Lou Hirsh, "Grocers, Union Still Negotiating Contract Issues," *Knight Ridder Tribune Business News*, June 5, 2007, pp. 1–2 at http://proquest.umi.com/pqdweb?did=1282329961&sid=1&Fmit=3&clientid=1997&RQT=309&VName=PQD; Carey W. English, "Two-Tier Pay Stirs Backlash among Workers," *U.S. News and World Report*, September 23, 1985, p. 61; and "IRRA Panelists Address the Two-Tier Implications for Fair Representation and Equal Opportunity," *Daily Labor Report*, January 10, 1985, pp. A 5–7.

48. Daniel J. B. Mitchell, "Two-Tier Compensation Structures: Their Impact on Unions, Employers, and Employees," *Industrial and Labor Relations Review* 45 (July 1992), pp. 814–815; James E. Martin and Melanie M. Peterson, "Two-Tier Wage Structures and Attitude Differences" in *Proceedings of the Thirty-Eighth Annual Meeting: Industrial Relations Research Association*, ed. B. D. Dennis (Madison, Wis.: Industrial Relations Research Association, 1986), pp. 78–79.

49. Frederick W. Cook, "Compensation Surveys Are Biased," *Compensation and Benefits Review* 26 (September–October 1994), pp. 19–22.

50. Sumner Slichter, *Basic Criteria Used in Wage Negotiation* (Chicago: Chicago Association of Commerce and Industry, January 30, 1947), p. 25.

51. Bachman, Wage Determination: An Analysis of Wage Criteria, pp. 251–258.

52. U.S. Bureau of Labor Statistics, "Productivity and Costs, First Quarter 2007, Revised," *News Release,* June 6, 2007, p. 5.

53. See for example: "The 'New Economy'—American Productivity," *The Economist* 368 (September 13, 2003), p. 62; Aaron E. Cobet and Gregory A. Wilson, "Comparing 50 Years of Labor Productivity in the U.S. and Foreign Manufacturing," *Monthly Labor Review* 125 (June, 2002), pp. 51–65.

54. Anne Marie Squeo, "Safe Harbor: How Longshoremen Keep Global Wind at Their Backs," *The Wall Street Journal,* July 26, 2006, pp. A1, A12; Aaron Bernstein, "Productivity—Not Pay Cuts—Will Keep Union Members Working," *BusinessWeek,* August 25, 1986, p. 32.

55. Madeline Zavodny, "Unions and the Wage-Productivity Gap," *Economic Review—Federal Reserve Bank of Atlanta* 84 (Second Quarter 1999), pp. 44–53; Thomas J. Volgy, John E. Schwarz and Lawrence E. Imwalle, "In Search of Economic Well-Being: Worker Power and the Effects of Productivity, Inflation, Unemployment and Global Trade on Wages in Ten Wealthy Countries," *American Journal of Political Science* 40 (November 1996), pp. 1233–1252.

56. Jeffrey B. Arthur and Linda Aiman-Smith, "Gainsharing and Organizational Learning: An Analysis of Employee Suggestions Over Time," *Academy of Management Journal* 44 (August 2001), p. 737.

57. Dong-One Kim, "The Benefits and Cost of Employee Suggestions under Gainsharing," *Industrial and Labor Relations Review,* 58 (4), July 2005, pp. 631–652; Omar Azfar and Stephan Danninger, "Profit-Sharing, Employment Stability, and Wage Growth," *Industrial and Labor Relations Review* 54 (April 2001), pp. 619–630; General Accounting Office, *Productivity Sharing Programs: Can They Contribute to Productivity Improvement?* (Washington, D.C.: U.S. Government Printing Office, 1981).

58. Woodruff Imberman, "Gainsharing: A Lemon or Lemonade?" *Business Horizons,* 39 (1), Jan/Feb. 1996, p. 38.

59. Jerome Rosow, "Productivity and the Blue-Collar Blues," *Personnel* 48 (March–April 1971), pp. 8–10.

60. William N. Cooke, "Employee Participation Programs, Group-Based Incentives, and Company Performance: A Union-Nonunion Comparison," *Industrial and Labor Relations Review* 47 (July 1994), pp. 594–609.

61. William F. Maloney, "Productivity Bargaining in Contract Construction," *Proceedings of the 1977 Annual Spring Meeting: Industrial Relations Research Association* (Madison, Wis.: Industrial Relations Research Association, 1977), pp. 533–534.

62. Robert J. Flanagan, "The Economics of Unions and Collective Bargaining," *Industrial Relations* 29 (Spring 1990), pp. 300–304; William W. Winpisinger, "Output:

Collective Bargaining and Productivity," in *Collective Bargaining: New Dimensions in Labor Relations,* ed. F. J. Havelich (Boulder, Colo.: Westview Press, 1979), pp. 25–28.

63. Maryellen R. Kelley and Bennett Harrison, "Unions, Technology and Labor-Management Cooperation," in *Unions and Economic Competitiveness,* eds. Lawrence Mishel and Paula B. Voos (Armonk, N.Y.: M. E. Sharp, Inc., 1992), pp. 247–250; Jacob Mincer, "Union Effects: Wages, Turnover, and Job Training," *Working Paper Series* (Cambridge, Mass.: National Bureau of Economic Research Inc., 1985), p. 42.

64. Michael H. Small and Mahmoud Yasin, "Human Factors in the Adoption and Performance of Advanced Manufacturing Technology in Unionized Firms," *Industrial Management + Data Systems* 100, no. 8 (2000), p. 389.

65. Susan McDowell and William Lesser, "The Effect of Unions on Productivity: An Analysis of the Cattle Kill Floor," *Agribusiness* 3 (Fall 1987), pp. 273–280; Ronald S. Warren, Jr., "The Effect of Unionization on Labor Productivity: Some Time-Series Evidence," *Journal of Labor Research* 6 (Spring 1985), p. 199; Charles Brown and James Medoff, "Trade Unions in the Production Process," *Journal of Political Economy* 86 (June 1980), pp. 355–359.

66. Hristos Douculiagos, Patrice Laroche, and T. D. Stanley, "Publication Bias in Union-Productivity Research?" *Relations Industrielles,* 60 (2), Spring 2005, pp. 320–344; Brian Chezum and John E. Garen, "Are Union Productivity Effects Overestimated? Evidence from Coal Mining," *Applied Economics* 30 (July 1998), pp. 913–918; Merwin W. Mitchell and Joe A. Stone, "Union Effects on Productivity: Evidence from Western Saw Mills," *Industrial and Labor Relations Review* 46 (October 1992), pp. 135–145; J. T. Addison and A. H. Barnett, "The Impact of Unions on Productivity," *British Journal of Industrial Relations* 20 (July 1982), pp. 145–149; John T. Addison, "Are Unions Good for Productivity?" *Journal of Labor Research* 3 (Spring 1982), p. 137; Robert S. Kaufman and Roger T. Kaufman, "Union Effects on Productivity, Personnel Practices, and Survival in the Automotive Parts Industry," *Journal of Labor Research* 8 (Fall 1987), pp. 332–349.

67. "Union Productivity Effects" *Monthly Labor Review* 108 (January 1985), p. 60; Richard B. Freeman and James L. Medoff, *What Do Unions Do?* (New York: Basic Books, Inc., 1984), pp. 162–190.

68. David A. Dilts, "The Consumer Price Index as a Standard in Negotiations and Arbitration," *Journal of Collective Negotiations in the Public Sector* 23, no. 4 (1994), pp. 279–285.

69. David S. Johnson, Stephen B. Reed, and Kenneth J. Stewart, "Price Measurement in the United States: A Decade After the Boskin Report," *Monthly Labor Review,* 129 (5), May 2006, pp. 10–19; John J. Greenlees and Charles C. Mason, "Overview of the 1998 Revision of the Consumer Price Index," *Monthly Labor Review* 119 (December 1996), pp. 3–9; Brent R. Moulton, "Basic Components of the CPI: Estimation of Price Changes," *Monthly Labor Review* 116 (December 1993), pp. 13–24; Alan B. Krueger and Aaron Siskind, "Using Survey Data

to Assess Bias in the Consumer Price Index," *Monthly Labor Review*, 121 (April 1998), pp. 24–33.

70. U.S. Bureau of Labor Statistics, "Consumer Price Index: May 2007," *News Release*, June 15, 2007, p. 1.

71. The Bureau of National Affairs, Inc., "Average Wage Increase of 3.3 Percent Reported in 2006," *Collective Bargaining Bulletin*, January 4, 2007, p. 4.

72. The Bureau of National Affairs, Inc., "2007 Employer Bargaining Objectives," p. S-13.

73. The Bureau of National Affairs, Inc., "2007 Employer Bargaining Objectives," p. S-12.

74. The Bureau of National Affairs, Inc., "Frequency of Lump-Sum Payments Declined in 2005 Contracts," *Collective Bargaining Bulletin*, February 16, 2006, pp. 21–22.

75. U.S. Bureau of Labor Statistics, "Employer Costs For Employee Compensation—March 2007," *News Release*, June 21, 2007, p. 11.

76. The Bureau of National Affairs, Inc., "2007 Employer Bargaining Objectives," pp. S-15–S-24.

77. Joshua Partlow, "Health Care a Growing Issue in Labor Talks," *The Washington Post*, June 18, 2003, p. E2; "Rising Health Care Costs Posing Challenges for Unions at the Bargaining Table," *The Labor Relations Research Association Online*, December 19, 2002, pp. 1–3.

78. "Healthcare Costs: More People in the U.S. are Dealing with the Financial Burden of Health Care Costs," *Health Insurance Week*, January 7, 2007, p. 37.

79. Vanesa Fuhrmans, "Health-Care Premiums Climb by 7.7 percent, Outstripping Inflation," *The Wall Street Journal*, September 27, 2006, p. A-2; Kathleen Day, "Health Insurance Rises Twice Rate of Inflation," *The Washington Post*, September 26, 2006, pp. 1–2 at http://www.washingtonpost.com.

80. The Bureau of National Affairs, Inc., "2007 Employer Bargaining Objectives," p. S-17.

81. The Bureau of National Affairs, Inc., "2007 Employer Bargaining Objectives," p. S-20.

82. Vanessa Fuhrmans, "Health Savings Plans Start to Falter; Despite Employer Enthusiasm for Consumer-Directed Approach, Patients Express Dissatisfaction with How the Accounts Work," *The Wall Street Journal*, July 2, 2007, p. D-1.

83. The Bureau of National Affairs, Inc., "2007 Employer Bargaining Objectives," p. S-25; Cristina Pita, "Advance Notice and Severance Pay Provisions in Contracts," *Monthly Labor Review* 119 (July 1996), pp. 43–50.

84. David DeKok, "Workers Advised to Weigh Benefits," *Knight Ridder Tribune Business News*, March 30, 2007, p. 1; Christina Salerno, "Hershey Workers to Receive Severance: Employees 55 and Older Will Keep Medical Benefits," *Knight Ridder Tribune Business News*, May 5, 2007, p. 1.

85. David Sherwyn and Michael C. Sturman, "Job Sharing: A Potential Tool for Hotel Managers," *Cornell Hotel and Restaurant Administration Quarterly*, 43 (5), October 2002, pp. 84–91; Joni McCollum and Cheryl Rice, "Use Partner Pairing to Boost Performance," *Nursing Management*, 34 (9), 2003, p. 14; Michael Huberman, "An Economic and Business History of Worksharing: The Bell Canada and Volkswagen Experiences," *Business and Economic History*, 26 (2), Winter 1997, pp. 404–415.

86. The Bureau of National Affairs, Inc., "2007 Employer Bargaining Objectives," p. S-23.

87. U.S. Bureau of Labor Statistics, *National Compensation Survey: Employee Benefits in Private Industry in the United States, March 2006* (Washington D.C.: U.S. Government Printing Office, 2006), p. 25.

88. Diane Stafford, "The Kansas City Star, MO., Workplace Column," *Knight Ridder Tribune Business News*, August 21, 2003, p. 1; "U.S. Short on Vacation Time," *The San Francisco Chronicle*, July 16, 1999, p. B4.

89. Joel Dresang, "Americans Get Less Time Off and Don't Use Up What They Get," *Knight Ridder Tribune Business News*, August 14, 2005, p. 1.

90. U.S. Bureau of Labor Statistics, National Compensation Survey: Employee Benefits in Private Industry in the United States, March 2006, p. 26.

91. National Center for Health Statistics, "Life Expectancy Hits Record High," *News Release*, February 28, 2005, pp. 1–2.

92. U.S. Bureau of Labor Statistics, National Compensation Survey: Employee Benefits in Private Industry in the United States, March 2006, p. 6.

93. Richard B. Freeman, "Unions, Pensions, and Union Pension Funds," *Working Paper Series* (Cambridge, Mass.: National Bureau of Economic Research Inc., 1983), p. 50.

94. *Ohio Public Employees Retirement System v. Betts*, 492 U.S. 158 (1989).

95. The Bureau of National Affairs, Inc., "2007 Employer Bargaining Objectives," p. S-21 and "Unions and Workers Often at Odds over Negotiation of 401(k)s," *Collective Bargaining Bulletin* 4 (December 30, 1999), p. 156.

96. Arleen Jacobius, "More Plan Sponsors Do Away with 401 (k) Match," *Pensions & Investments* 31 (August 18, 2003), p. 4.

97. Patrick P. McHugh, Joel Cutcher-Gershenfeld, and Michael Polzin, "Employee Stock Ownership Plans: Whose Interests Do They Serve?" *Proceedings of the 49th Annual Meeting of the Industrial Relations Research Association* (Madison, Wis.: Industrial Relations Research Association, 1997), pp. 23–32; Roger G. McElrath and Richard L. Rowan, "The American Labor Movement and Employee Ownership: Objections to and Uses of Employee Stock Ownership Plans," *Journal of Labor Research* 13 (Winter 1992), pp. 99–103.

98. James J. Choi, David Laibson, and Brigitte C. Madrian, "Are Empowerment and Education Enough? Underdiversification in 401k Plans," *Brookings Papers on Economic Activity*, 2005, pp. 151–213.

99. Joseph R. Blasi, Employee Ownership through ESOPs: Implication for the Public Corporation (New York: Pergamon Press, 1987), pp. 29–30.

100. Joseph Blasi, Michael Conte, and Douglas Kruse, "Employee Stock Ownership and Corporate Performance among Public Companies," *Industrial and Labor Relations Review* 50 (October 1996), pp. 60–79; Blasi, *Employee Ownership through ESOPs*, 1987, pp. 40–44.

101. Albert A. Okunade, "The Failing Pension System in the U.S. Private Sector: Have We Seen the Worst Yet?" *Business Perspectives*, 18 (2), Fall 2006, p. 10 and U.S. Bureau of Labor Statistics, *National Compensation*

Survey: Employee Benefits in Private Industry in the United States, March 2006, p. 7.

102. Charles Steindel, "How Worrisome Is a Negative Saving Rate?" *Current Issues in Economics and Finance,* 13 (4), May 2007, pp. 1–7; Christian E. Weller, "Need or Want: What Explains the Run-up in Consumer Debt?" *Journal of Economic Issues,* 41 (2), June 2007, pp. 583–591; and U.S. Department of Labor, "The State of Retirement Savings," *Saving for Your Golden Years: Trends, Challenges and Opportunities* (Washington, D.C.: March 1–2, 2006), p. 3.

103. Tom Groenfeldt, "Overcoming Underfunding," *Institutional Investor,* September 2006, pp. 1–3; James B. Davis, "The Pension Plan Crisis: Municipalities and Private Companies Share Woes," *Compensation and Benefits Review,* 38 (4), July/August 2006, pp. 52–56.

104. U.S. Department of Labor, *Types of Retirement Plans," Retirement Plans, Benefits & Savings,* December 14, 2003, pp. 1–4 at http://www.dol.gov/topic/retirement/typesofplans.htm; U.S. Department of Labor, *Frequently Asked Questions about Cash Balance Pension Plans,* December 14, 2003, pp. 1–2 at http://www.dol.gov.ebsa/FAQs/faq_compliance_cashbalanceplans.html; U.S. Department of Labor, *Fact Sheet: Cash Balance Pension Plans,* May 2003, pp. 1–9.

105. Curt Anderson, "Congress, Feds Examine Pension Plan," *Associated Press,* September 22, 1999, pp. 1–3 at http://www.washingtonpost.com/wp-srv/aponline/19990922/aponline 023454_000.htm.

106. Kathleen Day, "IBM Workers Continue to Fight Pension Changes," *The Washington Post,* April 18, 2001, p. E1; Albert B. Crenshaw, "Cash Balance Pension Plans Fall under Scrutiny," *The Washington Post,* September 21, 1999, p. E1; and Mike Hudson, "Pension Plans Spark Outrage," *Detroit Free Press,* September 22, 1999, pp. 1–3 at http://www.freep.com/business/qretire22.htm.

107. Richard J. Bottelli, Jr., "Born Again: Cash Balance Plans Get New Lease on Life with Latest Rulings, Pension Reform 2006 Legislation," *Benefits Quarterly,* 23 (1), 2007, pp. 28–33; *Cooper v. IBM,* 457 F.3d 636 (7th Cir. 2006); and Ellen E. Schultz and Theo Francis, "IBM Ruling Paves Way for Changes to Pensions," *The Wall Street Journal,* August 8, 2006, p. A-3.

108. Joint Committee on Taxation, *Technical Explanation of H.R. 4, The "Pension Protection Act of 2006,"* As Passed by the House on July 28, 2006 and as considered by the Senate on August 3, 2006, (JCX-38-06), August 3, 2006, pp. 233–234 and Mark J. Warshawsky, "The New Pension Law and Defined Benefit Plans: A Surprisingly Good Match," *Journal of Pension Benefits,* 14 (3), Spring 2007, pp. 14–27.

109. U.S. Department of Labor, *Compliance Assistance: The Family Medical and Leave Act,* December 15, 2003, pp. 1–11 at http://www.dol.gov/esa/regs/compliance/whd/1421.htm; Jane Waldfogel, "Family Leave Coverage in the 1990s," *Monthly Labor Review* 122 (October 1999), pp. 13–21; Tim Barnett, Winston N. McVea, Jr., and Patricia A. Lanier, "An Overview of the Family and Medical Leave Act of 1993," *Labor Law Journal* 44 (July 1993), pp. 429–433.

110. Jane Waldfogel, "Family and Medical Leave: Evidence from the 2000 Surveys," *Monthly Labor Review,* 124 (9), September 2001, pp. 17–23.

111. Charles L. Baum II, "The Effects of Government-Mandated Family Leave on Employer Family Leave Policies," *Contemporary Economic Policy,* 24 (3), July 2006, pp. 432–445 and Michael Prince, "FMLA Hasn't Been a Big Burden for Employers," *Business Insurance* 37 (September 29, 2003), pp. 1–4.

112. David Cantor, Jane Waldfogel, et. al., Balancing the Needs of Families and Employers: The Family Medical Leave Surveys, 2000 Update (Rockville, MD: Westat, 2000).

113. National Partnership for Women & Families, "America Celebrates Ten-Year Anniversary of the Family & Medical Leave Act," *Press Release,* August 5, 2003, pp. 1–2.

114. Lisa M. Cal and Brian H. Kleiner, "California's Recent Paid Family Leave Law," *Equal Opportunities International,* 24 (5/6), 2005, pp. 65–78; "California Authorizes Partially Paid Family and Medical Leave," *HR Focus* 79 (November 2002), p. 8.

115. Kenza Bemis Nelson, "Employer Difficulty in FMLA Implementation: A Look at Eighth Circuit Interpretation of 'Serious Health Condition' and Employee Notice Requirements," *Journal of Corporation Law,* 30 (3), Spring 2005, pp. 609–625; Margaret M. Clark, "FMLA Anniversary Events Focus on Workplace Flexibility Options," *HRMagazine* 48 (March 2003), p. 30; David L. Hudson, Jr., "Changing Act," *ABA Journal* 89 (September 2003), p. 15; Sheng Hengst and Brian H. Kleiner, "Implications of the Family and Medical Leave Act for Organizations," *Managerial Law* 44 (Number 1/2 2002), pp. 9–15.

116. David Cantor, Jane Waldfogel, et. al., Balancing the Needs of Families and Employers: The Family and Medical Leave Surveys, 2000 Update, 2000, Chapter 5.

117. AFL-CIO Working Women's Department, *Bargaining Fact Sheet: Family Leave and Expanding the Family and Medical Leave Act* (Washington, D.C.: AFL-CIO, 2001), pp. 1–4; Frederick L. Douglas, "Collective Bargaining under the Family and Medical Leave Act," *Labor Law Journal* 45 (February 1994), pp. 102–105.

118. Scott Smith, "Prepaid Legal Services Catching On: Plans Offer Low Cost Access to a Lawyer, but Experts Advise Caution," *Knight Ridder Tribune Business News,* February 12, 2007, p. 1; Ryan Mahoney, "Prepaid Legal Insurance Plans: Justice For All?" *Birmingham Business Journal* 20 (January 17, 2003), pp. 1–3; Charlotte Garvey, "Access to the Law," *HRMagazine* 47 (September 2002), pp. 82–92.

119. The Bureau of National Affairs, Inc., "2007 Employer Bargaining Objectives," p. S-24.

120. Fonda Phillips, "Employee Assistance Programs: A New Way to Control Health Care Costs," *Employee Benefit Plan Review* 58 (August 2003), pp. 22–24.

121. The Bureau of National Affairs, Inc., "2007 Employer Bargaining Objectives," p. S-24 and Cynthia J. Guffey, Judy F. West, and Charles S. White, "Employer Educational Assistance: An Assessment of the Impact on

Organizational Commitment," *Management Research News* 20 (1), 1997, pp. 12–30.

122. Amy Joyce, "Majority of Large Firms Offer Employees Domestic Partner Benefits," *The Washington Post,* June 30, 2006, p. D-3.

123. The Bureau of National Affairs, Inc., "2007 Employer Bargaining Objectives," p. S-24.

124. Greg Lewis, *Unionism and Relative Wages in the United States* (Chicago: University of Chicago Press, 1963).

125. David Neumark and Michael L. Wachter, "Union Effects on Nonunion Wages: Evidence from Panel Data on Industries and Cities," *Industrial and Labor Relations Review* 49 (October 1995), pp. 20–38; Richard B. Freeman and James L. Medoff, "The Impact of Collective Bargaining: Illusion or Reality," in *U.S. Industrial Relations 1950–1980: A Critical Assessment,* eds. Jack Stieber et al. (Madison, Wis.: Industrial Relations Research Association, 1981), pp. 53–54.

126. Susan Vroman, "The Direction of Wage Spillovers in Manufacturing," *Industrial and Labor Relations Review* 36 (October 1982), pp. 102–103.

Achieving a Competitive Wage Structure

CASE STUDY 7-1 In March 2007, the second largest retail consumer electronics company, Circuit City, announced a plan to terminate 3,400 employees out of an in-store work force of 40,000 (nine percent) in order to cut labor costs. The company stated the dismissals had nothing to do with individual employees' job performance but rather were simply designed to replace workers earning top pay rates with new employees who would be hired for less to do the same job. A terminated employee stated in an interview that he was told any employee who earned more than 51 cents above the pay rate established for their job at their store's location would be subject to termination. Terminated employees could reapply for any available positions after ten weeks. The terminations, along with other cost cutting actions, are expected to save the company $110 million in fiscal year 2008 and $140 million per year starting in fiscal 2009. Management believes the plan will enable Circuit City to compete better with rival firms such as Best Buy and RadioShack. Circuit City reported sales fell 4.3 percent in the quarter ending May 31, 2007, and sales at stores open at least one year fell 5.6 percent during the same time period.

Questions

1. Discuss your opinion regarding the merits of Circuit City's labor cost-cutting strategy. How might the strategy affect the following competitive issues: ability to cut prices on goods sold, customer service, and recruitment and retention of retail employees?

2. Circuit City employees are not represented by a labor organization and have no collective bargaining contract specifying terms and conditions of employment. How might Circuit City's labor cost-cutting strategy be affected if its retail employees were union members in a bargaining unit covered by an existing labor agreement?

SOURCE: Ylan Q. Mui, "Circuit City Cuts 3,400 'Overpaid' Workers," *The Washington Post*, March 29, 2007, p. D-1; Doug Desjardins, "Circuit City Re-Org Results in 3,400 Layoffs," *Retailing Today*, 46 (5), April 9, 2007, p. 3; and "Circuit City's Harsh Layoffs Give Glimpse of a New World," *USA Today*, April 3, 2007, p. A-14.

A Change in the Medical Insurance Plan

CASE STUDY 7-2 The employer designs, installs, and maintains private telephone systems for customers. Employees in the bargaining unit have been represented for many years by the union. The parties' current collective bargaining agreement provides for the following medical insurance benefits:

"**basic medical benefits covering reasonable and customary charges; and major medical benefits with an unlimited maximum benefit; a dental benefit plan; and long-term disability benefits. These benefits are described by the specific insurance contracts to be filed with the Union's district office.**"

The company had been experiencing declining profits for several months attributed to a general economic recession and the loss of a major client. In June, the management team reviewed the current situation and forecast for the firm's short-term future and decided to adopt a strategy of cutting operating costs. As part of this strategy, the three top managers of the firm, who were also its owners, agreed to eliminate their salaries and lay off two members of the administrative staff.

The company's principal source of capital funding was a loan arrangement with a local bank, which permitted the company to borrow up to 80 percent of the value of current accounts receivable. Whenever a customer paid a bill for which the receivables had been pledged to the bank as collateral for the loan, the payment had to be applied to reduce the amount of the outstanding loan. When new business was obtained, providing additional accounts receivables, the company could pledge these receivables to the bank and obtain additional loan capital to continue operations. The company's current loan was due to expire on September 1, and because of the company's current financial problems, the bank informed the company managers that the current loan must be fully paid by the end of September and no new loan would be issued by the bank.

At about this same time the company was notified by its current insurance carrier that medical insurance premium costs for the company's employee coverage would be increasing by 40 percent to a total of $28,000 per month. The insurance carrier also requested an advance payment equivalent to two months' premium expense to continue the coverage because the company had been late in making premium payments in the past. The company president did not believe the company could afford to make the higher insurance premium payments and, therefore, found another insurance company that would provide medical insurance coverage for employees at a cost of $22,000 per month. A meeting was requested by management officials with union representatives to inform the union about the new medical insurance plan.

The meeting occurred on October 8, at which time management explained the new medical insurance plan to union officials. The only significant difference between the old and new plans concerned the prescription drug benefit. Under the old plan employees were issued a prescription card that allowed the employee to fill any prescription for a cost of $4. The new plan would require each employee to pay a deductible amount before the insurance plan would cover any prescription drug expenses. Covered prescription drug expenses under the new plan would be reimbursed to the employee at the rate of 80 percent of the employee's actual cost. The company estimated the new plan would save the firm $26,000 annually in premium cost compared to the current cost of the existing medical insurance plan. Management further asserted that the new insurance plan complied with the parties' contractual language to provide medical insurance coverage. At this same meeting the company president also informed union leaders that management would like to reduce current employee wage rates by 20 percent to enable the firm to submit more cost-effective bids to obtain new customer orders.

Union representatives asked several questions about the medical insurance plan described by management officials, not all of which managers could answer. Company officials provided the union with the name and address of the new insurance carrier and suggested the union contact the carrier directly for detailed information about the plan. Union officials subsequently held a meeting with bargaining unit members at which the company's proposals to cut wages 20 percent and change insurance carriers was discussed. Employees voted unanimously to reject both proposed changes. Employees were particularly concerned about the lack of a drug prescription card under the new medical insurance plan. Union officials reported the results of the employees' vote to management.

Upon learning of the employees' negative vote, the company president told union leaders that they must not have explained the new medical plan to employees in the right way. Management requested that the union hold another meeting with employees at which management representatives could explain the new medical insurance plan to employees. Union officials agreed to the meeting, provided union officials were also present when managers spoke to the employees.

On the date of the scheduled employee meeting, the local union president was tied up on union business and did not arrive at the meeting until 25 minutes after it had begun. The local union president stated that when he arrived management officials were already in the process of explaining the new medical insurance plan to the assembled employees and had passed out enrollment cards for employees to fill out for the new plan. The local union president advised employees not to sign the enrollment cards because the union had not agreed to the new medical insurance plan. The company president replied that the change needed to be made quickly, and he had already decided to change carriers and adopt the new insurance plan.

Questions

1. In your opinion, was management's request to change the insurance carrier (plan) reasonable? Explain your reasoning.

2. In your opinion, was it reasonable for employees to oppose the new insurance plan because they perceived the prescription drug benefit would shift substantial new cost to them compared to the existing (old) plan? Explain your reasoning.

3. Is it the union's job to represent the views of the majority of its members to management or try

to change union member's views to be consistent with management's preferred business strategy?

4. Does the employer have a legal right to implement the change to a new insurance carrier (medical insurance plan) in this case without bargaining with the union? Why or why not?

Discontinuance of a Pay Practice

CASE STUDY 7-3 For a three-year period the employer granted no wage increases to employees due to the company's adverse financial situation. In July 1999, the employer implemented a new policy to provide an annual wage improvement for employees. Each employee's annual wage improvement was comprised of two components: (a) a fixed percentage of the employee's base hourly wage rate, which all employees received, and (b) an additional merit-based percentage increase, which varied depending upon management's evaluation of each employee's job performance. The employer considered factors such as the cost of living, the company's current and projected financial situation, and the amount granted by other employers in the industry to determine the amount of the across the board percentage increase.

On July 1, 1999 and 2000 employees received a three percent across-the-board increase and merit increases ranging from zero to two percent. On July 1, 2001 the employer granted a four percent across-the-board increase and merit increases ranging from zero to two percent.

In November, 2001 employees voted to elect the union as their bargaining representative. The union and company representatives began negotiations on an initial contract in January 2002. During 2002 the parties held 16 bargaining meetings, eventually reaching a final contract settlement in June 2003. The owner of the firm testified that some discussion had occurred among managers concerning whether to grant a wage increase on July 1, 2002. According to the owner, the company's attorney had advised against granting any wage increase as it might be interpreted as an unfair labor practice by the union. When union officials became aware that management was conducting employee performance evaluations in 2002, the union negotiator asked management if it intended to grant employees a wage increase on July 1, 2002 consistent with the firm's established past practice. The management negotiator responded that the parties were currently in negotiations over wages and the negotiations would take care of the wage issue. When employees asked the plant manager whether or not wage improvements would be granted on July 1, 2002, they were told by the plant manager that wages were frozen because of the negotiations with the union.

After the company failed to grant any wage improvement in July 2002 the union filed an unfair labor practice charge, alleging that the company's failure to grant the wage increase constituted a violation of the employer's duty to bargain in good faith. The union's position was that the employer had an established policy of granting a pay increase on July 1 of each year. According to the union, the failure to grant a wage increase on July 1, 2002 represented a unilateral change in an established term or condition of employment in violation of the employer's duty to bargain in good faith. The union had never agreed to suspend payment of the annual wage improvement plan nor had the parties already bargained in good faith to an impasse over the bargaining subject.

The employer maintained that the Labor Management Relations Act prohibits an employer from making a unilateral change in a mandatory bargaining subject such as wages for union-represented employees. The company was concerned that if management went ahead and granted a wage increase without having obtained the union's approval as to the amount and timing of such an increase, it would constitute a unilateral change in employees' wage rates. The company relied upon the advice of its legal counsel in making the decision not to grant any wage increase while negotiations were still underway with the union toward an initial labor contract.

Questions

1. Does the company's failure to make a wage adjustment consistent with past practice on July 1, 2002 constitute a violation of the employer's duty to bargain in good faith? Explain your reasoning.

2. If an employer were found guilty of bad-faith bargaining in a case like this, should employees be entitled to a back-pay remedy? If so, how could the NLRB determine the appropriate amount to be awarded?

Classroom Exercise

7.1
Employee Benefits

Directions:

A. From an *employee's* perspective, rank order the importance of the following employee benefits as a part of a compensation plan where 1 = the most important benefit and 16 = the least important benefit.

—— Employee assistance plan	—— Child-care assistance plan
—— Defined benefit pension plan	—— Education tuition aid
—— Defined contribution pension plan	—— Transportation reimbursement
—— Cash balance pension plan	—— Supplemental unemployment benefit
—— Major medical insurance plan	—— Paid holidays
—— Life and accidental death benefit	—— Paid vacation
—— Short-and long-term disability benefit	—— Paid sick leave
—— Prepaid legal service plan	—— Dental insurance plan

B. List the factors that were most important to you in determining your ranking priorities among the benefits listed above (e.g., age, sex, current job, prior work experience, marital status, number of dependents, expected time period until retirement, or knowledge of employment conditions at other firms).

C. If asked to perform the same ranking task from an *employer's* perspective, would your rankings change and if so, how or why?

CHAPTER 8
Administrative Issues

Most book chapters relate to a single topic, but this is one of those chapters that addresses several important administrative issues, each of which has important economic and work environment consequences for both labor and management. This chapter focuses on six broad areas that impact both contract negotiation and administration issues: (1) technological change and its impact on labor relations, (2) job security and seniority, (3) employee training, (4) work restructuring, (5) safety and health, and (6) accommodating employees with disabilities.

Management seeks flexibility in arranging work content and schedules to maximize efficiency. Unions seek to protect employees' job security and the conditions under which work is performed when workplace changes occur. The attempts of managers (owners) and union representatives (employees) to achieve their respective interests are discussed throughout this chapter.

TECHNOLOGICAL CHANGE AND JOB PROTECTION

Technological change refers to changes in the production process that result from the introduction of labor-saving machinery and changes in material handling and work flow. **Automation**, a type of technological change, goes one step further in that machines perform tasks formerly performed by humans, and the human operator is replaced by automatic controls.[1] Technological change may affect a job by altering the tasks or equipment used and thus the job skills required; the pace or scheduling of the work; or a job's characteristics (e.g., degree of exposure to health and safety hazards, frequency of interaction with co-workers, closeness of supervision, job stress level).

Use of new technology is a means by which firms and nations seek to gain a competitive advantage in the arena of international competition. Often the competitive advantage gained from the introduction of new technology is short lived. Such technology often becomes available to competitors fairly rapidly, lessening the competitive advantage of being the first to possess the technology. "Technology is being used to streamline and automate operations and reduce the need for labor, while also requiring remaining workers to do more."[2] Longer-term competitive advantage derives from the ability of workers to apply technology in a highly efficient manner. This requires workers who are well trained and motivated.

Technological change generally occurs in three phases: (1) the development phase, in which key choices about the design and configuration of the new technology are made; (2) the resource allocation phase, in which claims for resources by different organizational units are presented and evaluated against performance criteria; and (3) the implementation phase, in which the new technology is constructed, put into service, and modified if necessary. The third phase, implementation, is typically when a union enters the picture because implementation of new technologies affects the work structure and consequently the employees performing the job tasks. The consequences of the implementation of new technologies concern employees, as well as the union that represents their job-related interest.[3] Unions seek to protect the job interests of their members affected by technological change through (1) negotiating contract language (see later discussion of work scheduling, electronic monitoring, outsourcing, seniority rights); (2) lobbying for or against government legislation and assistance programs (see later discussion of Worker Adjustment Retraining and Notification Act); and (3) providing direct services to members (e.g., career counseling, job referral, short-term economic support, retraining, social-psychological support).

Unions and employers have a long history of bargaining over the effects of technological change. Approximately 26 percent of labor agreements contain some language that addresses in some manner the introduction of new technology. Only 17 percent of labor contracts provide for discussion with or advance notification to the union of the introduction of new technology, and only eight percent require an employer to retrain workers displaced by technological change.[4] Another study reported the elements of creating a new work system (e.g., team-based work system, job rotation, worker participation, pay for knowledge, profit sharing, or gain sharing) being discussed in one-third or fewer negotiations, with an agreement on these types of bargaining issues being reached in only 9 to 16 percent of contract settlements.[5]

These low percentages are partially due to the fact that current labor law classifies most decisions concerning the implementation of new technology as a nonmandatory bargaining subject.[6] This limits a union's bargaining role to issues regarding the *effects of technology* on members' interests after management decides what technology to use and when, where, and how to implement it. Essentially this forces a union to adopt a reactive rather than proactive stance in seeking to represent bargaining unit members' interests on technology change decisions. Critics of the current legal designation of technology issues as nonmandatory bargaining subjects argue that permitting unions to bargain over the full range of issues which arise concerning technology would provide valuable information to management from employees who work most closely with the technology, likely speed the adoption of new technologies, and enhance employees' acceptance of technological change efforts benefiting the interests of both management and employees.[7]

Some companies do see advantages in voluntarily involving employees and union representatives in the early stages of selecting new technology as a means of achieving a sustainable competitive advantage.[8] Employees and union representatives may accompany engineers on trips to vendors, provide input to assess the merits of available technologies, and render opinions on what types of equipment to purchase. Employees may contribute valuable insight into how to operate the equipment and how to organize the work process after the new technology is implemented. When a union is consulted early in the technology development process, it is more likely to become an advocate for the new technology and better able to assure its members that the technology will secure more jobs than it threatens.

The Joseph Abboud plant located in Bedford, MA, is an example of a labor-management relationship that has cooperated to implement a lean manufacturing system. This system features work teams and employee skill cross-training to ensure high-quality production and timely delivery of suits to retail merchants at a competitive price.[9] Local union representatives understood that low wage competition from imported clothing required a flexible approach to negotiating work rules to improve productivity and product sales, enabling the company to maintain higher employee compensation while adding additional jobs to the bargaining unit.

The International Association of Machinists (IAM) has adopted an integrated program with several employers with which the union has a bargaining relationship to create a **high performance work organization (HPWO)**, which is capable of saving and creating jobs while remaining globally competitive and stimulating company growth.[10] The HPWO envisions a partnership in which both management and labor take responsibility for ensuring that the firm will adapt to competitive market and technological demands by sharing information, continuously training workers, and adapting work rules to meet each firm's needs (see the following Labor Relations in Action feature). General Electric and Westinghouse negotiated provisions with the International Brotherhood of Electrical Workers that require advance notification of technology, committees, retraining, and safety measures for people who work with robots.[11]

Although more firms are seeking to involve and empower employees in adapting to technological change, many firms are not.[12] A bargaining relationship characterized by mistrust, leaders on either side not committed to developing a more cooperative relationship, or insecure in their own position will inhibit technology change efforts. The need for consultation with the work force may be viewed as a loss of authority by some supervisors and middle managers, who may resist transferring their power to employees. For innovative work practices to be effective, upper management and union leaders must communicate their commitment to cooperation to all employees within the organization.

Unions are often portrayed as being obstacles to technological change in the workplace because many Americans remember publicity given to railroad fireman who wanted to remain on diesel engines, the reluctance of plumbers to adapt to plastic pipes, airline crew members who resisted a reduction in the number of cockpit crew members needed to fly more modern aircraft, or the resistance of typographers to computerized typesetting in the newspaper industry. Unions are often depicted as negotiating complex work rules that restrict

LABOR RELATIONS IN ACTION
High Performance Work Organization (HPWO)
Partnership Principles

Copyright GettyImages

Union and management leaders responsible for their respective organizations are asked to write and sign a *Partnership Agreement* signifying a real commitment to partnership as a means of implementing meaningful change in the work environment. The following principles help define what components comprise a true partnership:

- **Shared decision-making** concerning issues critical to the competitiveness of the business, including costs and work processes.

- **Development of continuous learning and skill building** to meet the changing education needs of all employees.

- **Continuous integration of leading-edge technology** that utilizes the skills, knowledge, and insights of employees. Leading-edge technology includes equipment, new materials, work processes, and labor relations intended to both stabilize and grow the business and the work force.

- **A co-determined definition of quality and its continuous measurement and improvement.** Quality includes meeting customers' expectations and is critical to the ability of the firm to grow and its employees to prosper.

- **Shared technical and financial information.** Access to relevant and timely information is necessary for parties to make appropriate decisions. Open and honest communication between labor and management serves to build trust in a partner.

- **Ongoing joint determination of costs** such as design, prototype development, production, and administrative overhead. This requires a cost accounting system capable of assigning cost to various elements in the work process.

- **Acceptance of the union as an independently chosen representative of employees.** Through the collective bargaining process, including the use of a contract grievance procedure, the parties can seek to resolve conflicts of interests which may arise while seeking to expand opportunities for cooperation.

- **Union and management leaders willing to advocate the partnership concept and motivate all employees to participate in bringing about positive workplace changes.**

- **A jointly developed strategic business plan.** The plan should cover current products and services, development of new products and services, and the goals and direction to be taken by the partners to achieve future growth.

SOURCE: International Association of Machinists, *HPWO Components*, 2007, pp. 1–3 at http://www.goiam.org/content.cfm?cid=320.

management's ability to manage the workplace and management's right to introduce technological advancements. Yet some unions have clearly encouraged changes in job design, skills training, employee involvement in decision making, teamwork, gain sharing, improved labor-management communications, and more cooperative labor relations.[13] In fact, unions have generally accepted the doctrine of "high wages, high productivity, and low labor costs" as the best approach to maintaining income growth and employment stability for union members.[14] As Joseph Hunt, president of the Iron Workers' union has stated: "We have to make our contractors more competitive to gain market share. If they don't have a job, there's no job for us [our members] to work on."[15]

Technological change can have both positive and negative effects on employees, and a union must represent members affected by both types of change. In general, technological progress in the United States has resulted in higher productivity, the elimination of many menial and dangerous jobs, higher wages, shorter hours, and a higher standard of living.[16] Technological advances have brought about numerous positive effects, such as the ability to produce greater wealth with less effort; machinery performing tasks that humans cannot or performing tasks more reliably and efficiently, thereby lowering production costs and permitting products to be sold at lower prices; improved working conditions by minimizing backbreaking or hazardous work assignments; and improved skill levels for some workers leading to increases in pay.

Although technological change has many positive effects, it may also produce some negative effects. One explanation for the lack of job growth in recent years in the U.S. economy is the fact that due to technology advances, jobs are being eliminated at a faster rate than new jobs are being created without any decline in productivity.[17] Only a small percentage of jobs eliminated in the United States (approximately ten percent) are transferred to the global economy in the form of outsourcing or offshoring (e.g., sending work to countries such as Mexico, China, or India). Further, job elimination due to technological change is a phenomenon occurring in virtually every industrialized country in the world as employers adopt a similar competitive business strategy.

Technological advances also permit a reduction in the responsibility or skill level required to perform some jobs (**deskilling**), resulting in lower employee compensation and less job security for those employees holding such jobs. However, in some cases technology-enhanced machinery such as robotics may be less able to anticipate and adjust to unforeseen circumstances or changes in the operating environment compared to a well-trained human operator. Technology often carries higher capital costs to acquire it, which must be paid for through a combination of anticipated labor cost savings and a higher productivity rate. To the extent that competitors adopt similar technology, increasing productivity may flood the market with an excess supply of product relative to the market demand for such product. Such a supply-demand imbalance would likely result in a declining product price, thereby requiring additional time (expense) to recover a firm's capital investment in technology. This situation is exacerbated if a company is forced to borrow capital funds in an environment of rising interest rates in order to purchase technological enhancements.

Technology has also increased the sophistication of methods used to monitor employees at the workplace. A 2006 survey of 416 firms by the American Management Association reports that 76 percent of companies have e-mail usage and content policies, 24 percent have had employee e-mail subpoenaed in a legal dispute and 26 percent have terminated employees for e-mail misuse.[18] Just over half (51 percent) of 526 firms in another survey reported using video surveillance to monitor theft, violence, and sabotage; ten percent monitored on-the-job performance in certain job categories and six percent videotaped all employees.[19] Less than ten percent used Global Positioning Systems (GPS) to monitor cell phone usage or track company vehicles. Technology may be used to monitor an employee's e-mail or other computer files, employee location, telephone conversations, and Internet use to track employee productivity and activity, including counting keystrokes, error rates, time taken to complete tasks, and time away from a work station. Data collected might be used by managers to determine production standards and pay rates, monitor speed and accuracy of job performance, or take disciplinary or discharge action for failure to perform in a satisfactory manner consistent with company policies.[20]

Employers argue that electronic monitoring of employees is a useful way to objectively evaluate their performance, increase productivity, prevent theft or other unlawful activity on company property, avoid potential legal liability arising from a failure to reasonably monitor employee workplace activity, monitor compliance with safety regulations, and plan for future business needs. Union officials often respond that electronic monitoring can be a source of stress on employees, measures only quantitative aspects of job performance, erodes employees' dignity, and invades employees' privacy. Few federal or state laws provide any significant protection for employee workplace privacy rights. Employers are often encouraged to reduce employees' reasonable expectation of privacy in the workplace by adopting a policy "that clearly states all workplace technology, equipment and systems are the property of the company and should be used only for business related purposes."[21] Most employers inform their employees of company policies on monitoring activities as well as penalties for violating such policies.

Unions are often under pressure from members to negotiate work rules to provide reasonable privacy protections from employer monitoring activity. As a mandatory bargaining subject for unionized employers, a union negotiator might propose contract language to achieve one or more of the following employment terms or conditions:

- An outright ban on one or more types of unreasonable or obtrusive electronic monitoring activities.

- A requirement for advance notification to each employee whose performance will be subject to electronic monitoring.

- Imposing a "beep" provision requiring the employer to use a light or audible tone to inform employees when they are being monitored.

- Prohibiting management from collecting information not directly related to an employee's work performance.

- Prohibiting disclosure of employee information collected to other people or companies without prior employee approval unless in connection with a criminal investigation.

- Availability of counseling or other health-related services necessary to manage job stress or related conditions arising from exposure to electronic monitoring activities.

Management negotiators would want to ensure that any agreed-upon electronic monitoring work rule:

- Clearly inform employees that electronic communication equipment (e.g., computer, cell phone) cannot be misused for unprofessional or inappropriate communications (e.g., racial slurs, sexual harassment).

- Inform employees that electronic communication equipment necessary to perform assigned job duties will be provided by the company and represents company property.

- Inform employees that they have no reasonable expectation of privacy in the use of company property for electronic communications purposes.

- Require that employees sign a consent form or provide other evidence acknowledging they have read and understood all electronic monitoring work rules and the consequences for their violation.

JOB SECURITY AND PERSONNEL CHANGES

Most job growth over the next decade is expected to occur as the result of the need to replace employees who leave current jobs rather than the creation of additional (new) jobs. The shift in employment opportunities from goods-producing (manufacturing) to service-producing industries (e.g., retail trade; communications;

services; transportation; finance, insurance, and real estate) will continue with professional and service occupations projected to increase the most both in terms of percentage growth and the actual number of jobs created over the 2004–2014 period.[22] The 20 fastest percentage growth occupations through 2014 are concentrated in health care and computer-related jobs, while the 20 occupations expected to experience the largest numerical increase in jobs is spread over several occupations (e.g., retail salespersons, registered nurses, post secondary teachers, customer service representatives, and janitors and cleaners).[23] Twelve (60 percent) of the 20 fastest percentage growth occupations (e.g., network systems and data communications analysts, physician assistants, computer software engineers, occupational therapists) require a bachelor's or associate degree. In contrast, on-the-job training is the most significant source of education for 13 (65 percent) of the 20 occupations expected to experience the largest number of growth in jobs (e.g., physical therapist aides, medical assistants, home health aides, retail salespersons, waiters and waitresses, customer service representatives). Several occupations whose preparation for employment primarily consists of on-the-job training are expected to decline in the number of jobs available over the 2004–2014 period (e.g., farmers and ranchers, stock clerks and order filers, sewing machine operators, file clerks, computer operators, and telemarketers). One thing not likely to change for employees and the unions who represent them is a desire to obtain or enhance **job security**.

Job Security Work Rules

Much has been written about the decline of the "old social contract" whereby in exchange for good performance and loyalty, the employer promised to provide employees secure employment and periodic improvements in wages and benefits.[24] Motivated by a perceived need for flexibility to respond to changing market conditions and a desire to reduce labor costs, the "new employment contract" being offered by many employers shifts the risk and uncertainty of employment to each employee who is responsible for ensuring their skills and abilities stay current with available job requirements. Downsizing, outsourcing, and an expanding variety of contingent work arrangements are manifestations of the greater job insecurity facing many workers today.

A primary union concern is to ensure that members' jobs are protected from elimination resulting from technological change or unreasonable managerial decision making. Unions have been able to protect jobs by negotiating contract language concerning subjects such as job security guarantees, subcontracting, outsourcing, work assignments and jurisdiction, work scheduling, and the weight accorded seniority in personnel decisions.

Job security work rules are provisions that attempt to make jobs more secure, such as spreading the workload by placing limits on the load that can be carried, restricting the duties of employees, limiting the number of machines one operator can tend to, or requiring standby crews.[25] Such practices when carried to an extreme are known as **featherbedding**, which exhibits "unreasonable limits to the amount of work employees may do in a given period, ... payment for unneeded employees, unnecessary tasks, work not performed, or jobs duplicating those already done."[26] This practice is viewed negatively by managers and the public as a waste of resources, and unions have been forced to abandon or severely limit the use of such work rules in an era of global competition.

Congress attempted to help reduce featherbedding practices when it amended the Labor Management Relations Act (LMRA) to add Section 8(b)(6), which prohibits a labor union from causing or "attempting to cause an employer to pay or deliver or agree to pay or deliver any money or other thing of value, in the nature of an exaction, for services which are not performed or not to be performed."[27] Workload restrictions underlie many labor relations conflicts. From an overall (macro) viewpoint, union leaders agree that change is necessary for economic progress, but from an individual (micro) view, where significant adjustment would be necessary, change may be resisted by workers and their unions.[28]

A commitment to employment security has several advantages for both employers and employees. Such a commitment may motivate employees to support change, encourage employers to invest more in training employees, reduce costs associated with turnover, retain critical skills needed by the firm, and maintain employee morale. Building strategic partnerships with management based on a mutual recognition of the contributions that labor and management make to enhance a firm's competitiveness is one approach to improving job security.[29]

The collective bargaining process is a means by which union representatives and managers attempt to resolve conflicts between employees' desire for greater job security and employers' desire for greater flexibility and cost effectiveness in adjusting the size and duties of the labor force to the workload. Some examples of issues affecting job security covered by negotiated work rules include the following:

- *Job assignment*: Reducing crew size, adding duties, or eliminating unneeded jobs.

- *Job content*: Combining jobs such as millwright, welder, rigger, and boilermaker, or allowing journeymen to perform helpers' tasks.

- *Hours*: Clean-up time, flexible work schedules, mandatory overtime, advance notice of shutdown, or extending work time for the same pay.

- *Seniority*: Restricting the use of seniority in filling job vacancies, bumping, or determining work schedules.

- *Wages*: Permitting pay for knowledge, gain sharing, severance pay.

- *Training*: amount and type provided, employee eligibility criteria to receive training.

Union and management representatives must determine which job security work rules are appropriate in each bargaining relationship. Not all restrictive work rules intended to maintain a specified staffing level are illegal. Work rules negotiated between the longshoremen and shipping companies that prevent truckers and warehousemen from unloading cargo from containers within 50 miles of a ship docking pier were upheld by the U.S. Supreme Court because they were the product of voluntary bargaining between two informed parties. These work rules were designed to preserve a portion of the traditional longshore work that is dwindling because of the use of shipping containers.[30] In 2002 after an extended lockout by West Coast shippers and port terminal operators belonging to the Pacific Maritime Association, employers negotiated the right to implement new technology for loading and tracking cargo but the International Longshoremen's Association (ILA) negotiated the right of its union members to operate the new technology with no loss in the number of current jobs.[31] Since the labor agreement was signed, productivity improvements have helped support average earnings of $123,464 for full-time longshoremen working 2,000 hours per year and expanded the number of jobs available at West Coast ports.

Plant Closures, Downsizing, and WARN

In 1988 Congress enacted the **Worker Adjustment and Retraining Notification Act (WARN)** in response to data that showed large numbers of employers either shut down or initiated layoffs while giving employees or community leaders less than 14 days advance notice or no notice at all. The WARN act requires employers with 100 or more employees to give 60 days' advance notice of a plant closing or major layoff (i.e., termination of 50 or more workers at the same work location within a 30-day period or a major layoff affecting at least 50 employees who make up at least 33 percent of the workers at a work site), to employees (excluding those employed less than 20 hours per week), unions, and state and local governments.[32] In 2006, there were 7,201 mass layoffs recorded, affecting 935,805 employees.[33] WARN also allows negotiation of labor contract language requiring more than 60 days' advance notice.

Although providing workers with advance notice of shutdown has been shown to reduce the probability such notified workers will experience unemployment in transitioning to a new job opportunity, passage of the WARN has not had a substantial impact on increasing the number of employers providing or the number of displaced workers receiving advance notice of layoffs or plant closures.[34] In 2007, 57 percent of manufacturing and 40 percent of nonmanufacturing labor agreements surveyed provided for advance notice of shutdown.[35]

Several possible reasons exist for the failure of the WARN Act to provide more employees and community leaders with advance notice of significant job displacement events.[36] Some employers may be unaware or confused about their notification responsibilities under WARN, despite the U.S. Department of Labor's efforts to provide guidance to encourage voluntary employer compliance. The language of the act itself serves to undermine its potential. Exempting firms with fewer than 100 employees from coverage under the law eliminates a substantial portion of the labor force from receiving required advance notice. The WARN Act also has many exemptions applicable to covered employers. For example, an estimated 50 percent of layoffs involving 50 or more workers are exempt from any advance notice requirement because the number of affected employees is less than one-third of the employer's active work force (one-third rule). Seventeen states and the U.S. Virgin Islands have enacted state laws similar to the federal WARN Act. However, employers with as few as ten employees may be subject to coverage under state law and some states require employers to continue to provide group health care coverage or severance pay for affected employees.

WARN requires employers found liable for a violation to provide the affected employees up to 60 days' back pay and benefits.[37] Because the law designates no federal agency as responsible for enforcing the law, employees must take the expensive step of hiring an attorney to sue their employer in federal district court for any alleged violation of the WARN Act. A union may sue for damages on behalf of its members under the WARN Act, and state law determines the time limit imposed for filing such claims.[38]

On occasion, the rules under the WARN Act and the LMRA are intertwined. In 1991, the *Dallas Times Herald,* which had a long-standing bargaining relationship with the Dallas Typographical Union and Mailers Local, actively misled the unions about rumors of a closing during negotiations for a new contract. On the date the sale was finalized, the business was closed. The *Times Herald* then informed employees and the union. The National Labor Relations Board (NLRB) ruled that remedies (back pay) owed to employees under the LMRA were separate from payments required under the WARN Act. Therefore, an employer's payment for back pay and benefits arising from a violation of the WARN Act would not offset any back-pay liability arising from an unfair labor practice finding that involved the same affected workers under the LMRA.[39]

Subcontracting, Outsourcing, and Work Transfer

Subcontracting (also called "contracting work out") usually occurs when a firm determines that it cannot perform all the tasks that are necessary to operate its business successfully or that another firm can perform the needed tasks (janitorial and cafeteria services, equipment repair, parts production, and so on) better or at a lower cost. **Outsourcing**, a similar process, is a cost-cutting strategy of shifting work away from one's own firm to a different producer who may be located inside or outside the United States. **Offshoring** is a more recent term used to refer to the movement of work from a company location within the United States to locations outside of the United States (e.g., banking, information technology, telecommunications, engineering functions, tax preparation, medical services, manufacturing). The international producer who now performs the work may be owned in whole or in part by the U.S. firm from which the work came or may be a different company altogether. Approximately 25 percent of work relocation decisions involve movement of work outside the United States with Mexico and China being the most frequent recipient of that work.[40]

Advantages of subcontracting and outsourcing have been cited as lower costs (particularly labor costs); increased profitability, productivity, and quality improvements; increased operating flexibility, speed, and faster access to innovative technology with less capital risk.[41] Whereas many companies who outsource report achieving positive benefits, the magnitude of gains are often less than expected. A Dun & Bradstreet survey reported that 20 percent of outsourcing relationships fail in the first two years, and 50 percent fail within five years.[42] Several potential problems confront firms engaged in outsourcing, including loss of intellectual property or institutional knowledge, confidentiality risk, reduced ability to respond to market changes in a timely manner, employee concern over possible job loss, poor selection or monitoring of outsourcing suppliers, insufficient training provided to individuals responsible for managing outsourcing activities, and a failure to develop a clear plan detailing outsourcing objectives, expected benefits, and performance measures.

In recent years, auto manufacturers have been seeking to expand outsourcing of certain parts production and introducing less labor-intensive production methods, such as modular manufacturing, which permits various modules (e.g., dashboards, headliners, exhaust system) to be assembled by outside suppliers, requiring an auto manufacturer's workers to engage in only the final assembly of such preassembled modules.[43] The United Auto Workers (UAW) union has adopted a dual strategy of attempting to delay job cuts or limit such cuts to normal attrition rates at the Big Three auto plants while at the same time becoming more aggressive in seeking to organize nonunion auto supply plants to reduce the labor costs differential between primary auto manufacturers and auto suppliers.[44]

Use of the just-in-time inventory control method to minimize inventory carrying costs has left firms particularly susceptible to disruptions in the flow of parts caused by selective strike actions at key supplier's plants or their own plant. This increases the importance to management of developing stable and cooperative labor relations with workers and their union representatives. A strike by machinists at Boeing in 1995, the first since 1989, was caused in large part by outsourcing. Between 1989 and 1995, Boeing's worldwide work force had shrunk by 62,000, and forecasts for plane production were the lowest in 11 years. To help win orders in Asia, the aircraft industry's fastest growing market, Boeing agreed to farm out parts production to manufacturers in those countries (sometimes a requirement imposed by home countries in order for foreign firms to do business there). As an example, one supplier selected was Shanghai Aviation in China, with 2,000 employees who earned $120 per month compared to $3,530 per month earned by Boeing employees in Seattle, Washington, for producing 1,500 tail assemblies for Boeing. Although Boeing's aircraft are still assembled in Seattle, much of their fuselages and components, such as landing gear, are now produced in and imported from Asia.[45]

In some cases, the parties attempt to reverse outsourcing activities. For example, at the GM plant in Doraville, Georgia, the UAW and GM organized a joint union-management team to study the feasibility of keeping outsourced work. The committee found a way to produce seat cushions for one of GM's midsize models in-plant for less than the vendor charged. The team bid on the work and won the contract; now the cushions are produced at the Doraville plant. Despite such evidence that union labor can compete on a labor cost effective basis, in 2005 GM announced plans to close the Doraville plant by the end of 2008. United Auto Workers representatives called the announcement extremely disappointing and devastating to the thousands of workers, their families, and their communities affected, and expressed frustration that GM managers have failed to counter GM's declining market share by designing products that consumers want to buy.[46]

The subcontracting process can be a volatile and complicated collective bargaining issue. Unions often attempt to influence management's decisions to subcontract by restricting management's freedom to subcontract bargaining unit members' work in order to protect and maximize members' work and economic opportunities. Some contract language restricting management's right to subcontract is found in approximately 50 percent of labor agreements.[47] For example, a union might seek to have management agree not to subcontract or outsource work as long as necessary personnel and equipment were available to perform the work in a timely manner. Alternatively, a union might propose that there be no subcontracting or outsourcing of work without providing the union an opportunity to demonstrate how the work could be performed in-plant by bargaining unit members as cost effectively as it could if the work were outsourced to another supplier. A union may also request information from management to document the type and amount of bargaining unit work being subcontracted by the employer.

Negotiation practices involving subcontracting clauses may vary across industries because unions in the construction and apparel industries do not usually attempt to limit subcontracting. Instead, unions in these two industries often attempt to extend the provisions of the collective bargaining agreement to the subcontractors that are commonly used in those industries. Under the LMRA, subcontracting of bargaining unit work is considered a mandatory subject of bargaining. However, a company would not be required to bargain if all of the following conditions were met: (1) subcontracting was motivated solely by economic conditions, (2) subcontracting was a common method of doing business in the industry, (3) the current subcontracting decision did not differ much from similar decisions made by the company in the past, (4) there was no adverse impact on bargaining unit employees, and (5) the union had previously been given an opportunity to bargain over changes in established subcontracting practices.[48]

Arbitration likewise has played an increasingly important role in the subcontracting issue. In determining whether management had a contractual right to subcontract certain bargaining unit work, an arbitrator might consider several factors, such as the presence and clarity of contract language granting management a right to subcontract, any evidence of an established past practice regarding subcontracting, the history of the parties' prior negotiations over the issue of subcontracting, the intended duration of the subcontracting decision, the employer's business justification for contracting out, and any evidence of antiunion animus (i.e., a desire or intent to weaken the bargaining unit or union representative by subcontracting work).[49]

An employer who unilaterally transfers bargaining unit work to another location has a duty to bargain over the decision to relocate the work if the relocation decision does not involve a basic change in the nature of the employer's operation.[50] To avoid the duty to bargain, the employer must prove that (1) the work performed at the new location differs significantly from the bargaining unit work performed at the previous location, (2) labor costs were not a factor affecting the decision to relocate the work, or (3) the union representative of bargaining unit employees could not have offered sufficient labor cost concessions to reasonably justify any change in the employer's decision to relocate the work. Even where there is no duty to bargain over the decision to relocate bargaining unit work, an employer would still have a duty to bargain over the effects of the relocation decision on bargaining unit members (e.g., transfer rights, severance pay, pension rights).[51]

Even when a duty to bargain over the work relocation decision exists, an employer satisfies that duty by negotiating in good faith with the union until either a voluntary settlement or a bargaining impasse is reached, at which point the employer can legally implement the work relocation decision. This puts pressure on a union to adopt a reasonable approach in proposing alternative actions that might alter the employer's perceived need to relocate some or all of the planned work affected.

Arbitrators have also limited management's right to relocate bargaining unit work when they conclude that the parties have already placed limits on work relocation by including in their labor agreements the following standard contract provisions: (1) a recognition clause that acknowledges the union's status as representative of employees within the established scope of a bargaining unit, (2) clauses that establish job classifications and wage rates, (3) seniority clauses that include layoff and recall procedures, and (4) job security clauses that limit the circumstances in which employees can be terminated or jobs eliminated.[52] Practically speaking, there is usually good reason for an employer to bargain about a work relocation decision, as well as its effects. A union may offer helpful suggestions or concessions that make the relocation less necessary. More importantly, if the company acts unilaterally and its acts are later determined to be unlawful, it risks large back-pay awards and in isolated cases a costly order to reopen a closed operation.[53]

Work Assignments and Jurisdiction

When changes in technology, job descriptions, work materials, or processes occur sometimes labor disputes develop over which workers will be assigned to perform particular jobs or job duties. Such disputes may occur if: (1) two or more unions representing different bargaining units within the same firm claim jurisdiction for their members to perform the available work assignment; (2) bargaining unit employees believe their work is being assigned to other employees outside the bargaining unit, such as supervisors; or (3) a disagreement occurs within a union over which members should perform particular work assignments. These disputes over work assignments are called **jurisdictional disputes** (see Exhibit 8.1 for an example of a work jurisdiction clause in a labor agreement).

The LMRA, as amended, makes it unlawful for a union to engage in or encourage a work stoppage to force an employer to assign work to a particular union or craft. The LMRA provides a special NLRB procedure for resolving jurisdictional disputes within ten days after an unfair labor practice charge is filed. Factors considered by the NLRB in resolving these types of disputes are skills and work experience required to perform the work; any union certifications already awarded by the NLRB, industry, and local practice; prior arbitration decisions; the employer's desires; and cost effectiveness and operating efficiency of assigning the work to a particular bargaining unit or craft.[54] The AFL-CIO's Building and Construction Trades Department representing 12 affiliated national unions and several national contractors' associations have generally sought to avoid using the NLRB jurisdictional dispute procedure by voluntarily establishing a national joint board to consider and decide cases of jurisdictional disputes in the building and construction industry.[55] A 2003 agreement signed by management of the Philadelphia Convention Center and six unions representing convention center employees aimed at specifying how the six unions will work together to reduce jurisdictional disputes and labor costs has resulted in lower labor cost and stabilized labor relations, resulting in increased bookings for the convention center and a $700 million expansion project to add additional exhibition space.[56]

Some labor agreements require that bargaining unit work be performed only by bargaining unit employees except in instructional, experimental, or emergency situations. In instructional situations, there must be a clear, direct, and immediate connection between work done by members of management and instructions given to bargaining unit employees. Experimental work includes the introduction

Exhibit 8.1

Example of a Work
Jurisdiction Clause

It is the intent of the parties to this agreement to protect the work performed by employees in the bargaining unit.

The employer recognizes that it is important and desirable to use its own equipment and drivers to the greatest extent possible before using subhaulers and/or noncompany trucks.

The union recognizes that under certain conditions, such as those dictated by customer demands, equipment requirements, daily dispatch determinations, materials to be hauled and similar factors, that subhaulers and/or noncompany trucks are necessary and have been so used throughout the industry for many years.

The employer, in accordance with the above, must however, determine the number, type and location of its working equipment in conformity with its business requirements. The employer further must be able to determine, in keeping with sound business practices, the extent to which it will replace equipment that is too costly to operate, obsolete, or damaged.

Under these conditions, the employer agrees the subhaulers and/or noncompany trucks will not be used as a subterfuge to defeat the protection of the bargaining unit work.

In keeping with the above, the union recognizes that the employer will use such subhaulers and/or noncompany trucks as required by location and classification only after all the available company trucks at such locations and in similar classifications have been initially dispatched.

of a new technique, method, or procedure. Emergency situations might occur as the result of unforeseen circumstances, such as a tornado, fire, or power outage, that call for immediate action.[57] Unions generally don't object to bargaining unit work performed by supervisors in situations requiring only a few minutes of time but rather seek to prevent any transfer of work opportunities that might lead to the permanent elimination of one or more job positions held by bargaining unit members.

Intra-union work assignment problems, although not as critical and dramatic as other issues, are often very sensitive political matters for local union leaders. Conflicts between members of the same union over work assignments can cause problems, especially in industrial unions having both craft and semi-skilled employees as members. Whenever production processes are automated, reassignment of work from skilled employees to semi-skilled production employees can cause emotional conflicts within the union. For example, having pipe fitters do welding tasks when welding is not included in their job description gives rise to disputes.

To resolve these conflicts, unions favor specific, written job descriptions and a right to refuse to perform work outside those specified job descriptions. Management typically prefers increased flexibility in making work assignments provided by a more general job description that includes phrases such as able to "perform related duties" and "make minor repairs."[58] Companies implementing a team-based production system have been successful in getting unions to agree to more cross-functional training and broader multi-skill job descriptions that provide greater flexibility in assigning job duties to team members.

Work Scheduling

Collective bargaining agreements often deal with work scheduling, such as determining the timing or duration of a work shift, day, or week. Management has a right to determine work schedules unless restricted by negotiated language in the labor agreement. For example, management has a right to suspend operations temporarily, reduce the number of shifts, or change the number of days to be worked. Even when the labor agreement contains some restrictions on work scheduling, management can usually make unscheduled emergency changes in the work schedule if such changes are made in good faith and for reasonable cause, such as extreme weather conditions, bomb threats, or civil disturbances. The five-day, 40-hour workweek has been accepted as a standard work schedule in most U.S. industries since passage of the Fair Labor Standards Act (1938), requiring employers to pay time-and-one-half on a covered employee's regular rate of pay for hours worked in excess of 40 during the same workweek.

Unions in the United States and elsewhere have shown increasing interest in **flextime** work schedules, which allow an employee to start and finish work at his or her discretion, as long as the specified total number of hours per week or per day are worked and the employee is present at work during a core-hour period (e.g., 9:00 A.M. to 11:00 A.M. and 1:30 P.M. to 3:30 P.M.). Some employers use flexible work schedules as a hiring incentive to attract applicants in occupations with a current labor shortage. These programs are designed to better match job requirements with the personal needs of individual employees. Although flextime has much potential for meeting employee needs, some work operations require all workers to be present at the same time, and in these cases, work schedules cannot be altered unless the entire group accepts the alternative schedule.[59] Approximately 28 percent of union contracts contain language addressing flexible work scheduling.[60]

Another possible alternative work schedule is a **compressed workweek** consisting of four 10-hour work days with three days off each week or eight 9-hour days and one 8-hour day permitting one extra day off every two weeks.[61] For example, the National Treasury Employees Union and U.S. Food and Drug Administration negotiated contract language that permitted employees to work nine 9-hour days over a 14-day period or four 10-hour days per week with work hours being performed sometime between 6 A.M. and 6 P.M. Some authors have raised concerns about the possible negative health effects of non-standard work schedules, such as chronic sleep deprivation or the stress of being required to be "on call" during scheduled off hours.[62]

The Role of Seniority in Personnel Changes

Employers usually have a free hand in selecting initial hires that best fit the prescribed job requirements and needs of the firm. However, once any employee has been selected and placed on a job within a bargaining unit, the employer must abide by provisions of the labor agreement regarding personnel decisions such as promotions, transfers, and layoffs. The concept of **seniority** is often a factor used to determine personnel decisions that affect bargaining unit employees. Seniority has played a key role in labor relations since the 1920s, when foremen's discretion (often abused) in personnel decisions was replaced by seniority-based decisions affecting compensation or reward structures, promotion, transfer, layoff, and recall decisions.[63]

Seniority is usually measured by the length of an employee's continuous service in a company (plant) or in a specific department or job line-of-progression (e.g., welder 1, welder 2, etc.). Seniority may be used to determine **benefit rights** (e.g., vacation entitlement or scheduling) or **competitive job rights** (e.g., promotion, layoff or recall, work assignments, transfers, shift preference). When used to determine benefit rights, every employee's seniority is usually measured on the same basis from the date of initial employment in the company or specific plant location. Such a company or plant-wide measurement approach ensures equitable treatment of employees for entitlement to certain benefits that have no meaningful connection to the type of job or skill level the employee holds.

Determining who among competing employees will be entitled to a job promotion or transfer presents a different issue, because in determining competitive job rights the ability to perform the job is an important consideration. Management would generally prefer to measure seniority for determining competitive job rights on a department or job line-of-progression basis. This measurement approach gives more assurance that the most senior applicant will be qualified to perform the job and eliminates the risk of grievance claims filed by employees from other departments. If a contract grants **bumping rights**, in a layoff a more senior employee from one department might assert a claim to a job held by a less senior employee in a different department. Even if management wasn't sure the more senior employee could actually perform the job satisfactorily, the senior employee would likely insist on being granted a reasonable trial period to demonstrate his or her job ability.

Seniority provisions are found in most labor agreements and cover issues such as how seniority accrues, in what types of decisions it will be used, and in some cases, how it can be lost for a variety of reasons (e.g., layoff, failure to respond to recall, unauthorized absences, or taking a job elsewhere during a leave of absence). Seniority is considered very important by most union members, and managers seldom object to providing some sense of job security or benefit priority to productive long-service employees. Seniority serves as one of the few objective measures that can be used to distinguish between two or more employees, and is also used by nonunion employers in making some personnel decisions.[64] Seniority is not as commonly used outside of North America as a key factor in determining issues such as layoff or promotion decisions.[65] Arbitrators often consider an employee's seniority as a possible mitigating circumstance in deciding the appropriateness of a discharge decision where a long period of satisfactory performance would weigh in an employee's favor in determining whether the behavior violation alleged or proven is likely to occur again if the employee was given another chance to correct the behavior.

Some authors argue that the increasing level of organizational instability resulting from rightsizing, outsourcing, mergers, increased global competition, and declining union density have weakened employers' commitment to seniority and, in turn, weakened employees' loyalty and commitment to their current employer.[66] Individuals entering the labor force today can expect to work for multiple different employers over the course of their work career, making seniority with any single employer more difficult to attain. Other authors criticize seniority as a discriminatory concept because some groups with a higher proportion of more recent entrants to the labor force (e.g., women, minorities) are often among the first to be laid off when applying the "last-in-first-out" principle on which seniority preference is based.[67]

In some cases, union and management agree to include a seniority provision in the labor agreement called **superseniority**, which provides that highly skilled technical employees or union officials directly involved in contract negotiations or grievance handling will be the last ones laid off, regardless of their actual length of time on the job. This provision allows a company to retain essential skills and at the same time promote stable labor relations by ensuring individuals skilled in contract negotiation and grievance-handling techniques will remain available to resolve any labor disputes that might arise at the work place.

Seniority also plays a role in determining job promotion and transfer decisions. Personnel changes within an organization that advance an employee to a position of more responsibility, usually accompanied by a wage increase, are promotions. Promotion provisions usually rely on both ability and seniority as factors used to determine the personnel decision, but the weight accorded each factor can vary in different labor agreements. Although seniority can be easily and objectively determined, the measurement of ability is more complex. Job transfer provisions cover personnel changes from one job to another with relatively equal authority, responsibility, and compensation. Seniority and ability are also usually the determining factors in making a job transfer decision.

Four basic types of seniority clauses used in promotion and transfer decisions are presented here, with the approximate percentage of contracts using each:

- Seniority is the only determining factor (five percent).

- Among all employees who meet the minimum job requirements, seniority will be the determining factor (49 percent).

- Where the best qualified candidates are relatively equal in ability, seniority will be the determining factor (40 percent).

- Ability and seniority will be given equal consideration (two percent).[68]

Management would generally prefer to give ability to perform the job more weight than seniority in making promotion and transfer decisions to enhance potential productivity. Unions often argue that because the exact determination of ability is so complex, the emphasis should be on ensuring that each candidate is qualified to perform the job effectively, and among such qualified candidates, seniority is an objective means of determining the candidate selected. The use of only seniority to determine eligibility for promotions and transfers is objective and administratively easy, but it does not ensure that the more senior employee will always be qualified to perform the job. Union members and managers have a self-interest in ensuring that competent individuals occupy job positions within a bargaining unit, and thus ability to perform a job will almost always be a factor in any layoff or promotion decision. In the small percentage of contracts that apply equal weight to seniority and ability, arbitrators have concluded that when seniority between employees is relatively close, it is reasonable to use relative ability to perform the job as the determining factor. If candidates' seniority differs extensively, ability must be substantially greater to justify selection of a less senior candidate.[69]

Ability to perform a job includes measuring factors such as relevant job skills, knowledge, attitude, behavior, performance, pace, and production. Techniques most commonly used to measure these criteria include tests, work experience, education, production records, performance ratings, personality traits, and absence, tardiness, and discipline records.[70] Each of these criteria may be limited in its specific relationship to the needs of particular jobs, and thus the determination of employee qualifications is usually based on several criteria.

Although an employer may generally establish any valid criteria for assessing an employee's ability, promotion criteria and performance standards are mandatory bargaining subjects because they have the potential to directly impact both the employees' economic interests and job security. Promotion and layoff decisions must comply with any standards expressed in the parties' labor agreement. Selection and performance appraisal criteria and methods must also comply with the "Uniform Guidelines on Employment Selection Procedures" covering race, sex, national origin, and religious discrimination for covered employers.[71] Moreover, the provisions of the labor agreement itself must not be discriminatory or perpetuate past discriminatory practices.

Even though promotion and transfer procedures differ, most labor agreements require that job vacancies be posted for a specified time period to inform interested bargaining unit members about the employment opportunity. Interested employees are then permitted to bid for an available job vacancy within the reasonably specified time period. Other related labor agreement provisions may be included to prevent possible administrative problems. For example, agreements should prescribe whether an employee carries his or her seniority to a new position or whether seniority will be retained only after a predetermined period. Other provisions should specify whether an employee who transfers out of the bargaining unit or is promoted to a management position will be allowed to retain his or her seniority or lose it. Some contracts may also specify that if a promoted employee does not successfully perform his or her new job after a reasonable trial period, that employee may return to the previous position with no loss in previously accrued seniority. Management might well oppose such a contract provision since returning a previously promoted bargaining unit member to his or her prior job would cause a ripple effect, displacing the individual who had been promoted to fill the promoted member's vacated position.

Most union contracts also provide for recall of employees after layoffs in reverse order of layoff. This would mean more senior employees would be recalled before less senior employees. Increasingly, seniority has become the primary factor in layoff determination; however, contracts generally consider seniority as the determining factor for recall only if an employee is qualified for an available job.

Advance notice of a planned shutdown (e.g., one to five days) to the employees and their union is required in 46 percent of labor agreements, but is more common in manufacturing agreements (57 percent).[72] As previously discussed, the WARN Act requires covered employers to provide at least 60 days advance notice to the affected parties in the case of a plant closure or major layoff. Unionized firms experience only slightly higher layoff rates than nonunion firms in both manufacturing and nonmanufacturing industries.[73]

Alternatives to layoffs as a means of cutting labor costs include a pay freeze, pay cut, productivity improvement through work-rule changes, addition of new products or services, normal attrition and hiring freezes, voluntary leave, early retirement, a reduction in operating hours, rotating layoffs, work relocation, and **work sharing**. Work sharing where two or more employees share a job by dividing the standard total number of hours for the job between them is provided in three percent of labor agreements.[74] Work sharing agreements generally specify that the agreement will be implemented for a limited amount of time. Work sharing enables the employer to retain the skill mix of a full work force and consequently retain its investment in employee training, keeps the employer's unemployment compensation tax contribution rates from increasing, and is considered by many employers as more equitable than retaining some employees and laying off others. This approach was used successfully in the hospitality industry following the events of September 11, 2001, to retain key staff represented by the Hotel and Restaurant Employees Union.[75] Employers have no right to unilaterally institute work sharing arrangements without first bargaining to an impasse with the bargaining unit representative, unless such action is permitted by a labor agreement, such as in the management rights clause.[76]

Legal Issues Involving Seniority in Administrative Determinations

Job rights guaranteed an employee under a labor agreement may pose a potential conflict with other employees' legal rights. Use of seniority in administrative determinations such as promotions and layoffs has been the focus of much litigation. In some cases it has been shown that minorities have been locked in departments or jobs with unfavorable lines of progression, and these practices tend to perpetuate past employment discrimination.[77] Congress specifically granted legal protection to bona fide seniority systems that were not enacted for the intentional purpose of discriminating on the basis of race, sex, and so on, even though the operation of such a seniority system might tend to perpetuate different treatment of some employees.[78] Appropriate remedies for an unlawful seniority plan can include the award of retroactive seniority to employees who were discriminated against.

Although the Supreme Court encourages voluntary affirmative action plans, the high court upheld the right of white employees to challenge promotions made under a court-approved affirmative action consent decree when the white employees did not participate in the negotiation of the plan.[79] The white employees sued their employer, claiming reverse racial discrimination, alleging that they had been denied promotions that had been awarded to less-qualified black employees under an affirmative action consent decree entered into by the employer and minority employees to settle the black employees' discrimination claim.

Merely because an affirmative action plan grants a preference to a certain class of employees (e.g., minorities) for the purpose of addressing past discrimination practices does not mean the plan is unlawful. The Supreme Court upheld a voluntary affirmative action plan negotiated between an employer and union intended to increase minority participation in a skilled-trade apprenticeship training program because the parties' intent in establishing the plan was lawful, the plan was designed to be of a limited duration, and it did not unnecessarily harm the interests of non-minority employees (i.e., no non-minority workers lost employment because of the plan and 50 percent of available training slots were filled by non-minority applicants).[80]

The Supreme Court has tended to view permissible affirmative action in employee layoffs somewhat differently because layoffs represent the loss of something an employee already has and a potentially permanent loss of income, thereby representing greater potential harm to adversely affected employees' interests. In one decision the Supreme Court indicated that in fashioning a remedy for past discriminatory practices a court can only award "competitive" seniority (more days of service than they have actually worked) to individuals who were the actual victims of a discriminatory practice.[81]

The Supreme Court has also limited the use of racial preferences in layoff procedures intended to protect minority employees, even though the procedure is part of a negotiated labor agreement.[82] To ensure minority teachers' availability to serve as role models for minority students, a board of education and a teacher's union agreed that the order in which employees were laid off would be determined based on seniority, except that at no time would the percentage of minority personnel fall below the current percentage of minority students enrolled. In practice, the layoff procedure resulted in more senior non-minority personnel being laid off while less senior minority personnel were retained. The court recognized that the labor agreement provision represented an affirmative action effort. However, the provision could not be enforced because the presence of generalized societal discrimination is not a sufficiently compelling reason, absent evidence of specific discriminatory practices by the board of education or union, to warrant a special remedy such as racial preferences in layoffs. The court noted that the same affirmative action goal could be accomplished without adversely impacting current employees' interests by establishing future minority hiring goals and time tables.

Accommodating seniority and affirmative action interests presents difficult dilemmas for both employers and unions. Assuming that employers have increased the hiring of women and minorities in recent years, the firm's seniority list would consist of more non-minority and male employees toward the top and a greater proportion of minorities and women toward the bottom. If an employer was forced to lay off employees, it would impact minority and female employees more severely under a typical "last-hired, first-fired" seniority provision. In those cases where plant, department, or job line-of-progression seniority is used, a layoff could erase much of the employer's progress in its minority- and female-hiring affirmative action plan. An employer who fails to explain to an individual the reason for his or her layoff may increase the probability that the employee may challenge the lay off decision, alleging some form of discrimination as the basis for the lay off decision.[83] This issue represents an area of labor relations that afford both labor and management opportunities for a cooperative, mutual gain approach to resolving related issues in a fair and nondiscriminatory manner.

EMPLOYEE TRAINING

America's continued competitiveness in a global economy depends on how well our human resources are developed and managed. Many jobs in the future will require workers with higher levels of verbal, mathematical, organizational, and interpersonal skills. In 1964 less than 58 percent of U.S. workers had completed a high school education and less than 12 percent possessed a college degree.[84] By the year 2000, more than 90 percent of U.S. workers had obtained a high school degree. From 1980–2000 the number of workers with a post-high school degree increased 19 percent, but by 2020 that rate is expected to increase only an additional four percent.[85]

Despite an increase in the education and training level of American workers, an estimated 20 percent of the U.S. population still reads at or below a fifth-grade level.[86] The National Alliance of Business and the National Institute for Literacy estimate that basic employee skill deficiencies cost U.S. firms $60 billion in lost productivity annually.[87] The American Management Association reported that 36 percent of job applicants lacked the basic math and reading skills to perform the jobs for which they applied.[88] This places critical importance on the issue of employee training and retraining to ensure future competitiveness.

Training can occur in a formal, structured program, such as apprenticeship training, new employee orientation, safety and health, basic skills (e.g., reading, math, and computer) or job-specific skills training. Training can also occur on a more informal basis, such as on-the-job training or mentoring by a more experienced employee. The availability of formal training programs has been shown to be positively correlated with larger-size firms, the use of so-called high-performance work practices (e.g., total quality management, work teams), use of more capital intensive technologies, and workers' possessing higher levels of education.[89] Employees working in firms with a high turnover rate are less likely to receive training than those employed at firms with medium or low employee turnover.[90] Employers are often reluctant to invest in employees who aren't likely to remain on the job long enough to recoup the initial training investment. Because unionized firms tend to experience lower turnover rates compared to nonunion firms, over time union members have the ability to acquire more training related to a firm's specific job tasks and technologies, which can enhance productivity.

Most firms offer one or more types of formal training; however, the specific types of training and amount of training provided vary by industry.[91] The most common types of formal training programs focus on new employee orientation, safety and health, job skills, and workplace practices. The most common job skills taught are sales and customer relations, management skills, and computer skills. Although there is little difference in the total hours of formal training provided per employee between union and nonunion firms, unionized firms provide a greater percentage of training hours through formal, structured programs (36 percent) compared with nonunion firms (28 percent).[92] Greater employer willingness to invest in formal training programs in unionized firms reflects the longer tenure of unionized employees with the same firm (43 percent have ten or more years compared with 23 percent of nonunion employees with the same length tenure), making the training investment more cost effective.

U.S. employers now recognize that they are facing a training dilemma because advances in technology and global competition require a more highly skilled workforce. With the exception of the building trade unions that have long been providers of apprenticeship training, U.S. unions have traditionally left training activities to management. Joint union-management administered apprenticeship programs in the construction industry report higher rates of completion and greater participation by women and ethnic/racial minorities compared to programs run unilaterally by nonunion (open shop) employers.[93] "Many unions recognize that promoting a knowledge-based workforce is a critical strategy for economic development and employment security."[94]

Recently, unions have begun to take a more active role in response to increased interests from management in implementing new work practices such as continuous improvement in quality, productivity, and customer service. A survey of labor agreements scheduled to expire between 1997 and 2007 reported 154 (15 percent) contracts covering 854,803 workers contained language concerning high-performance work practices.[95] Ensuring that workers receive adequate training to meet current skills requirements and develop necessary future skills is important to any union seeking to base future economic gains and job security on productivity improvement.

For example, the United Auto Workers (UAW) union has joined Ford, GM, and Chrysler in developing an impressive set of programs for employees to upgrade their skills and further their education in personal and work-related matters. One program is the Paid Education Leave Program, which provides leadership training to both production and managerial employees to equip them to take an active role in the economic transformation occurring in the automobile industry.[96] Four unions, UAW, United Steelworkers of America, Communications Workers of America (CWA), and UNITE, in conjunction with the AFL-CIO's George Meany Center for Labor Studies and the U.S. Department of Labor, have organized the Labor Leadership Institute, designed to develop skills for co-management within these respective industries. In San Francisco, the Hotel Employees and Restaurant Employees Union negotiated an agreement with 12 hotels to create a $3 million training program directed toward employee empowerment, consensus decision making, and skill development in new technologies.

WORK RESTRUCTURING

Unions and companies are changing the nature of the work performed by employees.[97] **Work restructuring** programs have many different labels, such as employee involvement, worker participation, cross-training, multi-skills, or self-managed work teams. All such programs typically involve major departures from the traditional way of assigning specific tasks to each employee. For example, a work team may include five to 12 multi-skilled workers who rotate jobs and produce an entire product with a minimal amount of supervision. The team approach reduces the need for multi-level managerial tiers of authority and tears down bureaucratic barriers between departments. A team approach requires employees to improve their technical and behavioral skills. Some work teams not only gain a more direct voice in shop floor operations but also take over some managerial duties, such as scheduling work and vacations, hiring new members, and ordering materials. These programs have unleashed enormous energy and creativity in employees and increased their feelings of dignity and self-worth. Work restructuring programs have enjoyed success in companies like General Electric, Champion International, Lucent Technologies, and Harley Davidson Motor Company.

A study by the U.S. Department of Labor and Ernst & Young found that American companies have discovered that investing in employees and innovative workplace strategies pays off in profits.[98] Innovative work practices are most effective when implemented in conjunction with employee training and empowerment programs. The study found that those companies that adopted aggressive employee development and involvement practices, such as skill training and team-based management, made significantly larger productivity gains than those that did not.

Despite the advantages of adopting innovative workplace strategies, one survey reports that 35 percent of responding plant-level managers indicated employee empowerment or self-directed work teams had not been implemented at their firms and two-thirds of respondents who did confirm the use of such practices indicated they affected 25 percent or less of the firm's employees.[99] While innovative work practices may have a positive effect on firm performance, the exact magnitude of that effect and the ability to sustain performance gains over time have yet to be clearly demonstrated.[100] One study reported that the adoption of many high performance work practices actually resulted in greater wage inequality among employees within the firm over time.[101] There appears to be a gap between what some firms say about the importance of training and employee involvement and the commitment to expend scarce corporate resources and time to implement such practices.

One of the major efforts in work restructuring, particularly in the metals industry, has been the development of cell manufacturing. The need to improve product quality has driven companies to realize that using traditional functional layouts of similar machinery for batch manufacturing is costly and obsolete. Cell manufacturing involves placing groups of dissimilar machinery in a small, cell-like configuration dedicated to machining a particular part or family of parts. Cell manufacturing requires highly skilled employees who are generally more satisfied with their jobs because their tasks are varied and their authority is enhanced. Cell manufacturing is usually accompanied by just-in-time (JIT) inventory control and employee involvement (EI) programs. In cell manufacturing, employees are trained to perform new tasks, assume more responsibility, relinquish old habits and ideas, and become more involved in decision making through participation in work teams. Cell manufacturing is not an antiunion device, and unions around the United States are actively involved in these innovative efforts to make their companies more competitive. Active union involvement and cooperation in change efforts serve to reduce employee resistance to cell manufacturing.[102]

SAFETY AND HEALTH

Occupational safety and health clauses were found in 58 percent of labor agreements covering 1,000 or more employees scheduled to expire between August 1997 and July 2007.[103] The topics covered range from a pledge of cooperation on safety and health issues (64 percent) to the establishment of a joint local labor-management safety and health committee (50 percent), provision for protective clothing (41 percent), safety rules (36 percent), reporting of safety and health needs (31 percent), first aid and medical facilities (24 percent), the use of a separate grievance procedure for safety and health disputes (23 percent), joint labor-management involvement in conducting ergonomic evaluations and studies (23 percent), procedures for refusing to perform hazardous work (22 percent), and joint labor-management committee review of hazardous communication programs (22 percent). Many of these provisions have resulted from safety and health standards formulated under the 1970 **Occupational Safety and Health Act (OSHA)**; the emergence of new biological, ergonomic, and chemical hazards in the workplace (e.g., AIDS, cumulative trauma); rising health care treatment costs and greater awareness of the benefits of preventive health care; and an increase in legal claims filed by employees and attorneys related to occupational injury and disease.

The employer's overriding duty under OSHA is to furnish each employee with a work environment free from recognized hazards that may cause illness, injury, or death and to comply with all occupational safety and health standards adopted by the Department of Labor. In Fiscal Year (FY) 2007, the Occupational Safety and Health Administration (also known as OSHA, an agency within the U.S. Department of Labor responsible for administering the OSH Act) had an operating budget of approximately $487 million and 1,100 inspectors to cover 135 million employees at 8.9 million work sites.[104] In FY 2006, OSHA conducted 38,579 work site inspections, finding 89,913 violations resulting in penalties totaling $84.4 million. The majority (59.3 percent) of inspections occurred in the construction industry. In addition, 24 states, the Virgin Islands, and Puerto Rico operate OSHA-approved safety and health programs in lieu of direct federal agency oversight. In FY 2006, state programs conducted 58,058 inspections, finding 127,284 violations resulting in penalties of $71 million. Inspections typically target industries or specific employers that historically experience a higher rate of job-related injuries and illnesses. OSHA works with both employers and labor organizations through partnerships and cooperative programs to improve awareness of and compliance with guidelines and work practices designed to improve the safety and health of employees.

In 2005, 4.2 million private-sector nonfatal injuries and illnesses were reported, or 4.6 cases per 100 full-time employees.[105] Due to revised reporting requirements effective January 1, 2002, the current data gathered from the *Survey of Occupational Injuries and Illnesses* is no longer comparable to data gathered during prior survey years. Approximately 2.2 million cases (2.4 cases per 100 full-time employees) required an employee to miss work days, transfer to a different job, or have other restrictions placed on the work duties he or she could perform. Mid-sized firms (50 to 249 employees) recorded more cases (5.8 per 100 full-time workers) than small or large-sized firms. The majority (60.9 percent) of nonfatal injuries occurred in four industries: manufacturing (20.2 percent), health care and social assistance (15.7 percent), retail trade (14.8 percent), and construction (10.2 percent).

In 2005, fatal work injuries in the United States declined one percent to 5,702 deaths or 4.0 per 100,000 workers.[106] Transportation incidents (e.g., highway vehicle collisions) accounted for 43 percent of fatalities followed by contact with objects or equipment (18 percent), assaults and violent acts (14 percent), falls (13 percent), exposure to harmful substances or environments (9 percent), and fires and explosions (3 percent).

A study by the Congressional Office of Technology Assessment (OTA) revealed that OSHA has generally performed its regulatory tasks with "workable accuracy" and actual employer costs of compliance with OSHA standards were often less than the agency's initial estimates.[107] One reason for the lower than expected costs was employers' retooling and modernization efforts to meet OSHA standards. OTA reported, for example, that the costs of complying with OSHA's vinyl chloride standard was 25 percent less than initially estimated, and compliance with the cotton dust standard was 33 percent less than OSHA's estimate.

Employers must permit inspectors to enter their establishments and conduct inspections (although the employer may require the inspector to obtain a search warrant) and must post notices, provide equipment, and maintain records in accordance with OSHA's rules and regulations.[108] Employees have a right to refuse to perform work that they believe represents a serious threat to their safety or health.[109]

OSHA applies some safety and health standards across all industries while additional standards may be required for specific industries.[110] For example, employers are required to grant employees (or their designated union representative) access to the employee's medical records maintained by the employer or any records concerning the employee's exposure to toxic substances. As a general rule, OSHA does not require employers to measure employees' exposure to toxic substances or to conduct medical surveillance of employees to detect the effects of such exposure, but only to grant employees access to such information if such records are kept by the employer.

A second standard requires an employer to provide necessary personal protective equipment at no cost to the employee. This might include items such as protective helmets, eye and hearing protection, hard-toed shoes, or special goggles for welders. The hazard communications standard requires employers who manufacture or use materials to label all hazardous material containers, include a material safety sheet to inform customers about the nature and proper use of the hazardous materials, and train their employees to recognize and properly handle or avoid hazardous materials in the workplace. A fourth standard requires employers (except in certain low-hazard industries such as retail, insurance, and finance) to maintain an injury/illness log to record the occurrences and causes of anything beyond minor job-related injuries or illnesses. For example, injuries or illnesses that require more medical treatment than simple first aid or involve loss of consciousness, lost work time, or transfer to another job.

The Bush administration has implemented changes in the reporting of job related illness data so that it is no longer possible to track the occurrence of specific types of illness cases such as repetitive stress disorders (e.g., carpal tunnel syndrome). Because some occupational illnesses (e.g., long-term exposure to carcinogens) do not manifest themselves until years after initial exposure, data on occupational illnesses typically under-report such cases. There were 242,500 new cases of occupational illness reported in the U.S. private-sector in 2005, accounting for 5.8 percent of all occupational injuries and illnesses reported.[111] According to the AFL-CIO, "Musculoskeletal disorders caused by ergonomic hazards are the biggest job safety problem workers face today, accounting for an estimated 1.8 million injuries each year. According to the National Academy of Sciences, these injuries cost the country $45-$54 billion annually."[112]

In 1991 more than 30 labor organizations petitioned the administration of George H.W. Bush to enact a temporary emergency standard regulating ergonomic hazards in the workplace.[113] The petition was rejected by the Bush administration leading to an ensuing decade-long fight to have OSHA enact an ergonomic standard. Business interests generally oppose such mandated rules on the grounds that they are either unnecessary, too costly to implement, lack adequate scientific evidence on which to establish a required "safe level" of operation, or would be administratively burdensome on the employer. After OSHA proposes a health or safety standard, there is an extensive period of public comment in which interested parties may propose various changes in the proposed rule, resulting eventually in a final standard being adopted.

On January 8, 2001, the Clinton administration implemented a final ergo-nomic standard just 12 days prior to the start of the new George W. Bush admin-istration. Using the Congressional Review Act (passed in 1996 to give Congress the authority to overturn regulatory agency decisions within 60 days of imple-mentation) the Republican-controlled Congress passed a joint resolution repeal-ing the Clinton administration's ergonomic standard, which was signed by President Bush on March 20, 2001. OSHA has since issued voluntary guidelines to provide a flexible means to help employers identify and control ergonomic hazards in the workplace.[114] The OSH administration also decided it would not hold employers liable for OSHA standards regarding the estimated 20 million telecommuters who currently perform their jobs at home. However, OSHA does intend to enforce standards regarding manufacturing tasks that are performed in the home (e.g., manufacturing electronic components, lead fishing lures, clothing).[115]

The Bush administration approach of voluntary compliance and partner-ships with employers as a means of ensuring safe and healthy work environ-ments has been criticized by organized labor, which favors mandatory safety and health standards coupled with industry-wide enforcement initiatives. Peg Seminario, director of safety and health for the AFL-CIO, recently stated in tes-timony before Congress that OSHA under the Bush administration has totally failed to address the problem of musculoskeletal disorders such as back injuries and carpal tunnel syndrome that are caused by ergonomic hazards in the work-place. "Only three industry guidelines have been issued—on nursing homes, poultry, and retail groceries—the last one in 2004. Only 17 general duty cita-tions have been issued, the last one in 2005. The Bush administration has stated that 408 ergonomic hazard warning letters have been issued to employers since 2002. But to date no follow-up inspections have been done to determine if haz-ards have been abated."[116]

A controversial safety and health issue was decided by the Supreme Court when it ruled that companies could not bar women from jobs that may be haz-ardous to unborn children.[117] The court explained that decisions about the wel-fare of future children must be left to the parents. Unions and women's groups had challenged the policy of Johnson Controls, Inc., an automobile battery man-ufacturer, which banned women who could not prove they were infertile from working in areas of the plant where they were exposed to lead, the principal material used in making batteries. The challengers successfully argued that the company policy discriminated against female employees because they were blocked from being considered for higher-paying jobs. To reduce the possibility of potential employer liability, employers were advised to fully inform employ-ees of any potential health or safety risks involved in the performance of a par-ticular job.

The *Johnson Controls* (1991) decision, which permits the employee to decide if she is willing to risk exposure to potential hazards on the job, appears to be at odds with the Supreme Court decision in *Chevron U.S.A. Inc. v. Echazabal* (2002), where the court ruled an employer cannot be required to make a reason-able accommodation to enable the hiring of a disabled person under the Ameri-cans with Disabilities Act if the job tasks could be hazardous to the disabled person.[118] The job applicant in the case had a liver condition, which the employer argued would pose a direct health threat to the job applicant because of chemicals present in its oil refinery, even though the applicant had been previously employed by an independent contractor at the employer's oil refinery. The court stated that were an employer to hire a disabled person who knowingly consented to the particular hazards of the job, the employer might run afoul of the OSHA mandate to ensure the safety of every worker.

AMERICANS WITH DISABILITIES ACT

The **Americans with Disabilities Act (ADA)** of 1990, which covers an estimated 43 million Americans, went into effect in January 1992. Considered a "Bill of Rights" for Americans with a wide variety of disabilities, the act applies to employment, public accommodations, transportation, and telecommunications. In the United States, approximately 17 percent of the population have some type of a disability and two-thirds of disabled persons are unemployed, even though most indicate that they would prefer to be employed.[119] Labor force participation rates have increased for the moderately disabled (81.6 percent) but remain low (29.5 percent) for persons with severe disabilities.[120] Persons with disabilities not only report lower rates of employment and a higher probability of part-time employment but also are almost twice as likely as nondisabled persons to suffer job loss after becoming employed.[121]

In 2006, 15,575 discrimination claims were filed under the ADA representing 20.6 percent of all types of discrimination claims filed with the Equal Employment Opportunity Commission.[122] Courts have generally taken a restrictive approach to defining individuals and conditions covered under the ADA, which critics suggest has undermined the intent of the statute to promote more job opportunities for disabled persons.[123]

Unions represent both disabled and nondisabled individuals holding job positions in a bargaining unit. Passage of the ADA has made job restructuring to meet "reasonable accommodation" requirements a challenge for both employers and unions. A **person with disabilities** is broadly defined as (1) a person with a physical or mental impairment that substantially limits that person in some major life activity, (2) a person with a record of such a physical or mental impairment, or (3) a person who is regarded as having such impairment. Considerable controversy has occurred over the meaning and application of the term disabled person.[124] The U.S. Supreme Court has clarified this controversy to some extent by ruling that persons with impairments that are correctable are not disabled within the meaning of the Act.[125] For example, a vision impairment correctable through wearing eyeglasses or high blood pressure correctable through medication is not considered disabling.

Because most labor agreements do not include provisions on the initial selection of employees, ADA compliance in the hiring process is essentially the employer's obligation. However, employment decisions after initial hire, such as promotions, transfers, layoffs, and recalls, are addressed in most labor agreements and come under the employment provisions of ADA. Under ADA provisions, an employer must make **reasonable accommodation** for a person with a disability if that accommodation will allow the person to perform the "essential functions of the job." Thus, if an employer can make a modification in a job's requirements or structure that will not cause the employer "undue hardship" and that will allow a disabled employee to do the job, then that modification or change in the job must be made.

The Supreme Court has ruled that an accommodation requested by a disabled individual (e.g., assignment to a particular job) will not ordinarily be considered a "reasonable accommodation" under the ADA if such an assignment would conflict with the seniority rights of other employees.[126] A union has a legal duty to fairly represent both disabled and nondisabled members in a bargaining unit. Some national unions have prepared training manuals to aid local union representatives in anticipating and addressing ADA issues arising under a collective bargaining agreement.[127]

Job performance and other disciplinary problems relating to employee alcoholism or substance abuse are treated in a straightforward manner under ADA. Employers are not required to tolerate performance and disciplinary problems. Individuals who are currently using illegal drugs are excluded from coverage under ADA, although the following individuals would be protected under the act: (1) a person who has successfully completed a drug rehabilitation program or who has otherwise been rehabilitated and is no longer illegally using drugs, (2) a person who is currently participating in a rehabilitation program and is no longer illegally using drugs, and (3) a person who is erroneously regarded as illegally using drugs.[128]

An employer's responsibility toward employees impaired by alcohol or drugs primarily extends to accommodating treatment and recovery and not to accommodating diminished job performance or employee misconduct. The initiative to request an accommodation must come from the employee, not the employer. The employer's obligation in a unionized setting is significantly greater than in a nonunionized setting as a result of an established body of arbitration decisions going back many years. Not only must the employer comply with the ADA, but labor arbitrators will consider mitigating circumstances that may be present in a case such as an employee's long-term good service or when performance and disciplinary problems may have been caused by alcoholism or drug addiction.[129]

Although ADA encourages the use of alternative dispute resolution procedures, such as mediation and arbitration, to resolve ADA claims without resort to court action, employees covered under both ADA and a collective bargaining agreement containing a broad nondiscrimination clause may have the opportunity to file a contractual grievance, as well as pursue a discrimination claim under ADA. A denial of an employee's grievance claim arising under a collective bargaining agreement does not preclude the employee from subsequently pursuing a similar discrimination claim under ADA.[130] The Supreme Court has applied a similar principle in a nonunion context finding that the Equal Employment Opportunity Commission (EEOC) has a right to file a disability discrimination suit against a nonunion employer seeking employee-specific remedies (e.g., reinstatement and back pay) for proven violations of the ADA, even though all employees were required to sign an agreement to submit all employment related disputes to final and binding arbitration.[131]

Summary

This chapter has explored six general categories of administrative issues—technological change, job security and personnel changes, employee training, work restructuring, safety and health, and accommodating employees with disabilities. Each of these areas has many important facets that may be negotiated and become part of a labor agreement.

Technological change, an essential ingredient of a dynamic economic system, is broadly defined to include such activities as introduction of labor-saving machines, power-driven tools, and automatic loading equipment. Although unions generally accept technological change as inevitable with both positive and negative impacts on bargaining unit members' interests, they attempt to negotiate contract language which will protect members' present jobs, ensure appropriate compensation for work performed, and establish the means for ensuring future protection of members' interests.

Job security and personnel changes are two interrelated issues that raise challenges for both labor and management. Unions often seek to protect their members by negotiating workload restrictions, limiting management's right to subcontract or outsource bargaining unit work, demanding specific work assignments and jurisdiction, or structuring jobs and work schedules to benefit employees. When personnel changes occur (e.g., layoff, promotion, job transfer), seniority may become a key decision criterion. Employees like the objectivity of seniority determinations and generally believe long-term satisfactory performance should be rewarded. Both employers and unions must be concerned with ensuring that only qualified individuals are placed in job positions. Striking the appropriate balance between seniority and job performance as criteria in human resource decisions is a topic to be resolved through the negotiation process. Employers and unions must consider EEOC regulations and court rulings in addition to contractual language when deciding personnel changes.

Employee training has taken on increasing importance in maintaining competitiveness in today's global economy. Unions and employers alike expend much effort in providing training programs to match employees' skills with the requirements of work restructuring. Work restructuring efforts are often initiated by management, but union cooperation is essential to the complete success of such programs. Although some unions are reluctant to become involved with work restructuring initiatives, major breakthroughs have been identified involving some unions, such as the United Auto Workers and Machinists unions.

Safety and health issues have become more important since the passage of the Occupational Safety and Health Act of 1970. Safety and health is clearly an area with great potential for fostering union-management cooperation with tangible benefits accruing to both labor and management interests. Recent improvement in decreasing the frequency of workplace accidents and illnesses can be attributed in part to a greater awareness of the economic benefits of hazard prevention; better cooperation between government, employers, and unions regarding approaches to improve workers' safety and health; and the presence of safety standards provided by federal and state laws.

The chapter concludes with a discussion of the need to accommodate employee and employer interests under the Americans with Disabilities Act. The significance of the problems faced by disabled Americans and the potential benefits of addressing their problems by making reasonable work accommodations are addressed.

Key Terms

Technological change, p. 336
Automation, p. 336
High performance work
  organization (HPWO), p. 338
Deskilling, p. 340
Job security, p. 342

Featherbedding, p. 342
Worker Adjustment and Retraining
  Notification Act (WARN),
  p. 344
Subcontracting, p. 345
Outsourcing, p. 345

Offshoring, p. 345
Jurisdictional disputes, p. 348
Flextime, p. 349
Compressed workweek, p. 350
Seniority, p. 350
Benefit rights, p. 350

Discussion Questions

1. Why do unions' reactions to technological change vary in accordance with their industry affiliation?

2. Think of an industry or company with which you are familiar, and assume that you are the local union president. What types of clauses regarding technological issues would you attempt to negotiate with your employer?

3. Discuss the advantages and disadvantages of offshoring jobs.

4. Discuss some of the advantages and disadvantages of using seniority as a factor to determine shift preference or overtime assignments.

5. Explain why unions often place a priority on seniority in personnel decisions, whereas employers tend to emphasize ability to perform the job.

6. Who has the responsibility of ensuring a safe and healthy work environment? Should it be the employer, union, employees, or government?

7. To what extent are labor laws, such as those discussed in this chapter, still necessary today? What changes might occur if such laws were repealed?

8. Consider an organization with which you are familiar. What are some actions that could be taken on various jobs to reasonably accommodate an employee with a disability without causing undue hardship to the employer or unreasonably infringing on the collective bargaining rights of other bargaining unit members?

Exploring the Web

Administrative Issues

1. WARN. What is the WARN Act and when was it enacted? Under what circumstances is an employer not required to give notice of a plant closing? Where in the Code of Regulations may the regulations resulting from the Act be found? Use the Web site of the U.S. Department of Labor to answer these questions.

2. Safety and Health. Summarize the opinion from the Supreme Court case in 1991 involving Johnson Controls, Inc., United Automobile workers, and other unions (499 U.S. 1817). To locate the opinion, use the Supreme Court Collection at Cornell's Legal Information Institute or the Oyez Web site. What was the effect of the opinion on women in the workplace?

3. Electronic Monitoring. Following is a sampling of Web pages that offer publications on videotaping and use of e-mail and electronic communications as a way to monitor the activity of employees in the workplace.

Go to the Web site of the American Civil Liberties Union (ACLU) and search for the report, "Privacy in America: Electronic Monitoring." What features does the article suggest should be included in a "fair electronic monitoring policy"?

The American Management Association conducts a survey on electronic monitoring and surveillance. Search for a summary of the latest survey conducted by AMA. What percentage of the companies surveyed use video monitoring and what percentage of those companies notify their employees of the practice?

An article by Mark S. Dichter and Michael S. Burkhardt, "Electronic Interaction in the Workplace: Monitoring, Retrieving and Storing Employee Communications in the Internet Age" has been made available through the Internet. Locate the article and comment on the section that discusses the employer's rights to monitor an employee's electronic communications versus the employee's privacy rights.

4. Labor Unions and the ADA. Go to the Web site for the Institute for Legal Research at Cornell. In the Employment and Disability Institute Collection, search for the document, "The ADA and Collective Bargaining Issues" and find out the obligations that unions have under the Americans with Disabilities Act.

References

1. Julius Rezler, *Automation and Industrial Labor* (New York: Random House, 1969), pp. 5–6.
2. David T. Collins and Mike H. Ryan, "The Strategic Implications of Technology on Job Loss," *Academy of Strategic Management Journal,* 6, 2007, p. 29.
3. Daniel B. Cornfield, "Labor Union Responses to Technological Change: Past, Present, and Future," *Perspectives on Work* 1 (April 1997), pp. 35–38; and Robert J. Thomas, "Technological Choice and Union-Management Cooperation," *Industrial Relations* 30 (Spring 1991), pp. 189–190.
4. Editors of Collective Bargaining Negotiations and Contracts, *Basic Patterns in Union Contracts,* 14th ed. (Washington, D.C.: Bureau of National Affairs Inc., 1995), p. 81.
5. Joel Cutcher-Gershenfeld, Thomas A. Kochan, and John C. Wells, "How Do Labor and Management View Collective Bargaining," *Monthly Labor Review* 121 (October 1998), pp. 26–27.
6. Steven E. Abraham and Bart D. Finzel, "New Technology in Unionized Firms: Advantages of Mandatory Bargaining," *Employee Responsibilities and Rights Journal* 10 (March 1997), pp. 37–48.
7. Bart D. Finzel and Steven E. Abraham, "Bargaining over New Technology: Possible Effects of Removing Legal Constraints," *Journal of Economic Issues* 30 (September 1996), pp. 777–795.
8. John T. Delaney, "Workplace Cooperation: Current Problems, New Approaches," *Journal of Labor Research* 17 (Winter 1996), pp. 45–61.
9. Frank Langfitt, "Suit Maker Goes 'Lean' to Keep Jobs in the U.S.," *National Public Radio,* January 24, 2007, pp. 1–2 at http://www.npr.org/emplates/story.php?storyID=6968780.
10. Miriam Szapiro, "National Union Supports for New Work Systems and Technological Change," *Labor Studies Journal* 21 (Summer 1996), pp. 73–95.
11. Richard M. Cyert and David C. Mowery, eds., *Technology and Employment: Innovations and Growth in the U.S. Economy* (Washington, D.C.: National Academy Press, 1987), pp. 129–133.
12. Maury Gittleman, Michael Horrigan, and Mary Joyce, "Flexible Workplace Practices: Evidence from a Nationally Representative Survey," *Industrial and Labor Relations Review* 52 (October 1998), pp. 99–115.
13. Mark Kizilos and Yonatan Reshef, "The Effects of Workplace Unionization on Worker Responses to HRM Innovation," *Journal of Labor Research* 18 (Fall 1997), pp. 641–656; Jeffrey H. Keefe, "Do Unions Hinder Technological Change?" in *Unions and Economic Competitiveness,* eds. Lawrence Mishel and Paula B. Voss (Armonk, N.Y.: M. E. Sharpe, Inc., 1992), pp. 109–110.
14. *Collective Bargaining Negotiations and Contracts* (Washington, D.C.: Bureau of National Affairs Inc., 1992), p. 65:3.
15. Sherie Winston, "Ironworkers and Their President Are Polishing Up Performance," *ENR,* September 1, 2003, p. 1 at http://enr.construction.com/features/bizlabor/archives/030901.asp.
16. Richard M. Cyert and David C. Mowery, eds., *Technology and Employment: Innovation and Growth in the U.S. Economy* (Washington, D.C.: National Academy Press, 1987), p. 133.
17. David T. Collins and Mike H. Ryan, "The Strategic Implications of Technology on Job Loss," 2007, pp. 27–33.
18. American Management Association, "2006 Workplace E-Mail, Instant Messaging & Blog Survey: Bosses Battle Risk by Firing E-Mail, IM & Blog Violators," *News Release,* July 11, 2006, pp. 1–3.
19. American Management Association, "2005 Electronic Monitoring & Surveillance Survey: Many Companies Monitoring, Recording, Videotaping and Firing Employees," *News Release,* May 18, 2005, pp. 1–3.
20. Robert H. Moorman and Deborah Wells, "Can Electronic Performance Monitoring Be Fair? Exploring Relationships Among Monitoring Characteristics, Perceived Fairness, and Job Performance," *Journal of Leadership & Organizational Studies* 10 (Fall 2003), p. 2; Elise M. Bloom, Madeleine Schachter, and Elliot H. Steelman, "Justice in a Changed World: Competing Interests in the Post 9-11 Workplace: The New Line Between Privacy and Safety," 29 *William Mitchell Law Review* 897 (2003).
21. David S. Mohl, "Balancing Employer Monitoring and Employee Privacy," *Workspan,* September 2006, p. 69.
22. Daniel E. Hecker, "Occupational Employment Projections to 2014," *Monthly Labor Review,* 128 (11), 2005, pp. 70–101.
23. U.S. Department of Labor, Bureau of Labor Statistics, "Tomorrow's Jobs," *Occupational Outlook Handbook, 2006–07 edition,* Bulletin 2600, 2006, pp. 1–7.
24. William S. Brown, "The New Employment Contract and the 'At Risk' Worker," *Journal of Business Ethics,* 58, Spring 2005, pp. 195–201 and Jeffrey Pfeffer, *The Human Equation: Building Profits by Putting People First* (Boston, MA: Harvard Business School Press, 1998).
25. Summer H. Slichter, James J. Healy, and E. Robert Livernash, *The Impact of Collective Bargaining on Management* (Washington, D.C.: Brookings Institute, 1960), pp. 317–335.

26. Robert D. Leiter, *Featherbedding and Job Security* (New York: Twayne Publishers, 1964), pp. 32–33.

27. Benjamin Aaron, "Government Restraint on Featherbedding," *Stanford Law Review* 5 (July 1953), pp. 687–721.

28. William Gomberg, "The Work Rules and Work Practices," *Labor Law Journal* 12 (July 1961), pp. 643–653.

29. Peter Lazes and Jane Savage, "A Union Strategy for Saving Jobs and Enhancing Workplace Democracy," *Labor Studies Journal* 21 (Summer 1996), pp. 96–121.

30. *NLRB v. International Longshoremen's Association*, 473 U.S. 61 (1985).

31. Anne Marie Squeo, "Safe Harbor: How Longshoremen Keep Global Wind at Their Backs," *The Wall Street Journal*, July 26, 2006, pp. A-1, A12.

32. *The Worker Adjustment and Retraining Notification Act,* 29 U.S.C. 2101, et seq. (1988).

33. U.S. Department of Labor, Bureau of Labor Statistics, "Extended Mass Layoffs in the First Quarter of 2007," *News Release*, May 16, 2007, p. 2.

34. Parisis G. Gilippatos and Sean Farhang, "The Rights of Employees Subjected To Reductions in Force: A Critical Evaluation," *Employee Rights and Employment Policy Journal*, 6, (2002), pp. 324–326; John T. Addison and McKinley L. Blackburn, "A Puzzling Aspect of the Effect of Advance Notice on Unemployment," *Industrial and Labor Relations Review* 50 (January 1997), pp. 268–288; John T. Addison and Jean-Luc Grosso, "Job Security Provisions and Employment Revised Estimates," *Industrial Relations* 35 (October 1996), pp. 585–603.

35. "2007 Employer Bargaining Objectives," *Collective Bargaining Bulletin*, 12 (3), February 1, 2007, p. S-25.

36. Gerald E. Calvasina, Joyce M. Beggs, and I.E. Jernigan, III, "The Worker Adjustment and Retraining Notification Act: Policy and Practice Issues for Employers," *Journal of Legal, Ethical and Regulatory Issues*, 9 (1), 2006, pp. 31–48; John T. Addison and McKinley L. Blackburn, "The Worker Adjustment and Retraining Notification Act: Effects on Notice Provisions," *Industrial and Labor Relations Review*, 47 (4), July 1994, pp. 660–661.

37. U.S. Department of Labor, *Fact Sheet: The Worker Adjustment and Retraining Notification Act*, 2007, pp. 1–4 at http://www.doleta.gov/programs/factsht/warn.htm.

38. *United Food and Commercial Workers Union, Local 751 v. Brown Group, Inc.*, 517 U.S. 544 (1996); *North Star Steel Co. v. Thomas*, 515 U.S. 29 (1995).

39. *Times Herald Printing Company d/b/a Dallas Times Herald and Dallas Mailers Union, No. 20 affiliated with Communications Workers of America and Dallas Typographical Union, No. 173 affiliated with the Communications Workers of America*, 315 NLRB 700 (1994).

40. Sharon P. Brown and Lewis B. Siegel, "Mass Layoff Data Indicate Outsourcing and Offshoring Work," *Monthly Labor Review*, 128 (8), 2005, p. 5; Christian Zlolniski, "Labor Control and Resistance of Mexican Immigrant Janitors in Silicon Valley," *Human Organizations*, 62, Spring 2003, pp. 39–49; Kenneth L. Deavers, "Outsourcing: A Corporate Competitiveness Strategy, Not

a Search for Low Wages," *Journal of Labor Research*, 18, Fall 1997, 503–519; Murem Sharpe, "Outsourcing, Organizational Competitiveness, and Work," *Journal of Labor Research*, 18, Fall 1997, pp. 535–549.

41. Andrew R. Thomas and Timothy J. Wilkinson, "The Outsourcing Compulsion," *MIT Sloan Management Review*, 48 (1), Fall 2006, pp. 10–14; Dean Elmuti, "The Perceived Impact of Outsourcing on Organizational Performance," *Mid-American Journal of Business*, 18, Fall 2003, p. 33.

42. Deloitte Consulting LLP, *Calling a Change in the Outsourcing Market: The Realities of the World's Largest Organizations* (New York: Deloitte Development LLC, 2005), p. 6. See also: Phanish Puranam and Kannan Srikanth, "Business Insight (A Special Report): Global Business; Seven Myths About Outsourcing: No. 1: 'We Can Have It All'," *The Wall Street Journal*, June 16, 2007, p. R-6.

43. Gordon Fairclough and Jason Leow, "Chery Assembly Deal Makes Chrysler a Model in Exporting from China," *The Wall Street Journal*, July 5, 2007, p. A-12; Geri Smith, "Factories Go South. So Does Pay; Mexico's Auto Industry Is Booming, But Parts Outsourcing Is Keeping a Lid on Wages," *BusinessWeek*, April 9, 2007, p. 76; and Daniel Howes, "GM Sees Leaner Plants: Tough UAW Choice: Fight Automakers on Job Cuts or Work with Them to Organize Suppliers," *The Detroit News*, January 8, 1999, p. B-1.

44. Charles R. Perry, "Outsourcing and Union Power," *Journal of Labor Research*, 18, Fall 1997, pp. 521–533; Justin Hyde, "GM Applies Lessons to New Factory," *Associated Press*, January 31, 2000, pp. 1–3; Daniel Howes, "Leaner, Diversified Carmaker Likely to Emerge after Strikes: Wall Street Analysts Say Walkouts Increase the Pressure to Restructure," *The Detroit News*, July 26, 1998, p. A-3.

45. "Widgetless in Wichita," *The Economist*, October 14, 1995, p. 77.

46. "GM Doraville Facility to Shut Down in 2008," *Atlanta Business Chronicle*, November 21, 2005, p. 1 at http://atlanta.bizjournals.com/atlanta/stories/2005/11/21/daily1.html and Donald P. Crane and Michael Jay Jedel, "Mature Collective Bargaining Relationships," in *Arbitration 1988: Emerging Issues for the 1990s*, ed. Gladys W. Gruenberg (Washington, D.C.: Bureau of National Affairs Inc., 1989), p. 358.

47. "2007 Employer Bargaining Objectives," *Collective Bargaining Bulletin*, 12 (3), February 1, 2007, p. S-25.

48. Marvin J. Levine, "Subcontracting and 'Privatization' of Work: Private and Public Sector Developments," *Journal of Collective Negotiations in the Public Sector* 19 (4), 1990, pp. 275–277.

49. Marlise McCammon and John L. Cotton, "Arbitration Decisions in Subcontracting Disputes," *Industrial Relations*, 29, Winter 1990, p. 142.

50. *Dubuque Packing Company, Inc., and UFCW, Local 150A (Dubuque IL)*, 303 NLRB 386 (1991); enforced, 1 F.3d 24 (DC Cir. 1993).

51. Roger S. Wolters and Stewart D. Langdon, "The Duty to Bargain over Business Decisions," *Labor Law Journal*, 43, September 1992, pp. 583–587.

52. Kenneth A. Jenero and Patrick W. Kocian, "The Relocation of Work between Plants: A Planning Checklist of Statutory and Contractual Obligations," *Employee Relations Law Journal*, 20, Spring 1995, p. 622.

53. Leonard E. Cohen, "The Duty to Bargain over Plant Relocations and Other Corporate Changes: *Otis Elevator v. NLRB*," *The Labor Lawyer* 1 (Summer 1985), pp. 525–532.

54. James K. McCollum and Edward A. Schoreder IV, "NLRB Decisions in Jurisdictional Disputes: The Success of the 10(k) Process," *Employee Relations Law Journal*, 13, Spring 1988, pp. 649–652 and NLRB, *Seventieth Annual Report*, 2005, p. 130.

55. The Construction Users Round Table & The Building & Construction Trades Department, AFL-CIO, "Construction Industry Leaders Form Tripartite Initiative: Owners, Contractors, Unions Establish Collaboration to Improve Industry," *Joint News Release*, January 18, 2003, p. 1. This board uses two procedural rules that are worthy of note: (1) A request for a decision in a specific case does not have to wait until the dispute occurs. Once the contractor makes the initial work assignments, a request for a decision can be made. Thus, time is saved by facilitating the dispute-resolution process. (2) Decisions of the board are not precedent setting. This does not mean that similar decisions within an area are not based on patterns; it means that conditions vary from region to region, union to union, and even agreement to agreement. Therefore, the board is not bound completely by precedent, but past practice is a factor. Custom in the industry and skills, training, and job content are important elements that are considered.

56. Tom Belden, "The Big Groups Are Back in Philadelphia: The Convention Center is Doing Better in Key Bookings. Labor Peace Is Just Part of the Reason for the Gains," *Knight Ridder Tribune Business News*, January 29, 2007, p. 1.

57. Elvis C. Stephens, "A Supervisor Performs Bargaining-Unit Work: Is the Contract Violated?" *Labor Law Journal*, 31, November 1980, pp. 683–688.

58. Slichter, Healy, and Livernash, *The Impact of Collective Bargaining*, pp. 266–276.

59. Hal Walls, "Flex and the Married Worker," *Industrial Engineer*, 35, September 2003, p. 24; Gillian Flynn, "The Legalities of Flextime," *Workforce*, 80, October 2001, pp. 62–66; and Jeffrey M. Miller, *Innovations in Working Patterns* (Washington, D.C.: Communications Workers of America and German Marshall Fund of the United States, 1978).

60. "2007 Employer Bargaining Objectives," *Collective Bargaining Bulletin*, p. S-25 and United States Department of Labor, "Workers on Flexible and Shift Schedules in May 2004," *News Release*, July 1, 2005, pp. 1–14.

61. AFL-CIO Working Women's Department, "Bargaining Fact Sheet: Control over Work Hours and Alternative Work Schedules," Spring 2001, pp. 1–4.

62. Teresa Rivers, "Atypical Workdays Becoming Routine; Evenings, Some Weekends Are a Growing Part of Workers' Schedules," *The Wall Street Journal*, April 4, 2006, p. A-19; Linda J. Twiname, Maria Humphries, and Kate Kearins, "Flexibility on Whose Terms?" *Journal of Organizational Change Management*, 19 (3), 2006, pp. 335–338.

63. Frederic H. Harbison, *The Seniority Principle in Union-Management Relations* (Princeton, NJ: Princeton University Industrial Relations Section, 1939), pp. 21–23.

64. Slichter, Healy, and Livernash, *Collective Bargaining*, pp. 104–105; D. Quinn Mills, "Seniority –Versus Ability in Promotion Decisions," *Industrial and Labor Relations Review*, 38, April 1985, pp. 424–425.

65. Sangheon Lee, "Seniority as an Employment Norm: The Case of Layoffs and Promotion in the U.S. Employment Relationship," *Socio-Economic Review*, 2 (1), January 2004, pp. 65–86.

66. Andrew Sikula Sr., "The Five Biggest HRM Lies," *Public Personnel Management*, 30, Fall 2001, pp. 424–425.

67. Gangaram Singh and Frank Reid, "Are Seniority-Based Layoffs Discriminatory? The Adverse Impact of Layoffs on Designated Groups," *Relations Industrielles*, 53, Fall 1998, pp. 730–746.

68. Editors of Collective Bargaining Negotiations and Contracts, *Basic Patterns in Union Contracts*, pp. 85–87.

69. Roger I. Abrams and Dennis R. Nolan, "Seniority Rights Under the Collective Agreement," *The Labor Lawyer*, 2, Winter 1986, pp. 99–110.

70. William H. Holley, Jr., "Performance Ratings in Arbitration," *Arbitration Journal*, 32, March 1977, pp. 8–25.

71. Daniel A. Biddle and Patrick M. Nooren, "Validity Generalization vs. Title VII: Can Employers Successfully Defend Test without Conducting Local Validation Studies?" *Labor Law Journal*, 57 (4), Winter 2006, pp. 216–237; Robert D. Gatewood, Hubert S. Feild, and Murray Barrick, *Human Resource Selection*, 6th ed. (Mason, OH: Thomson/South-Western, 2008), pp. 50–57; and Equal Employment Opportunity Commission, 29 C.F.R. Part 1607—*Uniform Guidelines on Employee Selection Procedures* (1978) at http://www.access.gpo.gov/nara/cfr/waisidx_06/29cfr1607_06.html.

72. "2007 Employer Bargaining Objectives," *Collective Bargaining Bulletin*, p. S-25.

73. Mark Montgomery, "New Evidence on Unions and Layoff Rates," *Industrial and Labor Relations Review*, 44, July 1991, pp. 708–712.

74. "2007 Employer Bargaining Objectives," *Collective Bargaining Bulletin*, p. S-25; Mohamed Branine, "The Logic of Job-Sharing in the Provision of and Delivery of Health Care," *Health Manpower Management*, 24 (1), 1998, p. 20.

75. David Sherwyn and Michael C. Sturman, "Job Sharing: A Potential Tool for Hotel Managers," *Cornell Hotel and Restaurant Administration Quarterly*, 43 (5), October 2002, pp. 84–91.

76. Steven Briggs, "Allocating Available Work in a Union Environment: Layoffs vs. Work Sharing," *Labor Law Journal*, 38 (10), October 1987, pp. 650–657.

77. *Franks v. Bowman Transportation Co.*, 424 U.S. 747 (1976).

78. *Teamsters v. United States*, 431 U.S. 324 (1977); *American Tobacco Co. v. Patterson*, 456 U.S. 63 (1982).

79. *Martin v. Wilks*, 490 U.S. 755 (1989).

80. *United Steelworkers of America v. Weber*, 443 U.S. 193 (1979).

81. *Firefighters, Local 1784 v. Stotts*, 467 U.S. 561 (1984).

82. *Wygant v. Jackson Board of Education*, 476 U.S. 267 (1986).

83. Scott David Williams, William M. Slonaker, and Ann C. Wendt, "An Analysis of Employment Discrimination Claims Associated with Layoffs," *S.A.M. Advanced Management Journal*, 68, Winter 2003, pp. 49–55.

84. Daniel Aaronson and Daniel Sullivan, "Growth in Workers Quality," *Chicago Fed Letter*, February 2002, p. 1.

85. John A. Challenger, "Preparing for the Knowledge-Based Economy," *Vital Speeches of the Day*, 72 (13), April 15, 2006, p. 395.

86. U.S. Department of Labor, "Implications of Workplace Change," in *Futurework: Trends and Challenges in the 21st Century*, September 16, 1999, p. 3 at http://www.dol.gov.

87. Scott Hays, "The ABCs of Workplace Literacy," *Workforce*, April 1999, p. 71.

88. Kirstin D. Grimsley, "Applicants Not Making the Grade," *The Washington Post*, April 13, 1999, p. E1.

89. Lisa M. Lynch and Sandra E. Black, "Beyond the Incidence of Employer Provided Training," *Industrial and Labor Relations Review*, 52, October 1998, pp. 64–81.

90. Harley Frazis, Maury Gittleman, Michael Horrigan, and Mary Joyce, "Results from the 1995 Survey of Employer Provided Training," *Monthly Labor Review*, 121 (6), June 1998, p. 8.

91. Harley J. Frazis, Diane E. Herz, and Michael W. Horrigan, "Employer Provided Training: Results from a New Survey," *Monthly Labor Review*, 118 (5), May 1995, pp. 3–17.

92. Frazis, Gittleman, Horrigan, and Joyce, "Results from the 1995 Survey of Employer Provided Training," p. 8.

93. Robert W. Glover and Cihan Bilginsoy, "Registered Apprenticeship Training in the U.S. Construction Industry," *Education & Training*, 47 (4/5), 2005, pp. 337–349; Robert P. Mader, "Union Apprentices More Likely to Finish Training: GAO," *Contractor*, 52 (10), 2005, pp. 1, 20 & 54; and Gunseli Berik and Cihan Bilginsoy, "Do Unions Help or Hinder Women in Training? Apprenticeship Programs in the United States," *Industrial Relations*, 39 (4), October 2000, pp. 600–624.

94. Peter Lazes and Jane Savage, "Embracing the Future: Union Strategies for the 21st Century," *The Journal for Quality and Participation*, 23 (4), Fall 2000, p. 20.

95. George R. Gray, Donald W. Myers, and Phyllis S. Myers, "Cooperative Provisions in Labor Agreements: A New Paradigm?" *Monthly Labor Review*, 122 (1), January 1999, pp. 29–45; Pat Costine and Thomas N. Garavan, "Trade Union Attitudes to Training and Development: The Road to a More Positive and Proactive Approach?" *Journal of European Industrial Training*, 19 (10), 1995, p. 38; and John Hoerr, "What Should Unions Do?" *Harvard Business Review*, 69, May–June 1991, p. 42.

96. Henry P. Guzda, "Unions Active in Joint Training Programs," *American Workplace* (January 1995), pp. 1–4.

97. Chau-kiu Cheung, "Rational or Demoralized Responses to Work Restructuring in Hong Kong?" *Human Relations*, 58 (2), February 2005, pp. 223–247 and Paul S. Adler, "Work Organization: From Taylorism to Teamwork," *Perspectives on Work* 1 (April 1997), pp. 61–65.

98. "News Release: U.S. Department of Labor and Ernst & Young LLP Study Finds Competitive Gains from Innovative Workplace Practices," May 31, 1995 (Study conducted by Sarah C. Mavrinac, Neil R. Jones, and Marshall W. Mayer).

99. Patrick Herman, "The Untrained, Unempowered Masses," *Industry Week*, 248, December 6, 1999, pp. 94–96.

100. John Godard and John T. Delaney, "Reflections on the 'High Performance' Paradigm's Implications for Industrial Relations as a Field," *Industrial and Labor Relations Review*, 53, April 2000, pp. 491–493.

101. "Innovative Workplaces and Their Workers," *Monthly Labor Review*, 126 (5), May 2003, p. 32.

102. Noel Harvey, "How Unions Should Respond to Cells," *Labor Studies Journal*, 18, Winter 1994, pp. 21–31.

103. George R. Gray, Donald W. Myers, and Phyllis S. Myers, "Collective Bargaining Agreements: Safety and Health Provisions," *Monthly Labor Review*, 121 (5), May 1998, pp. 13–35.

104. U.S. Department of Labor, Occupational Safety & Health Administration, *OSHA Facts*, August 2007, pp. 1–4 at http://www.osha.gov/as/opa/oshafacts.html and John C. Bradbury, "Regulatory Federalism and Workplace Safety: Evidence from OSHA Enforcement, 1981–1995," *Journal of Regulatory Economics*, 29, 2006, pp. 211–224.

105. Bureau of Labor Statistics, "Workplace Injuries and Illnesses in 2005," *News Release*, October 19, 2006, pp. 1–29.

106. Bureau of Labor Statistics, "National Census of Fatal Occupational Injuries in 2005," *News Release*, August 10, 2006, pp. 1–16.

107. "OSHA Rulemaking Process Credible but May Overstate Costs, OTA Says," *Daily Labor Report*, October 25, 1995, p. A-9.

108. *Marshall v. Barlow's Inc.*, 436 U.S. 307 (1978).

109. *Whirlpool Corporation v. Marshall*, 445 U.S. 1 (1980); *Gateway Coal Co. v. United Mine Workers*, 414 U.S. 368 (1974).

110. U.S. Department of Labor, Occupational Safety & Health Administration, "OSHA Requirements That Apply to Most General Industry," *OSHA Compliance Assistance General Industry Quick Start*, 2007, pp. 1–10 at http://www.osha.gov/dcsp/compliance_assistance/quickstarts/general_industry/general_industry.html.

111. Bureau of Labor Statistics, "Workplace Injuries and Illnesses in 2005," p. 2, 28.

112. AFL-CIO, "Bush Administration Ergonomics Plan Fails to Protect Workers from Crippling Injuries," *AFL-CIO Safety and Health Fact Sheet*, April 2002, p. 2.

113. Stuart Shapiro, "The Role of Procedural Controls in OSHA's Ergonomics Rulemaking," *Public Administration Review*, 67 (4), July/August 2007, pp. 688–701.

114. U.S. Department of Labor, Occupational Safety & Health Administration, "A Four-Pronged, Comprehensive Approach," *OSHA Effective Ergonomics: Strategy for Success*, August 6, 2007, pp. 1–2 and U.S. Department of Labor, Office of the 21st Century Workforce, "Target Ergonomics: Workplace Guidelines for Repetitive Motion Injuries," *XXI Magazine*, Fall 2002, pp. 8–13.

115. Frank Swoboda, "OSHA Exempts White-Collar Telecommuters," *The Washington Post,* January 27, 2000, p. A1.

116. Testimony of Peg Seminario, Director Safety and Health, AFL-CIO Before the Senate Employment and Worker Safety Subcommittee of the Health, Education, Labor and Pensions Committee Hearing on "Is OSHA Working for Working People?" April 26, 2007, p. 3.

117. *United Automobile Workers Union (UAW) v. Johnson Controls, Inc.,* 499 U.S. 187 (1991).

118. *Chevron U.S.A. Inc. v. Echazabal,* 536 U.S. 73 (2002). See also Ronald Bayer, "Workers' Liberty, Workers' Welfare: The Supreme Court Speaks on the Rights of Disabled Employees," *American Journal of Public Health,* 93, April 2003, pp. 540–544 and Norman Daniels, "*Chevron v. Echazabal*: Protection, Opportunity, and Paternalism," *American Journal of Public Health,* 93, April 2003, pp. 545–548.

119. Gary F. Coulton and Roger Wolters, "Employee and Management Rights and Responsibilities under the Americans with Disabilities Act (ADA): An Overview," *Employee Responsibilities and Rights Journal,* 6, March 1993, pp. 55–56.

120. Thomas W. Hale, Howard V. Hayghe, and John M. McNeil, "Persons with Disabilities Labor Market Activity, 1994," *Monthly Labor Review* 121 (September 1998), pp. 3–12.

121. Edward H. Yelin and Laura Trupin, "Disability and the Characteristics of Employment," *Monthly Labor Review,* 126 (5), May 2003, pp. 20–31.

122. U.S. Equal Employment Opportunity Commission, *Charge Statistics FY 1997 Through FY 2006,* February 26, 2007, p. 1 at http://www.eeoc.gov/stats/charges.html.

123. Daniel Egan, "The Dwindling Class of 'Disabled Individual': An Exemplification of the Americans with Disabilities Act's Inadequacies in *D'Angelo v. Conagra Foods,*" *St. Johns Law Review,* 81 (1), Winter 2007, pp. 491–514; Nathan Catchpole and Aaron Miller, "The Disabled ADA: How a Narrowing ADA Threatens To Exclude the Cognitively Disabled," *Brigham Young University Law Review,* 5, 2006, pp. 1333–1379.

124. Deborah E. Knapp, Robert H. Faley, and Lori K. Long, "The Americans with Disabilities Act: A Review and Synthesis of the Legal Literature with Implications for Practitioners," *Equal Opportunities International,* 25 (5), 2006, pp. 354–372; Kelly C. Woodford and Thomas J. Woodford, "The Duty to Accommodate a Person Who Is Perceived as Disabled: Say It Isn't So," *Labor Law Journal,* 57 (2), Summer 2006, pp. 71–82; Suzanne M. Crampton and John W. Hodge, "The ADA and Disability Accommodation," *Public Personnel Management,* 32, Spring 2003, pp. 143–154; Jeffrey A. Mello, "The Rights of Employees With Disabilities: Supreme Court Interpretations of the American With Disabilities Act and Their Implications for Human Resource Management," *Employee Responsibilities and Rights Journal,* 13, December 2001, pp. 175–189.

125. *Toyota Motor Manufacturing, Kentucky, Inc. v. Williams,* 534 U.S. 184 (2002); *Sutton et al. v. United Airlines Inc.,* 527 U.S. 471 (1999); *Murphy v. United Parcel Service, Inc.,* 527 U.S. 516 (1999); and *Albertson's Inc. v. Kirkingburg,* 527 U.S. 555 (1999).

126. *US Airways, Inc. v. Barnett,* 535 U.S. 391 (2002).

127. Paper, Allied Industrial, Chemical, and Energy Workers Union (PACE), *The Americans with Disabilities Act: Collective Bargaining and Other Issues,* 1998, pp. 1–12. See also: AFL-CIO, *Discrimination: Disability,* 2007, p. 1 at http://www.aflcio.org/issues/jobseconomy/workersrights/rightsatwork_e/disc_disability.cfm.

128. Jeffrey A. Mello, "Employing and Accommodating Workers with Disabilities: Mandates and Guidelines for Labor Relations," *Labor Law Journal,* 44, March 1993, pp. 162–170.

129. James W. Bucking, "Beyond the ADA: Protection of Employees with Drug and Alcohol Problems in Arbitration," *The Labor Lawyer,* 11, Winter–Spring, 1995, pp. 1–5.

130. Coulton and Wolters, "Employee and Management Rights and Responsibilities," pp. 58–59.

131. *Equal Employment Opportunity Commission v. Waffle House, Inc.,* 534 U.S. 279 (2002).

ADA Claim for Reasonable Accommodation

CASE STUDY 8-1 Jack Hand was employed as a pipefitter's helper when he injured his back on the job. According to testimony from the neurosurgeon that treated Hand's injury, Hand was unable to lift more than 10 lbs. frequently or 20 lbs. occasionally, could not sit or stand more than one hour without a break, and could not stoop, crawl, climb ladders, or perform overhead work. These work restrictions were considered permanent due to the degenerative condition of Hand's lumbar region of the spine. Hand recognized that he could not perform the job he formally held at the time of his injury but did pursue other light-duty jobs (e.g., fire watch position or a job monitoring and checking for leaky pipes) at his employer's firm. After being repeatedly told that no light-duty jobs were currently vacant at the company, Hand quit and sued his employer for allegedly failing to provide him a reasonable accommodation under the ADA by refusing to assign him a light-duty job after his injury.

Questions

1. Does Hand meet the legal definition of a qualified individual with a disability who, with a reasonable accommodation, could perform the essential job functions of the light-duty position he seeks with the firm?

2. If an employer has some light-duty jobs in which individuals with injuries similar to Hand's have been previously or are currently employed, could the employer be required to create such a job vacancy for Hand to fill in order to provide him with a reasonable accommodation under the ADA?

The Outsourced Work

CASE STUDY 8-2 Rocket Motor Corporation (RMC) entered into a project labor agreement with 17 local building trades' unions concerning a building remodeling project at one of the company's manufacturing plants. As part of the project labor agreement, the unions agreed not to engage in any strikes, slowdowns, or other work stoppages and not to honor the picket lines established by any other labor organization at the job site. RMC agreed as part of the project labor agreement to hire contractors and subcontractors who would employ individuals to perform construction work from each specified type of trade represented by the 17 unions at terms and conditions of employment equal to the terms specified in any applicable union contract covering the type of work to be performed. The project labor agreement called for final and binding arbitration to resolve any disputes arising from the interpretation or application of the terms of the project labor agreement.

Bolton Engineering (BE) was one contractor hired by Rocket Motor Corporation to help remodel the company's paint facilities at the work site. As part of the contract entered into between RMC and BE, a pledge to adhere to the project labor agreement previously signed by RMC and the 17 unions was included. BE employed only a few supervisory employees of its own at the work site and relied upon unionized subcontractors to complete most of the assigned job site tasks. However, a significant portion of the metal fabrication work was subcontracted to two nonunion subcontractors whose employees performed the work offsite. All of the metal fabricated parts built offsite were eventually to be installed on the job site by union labor.

Local 82 of the Steel Fabricators Union (SFU) learned that BE was using nonunion labor at offsite facilities to perform metal fabrication work that could have been performed onsite by union members represented by the SFU. The prevailing wage for a steel fabricator under current area labor agreements covering SFU members was $20.73 per hour whereas the offsite nonunion workers were paid $9.00 per hour to perform the steel fabrication work. Local 82 leaders believed that BE was in violation of the project labor agreement by subcontracting steel fabrication work to nonunion subcontractors who were paying their employees substantially less than the prevailing wage rate called for under Local 82's current contract. Failing to resolve the issue voluntarily with BE, Local 82, SFU filed a grievance, which eventually went to final and binding arbitration. The union sought damages from BE in the amount of $1.6 million, the amount of the difference between the wages paid nonunion employees who performed the steel fabrication work offsite and what Local 82 members would have received had the work been performed by them on the work site.

Questions

1. Is BE bound by the terms of the project labor agreement, which it did not directly sign, including the duty to submit this labor dispute to final and binding arbitration for resolution?

2. Was the project labor agreement only meant to apply to work performed on the job site as BE contends, or could the terms of the project labor agreement also be applied to offsite work as well as the Union contends?

3. Is it legitimate for a labor organization to negotiate a work preservation clause which seeks to encourage contractors to perform work on the job site using union labor by imposing an economic incentive not to outsource the work elsewhere to lower paid employees?

4. What, if any, legitimate business interest of an employer is served by agreeing to a so-called work preservation agreement with one or more unions?

The Disputed Safety Bonus

CASE STUDY 8-3 Bob Dale and Sam Brady were employed as truck drivers by Jackson Transportation Inc. (JTI) a nonunion firm engaged in interstate commerce. JTI provided transportation services for nonunion Acme Steel Corporation (ASC) hauling steel coils between ASC's various plants and directly to various ASC customers. Dale and Brady performed all of their work assignments, transporting steel coils on ASC property.

To encourage safe trucking operations, ASC implemented a safety bonus program that paid trucking firms employed by ASC an amount equal to one dollar for each safe hour of work performed by each firm's employees. ASC strongly encouraged the transportation firms with whom it contracted for services to pass the $1 per safe hour of operation bonus on to their employees.

JTI decided to pass one half of the safety bonus payment (50 cents) on to its truck drivers and keep the remaining 50 cents to fund certain safety equipment purchases and the company's annual Christmas party. Bob Dale learned from talking to drivers at other firms employed by ASC that they were receiving the full $1 bonus from their employers. This upset Dale who thought his employer (JTI) should also be giving drivers the full $1 per hour bonus payment. Dale discussed his complaint with several other employees, including Sam Brady.

On December 9, employee Dale told Brady that he was on his way to see Phil Cook, ASC's transportation manager at the plant where both Brady and Dale were assigned. Brady said he would accompany Dale to the meeting as he didn't want to miss any of the fireworks. At the meeting, Dale explained to Cook his complaint about JTI not paying its drivers the full $1 bonus amount. Cook replied that essentially this was not a decision over which he had any control and any complaints should be delivered directly to JTI managers, not ASC. The meeting ended after about 15 minutes and Dale and Brady exited Cook's office. Cook then telephoned R. C. Ridley, the JTI terminal manager who supervised Dale and Brady, and explained to him the nature of the conversation Cook had engaged in with Dale in Brady's presence.

On December 19, Ridley, accompanied by a security guard, escorted Dale from the ASC property, explaining that he was being removed because "they believed that he was trying get a union started because he had talked to Cook." Ridley told Dale that ASC had barred Dale from its property. Dale responded that he was not trying to start a union and had never even spoken to anyone about doing so. Ridley stated the company would have to investigate the matter further.

On that same date (Dec. 19), Ridley, accompanied by a security guard, also escorted Brady from the ASC property. Ridley told Brady he was being removed from the property because he had been present when Dale met with Cook about the safety bonus issue. Brady indicated that he had not known in advance the specific nature of the statements that Dale planned to make that day in Cook's office.

On December 27, Ridley informed Dale that he was being terminated in the best interest of the company. Dale's written termination notice stated that he was terminated because he was "not able to function on ASC property." Ridley also informed Brady on the same date that he too was terminated because ASC did not want him back on their property. Brady's written termination notice stated the reason for termination was "not able to function on ASC property." Brady and Dale subsequently filed an unfair labor practice with the NLRB, alleging that JTI's discharge action represented unlawful discrimination against them under the LMRA, as amended.

Questions

1. Was the discharge of Dale and Brady a violation of Sec. 8 (a) (1) and (3) of the LMRA? If so, what should be the appropriate remedy?

2. Was the decision by JTI to award only half of the safety bonus money available to its truck drivers a lawful employer decision?

3. If you had been advising JTI on the safety bonus issue, would you have recommended the company retain half the bonus money for the purposes described by the company (i.e., buy safety equipment and pay for the annual Christmas party)? Why or why not?

Copyright GettyImages

CHAPTER 9

Resolving Negotiation (Interest) Disputes and the Use of Economic Pressure

Labor-management negotiations do not result in strikes very often. Only 20 major work stoppages involving 1,000 or more employees occurred in 2006, up slightly from the record low level of 14 recorded in 2003.[1] In recent years strikes and lockouts have accounted for .01 or less percent of the total hours worked. Media coverage of work stoppages which do occur is often intense and frequently fails to emphasize the important role that economic pressure tactics can play in helping negotiators to reach realistic settlement outcomes.

This chapter begins with a discussion of the alternative interest dispute resolution procedures involving third parties, such as mediation, fact-finding, and interest arbitration. The chapter also examines the use of economic pressure tactics (e.g., strike, lockout, boycott, picketing) as a means of encouraging the voluntary resolution of interest disputes.

IMPASSE-RESOLUTION PROCEDURES INVOLVING A THIRD-PARTY NEUTRAL

Usually both union and management representatives attempt to voluntarily resolve bargaining impasses, which can occur either before or after a contract's scheduled expiration date. In some cases, union and management officials need third parties either to facilitate the negotiation process or to render a final and binding decision to resolve an interest dispute. **Mediation, fact-finding,** and **interest arbitration** are three important impasse resolution procedures involving the aid of neutral, third parties in resolving interest (negotiation) disputes.

Mediation

Most union-management interest disputes are resolved voluntarily by the parties themselves without the need for assistance from an outside, third-party neutral. In 1947 as part of the Labor Management Relations Act, Congress created the **Federal Mediation and Conciliation Service (FMCS)**, an independent federal agency charged with helping to prevent or minimize labor disputes by providing mediation, conciliation, and voluntary arbitration services. In FY 2006, the FMCS was involved in 5,484 collective bargaining contract negotiations covering every major industry.[2] Mediation is the most commonly used third-party interest dispute resolution procedure, and the FMCS, along with some 18 state mediation agencies, help to achieve Congress' goal of fostering stable labor management relations in order to facilitate the free flow of commerce.

As part of the legal duty to bargain in good faith under the LMRA , bargaining parties are required to provide 30 days' advance notice to the FMCS or any other applicable state mediation agency that bargaining between the parties is ongoing but no settlement has yet been reached. This notice can be filed electronically, using a form available from the FMCS's Internet Web site at www.fmcs.gov. A mediator will contact the bargaining parties and offer his or her services in aiding the parties to reach a voluntary settlement. Deciding to use the services of a third-party mediator is voluntary on the part of the bargaining parties except in the rare case where the dispute involves a "national emergency" discussed more fully later in this chapter.

A mediator has no legal authority to impose a settlement on the parties, and thus functions more as an invited guest who can be required to leave if one or both bargaining parties no longer desire the mediator's continued involvement in the bargaining process. Mediators must rely on persuasion and their credibility as a facilitator in helping the bargaining parties reach agreement on their own. Mediators can perform a number of functions to assist the bargaining process including: assisting in scheduling meetings, keeping the parties talking, carrying messages back and forth, helping each party realistically assess their current bargaining position and alternatives, and suggesting possible new approaches or terms to facilitate settlement.[3] The mediation process is much more an art than a science. Mediation has been described as a process that "has been helpful in a haphazard way largely because of the talents of certain individuals who themselves would find it difficult to say why they had been successful."[4]

Several characteristics and practices of labor mediators have been associated with mediator effectiveness. Effective mediators have tenacity—they do not give up without exhausting themselves, the parties, and all reasonable avenues of settlement. A second characteristic is experience, which simply means that the more times a mediator is involved in mediating labor disputes, the more effective he or she is likely to be in settling one. Finally, mediators who are active, who pressure the parties to reach a settlement, who generate their own settlement terms, and who play an independent role in the mediation process are more likely to be effective mediators.[5]

Carl Stevens, in a study focusing on the mediator's functions and tactics, has identified several causal factors that lead to a negotiated settlement.[6] Timing of the mediator's involvement is one of the most important considerations. A mediator should enter the bargaining dispute before the parties become too fixed in their positions but not so early as to upset the power balance between the parties, causing them to harden their bargaining positions. In some instances, the mere entrance of the mediator may be sufficient for dispute settlement to occur. For example, assume that one of the chief negotiators leaves an active negotiation in a temper tantrum, vowing never again to return to the bargaining table. On subsequent reflection, the negotiator realizes a mistake was made but feels that calling the opposing negotiator would be embarrassing and perhaps indicate weakness. A common tactic used in such situations would be to call a mediator, who could schedule another meeting. Thus, mediation can represent a very important face-saving device for a bargaining party. In other cases, the parties do not desire any specific help from the mediator, but the availability of that mediator and the very existence of the mediation forum facilitate the bargaining process.[7]

Mediators are expected to possess a high level of knowledge concerning labor relations practices, economic and industry trends, labor and employment law, problem-solving techniques (e.g., interest-based bargaining), and best practices for building ongoing cooperative labor management relations (e.g., labor-management committees, partnership training).[8] Mediators vary in their roles, behaviors, and styles. Some have been characterized as "deal makers," entering the negotiations at an early stage and actively attempting to persuade the parties to accept the mediator's proposed settlement terms. Other mediators seem to prefer the role of "orchestrator," attempting to structure the negotiations to facilitate communication between the parties to provide greater insight into the issues in dispute. A mediator may become much more active in encouraging the parties to settle when a work stoppage appears imminent.[9]

A successful mediator is often an interpreter, who helps clarify the bargaining parties' perceptions of the bargaining climate and possible costs of failing to reach an agreement. For example, if the parties disagree on data about the cost of living, comparative wage rates, or productivity data, the mediator could assist in reaching agreement on what relevant sources to use to obtain statistical data. If a negotiator underestimates the cost of a strike or lockout or overestimates the cost of agreeing to another parties' proposed settlement terms, the mediator may be able to provide insights enabling the negotiator to evaluate his or her position more realistically. Often a mediator will hold separate meetings with each bargaining party before attempting to schedule a joint meeting between the parties. This provides the mediator a chance to better understand each party's rationale for current bargaining positions and the depth of commitment each party has for those positions. Developing trust between the mediator and each bargaining party is necessary before the mediator is likely to have much success helping the parties better understand and trust each other in the bargaining process.

Helping bargaining parties to better understand the tactics or intentions of each other can also aid the bargaining process. If management bluffs about its willingness to accept a strike or to allow an ongoing strike to continue indefinitely, the mediator may attempt to diagnose management's true intentions and then advise the union. On the other hand, if the union threatens a strike to obtain an excessive bargaining demand, the mediator could attempt to diagnose what the union is "really trying to say" and so inform the company negotiator. By holding private caucuses with each party, the mediator becomes privy to much confidential information. Although no mediator should reveal confidential information to the other party, he or she can provide insight to the parties regarding the magnitude of the differences that exist between them and encourage the parties that a settlement may be near if they continue bargaining in good faith. Mediators can apply pressure for settlement on one or both parties by using delays and deadlines in the mediation process, placing responsibility for settlement on the parties, engaging in marathon (round-the-clock) bargaining sessions, emphasizing the costs of a strike or lockout, and making settlement recommendations in a joint conference.[10]

The parties, however, play the dominant role in shaping the mediation process. Where experienced negotiators have a clear understanding of their bargaining objectives and strategies, the mediator is primarily the servant of the parties. However, where less experienced negotiators have not clearly defined their bargaining objectives, the personal qualities and actions of a competent mediator may be able to gain the trust of the parties and create the type of negotiating atmosphere that achieves a settlement.[11]

Because there is no widely adopted code of professional conduct for mediators, and because potentially great danger exists from inept and unscrupulous practitioners, national organizations led by The Association for Conflict Resolution (ACR) have developed a code of professional conduct to promote ethical behavior by mediators. This code articulates qualifications for mediators, standards of practice, and ethical behavior. It proscribes impermissible actions of mediators, such as holding meetings with one of the parties without prior consent of the other party and revealing to one party what would be considered an acceptable settlement to the other. The code is patterned after the widely accepted Code of Professional Responsibility for Arbitrators of Labor-Management Disputes, which has existed since 1951 (revised most recently in 1995) and has been adopted by the National Academy of Arbitrators, American Arbitration Association, and FMCS.[12]

Fact-Finding

Fact-finding is a semi-judicial process used primarily in the public sector to gather facts about a labor dispute for the purpose of publishing a public report containing the fact-finder's conclusions and often recommended terms of settlement. Like a mediator, a fact-finder has no legal authority to impose a final and binding settlement on the parties involved in a labor dispute. The fact-finder's purpose is to assess the facts and to organize and display them publicly in the hopes that the public will find the fact-finder's conclusions and recommendations to have merit and bring pressure on the parties in dispute to settle their differences.[13] Typically both public employers and public employee unions, recognizing the need to be responsive to taxpayers or consumers of public services, seek to use support from such groups to bolster their respective bargaining positions.

Fact-finding may be used in major disputes under the Labor Management Relations Act (LMRA) and the Railway Labor Act. In major disputes, fact-finding reports are useful to presidents in determining what actions to take in national emergencies, such as when to seek an injunction or recommend legislation to resolve the dispute. Because fact-finding lacks the ability to ensure a final end to the labor dispute, this process does not have a good record in resolving major disputes. However, there is some evidence that fact-finding when used as an intermediate step prior to some final resolution procedure (e.g., interest arbitration, legislative action) can increase the rate of negotiated settlements compared to the voluntary settlement rate achieved in the absence of fact-finding as an intermediate step.[14] The fact-finder's report and recommendations apparently serve as a focal point for negotiators, encouraging them to voluntarily agree to terms at or close to the fact-finder's recommendations, thus avoiding the need to turn the outcome of the interest dispute over to an outside party (e.g., arbitrator, legislature) to obtain a final dispute resolution.

Interest Arbitration

Traditional interest arbitration involves the selection of a neutral person or panel to hear the bargaining positions of the parties and make a final and binding decision on what should be included in a negotiated agreement. This process differs from grievance arbitration (see Chapter 11), which is concerned mostly with resolving rights-type disputes over the interpretation or application of existing contract terms.

Interest arbitration in the United States dates back to the eighteenth century in the copper mines of Connecticut. It is not used very often in the private sector (approximately two percent of negotiations) to resolve contract negotiation disputes with some notable exceptions, such as the Amalgamated Transit Union, which has arbitrated more than 700 cases, and the legal provision for interest arbitration of postal worker interest disputes.[15]

Management and union representatives in the private sector prefer to control the outcome of interests disputes which establish the terms or conditions of employment and are therefore reluctant to grant such authority to an outside arbitrator. Both parties have concerns about possible delay created in trying to schedule an arbitration hearing and the extra cost involved. In addition, management becomes particularly concerned if an arbitrator fails to take into account the economic effect of the arbitration decision on the employer's operations or if the award is above the industry average. Interest arbitration in the public sector is discussed more fully in Chapter 13.

Interest arbitration has been criticized on the assumption that arbitrators may tend to "split the difference," in resolving disputes, thereby causing the parties to take more extreme positions on issues in dispute. Whether an arbitrator has the flexibility to merely split the difference between the parties' offers is determined in part by the type of arbitration procedure used. Arbitrators have a number of criteria that can be used to determine what constitutes appropriate settlement terms of an interest dispute (see Exhibit 9.1). Most arbitrators will weigh the parties' positions and relevant supporting evidence in relation to specific criteria to determine the dispute outcome rather than mechanically splitting the difference to determine a dispute's outcome.[16] Because neutrals may vary in the norms of their decision making, the parties can exert some degree of control over the dispute outcome by defining the decision criteria to be used by an arbitrator in advance.[17]

Another criticism of interest arbitration is that it reduces the costs of not reaching agreement during face-to-face negotiations between the parties and thus exerts a so-called "chilling effect" on the parties' incentive to reach an agreement. Research supports a finding that fewer voluntary settlements are reached under a negotiation system that permits interest arbitration than under systems permitting a right to strike or lockout in the absence of a negotiated settlement.[18] If either party believes that it can gain a better settlement from an arbitrator than through negotiation, there may be an incentive to maintain unrealistic demands in the hope that an arbitrator might make a more favorable award than the other party is willing to offer at the bargaining table.

Exhibit 9.1

Some Relevant Criteria an Arbitrator May Use to Decide an Interest Bargaining Dispute

- Comparability of relevant employee wage, hours, or other working conditions with similar private- or public-sector employees within the same geographic area or industry.
- Current economic conditions (e.g., inflation, unemployment, product/service demand, productivity).
- Occupational or job requirements (e.g., physical or mental abilities, degree and variety of skills required, prior work experience or relevant training, hazardous or unpleasant working conditions, degree of responsibility, creativity, stress).
- The financial ability of the employer to pay for the costs of any proposed settlement terms (including an assessment of current and future projected revenues during the term of the labor agreement).
- Whether a bargaining proposal involves a new bargaining subject (i.e., a subject not previously agreed upon in a prior contract between the parties' or not common in other labor agreements in the industry or geographic area).
- The potential effect of the arbitrator's decision on the encouragement of effective and stable labor relations within the parties' bargaining relationship.
- The availability of recommended settlement terms from a mediator, fact-finder, or other similar board of inquiry concerning the interest dispute.
- The general welfare and interest of the public.

A third concern about interest arbitration is that the existence of the interest arbitration procedure may create a so-called "narcotic effect" on the bargaining parties. As the parties gain more knowledge of how arbitrators decide outcomes or experience actual gains through arbitration beyond what a party might have expected in the absence of an interest arbitration option, the parties may become increasingly reliant on interest arbitration to resolve bargaining disputes in subsequent negotiations.[19] In contrast, one study reported that knowledge gained by parties regarding arbitral preferences and decision criteria tends to make subsequent negotiations between the parties more realistic, producing settlements closer to the norms established by the arbitrator during prior contract negotiation disputes.[20]

In fact, studies of the existence of the "narcotic effect" in interest arbitration have produced mixed results. A study of the use of arbitration over an eight-year period under the Minnesota Public Labor Relations Act did not reveal its existence. However, earlier studies in New York and British Columbia had identified such an effect, although the effect seems to fade after several years as the parties gain experience with the process.[21]

THREE INTEREST ARBITRATION PROCEDURES

The interest arbitration procedure affording the arbitrator the greatest degree of flexibility to determine an appropriate settlement outcome is **conventional interest arbitration (CA)**.[22] Using this procedure, each party would present their proposed settlement terms and supporting evidence to the arbitrator who would have the authority to decide what final terms of settlement were most reasonable on a case-by-case basis. The arbitrator could select either party's proposal or some compromise settlement terms between or beyond those proposed by the parties themselves.

When an arbitrator is presented with two offers in which one offer differs substantially from what the arbitrator has determined to be a reasonable or preferred offer, the arbitrator will most often select the offer which is closer to his or her preferred offer.[23] This provides some incentive for parties to make reasonable offers in arbitration which may then become the basis for further voluntary negotiations resulting in settlement prior to an arbitrator rendering a final and binding decision.

Final-offer total package (FOTP) selection is a form of interest arbitration that restricts an arbitrator's authority to settle an interest dispute by requiring the selection of either the employer's or union's final proposal on all issues in dispute. This is in effect a "winner take all" proposition where one party's position will prevail on all issues in dispute. In theory, forcing one party to risk a total loss through FOTP arbitration provides a powerful incentive for parties to voluntarily negotiate an acceptable outcome to avoid risking the arbitrator's decision.[24] Neither party can guarantee that the arbitrator will select their proposal as the most appropriate or reasonable. FOTP also eliminates any chance for an arbitrator to simply split the difference between the union's and management's final proposed settlement terms. Theoretically, if both parties genuinely attempt to present acceptable proposals to the arbitrator, their positions will converge, enhancing the opportunity for them to settle their differences without third-party intervention.

A somewhat less risky alternative to FOTP is **final-offer issue-by-issue (FOIBI)** selection, where the arbitrator is restricted to selecting either the union's or employer's final proposal on each separate issue in dispute. The FOIBI procedure permits the arbitrator to assess each bargaining issue in dispute separately on its own merits to determine which party has the most reasonable proposal. While in theory one party could still be determined to have the most reasonable proposal on every issue in dispute, it is more likely that one party's proposal would be judged more appropriate on some issues in dispute whereas the other party's position might prevail on other issues.

FOTP selection arbitration has been used in determining baseball salaries for several years. Similar to a strike threat, the threat of arbitration imposes a cost risk on the player and team owner for continuing to disagree on settlement terms. Because the arbitrator may select only one of the two offers submitted by the opposing sides, the parties are motivated to reach a negotiated voluntary settlement. In a study of 1,774 final offers exchanged in professional baseball between the years 1981–2001, only 19 percent of cases actually resulted in an arbitration decision with the remainder being settled voluntarily by the parties prior to the arbitration hearing.[25]

Research on FOTP arbitration in baseball has revealed that typically only the high-quality baseball players file for arbitration and seek to have their salaries decided in arbitration. Because the salaries of baseball players who qualify for arbitration are 80 to 90 percent higher than those of comparable ineligible players, baseball clubs have an incentive to substitute players with cheaper salaries for players whose salaries are raised through arbitration beyond management's own valuation of a player's worth.[26] Arbitrators' preferred outcome in baseball salary arbitration tends to be based upon a weighted average of the player's salary from the previous season and the average free agent salary representing a compromise between the perspectives of owners and players.[27] While arbitration decisions do tend to select team owners' offers slightly more often than players' offers, one study reports such team proposals prevent players from receiving "true market wages," and this is particularly true for African-American and Latin-born players.[28]

Interest arbitration procedures do have some shortcomings, particularly if relevant criteria on which to base arbitration decisions are not agreed upon by the parties. More importantly, because labor negotiations usually involve multiple issues which may be in dispute between the parties, interest arbitration can become a very complex process. Under final offer arbitration procedures, if the parties do not compromise on significant differences between their bargaining positions prior to arbitration, then an arbitrator would be required to select one of the party's extreme proposals. This could heighten union-management tensions during the life of the contract and cause future difficulties in negotiating subsequent contracts.[29]

Mediation-Arbitration (Med-Arb)

Mediation-arbitration (or **med-arb**) is a variation on traditional mediation and interest arbitration procedures chosen by some bargaining relationships that seek to combine the two separate processes into one. Under the procedure, a third-party neutral selected by the bargaining parties will first function in the role of a mediator attempting to encourage the parties to reach a voluntary settlement. If no settlement occurs, the third-party neutral then switches hats to become an arbitrator empowered by the parties to make a final and binding decision to resolve the parties' interest dispute. Because the arbitrator would already be familiar with the parties' positions and supporting evidence on issues in dispute, less time would be required in the arbitration hearing to present those positions and have the arbitrator render a decision. By the same token, because the arbitrator has already functioned as a mediator in the dispute, one or both parties may be concerned that opinions formed during the mediation phase could influence the outcome of the arbitration phase since the same individual would be functioning as both mediator and arbitrator. In theory under a med-arb procedure, most issues will be resolved voluntarily by the parties because in addition to the traditional pressures of bargaining there is the pressure of knowing that the mediator-arbitrator will make a final and binding decision if the parties fail to reach a voluntary agreement.

The Use of Economic Pressure to Resolve Interest Disputes

The ability to raise a party's costs of continuing to disagree to current proposed terms of settlement is an important factor which can encourage that party to compromise in order to avoid such costs. In most cases, a credible threat of the costs associated with a work stoppage, whether initiated as a strike by employees or a lockout by an employer, is sufficient to motivate both union and management negotiators to seek a reasonable alternative. For such a threat to be perceived as credible, the party receiving the threat must believe that the party making the threat has both the ability and willingness to carry out the threat successfully. In commenting on the use of economic pressure tactics during good faith bargaining the Supreme Court stated:

The policy of Congress is to impose a mutual duty upon the parties to confer in good faith with a desire to reach an agreement, in the belief that such an approach from both sides of the table promotes the over-all design of achieving industrial peace.... The presence of economic weapons in reserve and their actual exercise on occasion by the parties, is part and parcel of the system that the Wagner and Taft-Hartley Acts have recognized.... In one aspect collective bargaining is a

brute contest of economic power somewhat masked by polite manners and volu-
minous statistics. Initially it may be only fear of the economic consequences of dis-
agreement that turns the parties to facts, reason, a sense of responsibility, a
responsiveness to government and public opinion, and moral principle; but in
time these forces generate their own compulsions, and negotiating a contract
approaches the ideal of informed persuasion.[30]

A **strike** is a temporary work stoppage by a group of employees for the purpose of expressing a grievance or enforcing a demand. Tactics often used to support a strike include picketing activity or a boycott of the primary employer's goods or services. The **primary employer** in a labor dispute is the employer with whom the striking employees (union) have a dispute and the employer who has the ability to end the dispute by agreeing to the employees' proposed settlement terms. The LMRA (Sec. 7 and 13) protects employees' right to strike so long as the strike is for a lawful purpose and is carried out using lawful means. Authorizing an illegal strike can have serious consequences for a union as the Transport Union Workers, Local 100 discovered when a judge fined the union $2.5 million and ordered the local union president to jail for ten days for calling an illegal strike which shut down New York City's mass transit system for three days during the Christmas holiday shopping season.[31]

A **lockout** is a temporary work stoppage caused by an employer's withdrawal of employees' opportunity to work for the purpose of enforcing a bargaining demand or minimizing the employer's potential loss should employees control the timing of a work stoppage by initiating a strike. Another reason an employer might initiate a lockout is to protect the integrity of a multi-employer bargaining unit. To counter a union's ability to selectively strike only certain competitors who may bargain together as a multi-employer unit, if one unit member is struck, the other employers agree to lockout their employees, thus making the union extend the scope of the bargaining dispute to a larger number of its members and forcing the union to expend resources at a faster rate to support members affected by the strike or lockout actions.

An example of a lockout occurred in the 2003–2004 interest dispute between some 70,000 Southern California grocery workers represented by the United Food and Commercial Workers Union and three employers.[32] After union employees initiated a strike on October 11, 2003, against two grocery store chains owned by Safeway, Inc., other grocery store chains owned by Kroger Co. and Albertsons Inc. responded by locking out their employees. The longest supermarket work stoppage in U.S. history, the dispute occurred principally over wage and health care benefit issues and featured mediation. Employers rejected a union proposal to submit disputed issues to final and binding interest arbitration, and only after four and a half months and millions of dollars in costs did the parties reach a negotiated contract settlement. In 2007, after four months of bargaining, these same parties reached settlement on a new four-year contract expiring in 2011 with the assistance of a mediator from the Federal Mediation and Conciliation Service.[33] The 2007 agreement was possible in part because the memory of costs associated with the 2004 work stoppage was still fresh in the minds of union and management negotiators.

During a lockout, an employer can attempt to continue normal business operations by using nonbargaining unit personnel or hiring temporary replacements for locked-out employees.[34] Since the employer initiated the work stoppage, permanent replacement of locked-out workers is not permitted. Otherwise, some employers might initiate a lockout as a means of replacing workers who had lawfully exercised their right to join a union and engage in collective bargaining. A locked-out employee always has the right to return to work at any time during the lockout by notifying management of the employee's voluntary acceptance of the employer's proposed terms and conditions of employment (termed an **unconditional request for reinstatement**). Any unreasonable delay in reinstating a locked-out employee following such an unconditional request for reinstatement would represent an unfair (illegal) labor practice by the employer.

It is useful to think about the concept of a strike along two dimensions. First, whether the strike is legal or illegal, which essentially involves examining the ends (purpose) of the strike action and the means (tactics) used to carry it out. A strike called for a lawful purpose does not become unlawful merely because one or more individuals engage in unlawful misconduct during the strike. Unlawful acts by individuals can be remedied without denying all participants their lawful right to strike. However, any employee who participates in an unlawful strike or engages in unlawful strike activity during an otherwise lawful strike forfeits the rights granted by the LMRA to lawful strikers (discussed further later in the chapter).

A second dimension used to classify strikes is whether the work stoppage involves an economic dispute or is caused by the commission of an employer's unfair labor practice (e.g., a refusal to bargain in good faith). Whether a work stoppage is classified as an **economic strike** or an **unfair labor practice strike** has important implications for the rights of both employers and employees participating in the strike. It is possible that a strike which began over a wage dispute (an economic strike) could be converted into an unfair labor practice strike if the occurrence of an employer's unfair labor practice prolonged the work stoppage by becoming a reason for the strike's continuation.

Most work stoppages are classified as lawful economic strikes involving a dispute over a mandatory bargain subject such as wages, benefits, hours of work, or management's rights. Sometimes bargaining unit members are asked to support a strike to gain improvements in desired terms or conditions of employment or to avoid (minimize) proposed management reductions in such terms or conditions. Additionally union members sometimes strike to achieve some institutional goal of their union such as a union security clause.[35]

Some types of economic strikes have been given their own special name. For example, the term **wildcat strike** generally refers to a strike which occurs in violation of an existing no-strike clause in a labor agreement and often without the approval or prior knowledge of union officials. Such a spontaneous work stoppage by one or more employees if in violation of current contract terms would be illegal and could result in the participating employees being subject to discipline or discharge by their employer. Some employees' refusal to work when confronted with perceived extremely dangerous and unsafe working conditions do not fit the definition of a wildcat strike because Section 502, LMRA specifically authorizes such concerted activity, which cannot be barred by the language of a contractual no-strike clause.[36]

A **sympathy strike** is a work stoppage by employees who have no dispute with their own employer but are striking to support another bargaining unit of their employer or a union representing employees at another employer. Standard no-strike/no-lockout clause language is generally interpreted to apply only to disputes between the parties to that contract and subjects which could be resolved through submission to the contract's final and binding grievance-arbitration procedure. An employer may seek to negotiate the addition of specific language to the parties' standard no-strike clause which would prohibit employees from engaging in a sympathy strike during the term of the labor agreement.

A **jurisdictional strike** involves a dispute between two or more unions over the assignment of work (see discussion in Chapter 8). It is an unfair labor practice under the LMRA for a union to strike or threaten such action to force an employer to assign work to that union's members rather than another work group.

Reasons for Strikes

Work stoppages in the United States since 1982 have been at or near historic low levels in terms of numbers of strikes, employees involved, and days idled (Exhibit 9.2). Although the number of major work stoppages in 2006 (20) declined from the prior year, the number of lost work days due to strike activity increased due to the length of those strikes.[37] The mean length of major work stoppages occurring in 2006 was 26.5 days compared to 20 days in 2005 and 14.6 days in 2004. Significant work stoppages occurring during 2006 involved Northwest Airlines and the Aircraft Mechanics Fraternal Association; AK Steel Corporation and the Armco Employees Independent Federation; and the Goodyear Tire and Rubber Company and the United Steelworkers of America.

Some researches have attributed the decline in the frequency of union strikes to their declining effectiveness as a means of placing economic pressure on an employer. An excess supply of labor in relation to the demand for labor in many occupations and geographic areas in recent years have made strike replacements both easier and less costly to obtain, dampening many union members desire to engage in a work stoppage.[38]

Work stoppages are not caused by one factor alone, although the most common issue over which strikes occur is wages, followed by plant administrative

Years	Employees Involved		Days Idled	
	Number per Year	Number (Thousands)	Number of Days	Percentage of Working Time
1947–1950	300.3	1,824.8	31,414	.29
1951–1960	331.5	1,508.2	24,902	.19
1961–1970	298.8	1,390.9	22,833	.14
1971–1980	269.4	1,320.5	22,818	.11
1981–1990	64.2	427.1	9,673	.04
1991	40	392	4,584	.02
1992	35	388	3,987	.01
1993	36	18	3,981	.01
1994	45	322	5,020	.02
1995	31	192	5,771	.02
1996	37	273	4,889	.02
1997	29	339	4,497	.01
1998	34	387	5,116	.02
1999	17	73	1,996	.01
2000	39	394	20,419	.06
2001	29	99	1,151	<.005
2002	19	46	660	<.005
2003	14	129	4,091	.01
2004	17	171	3,344	.01
2005	22	100	1,736	.01
2006	20	70	2,688	.01

Exhibit 9.2

Work Stoppages Involving 1,000 or More Employees in the United States, 1947 to 2006

SOURCE: U.S. Department of Labor, Bureau of Labor Statistics, "Major Work Stoppages in 2006," *News Release,* February 27, 2007, pp. 4–5.

issues, such as safety, promotion policies, and job assignments. In recent years several work stoppages have involved the issue of health care benefits as union members have sought to resist employer health care bargaining proposals aimed at reducing the employer's benefit cost for this item by shifting additional benefit cost to the employee or reducing the scope of health care coverage available (see Chapter 7). The decision to strike depends on the total environment in which bargaining takes place. Interrelated factors that can influence the decision to strike include the economic positions of the union and company, characteristics of the production or service delivery process, the firm's market structure, business location, and occupational and demographic characteristics of the workforce.[39]

Researchers have shown that before 1980, strikes and economic activity were highly correlated with strike activity rising during periods of economic growth and declining during economic recessions. During the 1980s this pattern did not occur with low levels of strike activity recorded despite eight straight years of economic expansion after 1982. Between 1982 and 1990, employees involved in work stoppages in communications, government, transportation equipment, transportation, and construction made up 63 percent of all employees involved in work stoppages.[40] Exhibit 9.3 presents several conclusions researchers have reached concerning the causes of work stoppages.

Although strikes have traditionally been viewed as economic or legal conflicts, the psychological aspects are important. Psychologically, strikes can be categorized as a protest or as a group process for organizational change. Protest strikes include actions by the membership such as walking off their jobs. Partial strikes occur in the form of work slowdowns where employees "work to rule," following every detail of proscribed work processes, which often slows the normal pace of work flow. These protests may be in reaction to a unilateral change by management, such as introducing production quotas or a change in working conditions such as lowering thermostat settings in winter months to save heating costs.

As a group process, strikes require an important issue around which to mobilize a union's membership and adequate strike resources. Effective union leadership is critical to the success of any strike. Union leaders must instill unity among the membership, control courses of action, respond to the feelings of

Exhibit 9.3

Conclusions from Research on Work Stoppages Regarding the Likelihood of a Strike

Strikes are more likely when:

- The duration of the preceding contract is longer.
- Negotiations serve as a pattern setter for other firms/union pairs.
- The bargaining units are larger.
- There is a large variance (sharp drops and increases in earnings) in the firm's financial performance.
- Firms and industries have risk of injury or fatalities.
- Firms can inventory or stockpile goods.

Strikes are less likely when:

- Fewer issues are being negotiated (such as in a contract reopener over wages).
- Firms and industries employ a large proportion of women.
- Firms and industries pay a higher wage rate than other firms or industries.

SOURCE: Bruce E. Kaufman, "Research on Strike Models and Outcomes in the 1980s. Accomplishments and Shortcomings," in Research Frontiers in Industrial and Human Resources, eds. David Lewin, Olivia S. Mitchell, and Peter D. Sherer (Madison, Wis.: Industrial Relations Research Association, 1992), pp. 110–111.

the group, and maintain communication with management. An individual union member's participation in a strike is often determined by perceived costs and benefits. If the perceived benefits are small and the costs are high, willingness to participate will be low. However, if the benefits are perceived to be high and the costs are low, willingness to participate will be high.[41] Employees who believe that their pay is inequitable are not very willing to strike for a small wage increase. On the other hand, employees may be willing to strike to support the union for a large increase. The degree of commitment (loyalty) an employee has toward his or her union also has an important effect on an employee's willingness to strike, even more so than the employee's perceived commitment to his or her employer. A union must help employees reduce the potential hardships of a strike (e.g., by providing strike benefits) to increase strike support.[42]

Strikes can have traumatic effects on the parties' attitudes; they can temper the militants with realism and radicalize the conservatives. Strikes may cause some members to question the credibility of their leaders or management. Most strikes end in some type of negotiated settlement. However, once a strike is over, much rebuilding must occur to restore good labor-management relations and co-worker relations between strikers and nonstrikers.[43]

Strategic Purposes of a Strike

Although the main purpose of the strike is to secure a contract, it may also serve other purposes. For example, a strike may be part of an overall union strategy to help resolve internal problems. A strike may have a cathartic effect on the union members, removing accumulated tensions and releasing frustrations resulting from monotonous work. In fact, strikes under these conditions might improve productivity when the strikers return to work. A strike might also help to unify members serving to rally diverse prestrike membership factions to work toward a common goal of winning the strike.

In some cases, a union may call a strike to show management it can unify the membership over a collective bargaining issue. Over time, frequent strike threats may lose their effectiveness. If such threats are never carried out, management may perceive the union leader's strike threat lacks credibility. Sometimes union members may view participation in a strike as an investment in the credibility of future strike threats intended to reduce the need for future strikes to occur.

Union leaders may also believe that their members might be more willing to accept a slightly modified company offer if employees have experienced the loss of wages during a brief strike. In this sense, strikes are used to "roll the steam" out of employees and force them to adopt a more realistic perspective on the possibility of attaining stated bargaining objectives.[44]

Unions also have to consider the effects of a strike on their institutional security. During a strike, some union members may accept jobs elsewhere and decide not to return after the strike. Sometimes employers hire permanent replacements for strikers, and the negotiations may never result in a collective bargaining agreement. Rival unions are sometimes waiting on the sideline for the legally recognized union to falter, hoping to get enough employees to shift their support to a rival union to win a union decertification election. With these considerations, a union must be aware that a decision to strike may be a risk to its own institutional security.

A strike may serve a strategic purpose for management as well. Although management cannot call a strike, it can take actions that it knows are likely to result in a strike. For example, management can demand that the union collect dues rather than have management deduct them from employee paychecks (the

LABOR RELATIONS IN ACTION
United Steelworkers' Strike at the Goodyear Tire and Rubber Company

In 2003, the United Steelworkers' Union (USW) agreed to labor cost concessions including the closure of an Alabama plant, which saved Goodyear Tire and Rubber Company an estimated $2 billion in an effort to make the company more competitive in the global tire market.[a] Negotiations occurred in the context of a bargaining environment dominated by a $1 billion company operating loss, an increasing debt load, and declining stock share value. Company management acknowledged the key role the union played in helping to implement a turnaround plan initiated by Goodyear chief executive Robert Keegan. In 2005 the company reported a net profit of $228 million, an increase of 98.3 percent over 2004 results.[b]

As the parties began preparations to renegotiate their labor agreement set to expire on July 22, 2006, the union membership expected the next contract to recognize their previous sacrifices with some tangible rewards. Union members were aware that the company had awarded top Goodyear executives with millions of dollars in bonuses in recognition of the company's improved financial performance. The company viewed the 2006 contract negotiation as an opportunity to expand upon the progress made in the previous contract, enabling the company to cope with rising raw materials cost (particularly rubber); offset higher health care and pension costs; address increased competition from major competitors such as Michelin and Bridgestone-Firestone; and to take advantage of opportunities to expand market share in developing world regions (e.g., China, India, Africa), where rising per capita income and improved road systems were reflected in increasing car and truck sales.

Formal negotiations began in June 2006, and it quickly became apparent to the parties that their expectations for the direction and outcome of negotiations differed substantially. The company requested significant health care and pension benefit changes, the closure of two additional U.S. manufacturing plants, and other work rule changes intended to further reduce labor cost while expanding operating profit margins, which the company argued were below those of its major competitors. The union proposed modest improvements in wages and benefits, no additional plant closures, and an increased commitment by the company to invest in its U.S. manufacturing facilities to ensure they would remain competitive. The union interpreted management's announced intention to close further plants as a sign the company planned to shift additional future tire production to some of its more than 100 production facilities located in 29 countries around the world.[c]

Both sides remained entrenched in their bargaining positions, and little bargaining progress towards settlement occurred. When the current contract expired on July 22, the parties agreed to extend the terms of the contract on a day-to-day basis with the provision that either party could end the extension by giving the other party 72 hours notice of its intent to do so.[d] The company continued to insist it would not agree to any new contract terms which did not permit the company to remain competitive in its industry. Union and management negotiators continued to disagree regarding what specific terms or conditions of employment would be required to provide the company a competitive edge. While both parties agreed that it was in their mutual interests to ensure the company remained competitive, there were sharp differences between the parties on the best means available to achieve that common goal.

Frustrated by the lack of significant progress in contract talks and seeking to change the existing bargaining dynamic by exerting additional economic pressure on management to compromise, the union provided Goodyear with the required 72-hour notice of its intent to terminate the existing labor agreement and on October 5, 2006, began a strike affecting some 15,000 USW-represented employees at 16 plants in the United States and Canada. According to USW executive vice president Ron Hoover, "The Company left us with no option. We cannot allow additional plant closures after the sacrifices we made three years ago to help this company survive. Closing more plants would not only cause more job losses and devastate the communities where the operations would cease, it would also threaten the long term viability of Goodyear by giving up market share."[e]

The company announced its intention to continue production operations through the use of supervisory personnel and the hiring of temporary replacement workers to perform bargaining unit work. Three weeks later the company announced a plan to close the plant at Tyler, Texas, eliminating 1,100 jobs and rejecting a $12 million dollar incentive plan offered by community officials to keep the plant operating.[f] Established in 1962, the Tyler plant produced 25,000 passenger and light truck tires per day. Talks between the company and union broke off, and both parties appeared ready to endure a protracted work stoppage.

Some Goodyear customers such as General Motors (GM) were surprised by the work stoppage, indicating that Goodyear had given its customers no advance warning that a work stoppage was likely or that it might last several weeks or months.[g] GM purchases approximately eight million tires per year ($350 million) from Goodyear, and by mid-October was down to a 25-day supply of tires. Both GM and Goodyear acknowledged that Goodyear continued to operate its tire production facilities during the strike, and Goodyear assured its customers it would be able to deliver customer orders on time.

The USW as a part of its national strike publicity campaign warned consumers that building tires was a highly skilled craft that could not be learned quickly by supervisors not used to performing daily production tasks or strike replacements recently hired without adequate prior tire building experience.[h] The USW cited the 14-million tire recall instituted by Bridgestone/Firestone in 2000 following safety issues that involved tires produced by strike replacement workers during a similar labor dispute. The company sought to assure consumers and government regulators that all appropriate safety standards would continue to be met at tire production facilities operating during the strike.

In November, the U.S. Army began complaining that Goodyear was not meeting its scheduled delivery dates for supplying tires for the Army's Humvee vehicles.[i] The Army went so far as to threaten to ask the President to invoke the National Emergency Dispute Procedure provided under the Labor Management Relations Act to force an end to the work stoppage. The Army's complaint undermined Goodyear's public claim that productivity levels had not been seriously impacted by the absence of striking workers during the labor dispute. Shortly thereafter, the company returned to the bargaining table, and negotiations with the USW resumed.

On December 22, 2006, after a 12-week strike, the USW and Goodyear reached a tentative contract settlement endorsed by the USW's Goodyear Policy Committee comprised of local union leaders from the 12 U.S. facilities covered by the labor agreement.[j] Key features of the settlement included a company pledge of $1 billion to establish a **voluntary employees' beneficiary association (VEBA)** trust controlled by the union who will use the funds' earnings to finance medical and prescription drug benefits for current and future retirees. This will permit the company to remove this debt liability from the firm's balance sheet, boosting firm performance. The USW is assuming the risk that the initial seed money provided by the company along with future investment earnings will be enough to keep up with any rise in future health care costs, allowing the union to maintain current medical benefit levels which otherwise would likely have been reduced if the company-sponsored health care plan had remained in effect. GM, Ford, and Chrysler LLC in the auto industry negotiations with the United Auto Workers union in 2007 were successful in emulating the USW-Goodyear health care approach as a way of coping with similar large unfunded health care liabilities (more than $90 billion) confronting auto industry company balance sheets.[k]

The Goodyear-USW tentative contract settlement also included an agreement by the company to delay the previously announced closure of the Tyler, Texas, plant for one year, during which time bargaining unit members of the plant could take advantage of sizable retirement buyout incentives provided by the company. Goodyear also agreed to commit $550 million in new capital investments to ensure that the firm's U.S. plants remained competitive in the global marketplace, helping to improve the job security of USW members employed at those plants.

The USW held a series of information meetings with local union members, during which the terms of the tentative contract settlement were explained. On December 28, the USW announced that the union's membership had approved the proposed contract settlement by a two-to-one margin. All striking workers were scheduled to return to work by January 2, 2007.

Goodyear management indicated satisfaction with the settlement and a desire to get back to focusing on business. "What we expect is that both Goodyear and its workers now get back to being one team. The focus is on serving the customer and beating the competition."[l] USW President Leo Gerard stated, "This agreement validates the solidarity of our members and their families who wouldn't allow the company to walk away from obligations earned through a lifetime of hard work and loyalty. We owe a debt of gratitude to the entire labor and activist communities, which rose with unprecedented solidarity to challenge Goodyear's assault on our members."[m] Some union members expressed disappointment they were not able to save the Tyler plant from closure but were looking forward to returning to work.

Union members were generally optimistic about the chances of rebuilding a good working relationship with management but understood the healing process after the strike would take some time. Some union members were less willing to forgive and forget, telling stories of some managers who passed workers on the picket line smiling and waving their pay checks at picketers. Plants where such incidents occurred will require more time to reestablish a positive working relationship based on mutual trust and respect between labor and management. Goodyear Tire and Rubber Company announced on February 16, 2007, that it had lost $367 million during the three-month period ending December 31 as a result of the strike.[n] Goodyear noted that the new three-year contract resulting from the strike is expected to save the company $70 million in 2007, $240 million in 2008, and $300 million in 2009.

SOURCES:

[a] Connie Mabin, "Goodyear Wants More Cuts," *Opelika-Auburn News,* October 7, 2006, pp. A 1 & 5.

[b] "Global—Tires & Rubber," *Datamonitor Industry Market Research,* March 15, 2007, p. 5.

[c] "Company Spotlight: The Goodyear Tire & Rubber Company," *Datamonitor,* 6 (5), May 2007, pp. 6–10.

[d] Jessica Marquez, "Goodyear Fight Hints at Rough Road for Unions," *Workforce Management,* 85 (22), November 20, 2006, p. 12 and United Steelworkers Union, "Company Provided No Option, says Steelworkers," Press Release, undated, at http://usw.org/usw/program/content/3461.php?lan=en.

[e] Ibid.

[f] "Goodyear to Close Tire Plant in Texas, Eliminating 1,100 Jobs," *Findlaw,* October 30, 2006, pp. 1–2 at http://news.findlaw.com.

[g] Robert Sherefkin, "Goodyear Strike Disappoints GM; Automaker: 'GM Does Not Like Surprises'," *Automotive News,* 81 (6225), October 16, 2006, p. 4.

[h] United Steelworkers Union, "USW Blasts Goodyear's Reckless Actions: Announcements of Plant Closing and Hiring Replacement Workers Will Only Make a Settlement More Difficult," *News Release,* undated, p. 1 at http://www.usw.org/usw/program/content/3502.php?lan=en.

[i] Sarah Lazare, "Goodyear Settles," *Multinational Monitor,* November/December 2006, p. 5.

[j] United Steelworkers Union, "USW Members at Goodyear Ratify New Three-Year Contract as 86-day Strike Ends," *News Release,* undated, at http://www.usw.org/usw/program/content/3671.php?lan=en.

[k] "GM's Plant Commitments in the Deal with the UAW," *USA Today,* October 1, 2007, pp. 1–2; Katie Merx, Tim Higgins, Sarah A. Webster and Joe Guy Collier, "UAW, GM Tentative Deal Ends Two-Day National Strike," *Detroit Free Press,* September 26, 2007, pp. 1–3; Tom Krisher, "Chrysler Union Local Leaders OK Contract," *The Washington Post,* October 15, 2007, pp. 1–2; and Sholnn Freeman, "Ford, Union Agree on Contract," *The Washington Post,* November 4, 2007, pp. 1–2.

[l] Joe Milicia, "Goodyear Workers Return to Work," *The Washington Post,* January 2, 2007, pp. 1–2 at http://www.washingtonpost.com/wp-dyn/content/article/2007/01/02/AR2007010200369_pf.html.

[m] United Steelworkers Union, "USW, Goodyear Reach Tentative Agreement," *News Release,* undated, pp. 1–2 at http://www.use.org/usw/program/content/3668.php?lan=en.

[n] "Goodyear Reverses After Earnings News," *Business Week Online,* February 27, 2007, p. 1.

union dues check-off procedure is discussed in Chapter 4). Unions view this demand as a threat to their security and will often strike in response to it. Management's demand to subcontract bargaining unit work at will or to substantially change the wage system to the perceived detriment of covered employees will almost certainly lead to a strike. Thus, management may attempt to cause a strike when a strike is to its advantage, such as when inventories are high and customer demand is low. If nonunion employees can produce at a sufficient level to maintain acceptable production, if the union is weak, or if management knows that all employees will not support a strike, management may force a bargaining impasse as a strategy to secure more favorable contract terms.

Strike Experiences and Preparation

Strikes can range from very peaceful conflicts of short duration to protracted conflicts involving unlawful acts on both sides lasting months or even years. Strikes have no uniform sequence of events, although strikers' enthusiasm is generally highest during the early days of a strike. Indeed, the first few days on a picket line often draw a large portion of union members in an almost carnival-like atmosphere. After several weeks, it may be more difficult for a union to recruit members to walk the picket line.

Frustrations, antagonisms, and anxieties usually increase as the strike continues, with increased membership pressure being placed on union leaders to resolve the impasse.[45] The relative peacefulness of a strike is influenced by the attitudes of community citizens, particularly merchants and creditors, toward the dispute. A striker's spouse is perhaps the most influential individual in shaping a striker's behavior and attitudes. It is of course much easier for a striker to sustain a long strike if her or his spouse lends moral and financial support to the cause. On the other hand, tensions created by the strike can create permanent divisions among family members, friends, and other groups in the community as the strike endures and as individuals are asked to demonstrate their support.[46] Tensions can be especially heightened if the company continues to operate the business with either supervisory employees or striker replacements.

Parties must prepare for a possible strike before the contract expiration date, whether a strike is called or a settlement is reached. Exhibit 9.4 presents some of the potential costs faced by employers, unions, or individual employees during a work stoppage as well as possible actions to minimize or limit the adverse effects of such costs.

Union leaders must be certain of the extent to which members will actively participate during a strike and present a unified front to the employer. Usually a strike vote will occur either days or weeks before the contract deadline to indicate the strength of the membership's willingness to strike and bolster the credibility of any union strike threat. Strike votes are typically supported by the overwhelming majority of union members voting, although management negotiators may place less credibility on the validity of such votes the earlier the vote is taken in advance of the contract expiration date.

As the strike date approaches, union leaders must schedule pickets, ensure appropriate support for those on the line (e.g., food, shelter, first-aid supplies), and properly prepare the pickets for various situations, such as what to do when strike replacements cross the picket line. The union also has to determine qualified recipients of strike benefits, as well as any available public aid. Communication channels (telephone hotlines, Internet Web sites, media news releases) must be created and maintained to keep union members and the general public informed about the progress of negotiations. Local 400, United Food and Commercial Workers in preparation for a potential strike against Safeway Inc. and Giant Food LLC in the Washington, D.C., area reported "selecting strike captains, handing out instructions for setting up picket lines, distributing the names of bail bondsmen, and establishing a local strike fund."[47] In coordination with other local unions, the AFL-CIO Metropolitan Washington Council, and community groups, Local 400 distributed leaflets inside and outside of Giant and Safeway stores as well as appealed for support from local political leaders in an effort to achieve a fair contract settlement.

Management often spends much time in its strike preparations, particularly if it is essential that the employer continue to operate during a strike, as public utilities or health care facilities must do. Management in manufacturing facilities must determine the feasibility of building inventories in advance of a possible strike or using a strategy of hiring striker replacements if the strike occurs. Continuing to operate during a strike may be a viable management alternative where the following conditions are met:[48]

- There is a high risk of loss of market share if the firm ceases operation.

- An adequate supply of labor is available to operate the firm at reasonable costs.

- The union's anticipated response to management's decision to continue to operate will be limited or manageable.

Exhibit 9.4

Some Potential Strike or Lockout Costs and Mitigating Actions

Some Potential Employer Strike or Lockout Costs

- Lost sales revenue
- Loss of customers/market share (temporary or permanent)
- Continued fixed operating costs (e.g., utilities, taxes, rent, maintenance, debt service)
- Nonbargaining unit employee payroll costs
- Recruitment, selection, and training costs for temporary or permanent replacement workers
- Shut-down and start-up costs
- Negative publicity
- Legal fees
- Damage to bargaining relationship or co-worker relations (temporary or permanent)
- Increased stress level on managers, employees, and their families

Potential Employer Actions to Minimize or Limit such Costs

- Build inventory in advance of an anticipated strike
- Notify customers and suppliers in advance of strike potential and help arrange alternative sources to meet customer needs
- Engage in a publicity campaign to inform the public (customers, civic leaders, and employees) about company efforts to resolve the labor dispute
- Shift the struck work to other primary employer-owned plants or outsource such work to other secondary employers
- Continue business operations using some combination of non-B.U. employees, B.U. employees willing to cross the union's picket line, and temporary or permanent strike replacements
- Existence of poor product market demand serves to decrease risk of market share loss and sales revenue
- Purchase strike insurance or enter mutual aid pact with other employers

Some Potential Union or Individual Employee Strike or Lockout Costs

- Loss of union members due to voluntary union membership resignation or permanent striker replacement
- Loss of wage income or employee benefits coverage
- Loss of union dues revenue
- Cost of strike benefits provided, if any
- Costs of operating a strike (e.g., printing costs, legal fees, picket-line supplies such as coffee, food, or medical aid)
- Political cost to union's leadership if strike isn't won or won "big enough"
- Damage to co-worker (peer) relationships between strike supporters and non-supporters
- Continuing personal debt payments (e.g., auto, home, credit card, insurance, and telephone)
- Increased level of stress on work stoppage participants, their families, and communities

(Continued)

Exhibit 9.4
(Continued)

Potential Union or Individual Employee Actions to Minimize or Limit Costs

- Ensure adequate membership support prior to initiating any strike action
- Solicit morale and financial support from outside organizations (e.g., other unions, community groups, general public)
- Increase individual savings rate in anticipation of income loss during work stoppage
- Work with creditors to delay or reduce monthly debt payments
- Ensure adequate funding of union strike benefit fund
- Engage in publicity to demonstrate the merits of union members bargaining positions at issue in the work stoppage and the effectiveness of strike efforts to impose added costs on the employer's ability to operate
- Recognize the potential effect of product market conditions (e.g., high product demand increases an employer's cost of lost sales, a high level of market competition increases an employer's risk of market share loss in the event operations are curtailed)
- Recognize the potential effect of labor market conditions (e.g., a relatively low supply of qualified labor reduces the risk of striker replacement)
- Establish support groups for strikers and their families to help maintain striker solidarity
- Keep strikers informed about the progress of efforts to resolve the labor dispute
- Encourage a consumer boycott of the primary employer's goods or services

The use of strike replacements (particularly permanent replacements) during an economic strike escalates the tensions between the parties and often prolongs the length of a strike's duration. For this reason, most employers when confronted with a work stoppage do not hire permanent strike replacements if a continuing operation strategy is implemented.

Many organizations have an emergency strike manual that provides specific and detailed plans in the event of a strike. The manual typically has two major components: (1) specific job assignments for non-striking employees, professional employees, and managers and (2) checklists of appropriate strike activities, such as notifying customers and suppliers, contacting law enforcement officials, and providing food and housing for those staying on the job. In cases where the work is highly automated, such as in the telephone industry, employees' strikes may be less effective because companies find it easier to continue to operate, at least during short strikes. Management might also seek professional assistance from employer colleagues, trade associations, or members of the Society for Human Resource Management.[49]

Although union and management officials carefully consider the advantages and disadvantages of work stoppage strategies and tactics, they are not entirely free to implement these activities as they please. While condoned as a viable part of the collective bargaining process, the use of economic pressure tactics are extensively regulated by federal, state, and local laws.[50] Knowledge of labor law principles is essential to developing and implementing effective strike strategies and tactics.

Reinstatement Rights of Unfair Labor Practice and Economic Strikers

Employees engaged in an unfair labor practice (ULP) strike cannot be permanently replaced but may be temporarily replaced by an employer for the purpose of continuing normal business operations. An unfair labor practice strike can occur at any time to protest the commission of an employer unfair labor practice and cannot be barred by language contained in a negotiated no-strike agreement. Participating in an unfair labor practice strike entails less risk for an employee in the sense that a striker knows he or she will eventually return to work when the dispute ends. Since the decision to participate in an unfair labor practice strike is voluntary, ULP strikers are not entitled to back pay for wages lost during their withdrawal of labor. An exception to this rule would occur if an employee's loss in pay was the direct result of an employer's unfair labor practice. For example, an illegally discharged employee would be entitled to back pay as part of a ULP remedy, but employees who subsequently engaged in a ULP strike to protest that illegal discharge would not be entitled to a back-pay remedy.

Economic strikers may be either temporarily or permanently replaced by an employer for the purpose of continuing normal business operations.[51] The threat of hiring permanent striker replacements can significantly increase employees' perceived risk of engaging in or continuing a work stoppage. The United States is one of the few industrialized countries in the world which permits the permanent replacement of lawful economic strikers during a labor dispute.[52]

Employers hire replacement workers in approximately 14 percent of strikes.[53] Temporary replacements are more likely to be hired than permanent replacements during a strike, which may help to reduce some of the risks associated with hiring strike replacements. The use of strike replacements both lengthens the duration of strikes and increases the chance that violent acts will occur, compared to strikes not involving the hiring of replacement workers.

If not permanently replaced, an economic striker has a right to be reinstated to his or her job at any time during a labor dispute after making an unconditional request for reinstatement to the employer. An economic striker's job is not considered to be filled on a permanent basis unless the employer indicates such an intent when hiring a replacement and the replacement is actually on the job performing a striker's job duties (as opposed to being in engaged in training in order to qualify to perform the normal job duties of a striking employee). If temporary replacement workers are hired during a strike, lawful strikers will go back to work after a settlement is reached and the temporary replacements will be dismissed.

An employer must be careful when hiring permanent strike replacements to ensure that no promise of continued or permanent employment is extended to replacements hired. Employees hired during a strike who receive a promise of permanent employment may sue an employer for breach of contract if subsequently laid off due to a negotiated strike settlement or NLRB-ordered unfair labor practice remedy requiring striking employees be reinstated.[54] Offering "regular" employment or "full-time" employment would not generally be considered equivalent to an offer of permanent employment. Other practical considerations may also discourage an employer from exercising the legal right to replace strikers. It is usually not easy to replace a large number of striking employees quickly, especially if work operations are complicated or employees require more than a short period of training to demonstrate the required level of job performance.

Efforts to enact a legislative ban on the use of permanent strike replacements, such as proposed in the *Workplace Fairness Act* in the early 1990s, have not been successful. Employers have argued that a legislative ban against hiring permanent striker replacements would drastically shift the balance of relative bargaining power to unions and would result in higher labor costs. However, in a Canadian study where the hiring of permanent striker replacements is banned by provincial law, no evidence was reported supporting the contention that striker replacement legislation alters the existing balance of power between management and labor.[55] Legislation to ban or restrict an employer's right to permanently replace lawful strikers is not likely to be enacted until Democrats regain control of the Congress and the presidency.

Even in cases where an economic striker is permanently replaced, the striker retains a right to be placed on a **preferential recall list**. The employer must fill any permanent vacancy occurring in a bargaining unit position thereafter by first offering the job vacancy to a qualified individual on the preferential recall list before the job vacancy can be filled by a job applicant not on the preferential recall list (**Laidlaw-Fleetwood doctrine**).[56] An employer and union may negotiate a reasonable time limit following a strike, during which permanently replaced economic strikers would be entitled to exercise their preferential recall rights.[57] Management would generally favor such a time limit to reduce the administrative burden of notifying qualified individuals on the preferential recall list each time a permanent job vacancy occurs. Factors which might affect what constitutes a "reasonable time period" could include:

- Historical data on normal employee attrition rates (e.g., voluntary turnover, discharge for cause, retirement, permanent disability).

- Future probability that new job openings may occur over some extended time period (e.g., new product development, plant expansion, industry economic forecast).

- The percentage of total employees eligible for recall who were actually recalled during the negotiated time limit.

An employer is not permitted to grant **superseniority** or retroactive seniority rights to permanent strike replacements in an effort to protect their recall rights in any future layoff situation where the labor contract calls for reinstatement to be accomplished according to seniority.[58] A grant of superseniority essentially exempts that individual from the normal application of seniority rights in making employment decisions. Since former economic strikers on a preferential recall list were hired before the permanent strike replacements, former strikers on a preferential recall list almost always have more seniority than replacement workers hired during a strike.

Unlawful Strike Misconduct

Employees who engage in an unlawful strike or **serious strike misconduct** during an otherwise lawful strike forfeit their normal rights to reinstatement. In addition to forfeiture of job reinstatement rights, some strike misconduct may also represent a violation of criminal or civil statutes, subjecting an employee to legal penalties such as a monetary fine or imprisonment. Serious strike misconduct would include:

- Acts of violence directed at managers, co-workers, customers, suppliers, or the general public.

- Intentional destruction of private property (e.g., acts of vandalism or sabotage).

- Verbal threats intended to intimidate or coerce an individual in the exercise of his or her lawful rights.

All strike misconduct is examined in light of the surrounding circumstances, and courts recognize the heightened emotions which exist and may affect the conduct of parties involved in a work stoppage. The use of derogatory language by picketers directed at individuals crossing a lawfully established picket line, although unpleasant or embarrassing for the target of such verbal abuse to endure, will not generally be classified as serious strike misconduct.[59]

Unions typically try to deter union members from crossing authorized union picket lines by adopting a rule permitting the union to impose a reasonable monetary fine on any union member who engages in such conduct.[60] Individual union members have a legal right to resign their union membership at any time including during a work stoppage authorized by their union.[61] To avoid the imposition of a monetary fine for crossing an authorized union picket line, a union member would simply need to resign from his or her union membership prior to crossing the picket line. Resigning one's union membership would not affect an employee's status as an employee of the company or as a member of the bargaining unit represented by the union from which the individual resigned.

Employee Picketing Rights

Employees have a right to publicize a labor dispute involving a primary employer in a peaceful manner to encourage public support for the striking employees' (union's) position.[62] Such publicity often takes the form of picket activity, which is primarily regulated by state and local laws. Efforts by state and local authorities to restrict employee picket activity requires a careful balancing of employee First Amendment free speech rights, employer property rights, and the government's interests in maintaining labor peace, the free flow of commerce, and protection of the public's interests.

Some reasonable restrictions on the right to picket during a labor dispute could include:[63]

- Banning picket activity conducted for an unlawful purpose or involving violence.

- Reasonable limits on the times when picketing may occur, noise level, number of picketers present at one time, or mandatory spacing between picketers to ensure reasonable entry or exit from the employer's property.

- Requiring that the content of picket signs be truthful and clearly identify the employer with whom the picketers have a labor dispute.

An employer generally has a right to establish reasonable rules to govern the exercise of free speech on private property. Union picket activity on the employer's private property may generally be banned if (1) the ban is applied in a consistent, non-discriminatory manner and (2) the union has other reasonable means of communicating its message to the intended audience.[64]

Secondary Strike, Boycott, and Picket Activity

Up to this point the discussion has focused on labor disputes between a primary employer and his or her employees. A **secondary employer** (i.e., one with no direct authority to resolve the labor dispute) may become involved in a labor dispute either voluntarily or involuntarily. A secondary employer who knows or reasonably should have known that engaging in certain conduct would aid a primary employer during a labor dispute is presumed to have voluntarily joined the labor dispute as a **business ally** of the primary employer, and therefore can be subjected to the same lawful economic pressure tactics that employees could engage in regarding the primary employer. A secondary employer who agrees to perform work normally done by striking employees (**struck work**) is the most common means of establishing ally status. A primary employer with several plants or ownership of separate firms may find non-struck entities enmeshed in the labor dispute as a business ally of the primary employer if a high degree of interdependence or co-mingling of assets is established between the various operations sharing common ownership. Where different operations function independent of each other, common ownership by itself would not be sufficient to establish business ally status of the non-struck operations, nor does carrying on an established business relationship with a struck employer by itself establish that a secondary employer has waived its neutral status in the labor dispute. Business ally status is determined case-by-case based on an analysis of the totality of relevant circumstances.

Section 8 (b)(4) of the LMRA makes it an unfair labor practice for a union to engage in tactics for the purpose of pressuring a neutral, secondary employer into becoming involved in a labor dispute. This includes prohibiting a union from discouraging employees of a neutral, secondary employer from performing their normal job duties. However, lawful picketing to publicize a labor dispute which has the effect of causing secondary employees to honor a picket line is not unlawful, so long as the intended purpose or object of such picketing is not to induce secondary employees to cease performing their regular job duties.[65]

In balancing the legitimate right of neutral, secondary employers not to be forced to participate in a labor dispute with striking employees' rights to use economic pressure tactics against the primary employer and publicize the existence of a labor dispute, Congress did not intend to guarantee neutral, secondary employers complete freedom from economic loss as the result of the lawful exercise of strike rights. For example, a neutral secondary employer's driver, who is scheduled to make a delivery to a struck employer's property but fails to make the delivery after encountering a union picket line at the struck employer's business is presumed to be acting in sympathy with the striking employees. The driver's voluntary decision not to cross the picket line represents a sympathy strike, and as a **sympathy striker** the driver's strike rights are equivalent to those of the picketers whose picket line the driver refused to cross.[66] If the picket line was part of a lawful economic strike, the neutral, secondary employer could temporarily replace the driver or permanently replace the driver if no other reasonable alternative action exists (e.g., reassignment of the driver to another delivery route which would not require him or her to encounter a picket line or rescheduling the delivery to another date when a driver willing to cross the picket line could be assigned to make the delivery). Even though the secondary employer may suffer some costs in the form of lost productivity, time delay, or even the loss of a sale, neither the primary employees' picket activity nor the secondary employer's driver's refusal to cross the picket line would become unlawful merely because the effect of their exercise of lawful strike rights caused an adverse economic impact on the neutral, secondary employer.

Common Situs Picketing

Common situs picketing occurs at a location where a primary employer and one or more neutral, secondary employers are engaged in normal business operations at the same site. Common examples of such sites would be a construction work site where several independent contractors are engaged in business or a shipping dock where several shipping companies may be engaged in business at the same time. The challenge becomes how to permit employees involved in a labor dispute with a primary employer at the site to engage in lawful picket activity without unnecessarily disrupting the ability of neutral, secondary employers to continue to operate at the work site without becoming enmeshed in the primary employer's labor dispute. The *Moore Dry Dock* doctrine establishes some guidelines for lawful picketing at a common site of a labor dispute.[67] Picketing at a common site is lawful if:

1. The primary employer is present and engaged in normal business operations as the common site. Presence can be indicated by the primary employer continuing to schedule deliveries to the site, maintaining equipment at the site, or having set-up or maintenance work continue to be performed at the site.

2. Picket signs must clearly identify the primary employer with whom the union has a labor dispute.

3. Picketing must occur at locations reasonably close to the primary employer's operations at the common site.

Sometimes a primary employer will provide a schedule to the union listing dates and times when the primary employer will be present at the site and thus union picket activity would be permitted. Of course, the primary employer would be required to adhere to the published schedule. If the primary employer maintains an intermittent presence at a work site so it is impossible for a union to know when the primary employer is or is not going to be present, the union is entitled to presume that the primary employer is present when conducting picket activity at the work site.

Unions have argued that the employers who occupy a common work site are so intertwined that a labor dispute with one employer is a labor dispute with all and, therefore, unions allege that there are no neutral employers on the site. The Supreme Court has rejected this union argument, ruling that general contractors and subcontractors on a building site are separate business entities and should be treated separately with respect to each other's labor controversies.[68] Picket activity at a common site of a labor dispute must meet the *Moore Dry Dock* standard to be lawful.

A union may lawfully picket under the *Moore Dry Dock* standard at the location of a neutral, secondary employer, so long as a primary employer is present and engaged in normal business operations at the neutral, secondary employer's site (so-called "picketing between the headlights"). This might occur where a struck primary employer is engaged in providing some service to its customers at the neutral, secondary employer's work site (e.g., computer repair service is struck by its employees but continues to service accounts at various neutral, secondary employers' business locations during the strike). The union representing the primary employer's repair technicians might follow the repair truck from the primary employer's business and picket at the entrance used by the primary employer's repair technician at the neutral, secondary employer's business while the repair person is inside the business. When the primary employer's technician leaves the neutral customer's location, the union's picket activity would also have to cease and the union's picketers would have to follow the repair truck to the next customer's location.

During a labor dispute, the **reserve gate doctrine** permits entrances to a work site to be clearly marked for the exclusive use of either a primary employer or neutral, secondary employer and their employees, customers, and suppliers.[69] Picketing by a union during a primary economic labor dispute at a gate reserved for the exclusive use of a neutral, secondary employer would generally be illegal, so long as the gate was properly marked, reasonably established, and used only by the neutral, secondary employer. A gate marked for the exclusive use of the primary employer involved in a labor dispute would not be reasonably established if the gate was located so as to unreasonably deny a union an opportunity to convey its intended picket message to the public (e.g., down a dead-end alley seldom used by customers or employees to gain entrance to the work site). Proper use of reserved gates helps to minimize the disruption in neutral, secondary employers' ability to continue normal business operations at a common site of a labor dispute while still permitting striking employees to picket the operation of the primary employer.

A situational application of the reserve gate doctrine occurs when a primary employer involved in an economic dispute turns his or her property into a common site by hiring a neutral, secondary employer to perform work on the primary employer's property during a labor dispute. Such work might involve construction of new buildings, installation of new equipment, major maintenance projects, or other tasks which could be accomplished, even though the employer's normal business operations have been curtailed due to the ongoing strike.

Striking employees of a primary employer normally have a right to picket at every entrance to a primary employer's property during a labor dispute. The *General Electric* **doctrine** establishes the conditions under which a primary employer could lawfully establish a gate on the primary employer's property reserved for the exclusive use of a neutral, secondary employer hired to perform some work for the primary employer during a labor dispute.[70] During a labor dispute, picketing may be prohibited at an entrance to the primary employer's property if the following conditions are met:

1. The gate must be reserved for the exclusive use of a neutral, secondary employer and only used by such employers, their employees, or suppliers. Once the neutrality of a reserved gate has been breached, the gate loses its neutrality and the union could lawfully picket the gate.

2. The work performed by the neutral, secondary employer on the primary employer's property cannot be struck work (i.e., work that except for the work stoppage would have been performed by bargaining unit members).

3. The work performed by the neutral, secondary employer cannot be work that would require a work stoppage to occur in order for the task to be completed. New construction projects, repairs on non-functional equipment, or installation of new equipment in a location not already occupied by existing equipment would generally meet this requirement. Major maintenance on equipment currently in use requiring such equipment to be taken out of service in order for the maintenance to be accomplished would not meet this third requirement. The purpose of this third requirement is to reduce management's incentive to force a strike as a means of avoiding payments due workers who were laid off as the result of equipment being taken out of service for maintenance.

Product Picketing Rights

Unions sometimes choose to picket the products or services of the primary employer involved in a labor dispute by picketing at the site of a neutral, secondary employer who sells the primary employer's product or service. **Product picketing** at a neutral, secondary employer's business is lawful for the purpose of encouraging consumers to boycott the products or services of the primary employer involved in a labor dispute.[71] Picket signs must clearly identify the primary employer as the target of the picket activity and only urge a boycott of the primary employer's products or services, not a total boycott of all products or services sold by the neutral, secondary employer. To the extent consumers heed the union's boycott request, the effect will be to impose economic pressure on the primary employer to resolve the labor dispute. Before initiating any product picket activity, the union may request a neutral, secondary employer to voluntarily cease selling the primary employer's products or services for the duration of the labor dispute, which would eliminate the need for the union to engage in any picketing activity at the neutral, secondary employer's business. While the secondary employer is not required to grant the union's request, a prudent employer will weigh the likely effectiveness or duration of such product picket activity against the potential costs (e.g., lost sales, customer dissatisfaction, or negative publicity) such picketing might entail for the neutral, secondary employer were it to occur.

There are two exceptions to a union's right to engage in product picketing at the business of a neutral, secondary employer. First, product picketing can be restricted or prohibited where evidence proves that the effect of such picket activity would cause a *near total boycott* (e.g., 90 percent or more loss of business) of the neutral, secondary employer.[72] This might occur in the case where the only products or services sold by the neutral, secondary employer consisted of the primary employer's products or services and the union's boycott appeal was very effective in causing customers not to purchase the primary employer's products or services. Since it may not be clear from the evidence how effective such a union product picket action might be prior to the onset of actual picketing activity, a neutral, secondary employer may have to bear some period of picket activity during which evidence as to the effectiveness of the union's picket action can be established and presented to a court to obtain a labor injunction or presented to the NLRB to support an unfair labor practice charge against the union.

A second exception to a union's right to engage in product picketing occurs if the product of the primary employer being struck and a neutral, secondary employer are so intertwined (**merged product doctrine**) that it would be impossible for a consumer to boycott the primary employer's product without inducing a near total boycott of the neutral, secondary employer.[73] For example, if the employees of a car battery manufacturer initiated a product picket at a new car dealer that used the primary employer's batteries in all of the vehicles on the sales lot, it would be impossible for a customer to refuse to buy the primary employer's battery without also refusing to buy the neutral, secondary employer's car in which the battery was located.

Handbilling Rights

Even where picket activity may be illegal, the LMRA permits other forms of publicity such as **handbilling** to communicate the existence of a labor dispute and seek public support. Attempting to hand a written notice to an individual is typically viewed as a less intrusive (and maybe less effective) means of communicating one's desired message than confronting that individual with picket signs carried by several individuals patrolling back and forth in front of an entrance. Shopping malls that include a multitude of separate employers give rise to some interesting questions about lawful union picket and handbilling activities. The Supreme Court has upheld the right of unions to peacefully distribute handbills urging customers not to shop at stores located in a mall (see, for example, the handbill shown in Exhibit 9.5) until all construction underway at the mall was performed by contractors paying "fair" wages. The Court ruled that the handbill used by the union truthfully revealed the existence of a labor dispute and urged potential customers of the mall to follow a wholly legal course of action, namely, not to patronize the retailers doing business in the mall. The handbilling was peaceful. No picketing or patrolling was involved. The union was within its members' right of free speech to encourage consumers to protest substandard wages by refusing to shop at a mall where such wages were paid.[74]

NATIONAL EMERGENCY DISPUTE RESOLUTION PROCEDURES

When labor disputes develop to a stage where they are regarded as having an adverse effect on the national interest, they assume a special significance. Strikes that have a substantial adverse impact on national economic or defense interests

---

Exhibit 9.5

Handbill Used at Shopping Mall to Influence Shoppers

PLEASE DON't SHOP AT EAST LAKE SQUARE.

The FLORIDA GULF COAST BUILDING TRADES COUNCIL, AFL-CIO is requesting that you do not shop at the stores in the East Lake Square Mall because of the Mall ownership's contribution to substandard wages.

The Wilson's Department Store under construction on these premises is being built by contractors who pay substandard wages and fringe benefits. In the past, the Mall's owner, The Edward J. DeBartolo Corporation, has supported labor and our local economy by ensuring that the Mall and its stores be built by contractors who pay fair wages and fringe benefits. Now, however, and for no apparent reason, the Mall owners have taken a giant step backwards by permitting our standards to be torn down. The payment of substandard wages not only diminishes the working person's ability to purchase with earned, rather than borrowed, dollars, but it also undercuts the wage standard of the entire company. Since low construction wages at this time of inflation means decreasing purchasing power, do the owners of East Lake Mall intend to compensate for the decreased purchasing power of workers of the community by encouraging the stores in East Lake Mall to cut their prices and lower their profits?

CUT-RATE WAGES ARE NOT FAIR UNLESS MERCHANDISE PRICES ARE ALSO CUT-RATE.

We ask your support in our protest against substandard wages. Please do not patronize the stores in East Lake Square Mall until the Mall's owner publicly promises that all construction at the Mall will be done using contractors who pay their employees fair wages and fringe benefits.

IF YOU MUST ENTER The MALL TO DO BUSINESS, please express to the store managers your concern over substandard wage and your support of our efforts. We are appealing only to the public—the consumer. We are not seeking to induce any person to cease work or to refuse to make deliveries.

SOURCE: Supreme Court decision in *DeBartolo v. Florida Gulf Coast Building & Construction Trades Council*, 485 U.S. 568 (1988).

are classified as **national emergency strikes** and the federal government has used three methods to deal with such strikes: (1) presidential seizure or other intervention, (2) procedures under the Railway Labor Act, and (3) procedures under the Labor Management Relations Act.

Presidential seizures or attempts at seizure where the government takes control of a company's assets and proceeds to operate the firm have occurred 71 times under four presidents—Lincoln, Wilson, Franklin D. Roosevelt, and Truman—in the interests of maintaining production when actual strikes or threatened strikes caused national emergencies. Most of these presidential seizure actions have occurred at a time when the United States was at war.

The Railway Labor Act provides a procedure for resolving national emergency work stoppages involving railroads or airlines that includes the following:

- The National Mediation Board (NMB) attempts to mediate the dispute, and if unsuccessful, recommends voluntary interest arbitration.

- If arbitration is rejected by one or both parties, a 30-day period is established during which wage rates, working rules, working conditions, and so forth would remain the same.

- If the dispute threatens to substantially interrupt essential transportation service to any section of the country, the president is notified by the NMB and can choose to appoint a Presidential Emergency Board (PEB). If the president chooses not to appoint a PEB, either union or management would be free after the conclusion of the 30-day cooling off period described in the previous step to pursue a strike or lockout action.

- Within 30 days, the PEB appointed to investigate the dispute must issue a written report containing findings of fact regarding the dispute and recommended settlement terms to the parties. Union and management then have an additional 30 days to try to reach a voluntary settlement before either party could resort to any strike or lockout action. During this time, the status quo regarding terms and conditions of employment is maintained. If no voluntary settlement is reached, the president could request Congress to enact legislation mandating settlement terms to resolve the bargaining dispute.

Since the RLA's passage in 1926, its emergency provisions have been invoked about 200 times, an average rate of four times per year, and work stoppages have occurred at the end of the 60-day period at a rate of one per year since 1947. However, government interventions in railroad disputes have averaged only about one per year since 1980 and only three PEBs have occurred in the airline industry since 1978.[75] Sixteen federal laws have been passed to deal with specific railroad labor disputes, usually by extending the strike date and involving a third-party mediator or arbitrator. The last time a federal law was passed to intervene was 1992, when Congress stopped a national rail strike and mandated mediation and arbitration of the dispute.

Sections 206-210 of the LMRA establish a procedure for managing a threatened or actual strike or lockout affecting an entire or substantial portion of a private-sector industry which, if allowed to occur or continue in the opinion of the President of the United States, would threaten the national health or safety. These provisions include a step-by-step procedure to halt the strike or lockout for 80 days and provide the parties assistance in resolving their disputes. Exhibit 9.6 displays the steps in the national emergency procedure of the LMRA. Prior to engaging in any lawful strike or lockout, the party initiating the work stoppage must

Exhibit 9.6
National Emergency Procedure under LMRA

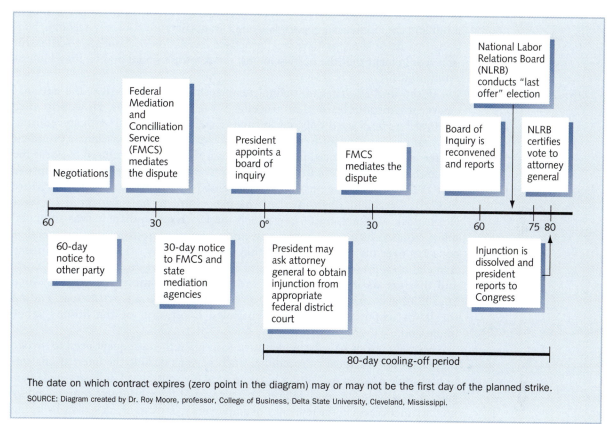

The date on which contract expires (zero point in the diagram) may or may not be the first day of the planned strike.

SOURCE: Diagram created by Dr. Roy Moore, professor, College of Business, Delta State University, Cleveland, Mississippi.

have bargained in good faith for 60 days, provided the FMCS at least 30 days' advance notice prior to the current contract's expiration that the parties' voluntary bargaining effort had not yet produced a settlement, and made sure that no contractual bar (e.g., a no-strike or lockout clause) was still in effect.

The first step in the national emergency dispute resolution procedure is for the president to appoint a board of inquiry when the actual or threatened strike is believed to be of sufficient severity to imperil the national health or safety. Because of the urgency of the matter, the board will investigate the mandatory bargaining subjects in dispute, gather relevant facts, and make a report to the president in a very short time, usually one to three days.

After the president receives and studies the report, he or she may direct the attorney general to secure an 80-day labor injunction from an appropriate federal district court to prevent or end the strike. Once the injunction is issued, the board of inquiry is reconvened, and after the first 60 days of the injunction period, it will be asked to report to the president on the employer's last offer and any other relevant factors. During those 60 days, the FMCS will attempt to mediate a voluntary settlement between the parties in the dispute. Assuming no voluntary settlement is reached, the board reports the final employer bargaining proposal to the president who will then instruct the NLRB to conduct and certify a secret ballot vote (between the 60th and 80th days of the injunction period), to determine if employees will accept management's final offer. If employees reject the offer, the attorney general must request the federal district court who issued the

80-day labor injunction to dissolve the injunction. After the 80th day, when the labor injunction has expired, the union could legally strike or the employer could initiate a lockout. The final step in the procedure calls for the president to submit a full and comprehensive report to Congress, accompanied by any recommendations that he or she may have (e.g. proposed legislation to mandate a settlement or a requirement that the parties submit the dispute to final and binding interest arbitration).

In the first 22 years following the enactment of the LMRA, the national emergency dispute resolution procedure was used 29 times. However, since 1960, it has been used only seven times (five times in 1971 with stevedoring and grain elevator operations). During a strike by eastern coal miners President Carter invoked the procedure in 1978, but a federal judge refused to grant the requested 80-day labor injunction because the attorney general failed to prove that the work stoppage actually represented a national emergency.[76] More recently, President Bush invoked the procedure to halt a lockout of West Coast dock workers in 2002 in which the key issue in dispute was shippers' plans to introduce new technology into port operations and union member concerns over the effect of such action on job security.[77] The Pacific Maritime Association representing shipping and cargo companies at 29 West Coast ports and the International Longshore and Warehouse Union representing some 10,500 dockworkers negotiated a voluntary contract settlement ending the labor dispute prior to the scheduled expiration of the 80-day labor injunction.

Several reasons have been identified to explain the infrequent need to invoke these national emergency procedures. Such reasons include the internationalization of some product markets; a breakup of many centralized, industry-wide bargaining arrangements; decline in the percentage of the work force represented by unions; an increase in the tendency of employers to seek to break strikes by hiring replacement employees; and increased employer willingness to operate during a work stoppage.[78]

Other critics argue that the use of national emergency dispute resolution procedures subverts the bargaining process by interjecting government action which alters the balance of bargaining power in the labor dispute and reduces the bargaining pressure on one party to reach an agreement at the bargaining table.[79] The National Emergency Dispute resolution procedure appears to work as effectively as Congress intended because of the rigidity and predictability of the procedures. When each step in the procedure is predictable, either party may include the issuance of a labor injunction as part of its bargaining strategy. The requirement that a secret ballot election on the employer's last offer be held often solidifies union members' opposition to management's proposal rather than facilitating the bargaining process toward settlement. Lastly, because the presidential boards of inquiry are prohibited from proposing settlements, their effectiveness in securing the necessary public support and pressure to move the parties toward settlement is limited.

Summary

Various third-party dispute resolution procedures to assist the parties in resolving negotiation disputes were presented; ranging from mediation (where a third party attempts to facilitate resolution by keeping the parties bargaining, acting as a go-between, and offering alternatives) to arbitration, a quasi-judicial procedure in which the bargaining positions are presented to an arbitrator who makes a final and binding decision. Within the range of dispute resolution procedures are the med-arb procedure (which attempts mediation first and then arbitration if mediation fails) and fact-finding (in which the parties present their positions to a fact-finder, other facts are collected, and a report, which includes a recommended resolution of the impasse, is written and publicized).

Although voluntary agreements are reached by the parties in the vast majority of negotiation disputes, sometimes one or both parties will resort to the use of economic pressure tactics (e.g., strike, boycott, picketing, lockout) to encourage a party to agree to proposed settlement terms. Work stoppages involve significant costs and risks for all participants and require careful consideration and preparation before embarking on such a course of action.

The right to strike or lockout for lawful reasons using lawful means is an intrinsic part of the labor relations process protected by law. It is a wise union or management representative who understands the difference between possessing a legal right and determining whether it makes practical sense to exercise such a right under the prevailing circumstances of a particular labor dispute. While data indicate that strike activity is less common in labor relations today, the potential threat of such action can still be a credible force encouraging the parties to carefully weigh the cost of agreement against the cost of continued disagreement. It is unfortunate that peaceful bargaining settlements do not attract the media or public attention that work stoppages engender.

Most strikes and related activities involve primary employers, but often secondary employers (not directly involved in the employer-employee relationship) are affected. A complex body of law and judicial decisions covers such activities as consumer and product boycotts and picketing, common situs picketing, and handbilling rights.

Strikes or lockouts that have an adverse effect on the national interest may be declared national emergency disputes. Procedures are available under the Railway Labor Act and the Labor Management Relations Act to facilitate their resolution. Although such impasses occur infrequently, they are significant when they do.

Key Terms

Discussion Questions

1. Define the major types of third-party interest dispute resolution procedures. How do they differ, and how are they similar?

2. What specific qualities should a mediator possess? Why do these qualities facilitate impasse resolution?

3. Why is interest arbitration used so infrequently in the private sector?

4. To what extent would you agree or disagree with the following statement: "Strikes are an intrinsic and essential element of the collective bargaining process." Explain your reasoning.

5. What types of preparation do management and union leaders need to engage in prior to a work stoppage?

6. What are some potential costs or risks parties face during a work stoppage, and how may such costs or risks be reduced or minimized?

7. Define and discuss the various types of economic pressure tactics union members may use during a primary labor dispute which could affect a secondary employer.

8. Should employees engaged in lawful strike activity be protected from permanent replacement? Explain your reasoning.

9. Reviewing the information presented in the "Labor Relations in Action" segment on the Goodyear strike, could the terms of the final contract settlement have been achieved by the parties without the union's use of the economic strike tactic? Explain your reasoning.

Exploring the Web

Strikes, Lockouts, and Collective Bargaining

1. Bureau of Labor Statistics Reports on Collective Bargaining. Go to the Collective Bargaining Agreements page on the BLS site and read the summary of the most recent annual Major Work Stoppages. Which strike created the most time lost for the year?

2. Collective Bargaining and the U.S. Code. Title 29 is the section of the U.S. Code that contains Federal law on labor. Go to Cornell's Legal Information Institute and search Title 29 for the following terms: picketing, strikes, advanced workplace practices. What is included in the list of unfair labor practices in Section 158?

3. Professional Sports Strikes and Lockouts. Return to the Web site for the Bureau of Labor Statistics. Search for the following articles written by Paul Staudohar and published in the *Monthly Labor Review*:

"The Baseball Strike of 1994–95" (March 1997)

"Labor Relations in Basketball: The Lockout of 1998–99" (April 1999)

"The Hockey Lockout of 2004–05" (December 2005) What were the causes of the lockouts and strikes? What is the difference between a lockout and a strike?

4. Mediation. The Federal Mediation and Conciliation Service is an "independent agency whose mission is to preserve and promote labor-management peace and cooperation." Locate the Code of Professional Responsibility for Arbitrators of Labor-Management Disputes on the FMCS Web site. Check the latest Annual Report for descriptions of FMCS involvement in major labor disputes.

5. Definitions of Labor Terms. Search the Web to find the definitions of the following terms used in labor relations. Be sure to use a credible Internet source with a glossary of labor terms or check to see if your college or university has a subscription to an online encyclopedia. Wikipedia is not a reliable source of information.

Boycott

Sympathy strike

Wildcat strike

References

1. Bureau of Labor Statistics, U.S. Department of Labor, "Major Work Stoppages in 2006" *News Release*, February 27, 2007, pp. 1–10.

2. Federal Mediation and Conciliation Service, *59th Annual Report, 2006* (Washington D.C.: FMCS, 2007), pp. 1–10.

3. Ruth D. Raisfeld, "How Mediation Works: A Guide to Effective Use of ADR," *Employee Relations Law Journal*, 33 (2), Autumn 2007, pp. 30–41; Carolyn Brommer, George Buckingham, and Steven Loeffler, "Cooperative Bargaining Styles at FMCS: A Movement Toward Choices," 2 *Pepperdine Dispute Resolution Law Journal* 465 (2002); William E. Simkin, *Mediation and the Dynamics of Collective Bargaining* (Washington, D.C.: Bureau of National Affairs, Inc, 1971), pp. 25–28.

4. Carl Stevens, "Mediation and the Role of the Neutral," in *Frontiers of Collective Bargaining*, eds. John T. Dunlop and Neil W. Chamberlain (New York: Harper & Row, 1967), p. 271.

5. Steven Briggs and Daniel J. Koys, "What Makes Labor Mediators Effective?" *Labor Law Journal*, 40 (8), August 1988, pp. 517–520.

6. Stevens, "Mediation and the Role of the Neutral," pp. 280–284.

7. Joseph Krislov and Amira Ealin, "Comparative Analysis of Attitudes towards Mediation," *Labor Law Journal*, 30 (3), March 1979, p. 173.

8. Patrice M. Mareschal, "Providing High Quality Mediation: Insights from the Federal Mediation and Conciliation Service," *Review of Public Personnel Administration*, 18, Fall 1998, pp. 55–67.

9. Richard B. Peterson and Mark R. Peterson, "Toward A Systematic Understanding of the Labor Mediation Process," in *Advances in Industrial and Labor Relations*, vol. 4, eds. David Lewin, David B. Kipsky, and Donna Sockell (Greenwich, Conn.: JAI Press, Inc., 1987), p. 145.

10. Richard B. Peterson and Mark R. Peterson, "Toward a Systematic Understanding," pp. 152–153.

11. Thomas A. Kochan and Todd Jick, "The Public Sector Mediation Process," *Journal of Conflict Resolution*, 22, June 1978, p. 236.

12. Robert A. Baruch Bush, "Efficiency and Protection or Empowerment and Recognition: The Mediator's Role and Ethical Standards in Mediation," *Florida Law Review*, 41, Spring 1989, pp. 253–286.

13. Michael Marmo, "The Role of Fact-Finding and Interest Arbitration in 'Selling' a Settlement," *Journal of Collective Negotiation in the Public Sector* 24 (1), 1995, pp. 78–82.

14. David L. Dickinson and Lynn Hunnicutt, "Does Fact-Finding Promote Settlement? Theory and a Test," *Economic Inquiry*, 43 (2), April 2005, pp. 401–416.

15. William H. Ross, Jr. "Situational Factors and Alternative Dispute Resolution," *The Journal of Applied Behavioral Science*, 24 (3), 1988, pp. 251–260.

16. Max H. Bazerman and Henry S. Farber, "Arbitrator Decision Making: When Are Final Offers Important?" *Industrial and Labor Relations Review*, 39, October 1985, pp. 76–89.

17. Max H. Bazerman, "Norms of Distributive Justice in Interest Arbitration," *Industrial and Labor Relations Review*, 38, July 1985, pp. 558–570.

18. Joseph B. Rose and Michael Piczak, "Settlement Rates and Settlement Stages in Compulsory Interest Arbitration," *Relations Industrielles*, 51, Fall 1996, pp. 643–645.

19. David E. Bloom and Christopher L. Cavanagh, "Negotiator Behavior under Arbitration," *The American Economic Review*, 77, May 1987, pp. 353–355.

20. Craig A. Olson and Barbara L. Rau, "Learning from Interest Arbitration: The Next Round," *Industrial and Labor Relations Review*, 50, January 1997, pp. 237–251.

21. David B. Lipsky and Harry C. Katz, "Alternative Approaches to Interest Arbitration: Lessons from New York City," *Public Personnel Management*, 35 (4), Winter 2006, pp. 266–267; Frederic Champlin, Mario Bognanno, and Paul Schumann, "Is Arbitration Habit Forming? The Narcotic Effect of Arbitration Use," *Labour*, 11 (1), 1997, pp. 23–42; James R. Chelius and Marian M. Extejt, "The Narcotic Effect of Impasse-Resolution Procedures," *Industrial and Labor Relations Review*, 38, July 1985, pp. 629–638.

22. Robert Herndon, "Public Sector Dispute Resolution in Transition," in *Public Sector Employment in a Time of Transition*, ed. by Dale Belman, Morley Gunderson, and Douglas Hyatt (Madison, WI: Industrial Relations Research Association, 1996), pp. 104–112.

23. Daniel R. Marburger and Paul L. Burgess, "Can Prior Offers and Arbitration Outcomes Be Used to Predict the Winners of Subsequent Final-Offer Arbitration Cases?" *Southern Economics Journal*, 71 (1), 2004, pp. 93–94.

24. Carl M. Stevens, "Is Compulsory Arbitration Compatible with Bargaining?" *Industrial Relations*, 5 (1), 1966, pp. 38–52.

25. Daniel R. Marburger and Paul L. Burgess, "Can Prior Offers and Arbitration Outcomes Be Used to Predict the Winners of Subsequent Final-Offer Arbitration Cases?" p. 102.

26. Daniel R. Marburger and John F. Scoggins, "Risk and Final Offer Arbitration Usage Rates: Evidence from Major League Baseball," *Journal of Labor Research*, 17, Fall 1996, pp. 735–741.

27. Daniel R. Marburger, "Arbitrator Compromise in Final Offer Arbitration: Evidence from Major League Baseball," *Economic Inquiry*, 42 (1) January 2004, pp. 60–68.

28. John D. Burger and Stephen J.K. Walters, "Arbitrator Bias and Self-Interest: Lessons from the Baseball Labor Market," *Journal of Labor Research*, 26 (2), Spring 2005, pp. 267–280.

29. David E. Feller, "The Impetus to Contract Arbitration in the Private Area," *Twenty-fourth Annual NYU Conference on Labor* (New York: Matthew Bender, 1972), pp. 95–98.

30. Excerpts from *NLRB v. Insurance Agents' International Union*, 361 U.S. 477 (1960).

31. "New York City Transit Union Fined $2.5 million for Illegal Strike," *Findlaw,* April 17, 2006, p. 1 and "Judge Rules Transit Union Boss Who Led NY Strike Should Get Jail," *Findlaw,* April 11, 2006, p. 1.

32. Alex Veiga, "California Grocery Workers Voting on Contract," *Associated Press,* February 28, 2004, pp. 1–2; Alex Veiga, "California Grocers Reject Binding Arbitration," *Associated Press,* February 4, 2004, pp. 1–2; "Secret Talks in California Grocery Strike Fail," *Associated Press,* January 11, 2004; Alex Veiga, "Labor Leaders to Assist Grocery Strikers," *Associated Press,* January 21, 2004, pp. 1–2.

33. "Southern California Grocers Reach Agreement with UFCW Members," *Progressive Grocer,* July 24, 2007, p. 1 and Federal Mediation and Conciliation Service, "FMCS Director Commends Parties in Southern California Grocery Talks," *New Release,* July 18, 2007, p. 1.

34. *Harter Equipment, Inc. and Local 825, International Union of Operating Engineers,* 280 NLRB 71 (1986; upheld, 829 F.2d 458 (3rd Cir. 1987); *NLRB v. Brown,* 380 U.S. 278 (1965); and *American Shipbuilding Company v. NLRB,* 380 U.S. 300 (1965).

35. James E. Martin and Robert R. Sinclair, "A Multiple Motive Perspective on Strike Propensities," *Journal of Organizational Behavior* 22 (June 2001), pp. 387–407.

36. *Gateway Coal Company v. United Mine Workers,* 414 U.S. 368 (1974) and B. A. Brotman, "A Comparative Analysis of Arbitration and National Labor Relations Board Decisions Involving Wildcat Strikes," *Labor Law Journal* 36 (July 1985), p. 440.

37. U.S. Department of Labor, Bureau of Labor Statistics, "Major Work Stoppages in 2006," *News Release,* February 27, 2007, pp. 1–10.

38. Michael H. LeRoy, "The Changing Character of Strikes Involving Permanent Striker Replacements, 1935–1990," *Journal of Labor Research,* 16, Fall 1995, p. 437.

39. Bruce E. Kaufman, "The Determinants of Strikes over Time and across Industries," *Journal of Labor Research,* 4, Spring 1983, pp. 173–174.

40. Bruce E. Kaufman, "Research on Strike Models and Outcomes in the 1980s: Accomplishments and Shortcomings," in *Research Frontiers in Industrial and Human Resources,* eds. David Lewin, Olivia S. Mitchell, and Peter D. Sherer (Madison, Wis.: Industrial Relations Research Association, 1992), pp. 78–79.

41. Marc Dixon and Vincent J. Roscigno, "Status, Networks, and Social Movement Participation: The Case of Striking Workers," *The American Journal of Sociology,* 108, May 2003, pp. 1292–1327; Bert Klandermans, "Perceived Costs and Benefits of Participation in Union Action," *Personnel Psychology,* 39, Summer 1986, pp. 380–381.

42. James E. Martin and Robert R. Sinclair, "A Multiple Motive Perspective on Strike Propensities," pp. 402–403; Aaron Cohen, "Attitudinal Militancy and Propensity to Strike Among Unionized Engineers and X-Ray Technicians," *Human Relations* 45 (December 1992), pp. 1333–1336; James E. Martin, "Predictors of Individual Propensity to Strike," *Industrial and Labor Relations Review,* 39, January 1986, pp. 224–225.

43. Nigel Nicholson and John Kelly, "The Psychology of Strikes," *Journal of Occupational Behavior,* 1 (4), October 1980, pp. 275–284.

44. William Serrin, *The Company and the Union* (New York: Knopf, 1973), p. 4.

45. Alex Veiga, "Strike, Lockout Hurting Grocery Workers," *Associated Press,* January 26, 2004, pp. 1–2 and George Getschow, "Strike Woes Pile Up for Leader of Local That Started It All," *The Wall Street Journal,* August 8, 1977, pp. 1, 17.

46. Ashly McCall, "Metal Workers Picket Home of Plant Manager in Nappane, Ind.," *South Bend Tribune,* January 16, 2003, pp. 1–2 and John R. Emshwiller, "Strike Is Traumatic for a Quiet Village in Michigan Woods," *The Wall Street Journal,* July 30, 1977, pp. 1, 24.

47. Michael Barbaro, "Sides Prepare for a Grocery Strike," *The Washington Post,* March 17, 2004, p. E01.

48. Charles R. Perry, Andrew M. Kramer, and Thomas J. Schneider, *Operating During Strikes: Company Experiences, NLRB Policies, and Government Regulations* (Philadelphia: University of Pennsylvania, 1982), p. 38.

49. William R. Crandall and Michael L. Menefee, "Crisis Management in the Midst of Labor Strife: Preparing for the Worst," *S.A.M. Advanced Management Journal,* 61, Winter 1996, pp. 11–15; L. C. Scott, "Running a Struck Plant: Some Do's and Don'ts," *S.A.M. Advanced Management Journal,* 38, October 1973, pp. 58–62 and John G. Hutchinson, *Management under Strike Conditions* (New York: Holt, Rinehart and Winston, 1966).

50. Julius G. Getman and F. Ray Marshall, "The Continuing Assault on the Right to Strike," *Texas Law Review,* 79 (3), February 2001, pp. 703–735.

51. *NLRB v. Mackay Radio & Telegraph Co.,* 304 U.S. 333 (1938).

52. George S. Roukis and Mamdouh I. Farid, "An Alternative Approach to the Permanent Striker Replacement Strategy," *Labor Law Journal,* 44, February 1993, pp. 81–88.

53. Peter Crampton and Joseph Tracy, "The Use of Replacement Workers in Union Contract Negotiations: The U.S. Experience, 1980–1989," *Journal of Labor Economics,* 16 (4), October 1998, pp. 674–676.

54. *Belknap, Inc. v. Hale,* 463 U.S. 491 (1983); and David B. Stephen and John P. Kohl, "The Replacement Worker Phenomenon in the Southwest: Two Years after *Belknap, Inc. v. Hale,*" *Labor Law Journal,* 37, January 1986, pp. 48–49.

55. John W. Budd and Wendell E. Pritchett, "Does the Banning of Permanent Strike Replacements Affect Bargaining Power?" *Proceedings of the 46th Annual Meeting of the Industrial Relations Research Association* (Madison, Wis.: IRRA, 1994), pp. 370–376.

56. *Laidlaw Corporation v. NLRB,* 414 F.2d 99 (7th Cir. 1969); *NLRB v. Fleetwood Trailer Company,* 389 U.S. 375 (1967).

57. *United Aircraft Corporation,* 191 NLRB 62 (1971).

58. *NLRB v. Erie Resistor Corporation,* 373 U.S. 221 (1963); and William T. Krizner, "The Mackay Doctrine: Much

More Than Mere Dicta," *Labor Law Journal,* 49, May 1998, pp. 997–999.

59. *North Cambria Fuel Co. v. NLRB,* 645 F.2d 177 (3rd Cir. 1981); see also: John R. Erickson, "Forfeiture of Reinstatement Rights through Strike Misconduct," *Labor Law Journal,* 31, October 1980, pp. 602–616.

60. *NLRB v. Allis-Chalmers Manufacturing Company,* 388 U.S. 175 (1967).

61. *Pattern Makers' League of North America v. NLRB,* 473 U.S. 95 (1985).

62. *Thornhill v. Alabama,* 310 U.S. 88 (1940).

63. *Lowe Excavating Company v. International Union of Operating Engineers, Local 150,* 327 Ill. App. 711 (2002) and Mary Swerczek, "Judge: Picketers Get 25 Seconds; Running Kaiser Strike Means Jail Time for 3," *The Times-Picayune,* May 13, 2000, p. B01.

64. *Lechmere Inc. v. NLRB,* 502 U.S. 527 (1992).

65. *NLRB v. International Rice Milling Company,* 341 U.S. 665 (1951) and *United Steelworkers of America v. NLRB,* 376 U.S. 492 (1964).

66. Bruce Feldacker, *Labor Guide To Labor Law, 4th edition* (Upper Saddle River, NJ: Prentice-Hall, 2000), pp. 276–278, 281–283.

67. *Moore Dry Dock Company and Sailors' Union of the Pacific,* 92 NLR 547 (1950); and *Sailors' Union of the Pacific v. NLRB,* 366 U.S. 667 (1950).

68. *NLRB v. Denver Building Trade & Construction Council,* 341 U.S. 675 (1951).

69. *Local 501, International Brotherhood of Electrical Workers v. NLRB,* 756 F.2d 888 (DC Cir. 1985).

70. *Local 761, International Union of Electrical, Radio & Machine Workers v. NLRB,* 366 U.S. 667 (1961).

71. *NLRB v. Fruit and Vegetable Packers & Warehousmen, Local 760,* 377 U.S. 58 (1964) and *NLRB v. Servette, Inc.,* 377 U.S. 46 (1964).

72. *NLRB v. Retail Store Employees Union, Local 1001, Retail Clerks International Association* (Safeco Insurance Co.), 444 U.S. 1011 (1980).

73. *The Kroger Company v. NLRB,* 647 F.2d 634 (6th Cir. 1980).

74. *Edward J. DeBartolo Corporation v. Florida Gulf Coast Building & Construction Trades Council ET AL.,* 485 U.S. 568 (1988).

75. General Accounting Office, *Airline Labor Relations: Information on Trends and Impact of Labor Actions* (Washington, D.C.: U.S. General Accounting Office, 2003), pp. 15–16.

76. C. Howard Davis, William M. Eisenberg, and Ronald E. Kutscher, "Quick Special Purpose Surveys Passed Test During Coal Strike," *Monthly Labor Review,* 102, February 1979, pp. 62–64.

77. Jim Puzzanghera, Jennifer Bjorhus, and Matt Marshall, "West Coast Ports to Reopen Today; Bush Uses Authority to Intervene in Dispute," *Knight Ridder Tribune Business News,* October 9, 2002, pp. 1–3 and J. Martin McOmber, "Six-Year Deal Ends West Coast Dockworker Dispute," *Knight Ridder Tribune Business News,* January 23, 2003, pp. 1–2.

78. Charles M. Rehmus, "Emergency Strikes Revisited," *Industrial and Labor Relations Review,* 43, January 1990, pp. 176–180.

79. Michael H. LeRoy and John H. Johnson IV, "Death by Lethal Injunction: National Emergency Strikes Under the Taft-Hartley Act and the Moribund Right to Strike," 43 *Arizona Law Review* 63 (Spring 2001).

The Aftermath of a Strike

CASE STUDY 9-1 On August 6, the collective bargaining agreement between the company and the union expired. Two days later, the union called a strike at the company's facilities, including those at 3303 Express Lane, St. Louis, Missouri. The strike ended on August 28 with the signing of a new three-year agreement. The following day, employees began returning to work. During the strike, a substantial number of bargaining unit employees at the plant crossed the union's picket line and continued to work.

On September 2, the union distributed materials to its union stewards for posting on bulletin boards maintained by the union at the company's facilities. One of the items posted was a commentary by author Jack London, entitled "Definition of a Scab":

> After God had finished the rattlesnake, the toad, and the vampire, he had some awful substance left with which he made a SCAB. A SCAB is a two-legged animal with a corkscrew soul, a water-logged brain, and a combination backbone of jelly and glue. Where others have hearts, he carries a tumor of rotten principles.
>
> When a SCAB comes down the street men turn their backs and angels weep in Heaven, and the devil shuts the gates of Hell to keep him out. No man has the right to SCAB, so long as there is a pool of water deep enough to drown his body in or a rope long enough to hang his carcass with. Judas Iscariot was a gentleman... compared with a SCAB; for betraying his master, he had the character to hang himself—a SCAB hasn't. Esau sold his birthright for a mess of pottage. Judas Iscariot sold his Savior for thirty pieces of silver. Benedict Arnold sold his country for a promise of a commission in the British Army. The modern strikebreaker sells his birthright, his country, his wife, his children, and his fellow man for an unfulfilled promise from his employer, trust or corporation.
>
> Esau was a traitor to himself. Judas Iscariot was a traitor to his God. Benedict Arnold was a traitor to his country. A strikebreaker is a traitor to himself, a traitor to his God, a traitor to his country, a traitor to his family, and a traitor to his class. THERE IS NOTHING LOWER THAN A SCAB....

Union steward Cora Able immediately posted the "Definition of a Scab" along with another article, entitled "From Cora's Desk," praising the strikers and criticizing those who remained on the job, on a union bulletin board in the computer terminal room, adjacent to Room 102 at the company's plant. Able posted the items in response to a memo from chief union steward, employee Anita Cain, requesting that she do so.

Able has been responsible for posting material on the union bulletin board in the computer terminal room since she became the union job steward three years ago. Able had previously posted campaign literature regarding candidates for union office, notices of union meetings, and articles from union newsletters on this bulletin board. Able had also removed comic strips from the bulletin board. Before September 2, no company supervisor had ever told Able what she could or could not post on the union's bulletin board, nor had any company supervisor ever removed anything from this board before this date.

The company had no written rules concerning the posting of literature on the union's bulletin boards on the company's premises. Neither the current nor previous collective bargaining agreements covering bargaining unit employees contained any provision regarding the union's bulletin boards at the company's facilities.

During the afternoon of September 2, company supervisor Joe Bay saw several employees near the bulletin board, apparently reading the posted articles. Supervisor Bay removed the "Definition of a Scab" and deposited it in a garbage can. Union steward Able noticed that the article had been removed and asked Bay where it was. Supervisor Bay told her he had removed it, balled it up, and thrown it into the garbage can.

Union steward Able took the sheet from the can, then got another copy from her desk, and hung it on the union bulletin board. In the presence of several other employees, supervisor Bay promptly snatched this copy down, telling Able, "this mess [isn't] going to hang up here." Bay then specifically prohibited Able from posting another copy and warned her of disciplinary action if she did so. Able called the chief union steward who spoke to supervisor Bay, requesting that he leave the literature on the bulletin board. Bay then told the chief union steward that the "Definition of a Scab" had no business on the board and was causing animosity among the clerks.

A half-hour later, supervisor Linda Trevino informed union steward Able that another supervisor, Ralph Coe, wanted to see her. Coe had a copy of the "Definition of a Scab" in his hand, and he told Able, "We're not going to have this mess hanging in this office." In the presence of supervisors Trevino and Bay, Coe also warned Able that she could be disciplined "for insubordination." Union steward Able asked to be excused and on returning to her desk called chief union steward Miller again.

Fifteen minutes later, supervisor Trevino told Able, "We would like to see you for five minutes." Able told Trevino that she did not want to go back to supervisor Coe's office. However, Able complied on Trevino's assurance that the return to Coe's office would take only five minutes, long enough to receive an apology. In Coe's office, Able was asked to tell her side of the incident. Supervisor Coe apologized, as did supervisor Bay, for the way they had treated Able in front of the other employees. Coe did not retract his support for supervisor Bay's action in removing the article and preventing its reposting.

On September 1, union job steward Milton Musk posted a copy of the "Definition of a Scab" on a union bulletin board located in a break room next to Rooms 208 and 209, the Switching Control Center, at the company's plant. Musk had been responsible for posting material on this bulletin board for the past three years. As a matter of practice, Musk had posted on the board notices of union meetings, listings of job vacancies provided to the union, lists of union officers' names, announcements for an employee charitable organization, and the campaign material of candidates for union office. Occasionally, Musk removed cartoons from the board that had been posted by employees. Before September 1, no supervisor had ever told Musk what he could or could not post on the union bulletin board.

The "Definition of a Scab" remained on the union bulletin board in the Switching Control Center break room until about 4 P.M., September 1. About that time, supervisor Wesley Vie directed Musk to remove "Definition of a Scab." Union steward Musk said he did not wish to do so. Supervisor Vie removed the printed copy of the "Definition of a Scab" as Musk watched.

The following day, before 7 A.M., the "Definition of a Scab" again appeared on the bulletin board. Supervisor Tom Davis summoned union steward Musk to his office at approximately 8 A.M. and told him to take down the "Definition of a Scab" from the union's bulletin board. Musk protested that he did not put it up, and he should not have to take it down. Supervisor Davis then warned Musk that he would suspend him if he continued to refuse to obey the order to take it down. Supervisor Davis asked for Musk's building pass and key, whereupon Musk requested permission to make a telephone call. After consulting a union district steward, Musk removed the "Definition of a Scab." Musk again told Davis that it was unfair that he had to remove the article when he had not posted it. Supervisor Davis told Musk that he "didn't want trash like that posted."

The union filed an unfair labor practice charge contending that the company violated Section 8(a)(1) of the LMRA by removing the "Definition of a Scab" from union bulletin boards and by threatening employees with punishment if they posted or reposted the item on those bulletin boards. The company denied that it violated the LMRA on the grounds that the posting of Jack London's pejorative appraisal of non-striking employees had disrupted the discipline of its employees and thus was beyond the protection of Sections 7 and 8(a)(1) of the act.

Questions

1. How does a union gain the right to use bulletin boards on a company's premises?

2. Why was the union so insistent on having the "Definition of a Scab" posted on the bulletin board?

3. Since the union is already recognized as the exclusive bargaining unit representative and the new contract terms have been settled, how or why does Section (8)(a)(1) apply to this case?

4. Did the supervisors' removal of the posted union material and threats to discipline union members for reposting the "Definition of a Scab" constitute an unfair labor practice under the LMRA? Explain your reasoning.

The Right to Strike

CASE STUDY 9-2 Seven of the employer's 11 concrete truck drivers met several times during the week of September 16 to discuss their current wage rates, the lack of a medical insurance plan, and whether they should consider joining a union. After meeting with a representative of the national truck drivers' union, four of the seven drivers signed union authorization cards. Employee Santos, one of the card signers, wrote a letter which the seven employees presented to the company's plant manager on Friday, September 20. The letter stated, in part, "Today all employees wish to express a silent strike in pursuance of the right that our salaries be increased to $5.75 per hour. We will not work today...until an accord is reached."

Later that Friday morning, the company president met with seven employees and told them that the company was in no position to give any wage increase; however, steps were already underway to establish a medical insurance plan by the end of the year. The seven employees met outside the plant and decided the company's position was unacceptable. The company president stated that the board of directors would be meeting the following day (Saturday) to consider the matter. The seven employees continued their walkout during the rest of Friday.

The board of directors met on Saturday and calculated the annual cost of the employees' wage demand to be $108,000. The board of directors found this unacceptable and decided to replace the seven drivers rather than agree to increase wages. Later on Saturday, the plant manager offered driver positions to three individuals who already had job applications on file with the company. All three applicants accepted the job offer and were scheduled to begin work the following week. On Monday, the seven drivers who had walked out on Friday returned to the company but remained outside the plant entrance.

Upon learning that the seven drivers had not reported for work at 8 A.M. on Monday morning but were instead congregating in front of the plant, the company president prepared a letter which was given to each of the seven drivers outside the company's entrance at 9:30 on Monday morning. The letter referred to the walkout on the previous Friday and stated in relevant part: "The circumstances of having abandoned your work without first holding a dialogue, then bringing later on some demands which we cannot face economically at this time, in addition to your refusal to work if your conditions are not met exactly the way [you] stated them, we have to interpret it as a resignation from your job, leaving us without alternatives and unfortunately we have to accept your decision effective today, Monday, September 23." The letter went on to state that the Friday work stoppage forced the company to fill some vacancies and curtail its operations in order to recover in part from the losses it had suffered.

After receiving the letters, the seven employees left the plant to attend a meeting with a union representative. Some time later on that Monday, three of the employees returned to the plant and requested reinstatement. The company reinstated the three drivers to their former jobs. The Union filed an unfair labor practice on behalf of the remaining four truck drivers, alleging that each had been unlawfully discharged in violation of the LMRA, as amended.

Questions

1. Does the work stoppage by the truck drivers in this case represent an economic strike or an unfair labor practice strike?

2. What is the difference between the reinstatement rights of an unfair labor practice striker and an economic striker?

3. Did the employer unlawfully discharge the four truck drivers who never returned to work? Explain your reasoning.

The Reinstatement Offer

CASE STUDY 9-3 On September 13 two employees went on strike to protest their employer's refusal to bargain in good faith. The two employees were approached on the picket line by the company's manager on September 13 and told they were fired for going on strike. On September 16, the company circulated a letter to building tenants stating: "Management has made it clear that any employee who decides to strike, his employment will be terminated immediately with no chance of reinstatement. The building superintendent has assured us he will continue to work. However, two porters have chosen their own demise. Their employment is hereby terminated!"

On September 23, ten days after the strike had begun, the company's manager sent a reinstatement offer to the two discharged employees by certified mail. The letter stated: "In view of your actions, management had no choice but to replace you. However, due to your fine performance at the position you held, management would be agreeable to reinstating you if you return to work immediately. Should you decide that you would like to return to work, please notify me within five (5) business days. If I do not hear from you I will have no choice but to search for permanent replacements." The two employees received the letter but made no response within the specified five business-day period or at any time thereafter.

The Union filed an unfair labor practice charge on behalf of the two employees, alleging that they had been engaged in an unfair labor practice strike and therefore the employer's discharge was illegal. Approximately two years and two months later, the NLRB upheld the union's unfair labor practice charge, finding the employer's discharge of the two employees was illegal.

At the unfair labor practice hearing, the employer argued that if it were found guilty of unlawfully discharging the two employees, any back-pay remedy should be limited to the first 15 days of the strike. The 15-day period covered the ten days prior to the date on which management sent the two employees the offer of reinstatement and the five business days in which the employees had the opportunity to accept the offer but chose not to do so.

Questions

1. Did the strike on September 13 by the two employees represent an economic or unfair labor practice strike?

2. Did the company make a lawful reinstatement offer to the two employees, thus terminating the employer's back-pay liability after 15 days from their original termination date? Explain your reasoning.

Denial of Health Care Benefits to Striking Employees

CASE STUDY 9-4 The employer operates two production facilities, one in Michigan and the other in Ohio. Employees at both plants are covered under separate, but similar labor agreements. On August 10, a lawful economic strike was initiated by local union members at the company's Ohio plant. The Ohio local union members established picket lines at both the Ohio and Michigan facilities of the employer. Picketing occurred at the Michigan plant on August 10–11; August 23–26; August 31–September 3; and September 7–9.

On August 5, the company sent a letter to all employees advising them of the status of negotiations at the Ohio plant and warning employees that "an employee's refusal to perform work under these circumstances could result in the immediate loss of all unaccrued benefits, including health care." The Michigan plant employees who honored the picket line established by the Ohio plant employees were subsequently denied health care benefits by the company on the days they participated in the strike by refusing to cross the picket line established at the Michigan plant.

Both the employer and union agree that the Michigan plant union members who honored the picket line established at their plant did not cease to be employees of the company as a result

411

of their refusal to cross the picket line. The language in the parties' contractual no-strike agreement covering the Michigan plant does not prohibit employees from engaging in lawful sympathy strike activity, and thus covered sympathy strikers cannot be disciplined or discharged for their refusal to cross a lawfully established picket line. Both the union and the employer agree that the Michigan plant labor agreement is silent on the specific question of whether health care benefits must be maintained or can be denied to employees who strike.

The only contract language with any possible relevance concerns the clause dealing with termination of employment, which states: "In the event of termination of employment other than normal layoff or retirement with pension, an employee's hospitalization, surgical and medical coverage and life insurance under the group arrangement shall be cancelled in thirty (30) days." The employer argues that this language is not applicable to the strikers in this case because none of the strikers were terminated. The union argues that if the parties clearly intended to permit a terminated individual to retain medical insurance benefits for at least 30 days after termination, then surely employees who were not terminated would have at least an equal right to continue health care coverage, even though they lawfully refused to work on certain dates in support of a lawful economic strike by other company employees.

The union filed a contractual grievance stating that the employer's withdrawal of medical benefits from Michigan plant sympathy strikers violated their contractual right to receive such benefits as provided under the health care benefits clause in the current labor agreement. The union asked the arbitrator to require the employer to reimburse all affected striking workers for all covered health care expenditures paid by the striking workers on dates when the company had suspended their health insurance coverage due to their refusal to cross a lawfully established union picket line at their place of employment.

Questions

1. Should the arbitrator uphold the union's grievance and find that the company's withdrawal of medical benefits from striking workers violated their contractual right to receive such benefits? If so, what should the appropriate remedy be? Explain your reasoning.

2. When the current contract governing the Michigan plant expires, would you advise the employer to negotiate specific contract language as part of a no-strike agreement clearly waiving bargaining unit members' right to engage in a sympathy strike during the term of the labor agreement? Explain your reasoning.

3. If the employer did propose a waiver of sympathy strike rights in the future, would this bargaining issue likely represent a **high, medium,** or **low priority item** for the union and its membership? Explain your reasoning.

Product Picket Activity

CASE STUDY 9-5 A union engaged in a lawful economic strike against the Brown Bag Company (the primary employer) decided to establish a product picket line at the site of the Stop & Shop grocery store, a secondary employer who used grocery bags produced by the Brown Bag Company. Although the Stop & Shop grocery store does provide boxes instead of bags to a few customers who specifically request a box, the vast majority of grocery items are carried from the store in bags produced by the Brown Bag Company.

The union's picket signs were carefully worded to identify the Brown Bag Company as the target of the picket action and to request customers of the Stop & Shop grocery store to boycott only bags produced by the Brown Bag Company. During the two days that picketing occurred, 150 of 4,300 customers who shopped at the Stop & Shop grocery store specifically requested a box to transport their groceries rather than a bag. Managers were able to provide enough boxes for about two-thirds of the customers who requested a box rather than use a grocery bag produced by the Brown Bag Company. A few customers brought their own containers from home (e.g., pillow case, bag, or box) to transport their grocery purchases. One customer, upon being told by a Stop & Shop manager that there were no more boxes available, left the store without purchasing or taking any of the grocery items she had brought to the checkout line.

The Brown Bag Company filed an unfair labor practice charge against the union alleging that the union's product picket action was a violation of Sec. 8 (b)(4), LMRA. The employer sought an order to prevent the union from engaging in further product picket activity at the Stop & Shop grocery store. The employer argued that it is impossible for a customer to comply with the union's boycott of Brown Bag Company grocery bags without also refusing to purchase grocery items sold by the Stop & Shop grocery store since the grocery store exclusively used grocery bags produced by the Brown Bag Company. As evidence, the employer pointed to the fact that there were only enough boxes available for approximately 2.3 percent of the total customers who shopped at the grocery store during the two days of product picket activity. The employer argued it was not reasonable to expect customers to bring their own containers with them to transport grocery items when shopping at the Stop & Shop grocery store.

Questions

1. Would the Stop and Shop grocery store in this case be classified as a **neutral, secondary employer,** or **business ally** of the Brown Bag Company? Explain your reasoning.

2. Should the **merged product** doctrine be applied in this case to declare that the union's product picket action was unlawful? Explain your reasoning.

Part 3: Administering the Labor Agreement

After the collective bargaining agreement has been negotiated and accepted by both union members and management, the day-to-day tasks of administering the agreement begins. Although not the most publicized nor the most dramatic part of labor relations, this process involves more union and management officials than contract negotiations and provides meaning and common law principles to the agreement. These chapters present the fundamentals of contract administration and labor and employment arbitration followed by a subject that relates to every workplace—employee discipline.

Copyright GettyImages

CHAPTER 10
Contract Administration

Labor agreements negotiation are usually the most publicized and dramatic aspect of labor relations. Strike deadlines, negotiators in shirtsleeves working around the clock to avert a possible strike, and the economic settlement of the labor agreement receive attention from the news media. The day-to-day administration of the labor agreement, on the other hand, receives little, if any, recognition beyond that given by the involved parties. Contract administration, however, involves more labor and management officials than does negotiations, and it applies meaning and common-law principles to negotiated labor provisions. In contract negotiations, the union is typically the initiator, but in contract administration, management assumes this role. In other words, management exercises its administrative initiative to make decisions and to direct the business operations.

During a typical year, managers in a large organization will make literally thousands of decisions on employment-related subjects, such as wage increases, promotions, discipline, work assignments, layoffs, performance appraisals, and so on. In small organizations, managers will make hundreds of these types of decisions. In organizations where there is a collective bargaining agreement that has been negotiated and agreed to by management and the union, rules, policies, and procedures contained in the collective bargaining agreement will guide the managers in their decisions.

Many times before a final decision is made, a designated person from management will be assigned the task of conducting an investigation to gather facts that will be used in the decision-making process. In fact, the largest portion of managers has their most frequent labor relations experience during the investigation phase and the decision-making process. In decisions on administrative issues (covered in Chapter 8), such as a promotion, the investigation will include the collection of information such as the job requirements, seniority (job, department, or company), performance appraisals, supervisor recommendations, test scores, and so on before the decision is made. In disciplinary matters (covered in Chapter 12) where there has been a major infraction, such as theft, fighting, carrying a weapon on the job site, threatening a supervisor, and so on, the employee may be suspended immediately, and the final decision of the type of discipline will be delayed until the investigation is completed. In disciplinary matters that are performance related, such as excessive absenteeism, failure to meet production standards, and so on, the investigation will be conducted prior to the disciplinary decision. Performance-related information includes any type of performance records, attendance and tardiness records, past discipline (check time limits to make sure the discipline has not been erased and check to make sure the discipline has been progressive), training received, the maintenance on the equipment to make sure the products is not the reason for the poor performance, and so on.

The investigation itself is simply a systematic collection of facts which will serve as the basis for making a decision. Since the employers are held accountable for their employment decisions, that is, compliance with the collective bargaining agreement or compliance with employment laws, the investigation should be speedy, thorough, and objective, and the employers should have a sound basis for making their employment decisions. The investigator will take many steps in completing the investigation. For example, in conducting an investigation of an altercation between employees, the investigator will interview witnesses and collect facts in order to describe and explain what occurred. As another example, if an employee falls on wet concrete on the job and seeks to be paid workers' compensation, the investigator will attempt to visit the scene of the accident as soon as possible after the fall to gather physical evidence, such as water on the floor, signs of leaking pipes, poor drainage, past requests to repair the leaking pipe, poorly lit stairwells, and so on.

After the investigator has gathered the facts, the investigator will then decide which pieces of information are important. The relevant facts are the pieces of information that have the potential of helping describe and explain what occurred. The pieces of information are referred to as evidence. There are four types of evidence that are used in investigations. The first type is *testimonial* evidence, which involves information gathered from witnesses to an incident. For example, if there are five witnesses to an incident, the investigator should interview all five witnesses. The witnesses simply tell the investigator about their observations and memories of the incident, and the investigator records the information.

If the investigator asks the witnesses to provide written statements or there is an audio and/or video made of the interview, this type of evidence is considered *documentary* evidence. Another type of evidence is *physical* evidence, which includes a broken chair that resulted from a fall, an item of clothing that contains blood as the result of an altercation, or a tool that was recovered from an employee engaged in theft of property. The final type of evidence is *demonstrative* evidence, which can be a diagram of the workplace where an incident occurred or a photograph that shows a cut to the lip of an employee who was engaged in an altercation.

LABOR RELATIONS IN ACTION
Rules Governing Workplace Investigations

1. The person assigned to be an investigator should not have an interest in the outcome of the case.
2. The investigator should interview the person who reported an incident first.
3. After the scene has been secured, the investigator should visit the scene before interviewing other witnesses.
4. The investigator should collect physical evidence at the scene and prepare demonstrative evidence for the use of those individuals who will evaluate the evidence and make the decisions about the validity of the findings.
5. The investigator should interview witnesses and take written statements immediately after visiting the scene (evidence becomes tainted from memory loss and influence of others who have interests in the outcome of the investigation).
6. The investigator should collect and review pertinent documentary evidence about the employee under investigation only after other types of information have been gathered.
7. The investigator should conduct background interviews with supervisors, coworkers, medical professionals, and others who may provide relevant information that could help describe or explain what occurred.
8. As the investigation nears completion, the investigator should conduct follow-up interviews to ask any question not thought of in the first interview, to discover additional information, and to help resolve conflicting evidence already gathered.
9. The investigator should write a final report, which includes a summary of the findings, details of the investigative activities, the conclusion, and attachments of the evidence.

SOURCE: Adapted from Antone Aboud, "Conducting a Fair Investigation," *The Dispute Resolution Journal,* Vol. 60, No. 3 (November 2004–January 2005), pp. 16–20.

As noted above, the investigation should contain three valuable characteristics: speed, thoroughness, and objectivity. *Speed* is important because the longer the evidence remains uncollected, the more likely it will be contaminated or lost. Witnesses may forget certain facts or may even fabricate their story of what happened. As an expert on investigation has claimed that the clock starts ticking at the time of occurrence and each tick represents a decay of evidence. Thoroughness is important because it is necessary to collect all relevant facts. If there are five witnesses, the investigator should interview all five witnesses, not a majority. Even when the first three witnesses tell the same story, the other two may have different versions. The three witnesses may have been standing in the same location or they may have a reason to tell consistent stories. Objectivity means that the investigator needs to conduct the fact-finding mission with a substantial degree of detachment. If the investigator is biased or prejudiced, the results of the investigation are less likely to contain the complete facts. If the investigator sympathizes with an employee who is being charged with a major infraction of company rules, the investigator may fail to ask tough and essential questions to obtain the truth. An expert on workplace investigation has formulated rules to govern investigations[1] (see Labor Relations in Action).

After management has made its decision, the union will monitor this decision to make sure that it is consistent with the collective bargaining agreement. If an employee or the union believes that management's decision has violated any provision of the collective bargaining agreement, either the employee or the union on behalf of an individual employee or a group of employees will file a grievance. The union will then conduct its own investigation.

This chapter defines employee grievances and explores their sources and significance. The next section examines the grievance procedure: its typical steps, the relationships among grievance participants, and theoretical as well as practical concerns involved in contract administration. Alternative dispute resolution (ADR), a process to resolve grievances with the assistance of a neutral third party, is discussed. The chapter concludes with a discussion of the union's duty of fair representation.

GRIEVANCES: DEFINITION, SOURCES, AND SIGNIFICANCE

A **grievance** represents the core of contract administration and is defined as an employee's (or employer's) alleged violation of the labor agreement that is submitted to the grievance procedure for resolution by the employee (or union representative or employer). A grievance is therefore distinguished from an employee's concern that is unrelated to labor agreement provisions and is not submitted to the grievance procedure. Grievances are usually written out at the first or second steps (Exhibit 10.1), which has several advantages for management and union officials:

1. Both union and management representatives need a written record of their daily problem resolutions. This record generates precedents that can guide future actions and save time in deciding similar grievances.

Exhibit 10.1
Examples of Incorrect and Correct Grievance Forms

THE WRONG WAY

FILL OUT IN TRIPLICATE

GRIEVANCE REPORT
USA Local Union No. ▆▆▆▆
Location ▆▆▆▆

Name ▆▆▆▆   Union Ledger No.   Age
Address ▆▆▆▆
Department ▆▆▆ Operation ▆▆▆ Check No. ▆▆
Service
Nature of Grievance

The foreman is against me. He always has it in for me. Lots of times he gives me dirty jobs. Now he refuses to give me holiday pay when I ought to get it. It's time he stopped discriminating against me.

WHEN? Be specific, give dates.

WHY? What section or sections of the contract are involved?

GET WHAT? Describe the adjustment sought.

SPELL IT OUT! Is this another grievance? What do these statements have to do with the Holiday Pay issue?

COPY FOR LOCAL UNION

THE RIGHT WAY

FILL OUT IN TRIPLICATE

GRIEVANCE REPORT
USA Local Union No. ▆▆▆▆
Location ▆▆▆▆

Name ▆▆▆▆   Union Ledger No.   Age
Address ▆▆▆▆
Department ▆▆▆ Operation ▆▆▆ Check No. ▆▆
Service
Nature of Grievance

I, the undersigned, a laborer in the Melt Department, claim that the Company violated Section 10 – Holidays, of the Basic Agreement when it failed to pay me for the July 4th unworked holiday even though I had satisfied the eligibility requirements. I request that the Company compensate me for 8 hours pay on July 4th as provided in Section 10 - Holidays.

COPY FOR LOCAL UNION

SOURCE: United Steelworkers of America, The Grievance Man's Handbook.

2. Written grievances tend to reduce the emotionalism present in many employee concerns. Verbal confrontation on an emotional issue can produce exaggerated accusations that may irreparably harm the relationship between the parties. Consequently, writing the grievance may be necessary for its rational discussion.

3. A written statement allows management and union representatives to focus on the employee's original grievance. As will be discussed further, a grievance can proceed through several steps that involve many more individuals than the aggrieved employee. Union officials may expand one employee's initial allegation into a broader philosophical issue. For example, a complaint over the company's unilateral increase in prices of candy bars for the vending machine could conceivably be magnified in subsequent steps to protest the company's arbitrary and capricious actions in other working conditions.

4. Written grievances can benefit management in cases where the employee is apprehensive about signing a written protest. One research effort found that supervisors react negatively in subsequent performance ratings of employees who file grievances against them that are decided in the employees' favor.[2]

5. Even though most labor agreements permit a union officer to file a grievance on behalf of the grievant, requiring grievances to be written probably reduces the total number that management representatives must administer.

There are two approaches to defining a grievance: therapeutic and legalistic. The therapeutic approach is extremely broad and hinges on the employee's perception that he or she has a grievance. Assume, for example, that Employee A protests Employee B's "immoral" behavior. This protest could be an oral complaint without reference to the grievance procedure. Conversely, the employee could insist the complaint represents a violation of the terms of the labor agreement (the legalistic approach). Management seeks to identify the cause of a grievance and resolve it. More common in unionized firms is the legalistic approach, which restricts a grievance to a perceived violation of the provisions of the labor agreement. Managers prefer the legalistic approach because it restricts possible arbitrator decisions to only those subjects covered in the parties' labor agreement, preserving management's right to control decisions affecting subjects not covered in the labor agreement.

Suppose the employee cites a contractual provision in the argument, such as an article stressing the "company's obligation to maintain a work environment in as safe a condition as possible." After unsuccessfully discussing the issue with Employee A, the supervisor has two options: (1) to refuse to accept the employee's grievance or (2) to accept the employee's grievance and deny it in the written grievance answer on the basis that there is no contractual violation. Not wishing to risk a time-consuming unfair labor practice charge, the supervisor will probably take the second alternative. There is a difference between accepting an employee's grievance and deciding the merits of an employee's grievance. Accepting an employee's grievance safeguards against unfair labor practice charges and at the same time preserves management's right to deny the grievance in its written answer.

In a typical collective bargaining agreement, there are multiple subjects negotiated by the parties and included in the agreement under the general subject of "wages, hours, and other terms and conditions of employment." Therefore, these provisions serve as the source of multiple grievances. Typical subjects of grievances are listed in Exhibit 10.2.

Exhibit 10.2

Potential Subjects for Grievances

Administrative Issues
  Use of seniority
  Promotion and Transfers
  Layoffs/Recall
  Work Assignments
  Training
  Job changes and work restructuring
  Safety and health
  Disability
  Discrimination

Economics Issues
  Wage rates
  Wage increases
  Job classifications
  Wage incentives
  Call-in pay
  Overtime assignments
  Shift differentials
  Merit pay
  Lump sum payments
  Past practice of benefits

Employee Discipline
  Reasonable rules
  Fair and thorough investigation
  Equal treatment/discrimination
  Due process rights denial
  Mitigating circumstances
  Excessive penalty
  Communication of the rules
  Abusive behavior
  Insubordination
  Falsification of company records
  Fighting on the job
  Workplace violence/threats
  Sexual harassment
  Absences/tardiness
  Use or possession of drugs or /alcohol

Reasons for Employee Grievances

Some research has focused on individual characteristics that predict who files a grievance. One such study found that employees who file grievances are younger; more active in their unions; and less satisfied with their job, supervisor, and union.[3] In a study of four organizations over ten years, researchers found that grievance filers had slightly higher performance ratings, substantially higher work attendance rates, and markedly higher promotion rates than nonfilers. However, following the grievance filings, the grievance filers had significantly lower promotion rates in all four organizations, significantly higher turnover rates in three organizations, and significantly lower performance ratings in two organizations. Differences in work attendance were not significant.

The research also shows that the step in the grievance procedure where there is a settlement and a decision in favor of the employer makes a difference. The performance ratings, promotion rates, and work attendance were higher for grievants whose cases were settled at the first step of the grievance procedure than at subsequent steps. As well, performance ratings were significantly higher for grievants whose cases were decided in favor of the employer rather than the grievants. Thus, the conclusion is that negative outcomes are more common for grievants whose cases are resolved at higher steps rather than lower steps of the grievance procedure, especially if the grievant wins the grievance.

Analysis of grievance filings appears to reflect the performance of first-line supervisors. During a ten-year period, supervisors against whom grievances were filed or settled had higher turnover rates (mostly involuntary), and lower job performance ratings and promotion rates than supervisors against whom grievances were not filed.[4]

Grievances have also assumed research significance. Many studies have examined how grievances relate to organizational characteristics and to outcomes.[5]

To better understand the reasons behind employee grievances, the following example is given. A first-line supervisor administers a labor agreement that has the following provisions pertaining to management's rights and the scheduling of work to be performed on a holiday:

Article III: Management Rights

Section 1. The Company's right to hire, fire, and direct the working force, transfer or promote is unqualified as long as this right is not used in any conflict with any provision of this contract.

Article IX: Holiday Scheduling

Section 1. When less than a normal crew is required to work on a holiday, the following procedure will apply:

(a) The senior employee working in the classification desired will be given the opportunity to work.

(b) Employees assigned holiday work will be paid a minimum of eight hours at time-and-one-half the contract rate of pay.

(c) If an employee works out of classification on the holiday, the senior employee in the appropriate classification will also be paid a minimum of eight hours at time-and-one-half his or her contract rate of pay.

Article XII: Bargaining-Unit Work

Section 1. Supervisors may perform bargaining-unit work only during emergencies.

With these provisions in mind, consider the following chain of events. A crane operator is needed to work the July 4th holiday. The senior employee in this classification starts work on his shift; however, after he has worked a half hour, the crane breaks down and can no longer be operated. Management believes the maintenance department will be able to repair the crane within two hours. All job classifications typically perform some minor housekeeping and clean-up work, such as dusting and picking up debris around the workstation; however, there is also a janitor's classification in the labor agreement.

The first-line supervisor has at least four options. First, the supervisor can send the employee home, although Section 1(b) of the labor agreement compels management to pay that employee eight hours at time-and-one-half the employee's hourly pay rate. Consequently, the first option is not attractive to management.

The second option would have the employee remain at work and do nothing until the crane is repaired. Because management is already obligated to pay the employee for the entire shift, it does not cost any additional money to have the employee sit in the work shed until crane operations can be renewed. The first-line supervisor is not likely to take this option, particularly if higher-level management officials and other hourly employees see this individual being paid while not performing work.

The third option would be to have the crane operator perform minor housekeeping chores until the crane is repaired. While the third option appears most beneficial to management, there is a good possibility that this action will result in a grievance from the senior employee in the janitorial classification, asking payment for eight hours at time-and-one-half because Section 1(c) would apparently have been violated. The fourth option for the supervisor is to help repair the crane to minimize the lost time. Because the agreement allows supervisors to perform bargaining-unit work only during emergencies, the supervisor must be prepared to convince the union that an emergency has occurred.

The employee could file a grievance for one or more of the following reasons.

1. To Protest a Contractual Violation

When labor and management officials negotiate a labor agreement, they are mainly concerned with agreement over the major issues. The negotiators are not concerned with determining the precise meaning of every word in the labor agreement, particularly if few or no previous problems have arisen from the contract language. Similarly, these officials cannot possibly anticipate all of the unique situations that could potentially destroy or add to the negotiated terms of the labor agreement. Consequently, union and management negotiators often gloss over the "unimportant" provisions, leaving potential interpretational problems to those who must live with and administer the labor agreement on a daily basis.

In the crane operator example, local union officials could contend that the crane operator did "work out of classification"—a clear violation of Section 1(c). Management, on the other hand, could contend that the needed holiday work was within the scope of a crane operator's job and point out the impracticality of paying an employee an amount equal to 12 hours' pay simply to dust or straighten up the workplace. Another management contention could be that minor housekeeping chores are performed by all employees; therefore, the crane operator did not work out of classification on the day in question. Hence, Article III, "Management Rights," would prevail in this situation. Even further, management could claim that the crane breakdown created an emergency situation.

2. To Draw Attention to a Problem in the Plant

Some grievances do not protest violation of the labor agreement; instead, they stress that management has obligations beyond the scope of the labor agreement. Most grievances over alleged safety hazards fall into this category because labor agreements may not specify management's detailed obligations in this area. The employee might file a grievance to communicate concern to management over a safety issue. In our example, the grievance over holiday scheduling might have been filed, not over receiving payment for the senior janitor in the classification but to give union officers a forum in which to stress the inadequate number of maintenance employees for equipment repair.

Unions quite often draw attention to a problem in the hopes of setting the stage for future labor agreement negotiations. A common union tactic is to file several grievances over a particular issue to buttress and document union demands during negotiation of the subsequent labor agreement. For example, labor unions adhering to a job-protection philosophy do not want supervisory personnel performing their members' work because these activities could reduce overtime opportunities or even result in employees being laid off. In the course of the workday, supervisors may perform several tasks that could be classified as bargaining-unit work. Employees file grievances whenever the supervisor engages in this practice no matter how minor that physical activity may be (e.g., changing a light bulb). Armed with several grievances, in formal contract negotiations the union can dramatize its concern that (1) performance of bargaining-unit work by supervisors is a widespread problem and (2) a contractual provision restricting supervisors from performing bargaining-unit work would save the company time and money by eliminating related grievances.

3. To Make the Grievant and Union Feel Important

In nonunion settings, the authority of managerial policies and actions often goes unchallenged. However, the grievance procedure permits and encourages an employee to protest an alleged wrong committed by management officials. Some employees raise their perceived organizational status by calling their organizational superiors on the carpet to explain their actions. Such grievances are often filed against a supervisor who flaunts authority unnecessarily, to protest the supervisor's personality as well as actions.

Similarly, some union officials wish to emphasize their importance through grievance involvement. Those falling into this category use grievances and contract administration problems to advance to high political office in the union. One research study found a positive relationship between encouragement of grievances and union rivalry as measured by closeness of vote in the most recent union election. "As incumbent union leaders contend with challengers for member support, they may seek to use the grievance process to extend support for themselves."[6] Grievances in these cases provide a forum where the union steward can demonstrate his or her verbal and intellectual capabilities to other management and union officials. Other union officials might wish to strengthen the union as an institution through the grievance procedure. Here, the importance of the union (not of the union official) is stressed—the union is safeguarding its members from management's arbitrary and capricious actions.

On some occasions, employees have a genuine belief that their supervisor is mistreating them in work assignments and pay raises. These employees want an opportunity to explain their feelings and vent their frustrations. If they are not allowed to be heard, the beliefs of mistreatment will escalate.

4. To Get Something for Nothing

Some managers believe that a few employees file grievances to receive pay related to their skill in formulating and writing grievances instead of their work efforts. The janitor in our crane operator example might not have been inclined to file a grievance at the time the work was denied. Indeed, he may have had previously scheduled holiday plans and refused to work if management had made the initial offer. However, assuming the janitor's classification paid $10 an hour, the janitor might have felt that time-and-one-half for eight hours ($120) was worth the effort to file a grievance. The payment could be particularly attractive to an individual who did not have to alter holiday plans to obtain it.

Employees filing grievances for this reason find opportunities in the area of overtime administration. A common labor agreement provision requires management to equalize overtime opportunity among qualified bargaining unit employees desiring overtime. In addition, management is often contractually required to pay the employee for the overtime worked by another employee if an administrative error was made. For example, assume the following list represents the names of employees in the electrician's classification who signed the daily overtime list, thereby volunteering to work overtime if the assignment occurs after the completion of their normal work shift.

Name of Employee	Number of Overtime Hours Worked and/or Refused Since January 1
A. Jones	89 hours
T. Grant	76 hours
B. Simms	43 hours

The figure to the right of the employee's name represents the number of overtime hours worked by the employee to date and also includes any overtime assignments refused by the employee—if Jones refused to work an eight-hour overtime assignment eventually worked by Grant, both employees are charged the eight hours. If an overtime assignment for electricians is needed on the day in question, the supervisor checks the overtime list and determines that Simms is lowest in overtime hours. Consequently, the supervisor would give Simms the first opportunity to accept or refuse the overtime assignment.

Suppose, however, that Simms desires to receive the overtime payment without having to work the overtime assignment. Simms could accomplish this by actively avoiding or hiding from the supervisor at the end of his or her shift when overtime assignments are determined. Confronted with an overtime emergency, the supervisor has to offer the assignment to Grant, the employee next lowest in overtime. The next day, Simms could file a grievance on the "administrative error" seeking to be paid the equivalent of Grant's overtime assignment for no corresponding work effort. Needless to say, this reason for filing a grievance draws management's ire, particularly because some employees appear to make a contest out of acquiring grievance "freebies," or payment for time not worked.

There are other reasons employees file grievances. Motives are as varied and complex as the employees' personalities and life experiences. For example, an argument with the employee's family, friends, or work associates might provoke a grievance. Other motives, such as poor employee/job match or a generally poor managerial climate, are perhaps more easily rectified by managerial action. Uncovering the motive behind a grievance may be helpful to management. However, it must be stressed that management must process the grievance even if it feels the employee's motives are illegitimate or improper.

Significance of Employee Grievances

Unresolved employee grievances can significantly affect both nonunion and union firms. In some cases, unsettled employee grievances have prompted successful union-organizing drives. Managers in nonunion firms might adopt some sort of grievance procedure to minimize discrimination suits, enhance employee input into organizational decision making, and minimize or eliminate the employee's desire to join a union. However, most nonunion grievance procedures do not enable the employee to have representation or to have his or her grievance decided by a third-party neutral, elements that are found in most grievance procedures in unionized firms.[7] (Other forms of dispute resolution in nonunion settings are covered later in this chapter.)

In unionized firms, employees often have unique concerns that are neither addressed in collective bargaining nor explicitly covered in the labor agreement. Union officials therefore demonstrate their intent to represent members' particular job interests against perceived arbitrary managerial actions through the use of the grievance procedure. A union not demonstrating its interest in union members through an effective grievance procedure runs the risk of lawsuits (discussed later in this chapter under "fair representation") or membership dissatisfaction with union leaders, which, in turn, can result in members voting leaders out of office or even decertifying the union.

Employee grievances and the grievance procedure can offer an organization two advantages, namely, *conflict institutionalization* and *open upward communication*. Employees who attempt to resolve grievances at an organization having no grievance procedure might participate in various job actions, such as sabotage, wildcat strikes, and job slowdowns, to solve the problem; or they might quit their jobs. Indeed, one study of New York state public school teachers under the age of 55 found that individuals with strong grievance procedures[8] in their labor agreements were less likely to quit than those working under weaker grievance procedures. All of these outcomes are costly to management, particularly when recruiting and training costs of employee replacements are considered.[9]

A grievance procedure, however, institutionalizes conflict. It recognizes that disagreements between employees, management, and the union are inevitable and provides an orderly, consistent approach for resolving differences. Grievances and related procedures represent a major upward communication forum for **employee voice**, whereby an individual has an opportunity to offer input into management's decision making and to discuss, even appeal, adverse employment actions.

Some think that grievances might assume even more significance because other employee-voice mechanisms are eroding as management, facing increased foreign and domestic competition, has become preoccupied with plant closings and large layoffs. Furthermore, many employees, while theoretically able to do so, are unwilling to pursue adverse job actions because of excessive costs and time delays.[10]

In one study, nearly half of the employees believed that the grievance procedure protected them against management high-handedness; however, these employees did not express a favorable opinion of the grievance procedure itself. Complaints included grievances that were not settled in a timely fashion; that if they filed a grievance, they would be exposed to management's reprisals; that the outcome of the grievance procedure was not fair and equitable; that the grievance procedure was not the best way to win one's case; and that once management made up its mind, it wasn't open to change. Surprisingly, 57.3 percent of employees chose not to file a grievance, even when they were in a position where they would have been able to do so.[11]

Preparation for Grievance Processing

During the grievance procedure, the grieving party, typically the union, must persuade management that one or more of the provisions of the collective-bargaining agreement has been breached. If management disagrees, management will attempt to persuade the union that management has complied with the provisions of the collective-bargaining agreement. For example, if the agreement states that overtime will be assigned to the most senior employee who is available, the union will file a grievance when a more junior employee is assigned overtime first. In response, management may claim that the more senior employees were not available. On the other hand, if management is convinced that the union's grievance has merit, then management will probably attempt to reach a settlement of the grievance. As an example, the collective-bargaining agreement provides that call-back assignments be offered first to the most senior employee. When a call-back assignment occurs, the supervisor calls the most senior employee at home, receives no answer, and then leaves a message on the answering machine. The supervisor then calls the second most senior employee and offers an early call-back assignment at double pay. When the most senior employee reports to work at the regular time, he observes that the second most senior employee is already working. The most senior employee files a grievance and claims that he was home and the phone did not ring. An examination of the telephone records shows that the supervisor had called an incorrect number and left the message on another person's answering machine. Under this discovery, management indicates its willingness to pay the grievant for the hours worked at the double time rate.

In processing a grievance, each party should approach the grievance just as if the grievance would be proceeding to arbitration. Essentially, every step in the grievance procedure prior to arbitration provides the parties an opportunity to negotiate a grievance settlement. There are several steps in building a persuasive case during the various meetings during the grievance procedure and in preparation for arbitration in the event the grievance is appealed to arbitration.[12] Exhibit 10.3 provides guidance in preparing for grievance meetings and for arbitration in the event the grievance is appealed to arbitration.

In preparation for grievance processing, the union may seek information from the company to assist the union in its preparation. Under the Management Labor Relations Act, the employer is required to provide information to the union that the employer has or can reasonably obtain, provided that the information requested is "relevant and useful" to the union in the processing of the grievance. If the employer refuses to supply such information to the union, the employer will be committing an unfair labor practice and the union may file an unfair labor practice charge against the employer and obtain the "relevant and useful" information through the National Labor Relations Board procedures (see Chapters 3 and 6). Examples of information that the union may request are listed in Exhibit 10.4.

Steps in the Grievance Procedure

The process for resolving employee grievances is specified in approximately 97 percent of existing labor agreements. However, the procedures are as varied as the labor agreements themselves. Some consist of only one step, whereas others contain as many as nine. Although no one grievance procedure is applicable to all labor-management relationships (21 percent of surveyed grievance procedures have two steps, and 51 percent have three steps), a four-step procedure illustrated in Exhibit 10.5 and discussed here is found in 19 percent of these procedures.

First Step of Grievance Procedure

The first step of the typical grievance procedure consists of two phases. First, the employee (with or without the union steward) discusses the alleged grievance with his or her first-line supervisor. Actually, the employee can file a grievance without any union endorsement. If agreement is not reached, then a written grievance is filed by the grievant or the union steward acting on the grievant's behalf. The supervisor then answers the employee's grievance in writing. Time limits for filing a grievance and managerial response exist in 69 percent and 63 percent, respectively, of grievance procedures. If management or the union does not follow the time limits, the grievance might be challenged by either party as not meeting the procedural requirements in the labor agreement.[13]

The purpose of the discussion is to resolve the grievance as early and as informally as possible. The union does not want to delay any remedy, particularly back pay owed its members or reinstatement. Management does not wish to incur any unnecessary continuing liability if back pay is owed an employee who is suspended or discharged and remains unemployed until the grievance is eventually resolved.

In some cases, the oral discussion is *pro forma*—the employee initiates this step with a written grievance on the assumption that no amount of discussion will change his or her mind. For example, the supervisor may have made the decision that led to the grievance and has no plans to change the decision. As is true with the next two steps of the grievance procedure, if the employee accepts management's answer to the written grievance, then the grievance is considered resolved and subsequent steps are unnecessary.

Exhibit 10.3

Preparation for Grievance Procedure Meetings (and for Arbitration Hearing)

Step 1: Gather Evidence
Since testimony of witnesses is the principal type of evidence, the investigator should identify persons on both sides of the grievance and interview all persons whose statements are relevant to the grievance. Often, the collective-bargaining agreement contains a provision requiring cooperation in developing the facts and contentions in order to increase the possibility that a resolution can be achieved at the initial steps of the grievance procedure. If relevant documents and other forms of physical evidence are not voluntarily offered, a written request with an explanation of why the documents are relevant should be mailed by registered mail. If the request is not honored, the arbitrator may draw adverse inferences about the withheld evidence in the event the grievance proceeds to arbitration.

Step 2: Determine the Facts and Substantiate Them
From the statements taken and evidence gathered, you should determine what facts the evidence establishes. Because the statements from witnesses will overlap, you should collate the statements in the following manner: (1) create a separate cover page for each fact established; (2) separate your witnesses' statements into the facts they address, noting the name of the witness on each; and (3) append the statement portions to the related fact cover pages.

Step 3: Assess the Facts for Credibility, Accuracy, Reliability, and Consistency
As you add factual claims, add your observation and conclusions about credibility, accuracy, and reliability furnished by each witness. Then compare each statement for consistency.

Step 4: Frame Your Arguments
The facts are obtained from the evidence and are what is objectively proven. Arguments are the way in which the facts show that the collective-bargaining agreement has or has not been breached and are reasons why those facts should affect the outcome of the grievance. For example, it is a fact that an employee had a satisfactory work record with the employer for 25 years; it is an argument that the employee's long-term record of satisfactory performance should mitigate the severity of any discipline imposed by the employer. Create a separate cover sheet for each argument and support each argument with a factual basis.

Steps 5 and 6: Seek Coherence, Consistency, and Credibility
Organize your arguments into a logical sequence. Then, make sure these arguments are coherent, consistent, and credible. For example, there is a contradiction when the union argues that the employee was defending himself if the union had earlier argued that the employee had been provoked.

Step 7: Prepare Witnesses Scripts
After a grievance meeting has been set up, outline the questions you will ask each witness. These questions will serve two purposes. (1) Establish the facts—you will ask unambiguous questions to which you already know the answer. If the answer is evasive, you should restate the question. If the answer is different from previous answers, you should remind the witness of an earlier statement. For example, "Mr. Jones, didn't you tell me when I previously asked you this very question...." (2) Impeach the credibility of the witness by showing inconsistencies with previous statements, indicating prior acts of dishonesty or untruthfulness, and asking detailed questions about testimony you believe to be perjurious. Witnesses have difficulty lying extemporaneously; liars are forced to remember details about previous lies instead of the truth that actually happened.

Step 8: Prepare Admissibility Challenges and Defenses
The fundamental rule is that evidence that is not reliable and not relevant should not be considered. Be prepared to argue that hearsay evidence should not prove the

(Continued)

Exhibit 10.3
(Continued)

truth of the matter asserted. For example, hearsay would be what one witness heard another person say. The other person would not be available to be cross-examined, and cross-examination is an important due process right.

SOURCE: Mark I. Lurie, "The 8 Essential Steps in Grievance Processing," *Dispute Resolution Journal* 54 (November 1999), pp. 81–86.

Second Step of Grievance Procedure

In addition to the individuals in the first-step grievance meeting, the union grievance committee members and management's labor relations representative are brought in to discuss the supervisor's first-step grievance answer. Both of these individuals are aware of administrative precedent throughout the entire facility; their main role is to determine whether the grievance should be resolved at this stage on the basis of this precedent.

For example, Employee A files a grievance protesting management's unilateral action in reducing wash-up time in her work area. The union grievance committee might be aware, however, that (1) the contract does not have a provision pertaining to wash-up time, and (2) employees in other departments do not receive any time before the end of the shift to clean their hands. Therefore, he or she would probably encourage the grievant to accept the reduction in wash-up time rather than risk losing the privilege entirely in subsequent steps of the grievance procedure.

On another issue—for example, an employee working out of his or her normal work classification and demanding an upgrade in pay for the time worked—the labor relations representative might reverse the supervisor's first-step answer to avoid sending the grievance to the third step, where it might affect employees

Exhibit 10.4

Examples of Information the Union May Request

- Accident records
- Attendance records
- Bargaining notes
- Company memos
- Contracts
- Correspondence
- Disciplinary records
- Equipment specifications
- Job evaluations
- Health and safety studies
- Inspection records
- Insurance policies
- Interview notes
- Job assignment records
- Job descriptions
- Videotapes

- Material safety data sheets
- Names of witnesses
- "Notes to file"
- Information details
- Payroll records
- Performance reviews
- Personnel files
- Photographs
- Reports and studies
- Salary records
- Security guard records
- Seniority lists
- Supervisor's notes
- Time study records
- Training manuals

SOURCE: http://www.ranknfile-ue.org/stwd_nlr.html

Exhibit 10.5

Example of a Typical Grievance Procedure

	Union Personnel Involved		Management Personnel Involved

First Step

Employee (with or without union steward) files the grievance within the required time limits ← Meeting to discuss grievance within 15 days → First-line supervisor

→ Resolved

↓

Unresolved

↓

The grievance is reduced to writing within five days and presented to management

↓

Management answers in writing in five days

↓

If management's answer is not accepted, the union has five days to appeal to Step 2

↓

Second Step

Addition of union grievance committee (President, Vice President, Shop Steward) ← Meeting to discuss grievance → Addition of plant labor relations representative

Unresolved → Resolved

↓

Management answers in writing in ten days

↓

If management's answer is not accepted, the union has ten days to appeal

↓

Third Step

Addition of international union representative ← Meeting to discuss grievance → Addition of company labor relations manager and general plant management official

Unresolved → Resolved

↓

Management answers in writing in 15 days

↓

If management's answer is not accepted, the union has 30 days to appeal

↓

Fourth Step

Resolution through a third-party neutral arbitrator

Fourth Step

The parties decide to use grievance mediation

↓

Fifth Step

Resolution through a third-party neutral arbitrator

with similar work experiences in other departments. The second-step written grievance answer is furnished by the Company's labor relations representative, and any precedent resulting from this answer usually applies only to the particular work department instead of the entire facility.

Third Step of Grievance Procedure

The third-step meeting involves the same individuals as the second step but also includes the labor relations manager and other management officials (such as a general foreman, superintendent, or assistant plant manager), members of the union's grievance committee (see Chapter 4), and the union's international union representative. These individuals are added because the grievance answer at this level could affect company-wide operations, and both management and union representatives wish to obtain as much input as possible before making the decision.

During the third step, meeting the union discusses the grievance and its related rationale, and management mostly listens and does not attempt to resolve the grievance in this meeting. This step offers union officials several advantages:

- It provides new union stewards who sit in on the meeting with free training—many labor agreements require paid time off for grievance meetings.

- It impresses the grievant that many union officials back his or her interests.

- It may serve as a buck-passing device for the grievant's shop steward, who claims that the union grievance committee, not he or she, decided not to pursue the grievance.

This step can also serve a therapeutic function for the grievant, who simply wishes to express concern to many levels of management officials. Perhaps the most important function of the third-step meeting is the inclusion of additional union and management officials who are not personally involved in the grievance outcome and can assess its merits with relative objectivity. The third-step grievance answer is usually written by the labor relations manager because the decision probably will have plantwide, even companywide, implications and applications.

Fourth Step of Grievance Procedure—Alternative Dispute Resolution (ADR)

In the fourth step, a third-party neutral may furnish either a final, binding **arbitration** decision or help the parties to resolve the issue themselves through **mediation**. (Arbitration is discussed in more detail in Chapter 11.)

Grievance Mediation

Grievance mediation is a formal step in the grievance procedure (before arbitration) designed to resolve grievances without the use of arbitration. Grievance mediation has several advantages over arbitration in the resolution of grievances.

Grievance mediation typically yields a voluntary agreement which is more satisfactory to both parties than arbitration where only one party wins. Mediators encourage the parties to trade low-priority items for higher-priority items. For example, a union representative in a mediation session could trade its demand that a discharged employee receive all back pay from the time of his termination (a low priority) in exchange for reinstatement (a high priority). The employer may have considered the avoidance of back pay as a high priority item due the high costs and the reinstatement as a low priority item because the employee had a reasonably good performance record prior to his termination. The settlement could result in a voluntary agreement which all parties can accept.

Grievance mediation is faster, less costly, and more informal than arbitration. In addition, it has the potential for long-term benefits. In mediation, the average time between the request for mediation and a final resolution was 43.5 days; in arbitration, the average completion time was 473 days. In arbitration, it usually takes one day for hearing each grievance; in mediation, several cases can be addressed in a single day. In mediation, there is no need for written transcripts, post-hearing briefs, or written decisions. The average amount paid to the mediator was $672 per case; the average paid to the arbitrator was $3,202, nearly five times as much. In mediation, the union and management representatives proceed without attorneys and participate in a facilitative process wherein each party has an opportunity to tell its story. The parties learn to develop communication skills and realize an understanding of the other side's position.

This understanding may be carried over to attempts to resolve future grievances. In fact, some of the residual effects of grievance mediation are improved relationships between the union and the company, better understanding of the needs and concerns of the other side, and a greater cooperative atmosphere, which creates an environment for mutual problem solving.[14]

Exhibit 10.6 demonstrates the difference between a grievance arbitration hearing and a grievance mediation session, both designed to involve a third-party neutral in reaching resolution of a grievance.

Exhibit 10.6

Grievance Arbitration vs. Grievance Mediation Scenarios

Grievance Arbitration: A hearing is scheduled eight months after the grievance was filed. The participants in the hearing are typically the grievant, the arbitrator, a court reporter, the union team (attorney, staff representative, local union officials, and witnesses to be called by the union), and the company team (attorney, human resource manager, line supervisor involved, and witnesses to be called by the company). During the hearing, witnesses are sworn, examined, and cross-examined and documents are submitted as evidence. Both attorneys make frequent objections, which are usually denied by the arbitrator. The hearing lasts from four to six hours; the court reporter may take two weeks to prepare a transcript; the two attorneys may take 30 days to prepare and submit written posthearing briefs; and the arbitrator will generally prepare a written decision in 30 days.

Grievance Mediation: A grievance mediation conference is set up about three months after the grievance was filed. In attendance are the mediator, representatives of the union, and the company (no attorneys and no court reporter). Each side provides a narrative description of the grievance, which summarizes its views of the facts and arguments supporting its position. Each group goes to separate rooms, and the mediator visits both rooms to discuss the strengths and weaknesses of their respective positions. In three hours, the parties agree on how the grievance should be resolved. After a break for lunch, the process is repeated with another grievance and another set of representatives. The mediator does not write up any decision. If no settlement is reached, the mediator advises the parties of the possible outcome of the grievance if it should proceed to arbitration. Then, the parties attempt once again to resolve the grievance.

SOURCE: Peter Feuille, "Grievance Mediation," *"Employment Dispute Resolution and Worker Rights in the Changing Workplace,"* ed. Adrienne E. Eaton and Jeffrey H. Keene, Champaign, IL: IRRA, 1999, pp. 187–188. Reprinted by permission.

Different Approaches by Grievance Mediators

Mediators take different approaches in assisting the parties in reaching a settlement of their differences. There are three categories of approaches; however, their distinctions are not "watertight," and the same mediator may shift from one type of approach to another during the same proceedings. Each of these approaches may be successful in different environments because the specific approach used by the mediator is highly dependent on the attitudes of the opposing parties.

The first approach is *transformation or collaborative mediation*. Here, the mediator tries to get the parties to discover their own separate and mutual resources and to understand the other party's point of view. This approach serves as a good starting point from which to move on, if necessary, to the other approaches to mediation. In the second approach, *evaluative mediation*, the mediator does not attempt to come up with a specific solution but concentrates on showing the respective strengths and weaknesses of each party's position. The mediator usually holds separate meetings with the parties in order to fully understand their positions. Then, effort is devoted to keeping the parties together, talking and listening, and moving toward a resolution.

The third approach is **directive or results-oriented mediation**. Here, the goal is to bring the parties to a certain agreement that the mediator believes is appropriate and achievable. The mediator first sits down with both parties who talk to the mediator directly, not to each other, with the agitated party going first. The ground rules require that no personal attacks be made and no interruptions are allowed from the listener. Caucuses are allowed from time to time to cool tempers, to permit confidential communications with the mediator, and to move the negotiations toward closure. In addition, the mediator will probably spend time meeting separately with the opposing parties in an effort to help each party understand the other's position.[15]

With the success record of grievance mediation but with only four percent of the collective-bargaining agreements containing mediation as a step in the grievance procedure,[16] the question is: Why isn't mediation more widespread? One reason is that only a small fraction of all grievances filed are ever taken to arbitration (usually fewer than 20 percent and often as few as 2 percent). In addition, the majority of grievances that are appealed to arbitration are not arbitrated but are resolved prior to an arbitrator's decision. Therefore, most parties have inadequate motivation to change their grievance resolution practice to incorporate mediation. A second reason is that mediation is a quite fragile process because mediation cannot guarantee resolved grievances, and the parties may still have to proceed to arbitration. In fact, the success of mediation depends on the continued existence of arbitration as the next step in the grievance procedure. A third reason that grievance mediation is not more widespread is that management is reluctant to accept it. Management appears to be the giving party, and the union has an opportunity to "get something" from the employer in return for resolving the grievance and avoiding arbitration. In most cases, the union is the party that files the grievance and is the party seeking a change in management's decision. For example, the union files a grievance when an employee is discharged, is not promoted, or does not receive a merit pay increase. Any compromise by the company to seek a settlement would be a change from management's initial decision. A final reason may be the self-interests of the arbitration advocates and arbitrators. Resolution of grievances through mediation infringes on the livelihoods of everyone who earns part or all of their professional income and status by arbitrating grievances. The vast bulk of the cost of arbitration is income to the arbitration professionals, and this income is lost if grievances are successfully mediated and not arbitrated.[17]

Successful grievance mediation depends on two key features. The first is the ability of the mediator. The experienced mediator will be able to point out the strengths and weaknesses of each party's position. Usually, there will be "side-bar" or "caucus" discussions with each party separately. If the parties do not reach a settlement, the mediator then provides an advisory opinion of the likely outcome if the grievance were appealed to arbitration. In other words, the mediator provides a "peek-a-boo" look at the likely outcome of an arbitration decision. The act itself creates substantial pressure on the party with the weaker position to reach a settlement in order to avoid the costs of losing in arbitration.

A second key feature for success is the motivation of the parties who have adopted the process. In cases where the parties are sufficiently motivated to try to improve their grievance resolution record, they tend to succeed because they have already decided to resolve differences on their own. Thus, "it may be more accurate to view mediation as a proxy for the positive grievance resolution attitudes held by the adopters than as a procedure which possesses some intricate ability to resolve grievances in a more cooperative manner than arbitration."[18]

The success of mediators has stimulated interest in adopting workplace ADR policies in other employment settings. Certainly the high number of employee complaints to government enforcement agencies, such as the Equal Employment Opportunity Commission (EEOC), has motivated many employers. The EEOC has jurisdiction over complaints of employment discrimination under the Civil Rights Act of 1991, the American with Disabilities Act, and the Age Discrimination in Employment Act. The number of employment discrimination charges filed with the EEOC averages over 70,000 each year. In addition, tens of thousands of charges over workplace disputes are filed with other federal, state, and local agencies each year. ADR has been introduced as a way of diverting these disputes from the courts and regulatory systems to an internal dispute resolution procedure. Additional stimulus has been provided by U.S. Supreme Court decisions that have upheld the validity of employment contracts that require employees to submit their discrimination claims to arbitration[19] (to be covered in Chapter 11).

During the first four years of the EEOC mediation program, over 52,400 mediations were held. The program was judged to be quite successful because more than 35,100 or 69 percent of the EEOC charges were successfully resolved in an average of 85 days.[20]

A comprehensive study of assessment of the participants in the program revealed that the participants had a positive experience with the procedure, the information provided, and the mediators. An overwhelming majority believed that mediation was fair, and they felt that they had a full opportunity to present their views. In addition, an overwhelming majority indicated that they would be willing to participate in the mediation program again if they were a party to an EEOC charge.[21]

As an example, the Americans with Disabilities Act encourages alternative dispute resolution (ADR) for resolving ADA claims. The mediator may help the parties reconcile their differences in making reasonable accommodation for the disabled employee. Types of reasonable accommodation may include one or more of the following: acquiring equipment, modifying equipment, making architectural changes, modifying the work environment, providing services, introducing flexible hours, restructuring jobs by assigning marginal functions to another employee, or reassignment to a vacant position.

In reaching a reasonable accommodation, the employer is excused if its action would result in an undue hardship or if placement of a disabled person may put that employee or other employees at risk of his or her health and safety. The mediator may help the parties in resolving their differences on the employer's financial capabilities, disruption to its business, nature and duration of the risks involved, the potential severity of harm to the employee and others, or the likelihood that harm will occur.

The United States Postal Service has over a decade of experience in **transformation mediation** and has the largest employment mediation program in the world. The mediation program is called REDRESS (which stands for Resolving Employment Disputes Reach Equitable Solutions Swiftly). In 2004, the participation rate of those employees who had complaints was 80 percent and there were over 1,000 disputes a month mediated in 90 different cities. This program required the training of 3,000 mediators who were committed to using the transformation model of mediation. The success of the program as measured by the settlement rate ("resolved at the table") of the employee's complaint was 54.4 percent. In addition, 64 percent of the employees and 69 percent of the supervisors reported that they were satisfied or highly satisfied with the outcome of the mediation and over 95 percent reported satisfaction with the mediator.[22]

Administrative Complexities of Processing Grievances

All grievance procedures—even though they may vary in terms of steps, time limits for the processing of each step, and participants—represent a progression of the initial grievance to higher-level management and union officials for consideration. These procedures can raise several administrative complexities (see the "Labor Relations in Action" box on page 438) and often appear inflexible. However, they also serve as the arena for the dynamic social relationships and interactions among management and union officials.

Other Forms of ADR

While arbitration and mediation are the most common forms of ADR, the parties have the flexibility to design ADR approaches to meet their needs. Other forms more likely to exist in nonunion organizations include (1) open-door policies, (2) ombudsperson, (3) peer review systems, (4) early neutral evaluation, and (5) multistep approaches.

The **open-door policy** means that supervisors and managers understand that part of their jobs is to solve workplace problems through open-door options, and the company prohibits retaliation against any employee who is trying to resolve a workplace problem through the open-door procedure. The first step encourages employees to resolve any workplace problems with their immediate supervisor because the supervisor is the person who is closest to the situation and may be aware of the problems and may be in a position to offer a new perspective or new facts that may be helpful. If the employee is not satisfied with the supervisor's response or the employee needs to talk to someone other than the immediate supervisor (who may be responsible for the problem), the employee may take the problem to the next higher level supervisor. At any time, the employee may choose to talk with someone in the Human Resources Department or the Employee Relations Department to seek advice or assistance or to conduct an investigation. Possible limitations to this approach are reluctance of employees to bypass their supervisors in fear of retaliation, problems with upper management overturning

The grievance procedure involves more than a number of steps and related participants and time limits for filing, answering, and appealing grievances. Union and management officials, and sometimes arbitrators, often have to resolve complex administrative issues during the process; these are reflected in the following questions:

1. Can management interrupt and order back to work employees who are also union officials investigating a grievance?
2. Does an employer have the right to charge the union a fee for processing requested information pertaining to a grievance?
3. Can employees be discharged for secretly taping a grievance meeting?
4. Do outside union representatives have the right to visit the facility to investigate a grievance?
5. Is a grievance "legitimate" if it is filed or appealed by someone not affected by the grievance? By a group of employees? By a union official over the original grievant's objections? By someone who states the grievance orally but not in writing?
6. Do clear time limits between grievance steps mean that a grievance cannot be processed if the union exceeds these limits? Must the employer agree to the grievance if it exceeds these limits?
7. Does the initial time limit in which a grievance may be filed start from the day of the incident or the date of the grievant's knowledge/discovery?
8. Does management have to pay union officials for all of the time spent investigating and processing grievances during company work hours?
9. Can the effective date of management's grievance adjustment (paying for an overtime administrative error, for example) precede the date the grievance was filed?
10. Can an employer file a grievance against the union even if the labor agreement does not specifically refer to this action?

The answer to all of these questions is "it depends." A specific "yes" or "no" answer at a particular facility depends on the formal (labor agreement language and/or memorandums or understanding) and informal (past practices) arrangements between union and management officials.

---

a supervisor's decision, unavailability of higher level managers due to other business duties, and fears by employees that the anti-retaliation policy will not hold up.

An **ombudsperson** is a person employed by a company to help resolve personnel disputes. The ombudsperson functions as a "go-between" the aggrieved employee and the company manager. The ombudsperson does not have independent authority to impose a resolution of the dispute but attempts to find a "common ground" on which all parties can agree. Some concerns about the ombudsperson approach to employees is whether the ombudsperson will be neutral in disputes with managers and whether the ombudsperson, who is on the company payroll, will keep information in confidence.

Peer review systems shift the personnel decisions, such as discipline, promotion denial, and so on, from management to the peers of the aggrieved employee. The **peer review panel** of employees and often a mix of managers and nonmanagers conducts a hearing in which the aggrieved employee tells his or her side of the story and presents witnesses. The company presents its version of the story and presents witnesses. Then, the peer review panel is empowered to recommend a solution, not to decide the issue. Employees tend to believe that the peer review system is fair, and employers like it because employees usually don't blame the employer for final decisions. Panel members may be chosen randomly or be selected from a specially trained group of employees. Most of the time, the type of grievance subjects which may be addressed is limited.

Early neutral evaluation is a process in which a neutral party is chosen jointly by the employee and the company to conduct an informal hearing at which the parties present their evidence and arguments. The purpose of the hearing is to narrow the issues and help the parties better understand the strengths and weaknesses of their positions. The neutral evaluator then renders a nonbinding, advisory opinion on the merits of the case. Assessment of early neutral evaluations shows no discernible effect on the amount of time needed to dispose of the case, litigation costs, and the parties' views of fairness or satisfaction with case management. In addition, the parties may be hesitant to reveal their "real" positions because either one or both may believe the case will end up in trial.[23]

GRIEVANCE RESOLUTION: RELATIONSHIPS AND FLEXIBILITY

A wide variety of activities, tactics, and relationships occur between the most frequently involved union and management participants: the union steward and the first-line supervisor.[24]

Codified Relationships

Codified relationships stress the rights and privileges of union stewards and first-line supervisors established through the labor agreement and various union and management publications. These publications urge the steward and first-line supervisor to treat each other as "organizational equals" in grievance resolution, and to realize that both benefit from resolving grievances at their level instead of involving higher-level and possibly disinterested officials.[25]

Supervisors and union stewards may be aware of normative philosophies and codes but often do not take them into account when interacting. For example, the *AFL-CIO Manual for Shop Stewards* strongly urges union stewards to present their grievances directly to the first-line supervisor in the first step of the grievance procedure.

It is important to observe the steps in the grievance procedure, even if the foreman has limited authority. Leapfrogging to a higher step may have undesirable effects. The lower level of management will resent this and will be more difficult to deal with the next time, or the company may seek to get the grievance thrown out because the proper steps were not followed.[26]

Yet many first-line supervisors maintain that they are often completely bypassed by the union steward in the grievance process. Indeed, the steward can also bypass the employee involved by filing a grievance in the name of the union. This "bypass capability" given to the union steward is not given to management.[27]

Many first-line supervisors do not implement another codified relationship aspect: treating the union stewards as "organizational equals" in the grievance process. It is often difficult for a first-line supervisor, accustomed to giving daily work orders to the union steward, to turn around in a grievance meeting and consider the union steward as a peer. Some first-line supervisors can accept this situation; others have problems:

This guy, Walker (union steward) here, doesn't realize that the gang is kidding him. They haven't got anything to kick about. All the stuff he is bringing up is old stuff. We've gone over it before with the other representatives. The other representative was sick of the job and gave it up. So the gang decided to elect this squirt because nobody else wanted the job. This fellow doesn't know anything about the department. He's only been there three months. He's only a kid and doesn't know what it's all about. I haven't got time to rehash this all over again....He's not qualified to talk about anything that happens in my department, and I haven't got time to waste with him. He brings up all this stuff and nonsense just so he can be a big shot.[28]

Codified relationships also suggest that first-line supervisors should have authority for resolving grievances at the first step of the procedure to give the employee a prompt response. Resolution of a grievance at the first step can also help prevent the plantwide precedents that are established in the third step. However, other management officials, who prefer to be kept informed on employee grievances, often instruct the supervisors to inform the labor relations representative of the situation before taking any action. Indeed, one study found that 27 percent of 800 first-line supervisors believed that higher-level managers sharply limited their authority to settle grievances informally or at the first step.[29]

Power Relationships

Conflicting **power relationships** develop in situations where the supervisor and union stewards pursue differing interests or goals. This situation has sometimes characterized shop-floor relationships in the steel industry:

The local unions became highly politicized; any leader who made peaceful overtures to the company was promptly denounced as a "sell-out artist." Union officials and supervisors conducted daily warfare over such matters as discipline, job assignment, and the handling of worker grievances. It was as though each side had to prove itself, day after day, that it had the capacity to hurt the other.[30]

Power relationships typically begin when both steward and supervisor are encouraged by their superiors to be attentive to problems in the department. The supervisor is encouraged to discover problems before they become grievances, whereas the steward is encouraged to talk to the potential grievant before that employee talks to the supervisor. Competition for the employee's attention might become particularly intense, as one research study found that stewards and supervisors are equally successful in communicating with employees.[31]

Another type of power relationship results from the union steward knowing the labor agreement better than the supervisor does. Many union stewards are long-term employees who have been involved in numerous grievance meetings. The new supervisor may be a recent college graduate who is having his or her first taste of an industrial setting. In addition, union stewards can concentrate on particular provisions of the labor agreement and their application to the shop. The supervisor, on the other hand, has major responsibilities for production scheduling, meeting departmental quality and quantity standards, participating in cost-reduction programs, and so on, which reduce the amount of time available for grievance and labor agreement analyses.

Intimidation is another power relationship strategy that can be employed by both the union steward and the supervisor. In some situations, the union steward anticipates that the supervisor is vulnerable when he or she receives an excessive number of grievances—the supervisor will be concerned with how management officials will react to this apparent inability to resolve labor relations problems. Even though the grievances might not be valid, some management officials might hold the following opinion:

A supervisor who is the subject of grievances creates red flags for us. We expect supervisors to be able to handle most employee relations issues, and if they can't, then we question whether or not they have a future with us. I know that grievances are sometimes filed with no justification whatsoever, but on the whole a supervisor who avoids formal grievances looks a lot better to management than a supervisor who's tying up his and our time in grievance hearings.[32]

Consequently, a union steward can use the threat of additional grievances (bogus or real) to persuade the supervisor to concede to the grievance in question or to alter the supervisor's overall approach to labor relations. The practice is explained by a union official:

A short time ago we had a lot of trouble with a certain foreman. . . . He was making them toe the line . . . no quitting early, work from whistle to whistle, no sitting down, no horseplay, this and that. I told the committeeman there, "You do the same thing. Every time he does any work, even if he picks up a box, write a grievance. . . ." The first thing you know grievances started mounting—finally had a pile like that.

Things got so bad . . . this foreman was removed from the department. He was moved to our department and it's his last chance. If he doesn't do good in this department, out he goes. So I went to the guy and told him, "It's your last chance here and you know it. You cooperate with us and we'll cooperate with you. If you don't we'll put the screws on you and out you go." Things are working out pretty good so far.[33]

Intimidation tactics are not always one-sided; a clever supervisor can make industrial life very difficult for the union steward, probably without incurring an unfair labor practice charge. For example, many job classifications have a wide variety of work assignments, with some of these assignments being less desirable than others. A supervisor could assign undesirable work assignments to the union steward, who would have little recourse as long as they were within his or her job classification. The supervisor could also undermine the steward's formal position in the union by (1) restricting the amount of freedom and time for the steward to investigate the grievance and (2) refusing to resolve any grievance in the first step when the union steward is present with the grievant. These tactics are usually successful only if the union steward is inexperienced. Regardless of the "success" of such actions, a grievance relationship governed by power and intimidation tactics distorts the primary purpose of contract administration: rational decision making.

Empathetic Relationships

Empathetic relationships occur between individuals when each is aware of the other's situation and is guided by an understanding appreciation. An example of this appreciation comes from a union steward's comment:

You can't have industrial relations without giving and taking on both sides. You'll always win more cases by getting along with supervision than by being tough. You've got to swap and make trades. . . . Sometimes I have to talk like hell to explain some of the deals I make with them and sometimes I keep what I'm doing to myself if I see a chance to get something good later on. The thing some grievers never get through their heads is that a lot of bosses are on the spot themselves. If you go a little easy on them when they're on the pan, by God—you make friends—they'll stand by you sometime when you're back of the eight ball. Sometimes when I have a rotten grievance, I'll take the case up to the supe [superintendent] and let him know I won't push it hard.[34]

Empathetic relationships are aided when the first-line supervisor and the union steward realize that they both occupy marginal positions within their own organizations. For example, one study found that first-line supervisors can have a rather loose identification with upper management. This might be due to several factors, including transient upper and middle management and reconsideration of the supervisor's original decision by other management officials.[35]

Union stewards have also experienced this situation in contract administration. On one hand, constituents expect their union steward to actively press every grievance because they think that the union should be attentive to their needs. Consequently, it is difficult for the steward to accept the supervisor's first-step rejection of the grievance, even if he or she thinks the supervisor is correct. On the other hand, union officials receiving the grievance in subsequent steps of the grievance procedure may tend to view the union steward as either ignorant of the labor agreement or gutless.

Flexible Consideration of Employee Grievances

The preceding varieties of interpersonal relationships reveal how individual objectives, strategies, and personalities force the contractual procedure to be more flexible in practice. This real-world consideration negates the theoretical principle that each grievance be considered on its individual merits. The grievant wishes to receive an answer uncolored by any political or tactical concerns, but the union must consider political influence and overall strategy in its determination of which grievances will be filed and pursued. Not all grievances are clear-cut issues; in fact, many involve confusing or opposing interpretations of the labor agreement. In these cases, management has two options—decide the grievance in the employee's favor, or appeal the grievance to arbitration. The latter alternative is not always attractive, particularly if management realizes there is little contractual guidance in the issue (as in the example of the holiday scheduling of a crane operator) and insufficient past practice or precedent to support the decision. Contract administration has many gray areas that are open to interpretation. This uncertainty is compounded when the parties solicit a neutral party to resolve the issue in binding arbitration. Also, the arbitrator's decision might refute management's action in terms that further erode management's discretion in future matters. Unions also tend to use arbitration only as a last resort because such cases can drain the union's treasury.

In these instances, flexibility may be possible with the addition of an informal **third-and-one-half step** in the grievance procedure. This may not be specified in the labor agreement but occurs after management's "final" third-step decision and before the third-party neutral hears the grievance. During the third-and-one-half step meetings, management and union representatives meet to discuss and trade grievances, dispatching several cases originally scheduled for arbitration. For example, they might trade a grievance requesting one-day pay upgrades for five employees who allegedly worked in a higher job classification for a grievance on management performing bargaining-unit work filed against a very unpopular first-line supervisor, which would give one union member a two-hour overtime payment as a remedy. Usually, the grievances involved in the negotiated package are settled "without prejudice" or without precedent to either party's position in future related issues. These settlements will not be binding in any future deliberations between the parties. However, settlement of the grievances preserves management's discretion on these issues and the union's right to file future related grievances. The union has to be careful because swapping grievances which are clearly meritorious may constitute a violation of the union's duty of fair representation (covered later in this chapter).

Opponents of this practice contend that valid employee grievances are bargained away for an expedient settlement. Grievance trading in the third-and-one-half step can also discourage first-line supervisors from actively trying to resolve grievances if they believe their efforts will be overturned in a mass grievance settlement. For example, the following remarks were made by a foreman who had sent an employee home for repeated tardiness. The employee filed a grievance with the foreman's supervisor, who sent the employee back on the job.

> I went over to O'Brien's [the superintendent's office] to find out why he had overruled me. He handed me a line of salve about "having to do it." Said, "It was a small item after all" and that he "might want a big favor from the union sometime in the future." He said, "We have to trade back and forth. Sometimes we give in; sometimes they give in. That's why we never have any big trouble!" Then he said he might have to reverse some of my decisions again sometime, but if he did, not to get sore about it, because he wouldn't mean no offense by it. Well damn that noise! If O'Brien wants to make me look like a fool every time I make a decision, why by God, he can make all the decisions. You know two can play that game. I can give the boys [workers] every damn thing he can give them. Then when they come up with a big one that I know well he can't give them, I'll tell 'em to take it up to him.[36]

As a result of management using the third-and-one-half step in the grievance procedure, unions might be encouraged to file more grievances in the belief that they can obtain more from a trade involving 50 fabricated grievances than they can from 5 legitimate ones. Furthermore, settlements "without prejudice" can result in more grievances of the same sort because the issues are not considered jointly resolved by management or union officials.

Advocates of settlements short of arbitration believe that this process merely represents another legitimate cooperative effort between labor and management officials in efficiently dealing with day-to-day administrative problems. These individuals indicate that the union's and management's organizational self-interests require considerations and possible use of the third-and-one-half step grievance trading session. Opponents state that the third-and-one-half step hinders the union's **fair representation obligation** discussed in the next section.

THE UNION'S DUTY OF FAIR REPRESENTATION

Thus far, grievance procedures have been discussed from the perspectives of the union, management, and employee participants. As is true with most labor relations activities, grievance resolution can be strongly influenced by a fourth participant, the government. As noted in Chapter 5, the union has the right to be the exclusive bargaining agent for all employees in the appropriate bargaining unit. This right has a corresponding legal duty to fairly represent all of the bargaining unit employees, union members and nonunion members alike, in both contract negotiation and administration. This section focuses on the extent of the union's obligation, particularly when some of the bargaining unit employees believe the union has acted in an unsatisfactory manner.[37]

Fair representation issues are very difficult to resolve. On the one hand, some individual freedom must be sacrificed if the union wishes to effectively represent its members. However, the individual member's right to dissent must also be protected, and all employees represented must be safe from negligent or corrupt union representatives. The Management Labor Relations Act adds to the complexity of the issues because it does not contain any explicit provisions obligating the union to represent fairly all bargaining unit employees. Therefore, jurisdictional disputes over fair representation issues have occurred between the governmental participants, more specifically the National Labor Relations Board (NLRB) and the courts.

The NLRB had for many years claimed that it alone had jurisdiction to determine fair representation issues because related unfair labor practices came under its statutory jurisdiction. However, the Supreme Court has indicated that district courts also have jurisdiction over such claims because the fair representation obligation is a fundamental part of federal labor relations policy and precedes the NLRB's statutory role in such cases.[38] A subsequent Supreme Court decision indicated that employees who claim breach of fair representation are also entitled to a jury trial if monetary losses (backpay) are claimed.[39]

Related court decisions have addressed the following question: How far must the union go in representing employees whose interests or claims could potentially disrupt union goals and policies? The importance of this question is magnified when we consider that many decisions help some members while hurting others.

Under the collective bargaining agreement, there are competitive rights involving subjects like promotions, transfers, and layoffs. If there is one vacancy, only one employee can be promoted. Those not promoted may believe that they have grievances.

Union actions pertaining to seniority (such as merging seniority rosters and calculating seniority credits for employees returning from leave) will hurt some bargaining unit members while helping others. As an example, after the terrorists attack on the New York World Trade Center on September 11, 2001, US Airways was forced to lay off many employees due to lack of business. The union agreed to a modified layoff plan which allowed US Airways to retain fewer senior employees at the Charlotte, NC, hub while laying off more senior employees who were assigned to the smaller air stations which were closed. Fifteen long-term passenger service employees sued the union and company. The court ruled that the anguish caused by the layoffs was not the result of the company and the union acting in bad faith, but by the tragic events of September 11. The court believed that the company and the union took reasonable measures amidst difficult and trying times.[40]

Not surprisingly, two Supreme Court cases involving fair representation concerned the seniority issue.[41] These decisions indicated that, although a bargaining unit employee has no absolute right to take his/her grievance to arbitration, the union satisfies its fair representation obligation in collective bargaining and grievance processing if it *considers the interests of all members* and *takes its ultimate position honestly, in good faith, and without hostility or arbitrary discrimination.*

These rather broad guidelines were also applied in a landmark Supreme Court decision, *Vaca v. Sipes,* which considered the union's fair representation obligation in the grievance procedure. A bargaining unit employee claimed that the union "arbitrarily, capriciously, and without just or reasonable reason or cause" refused to take his grievance to arbitration. The employee, a long-term high-blood-pressure patient, returned to work after a sick leave and was judged by the company's doctor as being unfit for reemployment. The employee's personal physician, as well as a second doctor, indicated that the employee was fit for work; therefore, the employee asked the union to seek his reinstatement through the grievance procedure. The grievance was processed; however, the union, in attempting to strengthen its case before going to arbitration, sent the employee to a third doctor. The third doctor did not support the employee's position; therefore, the union refused to take the employee's case to arbitration.

The Supreme Court decided that the union, in this case, acted in good faith and was neither arbitrary nor discriminatory. It also indicated (in this and in another case) the following[42]:

- The employee has the burden of proof of establishing that the union breached its fair representation obligation.

- Fair representation does not require the union to take every grievance to arbitration because this would create an intolerable expense for the union and management and would destroy the effectiveness of the lower steps in the grievance procedure.

- Courts should only examine the union's fair representation obligation, not the merits of the case.

In the event that a union is found guilty of breaching its duty of fair representation (actions are arbitrary, discriminatory, and/or in bad faith), the costs to the union may become quite expensive. In one case, the remedy assessed against the union was payment of the grievant's attorney fees, the costs of litigation, and back pay to the grievant from the date the grievant was dismissed to the date the grievant was either able to find employment or should have been employed in a substantially comparable job.[43] In a 2002 case, the U.S. Court of Appeals in the District of Columbia upheld a ruling of the National Labor Relations Board that allowed an employee to proceed with his grievance and directed the union to pay the grievant for his own lawyer to represent him.[44]

The U.S. Supreme Court decided that any judicial examination of a union's performance must be "highly deferential," giving "wide latitude" to union officials in the performance of their duties. A breach of fair representation has to be so far outside a "wide range of reasonableness" that it is wholly "irrational" or "arbitrary." Moreover, a union's decision is not irrational simply because it turns out in retrospect to have been a bad settlement.[45]

Currently, fair representation poses two difficult questions to the union and the employer. First, what specific types of conduct constitute violation of the fair representation duty? As previously noted, the Supreme Court has given only broad guidelines ("arbitrary," "bad faith," "dishonest," and so on). Sometimes these guidelines can be rather easily applied; for example, a union refusing to process grievances of any black, female, or nonunion employees is clearly guilty of a violation.[46] Other cases can become more complicated. The union, while not needing to take every grievance to arbitration, has an obligation to consider the merits of the grievance and effectively use the grievance procedure. In some cases, the courts have determined that union's *"perfunctory conduct"* (simply going through the motions) constitutes a breach of fair representation. Related actions include:

- Providing inadequate defense of the grievant at an arbitration hearing

- Delaying grievance processing until the time limits in the grievance procedure have expired

- Failing to inform the grievant that the union accepted a different remedy than that asked for by the grievant

- Failing to keep members informed about an arbitration award that affects members' seniority rights[47]

Yet, some courts have suggested that negligence or "honest mistakes" alone will not constitute a fair representation violation because union members always have the option of voting in new officers or even a new union to better represent them.

In an attempt to reduce the number of fair representation suits from members, unions include the subject of the duty of fair representation in their union steward training programs. While the exact content of these training programs may differ, unions focus on the Seven Golden Rules on the Union's Duty of Fair Representation provided in Exhibit 10.7.

A second question concerns employer and union liability if the union fails to fairly represent a bargaining unit employee who has been discharged. Employees currently can sue the union as well as the employer for breach of the labor agreement, including fair representation under Section 301 of the LMRA.

Assume, for example, that an employee is discharged, and then later establishes that the union breached its duty of fair representation and the employee was unjustly discharged. Both employer and the union can be liable according to the Supreme Court. An employee for the Postal Service named Bowen, was discharged for an altercation with another employee and filed a grievance. Bowen sued both the union and the employer in the district court. His evidence at trial indicated that the responsible union officer, at each step of the grievance procedure, had recommended pursuing the grievance but that the national office, for no apparent reason, had refused to take the matter to arbitration. The jury found that the Postal Service had discharged Bowen wrongfully and that the union had breached its fair representation obligation.

The Supreme Court eventually found that both the employer and the union contributed to this wrongful discharge. The employer, of course, made the initially wrong termination decision and therefore owed Bowen reinstatement with some of his back wages. However, the Court also agreed that the union also owed Bowen a portion of his lost wages because he could not have proceeded to arbitration independently of the union—and if the union had arbitrated his grievance, he would have been reinstated. Thus, the employer was responsible for the back wages from the termination date to the approximate date an arbitrator would have ordered reinstatement if the union had fairly represented the grievant and the case had been submitted to arbitration. The union was responsible for losses beyond that date. (See Exhibit 10.8 for determining the union's and the company's proportional liability.) The court also contended that joint employer–union liability might be in the interest of national labor relations policy.

Exhibit 10.7

Seven Golden Rules on the Union's Duty of Fair Representation

1. Consider all grievances solely on their merits.
2. Investigate each grievance promptly and vigorously.
3. Do not miss time limits.
4. Keep records.
5. Keep the grievant informed.
6. Have a valid reason for any action.
7. If the grievance lacks merits, drop it.

SOURCE: http://www.umass.edu/usa/dutyfairrep.htm.

Exhibit 10.8

Determination of the Union's and Company's Proportional Liability

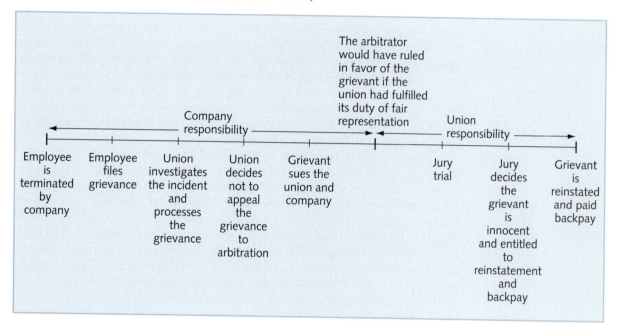

In the absence of damages apportionment where the fault of both parties contributes to the employee's injury, incentives to comply with the grievance procedure will be diminished. Indeed, imposing total liability solely on the employer could well affect the willingness of employers to agree to arbitration clauses as they are customarily written.[48]

Bowen has controversial implications for a labor–management relationship. Managers believe that they should not be held accountable for a union's errors, particularly because management is legally prohibited from dealing in the internal affairs of the union. However, it can easily be argued that the union would not have violated the law in the first place if the company had not wrongfully discharged the employee. There is also the possibility that this decision would encourage the union to take more marginal grievances to arbitration to avoid any possible breach of fair representation and related financial liability. In other words, the union may believe that it is less expensive to take the case to arbitration than to defend against a breach of contract suit before a jury. Research has yet to verify that this situation could be detrimental to the labor–management relationship.

Summary

Employee grievances and grievance administration extend collective bargaining by giving dynamic meaning to the negotiated terms of the labor agreement. A grievance is typically defined as any employee's concern over a perceived violation of the labor agreement that is submitted to the grievance procedure for resolution.

An employee might file a grievance for any of a variety reasons, such as to protest a contract violation, to draw attention to a problem in the plant, to get something for nothing, or to feel more important. Regardless of the reasons for filing grievances, management must process them through the grievance procedure specified in the labor agreement (legalistic approach).

Although no one grievance procedure applies to all labor–management relationships, two important aspects of a typical grievance procedure are inclusion of higher-level management and union personnel and, particularly in the private sector, binding arbitration by a third-party neutral. Grievance procedures typically offer an organization two major advantages: conflict institutionalization and open upward communication. However, the grievance procedure as actually carried out involves a variety of behavioral dimensions, including social relationships (codified, power, and empathetic) enacted among the grievance participants in resolving the grievance according to appropriate contractual provisions. The variety of personalities and motives of the participants suggests a flexible, pragmatic approach in grievance resolution may be best.

Grievance mediation, a form of Alternative Dispute Resolution (ADR) procedure, was discussed and compared to grievance arbitration, another ADR procedure. The advantages of grievance mediation, such as costs, informality, skills development, and others, were explained. However, despite these advantages, grievance mediation remains less frequently used than arbitration. The reasons for its less frequent use and the various approaches used were explained. As a result of its success, mediation is being used successfully by the EEOC to resolve employment discrimination disputes. Other forms of ADR—open-door policies, ombudsperson, peer review systems, and early neutral evaluation—were presented.

Unions have a legal obligation to fairly represent bargaining unit employees in the grievance procedure. Although unions are not legally required to take each grievance to arbitration, they must consider and process grievances in an effective, good faith manner. Legal and financial consequences to the union and the employer can arise when the union violates its duty of fair representation.

Key Terms

Grievance, p. 420
Employee voice, p. 428
Arbitration, p. 433
Mediation, p. 433
Grievance mediation, p. 433
Directive or results-oriented mediation, p. 435

Transformation mediation, p. 437
Open-door policy, p. 437
Ombudsperson, p. 438
Peer review panel, p. 438
Early neutral evaluation, p. 439
Codified relationships, p. 439

Power relationships, p. 440
Empathetic relationships, p. 441
Third-and-one-half step, p. 442
Fair representation obligation, p. 443

Discussion Questions

1. A thin line differentiates employee grievances and employee complaints. Discuss the problems involved in defining a grievance, indicating why a broad definition of employee grievances is both confusing and necessary.

2. Discuss two reasons grievances might be filed, furnishing examples of these reasons other than those found in the text.

3. Why does a typical grievance procedure have so many steps when the employee is either right or wrong and a one- or two-step procedure would

save time and money? In your answer, discuss the various functions, opportunities, and problems each of the grievance steps can offer.

4. Why is it difficult for union and management officials to resolve each grievance on its own merits?

5. Briefly discuss the broad judicial guidelines concerning unions' fair representation obligations to members. Also discuss the reasoning behind these obligations, furnishing some appropriate examples.

Exploring the Web

Grievance Procedures

1. Examples of Union Grievance Procedures. The Oil, Chemical and Atomic Workers International Union (OCAW) and the United Paperworkers International Union (UPIU) merged in 1999 to form PACE, the Paper Allied-Industrial, Chemical and Energy Workers International Union. In 2005 the United Steelworkers of American and PACE merged to form the largest industrial union in North America, the United Steel, Paper and Forestry, Rubber, Manufacturing, Energy, Allied Industrial and Service Workers International Union (USW). Find the Web site for USW and explore the Major Milestones in the USW History section. Discover, also, some of the crucial issues being addressed by the USW.

Locate the grievance procedures on the Web sites of the Industrial, Technical, and Professional Employees; the United Federation of Teachers; and the National Writers Union.

2. Shop Stewards. Find the section of the Web site for the International Brotherhood of Electrical Workers (IBEW) that discusses the rights of shop stewards. What are the "Weingarten rules" mentioned in the list of rights and why are they important to include in the discussion on shop stewards?

Explore the UNITE HERE Web site and find the Shop Stewards Resources which outline the shop steward's responsibilities in the grievance procedure.

3. Alternative Dispute Resolution and the USPS. The United States Postal Services alternative dispute resolution mediation program, REDRESS (Resolve Employment Disputes, Reach Equitable Solutions Swiftly) is recognized as one of the country's leading conflict resolution programs, according to the USPS Web site. Go to the FAQs and find out what happens if no settlement is reached in mediation.

4. Grievance Mediation and the EEOC. Mediation is a form of Alternative Dispute Resolution (ADR) that is offered by the U.S. Equal Employment Opportunity Commission (EEOC) as an alternative to the traditional investigative or litigation process. According to the EEOC, mediation is an informal process in which a neutral third party assists the opposing parties to reach a voluntary, negotiated resolution of a charge of discrimination. Explore the Commission's Web site and find what is said about the advantages of mediation. What groups are covered by EEO laws?

References

1. Antone Aboud, "Conducting a Fair Investigation," *The Dispute Resolution Journal*, Vol. 60, No. 3 (November 2004–January 2005), pp. 16–20.
2. Brian S. Klass and Angelo S. DeNisi, "Management Reactions to Employee Dissent: The Impact of Grievance Activity on Performance Ratings," *Academy of Management Journal* 32, no. 4 (1989), pp. 705–717.
3. Robert E. Allen and Timothy J. Keaveny, "Factors Differentiating Grievants and Nongrievants," *Human Relations* 38 (November 1985), p. 529.
4. David Lewin and Richard B. Peterson, "Behavioral Outcomes of Grievance Activity," *Industrial Relations* 38 (October 1999), pp. 554–566.
5. Chalmer E. Labig, Jr., and I. B. Helburn, "Union and Management Policy Influences in Grievance Initiation," *Journal of Labor Research* 7 (Summer 1986), pp. 269–284.
6. Douglas M. McCabe, "Corporate Nonunion Grievance Procedures: Open Door Policies—A Procedural Analysis," *Labor Law Journal* 41 (August 1990), pp. 551–557. See

also Mark J. Keppler, "Nonunion Grievance Procedures: Union Avoidance Technique or Union Organizing Opportunity?" *Labor Law Journal* 41 (August 1990), pp. 557–563; George W. Bohlander and Ken Behringer, "Public Sector Nonunion Complaint Procedures: Current Research," *Labor Law Journal* 41 (August 1990), pp. 563–568; Richard B. Peterson and David Lewin, "The Nonunion Grievance Procedure: A Viable System of Due Process," *Employee Responsibilities and Rights Journal* 3, no. 1 (1990), pp. 1–18; and Richard B. Peterson and Douglas M. McCabe, "The Nonunion Grievance System in High Performing Firms," *Labor Law Journal* 45 (August 1994), pp. 529–534.
7. "Strong grievance procedures" define a grievance as a dispute over any condition of employment that affects employee welfare and ends in arbitration no matter what the subject of the grievance. Daniel I. Reese, "Grievance Procedure Strength and Teacher Quits," *Industrial and Labor Relations Review* 45 (October 1991), p. 35.

8. Richard B. Freeman and James L. Medoff, *What Do Unions Do?* (New York: Basic Books, 1984), p. 10.

9. Richard B. Peterson, "Organizational Governance and the Grievance Process: In Need of a New Model for Resolving Workplace Issues," *Employee Responsibilities and Rights Journal* 7 (March 1994), p. 13.

10. Renaud Paquet and Sylvain Dufour, "Toward a Better Understanding of Grievance Procedure in the Public Service—A Canadian Example," *Journal of Collective Negotiations in the Public Sector* 28, no. 2 (1999), pp. 103–107.

11. For a fine research framework for grievances, see Michael E. Gordon and Sandra J. Miller, "Grievances: A Review of Research and Practice," *Personnel Psychology* 37 (Spring 1984), pp. 117–146. See also David Lewin, "Empirical Measures of Grievance Procedure Effectiveness," *Labor Law Journal* 35 (September 1984), pp. 491–496; Thomas R. Knight, "Feedback and Grievance Resolution," *Industrial and Labor Relations Review* 39 (July 1986), pp. 487–501; Casey Ichiowski, "The Effects of Grievance Activity on Productivity," *Industrial and Labor Relations Review* 39 (October 1986), pp. 75–89; Thomas R. Knight, "Correlates of Informal Grievance Resolution among First-Line Supervisors," *Relations Industrial* 41, no. 2 (1986), pp. 281–291; Brian Bemmels, Yonatan Reshef, and Kay Stratton-Devine, "The Roles of Supervisors, Employees and Stewards in Grievance Initiation," *Industrial and Labor Relations Review* 45 (October 1991), pp. 15–30; Jeanette A. Davy, Greg Steward, and Joe Anderson, "Formalization of Grievance Procedures: A Multi-Firm and Industry Study," *Journal of Labor Research* 13 (Summer 1992), pp. 307–316; Richard P. Chaykowski, George A. Slotsve, J. S. Butler, "Simultaneous Analysis of Grievance Activity and Outcome Decisions," *Industrial and Labor Relations Review* 45 (July 1992), pp. 724–737; Peter Capelli and Keith Chauvin, "A Test of an Efficiency Model of Grievance Activity," *Industrial and Labor Relations Review* 45 (October 1991), pp. 3–14; and Morris M. Kleiner, Gerald Nickelsburg, and Adam Pilarski, "Monitoring, Grievances, and Plant Performance," *Industrial Relations* 34 (April 1995), pp. 169–190.

12. Mark I. Lurie, "The 8 Essential Steps in Grievance Processing," *Dispute Resolution Journal* 54 (November 1999), pp. 81–86.

13. *Basic Patterns in Union Contracts* (Washington, D.C.: Bureau of National Affairs, 1995), pp. 33–39.

14. Stephen B. Goldberg, "How Interest-Based Grievance Mediation Performs Over the Long Term," *The Dispute Resolution Journal,* 60, (4) November 2004–January 2005, pp. 8–14; also, see Helen Elkiss, "Alternatives to Arbitration: Are Unions Ready for Change?" *Labor Law Journal* 48 (November 1997), pp. 675–690.

15. Theodore J. St. Antoine, "Introduction: What ADR Means Today," *How ADR Works* (Washington, D.C.: Bureau of National Affairs, 2002), pp. 4–5.

16. Nels Nelson and A. Meshquat Uddin, "Arbitrators As Mediators," *Labor Law Journal* 46 (April 1995), p. 205.

17. Peter Feuille, "Grievance Mediation," *Employment Dispute Resolution and Worker Rights in the Changing Workplace,* eds. Adrienne E. Eaton and Jeffrey H. Keene (Champaign, Ill.: IRRA, 1999), pp. 197–205.

18. Fueille, "Grievance Mediation," pp. 197–198.

19. Richard E. Dibble, "Alternative Dispute Resolution in Employment: Recent Developments," *Journal of Collective Negotiations in the Public Sector* 29, (3) 2000, pp. 247–248.

20. "History of the EEOC Mediation Program," http://eeoc.gov/mediate/history.html.

21. E. Patrick McDermott, Anita Jose, Ruth Obar, Mollie Bowers, and Brain Polkinghorn, "Has the EEOC Hit a Home Run? An Evaluation of the Equal Employment Opportunity Commission Mediation Program from the Participants' Perspective," *Advances in Industrial and Labor Relations,* eds. David Lewin and Bruce Kaufman (Amsterdam: JAI, 2002), pp. 2–34.

22. Lisa Bloomgreen Bingham, Cynthia J. Hallberlin, and Denise A. Walker, "Mediation of Discrimination Complaints at the USPS: Purpose Drives Practice," *Paper presented at the Annual Meeting of the National Academy of Arbitrators 2007.*

23. Laura J. Cooper, Dennis R. Nolan, and Richard A. Bales, *ADR in the Workplace* (St. Paul, Minn.: West Group, 2000), pp. 659–672.

24. Judith L. Catlett and Edwin L. Brown, "Union Leaders' Perceptions of the Grievance Process," *Labor Studies Journal* 15 (Spring 1990), p. 61.

25. See, for example, Ralph Arthur Johnson, "Grievance Negotiation: An Analysis of Factors Popularly Associated with Success," *Labor Studies Journal* 9 (Winter 1985), pp. 271–279.

26. *AFL-CIO Manual for Shop Stewards* (n.p., n.d.), p. 37.

27. William D. Todor and Dan R. Dalton, "Union Steward: A Little Known Actor with a Very Big Part," *Industrial Management* 25 (September–October 1983), pp. 7–11.

28. Paul Pigors, "The Old Line Foreman," in *Organizational Behavior,* eds. Austin Grimshaw and John Hennessey, Jr. (New York: McGraw-Hill, 1960), p. 98.

29. Michael E. Gordon and Roger L. Bowlby, "Propositions about Grievance Settlements: Finally, Consultation with Grievants," *Personnel Psychology* 41 (Spring 1988), p. 120. Another study also found that a high proportion of local union leaders believe that first-line supervisors have no authority to resolve grievances. See Catlett and Brown, p. 59.

30. John P. Hoerr, *And the Wolf Finally Came* (Pittsburgh: The University of Pittsburgh Press, 1988), p. 22.

31. P. Christopher Earley, "Supervisors and Stewards and Sources of Contextual Information in Goal Setting: A Comparison of the United States with England," *Journal of Applied Psychology* 71 (February 1986), pp. 111–117. See also Mick Marchington and Roger Armstrong, "Typologies of Union Stewards," *Industrial Relations Journal* (Autumn 1983), p. 44.

32. David Lewin and Richard B. Peterson, *The Modern Grievance Procedure in the United States* (New York: Quorum Books, 1988), p. 195.

33. Delbert C. Miller and William Forum, *Industrial Sociology,* 2d ed. (New York: Harper & Row, 1964), pp. 401–402.

34. Melville Dalton, "Unofficial Union-Management Relations," *American Sociological Review* 15 (October 1950), p. 613.

35. Marc G. Singer and Peter A. Veglahn, "Correlates of Supervisor-Steward Relations," *Labor Studies Journal* 10

(Spring 1985), pp. 46–55. For a study and related methodology revealing an empathetic relationship, see Brian Bemmels, "The Determinants of Grievance Initiation," *Industrial and Labor Relations Review* 47 (January 1994), pp. 293, 300.

36. Melville Dalton, "The Role of Supervision," in *Industrial Conflict,* eds. Arthur Kornhauser, Robert Dubin, and Arthur Ross (New York: McGraw-Hill, 1958), pp. 183–184.

37. For related legal violations (unfair labor practices), see Paul A. Brinker, "Labor Union Coercion: The Misuse of the Grievance Procedure," *Journal of Labor Research* 5 (Winter 1984), pp. 93–102.

38. Arthur Hamilton and Peter A. Veglahn, "Jurisdiction in Duty of Fair Representation Cases," *Labor Law Journal* 41 (September 1990), p. 668. See also Martin H. Malin, "The Supreme Court and the Duty of Fair Representation," *Harvard Civil Rights—Civil Liberties Law Review* 27.

39. "Decision of Supreme Court in *Teamsters Local 391 v. Terry,*" Bureau of National Affairs Inc., *Daily Labor Report,* no. 55 (March 21, 1990), pp. D-1–D-11. An appeals court decision interpreting a subsequent Supreme Court decision indicates the employee has a six-month period to sue starting from when he should have reasonably known about the union's alleged breach of duty. "Court Affirms That Fair Representation Claim over Abandoned Grievance Was Untimely Filed," Bureau of National Affairs Inc., *Daily Labor Report,* no. 151 (August 6, 1990), p. A-1.

40. Peter Geier, *The Daily Record,* Baltimore Maryland, January 5, 2004, p. 1. *Ford Motor Co. v. Huffman et al.,* 345 U.S. 320 (1953); and *Humphrey v. Moore,* 375 U.S. 335 (1964).

41. For examples of judicial decisions that have upheld and rejected unions' fair representation actions along these lines, see "Court Immunizes Union Failure to Pursue Grievance," Bureau of National Affairs Inc., *Daily Labor Report,* no. 48 (March 9, 1994), p. A-1; and "Court Finds UFCW Breached Duty, but Vacates Fee Award," Bureau of National Affairs Inc., *Daily Labor Report,* no. 101 (May 27, 1993), p. A-4.

42. *Vaca v. Sipes,* 386 U.S. 191 (1967); and *Amalgamated Association of Street, Electric, Railway and Motor Coach Employees of America v. Wilson p. Lockridge,* 403 U.S. 294 (1971).

43. "Union Must Pay Damages for Its Arbitrary Mishandling of Grievances," *National Public Employment Reporter,* July 5, 2001, p. 1.

44. "Unions under Scrutiny," *California Employment Law Letter,* May 13, 2002, p. 1.

45. "*Air Line Pilots Association, International v. Joseph E. O'Neill et al.,*" Bureau of National Affairs Inc., *The United States Law Week,* March 19, 1991, pp. 4175–4180.

46. For an example of a relatively straightforward breach of fair representation, see *Hines v. Anchor Motor Freight Inc.,* 424 U.S. 554 (1976).

47. "Union Failure to Publicize Award Held Fair Representation Breach," Bureau of National Affairs, *Daily Labor Report,* no. 112 (August 13, 1984), p. 1.

48. *Daily Labor Report,* June 11, 1983, p. D-5. See also T. Charles McKinney, "Fair Representation of Employees in Unionized Firms: A Newer Directive from the Supreme Court," *Labor Law Journal* 35 (November 1984), pp. 693–700.

Was This Grievance Arbitrable?

Issue

Was the grievance filed by Clinton Rowlett on May 5, 1996 processed in a timely manner in accordance with Section II of the labor agreement?

Background

On May 2, 1996, drivers of Delta Timberlands Corporation (the Company) were informed that they were being laid off because the paper mill located in Pine Bluff, Arkansas, was on strike.

On the following Monday, May 5, the vice president of the Paperworkers Union, Local No. 544, filed a Grievance on behalf of the drivers. His statement of the grievance was as follows:

> We, the drivers, feel that we are being discriminated against because we were laid off on May 2, 1996. The reason given by the supervisor was that the mill was blocked; however, on May 2, 1996, the independent contractors hauled 196 truckloads to the mill.

A Step 2 meeting was held on May 30, and the Company's answer was provided on June 12.

The final sentence of the letter essentially gives the Company's position on the grievance.

> The Company has not violated the contract and retains the right, power, and authority to schedule the sourcing and receipts of fiber into converting facilities.

The Union made a verbal appeal of the Grievance to Step 3 on July 9; however, no meeting was held and no written request for a grievance meeting was made until November 11. The Company responded to the Union's request for a meeting with a letter dated November 15, in which Mr. Jack Hopeful stated:

> The request for a third step meeting was untimely. The grievance was referred to the third step on July 9, 1996, after which the Company was not contacted again until November 11. However, the Company agrees to a meeting to be held on the afternoon of November 18.

At the November 18 meeting, the Grievance was restated and the answer that followed the Step 2 meeting was reviewed. In summary, the Company stated that it had not violated Sections 6 and 12 of the contract and retained the right, power, and authority to schedule the sourcing and receipts of fiber into converting facilities.

> The Grievance was then appealed to arbitration on February 2, 1997. A hearing was held on Thursday, April 23, 1997, and the parties agreed first to proceed with the issue of whether the case was arbitrable.

Pertinent Contract Provisions
Section II Grievance and Arbitration Procedures

The Union agrees to maintain during the term of this Agreement a Grievance Committee that shall meet with representatives of the Company to settle grievances. The committee shall be duly authorized and empowered at all times to represent employees and the Union in handling grievances with the Company. When meeting with the Company to settle grievances, the committee shall not exceed four members in number. The Company is agreeable to holding grievance meetings at mutually convenient times, normally during working hours.

> The settlement of such complaints or grievances shall be made in the following order and manner.
>
> **Step 1** The employee and/or his steward shall discuss his complaint with his immediate supervisor within five days following the date the incident occurred. If the employee was on an excused absence and he had no knowledge of it until his return to work, the five-day period shall begin on his first scheduled workday following the return from the absence. The supervisor shall reply to the employee within five days of the date the complaint was brought to his attention.
>
> **Step 2** An appeal of the supervisor's verbal answer may be made by reducing the grievance to writing on the form provided, signed by the employee, and transmitting it to the supervisor for referral to the department manager within ten days of the date the verbal answer was given. The department manager and/or his designated representative shall meet with the Grievance Committee within ten days of the date the written grievance was received. He shall give his written answer within ten days of the date of the meeting.

Step 3 An appeal of the department manager's answer must be made in writing to Step 3 within ten days of the date of the department manager's answer at Step 2. Within 30 days of the date the appeal notice was received, discussion of the appealed grievance shall take place at a meeting attended by the applicable manager and/or his designated representative together with the international union representative and the Union Grievance Committee. The manager shall give his answer within ten days of the date of the meeting.

Step 4 If no satisfactory settlement is reached on the matter within 15 days following the meeting, the Union may refer the matter to arbitration by notifying the Company in writing of such desire. The Union and the Company shall attempt to agree on an arbitrator within 14 days of receipt of a request to refer a dispute to arbitration. If the parties are unable to mutually agree on an arbitrator, the aggrieved party may request the Federal Mediation and Conciliation Service to submit the names of seven arbitrators to both parties. These parties agree to promptly select an arbitrator from the list to hear and decide the case, following the procedure of alternately striking names from the list. The arbitrator's decision shall be final and binding on all parties. A grievance must be filed and taken up in accordance with the time limits and procedures set forth in Steps 2 and 3 before it may be appealed to arbitration. The arbitrator shall hear the case as promptly as possible, affording each side reasonable opportunity to present witnesses and evidence in support of its case, and shall render an award in writing to both parties within 30 days following the last day of hearing on the matter. The fees of the arbitrator, including expenses, shall be paid equally by the Union and the Company. The award shall specify if reimbursement is intended and if so, to what extent, and shall otherwise provide a clear and concise decision on the matter. No more than one grievance shall be heard in any one arbitration hearing except by mutual consent of the parties. The arbitrator shall have no power to add to, subtract from, or change any of the provisions of this Agreement or any supplemental agreement hereto. Any of the time limits provided in the second, third, and fourth steps of the foregoing grievance and arbitration procedures may be extended by mutual agreement of the Company and appropriate Union before the expiration of the time limit. "Days" in the Grievance and Arbitration provision shall mean calendar days, excluding Saturdays, Sundays, and holidays. The time limits on the various steps of the grievance and arbitration procedures will be suspended during economic shutdowns and repair shutdowns.

The Company's Position

The Company argued that the maximum allowable number of days for processing a grievance in accordance with the labor agreement had been exceeded. This Grievance had taken 195 days to process. The Company provided data showing that the maximum number of days allowed to process a grievance under the contract is 95 days.

The Company contended that the Grievance was untimely processed between Step 2 and Step 3. The Step 2 meeting was held on May 30 and the Company response was given on June 12. However, only a verbal appeal was made by the Union on July 9. The verbal appeal did not comply with Step 3 of the labor agreement, which requires that an appeal to the Company's answer must be in writing and within ten days of the date of the Company's answer to the Step 2 meeting. Further, a meeting on the Grievance was not held until November 18, which was far beyond the 30 days required by Step 3 of the labor agreement. At the Step 2 meeting, the Company had challenged the timeliness of the Grievance and did not hear from the Union about this Grievance until November 11, during a contract negotiating session. Further, it was not until three months later, on February 2, 1997, that the Company was notified of the Union's request for an arbitration hearing.

The Company had granted a grievance extension to the Union in the middle of the summer during the strike at the mill. However, the Grievance had not been appealed further and no request for a meeting had been made. When the request for a grievance meeting was made in November, the Company challenged the timeliness of the Grievance.

In its opening statement at the arbitration meeting, the Company informed the arbitrator that both parties have a mutual obligation to abide by the contract. The Company spokesperson stated:

You negotiate a contract in good faith. I believe that the Company is certainly obligated to abide by the contract. But there are just a couple of clauses in the whole contract by which the Union has to abide. When it comes to their turn to abide by it, they don't want to. They want to hold the Company up to abide by everything in the contract; but they want to make exceptions.

The Company requested that its position be accepted because the maximum allowable days for processing grievances had been exceeded by 100 days. The Union had not complied with the labor agreement and the Grievance should be denied.

The Union's Position

The Union argued that the Grievance was timely filed after the May 2, 1996, notification of the layoff. A Step 2 grievance meeting was held on May 30, and the Company's response was given to the Union in a letter dated June 12, 1996.

Upon receipt of the Company's letter, the Union discussed appealing the Grievance further.

The local union president testified that:

I believe at this time that Sam (the union vice president) informed me that he had an agreement with the Company to extend the grievance because there was a strike out at the mill. Negotiations were continuing and they didn't have time to handle the grievance.

Further, the Union president was the person authorized to obtain an extension of the time limits and had stated at the hearing: "I was tied up in strike negotiations and got an extension on the time limit for the Grievance." It was not until around November 11 that the Union became aware of any problem concerning the timeliness of the Grievance.

The Union argued that there had been unusual circumstances surrounding this Grievance,

and these circumstances should be considered by the arbitrator. These unusual circumstances included a nine-week strike at the mill, which required heavy involvement by the Union president.

On several occasions during this strike, he assured the other union representatives that he had obtained an extension on processing this Grievance. Another set of unusual circumstances regarding this Grievance occurred on December 4, 1996, during the time when the Union could have processed the Grievance to Step 4 of the labor agreement. The local union president lost his bid for re-election and one day later suffered a heart attack that required an operation. Because the president was unable to process this Grievance during his recuperation and, although he was a lame-duck president, the Union contends that such unusual circumstances warrant an extension of time limits. (The former union president did not testify at the hearings.)

Thus, based on the unusual circumstances surrounding this Grievance and the mutual agreement to extend the Grievance, the Union requested that the challenge on the lack of timeliness be rejected.

Questions

1. To what degree does the Grievance procedure in this case meet the requirements for an effective Grievance procedure?

2. Assess the meaning of the last sentence in the Grievance procedure that states: "The time limits on the various steps of the grievance and arbitration procedures will be suspended during economic shutdowns and repair shutdowns."

3. Would the issue of whether the case was arbitrable be considered procedural or substantive? Why?

4. Assess the relative strengths of each party's position.

5. Decide whether the Grievance is arbitrable. If so, why? If not, why?

Must a Union Process a Grievance of a Nonunion Employee?

CASE STUDY 10-2 On August 15, employees Billie Green, Mary Swallows, Betty Jones, and Edie Barnett lunched together in the company's parking lot. The discussion centered on Barnett's pending grievance concerning her recently completed layoff. Green, a nonunion employee, asked Barnett if she had said that Green had not been laid off because she was providing sexual favors to a supervisor. When Barnett admitted that she had made the comment, Green asserted that Barnett's husband engaged in sexual conduct with Swallows, a union member. Swallows then slapped Green, and Green proposed that they leave the company property to settle the matter.

Swallows slapped Green again, and then turned and walked away. Green became infuriated, followed Swallows, and kicked her in the back. The two fought for about four minutes.

Later that day, human resource manager Joe Rogalski called Green and Swallows for separate meetings to talk about the incident. Rogalski had talked with witnesses to the incident and their accounts gave conflicting reports as to who had struck the first blow. Because he could not determine who had started the incident, he had no recourse but to fire both of them. He advised them that they could file a grievance if they chose. At the end of the day, Green and Swallows met at the time clock. Green accused Swallows of lying and told her, "Sooner or later I'll beat the hell out of you."

The next day, Green telephoned the plant and told the human resource department's secretary that she was going to file a grievance. The Union Grievance Committee was meeting that morning at the plant cafeteria. Green went to the meeting and spoke with grievance committee members Jack Nolan and Joe Caldwell about filing a grievance. Nolan told her to see union secretary Sue Cogdill. She spoke to Cogdill who told her, "We'll take care of it . . . just go up to the cafeteria and wait for me."

Earlier that same day, Swallows had met with the Union Grievance Committee in the cafeteria and had given her version of the incident. Green was later asked to give her version to the same group. Green believed that by meeting with the Grievance Committee she had officially filed a grievance. She then left the plant.

A week later, Swallows returned to work and Green was told by friends about Swallows's reinstatement. Green went to the plant to inquire about her grievance and was informed that no grievance had been filed on her behalf. She then confronted Cogdill and asked why her grievance had not been filed. Cogdill replied, "That's not normally my duty." Green then spoke to Rogalski, who explained that he could not rehire her because he had no written grievance from her. When she reminded him that she had told him earlier that she wanted to file a grievance, he responded that even if she had filed one, it would not have mattered because he and Cogdill had discussed the situation and decided to rehire Swallows. Green believed that her rights under the LMRA had been violated and filed a charge of an unfair labor practice with the NLRB, alleging lack of fair representation by the Union.

Questions

1. What are nonunion employee rights under the LMRA?

2. What is meant by the union's duty of fair representation?

3. When has the Union met its obligation of fair representation?

4. Has the Union in this case met its fair representation obligation? Explain.

Classroom Exercise

10.1
Arbitration Scenario

On Thursday, March 4, 2004, Juan Carlos, age 43, was on sick leave at his home. He went outside to feed his horses and noticed a pickup truck driving toward him. As the pickup came closer, Juan noticed that the driver was Billy Bob Jones, a former boyfriend of his ex-wife.

Billy Bob pulled up to Juan and the two of them had an exchange of words. This exchange led to Juan pulling out a pistol and shooting Billy Bob, who was taken to the hospital. Billy Bob was admitted and later released. A warrant for the arrest of Juan Carlos was issued by the Magistrate of the County District Court on March 5, 2004. Juan was arrested on March 5, 2004, made bail, and was released.

On Monday, March 8, Juan reported to work at the social service organization where he had worked for eight years. He asked for a meeting with his supervisor, Alice Smith, and department head, Larry Tate. Juan told them that he was involved in an altercation with Billy Bob Jones who had driven to his home, threatened to kill him, and grabbed his arm with his left hand from the driver's side of his pickup while the motoring was still running. When Billy Bob leaned to his right and reached down toward his car seat, Juan feared for his life and shot Jones in self defense. He told them that he was later arrested. After the meeting, Juan returned to his desk and continued his job of interviewing citizens who visited his office to apply for public assistance.

On the following day, Suzie Cue, a fellow employee, told Mr. Tate that she had read an article in the local newspaper that Juan had shot Billy Bob Jones and had been arrested. Suzie told Mr. Tate that she "was frightened having Juan in the same office." Mr. Tate knew that he had a potentially serious situation and he needed to investigate the situation. Mr. Tate first checked the Collective Bargaining Agreement. The relevant language is

Management may discipline employees for just cause.
The Agency may suspend an employee indefinitely if there is reasonable cause to believe that the employee has committed a crime for which a sentence of imprisonment could be imposed.

On March 10, 2004, Tate decided to propose to suspend Carlos indefinitely and Carlos was placed on administrative leave. After approval from his division head, Tate wrote a letter captioned, "Decision to Suspend Indefinitely," to Carlos. Upon receipt, Carlos began serving an indefinite suspension. On March 11, 2004, Carlos filed a grievance and also filed a charge of race and age discrimination with the EEOC. Management's preparation and decisions are only as good as its investigation. You be the investigator. What information will you seek? What actions will you take to obtain this needed information?

CHAPTER 11
Labor and Employment Arbitration

This chapter covers (1) traditional grievance labor arbitration, which involves the dispute-resolution procedures stemming from the last step in the grievance procedure, and (2) employment arbitration, which is initiated by the employer. The traditional labor arbitration procedures are negotiated between the employer and the union, the representative of bargaining unit employees. Employment arbitration is promulgated by the employer to resolve statutory claims, including employment discrimination and disputes over application of company personnel policies, such as promotion under an employer handbook or policy manual. These two arbitration procedures are covered separately because, although they have some commonalities, they are distinctly different.

The first difference is the presence of the union in the traditional labor arbitration procedure. The union's role is to represent all bargaining unit employees, and the union and the company bilaterally negotiate an arbitration procedure that will best reflect both the interests of the employees covered under the collective bargaining agreement and the interests of the employer. Under employment arbitration, the employer unilaterally designs the procedures and determines that disputes over employment subjects will be resolved in arbitration.

A second difference is the qualifications and selection of the arbitrators who hear the disputes. Arbitrators used in negotiated grievance arbitration have considerable experience and

Copyright GettyImages

expertise in labor and employment matters and are selected mutually by the parties, who research their backgrounds, education, experience, and so on before making the selection. In employer-promulgated employment arbitration, arbitrators may be selected only by the employer from commercial arbitration lists or lists developed by the employer. In fact, some employers refuse to use arbitrators who have experience in the labor relations arena because employers believe that these arbitrators are likely to use the same standards as used in labor–management arbitration, such as an employer having the burden of proof in a discharge case.

A third difference lies in the framework for decision making. Under a collective-bargaining agreement, arbitration involves issues that arise over the interpretation and application of the agreement. Therefore, the agreement negotiated by the union and company establishes the framework ("four corners of the agreement") for the arbitrator's decision. Under employment arbitration, the decision of the arbitrator involves interpretation and application of company personnel policy or a statute.[1]

DEVELOPMENT OF LABOR ARBITRATION
1865 through World War II

Arbitration first occurred in the United States in 1865, but it was used rarely before World War II, when it was used by the War Labor Board. In many cases employee grievances were resolved through sheer economic strength. For instance, a union desiring resolution of a particular grievance often needed to mobilize the entire workforce in a strike against the employer—a difficult task—before the company would attempt to resolve the grievance. Union and management officials were legally free to ignore the arbitrator's decision if they did not agree with it.

Other factors limiting the early growth of arbitration were the relatively few unionized facilities and the vague language found in labor agreements, which gave little contractual guidance for the arbitrator's decision. Consequently, the early arbitration process combined elements of mediation and humanitarianism in an effort to reach a *consensus decision,* one that would be accepted by both parties to a grievance. The arbitrator under these circumstances had to draw on diplomatic and persuasive abilities to convince the parties that the decision should be accepted.

Arbitration's popularity increased during World War II, when President Franklin Roosevelt's Executive Order 9017 provided for final resolution of disputes interrupting work that contributed to the war effort. Essential features of this order included a no-strike, no-lockout agreement and a **National War Labor Board (NWLB)** composed of four management representatives, four union representatives, and four representatives of the public—all presidential appointees. The Board was to encourage collective bargaining and, if necessary, resolve disputes over the terms of the agreements.

The advent of World War II encouraged the role of arbitration in several ways. Many union and management officials realized that uninterrupted wartime production was essential and that grievance resolution was more effectively accomplished through arbitration than through strikes. The NWLB urged labor and management officials to resolve their own disputes and encouraged the parties to carefully define the arbitrator's jurisdiction in the labor agreement. Thus, the Board gave any negotiated restrictions full force when deciding cases and denied arbitration where it was reasonably clear that the arbitration clause meant to exclude a subject from arbitral review. It further defined grievance arbitration as a quasi-judicial process, thereby limiting a decision solely to the evidence presented at the hearing.

Results of the NWLB's activities further popularized and enriched the arbitration process, as the Board resolved some 20,000 disputes during its tenure. In addition, these efforts served as a training ground for many arbitrators who were able to apply their newly acquired skills to the arbitration process throughout the United States after the war.

The Postwar Years and the Steelworkers' Trilogy

Although the use of arbitration increased during World War II, the role and authority of arbitrators were far from resolved.[2] Both parties in a labor dispute still remained legally free to ignore the arbitrator's award. In 1957, however, the Supreme Court declared in its *Lincoln Mills* decision that an aggrieved party could legally bring suit against a party that refused to arbitrate a labor dispute for violation of the labor agreement, under Section 301 of the Labor Management Relations Act. Thus, grievance procedures including arbitration could be subjected to judicial review, although much confusion remained over the court's role in these activities.

Either party could refuse to submit the grievance to arbitration if the labor agreement did not cover the issue in question. Some state statutes that made the agreement to arbitrate enforceable resulted in attempts to persuade the court to compel arbitration of various issues. Some courts then became involved in assessing the merits of a particular grievance and whether it should be arbitrated. These actions, of course, contradicted arbitral belief that arbitrators alone should rule on the merits of the grievance. Confusion resulted when labor and management representatives played the courts against the arbitrators in their attempts to obtain favorable decisions.

In 1960, the Supreme Court clarified and strengthened the arbitrator's role with three decisions commonly referred to as the *Steelworkers' Trilogy*. These decisions can be summarized as follows:

- The arbitrator, not the courts, determines the merits of a grievance. The courts have no business weighing the merits of a grievance.[3]

- Arbitrators have far more expertise than judges in interpreting the *common law of the shop* (experiences and past practices at a particular facility), which is fundamental to resolving existing grievances in a manner consistent with the continuing labor–management relationship.[4]

- Arbitrators have no obligation to the court to give their reasons for an award. Therefore, they have great latitude in fashioning a decision and its remedy.[5]

In summary, the *Steelworkers' Trilogy* greatly enhanced the authority and prestige of the arbitrator in interpreting the terms of the labor agreement and deciding the merits of a particular grievance. It also endorsed the arbitrator as most qualified to fashion a resolution of a grievance if it is based on the essence of the labor agreement. However, the Supreme Court has reaffirmed that the courts should determine whether a grievance should be submitted to arbitration when one party refuses, on the basis of its contention that the labor agreement excludes this particular subject from the arbitration procedure.[6] Other related decisions are presented in the next section.

Legal Obligations to Arbitrate and Enforce Arbitration Decisions

The Supreme Court has determined that the obligation to arbitrate a grievance cannot be nullified by a successor employer[7] or by the termination of a labor agreement. Management representatives in this latter situation argued that arbitration is a feature of the contract that ceases to exist when a contract terminates; therefore, a grievance cannot be processed to arbitration if the labor agreement is no longer in effect. Consequently, management representatives thought that the issue of severance pay was not subject to arbitration because the labor agreement had expired and management had decided to permanently close its operations. However, the Supreme Court indicated that arbitration was still appropriate because employee rights which arose during the life of the labor agreement were continuing rights.[8] Therefore, management had an obligation to honor a union's request for arbitration after the labor contract has expired only if the dispute either arose before the contract expired or concerned "a right that accrued or vested under the agreement."[9]

Another issue resolved by the Supreme Court concerns how far the courts are willing to go in enforcing the role of an arbitrator. More specifically, what happens when one party is willing to arbitrate a grievance while the other party prefers to use the strike or lockout to resolve a dispute? As previously mentioned, a strike was a plausible alternative in resolving a grievance in the early years of arbitration. Also, the *Trilogy* did not specifically consider this alternative in its conclusions.

The award enforceability issue was brought before the courts in 1969 when a union protested a work assignment given to nonbargaining unit personnel. The union expressed its concern by striking even though the labor agreement contained a provision for arbitrating disputes over the terms of the agreement. Management officials stressed that the union should use the contractually specified arbitration procedure and be enjoined or prevented from striking the employer, and the Supreme Court agreed in its *Boys Market* decision.[10]

ELEMENTS OF A TYPICAL ARBITRATION PROCEEDING
Selection and Characteristics of Arbitrators

When union and management need assistance in the selection of their arbitrator(s), the process usually begins with a request from the parties to an agency for a list of potential arbitrators. Annually, the parties will make approximately 30,000 requests for lists of arbitrators from which they make their selection. Unions and management rely primarily on three sources for lists of arbitrators. One source is the Federal Mediation and Conciliation Service (FMCS), an independent federal agency that provides computer-generated lists of arbitrators through its Office of Arbitration Services in Washington. About 43 percent of the requests for arbitrator lists are made to the FMCS. Its activity is limited to providing lists of arbitrators and biographical data on each arbitrator, informing arbitrators of their selection, and following up to assure that the selected arbitrator renders a timely decision. For these services, the FMCS charges each party $30 per case for an on-line request and $50 per case for request by mail or fax. Each arbitrator pays $100 per year to remain on the FMCS roster, and periodically, the FMCS reviews its roster of arbitrators and excludes those arbitrators who have been infrequently selected.

The parties will negotiate the specific procedure for selecting arbitrators and include the procedure in the collective-bargaining agreement. A common selection procedure is the *striking method*. For example, from a list of five potential arbitrators, one party will strike (mark through the name of the arbitrator so as to exclude) one arbitrator (usually the least desirable arbitrator) and then the other party will strike one arbitrator (usually the least desirable arbitrator from those remaining). The parties will continue to strike until there is one arbitrator (the least objectionable) remaining; the remaining arbitrator will be the one selected (unless both parties agree to request another list) and the arbitrator will be informed of the selection. Of course, if this procedure does not yield a selection, the parties may request another list or may ask the FMCS to make a direct appointment.

The second major source is the American Arbitration Association (AAA), a private, nonprofit organization that supplies hand-selected lists of arbitrators from regional centers. About 38 percent of the requests for arbitrator lists are made to the AAA. After selection, the AAA provides additional services, including establishing the location of the hearings, exchanging posthearing briefs, and forwarding the decision to the parties. The AAA offers a different range of services for which it charges from $50 to $350; the AAA charges each arbitrator $300 per year to remain on its list. Like the FMCS, it conducts a periodic review of its list to make sure that the arbitrators are considered acceptable to the parties.

The selection procedure used in AAA cases is called the *striking and ranking* procedure. Here, each party will strike the names of arbitrators who are not acceptable and then will rank (1 = most preferred, 2 = second most preferred, and so on) the remaining arbitrators. The arbitrator selected will be the one who receives the highest rank among those remaining. As under the FMCS procedure, if this procedure does not yield an arbitrator acceptable to both parties, then the parties may request another list or ask the AAA to make a direct appointment.

The third major source is the 26 state and local agencies located primarily in the northern and western states. The number of arbitrators on the agencies lists range from 270 with the New York Employment Relations Board to 15 with the North Carolina Department of Labor. About 18 percent of the requests for arbitrator lists are made to these agencies. The number of requests ranges from fewer than 50 to more than 300 per year, with 54 percent of the requests occurring in New York and New Jersey. The operational arrangements vary widely also. Some agencies provide lists of arbitrators to unions and management in both the private and public sector; some only to the public sector. Half of the agencies send out arbitrator lists on a random selection basis; half use a modified random, rotational, or discretionary system. Most agencies restrict membership on their arbitrator roster to state residents and residents of contiguous states. The Massachusetts Board of Conciliation and Arbitration, the New York State Employment Relations Board, the Washington Employment Relations Commission, and the Wisconsin Employment Relations Commission provide staff members to serve as grievance arbitrators at no cost to the parties, and the New York State Employment Relations Board has a roster of pro bono arbitrators who are seeking to gain experience as labor arbitrators. Under the state agencies, there are numerous and varied selection procedures.[11]

The Supreme Court by encouraging the use of arbitration contended that this essentially private, self-governing process is best suited to labor relations issues and to the unique needs of the parties at a particular facility. This means the particular arbitration procedures are essentially determined by the parties themselves, and there are no universally applicable rules concerning arbitration hearings. For example, the number of participants (even arbitrators) can vary; also, the location of the hearing might be at the plant conference room, a hotel room, or a courtroom. However, some considerations and procedures are acceptable for most, if not all, arbitration hearings. According to one study, only 16 percent of the grievances filed in the first step of the grievance procedure are eventually decided by arbitrators.[12]

First, the parties must decide the number of arbitrators needed to resolve a grievance. The most common method (approximately 82 percent of arbitration provisions) is for a single impartial arbitrator selected by management and union officials to be solely responsible for the decision, with no help from other individuals in formulating the written decision. In about 11 percent of cases, the labor agreement specifies a three-member (tri-partite) arbitration board or panel, with management and the union each selecting a member and these two individuals selecting the third member. Most decisions are made by this impartial arbitrator because the other two members of the panel are influenced by their respective management and union constituents, although the impartial arbitrator does consult with the other members. In either case, the arbitrator's decision is final and binding. In extremely rare circumstances, both management and the union agree to disregard or set aside the arbitrator's award or the courts overturn the decision.

Five percent of the labor agreements in the United States provide for a **permanent arbitrator** or umpire to resolve all disputes during the life of the labor agreement. Also in five percent of the agreements, there is a fixed list of arbitrators who serve on a rotating basis.[13] Usually, the use of permanent arbitrators applies to large companies or industries in which a large number of arbitration hearings are anticipated. Presumably, a permanent arbitrator can better allocate and schedule time to meet the grievance load of the union and employer so that settlements can be reached more promptly. This type of selection arrangement also allows the permanent arbitrator to become more knowledgeable of the complex and unique terms of the parties' labor agreement and industrial operations.

Assume, for example, that an arbitrator is hearing a grievance in the railroad industry for the first time. How long would it take for the arbitrator to accurately interpret the meaning of the following witness's testimony?

At 3 P.M. Mott Haven Yard was a busy place. A crew of gandy dancers tamped methodically on a frong near the switching lead. L.S. 3 was all made up and ready to be doubled over. She had forty-six hog racks on the head end and sixty-five empty reefers on the hind end. Her crew were all new men on the run. Mike Madigan, the hog head, had just been set up. Bill Blanchard, the fire-boy, was a boomer who had recently hired out. Jack Lewis, the brains of the outfit, had been a no bill since he was fired out of the Snakes for violating Rule "G." Brady Holms, the flagman, used to work the high iron in a monkey suit, and J.B. Wells was a "stu" brakeman, right off the street. Over the hump lead, the yard rats were riding 'em in the clear and typing 'em down. The east side switcher was kicking loaded hoppers around, despite the violent washouts of the yardmixer who had discovered a hot box. Two Malleys were on the plug and three more were at the coal pocket. Our train, Number B.D. 5, was all ready to pull out.[14]

The use of a permanent arbitrator saves time and expense because the parties do not have to repeatedly explain the meaning of these terms in the arbitration hearing or show the work location. Greater consistency can be attained where one individual applies the same decision-making criteria to all of the arbitrated grievances. Consistent decisions aid union and management officials in the day-to-day administration of the labor agreement. A permanent arbitrator should also enable the parties to better predict the arbitrator's subsequent decisions on similar issues, perhaps decreasing the number of frivolous grievances referred to arbitration as the parties become more certain of the arbitrator's reasoning.

Seventy-four percent of the labor agreements specify an **ad hoc arbitrator**, meaning that the arbitrator will be selected on an *ad hoc,* or case-by-case, basis; union and management representatives choose an arbitrator for a specific grievance, but may select other arbitrators for subsequent grievances arising during the life of the labor agreement. Particularly in the case of an established collective bargaining relationship, management and the union often reach an informal agreement on the appropriate arbitrator for a particular grievance. However, if they cannot agree, they usually obtain a list of arbitrators' names (a panel) from either the FMCS or the AAA. In some cases when the parties cannot agree on an arbitrator from the list provided, they might request that these organizations select an arbitrator.

Clearly, for unions and companies having few arbitration hearings, *ad hoc* arbitrators are less expensive than permanent arbitrators. Regardless of the grievance load, *ad hoc* arbitration offers the advantage of flexibility. Although permanent arbitrators usually are appointed by the parties for a specified period, either side can discontinue the appointment if it views the permanent arbitrator's decisions with disfavor. There is no obligation to retain the *ad hoc* arbitrator in future grievances if either side is displeased with the arbitrator's decisions.

Because some *ad hoc* arbitrators specialize in particular categories of grievances, such as job classification or wage incentives, they could be better informed than a permanent arbitrator on such issues. Permanent arbitrators may be more familiar with the parties but may have seldom encountered a particular issue in their arbitration experience. Because both types of arbitrators have comparative advantages and disadvantages, management and union officials will design the selection method that best meets their needs.

According to one survey, arbitrators are likely to be males over 50 years of age with more than 14 years of experience in arbitration and a law degree or a graduate degree.[15] (See Exhibit 11.1 for a profile of members of the National Academy of Arbitrators.) Arbitrators' characteristics can be significant for at least two reasons. First, union and management officials select an arbitrator who possess certain characteristics that might, according to one study, include name recognition, reputation for integrity, and a specific geographical location. Other studies found that employers tend to prefer arbitrators with training in economics, whereas union and management officials who have law degrees prefer arbitrators who also have law degrees.[16]

Second, there is at least the possibility that certain background characteristics might influence arbitrators' decisions. However, research studies have not

Exhibit 11.1

Profile of Members of the National Academy of Arbitration and Arbitration Data (462 responses from 600 members)

Age (average)	63
Years of arbitration	26
Percent of income earned by arbitration	76
Years as member at NAA	16
Education: Masters	12.6%
Law Degree	61.4%
Doctorate	22.6%
Number of arbitration cases per year	55
Number of cases mediated per year (50.8% mediated no cases)	5
Accepted and completed cases in nonunion employment arbitration	45.9%

SOURCE: Michel Picher, Ronald Seeber, and David B. Lipsky, *The Arbitration Profession in Transition,* Ithaca, NY: Cornell/ PERC Institute of Conflict Resolution, 2000, pp. 11–28; updated from http://www.fmcs.gov (accessed January 9, 2004).

established a strong relationship between arbitrators' age, experience, or education and decision outcomes[17] (e.g., upholding or denying the grievance).

Although grievance arbitration is typically considered a wholly objective proceeding in which an impartial neutral hears testimony, receives evidence from the employer and union representatives, and then makes a decision based solely on the facts, questions of acceptability often intrude on the process. Because arbitrators are selected by the parties, some believe that the arbitrators' decisions are occasionally influenced by their concern over being selected to arbitrate future cases. If and when one of the parties believes that the arbitrator is concerned about continued acceptability, that party may select the arbitrator because of the belief that the arbitrator may owe them a favorable decision, thereby contaminating the process. This concern is the reason that the National Academy of Arbitrators inserted into the *Code of Professional Responsibility for Arbitrators of Labor-Management Disputes* the following passage: "An arbitrator must be as ready to rule for one party as for the other on each issue, either in a single case or in a group of cases. Compromise by an arbitrator for the sake of attempting to achieve personal acceptability is unprofessional."[18]

Prehearing Activities

On occasion, the parties may decide to write a prehearing brief, which highlights the issues and positions of the parties before the arbitrator arrives at the hearing. The briefs alert the arbitrator to the matters he or she will face at the hearing. These optional briefs, although uncommon, vary in length from a one-page letter to an extensively footnoted document. Most of the time, the parties prefer to wait and introduce the subject matter of the arbitration to the arbitrator in the opening statements at the beginning of the hearing.

The prehearing brief might backfire for the presenting party, who is subject to challenges on the assumed facts and inconsistencies that may surface in the witnesses' testimonies. On the other hand, prehearing briefs can be viewed as keeping the parties honest—they tend to approach their contentions thoroughly and are forced to adhere to them during the arbitration proceedings.

Perhaps most arbitrators would agree to the value of *prehearing stipulations*— joint union-management statements as to the issues involved and certain applicable grievance "facts." This saves time in the arbitration hearing, for neither party feels obligated to repeat what the other has either previously said or agreed to in principle. In addition, through the process of working together to stipulate the issues and facts, the parties may be able to resolve the dispute without arbitration. If briefs or stipulations are not agreed to before the hearing, the parties will have to educate the arbitrator on the background of the case.

The Arbitration Hearing

Held on a date convenient to the arbitrator and parties, the **arbitration hearing** varies in length from half an hour to several days, with the average length being one day. Union and management officials who were involved in the grievance procedure (e.g., the international union representative and the labor relations manager) will likely present their versions of the arbitration case at the hearing. However, either party may decide to use attorneys to present their case. According to one recent research study, attorneys generally discourage pre-arbitration settlements between union and management and increase the use of prehearing and posthearing briefs.[19]

Variations also occur in the extent to which courtroom procedures and behaviors are used or required during the hearing. There are two perspectives on the arbitration process: (1) informal quasi-litigation (legalistic approach) designed to resolve a dispute between parties and (2) part of the ongoing collective bargaining process designed to facilitate conflict resolution (problem-solving approach). Those adopting the legalistic approach argue that a more formal and orderly proceeding improves the process. Frequently, however, the advocates view arbitration as an adversarial procedure and adopt tactics to win the decision without considering that the parties have to live with each other after the decision. From the second perspective, arbitration is viewed as serving more purposes than simply resolving disputes. For example, arbitration has "cathartic value" by allowing a grievant to openly air a complaint against a management decision. The belief is that complaints, if left unresolved, will become more serious and possibly counterproductive. In addition, the negotiators of the collective-bargaining agreement are not able to anticipate and address every possible future scenario in the relationship between the employer and the union. To do so would unnecessarily lengthen the negotiations and add significantly to the length of the collective bargaining agreement. Such actions would make the negotiations more complex and even jeopardize the possibility of reaching an agreement.[20] A comparison of example behaviors of the legalistic versus the problem-solving approaches is shown in Exhibit 11.2.

At the typical arbitration hearing, the first order of business is the introduction of joint exhibits. These exhibits usually include a copy of the relevant

Exhibit 11.2

Behavioral Examples of Legalistic Versus Problem-Solving Approaches

Legalistic Approach

Drafting the statement of the issue in such a way that there is a definite winner and a definite loser.

Looking for restrictions on the arbitrator's authority to hear issues not expressly stated in the written grievance.

Insisting on a specific burden of proof at the beginning of the hearing (preponderance of evidence, clear and convincing evidence, or beyond a reasonable doubt).

Harsh and aggressive (eat 'em alive) cross-examining in an attempt to destroy witness credibility. Objecting to any form of hearsay evidence.

Noting for the record objections to certain types of evidence, even though the arbitrator has allowed the evidence to be introduced.

Problem-Solving Approach

Acknowledging that the parties have a mutual obligation to bring out all relevant facts.

Citing custom and/or practice of the parties.

Arguing that the arbitrator should interpret provisions of the collective bargaining agreement in such a way that it will be reasonable and equitable to both parties.

Stipulating certain facts where the parties have no dispute.

Asking questions that call for a narrative answer, for example, asking the witness to tell the story about what happened in her own words.

Asking only a few nonthreatening questions on cross-examination.

Using friendly and dignified behavior toward the opposite party.

SOURCE: Adapted from Richard A. Posthuma and Maris Stella Swift, "Legalistic vs. Facilitative Approaches to Arbitration: Strengths and Weaknesses," *Labor Law Journal*, 52 (Fall 2001), pp. 181–182.

collective-bargaining agreement, which contains the provision(s) one of the parties (usually the union) alleges has been violated, a copy of the grievance and the written responses to the grievance, and stipulated facts that are not in contention.

Then, the arbitrator will ask the parties whether they have agreed to the wording of the issue to be addressed. If the parties cannot agree on the wording of the issue, they may request that the arbitrator frame the issue after hearing the evidence presented at the hearing. The issue is usually written in a one-sentence question to be answered by the arbitrator's award.[21] In a discharge case, the issue would typically be: "Did the Company terminate Betty Brooks for just cause? If not, what is the remedy?" In a typical non-discipline case, the issue would be: "Did the Company violate the Agreement when it promoted the least senior qualified employee? If so, what is the remedy?"

The major part of the hearing is devoted to the presentation of (1) union exhibits, management exhibits, and jointly agreed-on exhibits (such as the collective-bargaining agreement and the employee's written grievance); (2) the opening statements in which each party's spokesperson states what he or she plans to prove and highlights the major issues and background of the case; (3) union and management witnesses for testimony and cross-examination and related evidence to support union and management contentions (such as pictures of a job site, warning letters, performance ratings, and so on); and (4) summaries and closing statements by the union and management representatives. In 38 percent of cases, the parties agree to have a transcript of the hearing in order to have a written record of it. This written record may be desired for the convenience of the parties, for use in an appeal, and in the event the grievant has filed an EEO charge.

One or both parties may file a written posthearing brief after the hearing. The posthearing brief is actually a written summation of (1) the facts of the case, (2) the relevant contract language, (3) the arguments to support a position, (4) counterarguments to the opposing party's position, and (5) the requested decision from the arbitrator. The FMCS reports that in 77 percent of cases, posthearing briefs are filed.[22] A written *posthearing brief* can be helpful when the arbitration case is very technical or complicated or includes statistical data that are difficult to explain in an oral argument.[23] In many cases, however, a posthearing brief is unnecessary if the parties have prepared and presented their cases well during the hearing.

This summary of arbitration proceedings does not do justice to the considerable effort and drama shown in preparing and presenting an arbitration case. The Labor Relations in Action feature gives some techniques for preparing for an arbitration hearing.

Mental effort, skill, and tensions are not eliminated once the hearing begins. Assume, for example, that you are a labor relations manager charged with proving an employee deserved discharge for smoking marijuana on company premises. Consider the following:

- How do you prove the employee actually smoked the marijuana when the evidence was destroyed and it is the employee's word against supervisory observations?

- Can the supervisor convince the arbitrator that he or she had sufficient training to recognize the shape and smell of the object in a dimly lit location?

LABOR RELATIONS IN ACTION
Preparation Techniques for the Arbitration Hearing

1. Study the original statement of the grievance and review its history through every step of the grievance machinery.
2. Review the collective-bargaining agreement. Often, clauses that at first glance seem to be unrelated to the grievance will be found to have some bearing on the arbitrator's decision.
3. Assemble all documents and papers you will need at the hearing. Make copies for the arbitrator, for the other party, and the witness. If some of the documents you need are in the possession of the other party, ask that they be brought to the arbitration. Request that the arbitrator subpoena relevant documents and witnesses if they are not made available voluntarily.
4. Interview all of your witnesses. Make certain they understand the theory of your case, as well as the importance of their own testimony. Run through the testimony several times. Rehearse the anticipated cross-examination.
5. Make a written summary of the testimony of each witness. This can be useful as a checklist at the hearing to ensure that nothing is overlooked.
6. Study the case from the other side's point of view. Be prepared to deal with opposing evidence and arguments.
7. Discuss your outline of the case with others in your organization. A fresh viewpoint will often disclose weak spots that you may have overlooked.
8. Read published awards on the issues that seem to be involved in your case. Although awards by other arbitrators on cases between other parties are not binding in your case, they may be persuasive. The American Arbitration Association has published thousands of labor arbitration awards in its monthly publications. Bureau of National Affairs and Commerce Clearing House also publishes arbitrator awards. Use these decisions as a research tool.

SOURCE: Robert Coulson, *Labor Arbitration—What You Need to Know*, 3d ed. (New York: American Arbitration Association, 1981), pp. 51–52.

- Will the grievant's testimony be strengthened or broken under cross-examination?

- How long can the supervisor remain calm under cross-examination without becoming upset?

- What if the arbitrator gives little weight to the circumstantial evidence presented by the company and a great deal of weight to the grievant's previous long and exemplary work record with the company?

- Will the union introduce a surprise contention or witness not previously discussed in the grievance proceedings (e.g., that the grievant's discharge was due to the racial bias of the supervisor or because of a long-running dispute between the employee and supervisor)?

Management and union representatives often enter arbitration hearings emotionally charged and uncertain. These representatives are usually skillful in establishing their respective positions to the arbitrator's satisfaction and damaging their opponents' case by exploiting the opponents' weaknesses and uncertainties. The arbitrator must also display many skills in keeping an orderly hearing while at the same time objectively understanding and recording all of the facts presented.

One arbitrator has noted the following paradox: The union and management officials own the arbitration hearing, but the arbitrator is in charge of it. Union and management officials wrote the labor agreement and they hired the arbitrator. Therefore, arbitrators should not treat the process as theirs, act like judges, be arrogant, or talk too much.

> *Let the parties do the talking, work out the problems. You will be surprised how many knotty issues will be resolved during the hearing if you just ask the other side to respond, and then ask the original side to add something, and so on. By the time they have killed off each other's contrariness, the problem has disappeared.*
>
> *Do not try to take their procedure away from them. Give it back whenever they try to abdicate or place the burden of procedure on you. For example, it is an old ploy for one party or the other to say, Mr. or Ms. Arbitrator, do you want us to put in some evidence on this subject? This can put you into a trap. If your answer is no, then it is your fault when they lose the case because you excluded crucial evidence. If you say yes, then you are implying that the subject is important. Tell them it is up to them. Remind them that this is an adversary proceeding to elicit information and that it is their obligation to select whatever information they think is important.*[24]

For example, many arbitrators have suggested that eliminating posthearing briefs represents a major way to reduce arbitration costs.[25] Yet, they also indicate that posthearing briefs are significant in analyzing the case or writing the decision, and it is up to the union and management officials to determine if and when briefs are used.

COMPARISON OF ARBITRATION AND JUDICIAL PROCEEDINGS

The arbitration proceedings share some similarities with judicial proceedings, but their differences are profound. Many arbitration hearings differ from courtroom proceedings in that testimony of witnesses is not always taken under oath and transcripts of the proceedings are not always taken. Arbitrators may subpoena witnesses at the request of one of the parties. This is particularly true if management requests the subpoena to protect bargaining unit employee witnesses whose testimony is used to support management's position. This way other employees realize the employee had to testify because he or she was under subpoena. Although arbitrators have the legal authority to subpoena witnesses and documents in only a few states, the arbitrator may make an adverse inference if the subpoena is not complied with.

For over half a century, the fact remains that unions and companies have universally agreed that arbitration in the labor-management settings has advantages over litigation. These advantages are highlighted in Exhibit 11.3. The most significant difference between arbitration and judicial proceedings is the arbitrator's reliance on **common law of the shop** principles in the resolution of disputes. Arbitrators, unlike judges, are selected by the parties to the dispute, and they are responsible for interpreting contract provisions that were negotiated and written by the parties to cover wages, hours, and conditions of employment for an identified group of employees. Each of the over 150,000 separate labor agreements is different even though the subjects are similar. Judges are responsible for interpreting laws that are enacted by state and federal legislatures and that cover those individuals identified in the specific law.

Thus, the arbitrator's major responsibility is to resolve a dispute in a manner that the parties can live with. Unlike judicial decisions in lower courts, the arbitrator's decision is usually final and not subject to further appeals. Consequently, arbitrators must be concerned with the subsequent effects of their decisions on union–management relationships. A judge has no such allegiance to the

Exhibit 11.3

Advantages of Labor
Arbitration over Litigation

1. The parties themselves can potentially save money and time because there are fewer legal procedures, less discovery, and fewer appeals. Also, the parties are able to select the arbitrator and set up the hearing instead of waiting for the court to schedule a hearing. The parties can also require a decision by the arbitrator in 30 to 60 days.

2. Parties select an arbitrator who has expertise in labor–management relations as opposed to a judge assigned to the case who may or may not have any experience in labor–management relations.

3. Arbitration is a system of **self-government** in which the parties design the rules and procedures: how the arbitrator is selected, how many arbitrators, the authority of the arbitrator, and the like.

4. The parties negotiate and agree to the terms of their collective-bargaining agreement as opposed to a law enacted by a legislative body.

5. Labor arbitration is a private process between the union and the company as opposed to a public tribunal with a public record; the arbitrator's decision may be published only with the consent of both parties.

SOURCE: Adapted from *Elkouri & Elkouri How Arbitration Works*, 5th ed., eds. Marlin M. Volz and Edward P. Goggin (Washington, D.C. Bureau of National Affairs, 1985), pp. 10–15.

particular parties, the major responsibility being adhering to the statute in question, to established courtroom and legal procedures, and to precedent resulting from other applicable cases.

The common law of the shop often narrows the scope of arbitral decision making to the labor agreement language, intent of the parties, and past practices of the union and management officials at a particular industrial facility. The arbitrator uses these elements to convey to the union and management participants that their grievance is being resolved in terms of shop floor realities.

The distinction between judicial reasoning and common law of the shop principles can be shown through the following example. Assume that an employee has been discharged at Company A for drinking alcohol on the job. After an arbitral decision upholding the discharge has been reached, an employee at Company B is also discharged for drinking alcohol on the job. Strict adherence to judicial principles would uphold the second employee's discharge for drinking on the job. More specifically, the judicial principle of *stare decisis* (letting the decision at Company A stand in Company B's situation) would probably disregard the differences in work environments of the two companies.

However, the common law of the shop principles governing arbitration could lead the arbitrator to render a different decision at Company B than that reached at Company A. For example, supervisors at Company B may have been condoning this behavior, and other employees at this company may have been caught drinking on the job without being discharged for the infraction. Consequently, the arbitrator recognizes the two companies are independent with potentially unique circumstances and therefore deserve mutually exclusive decisions.

Evidence in Arbitration Versus in Judicial Proceedings

It is also important to note that arbitrators are much more liberal than the courts in the types of evidence permitted at the hearing. For example, lie detector tests (polygraphs) have been allowed by some arbitrators under certain conditions (having the administrator of the polygraph present for cross-examination), although their use and weight in the arbitrator's decision remains controversial.[26] Usually, arbitrators give this evidence little weight unless the obtained information is corroborated by supporting evidence. The rationale for liberal admission of evidence is that the parties are seeking a solution to their perceived unique problem. In addition, some arbitrators maintain that arbitration performs a therapeutic function, that the parties are entitled to air their grievances regardless of the eventual decision. Arbitrators may allow aggrieved employees to digress from the pertinent subject or "tell it like it is" in front of higher-level union and management officials to serve this function.

Occasionally, new evidence is introduced by one or both parties in the arbitration hearing. The arbitrator may accept or reject this new evidence, depending on the weight attached to the following, and sometimes conflicting, considerations: (1) the arbitrator's desire to learn all of the pertinent facts surrounding the grievance, (2) the need to protect the integrity of the prearbitral grievance machinery, and (3) general concepts of fairness.[27] Because union and management officials and their designated arbitration panels are entitled to receive all evidence presented at the hearing, the arbitrator will offer the opposing party additional time to review and respond to new evidence.

Offers of compromise settlements before the hearing are not accepted as evidence by arbitrators. For example, management officials with no major weakness in their original position might compromise their third-step discharge decision before arbitration by offering the grievant reinstatement with no back pay. A union could potentially use this evidence to indicate to the arbitrator that management admitted being wrong by revising its original decision. Since arbitrators maintain that the parties should make every effort to resolve their disputes internally instead of going to arbitration, an offer of settlement between the parties is viewed by the arbitrator as a genuine attempt to accommodate differences and save costs of going to arbitration, not an admission of guilt.

Other types of evidence are subject to varying arbitral consideration. Hearsay (second-hand) testimony might be allowed[28]; For example, Joe S. was told by Mary B. that he saw Jim M. stealing hammers and nails from the Company supply room. Hearsay evidence is typically given little or no weight unless it is corroborated by other credible testimony.

Arbitrators also vary in the weight they give to medical evidence presented in a grievance. Consider, for example, an employee who has her doctor testify that her previous back injury does not disqualify her from her present job. Management uses its doctor to counter the testimony, and the arbitrator now has to decide which doctor's testimony, if either, should be given the most weight. Exhibit 11.4 provides the

	1975 Study	1987 Study
1. Use specialist over nonspecialist	NA	77 (26%)
2. Use report that indicates most intensive examination	90 (51%)	133 (45%)
3. Use report that indicates most intimate knowledge of work performed	34 (19%)	79 (27%)
4. No response	53 (30%)	7 (2%)

SOURCE: Daniel F. Jennings and A. Dale Allen, Jr., "Arbitration and Medical Evidence: A Longitudinal Analysis," *Labor Law Journal* (June 1994), p. 352. Reprinted by permission of Daniel F. Jennings.

Exhibit 11.4
Survey of Arbitrators' Consideration of Conflicting Medical Opinions

results of two studies of arbitrators' use of medical evidence. Arbitrators are now more likely to rely on specialists' opinions, possibly because of the increase in the number of specialists over the past 20 years. However, these and other statistical changes might be more attributable to the arbitrators who answered the survey and the unique cases they were considering. Arbitrators' considerations of conflicting medical opinions can be further complicated by offsetting response categories. For example, how would an arbitrator who responded positively to the first two situations in Exhibit 11.3 handle the testimony of a nonspecialist who gave the most extensive examination?

THE ARBITRATOR'S DECISION

After the arbitration hearing, the arbitrator will render a decision (usually within 30 to 60 days). There are different ways in which arbitrators approach writing a labor arbitration decision. One is the "classic" approach which includes the following:

1. Names of union and management representatives involved in the case, along with others who gave testimony (e.g., employees or expert witnesses)
2. A statement of the issue(s)
3. A statement of the facts surrounding the grievance
4. Pertinent provisions of the labor agreement
5. A summary of the union and management positions
6. An analysis of the evidence and arguments in relation to the contract language
7. The arbitrator's decision (grievance upheld, grievance denied, or a decision between union and management positions)

Another common approach is a "narrative story-telling" approach wherein the arbitrator follows the sequence of events and the arbitrator explains what happened in "the story" and what should have happened (the arbitrator's decision). As one labor arbitrator said,

> Words are readily available to convey simple ideas. But transforming more complex ideas into persuasive written text is quite another level of achievement. This requires the arbitrator to use the exact words in a precise order—thus creating a unique expression, one that is inapplicable to any other situation, and exemplifies the wonder and diversity of the English language.[29]

Few prospective guidelines govern the form and content of the arbitrator's decision. However, the arbitrator should demonstrate through the decision a thorough understanding of all the facts and contentions raised in the arbitration hearing. Although arbitrators should address each argument and the evidence presented by both parties, some arbitrators address their decisions to the losing party because the winners do not have to be convinced they are right.

The necessity of the arbitrator's opinion has been the subject of considerable controversy. Some union and management officials basically look only at the arbitrator's final decision to see who "won" or "lost." Others read the decision to obtain principles and guidelines for future actions and to assess the arbitrator's interpretative abilities.

Controversy notwithstanding, the decision should tell the parties how the dispute was resolved and why. "Ideally, an opinion convinces the losing party that its arguments were heard, that the system used to decide the case is a fair one, and that the result makes sense."[30] An arbitrator's decision should explain the relative weight given to the parties' evidence and contentions and should indicate in clear language the benefits to which the parties are entitled and the obligations that are imposed on them. Thus, the arbitrator's decision should *educate* the parties (including other union and management officials, who often select an arbitrator after researching his or her published decisions) within the context of the common law of the shop and established arbitration principles.

In some cases, the arbitrator's analysis can be even more important than the decision. Assume, for example, the union grieves management's assignment of work normally performed in Job Classification A, loading trucks on Saturday, to an employee in Job Classification B, a laborer. Furthermore, the union seeks a remedy of eight hours at overtime rate of pay for the appropriate employee in Job Classification A, the senior employee in the shipping department, on the reasoning that the company's violation of the contract had deprived a Classification A employee of the overtime opportunity. However, the arbitrator denies the grievance and stresses the following in his opinion: "The various job classifications are for pay purposes only and do not restrict management's prerogative to assign work across different job classifications." This statement significantly harms the union in related matters, particularly if the language was not expressly stated in the labor agreement. Now the union will have a difficult time in grieving any work assignment controversy, even though the above decision pertained to one specific situation. Then, the union will attempt to change the contract language on work assignments in the next negotiations.

In other situations the arbitrator's gratuitous advice in the decision may harm one or both of the parties. There is often a thin line between advising management and union practitioners on more effective and humane ways to run the operation and arbitrating the grievance solely on the merits of the case. The latter approach does not advise but merely determines whether management's action was justified under the terms of the labor agreement and applicable *past practice* (which will be discussed later in this chapter).

Decision-Making Guidelines Used by Arbitrators

The arbitration decision is a deliberative process that requires on average about 2.4 days of the arbitrator's time to study the evidence and prepare a written decision.[31] The arbitrator's decision is particularly important to the parties because nearly all labor arbitration decisions issued in the private sector are final and binding. In fact, less than one percent of the arbitration decisions are appealed to the courts. Of those decisions that are appealed, less than one-third are overturned by the courts. Thus, it appears that the lower courts are complying with the U.S. Supreme Court's guidance that the lower courts should refrain from reviewing the merits of arbitrators' rulings and should overturn an arbitrator's decision only when the arbitrator's decision is not based on the "essence" of the collective-bargaining agreement.[32]

Although arbitrators do not follow precise or identical methods in making decisions, one study indicated that individual arbitrators have been consistent in the importance they assign to various decision-making criteria over the years.[33] The following generally accepted guidelines have been developed and serve as focal points subject to interpretation, consideration, and application by arbitrators in resolving grievances.

Burden of Proof, Witness Credibility, and Cross-Examination

When the union files a grievance claiming that management violated the spirit or letter of the labor agreement, the union is the charging party and has the burden of proof in convincing the arbitrator that management acted incorrectly. A major exception occurs in employee discipline and discharge cases, in which management is the charging party and has the burden of proof in establishing that its actions were correct.

The burden of proof is typically approached through evidence (discussed earlier in this chapter) and testimony from credible witnesses. Witness credibility is often assessed through rather subjective behaviors, such as talking softly or hesitantly, looking downward, or giving long, evasive answers to questions. The testimony is also subjected to cross-examination by the other party, who attempts to establish that the witness is inconsistent or unfamiliar with the facts or has bias or some other self-serving motive behind his or her testimony. A cross-examiner must avoid a major potential problem: namely, reinforcing the witness's testimony. This avoidance is easier said than done, as evidenced in Exhibit 11.5, which illustrates incorrect cross-examination after two direct questions.

Exhibit 11.5

Transcript from an Arbitration Hearing Reflecting Poor Cross-Examination

(Direct questions of employee witness by a union spokesperson)

Q: How did your supervisor sexually harass you?
A: He mooned me.
Q: Describe the circumstances to the Arbitrator.
A: I was working overtime and as far as I knew we were the only ones left in the laundry. As I was counting the inventory, the door to a broom closet opened, and there was this man's bare butt sticking out at me with his pants down around his ankles.

(Subsequent cross-examination of employee witness by a management spokesperson)

Q: Was the area near the broom closet well lighted?
A: No, it was rather dim.
Q: Was the broom closet well lit?
A: No, the light in the closet wasn't even lit.
Q: Was there a mirror that you could clearly see the face of the man?
A: No, I never saw his face when it happened. He stepped back into the closet, and I went and punched out right away.
Q: (Triumphantly) How then can you be sure that the bare fanny belonged to your supervisor?
A: Because of the tattoo.
Q: I've come this far so I might as well ask: what is the significance of the tattoo?
A: Well he was always bragging to us women about his tattoo, describing it and offering to show it to us. Of course, none of us ever took him up on it but there it was—just as he had pictured it. (Whereupon the grievant proceeded to describe in some detail the tattoo that had been so prominently displayed.)

SOURCE: John J. Flagler, "A Few Modest Proposals for Improving Conduct of the Hearing," in Gladys W. Gruenberg, ed., *Arbitration 1990: New Perspectives on Old Issues, Proceedings of the Forty-third Annual Meeting*, National Academy of Arbitrators (Washington, D.C.: Bureau of National Affairs, Inc., 1991), p. 55.

As noted earlier, participants' general characteristics (e.g., age and gender of the grievant or arbitrator) do not have a strong correlation to an arbitrator's decision. Arbitrators are, however, influenced by witnesses' credibility, which includes perceived mental attitudes of the grievance participants. A rambling, disjointed presentation by a witness, a union or management representative, or a grievant who comes across as insolent or sneaky will likely receive a strong, negative arbitral evaluation that might not be offset by other decision-making criteria.[34]

Clear and Unambiguous Language

One of the fundamental rules in labor arbitration is that, when the contract language is clear and unambiguous, the arbitrator must apply the language as it is written. The problem with this rule is that, if the parties have appealed to arbitration, one or both do not believe the contract language is clear and unambiguous. As demonstrated in the following Labor Relations in Action feature that discusses payment for jury duty leave, the negotiators of the collective bargaining agreement did not anticipate the specific dispute which arose or they would have addressed the issue at the bargaining table. There is always great potential for differences in contract interpretation and there exist several reasons for each party to take the position that the contract language is ambiguous. One reason is that the parties may allow less than explicit language to be included in the collective bargaining agreement when they are close to reaching a final agreement and they are working under pressure of a deadline. The negotiators may agree to ambiguous contract language because that is the only language on which they can agree, they want to save the rest of the agreement, and they don't want to have a strike or lockout over an issue which may not be significant. A second reason may occur during negotiations when the negotiators chose ambiguous language to memorialize their understanding. Each employer and each union negotiator independently knows what he/she has agreed to, but did not express his/her understanding in clear and concise contract language. A third reason is that the negotiators may have carried on complex negotiations over a long period of time, perhaps several weeks, and simply forgot about inconsistencies in different provisions of the agreement which may address the same issue.[35]

Adherence to common law of the shop principles stresses that the major function of the arbitrator is the interpretation of the labor agreement's provisions. Indeed, many arbitrators adhere at least in part to the **parole evidence rule**, which in its classic form holds that evidence, oral or otherwise, should not be admitted for the purpose of varying or contradicting written language recorded in the labor agreement. Consider, for example, the following labor agreement provision: "Notice of a promotional opening shall be posted for five working days." Even though "five working days" is clearer than "five days," a dispute could arise if the contract specified "working days" and the Saturday in question was a regularly unscheduled day on which certain employees were called in for emergency overtime. One of the parties might successfully argue before the arbitrator that the term "working day" is clear and applies to days on which work is performed and that this precludes any evidence that Saturday was unscheduled and never contemplated as a working day. Rationale for this rule is that the parties have spent many hours in negotiating standardized employment conditions; thus, disregarding negotiated terms would damage stable labor-management relationships and communicate to the parties that there is little or no point in reducing contract terms to writing.

A problem remains when the labor agreement language is ambiguous, because it normally cannot prescribe all essential rules or guidelines for day-to-day

LABOR RELATIONS IN ACTION
Example of Contract Language Ambiguity

Contract Language: "Any employee who is required to serve on jury duty who is unavoidably detained from his/her assigned shift shall be paid for the shift in question."

Facts: Employer operates 24 hours, 7 days a week.

Employee is a 3rd shift operator who works from 10:30 P.M. to 6:30 A.M.

Employee is required to report for jury duty on Tuesday at 9:00 A.M.

Employee reports at the required time and serves jury duty until 5:00 P.M.

Employee did not report for Monday evening shift prior to jury duty and did not report to work for the Tuesday evening shift.

Company does not pay the employee for either shift; the employee files a grievance seeking pay for both shifts.

Arguments:

The Company argued that the employee could have served jury duty and still worked both shifts. As an alternative, employee could have missed one shift of work and been paid for this one shift. The employer argues that "unavoidably detained from the employee's assigned shift" requires the employee to work the shift prior to jury service and the shift after jury service unless the jury service conflicts with the latter shift. The employer contends that "unavoidably detained" means "something not in the employee's control." Therefore, when the employee was released from jury duty in time to travel to work, the employee had no option except to return to work. If the employee did not work, the employee does not get paid.

The Union argued that the Company's position is neither reasonable nor practical. The Union claimed that, when the negotiators of the collective bargaining agreement used the word "detained," they meant that an employee cannot cover both the assigned shifts and jury duty in a single day.

SOURCE: Adapted from John B. LaRocco, "Ambiguities in Labor Contracts: Where Do They Come From?" *Dispute Resolution Journal,* vol. 59, No. 1 (February–April 2004), pp. 38–41.

---

administration of labor relations. Also, many labor agreement terms, such as "reasonable," "make every effort," "minor repairs," and "maintain the work environment as safely as possible" might have resolved negotiation impasses but still pose interpretive problems in contract administration and arbitration.

Some contract provisions that appear clear on the surface can cause differences of opinion among union and management officials as well as arbitrators. Consider the following three examples and related questions.[36]

Example 1: "The company will provide required safety clothing." Does the company have to pay for safety clothing or merely make it available for employees to purchase?

Example 2: "An employee must work the scheduled day before and after the holiday to receive holiday pay." What happens when the employee works three hours the day before the holiday, goes home because of sickness, and works the full eight hours the day after the holiday?

Example 3: "Management will distribute overtime as equally as possible." Does a supervisor making overtime request calls to employees' homes stop making such calls until contact is made with an employee whose telephone is busy or goes unanswered? Has the company met its obligation if the supervisor calls, leaves a message on the senior employee's answering machine, and then offers overtime to the next senior employee?

Arbitrators prefer to approach the ambiguity problem initially in terms of the labor agreement and to construe ambiguous language or provisions of the labor agreement so as to be compatible with the language in other provisions of the agreement. Thus, the contract should be viewed as a whole, not in isolated parts, and any interpretation that would nullify another provision of the contract should be avoided. When ambiguity remains, the arbitrator must seek guidance from sources outside the language in the labor agreement.

Intent of the Parties

Another guideline, the **intent of the parties**, refers to what union and management officials had in mind when they (1) negotiated the labor agreement or (2) engaged in an action that resulted in a particular grievance. Intent is entirely subjective; however, arbitrators consider observable behavioral manifestations of the intent to determine what a reasonable person would conclude from that behavior. For example, consider the previously cited holiday pay situation. To demonstrate that it intended for holiday pay to be given only to those individuals who worked a full eight hours the day before and the day after the holiday, management might supply the arbitrator with notes on various proposals and counterproposals made during labor agreement negotiations to prove what they intended the contract language to mean. Arbitrators are strongly influenced by this evidence of intent because they are reluctant to award a benefit that could not be obtained at the bargaining table.

An example of an action's intent considered in a grievance might occur when a supervisor believes an employee has stolen some company property. The supervisor approaches the employee, stating the following:

> *You and I both know you were caught stealing. Therefore, you have two options. You can file a grievance which will be denied in arbitration and the discharge on your record will make it difficult for you to find a job elsewhere. Or you can sign this resignation slip, quit, and we won't tell any other companies about the stealing incident.*

The employee hastily signs the slip and leaves the company premises. However, the next day the employee returns and informs management that she wants to work because she never really quit. If the company refuses the employee's request and a grievance is filed, the arbitrator would have to determine the grievant's and management's intent. Observable behaviors of an employee's intent to quit are cleaning out the locker, saying good-bye to colleagues, and asking management for the wages earned for that week. An employee usually resigns only after giving the decision careful thought and consideration. Because none of these behaviors were operative in this case, the arbitrator might attempt to assess management's intent in this action. Possibly, the supervisor was simply trying to do the employee a favor by letting her off the hook. However, management may have given the employee the alternative of quitting to avoid subsequent arbitration of the discharge and the risk of the discharge decision being overturned. The latter intent is viewed by arbitrators as being a *constructive discharge*.

Under this principle, the arbitrator would view the termination of employment as being subject to the employee discipline provisions of the labor agreement. These provisions usually call for union representation and a written notice of the reasons for the termination at the time of the employee's discharge. Because these procedures were not followed, many arbitrators would reinstate the grievant with full back pay.

Past Practice

The principle of **past practice** refers to a specific and identical action that has been continually employed over a number of years to the recognition and acceptance of both parties.[37] This decision-making criterion demonstrates to the arbitrator how the parties have applied the labor agreement. Management is usually more concerned about past practice because it administers the labor agreement through various supervisory directives to the hourly employees. Because established contractual provisions place restrictions on managerial discretion, management attempts to avoid further reductions on supervisory decision making by pressing for a "zipper" clause to be included in the labor agreement, similar to the following:

> Article XXVIII: Other Agreements
> Section 2.   The parties do hereby terminate all prior agreements heretofore entered into between representatives of the company and the unions (including all past understandings, practices, and arbitration rulings) pertaining to rates of pay, hours of work, and conditions of employment other than those stipulated in this agreement between the parties.*
>
> *This provision on past practice was taken from Walter E. Baer, *Practice and Precedent in Labor Relations* (Lexington, Mass.: Lexington Books, 1972), p. 8.

This clause does not guarantee that management does not add to its contractual restrictions by repeatedly handling a situation in a similar manner. A continued managerial practice of unilaterally giving employees a Thanksgiving turkey might become a binding, implied term of the labor agreement. Furthermore, management will likely have to negotiate a labor agreement provision to the contrary (even if the current labor agreement is silent on the subject) if it wishes to discontinue the gift in subsequent years.

In addition to interpreting ambiguous language or resolving problems not covered in the agreement, on rare occasions, past practices may even alter clear and convincing contractual provisions. At one company, it had been a practice for many years to require clerks to perform cleanup operations at the end of their workday and to pay them no money for up to 10 minutes' work, 15 minutes straight time for 11 to 15 minutes' work, and time and one-half for work of more than 15 minutes in duration. There was clear contractual language specifying that work in excess of eight hours per day would be computed at time-and-one-half overtime premium. The union eventually filed a grievance stating that clear contractual language compelled overtime payment for any amount of daily work exceeding eight hours. However, the arbitrator maintained that past practice was more significant than the express terms of the labor agreement in this case.

> The written contract is, of course, the strongest kind of evidence of what the parties willed, intended, or agreed upon. An arbitrator will not ordinarily look beyond its unambiguous language. Where, however, as here, the parties have unmistakably demonstrated how they themselves have read and regarded the meaning and force of the language, and where the meaning varies from its normal intendment, the arbitrator should not, indeed, cannot close his eyes to this demonstration.[38]

Past practice, although influential, is not interpreted the same by all arbitrators. For example, it is very difficult to determine in a consistent fashion how long or how frequently an action must be continued before it becomes a binding past practice.

Sometimes the nature of the issue further complicates the past practice criterion. Consider a situation in which management wants to unilaterally change a "clear" past practice of employee smoking at work. Some arbitrators have indicated that management could not unilaterally change this past practice, particularly if no specified evidence was presented to show that smoking adversely affected efficiency or productivity. However, some arbitrators have let management establish a no-smoking rule, thereby disregarding past practice, for the following reasons[39]:

- Past practice pertains to employee benefits, not management's direction of the workforce, and smoking is not an employee benefit.

- The past practice of permitting employee smoking can be broken because this activity has now proven to be detrimental to employees' health.

Previous Labor Arbitration Decisions

Also used as guidelines are previous arbitration decisions when they could bolster either party's position in the arbitration case. Similarly, the arbitrator may cite these decisions to refute the parties' contentions or to illustrate the arbitral opinion. Arbitrators accord some weight to prior arbitration decisions issued at the same facility, particularly if the situation and contractual language are similar. Of course, few prior arbitration decisions meet these requirements because the parties would be extremely reluctant to arbitrate the same issue a second time, given the first arbitrator's decision.

Arbitrators are far less likely to be influenced by decisions concerning different labor agreements by different parties at other facilities because, as arbitrators, they recognize the common law uniqueness and autonomy of a particular operation. In fact, arbitrators might give little weight to the admission of prior arbitration decisions into a current arbitration hearing.

> *Unwillingness to present a case solely on its own merits may come to be interpreted as a sign of weakness. Also it may be considered that citation of prior arbitration awards indicates either a lack of confidence in the judgment of an arbitrator or a belief that he may be swayed by irrelevant considerations. An attempt to induce an arbitrator to follow some alleged precedent may come to be recognized as at least bad etiquette.*[40]

Numerous factors influence the success of the parties in arbitration cases, including the burden of proof, the types of issues, and legal representation. The evidence suggests that management prevails more often in contract interpretation cases, and unions win more often in disciplinary cases. Because the employer has the burden of proof in disciplinary and discharge cases and the union has the burden of proof in contract interpretation and application cases, apparently the party having the burden of proof does not prevail in most of the arbitration decisions. In addition, evidence indicates that legal representation has a positive influence on the outcome of the arbitrator's decision. Furthermore, research has discovered that certain unions prevail more often than other unions. These unions include the Ladies Garment Workers; the Retail and Wholesale Clerks; the American Federation of State, County, and Municipal Employees; and the Operating Engineers. Possible explanations include that the union's duty to fairly represent all bargaining unit employees and the democratic nature of unions in determining which cases to take to arbitration may cause some unions to take some grievances to arbitration when they have little chance of prevailing in the decision.[41]

CURRENT ISSUES AFFECTING ARBITRATION

Legal Jurisdiction

As previously noted, the *Steelworkers' Trilogy* and other judicial decisions clarified and enhanced arbitrators' roles in resolving employee grievances. Yet, arbitration decisions can sometimes involve various government agencies and the courts, which might be concerned with specific aspects of a grievance. Consider, for example, a case in which an African American union steward is discharged for insubordination. A grievance is filed and proceeds to arbitration under the terms of the labor agreement. However, the employee claims that the discharge was prompted by racial bias and the fact that he was a union steward as well. Conceivably, the discharge grievance could claim the attention of a number of persons—the arbitrator and officials from the Equal Employment Opportunity Commission (EEOC) and the National Labor Relations Board (NLRB). The problem involves untangling the various jurisdictional squabbles that could arise over this one grievance.

Labor Arbitration and the Equal Employment Opportunity Commission

The passage of the 1964 Civil Rights Act (amended by the Equal Employment Opportunity Act of 1972), subsequent judicial decisions, and the passage of the 1991 Civil Rights Act have emphasized that management's well-meant intentions are not sufficient to preclude a charge of racial discrimination. Indeed, in administering this aspect of public law, the EEOC holds that employers must actively devise and implement employment procedures that remove present and possible residual effects of past discrimination. Hiring, promotion, and discipline procedures may be carefully scrutinized by the EEOC to protect employees from arbitrary and discriminatory practices when and if a charge of employment discrimination is filed. In a unionized facility, arbitrators also often assume a related decision-making role, particularly in grievances protesting discipline of an employee. This situation poses at least two questions:

1. Should management, the union, and the employee turn to the arbitrator, the EEOC, or both in resolving a minority employee's grievance?

2. How do the courts and the EEOC view the arbitrator's decision in terms of Title VII of the 1964 Civil Rights Act?

The first question was answered by the Supreme Court in its 1974 *Alexander v. Gardner-Denver Company* decision. The Court contended that the arbitrator's expertise pertains to labor agreement interpretation and not to resolving federal civil rights laws. Moreover,

> The fact-finding process in arbitration usually is not equivalent to judicial fact-finding. The record of the arbitration proceedings is not as complete; the usual rules of evidence do not apply; and rights and procedures common to civil trials, such as discovery, compulsory process, cross-examination, and testimony under oath, are often severely limited or unavailable.[42]

Consequently, a minority employee is almost encouraged to pursue both the arbitration process and appropriate judicial procedures.

Some predicted that the *Gardner-Denver* decision would create havoc as every discrimination grievance lost in arbitration would be overturned by the appropriate government agency or the courts. Yet, research does not support this prediction. One study found that a grievance reviewed by the EEOC or related agencies only stood a one in six chance of being reversed. Also, the chances of a trial court overturning a discrimination grievance heard by an arbitrator are slim, 6.8 percent according to one study and ten percent according to another.[43] Apparently, the courts believe that arbitrators are adequately covering the legal considerations of discrimination in their decisions.

The Supreme Court's *Gilmer* decision, discussed later in this chapter, might enable arbitrators instead of the EEOC and the courts to resolve a discrimination grievance filed under the terms of a collective bargaining agreement. However, this has not yet happened. The EEOC, while encouraging use of alternative dispute-resolution techniques, including arbitration, to resolve discrimination claims, has not yet waived its involvement on the issue. Moreover, Congress, in the passage of the 1991 Civil Rights Act, reinforced *Gardner-Denver*'s rationale for judicial oversight in unionized settings.[44]

Labor Arbitration and the National Labor Relations Board

Perhaps the most frequent supplements to arbitral decisions have come from the NLRB because the grievant could have been discharged for reasons pertaining to provisions of the labor agreement that are similar to laws, such as engaging in union activities on the job or acting overly aggressive in the capacity of a union official. Section 10(a) of the National Labor Relations Act provides that the NLRB "is empowered...to prevent any person from engaging in any unfair labor practice (listed in Section 8) affecting commerce. This power shall not be affected by any other means of adjustment or prevention that has been or may be established by agreement, law, or otherwise."

Although it has the power, the NLRB does not ignore arbitration decisions covering unfair labor practice issues. In fact, the NLRB often withholds its jurisdictional determination and investigation pending the arbitrator's decision. In 1955, the NLRB's deferral to arbitration policy was formulated in the *Spielberg Manufacturing Company* case. In that case, the Board honored an arbitration award that denied reinstatement to certain employees guilty of strike misconduct. Resulting deferral guidelines stressed that the arbitration proceedings must be fair and regular, there must be adequate notice and representation, the arbitrator must address the issue of the alleged unfair labor practice, and all parties must agree to be bound by the arbitration decision.[45] However, the Board will disregard the arbitrator's award if it is ambiguous or if the Board obtains pertinent evidence which was not presented in the arbitration proceeding.

The NLRB's deferral to arbitration policy was enhanced in the *Collyer* case, in which the NLRB administrative law judge found that the company had committed an unfair labor practice when it made certain unilateral changes in wages and working conditions.[46] The company maintained that the issues should be resolved through existing arbitration proceedings instead of the NLRB. The Board in essence agreed with the company's position. While reserving the right to investigate the merits of the issue, the Board maintained the following:

1. Related disputes can be better resolved through the special skills and experiences of the arbitrators.

2. The objectives of the National Labor Relations Act, industrial peace and stability, can be significantly realized through adherence to arbitration procedures established in the labor agreement.

Under *Collyer*, the employee was obligated to use the arbitration procedure before the NLRB would review the merits of the employee's unfair labor practice case.[47]

The NLRB's subsequent *Olin Corporation* and *United Technologies* decisions established new guidelines that make it even more likely that the NLRB will defer to arbitration decisions. Under *Olin*, the unfair labor practice does not have to be specifically considered in the arbitration hearing. The NLRB will still defer to an arbitrator's award "if the contractual and unfair labor practice issues were factually parallel and the facts relevant to resolving the unfair labor practice were presented generally to the arbitrator."[48]

Under this deferral policy, there is potential for abuse by either the union or the company. The arbitrator makes his or her decision based on the facts that the parties voluntarily choose to present at the arbitration hearing. Either of the parties could purposely withhold evidence and deny the arbitrator the full record for the purposes of undermining the NLRB's deferral to the arbitrator's decision. Such an incomplete record would preserve for one of the parties a "second bite at the apple," and the arbitrator would be hard pressed to produce a decision based on the record equivalent to the kind of record developed at an NLRB hearing.[49]

One research effort found that only about half of the arbitrators cited related external law in their decisions when at least one of the parties had filed an unfair labor practice charge with the NLRB. It also found that most of these arbitrators engaged in only brief consideration of relevant external law. The study urged that, at a minimum, arbitrators and union and management officials should be aware that they may provide the grievant his or her only opportunity to litigate a statutory claim; therefore, an explicit, informed choice should be made on "whether to vote, argue, discuss, and explore statutory issues in the arbitration forum, or to reject the discussion of such issues as inappropriate to the arbitration process."[50]

In summary, the Supreme Court has recognized the ability of arbitrators to interpret the labor agreement provisions and has even encouraged parties to arbitrate the issue before proceeding to the NLRB. However, this encouragement is not given to the same extent in disputes arising under Title VII of the Civil Rights Act.

Labor Arbitration, the Courts, and Public Policy: The *Misco* Decision

Federal courts can occasionally become involved when union or management officials request consideration of arbitration matters, particularly when a case heard by an arbitrator involves public policy considerations. The Supreme Court approached this situation in its *Misco* decision. Misco fired an employee who operated a "slitter-rewinder," which cuts rolling coils of paper, for allegedly smoking marijuana on company property. The grievant was arrested in his car in the company's parking lot. Police found a lit marijuana cigarette in the front ashtray of the car, and a subsequent police search of the car revealed marijuana residue.

The arbitrator reinstated the grievant because the evidence did not establish that the grievant smoked or even possessed marijuana on the company's premises. The arbitrator noted the grievant had been in the backseat of the car. The arbitrator also refused to consider the police report as evidence and ruled that the case must be limited to what the employer knew at the time of the firing. Management appealed the arbitrator's decision to the courts, claiming that bringing the employee back would violate public policy—operating dangerous equipment under the influence of drugs.

In *Misco*, the Court restated a principle established in an earlier decision *(W.R. Grace)*. It said that a "court may not enforce a collective bargaining agreement that is contrary to public policy." However, the Court noted that the public policy must be *"explicit," "well defined* and *dominant,"* and *"ascertained by reference to the laws and legal precedents and not from general considerations of supposed public interests."* The Supreme Court upheld the arbitrator's decision because none of these prerequisites were examined by the lower courts and would not likely be found in this situation.[51]

Misco therefore reinforces the wide latitude given to arbitrators' decision-making authority by the *Steelworkers' Trilogy.* It will probably reduce the number of instances in which the courts "second-guess" the arbitrator's award on public policy grounds. However, the public policy exception, although made narrow by *Misco*, still exists. An employer does not have to honor an arbitration decision that would require a violation of law (e.g., reinstating a bus driver who lacks a driver's license).[52]

Sexual harassment represents a controversial public policy issue that has been subsequently interpreted by arbitrators and judicial officials. The courts can have very different interpretations of this situation. For example, one federal district court vacated an arbitrator's award that reinstated an employee who allegedly harassed a female customer. The judge found that the arbitrator's decision contained some "disturbing comments" that evidenced bias in favor of the employee and insensitivity toward the customer-accuser. For example, the arbitrator noted that the employee was married and had children, whereas the customer weighed 225 pounds, "was unattractive and frustrated," and possibly fabricated the incident to attract her mother's caring attention. The judge ordered the case to be heard by a new arbitrator.[53]

Another federal court refused to set aside an arbitration decision, which reinstated an employee who, during a phone conversation, put down the receiver, approached a co-worker from behind, and grabbed her breasts. He then picked up the phone and said, "Yup, they're real." The court commented, "While we do not condone (the employee's) behavior, it was within the purview of the collective bargaining agreement and public policy for the arbitrator to order his reinstatement."[54]

Similar judicial rationale was used in the case of a trading-room secretary at a California brokerage firm. The secretary's boss admitted to calling her a "hooker" and a "bitch" and placing at least one condom on her desk. She filed a sexual harassment suit and was then told to submit her charge to an arbitration panel, which was mandated by the industry. The panel dismissed her charge, agreeing with the defendant that "[i]t's just the way that it is in every trading room."[55]

Appraising Labor Arbitration's Effectiveness

Although the courts have praised the effectiveness of arbitration, some critical assessments have come from participants—union and management officials and even some arbitrators (see Labor Relations in Action box for some related insights).

Arbitrators seldom, if ever, know why they were not chosen for a subsequent grievance. Little information is available concerning why the parties continually return to some arbitrators but not to others. Exhibit 11.6 approaches this void by grouping criticisms that several union and management practitioners have leveled at arbitrators. These criticisms apply to two general areas: arbitrators' capabilities and ethics, and the potential procedural problems in the arbitration process.

LABOR RELATIONS IN ACTION
Things They Never Told Me before I Became an Arbitrator

- The difficulty of setting up a hearing date when union and company representatives have such busy schedules.
- The ease of reading finished cases and the difficulty of writing one from scratch.
- The need to know about admission of evidence and reasons for sustaining and overruling objections at a hearing and making quick decisions about them.
- How physically tiring it is to fly or drive to some of the hearing sites.
- How unglamorous travel and hotels can be when all airports look alike and you are not even sure where you are.
- How mature and conscientious some parties can be in trying to do "what is right," while some parties enter the hearing armed for combat and confrontation.
- How much money, time, and effort could be saved if the parties prepared better and attempted to resolve their differences before arbitration.
- The role of the cancellation fee in making sure the parties are going forth to arbitration. (If there is no cost of canceling, one of the parties can abuse the arbitration process by canceling at a late date.)
- How one party will hold out for a compromise settlement until right before the hearing. When no settlement is forthcoming and their case is weak, the party will drop the grievance.
- How important the fee is to the parties—it cannot be too low because the parties think the arbitrator is not good enough; it cannot be too high because the arbitrator is priced out of a job.

SOURCE: From an experienced, somewhat weary arbitrator who enjoys relaxing in anonymity.

Exhibit 11.6

Summary of Criticisms Union and Management Practitioners Have toward Arbitrators

1. Fails to treat all parties with respect (e.g., has offensive personal traits, tends to apply his or her feelings of "fairness" or "justice" as opposed to applying the parties' intent, regularly exceeds his or her authority).

2. Cannot control the hearing properly (e.g., cannot rule on objections, is too legalistic or not legalistic enough, cannot stop gratuitous hostile exchanges or rambling or redundant testimony).

3. Awards are either too brief or too long, unclear, take a long time, emphasize compromise, evidence poor reasoning or writing skills, or fail to give parties direction on language issues.

4. Either too much experience with management or the union or insufficient experience with labor relations as a neutral or with the jobs and industry in question.

5. Decides cases on grounds other than those argued (e.g., fails to consider precedents, is too academic, fails to pay sufficient attention at hearing, reviews evidence not presented in hearing, discusses cases with uninvolved parties before decision being issued, does not address all facts or issues).

6. Too expensive (e.g., generally unavailable in a reasonable time frame, thereby increasing potential back-pay liability; cancellation policy is unreasonable).

SOURCE: Adapted from Thomas L. Watkins, "Assessing Arbitrator Competence: A Preliminary Regional Survey," *Arbitration Journal* 47 (June 1992), p. 43.

Arbitrators' Capabilities and Ethics

Some contend arbitrators might compromise their decisions to minimize or avoid displeasure from one or both of the parties or even to ensure reemployment in future arbitration cases. The following are examples of compromise decisions that might be used to appease both sides.[56]

- Reinstating a discharged grievant without any back pay awarded

- Changing the 50–50 outcome assessment of one case to 51–49 in favor of the party who had lost the other three cases heard at the hearing

In some instances, union and management representatives believe that the arbitrator "owes them one" because of their support (financial and otherwise). One arbitrator, who expressed surprise to officials at being selected to replace another prominent arbitrator, was given the following reason why the previous arbitrator was fired:

> *I'll tell you why we fired him. The last case he had ended here at about 4:00. Mr. _____ expressed considerable concern since he had to make a plane for New York and was running late. I assured him that he would have no problem. I carried his bags to his car, drove in excess of all the speed limits, went through back roads, even proceeded through changing traffic lights. After a hectic ride and at considerable risk, I got him to the airport just in time to make the plane. I parked my car in a no parking zone. I even carried his bags to the gate. After all this, you know, that [deleted] ruled against me.*[57]

Yet other participants or students of arbitration maintain that the arbitrator's indebtedness to the parties is a necessary ingredient of dispute resolution. The arbitrator owes allegiance to both union and management, thereby providing a well-formulated decision. The ethics issue has been directly approached by three organizations: the National Academy of Arbitrators, the FMCS, and the AAA. These organizations have come up with the following guidelines:

- An arbitrator, deciding that he or she does not have the technical competence to deal with the issue under consideration, is expected to withdraw from the case. Issues commonly included in this category are incentive systems, job evaluation plans, and pension and insurance programs.

- An arbitrator is not to make an award public without the consent of the parties.

- Before an arbitrator's appointment, the parties should be made aware of the arbitrator's fees for the hearing, study time, travel time, postponement or cancellation, office overhead expenses, and any work of paid assistants.

- If either party requests the arbitrator to visit the workplace, the arbitrator should comply.

- An arbitrator should not consider a posthearing brief that has not been given to the other party.

- If the arbitrator knows any of the parties or has any private issue in the organization, he or she must make disclosure of any potential conflict of interest before the hearing.

Other criticisms of arbitration have focused on the quality of the arbitrator's decision. The arbitrator's written opinion and award dissatisfy the parties if they do not reflect the original expectations and understandings of one or both regarding the nature or scope of the grievance. However, some arbitral decisions reflect legal considerations as much or more than union and management concerns expressed at the hearing. This potential "overlawyering" problem of arbitration decisions might be due to the large amount of legislation at the local, state, and federal levels that might pertain to the grievance, or the preferences of union and management officials and possibly the arbitrator[58] to minimize subsequent judicial reviews by considering related laws at the hearing and in the decision.

Management and union representatives might also obtain poor arbitration awards under the *garbage in, garbage out* theory. Because the arbitrator's decision is based on the merits of the grievance, a sloppy grievance formulation and presentation might result in a relatively lackluster arbitral decision. Sometimes, union and management officials present an arbitrator with poorly conceived grievances that should have been resolved before going to arbitration. Such grievances are often prompted by political considerations—the union or management officials take the grievance to arbitration to show support for their union stewards or first-line supervisors, even though they know them to be wrong. Arbitration in this sense serves as a buck-passing device; the errant union steward or supervisor is apparently given support, but in reality, is provided an education through the arbitrator's decision.

One almost inescapable concern arises from the finality of the arbitrator's award. Although the Supreme Court has encouraged single-person resolution of an industrial dispute, opponents of this practice suggest that an arbitrator has more authority than a judge, whose decisions may be overturned through judicial appeal. Unfortunately, many problems would result if arbitration awards were subjected to an appeals procedure. Any such procedure would be time consuming and expensive. If the arbitrator's award were reversed by a second arbitrator in the appeals procedure, it would be impossible to determine which arbitrator wrote the "correct" decision. Also, the "arbitrator as judge of last resort" situation might beneficially place pressure on the arbitrator to produce high-quality decisions.

Procedural Problems

The two general categories of procedural problems are time delay and expense of the arbitration proceedings. The FMCS reports that the average length of time between the filing of a grievance and an arbitrator's award is 315 days.[59]

Delay in arbitration is a concern of union and company advocates, especially in discharge cases. The discharged employee is likely to be unemployed after the discharge and faces an uncertain future. The employer probably has to fill the vacant position and faces the possibility of back-pay liability. Because it is a universally accepted principle that discharge decisions should be based on the facts known at the time of the decision and the passage of time does not alter the facts of the case, the length of time since the discharge should not affect the arbitrator's decision. However, research of arbitrators' decisions in discharge cases reveals that the longer the delay between an employee's discharge and the arbitrator's decision, the less likely the grievant will be reinstated.[60]

Although delay is harmful to employees, to the arbitration process, and to union–management relationships, a number of reasons have been identified as causes for this delay:

- Shortage of acceptable arbitrators coupled with the reluctance of the parties to take a risk on a new or inexperienced arbitrator

- Prearbitration activities, such as the steps in the grievance procedure and accommodating the schedules of busy advocates and arbitrators for the hearing

- Time after the hearing, which includes waiting on the preparation of the transcript of the hearing and any posthearing submissions by the parties, such as posthearing briefs; time taken by the arbitrator to review the evidence and arguments and to prepare the written decision

Although discharge cases are handled more expeditiously than nondischarge cases at every stage of the process, except for arbitrator selection, the parties have the power to address the causes of delay and are capable of moving more quickly because it is in their mutual interests to do so.[61]

Another criticism directed at arbitrators is that they split their decisions in discharge cases; that is, they reinstate the grievant but without back pay. Split decisions are not uncommon in discipline and discharge cases because arbitrators generally exercise the right to modify a penalty when the penalty is found to be too severe based on the facts of the case. The arbitrator may conclude that the employee's misconduct warranted some penalty, but short of removal from the job. The parties themselves have the power to avoid penalty modification by the arbitrator simply by negotiating language that directs the arbitrator either to uphold the penalty imposed by management or to sustain the grievance and return the grievant to the job with back pay—no split decision. One study of such contract language in the telecommunication industry showed that the grievant was more often reinstated with full back pay than under the traditional contract language when the arbitrator is allowed to modify the penalty. Thus, if the arbitrator has no authority to modify the penalty, the arbitrator must be convinced that the penalty of removal is the appropriate penalty.[62]

Time delay is only one of several expenses associated with arbitration. The FMCS reports that arbitrators' average per diem rate of $860 when applied to the arbitrator's average hearing time (1.11 days), travel time (.46 days), and study time (2.40 days), plus average expenses ($335.00), resulted in an average charge of $3,940.00 for an arbitrated grievance.[63] Although most labor agreements provide for the sharing of arbitration expenses between union and management organizations, each party can incur additional expenses, such as the fees for the parties' attorneys, which usually exceed the arbitrator's fee; wage payments to plant personnel who take part in the proceedings; and stenographic transcription costs, if a record of the hearing is desired.

Arbitral fees have increased over the years, which is understandable in view of inflation. In many cases, however, management and union officials bring added expenses on themselves when the parties require the arbitrator to review transcripts of the hearing, prior arbitration awards, testimony of superfluous witnesses, and prehearing and posthearing briefs. The parties may also insist on expensive frills, such as renting a hotel suite for a neutral arbitration site, that do not materially affect the quality of a decision.

Expedited Arbitration Procedures. Some union and management officials have reduced expenses by expediting the arbitration procedures before, during, or after arbitration hearings. Prehearing suggestions include (1) appointing a panel of arbitrators for the length of the contract rather than working through a new list of arbitrators each time an arbitration is scheduled, and (2) appointing a permanent umpire for a specific amount of time (e.g., 1 year or the life of the agreement). Hearings may be expedited by substituting tape recordings for transcripts. Posthearing expedition includes (1) setting a deadline for the decision to be returned to the parties, (2) reducing or eliminating the number of references for the arbitrator to research, and (3) setting a maximum on the length of the decision or establishing the maximum amount to be paid for the decision ahead of the hearing.[64]

Other possibilities also exist for streamlining the arbitration process. For example, some grievances solely concern interpretations of the labor agreement. Unlike discipline cases, these grievances do not personally involve employee grievants and thus do not entail related therapeutic or political considerations. Perhaps, these grievances could be argued on paper without the necessity of a hearing and related expenses.[65]

The use of expedited or experimental approaches illustrates two fundamental issues concerning arbitration:

1. This process, although not perfect, appears to offer great advantages over alternative methods of grievance resolution, such as sudden strike activity.

2. Union and management officials created the arbitration process and are charged with controlling it in accordance with their jointly determined needs. They must monitor the process as well as their related actions and attitudes, to ensure a relatively inexpensive, efficient, and objective means of dispute resolution.

Employment Arbitration

Recently, employers have initiated and used **employment arbitration** in situations such as the following:

- Employment discrimination claims in union or nonunion firms (instead of using the courts)

- Employee grievances in nonunion firms (instead of using unilateral management decision making)

It was reported that 62 percent of large corporations had used employment arbitration at least once. Between 1997 and 2001, the number of employees who had signed employment arbitration contracts had grown from three million to six million.[66]

See the Labor Relations in Action box (on pg. 490) for a summary of how employment arbitration differs from arbitration found in labor agreements.

The use of arbitration to resolve employment discrimination suits was enhanced in 1991 by the Supreme Court in *Gilmer v. Interstate Johnson Lane Corp* (500 U.S. 20, 1991). A securities representative signed an employment application (Form U-4, which is common in the securities industry) in part agreeing to arbitrate any dispute, claim, or controversy with his employer that was required to be arbitrated under the employer's rules. After being terminated at age 62, Gilmer filed an age discrimination complaint with the EEOC and subsequently in federal court. The Supreme Court agreed with Gilmer's employer that arbitration, not the courts, was both the agreed-on and proper dispute resolution forum that did not counter the legislative history of the Age Discrimination in Employment Act.[67] A subsequent Supreme Court decision seemed to recognize arbitration as a proper resolution of other employment discrimination claims in the securities industry and possibly other industries as well.[68]

The Supreme Court's *Gilmer* decision appeared to be inconsistent with its previous decision in *Alexander v. Gardner-Denver Company*. Questions arose as to whether mandatory arbitration of civil rights claims could be required under a collective bargaining agreement and whether a union through the collective bargaining agreement could waive an employee's right to a jury trial under the civil rights statutes. The *Gilmer* decision did not involve union–management relations, and the employee (Gilmer) had signed a Form U-4 agreement (known as the Uniform Application for Securities Industry Registration or Transfer).

In the *Wright* decision in 1998, Ceasar Wright injured his right heel and back, sought permanent disability, and ultimately settled for $250,000. Three years later, he asked to be returned to work through the union hiring hall, and presented his doctor's approval. Wright worked for nine days for four different companies, and none complained about his performance. However, when the employers realized that Wright had already settled a claim for permanent disability, they informed the union that they would no longer accept Wright for employment because a person certified as permanently disabled was not qualified to perform longshore work under the collective bargaining agreement. The union asserted that the employers had misapplied the collective-bargaining agreement and suggested that the American with Disabilities Act (ADA) entitled Wright to return to work if he could perform the duties of the job. The union contended that refusal of employment to Wright by the companies violated the collective bargaining agreement. When Wright contacted the union, the union advised him to file a civil suit under ADA, and Wright did so.

As their defense, the companies asserted that Wright had not exhausted his remedies under the collective-bargaining agreement. The Fourth Circuit Court of Appeals concluded that the language of the general arbitration clause in the collective-bargaining agreement was sufficiently broad to encompass a statutory claim arising under ADA.[69] However, the U.S. Supreme Court disagreed and decided that the contract language did not "contain a clear and unmistakable waiver of the covered employees' rights to a judicial forum for federal claims of employment discrimination."[70] Therefore, Wright was allowed to proceed with his civil suit under ADA.

In a 2001 case, *Circuit City Stores v. Adams*, the U.S. Supreme Court reconfirmed its position that there was a strong federal policy that supported arbitration and ruled that the Federal Arbitration Act applied to all contracts of employment except those applicable to employees working in transportation. The Court stated that arbitration was a desirable and workable forum for resolving employment disputes, including those under federal discrimination laws. In this case, Adams had signed an employment application form to "settle any and all previously unasserted claims, disputes, or controversies arising out of or relating to my application or candidacy for employment..." (see Exhibit 11.7). Then, in 2002, the Court clarified the role of the Equal Employment Opportunity Commission (EEOC) in cases where an employee had been required as a condition of employment to sign an agreement to arbitrate all employment discrimination claims. The Court ruled that the EEOC was not bound by an arbitration agreement because the EEOC had not been a party to such agreement. Therefore, the EEOC may go to court on a worker's behalf even though the employee had previously been required to sign an agreement to arbitrate all employment discrimination claims.[71]

In 2002, the U.S. Supreme Court held in *EEOC v. Waffle House, Inc.*, (534 U. S. 754) that an employee's agreement to arbitrate did not preclude the EEOC from suing the employer on behalf of the employee in order to enforce the Equal Employment Opportunity Act. The EEOC may attempt to recover

LABOR RELATIONS IN ACTION

How Employment Arbitration Differs from Arbitration Found in Labor Agreements

1. **What are the conditions under which the arbitration system is devised?**

   If the arbitration system is established to avoid a union, then many acceptable, well-qualified arbitrators will refuse to serve. If the employer designs a system for the purpose of providing a fair and equitable mechanism for employees to resolve their grievances by an independent neutral party, qualified arbitrators will be willing to serve. Under a collective-bargaining agreement, the union and company have negotiated and designed the arbitration procedure that best fits their purposes. In other words, the parties design a system of self-governance for resolving conflicts. In employment arbitration, the arbitration procedure is designed unilaterally by the employer.

2. **What subjects will be covered under the employment arbitration system, and will employees be required to waive their statutory rights, such as employment discrimination on the basis of race, gender, age, national origin, disability, and so on?**

   If the employees are required to waive their statutory rights as a condition of employment, the arbitration decision may not stand a court review. Under a collective-bargaining agreement, arbitration involves contract interpretation and application of provisions negotiated and agreed to by the parties. Various federal agencies have different policies on deferral to arbitration.

3. **How are the arbitrators selected? How long are they retained?**

   If the arbitrators are selected only by the employer and serve at the pleasure of the employer, then a perception may persist that the arbitrator is loyal to the employer and can be terminated if a decision unfavorable toward the employer is rendered. Under a collective-bargaining agreement, the arbitrators are selected and retained by a procedure negotiated and agreed on by the union and company. To avoid problems and misperceptions, selections may be made through independent agencies such as the American Arbitration Association and the Federal Mediation and Conciliation Service.

4. **What are the employee's due process rights, if any?**

   Employment arbitration systems contain no guarantees of due process; however, under collective bargaining agreements, arbitrators recognize these important employee rights that include:

   - Right to counsel by a union representative
   - Right to face one's accusers
   - Right to information to prepare for the arbitration hearing
   - Right to notice of hearing
   - Right to a copy of written charges against employee

5. **Who pays the arbitrator?**

   Under employment arbitration procedures, the employer typically pays the arbitrator. The concern is

judicial-specific relief, which may include back pay, reinstatement, and/or monetary damages.[72]

One study showed that, since the *Circuit City* decision by the U.S. Supreme Court, lower courts have enforced the majority of contested arbitration

Exhibit 11.7

An Employment Application Form under Mandatory Employment Arbitration

> I agree that I will settle any and all previously unasserted claims, disputes, or controversies arising out of or relating to my application or candidacy for employment, employment, and/or cessation of employment with XYZ Company, exclusively by final and binding arbitration before a neutral arbitrator. By way of example only, such claims include claims under federal, state, and local statutory or common law, such as the Age Discrimination in Employment Act, Title VII of the Civil Rights Act of 1964, as amended, including the amendments of the Civil Rights Act of 1991, the American With Disabilities Act, the law of contracts and the law of tort.
>
> SOURCE: *Circuit City Stores, Inc. v. Adams*, 532 U.S. 105 (2001).

that the arbitrator might show loyalty to the party who pays the fee. Under most collective-bargaining agreements, the union and the company jointly decide the method by which the arbitrator will be paid. Usually, the two parties share the costs; however, on a few occasions, the union and company negotiate the method whereby the loser pays. To avoid the perception of bias in favor of the payer of the fee, one organization designed a system whereby each employee pays a monthly fee to support an arbitration system; the arbitrator, then, is paid jointly by the employer and from employee fees.

6. **How final is the arbitrator's decision?**
Under employment arbitration, the arbitrator's decision is final if the employer wants the decision to be final. Although overturning the arbitrator's decision would be bad policy unless fully justified, no legal basis exists for prohibiting the employer from taking such action. Under collective-bargaining agreements, the arbitrator's decision will stand in nearly all cases, except in those limited cases where the arbitrator's decision is inconsistent with public policy, the arbitrator is incompetent, or the arbitrator has personal ties with one of the parties.

7. **How are employees who file grievances protected?**
Under the employment arbitration system, employee protection survives as long as the employer allows the system to survive. Under the collective-bargaining agreement, employees who file grievances are protected under the grievance and arbitration procedure, which lasts as long as the collective-bargaining agreement lasts.

8. **What issues are arbitrated under the arbitration systems?**
Under the employment arbitration system, the employer decides the issues that may be grieved and arbitrated. Under the collective-bargaining agreement, the union and company jointly decide; this usually includes conflicts over interpretation and application of provisions of the collective-bargaining agreement.

9. **What authority do arbitrators have to grant remedies?**
Under employment arbitration, the employer determines the extent of the arbitrator's authority. However, when there are statutory issues involved, such as gender discrimination, sexual harassment charges, and so on, remedial authority may include awarding attorney fees, punitive and compensatory damages, interest on back pay, and so on—in other words, issues normally decided by a jury. Under a collective-bargaining agreement, back pay, reinstatement, and "make whole" remedies are common. Interest may be paid where the parties have agreed to such payments. In the federal sector, arbitrators have authority to award attorney fees and interest on back-pay awards.

agreements. However, lower courts still are willing to deny enforcement of arbitration agreements which the courts believe are unfair to employees.[73]

Arbitral Dilemma

The EEOC's policy is that mandatory arbitration systems imposed as a condition of employment were fundamentally inconsistent with U.S. civil rights laws. However, the EEOC is on record in support of alternative dispute resolution (ADR), which includes arbitration and mediation that resolves employment discrimination in a fair and credible manner if entered into voluntarily or *after* the dispute arises. In other words, the EEOC's position is that claimants have a legal right to decide whether to pursue a judicial forum or voluntarily choose to resolve their claim through arbitration.[74]

Where a union exists and when there is an overlap between the language in a collective bargaining agreement and provisions in a law, the question arises as to what the parties and the neutral arbitrator should do. The conclusions drawn after analyzing court cases are as follows:

1. When the contract language and provisions of the Labor Management Relations Act apply (covered in Chapter 3), the statutory and contractual issues should be addressed, the arbitrator must write the award to confirm that the statutory provisions were addressed, and the arbitrator's decision must not be repugnant to provisions of the statute.

2. When the collective-bargaining agreement does not address any statute, arbitrators should decide the case based on the merits of the case and the contract language, not the law.

3. When the collective-bargaining agreement contains principles found in the statute without any specific reference to the statute (e.g., there shall be no discrimination against employees), the principles incorporated in the statute may enter into the arbitrator's award.

4. When the statute is explicitly included in the collective-bargaining agreement (e.g., this agreement must comply with provisions of the ADA) and instructs the arbitrator to apply the statute, the arbitrator should render his or her decision consistent with the statute.[75]

Several studies have shown that the typical rank-and-file employee with only a job and a small amount of money at stake finds it difficult to obtain an attorney to accept an employment discrimination claim and take it to court. The time and effort for the attorney is not worth it to an experienced practitioner who is probably operating on a contingency fee arrangement. The attorney prefers a professional or managerial employee who has the potential for a large payoff. As a result, only 1 in 20 discrimination claimants actually secure an attorney as counsel.

These studies also reveal rather startling results in the event the employee plaintiffs with job discrimination claims are actually able to reach court. These employees do not fare as well in court as do employees who take their cases to arbitration. In fact, claimants who take their cases to arbitration have won 55 to 63 percent of the time, while less than 20 percent of the claimants have prevailed in court. While claimants may obtain larger recoveries from a jury in court than in arbitration, for the mass of employees without large financial claims, arbitration may be the superior option. As one legal expert concluded:

> It gets them back to work sooner, more often, with less cost, and without the psychological pain of court litigation.
>
> In cases where the union represents the employees, unions have not been convinced that they should agree with the employers in making arbitration of discrimination claims the exclusive means of resolving such discrimination claims. Because unions have political characteristics wherein officers must stand for elections and many claimants are not yet aware (or satisfied) that, despite the statistics, they may fare better in arbitration than in court, there has not been a movement toward unions showing an interest in representing the bargaining unit employees with employment discrimination claims in arbitration. Employers who prefer arbitration have a selling task to perform to the skeptical employees as well as the union representatives. The employers must convince employees and union representatives that they are pressing for arbitration, not because they believe they will win more often, but that, win or lose, arbitration is less costly, less time consuming, and less disruptive than court litigation.[76]

Critique of Mandatory Employment Arbitration. Supporters of mandatory employment arbitration argue that arbitration is less expensive and more informal than the court system. Supporters also point out that arbitrators are significantly more predictable than juries, who have potential for rendering extraordinary monetary verdicts. Employers like mandatory employment arbitration because arbitration is a private process, which means that the hearings are private and the arbitrator's decisions are not made a public record.

Researchers have found that, while the court system from the outside appears to be the fairest way to adjudicate alleged mistreatment by employers, in reality the court system does not serve employees well. Plaintiff lawyers take only five percent of employment discrimination complaints, only three percent of those accepted ever go to trial and result in a verdict, and federal courts of appeal reverse 44 percent of appealed cases which had been won by employees in lower court. In other words, mandatory employment arbitration, although favoring the employer, provides a mechanism for employees to "have their day in court" to tell their side.[77]

The most controversial element of employment arbitration is that it is mandated by the employer as a condition of employment at the time of hire or after employment, but before there is a dispute. Predispute employment arbitration confronts job applicants with the choice of agreeing to arbitration with a chance of being hired on a new job or confronts current employees with agreeing to arbitration in order to continue their employment. There typically is no bargaining, and the job applicant or the current employees are required to agree to arbitration on a "take-it-or-leave-it" basis.[78]

Walter Gershenfeld, former president of the National Academy of Arbitrators, pointed out several additional deficiencies of a typical employment arbitration: (1) Many employment arbitrators also serve as advocates in other cases. This means that there is a question of whether these employment arbitrators are truly neutral, a core ingredient of a fair and impartial arbitration. In traditional labor-management arbitration, the arbitrator must be neutral. (2) In discipline/discharge cases in employment arbitration, the employee has the burden of proof. In traditional labor-management arbitration, the employer has the burden of proof in discipline/discharge cases. In other words, the employer must prove that the employee is guilty of the charges held against him. (3) The grievant has limited rights to appeal the arbitrator's decision in traditional labor-management arbitration. The grievant must prove that the arbitrator's decision was in manifest disregard to the collective bargaining agreement, the law, or public policy. In employment arbitration, the grievant must go to arbitration; the grievant who claims employment discrimination may take the case to arbitration, administrative agencies, and the courts, simultaneously or sequentially. In other words, the grievant in employment arbitration has more than one "bite at the apple."[79]

Mandatory employment arbitration procedures have given rise to major criticisms. Exhibit 11.8 highlights some reasons that courts have concluded that these procedures are not fair.

The Court's Observation of Arbitral Deficiencies. Even the U.S. Supreme Court has observed possible deficiencies in the arbitration process:

- The lack of legal expertise of arbitrators to analyze complex statutes

- Due process limitations with respect to discovery, examination of witnesses, remedies, compiling an official record of the hearing, and so on

- Ineffective communication of the reasoning behind the arbitrator's decision

Exhibit 11.8

Guidelines to Procedural Fairness in Arbitrating Statutory Discrimination Claims

Parties knowingly and voluntarily agree to submit their claim to arbitration.

Arbitration agreement contains specific language with sufficient notice that signing the agreement represents an agreement to arbitrate all statutory employment discrimination claims (with inclusion of a representative list of employment discrimination statutes for illustrative purposes).

Pre-hearing consultation addresses formulation of issues, production of evidence, witnesses lists, discovery, and application of rules of evidence.

Due process procedures provide that the employee has a right of representation of his/her choosing, adequate discovery of access to all information relevant to the employee claim, arbitrator authority to subpoena relevant information upon a specific request by one of the parties, and a reasonably timely hearing.

Impartial and competent arbitrator possesses personal qualities of honesty and integrity, and discloses any prior association that might represent a potential conflict.

Joint selection of the arbitrator allows each party to have adequate information about the potential arbitrators' organizational associations, biographical data, published case decisions, copies of recent decisions, etc. to avoid the advantage to the "repeat player" in the arbitration process.

Written opinions and awards that would include the issues decided, the findings of facts, conclusions of law, materials supplied by the parties, and information such as relevant decisions of courts and administrative agencies, cited by the parties demonstrate the arbitrator's reasoning in reaching the decisions, the remedies sought, and the remedies decided.

Publication of the decisions with the consent of the prevailing party serve as a deterrent to future similar discriminatory acts.

Payment of the costs of arbitration is shared by the parties to ensure impartiality, and are based on the employee's ability to pay and the relevant necessity of incurred expenses for adequate presentation of the employee's case.

SOURCE: Roger Wolters and William H. Holley, Jr., "Arbitration of Statutory Employment Discrimination Claims in a Nonunion Environment: A Guide to Procedural Fairness," *Employee Responsibilities and Rights Journal* 12, no. 3 (2000), pp. 174–175.

As a result of criticism, court decisions, and the Due Process Protocol for arbitration and mediation of statutory claims designed by the Task Force on Alternative Dispute Resolution (representatives of the most influential employment law and arbitration organizations),[80] several principles that provide a guide to procedural fairness have emerged (see Exhibit 11.8).

One circuit court judge has already addressed one of the controversial issues under mandatory employment arbitration procedures: the payment of the arbitrator's fee. Chief Judge Harry T. Edwards, a distinguished scholar and a former labor arbitrator, addressed this issue in one of his decisions. Judge Edwards wrote that the judicial system is supported by government through taxes paid by citizens. Litigants do not pay judges who hear their cases, but private arbitrators do not work for free. Judge Edwards required the employer to pay the arbitrator's fee based on the fact that the employee had been forced by a condition of employment to give up his or her right to pursue his or her statutory claims in court. Therefore, Judge Edwards reasoned, a beneficiary of a federal statute (the claimant) would not have been required to pay a judge in a judicial forum and therefore should not be required to pay an arbitrator to decide the merits of his or her claim.[81]

Repeat Players. In the absence of a union, the employment arbitration process is usually skewed against employees, particularly those who are not represented. When an employer is a repeat participant in the arbitration process, the employer has a distinct advantage over employees who are not likely to be involved in arbitration more than once or twice in their lifetimes. First, if the employer selects the arbitrator and pays the arbitrator for his or her services, the arbitrator may feel the pressure to rule in favor of the employer in order to be selected in future cases. For all practical purposes, the employer and the arbitrator are the "repeat players." Second, in the selection of the arbitrator, even when both parties participate in the selection, unrepresented employees have little information on which to base their selection. Even when an employee has legal counsel, the attorney may or may not have access to useful information about the arbitrator. In comparison, nearly all international unions and the American Federation of Labor–Congress of Industrial Organizations (AFL-CIO) have research staffs who can obtain evaluative information about arbitrators that would be useful in selection. Third, "repeat player" employers have certain strategic advantages because they have an institutional memory. Employers can keep records about the disposition of prior cases of the arbitrator; the unrepresented employee has no comparable resource. Because the union has a continuous relationship with the employer through the collective bargaining agreement, the union gains an institutional memory and becomes a "repeat player" in the arbitration process.[82]

Supporters of mandatory employment arbitration have reported two research studies that respond to two criticisms, i.e. inadequate representation and the repeat player criticisms. In a study of 200 arbitration decisions in 35 states, the research showed that employment arbitration can be affordable, even to lower-income employees, and arbitrators rule in favor of the employee in nearly half of the cases. This study rebutted the findings of an earlier study of 321 plaintiff attorneys, which revealed that plaintiff's counsel would not take on an employment discrimination case unless the case involved $60,000 or more in provable damages. For a low-income employee, the standard of $60,000 of provable damages might be too difficult to reach. The researcher found that 32 percent of the low-income employees paid nothing for arbitration, 29 percent paid only their attorney fees (average of $6,776 per case for all 200 cases studied), 13 percent paid their share of the filing fee, hearing costs, and arbitrator's fee (average of $2,292 per case), and 26 percent paid all their attorney's fees and their share of the filing fee, the hearing costs, and the arbitrator's fee. It might be worth noting that a plaintiff's attorney typically accepts a case with a contingency fee of 35 percent (on average) plus out-of-pocket expenses. Thus, the general conclusion was that mandatory employment arbitration was not beyond the means of a low-income employee.

In response to the "repeat player effect," which leads to the "repeat arbitrator effect," supporters of mandatory employment arbitration believe the repeat player effect theory is based on the belief that a repeat player (the employer) chooses the same arbitrator in several arbitration cases and therefore builds a relationship with the arbitrator, causing the arbitrator to rule in the repeat player's (the employer) favor. The research found no support for this theory. In the 200 cases studied, there were only two cases involving a second meeting between the same arbitrator and employer. On the employee side, it may also be argued that attorneys for grievants may become repeat players as more plaintiff attorneys accept employment arbitration assignments and as the number of employment arbitration cases grow.[83]

Public Policy Implications for the Future

A Comparison of Decisions by Employment Arbitrators, Labor Arbitrators, and Jurors in Employment Termination Cases.

In a study of 225 employment arbitrators, 200 labor arbitrators, and 112 jurors from a federal district court, the arbitrators and former jurors were asked to participate in a fairly extensive decision-making exercise that included 32 different case scenarios where an employee was challenging termination. Exhibit 11.9 highlights some of the significant differences between employment arbitrators, labor arbitrators, and jurors. Employment arbitrators, who usually have a management background, are usually selected solely by the employer and are less likely to rule in favor of the terminated employee. The employee has the burden of proof, which means that the employee must prove there was a violation of a Company rule or policy that was written by the Company. In addition, the employment arbitrator is not likely to consider mitigating circumstances, such as long service with the Company, a good work record, and so on. Because the Employer pays the arbitrator to serve and is selected by the Employer, some critics of employment arbitration would say that the employment arbitrator has allegiance to the Employer.

In comparison, the burden of proof in labor arbitration rests with the employer in the general principle that "a person is innocent until proven guilty." Since the labor arbitrator is selected and paid by both parties, the labor arbitrator must have a reputation of neutrality or he or she will not be selected by both parties. In addition, the labor arbitrator may find an employee guilty of wrongdoing, but due to a good work record of considerable years, may reduce the penalty from a termination to a disciplinary suspension without pay. Since the burden of proof rests with the employer and a labor arbitrator considers mitigating circumstances, the employee is more likely to receive a favorable decision from the labor arbitrator.

Exhibit 11.9

Differences between Employment Arbitration, Labor Arbitration, and Jurors Involving an Employee Discharge

	Employment Arbitration	Labor Arbitration	Jurors
1. Burden of Proof	Employee	Employer	Employee
2. Acceptability	Employer selects	Union and Employer	None
3. Professional Background	Management more than likely	Neutral	Public service
4. Consider Mitigating Circumstances	Not likely	Yes	Yes
5. Decision	Less likely employee will receive a favorable decision	More likely to receive favorable decision when represented by a union	More likely to receive favorable decision than by an employment arbitration
6. Who pays the arbitrator	Usually the employer	Usually the union and employer pay equally	Taxpayers a small fee for jury duty and expenses

SOURCE: Ideas from Brian S. Klass, Douglas Mahony, and Hoyt N. Wheeler, "Decision-Making about Workplace Disputes: A Policy Capturing Study of Employment Arbitrators, Labor Arbitrators and Jurors," *Industrial Relations*, Vol. 45, No. 12 (2006): 68–95.

In between, in a jury trial, the employee has the burden to prove that the employer violated the employer's rules or policies. However, since jurors will consider mitigating circumstances, they are more likely to render a favorable decision for the employee than an employment arbitrator. Since jurors serve as a public service, they are not concerned about acceptability and receive only a small fee for their time and reimbursement for their expenses.[84]

Summary

The arbitration process was little used during the period from 1865 to World War II; however, during World War II, the National War Labor Board encouraged its widespread use. Although the increased reliance on arbitration continued after World War II, a major problem of enforcing the arbitrator's decision remained. Either party could refuse to abide by the arbitrator's decision, with uncertain consequences from the courts. This problem was initially approached in the *Lincoln Mills* decision, which provided a judicial avenue for enforcement, and the *Steelworkers' Trilogy*, three cases that established the superiority of the arbitration process over the courts in resolving industrial grievances. Subsequent Supreme Court decisions have indicated that termination of the labor agreement does not eliminate the possibility of arbitration, and injunctive relief might be granted when one party refuses to arbitrate according to grievance procedures established in the labor agreement.

Before the arbitration hearing, arbitrators must be selected on either an *ad hoc* or permanent basis. Each of these selection techniques has unique advantages depending on the particular circumstances. The same can be said of prehearing and posthearing briefs. Other elements of an arbitration hearing include the grievance issue, presentation of witnesses for testimony and cross-examination, and presentation of separate and joint exhibits.

The hearing scene is a dramatic one; union and management officials display their skills in attempting to convince the arbitrator that their positions are correct. The arbitration hearing shares many similarities with a judicial trial but differs in several ways. Perhaps the most significant difference is the arbitrator's reliance on the common law of the shop.

Arbitrators consider the relevant provisions of the labor agreement, the intent of the parties, past practice, and to a much lesser extent, prior arbitration awards in arriving at their decisions. Because arbitration procedures differ in some respects from those used in a courtroom, various jurisdictional disputes can occur over interpretations of contract provisions by arbitrators and the legal interpretation of federal policy. For example, a discharge case decided by the arbitrator could be subsequently considered by the Equal Employment Opportunity Commission or the National Labor Relations Board.

Some criticisms directed toward arbitration pertain to the arbitrator's capability and ethics and potential procedural problems in the arbitration process. Certain arbitral problems, such as expense, time lag, and excessive formality, may be due to labor and management preferences rather than any characteristics inherent in the arbitration process. Management and union officials could reduce some of these problems by using expedited arbitration, new arbitrators, and grievance mediation.

Employment arbitration, which is used primarily with employees not represented by unions, was discussed. With favorable rulings from the U.S. Supreme Court, a growing number of employers have implemented mandatory employment arbitration for new hires as well as current employees. This type of arbitration requires an employee as a condition of employment to sign an agreement that requires all future employment disputes be resolved in arbitration. Views of supporters and critics of mandatory employment arbitration were presented. Attempts to rectify these deficiencies, such as guides to procedural fairness, were presented. Anticipated problems for the future of mandatory employment arbitration were also addressed and a comparison of decisions of employment arbitrators, labor arbitrators, and jurors were provided.

Key Terms

National War Labor Board (NWLB), p. 459
Steelworkers' Trilogy, p. 460
Permanent arbitrator, p. 463

Ad hoc arbitrator, p. 464
Arbitration hearing, p. 465
Common law of the shop, p. 469
Self-government, p. 470

Parole evidence rule, p. 475
Intent of the parties, p. 477
Past practice, p. 477
Employment arbitration, p. 488

Discussion Questions

1. How did World War II and the National War Labor Board greatly expand the use of arbitration?

2. The *Steelworkers' Trilogy* greatly enhanced the arbitrator's authority when compared with previous years, yet it did not give the arbitrator final jurisdiction over certain issues. Discuss the preceding statement in terms of the specific features of these judicial decisions; also consider current jurisdictional issues arbitrators face in terms of government agencies.

3. Discuss the similarities and differences between arbitration and judicial hearings with particular emphasis on the common law of the shop, admission of evidence, and the role of the arbitrator versus that of the judge.

4. Why are arbitrators' decisions usually lengthy when one sentence could indicate who was right and wrong? Your discussion of this question should include the purposes of arbitration and advantages, as well as disadvantages of an extensive arbitrator decision.

5. Discuss two decision-making guidelines used by arbitrators, furnishing specific examples (not mentioned in the text) of how these guidelines apply.

6. Cite and defend three specific methods you would use to make the typical arbitration procedure more effective. Also indicate the advantages and disadvantages of your suggestions.

7. Discuss the following: "The refusal to use grievance mediation as a step prior to arbitration illustrates the stubbornness of many union and management officials."

8. After reviewing Exhibit 11.9, would you rather be in an environment of labor arbitration or employment arbitration? Why? Why not?

9. Do you believe that labor unions should use the benefits of labor arbitration as part of the union's strategy to recruit new members? Give your reasons.

Exploring the Web

Labor and Employment Arbitration

1. Federal Mediation and Conciliation Service. The Federal Mediation and Conciliation Service (FMCS) was created by Congress in 1947 as an independent agency to the U.S. government and, according to the FMCS Web site, was "given the mission of preventing or minimizing the impact of labor-management disputes on the free flow of commerce by providing mediation, conciliation, and voluntary arbitration." What services does the agency provide?

Use the Web site to define the following terms: grievance mediation, preventive mediation, collective bargaining mediation, and alternative dispute resolution. What is the difference between mediation and arbitration?

2. Steelworkers' Trilogy. Using GPO Access or Findlaw, locate the three Supreme Court cases that are commonly referred to as the *Steelworkers' Trilogy*. Why are the cases important to labor arbitration?

United Steelworkers v. American Manufacturing (363 US 564)

United Steelworkers v. Warrior and Gulf Navigation (363 US 574)

United Steelworkers v. Enterprise Wheel and Car (363 US 593)

3. Arbitration and Title VII of the Civil Rights Act. The U.S. Court of Appeals for the Ninth Circuit ruled in 1998 that employees cannot be required, as a condition of employment, to arbitrate claims brought under Title VII of the Civil Rights Act. To read a discussion of the case, go to the Web site for the *Loyola of Los Angeles Law Review* and locate the article, "Arbitrary Civil Rights? The Case of *Duffield v. Robertson Stephens*" written by Robert S. McArthur. Use the link to Contents of Issues and scroll down to volume 32, issue 3.

4. American Arbitration Association. The Web site for the American Arbitration Association provides information on labor arbitration procedures and techniques as well as law and regulations. To find the statute on dispute resolution for your state, go to the Association's Web site, click on the links for Education, Laws and Statutes, and State. For example, the Florida Arbitration Code is under Section 682 of the Florida Code.

Just for fun, use the same Web site to look for information on the Association's role in settling sports disputes. What are the three major classes of disputes involving the Olympics that are resolved through arbitration?

References

1. Cynthia F. Cohen and Theresa Domagalski, "The Effects of Mandatory Arbitration of Employment Discrimination Claims: Perceptions of Justice and Suggestions for Change," *Employee Responsibilities and Rights Journal* 11, no. 1 (1998), pp. 27–40.
2. For a detailed historical perspective of labor arbitration, see Dennis R. Nolan and Roger I. Abrams, "American Labor Arbitration: The Early Years," *University of Florida Law Review* (Summer 1983), pp. 373–421.
3. *United Steelworkers of America v. American Manufacturing Company;* 363 U.S. 566–567 (1960).
4. *United Steelworkers of America v. Warrior and Gulf Navigation Company,* 363 U.S. 582 (1960).
5. *United Steelworkers of America v. Enterprise Wheel and Car Corporation,* 363 U.S. 598 (1960).
6. "*AT&T Technologies Inc. v. Communications Workers of America,*" *The United States Law Week,* April 8, 1986, p. 4341.
7. The case is *John Wiley and Sons v. Livingston* (1964), discussed in Ralph S. Berger, "The Collective Bargaining Agreement in Bankruptcy: Does the Duty to Arbitrate Survive?" *Labor Law Journal* 35 (November 1984), pp. 385–393.
8. *Nolde Brothers Inc. v. Local No. 358, Bakery and Confectionary Workers Union AFL-CIO,* 430 U.S. 254 (1977). See also Irving M. Geslewitz, "Case Law Development Since Nolde Brothers: When Must Post-Contract Disputes Be Arbitrated?" *Labor Law Journal* 35 (April 1984), pp. 225–238.
9. Paul F. Hodapp, "The U.S. Supreme Court Rules on Duty to Arbitrate Post-Contract Grievances," *Labor Law Journal* 42 (December 1991), pp. 827–829.
10. *The Boys Market Inc. v. Retail Clerk's Union, Local 770,* 398 U.S. 249, 250, 252–253 (1970). It should be noted that injunctive relief applies only when one party refuses to arbitrate issues that are subject to grievance procedures specified in the labor agreement. For additional details, see *Buffalo Forge Company v. United Steelworkers of America,* 428 U.S. 397 (1970).
11. Nels E. Nelson and Walter J. Gershenfeld, "The Appointment of Grievance Arbitrators by State and Local Agencies," *Labor Law Journal* 52 (Winter 2001), pp. 258–267.
12. Jeanette A. Davy and George W. Bohlander, "Recent Findings and Practices in Grievance Arbitration Procedures," *Labor Law Journal* 43 (March 1992), p. 187.
13. Bureau of National Affairs Inc., *Basic Patterns in Union Contracts* (Washington, D.C.: Bureau of National Affairs, 1995), p. 38.
14. Delbert C. Miller and William Form, *Industrial Sociology,* 2d ed. (New York: Harper & Row, 1964), p. 264.
15. Daniel F. Jennings and A. Dale Allen, Jr., "Labor Arbitration Costs and Case Loads: A Longitudinal Analysis," *Labor Law Journal* 41 (February 1990), pp. 80–88.
16. David E. Bloom and Christopher L. Cavanagh, "An Analysis of the Selection of Arbitrators," *American Economic Review* 86 (June 1986), pp. 408–422; and Arthur Eliot Berkeley and Susan Rawson Zacur, "So You Want to Be an Arbitrator: Update of a Guide to the Perplexed," *Labor Law Journal* 41 (March 1990), pp. 170–174. For a thorough analysis of arbitrator's backgrounds, experiences, and preferences, see Mario F. Bognanno and Charles J. Coleman, *Labor Arbitration in America* (New York: Praeger, 1992).
17. Clarence R. Deitsch and David A. Dilts, "An Analysis of Arbitrator Characteristics and Their Effects on Decision Making in Discharge Cases," *Labor Law Journal* 40

(February 1989), pp. 112–116; Brian Bemmels, "Gender Effects in Grievance Arbitration," *Industrial Relations* 29 (Fall 1990), pp. 513–525; Stephen M. Crow and James W. Logan, "Arbitrators' Characteristics and Decision-Making Records, Gender of Arbitrators and Grievants, and the Presence of Legal Counsel as Predictors of Arbitral Outcomes," *Employee Responsibilities and Rights Journal* 7 (1994), pp. 169–185; and Kenneth W. Thornicroft, "Gender Effects in Grievance Arbitration...Revisited," *Labor Studies Journal* 19 (Winter 1995), pp. 35–44.

18. Michael Marmo, "Acceptability As a Factor in Grievance Arbitration," *Labor Law Journal* 50 (Summer 1999), pp. 97–102.

19. Clarence R. Deitsch and David A. Dilts, "Factors Affecting Pre-Arbitral Settlement of Rights Disputes: Predicting the Method of Rights Dispute Resolution," *Journal of Labor Research* 12 (Winter 1986), p. 76.

20. Richard A. Posthuma and Maris Stella Swift, "Legalistic vs. Facilitative Approaches to Arbitration: Strengths and Weaknesses," *Labor Law Journal* 52 (Fall 2001), pp. 173–184.

21. For a fine conceptionalization of arbitrability's dimensions and implications, see Mark M. Grossman, *The Question of Arbitrability* (Ithaca, N.Y.: ILR Press, 1984).

22. http://www.fmcs.gov.

23. For guidelines pertaining to an effective management or union post-hearing brief, see Douglas E. Ray, "On Writing the Post-Hearing Arbitration Brief," *Arbitration Journal* 47 (December 1992), pp. 58–60.

24. Ronald W. Haughton, "Running the Hearing," in *Arbitration in Practice*, ed. Arnold M. Zack (Ithaca, N.Y.: ILR Press, 1984), p. 37.

25. Jennings and Allen, "Labor Arbitration Costs."

26. See, for example, James B. Dworkin and Michael M. Harris, "Polygraph Tests: What Labor Arbitrators Need to Know," *Arbitration Journal* 41 (March 1986), pp. 23–33; Kimberly Janisch-Ramsey, "Polygraphs: The Search for Truth in Arbitration Proceedings," *Arbitration Journal* 41 (March 1986), pp. 34–41; Herman A. Theeke and Tina M. Theeke, "The Truth About Arbitrators' Treatment of Polygraph Tests," *Arbitration Journal* 42 (December 1987), pp. 23–32; and Marvin F. Hill, Jr. and Anthony Sinicropi, *Evidence in Arbitration*, 2d ed. (Washington, D.C.: Bureau of National Affairs, 1987).

27. Frank Elkouri and Edna Asper Elkouri, *How Arbitration Works*, 4th ed. (Washington, D.C.: Bureau of National Affairs, 1985), p. 302.

28. See, for example, Cynthia L. Gramm and Patricia A. Greenfield, "Arbitral Standards in Medical Screening Grievances," *Employee Responsibilities and Rights Journal* 3, no. 3 (1990), pp. 169–184.

29. Herbert L. Marx, Jr., "Who Are Labor Arbitration Opinions Written For? And Other Musing About Award Writing," *The Dispute Resolution Journal*, vol. 59, No. 2 (May–June 2004), pp. 22–23.

30. Steven Starck, "Arbitration Decision Writing: Why Arbitrators Err," *Arbitration Journal* 38 (June 1983), pp. 30–33. See also David Elliot, "When the Hearing Is Over: Writing Arbitral Awards in Plain Language," *Arbitration Journal* 46 (December 1991), p. 53.

31. http://www.fmcs.gov.

32. Michael H. LeRoy and Peter Feuille, "Private Justice and Public Policy: Whose Voice Prevails in Arbitration?" *Proceedings of the 54th Annual Meeting of the Industrial Relations Research Association* (Champaign, Ill.: IRRA, 2002), pp. 219–221.

33. Daniel F. Jennings and A. Dale Allen, Jr., "How Arbitrators View the Process of Labor Arbitration: A Longitudinal Analysis," *Labor Law Journal* 44 (Winter 1993), p. 44.

34. Stephen M. Crow and James Logan, "A Tentative Decision-Making Model of the Strong and Weak Forces at Labor Arbitration," *Journal of Collective Negotiations in the Public Sector* 24, no. 2 (1995), pp. 111–120.

35. John B. LaRocco, "Ambiguities in Labor Contracts: Where Do They Come From? *Dispute Resolution Journal*, vol. 59, No. 1 (February–April 2004), p. 38–41.

36. The first two examples are from Allan J. Harrison, *Preparing and Presenting Your Arbitration Case: A Manual for Union and Management Representatives* (Washington, D.C.: Bureau of National Affairs, 1979), pp. 23–24. The third example is suggested by Thomas R. Knight, "Arbitration and Contract Interpretation: *Common Law v. Strict Construction*," *Labor Law Journal* 34 (November 1983), pp. 714–726.

37. For arbitration examples of these dimensions of past practice, see Arthur Dobbelaere, Williams H. Leahy, and Jack Reardon, "The Effect of Past Practice on the Arbitration of Labor Disputes," *Arbitration Journal* 40 (December 1985), pp. 27–43.

38. Ibid., p. 38.

39. Donald J. Petersen, "No Smoking! The Arbitration of Smoking Restricting Policies," *Dispute Resolution Journal* 50 (January 1995), pp. 45–50.

40. William H. McPherson, "Should Labor Arbitrators Play Follow the Leader?" *Arbitration Journal* 4 (1949), p. 170.

41. David Dilts, Mark Crouch, and Mashaalah Rahnama-Moghadam, "Effectiveness in Grievance Arbitration: Are There Differences in Unions?" *Journal of Collective Negotiations in the Public Sector* 26, no. 4 (1997), pp. 333–338.

42. *Harrell Alexander, Sr v. Gardner-Denver Company*, 415 U.S. 60 (1974).

43. Michelle Hoyman and Lamont E. Stallworth, "The Arbitration of Discrimination Grievances in the Aftermath of Gardner-Denver," *Arbitration Journal* 39 (September 1984), p. 55; Karen Elwell and Peter Feuille, "Arbitration Awards and Gardner-Denver Lawsuits: One Bite or Two?" *Industrial Relations* 23 (Spring 1984), p. 295; Aubrey R. Fowler, Jr., "Arbitration, the Trilogy, and Industrial Rights: Developments Since *Alexander v. Gardner-Denver*," *Labor Law Journal* 36 (March 1985), pp. 173–182. See also Elaine Gale Wrong, "Arbitrators' Awards in Cases Involving Discrimination," *Labor Law Journal* 39 (July 1988), pp. 411–417.

44. Stephen L. Hayford, "The Coming Third Era of Labor Arbitration," *Arbitration Journal* 48 (September 1993), p. 17. See also Martha S. Weisel, "The Tension between Statutory Rights and Binding Arbitration," *Labor Law Journal* 42 (July 1991), pp. 766–772.

45. *Spielberg Manufacturing Company*, 112 NLRB 1080 (1955). See John C. Truesdale, "NLRB Deferral to

Arbitration: Still Alive and Kicking," http://www.NLRB.gov/press/

46. *Collyer Insulated Wire and Local Union 1098, International Brotherhood of Electrical Workers*, 192 NLRB 150 (August 20, 1977).

47. Curtis L. Mack and Ira P. Bernstein, "NLRB Deferral to the Arbitration Process: The Arbitrator's Demanding Role," *Arbitration Journal* 40 (September 1985), pp. 33–43. For a related research effort, see Benjamin W. Wolkinson, "The Impact of the Collyer Policy on Deferral: An Empirical Study," *Industrial and Labor Relations Review* 38 (April 1985), pp. 377–391.

48. Pat Greenfield, "The NLRB's Deferral to Arbitration before and after Olin: An Empirical Analysis," *Industrial and Labor Relations Review* 42, no. 1 (1988), pp. 34–49. See also "Remarks of NLRB Chairman Gould on Deferral to Arbitration," Bureau of National Affairs Inc., *Daily Labor Report*, no. 114 (June 16, 1994), pp. E-1–E-3.

49. James L. Ferree, "National Labor Relations Board Deferral to Arbitration," *Dispute Resolution Journal* 52 (Summer 1997), pp. 31–35.

50. Patricia A. Greenfield, "How Do Arbitrators Treat External Law?" *Industrial and Labor Relations Review* 45 (July 1992), p. 695.

51. "Decision of Supreme Court in *Paperworkers v. Misco, Inc.*," Bureau of National Affairs, *Daily Labor Report*, no. 230 (December 1, 1987), pp. D-1–D-5. See also Bernard F. Ashe, "Arbitration Finality and the Public-Policy Exception," *Dispute Resolution Journal* 47 (September 1994), pp. 22–28, 87–89.

52. "Practitioners Assess Impact of Court Decisions Bolstering Finality of Labor Arbitration Awards," Bureau of National Affairs, *Daily Labor Report*, no. 238 (December 14, 1987), p. A-1. For additional consideration of public policy intertwined with arbitration decisions in drug testing, see Lorynn A. Cone, "Public Policies against Drug Use: *Paperworkers v. Misco Inc.*," *Labor Law Journal* 40 (April 1989), pp. 243–247. See also Bernard D. Meltzer, "After the Labor Arbitration Award: The Public Policy Defense," *Industrial Relations Law Journal* 10, no. 2 (1988), pp. 241–251; Robert F. Wayland, Elvis C. Stephens, and Geralyn McClure, "*Misco*: Its Impact on Arbitration Awards," *Labor Law Journal* 39 (December 1988), pp. 813–819; and Arthur Hamilton and Peter A. Veglahn, "Public Policy Exceptions to Arbitration Awards," *Labor Law Journal* 42 (June 1991), pp. 366–370.

53. "Court Vacates Reinstatement of Employee Charged with Sexual Abuse of Customer," Bureau of National Affairs, *Daily Labor Report*, no. 61 (March 29, 1991), pp. A-4–A-5. See also "Reinstatement of Sexual Harasser Overturned as Public Policy Violation," Bureau of National Affairs, Inc., *Daily Labor Report*, no. 204 (October 22, 1990), pp. A-8–A-9.

54. "Accused Sex Harasser Gains Reinstatement," Bureau of National Affairs, *Daily Labor Report*, no. 70 (April 10, 1992), pp. A-1, A-2. See also Thomas J. Piskorski, "Reinstatement of the Sexual Harasser: The Conflict between Federal Labor Law and Title VII," *Employee Relations Law Journal* 18 (Spring 1993), pp. 617–623; and Christie L. Roszkowski and Robert F. Wayland, "Arbitration Review: Is the Public Policy against Sexual Harassment Sufficient Cause for Vacating an Arbitration Award?" *Labor Law Journal* 44 (November 1993), pp. 707–717.

55. Margaret A. Jacobs, "Men's Club: Riding Crop and Slurs: How Wall Street Dealt with a Sex Bias Case," *The Wall Street Journal*, June 9, 1994, pp. A-4, A-6; Barbara Presley Noble, "Attacking Compulsory Arbitration," *New York Times*, January 15, 1995, p. F-21; and "Reinstatement of Alleged Sexual Harassers Does Not Violate Public Policy, Forum Told," Bureau of National Affairs, *Daily Labor Report*, no. 6 (January 10, 1994), pp. A-10, A-11.

56. Richard Mittenthal, "Self-Interest: Arbitration's 'Unmentionable' Consideration," *Dispute Resolution Journal* 47 (March 1994), pp. 70–72.

57. Harry J. Dworkin, "How Arbitrators Decide Cases," *Labor Law Journal* 25 (April 1974) p. 203.

58. "Arbitrator Traces Growing Legalism as Proceedings Are Modeled on Courts," Bureau of National Affairs, *Daily Labor Report*, no. 106 (June 3, 1991), p. A-6 and James Oldham, "Arbitration and Relentless Legalization in the Workplace," in *Arbitration 1990: New Perspectives on Old Issues*, ed. Gladys W. Gruenberg, Proceedings at the Forty-Third Annual Meeting, National Academy of Arbitrators (Washington, D.C.: Bureau of National Affairs, 1991), pp. 23–40.

59. http://www.fmcs.gov/.

60. Nels E. Nelson and A.N.M. Meshquat Uddin, "The Impact of Delay on Arbitrators' Decisions in Discharge Cases," *Labor Studies Journal* 23 (Summer 1998), pp. 3–19.

61. Allen Ponak, Wifred Zerbe, Sarah Rose, and Corliss Olson, "Using Even History Analysis to Model Delaying Grievance Arbitration," *Industrial and Labor Relations Review* 50 (October 1996), pp. 105–110.

62. Linda S. Byars, "Limiting an Arbitrator's Remedial Power," *Labor Law Journal* 48 (January 1997), pp. 29–33.

63. http://www.fmcs.gov.

64. Nancy Kauffman, "The Idea of Expedited Arbitration Two Decades Later," *Arbitration Journal* 46 (September 1991), p. 35.

65. Dennis R. Nolan and Roger I. Abrams, "The Future of Labor Arbitration," *Labor Law Journal* 37 (July 1986), pp. 441–442.

66. Elizabeth Hill, "AAA Employment Arbitration: A Fair Forum at Low Cost," *Dispute Resolution Journal*, Vol. 59, No. 2 (May–June 2003), pp. 9–15.

67. Thomas J. Piskorski and David B. Ross, "Private Arbitration as the Exclusive Means of Resolving Employment-Related Disputes," *Employee Relations Law Journal* 19 (Autumn 1993), p. 206; and Loren K. Allison and Eric H. J. Stahlhut, "Arbitration and the ADA: A Budding Partnership," *Arbitration Journal* 48 (September 1993), pp. 53–60.

68. Helen LeVan, "Decisional Model for Predicting Outcomes of Arbitrated Sexual Harassment Disputes," *Labor Law Journal* 44 (April 1993), p. 231. See also Robert A. Shearer, "The Impact of Employment Arbitration Agreements in Sex Discrimination Claims: The Trend Toward Nonjudicial Resolution," *Employee Relations Law Journal* 18 (Winter 1992–1993), pp. 479–488; Stuart L. Bass, "Recent Court Decisions Expand Role of Arbitration in Harassment and Other Title VII Cases," *Labor Law Journal* 43 (December 1992), pp. 772–779; Stuart H.

Bompey and Michael P. Pappas, "Is There a Better Way? Compulsory Arbitration of Employment Discrimination Claims after Gilmer," *Employee Relations Law Journal* 19 (Winter 1993–1994), pp. 197–216; and Evan J. Spelfogel, "New Trends in the Arbitration of Employment Disputes," *Arbitration Journal* 48 (March 1993), pp. 6–15.

69. George M. Sullivan, "*Alexander v. Gardner-Denver:* Staggered but Still Standing," *Labor Law Journal* 50 (March 1999), pp. 43–45. For a comprehensive analysis, see Donald J. Petersen and Harvey R. Boller, "Arbitral Responses to the Changing External Law of Discrimination," *Labor Law Journal* 49 (December 1998), pp. 1241–1253 and Harvey R. Boller and Donald J. Petersen, "Mandatory Arbitration Clauses," *Dispute Resolution Journal* 54 (February 1999), pp. 56–58.

70. *Wright v. Universal Maritime Service Corp.*, 119 S. Ct. 391 (1998).

71. Patricia Thomas Bittel, "Arbitration: Is This Where We Were Headed?" *Labor Law Journal* 53 (Fall 2002), pp. 130–131. Also see: *Circuit City Stores, Inc. v. Adams*, 532 U.S. 143 (2001); *EEOC v. Waffle House, Inc.*, 534 U.S. 279 (2002).

72. Patricia Thomas Bittel, "Arbitration: Is This Where We Were Headed?" *Labor Law Journal* 53 (Fall 2002), pp. 130–131. Also see: *Circuit City Stores, Inc. v. Adams*, 532 U.S. 143 (2001); *EEOC v. Waffle House, Inc.*, 534 U.S. 279 (2002).

73. Michael H. Leroy and Peter Feuille, "Short Circuiting *Circuit City*? Judicial Enforcement of Mandatory Employment Arbitration," Champaign, IL: *Proceedings of the 55th Annual Meeting of the Industrial Relations Research Association*, 2003, pp. 281.

74. Ellen J. Vargyas, "Verdict on Mandatory Binding Arbitration in Employment," *Dispute Resolution Journal* 52 (Fall 1997), pp. 10–14.

75. Charles J. Coleman and Jose A. Vazquez, "Mandatory Arbitration of Statutory Issues under Collective Bargaining: *Austin* and Its Progeny," *Labor Law Journal* 48 (December 1998), pp. 703–723. Also see Charles J. Coleman, "Invited Paper: Mandatory Arbitration of Statutory Issues: *Austin, Wright*, and the Future, in *Arbitration 1998: The Changing World of Dispute Resolution; Proceedings of the 51st Annual Meeting of the National Academy of*

Arbitrators, eds. Steven Briggs and Jay E. Grenig (Washington, D.C.: Bureau of National Affairs, Inc., 1999), pp. 134–159.

76. Theodore J. St. Antoine, "Mandatory Arbitration: Something Old, Something New," *Perspectives on Work* 7, no. 2 (Winter 2004), pp. 21–22.

77. Michael H. Leroy and Peter Feuille, "Short Circuiting *Circuit City*? Judicial Enforcement of Mandatory Employment Arbitration," Champaign, IL: *Proceedings of the 55th Annual Meeting of the Industrial Relations Research Association*, 2003, pp. 27–278.

78. Hoyt N. Wheeler, Brian S. Klaas, and Douglas M. Mahoney, *Workplace Justice without Unions*, Kalamazoo, MI: W. E. Upjohn Institute for Employment Research, 2004, p. 16.

79. Walter J. Gershenfeld, "Due Process in Employment Arbitration: Differential Coverage Is Not Due Process," Adrienne E. Easton, Editor, *Proceedings of the 57th Annual Meeting*, Champaign, IL: Labor and Employment Relations Association, 2005, pp. 259–269.

80. Lisa B. Bingham, "Emerging Due Process Concerns in Employment Arbitration: A Look at Actual Cases," *Labor Law Journal* 46 (February 1996), pp. 108–120; Marjorie L. Icenogle and Robert A. Shearer, "Emerging Due Process Standards in Arbitration of Employment Discrimination Disputes: New Challenges for Employers," *Labor Law Journal* 48 (February 1998), p. 84.

81. Morton H. Orenstein, "Mandatory Arbitration: Alive and Well or Withering on the Vine?" *Dispute Resolution Journal* 54 (August 1999), p. 86.

82. Lisa B. Bingham, "Employment Arbitration: Differences between Repeat Player and Nonrepeat Payer Outcomes," *Proceedings of the 49th Annual Meeting of the Industrial Relations Research Association* (Madison, Wis.: IRRA, 1997), pp. 201–207.

83. Elizabeth Hill, "AAA Employment Arbitration: A Fair Forum at Low Cost," *Dispute Resolution Journal*, 59 (May–June 2003), pp. 9–17.

84. Brian S. Klaas, Douglas Mahony, and Hoyt N. Wheeler, "Decision-Making about Workplace Disputes: A Policy Capturing Study of Employment Arbitrators, Labor Arbitrators and Jurors," *Industrial Relations*, 45 (2006). 68–95.

The Right To Contract Out

Background

This matter of arbitration stems from the following grievance: "The Company has unilaterally eliminated all janitor jobs and did not honor the contract. After foundry janitor jobs were evaluated, the Company informed the Union in a job evaluation meeting that the jobs would be cut. this action is in direct violation of the contract and did not comply with discussions between Company and Union over subcontracting during negotiations. Adjustment sought? Make employees whole."

William Ikerd, the Company HR manager, provided the Company Answer which was:

"The Company has honored the re-evaluation of the foundry janitor jobs and upgraded these jobs from Class L-1 to Class 1. We have also paid $.80 per hour more, effective 6/26/06, the date of the upgrade.

In 1989, the Company negotiated an L-1 rate for janitors to spread the pay scale through ten job classifications rather than eight. We agreed to "red circle" the wage rate of the employees who already held title to the Class 1 janitorial jobs. Effective 9/18/89, we agreed that all future janitors would be classified as Class L-1 with a lower pay scale. We agreed to an $.80 per hour lower rate for the Class L-1 job classification.

For 17 years, the L-1 rate has been sufficient pay for janitorial pay in our facility. However, in June of this year, the Union requested a re-evaluation of all class L-1 janitors.

On the morning of June 21, 2006, as we assembled to evaluate the L-1 janitor's job, I made statements that we already had the highest wages for janitors in our labor market. We had conducted a wage survey. We didn't evaluate the job that day. We waited until the following day so Roy Gander could be present. I voiced my concern about the wage rate being raised that day. the upgrade of the L-1 janitor to a Class 1 janitor meant an increase of $.80 per hour for seven employees. Two janitors continue to be "red circled" as Class 1. After 17 years, the Union wanted and successfully removed L-1 classification, which took out the low rate of pay we negotiated in 1989. The Company lost its right to hire any future foundry janitors at Class L-1. A newly hired foundry janitor would come off the street making $10.50 an hour and progress to $13.98, with a $.40 per hour increase due September 18, 2006.

After the evaluation meeting, Randy Elbert and I discussed the additional cost for janitorial service. We concluded we must consider contracting out the janitorial service.

I contacted the Union president, and he told me to hold off and let him talk to the janitors. After he talked with the janitors, the Union president called me back and said the janitors wanted the money. Our purchasing department contacted janitor vendors. On July 10, 2006, one of the senior janitors came to me and stated the janitors wanted to remain Class L-1 and not receive the raise. I told him the plant manager was on vacation, but I would talk to the purchasing manager, who took a sheet of paper to the senior janitor and asked the other janitors to sign to stay Class L-1. On July 12, 2006, the purchasing manager returned the paper. All janitors in the foundry had signed, except one. On July 18, 2006, when the Union president returned from vacation, he told me to honor the evaluation. The Company typed the payroll authorization and paid the foundry janitors back wages of $.80 per hour from 6/26/06 to current payroll date.

On August 11, 2006, we contracted with a vendor to supply janitorial service for the plant.

I notified the Union president that we would contract out janitorial work on August 14, 2006. On August 15, 2006, Larry Tate and I discussed the matter and I explained the events as they occurred. On August 22, 2006, Randy Elbert and I met with the Union president and vice president to discuss this matter.

The Company has contracted janitorial service for the front office, main cafeteria, and restrooms since January 1994.

The Company will save a substantial amount of money. The employees can now devote their time to meeting customer orders, maintaining an efficient operation, and shipping a quality product, etc.

Article 4.1.2 of the Contract Agreement provides the placing of production, service, maintenance, or distribution work with outside contractors or subcontractors due to the savings and the ability to spend more time operating the plant, the Company will contract out janitorial services effective September 2, 2006."

The Grievance was appealed. Mr. Ikerd provided the Company's Step 4 Answer. In addition to the company's previous response, Mr. Ikerd wrote:

"The maintenance laborers used to do the yard work. We have contracted out that work for many years. the Company has contracted out janitorial service for the front office, main cafeteria, and restrooms since January 1994.

The Company will save a substantial amount of money. Employees can devote their time to meeting customer orders, maintaining an efficient operation, and shipping a quality product, etc.

The Company has honored the change in evaluation of the foundry janitor job and upgraded it from Class L-1 to Class 1. We have paid an additional $.80 per hour since effective date of June 26, 2006.

All the janitors who are able to perform jobs have bid jobs to return to work for the Company and they have returned to jobs with higher wage rates.

The Union and the company recognize that the success of the business is vital to all concerned. Increasing the wage rate of janitor job to $13.89 effective June 26, 2006, and effective September 18, 2006, to $14.38 will not allow the Company to be successful.

The grievance is denied."

Mr. Larry Tate, International Union Representative, appealed the grievance. he stated:

> "In Article 2.1.1 the Company recognizes the Union as the sole and exclusive bargaining agent with respect to rates of pay, wages, hours, and all other conditions of employment for all employees covered by this Agreement.

For the Company to eliminate the janitors from the contract is a violation of the contract. In 2004 the Company and the Local Union were in negotiations. during the negotiations the subject of subcontracting came up. The Company said it would be necessary from time to time to contract out some maintenance work, because we did not have the time or the manpower to do all the work that had to be done. Robert Holcomb, the plant manager at the time, made a statement in the negotiations that the Company would not eliminate any jobs, that was a very strong statement on the word of the plant manager, and the Local Union decided to trust the Company. Less than two years later the Company eliminated the janitors from the Contract.

It has always been established that, if the Union could show enough change in a job, the Company would agree to reevaluate the job. When the Union approached the Company about the evaluation, the Company did not state that there had not been enough change to warrant a reevaluation. After the evaluation was done, the Company notified the Union that they were going to contract out the jobs. The Union considered the evaluation binding on both the Union and the Company, as stated in Article 29. If the Company can contract out jobs just because they do not like the rating, then the contract has been bastardized. How can the Company expect the Union to ever evaluate another job for fear of retaliation? If the Company does not like the results, then the next step is to do away with the job.

The Union had offered a solution that was to remove some of the duties that had been added to cause the reevaluation, and reevaluate the job. The company refused to do this.

Just as the Union did during the negotiations, the Company had the right to make proposals. if the Company had wanted to exclude the L1 rate from the evaluation process, then it should have made such proposals. By trying to exclude the L1 rate in the middle of a contract is like trying to slip in the back door without getting caught. For the Company to eliminate the jobs because of the job evaluation is a violation of the contract.

Therefore, the Company leaves me no choice but to appeal this grievance to arbitration."

Issue

Did the Company violate the Agreement when it contracted out the janitorial jobs? If so, what is the remedy?

Relevant Provisions of the Agreement

Article 2–Recognition

2.1.1 The Company recognizes the Union as the sole and exclusive bargaining agent with respect to rates of pay, wages, hours, and all other conditions of employment for all employees covered by this Agreement.

2.1.2 The term "employee" as used in this Agreement shall mean and include: All production and skilled trade employees employed by the employer, including all plant clerical employees, but excluding all office clerical employees, confidential employees, professional employees, technical employees, inspectors, managerial employees, guards, and supervisors as defined in the Act.

Article 4–Managerial Functions

4.1.2. Without limiting the generality of the foregoing, and subject to the other provisions of this Agreement, as used herein the term "rights of management" includes: The right to manage the plant; the right to direct the working forces, including the right to hire, promote, or transfer any employee, . . . introduction of new, improved, or different production, maintenance, service, or distribution methods or facilities; the placing of production, service maintenance, or distribution work with outside contractors or subcontractors; the determination of the amount of supervision necessary; the right to terminate, merge, or sell the business, or any part thereof.

Article 6–Grievance and Arbitration

6.4.3 The powers of the Arbitrator are limited as follows:

(1) He shall have no power to add to, subtract from, or modify any of the terms of this Agreement.

(2) He shall have no power to substitute his discretion for the Company's discretion in cases where the Company is given discretion by this Agreement, except where the issue before him involves discharge for "just cause" and the Union is seeking to mitigate the discharge penalty.

Article 19–New Departments

19.1.1 Whenever the company establishes a new department and/or jobs, the new jobs resulting from this establishment shall be described and evaluated by the Company. These descriptions and evaluations shall be presented to the Union and discussed with Union representatives. Following such discussions, the descriptions and evaluations will be implemented. If the Union believes that any of the jobs have been evaluated improperly, the evaluation committee will convene to discuss any alleged specific errors in the evaluation. The dispute will be resolved by the evaluation committee, either by mutual agreement or reevaluation as soon as feasible. If there is a change in pay, it will become effective on the first day of the following week of the evaluation by the committee.

19.1.2 The new jobs so established will be subject to Article 19 dealing with job bidding.

Article 25–Wages

25.3.1 Job Descriptions. Job descriptions have been developed for existing jobs in the plant and new or revised job descriptions will be developed when new jobs are introduced or existing jobs are changed substantially. It is specifically recognized by the parties that job descriptions are for the sole purpose of assisting in the proper evaluation of jobs for wage rates, and in no way constitute a limitation or restriction on the Company's right to assign employees to various tasks, duties, or jobs as the company deems necessary or desirable.

Article 29–Job Evaluation Committee

29.1.1 It is the intent of the Union and the Company to evaluate plant jobs in a fair and consistent manner in order to promote harmony and efficiency in the plant. The evaluation committee will consist of three voting delegates from the Union and three from the Company.

29.1.2 The Union will submit a list of two employees for the Company to select one member of the Union committee when and if a change from the current members is necessary. In no case will there be more than one delegate from a department. It shall be the aim of both parties to settle evaluation conflicts in an expedient manner.

29.1.3 Any new job evaluation delegate shall be trained by the committee in the principles of the job evaluation as it relates to the company plan. The job evaluation delegates will be paid by the company for all time served as a delegate.

29.1.4 The evaluation committee's decisions in evaluating jobs will be binding on the Union and the Company since the parties at the local level have more knowledge of the jobs and job duties.

29.1.5 When a job evaluation meeting is scheduled, the Union will invite one employee from the job being evaluated to explain the job duties to the committee.

Positions of the Parties

The Union:

The Union stated that it approached the Company in June 2006 and requested a re-evaluation of the janitorial job in the foundry department. This department employs seven janitors at labor grade L1. The Union presented the Company with a list that consisted of current job duties and job duties that had been added over the years. This process has always been used to request an evaluation of any job in the plant. The Company never told the Union that the janitors in the foundry should not be evaluated. On June 21, 2006, the Company and Union evaluation committee convened to evaluate the janitorial job in the foundry department. On this day, the Company and Union attempted to evaluate the job; however, the absence of one committee member, Ronald Gander, halted the evaluation until all committee members could be present. During this meeting, the Company informed the Union that it really did not want to evaluate the janitorial job because a wage survey had been conducted and the survey showed that the foundry janitors were the highest paid in the area.

On the following day, the committee evaluated the job. This job evaluation method has 11 different categories with five degrees of difficulty and a range of points in each degree. For each category, the six voting members discussed how each category related to the job being evaluated. After the discussion, each member assigned a point value for the degree most suitable for the job. After all members had assigned a point value to each category, the points were added up and the average of all the scores became the points given to each category.

There didn't appear to be any real disagreements in how the points were assigned. Then one company representative said "These jobs are probably gone." The Company could have done what had reasonably been done in the past, that is, discuss the importance of the job remaining an L1 in classification with the committee. Tim Adams testified that, in other evaluations, if the Company did not feel the points fit the job, the Company requested that the committee review the evaluation in order to determine whether adjustments could be made. In this case, Company officials could have requested a way to lower the points as it had in the past or increase the points on previous jobs. The Company did not make a request to lower the points so the Company's actions proved that the evaluation must have been fair, even in the Company's eyes.

After the Company announced the jobs would be eliminated, the Union requested that the Company review Article 19 Section 19.1.1 to determine whether another evaluation would be warranted. The Company made no attempt. Instead, the Company decided to contract out the janitorial jobs.

The Union stated that it made several attempts to retain the janitorial jobs in the bargaining unit. The Company's response was that it was too late because the Company had already signed a contract with the outside contractor. This turned out not to be true. The Company had an oral agreement with the contractor, but not a contract. Further, the agreement for its services was on a month-to-month basis.

The Company stated that the only reason for removing the jobs from the bargaining unit was cost. If cost was the only reason, the Union asked, then: "Why did the Company wait until after the re-evaluation to eliminate the janitorial jobs?" The Company stated it was obtaining the same janitorial services at less cost. The Union claimed that the contractor's janitors were not performing the same duties as the bargaining-unit janitors. There were several duties identified. These included weekly checks of the fire extinguishers, operation of the trash compactor, cleaning of mirrors in the forklift aisles, and cleaning in the assembly bays. The contractor's employees are now performing all of these jobs. this work takes away from employees' core duties and this means less production and less profit for the Company. If the Company had contracted out all the work that the bargaining-unit janitors were performing, the Union asked: "How can the Company say they are getting the same work done at less cost when the contractor employees are not doing all the work the bargaining-unit janitors were doing (apples for apples)?"

The Union argued that the Company accused the Union of using the contract to "backdoor a wage increase for the janitors." The Union stated that it was not the Union's fault if the Company did not secure language during contract negotiations to prevent the janitorial job from being reevaluated.

The Union stated:

> *Some people may say they're just janitor jobs, not jobs that require a lot of skill. Good jobs in the United States are hard to come by. The Union has always known the janitorial jobs could be contracted out for less than the labor agreement called for, but the Union took pride that our janitors were paid a fair wage. What will be next, the shipping department, the maintenance department, or maybe the tool and die department? These particular departments are not on a wage scale as the janitors are not; however, the above-mentioned departments as well as the janitors are still part of the current labor agreement. If the Company wants to contract out our jobs, then do it at the bargaining table. At least give the Union a chance to retain the jobs.*

The Union claimed that the Company had no intention of honoring Article 19 and Article 29. The Company led the Union into the evaluation so the Company could justify eliminating the janitorial jobs "just as you would lead a lamb to slaughter." The Company allowed the evaluation to happen without complaining and went through the process without problems. Then, it took the jobs out from under the Union, claiming it was a management right. The Union asked: "Why does the Company say it's too late? There is no contract with the contractor." The Union argued that it can never be too late to do what is right. In Article 2 of the Agreement, the Union retained the right to be the sole and exclusive bargaining agent for all jobs in the contract, not just the ones the Company chooses to allow the Union to represent.

The Union concluded:

> *The Union has shown the Company was in violation of the current labor agreement. Therefore, the Union would respectfully request(s) the arbitrator to sustain the grievance and order the return of the foundry janitor jobs to the bargaining unit and make whole all employees affected by the elimination of the foundry janitor jobs.*

The Company:

The Company stated that the "very broad Management Rights clause" contained in the current Collective Bargaining Agreement was set forth verbatim in the first agreement between the Company and Union dated January 29, 1977. The Company and Union representatives both acknowledged that the Union has proposed changing or limiting this broad language on numerous occasions in contract negotiations over the past 30 years, but no change has ever been effected. In the contract negotiations in 2004, the Company's response to the Union's perennial proposal in this regard was to note that the clause is as sacred to the Company and is as important to the Company as seniority is to the Union.

The Company stated that jobs have been evaluated to fit within its wage scale since 1980. At that time, the Company had eight job classifications. The jobs were evaluated in accordance with the Company Job Evaluation Method. The evaluation was carried out by the Company representatives. The lowest rated job in the plant was the janitor, and the highest rated jobs in the plant were maintenance or tool and die maker. The janitor job was a Class 1; the maintenance and tool and die jobs were Class 8; the other jobs in the plant would be spread evenly throughout the classifications by dividing up the point differential between the rating of the janitor's job and the rating of the maintenance and tool and die jobs equally.

In 1989, the company conducted a wage survey of the jobs in the area and determined that the wages paid to janitors were much higher than average. Also, the company found that its wage rate for the most highly skilled workers was lower than in the region. To correct this situation, the Union and the Company agreed in 1989 that there would be 10 job classifications. The janitorial job was changed from Class 1 to L-1, and the most highly skilled jobs were moved up to a Class 9. The parties agreed that any janitors at the plant at the time of the change would be "red circled" and would continue to be paid as though they were in Class 1.

The Management Rights clause has been the basis for the Company's decision to contract out certain work formerly performed by bargaining unit employees over the years. In 1994, the company subcontracted out the janitorial work for the front office. The Union grieved that decision, but withdrew the grievance prior to arbitration.

Mr. Ikerd, HR Manager, stated that over the years the Company had contracted out the lawn and landscaping work, some machining work, and certain maintenance and installation work. None of these decisions were challenged by the Union. All agreed that the Management Rights clause has never been abrogated or limited, either with respect to contracting out or anything else. Every decision by the Company to contract out has either not been challenged by the Union or the challenge has not been successful.

In 2000, the Joint Job Evaluation Committee was established and included representatives from both the Union and the Company. This committee continues in operation today. However, the Committee is limited in the jobs it may consider. It evaluates jobs when new jobs are added at the plant (Article 19), and when existing jobs are "changed substantially" (Article 25).

A number of jobs have been evaluated over the years. the ratings of some jobs have gone down, while others have gone up. Until this situation, no job had ever been contracted out after an evaluation had changed its rate.

In the summer of 2006, the Company stated that the Union requested that the foundry janitor job be re-evaluated. The Company's initial response was that evaluation was not appropriate because none of the duties were new and the job had not changed substantially as required by the contract. However, the Union insisted that the re-evaluation go forward and the re-evaluation was carried out on June 21 and 22, 2006.

Mr. Ikerd informed the evaluation committee that the Company did not want the wage rate of the foundry janitor job to go up and did not feel that was reasonable. Ikerd stated that the Company might take other measures if that occurred. When the evaluation was completed, to no one's surprise, the janitor's job was reclassified from Class L-1 to Class 1 and the wage rate increased.

The Company felt that the result of this evaluation caused the janitors' wage rate to be badly out of line with prevailing wages in the labor market area for janitors. The Company also felt that the Union was using the evaluation system to get around its previous agreement, which established the L-1 classification. After giving the Union several opportunities to withdraw its request, the Company implemented the Evaluation Committee's decision, but, shortly thereafter, contracted out the work of the foundry janitor.

Mr. Ikerd presented the cost information that was available to him at the time the decision was made. This information showed an annual cost savings of over $370,000 due to the change.

The Company claimed that none of the janitors at the plant suffered financially from this decision. Two of them quit for reasons unrelated to the decision. The other five were all still employed at substantially higher hourly rates. No one lost any wages.

The Company stated that the question in this decision is whether the Company violated the Collective Bargaining Agreement in contracting out the foundry janitorial work. The clear language of the contract allowed precisely the action taken by the Company. The Union attempted to circumvent its own agreement, which led directly to the action of which it now complains.

The Company stated:

> The Management Rights provision in the Collective Bargaining Agreement unequivocally states that the Company has the right to place "production, service, maintenance, or distribution work with outside contractors or subcontractors." This provision has been in every Collective Bargaining Agreement between the Company and the Union, and has survived numerous attempts by the Union to have it modified in negotiations. The negotiation notes introduced by the Union demonstrate that the Management Rights clause is "sacred" to the Company. Mr. Ikerd testified that the Company would take a strike over removal of that language. There would be no point in taking such a strong position on the language unless the Company intended to be able to utilize it, at least on occasion. On that ground alone, there can be no contract violation here.

The Company contended that the Union appeared to claim that the Company's actions are "unfair" and in retaliation for the Union's rightful use of the job evaluation procedure. The Union appeared to claim that it would be unwilling to use the evaluation procedure in the future because of these actions, but neither of these positions is justified. First, the union's use of the job evaluation procedure for these positions can hardly be characterized as "in good faith." In 1989, two new job classifications were created to broaden the spectrum at the Company. By agreement, janitors were placed in a lower L-1 classification with protection for those who currently held the job. At the time, everyone knew that this was being done because janitors' wage rates were so out of line with the norm for the labor market.

The Company argued that the Union appeared to argue that the Company should have bargained and changed its mind after the contracting out decision was made. This argument comes too late. During the evaluation process, Mr. Ikerd told the Union plainly that the Company viewed the evaluation as improper and would consider its options, including contracting out if the Union persisted. Undeterred, the Union went forward with the evaluation procedure, which inevitably resulted in the janitor's job being upgraded to a Class 1 job. Afterwards, the Company held off on implementing the decision to give the Union an opportunity to reconsider. Despite that opportunity and despite the fact that all but one of the janitors signed a sheet which indicated that they did not want the raise and in fact were perfectly content with their current situation, the Union still insisted that the change be made. Despite all of these warning signs, the Union never considered or offered any sort of compromise in its position. When the work was contracted out, the Union began to complain loudly that the Company refused to negotiate, bargain, or compromise. In fact, the Company's decision was caused by the conduct of the Union.

The Company stated that it chose to contract out this work because of the enormous cost savings involved. Of course, that is almost always the reason for decisions to contract out and is clearly understood to be the reason for having such a right in the labor agreement in the first place. Mr. Ikerd did not conduct a cost comparison until the Union pushed forward with the evaluation. If the Union had not improperly raised the issue, things would probably still be as they were in the spring of 2006. However, once the Union opened the Pandora's Box of re-evaluating the janitor's jobs, the Company considered its options and found to its surprise that the savings were very significant. What this demonstrates primarily is the fact that the janitor's wage rate was grossly inflated from a market standpoint. The cost comparison showed annual savings of $370,000. Those savings provide ample justification for the Company's decision, which in any event is left to its sole discretion according to the labor agreement.

The Company noted that no one has been damaged by this action; all are still at work, and are making substantially more money. Some may prefer to have their old jobs back. What that primarily suggests is that their old jobs (at least as they performed them) were so easy that they didn't mind the lower wage rate. In any event, none of the Union's membership has been harmed financially and that hardly demonstrates a retaliatory motive.

Questions

1. Which party has the burden of proof? Which level of proof should be used? Why?

2. Is this case a matter of "good faith" on the part of the Company or a contract interpretation issue? Why? Why not?

3. Develop some general guidelines for companies to retain the right to contract out bargaining unit work.

4. When a company contracts out work formerly performed by bargaining unit employees, is the company violating the recognition clause of the Labor Agreement?

5. Be the arbitrator. How do you rule? Why?

Did the Company Violate the Agreement When It Did Not Pay Holiday Pay?

CASE STUDY 11-2
Background

During September 2005, the parties were negotiating the Labor Agreement due to expire on October 31, 2005. The Union had proposed to add Martin Luther King, Jr.'s birthday and Memorial Day as non-work holidays. The Company countered with a proposal to "Swap George Washington's birthday for Memorial Day." On October 25,

2005, the parties agreed to a Contingent Agreement on Contract Extension, which stated:
It is understood by all parties that:

1. The current Labor Agreement expires at midnight on October 30, 2005;

2. The parties are negotiating in good faith to reach a new Agreement;

3. The parties wish to provide every opportunity for the bargaining unit's voters to consider the negotiation proposals while work under the existing Agreement continues uninterrupted and without threat of interruptions; and

4. The parties do not wish for the current Agreement to expire without a new Agreement in place unless and until all reasonable efforts to avoid operating without an Agreement have been pursued.

As such, the parties agree as follows:

1. The current Agreement will remain in full force and effect until midnight November 15, 2005, unless a new Agreement is substituted for the current Agreement or the parties mutually agree in writing to end the Agreement earlier;

2. After November 15, 2005, either party may terminate the current Agreement's extension by written notice to the other of at least seven (7) calendar days;

3. The parties agree to apply the terms of any wage or benefit change agreed upon during the extension of the current Agreement back to the expiration of that Agreement on October 30, 2005.

On November 10, 2005, a Negotiation Proposal Status and Counter Proposals Report was prepared. In reference to holidays, the Union proposal was: "Add Memorial Day and MLK's birthday as non-work holidays." The Company proposal was: "Exchange GW's (George Washington) birthday for Memorial Day."

On January 20, 2006, the Company presented its final proposal. Article 6 Holiday, paragraph 12 included:

> *Article 6 Holidays*
> *Paragraph 12*
> *Exchange George Washington's birthday for Memorial Day.*

On February 14, 2006, Jim Fulgham, HR Manager, posted the following notice:

> *Effective immediately, the Company-paid George Washington's birthday holiday has been swapped for the Memorial Day holiday, as agreed upon with the Union.*
>
> *This means beginning this year (actually next week), George Washington's birthday will not be a Company-paid holiday. Memorial Day, Monday, May 29, 2006, will be a Company-paid holiday.*

On February 15, 2006, Mr. Marty H. Stokes, company attorney, sent an e-mail to Mr. Jim McBride, the Union's staff representative. Mr. Stokes stated:

> *Holidays*
> *Memorial Day will become a paid holiday in exchange for the current George Washington's birthday holiday.*

On February 23, 2006, Mr. Stokes sent a second e-mail message to Mr. McBride, which stated:
This is to confirm our discussions from yesterday:

1. The retro pay of $150 per person eligible will be paid no later than March 10, 2006, presuming a ratification by this weekend;

2. The $150 will be paid either in a separate check or noted in a single, regular check and programmed so as to note the additional amount and so as to avoid the extra taxes paid if the retro pay was combined as ordinary income with the regular check;

3. The "show up pay" will also be paid no later than 3/10/06. These amounts will be paid in a regular check with a notation of the additional amount, or in a separate check. Since this must be included in ordinary income, the amount will be paid at 100 percent [rather than 80 percent, with no deductions], and normal deductions will be made;

4. The terms and conditions offered for the final offer are as spelled out in our memo dated 2/14/06.

On February 24, 2006, Mr. Stokes sent an e-mail message to Mr. McBride, which contained the Labor Agreements Final Proposal. Included was:

> *Holidays*
> *Memorial Day will become a paid holiday in exchange for the current George Washington's Birthday holiday.*

The Company did not pay its employees holiday pay for George Washington's birthday and the following Grievance was filed by Jim McBride on March 6, 2006:

Statement of Grievance:

> The Company scheduled the bargaining unit employees to work on George Washington's Birthday and did not pay them their proper holiday pay.

Articles & Sections of Contract Alleged Violated Including, But Not Limited To:

Article 6 Holidays, Paragraph 12 and Paragraph 14 of the extended Agreement.

Settlement Desired:

> Make the bargaining unit employees whole by paying everyone who worked four (4) hours pay for working and eight (8) hours holiday pay. Employees who did not work the holiday to be paid eight (8) hours holiday pay only.

The Company response was provided by Jim Fulgham, HR Manager, who wrote:

Disposition of Grievance:

> George Washington's Birthday was paid in accordance w/the ratified agreement.

The grievance was appealed to arbitration.

Issue

Were the employees entitled to holiday pay for George Washington's birthday, 2006?

If so, what is the remedy?

Relevant Provisions of the Agreement

Article 6, Section 12b–Holidays
Recognized Holidays–The holidays to be recognized are New Year's Day, Memorial Day, July 4th, Labor Day, Thanksgiving Day, Christmas Day, Martin Luther King, Jr.'s Birthday, and the employee's birthday. The Company retains the right to schedule work on the holidays enumerated above with the exception of Christmas and Thanksgiving. (When one of the named holidays falls on Saturday it shall be celebrated on the preceding Friday. Holidays falling on Sunday shall be celebrated on Monday.)

Article 22–effective Dates of Agreement
In witness whereof, the parties hereto have signed and executed this Agreement effective this 1st day of November 2005.

Positions of the Parties

The Union:

The Union stated that during the most recent contract negotiations, the Company proposed eliminating George Washington's birthday as a paid holiday and making Memorial Day a paid holiday instead. The Union countered with a proposal to have both days as paid holidays. The parties were unable to conclude a new agreement prior to October 31, 2005, the expiration date of the previous agreement. On October 25, 2005, the parties entered into a contingent agreement that extended the previous agreement subject to termination by either party with seven days' notice. The contingent agreement provided that the parties agreed "to apply the terms of any wage or benefit change agreed upon during the extension of the current Agreement back to the expiration of the Agreement on October 31, 2005."

In January 2006, the Company presented an offer that Memorial Day would be a paid holiday, but not Washington's birthday. On January 15, 2006, the Union membership voted and rejected that offer. One of the issues that especially concerned the membership was the loss of Washington's birthday as a paid holiday. After several more negotiation sessions, the Union scheduled a vote on the Company's final offer for Sunday, February 19, 2006. Because the Company scheduled that day as a workday, the date for the Union ratification vote was rescheduled to Sunday, February 26, 2006. On that day, the membership voted to ratify the agreement.

On February 14, 2006, the Company had posted a notice which stated that the Company and Union had agreed to swap the holidays. The notice stated that "beginning this year (actually next week), George Washington's birthday will not be a company-paid holiday." When the notice was posted, union representative Jim McBride called HR manager Jim Fulgham and told him that the notice should not have been posted because the Union had not ratified the Labor Agreement. As a result of that call, Mr. Fulgham took the notice down.

The Company did not treat Washington's birthday as a paid holiday and a Grievance was filed on March 6, 2006. Afterwards, the Company did treat Memorial Day as a paid holiday.

The Union stated that the Company's position was that the Contingent Agreement provided that wages and benefits agreed to subsequent to the expiration of the prior agreement would be applied retroactively to the expiration date of the prior agreement, the holidays were swapped, and the employees were entitled to pay for Memorial Day, but not Washington's birthday. That position, however, is unreasonable and not supported by the facts and should be rejected.

The Union argued that the Company's position emphasized the wrong clause of the Contingent Agreement. The first enumerated item of the parties' agreement provided that the previous agreement would remain in effect following its expiration. The agreement provided three methods for terminating the extension: (1) substitution of a new agreement; (2) a mutual agreement in writing to end the Agreement; (3) termination by either party on seven days written notice. By Washington's birthday, February 22, 2006, none of those actions had occurred. the previous contract was still in effect and there was no dispute that the previous agreement provided that Washington's birthday would be a paid holiday. The right of the employees to have that day treated as a paid holiday vested on that day. Obviously, a retroactivity clause cannot erase events that have already occurred. Therefore, the only reasonable construction of the Contingency Agreement is that the retroactivity clause was not applicable to that event. The Union claimed that in construing ambiguous contractual language, nonsensical results are to be avoided.

The Union stated that the Company will no doubt make the argument that it is unfair for the employees to receive pay for Washington's birthday in 2006 in light of the fact that they were paid for Memorial Day in 2006. That argument should not carry any weight. It is well settled that clear and unambiguous contractual language should be construed according to its plain meaning. In this case, the Company does not even contend that the prior Agreement which was extended and was in effect on February 22, 2006, did not clearly and unambiguously provide that Washington's birthday was a paid holiday. That was the effective language on February 22, 2006, and it should be applied.

The Union concluded:

> Based upon the foregoing, the Union urges that its grievance should be sustained and that as a remedy, the Arbitrator should award back pay plus interest.

The Company:

The Company stated that the Union demands that eligible employees be paid "Holiday Pay" for George Washington's birthday of 2006. The Company contended that the issue is whether the Grievance should be granted or denied and, if granted, employees otherwise eligible for holiday pay for George Washington's birthday would be compensated according to the previous Labor Agreement, which expired on October 30, 2005.

The Company stated that it never offered to add a new holiday benefit; just exchanged one for another, something agreed upon and ratified by the parties. For the past 15 years, the current and all preceding Collective Bargaining Agreements (CBAs) provided eight paid holidays. The previous CBA, which expired on October 30, 2005, had provided for eight paid holidays, but included George Washington's birthday. The current Agreement exchanged that holiday for the current CBA's Memorial Day. During the entire history of these last negotiations, the Company never indicated a willingness nor offered to increase the number of paid holidays beyond eight in a year. Beginning on October 18, 2005, when the Company substituted George Washington's birthday for Memorial Day, all offers and the final Agreement involved no increase in paid holidays, only this holiday exchange. There is no dispute that the final Agreement ratified on February 26, 2006, was consistent with the Company's long-standing and unwavering offer as to eight paid holidays per year.

The Company argued that the parties agreed to apply retroactively the terms and conditions of the new Agreement's wage or benefit change back to October 30, 2005. On October 25, 2005, the parties agreed to extend the expiring CBA until a new Agreement could be negotiated. This practice is not unusual, especially in more long-standing relationships such as this one. This practice benefits all parties by stabilizing the labor relations scene while allowing for a less hectic conclusion to negotiations. In such extensions, it is common to provide for some retroactivity, especially as to wages and, sometimes, benefits. This practice stabilizes conditions and avoids the temptation of employers to "drag things out" for financial gain.

The negotiations at issue contained three significant "wage and benefit" issues which were implemented during the first year of the new Agreement:

- A 40¢ per hour wage increase and some wage classification changes

- An $8.00 per week employee contribution for health insurance.

- A change in scheduled holidays.

The retroactivity of any "wage and benefits" back to the expiration of the prior CBA's expiration is clearly spelled out in the "Contingent Agreement on Contract Extension" signed on October 25, 2005. This Contingent Agreement assured both parties that the wage and benefit changes negotiated during any interim extension would be effective as of October 30, 2005, unless no new CBA was reached or either party terminated the Contract Extension with seven days' written notice. No such nullification occurred and the ratified CBA was made retroactive, as agreed.

The Company claimed that the parties did apply all the new "non-holiday" wage and benefit terms retroactively without dispute. The new CBA was ratified on February 26, 2006. Measuring from the expiration of the previous Agreement, this was 17 pay weeks. If one assumes the normal 40 hour work week, the 40 cents per hour retroactive pay increase would have amounted to $272.00 per employee ($17 \times 40¢ \times 40$ hrs). Employees were paid approximately $150.00 in retroactive pay. This was to account for the CBA's new $8.00 a week insurance payment of $136.00 ($8 \times 17$ weeks), while allowing for possible additional hours worked and other pay changes. Employees were paid a slightly "rounded up" amount of $150.00 to deal with all retroactive pay and benefit changes under the new CBA. As such, all other wage and benefit items in the CBA were applied retroactively to October 30, 2005.

The Company stated that the CBA ratification meeting was originally scheduled for February 19, 2006, prior to the George Washington holiday and the accident of a later meeting date must not have the unintended consequences sought in the Grievance. The original ratification date was set for February 19, 2006, and was delayed a week for scheduling convenience. In the interim between

February 19, 2006, and the ratification vote for February 26, 2006, there were no substantive changes to the proposal.

The later vote date did come after the holiday on February 22, 2006, but before the holiday was paid. While the actual pay date was not referenced, the arbitrator should take "judicial notice" of the fact that large companies do not pay employees for hours worked during the same work week; there was a delay of one or more weeks, as in this case. This was necessary in order to calculate overtime and to prepare and distribute checks. This time lag would have allowed the Company to pay the George Washington holiday pay if there had been no ratification and no retroactivity.

The Company explained that, in anticipation of the ratification vote on February 19, 2006, and so as to avoid any possible confusion, Mr. Fulgham posted a short notice to employees on February 14, 2006. This notice informed the employees that the new CBA would not have George Washington's birthday as a paid holiday, but would have Memorial Day as a paid holiday instead. This notice was taken down later on the day it was posted. There was no dispute that this notice was accurate, only that the CBA had not yet been ratified. Since the vote was then scheduled for the February 19, 2006, ratification was anticipated at that time. With the later ratification vote, an intervening holiday, George Washington's birthday, under the previous Agreement had occurred. The Union accepted that the current CBA became retroactive at the time of ratification vote on February 26, 2006, back to the old expiration date of October 30, 2005, by the time the obligation to pay for the prior week's work had occurred. The CBA in effect did not include an obligation to provide holiday pay for February 22, 2006.

Under the totality of circumstances, granting the Union's Grievance would have a harsh and unjust result. The cost of an additional paid holiday for the Company approaches $100,000.00. This is far more than a token amount, even for large plant. Consequently, it would be unreasonable and inequitable for the Company to be saddled with this obligation absent an unambiguous intent and mandate to do so. The Company contended that, furthermore, if the Union really believed that the information in Mr. Fulgham's posting was inaccurate, it should have clarified its position before all other retroactive payments were made. In this case, the Company asserted that there is no such clear obligation as the "Contingent Agreement on Contract Extension" signed by the parties applies the wage and benefit terms of the new agreement retroactive to October 30, 2005. This eliminates any obligation to provide holiday pay for George Washington's birthday in 2006.

The Company argued that the Union seeks to have it both ways by:

(a) allowing the retroactive application of other wages and benefits at considerable expense, plus;

(b) the payment of an extra 9th holiday.

Such a result is just too much of "having your cake and eating it, too."

As noted in the Sixth Edition of *How Arbitration Works* by Elkouri & Elkouri (BNA, Washington, D.C.):

> When an interpretation of an ambiguous contract would lead to harsh, absurd, or nonsensical results, while an alternative interpretation, equally plausible, would lead

to just and reasonable results, the latter interpretation will be used (at pgs 470–71).

The Company strongly contended that the terms of the Contingent Agreement on Contract Extension are unambiguous when read reasonably and nullify the George Washington's birthday holiday for 2006. The equitable application of normal contract interpretation rules would not allow the double rewards sought by this Grievance.

For the reasons stated above, the Company concluded that this Grievance should be denied.

Questions

1. Which party has the burden of proof in this case? Which level of proof will be used? Why?

2. Evaluate the Union's argument that, since George Washington's birthday holiday had occurred before the Agreement was ratified, employees were entitled to holiday pay.

3. Evaluate the Company's argument that the parties agreed to make the effective date retroactive.

4. Should the holiday pay be included in the category of "wages and benefits"?

5. Be the Arbitrator. How would you rule? Give your reasons.

Must Employee Take Assessment Test To Be Considered for Transfer?

CASE STUDY 11-3 This matter of arbitration stems from a bid on a job posting for the extra-hand position in the Technical Department on August 5, 2004. Ms. Pat Boone was notified that she was the senior bidder and was required to take a Work Keys test. Ms. Boone took the test, but did not score high enough to be awarded the job. She filed the following Grievance:

Nature of Grievance:

> Pat Boone was the successful bidder for a job posting in the Technical Dept. and was disqualified without any opportunity to train for the job.

Date of Occurrence:
August 5th, 2004
Settlement Desired:

> Allow Pat Boone to train for the job in question as specified in the Labor Agreement and allow her to accept the job if qualified. Make Ms. Boone whole.

Provision of Labor Agreement Alleged to be Violated:

Section VI. 10. And Addendum 22

In a letter dated October 8, 2004, Mr. Dan Keel, technical manager provided the Company response:

This grievance was filed after Pat Boone did not meet the Work Keys skill levels required for transfer to the Technical Department, and the bid was awarded to the next senior bidder, who did meet the skill levels. After a thorough review of the facts, the company finds there was no violation of the labor agreement.

Therefore, the company respectfully denies the grievance.

The Grievance was appealed. In a letter dated April 7, 2005, Mr. Mike Senter, plant manager, provided the Company's Step 3 Answer:

The company is willing to meet with the union to discuss the issues raised by this grievance in a good faith effort to reach a mutually acceptable agreement that will resolve the subject grievance.

The Grievance was appealed to arbitration.

Issue

Did the Company violate the CBA when it denied Pat Boone the extra-hand job bid in the Technical Department?

Relevant Provisions of the Agreement

Section VI. Determination and Application of Seniority Rights:

10 Filling Vacancies

B General

Seniority shall operate according to lines of progression agreed upon between the local Unions and Mill Management. Such lines of progression shall be subject to change only by mutual agreement of the two parties.

In the consideration of seniority for promotions, first preference shall be given job seniority. Where job seniority is equal, departmental seniority shall prevail. If job and departmental seniority are both equal, then Mill seniority shall determine the promotion. In filling subsequent vacancies in lines of progression, the senior qualified employee shall be promoted. Should a question arise as to whether or not the senior employee is qualified, and it cannot be resolved in agreement between the Union and Management, the senior employee will be given a trial period of up to thirty (30) days on the job in question.

If, during the trial period, it is found that the employee is not performing satisfactorily, he or she will be returned to his or her former job and become junior to the employee that bypasses him or her; the job will then be filled by the next senior qualified employee....

D. Job Vacancies and Qualifications

Notice of permanent vacancies in entry level jobs (bottom job classification) in all lines of progression and in single jobs not in line of progression shall be posted for seven calendar days on the Personnel Department bulletin board with the further understanding that copy of the notice will be given to each of the local unions. Employees who wish to bid on such job openings can do so by completing the appropriate bid form from the Personnel office during the bid posting period. Employees who are selected as successful bidders may not bid on other jobs for the next nine-month period commencing on the date of starting on the new job.

In implementing this Agreement, the Company shall take into consideration ability to do the job in question.

All employees covered by this agreement shall not be deemed unqualified for the job opening if their qualifications are as high as the minimally qualified employee currently on the job.

If any employee is found not to be qualified for a job after being transferred or promoted to that job and has had a reasonable opportunity of up to 30 days to train or if he, or she voluntarily chooses to do so within 30 work days after the transfer, the employee shall return to the employee's former job without loss of any seniority.

ADDENDUM

22. Before hiring from the outside, it is agreed that job openings within the mill will be filled in accordance with qualifications and seniority from employees who bid on posted job openings for transfer from another department in the mill and who are qualified at the time the job opening occurs. Management retains the right to determine the best qualified applicant.

Positions of the Parties

The Union:

The Union stated that this plant has established lines of progression wherein an employee can bid into the bottom job, which is called the extra-hand job, and move up the line of progression to the top job. For many years, the Company has required employees in the Maintenance and Electrical and Instrumentation (E&I) departments to take a qualification test of some sort to determine their eligibility. However, a production employee has never been required to take any type of test to be awarded a job bid into an entry level position. This procedure has always been done by seniority, Section 10 of the Collective Bargaining Agreement.

In August 2004, Ms. Pat Boone bid on a job posting for the extra-hand position in the Technical Department. Upon being notified she was the senior bidder, Ms. Boone was required to take a Work Keys test. Ms. Boone notified the president of the Local #986, Jim Kelter, about her requirement to take the test. Mr. Kelter went to the Human Resource Department to notify them of the Grievance. Ms. Boone failed the test per the requirements of the Company and was not awarded the bid.

The Union claimed that the Company violated the Collective Bargaining Agreement when it denied the Grievant the job bid for the Technical Department in August, 2004. Ms. Boone was the senior bidder on the job bid, was equally qualified compared to the person holding the position, and should have been awarded the position.

The Union stated that prior to establishing this Work Keys test for the extra-hand position in the Technical Department, the Company had never required production employees to qualify for an extra-hand job in any line of progression outside the traditional skilled jobs in the mill. In 2002, Norman Bear, HR manager, approached the president of Local #986, Jim Kelter and vice president, Tommy Sweats about establishing a Work Keys test for the entry level job in the Technical Department. during that meeting, the Union officials stated without dispute that they were not interested in a Work Keys test. At no time after that meeting did the Company say it wanted to do it anyway or offer to negotiate over the issue. The Company failed to provide any documentation and it did not notify the Union of its intentions. Also, the Company did not provide any documentation of proposals for determining the reason for needing this change.

The Union argued that the Company is well aware of the procedure for negotiating changes to working conditions, more specifically establishing a Work Keys test. In 2000 and 2001, the Company met with, proposed, and negotiated the Work Keys test for the various Maintenance Level Skill Sets with the Maintenance Local #505. The Union is clearly not opposed to Work Keys tests so long as the Union is utilized appropriately. When establishing the Work Keys test for Maintenance A, B, C, D, the Company was diligent in involving Ed Moore, president of the Maintenance Local #505.

The Union stated that Company witness, Norman Bear, said that the Company had been requiring tests for many years. However, it is clear that this testing has been done only for the skilled trade groups: Maintenance and Electrical and Instrumentation (E&I) departments.

The Union argued that the procedure for filling the extra-hand jobs in the bottom jobs in the lines of progression has always been filled per Section IV, 10, Job Vacancies and Qualifications. Bidders for these unskilled jobs have never been required to take a test to determine their qualifications. The sole purpose of seniority is to give senior employees the first opportunity to prove themselves to perform a specific task or duty. The Company could not prove it was having difficulty filling this position or the position of extra hand because no one had ever been disqualified. The true qualification standard for the production department lies within the language; Section VI, Section 10-D.

All employees covered by this agreement shall not be deemed unqualified for the job opening if their qualifications are as high as the minimally qualified employee currently on the job.

At the time Ms. Boone bid for the job, she was an extra hand in another department. This job was the same as the person holding the job at the time she bid. The job Ms. Boone bid on was an extra-hand job in the Technical Department.

ADDENDUM states:

> Before hiring from the outside, it is agreed that the job openings within the mill will be filled from the employees in accordance with qualifications and seniority from employees who bid on posted job opening for the transfer from another department in the mill and who are qualified at the time the job openings occurs. Management retains the right to determine the best qualified applicant.

The Company has claimed that it retained the rights to determine qualifications for job bidders under this section of the Agreement. However, it is the Union's position that this language is consistent with the Company's right to determine the best qualified applicant when hiring from outside the mill as the paragraph begins. This particular section clearly discusses determining applicants from outside the mill. *Webster's New World Dictionary: Second College Edition* defines the word, applicant, as a "person that applies for employment, help, etc." Ms. Boone was already employed; she bid on a different job; she was not an applicant for employment.

If this language applied to job bids and filling vacancies, the Union asked: "Why wouldn't it be placed in Section VI, Subsection 10-D, Job Vacancies and Qualifications, instead of in an Addendum, which references, 'hiring from outside the mill'." The Union concluded:

> The Company violated Ms. Boone's rights under the CBA by denying her the opportunity to train in an extra-hand position in the Technical Department. She was the senior bidder and was as qualified as an extra hand in another department. Ms. Boone was never given an opportunity to train and should have been allowed 30 days to prove she could perform the job.
>
> The Company clearly established the past practice of allowing the senior bidder in a production line of progression to be awarded the job and could not and did not show otherwise. The Company had no reason to establish a Work Keys test for this job, because there was no justified reason. No one had even been disqualified for the position of extra hand. Ms. Boone met the qualification requirement under Section 6, Subsection 10-D of the CBA. She should have been awarded the job.

As remedy, the Union requested the grievances should be sustained and to make the grievant whole, to direct the Company to allow the grievant to train in the position of extra hand in the Technical Department line of progression, and to stop requiring future job bidders to pass a Work Keys test to qualify for this position.

The Company:

The Company claimed that the use of the Work Keys system is designed to objectively determine whether employees have the minimum qualifications and job skills necessary for transferring into various jobs in the plant. The Company began utilizing the Work Keys system in the fall of 2000. By

the time the Grievant took the Work Keys assessment in an effort to transfer into the Technical Department, Work Keys assessment had been utilized in the plant for nearly four years.

The Union contended that the Company violated the Collective Bargaining Agreement by not allowing Ms. Boone who did not pass her Work Keys assessment to train for the position for 30 days to determine whether she would be able to become qualified after this training.

The Company argued that neither the Labor Agreement nor past practice supports the Union's position. Management has always had the exclusive right to determine whether employees are qualified to do a job and it has utilized various objective "paper-pencil" tests over the years to make those determinations. The Labor Agreement gives it complete discretion to determine whether an employee is qualified. Seniority comes into play only if the employee is qualified at the time the job opening occurs. The Work Keys assessment system is a fair and objective way to measure the necessary job skills and qualifications of employees and it is consistent with the parties' CBA.

Mr. Bear explained that the Company has utilized various objective tests over the years to determine the qualifications of applicants and employees. Mr. Bear was impressed by the Work Keys assessment system when he first became aware of it in the summer of 2000. Work Keys is a skills assessment system that determines an individual's level of proficiency in a given skill area and identifies pools of qualified applicants who have achieved the levels of proficiency needed to perform a job as determined through job analysis. Work Keys is not a test, per se; it is criterion-based. Work Keys assessment scores reflect what individuals can do relative to job requirements, not relative to scores of other individuals who have been assessed.

Mr. Bear was impressed by the Work Keys job analysis profiling procedure, which is conducted by the employees who have performed the job in question. The benefit of having employees determine the skill levels necessary to perform a job is obvious. Experienced employees have knowledge of the job; they are referred to as Subject Matter Experts (SMEs). Mr. Bear recognized that this unique aspect of the Work

Keys assessment system was particularly valuable to the Company because it was perfectly tailored to the Labor Agreement which states: "All employees covered by this Agreement shall not be deemed unqualified for the job opening if their qualifications are as high as the minimally qualified employee currently on the job." The Company asked: "Who better to determine the tasks and skills required for an entry-level position than those who have performed it?"

After reviewing an initial task list for relevance and comprehensiveness, the SMEs delete tasks they consider not applicable, revise some tasks, and add new tasks considered important to the job in question. The SMEs consider and refine the initial task list thoroughly to make certain that the list accurately reflects the job requirements. The SMEs then evaluate each task in terms of its importance and the time they spend on the task relative to the time they spend on other tasks to determine which tasks are most critical and least critical, day in and day out.

After reviewing and discussing the examples associated with Work Keys skill levels, the SMEs arrive at a consensus as to the skill level necessary for each task required by the position. The SMEs rank the various skills to determine their criticality to performing the position.

Mr. Bear discussed the Work Keys system with Union officials and by fall 2000, every local Union knew about the system. Local 986 requested information from the Company about Work Keys after it was first given for the Class D Mechanic position. Afterwards, the Company expanded the use of Work Keys for Class C Mechanics, Class B Mechanics, Class A Mechanics, and E&I Class C Mechanics, E&I Class B Mechanics, and E&I Class A Mechanics.

In spring 2002, Mr. Bear discussed utilizing the Work Keys system for the entry-level position, extra hand, in the Technical Department. Mr. Jim Kelter, President of Local 986, was "lukewarm" about the idea, but others liked it because it gave equal treatment to everybody.

Six SMEs conducted the extra hand job profiling process on May 23, 2002. These SMEs had been with the Company for an average of more than 17 years and in their present positions for approximately 4½ years. Using the job profiling procedures, the group determined the necessary skill levels for entry and effective performance in the extra hand position. The SMEs ranked the skills according to their criticality to performing the job in the following order: (1) reading for information, (2) applied mathematics, (3) locating information, (4) observation, (5) applied technology, (6) teamwork, (7) listening, and (8) writing.

The first extra hand Work Keys assessment was administered on June 19, 2003. Kelly Hardy, an external applicant and Dan Conners, a transfer bidder from another department, passed the assessment and were employed in the Technical Department on July 27, 2003. Neither the Union nor any other person raised objections to the first two extra hand Work Keys assessments.

On July 26, 2004, the Company posted another opening for the extra hand position in the Technical Department. Ms. Boone did not file a Grievance because the job bid required her to take the Work Keys assessment. Instead, Ms. Boone and the Union waited for the results of her Work Keys assessment before a Grievance was filed. As such, Ms. Boone waived her right to argue that she should not have been given the Work Keys assessment. The Agreement requires Grievances to be filed within five days to be timely. The Union acknowledged that the Union failed to file a timely Grievance within five days of the job bid being posted and Ms. Boone being tested.

Ms. Boone was the most senior employee to bid for the position, but she only passed two out of the four areas assessed. Because she was only qualified in two of the four skills assessed, she was disqualified for the extra hand position. Ms. Boone achieved a level four in applied mathematics, but a level five was required. Ms. Boone achieved a level four in locating information, but a level five was required. Ms. Boone demonstrated the requisite levels for observation and reading for information. To qualify for the position, employees must have qualified in three out of four skill areas. Brad Henry, the next most senior bidder for the position, passed the Work Keys assessment by qualifying in three out of four areas. Henry was then transferred into the Technical Department on August 15, 2004.

The Union claimed that Ms. Boone was the "successful bidder" and that the term "successful" really just means "most senior." The viewpoint that seniority alone should determine who fills vacant positions ignores the clear language of the Labor Agreement and the longstanding past practice at the plant that employees must first be qualified for the position in question. If seniority alone determined how vacant positions were to be filled, the Labor Agreement would not state, as it does: "Job openings within the mill are filled in accordance with qualifications and seniority from employees...who are qualified at the time the job opening occurs."

The Union argued that Ms. Boone should have been allowed to train for the job in question and accept the job if she became qualified after training. The Union referred to the 30-day training period, but that section applies only if:

1. the Company has already determined that the employee was qualified at the time of the job opening;

2. the employee has already transferred into the position; and

3. after training in the new position (for up to 30 days), either the Company or the employee decides that the employee should return to his former position.

Mr. Bear explained that the purpose of this section is to protect the employee's seniority in the former position. this section does not provide, nor has it ever provided, for a 30-day trial or training period. In fact, the Union has lost this same argument in a prior arbitration. In 1987, Arbitrator J. Marler ruled that "there was no implied right to a trial period in the contract, that the Company and the Union were capable of, but had not, contracted for such a trial period, and that adding a trial period would be inconsistent with the contract."

Under the Labor Agreement, the Company claimed it has the right to determine whether an employee is minimally qualified at the time the job opening occurs and up to 30 days after the qualified senior bidder goes into the position and trains. this is a two-part process. According to the clear language of the Labor Agreement, the Company has the exclusive right to determine the best-qualified applicant at the time the job is posted. The Union cannot point to any contract language that requires employees to be given 30 days to train to become qualified. The Labor Agreement is simple. To fill a vacancy, one must be (1) qualified for the position, (2) as determined by the Company, (3) at the time the job opening occurs.

The Company claimed that, even in the absence of a specific contract provision, Management had been entitled to give reasonable and appropriate written, oral, performance, aptitude, and physical abilities tests relative to job performance, as an aid in determining the ability of competing employees. Recognizing the Company's authority to institute and utilize tests, the Company is vested with continuing authority to change its testing methods and procedures in accordance with the exercise of sound judgment. Mr. Bear informed the Local #986 about the Work Keys system, not because he was obligated to negotiate its use, but in the spirit of cooperation.

The Company contended that the use of a fair and objective test, such as Work Keys Assessment, helps avoid the appearance of favoritism or discrimination in the employee selection procedure. The employment of tests, fairly and objectively administered, should appear to be desirable and in the interests of the employees, the Company, and the Union. A sound testing procedure should serve to allay any suspicion among competing employees as to favoritism or discrimination in awarding jobs. The use of tests constituted an effort to apply objective measures of qualifications, rather than to leave the determination to the general judgment and subjective reactions of Management.

The Company stated that Ms. Boone has not been denied the extra hand position in the Technical Department because she did worse on a test than other people. At the time the job was posted, she did not have the minimum skills required to be an extra hand, according to the Technical Department SMEs. The key to the whole Work Keys system is the job analysis and job-profiling procedure because the employees who were already experienced extra hands determined the tasks required by the job and the level of skill needed to perform the job effectively. This detailed and prolonged process is the heart of the Work Keys system and what makes it different and better than all its "paper/pencil" predecessors. With Work Keys, it is not the Company or outside consultant who says, "You need to be able to do x" or "you should be this smart to hold this job." Work Keys is different because the SMEs set the bar. The Union did not question

Work Keys' validity, but raised some questions about its use. The Union claimed that it was okay for the Company to use Work Keys assessment for the "skilled" Mechanic positions, but it was not appropriate for the "unskilled" extra hand position. This Union position is not based on contract language. First, there is no contractual language which distinguishes the Company's right to determine an employee's qualifications to be a mechanic versus an extra hand. The Company has an exclusive right to make this determination for all job openings in the Mill. The Company concluded that Ms. Boone's grievance should be denied because:

1. Ms. Boone was not qualified for the extra hand job opening posted on July 26, 2004;

2. The Company did not violate the CBA by not allowing Ms. Boone to assume the extra hand position for training;

3. The CBA does not require or imply that employees are entitled to a 30-day trial period; and

4. The Company was within its contractual rights to utilize the Work Keys system to determine qualifications of employees.

Questions

1. Which party has the burden of proof? Which level of proof will be used? Why?

2. Evaluate the Union's past practice argument.

3. Does it matter which type of assessment is used by the Company?

4. If the Union alleged that the Work Keys Assessment was not valid, which party would have to prove the validity?

5. You are the arbitrator. What is your decision? Why?

Copyright GettyImages

CHAPTER 12

Employee Discipline

We devote an entire chapter to employee discipline, an important union–management issue, for the following reasons:

- It is the most commonly heard grievance in arbitration, making up approximately 40 percent of the decided cases.

- It is approached consistently by arbitrators, who typically rely on established principles to make their determinations.[1]

- It is the most likely to involve readers of this book, who are likely to discipline employees in their careers in unionized or nonunionized settings and have that action challenged by a union, employees, government agencies such as the Equal Employment Opportunity Commission (EEOC), or the courts.

Employee discipline is approached in this chapter by discussing its changing significance over time and its various elements, thereby enabling the reader to apply considerations discussed in Chapter 11 to this issue.

THE CHANGING SIGNIFICANCE OF INDUSTRIAL DISCIPLINE

Employee discipline represents both organizational conditions and actions. Organizational conditions can lead employees to form a disciplined work group that is largely self-regulated and willingly accepts management's directions and behavioral standards. Managerial actions are taken against an employee who has violated organizational rules.[2] This dimension has changed over time.

Historical Overview of Employer Disciplinary Policies

During the eighteenth and nineteenth centuries, the employer exercised "unrestricted discretion" in directing the work crew.

In 1884, a judge in the State of Tennessee wrote the following:

> All may dismiss their employees at will, be they many or few, for good cause, for no cause[,] or even for cause morally wrong, without being thereby guilty of legal wrong.[3]

This judge's statement laid the foundation for the common law employment-at-will doctrine, which will be covered next in this chapter.

Discipline during this time was sometimes harsh. Employees who were verbally insolent to employers could have their tongues burned with a hot iron or be subjected to public humiliation (e.g., a public whipping in the town square).

By 1935, management's total discretion to discipline employees was challenged on pragmatic and legal grounds. Frederick Taylor's theory of *scientific management,* popular by 1920, stressed the financial waste that occurred when employees were discharged in an arbitrary or capricious manner. According to Taylor, management had an obligation to determine and obtain desired employee work behavior and to correct, rather than discharge, the employee who deviated from managerial standards.

The Wagner Act of 1935 legally shaped management's disciplinary policies. A primary feature of this legislation was the prohibition of discriminatory discipline of employees because of their union activities or membership. An independent agency, the National Labor Relations Board (NLRB), was created, in part, for enforcement purposes. Management often had to defend disciplinary actions against charges filed with this agency, with a potential remedy being reinstatement with back pay. This was the first time that management could be legally held accountable for employee discipline, a situation that encouraged further development of corrective disciplinary principles and policies.[4] The NLRB also affected organizational discipline procedures indirectly when it ruled that discipline and grievance procedures were mandatory issues subject to collective bargaining. As a result of this NLRB decision, nearly all existing collective bargaining agreements now have both a provision regulating discipline and a grievance procedure that makes possible the submission of discipline issues to arbitration.

From the 1940s to the present, managerial policies on employee discipline were greatly influenced by the growth and development of labor arbitration. Currently, arbitrators have the following three broad powers on discipline:

1. To determine what constitutes "just cause" for discipline.

2. To establish "standards of proof and evidence."

3. To review and modify or eliminate the penalty imposed by management when warranted.

Employment-at-Will Doctrine and Wrongful Discharge Consideration in Nonunion Employees

In 2007, the number of union members in the workforce was 15.7 million, or 12.1 percent of the workforce, and unions represented another 1.5 million workers who were not members. In other words, today more than 85 percent of the U.S. workforce is not afforded the protection of a union contract or a collectively bargained grievance-arbitration procedure. Most of these nonrepresented employees are "employment-at-will" employees and may be discharged at will.[5]

Under the *public policy exception* to the employment-at-will doctrine, an employee is **wrongfully discharged** if and when the discharge is inconsistent with an explicit, well-established public policy of the state. As an example, an employer cannot discharge an employee for filing a workers' compensation claim after being injured on the job or refusing to break a law at the direction of the employer. (Forty-four states have made one or more public policy exceptions to the employment-at-will doctrine. Not all states recognize the same number or type of public policy exceptions.)

The *implied contract exception* to the employment-at-will doctrine occurs when an employer and employee form an implied contract, even though there is no express, written instrument regarding the employment relationship. For example, an employer makes oral or written representations to employees about job security or procedures that will be followed before adverse actions (discharges) are taken. These representations may create an employment contract. (Forty-one states have recognized the implied contract exception to the employment-at-will doctrine.)

The *covenant-of-good-faith and fair dealing* exception to the employment-at-will doctrine means that employer personnel decisions are subject to the "just cause" standard, prohibiting terminations made in bad faith or motivated by malice. (Twelve states have recognized the covenant-of-good-faith and fair dealing exception to the employment-at-will doctrine.[6]) See Exhibit 12.1 for the listing of states that have exceptions to the employment-at-will doctrine.

A RAND Corp. study has found that employers overestimate the potential costs of a wrongful discharge suit and incur indirect costs that are 100 times higher when they attempt to avoid these suits. These indirect costs occur when employers do not terminate employees who perform poorly, establish complex and more costly hiring and decision-making processes, or use severance payments to deter wrongful termination claims.[7]

In 1987, Montana became the first (and still the only) state to have passed legislation (Wrongful Discharge from Employment Act) which adopted a "good cause" standard for discharge of employees with contracts of an unspecified duration. Under the Act, a discharge is wrongful only if (a) the discharge is in retaliation for the employee's refusal to violate a public policy or reporting a violation of public policy, (b) the discharge is not for "good cause" and the employee had completed his/her probationary period, or (c) the employer violated an expressed provision of its own written personnel policy. Under the Montana Act, if a discharged employee makes a valid offer to arbitrate and the employer accepts, the arbitrator's decision will be final and binding and there is no right for the employee to bring a lawsuit. If the employee prevails, the arbitrator will issue an appropriate remedy and the employer must pay the arbitrator's fee and all costs associated with the arbitration. Due to Montana having less than a million employees in its workforce, broad application of the results cannot be applied across the United States.[8]

Exhibit 12.1

Recognition of Employment-at-Will Exceptions, by State

State	Public-Policy Exception	Implied-Contract Exception	Covenant of Good Faith and Fair Dealing
Total	45	41	12
Alabama	yes	yes	no
Alaska	yes	yes	yes
Arizona	yes	yes	yes
Arkansas	yes	yes	no
California	yes	yes	yes
Colorado	yes	yes	no
Connecticut	yes	yes	yes
Delaware	no	no	yes
District of Columbia	yes	yes	no
Florida	no	no	no
Georgia	no	no	no
Hawaii	yes	yes	no
Idaho	yes	yes	yes
Illinois	yes	yes	no
Indiana	yes	yes	no
Iowa	yes	yes	no
Kansas	yes	yes	no
Kentucky	yes	yes	no
Louisiana	no	no	no
Maine	no	yes	no
Maryland	yes	yes	no
Massachusetts	yes	yes	yes
Michigan	yes	yes	no
Minnesota	yes	yes	no
Mississippi	yes	no	no
Missouri	yes	yes	no
Montana	yes	yes	yes
Nebraska	yes	yes	no
Nevada	yes	yes	yes
New Hampshire	yes	yes	yes
New Jersey	yes	yes	no
New Mexico	yes	yes	no
New York	no	yes	no
North Carolina	yes	no	no
North Dakota	yes	yes	no
Ohio	yes	yes	no
Oklahoma	yes	yes	yes
Oregon	yes	yes	no
Pennsylvania	yes	no	no
Rhode Island	no	no	no
South Carolina	yes	yes	no
South Dakota	yes	yes	no

(Continued)

State	Public-Policy Exception	Implied-Contract Exception	Covenant of Good Faith and Fair Dealing
Tennessee	yes	yes	no
Texas	yes	yes	no
Utah	yes	yes	no
Vermont	yes	yes	no
Virginia	yes	no	no
Washington	yes	yes	no
West Virginia	yes	yes	no
Wisconsin	yes	yes	no
Wyoming	yes	yes	yes

Exhibit 12.1
(Continued)

SOURCE: Charles J. Muhl, "The Employment-at-Will Doctrine: Three Major Exceptions," *Monthly Labor Review* 124 (January 2001), pp. 3–11; David J. Walsh and Joshua L. Schwarz, "State Common Law Wrongful Discharge Doctrines: Up-Dates, Refinement, and Rationales", 33 *American Business Law Journal* (Summer 1996); David Autor, "Outsourcing at Will: Unjust Dismissal Doctrine and the Growth of Temporary Help Employment," *Journal of Labor Economics*, Vol. 21, No. 1, January 2003, pp. 1–42.

In an address to the National Academy of Arbitrators in 2006, former president George Nicolau noted that more than one million employees are discharged in the United States annually without the right to appeal the discharge decision. Nicolau called for a National Unfair Dismissal Statute which would provide protection against unfair dismissal to those employees who have worked for an employer (15 or more employees) for a period of one year. Nicolau believed that a one-year period should provide ample time for the employer to assess the performance of an employee and determine the needs of the company. After one year of continuous employment, a covered employee would have protection against an unfair dismissal by an employer.[9]

Present-Day Significance of Discipline

Disciplinary systems are designed to discourage problematic behavior and to quickly correct problems when they are discovered. The first-line supervisor is usually the first person to become involved in disciplinary action. The first-line supervisor usually conducts the initial investigation of the facts surrounding the employee's misconduct. Furthermore, it is usually the first-line supervisor who recommends disciplinary action or has the authority to take disciplinary action. Because certain employee rights must be protected, employers may decide to have an oversight of the supervisor's decisions to discipline and require higher-level approval before disciplinary action is taken. Therefore, it is possible to introduce some level of restriction on supervisors to protect employee rights without adversely affecting supervisors' belief in the effectiveness of the disciplinary system.[10]

Management, union officials, and employees at unionized firms are strongly affected by disciplinary actions and arbitrators' decisions concerning disciplinary actions. (See the Labor Relations in Action feature on page 526 for potential disciplinary situations that have occurred on an automobile assembly line.) An arbitrator has two typical options in a case involving a discharged employee. The arbitrator can (1) uphold management's discharge decision or (2) reinstate the employee with some or all back pay for wages lost as a result of the employee's forced absence.

LABOR RELATIONS IN ACTION
Disciplinary Possibilities on the Assembly Line

The following excerpts are taken from *Rivethead* (New York: Warner Books, 1992), written by Ben Hamper concerning his work experiences on an automobile manufacturing line. These situations reflect vivid, real-world employees' behaviors that management attempted to correct through disciplinary actions. Unions could claim management's response to each of these actions was inappropriate by filing a grievance that might, in time, be resolved by an arbitrator. The first five considerations involve employees Hamper knew on the line; the remainder of the events were perpetrated by Hamper and co-workers.

- Roy captured a tiny mouse at work and built a home for the rodent. He took care of the mouse until one lunch break, when he claimed it was mocking his job performance. He then grabbed the mouse by the tail, took a brazing torch, and "incinerated his little buddy at arm's length."
- Lightnin' had no known job assignment but would spend each workday in the men's washroom leaning up against the last urinal wall, asleep.

- Jack hated the company and thought management was out to get him. One night he claimed that the company purposefully robbed him by not returning cigarettes for cash he placed into a vending machine. He then took a sledgehammer (which he labeled "the Better Business Bureau") and beat the vending machine to a glass and metallic pulp.
- Franklin was a man who took real pleasure in beating up other employees. He snuck up on one employee who refused to give him an extra pair of safety gloves and "smashed him over the head with a door latch." The employee received a dozen stitches in his head, and Franklin received a 30-day suspension.
- Louie peddled half pints of Canadian Club and Black Velvet at the workplace, delivering the alcohol to the customer's work station.

Mr. Hamper also admitted to drinking rather substantially at work. His regular intake included "a forty ouncer at first break, another one at lunch, then . . . a pint or two of whiskey for the last part of the shift."

He and another employee also doubled up on the job, where one employee would perform both jobs, allowing the other employee to sleep in a hiding place. This practice basically gave each employee a four-hour nap during the work shift.

In a 1987 study, researchers found that management loses more discipline cases than it wins, as arbitrators follow the second alternative in a majority of their decisions.[11] This loss is advertised when the reinstated employee is brought back to the shop floor. Reinstatement of the employee with back pay represents a financial loss to management and supervisory authority may also be reduced. It is rare for a supervisor who experiences the return of a disciplined employee to his work group with a large back-pay check to pursue subsequent disciplinary action with as much vigor and initiative.[12]

In a more recent study involving 85 employers and a total of just over 2,000 arbitration cases over termination, 767 or 63 percent of the termination were sustained by the arbitrators. This percentage is considerably higher than the percentages in studies conducted between 1942 and 1967 where the discharges upheld by arbitrators ranged from 39 percent to 46 percent. There are two explanations for the increase: (1) previous studies were based on published decisions and (2) over the last 40 to 60 years, a body of "common law of the shop" has been developed as reasonable guides on the definition of the "just cause" standard in a wide variety of circumstances and are now being used by managers.

Of the 767 employees who were terminated and then offered reinstatement, nearly 100 percent accepted reinstatement; only one percent agreed to a monetary buyout. After one year from their reinstatement, only ten percent had been terminated again and four percent had quit their jobs. The vast majority (86 percent) remained on the job, and more than half of these employees had better disciplinary records than before their terminations. Interestingly, of the 1,303 cases in which the discharge decision was upheld by the arbitrators, only 12 employees (less than one percent) who did not prevail in their arbitration filed a duty of fair representation (dfr) suit against the union. As a result, it may be concluded that discharged employees were satisfied with their unions' representation in the arbitration hearing.

In these same 85 employers, there were 1,113 suspension arbitrations (five days or more). Arbitrators upheld 72 percent of the suspensions. The employers reported that the disciplinary records of these employees were the same or better after the arbitration than before. Only 25 percent of the employers reported that arbitration had a negative effect on workplace relationships. In general terms, the negative effect was expressed as "low morale." More specific comments included: co-workers became angry with each other, company witnesses were harassed, reinstated employees were bitter against the company, and overturning the disciplinary action undermined the supervisor's authority.[13]

There is also no guarantee that the reinstated employee will perform well when returned to the job. Two studies have found that 51 to 62 percent of the reinstated employees performed their work in a below-average capacity, with a majority having subsequent disciplinary problems.[14] Moreover, the seniority of the discharged employee (often considered an influential mitigating circumstance by arbitrators) was insignificant in predicting the employee's performance after reinstatement.[15]

Arbitral reversal of management decisions can also create tensions between different levels of management officials. As noted in Chapter 1, management participants in the labor relations process do not constitute a unified group. The first-line supervisor is often most involved in employee discipline, having typically trained the employee; created past practices in the department that might influence the arbitrator's decision; and witnessed, reported, and in some cases, participated in the events resulting in discipline. The supervisor also is the management official who directly administers discipline to employees.

Other management officials, such as labor relations representatives, monitor these activities to make sure that supervisory actions are consistent with company policy, reversing them if they are not, to avoid adverse arbitration decisions. This reversal can cause tensions, as indicated in the following remarks of a first-line supervisor:

> I had this one troublemaker. He was a solid goldbricker. He couldn't cut the buck on any job. I tried everything, but he was lazy and he was a loudmouth. I caught him in the toilet after being away from his machine for over an hour. I told him he was through and to go upstairs and pick up his check. And [deleted]. Do you know what those college boys in personnel did? He gives them some bull about being sick and weakly and the next day he is sitting on a bench in the department next to mine. He says to me, "Well, wise guy you don't count for nothin' around here. Every time I see you, I'm going to call you 'Mr. Nothin'."[16]

What management loses in arbitration hearings appears to be the union's gain. Most if not all union members believe the union should be responsive to problems arising from their day-to-day working conditions that remain after the formal labor agreement has been negotiated. There is no more dramatic example of union concern for its members than "saving" an employee's job. Almost every union newspaper contains at least one article per issue that describes (along with appropriate pictures of union representatives, the grievant, and the back-pay check) how the union successfully defended an employee against an unjust act of management. A representative article from one union newspaper proclaimed in bold headlines, "Worker Wins $5,895 in Back Pay When Fired for Opening Beer Can."[17]

Perhaps a disciplinary action carries the most significance for the affected employee. Discharge has been viewed by unions as *economic capital punishment*, for it deprives the employee of currently earning a livelihood and at the same time (with the discharge on his or her work record) makes it difficult to find future employment elsewhere. Any form of discipline represents an embarrassment to individuals who do not like being told they are wrong and, in some instances, have to explain their unpaid removal from work to their friends and family.

ELEMENTS OF THE JUST CAUSE PRINCIPLE IN EMPLOYEE DISCIPLINE

Discipline for Just Cause and Discipline's Legitimate Purpose

Management has always insisted that there be order in the workplace. In reaching this goal, management has developed work rules with respect to employee conduct and included some form of discipline, including discharge, for misconduct. Unions almost always accepted these themes; however, unions have insisted that a disciplinary system be fair in principle and in application. Management and unions have agreed to a verbal formula which would require management to show a valid reason (cause) for imposing discipline and to show that the penalty imposed was appropriate (just) given the nature of the offense and the surrounding circumstances, including the employee's years of service and employee's disciplinary history. Through the application of this language, third-party arbitrators (neutrals) determine not only the propriety of a given disciplinary action, but also the standards of conduct that employers may require, and how far, and in what manner, they may regulate employees' lives.[18]

In addition, government agencies such as the EEOC and the NLRB indicate that employee discipline must be for **just cause**, which must meet all of the following criteria[19]:

1. There is clear and convincing evidence that a disciplinary offense was committed by the grievant.

2. The disciplinary action taken by management was appropriate for the offense committed.

3. The discipline cannot be arbitrary or discriminatory; instead, it must be applied consistently to employees given similar circumstances.

Although there is no legal or standard definition of "just cause," arbitrator Harry Platt might have said it best when he wrote:

> It is ordinarily the function of an Arbitrator in interpreting a contract provision which requires "sufficient cause" as a condition precedent to discharge not only to determine whether the employee involved is guilty of wrongdoing ... but also to safeguard the interests of the discharged employee by making reasonably sure that the causes for discharge were just and equitable and such as would appeal to reasonable and fair-minded persons as warranting discharge. To be sure, no standards exist to aid an Arbitrator in finding a conclusive answer to such a

question and, therefore, perhaps the best he can do is to decide what a reasonable man, mindful of the habits and customs of industrial life and of the standards of justice and fair dealing prevalent in the community, ought to have done under similar circumstances and in that light to decide whether the conduct of the discharged employee was defensible and the disciplinary penalty just.[20]

Arbitrators have long held that management has the right to direct the work force and manage its operations efficiently. Indeed, inefficient operations harm both the employer and employees because higher costs and subsequent reduced profits can result in employee layoffs. Discipline can improve efficiency by accomplishing the following interrelated purposes:

- *To set an example of appropriate behavior.* For example, management impresses on its employees the seriousness of being tardy by giving one tardy employee a five-day suspension.

- *To transmit rules of the organization.* As illustrated in the preceding purpose, management has transmitted a rule of the organization—lateness will not be accepted.

- *To promote efficient production.* Discipline those employees who either cannot or will not meet production standards.

- *To maintain respect for the supervisor.* In a sense, discipline shows the employee who is the boss. A supervisor who does not discipline poor employees weakens managerial authority.

- *To correct an employee's behavior.* Indicate what is expected, how the employee can improve, and what negative consequences might result in the future if the behavior does not change. The assumption here is that most employees have good intentions and will improve if management will simply show them the error of their ways.

Discipline can accomplish all these purposes, but arbitrators must be convinced that management based its action on "correction," which is discipline's only legitimate purpose. Because discharge is a terminal rather than a corrective action, it is appropriate only when all other attempts at correction have failed or the nature of the offense is so heinous, such as theft, attacking a supervisor, and so on, as to make lesser forms of discipline inappropriate. Correction permeates the elements of the just cause principle of employee discipline as shown in Exhibit 12.2,[21] which is a guide for management in employee disciplinary cases.

Collective bargaining agreements usually do not include a disciplinary structure that calls for specific penalties for specific offenses. Such arrangements have limited feasibility in today's complex workplace. Employee misconduct, such as insubordination, fighting, stealing, and so on takes many forms, and the circumstances surrounding an act of misconduct have a multitude of variations, such as provocation, horseplay, and so on. In addition, each wrongdoer has his or her own explanations for behavior, experience, and work history. Unions tend to resist a Table of Penalties, such as shown in Exhibit 12.3, because they believe such prescriptions are overly strict and inflexible. Unions prefer that consideration be given to fairness and equity at the workplace. On the other hand, management prefers consistency in approach and seeks to preserve a large measure of discretion in determining the penalty in any given case. Since management's goal is usually not achieved in bargaining, management usually establishes rules of conduct unilaterally

Exhibit 12.2

Seven Tests for "Just Cause" Employee Terminations

If the answer is "no" to one or more of the following questions, just cause for termination is not present or is seriously weakened.

1. *Notice.* Did the employer give to the employee forewarning or foreknowledge of the possible or probable consequences of the employee's disciplinary conduct?
   If no, the grievance is sustained.

2. *Reasonable rule or order.* Was the employer's rule or managerial order reasonably related to (a) orderly, efficient, and safe operation of the employer's business, and (b) performance that the employer might properly expect of the employee?
   If no, the grievance is sustained.

3. *Investigation.* Did the employer, before administering the discipline to an employee, make an effort to discover whether the employee did in fact violate or disobey a rule or order of management?
   If no, the grievance is sustained.

4. *Fair investigation.* Was the employer's investigation conducted in a fair and objective manner?
   If no, the grievance is sustained.

5. *Proof.* At the investigation, did the decision maker possess substantial evidence or proof that the employee was guilty as charged?
   If no, the grievance is sustained.

6. *Equal treatment.* Has the employer applied its rules, orders, and penalties even-handedly and without discrimination to all employees?
   If no, the grievance is sustained.

7. *Penalty.* Was the degree of discipline administered by the employer in a particular case reasonably related to the seriousness of the employee's proven offense?
   If no, the grievance is sustained.

If the answers to the questions above are YES, then additional questions are considered in determining the degree of penalty:

1. Are there any due process procedural violations of the employee's rights, such as failure to give notice of charges, not allowing the employee to face his or her accusers, or lack of counsel?

2. Are there any mitigating circumstances, such as a record of long-term service with the employer or fault on the part of management which may result in a penalty less than termination, such as reinstatement without back pay?

SOURCE: Adapted from *Enterprise Wire Co. and Enterprise Independent Union,* 46 LA 359, 1996 (Carroll R. Daugherty). Also see Adolph M. Koven and Susan L. Smith, *Just Cause: The Seven Tests,* revised by Donald F. Farwell (Washington, D.C.: Bureau of National Affairs, 1992); Jack Dunsford, "Arbitral Discretion: The Tests for Just Cause," *Proceedings of the 42nd Annual Meeting of the National Academy of Arbitrators* (Washington, D.C.: Bureau of National Affairs); also see Adolph M. Koven and Susan Smith, *Just Cause: The Seven Tests,* Third Edition by Kenneth May, Washington, D.C.: Bureau of National Affairs, Inc., 2006.

under its management's rights clause and describes each prohibited offense and the corresponding penalty to be assessed for committing each separate offense.[22]

Degree of Proof in Disciplinary Cases: Nature of the Evidence and Witness Credibility

An overriding consideration in discipline and discharge cases is management's burden of proof to establish that the employee committed an infraction. Such proof is easier to establish in situations having objectively measured indicators

Offense (Cause of Action)	First Offense	Second Offense	Third Offense
1. Tardiness–less than one hour	Reprimand	1-day suspension	3-day suspension
2. Unauthorized absence	Reprimand	14-day suspension	Discharge
3. Sleeping on duty	Reprimand	14-day suspension	Discharge
4. Gambling during working hours	Reprimand	5-day suspension	Discharge
5. Working while intoxicated	Discharge		
6. Use or possession of illegal drugs	Discharge		
7. Selling or transfer of illegal drugs	Discharge		
8. Theft	Discharge		
9. Discourteous conduct	Reprimand	14-day suspension	Discharge
10. Failure to observe safety rules	Reprimand	14-day suspension	Discharge
11. Falsifying company records and documents for personal gain	Discharge		
12. Failure to report accident	Reprimand	14-day suspension	Discharge

SOURCE: Taken as examples from various company rules and collective bargaining agreements.

Exhibit 12.3
Table of Penalties

(e.g., absenteeism and related attendance records) than those that do not (e.g., insubordination).[23]

Subjective standards can also apply to other employee infractions. For example, one arbitrator contends that a major difference exists between "nodding off" (eyes closed, head nodding lower and lower, jerking up, and then nodding again) and "sleeping on the job," because the former condition, if successfully fought by the person, "would lead to completely restored wakefulness."[24]

Arbitrators use three levels of proof. The most often used level of proof by arbitrators is **preponderance of evidence**, wherein testimony and evidence must be adequate to overcome opposing presumptions and evidence. The second, **clear and convincing evidence**, is shown where the truth of the facts asserted is highly probable. The third, **beyond a reasonable doubt**, represents a higher degree of proof, which some arbitrators use in "criminal" cases, such as selling illegal drugs on company property, or stealing, that can more adversely affect the grievant's chances of finding subsequent employment. Some believe that this level of proof is extraordinarily high and should not be used in arbitration because the level of proof used in NLRB and unemployment insurance cases do not require proof beyond a reasonable doubt.[25]

In more recent years, the use (or misuse) of e-mail and the Internet for non-business purposes has led to employee discipline. Misuse of e-mail or the Internet has been placed into three categories: (1) minor "personal" use, which the employer permits or ignores, (2) use without permission or improper use which warrants discipline, (3) serious misuse which the employer believes warrants discharge. Misuse requires that the employer promulgate company rules about the use of e-mail and/or Internet, to communicate the rules, and to enforce the rules evenly and consistently. The question of whether a particular e-mail message warrants discipline depends on the magnitude of the distribution, the effect on the employer, and the employee's intent in sending the message. The charge of misuse is more serious when the employee sends e-mails than when the employee receives the e-mail message, and when the employee seeks out material on the Internet, such as pornographic materials.[26]

Another problem can occur when management uncovers the evidence while using search-and-seizure techniques. Few arbitrators deny the employer's right to impose, as a condition of employment, an inspection of the employee's clothes and packages on entering and leaving the plant. However, a problem arises when company officials search an employee's locker or, in some cases, home, with or without the employee's permission. Many arbitrators (and the Supreme Court in *Dennis O'Conner v. Magno Ortega*, 480 U.S. 709 (1987)) permit evidence obtained without the employee's knowledge if it is from company property, even if the property (such as a locker or tool chest) is momentarily under the control of the employee. On the other hand, few, if any, arbitrators believe evidence should be accepted if management obtained the evidence by forcibly breaking into the employee's personal property, even if the property is located on company premises.

Arbitrators often have to assess witnesses' testimony in a discipline case. These individuals are deemed "credible" if they had neither motive for an incorrect version (e.g., personal bias against the grievant) nor physical infirmity (e.g., poor hearing).[27] Yet one arbitrator notes:

> *It is simply impossible to tell by observation if someone is lying under oath. You cannot tell by looking at and listening to the person. A trial judge in Chicago once compiled a list of tests to see if a witness is telling the truth: does he perspire; lick his lips; fidget in his seat; is he shifty-eyed? From my experience as an arbitrator, I can tell you that shifty-eyed people often tell the truth, while most honest-looking people will lead you by the nose right down the primrose path.*[28]

Documented and credible evidence is necessary to bolster the company's decision to discipline/discharge an employee.

Effect of Work Rules on Discipline

Management's right to establish (even without initially advising the union) and administer work rules is generally acknowledged as fundamental to efficient plant operations. Yet, managerial administration of work rules also assumes some fundamental responsibilities and obligations that, if not followed, may affect management's disciplinary efforts.

A first question that arises is, what happens if management has no rule governing the alleged offense committed by the employee? Such an event is not uncommon because employers cannot possibly anticipate the endless variety of employee misbehaviors. Arbitrators, for example, have upheld the discharges of employees who have done the following:

- Watched a fire develop and destroy a portion of a company over a lengthy period without notifying the company[29]

- Called management officials in the early morning hours to belch over the telephone[30]

- Urinated on the floor of a delivery truck even though there were restroom facilities nearby

- "Streaked" (ran naked) through a portion of an airport[31]

Needless to say, management had no previously established work rules covering these behaviors. Arbitrators have also upheld management's right to discipline employees for those offenses that are commonly regarded as unwritten laws—prohibitions against stealing or striking a supervisor, for example.

In most disciplinary situations, particularly those cases that are somewhat common in industry (poor performance, absenteeism, insubordination, and so forth), management is on weak grounds with the arbitrator when it does not have established work rules. Furthermore, written work rules must be *reasonable, clear,* and *state the consequences of their violation.* Reasonable rules are related to the orderly, efficient, and safe operation of the employer's business and the performance that the employer might properly expect of an employee. Unions will contend a rule is unreasonable if it is unrelated to business operations or outweighed by the employee's personal rights on and off the job.

Determining a rule's reasonableness can be complicated. For example, some arbitrators view a unilateral rule prohibiting smoking as "reasonable," particularly if management presents evidence that nonsmoking employees can be harmed by being exposed to secondhand smoke. However, other arbitrators regard a no-smoking rule to be unreasonable, particularly if a clear past practice has permitted this activity.[32] The reasonableness of an industrial work rule can vary according to industrial or company differences. A unilateral ban on moonlighting (working a second shift with another employer) is regarded as reasonable in the utility industry, which often needs emergency work performed during off shifts. Other industries not having emergency-related concerns might have a difficult time establishing the appropriateness of this rule.[33] Rule reasonableness can also vary within an industrial production facility. For example, an employer might reasonably require a long-haired employee working in the cafeteria to wear a hair net (for sanitary reasons); it would be unreasonable to request the same compliance if the employee worked in the shipping department. Further complications regarding rule reasonableness can occur when an employee is disciplined for off-the-job conduct. At first glance, this infraction would not appear to be job related; however, discipline would be appropriate if management establishes that it adversely affected the employer (e.g., damaged its reputation or standing in the community or had a negative effect on other employees' performance caused by their fear of working beside the individual who had shot another person). In other words, management must establish that there is a "nexus" (connection) between the off-the-job behavior and the employee's job performance, the employer's business, and/or other employees' performance.[34]

The clarity of a work rule is also an important issue in corrective discipline because employees cannot adequately perform or correct behavior if they do not know what is expected. Management officials can create a problem when they discipline employees for infractions of a vague or confusing work rule, such as discharge for "gambling on company premises," or "falsifying an employment application." These rules may, at first glance, appear clear and conclusive; however, their vagueness becomes apparent to any first-time supervisor who tries to enforce them. "Gambling" poses a managerial problem, particularly if employees are disciplined for participating in a card game on company premises while a management representative is sponsoring a World Series pool with hourly employee participants. Also, does gambling occur when employees are playing cards during their lunch break for matches or a numerical score that management (perhaps correctly) assumes will be converted into cash payments once the employees are off the company premises?

In another example of a vague work rule, does omitting application information constitute "falsification"? Some arbitrators would say yes, particularly if the omissions are numerous and job related. Other arbitrators maintain that "falsification" involves a definite response and might not accept discharge, much less discipline, of an employee if management did not promptly seek an explanation for any blank application items.[35]

The existence of work rules carries the implicit, if not explicit, obligation for management to inform its employees of the rules and the consequences of their violation. Sometimes an employee disciplined for violating a rule contends that he or she was unaware of the directive from management. Management then usually has the difficult task of proving otherwise. Some arbitrators have even suggested that a card signed by an employee indicating he or she had read the rules is insufficient because it is signed in haste as part of the employee's orientation, and the signed card does not indicate that management has explained each rule to the employee, allowing time for questions. Many times management indicates in rules or warnings that an employee's continued misconduct could be "subject to dismissal." However, arbitrators regard this term as carrying the potential for lesser penalties such as written warnings or suspensions.

Finally, management must administer the rules consistently for those employees who violate the rules under similar circumstances. Management will likely have its disciplinary action reduced or eliminated by the arbitrator if the union establishes that the employer was inconsistent or lax in enforcing the rule for the same misconduct on previous occasions or gave different penalties to employees who were involved in the misconduct.[36] Problems can also occur if management did not take different circumstances into account. In one case management stressed its consistent anti-horseplay approach by indicating that it had discharged not only the grievant in the current situation but also another employee who engaged in horseplay in the past. The arbitrator overturned management's action, however, noting that the horseplay committed in this case was far less serious than in the previous situation, where another employee placed razor blades in a doughnut.[37]

In assessing the degree of consistency, arbitrators place particular emphasis on past practice, which refers to the customary way similar disciplinary offenses are handled and penalized. Some organizations seek to impose consistent discipline by including a **price list** in the labor agreement; which lists specific rules and furnishes uniform penalties for single or repeated violations (refer to Exhibit 12.3). This form of rule making has advantages: (1) the employee is clearly informed of the specific rules and consequences of violations, (2) the standardized penalties suggest consistent disciplinary action is implemented, and (3) if agreed to by the union, the price list assumes more legitimacy than a unilateral work rule posted by management. However, some individuals contend that the price list represents a mechanical imposition of discipline that runs counter to the corrective philosophy because it does not consider each case on its own merits. Say, for example, management finds two employees fighting—one a short-term employee, the other a long-term employee with a fine work record. According to the price-list approach, management is obligated to discharge both employees, yet it is likely that the arbitrator will reinstate the long-term employee who has an excellent performance record and who would typically respond to corrective measures to retain job seniority credits.

Progressive Discipline

Progressive discipline refers to increasingly severe penalties corresponding to repeated identical offenses committed by an employee. It relates to correction in at least two ways: (1) by impressing on the employee the seriousness of repeated rule infractions and (2) by providing the employee with opportunities to correct his or her behavior before applying the ultimate penalty of discharge. Management might have to give an oral warning, a written warning, and at least one suspension before it can discharge an employee for repeatedly committing a similar offense, such as failure to wear safety equipment, poor attendance, or ineffective performance. An exception to progressive discipline occurs when the nature of the offense is so heinous (stealing, striking a supervisor, setting fire to company property) as to make corrective discipline inappropriate.

An **oral warning** (or reprimand) represents an informal effort to correct and improve the employee's work performance. The informality of this oral warning is for corrective training purposes; however, the oral warning can be prejudicial to the employee if it is entered as evidence in arbitration hearings. This disciplinary action, however, is subject to the following employee defenses: (1) the employee might have thought the supervisor's remarks were instructional and been unaware of the disciplinary aspects or consequences of the warning, and (2) an oral warning given in private can lead to conflicting testimony—the employee can state that the supervisor never gave an oral warning. However, because of its relative harmlessness, the union seldom contests this form of discipline.

A **written warning**, the next step in progressive discipline, is a more serious matter because it summarizes the previous oral warnings to correct the employee's behaviors and is entered in the employee's work record file.

More official than an oral warning, it brings disciplinary actions into focus by warning the employee of consequences of future rule violation.

If the written warning is not successful in correcting the employee's adverse behavior, a suspension is used.

A **suspension** is a disciplinary layoff without pay given by management to impress on the employee the seriousness of the offense. Although oral and written reprimands might also achieve this purpose, they do not involve a financial penalty to the employee. A suspension serves as an example of the economic consequences associated with discharge and at the same time indicates that management is willing to retain the employee if he or she will comply with directives and change errant ways. Management initially imposes a mild suspension (one to three days) and will then impose a suspension greater than ten days for a repeated offense. Arbitrators are reluctant to reduce the suspensions unless it can be shown that other employees were given lesser penalties for identical offenses under similar circumstances.

Discharge, unlike suspension or warnings, is not a corrective measure because it means the employee is permanently removed from the company. As mentioned earlier, arbitrators have attached tremendous significance to the effects of discharge on the employee, regarding it as a last resort to be used when all other corrective attempts have failed and the employee totally lacks usefulness to the firm.

Progressive discipline also implies a *statute of limitations*. For example, it would be difficult to discharge an employee who has previously received two suspensions for failing to report an absence to management if the worker has worked for a fairly long time (say, three to five years) before committing a similar present offense. Management is usually not obligated to return to the first step, that is, an oral warning; however, discharge is not warranted—the employee's offense-free period indicates that corrective measures did have some effect and should be tried again before terminating the employee. Some unions have been able to negotiate clauses which erase earlier disciplinary actions after a certain period of time (e.g., first disciplinary action is erased if no other incident occurs in two years).

A discipline price list does not take the statute of limitations into account—its penalties are for repeated infractions regardless of the intervening period. In these circumstances, should management negate its own price list by returning to a suspension, even though discharge is the next step in the procedure? Or should it proceed with the discharge, knowing that many arbitrators, employing a statute of limitations, would reinstate the employee because of the period between his or her previous and recent offenses? Both courses of action have risks. In the first case, management might establish precedent that can adversely affect other cases; in the second, management might appear arbitrary in its discipline administration.

Last Chance Agreements

After the company gathers sufficient evidence to justify a "just cause" discharge and before issuing the removal notice, the union and the company may agree on a last chance agreement (see Exhibit 12.4).

A **last chance agreement** is a negotiated written agreement signed by an employer, union, and employee whose conduct has been determined to be unacceptable. Its purpose is to settle a grievance over an employee's termination and to hold the removal in abeyance. It sets strict conditions for continued employment in return for the employer's agreement not to discharge the employee immediately. Because these types of cases are usually performance related (such as poor performance, excessive absences, being under the influence of illegal drugs), one goal of the last chance agreement is to rehabilitate the employee and provide an opportunity for the company to keep an employee who has skills and training that cannot be easily replaced and for the union to save the job of one of its members. A successful last chance agreement tends to use shock value to motivate an errant employee to rehabilitate himself or herself. If the employee violates the last chance agreement, progressive discipline is not used. If the discharge is appealed to arbitration, the arbitrator is generally limited to determining whether the last chance agreement was valid and whether the terms of the agreement were violated.[38]

One study in one plant over a 15-year period revealed that the use of last chance agreements was effective in a majority of cases. Most employees who signed last chance agreements and who were returned to work became effective, rule-abiding employees, at least in the short term. Because the discharged employee is costly to replace and there is no guarantee that the replacement will be equal in performance to the rescued employee, the last chance agreement strategy appears to be justifiable to the employee, the employer, and the union.[39]

Disciplinary Penalty and Mitigating Circumstances

Arbitrators will determine whether management was correct in assigning a particular disciplinary penalty for an employee found guilty of an infraction. Researchers who have attempted to identify the relevant factors which influence arbitrator decisions found that work history, particularly seniority, is an important factor. Arbitrators tend to treat employees with long-term service more leniently than their junior counterparts. Other factors include the grievant's disciplinary record and prior job performance; this finding suggests that arbitrators give weight to the grievant's rehabilitation potential as an important factor in the decision. Thus, a long-term employee with little or no prior discipline

Exhibit 12.4
Last Chance Agreement

1. I understand and voluntarily agree that my continued employment by the company is based upon and constrained by the following terms:

2. I accept admission to the Employee Assistance Program and/or an accredited rehabilitation program as approved or recommended by the EAP.

3. As a condition of my continued employment, I will comply with all of the rehabilitation program's requirements to their successful conclusion. This includes but is not limited to attendance at all required meetings.

4. I recognize that my reinstatement may require participation of my spouse and adult children in my recovery program if so directed by the EAP.

5. I understand that my previous conduct/job performance warrants close supervision upon my return to work and will accept such supervision as a constructive part of my recovery and also give my consent to searches of my person or any property under my control or in my possession.

6. I understand that upon return to the workplace I must meet all established standards of conduct and job performance and that I will be subject to the Company's disciplinary procedures for any failure to meet the standards. If discharge is determined to be the appropriate penalty for any failure to meet the standards of conduct and job performance by the Company, I specifically acknowledge and agree that the Company need not satisfy the "just cause" standard set forth in the collective bargaining agreement between the Company and the Union (if applicable to me) as applicable to other bargaining unit employees of the Company.

7. I agree to submit to alcohol/drug tests at any time the Company requests during the life of this Agreement.

8. I agree to waive my right to work overtime should I have a rehabilitation meeting scheduled that would be in conflict with the overtime assignment. Also, I understand that I may have to waive all overtime if my EAP counselor determines that in order to accomplish rehabilitation goals my hours of work should be limited, and I agree to comply with any request by the EAP counselor to do so.

9. I understand that I will be subject to the terms of this rehabilitation agreement until I have completed at least twenty-four (24) months of work following my return without further incidents of the conduct that led to this agreement (drug and/or alcohol use or job performance).

10. I agree that this constitutes my final opportunity for treatment and rehabilitation while employed by the Company. I further agree that any future alcohol or drug problem, positive drug and/or alcohol test (an alcohol test is positive if the level is equal to or greater than 0.02G/210L), refusal to be tested, or sample alteration will result in my immediate termination even though such may occur after the expiration of this agreement. I do understand what constitutes a positive alcohol/drug test.

11. I authorize and direct the Employee Assistance Provider, Substance Abuse Rehabilitation Provider, and all other Health Care and Insurance Providers to release to my Employer all information concerning my assessment, participation, attendance, progress, and any other information or records that may relate to my evaluation and rehabilitation, and I release and hold harmless such providers and the Company for any employment actions resulting from the release of such information.

12. I understand and agree that my reinstatement and continued employment are contingent upon my meeting satisfactorily all of the above, and that my failure to fulfill each and every provision of the Agreement relinquishes all defense on

(Continued)

Exhibit 12.4
(Continued)

my part and subjects me, without recourse, to the immediate termination of my employment with the Company. If pursued through the grievance procedure established under the collective bargaining agreement (if applicable) to arbitration, the Arbitrator can only decide if this Agreement was violated. If this Agreement was violated, then the discharge must stand. If I am not subject to the terms of the collective bargaining agreement, I acknowledge and agree that I have no right to appeal a termination decision.

Employee Signature:_____

Date:_____

Company Representative Signature: _____

Date:_____

Union Representative Signature:_____

Date:_____

problems and a good performance record frequently has his or her discipline reduced.[40]

In making their determinations, arbitrators use several arbitral principles that have been developed over the years for considering management's discharge decisions (see the Labor Relations in Action feature on pg. 540 for examples of typical cases). Arbitrators often consider **mitigating circumstances (factors)**, which might reduce management's assigned penalty (e.g., from a discharge to a suspension), based on one of three assumptions:

1. Management contributed to a problem and must therefore assume part of the responsibility for the wrongdoing.

2. The circumstances of the case were so unusual as to give great doubt that it will occur again, particularly if management uses corrective techniques instead of discharge.

3. Personal factors (such as marital, financial, or substance abuse problems) caused a stressed or troubled employee to perform the disciplinary incident (e.g., absenteeism, poor work performance, or insubordination). Therefore, the employee will not continue these infractions once his or her personal problems are identified and resolved.

An example of mitigating circumstances under the first arbitral assumption occurs when management has provided the employee with faulty tools and equipment and subsequently disciplines the employee for low production output. A more common example of mitigating circumstances occurs when a management representative provokes the employee into committing physical or verbal abuse. In a representative discharge grievance, an arbitrator reinstated an employee who was discharged for striking his supervisor after he found out that the supervisor was asking other employees questions about his wife's fidelity.[41]

Management might also contribute to a disciplinary infraction by condoning, either openly or tacitly, offenses committed in the shop. Related examples include supervisors observing employees engaged in horseplay without attempting to stop the situation and subsequently disciplining employees for the action, and supervisors encouraging employees to violate quality standards in the name of production efficiency.

A thorough discussion of the numerous mitigating circumstances suggested by the second arbitral assumption regarding unusual circumstances is beyond the scope of this chapter, but the following example is illustrative: An employee has been repeatedly warned and suspended for failure to report his absence to management when he is unable to work a production shift; at the last suspension the grievant was informed that another infraction would result in discharge. One month after suspension, the employee again failed to report his absence to management and was discharged when he reported to work the following morning. The employee contended (and added evidence in the form of a doctor's slip) that his wife became suddenly and seriously ill and that his concern for his wife, coupled with no telephone in the apartment, resulted in his failure to report his absence to management. Here, management has followed all the principles of progressive discipline; however, the employee's discharge might be set aside if the arbitrator concludes that the circumstances were so unusual as to give management no reason to think it will happen again in the future.

Arbitrators often consider the mitigating effects of the grievant's role as a union officer. Compared with other employees, union officials usually have special rights and privileges, particularly when conducting union business. Many arbitrators consider the union steward and foreman as organizational equals in discussion of union matters. Arbitrators therefore give the union steward leeway if harsh words are exchanged in these grievance meetings, whereas other employees might be successfully charged with insubordination for identical actions.

Union officers also have greater responsibilities that correspond to their rights. For example, arbitrators and the NLRB have upheld more serious disciplinary action for union officers who failed to prevent a wildcat strike than for employees who actually participated in the strike, if the union officers knew in advance of the strike and failed to stop it. This differential penalty implies that union officers should be more knowledgeable about contractual prohibition against a wildcat strike and thus should uphold their contractual obligation to maintain uninterrupted production during the term of the labor agreement when there is a no strike clause in the labor agreement.

Perhaps the most common mitigating factor in discharge cases is the employee's work record. An arbitrator will likely consider reinstating a discharged employee who violated a work rule (e.g., one that prohibits insubordination) if that employee has a long and satisfactory work record with the company. The arbitrator in this situation realizes the potential of the employee returning to previous work habits, so he or she might reinstate the employee with no back pay, which would represent a disciplinary suspension. One study has shown that discharges of grievants with little seniority (less than two years' service with the organization) are more likely to be upheld than discharges of grievants having more than 11 years of service.[42]

The most complicated and controversial mitigating circumstances are found with troubled employees. Many management officials contend that arbitrators exceed their authority to interpret the labor agreement in these discipline cases and instead assume the roles of clergymen, psychiatrists, and medical doctors in indicating that management has an obligation to nurture these employees, even though this is not required by the contract language. One arbitrator acknowledged that he and some of his peers have addressed one troubled employee issue, alcohol abuse, with little medical or scientific foundation:

Curiously, published arbitral decisions involving alcohol abuse rarely distinguish between social drinking, heavy drinking, and alcoholism—distinctions that are crucial in the mental health field. Moreover, although hundreds of arbitration decisions have adopted the popular view that alcoholism is a "disease" that involves "loss of control" over drinking, I am unaware of any decisions (including my

LABOR RELATIONS IN ACTION
Examples of Employee Misconduct and Mitigating Factors to Consider in Employee Discipline

Abusive behavior (a form of insubordination) occurs when an employee directs profanity, epithets, or verbal abuse toward a supervisor. Employees' defenses have included (1) no intent of hostility or anger, (2) provocation from the supervisor, and (3) words used were "shop talk," which are frequently used in the department.[a]

Aggression toward supervisors includes verbal and physical abuse by subordinates that demean supervisors, undermine their authority, induce fear, and cause injuries. Reasons for setting aside employer-imposed discipline are severity of the infraction; provocation by the supervisor; the grievant's status, such as mental condition; employee's work history and seniority; lack of convincing evidence that the disciplinable offense occurred; and breach of contractual or due process requirements.[b]

Alcohol-related discipline occurs when an employee consumes alcohol on the job, possesses alcohol on the job, or reports to work under the influence of alcohol. Issues may involve whether there exists a "reasonable suspicion" that the employee was under the influence of alcohol, the employee refused to submit to an alcohol test, the employee failed the alcohol test, the employee was found drinking on the job or possessed alcohol on the job, or consumed alcohol off the job and then reported to work under the influence of alcohol. Another consideration may be the existence of a last chance agreement that contains conditions with which the employee must comply in order to continue employment, such as testing for drugs/alcohol without warning, participation in a rehabilitation program, and so on.[c]

Falsification of employment application occurs when an applicant writes incorrect information on an application for employment. Arbitrators consider a four-part test: Was the misrepresentation willful? Was it material to the decision to hire? Was it material to the employer at the time of discharge? Did the employer act promptly and in good faith when it discovered the misrepresentation? Mitigating circumstances include the following: The employee did not understand the question or made an honest mistake; lack of connection (nexus) between the answer given and the employee's ability to perform the job; the employee had worked successfully over a long period of time; and the employer did not act promptly when the misrepresentation was discovered.[d]

Fighting on the job occurs when one employee physically attacks another employee on the job. Prohibitions against fighting in the workplace are considered a legitimate employer interest because employers are obligated to provide employees with a safe working environment. Reasons for modification of penalties include the following: Employee was provoked by another employee, employee was a victim of another employee's violent act, penalty was too severe given the nature of the fight, management in some way contributed to the problem that caused the fight, or the grievant had a long-term service record without discipline.[e]

Insubordination is the refusal of an employee to work or follow a direct order given by a supervisor. The employee is to obey now and grieve later. There are several qualifications: The employee's act must be knowing, willing, and deliberate; the order must be explicit and clearly given so that the employee understands its meaning and intent; the order must be work related and reasonable; the order must be given by someone with appropriate authority; the employee must be made aware of the consequences of failure to follow the supervisor's direct order. An employee is not obligated to follow an order that threatens the employee's health or safety or to engage in illegal or immoral behavior. An employee may refuse to

own) that express an understanding of what arbitrators actually mean when they call alcoholism a "disease." Even in the literature of arbitration, there is little recognition of whether alcoholism is a medical disease, a social disorder, or some complex combination, and whether it has a natural progression and a unitary etiology.[43]

Application of the Just Cause Standard

In general, the arbitrator has the responsibility in discipline cases to determine whether an employer has applied the just cause standard. Just cause is generally considered a universal standard by which to evaluate an employer's

participate in an investigative interview in the absence of a union representative after the employee has exercised his or her *Weingarten* rights.[f]

Refusal to work overtime occurs when an employee is scheduled to work overtime or the employee is required to work overtime because of skill requirements, emergencies, short-term labor demands, or interdependencies of operations and then the employee refuses to work. Penalties may be reduced or overturned for several reasons including: no warning of the consequences of the overtime refusal; the order to work overtime was not clearly given, or lack of proper advance notice, failure to apply progressive discipline, no previous discipline, or the employee offered a reasonable excuse for not working overtime.[g]

Sabotage is the willful destruction of company equipment, machinery, or property by an employee who has motive or opportunity to commit the act. Because sabotage is a criminal act, the burden of proof is usually beyond preponderance of the evidence. These cases may involve direct evidence (an eyewitness account) or circumstantial evidence. As an example of circumstantial evidence, a foreman sees an employee with a hose in one hand and a knife in the other. The foreman then observes that the hose is cut. The foreman did not see the employee cut the hose, but circumstantial evidence leads the foreman to the conclusion that the employee cut the hose.[h]

Sexual harassment misconduct occurs when one employee creates a hostile work environment for another employee or employees. Arbitrators evaluate the degree to which the alleged misconduct is severe or pervasive, and the degree of discipline follows the Seven Tests of Just Cause[i] in Exhibit 12.2 on pg. 530.

Striker misconduct occurs when violence is directed toward strikebreakers or when strikers cause damage to nonstrikers' property or the employer's property. Factors that may modify the penalty include the following:

The employee actions were not exceptionally vicious or willfully malicious; the grievant engaged in a single incident, not multiple incidents of physical violence; no damage was done to the employer–employee relationship; there was provocation to cause the misconduct; disparate or discriminatory treatment had occurred; and the employee has a long service or good work record.[j]

Tardiness occurs when an employee is late for work, is not ready for work at the starting time, or is not at his or her work station at the scheduled starting time. Factors considered in determining the degree of discipline are the definition of tardiness, the number of tardies and the period of time over which the tardies occurred, and the appropriateness of the penalty under the circumstances.[k]

---

[a]Stanley J. Schwartz, "Insubordination: A Cardinal Sin in the Workplace," *Labor Law Journal* 48 (December 1993), pp. 756–770.

[b]Margaret A. Lucero and Robert E. Allen, "Aggression against Supervisors," *Dispute Resolution Journal* 53 (February 1998), pp. 57–63.

[c]Donald J. Petersen, "Arbitration of Alcohol Cases," *Journal of Collective Negotiations in the Public Sector*, 29, no. 3 (2000), pp. 175–193.

[d]Donald J. Petersen, "Trends in Arbitrating Falsification of Employment Application Forms," *Arbitration Journal* 47 (September 1992), pp. 36–37.

[e]Margaret A. Lucero and Robert E. Allen, "Fighting on the Job: Analysis of Recent Arbitration Decisions," *Dispute Resolution Journal* 5 (August 1998), pp. 51–57.

[f]*Discipline and Discharge in Arbitration*, ed., Norman Brand (Washington, D.C.: Bureau of National Affairs, 1998), pp. 156–161.

[g]Donald J. Petersen, "Arbitration of Employee Refusal to Work Overtime," *Dispute Resolution Journal* 52 (January 1997), pp. 21–27.

[h]Donald J. Petersen and Harvey R. Boler, "The Arbitration of Sabotage Cases," *Employee Relations Law Journal*, 30 (Winter 2004), pp. 52–64.

[i]Mollie H. Bowers, W. Sue Reddick, and E. Patrick McDermott, "Just Cause in the Arbitration of Sexual Harassment Cases," *Dispute Resolution Journal* 55 (November 2000/January 2001), pp. 40–85.

[j]Donald J. Petersen, "Arbitrating Cases of Employee Misconduct in Work Stoppages." *Dispute Resolution Journal*, 5 (February 1998), pp. 44–52.

[k]Donald J. Petersen, "The Arbitration of Tardiness Cases," *Journal of Collective Negotiations in the Public Sector*, 29, (2000), pp. 167–174.

---

disciplinary action. In almost 50 percent of all discipline and discharge arbitration cases, arbitrators have reversed or modified the employer's disciplinary action for failing to meet at least one of four just cause standards. Of those, the reasons were:

- 20 percent for failure to conduct a full and fair investigation of the employee's misconduct that yielded supporting evidence of the misconduct charge.

- 20 percent for mitigating circumstances, such as the grievant had a lengthy and unblemished past disciplinary record.

- 16 percent for arbitrary, capricious, discriminatory, or disparate treatment, which means the employer did not act evenhandedly and uniformly in determining the discipline.

- 14 percent for improper administration of the employer's rules and requirements, which includes failure to inform an employee of applicable standards, lack of reasonableness in rules and job requirements, and lax enforcement of standards.

Arbitrators have reversed the employer's disciplinary action because of failure to provide due process standards in 15 percent of disciplinary cases. Due process and procedural errors committed by employers include failure to follow progressive disciplinary procedures, failure to adhere to contractual notice requirements, denial of representation rights, excessive delay in imposing penalty, and failure to provide a formal charge of wrongdoing.[44]

Possible Collision between Discharge Decisions and Public Policy

As a general rule in arbitration of disciplinary cases, the parties depend on the finality of the arbitrator's decision. If the employer proves just cause for its disciplinary action, the arbitrator upholds the employer's disciplinary action. If the employer fails to prove just cause, the employee is returned to the workplace with an appropriate make-whole remedy. In disciplinary cases involving just cause determinations on sexual harassment charges, the finality of the arbitrator's decision becomes more complicated. After an alleged sexual harasser is disciplined and files a grievance, he is subject to the traditional application of the just cause principles whereby the grievant would be entitled to a due process hearing with the presumption of innocence. Furthermore, the arbitrator may consider the severity of the conduct, the employee's work and discipline record, length of service, potential for rehabilitation, proper investigation of the matter, and mitigating circumstances. However, courts may vacate an arbitrator's decision if the decision contravenes a significant public policy. Therefore, a court may vacate an arbitrator's decision if the court finds that an employee had engaged in illegal sexual harassment activities on the job.[45]

Due Process and the Weingarten Decision

Due process has both substantive and procedural aspects. Substantive due process focuses on the purpose or rationale of the work rules to ensure that an employee has not been arbitrarily disciplined or discharged. This aspect is reflected in the previously discussed purposes and elements of discipline. Procedural aspects of due process are usually covered in labor agreements and include the following:

- The existence of a procedure that has rules, is known, is predictable, and is not arbitrary.

- Is applicable and administered equitably to all employees.

- Includes the right to be represented; the right to present evidence and rebut charges; the right to know the charges, and the right to relevant information concerning the charges.

- The right to a fair and impartial fact-finding process and hearing.

- To be free from retaliation.

- The right to as much privacy and confidentiality as is practicable.[46]

Other due process requirements which may be written in the labor agreement include:

- The discipline process will follow certain time limits specified in the labor agreement.

- The employee will be entitled to union representation, if requested, when discipline is being administered, and will be given an opportunity to respond (defend himself or herself).

- The employee will be notified of the specific offense in writing.

The due process procedure of union representation has been influenced by NLRB decisions and by the Supreme Court in its *Weingarten* decision. This decision will be discussed in detail because it illustrates the model of the labor relations process presented in Chapter 1 (see Exhibit 1.2) and because it illustrates the impact of the fourth participant, the government, on labor–management relations.

The *Weingarten* decision pertained to an employee who was believed to have paid only a fraction of the price of food she took out of the store. During the interview with management representatives she repeatedly asked for a union representative to be present but was denied. Management subsequently found her version of the incident to be supported, but in her emotional state, she admitted that over a period of time she had taken free lunches (totaling approximately $160) from the store, something a management official and other employees had also done. She was not disciplined for her actions; however, she informed her union representatives of the events and an unfair labor practice was filed. The NLRB decided that management did commit an unfair labor practice, violating Section 8(a)(1) of the National Labor Relations Act (mentioned in Chapter 3), by denying the employee union representation.

Union representation must be given to the employee at an employee's request when the employee reasonably believes an investigation could result in disciplinary action. The employer has no legal requirement to bargain with any union representative who attends the interview.

The NLRB's *Weingarten* decision was appealed through the courts, and eventually upheld by the Supreme Court. Rationale for this decision was in part based on the union official's potential contribution to the disciplinary investigation:

A single employee confronted by an employer investigating whether certain conduct deserves discipline may be too fearful or inarticulate to relate accurately the incident being investigated, or too ignorant to raise extenuating factors. A knowledgeable union representative could assist the employer by eliciting favorable facts, and save the employer production time by getting to the bottom of the incident occasioning the interview. Certainly [the union representative's] presence need not transform the interview into an adversary contest.[47]

Earlier arbitrator decisions formed the foundation for the Supreme Court's opinions on an employee's right to union representation. Justice Brennan observed that "even where such a right is not explicitly provided in the agreement a 'well-established current of arbitral authority' sustains the right of union representation at investigatory interviews, which the employee reasonably believes may result in disciplinary action against him."[48]

The Supreme Court ruled that an employee has the legal right to have a union representative present during an investigatory interview if the employee has reason to believe that the investigation will result in disciplinary action. The Court and NLRB adopted the several principles highlighted in Exhibit 12.5.

The *Weingarten* decision also refuted the company's contention that union representation is necessary only after the company has made its discipline decision. The Supreme Court contended that this practice would diminish the value of union representation, thereby making it increasingly difficult for the employee to vindicate himself or herself in the subsequent grievance proceedings. NLRB cases indicate that an employee who is discharged for just cause will not be reinstated solely because the employer violated his or her *Weingarten* rights. This means that if the employer has obtained evidence from sources other than from the illegal interview, the employee's discharge will stand.

Union's Communication with Members on Weingarten Rights

Unions continually attempt to inform their members of their *Weingarten* rights. Not only are these rights important to the individual member who needs representation by an experienced union representative, but the exercise of these rights play an important part in the union's role of representing members. For example, one union provides wallet-sized cards for members to carry with them (see Exhibit 12.6, The Weingarten Card: Don't Leave Home without It!). The Teamsters have developed an Awareness Quiz on *Weingarten* rights on its

Exhibit 12.5

Application of Weingarten Rights

1. The employee's right to union representation stems from Section 7 of the Labor Management Relations Act, which allows the employee to engage in concerted activities for mutual aid and protection.

2. The right can be exercised only if the employee chooses to request representation; the employer is not obligated to inform the employee of his or her legal right to union representation.

3. The employee must reasonably believe that disciplinary action could follow before requesting the presence of a union representative.

4. If the employee refuses to go through the interview, the request for representation having been denied, the employer may continue the investigation without the input of the employee.

5. The employer is not obligated to bargain with the employee's union representative during the interview.

6. If the employer denies the employee his or her right to union representation after the employee makes a legitimate request and continues the investigatory interview, the interview is considered an illegal interview, and any information gained by the employer, even a confession to a misdeed such as theft, should not be allowed in a subsequent procedure, such as arbitration. Not to be confused, such rulings do not prove that the employee is innocent of the alleged crime; simply, the employer must prove the employee's guilt with some other evidence. For example, another employee may be willing to come forward as a witness to the employee's theft.

7. *Weingarten* rights do not apply if management had already decided to impose discipline and the purpose of the meeting with the employee is for management to communicate the disciplinary decision.

SOURCE: Neal Orkin and Miriam Heise, "*Weingarten* through the Looking Glass," *Labor Law Journal* 48 (March 1997), pp. 157–159. © 1994, 1997, & 2000, CCH Incorporated. All Rights Reserved. Reprinted with permission from *Labor Law Journal*.

Exhibit 12.6
The Weingarten Card: Don't
Leave Home without It!

"If this discussion could in any way lead to my being disciplined or terminated, or affect my personal working conditions, I request that my UE steward or union officer be present at the meeting. Without representation, I choose not to answer any questions."
(This is my right under a Supreme Court decision called *Weingarten*) http://www.ranknfile-ue.org/stwd_wei.html

Web page to better educate its members (see Exhibit 12.7 for the Web site address of the interactive Awareness Quiz and see how you score).

The NLRB has a history of extending and then rescinding the rights of unrepresented employees to have a co-employee present during an investigatory interview which he or she reasonably believes could result in disciplinary action. On July 10, 2000, the NLRB decided that *Weingarten* rights should be extended to employees in nonunion workplaces to afford them the right to have a co-worker present at an investigatory interview that the employee reasonably believes could result in disciplinary action.[49] Then, in 2004, the NLRB (with a majority of the Board appointed by President George W. Bush) flip-flopped again and returned to the 1985 position, meaning that currently unrepresented employees *do not* have the same rights of representation under the U.S. Supreme Court's *Weingarten* decision as are guaranteed employees who are represented by a union.[50] Exhibit 12.8 shows how the National Labor Relations Board has changed its position on unrepresented employee *Weingarten* rights since 1982.

If a Democrat becomes president in 2008 and appoints the majority of the Board, the NLRB's policy is likely to change again. During the years in which *Weingarten* rights were extended to nonunion employees, several interesting issues were raised.

First, there is a question of whether the rules developed by decisions of the National Labor Relations Board since the Supreme Court's 1975 *Weingarten* decision will be applied to nonunion settings. For example, an employee in a unionized setting does not have the right to union representation when the sole purpose of a meeting called by a management official is to communicate a previously determined disciplinary action.

Second, there is a question of who will serve as a witness. Although the decision that extended *Weingarten* rights to nonunion employees refers to a co-worker as a witness, questions that may be raised are: May an employee bring in his or her attorney as a witness? May the employee call in another supervisor? What if the employee wants to bring in a co-worker who is under investigation for the same wrongdoing? What happens if the employee calls for a co-worker who is not readily available, for example, is on layoff or vacation, or has been suspended pending a more thorough investigation?

Third, there is a question of the role of the witness in a nonunion setting. In a unionized setting, a union representative may ask questions for clarification and consult with the employee. If there is an emotional confrontation, the union representative will try to defuse it. In a unionized setting, the union representative possesses knowledge of the grievance procedure and past practices of the parties and will be able to articulate the "common law of the shop" with the employer. A co-worker witness no doubt will not have such knowledge and expertise. In fact, a co-worker may be reluctant to serve as a witness because he or she may fear retribution from the employer, and the co-worker is left unprotected because there is no collective-bargaining agreement that provides protection.

Exhibit 12.7

Weingarten Rights Quiz—
Interactive Exercise

Check Your Weingarten Awareness

Click on the answer you think is correct. When you're done, click the "How do you score?" button at the bottom to see how well you know your *Weingarten* rights.

1. A steward sees a member being interviewed in the supervisor's office. Should he demand to attend?

   A. YES

   B. NO

2. Larry is being questioned about a workplace theft and is asked to provide information about his co-worker Roger, who is suspected. Should Larry have union representation?

   A. YES

   B. NO

3. Management asks an employee to submit to a urine test. Does *Weingarten* apply?

   A. YES

   B. NO

   C. YES AND NO

4. Can management pressure an employee to drop a *Weingarten* request?

   A. YES

   B. NO

5. An employee is called to his supervisor's office, but the steward is on vacation. Can that employee insist that an interview be delayed until the steward's return?

   A. YES

   B. NO

6. I am a steward. If called in by my supervisor to discuss a problem with my work, can I bring my chief steward?

   A. YES

   B. NO

7. Can an employee ask for a lawyer during an investigatory interview?

   A. YES

   B. NO

8. The plant manager telephones a member at home to ask about missing tools. Does the member have to answer?

   A. YES

   B. NO

9. A manager denies an employee his/her *Weingarten* right, yet continues to ask questions. Can the employee just walk out?

   A. YES

   B. NO

   C. IN SOME CASES

10. Can *Weingarten* be invoked during a polygraph examination?

   A. YES

   B. NO

(Continued)

Exhibit 12.7
(Continued)

11. Can management order an employee to open their locker without a steward present?

    A. YES

    B. NO

12. If an employee is asked to sign an acknowledgment upon receiving a warning slip, must management allow union representation?

    A. YES

    B. NO

To see how you score, go to http://edu.teamster.org/quizzes/weingartenquiz.htm.

SOURCE: http://edu.teamster.org/quizzes/weingartenquiz.htm. Reprinted by permission.

Fourth, there is a question concerning the employer's actions when an employer asserts *Weingarten* rights and requests a co-worker as a witness. One choice for the employer is simply to grant the request; this may be appropriate when the co-worker's presence may be beneficial to the investigation. A second choice is to discontinue the interview and continue the investigation without an interview with the suspected employee. If the employer rejects the employee's request for a co-worker representative and continues the interview, the interview would be considered an illegal interview and no information learned in the

Exhibit 12.8
Evolving NLRB Policy on
Employee *Weingarten* Rights

1975—The U.S. Supreme Court held that a unionized employee has the right to union representation at an investigatory interview when the employee reasonably believes that the investigatory interview could lead to disciplinary action. *NLRB* v. *J. Weingarten, Inc.,* 420 U.S. 251.

1982—The Board held that nonunion employees had *Weingarten* rights because Section 7 of the National Labor Relations Act gives employees the right to engage in protected concerted activities for mutual aid and protection. *Materials Research Corp.,* 262 NLRB 1010.

1985—The Board reversed itself and held that nonunion employees did not have *Weingarten* rights because such rights stem from the union's right to represent employees and *Weingarten* rights extend to employees only when there is an exclusive bargaining representative (union). *Sears Roebuck & Co.,* 274 NLRB 230.

1985—*Weingarten* rights are not applicable to nonunion settings. *E. I. DuPont De Neumours & Co.,* 289 NLRB 627 (*DuPont III*).

2000–2001—The Board reversed itself again and held that nonunion employees had *Weingarten* rights. Employees are afforded the right to have a co-worker present at an investigatory interview when the employee reasonably believes the investigatory interview could lead to disciplinary action. *Epilepsy Foundation of Northeast Ohio v. NLRB,* 331 NLRB 92, upheld by the U.S. Circuit Court of Appeals, No. 00-1332 (November 2, 2001) 2001 U.S. App. LEXIS 23722 (D.C. Cir. 2001).

2004—For the fourth time, the NLRB changed its position. In *IBM Corp.,* 341 NLRB 148 (June 9, 2004), the Board ruled that rights afforded to unionized workers by the U.S. Supreme Court's decision in *NLRB v. J. Weingarten, Inc.,* 420 U.S. 251 (1975) are not extended to nonunion employees.

SOURCE: Michael J. Soltis and Alexandra M. Gross, "*Weingarten* Redux: An Employer's Manual," *Labor Law Journal,* 51 (Winter 2000), pp. 179–180; James F. Morgan, James M. Owens, and Glenn M. Gomes, "Union Rules Intrude Upon the Nonunion Domain: Workplace Investigations and the NLRB," *Employee Responsibilities and Rights Journal,* 14 (March 2002), p. 36; "*Weingarten* Rights, Labor Law & Due Process," *Center for Labor Relations and Research,* Pearl City, Hawaii, University of Hawaii, West Oahu, http://www.homepages.uhwo.hawaii.edu/~clear/wein.html, pp. 1–2.

interview could be used to support the disciplinary action. However, the employer may discipline the employee on facts found through means other than the interviews. Moreover, if the employee is considered an at-will employee, the employee may be disciplined for "any reason or no reason" and probably will not have access to a grievance procedure or other forms of protection.[51]

A fifth dilemma for the employer is the pay for the co-worker representative. In a unionized setting, the collective-bargaining agreement usually addresses whether union officials will be paid for time spent on union representational activities and at what rate. In a nonunion setting, since there is no collective-bargaining agreement, the employer may attempt to avoid the issue by scheduling interviews after hours. Then, the employer may contend that the co-worker is not entitled to any pay because the employer did not ask the co-worker to attend the interview. The co-worker representative's appearance at the interview was at the request of the employee being investigated.[52]

Another element of due process, written notice, has caused some problems for management and is a major reason for the involvement of labor relations representatives in the discipline process. For example, if an employee gets into a heated argument with a supervisor, refuses to work an assignment, and shouts an obscenity at the supervisor, the foreman could discipline the employee for "directing obscene and profane language toward a management representative." Once the charges are in writing, management may be required to convince an arbitrator that this charge warrants discipline, a task that is not easy if the arbitrator concludes that obscene language is regarded as common shop talk at the location. In this instance, management would have been wiser to have disciplined the employee for a more serious offense: "Insubordination: refusal to follow supervisory orders." Since management can seldom change the offense once it is in writing and handed to the grievant, a member of the industrial relations department is usually present for consultation or direction before the charges are reduced to writing.

Another related element of due process is *double jeopardy*—assigning an employee a more severe penalty than the one originally given. The rationale against double jeopardy is that management is held to any decision that purports to be final; therefore, it is important that it act only after ascertaining all relevant facts and determining the magnitude of the offense. Management can avoid the problem of double jeopardy if it makes clear to the grievant that the action taken in the first instance is tentative, pending further investigation by higher company officials. Usually, this takes the form of an indefinite suspension that, pending a subsequent investigation, can be converted to discharge without arbitral disapproval. A final element of due process is the keeping of secret records on the employee, which most arbitrators maintain is worse than keeping no records at all.

One arbitrator notes three alternative positions that the arbitrator can take on procedural or due process irregularities:

> *(1) [T]hat unless there is strict compliance with the procedural requirements, the whole action will be nullified; (2) that the requirements are of significance only where the employee can show that he has been prejudiced by failure to comply therewith; or (3) that the requirements are important, and that any failure to comply will be penalized, but that the action taken is not thereby rendered null and void.*[53]

Arbitrators tend to favor the third alternative, reasoning that management should suffer the consequences of its errors, but not to the point of exonerating an employee who is guilty of a serious offense (particularly if it has not prejudiced the employee's case).

Summary

In many respects, employee discipline represents the most significant day-to-day issue in administering the labor agreement. For the union and management organizations, administration of discipline is a key factor related to control and production; the supervisor and the affected employee are even more directly and personally affected.

Management had a unilateral right to discharge or discipline employees until the 1930s, although psychological reform and efficiency movements in the early 1900s urged management to critically examine its disciplinary policies. Some managers realized that an employee represented an investment that could be unnecessarily lost because of whimsical disciplinary actions. These individuals realized that they had an obligation to provide employees with clear work rules and proper training that would minimize the number of discipline problems and lead to increased productivity. The establishment of the NLRB further refined employers' disciplinary policies, as employees discharged for union activities could be reinstated to their jobs with back pay.

Discipline in unionized settings must be for just cause, a concept consisting of several dimensions. Management has the burden of proof to establish that an employee committed an infraction. Although discipline can accomplish several purposes for the organization, management may have to prove that its actions were taken to correct an employee's behavior. Correction suggests that an employee must be aware of work rules that are clear in their content, as well as consequences for their infraction. The work rules must also be reasonable—that is, related to the job—and consistently applied to all employees under similar circumstances.

Discipline's corrective emphasis also suggests progressive penalties be given to an employee for repeating a similar offense. Progressive discipline impresses on the employee the seriousness of repeated rule infractions while giving the employee additional opportunities to correct work behavior. Unless the infraction is heinous, such as stealing property, management usually has to give an employee an oral warning for the first offense, then a written warning and suspension for subsequent, similar offenses. Discharge is a last resort, used only when all other attempts at correction have failed or the nature of the offense is so unacceptable as to make corrective efforts inappropriate.

Management must also establish that the penalty fits the crime and that it considered all possible mitigating circumstances before imposing discipline. Management must also provide the employee with due process in the disciplinary procedure; that is, it must ensure that the appropriate contractual provisions are upheld. The employee usually has the right to union representation and the right to be notified of the offense in writing.

The U.S. Supreme Court has ruled that an employee has the legal right, a *Weingarten* right, to have a union representative present during an investigatory interview if the employee reasonably believes that the investigation could result in disciplinary action. Since this decision, the NLRB has provided guidance to the parties through case decisions. The policy of the NLRB has changed over the years and has resulted in several questions of application. Unions have attempted to inform their members on how to use their *Weingarten* rights.

Key Terms

Wrongfully discharged, p. 523
Just cause, p. 528
Preponderance of evidence, p. 531
Clear and convincing evidence,
     p. 531
Beyond a reasonable doubt, p. 531

Price list, p. 534
Progressive discipline, p. 534
Oral warning, p. 535
Written warning, p. 535
Suspension, p. 535
Discharge, p. 535

Last chance agreement, p. 536
Mitigating circumstances (factors),
     p. 538
Due process, p. 542

Discussion Questions

1. Why is discipline the most significant issue for the union and management organizations? Describe how this significance has shifted over time.

2. One union newspaper indicated how it saved an employee's job. The employee was in the mechanic's classification and was discharged for refusing to comply with management's sudden, unilateral rule that mechanics must perform janitorial duties. Given this sketchy situation, discuss the many possible reasons for the disciplinary action, indicating why the arbitrator might not have been convinced that management's discipline was for a legitimate purpose. (You are free to make and state assumptions in your answer.)

3. Explain in some detail the difficulties management would have in administering the following work rule in accordance with the disciplinary principles established in the chapter: "Any employee reporting to work under the influence of alcohol will be subject to discharge."

4. Indicate the comparative advantages and disadvantages of a disciplinary price list (see Exhibit 12.3 on pg. 531) of disciplinary prerogatives in the labor agreement and a one-sentence contractual provision indicating "management has the right to discipline or discharge an employee for cause."

5. Although not subject to judicial scrutiny, evidence in an arbitration hearing still has its complexities. Discuss related considerations that could be involved in an arbitration hearing involving an employee who was discharged for smoking marijuana on the job.

6. Assume you are in charge of establishing a training program for supervisors in administering discipline. Based on the supervisor's potential role in the disciplinary process, formulate and discuss three major principles you would stress in this session.

Exploring the Web

Employee Discipline

1. **Wrongful Discharge.** A reference is made in this chapter to a RAND study on the economic consequences of wrongful termination. Find an abstract of the study on RAND's Web site. What effect does the abstract indicate that fear of wrongful termination suits could have on managers? Go to "About RAND" from the home page to find the meaning of the acronym. What other studies have been done by RAND on labor relations?

2. Evidence in Disciplinary Cases. The OYEZ Project is a multimedia archive devoted to the Supreme Court of the United States and its work. According to the OYEZ Web site, it "aims to be a complete and authoritative source for all audio recorded in

the Court since the installation of a recording system in October 1955." The site provides information on justices along with audio and text of opinions.

Locate the case, *O'Conner v. Ortega*, in which Magno Ortega is the plaintiff against the executive director of the hospital where Ortega was employed. The case involved management's methods used in an investigation on Ortega's acquisition of a computer and sexual harassment and is an illustration of one of the problems that can occur when management seeks evidence for disciplinary action.

3. Employment Discrimination. The Legal Information Institute at Cornell has an excellent Web site that allows for searching federal and state statutes and case law and provides additional Web links by subject. Search on "employment discrimination" and find a recent Supreme Court case.

You may want to click on "Law about . . . articles" and then choose "Employment discrimination." Investigate the overview and various sources of law.

4. Seven Tests for Just Cause. A common test for determining whether just cause exists for imposing disciplinary actions was developed by arbitrator Carroll Daugherty in 1966. The standard is known as "The Seven Tests for Just Cause." Go to the Web site of the International Brotherhood of Teamsters and read the seven tests under Educational Resources. Discuss the test of reasonable rule or order.

5. Work Rules. CCH, a Wolters Kluwer company, provides a business owner's toolkit through their Tax and Accounting service. CCH is a leading provider of business, legal, and tax information. Locate the sample work rules provided by CCH. Work rules established by management must be clear and understandable and communicated effectively to employees. Comment on the reasonableness and clarity of the sample work rules from on the CCH site.

References

1. Ahmad R. Karim, "Why Arbitrators Sustain Discharge Penalties," *Labor Law Journal,* 45 (June 1994), pp. 374–378; and Stephen M. Crow, Elvis C. Stephens, and Walton H. Sharp, "A New Approach to Decision-Making Research in Labor Arbitration Using Alcohol and Drug Disciplinary Cases," *Labor Studies Journal,* 17 (Fall 1992), pp. 3–18.

2. For consideration of other, more informal disciplinary actions taken by management, see Bruce Fortado, "Informal Supervisory Social Control Strategies," *Journal of Management Studies,* 31 (March 1994), pp. 251–275.

3. *Payne v. Western & Atlantic Railroad Co.,* 81 Tenn. 507, 519–520, 1884 WL 469 at *6 (Sep. term 1884).

4. For an example of how the NLRB can alter an organization's decision policies, see Marcia A. Graham, "Obscenity and Profanity at Work," *Employee Relations Law Journal* 11 (Spring 1986), pp. 662–677.

5. Richard E. Dibble, "Alternative Dispute Resolution in Employment: Recent Developments," *Journal of Collective Negotiations in the Public Sector,* 29, (2000), pp. 245–257.

6. Marvin J. Levine, "The Erosion of the Employment-At-Will Doctrine: Recent Developments," *Labor Law Journal* 45 (February 1994), pp. 79–89. See also William H. Holley, Jr., and Roger S. Wolters, "An Employment-At-Will Vulnerability Audit," *Personnel Journal* 66 (April 1987), pp. 130–138; and William H. Holley, Jr., and Roger S. Wolters, *Labor Relations: An Experiential and Case Approach* (Hinsdale, Ill.: The Dryden Press, 1988), pp. 33–35. See also Giles Trudeau, "Is Reinstatement a Remedy Suitable to At-Will Employees?" *Industrial Relations,* 30, (Spring 1991), pp. 302–315; Jay E. Grenig, "Dismissal of Employees in the United States," *International Labor Review,* 130 (1991), pp. 569–581; Marcia P. Miceli, Janet P. Near, and Charles R. Schwenk, "Who Blows the Whistle and Why?" *Industrial and Labor Relations Review,* 45 (October 1991), pp. 113–130; Lisa B. Bingham, "Employee Free Speech and Wrongful Discharge," *Labor Law Journal,* 45 (July 1994), pp. 387–400; and Melissa S. Baucus and Terry Morehead Dworkin, "Wrongful Firing in Violation of Public Policy: Who Gets Fired and Why," *Employee Responsibilities and Rights Journal,* 7 (1994), pp. 191–206; Charles J. Muhl, "The Employment-at-will Doctrine: Three Major Exceptions," *Monthly Labor Review,* 124 (January 2001), pp. 3–11.

7. "RAND Corp. Study Links Job Losses to States' Wrongful Termination Rules," Bureau of National Affairs, *Daily Labor Report,* no. 142 July 23, 1992, p. A-2. For somewhat similar conclusions reached by another survey, see "Wrongful-Discharge Claims Increasing, Management Association Survey Finds," Bureau of National Affairs, *Daily Labor Report* no. 25 February 6, 1990, pp. A-8, A-9.

8. Bradley T. Ewing, Charles M. North, and Beck A. Taylor, "The Employment Effects of a 'Good Cause' Discharge Standard in Montana," *Industrial and Labor Relations Review,* 59 (October 2005), pp. 17–33.

9. George Nicolau, "Is It Time for a National Unfair Dismissal Statute?" *Paper Presented at the Annual Meeting of the National Academy of Arbitrators,* May 27, 2006, pp. 2–9.

10. Brian S. Klaas, Thomas W. Gainey, and Gregory G. Dell'Omo, "The Determinants of Disciplinary System Effectiveness: A Line-Management Perspective," *Industrial Relations,* 8 (October 1999), pp. 542–550.

11. See Kenneth M. Jennings, Barbara Sheffield, and Roger S. Wolters, "The Arbitration of Discharge Cases: A Forty Year Perspective," *Labor Law Journal,* 38 (January 1987), p. 35. See also Ahmad Karim and Thomas H. Stone, "An Empirical Examination of Arbitrator Decisions in Reversal and Reduction Discharge Hearings," *Labor Studies Journal,* 13, (Spring 1988), p. 47.

12. See, for example, Thomas R. Knight, "The Impact of Arbitration on the Administration of Disciplinary Policies," *Arbitration Journal,* 39 (March 1984), pp. 43–56.

13. Stephen B. Goldberg, "What Happens after the Arbitrator's Award?" *Paper Presented at the Annual Meeting of the National Academy of Arbitrators,* May 25, 2006, pp. 7–7 to 7–10.

14. Arthur Anthony Malinowski, "An Empirical Analysis of Discharge Cases and the Work History of Employees

Reinstated by Labor Arbitrators," *Arbitration Journal,* 36 (March 1981), p. 39; and William E. Simkin, "Some Results of Reinstatement by Arbitration," *Arbitration Journal,* 41 (September 1986), p. 56.

15. Chalmer E. Labig, Jr., I. B. Helburn, and Robert C. Rodgers, "Discipline, History, Seniority, and Reason for Discharge as Predictors of Post-Reinstatement Job Performance," *The Arbitration Journal,* 40 (September 1985), p. 49. For additional considerations of this relationship, see Robert C. Rodgers, I. B. Helburn, and John E. Hunter, "The Relationship of Seniority to Job Performance Following Reinstatement," *Academy of Management Journal* 29 (March 1986), pp. 101–114; and I. B. Helburn, "Seniority and Postreinstatement Performance," in *Proceedings of the Forty-Third Annual Meeting, National Academy of Arbitrators,* ed. Gladys W. Gruenberg, (Washington, D.C.: Bureau of National Affairs, 1991), pp. 141–149.

16. D.C. Miller, "Supervisor: Evolution of a Forgotten Role," in *Supervisory Leadership and Productivity,* eds. Floyd Mann, George Homans, and Delbert Miller (San Francisco: Chandler, 1965), p. 113.

17. "Oil, Chemical, and Atomic," *Union News,* July 1970, p. 9.

18. Richard Mittenthal and W. David Vaughn, "Working at the Margins of 'Just Cause', The Never-Ending Dispute over Arbitral Discretion on the Discharge Penalty," *Paper Presented at the Annual Meeting of the National Academy of Arbitrators,* May 25, 2006, pp. 3–9 to 3–35; Clarence R. Deitsch, "Seniority Clauses: An End Run Around Just Cause?" *Dispute Resolution Journal,* 60 (November 2005–January 2006), pp. 31–34.

19. *Hoosier Panel Co., Inc.,* 61 LA 983 (M. Volz, 1973). Marvin Hill, Jr. and Diana Beck, "Some Thoughts on Just Cause and Group Discipline," *Arbitration Journal,* 41 (June 1986), pp. 60–62.

20. *Riley Stoker Corp.,* 7 LA 767 (Platt, 1947).

21. For more thorough explanations of this exhibit, see Donald S. McPherson, "The Evolving Concept of Just Cause: Carroll R. Daugherty and the Requirement of Disciplinary Due Process," *Labor Law Journal,* 38 (July 1987), pp. 387–403; and Adolph M. Koven and Susan L. Smith, *Just Cause: The Seven Tests* (San Francisco: Kendall/Hunt, 1985).

22. Richard Mittenthal and W. David Vaughn, "Working at the Margins of 'Just Cause', The Never-Ending Dispute Over Arbitral Discretion on the Discharge Penalty," *Paper Presented at the Annual Meeting of the National Academy of Arbitrators,* May 25, 2006, pp. 3–11.

23. David A. Dilts, Ahmad Karim, and Mashalah Kahnama Moghadam, "The Arbitration of Disciplinary Matters: Do Objective Standards Make a Difference in Proof?" *Labor Law Journal,* 42 (October 1991), pp. 708–712.

24. Arthur Eliot Berkeley, "Asleep at the Wheel: How Arbitrators View Sleeping on the Job," *Arbitration Journal,* 46 (June 1991), p. 48.

25. Randall M. Kelly, "The Burden of Proof in Criminal Offenses of 'Moral Turpitude' Cases," *Arbitration Journal,* 46 (December 1991), pp. 45–48.

26. Ayelet "Ellie" Lichtash, "Inappropriate Use of E-Mail and the Internet in the Workplace: The Arbitration Picture," *Dispute Resolution Journal,* 59 (February-March, 2004), pp. 26–37.

27. Laura Davis, "Discipline and Decisions: A Study of Arbitration Cases Dealing with Employee Discourtesy," *Labor Law Journal,* 46 (February 1995), p. 84.

28. Edgar A. Jones, Jr., "Selected Problems of Procedure and Evidence," in *Arbitration in Practice,* ed. Arnold M. Zack (Ithaca, N.Y.: ILR Press, 1984), p. 62.

29. *Buick Youngstown Company,* 41 LA 570–753 (H. Dworkin, 1963).

30. *Buick Youngstown Company,* 41 LA 570–753 (H. Dworkin, 1963).

31. Terry L. Leap and Michael D. Crino, "How to Deal with Bizarre Behavior," *Harvard Business Review* (May–June 1986), pp. 18–25. This article also furnishes eight criteria for management in determining whether discharge for previously unconsidered disciplinary infractions is justified.

32. Donald J. Petersen, "No Smoking!" *Dispute Resolution Journal,* 50 (January 1995), p. 48.

33. For additional consideration of the "moonlighting" employee, see Muhammad Jamal, "Moonlighting Myths," *Personnel Journal,* 67 (May 1988), pp. 48–53.

34. Robert A. Kearney, "Arbitral Practice and Purpose in Employee Off-Duty Misconduct Cases," *Notre Dame Law Review* 69 (1993), pp. 135–156; and Janie L. Miller, David B. Balkin, and Robert Allen, "Employer Restrictions on Employees' Legal Off-Duty Conduct," *Labor Law Journal,* 44 (April 1993), pp. 209–219.

35. Donald J. Petersen, "Trends in Arbitrating Falsification of Employment Application Forms," *Arbitration Journal* 47 (September 1992), pp. 32–33.

36. Gregory G. Dell'Omo and James E. Jones, Jr., "Disparate Treatment in Labor Arbitration: An Empirical Analysis," *Labor Law Journal,* 41 (November 1990), pp. 739–750.

37. Lisa Davis and Ken Jennings, "Employee Horseplay and Likely Managerial Overreaction," *Labor Law Journal,* 40 (April 1989), pp. 248–256.

38. Kenneth Grinstead, "The Arbitration of Last Chance Agreements," *Arbitration Journal,* 48 (March 1993), p. 71; Norman Brand, ed., *Discipline and Discharge in Arbitration* (Washington, D.C.: Bureau of National Affairs, 1998), pp. 303–315.

39. Peter A. Bamberger and Linda H. Donahue, "Employee Discharge and Reinstatement: Moral Hazards and the Mixed Consequences of Last Chance Agreements," *Industrial and Labor Relations Review,* 53 (October 1999), pp. 3–19.

40. Patricia A. Simpson and Joseph J. Martocchio, "The Influence of Work History Factors on Arbitration Outcomes," *Industrial and Labor Relations Review,* 50 (January 1997), pp. 252–266.

41. *Gindy Manufacturing Company,* 58 LA 1038–1040 (M. Handsaker, 1972).

42. Jennings, Sheffield, and Wolters, "The Arbitration of Discharge Cases," p. 43.

43. Tim Bornstein, "Getting to the Bottom of the Issue: How Arbitrators View Alcohol Abuse," *Arbitration Journal,* 44 (December 1989), p. 47.

44. George W. Bohlander and Donna Blancero, "A Study of Reverse Determinants in Discipline and Discharge Arbitration Awards: The Impact of Just Cause Standards," *Labor Studies Journal,* 21 (February 1996), pp. 3–10.

45. John B. LaRocco, "Just Cause Collides with Public Policy in Sexual Harassment Arbitrations," *Proceedings of the*

49th Annual Meeting of the Industrial Relations Research Association (Madison, Wis: IRRA, 1997), pp. 211–216.

46. Hoyt N. Wheeler, Brian S. Klass, and Douglas M. Mahoney, *Workplace Justice without Unions*, Kalamazoo, MI: W. E. Upjohn Institute for Employment Research, 2004, p. 7. *NLRB v. J. Weingarten, Inc.*, 420 U.S. 262, 1974. See also M. J. Fox, Louis V. Baldovin, Jr., and Thomas R. Fox, "The *Weingarten* Doctrine," *The Arbitration Journal,* 40 (June 1985), pp. 45–54. The Weingarten decision has also been held by an appeals court to be applicable in at least some federal sector situations. See "Court Permits Union Representation at Meetings with DOD Investigators," Bureau of National Affairs, *Daily Labor Report,* no. 173 (September 7, 1988), A-1.

47. Ibid.

48. Ibid.

49. *Epilepsy Foundation of NE Ohio and Borgs and Hassan,* 331 NLRB 92 (July 10, 2000).

50. Clarence R. Deitsch, David A. Dilts, and Francice Guice, "*Weingarten* Rights in the Non-Union Workplace: A Merry-Go-Round of NLRB Decisions," *Dispute Resolution Journal,* 61 (May-July 2006), pp. 46–49.

51. Ann C. Hodges, Courtney Mueller Coke, and Robert R. Trumble, "*Weingarten* in the Nonunion Workplace: Looking in the Funhouse Mirror," *Labor Law Journal,* 54 (Summer 2002), pp. 94–95.

52. James F. Morgan, James M. Owens, and Glenn M. Gomes, "Union Rules Intrude Upon the Nonunion Domain: Workplace Investigations and the NLRB," *Employee Responsibilities and Rights Journal,* 14 (March 2000), pp. 36–39.

53. R. W. Fleming, *The Labor Arbitration Process* (Champaign: University of Illinois Press, 1965), p. 139.

Is an Indefinite Suspension for Just Cause?

CASE STUDY 12-1
Background

On March 30, 2006, David Gates was arrested and charged with felony Conspiracy to Distribute Schedule II Narcotics and Felony Possession of Schedule VI Marijuana.

In a letter dated March 31, 2006 Mr. Jamie Calvin, plant manager, wrote to Mr. Gates:-

> This letter is to inform you that you are suspended until further notice from employment effective this date as a result of your arrest for 1) Conspiracy to Distribute Schedule II Drugs and; 2) Possession of Schedule VI Marijuana–both felonies in the State of Tennessee.
>
> Your continued employment status will be determined based upon the disposition of these charges.

On April 3, 2006, Mr. Eddie Albert, vice president, Local 345, filed the following Grievance:

> Step 1. Statement of Grievance:
> Mr. Gates was suspended on March 31, 2006. The Union asks that Mr. Gates be reinstated and be made whole for all lost wages and benefits.

The Grievance was denied and the Union appealed. In a letter dated June 6, 2006, Mr. Gary Folkes, manager employee relations, provided the Company's response:

> The Company has an obligation to provide a safe work environment for all employees. It is the Company's position that the grievant presents significant risk to both himself and his fellow employees and, therefore, should not be allowed to work until the felony charges against him are resolved by a court of law. Grievance denied.

In a letter dated June, 19, 2006, Mr. Joe Blackwater, president, Local 345, responded to Mr. Folkes. He wrote:

> The Union rejects the Company's answer. Appeal to arbitration.

Issue

Did the Company violate the Agreement when it indefinitely suspended the Grievant? If so, what is the remedy?

Relevant Provisions of the Agreement

Article 2—Management Rights

The Union agrees that the Company is vested exclusively with the management of the business, including the direction of the working force; the right to plan, direct, and control all plant operations; the right to relieve employees from duty because of lack of work or for any other legitimate reason; the right to establish, change, or introduce new or improved production methods or facilities; and, except as expressly limited by the provisions of this Agreement, the right to hire, promote, suspend, demote, discipline, or discharge employees for just cause.

All authority normally exercised by management is and shall remain the exclusive prerogative of the Company, except where such authority is expressly limited by the terms of this Agreement.

Article 16—Rules of Conduct

For the purpose of plant discipline, the Company shall have the right to make and, after publication thereof, to enforce reasonable factory rules, not otherwise inconsistent with the terms of this Agreement.

The purpose of disciplinary action is not to punish, but to discourage repetition of misbehavior by the offender.

If the Company should post a new rule that the Union should consider unreasonable, it shall be subject to the grievance procedure.

The reasonableness of the following factory rules are agreed to by the parties and shall be subject to the following outlined disciplinary action.

NOTE: The Company does not waive its right to make rules during the term of the labor agreement.

CATEGORY C: This covers the disciplinary action for offenses listed below:

First offense-Discharge . . .

(10) Conviction of a felony

Positions of the Parties

The Company:

The Company stated that the Union believes the contract somehow obligates the Company to keep Gates in the plant. However, the Company believes that the Contract does not address the issue. An employee convicted of a felony is to be terminated pursuant to Category C (10). Gates was not terminated by the Company; rather he was suspended. The Contract is silent; therefore, the Management

Rights Clause of the Contract controls. The Management Rights Clause reads:

The Union agrees that the Company is vested exclusively with the management of the business, including the direction of the working force; the right to plan, direct, and control all plant operations; the right to relieve employees from duty because of lack of work or for any other legitimate reason; the right to establish, change, or introduce new or improved production methods or facilities; and, except as expressly limited by the provisions of this Agreement, the right to hire, promote, suspend, demote, discipline, or discharge employees for just cause.

Therefore, so long as the suspension was for "just cause," the Grievance must be denied and the suspension must stand. The relevant inquiry is what constitutes "just cause" within the parties' relationship and within the context of arbitration legal authority in general.

The Company stated that its arbitration history between the parties is long. Many cases that have defined just cause have been arbitrated. Just cause within the parties context is best and most recently defined in the recent grievance over the termination of David DeRoot. In the analysis of just cause, the Arbitrator cited the opinion of Arbitrator McCoy in *Stockham Pipe Fittings* Co. 1 LA 160 (1945). The opinion defines just cause analysis in the penalty context:

The only circumstances under which a penalty imposed by management can be rightfully set aside by an arbitrator are those where discrimination, unfairness, or capricious and arbitrary actions are proved–in other words, where there has been an abuse of discretion.

The Arbitrator defined the responsibility of the arbitrator when making a just cause determination:

Admittedly, since management is the one saying it had just cause here, it is necessary for an arbitrator to make an objective review of the evidence to make certain that management did not act arbitrarily or capriciously.

As to the necessary standard of proof, the Company argued that it was not judging the innocence or guilt of Gates. The Company is not charged with the responsibility of making any determination of the guilt or innocence of the accused felon. The issue in arbitration is not whether the accused felon committed the act. The issue is not whether the grievant was arrested and accused. As to that point, there is no dispute. Gates was arrested and accused of felonies. The proper issue is whether the Company may suspend an accused felon from employment pending the outcome of the felony criminal charges.

The Company claimed that the only issue for determination is whether the Company had just cause to suspend the employee. The employee was not charged with a misdemeanor. The employee was charged with a felony, a very serious felony, which involved a very significant amount of drugs. Other employees have reported Gates selling drugs to other persons in the plant, but are not willing to testify in an arbitration hearing. Gates was caught and arrested for possession of about 60 lbs. of marijuana. These arrests generally do not happen by accident. Therefore, the Company has numerous compelling reasons for suspending Gates.

The facts of the matter certainly appear as though Gates is a drug dealer. The Company has a legitimate interest in keeping drugs out of its plant. There are obvious concerns in the Company about possible drug usage and sales in the plant. It is certainly not arbitrary or capricious for the Company to keep a suspected and charged drug dealer out of its plant. If Gates is indeed a drug dealer, as it certainly appears he is, then employee safety is another legitimate concern. An employee under the influence of drugs could seriously injure himself, but more importantly, another employee in the plant.

An employee under the influence who works in production, drives fork trucks, and operates heavy machinery could cause injury or even death. It is not arbitrary or capricious to keep such a suspected and charged person out of the plant facility pending the resolution of the charges. The Company did not terminate Gates upon the charge; the Company suspended him. The suspension is absolutely a legitimate penalty.

The Company stated that the Union argued that an employee Jackie Johnson was allowed to stay in the plant in 1981 or so after a felony charge. The irrelevance of a matter 25 years old notwithstanding, the evidence shows beyond a shadow of a doubt that Johnson was allowed to stay in the plant on a last chance agreement.

Rather than terminate or suspend the employee, the Company allowed him to stay in the plant on a last chance agreement. The Union was a party to that agreement and its non-precedent effect is noted on the face of the documents. Johnson cannot be considered as a precedent, and it is highly suspect for the Union to bring the matter to the attention of an arbitrator and attempt to use as a precedent. Union President Blackwater testified that there have been other persons who have been allowed to stay in the plant (i.e. not suspended) with a pending felony. However, Blackwater was not able to name any persons who were allowed to stay without a last chance agreement.

The Company stated that the Union seemed to argue that the Company had placed Johnson on a Last Chance Agreement; therefore, it should be bound to place Gates on a Last Chance Agreement. Such an obvious misunderstanding of the concept of "Last Chance" is stunning. In 1981 that, in order to save the job of Johnson, the Union had no arguments with regard to the Company's right to terminate. The Company forfeited its right to terminate Johnson and the Union agreed. Now, 25 years later, the Union is asking the arbitrator to rule that not only did the Company forfeit its right to terminate Johnson in 1981, but it forfeited its right to discipline anyone in regard to a felony, (i.e., it obligated itself to offer Last Chance Agreements to any employees charged with a felony into the future). That assertion is obviously ridiculous.

The Last Chance Agreement for Johnson was a modification to the Master Collective Bargaining Agreement and an application to a specific employee (Johnson). The Last Chance Agreement has no effect as precedent, does not change the relation between the parties (except as to the affected employee), and cannot be considered as precedent in an arbitration context. The Last Chance Agreement is a signed written modification of the relationship between the parties; it modifies the Collective Bargaining Agreement as to the particular employee or employees addressed in the Last Chance Agreement. To allow Last Chance Agreements to serve as a precedent would be to terminate the use of Last Chance Agreements and would thereby defeat the beneficial purpose served through the use of Last Chance Agreements.

The Company stated that the evidence collected by the police showed Joe Stone, a friend of Gates from his hometown, called Gates and told Gates to pick up a package at the house of Gates's girlfriend Teresa Clem. Gates told the police that Stone was having the package delivered to the house of Clem because Stone had no fixed address; Stone was "somewhat of a drifter." Gates told police that he and Stone were friends from years ago in Kentucky. Gates said he did not know what was in the package when he picked it up at his girlfriend's house. Gates testified that he had introduced Stone to his girlfriend a couple of years ago. The Company asked: "Why would Stone have a package delivered 2 ½ hours drive away? Why would Stone not have the package delivered to Gates's house if he expected Gates to pick the package up for him?" The story is obviously disingenuous on its face.

The Company concluded:

> The Company suspended David Gates because Gates was charged with a felony. Gates was not charged with just any felony. He was charged with a drug-related felony.
>
> The Company has received numerous complaints about drug usage and sales in the plant. The circumstances of Gates's case appear beyond much doubt that he is guilty, but that is not for the Company to determine, nor has the Company made a determination on his guilt or innocence. The Company's only concern is keeping an accused drug dealer out of its plant. The Company's only charges do not contemplate a small amount of marijuana for his own personal use. Gates's charges involve approximately sixty (60) pounds of marijuana. The amount alone makes it obvious that Gates is apparently a drug dealer and had designs on selling a great deal of marijuana. It would be irresponsible of the Company to allow someone such as the accused in its plant until the conclusion of the criminal issues,—just as it would be irresponsible for the Company to allow an accused murderer or rapist to work pending the outcome of the charges. The newspaper article exhibit references a street value of $90,000 for the marijuana retrieved. The Company has a legitimate business reason due to safety and preventing illegal activity in its plant to keep Gates out of the plant on suspension until resolution of the charges. For all of the foregoing reasons this grievance must be denied.

The Union:

The Union argued that Gates had already been disciplined for a long period of time (nine months by the date of the arbitration hearing) and Gates should be presumed innocent until proven guilty. The Union claimed that Rule 10, Category C requires "conviction of a felony." Gates had not been convicted. Gates was arrested and charged, but not convicted. In fact, Gates had a good work record. Mr. Colbert, plant manager, testified that Gates had no performance issues.

The Union stated that the Company had allowed other employees who were convicted of felonies to continue to work. The Union presented a document which involved Jackie Johnson who was convicted of a felony and who was allowed to continue to work at the Company. In addition, Mr. Blackwater, president, Local No. 345, identified other similarly situated employees—Marvin Holden, Bob Cooper, and Troy Lode—who were convicted of felonies, but who were allowed to continue to work.

The Union stated that Gates tested negative for illegal drugs in his system. Gates's personal locker and vehicle had been searched and no illegal drugs were found.

The Union stated that Mr. Colbert made the decision to permanently suspend Gates. Mr. Colbert said that if the charge is reduced or the Grievant is found not guilty, the Company knows that Gates will be brought back to work and made whole for any losses.

The Union contended that Gates agreed to go to his girlfriend's house to receive the package. Gates did not open the package, but put it in the back of his truck. Gates told the police that the package was not his, and he did not know the package contained drugs. The Union stated that Gates cooperated with the police in order to secure the arrest of Stone, the addressee of the package containing the illegal drugs. The Union stated that Gates knew Stone as a childhood friend in Kentucky. However, Stone was a drifter who lived in Kentucky and who had an address in West Virginia.

The Union concluded that Gates did not violate Rule 10 of Category C, there was no just cause for this indefinite suspension, and Gates should be reinstated and made whole for any losses.

Questions

1. Which party has the burden of proof in this case? Why?

2. What is the rule about off-duty conduct in regard to employee discipline?

3. What type of evidence are the e-mails received from employees about Gates's on-duty behavior? Should this evidence be considered by the arbitrator? Why or why not?

4. Should the Company's offer to pay back pay and to restore seniority and benefits if Gates is found not guilty be considered by the arbitrator? Why or why not?

5. You be the arbitrator. Should the Grievance be sustained or denied? Explain your reasoning.

Last Chance Agreement Versus Just Cause–Progressive Discipline

CASE STUDY 12-2
Background
On March 27, 1998, the Company, the Union, and Mr. Danny Webb, the Grievant, entered into and signed the following Agreement:

Without precedent, the Company, the Union, and Mr. Danny Webb agree to the following:

1. *Mr. Webb has reached the discharge step for progressive discipline under Category "B" rules. He is, hereby, given a final opportunity to save his job by compliance with conditions set forth in this agreement.*

2. *There will be a suspension from 3/27/98 to 4/20/98. Mr. Webb will return to work the week of 4/20/98.*

3. *There will be a probationary period of 18 months, which will expire September 27, 1999.*

4. *The violation of any plant rule during the probationary period will result in immediate discharge.*

5. *Any absence of scheduled work time, including tardiness, during the probationary period will result in immediate discharge, unless determined by supervision to be beyond Mr. Webb's control.*

6. *Mr. Webb understands that overtime is a part of his job.*

7. *Mr. Webb has been made aware of the Employee Assistance Program, for help with the anger problem he says he has.*

On April 27, 1999, Warehouse Supervisor Mr. Ted Holt wrote the following Notice:

Reason for Warning or Reprimand:
Violation of plant rules including negligent act resulting in damage to company property. Category B (12) Danny flipped over (2) crates of 1/8" × 48" × 60" heavy case (HC) glass in zone #326 on the top row and then took (1) crate of HC from the bottom and placed it in front of the damaged crate. This hid the flipped-over crate. He went home without reporting the incident. Other employees observed the incident and reported to Tommy Biggers.

Supervisor's Comments:
Danny did not report the incident to any supervisor. He placed a crate in front of the two crates that he caused to flip over to hide the damage and presented a hidden danger to other employees. This is in violation of his Last Chance Agreement dated March 27, 1998, and therefore results in discharge.

On the same day, Mr. Joe Broadway, first vice president, Local Union no. 911, filed the following Grievance:

Statement of Grievance:
The Union asks that Mr. Webb be put back to work and made whole for any lost wages.

The Company denied the Grievance in a letter dated June 11, 1999, to Mr. Thomas Rowe, president, Local Union no. 911. The reason given was:

The facts of the case indicate that Mr. Webb did indeed tip two crates of glass, knowingly concealed the damage, and failed to report the incident to his supervisor. The disciplinary action taken was appropriate given the facts. Grievance denied.

The Grievance was appealed in a letter dated June 16, 1999. The appeal stated:

L-26-9—The Union is in dispute with the Company's position pertaining to the discipline of this Grievant; therefore this grievance is appealed to arbitration.

Issue
Was the Grievant's discharge for just cause? If not, what is the remedy?

Relevant Provisions of the Agreement

Article 2—Management
2.01   The Union agrees that the Company is vested exclusively with the management of the business, including the direction of the working force; the right to plan, direct, and control all plant operations; the right to relieve employees from duty because of lack of work or for any other legitimate reason; the right to establish, change, or introduce new or improved production methods or facilities; and, except as expressly limited by the provisions of this Agreement, the right to hire, promote, suspend, demote, discipline, or discharge employees for just cause.

2.02   All authority normally exercised by Management is and shall remain the exclusive prerogative of the Company, except where such authority is expressly limited by the terms of this Agreement.

2.03   Any alleged discrimination or violation of the terms of this Agreement deemed to exist as a result of the exercise of these prerogatives by the Company shall be subject to the Grievance Procedure of this Agreement.

Article 5—Settlement of Grievances
(e) Step 5: Arbitration
   ...The arbitrator shall have jurisdiction and authority only to interpret, apply, or determine compliance with the provisions of this Agreement insofar as shall be necessary to the determination

of the grievance submitted to him, but he shall not have jurisdiction or authority to add to, subtract from, or alter in any way, the provisions of this Agreement. . . .

Article 32—Rules

32.01 For the purpose of plant discipline, the Company shall have the right to make and, after publication thereof, to enforce reasonable factory rules, not otherwise inconsistent with the terms of this Agreement.

32.02 The purpose of disciplinary action is not to punish, but to discourage repetition of mis-behavior by the offender.

32.03 If the Company should post a new rule that the Union should consider unreasonable, it shall be subject to the grievance procedure.

32.04 The reasonableness of the following factory rules are agreed to by the parties and shall be subject to the following outlined disciplinary action.

Category B—This covers the disciplinary procedure for handling those types of offenses that require more severe penalty:

First Offense—Five-day suspension (working days)

Second Offense—Discharge

(12) Negligent acts resulting in loss of production or damage to Company property.

Positions of the Parties

The Company:

The Company stated that on April 27, 1999, Mr. Webb, a forklift operator in the Shipping Department, was working the day shift pulling orders for glass crates from the warehouse. The order list from which the Grievant was working called for one crate of 1/16" × 48" × 84", heavy case (HC) gray glass located in Zone no. 326. The Grievant proceeded to this location and was removing a two-crate pack (banded together) of the required glass when he accidentally tipped over a second two-crate pack, which was located immediately behind the first one. The tipped-over pack made a loud noise when it fell, and the noise was heard by both the Grievant and two employees who were working in the "repair" area some 25 to 30 feet away. Instead of stopping to check to see what had happened, the Grievant proceeded to lower the two-crate pack he had on his forks, cut the band holding them together, set one single crate back on top of a three-tier stack, and drove off to the dock staging area with the single crate. His actions were observed by two other hourly employees who were working in the "repair" area and who subsequently reported the incident to supervision. Mr. Webb never reported the incident to any member of supervision. In fact, the Grievant created a safety hazard for his fellow employees by setting a single unbanded crate on a three-tier stack.

On investigation of the incident by area supervision, the Company determined that Mr. Webb had acted negligently in the performance of his duties. His failure to report the accident and making the situation a dangerous one by stacking a single unbanded crate on the three-tier stack reflected a total disregard for his job responsibilities and the safety of his fellow employees.

The Company argued that the Grievance is without merit. At the time of his discharge, Mr. Webb was working in a probationary status under the terms of a last chance agreement dated March 27, 1998. The terms of this agreement specifically state that "the violation of any plant rule during the probationary period will result in immediate discharge." The probationary period extended from March 27, 1998, through September 27, 1999. The present incident occurred on April 27, 1999, well within the probationary period. The last chance agreement was a final opportunity for the Grievant to preserve his job. Mr. Webb, the president of Local 911, and the vice president of Local 911 all signed the agreement. The agreement has both a starting and ending time frame, and its probationary period does not exceed any of the probationary time frames outlined under Article 32—Rules of the Labor Agreement.

The Company argued that Mr. Webb had been given an opportunity to retain his job. The Company went beyond what the Labor Agreement demands in the way of "second chances." This is evidenced by the fact that a last chance agreement was entered into with the Grievant. Although the Company was well within its rights and the provisions of the Labor Agreement to discharge the Grievant in March 1998, it gave the Grievant a final opportunity to save his job. The last chance agreement was above and beyond the requirements of the Labor

Agreement and demonstrates that the Company was not "out to get" the Grievant.

Eyewitness testimony from fellow employee Donnie Ossie indicated that he saw the Grievant tip over the two crates of glass in question. Although fellow employee James Staples did not see it, he testified that he heard a loud noise where Mr. Webb was working and asked Donnie Ossie if "Danny had turned over some glass." Even Mr. Webb himself admitted that he heard a loud noise when he attempted to lift two crates of glass (banded together) from the third tier, but he did not check to see if there was any damage. This action goes to the very heart of why the Grievant was charged for performing his job in a negligent manner. Basic common sense would dictate that a person would check to see if he had caused an accident and, if so, to report it to the proper authority.

The Company claimed that Mr. Webb is not an inexperienced novice in the workplace who can claim he did not know what he was supposed to do in such a situation. Webb confirmed that he had worked at the Company since 1973, that he was aware of the fact that he was supposed to report all accidents to supervision, and if cleanup was involved, that the person causing the damage was the one who was supposed to clean it up. Yet, despite his understanding of the rules, he failed to report the accident and clean up his mess. Furthermore, he exacerbated the situation by creating a safety hazard by placing a single crate of glass (unbanded) on the third tier.

The Company claimed that Mr. Webb did not admit to nor deny that he "could have" tipped over the two crates of glass. Webb's lone defense was that he just did not know whether he had tipped the glass over. Webb did admit to hearing a loud noise as he was removing two other crates of glass. Again, the fact that the Grievant was experienced on the job and the fact that basic common sense would prompt any prudent person to check to see what had caused the noise calls into question the credibility of the Grievant. The Grievant confirmed that the lone eyewitness was positioned at a location where he could have observed if any crates had been turned over. The noise created by the falling glass was of sufficient volume that another employee in the "repair" area heard and reacted to it. All these facts paint an undeniable picture that Mr. Webb acted negligently.

The Company stated that the Union alleged that forklift operators had been told by supervisors to stack single crates on the third tier. The Grievant testified that supervisors had instructed them to "pack the crates tight" against one another. When Mr. Webb was asked if any supervisor had ever told him to stack single crates on the third tier, Mr. Webb said that he had been told to pack them tight. When pressed further, Mr. Webb admitted that he had never been told directly by any member of supervision to stack single crates on the third tier. In fact, Mr. Webb confirmed that the standard method of operation was to stack two-crate packs of glass, which are banded together, when stacking three tiers high.

The Grievant was asked if he thought that stacking single crates, three tiers high presented a safety hazard to himself or to others. The Grievant said, "No." He further stated that on April 27, 1999, he broke the band on a two-crate pack, took one crate out, and returned the single crate to its former position on top of the third tier. Mr. Webb stated that the total width of a single crate was 12 to 13 inches wide and that the weight of a single crate would exceed 4,000 pounds. It is clear that such a crate would be less stable than a two-crate banded pack, yet Mr. Webb maintained that he did not believe this to be a safety hazard. In fact, he admitted to setting a single crate on the third tier as a freestanding object with no other standing crate behind it. This action violates even the Grievant's own version of the stacking instructions, which was to pack single crates tight against other crates. There were no standing crates behind the single crate that the Grievant placed on the third tier. This illustrates that Mr. Webb was negligent in the performance of his job and that he did indeed create a real safety hazard for himself and other employees.

Supervisor Brian Waters testified that the two crates of glass that were tipped over by the Grievant were valued at $2,320. This figure did not include the cost associated with removal and disposal of the broken glass. Mr. Waters testified that both of the crates of glass were total losses. Supervisor Waters pointed out that the proper way to handle crates of glass would have been to insert the forks of the forklift under the two-crate pack to be loaded but not to the point that the forks would extend beyond the two-crate pack being lifted. If the forks were fully inserted, they would extend below the next two-crate packs behind the two-crate pack being lifted. When the driver raised the forks to lift the front two-crate pack, the tips of the protruding forks would act as a lever on the second two-crate pack and cause it to topple. The Company's position is that this is exactly what Mr. Webb did when he toppled the crates of glass.

The Company concluded that it had presented unrefuted evidence that:

- The Grievant was given one more chance to save his job than was required by the labor contract.

- The Grievant had previously reached the discharge step for progressive discipline under Category B rules.

- The Grievant was working under a last chance agreement in which any violation would subject him to immediate discharge.

- The last chance agreement was agreed to by the Company, the Grievant, and the Union as evidenced by their signatures on the document.

- The last chance agreement specified a beginning and ending date, set a probationary period that was in line with the probationary periods used elsewhere in the labor contract, and specified that violation of any plant rules during the probationary period would result in immediate discharge.

- The incident that occurred on April 27, 1999, was within the probationary period of the last chance agreement (March 27, 1998, to September 27, 1999).

- The incident was witnessed by bargaining unit employee Donnie Ossie and heard by bargaining unit employee James Staples, as well as the Grievant himself.

- The Grievant removed a two-crate pack from the third tier, broke the band, removed a single crate, and set a single crate back on the third tier, thus creating a safety hazard.

- The grievant was never instructed by any member of supervision to stack a single crate on the third tier of any stack.

- The Grievant acted negligently in the performance of his job.

Therefore, the Company respectfully requests that the Arbitrator deny this grievance.

The Union:

The Union stated that Mr. Webb was hired by the Company into the Flat Glass Department on April 23, 1973. Webb worked packing glass for three years and drove a forklift approximately eight years. Webb had been working in this shipping department since 1991 and has worked all the jobs in the department. At the time of his discharge, he was a forklift driver, pulling stock.

On April 28, 1999, the Grievant worked the day shift (7:00 A.M. to 3:00 A.M.). Near the end of the shift, the Grievant was told by his supervisor that he was required to work overtime on the next shift. Webb was not the lowest in used overtime and went looking for Mr. Bob Crain, the Union Steward for the department on that shift. While he was looking for Mr. Crain, Webb saw Mr. Joe Broadway, the Local Union vice president. Mr. Broadway told the Grievant that Mr. Crain was in the personnel office to talk to the Grievant. Mr. Broadway told the Grievant that the Company was going to fire him for turning over some glass the day before. Mr. Webb told Mr. Broadway he did not know anything about it. The Grievant went back to his department, and his supervisor told him that he was wanted in Mr. Don Grey's office. The Grievant and his supervisor went to Mr. Grey's office, where the Grievant was discharged for "violation of plant rules including negligent act resulting in damage to Company property. Category B (12)" and "violation of last chance agreement dated March 27, 1998."

The Union stated that Mr. Donnie Ossie testified that he and Mr. James Staples were working in the "repair" area of the shipping department approximately 30 to 40 feet from where the Grievant removed two crates of HC glass from the third stack with a forklift. The two crates were banded together. Ossie stated that when the Grievant was getting the two crates down, the fork on the forklift tipped over two other crates of glass and that he heard glass breaking. Ossie stated that the Grievant cut the bands of the two crates, put one crate back up where the two crates had been, and carried the other crate of glass with him. Ossie testified that the Grievant said something to him, but he could not hear what he said because of the noise. Ossie testified that there was space behind the two crates that were tipped and that, if they had been stacked properly, the two crates could not have fallen. Ossie indicated that the two-crate pack that was tipped over was next to and behind the two-crate pack that the Grievant removed from the stack.

Mr. Ossie testified that the glass in question had been shipped from Mexico, that the crates were not very steady, and that the crates of glass from Mexico would sometimes fall if you looked directly at them. Ossie testified that everyone who worked in shipping had broken some glass and that employees had to do the best they could. Mr. Ossie admitted that he did not see any broken glass in the area.

Mr. James Staples testified that he and Mr. Ossie were in the "repair" area and that he heard a noise and determined that it came from the area where Mr. Webb was loading crates of glass. Staples did not see any crates of glass fall and could not see the two crates that were laying flat. Staples admitted that it was common for people to break glass and that it was a noisy work area.

The Company had stated that the Grievant said that he had an order for one crate of 1/16" × 48" × 84" glass and went into the area and pulled a two-crate pack of 1/16" × 48" × 84" glass from the third tier, cut the bands, and put one crate back on the third tier as he had been instructed to do by his supervisor. Webb then carried one crate with him and put it in the dock area. The Grievant testified that, when he was loading the two-crate pack of 1/16" × 48" × 84" glass, he heard a noise but could not see what had caused the noise and that he did not know whether or not he had turned over the two-crate pack of glass. Webb stated that he had to drive down the aisle before he could see the two crates laying flat on the top of the other crates. He did not know if they were laying flat before he got the two crates or not. Webb testified that he asked Mr. Ossie and Mr. Staples if they had heard the noise, but they could not hear him

because of the noise in the plant, and he did not pursue it. Webb stated that he saw an empty space behind the two-crate pack of glass that he loaded but could not see any other crates behind on the third tier. The Grievant testified that he had broken glass before and that everyone who drove a forklift had broken glass. To his knowledge, no one had ever been disciplined for breaking glass. Webb stated that no one from Management ever talked to him about the alleged incident until the meeting near the end of the shift on April 28, 1999, and he knew nothing about the alleged incident until that meeting. Each employee testified that, if the two crates of glass in question had been stacked properly, they would have been against the wall and could not have fallen.

The Union argued that the Company did not afford the Grievant anything that even slightly resembled due process. Mr. Crain testified that he made up his mind to discharge the Grievant at about 6:00 P.M. on April 27, 1999. At that time, Crain had talked only to his supervisors, none of whom had any direct knowledge of what had or had not happened. Until the meeting on April 28, 1999, the only supervisor who possibly had any direct knowledge of what happened was the supervisor to whom Mr. Ossie reported that the glass had been tipped over by Mr. Webb. There was no evidence that any Company official ever talked to Mr. James Staples until the day of the arbitration hearing. In other words, Mr. Crain made the decision to discharge Mr. Webb at 6:00 P.M. on the April 27, 1999, without talking to anyone other than Mr. Ossie, who could not have possibly seen the forks on the Grievant's forklift tip over the two-crate pack of glass in question. There was no evidence that any member of management checked the wood on the crates to see whether there were marks other than those made by the forks on the lift truck. The Union argued that Mr. Crain made the decision to discharge Mr. Webb on April 27, 1999, at 6:00 P.M. and was not going to change his mind.

The Union stated that it is clear that the Company did not conduct a fair investigation and did not afford the Grievant due process by any stretch of the imagination. As such, there are grounds to sustain the Grievance. The majority of arbitrators have reversed discipline and discharge of employees when the employer has violated the basic notion of fairness and due process.

The Union stated that Mr. Webb testified that, when he was getting the two-crate pack of $1/16" \times 48" \times 84"$ glass, he could see empty space behind them, that he could not see any other crates behind them, and that during the time he was removing the two-crate pack he heard a noise but could not tell what had caused it. Mr. Staples testified that he heard a noise but that it did not sound like glass breaking. Mr. Webb testified that he broke the bands on the two-crate pack of glass, cut the band, set one crate back on top, and took the one crate he needed with him to the dock area. Webb stated that as he was backing up with the two-crate pack of glass, at some point he could see the two crates laying flat on top of the stack. The Grievant stated without reservation that he did not know if the two crates of glass were laying flat when he came to the row or if he had accidentally tipped them over.

The Union argued that the evidence clearly shows that the glass fell over on its own as a result of the Grievant possibly bumping the front of the stack or that the movement of the glass being lifted caused the row to move, causing it to tip over. Mr. Ossie testified that the glass packed at the Mexico plant would fall over if you looked at it. It is clear that the fork of the forklift could not have possibly tipped over the glass.

The crate extended eight to ten inches beyond the end of the forks. According to the order list, the glass was 48 inches wide. Allowing two inches on each side for the crate, the total width of the crates would be 52 inches. The forks were approximately 46 inches long. If two of the crates are 24 to 26 inches across, the forks would not go all the way through the four crates. If the Grievant had attempted to raise the four crates up as described by Mr. Ossie, they would have had to have been stacked close together. If the two crates were set up from where they are shown to be laying, there is no possible way the forklift could have touched them. If the forks had gone under all four of the crates as described by Mr. Ossie, the forklift could not have lifted them, and they surely could not have fallen off the forks.

The Union stated that there were no marks of any kind anywhere on the wooden crates that could have been made by the forks on the forklift. If they had been tipped over by the forks, there would have had to be some type of marks on the wood. Thus, the crates could not possibly have been turned over or tipped over by the forklift driven by Mr. Webb.

The Union stated that the Company position that Mr. Webb set the single crate of glass back on top was destroyed by the testimony of the Grievant that just a few days before the alleged incident his supervisor had told him to do exactly as he did in this case. Therefore, the Company presented no evidence whatsoever that the Grievant was negligent or that he tried to hide anything.

The Union closed by stating:

For all of the above, the Union requests that the arbitrator sustain the grievance, order the Company to reinstate the Grievant to his job without loss of seniority and make him whole for all wages and benefits lost.

Questions

1. What is a last chance agreement?

2. Does a last chance agreement limit the arbitrator's authority? If so, how? If not, why not?

3. Is the length of the probationary period in the last chance agreement reasonable? If not, does this period make the last chance agreement unreasonable?

4. What proof does the Company have that the Grievant did what he was accused of?

5. What are the mitigating factors in this case? Should the arbitrator consider these mitigating factors in reviewing the penalty assessed by the Company?

6. You be the arbitrator. You decide and give your reasoning.

Is an Employee Entitled to Have a Witness at a Disciplinary Interview?

CASE STUDY 12-3 Terry Williams is an employee at a unionized plant in Memphis, Tennessee. Williams is a member of and represented by Local #10 of the United Brotherhood of America. Williams clocked out on Friday afternoon at 3:30 P.M., half an hour before his regular workday ended. Williams was later seen distributing union leaflets on the sidewalk near the main plant in Southhaven, Mississippi, eight miles south of Memphis, by plant manager Otto Payonzeck. Payonzeck confronted Williams and asked him what he was doing at the Southhaven, Mississippi, plant. Payonzeck then called the personnel office at the Memphis plant to see if Williams had permission to be at Southhaven.

When Williams reported to work the next day, he was called to a meeting with supervisors Fisher and Gray and personnel administrator Harless. As soon as Williams entered the room, he recognized the people and asked to be permitted to call another employee into the room as a witness. Harless responded that it was not necessary because they were only going to ask him some questions and therefore he did not need a witness. Williams then asked to make a phone call, and this request was likewise rejected.

The supervisors and Harless proceeded to ask Williams questions about what he did after he left work early on the previous workday. The meeting lasted 15 minutes, and Williams refused to answer any questions. In fact, Williams' response to most questions was that it was none of their business. Williams was permitted to leave the meeting and was told to return at 10:00 A.M. During the break, Williams called the NLRB's regional office. At 10:00 A.M., Williams returned to the meeting and was told that he was being suspended for three days.

Supervisor Fisher said that on the morning of the day that Williams was suspended, he met with Harless to determine disciplinary action. Gray had suggested discharge; however, it was decided to suspend Williams for three days. Fisher said that Williams was refused a witness and the telephone call because they were not going to fire him, they were just going to suspend him. In fact, Williams refused to answer any questions about the rule infraction of leaving early to distribute union literature.

Supervisor Gray's version of the incident varied slightly from Fisher's. Gray recalled that Harless told Williams, after denying his request to use the telephone, that he was being suspended for three days, but Harless would continue to investigate the matter.

Questions

1. Was Williams entitled to have a witness at the meeting with Harless, Gray, and Fisher? Explain.

2. To what remedy is an employee entitled if his or her rights have been violated?

3. What would be your ruling if the plant in Memphis had no union? Explain.

4. Should this suspension be upheld? Explain.

Part 4: Applying the Labor Relations Process to Different Labor Relations Systems

Part 4 presents the opportunity to apply the previous chapters' discussions of the labor relations process to various labor relations situations. Collective bargaining in the public sector at all governmental levels is discussed, and a discussion of foreign labor relations systems is presented for comparative purposes.

 Copyright GettyImages

Chapter 13
Labor Relations in the Public Sector

Chapter 14
Labor Relations in Multinational
Corporations and in Other Countries

Labor Relations in the Public Sector

The public sector has become an important factor in the U.S. labor scene. As the number of public employees has increased, so has the number of these employees joining unions. This chapter presents an overview of labor relations in the public sector and provides a brief summary of the similarities and differences in public- and private-sector labor relations. It also examines public-sector bargaining at the local, state, and federal levels. The chapter concludes with a discussion of labor challenges and opportunities, public-sector unions, and prospects for the future.

SIGNIFICANCE OF PUBLIC-SECTOR LABOR RELATIONS

The field of public-sector labor relations has developed from a time when public employees were required to lobby their respective legislators for favorable employment terms to one in which bona fide collective bargaining occurs. Public-sector labor relations has moved from an earlier period characterized by rapid union growth, management's inability to react to collective bargaining, and a fear of strikes to a period characterized by slower union growth, most states providing public employee bargaining rights, and a willingness on the part of public employers to take strikes.[1] With many state legislatures and the U.S. Congress interested in reducing government costs, management strategies, such as downsizing and privatization of public services, have caused many public employees to become more concerned about their job security and welfare.[2] Therefore, union leaders are showing increased attention to public employees' concerns in these areas (see the Labor Relations in Action feature on page 574).

In 2007, 7.4 million union members made up 35.9 percent of total public-sector (federal, state, and local) employment.[3] About 32 percent of federal employees, 34 percent of state employees, and 46 percent of local government employees are represented by unions. This union density level is much higher than the 8.2 percent of private-sector employees represented for purposes of collective bargaining.

In terms of government function, unions represent a majority of postal employees, teachers, firefighters, police, and bus and urban transit employees. There are also major differences in public-sector union membership based on geography. Public-sector union membership is much greater in the Northeast, North, and West than in the South and Midwest. For example, public-sector union membership is over 60 percent in New York, Rhode Island, Hawaii, and New Jersey as compared with less than ten percent in Mississippi, North Carolina, and South Carolina.[4]

Exhibit 13.1 presents a listing of some national unions representing public-sector employees. Some national unions (e.g., United Auto Workers, International Association of Machinists), which predominantly represent private-sector employees, have also diversified their organizing efforts in recent years to attract public-sector employees. The Service Employees International Union (SEIU) now represents over 600,000 public-sector employees in the United States, Canada, and Puerto Rico.[5]

The so-called "free rider" issue mentioned in the discussion of private-sector union security issues in Chapter 4 is an important factor affecting union membership among federal employees.[6] Under the Civil Service Reform Act (CSRA) of 1978 and the Postal Reorganization Act, union security clauses, such as a union

Exhibit 13.1
Some Unions Representing
Public Employees

Union	Number of Public Employee Members
American Federation of Government Employees (AFGE)	229,248
American Federation of State, County, and Municipal Employees (AFSCME)	1,470,095
American Federation of Teachers (AFT)	822,504
American Postal Workers Union (APWU)	283,279
Fraternal Order of Police (FOP)	240,000
International Association of Firefighters (IAFF)	277,464
National Air Traffic Controllers Association (NATCA)	14,571
National Association of Letter Carriers (NALC)	287,036
National Education Association (NEA)	2,767,696
National Federation of Federal Employees (NFFE, IAM)	7,500
National Rural Letter Carriers Association (NRLCA)	107,564
National Treasury Employees Union (NTEU)	77,707

SOURCE: *Directory of U.S. Labor Organizations, 1997 edition*, ed. C. D. Gifford (Washington, D.C.: The Bureau of National Affairs, 1997), pp. 47–78; Updated from the Forms LM-2 Reports by U. S. labor unions, which can be found at http://www.dol.gov/esa, the home page of the U.S. Department of Labor.

or agency shop, are prohibited. Therefore, unions are required to represent all employees in recognized bargaining units but receive no fees or dues from those who choose not to be union members. Because the so-called free riders receive benefits at no cost to them, there is not a significant incentive to join and pay dues.

Overall, 7.4 million public-sector employees are union members who pay dues to be represented by unions, but nearly 800,000 are not union members and do not pay dues. Still, these nonpaying employees must be represented in collective bargaining, grievance administration, and arbitration by the unions.[7]

The American Federation of Government Employees (AFGE) is the largest union representing federal government employees. Although its membership is 229,248, the AFGE is legally required to represent nearly 600,000 federal government employees and negotiates over 300 collective bargaining agreements. In other words, 62 percent of the federal government employees who are represented by the AFGE do not pay dues; therefore, 38 percent of those who are members pay dues to provide representational services (bargaining, grievance handling, arbitration, etc.) for the other 62 percent (see Chapter 4 for discussion of union security issues). As a result, the U.S. federal government is the nation's largest "open shop" employer.[8]

Labor Legislation in the Public Sector

The presence of a strong public-sector bargaining law may be influenced by the general public's attitude toward collective bargaining, the degree of private-sector employers' opposition to unions, and the degree to which state legislators are viewed as being more "liberal," among other factors.[9] Favorable legislation protecting employees' right to bargain, regulating unfair labor practices, and establishing impasse procedures to resolve both interests and rights-type labor disputes is a significant factor encouraging the growth of public-sector bargaining within a state.[10]

As shown in Exhibit 13.2, 23 states have passed legislation allowing collective bargaining, which covers police and fire, state, education, and municipal employees. Twelve states (Alabama, Arizona, Arkansas, Colorado, Louisiana, Maryland, Mississippi, Missouri, North Carolina, South Carolina, Virginia, and West Virginia) have no legislation that allows these types of public employees to participate in collective bargaining. The remaining states have legislation that allows collective bargaining for one or more of the police and fire, state, education, and municipal employee groups. Thirty-two states provide bargaining rights to police and firefighters, 35 states provide bargaining rights to public education employees, 26 states provide bargaining rights to municipal employees, and 23 states provide bargaining rights to state employees.[11]

Forty-one states have enacted statutes permitting public school employees to bargain collectively with boards of education, and over 80 percent of the teachers

Alaska	Massachusetts	New York
Connecticut	Michigan	Ohio
Delaware	Minnesota	Oregon
Florida	Montana	Pennsylvania
Hawaii	Nebraska	Rhode Island
Illinois	New Hampshire	Vermont
Iowa	New Jersey	Wisconsin
Maine	New Mexico	

SOURCE: Bureau of National Affairs, "Public-Sector Bargaining—State Comparison Chart," in *Collective Bargaining Negotiating and Contracts*, May 18, 2000, pp. 8:2901–2952; updated by "State Labor Laws," *BNA Labor Relations Reporter*, Washington, D.C., 2007.

Exhibit 13.2

Public-Sector Collective Bargaining Laws Covering Police and Fire, State, Education, and Municipal Employees

are covered by collective-bargaining agreements.[12] Although the content of these agreements may vary, the typical agreement includes provisions such as those found in Exhibit 13.3.

The scope of bargaining subjects covered under most state bargaining laws include wages, hours, and other terms or conditions of employment similar to the scope of bargaining under the private-sector LMRA. However, a majority of the states have some statutory limitations on the scope of collective bargaining, such as limitations guaranteeing management rights. Another important element of labor legislation is unfair labor practices. Although these vary somewhat from state to state, most states have legislation defining unfair labor practices for some or all public employees that are similar to the types of discrimination banned under the private-sector LMRA (e.g., bad-faith bargaining, threats or reprisals for engaging in concerted and protected activity).

Thirteen states permit public-sector strikes by some groups of public employees either by statutory law or judicial decision.[13] These states are Arkansas, California, Colorado, Hawaii, Idaho, Illinois, Louisiana, Minnesota, New Jersey, Ohio, Oregon, Pennsylvania, and Vermont. For example, in California, the state supreme court ruled that strikes by public employees other than police or firefighters were not illegal as long as they did not represent a substantial or imminent threat to the public's health or safety.[14] Most states prohibit public employee strikes and may authorize a variety of potential sanctions for illegal

Exhibit 13.3

Provisions in a Collective-Bargaining Agreement between Teachers and Boards of Education

A *management rights clause* is designed to clarify and protect the rights of the employer and to limit the authority of an arbitrator. Such a clause would include the right to supervise all operations; determine the size of the workforce; introduce new methods, programs, or procedures; hire and discharge employees for just cause; and maintain an orderly, effective, and efficient operation.

A *grievance procedure* is a step-by-step sequence of steps for resolving allegations of violations of the provisions of the collective-bargaining agreement.

A *no strike and no lockout provision* is included to guarantee continued operation for the life of the agreement. Some agreements provide for discipline of employees who participate in a work stoppage in violation of the no strike clause and penalties to the union that encourages a work stoppage.

A *zipper clause* stipulates that the written agreement is the complete and full contract between the parties and that neither party is required to bargain over other items during the term of the agreement.

Maintenance of standards incorporates a school district's current and past practices, such as teaching hours, relief periods, leaves of absence, extra compensation for work outside regular teaching hours, etc.

A *reduction-in-force* provision provides the criteria used in layoffs. Usually seniority in a certified field is used in layoff and recall, and some agreements provide for bumping rights.

A *wages and benefits* provision addresses wage increases, such as across-the-board increases, step increases, cost-of-living increases based on the Consumer Price Index, and merit increases. Benefits would include insurance (life, health, and dental), pensions, sick leave, personal days, funeral leave, holidays, etc.

Other issues include grievance arbitration, teacher evaluation, class size, school calendar, etc.

SOURCE: Fred C. Lunenburg, "Collective Bargaining in the Public Schools: Issues, Tactics, and New Strategies," *Journal of Collective Negotiations in the Public Sector* 29, no. 4 (2000), p. 259.

strike activity varying from injunctions to dismissals, jail sentences, substantial fines, and loss of union recognition. Decreasing use of the strike as a bargaining tactic has occurred in recent years in the public sector, similar to the trend in the private sector. Unionized public-sector employees in states that grant a legal right to strike are only slightly more likely to be involved in strikes compared with states that ban public employee strikes. Educators are the employee group most likely to participate in strikes, and strikes in education are more likely to occur in five states (California, Illinois, Michigan, Ohio, and Pennsylvania).[15]

In states that allow some public employee groups to strike, certain employees, such as police, firefighters, hospital employees, and correctional employees, are usually prohibited from striking under any circumstances. Services of these employees are often deemed to be critical to the health and safety of the citizens. Police, firefighters, and teachers are the public-employee groups most likely to be offered an alternative dispute resolution procedure to the strike, such as mediation, fact-finding, or interest arbitration (discussed later in this chapter).

Most federal employees' bargaining rights are governed by Title VII of the CSRA. One group of federal workers, U.S. Postal Service employees, are the only public employees covered under the private-sector Labor Management Relations Act (LMRA) as specified in the Postal Reorganization Act of 1970.[16] Unlike other employees covered under the LMRA, postal workers are not permitted to legally strike but are granted access to final and binding interest arbitration as a means of resolving bargaining disputes.

FEDERAL-SECTOR LABOR RELATIONS LEGISLATION

Federal-sector labor relations are governed by the CSRA, which was passed in 1978. Although the CSRA retained many provisions of previous executive orders, the following discussion centers on the provisions of Title VII, "Federal Service Labor–Management Relations." Also important to remember is that the CSRA is applied within a framework of federal personnel rules and policies affecting merit system principles, civil service functions, performance appraisal, staffing, merit pay, senior executive service, and adverse employment actions such as discipline or discharge.

The CSRA established the **Federal Labor Relations Authority (FLRA)**, an independent, neutral agency that administers the federal labor relations program and investigates unfair labor practices. The FLRA oversees the creation of bargaining units, supervises elections, prescribes criteria for determining national consultation rights, conducts hearings and resolves complaints of unfair labor practices, resolves exceptions to arbitrator awards, and assists federal agencies in dealing with labor relations issues. It is headed by a chairperson and two members, appointed on a bipartisan basis for five year terms.

The FLRA's structure provides for a General Counsel whose office prosecutes unfair labor practice charges and incorporates the existing **Federal Service Impasse Panel (FSIP)**, which provides assistance in resolving negotiation impasses. The General Counsel prosecutes unfair labor practice complaints under the act and exercises such powers as the FLRA may prescribe.[17] The role of the FSIP is to resolve bargaining impasses between federal agencies and unions in the federal government that arise over the negotiation of terms and conditions of employment. The FSIP is composed of a chairperson and at least six other members who are appointed by the president for five-year terms, are familiar with federal government operations, and are knowledgeable about labor–management relations.

LABOR RELATIONS IN ACTION
Privatization of the Public Sector

Privatization of public-sector services or transfer of governmental services to the private sector has received much attention over the last two decades. This focus is due largely to perceived cost differences between public- and private-sector service delivery. However, an important consideration is the role of public employee unions in the privatization process as an interest group and as political actors in blocking the privatization efforts.

A hallmark of the conservative agenda begun in the Reagan administration in the 1980s was the initiative to reduce the scope and size of government. This initiative was manifested in the call for privatization of services formerly provided exclusively by government agencies. Privatization has come in many forms: contracting out or outsourcing of support services, such as janitorial or maintenance services; vouchers for use in education; and management contracts to operate organizations such as airports or prisons. Needless to say, public-sector unions have strongly opposed privatization and feel threatened with the loss of jobs to private-sector employees. In addition, privatization has already caused a reduction in the percentage of union membership in hospitals, bus and urban transit, sanitary

services, and education. Privatization will likely remain a contentious issue in the public sector, particularly because of the charter school movement in elementary and secondary education and the two-front assault from the Bush administration: (1) an announcement that the administration planned to place as many as 850,000 jobs, half of the federal work force, up for bids to private contractors and (2) limitations on collective-bargaining rights for employees of the Department of Homeland Security.[a]

One consideration in the decision whether to privatize is the differing labor laws that cover private- and public-sector employees. Collective bargaining rights for employees in the private sector are covered primarily under the Labor Management Relations Act (LMRA); employees of interstate carriers in the railroad and airline industries are covered under the Railway Labor Act (RLA). Collective bargaining rights for state and local public employees are covered under various local ordinances and state laws; and federal government employees are covered under the Civil Service Reform Act. When government services are contracted to private firms, employees performing such services are covered under different statutes. This means that in some states in which no laws are in place to protect public employees' right to bargain, employees of the private contractor will be covered. Also, in some states where a public-sector labor law provides bargaining rights to public employees, the employees of firms contracting government services

The FSIP has jurisdiction over 71 federal departments and agencies representing 1.8 million federal employees. The FSIP appoints an executive director, who is responsible for the day-to-day operations.[18]

Although the Federal Mediation and Conciliation Service (FMCS), the federal agency established in 1947 by the LMRA, is required to assist the parties in resolving negotiation impasses, either party may request that the FSIP consider the matter or pursue binding arbitration. The panel must investigate the impasse and recommend a procedure for resolution or assist the parties through whatever means necessary, including fact-finding and recommendations. If these actions fail, the FSIP may conduct a formal hearing and take legal action to settle the dispute.

Appropriate Bargaining Units and Union Recognition in the Federal Sector

An appropriate bargaining unit for exclusive union representation purposes may be established on an agency, plant, installation, function, or other basis to ensure a clear and identifiable community of interests among employees and to promote effective federal agency operations. The criteria used for determining the extent to which employees in different federal jobs share a sufficient community of interests now have to seek union representation through the procedures of the LMRA or the Railway Labor Act (RLA), whichever is applicable.

Another issue in privatization is that a different employer takes over the responsibilities for the contracted public service, and this employer is responsible to the contracting agency for the performance of the public service, not directly to the citizens. The private employer takes over the publicly owned buildings and equipment either by renting or purchasing them or, in regard to small contracts, provides equipment and building space already owned but charges overhead costs to the public employer.[b] Although the advantages of privatization should be similar for the same type of public service whether currently provided by a unionized or unrepresented (nonunion) public workforce, the type of relationship between the union and city management is a significant factor. If the union–management relationship is very cooperative, the probability of the city contracting out services currently performed by union-represented employees is lower than in a nonunion city. On the other hand, the probability of a city considering privatizing when a bargaining relationship is very adversarial is higher than in a nonunion city.[c]

Another interesting dilemma is the difference in employees' right to strike. In most public-sector jurisdictions, the right to strike has been eliminated or limited. If services performed by public employees were contracted to a private employer covered by the LMRA or the RLA, employees now performing such services would have a legal right to strike under those statutes.[d]

In recent years, more public-employee unions have been accepting the challenge of demonstrating that they can compete successfully with private-sector employers who offer similar services.[e] Phoenix, Arizona; Indianapolis, Indiana; Charlotte, North Carolina; and Philadelphia, Pennsylvania are examples of communities in which public-employee unions have demonstrated their ability to deliver more cost-effective, higher-quality, and more effective public services than competing private-sector firms.[f]

[a]Terry Thomason and John F. Burton, Jr., "Unionization Trends and Labor–Management Cooperation in the Public Sector," *Going Public: The Role of Labor–Management Relations in Delivering Quality Government Services,* eds. Jonathan Brock and David B. Lipsky (Champaign, Ill.: Industrial Relations Research Association, 2003), pp. 94–100.

[b]Timothy D. Chandler and Peter Feuille, "Municipal Unions and Privatization," *Public Administration Review* 51 (January/February 1991), pp. 15–22.

[c]David A. Dilts, "Privatization of the Public Sector: De Facto Standardization of Labor Law," *Journal of Collective Negotiations in the Public Sector* 24, no. 1 (1995), pp. 37–47.

[d]Chandler and Feuille, 1994.

[e]Robert Hebdon, "Contracting Out in New York State: The Story the Lauder Report Chose Not to Tell!" *Labor Studies Journal* 20 (Spring 1995), pp. 3–10.

[f]Lawrence L. Martin, "Public-Private Competition: A Public Employee Alternative to Privatization," *Review of Public Personnel Administration* 19 (Winter 1999), pp. 59–70; Also see: Richard W. Hurd and Sharon Pinnock, "Public Sector Unions: Will They Thrive or Struggle to Survive?" *Journal of Labor Research,* Vol. XXV, No. 2 (Spring 2004), pp. 211–221.

are similar to those used by the National Labor Relations Board (NLRB) in the private sector. These include comparing jobs to identify common duties and skills, similar working conditions, common supervision, degree of work interdependence, and physical proximity of the jobs. No single factor determines the decision, but rather an evaluation is made based on a preponderance of the evidence. Similarly, certain positions are generally excluded from the bargaining unit, such as confidential employees, management and supervisory personnel, human resource management employees, and professionals, unless they vote in favor of inclusion. About 60 percent of all eligible employees are represented by various labor organizations in over 2,000 bargaining units, and nearly 60 percent are covered by labor agreements.[19] A federal agency accords **exclusive recognition** to a labor union if the union has been selected as the employee representative in a secret-ballot election by a majority of the employees in the appropriate unit who cast valid ballots.

Negotiable Subjects in the Federal Sector

In the federal sector, the agency and the exclusively recognized union have a duty to meet at reasonable times and confer in good faith with respect to *mandatory* subjects of collective bargaining, such as certain personnel policies and practices and working conditions, to the extent that appropriate laws and regulations allow such negotiations. The parties may voluntarily agree to bargain over certain *permissible* subjects, but the CSRA does not require negotiation over such subjects—one party can legally refuse to negotiate these issues. Permissible subjects include numbers, types, and grades of positions assigned to any organizational unit, work project, or tour of duty; technology of the workplace; and methods and means of performing the work. Subjects *prohibited* from negotiations include wages (except for certain blue-collar employees) and the following management rights:

- To determine the mission, budget, organization, number of employees, and internal security practices

- To hire, assign, direct, lay off, and retain employees in accordance with applicable law

- To suspend, remove, reduce in grade or pay, or take other disciplinary action

- To assign work, subcontract, and select employees for promotion from properly ranked and certified candidates and other appropriate sources

- To take whatever actions may be necessary to carry out the agency's mission during emergencies

Although the CSRA limits the scope of negotiable subjects, the parties have ample opportunity to negotiate many issues, as illustrated in Exhibit 13.4. The fact that management and the union are required to bargain in good faith does not mean that the parties must reach an agreement on these issues but only evidence a good-faith intent to do so.

Under the CSRA, the FSIP is responsible for resolving interest disputes that result in an impasse during negotiations. If mediation or fact-finding fails to resolve the dispute, the FSIP may use arbitration to render a final and binding decision to resolve the interest dispute. Management's position tends to prevail in 58 percent of disputes resolved through arbitration conducted by the FSIP, a higher management win rate than typically prevails under state and local interest arbitration procedures (see discussion later in this chapter).[20]

Unfair Labor Practices in the Federal Sector

The CSRA specifies unfair labor practices to protect the rights of individual employees, labor organizations, and federal agencies. Employee grievances over matters concerning adverse action, position classification, and equal employment opportunity are covered by other laws, statutes, or agency rules and cannot be filed as an unfair labor practice charge under the CSRA.

Exhibit 13.4

Subjects That Could Be Included in a Master Labor Agreement in the Federal Sector

Union recognition	Sick leave
Official time	Health and safety
Discipline and counseling	Contracting out
Grievance procedure and arbitration	Child care services
Dues withholding	Call-back, standby, and on-call duty
Employee performance	Workers' compensation
Merit promotion	Performance appraisal
Training	Hazard and environmental pay
Equal employment opportunity	Reduction-in-force
Travel time and pay	Position classifications
Annual leave	

The CSRA prohibits unfair labor practices very similar to those prohibited under previous executive orders and the LMRA. For example, prohibited management activities include restraining and coercing employees in the exercise of their rights; encouraging or discouraging union membership; sponsoring, controlling, or assisting a labor organization; disciplining union members who file complaints; and refusing to recognize or negotiate with a designated labor organization. The CSRA prohibits unions from interfering with, restraining, or coercing employees in the exercise of their rights; attempting to induce agency management to coerce employees; impeding or hindering an employee's work performance; calling for or engaging in job actions (e.g., work slowdown or strike); and discriminating against employees or refusing to consult, confer, or negotiate with the appropriate federal agency. Unfair labor practice remedies available to the FLRA include the issuance of a cease-and-desist order and/or an appropriate make-whole type of remedy, such as requiring that an employee be reinstated with back pay.

The CSRA makes it an unfair labor practice to refuse or fail to cooperate in impasse procedures and decisions. The FLRA has authority to revoke recognition of a union that commits an unfair labor practice or encourages a strike or slowdown. The FLRA can also require the parties to renegotiate a labor agreement in accordance with an FLRA decision and seek a temporary restraining order to halt suspected unlawful conduct while an unfair labor practice case is pending.

The CSRA requires that all negotiated agreements in the federal sector include a grievance procedure with binding arbitration as its final step. A grievance is broadly defined to include any complaint by an employee, labor organization, or agency relating to employment with an agency and any claimed violation, misinterpretation, or misapplication of any law, rule, or regulation affecting conditions of employment. Certain issues are exempt from the grievance procedure, such as employee appointment, certification, job classification, removal for national security reasons or political activities, issues concerning retirement, and life and health insurance. However, the scope of grievance procedure coverage has been extended considerably. In fact, all matters within the allowable limits of the CSRA are within the scope of any grievance procedure negotiated by the parties, unless the parties have specifically agreed to exclude certain matters from coverage. Thus, unlike private-sector negotiations, which often focus on union efforts to expand the scope of grievance subjects, federal sector negotiators often focus on management proposals to remove specific items from the scope of grievable subjects. Negotiated grievance procedures serve as the exclusive forum for bargaining unit employees in most cases; however, in cases of adverse employment action (e.g., suspension, reduction in grade, or discharge for poor performance), the employee may choose either the negotiated grievance procedure or an applicable statutory procedure, but not both. Depending on the nature of the employee's grievance claim, the employee might receive a hearing before the FLRA, the Equal Employment Opportunity Commission (EEOC), Merit Systems Protection Board (an independent agency established to hear federal employee grievances under CSRA), or a federal court.[21]

Labor–Management Partnerships in the Federal Government

In 1993, President Clinton directed Vice President Gore to conduct a six month National Performance Review of the federal government. The results of this review led President Clinton to issue Executive Order 12871, which established the National Partnership Council (NPC) composed of federal agency and union officials, with the purpose of recommending reforms to empower federal employees as full partners with management to promote labor–management cooperation and improve the delivery of government services.[22] Federal negotiators were to be guided by a legislatively mandated "good government" standard, the pursuit of increased quality and productivity, customer service, employee empowerment, mission accomplishment, efficiency, organizational performance, and, in the case of the Department of Defense, military readiness. Specific examples of successes of labor–management partnerships included:

- Partnership between the Internal Revenue Service (IRS) and the National Treasury Employees Union (NTEU) modernized and restructured the IRS and resulted in measurable improvements in customer service and job satisfaction.

- Partnership between the American Federation of Government Employees (AFGE) and Defense Contract Management Command resulted in overwhelming improvement in customer service ratings as the workload increased 100 percent and the work force was downsized, with $900,000 saved from a reduction in labor–management litigation.

- Partnership between the James A. Haley Veterans' Hospital and AFGE Local 547, the Florida Nurses Association, and the Tampa Professional Nurses Unit reduced delivery time for critical medication from 92 minutes to 20 minutes, cut turnaround time for X-ray reports from eight days to one day, and reduced processing time for pension and compensation exams from 31 days to 18 days.

- A NTEU–Customs Service partnership yielded a seven-step strategy to increase seizures of illegal drugs. During the first six months, narcotics seizures increased by 12 percent and drug currency seizures increased by 74 percent.

- Partnership between the Defense Distribution Depot in San Joaquin and AFGE 1546 saved $950,000 per year by reducing workplace accidents by 20 percent and ergonomic injuries by 40 percent, reduced overtime expenses from $9.8 million to $1.4 million, and reduced production costs from $25.42 per unit to $23.48 per unit.[23]

Within a month after taking office, on February 17, 2001, President Bush signed Executive Order 13203, which immediately dissolved the National Partnership Council and revoked any "orders, rules, regulations, guidelines, or policies implementing or enforcing Executive Order 12871." The current director of the Office of Personnel Management informed the federal government department heads that President Bush was motivated by his conviction that a partnership was not something that should be mandated for every agency in every situation. However, while agencies were no longer mandated to form partnerships with their unions, they were strongly encouraged to establish cooperative labor–management relations.

In a study of 60 labor–management partnership councils in eight federal agencies employing more than 310,000 bargaining unit employees, researchers found:

First, partnership can improve labor–management communications.
    Second, it can also contribute to the enhancement of the labor relations climate.

> *Third, partnership has the potential to improve agency performance.*
>
> *Fourth, management commitment and commensurate union strength are essential to realizing the potential of collaboration.*[24]
>
> *Fifth, partnerships contributed to costs savings due to reduced workplace disputes.*
>
> *Sixth, partnerships were most effective when the efforts were precisely targeted.*

For example, partnership councils which focused on improving customer satisfaction, reducing workplace disputes, and improving productivity achieved demonstrable results.[25]

Homeland Security Act

In November 2002, Congress passed and President Bush signed the Homeland Security Act (HSA). This act transferred several existing agencies into the Department of Homeland Security (DHS), which would operate along four functional lines: Border and Transportation Security, Emergency Preparedness and Response; Chemical, Biological, Radiological and Nuclear Counter-Measures; and Information Analysis and Infrastructure Protection. The total work force of the DHS is over 200,000 federal government employees. From a labor–management relations standpoint, over 40,000 of these employees were members of preexisting bargaining units. These included 24,000 employees within the Immigration and Naturalization Service (Justice Department); 12,000 in the Customs Service (Treasury Department); 3,500 in the Coast Guard (Department of Transportation); and 2,500 in Animal and Plant Health Service (Department of Agriculture). The provision that makes labor unions nervous is Section 730, which states:

> *Notwithstanding any other provision of this title, the Secretary of Homeland Security may, in regulations prescribed jointly with the Director of the Office of Personnel Management, establish, and from time to time adjust, a human resources management system for some or all of the organizational units of the Department of Homeland Security, which shall be flexible, contemporary, and grounded in the public employment principles of merit and fitness.*

Under the Civil Service Reform Act, the president has authority to exempt from coverage any group of federal employees for national security purposes. Under the Homeland Security Act, the president may waive employee and union rights granted under the Civil Service Reform Act if such application would have a substantial adverse impact on the ability of the department to protect homeland security and/or the agency, subdivision, or unit's mission and responsibilities are materially changed and a majority of the affected employees are assigned intelligence, counterintelligence, or investigative work directly related to terrorism investigation as their primary duty.[26]

In 2003 as part of the National Defense Authorization Act, Congress authorized the Department of Defense (DoD) to create a new personnel system. DoD created the National Security Personnel System (NSPS) which covers 700,000 employees, 40 percent of the federal government civil service work force. The NSPS includes changes in such personnel matters as pay for performance, performance appraisals, training, promotion, pay classifications, labor relations, and employee appeals.

On November 17, 2005, several DoD unions sued to block the portions of NSPS regulations which dealt with labor relations, discipline, and employee appeals. DoD agreed to delay implementation of those portions of NSPS until February 1, 2006. DoD and the unions agreed to request that a Court set a hearing in early 2006. On February 27, 2006, District Court Judge Emmet Sullivan ruled that several portions of NSPS that dealt with labor relations were illegal. Judge Sullivan ruled that NSPS failed to ensure that employees can bargain collectively, failed to provide fair treatment of employees in the appeals process, and did not create a third-party independent review of labor relations decisions. DoD appealed the decision. On May 18, 2007, the U.S. Court of Appeals for the District of Columbia reversed Judge Sullivan's decision. The Court ruled that the Defense Authorization Act permitted DoD to create a new labor relations system and to curtail collective bargaining through November 2009. The Court ruled that the unions had not proven the newly created National Security Labor Relations Board lacked independence. The Court concluded that the portions of the NSPS which dealt with discipline and employee appeals were "not ripe for judicial review."

In 2005, the Department of Homeland Security (DHS) had established a new Human Resource Management System (Transportation Security Administration not included) which included occupational clusters, pay bands, pay ranges, and pay for performance. DHS created a Homeland Security Labor Relations Board but also issued regulations in labor relations, which included an expansion of management rights, limited bargaining on the impact of management's actions, prohibited bargaining on procedures, changed the burden of proof to a single "preponderance of evidence" standard, and permitted arbitrators to mitigate discipline only "when the penalty was wholly without justification." The DHS had reserved for itself the right to declare any part of any collective bargaining agreement "null and void" by issuing directives or taking whatever actions may be necessary to carry out DHS's mission.[27]

POSTAL REORGANIZATION ACT OF 1970

The Postal Reorganization Act (PRA) signed by President Nixon on August 12, 1970, fulfilled the desires of the postal unions to have their labor–management relations programs established by statute. Under previous presidential executive orders authorizing bargaining by federal workers, the Post Office Department never fully accepted collective bargaining, even though it was the largest single employer in the United States and had the largest proportion of employees belonging to unions. Another interesting note is that the legislation placing postal employees under the private-sector LMRA was proposed by President Nixon and adopted by Congress to resolve an illegal strike by postal workers—a far different approach than that used by President Reagan during a similar illegal strike by air traffic controllers in 1981 wherein all strikers were terminated.[28]

The PRA created the U.S. Postal Service (USPS) as an independent entity within the executive branch of the federal government. The office of postmaster general, previously a position in the cabinet, was made independent of Congress and the president. The postmaster general was selected by an 11-member board of governors. Under the PRA, wages, hours, benefits, and other terms and conditions of employment are mandatory bargaining subjects to be determined through collective bargaining. Grievance and arbitration procedures are also subject to negotiation. The NLRB supervises representation elections and prosecutes unfair labor practices. Although the right to strike was denied postal employees, a fact-finding and binding interest arbitration procedure was made available if a bargaining impasse persisted longer than 180 days after bargaining began. Since the PRA was passed, contracts have been negotiated without any major disruption in the delivery of postal services.

The parties have often relied on the arbitration provisions of the PRA to resolve one or more bargaining issues. The Postal Service and one or more of the postal unions submitted their unresolved issues to third-party neutrals in 1978, 1984, 1991, 1995, and 1998. In 2002, the U.S. Postal Service and each of its major unions (the American Postal Employees Union, the National Association of Letter Carriers, and the Postal Mail Handlers Union) reached agreement to extend their respective collective-bargaining agreements to 2004. In 2007, each of the postal unions, except the National Rural Letter Carriers, reached agreement with the U.S. Postal Service. The American Postal Workers Union and National Postal Mail Handlers Union reached agreements through typical negotiations. The National Association of Letter Carriers reached agreement with the U.S. Postal Service after the parties had selected Rich Bloch to be the neutral arbitrator and after the parties had scheduled hearing dates.[29]

SUMMARY OF THE MULTIPLES OF LABOR–MANAGEMENT MODELS IN THE FEDERAL SECTOR

Since September 11, 2001, labor relations in the federal sector has evolved into a multitude of labor–management relations models. The Postal Reorganization Act of 1970 had established a labor–management relations model for postal employees under the Labor Management Relations Act. The Civil Service Reform Act of 1978 established the basic labor law for non-postal federal employees. In 1996, as part of the Department of Transportation appropriations, Congress directed the FAA to negotiate labor–management relations reform, which provided for salary negotiations with the air traffic controllers union. In 2001, the Aviation and Transportation Act created the Transportation Security Administration (TSA), which federalized airport screeners and gave the TSA the same personnel flexibilities afforded the Federal Aviation Administration. Further, the TSA was authorized to determine whether the airport screeners could unionize and the TSA decided they could not unionize. In 2002, the Department of Homeland Security (DHS) was created and, with assistance from the Office of Personnel Management, was granted authority to develop a new personnel system. In 2003, the Department of Defense (DoD), again with assistance of the Office of Personnel Management, was authorized to design and implement a new personnel system (called the National Security Personnel System). Thus, at one extreme are the labor–management models, which allow unionization and bargaining over wages (as the Federal Aviation Administration and air traffic controllers). At the other extreme is the prohibition of unionization and collective bargaining (as with the TSA). Then, in between these two extremes are the DHS and DoD labor–management relations models, which are very similar.[30]

SIMILARITIES BETWEEN PRIVATE- AND PUBLIC-SECTOR BARGAINING

Although differences are found between private- and public-sector labor relations, similarities also exist. First, many of the participants in public-sector bargaining are trained and gain their experience in the private sector. Labor relations practitioners in the public sector tend to rely on the private-sector approach to labor relations with appropriate modification as needed. State and local bargaining statutes often use NLRB criteria for appropriate bargaining units, subjects for collective bargaining, use of labor injunctions, and standards for arbitration. Some unions, such as the SEIU and the Teamsters that represent a significant number of public employees, have much experience in private-sector labor relations. Other unions (such as the National Education Association; the American Federation of Teachers; the American Federation of State, County, and Municipal Employees; and civil service employee groups) often hire professional staff members with private-sector labor relations experience.[31]

A second similarity is the reason why employees form and join unions. Public employees, like their private-sector counterparts, form and join unions when they are dissatisfied with some term or condition of employment, which includes their work, supervision, and promotional opportunities; have a favorable attitude toward unions as institutions; and believe that unionization will be instrumental in yielding positive outcomes.[32] In fact, public employees tend to hold more favorable attitudes toward a desire for union representation than do private-sector workers and perceive public managers to be less hostile toward unionization compared with their private-sector counterparts.[33]

A third similarity is that the collective-bargaining settlement will often be influenced by the personalities of the negotiators and their abilities to increase their bargaining power relative to the other party (the bargaining power model was discussed in Chapter 6). To reiterate briefly, each party increases bargaining power over the opponent by either increasing the cost to the opponent of disagreeing or reducing the cost to the opponent of agreeing. Public opinion represents a most significant cost item in public-sector labor relations—both union and government officials often structure their tactics in a manner intended to gain public support for their position, which places pressure on the other party to concede negotiation items.

However, public opinion and political support can be a double-edged sword in the bargaining process. Public unions can use at least three general strategies to increase management's cost of disagreeing with the union's position.[34] The first technique is a union threat to "blow the whistle" on a questionable practice unless the government agency agrees with the desired settlement. Examples include threatening to release information on the unpublicized practice of dumping raw sewage in a river or on the dollar amount of government officials' liquor bills, which are paid by the taxpayers. Of course, the union is hoping that government officials will capitulate, rather than risk vote loss in subsequent elections as a result of the public revelation of such information. Management's cost of disagreeing can be more directly increased by a union's threat of withdrawing political support.[35] Public employees tend to vote at a higher rate than other individuals. A threat to withhold candidate endorsements or campaign support, both manpower and financial, may also be used to increase pressure on elected officials in a position to influence bargaining outcomes. The success of this tactic depends on the number of union members and the ability of the union to mobilize a cohesive voting bloc.

The union can also use various job action techniques to raise management's cost of disagreeing. Strikes by public employees have occurred often despite legal sanctions. Perhaps these actions are taken under the assumption that most public-sector strikes have eventually been resolved without fines or other sanctions, even though they are illegal. Some other job actions that have been used are also outside the law or proscribed by the job requirements (for example, government employees in New York raising the toll bridges at rush hour when walking off the job), whereas others are marginally outside the law or job requirements (for example, all public employees calling in to say they are too sick to work—"blue flu").[36]

From the union standpoint, a most promising job action is working within the law while placing pressure on management to resolve the dispute. Job slowdowns fall marginally into this category because most public-sector labor agreements give management the right to discipline employees for poor performance. Yet, there is a thin line between a job slowdown and malicious obedience (also called **work-to-rule**) by which the employees follow the agency's rules to the letter. For example, a fingerprint technician is charged with verifying an individual's address during his criminal booking. This could be done by simply telephoning the individual's purported residence. However, a more time consuming but accurate verification method would be for the fingerprint technician to personally visit the individual's residence. Needless to say, the home visit approach would create an assignment backlog. Other public employees can also use bureaucratic rules to their advantage. For example, tollbooth employees could check paper currency serial numbers against a list of counterfeit bills, or postal workers could check each item to ensure a proper ZIP code. Malicious obedience has the tactical advantage of cutting back on the delivery of public services. More importantly, employees continue to receive wages under this tactic while being relatively immune from disciplinary actions.

Public-sector unions can also reduce management's cost of agreeing with the union by campaigning for referendums to fund the negotiated labor settlement or eliminating some of their initial proposals.[37] Public employee unions can also push for certain issues that contribute significantly to their economic well-being at little cost to the political incumbents. Employee pensions usually fall into this category because they can be increased without immediate cost implications; the bulk of pension costs would be incurred under some future politician's budget.

Management can reduce its political cost of agreeing on wages by publicizing a rather low across-the-board settlement along with general improvements in the pay step plan. This plan usually gives progressive salary increases to each job classification. For example, an employee in a particular classification might receive a five percent wage increase after three years' service in that classification. Management can improve the employee's situation by either raising the percentage increase or reducing the number of service years needed to qualify for a step wage increase. However, it is difficult to determine and report the precise cost of these changes. Most news media presentations are limited to specific reports on the average wage gain of public employees and ignore the more detailed cost implications of a modified pay step plan.

Another similarity is the continuing controversy over nonunion employees' obligation to pay for their representational rights. Public-sector employees not joining unions may be required to pay for representational services provided by the union (collective bargaining, grievance handling, arbitration, and so on) but not for non–collective bargaining activities (such as political action committees, lobbying, or public relations activities).[38] The nonmember has the burden of objecting to inappropriate expenditures of his or her agency or fair-share fee, but the union must provide written notice to nonmembers of their right to raise objections and provide sufficiently detailed information about the nature of dues expenditures to permit the nonmember to make a reasonable determination whether to challenge a particular expenditure as chargeable.

On June 14, 2007, the U.S. Supreme Court ruled in *Davenport et al. v. Washington Education Association* that the First Amendment prohibits public-sector unions from using nonmember fees collected under an agency shop agreement for purposes not germane (such as the union's political agenda) to the union's collective bargaining duties. The Court further ruled that unions must have procedures to obtain the nonmembers' affirmative authorization (opt-in) before using their fees for election-related purposes.[39]

In summary, public-sector collective bargaining has some similarities to the process found in the private sector. In both situations, the parties are trying to increase their bargaining power relative to the other party's by increasing the other party's cost of disagreeing with their party's position or by reducing the other party's cost of agreeing with their party's position. There are several differences between public- and private-sector bargaining processes; however, once these differences are acknowledged and understood, one can better appreciate the public sector as it fits into the overall framework of labor–management relations in the United States. Moreover, skills learned in private-sector labor relations are easily transferred to the public sector.

DIFFERENCES BETWEEN PRIVATE-SECTOR AND PUBLIC-SECTOR BARGAINING

An understanding of public-sector labor relations requires recognition of some of the differences as well as the similarities between the public and private sectors.

Market Economy Does Not Operate in Public Sector

One difference between the public and private sectors can be explained in terms of the economic system and the market economy. Unlike the private sector, many public services (such as public education, welfare services, police and fire protection) are provided to the citizens at little or no additional cost (beyond taxes). The cost of such services is spread across many individuals rather than expecting each customer to pay the entire cost of the services used or available for use. The market economy therefore does not operate in the public sector and cannot act as a constraint on union and management negotiators.

Moreover, monopolistic conditions often exist in the public sector, and public organizations often control the services rendered or the products offered. For example, the police and fire departments are the primary organizations that provide certain types of security protection. Public education has very little real competition from the private sector, and even that is usually among only more affluent families. Thus, products and services provided by the government cannot be readily substituted if they become more costly.

The lack of substitute goods or services distinguishes public-sector collective bargaining from related activities in the private sector and adds to the critical nature of public services. For example, citizens usually take sanitation services for granted; yet a strike by city garbage collectors would be regarded as a public crisis because there is no immediate alternative means for garbage disposal. The lack of substitute services also eliminates one of management's strike costs: loss of business to a competitor. In fact, some union leaders contend that municipal leaders use a strike to their advantage by transferring payroll savings resulting from a strike to other government budgetary accounts.

Finally, the relatively vague aspects of particular public service institutions may make productivity bargaining difficult. Clear and precise productivity measures are a necessary first step in productivity bargaining (although many private-sector companies have these figures and do not engage in productivity bargaining). Most public-sector bargaining parties do not have specific productivity measures at their disposal and could not engage in productivity bargaining even if they desired this approach. Many public services are provided regardless of customer use. Police officers and bus drivers can legitimately contend that they should not be financially punished for nonuse of their services; their salaries should not be a direct function of the number of crimes detected or riders served, respectively, if the service is available for all. Hence, much of the public-sector wage determination process is based on a comparison of similar jobs in the public and private sectors rather than on employee performance records. Because the market does not act as a significant moderator in the public sector, budgetary limitations, public attitudes, and administrative discretion must operate to successfully maintain order, equity, and balance in collective bargaining relationships.[40]

Relationship between the Budget and Public-Sector Bargaining Processes

The budget tends to play a more conspicuous role in public-sector collective bargaining than in private-sector bargaining. In recent years, public employers have been under severe budget constraints, necessitating an increased emphasis on costs reduction. To the extent taxpayers are unwilling to approve revenue increases through the political process, cost reductions must come from curtailing public services or finding more cost-efficient ways of providing public services at current levels. Public employers have experienced increased pressure to emulate changes in labor relations practices occurring in the private sector by privatizing (i.e., outsourcing or subcontracting) some public services, broadening job classifications and multi-skill job descriptions, using more part-time or contingent employees, paying for performance, adopting flexible and alternative work schedules, reducing supervision and encouraging employee involvement and empowerment, decentralizing and streamlining bureaucratic operating structures and methods, and increasing labor–management cooperation.[41]

Most municipal budgets are published in advance before public hearings and subsequent adoption. Although many citizens ignore public hearings, key taxpayers, such as local companies, give close attention to the budget in terms of its implication for increased property or business taxes. The anticipated salaries for public employees are recorded as separate line items on the budget, something not done in the private sector. Thus, the opportunity exists for concerned taxpayers to pressure city officials in the hopes of keeping the budget and subsequent taxes at a minimum.

The specific influence of the budget on the public-sector bargaining process remains uncertain. Some suggest that a great deal of flexibility exists in the budget bargaining relationship in terms of budget padding, transfer of funds among line items, and supplemental or amended budgets that can often be filed after the final approval date.[42]

Union negotiators' major concerns pertain to securing benefits for their members; it is up to management to find sufficient funds for an equitably negotiated settlement. Thus, there is little union–management agreement over the budget's significance in contract negotiations. Few if any public-sector collective bargaining agreements have provisions specifying the role the budget will assume in the collective bargaining process.

Employee Rights and Obligations

Another way that public employment differs from private employment is that public employees have some legal rights and obligations that private employees do not. Numerous laws and executive orders pertain only to public employees. Public employees' political activities, personal appearance, place of residence, and off-the-job behavior are regulated more closely than most private-sector workers. For example, public employees in particularly sensitive jobs and those whose misdeeds are most susceptible to adverse publicity, such as teachers, police officers, and firefighters, are held to a higher conduct standard than most other employees.[43] Because citizens pay the taxes that pay public employees' salaries, employers have to be careful of the image employees project.

Although freedom of speech and association are constitutional rights, there are limits to their exercise by public employees. The Supreme Court has identified several reasons for which these rights may be limited, including the need to maintain discipline and harmony in the workforce, the need for confidentiality, and the need to ensure that the proper performance of duties is not impeded.[44] However, public employers cannot give priority to efficient work operation over an employee's First Amendment right to expression about a matter of public concern.

Generally, the courts have not attempted to substitute their judgment for that of executive branch officials about whether an individual public employee should be dismissed. Rather, courts have sought to establish guidelines for the constitutional treatment of public employees in adverse action cases, such as a discharge. Procedural due process requires the right of notice of the proposed government action; the reasons for the action; the opportunity to respond; the right to a hearing before an impartial official; and the rights to counsel, to confront accusers, and to cross-examine and subpoena witnesses.

In *Board of Regents v. Roth* (1972) the Supreme Court delineated the following grounds on which a public employee whose employment has been terminated could assert the right to procedural due process[45]:

- Where an employee had a property right to the job

- Where the termination harmed the individual's reputation and/or adversely affected his or her future employability

- Where termination was in retaliation for an exercise of a protected constitutional activity, such as the freedom of speech or freedom of assembly

In the case of *Cleveland Board of Education v. Loudermill* (1985), the Supreme Court held that, before tenured public employees can be fired, they must be informed of the charges against them and be given an opportunity to respond.[46] Tenured employees' due process rights under the U.S. Constitution include written or oral notice of the charges against them, an explanation of the employer's evidence, and an opportunity to rebut the evidence.

COLLECTIVE BARGAINING STRUCTURES AND DECISION-MAKING PROCESSES

The bargaining structure within municipal governments is very decentralized, and with few exceptions, negotiations are conducted on a single-employer basis. The bargaining unit coverage extends only as far as the municipal jurisdiction, and municipal officials are reluctant to relinquish their political autonomy and decision-making authority. The city manager or chief administrative officer of the municipality will often serve as chief negotiator, followed by the personnel director or an attorney retained by the city.[47] An increased level of political activity by public employees, increased level of strike activity, and occurrence of prior job actions by organized public employees are factors that increase the likelihood that a labor relations specialist will be included on the negotiations team. However, if the negotiation activities become complex, the city is more likely to employ a labor relations professional as the chief negotiator.[48]

Defining the appropriate bargaining unit in the public sector is more difficult than in the private sector. In the private sector, legislation and related enforcement agencies provide direction for determining an appropriate bargaining unit. For example, plant guards in the private sector are required to be in separate bargaining units, and supervisors are not eligible for membership in a bargaining unit. The public sector, especially at the state and local levels, experiences many different combinations of appropriate bargaining units. Depending on the particular applicable state law or administrative determination, public-sector supervisors can be prohibited from joining unions, they can be in the same bargaining units as other employees, or they can join unions in separate bargaining units.[49]

Of the differences between public- and private-sector labor relations, one of the potentially most important, but often ignored, is the unionization of supervisors and other managers. While private-sector supervisors and managers lack representational rights under the Labor Management Relations Act, public-sector supervisors and other lower- to middle-level managers have the right to engage in collective bargaining in more than a dozen states, including the most highly populated states. There have been questions about the loyalty, identity, and organizational commitment of public-sector supervisory unions, and the logic for exclusion is rooted in the need of the employer to have the undivided loyalty of supervisors and other managerial employees. However, research has identified little negative effect from the unionization of supervisors. Potential problems seem to arise with the highest-level supervisors on issues concerning strikes and discipline, especially when supervisors are in the same bargaining units as employees. Based on research in New Jersey, supervisors could both receive representation in their role as employees and act on the job in a managerial capacity. In other words, supervisors can "wear two hats"; they are loyal to the mission of the agency and act as supervisors to further the mission of the agency while they are also union members.[50]

Another organizational difference applies to the chief negotiator in the public sector, who often lacks authority to reach a final and binding agreement with the union on behalf of the public organization. The **sovereignty doctrine** makes it difficult to delegate decision-making authority to specific administrative officials. Many elected officials still refuse to give up their legislative authority to make final decisions on matters that they believe are important to effective government operations because they feel responsible directly to the electorate. Elected officials do not want appointed negotiators to bind them to wage settlements and other provisions of collective bargaining agreements that they believe are unworkable.[51] For example, unionized schoolteachers might encounter a variety of managers in collective negotiations—the school principal, the superintendent of schools, the school board, and possibly state education officials. The problem of determining "who speaks for management" can negatively affect the negotiation process in two ways:

1. Management negotiators at the bargaining table can defer to other management officials in the bargaining process. Union officers are often

shuffled off to a variety of government officials in collective bargaining on the premise that another individual has specific authority for a particular issue or a portion of available funds. Often, political rivalries prompt certain government officials to either intervene or pass the buck in the hopes of looking good at another official's expense. This situation can result in a more confusing collective bargaining relationship than is typically found in the private sector. In some cases, it can almost entirely prevent serious collective-bargaining efforts between management and the union.

2. The unwillingness of some government agencies to delegate sufficient authority to a labor relations representative can result in a lack of labor relations' understanding on management's side of the negotiation table. In some cases, taxpayers are affected if unions take advantage of the inexperienced management negotiators. Perhaps in other cases a public strike could have been avoided if the parties had adopted a more realistic understanding of the collective-bargaining process.[52]

Research has shown that when the chief negotiator is a higher-level position in the organizational structure, the parties are less likely to reach an impasse. This is because the chief negotiator from a higher-level position has greater authority to make crucial decisions during the negotiations, thereby simplifying the process. Where outside consultants serve as the chief negotiator, public-sector unions are more likely to make "end runs" to higher-level government officials whom the union negotiators perceive as having greater authority to make binding decisions in the negotiations. Such activity occurs away from the bargaining table and makes the negotiations between the parties at the bargaining table more difficult. In reference to bargaining strategies covered in Chapter 6, chief negotiators who use the "mutual gain bargaining strategy" decrease the likelihood of an impasse, and the negotiators who use a "distributive strategy" increase the likelihood of a bargaining impasse. In reference to impasse procedures covered in Chapter 9, prior use of arbitration increases the likelihood of a bargaining impasse.[53]

Negotiable Issues and Bargaining Tactics

Exemption by statute of many traditional collective bargaining subjects (particularly at the federal level) limits the ability of both unions and managers to resolve some disputes through the bargaining process. Under the CSRA, most compensation issues affecting federal budgets are excluded from the scope of mandatory bargaining subjects (except for postal workers and air traffic controllers). In many states operating under merit system rules and regulations, related subjects such as promotion, pension plans, and layoff procedures cannot be negotiated.[54] Merit or civil service systems establishing rules for governing terms and conditions of employment existed before the passage of state laws authorizing collective bargaining as a procedure for determining work rules affecting public employees. This situation sometimes can lead to conflicts over which system should take precedent in deciding the outcome of disputes over the determination or application of particular work rules. Legislators should clearly address this potential dilemma when drafting public-sector bargaining laws to minimize conflicts over whether collective bargaining or civil service procedures should take precedent.[55]

Some public-sector bargaining relationships attempt to get around statutory limitations on bargaining subjects by removing such discussions from the formal bargaining process. One study found that some public-sector labor agreement provisions are not actually negotiated between the parties, whereas other decisions are jointly determined but not included in the formal labor agreement.[56] Thus, relatively few generalizations can be made on the scope of collectively bargained items in the public sector.

Public-sector bargaining tactics also differ from those in the private sector. Negotiations in the private sector stem from a bilateral relationship— management and union representatives negotiate the terms of the labor agreement with little involvement from outside groups. **Multilateral bargaining** is a term used, particularly at the state and local levels, to describe the involvement of multiple parties in the collective bargaining process.[57] For example, elected (e.g., mayor, city council member) and administrative (e.g., city manager, police chief) officials may share decision-making responsibility over some issues on the employer side. Various community interest groups (e.g., taxpayer, minority, environmentalist, business) perceive themselves as stakeholders potentially affected by the outcomes of negotiations and may also seek to actively influence the bargaining process by bringing pressure on either the employer or union(s) to approve acceptable bargaining terms. The outcomes of the negotiating process may affect the need for additional revenues (e.g., taxes) to fund improved employment terms or the quantity or quality of public services provided citizens.

The ability to impose political costs or rewards on a bargaining party often becomes as important in determining public-sector bargaining outcomes as the ability to impose or minimize economic costs affects bargaining power in the private sector. Thus, public-sector negotiations often become an exercise in politics— who one knows and what one can do to help or hurt a government official's political career. Public unions have demonstrated an ability to use multilateral bargaining and political pressure to increase economic gains and job security for their members.[58]

Public-sector unions often have opportunities to engage in **end-run bargaining** before, during, or after negotiations, which involves a union making a direct appeal to a legislative body or government official who has the final decision-making authority rather than dealing exclusively with the designated management negotiator present at the bargaining table. For example, one mayor made concessions to a police association in return for its endorsement in the gubernatorial primary. The mayor changed the regular police work schedule from five days on and two off to four days on and two off (increasing the annual days off by 17), guaranteed two patrol officers in every car, and agreed that 50 percent plus one of the patrol cars in each police district would be on the street during night hours.[59] Because public-sector unions are often politically potent, elected officials are generally more receptive to this end-run tactic than a private-sector corporation president or majority stockholders of a corporation might be. In fact, such attempts by a union to bypass the designated management negotiators of a private-sector organization would probably result in an NLRB unfair labor practice finding of refusal to bargain in good faith.

Occasionally, the media aids a party's use of the end-run tactic by allowing management and union negotiators to present their positions through the press rather than to the other party at the bargaining table. Public-sector bargaining usually receives more press coverage than similar activities in the private sector because more information is typically furnished to the media by the bargaining parties and the eventual settlement has a more direct impact on the government's constituents. Use of the end-run tactic can harm the collective bargaining process, as evidenced by a union leader's account of one contract negotiation between New York City and its uniformed forces:

> *All of this [bargaining issues] should have been brought to the bargaining table. It would have given both labor and management a chance to work out of these very difficult trouble spots....But, almost nothing was done at the table; instead both sides took to the television, advertising, and the loud and dramatic press releases....*
>
> *Experts...know the best way to insure trouble is to bring collective bargaining into the public arena. Instead of labor and management representatives talking to each other, they will talk to the public and to their principals only. Invariably, the wrong things will be said.*
>
> *Management will talk of the "irresponsibly high demands" of the workers, and about how services will have to be cut back or taxes raised....The labor leader now has to talk tough. The strike threat becomes almost obligatory, because he is now put in an impossible squeeze. When the union leader goes public he first must talk to the people he represents, and retain their confidence. Understandably, the public responds not to the facts of the situation but to the militant rhetoric. Everybody loses in the process, a process that has little or nothing to do with collective bargaining.[60]*

The media play an important role in determining the priority issues, providing information about bargaining issues, and helping the public formulate its attitudes toward the negotiating parties. The local media is highly influential because many times it is the primary source of information for the general public. Because voters cannot directly observe union and management interactions, they rely on the media, which itself has biases. These biases include personal beliefs, ideologies and prejudices, budgetary and technological constraints, and a tendency to deal with problems stereotypically.

During negotiations, both parties try to manipulate the media because the negotiation outcomes are often shaped as much by people's perceptions of what is reasonable or necessary as they are by the factual merits of a bargaining position. In fact, sometimes the parties jointly manipulate the media to their own advantage. The union may blame city officials for its members receiving less than the wage increase they demanded; city officials in turn blame the union for a tax increase needed to pay for a wage increase that was given.[61]

Accompanying the growth of collective bargaining in the public sector have been efforts to open up the bargaining process to citizen observation and participation through the enactment of so-called **sunshine laws**. The rationale for this approach is that citizens can provide more input into how tax dollars are spent by their involvement, and openness reduces public distrust of the bargaining process. Although every state has some form of sunshine law, 25 states require labor negotiations to be conducted in the open, and 12 states even require that the strategy sessions in preparation for labor negotiations be open.[62] The open approach to public-sector bargaining differs widely from the private sector in that a private enterprise's owners (stockholders) are excluded from collective bargaining sessions.

Negotiators often seek to avoid "bargaining in the sunshine" because it becomes more difficult to make necessary trade-offs amongst bargaining priorities and terms when every constituent affected by those trade-offs can observe the deliberations. Negotiators may spend too much time posturing for the benefit of key constituents in the public audience, thereby prolonging the amount of time required to get down to the parties' "bottom-line" bargaining interests and positions. One study found the presence of a sunshine law to have no significant effect on bargaining outcomes in a national cross-sample of police and firefighter negotiations.[63]

Grievance Administration

The public sector has widely accepted the grievance procedure with binding arbitration as the mechanism for resolving conflicts over the interpretation and application of the collective bargaining agreement. Although most grievance procedures are multi-step, unlike in the private sector, most grievances are not settled at the first step. Instead, grievance disputes tend to be settled at the second or third step. Some evidence indicates that where there are fewer steps in public-sector grievance procedures, grievances are resolved more quickly. Once a grievance is appealed to arbitration, the parties make a significant effort to resolve the grievances before the formal arbitration hearing. At an arbitration hearing, labor and management representatives are most likely to present their own case rather than rely upon an outside attorney to represent their party, as is common in the private sector.[64]

Similar to the private sector, legalism is creeping into the arbitration process in the public sector. Increased legalism means greater use of attorneys, posthearing briefs, written transcripts, and over adherence to formal rules of order. Although grievance arbitration (as well as conciliation, mediation, and fact-finding) initially was intended to avoid legalism, the process of arbitration appears to be evolving as part of the problem rather than part of the solution. In addition, labor and management initially viewed the informality of the arbitration process as the primary reason for its effectiveness; however, the increase in formality has caused a decline in the willingness of the parties to use arbitration as an alternative dispute resolution process.[65]

The types of grievance subjects arbitrated in the public sector do not vary significantly from the private-sector experience, and in both sectors, discipline and discharge cases constitute the largest single category of grievance disputes.[66] Public-sector union stewards may be less likely to file a written grievance if a cooperative bargaining relationship exists, which provides and encourages informal methods of resolving employment disputes.[67] A number of alternative dispute-resolution methods are being encouraged on the federal, state, and local levels to ensure fair and cost-effective resolution of employee grievances. Among techniques being used are mediation, peer review panels comprised of employees or employees and managers, and arbitration.[68] Mediation programs typically report dispute settlement rates in the 75 to 90 percent range, and arbitration may reduce attorney fees and settlement costs by 20 percent.[69]

The Right-to-Strike Controversy

The right to strike, considered by many a vital instrument for successful collective bargaining, is usually prohibited by statute in the public sector.[70] Even though public employee strikes are illegal in most states, there appears to be no research evidence to support the proposition that the presence of a statutory strike ban significantly reduces the occurrence of public employee strike activity.[71]

The basic argument given for legislative prohibition of strikes is that the services provided by public organizations are essential to the general welfare of the citizens. Work stoppages or refusals to work would adversely affect the delivery of such vital services and create disorder in the community. As is true with many industrial relations concepts, the words *essential services* are subject to many diverse interpretations. Some maintain that all public services are essential, whereas others suggest that many public employee classifications (such as clerks, mechanics, and librarians) are no more essential than their counterparts in the private sector who are granted a right to strike. Police and firefighters are almost always viewed as crucial for public safety; however, at least one police strike saw no increase in the area's crime rate. One political official, believing that criminals fear irate citizens more than they fear the police, commented, "Hoods have no rights without police protection. Shop owners will use their shotguns."[72]

The right to strike in the public sector has other debatable dimensions. Some would prohibit public-sector strikes because they would place too much power in the hands of a union relative to taxpayers. Also, unions would unnecessarily benefit at the expense of other groups that are dependent on government revenues but do not have a right to strike or participate in power ploys with public officials.[73]

One research study found that successful bargaining gains in the public sector occur when unions either use the threat of a strike despite its illegality or intertwine themselves closely with their employers by exchanging patronage for political support.[74] Some contend that the right to strike in the public sector is not essential to collective bargaining because public-sector unions are already influential interest groups and effectively use their lobbying and political support techniques to obtain collective bargaining goals.

Regardless of the arguments for or against the right to strike or statutory penalties imposed for illegal strike activity, significant strikes have occurred in the public sector. When illegal strike activity occurs or management permanently replaces lawful strikers, strike settlements may be delayed as union representatives seek to negotiate terms granting all strikers or discharged employees amnesty or reinstatement to their former jobs. Although there would generally be no legal obligation for a public employer to bargain over or grant such a union proposal, public or political pressure to end the strike may cause a public employer to voluntarily agree to such a proposal.[75]

Discipline of Public-Sector Employees

Although private-sector employees may be disciplined or discharged for off-duty misconduct, employers in the public sector have a heightened sensitivity about off duty misconduct of their employees, especially public school teachers, firefighters, and police officers. As a general rule, in both the private and public sector, the employees retain the right to conduct their private lives as they see fit without the interference of their employer, and the employer has just cause to discipline employees *only* if there is a nexus (connection) between the off-duty conduct and the employment. However, it is well established that off-duty conduct of public employees is subject to closer employer scrutiny, and discipline is more likely than for similar conduct in the private sector. Police officers are held to a more rigid standard of conduct since they are sworn, uniformed, and armed employees. Firefighters are frequently disciplined for unbecoming off-duty conduct. School teachers who are certified professionals have important responsibilities for nurturing the community's youth and serving as role models for their students. Publicized criminal convictions for such illegal activities as drug use and selling drugs by school teachers will very likely lead to termination of employment. In the private sector, the employer may discipline the employee, but will be required to prove that the off-duty conduct had harmed productivity, adversely affected the business, and/or other employees refused to work with the convicted employee. In addition, employees in the private sector may be employed under a collective bargaining agreement which requires entry to a rehabilitation program for a first offense.[76]

Interest Dispute Impasse-Resolution Procedures in the Public Sector

Because legislation usually prohibits public employees from striking or requires participation in impasse-resolution procedures before striking, these procedures play an important role in resolving interest disputes over what the terms and conditions of employment will be in the public sector. Because multiple laws exist that govern labor relations in different governmental jurisdictions, many different impasse-resolution procedures may be mandated or encouraged. These procedures normally involve a third party, who assists the parties in reaching an agreement without interrupting services or endangering the public interest (see discussion of **mediation**, **fact-finding**, and **interest arbitration** in Chapter 9).

Public-sector impasse-resolution procedures are controversial and have received considerable attention. Impasse-resolution procedures may combine mediation, fact-finding, and conventional or final-offer arbitration.[77] For example, Connecticut has mediation, fact-finding, and arbitration for state employees; fact-finding and arbitration for municipal employees; and mediation and fact-finding for teachers. Mediation is a legislatively mandated mechanism in public-sector bargaining in 35 states, followed by fact-finding which is required in 31 states.[78] Some form of interest arbitration is provided for firefighters in 21 states and the District of Columbia, for police in 20 states, for educators in 8 states, for municipal employees in 6 states, and for state employees in 5 states.[79] In all, 28 states have legislation that provides for interest arbitration for some employees (see Exhibit 13.5).[80]

Mediation

Mediation involves a third-party neutral who has no binding authority to decide a dispute but assists the parties' efforts to reach a voluntary agreement. Of the impasse-resolution procedures used in the public sector, mediation is the least intrusive and is little more than an adjunct to the negotiation process.[81] "Mediation is probably the most used and least studied dispute resolution procedure. This is because the mediation process is relatively informal and unstructured, reflecting the personal style of the mediator, the preferences of the union and employer representatives, and the intensity of the dispute."[82] The key ingredient for mediator effectiveness is experience, with related mediator training and knowledge. Effective mediators need tenacity—for example, not taking "no" for an answer—and they need to take an active role in the process by such actions as pressuring the

Alaska	Maine	New Mexico	Tennessee
California	Massachusetts	New York	Texas
Connecticut	Michigan	Ohio	Utah
Delaware	Minnesota	Oklahoma	Vermont
Hawaii	Montana	Oregon	Washington
Illinois	Nevada	Pennsylvania	Wisconsin
Iowa	New Jersey	Rhode Island	Wyoming

SOURCE: Committee Report of the Public Employment Disputes Settlement Committee of the National Academy of Arbitrators, May 9, 2007, Joyce M. Najita, Chair.

Exhibit 13.5

States with Legislation for Interest Arbitration Covering Some Public Employees

parties with successive proposals for compromise rather than simply relaying messages back and forth to the parties.[83]

Mediation tends to be more successful when the parties are unsure of themselves or have personality conflicts. Mediation is generally less effective when followed by fact-finding, but more effective when followed immediately by arbitration.[84]

Fact-Finding and Arbitration of Interest Disputes

Fact-finding and arbitration are separate impasse-resolution procedures; however, they are discussed and assessed jointly because of their many similarities. Both involve a third-party neutral who conducts a quasi-judicial hearing to assess union's and management's collective bargaining positions on issues in dispute. Those neutrals who are generally accepted to serve as fact-finders or arbitrators are likely to have much labor relations experience, as evidenced by their membership in the National Academy of Arbitrators, and are more likely than not to be attorneys trained in the evidentiary process.[85]

Fact-finders have multiple roles in the impasse-resolution process. A fact-finder must interpret data and information presented and recommend settlement positions to the parties.[86] Fact-finding is intended to encourage a voluntary settlement by the parties by providing an objective assessment of the dispute from a credible and neutral third party. However, the fact-finder's recommendations are not binding on the bargaining parties.

Unlike mediation or fact-finding, arbitration entails a binding decision by a third-party neutral who settles the negotiation impasse. The degree of flexibility an arbitrator has in resolving the bargaining dispute depends on the procedure adopted by the parties or mandated by applicable law. Conventional arbitration permits the arbitrator to decide the most appropriate outcome based on the evidence presented. The arbitrator's discretion is more restricted under a final-offer arbitration (FOA) procedure, which typically has two variations. Total package selection FOA requires the arbitrator to choose either the union's or employer's final offer covering all disputed issues. Issue-by-issue FOA still requires the arbitrator to select either the union's or employer's final offer on an issue-by-issue basis. In both cases, FOA means the arbitrator can select only one party's final offer; there is no compromise or splitting the difference.[87]

Fact-finding and arbitration are successful in resolving impasses because these techniques provide deadlines for the parties to resolve their differences, fresh knowledgeable perspectives, and political advantages because negotiators can blame the neutral for the eventual settlement. Politicians sometimes criticize fact-finders or arbitrators, calling them "outsiders" or "limousine liberals" who have no accountability to taxpayers—they make the decisions and then leave town. The mere possibility that these procedures might be used to determine negotiation outcomes is intended to pressure the negotiators to resolve their differences voluntarily for fear that the third-party neutral might not understand or agree with their bargaining proposals.

These techniques can also carry some disadvantages. For example, the fact-finder's recommendation and arbitrator's decision may lead to settlement terms but may not resolve the genuine union–management differences underlying the interest dispute. These techniques might cause the parties to cement their respective positions during negotiations because negotiators believe they can get a better deal from the arbitrator or more favorable recommendations from the fact-finder. Instead of earnestly attempting to resolve differences during negotiations, negotiators focus their time and thoughts on preparing for the fact-finder or arbitrator, thus producing a so-called **chilling effect** on the bargaining process. Rather than being viewed as a risk to be avoided, fact-finding or arbitration simply becomes another bargaining strategy. If either party believes that it could get a better settlement from an arbitrator than from negotiation, an incentive exists to maintain excessive demands in hopes that the arbitrator may "split the difference" and make a favorable award. When one side acts in such a manner, the other side has no realistic choice but to respond similarly, widening the gap between the parties and chilling the prospects for reaching a voluntary settlement.[88]

Research into this aspect of interest arbitration has produced mixed results. Analysis of arbitral decisions involving police impasses revealed that some management officials are reluctant to reveal their final offer before arbitration because the arbitrator will use management's final offer as a starting point in his/her decisions.[89] Yet this concern appears less relevant in a study of several arbitration awards in firefighters' interest disputes, for which the majority of arbitrators took an intermediate or compromise stance on negotiation issues, such as wages and clothing allowances, but did not compromise on other issues, selecting either management's or the union's final position.[90]

Another concern about public-sector interest arbitration is that the mere existence of impasse-resolution procedures could create a so-called **narcotic effect**. Once the parties start using fact-finding or interest arbitration procedures, they may become increasingly reliant on them in subsequent negotiations. Research studies find that this frequently expressed concern is not warranted, and the so-called narcotic effect tends to dissipate over time in subsequent contract negotiations.[91]

Effectiveness of Fact-Finding and Arbitration of Interest Disputes

Many variables influence the bargaining process and outcomes. One general measure of effectiveness is the "cost to at least one of the parties of continuing to disagree while lowering the cost to the other party of agreeing voluntarily."[92] Union and management officials are likely to push disputes to the last step of an impasse-resolution procedure when one or both parties:

- Are uncertain of future costs or continued collective bargaining (a situation that particularly applies to inexperienced negotiators)[93];

- Expect to receive a better settlement through the impasse procedure; or

- Need to pass the blame for an "unfavorable" settlement to a third-party neutral instead of accepting personal responsibility for the results.[94]

Assessing fact-finding is particularly difficult. Its effectiveness does not hinge on the fact-finder's ability; this individual is presented facts by the parties in hopes that he or she will agree with their respective positions. The success of such a procedure is based on the assumption that the fact-finder's report will structure public opinion, which will in turn place pressure on the parties to resolve their differences in accord with published recommendations. Thus far, no concrete evidence shows that public pressure has noticeably affected public-sector management and union officials. The views of the participants themselves appear to be divided, with time delays and disagreement over the weight attached by the fact-finder to factors, such as wage comparability being among the criticisms voiced.[95]

In general, participants, as well as analysts, appear to be satisfied with interest arbitration procedures used in the public sector. Compulsory arbitration of interest disputes does reduce the occurrence of public-sector strikes.[96] Voluntary settlement rates of interest disputes tend to be highest when the parties have a legal right to strike (94.7 percent of cases), followed by the availability of FOA issue-by-issue selection (87 percent), FOA total package selection (84.1 percent), and conventional arbitration (75.7 percent).[97] Compulsory interest arbitration also appears to have a small positive effect on wage and benefit improvements for affected employees.

Arbitrators in interest disputes tend to rely on three major wage standards: ability to pay, cost of living, and prevailing practice. Several minor standards—productivity, past practice and bargaining history, geographic differentials, and steadiness of employment—are also considered if presented. Each party presents evidence on these standards, and the final determination is based on the quality of the evidence on those standards.[98]

Interest arbitrators view their role in the arbitral process as continuing the existing nature of the parties' relationship, which has stemmed from the bilateral process of negotiations. Arbitrators believe that any major deviations from this relationship must come from the parties, not the arbitrator.[99] In wage disputes using FOA, evidence suggests that arbitrators are heavily influenced by wage settlements in comparable units of government. As a result, national unions discourage their local union affiliates from settling for a wage less than the targeted statewide settlement terms.[100]

Even though some management officials may fear arbitration, arbitrators have not stripped them of their rights and authority. Interest arbitration settlements have not proven to be significantly different from outcomes reached through voluntary negotiations under similar circumstances. The public, in general, has accepted the use of alternative dispute-resolution procedures to avoid public-sector strikes, and most significantly, arbitration has been increasingly adopted as an impasse-resolution procedure throughout the public sector.[101]

A derivative of FOA, called "Night Baseball Arbitration" has been proposed. Here, each party has an incentive to settle and each party has an incentive to present reasonable proposals. The parties do not present specific proposals at the arbitration hearing as they do with FOA, but present their respective final offers in sealed envelopes. Evidence and testimony from witnesses, which support each side's position, are presented to the arbitrator, and both sides may specifically point to the preferred resolution to the dispute. After the hearing, the arbitrator examines the evidence and testimony, renders a nonbinding ruling, and then opens the two parties' envelopes. The arbitrator then endorses the proposal that is closest to the arbitrator's ruling. Thus, like FOA, the final contract language is from the proposals crafted by one of the parties, not from the ruling crafted by the arbitrator.[102]

Referendum

One final impasse-resolution procedure that is sometimes used to resolve public-sector interest disputes is to submit unresolved issues to a taxpayer referendum or vote. The following item, for example, might be placed on a ballot: "Do you approve of granting a wage increase of X cents per hour to our police officers at an estimated additional annual cost to property taxpayers of Y million dollars?"[103]

One advantage of the referendum procedure would be to avoid having an outsider (fact-finder or arbitrator) determine the cost of a negotiated settlement. Citizens should complain less if the union's settlement was achieved in a democratic manner. Similarly, a union's integrity would be at stake if it refused to abide by the "will of the public." Yet, this procedure could turn collective bargaining into a public relations campaign directed at a body of individuals (citizens) largely unfamiliar with labor relations' complexities. This procedure has no precedent in private-sector labor relations because no practical company would agree to submit labor agreement proposals to stockholders or consumers for approval.

Referendum, or direct submission to the electorate for final and binding settlement of interest disputes, has been used in several Texas cities. Employees have won over two-thirds of the elections that involved civil service and bonus issues, but lost 56.6 percent when the issue was pay parity, such as raising the firefighter pay scale to the level of the police.[104] Use of a referendum has the potential advantage of motivating citizens to take an active interest in the matter of public employment.[105] However, in cities where the referendum method has been used, the assessment of this approach has not been favorable. First, the electorate has little understanding of the law and the issues, and it is highly susceptible to propaganda campaigns by both parties. Second, the referendum appears to help make the strong stronger and the weak weaker without regard for what is equitable or reasonable for all the parties involved.[106]

In conclusion, there are many varieties and combinations of public impasse-resolution procedures. Yet, the objectives remain the same: to avoid strikes, to minimize dependence on outsiders, to maximize good faith bargaining between the parties, to protect the public interest, and to build labor–management commitment to accountability and mutual problem solving.

Challenges and Opportunities for Public-Sector Unions

Although the public sector union density has been above 35 percent for over 20 years, public-sector unions must be conscious of the external and internal influences that could affect their strength and stability. Public-sector unions are presented with many challenges and opportunities, some of which are:

- *Privatizing of public services.* Political candidates and elected officials who advocate privatization usually argue for cost savings; however, beneath the surface, they are attempting to do away with jobs held by union members. Unions will have to challenge these approaches and promote the value of public services reaching out to political leaders who embrace that appeal.

- *Extending bargaining rights* by law, executive order, or municipal ordinance to the dozen-plus states that do not have legislation that grants rights to public employees to join unions and to bargain collectively. Although over the last few years there have been bills in Congress to establish minimum standards to extend employee rights to join unions and to bargain collectively for all state and local government employees, no law has been passed. Thus, unions must continue their political efforts at every level.

- *Unionizing the unrepresented professionals* who make up 37 percent of government jobs. Organizing campaigns will increasingly rely on the Internet and Web-based technologies because nearly all of the professional employees have computers at their work stations. In addition, unions will need to experiment with alternative forms of representation, such as associate memberships, minority unions, and legal assistance.

- *Moving beyond the traditional adversarial approaches.* Because public-sector employees and managers share a common commitment to serve the public, they want to secure and defend the missions of their agencies. This common ground will create opportunities for interest-based bargaining, labor–management partnerships which were successful in the federal sector during the Clinton administration, self-directed work teams, labor–management commitments, and full partnerships.

- *Seeking new approaches and subjects for bargaining.* Unions and management must become innovative in their negotiations. The parties might negotiate "evergreen contracts" which have no fixed expiration date so the parties are allowed to modify their collective bargaining agreements at any time in order to keep pace with technological changes and conditions. Subjects such a quality of work life, family and work life, and telecommuting create opportunities to address the contemporary working lives of employees.

- *Recruiting a new cadre of leaders.* At all levels of unions, those experienced leaders who helped build their organizations in the 1960s and 1970s are reaching retirement age. Unions will have to devote more attention to leadership training and management skills in the context of union values. Unions will need a more diverse set of leaders who will reflect a membership that is diverse occupationally, ethnically, and chronologically.[107]

PROSPECTS FOR FUTURE PUBLIC-SECTOR LABOR RELATIONS

Labor relations expert James Craft has projected 20 years into the future of public-sector labor relations and forecasts the following.

- There will be intense emphasis at all levels of government on reducing costs and improving efficiency. The private sector will continue to serve as a model to reshape government with goals of improving cost efficiencies, reducing size of government, stimulating an entrepreneurial spirit, and creating a customer orientation. Governments at all levels will continue to contract out services to the private sector and use competitive bidding to control costs. These actions will have direct implications on labor relations in the public sector.

- The number and percentage of public-sector employees who will be union members will increase. Among the reasons are (1) a more favorable general image of unions; (2) public-sector employees perceive unions as having greater influence in providing job security and greater protection of their general benefits and welfare; (3) the attitudes and behavior of public-sector managers, unlike the private-sector managers, are less resistant to employees being represented by unions; and (4) there are many opportunities in the public sector for unions to organize those who are not presently well represented, such as public-sector nurses and doctors, college professors, home-care workers, and increased numbers of security employees.

- There will be increased rivalry among unions who react to the changing operations of governments. For example, when a government contracts out services to a private employee, it creates employment in the private sector, which creates opportunities for private-sector unions to represent the new employees. Such actions may create tensions between the American Federation of State, County, and Municipal Employees, which represents primarily public-sector employees, and other unions, such as the Communications Workers of America and the United Food and Commercial Workers, which represent primarily private-sector employees.

- There will be few, if any, totally new union tactics and actions. The unions will rely less on the use of formal strikes, and more emphasis will be placed on political actions for several reasons: (1) there is greater maturity in the relationships between the parties and understanding of the collective bargaining process; (2) there is concern among employees in the nonessential services that they may create interest in contracting out their jobs; and (3) there is less tolerance among the public for strikes by employees in the public sector.

- There will be increased interest in merit-, market- and performance-based compensation models, which include group-based incentive pay that potentially can reduce costs and reward employees for savings.

- There will a growing emphasis on the development of labor management cooperation and collaboration at all levels of governments. Both unions and employers will recognize the mutual benefits of a more cooperative relationship and move toward constructive processes such as interest-based bargaining, as described in Chapter 6.[108]

Summary

Public employee unions over the past 40 years have grown to represent a majority of employees in education, police, and fire protection in state and local governments and a significant proportion of workers in the federal sector. Public employers and employees are under pressure to deliver an increasing variety of public services in the most cost-efficient and timely manner possible. Concepts familiar to private-sector labor relations over the past 20 years, such as downsizing, cost reduction, outsourcing, and productivity improvement, have made their way into the bargaining reality of public-sector labor relations as well.

Most states have one or more comprehensive laws regulating state and local public-sector labor relations. Such legislation typically specifies the administrative setup, union recognition procedure, bargaining rights, impasse procedures, unfair labor practices, and strike provisions applicable to covered employees. The Civil Service Reform Act (CSRA) of 1978 regulates federal employee labor relations. The administrative structure under the CSRA includes the Federal Labor Relations Authority, the General Counsel, and the Federal Service Impasse Panel. Within this framework, the parties attempt to negotiate and administer labor agreements covering mandatory and permissible bargaining subjects. Also available for assistance are the Federal Mediation and Conciliation Service, labor arbitrators, and fact-finders who provide important dispute resolution services for the parties.

Public- and private-sector labor relations differ in several ways: (1) by its very nature, public service differs from private-sector services economically and in its demand characteristics; (2) the effect of the budget on bargaining processes differs; (3) the bargaining structure differs, affecting decision-making processes; (4) negotiable issues and bargaining tactics different; and (5) the right to strike is usually prohibited by law. Public- and private-sector similarities include the role of personalities and skills of negotiators and the interplay of bargaining power model variables, such as public opinion, political support, and various forms of job actions.

Since September 11, 2001, Congress has passed a series of laws that have affected labor management relations in the federal sector. In 2001, the Aviation and Transportation Act created the Transportation Security Administration (TSA) which federalized airport screeners and gave the TSA the same personnel flexibilities afforded the Federal Aviation Administration. In 1996 as part of the Department of Transportation appropriations, Congress had directed the FAA to negotiate labor management relations reform, which provided for salary negotiations with the air traffic controllers union. The TSA was also authorized to determine whether the airport screeners could unionize, and the TSA decided they could not unionize. In 2002, the Department of Homeland Security (DHS) was created and with assistance from the Office of Personnel Management, was granted authority to develop a new personnel system. In 2003, the Department of Defense (DoD), again with assistance of the Office of Personnel Management, was authorized to design and implement a new personnel system (called the National Security Personnel System).

Impasse-resolution procedures often established as a substitute for public employees' lack of a legal right to strike include mediation, fact-finding, arbitration, and various combinations of these. Such terms as *chilling effect* and *narcotic effect* have become common in assessing the effectiveness of these procedures. Public employee unions do appear to have had a positive impact on raising wage and benefit levels for public employees and in garnering a larger proportion of public-sector budgets to address employee interests. Although public-sector union membership growth rates are likely to moderate in future years, public employee unions will continue to play an important role in determining labor relations policy and outcomes in the public sector.

Key Terms

Federal Labor Relations Authority (FLRA), p. 573
Federal Service Impasse Panel (FSIP), p. 573
Exclusive recognition, p. 575

Work-to-rule, p. 583
Sovereignty doctrine, p. 587
Multilateral bargaining, p. 589
End-run bargaining, p. 589
Sunshine laws, p. 590

Mediation, p. 593
Fact-finding, p. 593
Interest arbitration, p. 593
Chilling effect, p. 595
Narcotic effect, p. 595

Discussion Questions

1. Think of a public organization with which you are familiar. Explain how it differs from a private company in terms of the following:

   a. Nature of its service

   b. Relationship between its budget and collective bargaining processes

   c. Bargaining structure and decision-making processes

   d. Negotiable issues and bargaining tactics

   e. The right to strike

2. Using the same public organization as in Question 1, discuss the similarities between collective bargaining in this organization and a typical negotiation between a private company and its union.

3. Explain why some states do and other states do not have a public-sector bargaining law or laws that cover some public employees but not others.

4. Describe the different types of impasse-resolution procedures used in the public sector and discuss the relative effectiveness of each.

5. What are the advantages of "Night Baseball" arbitration over conventional interest arbitration and FOS arbitration?

6. What are some possible advantages or disadvantages of expanding the scope of bargaining in the federal sector to include issues such as wages and benefits?

7. Why does the federal government have multiple labor management relations models?

8. Should public employees have the same right to strike as private-sector employees are granted under the Labor Management Relations Act? Why or why not?

9. Should all public employees have a right to submit interest disputes to final and binding arbitration in exchange for giving up the right to engage in legal strike activity? Why or why not?

Exploring the Web

Labor Relations in the Public Sector

1. Federal-Sector Labor Relations Legislation. The Federal Labor Relations Authority is an independent agency responsible for administering the labor management relations program for Federal non-postal employees. Go to the Web site of the Authority and find the section that describes the purpose of the Federal Service Impasses Panel. Who are the members of the Panel?

How did the Postal Reorganization Act of 1970 affect labor management relations in the Postal Service? Look for the history of the USPS on the Web site of the Postal Service.

2. Articles on Public-Sector Unionism. The Public Service Research Foundation, a private nonprofit organization, makes available papers and pamphlets that "address a variety of issues related to public-sector unionism and union influence on public policy." Locate the article, "Beyond Public Sector Unionism" in which president David Denholm

discusses the differences between public- and private-sector unionism. How does he argue that public-sector collective bargaining goes against the public interest?

3. Labor Relations and Teachers. Locate and read David Denholm's "The Impact of Unionism on the Quality of Education" as well.

The Education Policy Institute in Washington, D.C., provides links to information on teacher unions. What are some of the differences between the National Education Association (NEA) and the American Federation of Teachers (AFT)?

4. Bureau of Labor Statistics on Work Stoppages in the Public Sector. The BLS reports "major work stoppages," which include worker-initiated strikes and lockouts by their employers involving 1,000 workers or more. What percentage of the total work stoppages in 2006 occurred in the public sector?

References

1. David Lewin, Peter Feuille, and Thomas Kochan, *Public Sector Labor Relations: An Analysis and Readings,* 2nd ed. (Glen Ridge, N.J.: Thomas Horton & Daughters, 1988), pp. 1–5.

2. Dale Belman, Morley Gunderson, and Douglas Hyatt, "Public Sector Employment Relations in Transition," in *Public Sector Employment,* eds. D. Belman, M. Gunderson, and D. Hyatt (Madison, Wis.: Industrial Relations Research Association, 1996), pp. 1–9.

3. Bureau of Labor Statistics, "Union Members in 2007," *News Release,* January 25, 2008 at http://www.bls.gov/.

4. Terry Thomason and John F. Burton, Jr., "Unionization Trends and Labor Management Cooperation in the Public Sector," *Going Public: The Role of Labor Management Relations in Delivering Quality Government Services,* eds.

Jonathan Brock and David B. Lipsky (Champaign, Ill.: Industrial Relations Research Association, 2003), pp. 69–83.

5. Service Employees International Union, "SEIU's Public Service Employees," 2002, pp. 1–2 at http://www.sein .org/public_employee/abtpubemp.html.

6. James L. Stern, "Unionism in the Public Sector," in *Public Sector Bargaining,* 2nd ed., eds. Benjamin Aaron, Joyce M. Najita, and James L. Stern (Washington, D.C.: The Bureau of National Affairs, 1988), pp. 66–67; Marick F. Masters and Robert S. Atkin, "Reforming Federal Sector Labor Relations: Recommendations of President Clinton's National Partnership Council," *Labor Law Journal* 45 (June 1994), pp. 353–354.

7. http://www.bls.gov/news.release/union2.t03.htm.

8. James T. Bennett and Marick F. Masters, "The Future of Public Sector Labor Management Relations," *Journal of Labor Research* 24 (Fall 2003), pp. 537–538.

9. Heejoon Park, "State Legislation of Public Sector Collective Bargaining: An Event History Analysis," in *Proceedings of the Fiftieth Annual Meeting, Industrial Relations Research Association* (Madison, Wis.: Industrial Relations Research Association, 1998), pp. 23–32; Susan Schwochau, "Interest Group Tactics and Public Sector Labor Relations Policy," *Journal of Labor Research* 15 (Fall 1994), pp. 331–354.

10. Jeffrey S. Zax and Casey Ichniowski, "Bargaining Laws and Unionization in the Local Public Sector," *Industrial and Labor Relations Review* 43 (April 1990), pp. 447–463; Greg Hundley, "Who Joins Unions in the Public Sector? The Effect of Individual Characteristics and the Law," *Journal of Labor Research* 9 (Fall 1988), pp. 301–306; Richard B. Freeman and Casey Ichniowski, "Introduction: The Public Sector Look of American Unionism," in *When Public Sector Workers Unionize*, eds. Richard B. Freeman and Casey Ichniowski (Chicago: The University of Chicago Press, 1988), p. 3.

11. Bennett and Masters, "The Future of Public Sector Labor Management Relations," pp. 534–536.

12. Fred C. Lunenburg, "Collective Bargaining in the Public Schools: Issues, Tactics, and New Strategies," *Journal of Collective Negotiations in the Public Sector* 29 (2000), p. 259.

13. John Lund and Cheryl L. Maranto, "Public Sector Labor Law: An Update," in *Public Sector Employment in a Time of Transition*, eds. Dale Belman, Morley Gunderson, and Douglas Hyatt (Madison, Wis.: Industrial Relations Research Association, 1996), p. 48.

14. *County Sanitation District No. 2 of L.A. County v. L.A. County Employees Association*, 699 P.2d 835 (1985); Raymond L. Hogler, *Public Sector Strikes: Employee Rights, Union Responsibilities, and Employer Prerogatives* (Alexandria, Va.: International Personnel Management Association, 1988), pp. 5–6.

15. Robert Hebdon, "Public Sector Dispute Resolution in Transition," in *Public Sector Employment in a Time of Transition*, eds. Dale Belman, Morley Gunderson, and Douglas Hyatt (Madison, Wis.: Industrial Relations Research Association, 1996), pp. 87–92.

16. Charles J. Coleman, "Federal Sector Labor Relations: A Reevaluation of Policies," *Journal of Collective Negotiations in the Public Sector* 16 (1987), pp. 37–52.

17. Ibid.

18. George W. Bohlander, "The Federal Service Impasse Panel: A Ten-Year Review and Analysis," *Journal of Collective Negotiations in the Public Sector* 24 (1995), pp. 194–195.

19. Ibid.

20. Charles G. Smith, "Winning and Losing in Federal Sector Dispute Resolution," *Public Personnel Management* 23 (Summer 1994), pp. 301–319.

21. Peter Feuille, "Unionism in the Public Sector: The Joy of Protected Markets," *Journal of Labor Research* 12 (Fall 1991), pp. 351–353 and Jill Kriesky, "Trends in Dispute Resolution in the Public Sector," in *Employment Dispute Resolution and Worker Rights in a Changing Workplace*, eds. Adrienne E. Eaton and Jeffrey H. Keefe (Champaign, Ill.: Industrial Relations Research Association, 1999), pp. 249–250.

22. William J. Clinton, *Presidential Executive Order No. 12871: Labor Management Partnerships*, October 1, 1993 at http://www.opm.gov/npc/html/eo12871.htm; William J. Clinton, "Memorandum for the Heads of Executive Departments and Agencies," *News Release*, October 28, 1999, pp. 1–2 at http://www.opm.gov/pressrel/1999/pres_statement.htm.

23. Martin H. Malin, "Public Sector Labor Law Doctrine and Labor Management Cooperation," *Going Public: The Role of Labor Management Relations in Delivering Quality Government Services*, eds. Jonathan Brock and David B. Lipsky (Champaign, Ill.: Industrial Relations Research Association, 2003), pp. 278–279.

24. Marick F. Masters and Robert B. Albright, "Federal Labor Management Partnerships, Perspectives, Performance, and Possibilities," and Terry Thomason and John F. Burton, Jr., "Unionization Trends and Labor–Management Cooperation in the Public Sector," *Going Public: The Role of Labor Management Relations in Delivering Quality Government Services*, eds. Jonathan Brock and David B. Lipsky (Champaign, Ill.: Industrial Relations Research Association, 2003), pp. 177–207.

25. Marick F. Masters, Robert R. Albright, and David Eplion, "What Did Partnerships Do? Evidence from the Federal Sector," *Industrial and Labor Relations Review*, 59 (April 2006), pp. 367–382.

26. Marick F. Masters and Robert R. Albright, "Labor Relations in the Department of Homeland Security: Competing and Perspectives and Future Possibilities," *Labor Law Journal* 54 (2003), pp. 66–83.

27. http://www.cpms.osd.mil/nsps/lr.html; http://www.opm.opm.gov. See: Douglas A. Brook and Cynthia L. King, "Civil Service Reform as National Security: The Homeland Security Act of 2002," *Public Administration Review*, 67 (May-June 2007), pp. 399–407.

28. Richard W. Hurd and Jill K. Kriesky with reply by Herbert R. Northrup, "The Rise and Demise of PATCO," *Industrial and Labor Relations Review* 40 (October 1986), pp. 115–127; Herbert R. Northrup, "The Rise and Demise of PATCO," *Industrial and Labor Relations Review* 37 (January 1984), pp. 167–184.

29. http://www.apwu.org/; http://www.nalca.org/; http://www.npmhu.org; http://www.nlrca.org/.

30. Marick F. Masters, "Reforming Human Resource Management in the Federal Sector," *Perspectives on Work*, 9 (Winter 2006), pp. 29–30; Jean Lenderking and Robert Albright, "Human Capital Reform and Pay Bargaining: The FAA Experience," *Perspectives on Work*, 9 (Winter 2006), pp. 31–32.

31. Tim Bornstein, "Legacies of Local Government Collective Bargaining in the 1970s," *Labor Law Journal* 31 (March 1980), pp. 165–173.

32. Jack Fiorito and Lee P. Stepina, "Explaining the Unionism Gap: Public–Private Sector Differences in Preferences for Unionization," *Journal of Labor Research* 17 (Summer 1996), pp. 463–478; Kate Bronfenbrenner and Tom Juravich, *Union Organizing in the Public Sector* (Ithaca, N.Y.: Cornell University Press, 1995); Lee A. Graf, Masoud Hemmasi, Kenneth E. Newgreen, and Warren R. Nielsen, "Profiles of Those Who Support Collective

Bargaining in Institutions of Higher Learning and Why: An Empirical Examination," *Journal of Collective Negotiations in the Public Sector* 23 (1994), p. 155.

33. Richard Freeman, "Through Public Sector Eyes: Employee Attitudes toward Public Sector Labor Relations in the U.S.," in *Public Sector Employment in a Time of Transition,* eds. Dale Belman, Morley Gunderson, and Douglas Hyatt (Madison, Wis.: Industrial Relations Research Association, 1996), pp. 71–73.

34. These techniques were formulated in various discussions with Paul Gerhart of Case Western Reserve University.

35. Kevin M. O'Brien, "Compensation, Employment, and the Political Activity of Public Employee Unions," *Journal of Labor Research* 13 (Spring 1992), pp. 189–203; Michael Marmo, "Public Employee Unions: The Political Imperative," *Journal of Collective Negotiations in the Public Sector* 4 (1975), p. 371.

36. Paul D. Staudohar, "Quasi-Strikes by Public Employees," *Journal of Collective Negotiations in the Public Sector* 3 (Fall 1974), pp. 363–371.

37. Richard B. Freeman and Casey Ichniowski, "Introduction: The Public Sector Look of American Unionism," in *When Public Sector Workers Unionize,* eds. Richard B. Freeman and Casey Ichniowski (Chicago: The University of Chicago Press, 1988), pp. 1–13.

38. John Lund and Cheryl L Maranto, "Public Sector Law: An Update," pp. 39–47.

39. http://www.lawmemo.com/sct/WEA/.

40. Michael Moskow, J. J. Loewenberg, and E. C. Koziara, *Collective Bargaining in Public Employment* (New York: Random House, 1970), pp. 14–18; H. H. Wellington and R. K. Winter, Jr., "Structuring Collective Bargaining in Public Employment," *Yale Law Journal* 79 (April 1970), pp. 806–822.

41. Dale Belman, Morley Gunderson, and Douglas Hyatt, "Public Sector Employment Relations in Transition," in *Public Sector Employment in a Time of Transition,* eds. D. Belman, M. Gunderson, and D. Hyatt (Madison, Wis.: Industrial Relations Research Association, 1996), pp. 4–5.

42. Milton Derber, Ken Jennings, Ian McAndrew and Martin Wagner, "Bargaining and Budget-Making in Illinois Public Institutions," *Industrial and Labor Relations Review* 27 (October 1973), pp. 49–62; Kenneth M. Jennings, J. A. Smith, and Earle C. Traynham, Jr., "Budgetary Influences on Bargaining in Mass Transit," *Journal of Collective Negotiations in the Public Sector* 6 (1977), pp. 333–339.

43. Michael Marmo, "Public Employees: On-the-Job Discipline for Off-the-Job Behavior," *The Arbitration Journal* 40 (June 1985), p. 23; Marvin Hill, Jr., and Donald Dawson, "Discharge for Off-Duty Misconduct in the Private and Public Sectors," *The Arbitration Journal* 40 (June 1985), pp. 24–33.

44. Kevin A. Banasik, "Government Regulation of Federal Employee Speech: *United States v. National Treasury Employees Union,* 115 S.Ct. 1003 (1993)," *Harvard Journal of Law & Public Policy* 19 (Fall 1995), pp. 200–209; David H. Rosenbloom, "Public Personnel Administration and the Constitution: An Emergent Approach," *Public Administration Review* 35 (February 1975), pp. 52–59.

45. *Board of Regents v. Roth,* 408 U.S. 564 (1972); *Perry v. Sindermann,* 408 U.S. 593 (1972).

46. *Cleveland Board of Education v. Loudermill,* 470 U.S. 532 (1985).

47. Timothy D. Chandler and Timothy A. Judge, "Management Chief Negotiators, Bargaining Strategies, and the Likelihood of Impasse in Public Sector Collective Bargaining," *American Review of Public Administration* 28 (June 1998), pp. 146–166.

48. Rafael Gely and Timothy D. Chandler, "Determinants of Management's Organizational Structure in the Public Sector," *Journal of Labor Research* 14 (Fall 1993), pp. 381–397.

49. Stephen L. Hayford, "An Empirical Investigation of the Public Sector Supervisory Bargaining Rights Issue," *Labor Law Journal* 26 (October 1975), pp. 641–652; Alan Balfour, "Rights of Collective Representation for Public Sector Supervisors," *Journal of Collective Negotiations in the Public Sector* 4 (1975), pp. 257–265; and William H. Holley, Jr., J. Boyd Scebra, and William Rector, "Perceptions of the Role of the Principal in Professional Negotiations," *Journal of Collective Negotiations in the Public Sector* 5 (1976), pp. 361–369.

50. Adrienne E. Eaton and Paula B. Voos, "Wearing Two Hats: The Unionization of Public Sector Supervisors," *Going Public: The Role of Labor–Management Relations in Delivering Quality Government Services,* eds. Jonathan Brock and David B. Lipsky (Champaign, Ill.: Industrial Relations Research Association, 2003), pp. 295–309.

51. Louis V. Imundo, Jr., "The Federal Government Sovereignty and Its Effect on Labor–Management Relations," *Labor Law Journal* 26 (March 1975), pp. 145–152.

52. Milton Derber, "Management Organization for Collective Bargaining in the Public Sector," in *Public Sector Bargaining,* eds. Benjamin Aaron, Joseph Grodin, and James Stern (Washington, D.C.: Bureau of National Affairs, 1978), pp. 80–117.

53. Timothy D. Chandler and Timothy A. Judge, "Management Chief Negotiators, Bargaining Strategies, and the Likelihood of Impasse in Public Sector Collective Bargaining," *Annual Review of Public Administration* 28 (June 1998), pp. 160–161.

54. I. B. Helburn and N. B. Bennett, "Public Employee Bargaining and the Merit Principle," *Labor Law Journal* 23 (October 1972), p. 619; I. B. Helburn, "The Scope of Bargaining in Public Sector Negotiations: Sovereignty Reviewed," *Journal of Collective Negotiations in the Public Sector* 3 (Spring 1974), pp. 147–166.

55. Richard C. Williams, "Resolution of the Civil Service–Collective Bargaining Dilemma," *American Review of Public Administration* 24 (June 1994), pp. 149–160.

56. Paul F. Gerhart, "The Scope of Bargaining in Local Government Negotiations," *Labor Law Journal* 20 (August 1969), pp. 545–552.

57. Margorie Sarbaugh-Thompson, "Bargaining Over Education Policy: Who Represents the Community?" *Journal of Collective Negotiations in the Public Sector* 26 (1997), pp. 223–245; Thomas A. Kochan, "A Theory of Multilateral Collective Bargaining in City Governments," *Industrial and Labor Relations Review* 27 (July 1974), pp. 525–542.

58. Marick F. Masters, "AFSCME as a Political Union," *Journal of Labor Research* 19 (Spring 1998), pp. 313–349; Marick F. Masters and Robert S. Atkin, "Financial and Political Resources of Nine Major Public Sector Unions in the 1980s," *Journal of Labor Research* 17 (Winter 1996), pp. 183–198; Rafael Gely and Timothy D. Chandler, "Protective Service Unions' Political Activities and Departmental Expenditures," *Journal of Labor Research* 16 (Spring 1995), pp. 171–185; Robert G. Valletta, "The Impact of Unionism On Municipal Expenditures and Revenues," *Industrial and Labor Relations Review* 42 (April 1989), pp. 430–442.

59. Peter Feuille, "Police Labor Relations and Multilateralism," *Journal of Collective Negotiations in the Public Sector* 3 (Summer 1974), p. 216.

60. Victor Gotbaum, "Collective Bargaining and the Union Leader," in *Public Workers and Public Unions,* ed. Zagoria, pp. 83–84.

61. Michael Marmo, "Public Employee Collective Bargaining: A Mass-Mediated Process," *Journal of Collective Negotiations in the Public Sector* 13 (1984), pp. 291–307.

62. "Characteristics of 'Sunshine' Laws in the 50 States," *The Chronicle of Higher Education,* October 10, 1984, p. 18.

63. Kevin M. O'Brien, "The Impact of Sunshine Laws on Police and Firefighter Bargaining Outcomes," *Applied Financial Economics* 5 (December 1995), pp. 425–432.

64. George W. Bohlander, "Public Sector Grievance Arbitration: Structure and Administration," *Journal of Collective Negotiations in the Public Sector* 21 (1992), pp. 282–283; Greg Stewart and Jeanette A. Davy, "An Empirical Examination of Grievance Resolution and Filing Rates in the Public and Private Sectors," *Journal of Collective Negotiations in the Public Sector* 21 (1992), pp. 331–334.

65. Barry M. Rubin and Richard S. Rubin, "Creeping Legalism in Public Sector Grievance Arbitration: A National Perspective," *Journal of Collective Negotiation in the Public Sector* 30 (2003), pp. 3–12.

66. Debra J. Mesch and Olga Shamayeva, "Arbitration in Practice: A Profile of Public Sector Arbitration Cases," *Public Personnel Management* 25 (Spring 1996), pp. 119–132.

67. Michael J. Duane, "To Grieve or Not to Grieve: Why Reduce It to Writing?" *Public Personnel Management* 20 (Spring 1991), pp. 83–88.

68. Jill Kriesky, "Trends in Dispute Resolution in the Public Sector," in *Employment Dispute Resolution and Worker Rights in the Changing Workplace,* pp. 251–254.

69. Joseph I. Goldstein and Martin F. Payson, "Alternate Dispute Resolution of Employment Matters in the Public Sector," *Spectrum: The Journal of State Government* 68 (Fall 1995), pp. 36–42.

70. Michael H. Cimini, "1982–97 State and Local Government Work Stoppages and Their Legal Background," *Compensation and Working Conditions* 3 (Fall 1998), pp. 32–34; John Lund and Cheryl L. Maranto, "Public Sector Labor Law: An Update," in *Public Sector Employment in a Time of Transition,* p. 30.

71. Dane M. Partridge, "The Effect of Public Policy on Strike Activity in the Public Sector," *Journal of Collective Negotiations in the Public Sector* 19 (1990), pp. 87–94; Robert E. Doherty, "Trends in Strikes and Interest Arbitration in the Public Sector," *Labor Law Journal* 37 (August 1986), pp. 473–475; Craig Olson, "Strikes, Strike Penalties, and Arbitration in Six States," *Industrial and Labor Relations Review* 39 (July 1986), p. 539.

72. "Crime Rate Is Same Despite Police Strike," *Miami Herald,* July 20, 1975, p. 15-A.

73. Paul D. Staudohar, "Reappraisal of the Right to Strike in California," *Journal of Collective Negotiations in the Public Sector* 15 (1986), p. 91.

74. Theodore Kheel, "Resolving Deadlocks without Banning Strikes," *Monthly Labor Review* 91 (July 1969), pp. 62–63.

75. Michael H. Cimini, "1982–97 State and Local Government Work Stoppages and Their Legal Background," 1998, p. 34.

76. William Walsh and Sheila Vicars-Duncan, "Disciplining Public School Employees for Off-Duty (Mis)conduct: A View for Arbitration Decisions," *Journal of Collective Negotiations in the Public Sector,* 30 (2005), pp. 329–336.

77. U.S. Department of Labor, Labor–Management Services Administration, *Summary of Public Sector Labor Relations Policies, 1976* (Washington, D.C.: Government Printing Office, 1976), pp. 1–126.

78. Mark D. Karper, "Fact Finding in Public Employment: Promise or Illusion, Revisited," *Journal of Collective Negotiations in the Public Sector* 23 (1994), pp. 288–296.

79. John Lund and Cheryl L. Marnto, "Public Sector Labor Law: An Update," in *Public Sector Employment in a Time of Transition,* pp. 31, 48, 50–54.

80. Committee Report of the Public Employment Disputes Settlement Committee of the National Academy of Arbitrators, May 9, 2007, Joyce M. Najita, Chair.

81. David A. Dilts, Ahmad Karm, and Ali Rassuli, "Mediation in the Public Sector: Toward a Paradigm of Negotiations and Dispute Resolution," *Journal of Collective Negotiations in the Public Sector* 19 (1990), pp. 49–50.

82. David Lewin, Peter Feuille, Thomas A. Kochan, and John T. Delaney, *Public Sector Labor Relations: Analysis and Readings* (Lexington, Mass.: D.C. Heath, 1988), pp. 334–335.

83. Steven Briggs and Daniel J. Koys, "An Empirical Investigation of Public Sector Mediator Effectiveness," *Journal of Collective Negotiations in the Public Sector* 19 (1990), pp. 121–126.

84. Thomas A. Kochan, "Dynamics of Dispute Resolution in the Public Sector," in *Public Sector Bargaining,* eds. B. Aaron, J. R. Grodin, and J. L. Stern (Washington, D.C.: Bureau of National Affairs, 1979), pp. 150–190; Thomas P. Gilroy and Anthony Sinicropi, "Impasse Resolution in Public Employment: A Current Assessment," *Industrial and Labor Relations Review* 25 (July 1972), pp. 500–501.

85. Stanley W. Elsea, David Dilts, and Lawrence J. Haber, "Factfinders and Arbitrators in Iowa: Are They the Same Neutrals?" *Journal of Collective Negotiations in the Public Sector* 19 (1990), pp. 61–81.

86. Debra J. Mesch, "A Union-Management Cooperative Program Gone Wrong: Some Unintended Consequences of a Fact-Finding Program," *Journal of Applied Behavioral Science* 30 (March 1994), pp. 43–62; Kenneth

M. Jennings, Steve K. Paulson, and Steven A. Williamson, "Fact-Finding in Perspective," *Government Union Review* 8 (Summer 1987), pp. 54–70; Nels Nelson, "Fact-Finders View the Factfinding Process," *The Journal of Collective Negotiations in the Public Sector* 19 (1990), pp. 141–149.

87. For an excellent review of the distinctive nature of arbitration in the public sector, see Helen LaVan, "Arbitration in the Public Sector: A Current Perspective," *Journal of Collective Negotiations in the Public Sector* 19, (1990), pp. 153–163.

88. Lewin, Feuille, and Kochan, *Public Sector Labor Relations*, p. 229; Frederic C. Champlin and Mario F. Bognanno, "Time Spent Processing Interest Arbitration Cases: The Minnesota Experience," *Journal of Collective Negotiations in the Public Sector* 14 (1985), pp. 53–64; Charles M. Rehmus, "Public Employees: A Survey of Some Critical Problems on the Frontier of Collective Bargaining," *Labor Law Journal* 27 (September 1976), pp. 588–599.

89. Craig E. Overton and Max S. Wortman, "Compulsory Arbitration: A Strike Alternative for Police?" *Arbitration Journal* 28 (March 1974), p. 40.

90. Hoyt N. Wheeler, "Is Compromise the Rule in Fire Fighter Arbitration?" *Arbitration Journal* 29 (September 1974), pp. 176–185.

91. James R. Chelius and Marian M. Extejt, "The Narcotic Effect of Impasse Resolution Procedures," *Industrial and Labor Relations Review* 38 (July 1985), pp. 629–637; Marian M. Extejt and James R. Chelius, "The Behavioral Impact of Impasse Resolution Procedures," *Review of Public Personnel Administration* 5 (Spring 1985), pp. 46–47.

92. Paul F. Gerhart and John E. Drotning, "Do Uncertain Cost/Benefit Estimates Prolong Public-Sector Disputes?" *Monthly Labor Review* 103 (September 1980), pp. 26–30; Frederic Champlin and Mario F. Bognanno, "'Chilling' under Arbitration and Mixed Strike-Arbitration Regimes," *Journal of Labor Research* 6 (Fall 1985), pp. 375–386.

93. David E. Bloom, "Is Arbitration Really Compatible with Bargaining?" *Industrial Relations* 20 (Fall 1980), pp. 233–244.

94. Henry S. Farber, "Role of Arbitration in Dispute Settlement," *Monthly Labor Review* 104 (May 1981), p. 34.

95. Hebdon, "Public Sector Dispute Resolution in Transition," pp. 102–103.

96. Morley Gunderson, Robert Hebdon, and Douglas Hyatt, "Collective Bargaining in the Public Sector: Comment," *American Economic Review* 86 (March 1996), pp. 315–326.

97. Hebdon, "Public Sector Dispute Resolution in Transition," pp. 110–112; Michael A. Zigarelli, "Dispute Resolution Mechanisms and Teacher Bargaining Outcomes," *Journal of Labor Research* 17 (Winter 1996), pp. 135–148.

98. David A. Dilts, Mashaalah Rahnama-Moghadam, and Tedessa Mengestu, "Institutional Wage Standards in Public Sector Interest Arbitration," *Journal of Collective Negotiation in the Public Sector,* 30 (2005) pp. 339–348.

99. Richard A. Turpin, "An Analysis of Public Sector Interest Arbitrators' Assessments of Wage Comparability," *Journal of Collective Negotiations in the Public Sector* 27 (1998), pp. 45–51; Richard A. Turpin, "Factors Considered by Public Sector Interest Arbitrators in Assessing Ability to Pay," *Journal of Collective Negotiations in the Public Sector* 26 (1997), pp. 1–7; Gregory G. Dell'omo, "Wage Disputes in Interest Arbitration: Arbitrators Weigh the Criteria," *The Arbitration Journal* 44 (June 1989), pp. 4–8; Susan Schwochau and Peter Feuille, "Interest Arbitrators and Their Decision Behavior," *Industrial Relations* 27 (Winter 1988), pp. 37–55.

100. Craig A. Olson and Paul Jarley, "Arbitration Decisions in Wisconsin Teacher Wage Disputes," *Industrial and Labor Relations Review* 44 (April 1991), p. 546.

101. Karl O. Magnusen and Patricia A. Renovitch, "Dispute Resolution in Florida's Public Sector: Insight into Impasse," *Journal of Collective Negotiations in the Public Sector* 18 (1989), pp. 241–252; J. Joseph Loewenberg, "Compulsory Arbitration in the United States," in *Compulsory Arbitration,* ed J. J. Loewenberg et al. (Lexington, Mass.: D.C. Heath, 1976), p. 166; Hoyt N. Wheeler, "An Analysis of Fire Fighter Strikes," *Labor Law Journal* 26 (January 1975), pp. 17–20.

102. William H. Ross, "Should 'Night Baseball' Arbitration Be Use in Lieu of Public Sector Strikes? Psychological Considerations and Suggestions for Research," *Journal of Collective Negotiations in the Public Sector,* 31 (1), 2006, pp. 45–47.

103. J. H. Foegen, "Public Sector Strike-Prevention: Let the Taxpayer Decide," *Journal of Collective Negotiations in the Public Sector* 3 (Summer 1974), p. 223.

104. I. B. Helburn and J. L. Matthews, "The Referendum as an Alternative to Bargaining," *Journal of Collective Negotiations in the Public Sector* 9 (1980), pp. 93–105.

105. Raymond L. Hogler and Curt Krciksciun, "Impasse Resolution in Public Sector Collective Negotiations: A Proposed Procedure," *Industrial Relations Law Journal* 6 (1984), pp. 481–510.

106. Donald T. Barnum and I. B. Helburn, "Influence the Electorate Experience with Referenda on Public Employee Bargaining," *Industrial and Labor Relations Review* 35 (April 1982), pp. 330–342.

107. Richard W. Hurd and Sharon Pinnock, "Public Sector Unions: Will They Thrive or Struggle to Survive?" *Journal of Labor Research,* 25 (Spring 2004), pp. 211–221.

108. James A. Craft, "Future Directions in Public Sector Labor Relations: A 2020 Perspective," *Journal of Labor Research* 24 (Fall 2003), pp. 543–558.

Transfer Instead of a Promotion

CASE STUDY 13-1
Background

At the Coral Gables VA Medical Center, the position for Gardener Leader PD#086550, WL-5003-08, Engineering & Construction Dept. FAC was posted with an opening date of June 12, 2006, and closing date of June 30, 2006. Mr. Mike Box, lead gardener at the U.S. Air Command in Miami, Florida, and Mr. James Mitchell, tractor operator at the Coral Gables VA Medical Center, were selected to be interviewed by a three-person panel. The panel ranked Mr. Box No. 1. Mr. Box was offered the position, and he accepted.

On September 15, 2006, Mr. Mitchell filed the following Grievance:

Employee's statement of grievance:

I am aggrieved due to violation of the following article of the Master Agreement:

Article 22—Merit Promotion

Disposition of Case:

The resolution I am seeking includes:

Upgrade to WL-8 salary or salary equivalent to the WL-8 in the WG pay scale.

In a letter dated October 6, 2006, Mr. Pat Moore, director, Facility Management Services, provided the Agency's response which was:

1. On September 19, 2006, I met with you and your Union Representative, Tom Ryan, to discuss the grievance regarding "violation of the following article of the Master Agreement: Article 22" you filed on September 15, 2006. This meeting was held in order to hear your grievance and give you an opportunity to present any information that would be relevant.

2. The HR Department has reviewed the recruitment action carefully in conjunction with pertinent VA staffing policies and procedures and Article 22 of the Master Agreement. They have determined that a procedural error was made when Mr. Box was referred for the gardener leader position. Mr. Box was a transfer candidate to a higher graded position. As such, he should have been in the third area of consideration for promotion candidates but had been referred along with the promotion candidates from the first area of consideration.

3. As a result of this error, you will be given priority consideration for the next promotion opportunity up to the pay rate of a WG-8 or WL-8 position for which you qualify and wish to be considered at this Medical Center. You will be provided with more detailed information about this in a separate memorandum from the HR Department.

On October 10, 2006, Mr. Mitchell appealed his Grievance. He wrote:

My grievance was not resolved to my satisfaction at Step 2. I am proceeding to Step 3 with my grievance.

On October 25, 2006, Mr. John Goodman, deputy director, provided the Agency's response to the Step 3 Grievance. He wrote:

1. I held a meeting with you and your representative, Tom Ryan, on October 17, 2006 to discuss your grievance regarding a violation of Article 22 of the Master Agreement between VA and Government Employees Union. Your requested resolution to be promoted to either the W-8 or WL-8 was also discussed.

2. As I stated in our meeting, I agree that Article 22 was violated. It was inappropriate for the selectee, a transfer candidate to a higher graded position from the third area of consideration, to have been referred for the position, when the vacancy announcement did not indicate that the area of consideration for promotion candidates was being expanded.

3. I have carefully considered all of the options we discussed in our meeting. You cannot be promoted to the WG-8 grade levels without there being a vacant position for which you qualify at one of those grades levels. At this time, there are no vacancies at either of those grade levels. In accordance with Section 13 of Article 22, when an employee fails to receive proper consideration for selection because of a procedural, regulatory, or program violation, the employee should be given priority consideration for a vacant position that leads to the same grade level as the vacancy for which proper consideration was not given. In your case, I support giving you priority consideration for any vacant position in the Federal Wage System up to the pay rate of a WL-8 position for which you qualify and wish to be considered at this Medical Center.

On October 31, 2006, Ms. John Harden, director, Human Resources Management Services, wrote the following letter to Mr. Mitchell:

1. Due to a procedural error, a promotion candidate from the third area of consideration was referred for the gardener leader, WL-5003-8, Vacancy No. TUS-06-FAC-088, when the vacancy announcement did not indicate that the area of consideration for promotion candidates was being expanded. In accordance with Section 13 of Article 22, when an employee fails to receive proper consideration for selection because of a procedural, regulatory, or program violation, the employee should be given priority consideration for a vacant position that leads to the same grade level as the vacancy for which proper consideration was not given. In your case, the deputy director supports giving you priority consideration for any vacant position in the Federal Wage System at this Medical Center up to the pay rate of WL-8 position for which you qualify and wish to be considered at this Medical Center.

2. The following are the procedures for exercising your right to priority consideration:

   a. You will need to continue to review the vacancy announcements posted on the official bulletin boards or on the VISN 7 Job Bank.

   b. Once you see a posted vacancy announcement for a position for which you are interested in exercising your priority considerations, you must notify in writing the HR staff member who is handling the recruitment for the position. In addition, you must submit all of the required application materials as stated in the posted vacancy announcement.

   c. If the position is determined to be an appropriate vacancy for which you may exercise your priority consideration (i.e., a vacancy for which you meet all qualification and eligibility requirements and does not exceed the WL-8 pay rate), you will be referred for the position prior to the evaluation of any other applicants. If the position is determined not to be an appropriate vacancy, you will still have priority consideration for the next appropriate vacancy at this Medical Center for which you are interested.

   d. The selecting official for the position will make a determination whether or not to select you for the position prior to evaluating other applicants for the position.

   e. HR will notify you of the selecting official's decision.

   f. There is no specific timeframe during which you must exercise your priority consideration. The exercising of your priority consideration does not preclude you from also filing an application through the regular application procedures.

3. If you have questions about the priority consideration process, please contact one of the HR Specialists in Staffing.

In a letter dated November 16, 2006, Mr. Tom Ryan, president, AFGE Local #131, appealed the Grievance to arbitration. He wrote:

> We are not satisfied with the resolution at Step 3 of the grievance filed on behalf of James Mitchell. This is to notify you that we are invoking arbitration in this case.

The Grievance was appealed to arbitration.

Issue

The parties agreed to the following:

> Whether there was a violation of Article 22 of the Master Agreement between the Department of Veterans Affairs and the Government Employees Union; in particular, Section 8, paragraph C and Section 12, paragraph D.

Also, the Agency submitted:

> Is priority consideration a proper remedy for a violation of Article 22, Section 8C2 when Management failed to identify the expanded area of promotion consideration in the internal vacancy announcement?

Relevant Provisions of the Agreement
Article 22—Merit Promotion
Section 7—Applicability of Noncompetitive Actions

D. Other Noncompetitive Actions:

    3. Transfer of a Federal employee or reinstatement of a former Federal employee (including conversion to reinstatement from a temporary appointment) to a position at the same or lower grade than the highest permanent grade held under a career or career-conditional appointment provided the candidate was not demoted or separated for personal cause from a higher grade and also provided that the position does not have known promotional potential to a grade higher than the highest permanent grade held.

    Section 8—Vacancy Announcements and Areas of Consideration

    B. Prior to considering candidates from outside the bargaining unit, the Employer agrees to first consider internal candidates for selection.

    C. Areas of Consideration:

    The areas of consideration will be:

    First—Facility-wide (including satellites) except:

1. This area may be made more narrow or expanded through mutual agreement.

2. Where evidence suggests that the area of consideration is not expected to produce at least three qualified candidates, it may be expanded. The vacancy announcement will identify the expanded area of consideration.

3. For VA Headquarters unit positions, GS-12 and above, the area of consideration may be expanded.

    However, in all cases, (1, 2, and 3 above), first and full consideration shall be given to any best qualified candidates within the facility (or more narrow area).

    Second—Any other promotion candidate or candidates required to compete from other VA facilities.

    Third—

1. Reassignments/demotions to positions with higher known promotion potential.

2. Reinstatements to positions at a higher grade or with higher known potential.

3. Transfers to positions at a higher grade or with higher known potential.

D. Consideration of VA employees as promotion or promotion-potential candidates outside the normal area of consideration for positions covered by this article will be considered as follows:

    The employee can submit an application and supporting attachments, designated on the form, to the appropriate Human Resources Management (HRM) Office. The applicant should indicate thereon the specific position or types of positions, and location(s) for which the employee wants to be considered. To ensure full consideration, employees should include on their applications information relevant to the assessment criteria for the position in which they may be interested. In order to be considered for a particular vacancy, the employees must have the form on file with the HRM Office prior to closing of the announcement.

    Section 12—Selection

    D. Management recognizes that it is important for maintaining high morale to try to select from within the facility when the candidates are equally qualified to those candidates available from outside sources. Thus, management will agree to look closely at the relative qualifications of candidates from outside and within and shall exercise good faith in the selection.

    Section 13—Priority Considerations

    A. Definition—For the purpose of this article, a priority consideration is the bona fide consideration for noncompetitive selection given to an employee as the result of a previous failure to properly consider the employee for selection because of procedural, regulatory, or program violation. Employees will receive one priority consideration for each instance of improper consideration.

    B. Processing—The procedures for processing a priority consideration shall be:

1. Employees will be notified in writing by the authorized management official of entitlement to each priority consideration. Such notice will advise employees that if a vacancy is announced and posted and the employee wishes to exercise their priority consideration, the employee should submit the necessary application to HRMS with a written request that they wish priority consideration for the vacancy.

2. Priority consideration is to be exercised by the selecting official at the option of the employee for an appropriate vacancy. An appropriate vacancy is one for which the employee is

interested, is eligible, and which leads to the same grade level as the vacancy for which proper consideration was not given.

3. Prior to the evaluation of other applicants, the name(s) of the employee(s) requesting to exercise priority consideration will be referred to the selecting official. The selecting official will make a determination on the request prior to evaluating other applicants.

4. The fact that the employee chooses to exercise a priority consideration does not preclude that employee from also filing an application through the regular posting process.

C. Union Notification—In order to assure compliance with this section, the Union will be furnished statistics on priority considerations granted and exercised and the results. Statistics will be kept and provided to the Union on a quarterly basis. The Union will also be notified in writing of each individual priority consideration completed.

Section 16—Union Review of Competitive Actions

A. The Union will be permitted to conduct audits of promotion packages for all bargaining unit positions when it has reason to believe a discrepancy exists or when requested to do so by an employee.

Positions of the Parties

The Union:

The Union contended there was willful neglect and manipulation of the U.S. Civil Service Merit System principles and relevant sections of the Master Agreement on the part of Management in selecting a candidate for the position of gardener leader. The Union focused on the following:

1. Did Management exercise good faith in its selection of a candidate for the position?

A. Did Management pretextually utilize non-competitive selection in an attempt to explain the selection of Mr. Box?

B. Did Management pretextually utilize the "leadership abilities" in order to justify their selection of Mr. Box?

When Mr. Mitchell found out that he was not selected and that an external candidate had been selected, he brought the issue to the attention of the Union. Mr. Mitchell believed that there was a discrepancy in the promotion process. The Union reviewed the promotion package in accordance with Article 22, Section 16, paragraph A. After

the package was reviewed, the Union informed Mr. Mitchell that it also believed there was a discrepancy. Mr. Mitchell felt that violations of the Master Agreement had occurred and decided to proceed with the filing of his Grievance. Mr. Pat Moore, the director for Facilities Management Services at the time, was the selecting official.

The Union felt that violations of Article 22, Section 8, Paragraph C and Section 12, Paragraph D had occurred. The Union felt that Mr. Mitchell was equally, if not more qualified, than Mr. Box. In Mr. Moore's response, he acknowledged that the only error was referring the external candidate from the third area of consideration. Mr. Box did not even fall into the third area of consideration (Article 22, Section 8, paragraph C) because Agency employees are not external candidates. This was the third error. No mention was made in Mr. Moore's response as to the qualifications of Mr. Mitchell as not being equal to Mr. Box's qualifications.

The Union stated that the Grievance was elevated to Step 3. Mr. Mitchell did not agree to the paltry sum of a $0.61 per hour raise. Ms. Smyth did not recount Mr. Goodman's remarks about "not wanting to go to arbitration" and "we just want to do what is fair." The Union did not recall her statements to the effect that there was "no reason to assume that Mr. Mitchell would have been selected," or that Mr. Goodman agreed with her statement. Ms. Smyth and Mr. Goodman stepped out into the hallway to talk privately at one point in the meeting, and these statements may have been made between the two of them. During the meeting, Mr. Ryan read the relevant portions of Article 22, Section 8, Paragraph C and Section 12, paragraph D. Mr. Mitchell offered to assume extra duties in order to be paid at the WG-8 level. He left the meeting feeling that there was good reason to believe that a satisfactory resolution would be offered. Upon receiving the response to Step 3, it was discovered that the same resolution (as previously offered in Step 2) was offered, namely "priority consideration."

The Union stated that Management argued that Mr. Box's appointment was a non-competitive appointment and claimed that Management only knew after he arrived that he had been promoted, rendering the "non-competitive" argument null and void. Non-competitive appointments in Mr. Box's case would have occurred only in the event of a transfer to a position of same or lower grade, as outlined in Article 22, Section 7, paragraph D.3. There was an e-mail between officials at Mr. Box's previous facility that showed that Management was aware of the fact that this was a promotion for Mr. Box at least by August 22. Management did not offer priority consideration at the time it was discovered that Mr. Box had been promoted in violation of Article 22, Section 7; thus this was the fourth error.

The Union claimed that at no time prior to arbitration did Management officials stress the issue of leadership ability as being the most important factor in their decision. Management officials who were responsible for recommending the hiring of Mr. Box added the "leadership ability" phrase. These officials pointedly either ignored or made light of Mr. Mitchell's leadership experience. Ms. Smyth attempted to prove Mr. Box's previous job "should have been rated a WL-8," but this is irrelevant in these proceedings. The fact remains that Mr. Box was not a WG-8 employee in a WG-8 job at another federal installation. It appears that the Human Resources specialist at Mr. Box's previous facility was just as clueless about his position as our specialists are. A job can be titled anything, but it doesn't change the grade.

The Union argued that Mr. Moore, as acting associate director, has recently offered to assist the Union in possibly resolving another Grievance matter if the Union would "drop" its case for James Mitchell. The Union has ethically chosen not to "Rob Peter to pay Paul." This case is a pure matter of justice and is not an item upon the auction block."

The Union argued that the director of facilities management, Mr. Paul Moore, was questioned about the size of the applicant pool. Moore stated that this was dependent upon the expressed qualifications of those within the pool at any given time. In other words, there are no minimum requirements for any number of applicants. The Union asked: "Why was it not ascertained that Mr. Mitchell, the only internal applicant, was best qualified for the position?

Why was it deemed necessary to seek applicants from outside the unit? What has it done to the employees of the Medical Center Facilities to witness one of their own shunned and bypassed, as has happened in so many instances heretofore? 'Priority Consideration' or not, it may be years, if ever, that another similar position will be available to Mr. Mitchell."

The Union asked: "How many procedural errors have to be committed before a rational observer is to believe that such a phenomenon is humanly impossible on a professional level, and is blatantly secondary to an intentional design?"
The Union concluded:

> The remedy being sought is salary equivalent to the WL-8 salary that Mr. Mitchell would have received had he been promoted. While we realize that two WL-8 jobs may not be possible due to regulations, Mr. Mitchell is still willing to take on added duties in his current position in order to justify a salary on the WG-8 pay scale equivalent to the salary he would have made had he been promoted to the WL-8 position.

The Agency:

The Agency stated that Article 22, Section 12D, of the Master Agreement states, "Management recognizes that it is important for maintaining high morale to try to select from within the facility when the candidates are equally qualified to those candidates available from outside sources. Thus, Management will agree to look closely at the relative qualifications from outside and within and shall exercise good faith in the selection."

The Agency claimed that it did not violate Article 22. Management examined closely the relative qualifications of the Grievant, Mr. Mitchell, and the external applicant, Mr. Box. Mr. Mitchell was not equally qualified to Mr. Box for the gardener leader position. Mr. Box had the most desirable qualifications, including demonstrated leadership experience and gardener/landscaping skills which he attained during his 14 years as a gardener leader at another large installation. Mr. Box's qualifications significantly exceeded the requirements of the gardener leader position at issue as he was experienced in performing duties, such as counseling employees, approving employees' leave requests, completing employees' performance evaluations, and procuring supplies and parts with a government credit card. Although these duties normally exceed the authority of work-leaders at the present facility and are usually assigned to supervisors, the fact that Mr. Box has this experience and skills made him an even greater asset to the organization.

While it is unusual for Mr. Box to have been assigned to the wage grade (WG) pay plan, instead of the wage leader (WL) pay plan in his former position of gardener leader with the U.S. Air Command; it is not true or supported, as the Union and one of its witnesses, Mr. Michal, contend, that Mr. Box was not a work-leader if he was not assigned to the WL pay plan. The duties and responsibilities that Mr. Box performed and documented in his application were verified by his previous supervisor and clearly indicate that he performed in a highly responsible leadership role. Dennis Benoit, human resources specialist with the Office of Civilian Personnel Southeast Branch, Department of Homeland Security, confirmed that Mr. Box was classified as a gardener leader, and had been classified as such at different grade levels since September 1992. The Agency claimed that Mr. Mitchell was a good worker, but has never occupied a gardener leader or related position. Although Mr. Mitchell had previous experience in leadership roles in the military a number of years ago and may have briefly performed some basic work leader functions on an intermittent basis during his employment at this facility, the recency and/or quality of his experience was significantly less than that of Mr. Box's experience.

The Agency argued that Management exercised "good faith" in its selection and selected the best qualified candidate for the position. Article 22 of the Master Agreement does not restrict Management's ability to consider other applicants or to expand the area of consideration or otherwise interfere with Management's rights to select from any appropriate source. Section 8C2 of Article 22 states, "Where evidence suggests that the area of consideration is not expected to produce at least three qualified candidates, it may be expanded. The vacancy announcement will identify the expanded area of consideration." The Agency claimed that it had sufficient evidence to expand the area of consideration. There was only one promotion candidate available for the position.

The Union officials stated that they had not been consulted nor had they agreed to an expansion to the area of consideration. In accordance with Section 8C2, there is no requirement for Management to consult or obtain agreement from expanding the Union before the area of consideration. If Management realized that Mr. Box was not a noncompetitive transfer candidate, but a promotion candidate at the time of his referral for the gardener leader position, Management would have reposted the internal merit promotion announcement, identified the expanded area of consideration, and then referred Mr. Box along with any additional qualified candidates who applied under the reposted announcement. The selecting official, Mr. Moore, testified that he would not have accepted only one applicant as his candidate pool for the position, but would have requested additional recruitment for the position. The fact that Management did not re-post an internal announcement with an expanded area of consideration prior to referring Mr. Box did not adversely affect Mr. Mitchell. Mr. Mitchell received bona fide promotion consideration for the position. The Agency stated that Management acknowledged that Section 8C2 was violated. In accordance with Section 13 of Article 22, priority consideration is the appropriate remedy for this type of procedural error and has been offered by Management to Mr. Mitchell, and the Grievance should be denied.

Questions

1. Which party has the burden of proof in this case? Which level of proof will be used?

2. Since the Priority Consideration under Article 22, Section 13 is included by the parties as a solution to a selection violation, is this priority selection the proper remedy? Why? Why not?

3. If there is a contract violation found and the arbitrator sustains Mr. Mitchell's Grievance, should he be promoted and receive back pay for the failure to promote him? Why? Why not?

4. You be the arbitrator. How will you rule? Give your reasoning.

Discharge of Postal Letter Carrier for Off-Duty Conduct

CASE STUDY 13-2
Background

This matter of arbitration stems from an indictment of Thomas Allen for one count of arson–first degree and ten counts of burglary in Quitman County, Mississippi, on March 28, 1999. In a letter dated March 30, 1999, Billy Como, postmaster, wrote:

> This is written notice that you have been removed from employment with the Postal Service. This action is being taken in accordance with Article 16 of the Agreement.
>
> There is reasonable cause to believe you have committed a crime for which a sentence of imprisonment may be imposed.
>
> Specifically, by the indictment dated March 28, 1999, you were indicted in the Superior Court of Quitman County for one count Arson–First Degree and ten counts of Burglary.
>
> These aforementioned charges are so egregious in nature that retaining you in postal employment would not be in the best interest of the Service.

In a letter dated April 9, 1999, Mr. Jesse G. Bolton, attorney for Mr. Allen, wrote to Walter E. Flatten, human resources manager:

> I have been asked to assist Mr. Allen in regard to his removal from the Postal Service.
>
> Although there has been an indictment of Mr. Allen by the Superior Court of Quitman County, MS, it is probable that the indictment has overstated the underlying facts and it is also possible that some or all of the charges could be dropped or minimized.
>
> The arraignment date in the case was set for March 28th, 1999, and this was suspended or continued on an indefinite basis.
>
> Mr. Allen is 47 years old and has never been charged with any criminal offense involving moral turpitude. He has only had one speeding ticket, in the year 1968, while in the service of the United States Air Force.
>
> His character and reputation in the community in which he lives are exceptional, and there is a reasonable possibility that a sentence of imprisonment will not be imposed. From the earliest days of the charges, restitution was made by the subjects and accepted by the affected party or parties. The hunting cabin for which the one count of arson was made, according to my information, was unoccupied at the time, and restitution for damage to that house has largely been accomplished by and through the replacement of the house and acceptance of the same by the owner. The only reason that rebuilding the cabin has been delayed is because the accused parties have been doing all the physical labor themselves.

On April 13, 1999, Mr. Allen filed the following Grievance:

1. Nature of Grievance: (Be specific: what, where, when, etc.)

    This is a Step 2 Appeal filed on behalf of Thomas Allen, a reg. carrier at the Marks, Mississippi, post office, from an adverse decision rendered at Step 1. Mr. Allen was issued a Notice of Removal on March 30, 1999 in accordance with Article 16 of the National Agreement. Mr. Allen received the letter on April 4, 1999.

2. Contract Violation: This action is a violation of Article 16 of the National Agreement.

3. Corrective Action Requested:

    The Union respectfully requests that the Notice of Removal be rescinded and the Grievant be made whole for all lost wages and benefits. The facts do not reveal reasonable cause to believe the Grievant is guilty.

On April 21, 1999, Mr. Flatten wrote the following letter to Mr. Bolton. This letter stated:

> In accordance with Article 1, Section 1 of the National Agreement, the Rural Carriers' Union is the exclusive bargaining representative for Mr. Allen. As such, I cannot grant your request for a summary outline of the evidence the Postal Service has obtained.
>
> In accordance with Article 15, Section 3, Step 1 of the National Agreement, Mr. Allen has a contractual right to file a grievance on any action taken by the Postal Service. In the event Mr. Allen exercises this right, he would be represented by the Rural Carriers' Union.

On the same date, Mr. Flatten wrote a letter to Mr. Allen. This letter stated:

> On April 4, 1999, you received a Notice of Removal from the Postal Service based on charges listed in indictment bill dated March 28, 1999. These charges included one count of Arson–First Degree and ten counts of Burglary.

You have not presented any rebuttal evidence on your behalf and the Postal Service has reason to believe that you are guilty of a crime for which a sentence of imprisonment may be imposed. Therefore, I find no basis to alter your removal.

You have the right to appeal this action in accordance with Article 15, Section 3 of the National Agreement within 14 days of your receipt of this decision.

In a letter dated May 22, 1999, Robert Thorne, state steward of the Rural Carriers' Union, appealed the Grievance. In a letter dated May 13, 1999, Mr. Statten, labor relations, gave Management's answer. Statten stated:

In the instant case management contends that the employee was given the benefit of the doubt. Since we have a copy of the indictment, we have reason to believe that the grievant may be guilty of a crime for which a sentence of imprisonment may be imposed. Arbitrators have consistently ruled that by having an indictment, we have met the burden of having reasonable cause to believe that the grievant is guilty of a crime for which a sentence of imprisonment may be imposed. The grievance is therefore denied.

On September 26, 1999, the Union appealed the Grievance to Arbitration.

Issue

Did the Postal Service violate Article 16 of the Agreement when it suspended Mr. Thomas Allen indefinitely? If so, what shall be the remedy?

Relevant Articles of the Agreement

Article 16—Discipline Procedure

Section 1. Statement of Principle

In the administration of this Article, a basic principle shall be that discipline should be corrective in nature, rather than punitive. No employee may be disciplined or discharged except for just cause such as, but not limited to, insubordination, pilferage, intoxication (drugs or alcohol), incompetence, failure to perform work as requested, violation of the terms of this Agreement, or failure to observe safety rules and regulations. Any such discipline or discharge shall be subject to the grievance-arbitration procedure provided for in this Agreement, which could result in reinstatement and restitution, including back pay.

When there is reasonable cause to believe an employee is guilty of a crime for which a sentence of imprisonment can be imposed, the advance notice requirement shall not apply and such an employee may be immediately removed from a pay status.

Position of the Parties

The Agency:

Management stated that Mr. Allen was indicted on one count of arson in the first degree and 10 counts of burglary by a Grand Jury of Quitman County, Mississippi, on March 28, 1999. Each of the eleven counts carries a maximum sentence of 20 years' imprisonment as provided by Mississippi State Law. The total would equate to 220 years' imprisonment for the alleged crimes if he were convicted and given the maximum sentence.

The Postal Service obtained a copy of this indictment and questioned Mr. Allen. After he was removed from employment, a letter from Mr. Jesse G. Bolton, attorney at law, on Allen's behalf was forwarded to Mr. Flatten. This letter advised Mr. Flatten of arguments he thought were pertinent to Allen's case and requested information relative to the case at hand. Mr. Flatten advised Mr. Bolton that the Union was the authorized bargaining agent recognized to represent Allen and that no documents would be forthcoming.

Management argued that arbitral precedent had established that the burden of proof does not encompass the normal "doctrine of just cause" in these types of cases. Arbitral precedent has established that the proof required in similar cases requires that Management has only to establish that it had reason to believe that Mr. Allen was guilty of a crime for which a sentence of imprisonment may be imposed. Arbitral precedent has established that the proof required comes in the form of an indictment by a grand jury composed of the defendant's peers. Management removed Allen based on an indictment for which the charges have not been denied.

Management stated that Billy Como, postmaster, had obtained a copy of the indictment on the advice of Labor Relations. Allen was given an opportunity to respond to the indictment and did not deny any of the charges. Mr. Como testified that he had copies of two newspaper articles from adjoining counties that pertained to Allen's situation before issuing him his removal notice. At no time did Allen ever profess his innocence of the charges.

Management explained that Mr. Allen and an accomplice burglarized a hunting cabin, took items, which according to a newspaper article, included a shotgun, and then burned down the cabin. The charge of first-degree arson indicates that the cabin was completely burned. The charges have yet to be dropped and are still pending.

The Grievant had his chance to convince Management that the charges were ill-founded, and he did not. Management argued that it has more than met its required burden of proof. Management proved that it had reason to believe that Allen was guilty of a crime for which a sentence of imprisonment may be imposed. Thus, removing the Grievant was done to protect the integrity of the Postal Service.

Management argued that it has been well established through arbitral precedent that a party cannot make its case at arbitration. The Union has attempted to do so by bringing in character witnesses who testified on the Grievant's behalf. The Union presented the testimony of Mr. Como about his reluctance to remove Allen; this should not be considered in the ninth hour. These had not been contentions during the processing of the Grievance. If these had, Management may have provided rebuttal testimony. Other members of the community who may not have known Allen as intimately as the witnesses could have offered their opinions about suspending someone who had been indicted on 10 counts of burglary, stealing a shotgun, and burning down someone's property. Management could have provided Mr. Jim Smith, a labor relations specialist, to testify as to what advice he gave Mr. Como and whether he had the authority to make or instruct Mr. Como in either of these official capacities.

Management claimed that the only argument raised in Allen's defense during the processing of this Grievance was that Allen had made restitution and that the charges levied against Allen would be dropped; however, the charges have not been dropped. Mr. Robert Thorne testified that at Step 2 of the Grievance Procedure,

the Union did not mention anything about the community wanting Allen returned to work. Nothing pertaining to these arguments was raised before arbitration.

Management argued that Allen's character and standing in the community are irrelevant and have nothing to do with the action that Management took. Management's action was based on an indictment that was instituted by a jury of his peers, based on evidence examined pertaining to his alleged involvement of a crime for which a sentence of imprisonment may be imposed. Management gave Allen ample time to offer a rebuttal to the charges or time to have the charges dropped. Management did not profess the guilt or innocence of the Grievant. The Mississippi Bureau of Investigators evidently still believes that other matters have yet to be resolved because Allen may still face possible other charges for the indictment.

Management stated that the overwhelming majority of Arbitrators have consistently ruled that the standard of proof required to be sustained by Management in cases where the issue in dispute had criminal connotations is "reasonable cause." Where Arbitrators sometimes use the words "just cause," the burden of proof still does not rise to the level of the traditional doctrine of just cause.

Management addressed the principle of "nexus." Pertinent considerations on the disposition of this case are as follows:

1. Whether there in fact was a reasonable basis to believe Allen guilty of the alleged crime.

2. Whether there was a sufficient relationship between the alleged crime and Allen's job as a carrier or such other jobs to which he might be assigned in accordance with his seniority that would warrant removal.

Management has stated consistently that, if the charges had been dropped and evidence furnished stating the same, Allen would have been returned to work. In regard to establishing a nexus, Allen is a rural letter carrier and meets the public each day. His job requires constant contact with the public.

Management stated that Marks is a small rural community with about 2,200 to 2,300 residents who know of the charges brought against Allen. Allen was indicted by a grand jury of his peers. Evidently, they were not persuaded that his former image should cloud their duty; others may not also. The Postal Service has a responsibility to maintain the public's confidence. The drafters of the National Agreement recognize this responsibility and provided language in the form of Article 16.

Management admitted that Mr. Como initially testified that he had been directed by Management to take this action and would not have done so if he had not been directed. On cross-examination, Como was asked for whom he worked. Under oath, he said his boss was Mr. Jimmy Whitestone, manager of Post Office Operations. Whitestone directed Como in the performance of his duties to do what was expected of him. Labor Relations has a responsibility to advise Management officials of the proper procedures to take in disciplinary matters that are consistent with postal policies and contractual procedures. Mr. Como stated that Labor Relations advised him on how this type of situation is normally handled. Mr. Como read Article 16 in the National Agreement, and he was satisfied that he complied with Article 16.

Mr. Como testified that he felt like Allen and other employees of the Marks Post Office were family. This explained Como's reluctance to remove Allen. Como stated that he had no problem upholding Postal Service's policies once it was explained to him that the action taken was consistent with the postal policy on how to handle situations wherein an employee had been indicted for a crime for which a sentence of imprisonment may be imposed. Como issued the removal based on the indictment after he gave Allen an opportunity to respond.

Mr. E. L. Elton, the mayor of Marks, testified that he was surprised when he learned that Allen was the accused; however, he did not condone these types of actions. Mr. Willie Andrews, a postal customer on Allen's route, testified that he was shocked when he learned that Allen was the accused. Andrews also did not condone these types of actions. These individuals knew Allen on an individual, personal basis. They stated that they were speaking on his behalf for personal reasons. Management asked: "What about those who do not know the Grievant on a personal basis? I wonder what they might say?"

Management stated that this Grievance should still be denied if this higher form of just cause is applied. Arbitrators have ruled consistently that the "reasonable cause" standard is the only proof required before removing an employee for criminal considerations. Arbitral jurisprudence has established the reason for the position taken by Management.

Management closed by stating:

> Management has stated consistently that management based its decision to remove the grievant on an indictment. Proof of the grievant's guilt, innocence, former standing in the community, or whether restitution has been made is irrelevant to this proceeding. What is relevant is, whether Management had substantive information in hand, prior to removing the grievant. Based on arbitral precedent, an indictment has been deemed to be the proper information on which one should base a decision of this nature.
>
> The Union offered, in the grievant's defense, that the charges either would be dropped or are in the process of being so. However, they have not. If they are dropped the grievant will be put back to work. If not, our final decision will be predicated on the outcome of his arbitration. The grievant still faces the possibility of criminal conviction with sentencing ranging from 1 to 220 years imprisonment.
>
> Whether the Arbitrator applies the reasonable cause or the just cause standard, Management has proven that the action taken was proper in accordance with Article 16 of the National Agreement. Management asks that the Arbitrator find the same and deny this grievance in its entirety.

The Union:

The Union claimed that Billy Como, postmaster and Allen's immediate supervisor, testified that it was not his decision to remove Thomas Allen. Como testified that he did not notify the Labor Relations office in Jackson, Mississippi, after Allen was indicted. The Labor Relations office was informed about the indictment by a relative of Mr. Flatten, who attended a church service in Marks. When the Labor Relations office learned of Mr. Allen's indictment, it directed Como to obtain a copy of the indictment and forward it to Jackson. Como dutifully obtained a copy of the indictment, which is public record.

Como testified that, if it had been up to him, he would not have removed Allen, and Allen would still be working. Como testified that he did not draft the notice of removal; he was told by the Labor Relations office to sign and deliver it to Allen. Como clearly indicated that this entire matter was handled by the Labor Relations office in Jackson, Mississippi.

The Union stated that where the imposition of discipline is not recommended or initiated by the employee's first-line supervisor, the discipline cannot stand. When higher-level authority does more than advise and when it takes over the decision-making role and eliminates the contractual responsibility of local supervision—and then concurs in its own decision—a substantive due process violation occurs. Such violation cannot be overlooked as a mere technicality. The bi-level disciplinary procedure provides a unique protection for employees. It cannot legitimately be disregarded, and the employer's neglect to follow it creates a breach of contractually established due-process requirements of such importance as to require that the resulting discipline be overturned.

The Union argued that the Postal Service did not have just cause to remove Thomas Allen. The record reflects that the Postal Service did not carry its burden in showing that just cause existed for Allen's removal. Throughout the Grievance Procedure and at the hearing, the Postal Service took the untenable position that, because Allen had been indicted, the Postal Service was privileged to remove him pursuant to Article 16 of the National Agreement. Article 16 only allows the Postal Service to immediately remove an employee from pay status when there is "reasonable cause to believe an employee is guilty of a crime for which a sentence of imprisonment can be imposed."

The Postal Service has taken the position that standards of just cause did not apply to this case, and the Postal Service made no serious efforts to show that just cause existed. The Postal Service is mistaken that "reasonable cause to believe" eliminates the overriding principle of Article 16 that all discipline must be for just cause.

The Union argued that the relationship between the "reasonable cause to believe" language and the "just cause" principles that underlie the party's discipline procedure was the subject of a previous arbitration decision. The Arbitrator stated that the parties appeared to recognize that in a criminal case, disciplinary action must be for "just cause."

The Union claimed that the Postal Service cannot carry its burden and show either that it had "reasonable cause to believe" or that it had just cause to remove Mr. Allen. The Postal Service essentially admitted that it did nothing but rely on the indictment in removing Mr. Allen. The Postal Service offered no evidence that an independent investigation of any kind was ever considered or carried out. Thus, it is difficult to see how the Postal Service could have had "reasonable cause to believe."

The Union contended that the charges contained in the indictment remain allegations and in no way prove that Mr. Allen is guilty of them. The Postal Service was provided with information from Mr. Allen's criminal attorney, who represented that "it is probable that the indictment has overstated the underlying facts, and it is also possible that some or all of the charges could be dropped or minimized." This information was obviously discounted by the Postal Service; no reasonable explanation has even been offered as to why. Any suggestion that this information was less valuable or could not be considered because it did not come from Mr. Allen's collective bargaining representative is ridiculous. This information goes directly to the question of "reasonable cause to believe." It is noteworthy that the Labor Relations office in Jackson had caused the removal letter to be issued to Mr. Allen within 48 hours of the issuance of the indictment, thus making it difficult, if not impossible, to engage in a meaningful investigation. The sequence of events is clear. The Labor Relations office in Jackson fortuitously learned of Mr. Allen's indictment and then required Postmaster Como to issue a notice of removal.

The Union stated that the Postal Service is required to demonstrate that Allen's alleged criminal conduct had a significant bearing on his ability to perform his job as a rural letter carrier. It is well established that the Postal Service may discipline an employee for off-duty misconduct only when it affects the employer–employee relationship. In this case, the Postal Service made little effort and was unable to show that Mr. Allen's indictment had any negative effect on the efficiency of the Postal Service's operations or its image.

Postmaster Como testified that Mr. Allen was a very good employee with no disciplinary history. There was no evidence that any of Allen's co-workers did not want to work with him or that any customers would object to his return to the route. Mr. Como testified that there was overwhelming community support for Allen. When the Postal Service attempted to remind Mr. Como of a conversation the day before the hearing at the Marks Post Office, where a female customer apparently had something negative to say about Allen, Mr. Como explained that the customer was not upset with Allen because of the indictment but because Allen was an outspoken supporter of the construction of a nearby medical waste incinerator. The female customer was one of the incinerator project's most vocal opponents. Thus, the Postal Service has been unable to produce a shred of evidence indicating any opposition to Allen's continued employment with the Postal Service. The Postal Service's own witness, Postmaster Como, suggested that there was overwhelming support for Allen.

The Postal Service introduced three newspaper articles to show that the Postal Service's image had been tarnished by the indictment. One article with the headline, "Ming: No arrests yet in arson case," made no mention of Allen. The other two articles indicated only that Allen had been indicted. Neither article made any mention that Allen was a postal employee. Marginal newspaper coverage, especially with no reference to the Postal Service, is meaningless. The newspaper clippings clearly were not considered when the Labor Relations office in Jackson issued the notice of removal. Mr. Como indicated that he had not sent the articles to the Labor Relations office at that time and that he had only shown them to the Management Advocate the day before the arbitration hearing.

The Postal Service was unable to show that Allen's indictment poses a threat to himself, his co-workers, or his customers or that the image of the Postal Service will be tarnished by his employment. Mr. Allen is well liked, the community wants him back on his route, and the image of the Postal Service will not suffer if he remains on the job.

The Union presented three witnesses on behalf of Mr. Allen. Mr. Willie Andrews, a psychiatric social worker and Quitman County Board of Education member, testified that Allen was an excellent carrier who often went beyond the call of duty. Andrews stated that he was happier with his mail service when Allen was carrying the route. Mr. Andrews had known Allen for 10 or 15 years and stated that he was shocked when he learned of

Allen's arrest and indictment. He indicated that the Postal Service's image would be improved if Allen were returned to work.

Mayor E.L. Elton testified that he has known Allen all of his life and was in disbelief when told that Allen had been indicted. Mr. Elton was a very satisfied customer and would like to see Allen return to his duties. As mayor, Mr. Elton was in a unique position to gauge community sentiment and testified credibly that there was "very strong support" for Allen's return to work. He believes that the image of the Postal Service will not be tarnished if Allen returns to work.

Ms. Hortense Balk, a lifelong Marks resident, owned the property that was destroyed in the fire that Allen is accused of intentionally setting. The destroyed property was a hunting cabin that Ms. Balk rented to hunters. Ms. Balk was shocked when she learned that Allen had been indicted because she had known Allen all of his life. Ms. Balk testified that she did not press charges against Allen and noted that Allen had already rebuilt the hunting cabin. Ms. Balk testified that he did such a great job that she thought about moving into it. The Union noted that the fact that Allen made restitution to Ms. Balk should not be construed as an admission that he is guilty of a crime for which a sentence of imprisonment can be imposed. If anything, Allen's gesture reflects favorably on his character. Despite the personal loss felt by Ms. Balk, she does not believe that Allen should lose his job.

The Postal Service did concede that if the indictment is dropped or Allen is acquitted in a trial, he will be returned to work immediately. The Postal Service must do its part in managing its employees and imposing discipline where appropriate. The Postal Service has ceded all judgment to the criminal process and to a district attorney who has sat on this indictment for almost ten months with no specific date set for trial. During these ten months, Mr. Allen has been an effective postal employee, and no other employee's performance has been affected.

The Union stated that the Postal Service had an affirmative duty to investigate on learning of the indictment but did not. The Postal Service is required in cases of alleged off-duty misconduct to determine whether that alleged misconduct would affect the integrity of the operations of the Postal Service. If the Postal Service had been able to offer credible testimony in this regard, it may have met its burden under just cause. However, the Postal Service made no efforts to address these issues.

The Union concluded:

> *The removal of Thomas Allen was not properly initiated by Mr. Allen's supervisor, Postmaster Como. Instead, the removal was forced on Postmaster Como by the Labor Relations office in Jackson. This is a clear violation of Article 16 of the National Agreement. There is no exception that allows the Postal Service to ignore the judgments and desires of its front line supervisors, even in cases where employees have been indicted for off-duty misconduct.*
>
> *The record reveals that the Postal Service failed to meet its burden to show that it had "reasonable cause to believe that Mr. Allen was guilty of a crime for which the sentence of imprisonment could be imposed." The Postal Service also failed to show that removal was for just cause.*
>
> *The record reflects that Thomas Allen is an Air Force veteran and an exemplary 18-year postal employee. He does not pose a threat to his postmaster, his co-workers, or his customers. Indeed, these people want him back on the route. The Postal Service never had and does not now have a valid reason for removing Allen.*
>
> *The Union requested that the Arbitrator hold the Postal Service to its contractual promise that all removals be supported by just cause. As none exists here, it is requested that the grievance be granted and that Mr. Allen be reinstated with full*

back pay with interest and benefits to the date of his removal.

Questions

1. Explain the principle of "nexus" as it applies to off-duty misconduct. How does it apply in this case?

2. Distinguish between arrests, indictments, and convictions.

3. How much weight should be given to the following:

   a. Mr. Como's testimony that he did not make the decision to remove Allen

   b. Ms. Balk's testimony that Mr. Allen has restored the burned cabin

   c. The district attorney has not taken the case to trial

   d. The support from Allen's customers and community support

   e. The effect on Allen's co-employees

4. Does it make any difference that Mr. Allen is employed in the public sector, instead of the private sector? Give your reasoning.

5. Did the Postal Service act appropriately when it did not grant Mr. Bolton's (attorney for Mr. Allen) request for information relevant to Mr. Allen's Grievance? If so, explain. If not, explain.

6. Should the Union be allowed to provide "character" witnesses on behalf of Mr. Allen? If so, why? If not, why not?

7. What level of proof should be used in this matter? Why?

8. Weigh the evidence and consider the burden of proof and the levels of proof. Be the arbitrator and support your decision.

CHAPTER 14

Labor Relations in Multinational Corporations and in Other Countries

With the development of a global economy, movement in Eastern Europe and China toward greater political democracy and market-oriented economies, and the reduction of trade and travel restrictions within the Western European and North American countries, the study of labor relations within multinational corporations (MNCs) and foreign countries becomes imperative to today's student. This chapter begins with a general discussion of the operations of MNCs in a global economy and unions' approaches and problems in dealing with MNCs. Concerns about globalization and free trade are addressed and principal characteristics of the labor relations systems of the major trading partners of the United States are also presented.

MULTINATIONAL CORPORATIONS AND TRANSNATIONAL COLLECTIVE BARGAINING

The growing interdependency among nations and the activities of **multinational corporations (MNCs)** have become important facets of economic life. Although multinational corporations have existed for more than 150 years, their numbers and share of world output have expanded their importance and visibility in recent years.

MNCs are now producing and marketing their products in several countries, instead of producing only at the home base and selling abroad, and they are doing so with increasing impact. Many of the largest MNCs have been labeled "stateless corporations" because a high percentage of their assets are outside their home country.

U.S. multinational corporations are enormous in size. As examples, the annual revenue of Wal-Mart ($351 billion in 2006) is greater than the gross national product of each of the following countries: Austria, Norway, and Poland. The annual revenues of Exxon Mobil ($347 billion) in 2006 were greater than both Belgium and Sweden.[1]

To indicate the enormousness of MNCs, the following are facts to consider:

- Of the top 100 MNCs in the world, 25 percent are corporations based in the United States, and the proportions of their overseas operations and employment are increasing. For example, IBM and McDonald's have more employees outside the United States than inside.[2]

- Of the largest 100 largest economies in the world, 53 are MNCs and 43 are countries.

- ExxonMobil, the world's largest company in terms of sales, has annual revenues greater than the gross national product (GNP) of all but 20 of the 220 nations in the world.

- The 1,000 largest MNCs account for 80 percent of the world's industrial production.

- In 1962, almost 60 percent of the largest MNCs were U.S. based; in 2004, of the largest 500 MNCs, only 185 were headquartered in the United States, 126 were headquartered in the European Union, and 108 were headquartered in Japan.

- MNCs and their subsidiaries employ 90 million total workers with 20 million in developing countries; they pay more than $1.5 trillion in wages, more than $1.2 trillion in taxes, and contribute 25 percent to the gross world product.[3]

The enormousness of international trade and investment activities may be measured by gross product, employment, exports and imports, and direct foreign investments. In 2004, the dollar gross product of U.S. affiliates of foreign companies was $515 billion; seven countries—Canada, France, Germany, Japan, the Netherlands, Switzerland, and the United Kingdom—accounted for more than three-fourths of the gross product. Manufacturing accounted for nearly half of this gross product and the U.S. affiliates of foreign companies had 5.2 million employees. Exports of goods by U.S. affiliates were $154 billion and imports were $378 billion.[4] Outlays by foreign direct investors to acquire or establish U.S. businesses amounted to $161.5 billion in 2006 (up from $91.4 billion in 2005).[5]

Because of their size, MNCs appear intimidating to smaller countries. For example, foreign firms account for almost half of Ireland's employment and two-thirds of its output. In some larger countries, concern has been raised about the economic influence of MNCs. In Australia, each of the ten largest industrial MNCs has annual sales larger than the government's tax revenue. Still, on average, MNCs employ two-thirds of the workforce in their home country and produce two-thirds of their output at home. In addition, MNCs usually pay better wages than their domestic counterparts and create jobs faster. For example, in poorer countries such as Turkey, wages paid by foreign firms are 124 percent above average, and their workforces have expanded by 11.5 percent per year, compared with 0.6 percent by local firms.[6]

Exchange rates have a great deal to do with the trade between countries and production within a specific country. The importance of fluctuating exchange rates is reflected in Exhibit 14.1, which shows the indexes of hourly compensation

Exhibit 14.1

Indexes of Hourly Compensation Costs for Production Workers in Manufacturing for 31 Countries or Areas, 1980–2005

Country or Area	Percentage of Workforce in Unions	Index (United States = 100)					Compensation Costs in 2003 U.S. Dollars	Compensation Costs in 2005 U.S. Dollars
		1980	1990	1998	2002	2005		
United States	12.0	100	100	100	100	100	$21.33	23.65
Canada	30.8	92	107	85	75	101	16.02	23.82
Brazil	35.4	14	17	—	12	17	2.57	4.09
Mexico	20.0	30	12	10	11	11	2.38	2.63
Australia	25.0	82	88	80	73	105	15.55	24.91
Hong Kong	18.0	15	22	29	27	24	5.83	5.65
Israel	56.0	39	57	65	57	53	12.14	12.42
Japan	18.7	57	87	97	88	92	18.83	21.76
Korea	11.2	0	28	27	43	57	9.16	13.56
New Zealand	34.3	54	56	50	42	63	8.89	14.97
Singapore	14.5	15	22	42	34	32	7.27	7.66
Taiwan	34.9	10	27	28	25	27	5.41	6.38
Austria	53.0	87	114	119	99	124	21.07	29.42
Czech Republic	—	—	—	—	18	26	—	6.11
Belgium	76.6	134	127	127	107	130	22.79	30.79
Denmark	75.2	111	126	122	114	150	24.23	35.47
Finland	85.0	84	139	116	101	135	21.56	31.93
France	8.3	91	103	98	82	104	17.42	24.63
Germany	25.0	125	144	151	118	140	25.08	33.00
Greece	30.0	38	45	48	—	—	—	—
Ireland	55.0	60	79	72	71	96	15.09	22.76
Italy	40.0	81	119	92	70	89	14.93	21.05
Luxembourg		122	110	—	89	117	18.91	27.68
Netherlands	28.0	123	125	111	102	135	21.74	31.81
Norway	65.8	119	147	128	128	166	27.40	39.14
Poland	—	—	—	—	15	19	—	4.54
Portugal	42.0	21	24	30	23	31	5.07	7.33
Spain	11.0	61	78	65	56	75	12.04	17.78
Sweden	78.0	127	141	119	95	121	20.18	28.73
Switzerland	32.4	113	139	131	113	129	24.11	30.50
United Kingdom	32.0	76	84	89	82	109	17.47	25.66

Note: Dash indicates data not available.

SOURCE: "International Labor Comparisons of Hourly Compensation Costs for Production Workers in Manufacturing," 2005, U.S. Department of Labor, *Foreign Labor Trends* (Washington, D.C.: U.S. Department of Labor, Bureau of International Labor Affairs, http://www.bls.gov/fls).

costs for production workers in manufacturing for 31 countries during periods from 1980 to 2005. In 2005, hourly compensation costs for manufacturing production workers in Belgium, Germany, Denmark, Norway, and Switzerland were 29 to 66 percent higher than those in the United States. Compensation costs were 109 percent of the U.S. figure in the United Kingdom, 105 percent in Australia, 75 percent in Spain, 24 percent in Hong Kong, 57 percent in Korea, 27 percent in Taiwan, and 11 percent in Mexico.

In 1980 Japan's hourly cost was 57 percent of that of the United States; however, it increased to 97 percent by 1998 and then dropped to 92 percent by 2002. In Germany in 1980, the cost was 25 percent higher than the United States; but by 1998 it rose to 151 percent of U.S. compensation costs and then fell to 140 percent by 2005.

Operating in different countries creates opportunities for MNCs to bypass protective tariffs by making parts in one country and assembling the final product in another. For example, the European Union accused Ricoh, a maker of photocopiers, of making 90 percent of its parts in Japan, doing the assembly work in the United States, and shipping products from the United States as U.S. exports. Such situations create other possibilities in the auto industry because England, France, and Italy limit the Japanese share of its auto market. With Japanese automakers locating in the United States, such issues provide challenges in trade between countries.[7]

U.S. MNCs prefer to locate production facilities in foreign countries that have a decentralized bargaining structure, like that in the United States. Labor relations features like union density and strike intensity do not appear to be nearly as important. The most important reason for locating production facilities are the national resources of the particular country.[8]

MNCs have the capacity to force concessions from unions by threatening to shift production to another country and essentially pit one group of employees against another. One automaker that operates a plant in Ohio sought to introduce new technology; the union resisted because the membership would lose jobs. The company then took a number of the union leaders to a new plant in Juarez, Mexico—just across the border from El Paso—showed them the technologies used in the plant, and said: "It is your choice. Either you concede what we are asking in terms of bargaining or the work that you do in Ohio will be transferred to Juarez. If you think this is an idle threat, this is the plant. This is the production process."[9]

Organized labor has been critical of the effect of U.S. MNCs on employment and labor relations for the following reasons:

- U.S. MNC's foreign investments deplete capital resources needed for domestic investment and undermine economic growth and new job creation at home.

- U.S. MNCs export U.S. technology to exploit low-cost foreign labor, depriving American employees of their rightful share of the rewards of technology.

- U.S. MNCs substitute imports from their affiliates in low-wage countries for American-made goods, thereby undermining the American wage standard, depressing economic conditions at home, and decreasing employment and payrolls.

- U.S. MNCs displace U.S. exports with foreign-produced goods from their foreign affiliates, thereby adversely affecting the U.S. trade balance.[10]

Foreign MNCs have grown rapidly and installed facilities in the United States. Unions have often viewed these MNCs with suspicion, but the management and employment practices tend to be more similar to those of home-based firms. The labor relations activities and decisions tend to be locally determined and highly decentralized. American unions have found that organizing foreign-based MNCs has been just as difficult as organizing a home-based company. In addition, the management of the various plants of foreign-based MNCs uses essentially the same tactics to keep unions out of the plant. These tactics include use of lawyers and management consultants, positive human resources management, consultation with employees on decisions, delays allowed under National Labor Relations Board procedures, and local politicians making statements to support the company. Unions essentially use the same organizing tactics, with the addition of negative publicity directed toward the foreign owners and appeals to American patriotism. With these counteractive tactics, the results of elections have not been significantly different—approximately 50 percent wins for the unions. Whenever American unions have contact with foreign-based unions, these contacts are generally of the information-sharing nature.[11]

In some cases, MNCs transplant their management practices into their foreign affiliates. In recent years, Japanese MNCs have been successful in making this transfer in unionized plants. In Fremont, California, New United Motor Manufacturing, Inc., the joint venture between General Motors and Toyota, was successful. The Fremont plant had one of the worst labor relations records in the United States, but its performance has become one of the best in the industry. Successes have also been noted by the Japanese-owned MNC Sumitomo Rubber, which purchased the Dunlop tire plant in Birmingham, England.

Japanese practices that have been introduced include elimination of executive perks, such as reserved parking places and separate cafeterias, work teams of six to eight members who rotate jobs, emphasis placed on trust between managers and employees, managers spending more time on the shop floor with the employees, regular meetings to inform employees about production and financial results of the company, wearing of "team" jackets by managers and employees, flexibility in job assignments, and holding each employee responsible for the quality of products produced.

Not all results of management transfer are positive, however, especially when sales decline, the foreign manager may not speak the local language, or employees may resist imposition of a new way of doing things. In Forrest City, Arkansas, for example, the Sanyo Company, maker of televisions and microwave ovens, had only one Japanese manager who spoke English, so every meeting required an interpreter. When sales lagged, the company demanded medical insurance cuts, changes in the seniority system, and the right to shift employees from job to job. The union reacted by striking for three weeks, and there were incidents of stone throwing, tire slashing, and charges of an attempted firebombing, resulting in 39 persons arrested.[12] The plant has since closed.

Unions particularly have difficulty dealing with MNCs for the following reasons:

1. *If a strike occurs,* the union cannot shut down the flow of financial resources to the struck plant. Operations of the MNCs in other countries continue to function and generate profits, which may relieve management of much pressure in negotiations and reduce the costs of the strike.

2. *MNCs have an internal source of products* from facilities in several countries and use this position as leverage to bargain down wages, benefits, and other conditions of employment (called **whipsawing** the union). If a strike occurs at one facility, the MNCs increase production at other units,

destroying the potency of the strike.[13] Many specific examples of whipsawing can be identified. General Motors (GM) was able to expand the work week from 37.5 hours to 40 hours by convincing the union in Germany that it must increase hours to retain competitiveness. GM has considered increasing its auto production in Brazil and Mexico as part of its wage concession demands, and when Canadian unions resisted wage concessions, GM considered shifting production back to the United States.

3. *MNCs with complex tiers of management* do not delegate authority to local management to make labor relations decisions, thereby complicating the negotiation process because unions do not know who is in charge.[14] Empirical evidence indicates that most unions have not encountered different behavior between domestic and foreign-owned MNCs, but there seems to be a wider variation in behavior among the MNCs than among single-nation corporations in terms of grievance settlement before arbitration, amount of local autonomy in negotiations, and difficulty in negotiating the first agreement.[15] However, because budget and investment decisions are made at the home office, local negotiations are certainly affected.

4. *MNCs shift profits to different facilities,* manipulate prices on internal transactions, and change marketing emphasis, confusing the unions in negotiations when they seek the facts necessary to address and resolve collective bargaining issues.

Because U.S. unions are accustomed to bargaining on ability to pay and are entitled to wage and financial information that allows them to conduct informed negotiations, they are frustrated when MNCs furnish only information that is required by law. Such information about MNCs locating plants in foreign countries and operating data on these plants may be refused by the MNCs with the approval of the NLRB.[16]

UNION APPROACHES TO MULTINATIONAL BARGAINING AND EMPLOYER REACTIONS

A primary motivator for American and foreign-based unions to seek transnational bargaining and to standardize labor conditions among the MNCs is to lessen competition from lower-wage areas and to protect their own standards—in other words, to take wages out of competition. To combat the power of the MNCs and to seek objectives that are mutually beneficial to the unions and their members, union leaders have tried two main approaches: (1) collective bargaining and (2) legislative enactment. Through collective bargaining, unions have either attempted to bargain directly with the MNCs or coordinate their bargaining activities with unions in other countries by sharing information and supporting one another's activities.

In 1995, the International Labor Organization (ILO) promulgated a group of Eight Fundamental Conventions. These conventions include the freedom of association and the right to collective bargaining, the abolition of forced labor, equality and elimination of discrimination, and elimination of child labor. Recognizing that colleges and universities spend $5 billion a year on logo clothing, student groups, consumer groups, and unions have pressured copyright logo owners to require that their brand name products only be produced and sold by firms that adhere to the ILO conventions. With the increased pressure on brand name companies, a ten year Multifibre Agreement was reached in 1994. This agreement meant that garments manufactured in Cambodia, Sri Lanka, Viet Nam, Indonesia, and Bangladesh would conform to the ILO conventions. The result has been to extend workplace protections to 30 million workers in those countries. Although the Multifibre Agreement ended in 2004, most U.S. garment manufacturers issued Codes of Conduct that subscribe to fair labor standards on their own.

As good as the garment arena has been in providing fair labor conditions, this segment represents only five percent of world trade. The manufacturers of tire rims, automobiles, microwaves, TV sets, and other consumer items make up the remaining 95 percent. Now China has lured U.S. factories to employ their billions of workers to produce products in China and sell their products in the United States where the products were once made by U.S. workers. For example, in one city, Guangdong, China, there are 1,400 shoe factories, and these factories export 5.6 billion pairs of shoes each year. China currently produces 60 percent of the world's furniture and more than half of its TVs, microwaves, refrigerators, toasters, and on and on. Although more and more companies are adopting Codes of Conduct because of the positive experience in the garment industry, it is still uncertain how much leverage these companies will have with the Chinese government and the government's All Chinese Trade Union Association (the only permitted union because independent unions are prohibited in China). As one recent visitor to a modern auto factory found, the law provides for a 40-hour work week, but the normal work week is 6 days/66 hours for employees who work "totally voluntary."[17]

Another mechanism for securing workers' rights has been the International Framework Agreements (IFAs). These IFAs are agreements on minimum labor standards negotiated between Global Union Federations and multinational corporations. These agreements usually include freedom of association, the right to collective bargaining, a formalized procedure for union representation, and a procedure for monitoring compliance with the agreement. By 2005, at least 30 IFAs have been negotiated. Although most of these agreements have been negotiated in Europe, one noteworthy IFA (with Chiquita Brands International to cover Latin America banana operations) has been negotiated in the United States.[18]

Unions, as well as some governments, have asserted that collective bargaining on a national basis has considerable limitations in facing MNCs. This assertion is based on the belief that MNCs have adopted global strategies, so a union acting alone within one nation cannot effectively respond. Likewise, some governments are uneasy about the fact that MNCs cannot easily be made accountable to any one country's economic and social policies. Moreover, there has been persistent fear that, if a union or government in one country acted without the support of unions or governments in other countries, it would risk transfer of operations by the MNC to a more hospitable nation.[19]

The creation of the European Union has led to a resurgence of interests in prospects of transnational collective bargaining. However, recent initiatives have taken the form of joint consultation and adherence to labor rights principles at a transnational level rather than true collective bargaining.

The aim of European trade unions is to achieve European-level collective bargaining. Despite the long recognized hurdles, there have been positive steps toward this end. First, the European Trade Union Confederation (ETUC) has become an effective voice for trade unions in the political arena and has the potential to become the spokesperson for European trade unions in collective bargaining. Second, new agreements between trade unions in two countries have been signed. These agreements grant reciprocal memberships to members in both unions and provide for cooperation between these unions in exchanging information, developing closer coordination with respect to European **works councils,** harmonization of pay demands, and training. Third, cross-national coordination of collective-bargaining strategies is taking place. Trade unions are agreeing on a common bargaining strategy and exchange of information. In 1998, trade unions in Germany, Netherlands, Belgium, and Luxembourg agreed to make pay demands reflect inflation and productivity gains and agreed to bargain on reducing the hours of work. The ETUC has established bargaining committees comprised of officials from European-level federations who are responsible for collective bargaining. The intent is to achieve some consistency in collective bargaining across national boundaries.[20]

In the past few years, the number of global agreements signed by MNCs has increased. These agreements between MNCs and international trade union organizations commit the companies to observing standards and principles in their operations worldwide. These principles generally relate to various aspects of worker rights, employment, and other areas of corporate social responsibility. There are 30 global agreements in place. Although the number is small, the companies involved include some of the world's largest, most high-profile and "internationalized" MNCs. For example, DaimlerChrysler employs 370,000 worldwide, Volkswagen employs 320,000, French retailer Carrefour employs 300,000, and Danish business services organization ISS employs 250,000. In total, the 30 companies including General Motors Europe that have signed the global agreements employ around 2.5 million.[21]

Most MNCs generally consider transnational labor relations a distant prospect and one that will not be lightly entertained by management. Part of management's opposition stems from the unions' potential for shutting down production internationally. Furthermore, transnational bargaining would introduce a tri-level structure of bargaining that would include multinational negotiations, followed by national, and then local. This additional level would increase the complexity of negotiations, as well as companies' vulnerability to strikes at the international level without a comparable reduction in vulnerability at the national and local levels.

In some cases, countries themselves are not encouraging investments by MNCs by using taxation policies, building limitations, requirements for local partners, the possibility of nationalization and expropriation of facilities, and the risks of political uncertainties to deter MNC investments. Less-developed countries seek additional investments by MNCs for economic stimulus to the countries' development, income, employment programs, and so on. MNCs find these countries attractive because of the low wage structure, tax incentives, and political guarantees. Such advantages are particularly appealing to the MNC that must operate in a very competitive product market. However, when unions press via transnational bargaining for improved wages, benefits, and working conditions—all socially desirable goals for the populace—they become a force running counter to the short-run national economic goals of the country. The economic boost MNCs can give a developing nation will not occur if firms fail to locate there. MNCs might well decide to avoid countries with the high wages and benefits that transnational bargaining has instituted.[22]

Obstacles for Unions in Bargaining with Multinational Corporations

American and foreign unions face formidable tasks in their efforts to arrange transnational bargaining because they must be successful in mediating and balancing the conflicting interests of different groups encompassed by the MNCs' employees, labor leaders, companies, and governments. In fact, unions them-selves provide some of the more important obstacles to transnational bargaining; however, these obstacles are not insurmountable. Only when these obstacles are overcome can attention be turned to external factors.

Differences in Labor Relations Laws

Legal systems for labor relations vary widely among countries. There are differ-ent methods for determining union representation, different union jurisdictions and structure, and differences in the scope of bargaining.[23]

Absence of a Central Authority

Unions lack strong, centralized decision-making authority on transnational affairs, and most national union leaders are reluctant to allow a transnational body to make decisions that affect their unions and members.

Cultural Differences

Among complicating factors are the differences in ideological and religious beliefs among, for example, free trade unions and socialist- or communist-linked unions. Such differences have made joint undertakings between unions in the free world and elsewhere almost impossible.

Lack of Coordination of Activities

Unions have not been very successful in coordinating their transnational bargain-ing, boycott, and strike activities. An excellent example occurred in the last major rubber strike of Goodyear, Uniroyal, B.F. Goodrich, and Firestone. Each had extensive overseas operations. Support for the U.S. strikes came from the Inter-national Federation of Chemical, Energy, Mining, and General Workers Unions (ICEM), which has affiliates in Europe, North America, and Japan. The ICEM Rubber Division approved a ban on overtime by employees of nonstruck compa-nies and a system of monitoring and preventing shipments to the United States. At the end of the strike—the longest rubber strike in U.S. history—the ICEM claimed that its efforts had had a significant effect on the bargaining outcome; how-ever, the facts seemed to contradict this claim. A study by Northrup and Rowan of the U.S. rubber workers' strike did not reveal a single instance of interference with tire shipments from Europe, Japan, or North America; in fact, they found that imports jumped substantially in anticipation of the strike and never fell below the prestrike level. Furthermore, even Canadian imports were significantly in-creased during the strike, reversing what had occurred several years before, when U.S. rubber workers refused to support a strike by Canadian rubber workers.[24]

Differing National Priorities

The economic, social, legal, and political differences among countries serve as yet another obstacle to transnational bargaining. Few, if any, countries would sub-vert their national needs to the interest of developing an international system of labor relations.

Employer Resistance

Employer resistance is less obvious than other obstacles at this time, mostly be-cause of the inability of the unions to overcome the other hurdles that they face. Once the initial hurdles are overcome, employers' opinions and attitudes concern-ing transnational collective bargaining will no doubt emerge, but in the meantime, MNCs may sit idly by until the unions are able to eliminate the initial hurdles.

Effects of Unions on Multinational Corporations

Research conducted mostly in European countries has indicated that unions have had little direct effect on investment and production allocation policies of MNCs. However, unions have had considerable indirect effect because labor relations with employers help shape the investment climate of a country. Thus far, MNCs rarely have been able to afford to switch production to other countries as a bargaining or union intimidation tactic because of the costs involved. MNCs no doubt would shift production to another country in cases where a labor dispute stops production and the move is economically and practically possible. However, such decisions are considerably limited because companies must have the necessary excess production capacity available and management must expect the labor dispute to last sufficiently long enough to justify a shift in production before it would be feasible.

Overall, little evidence exists of substantial negative effects of MNCs on labor relations in countries in which they operate. MNCs usually offer prevailing or superior wage standards and provide comparable working conditions for several reasons. The strengths of unions in the respective countries, the highly integrated and institutionalized nature of labor relations systems, and the socioeconomic and political climates of the countries have clearly constrained the potential for direct adverse effect.[25]

Conclusions and Predictions on Transnational Bargaining

Systematic investigations of transnational collective bargaining reveal that it does not yet exist in any realistic form and is not likely to occur in the immediate future. MNCs are generally opposed to it, and trade unions are not of a single mind on its desirability. Although there have been several cases of information exchange between multinational unions and a few instances of union–management consultation, only one trade union secretariat—the International Transport Workers Federation (ITF)—has actually negotiated an agreement (with shipping companies). Furthermore, only in the unique U.S.–Canadian and European Union environments do much transnational activities occur.

There has been no identifiable trend toward transnational collective bargaining by companies and unions in the United States, Europe, or Japan. Some believe that no effective transnational collective bargaining will occur in the near future. However, others believe that such collective bargaining is inevitable. It will probably develop first either in the European Union, North America, or Central America and deal initially with general topics, such as employment protection, investment policies, and codes of fair practices, before broadening into other bargaining topics.

GLOBALIZATION AND CONCERNS ABOUT FREE TRADE

The net effect of free trade—globalization—has been gains to consumers in lower prices, greater efficiency in the overall economy, and reduced poverty in developing nations. However, the distribution of the net benefits of free trade and globalization has been uneven. American jobs have been lost in major industries, such as the automobile, steel, textile, footwear, and consumer electronics, whereas jobs in the aircraft, computers, entertainment, and finance industries have increased.

There is concern in the United States, the European Union, and Australia that Ireland, South Africa, Russia, and India (where there are two million college graduates per year and 80 percent speak English) may do for the service sector what China has already done for manufacturing. (Japan has similar concerns about northern China, where Japanese is spoken.) In the near future, competition will come from the Philippines, where there are 300,000 college graduates each year who speak English and Malaysia. Also, any product can be manufactured in China less expensively than in the richer, high-wage countries. Now, it is just a matter of time before any service that can be electronically transmitted will be produced in India more cheaply. Cheaper communications allow companies to move back-office tasks such as data entry, call centers, and payroll processing to poorer countries, such as India, which has three huge advantages for companies: a large pool of well-educated young workers, low wages, and the use of the English language.[26]

One of the free trade agreements signed by the United States is the **North American Free Trade Agreement (NAFTA)**, an agreement between Canada, Mexico, and the United States that removed most barriers to trade and investments between these three countries. Many of the tariffs were eliminated immediately, and the others were to be phased out over 5 to 15 years. NAFTA was approved by Congress in 1993, signed by President Clinton in 1993, and took effect on January 1, 1994. Under NAFTA, three countries became a single, giant, integrated market of over 400 million people with $11.4 trillion worth of goods and services traded annually.

Since President George W. Bush's election, the United States has signed other free trade agreements, with countries such as Australia, Korea, and the Dominican Republic/Central America. These agreements are similar to NAFTA whereby tariffs on trade with the United States are eliminated. In addition, discussions began on a Free Trade Area of the Americas that would cover 34 North, Central, and South America countries, extend trade agreements similar to those under NAFTA, and cover a population of over 800 million.[27]

The promises of NAFTA included creation of new and better jobs, rising incomes, and economic growth acceleration to underdeveloped countries in Central America. Whereas there would be environmental challenges, extra resources would be made available to address those challenges. Economists have attempted to identify the effects of NAFTA on the economies of the United States, Canada, and Mexico. After 13 years, there has been expansion in trade and foreign investment; in fact, U.S. exports to and imports from Canada and Mexico now account for about one-third of U.S. trade (up from one-fourth in 1990). However, there has been a contraction in manufacturing employment in the United States and economic stagnation in Mexico.

In fact, Mexico wages have declined relative to U.S. manufacturing wages (see Exhibit 14.1). In Mexico, productivity rates have improved; however, real wages have risen only slightly. In several areas of the agricultural sector, there has been a near disaster for most farmers, who have to compete with America's government-subsidized products, such as corn. Up to 90 percent of the heads of families in some communities now spend at least six months per year working in the United States and Canada where they earn in four months the amount they would earn in Mexico in an entire year. Mexican producers of horticultural products, fresh vegetables, and fresh fruits have nearly doubled their exports to the United States. Sadly, successive Mexican governments have failed to deal with structural problems of corruption, poor education, red tape, crumbling infrastructure, lack of credit, and an inadequate tax base.[28]

Since the 1990s, about 600,000 Mexican farm jobs have been lost due to lower import barriers for beans, apples, grapes, and other crops. In 2010, tariffs on imported corn will be eliminated, and loss of jobs will increase. These job losses in agriculture have fueled migration into urban areas, where 80 percent of the population now resides. Migration to the cities is much faster than the rate of new job creation. Investments encouraged by NAFTA have produced 300,000 jobs, mostly in the northern cities. However, since a million people enter the labor force each year in Mexico, there is an annual deficit of 700,000 jobs. As a result, 40 percent of the labor force—about 12 million workers—do not have stable employment. Most of them work in the informal sector as street vendors, maids, and short-term workers—jobs that provide no social security protections. As a result, the loss of rural jobs in Mexico has swelled the ranks of undocumented Mexican workers in the United States.

While the value of exports was ten times greater than in 1990, the total compensation of these workers in Mexico is still nearly one-tenth of what similar workers in the United States earn. Factories continue to use outdated equipment and inefficient work systems, and technological improvements have been concentrated in the export-oriented plants owned by global corporations, particularly in the electronics and automobile industries. Managers realize that they must adapt to new work arrangements and improve the skills of their employees; however, only a few companies, usually foreign-owned, have introduced quality control methods and workplace systems that promote efficiency or provide formal training for employees. Until changes are implemented, Mexican workers will see few gains from free trade.[29]

Along the border with the United States, the number of *maquiladoras* plants (assembly plants for export using imported parts and components) rose 67 percent to 3,655 during the first seven years after NAFTA was enacted in 1993. However since 2000, more than 850 have shut down and employment is down more than 20 percent from its peak of 1.3 million. Companies like Delphi are courted by China with tax incentives, low wages (assembly workers earn $0.57 per hour), worker training, and access to the latest technology.[30]

One disputed study estimated that 110,000 jobs per year have been lost in the United States due to NAFTA; however, the United States generates an average of more than two million jobs per year, and a great majority of these new jobs pay above the median wage. In Canada, there were initial concerns about the flight of low-skilled manufacturing jobs to Mexico and a depressing effect on the Canadian tax base; however, unemployment rates were 11 percent in 1990 and were seven percent in 2000, and Canada has actually experienced a budget surplus. The end result is that NAFTA did not achieve as much as the politicians promised, but neither was there the "giant sucking sound" of work moving south that presidential candidate Ross Perot predicted.[31]

North American Agreement on Labor Cooperation (NAALC)

The North American Free Trade Agreement provided several side agreements that were designed to protect employees and the environment. The North American Agreement on Labor Cooperation (NAALC), one of the two side agreements, commits the United States, Canada, and Mexico to implement, enforce, and improve labor principles through national legislation and institutions. Its objectives are to be furthered by intergovernmental cooperation and by a procedure established to resolve complaints based on a monitoring system and a series of steps to resolve unsettled disputes (up to arbitration). Two dozen complaints (7 against the United States; 2 against Canada; 15 against Mexico) have been submitted. These complaints included infringements on the right to freedom of association, charges of employment discrimination, and occupational health and safety violations. Thus far, the NAALC has failed because the three countries disagree on its aims. Canada and Mexico consider the NAALC a way to achieve greater intergovernmental cooperation; the United States focuses on the dispute-resolution mechanisms. As a result, limited success has been achieved on either front because the parties seldom engage in active cooperation and are reluctant to use the conflict resolution mechanisms.[32]

Thus far, the NAALC has fallen far short of the expectations of Canadian and U.S. labor organizations. First, it does not offer remedies to workers whose legal rights have been violated. Second, it is procedurally difficult to sanction NAFTA governments that fail to enforce their own labor laws and violate the NAALC's 11 labor principles (see Exhibit 14.2). Whereas arbitration offers sanctions, the procedures are cumbersome, and only occupational safety and health, child labor, and minimum wage issues may be arbitrated. Core labor rights of freedom of association, bargaining collectively, and striking are not subjects for arbitration. So far, no arbitration panel has been called into service. Although the NAALC has not met expectations, it has provided an important education and research role. Trade unions have publicized abuses for all to see and have brought together cross-border coalitions among unions that would have otherwise not been formed. Of the 24 union submissions of alleged violations, four were brought to an equitable resolution after widespread negative publicity or threat of negative publicity. The conclusion of one study is:

> *The labor law side agreement is withering as an effective labor law enforcement and MNC compliance strategy. To sustain as an institution designed in part to motivate labor law enforcement and business compliance with labor policy, the remedy and penalty aspects of the NAALC will need to be revisited.*[33]

Jon Hiatt of the AFL-CIO concluded that the case history of NAALC has indicated that, even "when workers win, they still lose." He concluded that no workers have been reinstated in any NAALC cases, there have been no concrete remedies ordered, and no financial sanctions imposed. In fact, he concluded that corporate or government behavior has changed very little as a result of any cases brought under the NAALC. Hiatt recommends several specific actions:

- The NAALC, instead of being a side agreement, should be made a part of NAFTA, which does not address worker rights.

- All 11 principles of worker rights covered by NAALC (see Exhibit 14.2) should be subject to final and binding dispute resolution and to possible sanctions.

Exhibit 14.2

Eleven Principles of the North American Agreement on Labor Cooperation

1. Freedom of association and protection of the right to organize
2. Right to bargain collectively
3. Right to strike
4. Prohibition of forced labor
5. Labor protection for children and young persons
6. Minimum employment standards, such as minimum wages and overtime pay
7. Elimination of employment discrimination
8. Equal pay for women and men
9. Prevention of occupational injuries and illnesses
10. Compensation in cases of occupational injuries and illnesses
11. Protection of migrant workers

SOURCE: http://www.mac.doc.gov/nafta/3006.htm (December 15, 2003).

- The NAALC should address the need to raise a country's labor standards where inadequate, not just the obligation to adhere to a country's existing laws.

- The time frame for dispute resolution should be shortened.

- Where a dispute involves an allegation that a company has violated the law, that company should be required to participate in the hearing.[34]

Another assessment of the NAALC found five general trends. First, most of the alleged violations of the NAALC side agreements have involved lack of or improper enforcement of labor laws in Mexico. Second, labor unions and human rights groups in one of the NAFTA countries are more likely to file the complaint in their own country against another country. Third, most of the complaints allege violations of workers' rights to organize labor unions in Mexico, where independent unions have tried to organize workers. Fourth, the submission process has resulted only in conferences, seminars, and public reports. While these are not effective remedies, employers' desire to avoid public attention has facilitated resolution in those cases where the submissions were voluntarily withdrawn. Fifth, the dispute resolution procedure has provided a platform for those parties who want to raise concerns about the enforcement procedures in the NAFTA member countries.[35]

UNIONS IN OTHER COUNTRIES

With the growing interdependency among nations, major improvements in communication and travel between countries, and the increasing role of MNCs, the need to learn more about labor relations systems in other parts of the world is imperative. Books have been written about many of the specific topics in this chapter, so no attempt is made to present detailed descriptions or analyses of labor relations systems in the countries mentioned. This section presents unique and interesting features of a variety of countries with the hope of encouraging readers to pursue more thorough investigation further. The chapter's coverage ranges from the developing countries of Central and South America to the countries nearest our borders—Mexico and Canada—to the major trading partners of the United States such as Japan and the Western European countries. The extent of discussion of each country's labor relations system is determined by its proximity to the United States; its trade, economic, and political relationships with the United States; and its uniqueness among the world's labor relations systems.

Many U.S. residents tend to view the rest of the world in terms of their own patterns of living. The fact is that virtually no country has a labor relations system like ours. One example of the differences between countries is the degree of employee protection against termination without cause. In the United States, only 20 percent of employees have such protection. In other words, the majority of American employees can be terminated from their employment without any justification unless termination is a violation of a contractual agreement, such as a collective bargaining agreement, or a law. As shown in Exhibit 14.3, 50 percent of Canadian employees are protected, and 90 percent of employees in Australia and the United Kingdom are protected. In Belgium, France, Germany, Italy, and Spain, 100 percent of employees are protected against termination without cause. As discussed in Chapter 12, there are basic principles for terminating employees for cause.[36]

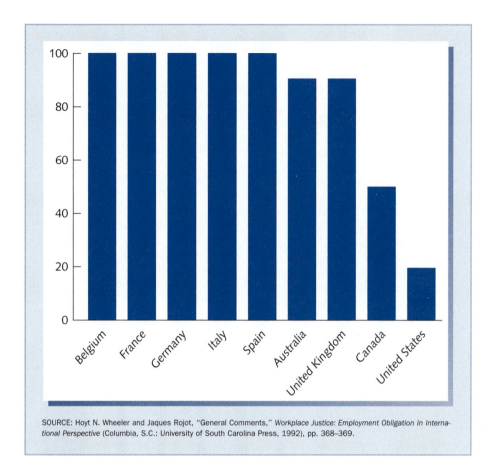

Exhibit 14.3

Percentage of the Labor Force That Is Protected against Termination without Cause

SOURCE: Hoyt N. Wheeler and Jaques Rojot, "General Comments," *Workplace Justice: Employment Obligation in International Perspective* (Columbia, S.C.: University of South Carolina Press, 1992), pp. 368–369.

Canada has several major departures from typical U.S. labor relations practices. Unions of Europe have much closer ties to political parties; Japanese unions are organized on the enterprise level; and Central American unions are split along ideological lines. By contrast, the U.S. labor relations system is based on majority rule, exclusive representation for bargaining agents, and political independence. Exhibit 14.4 presents an overview of distinguishing features of foreign labor relations systems; the following discussion briefly explains these systems.

Another distinguishing feature between labor relations in the United States and that of other countries of the world is the percentage of employees who are union members. Exhibit 14.5 shows that the United States is classified among the least unionized countries, such as France and Spain. Denmark, Belgium, Finland, and Sweden are the most unionized countries, with 75 percent or more of the workforce being unionized.

Canada

Canada's labor relations system is affected by a number of variables: foreign influences, climate, natural resources, and two major linguistic and cultural groups. Its economy is subject to cyclical fluctuations resulting from harsh winters, seasonality of its industries, and foreign influences (mostly the United States). In addition, Canada's geographical spread, labor laws within the provinces, regional concentration of resources and production have led to decentralized and fragmented collective bargaining. The penetration of U.S. corporations into Canada has had a significant effect on Canadian labor relations because many major decisions still

Exhibit 14.4

Overview of Distinguishing Features of U.S. and Foreign Labor Relations Systems

United States
Exclusive bargaining representation
Majority rule
Political independence

Canada
Influence by unions and companies from United States
Two major linguistic and cultural groups
Decentralized and fragmented collective bargaining
Legal influence within provinces

Central and South America
Wide variation in the degree of sophistication in labor relations systems
Close connection between trade unions and political parties
Voluminous labor codes and government regulations that cover wages and terms of employment
Negotiations predominantly at plant level only

Western Europe
Exclusive bargaining representation nonexistent
Much negotiation between employer association and union confederation with individual bargaining under the resulting agreement
Many fringe benefits established by law
Worker participation mandated in many countries

Japan
Labor–management consultation/teamwork
Lifetime employment in large firms
Enterprise unions
Wage system with much weight on seniority

Australia
Decentralized bargaining
Nonunion bargaining
Unfair dismissal law

Eastern Europe
Little collective bargaining
No labor agreements

are made in the United States. The French- and English-speaking division of Canada has produced two distinct labor movements. Relationships between management, which is primarily unilingually English-speaking, and the predominantly French-speaking workforce have not been ideal.[37] In 1995 the citizens of Quebec, Canada's predominantly French-speaking province, voted by a slight margin to remain in Canada. Of the four largest labor unions in Canada, three are in the public sector. Half of the largest 16 unions have their headquarters in the United States. The Canadian Autoworkers and the Canadian Paperworkers are two of the largest unions and were formerly affiliated with U.S.-based unions.

Although the public-sector unions continue to represent 75 percent of public employees, private-sector unions have begun to recruit members outside their traditional jurisdictions to offset their decline in membership. The Steelworkers now represent many hotel and restaurant employees, and the Canadian Autoworkers represent fishermen on the East Coast of Canada. In addition, some significant mergers have taken place, such as the Canadian Retail, Wholesale Union (formerly part of a U.S. union) with the Canadian Autoworkers.[38]

In 1956, union membership in Canada and the United States was about one-third of the labor force. Union membership in Canada has remained at about the same strength, whereas the United States has faced serious membership erosion. In 2006, there were 4.4 million union members in Canada, an increase of 60,000 since 2005. The union density was 30.8 percent (25.2 percent of the private workforce), about two and one-half times the union membership percent in the United States. Seventy-two percent of the union members belonged to unions that were affiliated with the Canadian Labour Congress, the major union federation in Canada.[39]

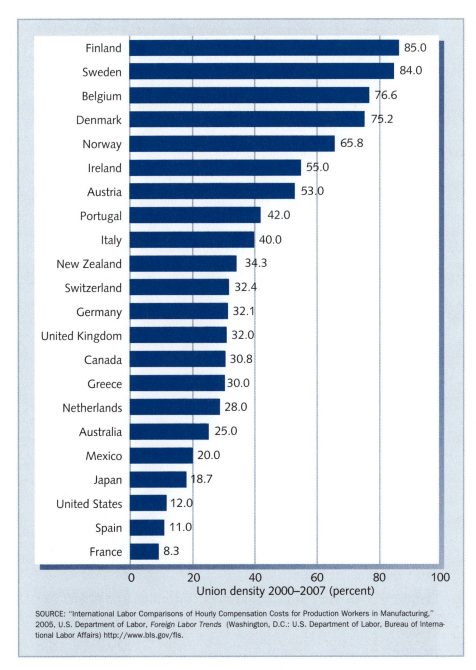

Exhibit 14.5
Comparison of Worldwide
Union Density: 2000–2007

SOURCE: "International Labor Comparisons of Hourly Compensation Costs for Production Workers in Manufacturing," 2005, U.S. Department of Labor, *Foreign Labor Trends* (Washington, D.C.: U.S. Department of Labor, Bureau of International Labor Affairs) http://www.bls.gov/fls.

The differences between the membership success of Canadian unions and U.S. unions can be attributed to several interrelated factors: favorable Canadian labor laws and court decisions; more aggressive union organizing; less employer opposition, and supportive public policy. Favorable labor laws contribute to union organizing and success (a rate of about 70 percent in Canada, compared with around 58 percent in the United States) Canadian legal restrictions on employer opposition to unions also contribute toward a higher union density (30.8 percent in Canada versus 12.1 percent in the United States).

In addition to supportive pro-collective bargaining legislation, the Supreme Court of Canada in 2001 proclaimed that all Canadian workers possessed the constitutional right to organize, to pick their leaders, to devise a program to advance their interests, and to represent these interests to their employers. The Supreme Court further recommended firmly that employers have a constitutional duty to acknowledge and work with the employees' representatives in order to address workplace issues.[40]

As a result of greater union membership, unions are able to mobilize greater resources (such as financial resources, union staff, member participation and voting) to achieve greater effectiveness in terms of organizing and bargaining successes and to have greater political influence.

Since 1980, unions in the United States have been unable to recruit sufficient members to offset job losses, and union membership has fallen to 12.1 percent of the total labor force. At the same time, Canadian unions have gained 700,000 members, an increase of 20 percent.[41] Unions in Canada have used their strength to achieve major bargaining gains and have wielded significant political influence, while the U.S. unions have been placed in a defensive bargaining and political position.

Some other factors that contribute to greater Canadian union density are:

- Canadian unions have exhibited greater activity in recruiting new members and have assigned a higher priority to organizing than in the United States.

- Faster union certification procedures and fewer legal procedural delays than in the United States.

- Greater job protection for striking workers, and the use of replacement workers during strikes and lockouts is restricted in some provinces.

- There is widespread use of card-based certification rather than secret-ballot votes in some of the largest jurisdictions.

- Some Canadian labor boards in the provinces have greater remedial powers, for example, to certify the union without a vote or to order a first collective bargaining agreement.

- In some provinces, there is arbitration available for the first contract.

- Employer campaigning activities during union representation attempts are more restrictive, e.g. more restrictions on the content of employer captive audience speeches.

- There is no such thing as a right-to-work law in Canada; in fact, 7 of 11 provinces in Canada have made the agency shop (see Chapter 4) the statutory minimum.[42]

- The scope of bargaining is greater because the distinction between mandatory and voluntary subjects for collective bargaining has never been adopted in Canada. Therefore, all subjects except those which are illegal may be negotiated.

In 1991 the Supreme Court of Canada rendered a ruling opposite to the *Beck* decision in the United States (see Chapter 4). Unions can use membership dues for activities not directly related to collective bargaining, including political contributions. If the decision had gone the other way, unions would have seen their political activities thwarted by lack of funds and a restriction on their support for the New Democratic Party (NDP).[43]

In 2007, the U.S. House of Representatives passed the Employee Free Choice Act (the U.S. Senate failed to pass the Act) which would have allowed card checks for employees to gain union recognition. Canada has had much experience with card checks in union recognition campaigns. In Canada, five provinces require secret ballot elections and five provinces allow card-check union recognition. The province of British Columbia allowed card checks until 1984; then from 1984 to 1992, secret ballot elections were required. In 1992, card checks were allowed again. During the period when card checks were allowed, the union success rate was 91 percent; when secret ballot elections were required, the success rate was only 73 percent. Also, during the period where card checks were allowed, there was an average of 531 union organizing drives per year; during the period when secret ballot elections were required, the average was only 242.[44]

Mexico, Central America, and South America

Collective bargaining in Central and South America is less extensive and sophisticated than corresponding activities in the United States; however, the number of labor agreements has been increasing. About one-fifth of the employees are covered by labor agreements in Mexico, Venezuela, and Argentina—much more than in the United States. This amount reflects more of a government extension of contract terms than actual industry-wide bargaining patterns. The extent of development of collective bargaining may be illustrated in three categories:

1. The advanced group, as exemplified in parts of Mexico and Argentina.
2. A much larger middle group in which bargaining ranges from advanced collective bargaining with larger firms to very simple or no bargaining in smaller firms, as in Chile and Brazil.
3. A large third group in which collective bargaining is not widespread, as in Costa Rica, Ecuador, and Nicaragua.

Mexico is the second largest trading partner of the United States and has the twelfth largest economy in the world. Mexico has paid a high price for its stability in terms of corruption and lack of democratic processes due to decades of one-party rule by the Institutional Revolutionary Party (PRI). However, Mexico is a model of stability when compared to many Latin American countries. Union membership in Mexico has declined from over 30 percent in 1984 to 20 percent in 2000. However, because of the variety of unions in Mexico, sometimes it is difficult to determine whether a worker is really a union member. Confounding the determination of the number of union members is the presence of "company unions" (ghost unions) which negotiate protection contracts with employers whereby the union collects dues from workers but protects the company from organizational campaigns by other unions. By allowing the less intrusive "ghost unions" to organize, the company is not subject to organizing campaigns from legitimate unions.

Most unions are in confederations that have traditionally been in alliance with the PRI. The largest is the Confederation of Mexican Workers (CTM), which claims 5.5 million members. The Revolutionary Workers and Peasants Confederation claims between two and four million. Teachers are the most heavily unionized at 65 percent, and the dominant teachers union is the National Union of Education Workers which is affiliated with the independent Democratic Federation of Unions of Public Servants.[45]

The traditional labor union centrals have long sacrificed freedom of action to gain political influence and position. However, the importance of political influence to workers has declined as the economy has decentralized and privatized. Today, unions must obtain more for workers through enterprise collective bargaining and less through influence with the government. With NAFTA and facing international competition, unions and employers are finding it increasingly necessary to work together to improve productivity, competitiveness, and quality if companies and jobs are to survive and profits and wages are to increase.

Mexico has undergone profound changes over the last 20 years. It has changed from a closed, import-substitution economy to become part of the open, market economy. It has joined the Organization for Economic Cooperation and Development (OECD) and entered into the North American Free Trade Agreement (NAFTA) in 1994. Mexico is experiencing a dramatic political change from a system dominated by the Institutional Revolutionary Party (PRI) for more than 70 years with strong worker and peasant sectors and featuring leftist, nationalist, and often anti-American rhetoric, to a more multi-party, democratic system, with a closer relationship with the United States.

Of the over 40 million in the economically active population, about 39 percent are employed in the formal sector. These jobs are covered by social security and related programs funded through employer and smaller worker contributions (medical care, small pension, and IRA-like compulsory retirement savings plan, and a housing loan fund). The formal sector workers also receive profit sharing. Another 20 percent of the economically active population works in tiny enterprises in the semiformal sector, where few are covered by social security. The remaining 40 plus percent are marginally underemployed or self-employed in the informal sector.

Mexico has comprehensive, progressive labor laws; however, there are many enforcement deficiencies. Its constitution and laws provide extensive rights and protections for labor and favor union organization. Mexico has ratified 78 International Labor Organization (ILO) Conventions, and 68 are currently in force. The legal protections for union organization also can unintentionally protect and facilitate racketeering, sweetheart protection contracts, and undemocratic practices in many unions. These practices have been fairly widespread, but not universal. The CTM has recognized the need to address corrupt practices and has agreed to promote changes that would lead to the elimination of protection contracts. Nevertheless, such contracts are with respected businesses and more than 50 percent of all labor contracts contain sweetheart protection clauses.[46]

One of the most important developments in the past decade has been the Mexican Supreme Court's decision on May 11, 1999, which recognized the legitimacy of independent unions that were not affiliated with the CTM. This decision allows employee groups of 20 or more the right to form unions on their own. To obtain protection under the law and to conduct collective bargaining, the unions are required to register with the Secretary of Labor and Social Welfare. However, the government has been willing to deny some new union registrations, and this denial has become a weapon to be used to prevent the more activist independent unions from representing workers. In addition, labor laws in Mexico permit exclusion clauses, which allows for restrictions on hiring (essentially a closed shop [see Chapter 4] that requires potential employees to become union members before they can be employed. Thus, the "ghost unions eliminate") can control jobs of potential employees.[47]

The Mexican Constitution and the Federal Labor Law guarantee the right to strike; however, a six to ten days' notice is required, followed by government mediation. If a strike is ruled nonexistent or illicit, employees must remain at work, return to work within 24 hours, or face dismissal. If the strike is ruled legal, the company must shut down totally, management may not enter the premises until the strike is over and striker replacements may not be hired. In the administration of these laws, unions have accused government authorities of stretching the legal requirements to rule that strikes are nonexistent or illicit so that they can prevent potentially damaging strikes.

Under Mexican law, closed shops are allowed in collective bargaining agreements, as are exclusion clauses, which allow union leaders to veto new hires and force the firing of anyone the union expels. Under Mexican law, several mandatory benefits and protections are provided. Work shifts are eight hours for the day shift, seven hours for the night shift, and seven and one-half hours for a mixed shift. The work week is 48 hours with a full day of rest. Workers are paid double for overtime and triple for more than nine hours. Overtime is voluntary and often refused. A Christmas bonus equal to at least two weeks' wages must be paid to employees in December of each year. Mexican workers are guaranteed seven holidays per year and are paid double time for work on holidays. Employees are entitled to six working days of paid vacation after one year of service, with more days added as the years of service increase. Employees are entitled to a vacation bonus equal to 25 percent of the weekly salary. Employees are also entitled to severance pay when termination is without "just cause"; however, this money is usually paid any way rather than the employer trying to prove "just cause" to the labor board.[48]

Under Mexico's constitution, workers are entitled to participate in the profits of the enterprise. Employees participate in the profits at a percentage rate fixed by the National Committee for Workers' Profit-Sharing in Enterprises. This committee is required to consider the general condition of the Mexican economy, the promotion of industrial development, the right of capital to obtain reasonable interest, and the necessity of reinvestment of capital. Fifty percent of the profit shared is distributed equally among employees in accordance with the number of days worked during the year. The remaining 50 percent is distributed among eligible workers in proportion to the earnings for the year.[49]

The opening of the Mexican markets to NAFTA and international trade, the devaluation of the peso, plant closings, and corporate downsizing to become more competitive have created an economic challenge for the entire country. Free collective bargaining in the last few years has been limited voluntarily and replaced by annual national pacts negotiated by the government, the major trade unions, and employers with the major goal of controlling inflation. Many efforts have been made by employers, unions, and the government to create greater flexibility and labor–management cooperation to improve productivity, quality, and employee renumeration.[50]

Since NAFTA, there have been numerous alliances and exchanges between Mexican, U.S., and Canadian unions. AFL-CIO president John Sweeney visited Mexico and met with Mexican union officials. They agreed to exchange visits of union officials and labor lawyers. The United Auto Workers and Canadian Auto Workers have conducted safety and health training in Mexico. The Steelworkers have provided financial assistance to Mexican unions to assist their organizing efforts. There have been worker-to-worker exchanges which help to erase stereotypes of both U.S. and Mexican workers by providing workers on both sides with opportunities to cross the borders and tour plants, attend union meetings, work on organizing drives, and walk picket lines. As an example, union organizers from Mexico went to Milwaukee to meet with Mexican workers to speak of their own experience in telling them that the U.S.-based United Electrical Workers was a democratic union, unlike some unions (ghost unions) in Mexico.[51]

In Central and South America, negotiations between unions and employers take place primarily at the plant level. Only Argentina, Venezuela, and Mexico have widespread industry-wide bargaining. The principal reason for this arrangement is that legislation in the various countries typically does not require employers to bargain except at the plant level.

An interesting departure from most of the rest of the world is the important role of collective bargaining between employers and nonunion employees. In fact, over 25 percent of the labor agreements in Columbia and Venezuela are negotiated without trade unions. Obviously, the unions look with disfavor on this arrangement because employers use the nonunion groups as a means to bypass trade unions.

In the more industrialized countries of the world, people interpret labor–management relations to mean the wide range of relationships between employers and employees. However, people of Central American countries tend to define labor relations in terms of the voluminous labor codes and government regulations.

Labor relations vary widely among the countries in Central America, but they have one common feature: a close connection between trade unions and political parties. For example, in Mexico, unions constitute a large section of a political party and therefore are assigned a quota of candidates on the party's ticket for office. Thus, unions have some assurance of having a voice in the party's program and on its council. Some unions have been very effective in gaining relatively high wages for members. For example, the electrical workers in Mexico earn two to three times more than the urban working class.[52] Likewise, unions have been criticized because they have made gains for their own members while neglecting the interests of the great mass of people, including the peasants, who are terribly poor.

Labor agreements vary in content both within countries and among countries. In Argentina, labor agreements include provisions that set forth in some detail the employment conditions and establish a highly developed shop steward system to administer grievances and ensure that employers abide by the agreements. In Chile, labor agreements are more general, but they do establish certain minimum rules and include a grievance mechanism to enforce the agreement. In Brazil, where unions have struggled since 1945 to have a greater say in determining employment rules and conditions for their members, they have achieved more through labor legislation than by engaging in collective bargaining.

In Central American countries, political parties maintain close ties with unions for their support, votes, and influence. Likewise, trade unions depend on the politicians for laws to protect their members, to legalize their organizations, and to regulate their relations with employers. On the other hand, political parties have appealed to organized labor to favor their own policies, and in some cases, they have accommodated organized labor in hopes that it will remain satisfied and continue to support the existing economic and political system.[53]

The United States has signed a free trade agreement, the Dominican Republic–Central America Free Trade Agreement (DR-CAFTA), with the countries of Costa Rica, El Salvador, Guatemala, Honduras, Nicaragua, and the Dominican Republic. Eighty percent of U.S. exports of consumer and industrial goods from Central America and the Dominican Republic will become duty free immediately with the remaining tariffs phased out over ten years. U.S. exports that will benefit are information technology, agriculture, construction equipment, paper, pharmaceuticals, and medical and scientific equipment. Tariffs on U.S. autos and auto parts will be phased out within five years. DR-CAFTA addresses worker rights protections with a three-part strategy intended to ensure effective enforcement of domestic laws, establish a cooperative program to improve labor laws and enforcement, and build the capacity of Central America and the Dominican Republic to monitor and enforce labor rights.[54]

Cuba

Although not a major trading partner of the United States, Cuba, the largest island nation in the Caribbean Sea, is on the brink of social, economic, and political change. With the Helms-Burton Law designed to discourage foreign investments and the demise of the Soviet Union (Cuba's major source of economic subsidies), Cuba has been struggling to survive, and its future direction is not entirely clear. As with the former Soviet bloc countries in Eastern Europe, an option for change is toward economic privatization and political democracy. If this occurs, the developing relationships between government, business, and labor will need to be examined.

Before the 1959 revolution, Cuba had more organized workers than any other Central American country, except Mexico, Brazil, and Argentina. In the 1960s, labor unions were replaced by the Advanced Workers' Movement, which comprised between 10 and 15 percent of the workforce. The role of labor unions was curtailed, and unions were not deeply involved in defending workers' rights and had little input on employment-related matters. As labor became dormant, Cuba attempted to transition to a "planned" market economy, which had limited success. With failures in agriculture in the 1970s, Cuba began to reactivate the role of labor unions by encouraging worker input into decision making, defending workers' rights, and informing managers of current and impending problems in the production process.

Despite the "union reactivation," Cuba retained a fundamentally Stalinist approach to labor well into the twenty-first century. Nonpaid voluntary work is encouraged, strikes are prohibited, free collective bargaining does not exist, and workers remain militarized to sustain the "heroic" tempo of the revolution. Only a small semi-free market in the tourism industry exists. However, tourist dollars are paid to the government, and employees are paid in devalued pesos (in 1958 the peso and the U.S. dollar were equivalent; today the peso is less than one-quarter the value of the dollar).

As countries in Eastern Europe have moved toward more democratic and pluralistic economies, so shall Cuba in time. The future choices will then be the various forms of labor participation programs, such as work councils, employee collectives, and greater reliance on collective bargaining at the enterprise level. Unions have become the primary means by which workers are represented. Unions represent a broader segment than their membership; they represent retired pensioners, the unemployed, and so on. Unions in Eastern Europe have become political partners within the framework of tripartite arrangements (government, labor, and management). Whether these approaches are suitable for Cuba after the transition from Fidel Castro will be open for debate. What is certain is the economic globalization trend will continue, posing the question to what extent Cuba will participate in that process.[55]

Western Europe

In Western Europe unionization is significantly greater than in the United States, with the exception of France and Spain. Of the largest countries, the range is from less than ten percent in France to over 75 percent in Belgium, Denmark, Finland, and Sweden. Unions have been able to use this membership strength to accumulate political influence at the national level. Furthermore, they have been able to coordinate their efforts with large, well-established labor parties in government to achieve their goals.

As in the United States, union membership in Western Europe has declined. Nationwide and industry-wide bargaining is less frequent, and employers are winning more concessions for efficient work rules and wages. Also, as in the United States, unions are trying to sign up new members in growing industries, such as leisure and finance, where technological change has fueled worries about job security.[56] Unions have achieved significantly greater worker participation in the operation of the firm—many times through legislative mandate and sometimes through management reaction to wildcat strikes and worker dissatisfaction. In addition, public opinion in these countries strongly supports the idea that worker participation enhances production, fosters harmony, and enriches the workers personally.

The labor relations system in Western Europe can be contrasted with that of the United States in a number of ways.[57]

1. In the United States, unions are selected by the majority of the appropriate bargaining unit and certified as the exclusive bargaining representative, whereas in Western Europe, exclusive representation is not a common concept.

2. In the United States, the exclusive bargaining representative has a monopoly over all employee bargaining, and the employer is required to bargain only with the legally certified union. In Western Europe, the employer often bargains with a number of unions in addition to worker councils elected by the employees.

3. In Western Europe, negotiations take place between representatives of employer associations and those representing a confederation of unions; in the United States, this bargaining arrangement is adopted in only a few industries, primarily construction.

4. In North America, the focus of union–management interaction is the shop floor, whereas in Europe, bargaining at national levels is the major focus of most unions.[58]

5. More fringe benefits are established by law in Europe than in the United States; therefore, trade unions have found that they can obtain benefits more quickly through the political process and have tied themselves more closely to political parties.

6. Western European countries have a greater commitment to employee training. For example, German firms spend twice as much on this activity as U.S. firms, or nearly 17 times as much per apprentice. About 65 percent of each class of middle school graduates in Germany enter apprenticeship training. In contrast, 57 percent of high school graduates in the United States enroll in postsecondary education, and the majority drop out before graduation.

One major reason for the disparity in support for employee training between Germany and the United States is the role of unions and employer associations. German companies band together in employer associations to negotiate with unions over wages and other personnel matters, such as training. Because unions represent 25 percent of the labor force and unions are stronger in Germany, the labor agreements require investments in training, and collective bargaining provides the mechanism for collecting union dues and fees. This approach is similar to the high-quality apprenticeship programs financed by contracts between craft unions and employer associations in the U.S. construction industry.[59]

European Union (EU)

By 1992 the economies of 12 countries in Western Europe (Belgium, Denmark, Germany, Greece, France, Ireland, Italy, Luxembourg, the Netherlands, Portugal, Spain, and the United Kingdom) were joined together as the European Union (EU) (see Exhibit 14.6). In 1995, Austria, Finland, and Sweden joined the EU. By 2007, the EU had a membership of 27 countries with a combined population of 490,426,060 and an economy of $15.7 trillion, the largest in the world (see Exhibit 14.6).

The EU's goal is the gradual elimination of economic barriers among member countries and of restrictions on the movement of goods, capital, and labor

Exhibit 14.6
The European Union

across national borders.[60] The EU constitution will include employment and social issues (see Exhibit 14.7 for the draft of employment-related issues).

The Charter of Fundamental Social Rights (called the "Social Charter") was approved by all EU countries except Great Britain. This arrangement establishes certain standards for working conditions throughout the EU so that some countries cannot attract industry merely because their pay and working conditions are below those of other countries. The charter stipulates statements of principles on fundamental rights that include freedom of association and encourages collective bargaining, vocational training, equal treatment for men and women, health and safety, child protection, and rights of information, consultation, and participation for workers.[61]

Critics of the Social Charter have argued that the EU has returned Western Europe to a re-regulation phase that will raise labor costs, inhibit employment growth, and disproportionately affect the poorer employees. Critics contend the end result of mandated benefits in the Social Charter will lead to higher costs and an erosion of their external competitive position.[62]

Companies are already considering the effects of the EU, which could include increased mobility of employees among operations in the various countries, more recruiting from overseas, more active monitoring of pay and benefits developments in other countries, and increased language training, as well as a premium placed on language skills. These areas and others will provide much opportunity for trade unions to be involved at the bargaining table.

The European Works Council (EWC) Directive was adopted in 1995 to provide a legal right for workers and their representatives to be consulted and informed about MNCs operating in more than one country in the EU. Any MNC employing more than 1,000 workers in the European Economic Area (EEA includes the EU countries plus Norway, Iceland, and Liechtenstein) and with 150 workers in at least two member states have to establish a procedure for informing and consulting employees when the workers asked for it. Estimates of the number of MNCs covered by the directive range from 860 to 1,500. By 1996, it was estimated that close to 500 MNCs had negotiated voluntary

Exhibit 14.7

Employment-Related Elements of the Charter of Fundamental Rights

Prohibition of slavery and forced labor
Protection of personal data
Freedom of assembly and association, including trade union matters
Freedom to choose an occupation and the right to engage in work
Equality in employment matters including prohibition against employment discrimination based on sex, race, color, ethnic or social origin, nationality, genetic features, language, religion, disability, age, sexual orientation
Information and consultation
Right of collective bargaining and action
Right of access to placement services
Unjustified dismissal
Fair and just working condition including health, safety, and dignity
Child labor and protection
Family and professional life including protection against dismissal connected to maternity and the right to paid maternity leave and parental leave following birth or adoption of a child
Social security and assistance in cases such as maternity, illness, industrial accidents, dependency or old age and loss of employment

SOURCE: *European Union 2003*, Washington, D.C.: U.S. Printing Office, 2003, pp. 17–19.

agreements. Although these agreements are indeed transnational, their effect on worker representation, unions, economic performance, and labor markets has yet to be determined.[63]

Each of these EWCs meets at least once a year to discuss the firm's changes, its business environment, employment issues, and future plans. Senior managers present information to employee representatives who are asked to respond, and consultation takes place over corporate decisions that affect workers in more than one country. Most EWCs allow employee representatives to hold their own meetings before and after the main sessions, and some EWCs are developing new forms of communication between the annual events. Although EWC activities are separate from trade union activities and European trade unions are not actively involved, the EWC provides a mechanism for promulgating industrial relations policy initiatives across national boundaries and implementing new regulatory measures in industrial relations within the European Union.[64]

In 2002 the euro, the new common currency of the EU, replaced the national currencies, and identical notes and coins are used within the EU countries. The single EU currency (currently adopted by 13 of the 27 member countries) will encourage the formation of a single European economy as the corollary of a single European market. A single currency is expected to make European markets for goods and services more integrated and efficient. Therefore, European firms will need to become more integrated and efficient to compete against each other and foreign competitors, who will be attracted to the EU as the internal barriers disappear. A wave of consolidations which is expected among businesses has already begun in banking, retailing, and manufacturing. As in the United States during the 1990s, the mergers and consolidations have evoked cost-cutting and major layoffs. Unions and governments will have to be attentive to the problems that coincide with these events.[65]

Great Britain

Like membership in trade unions in other countries, the number of union members in Great Britain has declined since their overall peak in 1980 of over 13 million members and 56 percent of the workforce. The decline in membership during the 1980s and 1990s can be attributed to industrial change, particularly manufacturing, and government policies established particularly during the term of Margaret Thatcher. In recent years, there have been promising signs of a resurgence, due to the passage of the Employment Relations Act of 1999 and the recent growth in trade union recognition, particularly in professional unions (teachers, nurses, and doctors).

Membership in unions in Great Britain's public sector (about 60 percent) is greater than the private sector (about 20 percent). The Trade Union Congress (TUC) continues to be largest labor organization, and the TUC has 11 unions with each having over 100,000 members. Two other unions with over 100,000 members, the British Medical Association (doctors) and the Royal College of Nurses (nurses), are not in the TUC.[66]

The traditional system in Great Britain is characterized by voluntary collective bargaining, implemented without legal compulsion through unenforceable labor agreements that have been negotiated by a large number of multiunion–multiemployer negotiating committees. The United Kingdom has nearly 600 labor unions, over three times the number in the United States, and a manufacturing firm typically negotiates with about seven unions. One of the most important negotiations involve the Engineering Employers' Federation, representing 5,000 companies, and the Confederation of Shipbuilding and Engineering Unions, representing 34 unions and over two million employees. This general agreement sets forth guidelines that establish the floor for additional bargaining at the plants. Labor agreements are negotiated and administered at the plant level; however, they are not enforceable by law and grievances are not subject to private arbitration.

Shop stewards are volunteers who serve without pay. Unlike their U.S. counterparts, they cannot be removed by union executives. Often, shop stewards accumulate much authority and influence at the plant and have more control over local union affairs than any national union official. Steward councils composed of union stewards from various unions and work councils representing members of the various departments are important in the labor relations system.

Labor agreements at the plant level are often negotiated by representatives of the national union, steward councils, and work councils. These agreements usually have no fixed term and include letters of understanding, minutes of meetings, and oral understandings. Although there is no legal obligation to negotiate, unions have gained extensive power and control over jobs by refusing to work with any employer whom they find in bad standing and maintaining strict membership discipline.

From 1979 to 1999, under the British conservative party's leadership, union membership in Great Britain was nearly halved. In 1979, 90 percent of workers had their pay determined by collective bargaining; now, less than 30 percent are covered by such agreements. An explosion of contingent pay plans has occurred, such as profit sharing, employee stock ownership, and merit pay. This era of deregulation included new industrial relations legislation being passed every two years, with changes affecting these areas. The responsibility for industrial relations was placed at the company level, and any collective bargaining agreement would cover only a single firm. Before, there had been multi-employer bargaining.[67]

In 1999, the British parliament passed the Employment Relations Act where "for the first time in a generation unions were given legislative support to establish themselves as key partners at the workplace, working with employers for greater productivity and better work practices." The centerpiece of the Act is the inclusion of a statutory procedure for the recognition of trade unions for collective bargaining purposes. Applications are made to the Central Arbitration Committee (CAC). The Act encourages voluntary settlement of recognition claims either following application to the CAC or without any involvement of the CAC. The Act provides individual worker protections against unfair dismissal and protections for supporting union recognition. After the CAC grants recognition, the employer must bargain over pay, hours, and holidays, but may bargain over other issues as they wish. The Act also introduced new protections from dismissal of striking workers and established an Employment Appeal Tribunal procedure for unfair employee dismissals. After the first four years, 79 percent of the parties to CAC cases expressed satisfaction with the procedures.[68]

Germany

The German model of labor–management relations rest upon two pillars: (1) centralized industry-level collective bargaining and (2) plant-level codetermination committees or works councils. The central wage agreements are designed to take wages out of competition and the works councils are designed to facilitate implementation of the master agreements and represent workers' interests at the workplace. Collective bargaining in Germany occurs between trade unions and employer confederations at the industry and regional level. With the exception of Volkswagen, which negotiates its own collective bargaining agreements with their unions, collective bargaining over wages and conditions of employment (job classification, working time, and working conditions) occurs formally outside the plant. Decisions on strikes (among the lowest in the world; only four between 2000 and 2003) and lockouts are not made at the local level.

Works councils at the workplace focus on production issues, handle individual grievances, and are charged with the implementation of the collective bargaining agreements. Works councils may negotiate plant agreements with local management on matters that are not covered by the collective bargaining agreements. Works councils have actively participated in the fixing of wages above the formal wage schedule set under the collective bargaining agreements and have negotiated provisions for special bonuses and allowances at the plant. These types of provisions are allowed in Germany.

The role of the works councils was determined by the Works Constitution Act of 1952 (amended in 2001). Under this law, works councils are set up in any establishment with at least five permanent employees after a petition is filed by a small group of workers or a trade union representing the workers. While mandatory, they are not automatic. In fact, works councils are found in only ten percent of German establishments in the private sector. However, their presence rises sharply with plant size, and the number of employees covered considerably exceeds their frequency. Members of the works councils are elected by secret ballot for a four-year term and represent all workers, not just union members. While works councils are formally independent of unions, as a practical matter, the ties are usually close because three of the five works councilors are union members. Typically, works councilors assist in recruiting union members at the workplace and are considered "pillars of union security."

The law provides works councils with rights to information and consultation on subjects such as manpower planning, change in work processes, working environment, and job content. There is a set of rules on codetermination or joint-management rights on so-called social matters, which include subjects such as working hours, principles of remuneration, holidays, health, and safety. The works councils also have "consent rights" on hiring and firing decisions.

Like most of the developed countries, union membership in Germany has been declining and has fallen from 33 percent in 1980 to 25 percent today. However, the percent of employees covered by collective bargaining agreements is still quite high, 68 percent in Western Germany and 53 percent in Eastern Germany. The major federation is the German Federation of Trade Unions, which includes eight major unions representing 80 percent of all union members. These unions bargain at the industry and regional levels with the manufacturing union taking the lead and setting the wage standard for others to follow. For example, IG Metal, the German metalworkers union, represents 2.4 million metalworkers and is the dominant wage trend setter in national bargaining. Interestingly, Eastern German manufacturers, which are still adjusting to a competitive market economy, are allowed to enter into "hardship agreements" that exempt them for a period of time from the industry wage standard. Companies seeking these agreements must prove they are close to bankruptcy and must demonstrate a strategy for economic recovery by opening their books to scrutiny.[69]

Central and Eastern Europe—Former Soviet Bloc Countries

Trade unions represent workers all over the region; however, their major role in many countries has been to exert political pressure. For instance, solidarity in Poland, the original independent union in Eastern Europe, has 2.5 million members and played a major role in the breakup of the Soviet bloc. Trade unions in Czechoslovakia led the revolution, and then members voted out the old leadership and democratized the union movement. The unions wanted the country to be divided along Czech and Slovak ethnic lines, thereby creating the Czech Republic and Slovakia. In the former Soviet Union, the trade union movement has been in a state of rapid flux; however, coal miners have maintained their relative strength throughout the developments.[70]

Some countries in the former Soviet bloc are enjoying success in attracting new industries. Offering lower wages and lower manufacturing costs, businesses primarily from Western Europe are investing in central Europe particularly. The transition to a market economy has been slow and judged not yet successful. Factories do not have the funds to upgrade their plants, buy products from one another, or make payrolls. Faced with massive restructuring and operational inefficiencies that have been allowed to develop over the years, unemployment remains high.[71]

The transfer of labor institutions from Western Europe to central and Eastern Europe has been slowly progressing. Although central and Eastern Europe represent only 5.7 percent of Germany's foreign investments, the Czech Republic (10th) and Poland (5th) are among the ten most attractive locations for Germany's direct investors. Germany has become the leading direct investor in Hungary and the Czech Republic, where it competes with the United States and France for the leading position. However, there is no evidence that these German companies are exporting the "German model" of labor relations to Eastern European countries. Instead, the German companies have adapted to the host country's institutions and environment and transferred only those labor relations practices, such as heavy emphasis on vocational training, long-term employment commitment, and consensual work organizations, which are acceptable in the host country.[72]

The cultures, traditions, and beliefs of West Germans have been slowly introduced in East Germany. Works councils have been introduced in Hungary, and German labor legislation has been introduced in Slovenia. The nature of collective bargaining varies widely from merely endorsing legislation for consultation only to regulation of conflict. Collective agreements on pay appear to be widespread in the unionized sectors; however, employers refuse to negotiate on any other issues. Hungary and the Czech Republic have had the most employment deregulation and workplace change, but unions exercise few controls over employment contracts and working hours.

Collective bargaining varies across countries and companies. These differences in collective bargaining are determined in part by the dissimilarities in legislation, nationally inherited legacies, and the progress made toward economic reform. In Eastern European countries such as Romania, there is a trend toward decentralization of bargaining, thereby establishing terms and conditions of employment at the company level with more authority delegated to managers and union officials at that level. Also, the strike as a power source for the union is a new phenomenon.[73]

In Russia, where the market economy is still in its infancy, lawmakers decided in 2002 to adopt a Labour Code that would present a reassuring face to millions of workers whose cultural and psychological environment was thrown into disarray by the collapse of the Soviet system. The new Labour Code marked a further step in Russia's process of legislative and institutional reform in the field of labor relations. While the new Code stops short of making a clean break with the past, it reflects a radical departure from the former Soviet system. Under the Soviet system, the purpose of a collective bargaining agreement was to spell out in writing the mutual obligations of management and workers in the execution of the production plans, introduction of new equipment, raising labor productivity, improvement in quality standards, lowering production costs, strengthening production and labor discipline, and training of supervisory personnel.

Under the new Code, there is greater flexibility given to the parties with guaranteed protections provided to workers (safety and health, minimum wages, etc.). The new Code covers contracts of employment, dismissal rules and procedures, and dispute resolution procedures. The parties decide the appropriate level for collective bargaining; they may choose to bargain at the enterprise, regional, industry, or federal level. The parties to collective bargaining have chosen enterprise bargaining far more frequently (161,700 enterprise level collective contracts, 77 regional agreements, 2,293 industry, and 61 federal). Bargaining procedures, schedules, and duration of the labor agreements are decided by the parties. Under the new Code, unions have the right to strike, but only after a long detailed procedure of attempts at mediation and advanced notice. In addition, strikes in the public services industries and in industries that would pose a threat to the country are prohibited. During strikes, the freedom to work by non-strikers must be guaranteed.[74]

Japan

Japan's labor relations system has five distinguishing characteristics: labor–management consultation and teamwork, lifetime employment, a wage system based on seniority, enterprise or company unions and a higher status for the human resources department. Management and employees communicate considerably more in Japan than in most other countries. Ninety percent of all Japanese companies have some sort of labor–management consultation. The flow of information is extensive. As examples, management reports to employees on the company's financial status, its problems, its expectations and plans, and on contemplated technological innovations before they occur. All aspects of employment, training, discipline, working conditions, and employee benefits are open for examination. Joint consultation includes subjects that a U.S. manager would classify as management prerogatives.[75] Research has shown that when Japanese firms increase their information sharing with employee unions, the negotiations are shorter and easier, unions tend to demand and accept lower wage increases,[76] and profitability and productivity are improved.[77]

Teamwork and consensus building are a cultural heritage in Japan. Japanese employees feel comfortable with this approach, and both sides stress sharing of goals, responsibilities, and rewards. The communication links are through the normal channels at work, such as meetings, newsletters and bulletins, labor unions, and labor-management councils.[78]

Lifetime employment, a standard in Japan since the 1950s when employers agreed to this arrangement to quell labor unrest, has been applied to regular employees of large employers (500 or more employees), which make up about one-third of the nonagricultural workforce. These "regular employees" are hired after completing high school or college, with the expectation that they will be retained by the company until they reach the mandatory retirement age of 60. Legal, written contracts are nonexistent; however, unacceptable behavior may lead to a suggested voluntary resignation or a "hidden discharge." Lifetime employment has encouraged employers to invest in training these long-term employees and responsiveness by employees not only to participate in training but to willingly accept innovation and technological advancement, knowing that they will not be adversely affected by a layoff.[79]

When Japanese companies locate a plant in the United States, they most likely do not adopt the lifetime employment concept. Although over half of the Japanese plants have explicit "no-layoff" policies, only five percent of their plants located in the United States have a similar policy. The Japanese plants use temporary workers as a buffer to enhance employment security for their core workforce, whereas the U.S. counterparts use layoffs to adjust to a shortfall in demand for workers. For example, auto parts plants typically lay off employees for one month when retooling is required to meet new customer specifications. In Japan, companies tolerate periods of substantial underemployment to avoid layoffs. In fact, some Japanese companies donate their employees to perform community service during temporary slowdowns.[80]

The **wage system** in Japan has several distinguishing characteristics:

1. Salaries are paid monthly, even if the employee has been absent (with justification) from work.

2. Wage differentials are small between regular line employees and staff personnel, all of whom are members of the same union.

3. Wage distinctions exist between amounts earned for one's work (for example, efficiency output) and amounts earned for just being an employee (such as allowances for housing, transportation, and dependents).

4. Wages are accepted as permanent and last for the employee's entire career, including a minimum annual increase and a lump sum at retirement.[81]

Length of service and age are more highly correlated with wages in Japan than in other industrially developed countries. For example, between the ages of 40 and 50 the Japanese workers' wages are 67 percent greater than those of 21- to 24-year-old employees, whereas in the United States, the older employees' wages average only 23 percent more than those of younger workers. The smaller difference in income levels between managers and workers than in other countries contributes to the sense of unity among employees. Wage increases and promotions are primarily governed by the employee's age and the length of service in the company. The seniority-based wage system serves as a means of guaranteeing stability of employment throughout employees' careers within the company and is closely connected to the lifetime employment concept. In addition to wages, employees are provided fringe benefits that enable them to enjoy recreation and leisure activities, such as athletic competition, employee excursions, and so on. Employees have access to facilities for hobbies, including sports, reading, and board games. Companies offer special allowances for company-owned housing, dormitories for single workers, and various health and welfare benefits. Workers in smaller companies (who make up 60 percent of the total workforce) do not receive the same benefits or job security as those who are employed in the larger companies.[82]

By 2006, long-term employment practices and seniority-based wage system were being re-evaluated by employers due to changes in the labor market structure caused by a decreasing birth rate and rapidly aging society. The rise in the employment of part-time workers also has imposed a tremendous influence on collectively bargained labor agreements. The overall unionization rate had fallen to 18.7 percent by 2005 (16.4 percent in the private sector and only 3.3 percent among part-time workers). However, the unionization rate among corporations with more than 1,000 employees remained high at 47.7 percent, but with employers with less than 99 employees, the rate was only 1.2 percent.[83]

Enterprise unionism implies at least three practices: (1) employees of a single firm organize their own union and include all employees, except managers and temporary employees, (2) there is no segregation based on employees' occupation classification or job categories, and (3) collective bargaining takes place at the firm level, which leads to a decentralized bargaining structure in Japan. Thus, in Japan, the enterprise unions have functioned both as labor unions for gaining higher wages and improving working conditions in negotiations with management and also as the employee representative bodies, which promote participation and cooperation with management.[84] Thus, the individual employee identifies more closely with the company than does the typical employee in many Western countries.

The enterprise unions are affiliated at the national level and have national organizations in the textile, electricity, shipbuilding, automobile, steel, appliance, and chemical industries which hold conferences to discuss industrial policies. National organizations do not discuss such topics as wages, working conditions, and other employment policies. These topics are discussed within the enterprise union. At the national level, industrial problems are discussed in a more general context, and issues such as economic growth, employment forecasts, retirement ages, and improved communications are addressed.[85]

In Japan, the human resources (HR) department has a higher status in corporations than in the United States. The HR department is in charge of rotating managers around the company and identifying people for senior positions. Managers view HR as a beneficial position because it is a place to network with other managers and is a good springboard for top corporate positions. HR is linked to corporate governance indirectly by grooming people for the board of directors which is comprised of management insiders. On the board, the HR executive voices employee concerns to other executives and serves as the advocate for career employees in strategic decision-making. In the last 40 to 50 years in the United States, the powerhouse function has been finance, not human resources.[86]

In comparison to the United States (see Chapter 5), it is relatively easy for a group of workers to establish a trade union. The Japanese Trade Union Law requires neither majority support for certification nor the recognition of exclusive bargaining rights. Instead, under the Trade Union Law, when a group of workers wishes to form a so-called "statutorily qualified union" and receive legal protection under the law, an application is filed with the Labor Commission. The Commission then conducts a "qualification examination" with rules set forth by the Labor Commission. When the group of workers is qualified as a union, the employer is required by law to engage in collective bargaining even though the union represents only a very small number of workers. In practice, prior to filing with the Labor Commission, union organizers usually visit the employers and obtain their consent. This consent is important because many workers will not want to join a union that is opposed by their employer. Unlike in the United States, it is rare that an employer will engage in activities that are regarded as active union opposition or suppression.[87]

Japan has over 70,000 unions; however, only 18.7 percent of the workforce belongs to a union (far less than the 35 percent in 1975). The decline in union density is due in part to the reduction in the percentage of workers employed in manufacturing and other industries that tend to be highly unionized.

Unions have received low wage increases in the last several years and are becoming more adversarial. Although the work days lost because of strikes in Japan average less than in Canada, Australia, and the United States, work day losses are greater than those of Sweden, Norway, Germany, Austria, and the Netherlands, where work council systems prevail.

In the private sector, collective bargaining covers almost every conceivable aspect of labor–management relations. The results are formalized into a "comprehensive labor agreement." Issues that affect management and production, such as new plants and equipment and subcontracting, are normally handled in the process of the regular consultations between the union and management. The comprehensive labor agreements normally do not cover wages because wages are determined in separate annual negotiations held during the *Shunto* (spring labor offensive). Wage negotiations are conducted by individual enterprises and their respective unions with coordination within an industrial group. In the public sector, both wages and employment conditions are determined by law. The National Personnel Authority makes annual recommendations (based on salary surveys) for salary increases for public employees to the Cabinet and national legislature, which makes the final determination.[88]

Entering the twenty-first century, labor unions with their annual Shunto found it difficult to maintain its so-called annual pay increases of two percent due to Japan's long recession and increased pressure by employers to implement performance-based pay systems. Since 2002, the Japan Council of Metalworkers' Unions (composed of steel, ship-building and engineering, electric, and autoworkers unions) discontinued making a unified request for wage hikes in their base pay, and the phenomenon of Shunto ceasing to seek wage hikes continued. In response, a manager was quoted as declaring that "Shunto is dead." Either way, it must be concluded that the bargaining power of labor unions in Japan has been weakening during the 1990s and into the 2000s.[89]

In the final analysis, Japanese employers and unions eventually will have to face many critical issues that may cause a change with the traditional labor relations system. These issues include early retirement, higher unemployment, elimination of automatic pay increases and promotions, introduction of labor-saving devices, union emphasis on job security rather than wage hikes, decline of employee loyalty to the firm, and Japan's declining competitiveness with rapidly developing countries such as Brazil, China, South Korea, Singapore, and Taiwan.[90]

Korea[91]

On June 30, 2007, the United States and Korea signed a free trade agreement (Korea-United States Free Trade Agreement (KORUS FTA)) which will expand bilateral trade and investment opportunities in both countries. Korea is the world's tenth largest economy and the United States' seventh largest goods-trading partner, with two-way goods trade of $78 billion in 2006. Under KORUS FTA, 64 percent or $1.91 billion of agricultural products from the United States will be duty free immediately and the remainder will be phased out over time. Nearly 95 percent of consumer and industrial goods will be duty free within three years and the remaining tariffs will be eliminated in ten years. KORUS FTA removes tariffs and non-tariff barriers that U.S. automakers have identified as impediments to their success in Korea's markets. KORUS FTA also incorporates provisions to safeguard workers' rights and provides environmental protections that are consistent with internationally recognized standards.[92]

Korea has a tripartite labor relations system in which the Ministry of Labor serves as the governmental agency that formulates labor relations policy and implements and enforces labor relations laws, including child labor, forced labor, employment equality, wages, hours of work, and safety and health. The government continues to receive criticism of its policies concerning freedom of association and the right to organize because the government refuses to register new trade unions in the public sector and arrests and imprisons trade unionists who participate in strikes.

The other parties, trade union federations and employer organizations, represent their constituents concerning labor relations matters by giving advice and guidance and serving on government advisory commissions. The Korean Employers' Federation (KEF) serves as an umbrella organization representing 13 regional employers' associations, 30 trade associations, and about 4,000 enterprises. The KEF claims industrial peace and national economic development as its primary objectives and advocates its members' interests to the government and legislative bodies. In addition, the KEF provides advice to its members on labor laws and industrial relations matters.

The 6,150 unions in Korea, with a membership of 1.6 million, may be organized by company, by occupation, by region, or by industry. While the majority of unions in Korea are enterprise-based unions, there are 44 industrial federations and two national federations: the Federation of Korean Trade Unions (FKTA) and the Korea Confederation of Trade Unions (KCTU). The FKTU is the largest labor organization in Korea and represents nearly one million workers in 3,408 unions. The KCTU now represents about 600,000 workers in 16 industrial federations.

Korea is governed by numerous labor laws. The Korean constitution guarantees freedom of association, the right to bargain collectively, and the right to collective action. However, strikes are prohibited in government agencies, state-owned enterprises, and defense industry companies. A majority of union members must vote in favor of striking by direct, secret, and unsigned balloting, and the union must report the planned strike in advance and in writing to the appropriate administrative agencies.

Labor relations is governed by five separate laws; the most comprehensive is the Trade Union and Labor Relations Adjustment Act (TULRAA), which among other provisions protects workers from dismissal for organizing and joining unions and for participating in union activities. A worker may seek relief for any such unfair labor practice by filing a complaint with the Labor Relations Commission (LRC) or by bringing a civil suit against the employer. Employers who are found guilty of an unfair labor practice can be required to reinstate the worker and provide back pay.

Individual and collective labor disputes are adjudicated and mediated or arbitrated by the LRC, which operates at the regional and national levels. As a general rule, collective bargaining takes place at the enterprise level, but a union may delegate negotiation responsibility to the trade union federation with which it is affiliated. Collective bargaining usually covers wages, hours of work, workers' welfare, and other employment conditions. The collective bargaining agreements are valid for up to two years; however, if a new agreement is not concluded by the expiration date of a current agreement even though the parties are engaged in negotiations, the existing agreement will remain in effect for another three months. Negotiations may extend to trade union activities during working hours and issues concerning full-time union officers. Within 15 days following completion of negotiations, the collective bargaining agreement must be submitted to the appropriate administrative agencies. If any provision of the agreement is determined to be unlawful, the parties may be ordered to amend the unlawful provision(s).[93]

Australia

Until recently, the Australian labor relations system was characterized by industry-wide or company-wide "awards," which were negotiated by company, union, and sometimes government officials and then submitted to the federal Australia Industrial Relations Commission (AIRC) for ratification or resolution of differences. Such "awards" establish minimum wages and working conditions for specific categories of workers and are the approximate equivalent of an American collective bargaining agreement. As an example, if a union claims a wage for one class of worker, such as a metal machinist, an "award" for a wage increase would apply to all machinists in the same class throughout Australia. This mechanism led to rampant wage-push inflation in the 1970s as unions fought to protect the value of workers' real wages. In the 1980s, the government restricted wage claims and price increases by companies.[94]

When the Conservative Liberal-National Party Coalition won power in 1996, the new Prime Minister John Howard made it clear that reducing trade unions' power would be one of his objectives. The Coalition quickly passed the Workplace Relations Act of 1996 (WRA) which overturned a century of law and practice that took collective regulation of workplaces as the norm. The WRA introduced individual contracts called Australian Workplace Agreements (AWAs) to enhance "choice" by placing individual and collective agreements on an equal footing. Absent was any mechanism for union recognition or good faith bargaining. As a result, the absence of statutory protection against coercion or inducement allowed employers to pressure or compel employees into signing AWAs. Union rights, including rights to workplace entry, were curtailed. While a right to strike was legislated for the first time, the practical effect was to limit the circumstances under which unions could take industrial action.

For the first time in Australian history, employers had the right to lockout employees, including "AWA lockouts" which are used to induce employees to sign individual agreements. Under the WRA, employers may use two types of lockouts: (1) "Big Bang" and (2) "Bargaining.". With the longer running "Big Bang" lockout, the employer coerces a unionized workforce via an ultimatum that employees cannot return to work until they sign individual agreements and/or agree to cuts in their wages and conditions. Employers often gamble on such lockouts when they want to restructure the business and/or remove a union from the workplace. The shorter term "Bargaining" lockout is used by employers to counter a well-organized unionized workforce that employs rolling campaigns of selective work bans, slowdowns, and brief work stoppages. Employers are able to regain an element of control by locking out employees who are likely to extended stoppages that could mean a loss of business to other plants of the same employer or to other employers.

A group of researchers concluded:

> Australia was once regarded as a progressive, union-friendly "social laboratory." The prolonged and marked decline in Australia's union density, however, marks a fundamental shift in the nature of employment relations. Moreover, the agency of the state has allowed Australian employers to use a range of strategies and tools when pursing their aim of reducing union influence.[95]

Australia has experienced significant changes in bargaining structure and coverage between the 1990s and 2005. In the 1990s, 80 percent of the workers had their wages and conditions determined by awards. By 2005, the awards covered only 20 percent of the workers and the coverage of enterprise collective bargaining agreements had increased to 38 percent. Most of the growth in enterprise-level bargaining from 1995 to 2004 was in nonunion collective agreements.[96]

Over this period, union membership declined dramatically from over 40 percent in the early 90s to 25 percent currently. The decline in union density and reforms in industrial relations have significantly altered the pattern of union/nonunion wage differentials, especially in industries with higher union densities, such as mining, utilities, communication, transport, and manufacturing. The unions in these industries have retained the power to raise wages for their members, but unions have had less effect on the wages of nonunion workers in other industries, such as services, trade, accommodations, public administration, and education.[97]

In 2005, the Workplace Relations Act of 1996 was amended by the Work Choice Act of 2005. The "Work Choices" reform represents a most fundamental revolution in the Australian industrial relations system. Although the government emphasizes that the new laws are designed to increase choices to employers and employees, the main beneficiaries of the reform appear to be employers. Employers are now able to access a wide range of industrial agreements. In addition to the AWAs, employers can now choose to negotiate union or nonunion collective agreements or union or employer "Greenfield agreements" which enable an employer to unilaterally determine the terms and conditions of employment that bind all future employees of a new work site for a period of up to 12 months. The employer may simply elect not to bargain with their employees and remain within the law, provided the conditions they offer meet the minimum standards established by the new Fair Pay and Conditions Standard. Further, wage rates of employees covered by awards will not be increased until their wage rate falls below the minimum wage set by the new Australian Fair Pay Commission. Employees who are left on awards will, over time, become dependent on the minimum set by the Australian Fair Pay and Conditions Standard unless they are able to negotiate a collective agreement or an individual contract or accept an AWA that might be offered by their employer.

The "Work Choices" dramatically recast the role of the Australian Industrial Relations Commission (AIRC) by all but removing its compulsory arbitral power. Now, instead of the parties going to the AIRC to resolve their disputes, the parties are required to agree on a dispute resolution procedure of their own. The government's Workplace Relations Minister can also declare an end to a bargaining period on a wide range of grounds, thereby rendering any industrial action, such as a strike, illegal. Under "Work Choices" reform, terminated employees' right to bring an action for unfair dismissal has been severely restricted. Employees of corporations with fewer than 100 employees now have no right to bring action. Larger employers are protected from the risk of an unfair dismissal claim where they can establish that at least one of the grounds for dismissal was a "genuine operational reason." As one commentator stated:

> *Over time, the Work Choices laws will increase the size of the low-wage sector, further individualize industrial relations and bargaining, and encourage a "low road" labor market development path in Australia.*[98]

In the November 2007 federal election, the Liberal Party led by John Howard was soundly defeated by the Australian Labor Party led by Kevin Rudd, the new prime minister. In fact, John Howard lost his seat in the Australian House of Representatives. Key differences by the political parties included environment, health, and educational issues, Australian participation in the war in Iraq, the Kyoto Protocol on global warming, and Howard's unpopular labor law reforms since 1996. As a result, there are high expectations that change is on the way on a broad front of issues.

China

Before China opened to the rest of the world and engaged in reform, labor relations in China were unusual. Labor relations essentially involved relations between the employee and the government, instead of between work units and laborers. The Premier of the State Council was the only boss and the only authoritative labor relationship was formed between the central government and the workers. This abnormal arrangement has come to an end in the last two decades. However, the Chinese employment system is more complex now than it was in the late 1970s. There are 730 million employees in China; 240 million in urban areas and 490 million in rural areas. Within the urban areas, there are many types of employers: state-owned enterprises, state units, collective units, private and individually owned enterprises, and foreign-owned enterprises. The government is not involved in hiring among the collective units and private enterprises, and the state-owned enterprises now have more autonomy in employment decisions. Although employment remains rather stable, employers now treat staffing levels more flexibly than in the past. In 2001 alone, employers terminated their relationship with 1.4 million workers, and these workers had no right to appeal their employment decisions.[99]

The leading trade union organization is the All-China Congress of Trade Unions (AFCTU), which was founded in 1921, one year after the founding of the Communist Party of China (CPC). When the CPC took over, trade unions were one of the three Leninist Mass Party organizations, but they were not given any bargaining status at the national or enterprise level. In the 1950s, the trade union movement helped the CPC bring industry under state control. In the early 1960s, the AFCTU sought and achieved a short-lived institutional upgrade; however, the Cultural Revolution in 1965 brought about a purge of the AFCTU and its disbandment. In 1978, with the removal of the Maoist regime and the launching of the modernization of China with a goal of quadrupling China's GNP by 2000 coupled with ownership, enterprise management, and distribution era in wealth, trade unions were once again reconstituted to play a more appropriate role.

Trade unions in China had been dominated by "welfarism" and played a role in surveillance and control of the workers rather than serving as a political representative of the working class. Trade unions were viewed more as a "caretaker" of workers that channeled their grievance to higher authorities. In China, the CPC controlled the unions and dictated the unions' programs. The CPC held absolute control of the union, and the union leaders remained answerable only to the heads of state, not the working population. In 1992, the National People's Congress passed amendments to the Trade Union Law in which unions were given consultative status, rather than collective bargaining power. Trade unions were given the task of supporting the state's economic program.[100]

The Chinese economic system has evolved from a centrally planned economy to a guided market economy open to foreign investments. Under the centrally planned economy, employees were assigned to state-owned enterprises that guaranteed lifetime employment and a wide range of benefits, including housing and education. Wage levels were set centrally, and the Communist Party served in a supervisory capacity in the factory. In the 1980s, changes in employment relations began to align with an emerging market economy; that is, enterprises attempted to become more competitive, and firms with foreign investments were allowed to operate without undue state interference. Centralized job allocation and state guarantees of lifetime employment were relaxed and firms no longer were required to provide social welfare benefits. In the mid-1980s, employment laws required that new workers be hired on fixed-term contracts, but the terms could not exceed four years. In addition, employers were authorized to dismiss employees under certain circumstances, such as stealing. The authority of factory managers was increased, and pay linked to performance was introduced. In the early 1990s, new regulations allowed factory managers to lay off surplus workers through voluntary resignations, but required the firms to try to find work for these employees and/or train them for new jobs. Meanwhile, the government did not allow independent unions or any form of collective action in industrial disputes. State-controlled trade unions continued to exist at the enterprise, industry, and regional levels. A dispute settlement law that applied to a broad range of issues was passed, and arbitration tribunals were also established. However, individual disputes accounted for 93 percent of the disputes, and work stoppages were likely to come in the form of spontaneous actions in the outlying provinces, which are less subject to control from Beijing and foreign-owned enterprises. In recent years, there have been rising protests against unemployment and job insecurity, thereby suggesting a role for dispute-resolution procedures designed to secure and maintain industrial peace.

In 1994, China consolidated its labor laws and applied them to domestic and foreign-invested enterprises. The 1994 act gave the state-controlled unions the right to bargain in collective with employers on a prescribed range of matters, including wages and working conditions. Technical assistance on collective bargaining and dispute-settlement procedures was provided by the International Labor Organization (ILO). Minimum standards on wages, hours of work, health and safety, and discrimination against women and young workers were established. By 1995, there were fewer than 11,000 collective bargaining agreements, but it is unclear to what extent bargaining actually took place. In fact, the Chinese workers appear to have little faith in their unions, which perform primarily a social welfare function.[101]

In China, the formal system of laws and regulations is supplemented by local interpretation and is unevenly enforced. For example, it is easier for workers in some provinces to obtain and extend work permits than others. Also, the working hours differ; in several districts of the Guangdong province, firms are able to extend working hours beyond the 60 hours per week maximum by seeking permission (which is rarely denied) from the local government labor authority. Throughout China, local officials will sacrifice enforcement of labor standards in order to attract investment and to generate additional jobs. There has been increased labor unrest and a growing number of labor disputes, which are usually spontaneous actions and have more frequently occurred in the outlying provinces, less subject to control from Beijing and by foreign-owned enterprises.[102]

The economic conditions in China have drastically changed over the last two decades. Total accumulative foreign direct investment in China has risen from $1.8 billion in 1983 to $691.9 billion in 2006. While these numbers are impressive, these investments create an enormous challenge because the Chinese economy will need to absorb ten million new job seekers who are expected to enter the labor market between now and 2010.

There are two contrasting narratives on the effect of investments of MNCs on China labor practices. On the one hand, it has been argued that MNCs transfer their best labor practices to China and therefore the labor practices in China are quite similar to those at home. On the other hand, there is a growing body of research which shows that foreign MNCs are exploiting China's weak and unprotected workforce, particularly the migrant rural workers. As a result, the ACFTU has been forced to take a more proactive stance toward foreign MNCs. This stance has resulted from the growing number of employees of foreign MNCs, the decline in the number of state-owned enterprises, and the limited, but growing, trend of independent union organizing outside of the ACFTU. Currently, the ACFTU still has to perform a dual function: an instrument of the state and a labor organization that represents its members.

There are three fundamental developments that will shape labor relations within foreign MNCs in China. First, the ACFTU will have to continue to engage in grassroots organizing to counter management opposition to trade unions. The most publicized has been Wal-Mart, which refused to recognize a union until the ACFTU was able to obtain the signatures of at least 25 workers at each Wal-Mart store. By September 2006, all 62 Wal-Mart stores in China were unionized (unlike Wal-Mart stores in the United States). Second, there is a growing trend within ACFTU for direct election of trade union leaders at the workplace levels. Although the direct election is still a contested issue, there is much experimentation going on among union members who are employed by foreign MNCs. Third, within the new labor arbitration system, which includes 3,000 arbitration committees, the ACFTU representatives have become more involved at the workplace levels. The ACFTU officials are more likely to confront managers in order to protect workers' rights.[103]

In August 2007 after embarrassing reports of slave labor camps in the Henan and Shanxi Provinces and massive recalls of defective products made in China (food, toys, and tires), China President Hu Jintao announced that the central government would have a more active role in monitoring compliance with labor, safety, and environmental regulations at the local levels where local officials have been lax in compliance.[104] China's legislature enacted a sweeping new law that strengthens protections for workers. This enactment was a response to increasing signs of restiveness among tens of millions of migrant laborers and a news release of widespread slave labor in as many as 8,000 brick kilns and small coal mines in the Shanxi and Henan Provinces. The law requires employers to provide employees with written employment contracts which comply with minimum wage and safety regulations. The law restricts use of temporary laborers and helps give more employees long-term job security. Under the new law, employees with short-term contracts become full-time employees with lifetime benefits after a short-term contract is renewed twice. In addition, companies must consult with the state-run monopoly union (All-China Federation of Trade Unions—ACFTU) if they plan to lay off any employees. The law, which takes effect in 2008, enhances the role of the ACFTU and allows collective bargaining for wages and benefits. In the past, workers have been required to negotiate wages with their employers individually, and the ACFTU has had almost no involvement in setting wages and benefits.

This new law may not improve conditions for the low wage workers unless it is enforced more rigorously than the present laws, which already offer protections that on paper are similar to those in developed countries. In China, the present laws have not been enforced. In the past, the ACFTU has served more in the role of an official state organization charged with overseeing workers. Its practice has been either to play no role or to assist managers in monitoring and controlling workers. The new law continues ACFTU's monopoly status and does not allow workers to form independent unions. In the past, the ACFTU has rarely pressed companies for higher wages or better benefits, and the ACFTU does not permit strikes.

Some foreign executives have commented that they are worried about the new law because their companies already comply with existing laws more rigorously than some of their competitors. Thus, their disadvantage of compliance and the tendency of local governments to bend the rules make the new law more complicated and result in a competitive disadvantage to those companies that comply with the laws.[105]

In the Western world, labor and management enter negotiations, which typically lead to collective bargaining agreements. In China, autocratic management, nepotism, and unprofessional, undisciplined management techniques have dominated the workplace. Managers have viewed their firm as their personal kingdom, and paternalism has led workers to expect a certain level of economic and noneconomic support from their employers. Unity of labor–management interests has usually been more important than personal disagreements. While there has been significant change in China since 1988, China is a long way from embracing Western-style employment relations, strong unions, and collective bargaining. China remains constrained by its cultural and political history and by a large supply of low wage workers. Moreover, its labor relations system does not appear likely to demonstrate major changes for many years.[106]

Summary

Multinational corporations and transnational collective bargaining are becoming increasingly important topics of labor relations. Although multinational corporations continue to grow in sales volume, capital investments, and economic influence, they have also aroused trade unions in various countries to combine their energies, skills, and power in an effort to negotiate on an equal footing. Thus far, little success has been achieved because of legal, political, social, economic, and organizational obstacles. However, it is obvious that transnational collective bargaining could have a tremendous impact on the world's economy if the obstacles can be eliminated. Time will tell whether unions will be able to overcome the obstacles.

With the growing interdependency among nations, it is imperative that students who study labor relations learn more about labor relations systems throughout the world. This chapter highlights the main features of the labor relations systems of the major trading partners of the United States. Unions in Canada have expressed concern over the United States' economically dominant role in North America and its influence in the internal affairs of that country. Canada's system features two major linguistic and cultural groups and highly decentralized collective bargaining activities that are governed by provincial law. Mexico, the other partner with Canada and the United States in the North American Free Trade Agreement (NAFTA), has fairly well-developed labor laws but has major deficiencies in their administration and enforcement. The effects of NAFTA on jobs and trade unions were discussed.

Cuba, the largest Caribbean island, has a labor relations system that has suffered under the Castro regime but is showing signs of change. Labor relations vary widely among the countries in Central and South America, but they have one common feature: a close connection between trade unions and political parties.

Unionization in most of Western Europe is significantly greater than in the United States, and there is wide implementation of co-determination and employee participation policies. By 2007, 27 countries in Europe with a market of 490 million consumers had joined together to form the European Union (EU), which provides for greater deregulation and a decrease in trade and travel barriers between member countries. The formation of the EU increases the need to learn more about the labor relations system in each of these countries and will probably bring these countries closer together. In the past, the labor movements in many Eastern European countries were dominated by the Soviet Union. The countries of the former Soviet bloc are now trying to adjust to a market economy.

Unique features of the Japanese system include labor–management consultations, teamwork, a lifetime employment policy of the largest firms, a wage system primarily based on seniority, enterprise unions, and higher status accorded human resource managers. However, international money exchange rate fluctuations and recession could quickly alter these special union–management relationships of the Japanese system.

Korean labor relations have developed rapidly from a strike-ridden system in 1987 to more successful collective bargaining. With high growth rates, Korea still has problems of discrimination against women and employment of child labor.

The Australian system has evolved from a highly centralized system in which unions had much power to a pro-employer, more decentralized system. With a recent election, change is on the way.

The chapter ends with a description of the Chinese labor relations system, which has experienced rapid change in recent years, including the passage of new labor legislation in 2007.

Key Terms

Multinational corporations (MNCs), p. 619

Whipsawing, p. 623

Works councils, p. 626

North American Free Trade Agreement (NAFTA), p. 629

Wage system, p. 650

Enterprise unionism, p. 651

Discussion Questions

1. Although we share a common border with Canada, its labor relations system is affected by a number of variables that do not greatly affect the United States. Enumerate and explain these variables.

2. Explain why labor unions in many Central American countries have developed more slowly than those in the United States.

3. Western Europe seems to be uniquely involved with various forms of worker participation. What are some reasons that these worker participation systems have developed so fully there instead of elsewhere?

4. What are the five special features of the Japanese system? Why haven't these features been widely adopted in the United States?

5. Although multinational corporations seem to be growing in size and influence, what must occur before transnational collective bargaining can be effectively carried out?

6. Which features of Canada's labor relations system would you transfer to the United States?

7. Assess the transformation of the Australian labor relations system.

8. Give your assessment of the requirements for Cuba to develop a free, independent trade union. Is it essential for a free society?

9. Assess the strategy of Wal-Mart in China where the company has recognized unions in all 62 stores, to its strategy in the United States, which is to combat any type of union representation.

Exploring the Web

Labor Relations in Multinational Corporations and in Other Countries

1. The International Labour Organization. The International Labour Organization (ILO) has established labor standards for 150 countries represented by the organization. Locate the Web site for the ILO and comment on how these standards are created and how they are used. What is the Declaration of Philadelphia?

Locate the section on National Labour Law Profiles, select a country, and read the section on collective bargaining for that country.

2. Foreign Labor Trends. Search the Foreign Labor Statistics home page of the Bureau of Labor Statistics to find the following information:

Hourly compensation costs in U.S. dollars for production workers in manufacturing in 2005 for the United States, France, Canada, Mexico, and Ireland.

How did the employment rate in Canada compare with the rate in the United States in July 2007?

Using LABORSTA Internet, the service from the ILO Bureau of Statistics, compare statistics on strikes and lockouts in 2006 for two countries of your choice.

3. Guidelines for Multinational Corporations. The guidelines for Multinational Enterprises established by the Organization for Economic Cooperation and Development and presented on the OECD Web site are recommendations addressed by governments to multinational enterprises. The guidelines provide voluntary standards for responsible business conduct in a variety of areas, including employment and industrial relations. Locate "OECD Guidelines: Useful for Workers' Rights?" on the Clean Clothes Web site. How do unions go about filing a complaint against companies that are in violation of the guidelines?

4. Multinational Labor Organizations. Search for the history and mission statements for the following organizations:

International Federation of Airline Pilots Association (IFALPA)

International Metalworkers Federation (IMF)

International Federation of Chemical, Energy, Mine and General Workers (ICEM)

References

1. "Fortune Global 500," http://bookofup.com/meagagines/fortune/.
2. Anthony Ferner and Phil Almond, "Managing People in U.S.-Multinationals: The Case of Europe," *Perspectives on Work,* 11, (Summer 2007), p. 4.
3. George Melloan, "Feeling the Muscles of the Multinationals," *The Wall Street Journal,* January 6, 2004, p. A19.
4. Thomas W. Anderson and William J. Zeile, "U.S. Affilitates of Foreign Companies," *Survey of Current Business* 86 (August 2006), p. 195–206.
5. Lawrence McNeil, "Foreign Direct Investment in the United States," *Survey of Current Business* 87 (June, 2007), pp. 44–46.
6. "The World's View of Multinationals," *The Economist,* January 29, 2000, p. 21.
7. Thane Peterson, "Is Japan Using the U.S. as a Back Door to Europe?" *BusinessWeek,* November 14, 1988, p. 57.
8. Mario F. Bognanno, Michael P. Keane, and Donghoon Yang, "The Influence of Wages and Industrial Relations Environments on the Production Location Decisions of U.S. Multinational Corporations," *Industrial and Labor Relations Review,* 58 (January 2005), pp. 171–200.
9. Harry Shaiken, "Globalization and the Worldwide Division of Labor," *Monthly Labor Review* 110 (August 1987), p. 47.
10. Marvin J. Levine, "Labor Movements and the Multinational Corporation: A Future for Collective Bargaining?" *Employee Relations Law Journal* 13 (Winter 1987–88), pp. 382–398.
11. Rajib N. Sanyal, "Unionizing Foreign-Owned Firms: Perceptions of American Union Officials," *Labor Studies Journal* 14 (Winter 1989), p. 66.
12. "Hands across the Workplace," *Time,* December 26, 1988, pp. 15–18; "Working for the Japanese," *Time,* September 14, 1987; Paul Hemp, "Britain's 'Intransigent' Rubber Workers Bow to Japanese Management Practices," *The Wall Street Journal,* March 29, 1988, p. 26.
13. "Canada's UAW Thumbs Its Nose at Concessions," *BusinessWeek,* July 26, 1982, p. 23.
14. Charles R. Greer and John Shearer, "Do Foreign-Owned U.S. Firms Practice Unconventional Labor Relations?" *Monthly Labor Review* 104 (January 1981), pp. 45–47.
15. Duane Kujawa, "Collective Bargaining and Labor Relations in Multinational Enterprise: A U.S. Public

Policy Perspective," in *Research in International Business and Finance,* ed. Robert G. Hawkins (Greenwich, Conn.: JAI Press, Inc., 1979), p. 37.

16. Robert F. Banks and Jack Stieber, "Introduction," in *Multinationals, Unions, and Labor Relations in Industrial Countries* (Ithaca, N.Y.: New York State School of Industrial and Labor Relations, 1977), p. 1.

17. Arnold M. Zack, "Globalization and Its Effect on Collective Bargaining and Labor Arbitration," *Presentation to the Annual Meeting of the National Academy of Arbitrators,* May 26, 2006, pp. 10-8 to 10-12.

18. Lone Riisgaard, "International Framework Agreements: A New Model for Securing Workers' Rights," *Industrial Relations,* 44, (October 2005), pp. 707–736.

19. Geoffrey W. Latta and Janice R. Bellace, "Making the Corporation Transparent: Prelude to Multinational Bargaining," *Columbia Journal of World Business* 18 (Summer 1983), p. 73.

20. Hoyt N. Wheeler, *The Future of the American Labor Movement* (Cambridge, Mass.: Cambridge University Press, 2002), pp. 160–162.

21. "Update on Global Agreements," *European Industrial Relations Review,* June 2003, pp. 26–29.

22. Robert F. Banks and Jack Stieber, "*Multinationals, Unions, and Labor Relations in Industrial Countries* (Ithaca, N.Y.: New York State School of Industrial and Labor Relations. 1977), p. 11–12.

23. Levine, "Labor Movements and the Multinational Corporation," pp. 392–398.

24. G. B. J. Bomers, *Multinational Corporations and Industrial Relations* (Amsterdam, The Netherlands: Van Gorcum, Assen, 1976) p. 179.

25. Herbert R. Northrup, "Why Multinationals Bargaining Neither Exists Nor Is Desirable," *Labor Law Journal* 29 (June 1978), pp. 330–331.

26. "Stolen Jobs?" *The Economist,* December 13, 2003, pp. 13–15; "Relocating the Back Office," *The Economist,* December 13, 2003, pp. 67–68; Charles Schumer and Paul Craig Roberts, "Second Thoughts on Free Trade," *The New York Times,* January 6, 2004, p. A27.

27. http://www.fas.usda/gov/info/factsheets/nafta.

28. "Free Trade on Trial," *The Economist,* January 3, 2004, pp. 13–16; Joseph E. Stiglitz, "The Broken Promise of NAFTA" *The New York Times,* January 6, 2004, p. A27.

29. Francisco Zapata, "NAFTA: Few Gains for Mexico's Workers," *Perspectives on Work* 6 (2002), pp. 22–24.

30. "Mexico: Was NAFTA Worth It?" *BusinessWeek,* December 22, 2003, pp. 66–72.

31. "Free Trade on Trial," *The Economist,* January 3, 2004, pp. 13–16; Joseph E. Stiglitz, "The Broken Promsie of NAFTA" *The New York Times,* January 6, 2004, p. A27.

32. Rainer Dombois, "The North American Agreement on Labor Cooperation: Designed to Fail?" *Perspectives on Work* 6 (2002), pp. 19–21.

33. Mario F. Bognanno and Jiangfeng Lu, "NAFTA's Labor Side Agreement: Withering as an Effective Labor Law Enforcement and MNC Compliance Strategy?" *Multinational Companies and Global Human Resource Strategies,* ed. William N. Cooke (Westport, Conn.: Quorum Books, 2003), pp. 391–393.

34. Jon Hiatt, "Discussion," *Proceedings of the 52nd Annual Meeting of the Industrial Relations Research Association,* ed. Paula B. Voos (Champaign, Ill.: IRRA, 2000), pp. 278–280.

35. Diana Chew and Richard A. Posthuma, "International Employment Dispute Resolution under NAFTA's Side Agreement on Labor," *Labor Law Journal* 53 (2002), p. 45.

36. Hoyt N. Wheeler and Jaques Rojot, "General Comments," in *Workplace Justice: Employment Obligations in International Perspective* (Columbia, S.C.: University of South Carolina Press, 1992), pp. 368–369. Also see: Hoyt N. Wheeler, Brian S. Klass, and Douglas M. Mahoney, *Workplace Justice without Unions.* (Kalamazoo, MI: W. E. Upjohn Institute for Employment Research), 2004.

37. Joseph B. Rose and Gary N. Chaison, "Union Density and Union Effectiveness: The North American Experience," *Proceedings of the 9th World Congress of the International Industrial Relations* Association (Sydney, Australia: International Industrial Relations Association, 1992), p. 528.

38. Jean Boivin, "The Transformation of Canadian Employment Relations," *Perspectives on Work* 1, no. 2 (1997), pp. 40–44.

39. *Union Membership in Canada—January 1, 2006,* Labour Policy and Workplace Information, Labour Program, Human Resources and Skills Development Canada, http://www.hrsdc.gc/.

40. Victor G. Devinatz, Book Review: Labour Left Out: Canadian's Failure to Protest and Promote Collective Bargaining as a Human Right, by Roy J. Adams, *Journal of Labor Research,* 27 (Spring 2007), pp. 413–415.

41. Joseph B. Rose and Gary N. Chaison, "Canadian Labor Policy as a Model for Legislative Reform in the United States," *Labor Law Journal* 46 (May 1995), p. 259. See Richard N. Block and Karen Roberts, "An Overview of Labor Standards in the United States and Canada" *Labor Law Journal* 49 (September 1998), pp. 1127–1133.

42. Daphne G. Taras, "Explaining Canadian-American Differences in Union Density," *Proceedings of the 53rd Annual Meeting of the Industrial Relations Research Association,* ed. Paula B. Voos (Champaign, Ill.: IRRA, 2001), pp. 153–159.

43. Joseph B. Rose and Gary N. Chaison, "Linking Union Density and Union Effectiveness: The North American Experience," *Industrial Relations* 35 (January 1996), pp. 78–105.

44. Gerald Mayer, "Labor Union Recognition Procedures: Use of Secret Ballots and Card Checks," *Congressional Research Service,* The Library of Congress, 2005 (http://digitalcommons.ilr.cornell.edu/key workplace/237).

45. Charles R. Greer, Charles D. Stevens, and Gregory K. Stephens, "The State of the Unions in Mexico," *Journal of Labor Research,* 28 (Winter 2007), pp. 69–92.

46. *Mexico* (Washington, D.C.: U.S. Department of Labor, Bureau of International Labor Affairs, 2002), pp. 4–6. For more information about Mexican legislation involving employment security and employment discrimination, see: Charles Hollon, "Discrimination in Employment Provisions in the Mexican Federal Labor Law," *Employee Responsibilities and Rights Journal,* 11 (1998),

pp. 65–70; Charles Hollon, "Individual Employee Employment Security under Mexican Federal Labor Law," *Labor Law Journal* 47 (October 1996), pp. 648–656.

47. Charles R. Greer, Charles D. Stevens, and Gregory K. Stephens, "The State of the Unions in Mexico," *Journal of Labor Research,* 28 (Winter 2007), pp. 69–92.

48. *Mexico,* Washington, D.C.: U.S. Printing Office, 2002, pp. 4–6.

49. Charles J. Hollon, "Employee Profit Sharing under the Mexican Labor Law," *Labor Law Journal* 47 (May 1996), pp. 323–326.

50. Craig Torres, "Mexico Reaches Wage and Price Accord," *The Wall Street Journal,* October 30, 1995, p. A14.

51. Charles R. Greer, Charles D. Stevens, and Gregory K. Stephens, "The State of the Unions in Mexico," *Journal of Labor Research,* 28 (Winter 2007), pp. 69–92.

52. Everett M. Kassalow, *Trade Unions and Industrial Relations: An International Comparison* (New York: Random House, 1969), pp. 302–303.

53. "Europe's Unions Are Losing Their Grip," *BusinessWeek,* November 26, 1986, pp. 80–84.

54. *Free Trade with Central America and the Dominican Republic,* Office of the United States Trade Representative, February 2005, pp. 1–2.

55. Karl O. Magnusen and Leonardo Rodriguez, "Cuba, Labor, and Change," *Labor Studies Journal* 23 (Summer 1998), pp. 22–39.

56. Everett M. Kassalow, "Conflict and Cooperation in Europe's Industrial Relations," *Industrial Relations* 13 (May 1974), pp. 156–163.

57. "Eleven European Leaders Endorse EC Worker Rights Code, Thatcher Objects," *Daily Labor Report,* December 12, 1989, p. A-3; "Social Charter: Action Programme Released," *European Industrial Relations Report* no. 112 (January 1990), pp. 11–14.

58. Roy J. Adams, "Industrial Relations in Europe and North America: Some Contemporary Themes," *European Journal of Industrial Relations* 1 (1995), p. 50.

59. Margaret Hilton, "Shared Training: Learning from Germany," *Monthly Labor Review* 114 (March 1991), pp. 33–35; Robert J. Gitter, "Job Training in Europe: Lessons from Abroad," *Monthly Labor Review* 115 (April 1992), pp. 25–27.

60. "Europe's Union to Grow by 10," *The New York Times,* December 2, 2003, p. C-4; *European Union 2003,* (Washington, D.C.: U. S. Printing Office, 2003), pp. 17–19.

61. "Introduction—Special Report," *Daily Labor Report,* June 22, 1990, p. 3.

62. John T. Addison and W. Stanley Siebert, "The Social Charter of the European Community: Evolution and Controversies," *Industrial and Labor Relations Review* 44 (July 1991), pp. 597–623.

63. Trevor Bain and Kim Hester, "Similarities and Differences in a Sample of European Works Council Agreements," *Proceedings of the 52nd Annual Meeting of the Industrial Relations Research Association,* ed. Paula B. Voos (Champaign, Ill.: IRRA, 2000), pp. 45–47.

64. Paul Marginson, "The Eurocompany and Euro Industrial Relations," *European Journal of Industrial Relations* 6 (2000), pp. 9–30; Jane Wills, "Great Expectations: Three Years in the Life of a European Works Council," *European Journal of Industrial Relations* 8 (2000), pp. 85–107.

65. "A Work in Progress: A Survey of Europe," *The Economist,* October 23, 2000, pp. 3–18.

66. Paul Willman and Alex Bryson, "Union Organization in Great Britain," *Journal of Labor Research,* 28 (Winter 2007), pp. 93–111; Gregory Fall, "Trade Union Recognition in Britain: Is a Corner Being Turned?" *Proceedings of the 57th Annual Meeting of the Labor and Employment Relations Association,* Editor, Adrienne E. Easton, Champaign IL, LERA, 2006, p. 216.

67. David Metcalf, "Prime Minister Blair's New Labor Industrial Relations Program," *Perspectives on work* 3 (1999), pp. 12–17.

68. *Review of the Employment Relations Act of 1999,* Department of Trade and Industry, February 2003, pp. 7–19.

69. John T. Addison, Claus Schnabel, and Joachim Wagner, "Te (Parlous) State of German Unions," *Journal of Labor Research,* 28 (Winter 2007), pp. 3–16.

70. *World Labor Report* 1992 (Geneva: International Labour Office, 1992), p. 57.

71. Peter Galuszka, "Toss another Match into the Russian Tinderbox: Labor," *BusinessWeek,* June 6, 1994, p. 51.

72. Katharina Bluhm, "Exporting or Abandoning the 'German Model'?: Labour Policies of German Manufacturing Firms in Central Europe," *European Journal of Industrial Relations* 7 (July 2001), pp. 153–168.

73. Aurora Trif, "Collective Bargaining in Eastern Europe: Case Study Evidence from Romania," *European Journal of Industrial Relations,* 13 (July 2007), pp. 236–254.

74. Arturo Bronstein, "The New Labour Law of the Russian Federation," *International Labour Review,* 133, (2005), 291–318. Also see: Simon Clarke, "The State of the Russian Unions," *The Journal of Labor Research,* 28 (Spring 2007), pp. 275–299.

75. Joseph Krislov, "How Does the Japanese Industrial Relations System Differ?" *Labor Law Journal* 40 (June 1989), pp. 338–344.

76. Motohiro Morishima, "Information Sharing and Collective Bargaining in Japan: Effects of Wage Negotiations," *Industrial and Labor Relations Review* 44 (April 1991), pp. 469–482.

77. Motohiro Morishima, "Information Sharing and Firm Performance in Japan," *Industrial Relations* 30 (Winter 1991), pp. 37–57.

78. Kiyoshi Kawahito, "Labor Relations in the Japanese Automobile and Steel Industries," *Journal of Labor Research* 11 (Summer 1990), pp. 232–237.

79. Katsumi Yakabe, *Labor Relations in Japan* (Tokyo: International Society for Educational Information, 1974), pp. 1–14; Hisashi Kawada and Ryuji Komatsu, "Post-War Labor Movements in Japan," in *The International Labor Movement in Transition,* eds. Adolph Strumthal and James G. Scoville (Urbana, Ill.: University of Illinois Press, 1973), pp. 122–148; and Tadashi A. Hanami, "The Multinational Corporation and Japanese Industrial Relations," in *International Labor and Multinational Enterprise,* ed. Duane Kujawa (New York: Praeger Publishers, 1975), pp. 183–185.

80. Peter B. Doeringer, Christine Evans-Klock, and David G. Terkla, "Hybrids or Hodgepodge? Workplace Practices of Japanese and Domestic Startups in the United States," *Industrial and Labor Relations Review* 51 (January 1998), pp. 171–177.

81. Krislov, "How Does the Japanese System Differ?" p. 340.

82. JIM: Japan Information Network, http://www.jinpapn.org/access/employ/index.html (January 4, 2004).

83. JIM: Japan Information Network, http://www.jinpapn.org/access/employ/index.html (January 4, 2004).

84. Tsuyoshi Tsuru and Motohiro Morishima, "Nonunion Employee Representation in Japan," *Journal of Labor Research*, 20 (Winter 1999), pp. 94–96.

85. Glenn Halm and Clinton R. Shiels, "Damage Control: Yen Appreciation and the Japanese Labor Market," *Monthly Labor Review* 111 (November 1988), pp. 3–5.

86. Sanford M. Jacoby, Emily M. Nason, and Kazuro Saguchi, "The Role of the Senior HR Executive in Japan and the United States: Employment Relations, Corporate Governance, and Values" *Industrial Relations*, 44 (April 2005), pp. 207–241.

87. Tsuyoshi Tsuru and Motohiro Morishima, "Nonunion Employee Representation in Japan," *Journal of Labor Research*, 20 (Winter 1999), pp. 94–96.

88. *Japan* (Washington, D.C.: U.S. Department of Labor, Bureau of International Labor Affairs, 1996), pp. 10–15.

89. *Labor Situation in Japan and Analysis: General Overview 2006/2007*, The Japan Institute for Labour Policy and Training, November 2006, pp. 67–82.

90. "An Aging Workforce Strains Japan's Traditions," *BusinessWeek*, April 20, 1981, pp. 72–85.

91. Drawn primarily from Mario F. Bognanno, *Korea's Industrial Relations at the Turning Point* (Seoul: Korea Development Institute, 1988), pp. 4–90; Mario F. Bognanno, John W. Budd, and Young-Myon Lee, "Institutional Turmoil and Strike Activity in Korea," *Journal of Industrial Relations* 36 (September 1994), pp. 360–367; *Korea* (Washington, D.C.: U.S. Department of Labor, Bureau of International Labor Affairs, 1998), pp. 8–9; Mario F. Bognanno, Michael L. Bognanno, and Young-Myon Lee, "Incomplete Information and Conversion to a 'No Work—No Pay' Strike Policy: Their Effects on Wage Settlements and Strikes in Korea," *Working Paper*, July 1998, p. 1.

92. "United States and the Republic of Korea Sign Landmark Free Trade Agreement," *Office of United States Trade Representative*, http://www.ustr.gov/.

93. *Korea,* (Washington D.C.: U.S. Government Printing Office, 2003), pp. 1–19.

94. *Australia,* (Washington, D.C.: U.S. Printing Office, 2003), pp. 3–7.

95. Rae Cooper, Chris Briggs, Bradon Ellem, and Diane Van Den Broek, "The New Australian Employer Militancy," *Work on Perspectives,* 11 (Summer 2007), pp. 39–41.

96. Russell B. Lansbury and Nick Wailes, "Different Paths to Similar Outcomes: Industrial Relations Reform in Australia and New Zealand," *Work on Perspectives,* 11 (Summer 2007), pp. 29–34.

97. C. Jeffrey Waddoups, "Trade Union Decline and Union Wage Effects in Australia," *Industrial Relations,* 44 (October 2005), pp. 607–624.

98. Richard Hall, "The 'Work Choices' Revolution in Australia: Recent Legislative Reforms and Their Consequences," *Work on Perspectives,* 11 (Summer 2007), pp. 35–38.

99. Jihi Xia, "Reforming China's Systems of Employment and Labor Relations," *Perspectives on Work* 7 (Winter 2004), pp. 28–30.

100. Stephen Frenkel and Sarosh Kuruvilla, "Logic of Action, Globalization, and Changing Employment Relations in China, India, Malaysia, and the Philippines," *Industrial and Labor Relations Review* 55 (April 2002), pp. 398–401.

101. Trini Wing-Yue Leung, "Trade Unions and Labor Relations Under Market Socialism in China," *Industrial Relations between Command and Market: A Comparative Analysis of Eastern Europe and China*, eds. Gerd Chienstock, Paul Thompson, and Franz Traxler (New York: Nova Science, 1997), pp. 2347–280.

102. Stephen Frenkel and Sarosh Kuruvilla, "Logics of Action, Globalization, and Changing Employment Relations in China, India, Malaysia, and Philippines," *Industrial and Labor Relations Review* (in press), pp. 26–30.

103. Christain Levesque and Hao Hu, "Multinationals and Employment Relations in China," *Perspectives on Work,* 11 (Summer 2007), pp. 13–15.

104. Andrew Batson, "China Tightens Local Oversight," *The Wall Street Journal*, August 10, 2007, p. A5.

105. Joseph Kahn and David Barboza, "As Unrest Rises, China Broadens Workers' Rights," *The New York Times*, June 30, 2007, p. A-1 and A-5.

106. Trevor Bain and Chyi-Herng Chang, "Revisiting China and Taiwan," *Perspectives on Work* 7 (Winter 2004), pp. 34–35.

Classroom Exercise

14.1
Mobile Factory

You are the owner of a small North Carolina factory that makes T-shirts for international distribution. You have observed that your sales have declined by about ten percent for each of the last three years. You believe that the reason is that you are being underpriced by your international competitors even though your market is in the United States and your competitors are required to pay transportation costs from their factories in other countries to the United States.

You have been reading several articles about exchange rates and the weakening of the dollar in comparison with many foreign currencies and believe you have come up with a unique solution to your problem. You have surveyed your 50 employees and found that most of them are single and love to travel. Therefore, you have decided to purchase a ship and transfer your machinery and office equipment to the ship. Since you pay employees and sell your goods based on where you dock your ship, you have considerable flexibility on the country in which you conduct business. When the exchange rates change, you will simply move to another location where the exchange rates are more favorable. As an example, in 2002, the 100 U.S. dollars were trading for about 90 euros; in early 2008, 100 U.S. dollars would trade for 68.1 euros. That means that U.S. manufacturers were much more competitive internationally in 2008 than in 2002, when the U.S. dollar was stronger internationally.

You have to decide where in the world you would like to dock your ship in order to take advantage of the exchange rates and wage rates of the country where you dock.

Questions
1. Evaluate the exchange rates and wage rates shown in Exhibit 14.1 and decide where you should dock your ship for local production.
2. Review the index of wage rates of 1980, 1990, 1998, 2002, and 2005 and determine whether the strategy and decision in 2008 would be the same as in the previous years.

Collective Bargaining Negotiations Exercise: QFM Company and IWU

Simulation Contributor: Charlie T. Cook

LEARNING OBJECTIVES

1. To gain an understanding of negotiation preparations, actual negotiations, and assessment of negotiations' outcomes.
2. To develop an appreciation for the psychological interactions and the realism of contract negotiations.
3. To learn the mechanics of give-and-take, compromise, trading issues, and the art of negotiation.
4. To familiarize the participants with the issues in collective bargaining and the challenge of writing provisions acceptable to both parties.
5. To realize the importance of and problems associated with teamwork and intra-organizational bargaining.
6. To gain an appreciation for the application of bargaining theories to negotiations.

RULES OF THE NEGOTIATIONS EXERCISE

1. Participants must not discuss the exercise with anyone except their assigned team members.
2. Each participant will be assigned a role (organization position) by the instructor.
3. The negotiations must take place within the framework of the present company and union at the St. Louis plant. Creativity is encouraged, but a realistic and pragmatic approach is recommended.
4. Data, materials, and information used for each position or argument on behalf of a proposal should not be falsified.
5. Each team may have as many meetings *outside* class as are needed and desirable.
6. Team members must follow the instructions of their respective team leaders.
7. All activities of team members should be directed toward negotiating an agreement that is mutually acceptable and that the parties can live with, survive on, and prosper under.

Instructions to the Participant

1. Participants will be assigned to either the management or the union bargaining team. Each team will be responsible for determining the specific tasks or roles assigned to individual team members.

2. The team leaders—the president of the Industrial Workers United (IWU) and the labor relations director of Quality Furniture Manufacturing (QFM) Company—will call separate meetings to discuss and prepare for the upcoming negotiations and anticipate each other's proposals. Major issues for negotiations could include:

   a. Union security (e.g., dues checkoff, union shop)

   b. Wages, job classes, premiums

   c. Management's rights

   d. Promotions and layoffs (use of seniority)

   e. Grievance procedure and arbitration

   f. Affirmative action plans

   g. Pension plans

   h. Health insurance

   i. Vacations

   j. Holidays

   k. Sick leave

   l. Other issues allowed by instructor

3. In bargaining preparation meetings, each team should study the present agreement to identify contract language in need of improvement or deletion; identify key subjects not covered by the expiring contract's terms which should be included in any new (renegotiated) labor agreement; determine relevant information sources and gather materials, data, and information necessary to support the team's proposals and positions or address bargaining subjects expected to be raised by the other party during negotiations.

4. Based on study and analysis, each team must determine its bargaining strategy and goals.

5. Each team must complete the first four columns of Form 1 (on page 678) and give it to the instructor prior to the first scheduled face-to-face bargaining meeting between union and management teams. (The form should not be shown to anyone else.)

6. The union and management teams will meet at a time and location specified by the instructor for the purpose of negotiating a new agreement to replace the expiring contract's terms.

7. At the first meeting, the union will present and explain its proposals first. Management will then present its proposals or counterproposals and explain each proposal.

8. Actual negotiations will begin after the proposals are exchanged and will continue until a new agreement is negotiated and signed or the present contract expires. The instructor will specify the current contract's expiration time and date as well as the schedule for formal bargaining meetings between union and management teams.

9. On completion of the negotiations, each team will project the total annual costs of the new agreement. If assigned by the instructor, the teams will submit a written agreement.

10. Additional instructions may be given to the participants by the instructor.

SOURCES OF MATERIALS FOR PREPARATION

Government publications: U.S. Department of Labor, Bureau of Labor Statistics, *Area Wage Surveys, Employment and Earnings, Handbook of Labor Statistics, Monthly Labor Review, Characteristics of Major Collective Bargaining Agreements.*

U.S. Department of Commerce, *U.S. Industrial Outlook* (published every year).

Binder services of Bureau of National Affairs, Inc. (BNA) and Commerce Clearing House. Especially helpful is the BNA *Collective Bargaining Negotiations and Contracts.*

Business publications: *BusinessWeek* and *The Wall Street Journal.*

Professional labor relations journals: *Collective Bargaining Bulletin, Dispute Resolution Journal, Employee Relations Law Journal, Industrial and Labor Relations Review, Industrial Relations, Berkeley Journal of Employment and Labor Law, Journal of Collective Negotiations in the Public Sector, Labor Law Journal,* and *Monthly Labor Review.*

Proceedings: Labor and Employment Relations Association, Labor Law Developments, National Academy of Arbitrators, and NYU Conference on Labor.

Current labor agreements between companies and unions (as available).

THE FURNITURE MANUFACTURING INDUSTRY

U.S. furniture manufacturers generated about $65 billion in sales of all furniture types in 2006—the market for household furniture was $31.5 billion.[1] The highly fragmented household furniture industry is segmented into wood furniture ("case goods") at 60 percent of sales, upholstered furniture (primarily sofas and recliners) at 30 percent of sales, with metal furniture, mattresses, and other products accounting for the remaining ten percent. Case goods include kitchen and dining room sets, china cabinets, dressers, and home entertainment/media centers. Products are sold either finished or in ready-to-assemble form. Competition in the industry is among purely domestic manufacturers, domestic manufacturers that import specific product lines, and foreign producers.[2]

Global competition has severely impacted the U.S. furniture manufacturing industry for the past decade. In a near-complete reversal, over half of all wood furniture sold in U.S. markets today is imported.[3] Once global competitors began rapidly entering U.S. markets, American manufacturers responded by consolidating or closing U.S. operations, acquiring or building overseas plants, and contracting with foreign companies to produce piece goods for the U.S. market. The number of domestic manufacturers has fallen rapidly as weaker firms have exited the industry or have been acquired by the remaining competitors. Furniture imports into the U.S. market over the last decade have increased at annual rates as much as ten times the increase in American exports to foreign markets even though shipping costs can total as much as one-fourth of the value of the shipped products.[4]

Labor-intensive production operations have been outsourced to China, Vietnam, Indonesia, Taiwan, Eastern Europe, and Mexico to take advantage of lower labor costs. American furniture workers earn an average hourly wage of about $12 while Chinese workers receive less than $1.[5] Employment in the industry peaked in 2000 and has declined steadily since.[6] Conversely, some jobs in the industry are beginning to go begging. Skilled upholsterers, who can earn $35,000 to $45,000 per year doing piece rate work for domestic manufacturers, are in high demand. Average annual revenue per worker is about $130,000, dropping to only $100,000 per worker in the household furniture segment.[7]

The upholstered furniture product segment has, for now, been largely unaffected by the competitive forces in the furniture industry. Almost half of all upholstered items are custom ordered. The extended delivery lead times involved in foreign manufacturing cannot satisfy customers who want their furniture sooner rather than later. Competitors in this segment that can efficiently produce and quickly deliver high quality custom furniture at attractive (and profitable) price points will have a sustainable competitive advantage that will be difficult for overseas producers to overcome.[8]

To control costs and stay profitable, U.S. furniture manufacturers have adopted the lean manufacturing methods of Toyota Motor Corporation's production system. This system focuses on continuous improvement in production processes, elimination of waste, inventory reduction, and speed of delivery.[9] Another challenge for the household furniture industry is the urgent necessity for a radical restructuring of traditional supply and distribution channels to further lower costs as overseas producers continue to improve their product quality and distribution efficiencies. Developing strong brands to sell in branded retail stores will help shield some competitors from direct competitive threats; others will fall victim to the rising industry trend of ever fewer supply-chain intermediaries between overseas manufacturers and domestic big-box and specialty retailers. An accompanying trend is the spreading use of the Internet by furniture consumers, furniture distributors, and manufacturers, and the use of e-procurement between manufacturers and suppliers.[10]

The household furniture industry is headed for difficult times as the U.S. residential housing market's boom appears to have run its course. Consumers, when faced with higher mortgage payments as interest rates rise, will likely delay household furniture purchases, and those who do purchase will have become much more price sensitive. Until better economic times return, home furniture retailers are expected to tighten inventories and to narrow product selections to focus on higher-margin quality goods. These actions and the threat of office furniture manufacturers diversifying beyond home office products will create increased competition in the industry's value/activity chain of vendors, suppliers, and manufacturers. A deteriorating economy and continued increases in better quality imports will put additional pressure on all industry competitors to reduce prices to maintain sales and market shares while simultaneously keeping up capacity utilization of manufacturing assets to reduce largely fixed overhead costs through volume production. If the economy improves, then consumers will once again begin to furnish their homes.

THE QFM COMPANY AND THE UNION

QFM Company began in 1820 in Laconia, New Hampshire, as a family-owned and operated furniture manufacturer. It was headed by Herman Sweeny, one of the early settlers in Laconia. The company grew to 30 employees by 1920, but at that time, Ben Franklin Sweeny, Herman's son, decided to move the firm to

St. Louis, Missouri—a location more central to the firm's market. Barely surviving the 1930s depression, QFM was one of the first companies to convert its manufacturing processes to the production of war materials. The company prospered during the war, and afterward, Sweeny decided to expand, sell stock publicly, and focus on producing metal and plastic-laminated furniture. With the production experience it had gained during the war and with its location some distance from the predominantly wood-furniture manufacturers, QFM Company launched a new era for itself in 1946.

By 1970 the St. Louis plant of QFM Company had 1,300 employees and was producing 450 dinette sets, 200 sets of lawn tables and chairs, and 300 bar stools and miscellaneous furniture daily. During the 1971–1973 furniture boom with its expectations of continuous growth, QFM's new president, Gerald Brooks, decided that a new, modern plant and more diversity in the product line were necessary to meet the expected demand. Taking into consideration location, material supply, transportation, markets, labor costs, and other factors, Brooks decided to build the new plant in Dallas, Texas. This plant was to specialize in the new product lines, and the St. Louis plant was to concentrate only on dinette sets. In 1972, 200 employees were transferred from St. Louis, and another 200 were hired from the Dallas–Fort Worth area. The Dallas plant started with no union and 400 employees. In 1993 the founder's granddaughter, Bethany Sweeny, became plant manager, and the plant size grew to the current 894-employee non-union workforce.

The company pays its Dallas employees at least $1 less per hour than it pays the St. Louis employees in comparable jobs which the company has always attributed to the lower cost of living in the Dallas-Ft. Worth area. The St. Louis plant continues to produce 450 dinette sets per day, mostly for chain retailers (e.g., Wal-Mart, Babcock Home Furnishing, Home Depot), and employs about 1,000 employees in the bargaining unit represented by the IWU. During the past year the St. Louis plant has begun producing high-end custom wood entertainment centers designed to cater to consumer demand fueled by high definition, flat panel televisions and home theater sound systems. Initial customer reaction to the new product line has been positive. Employment levels at the St. Louis plant have remained relatively stable over the past 30 years.

The company has invested in modernizing plant equipment and production methods at both the St. Louis and Dallas plants since the mid-1980s. The Dallas plant has started producing a new high-end product line—dinette sets under the Eagle brand name aimed at capturing higher income consumer demand. Consumer response has been positive, and the Dallas plant's future looks very promising. With increasing import competition, the company is investigating the possibility of locating a production facility in China or Mexico, but no final decision has been reached yet on whether to initiate such an expansion. Throughout its history, QFM Company has prided itself on being a progressive employer.

The Industrial Workers United (IWU) first sought to represent QFM employees at the St. Louis, MO plant in 1975. The building of the Dallas plant, increasing employment at the Dallas plant rather than at the St. Louis plant, and employee complaints about lower than average area wage rates were all issues in the 1975 representation election campaign at the St. Louis plant. After a heated campaign by both management and the Union, NLRB investigations of unfair labor practices, and challenged ballots, the union lost the election by a vote of 497 to 481. Two years later, the union returned and won an NLRB-supervised representation election by a vote of 611 to 375. The election campaign was bitter, and the negotiations that followed were even more contentious. After a six-week strike, the company and union reached agreement on their first labor contract. There have been nine subsequent contracts negotiated between the parties without the occurrence of a work stoppage. The current labor agreement covering the St. Louis plant is close to its expiration date, prompting the union to notify management requesting the company renegotiate the terms of the existing contract. Although company officials have expressed a desire to return to the era when management and labor trusted each other, worked cooperatively, and shared mutual goals and benefits, the union's leaders are taking a wait-and-see attitude, believing that actions speak louder than words.

The company's insurance carrier recently announced a 15 percent increase in the annual health insurance policy premium cost covering bargaining unit members to take effect on April 15, 2008. The current (about to expire) contract calls for health insurance policy premium costs to be split, with the employer paying 90 percent and the employee the remaining ten percent of the total premium cost. Currently, 75 percent of bargaining unit members are covered under a family health care plan at an annual premium cost per employee of $2,970. Twenty-five percent of bargaining unit members have single employee coverage at a total annual premium cost of $1,412 per employee. Union members believe the company could easily afford to absorb the announced 15 percent health insurance premium cost increase without having to pass any of the increase along to bargaining unit members.

The upcoming negotiations will determine the company's commitment to improving labor relations at the plant. The union believes it is entering negotiations in a strong bargaining position with 95 percent of the bargaining unit now enrolled as union members.

References

1. Fast Facts 2007, http://www.exportvirginia.org/FastFacts/FastFacts_2007/FF_Issues_Furniture_Lumber_07.pdf
2. Bryson, Lanzillotti, Myerberg, Miller, and Tian, "The Furniture Industry (Case Goods), The Future of the Industry, United States versus China," *Industry Economics*: March 7, 2003.
3. Vlosky, Richard, "Dynamics and Trends in US Furniture Markets," Louisiana State University Agricultural Center, School of Renewable Natural Resources, June 7, 2005.
4. Al Schuler and Steve Lawser, "The U.S. Furniture Industry: Yesterday and Today Will There Be a Tomorrow?" *Wood Digest*, June 2007.
5. Schmid, John and Romell, Rick, "Furniture, China, and the End of an Era," *The Morning Journal*, February 1, 2004.
6. *Industry Overview: Furniture Manufacturing*, http://www.hoovers.com/furniture-manufacturing/–ID__49–/free-ind-fr-profile-basic.xhtml, last accessed January 01, 2007.
7. *Current Trends in Furniture Production and Sales*, AKTRIN Furniture Information Center, January 2006.
8. www.duke.edu/web/mms190/furniture/dimensions.html.
9. *The Impact of Globalization on NC's Furniture Industries,* (Buehlmann, Urs; Schuler, Al; Nwagbara, Ucheoma) 2002.
10. Jon Chavez, "Overseas Competition Challenges Furniture Industry," *Toledo Blade*, Thursday, March 22, 2007.

The Labor Agreement between Quality Furniture Manufacturing Company (QFM) and Industrial Workers United (IWU), AFL-CIO

This agreement is entered into on _____ by the Quality Furniture Manufacturing Company (QFM), located in St. Louis, Missouri, and Industrial Workers United (IWU). This agreement covers employees at the St. Louis plant only.

Article I—Recognition

The company recognizes the IWU as the sole and exclusive collective bargaining agent in all matters pertaining to rates of pay, wages, hours of employment, and other conditions of employment for all production and maintenance employees, excluding professional employees, storeroom employees, office clerical employees, guards, and supervisors, as defined in the Labor Management Relations Act.

Article II—Union Security

The company agrees not to interfere with the right of employees to join the Union and will not discriminate against employees who are Union members. Employees in the bargaining unit are completely free to participate in the affairs of the Union, provided that such activities do not interfere with their work duties and responsibilities.

While no employee will be required to join the Union as a condition of employment, union dues will be deducted from any bargaining unit employee's pay check, provided proper written notification is given to the Company. At the end of each pay period, the Company will forward the collected dues, minus a three percent administrative fee, to the Union.

Article III—Management Rights

All management functions of the enterprise that are not specifically limited by the express language of this agreement are retained by the Company. The functions and rights listed here are examples of the exclusive responsibilities retained by the Company and are not intended as an all-inclusive list: to manage the manufacturing operations and methods of production; to direct the workforce; to decide what work shall be performed in the plant by subcontractors or by employees; to schedule working hours (including overtime work); to hire, promote, demote, and transfer; to suspend, discipline, and discharge for cause; to relieve employees due to lack of work or for other legitimate reasons; to create and enforce reasonable shop rules and regulations; to establish production standards and rates for new or changed jobs; to introduce new and improved methods, materials, equipment, and facilities; to change or eliminate existing methods, materials, equipment, and facilities.

Article IV—No Strike and No Lockout

The company agrees that during the life of this agreement there shall be no lockout of bargaining unit employees. The Union agrees that during the life of this agreement there shall be no strike, work stoppage, slowdown, work refusal, delay of work, refusal to report for work, or boycott.

Article V—Hours of Work

The normal workweek shall consist of eight (8) hours per day, forty (40) hours per week, for a five (5) day week, from Monday to Friday. The starting time shall be made by the Company, and it can be changed by the Company to suit varying conditions of the business. Such changes in working schedules shall be made known to the Union representative in the plant as far in advance as possible. Employees shall be notified by a written bulletin or other communications medium.

Article VI—Grievances and Arbitration Procedures

Grievances arising out of the operation and interpretation of this agreement shall be handled and settled in the following manner:

Step 1: The aggrieved employee and/or shop steward shall discuss the grievance with his or her supervisor.

Step 2: Should the answer provided by the supervisor not produce a satisfactory solution to the grievance, the grievance shall be reduced to writing and shall state the provision of the agreement which has been violated. The department head shall arrange for a meeting of the aggrieved employee, the shop steward, the supervisor, the employee relations supervisor, and himself or herself for the purpose of discussing the grievance. The department head shall provide a written answer to the grievance after the close of the meeting.

Step 3: If a satisfactory conclusion is not reached, the grievance can be referred to the plant manager by the Union. The plant manager shall schedule a meeting to discuss the grievance with the Union. The local Union can bring in a representative of the International Union at this step, and the plant manager can bring in anyone who he or she feels may aid in the resolution of the grievance.

Step 4: If a grievance is appealed to arbitration, the Company and the Union shall attempt to select an arbitrator. If this attempt fails, the Company and/or Union shall ask the Federal Mediation and Conciliation Service to submit a list of seven (7) arbitrators. Each party shall eliminate three (3) names from the list by alternately striking one name at a time, and the person whose name remains shall serve as the arbitrator.

The arbitrator shall render a decision in writing that shall be final and binding upon the parties. The arbitrator to whom any grievance is submitted shall have the authority to interpret and apply the provisions of this agreement, and the arbitrator's decision must be in accordance with and based upon the terms of this agreement or any written amendment thereto. The arbitrator shall have no jurisdiction or authority to add to, subtract from, or modify any of the terms of this agreement.

The Company and local Union shall each pay its own expenses incurred in connection with the arbitration and one-half of the expenses and fees of the arbitrator and the facilities used in the arbitration hearing.

Article VII—Seniority

"Seniority" as used in this agreement shall be the period of continuous service in the job or plant from the date of the employee's appointment.

"Probationary employment" consists of a period of one hundred twenty (120) days of employment.

Layoffs shall be made in the following order:

a. Probationary employees

b. Other employees in order of job seniority

Recall shall be made in the following order:

a. Employees in order of job seniority, given equal job ability

b. Probationary employees

Promotions shall be made on the basis of qualifications, merit, and seniority. Promotions out of the bargaining unit remain management's prerogative.

An employee who quits or is discharged for cause shall lose all seniority rights.

If the Company decides to terminate any operation or job and the employees remain on layoff for a period of twelve (12) months, the employees shall be considered to have been terminated for cause at the expiration of said twelve (12)-month period.

Article VIII—Wages and Classifications

Job classifications and a wage schedule setting forth the rates of pay of the various job classifications are included in **Schedule A** and are hereby made part of this agreement.

If and when the Company creates a new job classification or modifies, alters, amends, or combines existing jobs, or revises the skills and responsibilities of a job, job descriptions will be drawn and a wage rate assigned. The Union shall have a maximum of five (5) working days to examine the job description to determine whether it accurately describes the principal functions and whether the pay range is consistent with established job classification pay ranges.

If the Union takes exception, it can review both factors with the Company. If the issue cannot be resolved, the Union can take the issue through the grievance procedure.

Job classifications are for pay purposes only and do not pertain to whoever might perform the work in that classification—unless modified by the terms of the agreement.

Article IX—Insurance

An employee who has completed ninety (90) days of employment is eligible for enrollment in the company group insurance programs on the monthly premium date for each particular insurance coverage that next follows the completion of ninety (90) days of employment.

1. **Group Life Insurance**   **Accidental Death and Dismemberment**
   $20,000 $20,000

2. **Accident and Health Insurance**

Lost income due to a covered condition equals one-half of the employee's weekly pay up to a maximum of $150. It is understood and agreed that the cost of the hospitalization, medical and health insurance, major medical insurance, accident and health and life insurance will be paid 90 percent (90%) by the Company and 10 percent (10%) by the employee, when subscribed to by the employee.

It is understood and agreed that in the event that the Company wishes to change carriers, there is no obligation to negotiate with the Union prior to instituting the change.

Employees on medical leave for a period in excess of ninety (90) consecutive days may continue to be covered under the group insurance program after the first ninety (90) days, providing the employee pays the total insurance premium.

Article X—Pension Plan

A defined benefit pension plan for bargaining unit employees of the company is hereby made a part of this agreement. The normal monthly retirement benefit for all years of service is $30 per month per year of service.

Article XI—Holidays

All employees, after completing six (6) months of service with the Company, shall be paid eight (8) hours pay for the following holidays:

- New Year's Day
- Independence Day
- Labor Day
- Thanksgiving Day
- Day after Thanksgiving Day
- Christmas Eve Day
- Christmas Day

To be eligible for holiday pay, the employee must have worked the days immediately preceding and following the holiday. Legitimate excuses for absences will be considered.

Article XII—Vacation

Employees shall qualify for vacation with pay in accordance with the following (determined June 1 of each year):

Continuous Service	Vacation with Pay
More than 1 but less than 5 years	1 week
5 years but less than 10 years	2 weeks
10 years but less than 20 years	3 weeks
20 or more years	4 weeks

Vacation pay shall be computed on the basis of each employee's average weekly earnings from June to June. Payment will be made on the work day prior to the vacation period.

Article XIII—Sick Leave

A full-time employee is eligible for sick leave after completing six (6) months service with the Company. An eligible employee will accumulate sick leave at the rate of one-half day per month of service from date of hire. Sick leave will not be carried over from one year (January 1 to December 31) to the next, and it can be used only for personal illness not covered by workers' compensation. The Company retains the right to require a doctor's certificate as proof that an absence was due to a legitimate injury or illness.

Article XIV—Nondiscrimination

The Company and the Union mutually agree not to discriminate in making decisions and determinations concerning hiring, promotion, employment termination, transfer, compensation, and terms or conditions of employment. Both parties agree that all such decisions and determinations will be made without regard to race, color, religion, sex, age, disability not related to job performance, national origin or ancestry, or because an individual is disabled or a Vietnam-era veteran.

Article XV—Complete Agreement

This agreement is complete. It may be amended by mutual agreement in writing. Such amendment may be effective during the term of this agreement and may extend the term of this agreement. This agreement does not operate to include, nor does it obligate the Company to continue in effect, any working condition, benefit or past practice which is not covered or contained in the agreement.

Article XVI—Duration of the Agreement

This agreement shall become effective as of _____, and shall continue in effect until _____. Thereafter, it shall renew itself for yearly periods unless written notice of termination is given by one party to the other not less than sixty (60) nor more than ninety (90) days prior to the expiration of this agreement.

Schedule A: Current Wages and Classifications

Wage Grade	Job Title	Wage Rate
1	Janitor	$8.65
2	Packer	9.15
3	Materials handler	10.50
	Woodworking machine operator B	10.75
	Maintenance worker B	10.75
	Furniture finisher	10.80
4	General laborer	11.24
	Team assemblers	11.60
	Industrial truck & tractor operator	12.81
	Woodworking machine operator A	12.65
5	Welder	13.34
	Electrician B	13.35
	Tool grinder	13.45
	Wood worker, general	13.93
6	Maintenance worker A	15.40
	Machinists	15.45
7	Inspector	15.90
8	Painter	17.20
	Electrician A	17.50
9	Lead person	18.65
10	Tool and die maker	19.68

Form 1: Pre-bargaining Preparation Form

Each bargaining team must complete both parts A and B of Form 1. Part A is for each team's own strategic planning and should **not** be revealed to any other bargaining team. Part B contains your team's initial written bargaining proposals to be presented to the other bargaining team with whom you will be negotiating during the first bargaining meeting. Each bargaining team will turn in a completed copy of Form 1 (parts A & B) to the instructor prior to the initiation of face-to-face bargaining between union and management teams.

In column 1, briefly label the bargaining subject (e.g., wages, holidays, health insurance, pension, etc.). In column 2, identify the priority rank of that bargaining subject to your bargaining team. In column 3, describe in detail the specific outcome your bargaining team expects to achieve on each identified bargaining subject.

Part A

Bargaining Subject Area	Bargaining Priority (rank in order each subject from 1 to n, with 1 being the highest priority subject)	Realistic Expected Bargaining Outcome

Form 1, Part B: Initial Bargaining Proposals

Instructions: For each initial bargaining proposal or counterproposal that your team intends to introduce as part of the bargaining agenda at the first joint negotiation meeting, include the complete, specific, and clear wording of each initial bargaining subject proposal. Proposals should be stated using the exact contract language your party would prefer to appear in the labor agreement (contract).

Exhibit 1
QFM Company Balance Sheet, 2007

Assets		
	Current Assets:	
Cash		$ 2,420,659
Notes and accounts receivable		55,972,823
Inventories		70,720,456
Prepaid expenses		927,138
Total current assets		$130,041,076
	Fixed Assets:	
Land		$ 11,273,570
Buildings		28,183,925
Machinery and equipment		22,140,388
Total fixed assets		61,597,883
Total assets		$191,638,959
Liabilities and Stockholders' Investment		
	Current Liabilities	
Notes and accounts payable		$ 18,611,307
Accrued payroll		7,440,556
Taxes (local, state, federal)		59,749,921
Total current liabilities		$ 85,801,784
	Stockholders' Investment	
Common stock (common @ $20 per share)		$ 45,095,086
Earned surplus		60,742,089
Total stockholders' investment and earned surplus		$105,837,175
Total liabilities and stockholders' investment		$191,638,959

Exhibit 2
QFM Company Income Statement

	2006	2007
Net Sales	$216,468,226	$238,115,271
Costs of Goods Sold		
Production (labor, materials, overtime)	$174,515,138	$182,314,515
Administrative	14,792,253	15,806,447
Sales	7,215,085	9,469,799
Other	1,831,306	2,077,494
Total Cost of Goods Sold	$198,353,782	$209,668,255
Income before taxes	18,114,444	28,447,016
Taxes (local, state, federal)	5,262,503	7,015,580
Net Income	$ 12,851,941	$ 21,431,436

Exhibit 3
QFM Company Net Sales and Income

	Net Sales	Net Income
2006	$216,468,226	12,851,941
2007	238,115,271	21,431,436
2008 (estimated)	254,826,000	26,147,000

Exhibit 4
Number of QFM Production and Maintenance Employees by Seniority in St. Louis and Dallas Plants

Years	St. Louis	Dallas
Less than 1	10	100
1–2	45	150
3–4	50	90
5–6	120	135
7–10	165	165
11–15	128	84
16–20	190	60
21—25	105	58
26–30	120	45
more than 30	67	7
Total	1,000	894

Exhibit 5
Number of QFM Employees in Each Job Title, by Wage Grade

Wage Grade	Job Title	St. Louis	Dallas
1	Janitor	12	9
2	Packer	66	54
3	Materials handler	60	53
	Woodworking machine operator B	85	68
	Furniture finisher	72	68
	Maintenance worker B	15	13
4	General laborer	56	49
	Team assemblers	305	295
	Industrial truck & tractor operator	20	18
	Woodworking machine operator A	45	40
5	Welder	16	13
	Electrician B	14	10
	Tool grinder	5	5
	Woodworker, general	85	78
6	Maintenance worker A	10	8
	Machinists	15	12
7	Inspector	29	25
8	Painter	35	32
	Electrician A	15	12
9	Lead person	28	24
10	Tool and die maker	12	8
TOTAL		1,000	894

Exhibit 6

Average Hourly Earnings, Excluding Overtime, for Selected Industries (Not Seasonally Adjusted)

NAICS	Industry	2004	2005	2006	2007*
N/A	**Manufacturing**	15.29	15.68	15.95	16.52
N/A	**Durable Goods**	15.92	16.41	16.78	17.43
321	Wood Products	12.36	12.52	12.78	13.07
327	Nonmetallic Mineral Products	15.17	15.45	15.56	15.83
331	Primary Metals	17.26	17.65	18.05	18.49
332	Fabricated Metal Products	14.51	14.97	15.33	15.72
333	Machinery	15.78	16.07	16.31	16.93
334	Computer and Electronic Products	16.52	17.61	18.71	19.32
335	Electrical Equipment and Appliances	14.20	14.56	14.80	15.29
336	Transportation Equipment	20.17	20.80	21.19	21.94
337	Furniture and Related Products	12.58	12.92	13.28	13.75
339	Miscellaneous Manufacturing	13.30	13.50	13.84	14.27
N/A	**Nondurable Goods**	14.27	14.47	14.54	14.97
311	Food Manufacturing	12.25	12.30	12.39	12.82
312	Beverage and Tobacco Products	18.16	17.52	17.04	16.69
313	Textile Mills	11.50	11.80	11.99	12.65
314	Textile Product Mills	10.97	11.04	11.32	11.40
315	Apparel	9.47	9.96	10.29	10.66
316	Leather and Allied Products	11.32	11.19	10.94	11.79
322	Paper and Paper Products	16.83	16.88	16.89	17.33
323	Printing and Related Support Activities	15.05	15.10	15.12	15.71
324	Petroleum and Coal Products	22.35	22.37	22.18	23.42
325	Chemicals	18.13	18.65	18.69	18.65
326	Plastics and Rubber Products	13.88	14.09	14.27	14.66

*Preliminary

SOURCE: Bureau of Labor Statistics, U.S. Department of Labor, on the Internet at http://data.bls.gov/PDQ/outside.jsp?survey=ce (visited October 11, 2007).

Exhibit 7
Mean Hourly Earnings of Selected Manufacturing Plant Employees in Texas and Missouri, November, 2004

Job Titles	Texas	Missouri
Team assemblers	$9.94	$11.90
Wood worker, general	$7.93	$14.60
Electrician	$17.86	$24.16
Inspector	$14.71	$16.23
Woodworking machine operator	$9.57	$11.02
Inspectors	$14.71	$16.23
Industrial truck and tractor operator	$11.48	$13.00
Furniture finisher	$10.10	$11.53
Packer	$8.27	$9.14
Material handler	$9.58	$10.95
Welder	$12.67	$13.39
Janitor	$8.25	$9.14
Laborer	$8.53	$11.97

SOURCE: U.S. Department of Labor, Bureau of Labor Statistics, *November 2004 State Occupational Employment and Wage Estimates* at http://www.bls.gov/oes/current/oes_tx.htm and http://www.bls.gov/oes/current/oes_mo.htm.

Exhibit 8
Consumer Price Index (CPI) for Urban Wage Earners and Clerical Workers Base Period: 1982–84 = 100 (Not Seasonally Adjusted)

Index	2004	2005	2006	2007*
Dallas-Fort Worth, Texas	179.0	185.6	191.6	192.9
Saint Louis, Missouri–Illinois Area	178.7	184.9	188.5	190.9

Percent Change in Index from Previous Year	2004	2005	2006	2007*
Dallas-Fort Worth, Texas	1.8	3.7	3.2	.60
Saint Louis, Missouri–Illinois Area	4.0	3.5	1.9	1.3

*Preliminary

SOURCE: Bureau of Labor Statistics, U.S. Department of Labor, on the Internet at http://www.bls.gov/cpi/home.htm (visited October 11, 2007).

Exhibit 9

Average Hourly and Weekly Earnings for All Private Workers and for Production Workers (Not Seasonally Adjusted)

Hourly Earnings					
NAICS	Industry	2004	2005	2006	2007*
N/A	Total Private	15.69	16.13	16.76	17.63
N/A	Manufacturing	16.15	16.56	16.80	17.39
3371	Household and Institutional Furniture	12.81	13.15	13.65	14.07

Average Weekly Earnings					
NAICS	Industry	2004	2005	2006	2007*
N/A	Total Private	529.09	544.33	567.87	602.95
N/A	Manufacturing	658.59	673.37	690.83	725.16
3371	Household and Institutional Furniture	510.78	517.27	524.27	557.17

Average Weekly Hours					
NAICS	Industry	2004	2005	2006	2007*
N/A	Total Private	33.7	33.8	33.9	34.2
N/A	Manufacturing	40.8	40.7	41.1	41.7
3371	Household and Institutional Furniture	39.9	39.4	38.4	39.6

*Preliminary

SOURCE: Bureau of Labor Statistics, U.S. Department of Labor, on the Internet at http://data.bls.gov/PDQ/outside.jsp?survey=ce (visited October 11, 2007).

Index

Haywood, William "Big Bill,"
defined, 51
Health care cost
containment, 312
Health maintenance
organization (HMO), 313
HealthSouth, 157, 292
Heartland Labor Capital
Project, 18
HERE, 148
Hershey Foods Corporation,
312, 313
Hiatt, Jon, 631
High performance work
organization (HPWO), 338
partnership principles, 339
Hillman, Sidney, 59
HMO. See health maintenance
organization.
Hoffa, James, 61, 84, 157
Hoffman Plastic Compounds,
Inc. v. NLRB, 86
Holiday pay, 315
Holly Farms Corp. v.
NLRB, 86
Holt-Baker, Arlene, 152
Home computer
assistance, 321
Home Depot, 670
Homeland Security Act (HSA),
579–580
Homestead Incident, 38, 48–49
Hoover, Ron, 386
Hotel and Restaurant
Employees Union,
353, 356
Hourly compensation, various
countries, 621
Howard, John, 654, 655, 656
HPWO. See high performance
work organization.
HSA. See Homeland Security
Act.
Human Resource Management
System, 580
Human Rights Watch, 120
Hunt, Joseph, 339
Hurricane Katrina and Rita, 24

I

Iacocca, Lee, 267
IAM. See International
Association of Machinists
& Aerospace Workers.
IBEW. See International
Brotherhood of Electrical
Workers.
IBM Corporation, 88, 547
IBM, 122, 319, 620
IG Metal, 647

ILA. See International
Longshoremen's
Association.
Illegal bargaining subject, 268
ILO. See International Labor
Organization.
Immigration and
Naturalization
Service, 579
Immigration Reform and
Control Act, 86
Impasse-resolution procedures
involving third-party
neutral, 373–378
Implied contract exception, 523
Improshare, 324
Improshare plan, 299
Inability to pay, 270
Income maintenance, 313
Independent unions, 149
Indicators of state of
economy, 15
Industrial,
discipline, changing
significance of, 522–528
spies, 56
unionism, CIO and, 58–61
unions, 136
wage differentials, 292–294
Industrial Workers of the
World (IWW), 37, 38, 39,
51–54, 60, 220, 626
reasons for decline, 52–53
Industry level bargaining, 246
Ingersoll-Rand Company, 122
Institutional Revolutionary
Party (PRI), 637, 638
Insurance, 312
Intel Corporation, 24
Intent of the parties, 477
Interboro doctrine, 92
Interest arbitration, 374,
377–378, 593
conventional, 378
procedures, 378–380
Interest dispute, 6, 244
economic pressure used to
resolve, 380–383
impasse-resolution
procedures in public
sector, 593–596
Interest-based bargaining, 260
Internal Revenue Service
(IRS), 578
International Association of
Machinists & Aerospace
Workers (IAM), 211, 245,
338, 570
International Brotherhood of
Electrical Workers
(IBEW), 17, 200, 216, 338

International Brotherhood of
Teamsters, 61, 66, 84,
143, 157, 193, 204, 313,
544, 551, 582
International Congress of Staff
Unions (ICSU), 145
International Federation of
Airline Pilots Association
(IFALPA), 661
International Federation of
Chemical, Energy,
Mining, and General
Workers Unions (ICEM),
627, 661
International forces, 20
International Framework
Agreements (IFAs), 625
International Harvester, 299
International Labor
Organization (ILO), 22,
624, 638, 657, 661
International Ladies Garment
Workers Union, 149
International Longshore and
Warehouse Union, 401
International Longshoremen's
Association (ILA),
307, 343
International Metalworkers
Federation (IMF), 661
International Monetary
Fund, 23
International trade, 22
International Transport
Workers Federation
(ITF), 628
International unions, 140–148
organizational chart, 134
representative of, 138
Internet and e-mail, union use
of, 211–212
Interstate Commerce
Commission, 101
Intraorganizational
bargaining, 266
Iron workers, union, 339
IWW. See Industrial Workers
of the World.

J

Japan, 649–652
Japan Council of Metal
workers' Unions, 652
Japanese Trade Union Law,
651
Jintao, Hu, 658
Job analysis, 295
Job characteristics,
differing, 137
Job evaluation, 294

differential feature of work,
301–311
occupational wage
differentials and,
294–301
Job growth, 16
Job protection, technological
change and, 336–341
Job rights, competitive, 350
Job security, 177, 342
and personnel changes,
341–355
Job security work rules,
342–343
Job skills, differing, 137
Job Training Partnership Act
(JTPA), 104
Jobs within the organization,
evaluating, 294–296
Johnson Controls decision, 360
Johnson Controls, Inc., 360, 364
Joint councils, 149
Journeymen Bootmakers'
Society, 76
Judicial proceedings,
comparison to arbitration,
469–472
vs. arbitration, evidence in,
470–472
Jurisdiction,
exclusive union, 48
work assignments and,
347–349
Jurisdictional,
disputes, 348
strike, 383
Just cause,
employee termination, tests
for, 530
principle in employee
discipline, 528–548
standard, application of, 540

K

Kaiser Steel, 62
Keegan, Robert, 386
Kennedy, John F., 40
Kerry, John, 66
King, Martin Luther, 40
Kirkland, Lane, 152
Kmart, 317
Knight-Ridder, 21
Knights of Labor (KOL), 37,
38, 41–44, 46, 48, 52,
53, 60
effectiveness of, 45
reasons for failure and
demise, 43
strategies to accomplish
goals, 42